DICTIONARY OF
IRISH LITERATURE

DICTIONARY OF IRISH LITERATURE

Revised and Expanded Edition

M–Z

ROBERT HOGAN, EDITOR-IN-CHIEF

ASSOCIATE EDITORS: Zack Bowen,
Richard Burnham, Mary Rose Callaghan,
Anne Colman, Peter Costello, William J. Feeney,
Maryanne Felter, James Kilroy, Bernard McKenna,
and Marguerite Quintelli-Neary

GREENWOOD PRESS
Westport, Connecticut • London

Library of Congress Cataloging-in-Publication Data

Dictionary of Irish literature / Robert Hogan, editor-in-chief ;
   associate editors, Zack Bowen . . . [et al.].—Rev. and expanded ed.
      p.   cm.
   Includes bibliographical references and index.
      ISBN 0–313–29172–1 (alk. paper : set).—ISBN 0–313–30175–1 (alk. paper : A-L).—
ISBN 0–313–30176–X (alk. paper : M-Z)
      1. English literature—Irish authors—Dictionaries. 2. Ireland—
In literature—Dictionaries. 3. Irish literature—Dictionaries.
   I. Hogan, Robert Goode. II. Bowen, Zack R.
   PR8706.D5   1996
   820'.99415—dc20   95–50428

British Library Cataloguing in Publication Data is available.

Library of Congress Catalog Card Number: 95–50428
ISBN: 0–313–29172–1 (set)
        0–313–30175–1 (A-L)
        0–313–30176–X (M-Z)

First published in 1996

Greenwood Press, 88 Post Road West, Westport, CT 06881
An imprint of Greenwood Publishing Group, Inc.

Printed in the United States of America

The paper used in this book complies with the
Permanent Paper Standard issued by the National
Information Standards Organization (Z39.48–1984).

10 9 8 7 6 5 4 3 2 1

Every reasonable effort has been made to trace the owners of copyright materials in this
book, but in some instances this has proven impossible. The author and publisher will
be glad to receive information leading to more complete acknowledgments in subsequent
printings of the book and in the meantime extend their apologies for any omissions.

REF
PR
8706
.D5
1996
v. 2

CONTENTS

CONTRIBUTORS

Jonathan Allison
University of Kentucky

Mary Ball
Dublin

Ivy Bannister
Dublin

John Barrett
University College, Dublin

Sheila Barrett
Dublin

Kate Bateman
Dublin

Jerry C. Beasley
University of Delaware

Paul Bew
Queen's University of Belfast

John Boyd
Belfast

Zack Bowen
University of Miami

Terence Brown
Trinity College, Dublin

Richard Burnham
Dominican College

Mary Rose Callaghan
Bray, Co. Wicklow

Anne Clune
Trinity College, Dublin

Anne Colman
*Institute of Irish Studies,
Queen's University, Belfast*

Evelyn Conlon
Dublin

Peter Costello
Dublin

Dennis Cotter, Jr.
Dublin

Jane Cunningham
Dublin

Kathleen Danaher
Wilmington, Delaware

John F. Deane
Dedalus Press

Seamus de Burca
Dublin

Celia de Fréine
Dublin

Tim Dennehy
Mullagh, Co. Clare

Alan Denson
Aberdeenshire

Barbara DiBernard
University of Nebraska

William G. Dolde
University of Iowa

Mary E. Donnelly
University of Miami

Aileen Douglas
Trinity College, Dublin

James Douglas
Bray, Co. Wicklow

Rachel Douglas
Bray, Co. Wicklow

Paul A. Doyle
Nassau Community College

Peter Drewniany
Germantown Academy

Seán Dunne

Grace Eckley

Owen Dudley Edwards
University of Edinburgh

Antony Farrell
Lilliput Press

Christopher Fauske
University of New Hampshire

William J. Feeney
Oak Park, Illinois

Maryanne Felter
Cayuga Community College

Deborah Fleming
Ashland University

John Wilson Foster
University of British Columbia

Jean Franks
Anaheim, California

Barbara Freitag
Dublin City University

Helmut E. Gerber

Priscilla Goldsmith
University of Delaware

Eamon Grennan
Vassar College

Christopher Griffin
Strayer College, Washington, D.C.

Patricia Boyle Haberstroh
La Salle University

Andrew Haggerty
Miami University

Jay L. Halio
University of Delaware

Jack Harte
Lucan Community College

Mark D. Hawthorne
James Madison University

Rüdiger Imhof
University of Wuppertal

K.P.S. Jochum
University of Bamburg

Fred Johnston
Galway

Richard M. Kain

Colbert Kearney
University College, Cork

A. A. Kelly
Lymington, Hampshire

Kevin Kerrane
University of Delaware

Frank Kersnowski
Trinity University

James Kilroy
Tulane University

Thomas Kinsella
County Wicklow

James Liddy
University of Wisconsin–Milwaukee

Nora F. Lindstrom

William J. Linn
University of Michigan–Dearborn

Victor Luftig
Brandeis University

M. Kelly Lynch
Babson College

J. B. Lyons
Royal College of Surgeons, Dublin

Dolores MacKenna
Dublin

Alf MacLochlainn
County Galway

Bryan MacMahon
Listowel, County Kerry

Michael McDonnell
Fairfield University

Patricia McFate

Nora McGuinness
University of California-Davis

Bernard McKenna
Middletown, Delaware

Sean McMahon
Derry

Donald McNamara
Catholic University of America

Andrew Marsh (John O'Donovan)

Augustine Martin
University College, Dublin

James H. Matthews

D.E.S. Maxwell
Belfast

Donald C. Mell
University of Delaware

Thomas F. Merrill
Sanibel, Florida

Liam Miller

Sven Eric Molin

Christopher Murray
University College, Dublin

Jerry H. Natterstad
Framingham State College

John Nemo

James Newcomer

Eilís Ní Dhuibhne
National Library of Ireland

Johann A. Norstedt
Virginia Tech

Micheál Ó hAodha
Dingle, County Kerry

Shawn O'Hare
Florida State University

Seamus O'Neill

Cóilín Owens
George Mason University

Christopher Penna
University of Delaware

Åke Persson
*Sigturna International College of the
Humanities, Uppsala*

Richard Pine
Dublin

Raymond J. Porter

Victor Price

Kathleen A. Quinn
Queen's University, Belfast

Marguerite Quintelli-Neary
Winthrop University

Dorothy Robbie
Greystones, County Wicklow

Peter Robbie
Greystones, County Wicklow

Helen Ryan
Children's Literature Association of Ireland

Martin Ryan
Dublin

Ann Saddlemyer
University of Toronto

George Brandon Saul

N. A. Saunders
*Convent of Mercy,
Callan, Co. Kilkenny*

Bonnie Kime Scott
University of Delaware

Colin Smythe
Colin Smythe, Ltd.

Bruce Stewart
University of Ulster, Coleraine

Mary Helen Thuente
*Indiana University/Purdue University,
Fort Wayne, Indiana*

Alan Titley
St. Patrick's College, Drumcondra

Terence Winch
Smithsonian Institution

Terence de Vere White

PREFACE

A preliminary word seems necessary about the plan of this book.

The Introduction might really be titled "The Literary Uses of Ireland," for the principal characteristic of writing in Ireland is its Irishness. While this statement may seem obvious, it also is obvious that, since the Renaissance, nationality, as expressed in literature, has been increasingly diminished by internationality. For instance, the excellence of what D. H. Lawrence called "Classic American Literature" was considerably diluted by an international, and particularly an English, influence. The inimitable excellence of the nineteenth-century American authors Emerson, Thoreau, Poe, Hawthorne, Melville, and especially Walt Whitman appears to lie mainly in the extent to which they resisted that influence and allowed themselves to be receptive to their own native milieu. The triumphant progression of Russian literary masters in the nineteenth century, from Pushkin to Gogol to Tolstoy and Dostoyevsky, Turgenev, and Chekhov, certainly must be attributed to the backwardness, the provinciality, the isolation, and the ingrown "Russianness" of their society.

Irish society also, until the very recent past, remained surprisingly insulated from the modern world. Although in many ways pernicious, that isolation did have the effect of intensely focusing the attention of the Irish writer on the little world of his Four Green Fields. Even now, when Ireland is a much more outward-looking society, the effects remain dramatically evident. The Introduction, then, is an attempt to chart how the Irish writer used this narrow, but rich, subject matter—the landscape, the climate, the history, the manners, the morals, the customs of his native land.

The Introduction is not a capsule review of Ireland past and present, as any attempt to compress so much information into so little space would be to court superficiality with a vengeance. Rather, it deals with those facets of Ireland that the writers themselves have thought the most salient and that have appeared so constantly in their work. As a historical or sociological or even literary survey, the Introduction is too short and malproportioned to serve; but as a not wholly subjective view of how Ireland's writers have portrayed their country, and of what those writers have thought important, it may introduce the reader to at least the primary preoccupations of Irish literature.

In planning this dictionary, the most difficult editorial question to resolve has been how to treat literature written in the Irish language. Such literature is centuries-old and continues to be written even today. The range of that literature, from saga to satire, is broad indeed, and the quality of much of that literature is brilliant. However, the fortunes of the Irish language have been wedded to the fortunes of the Irish nation. As England's power waxed in Ireland, the old Irish culture waned and Irish as a living language progressively decayed. The year 1800 may be taken as symptomatic of the triumph of the English language in Ireland. In that year, the Act of Union abolished the separate Irish Parliament and included Irish representatives in Westminster. Irish, of course, was still spoken, but as the sole language it survived only in secluded rural pockets. An Irish language revival around the turn of the twentieth century was a harbinger of the secretly growing political revival that was to culminate in the Easter Rising of 1916, in the Irish Free State, and finally in an independent republic that comprised most of the island. However, political independence did not mean that the Irish language could be restored as the living language of the people. Ireland became nominally bilingual, but, despite great dedication and immense effort, it was impossible to go back.

Today, Irish alone is spoken in a few small sections of the country. The language is studied in the schools from an early age, and some modern books of merit have been written in Irish. Nevertheless, it remains true that the great works of modern Irish literature have been written in English. It is also lamentably true that the classic works of the Irish language are to be perceived, even by the Irish themselves, mainly through their influence on modern Irish writing in English. Whether in direct translation, adaptation, or even simply as a fecund source of allusion and inspiration, that influence is profound and pervasive, but it is an influence at one remove.

A dictionary of Irish literature assuredly must deal with writing in Irish. Apart from its own extraordinary merits, literature in Irish remains the bedrock foundation for much, if not most, modern Irish writing in English. Nevertheless, it seemed that this work must stress Irish writing in the English language. After all, W. B. Yeats, James Stephens, and James Joyce are the mirrors in which the entire world, including Ireland itself, sees reflected the old Ireland that was. Consequently, we have adopted a compromise by reprinting from the first edition the lengthy critical and historical survey of writing in Irish. This survey was written by the late Seamus O'Neill, himself a distinguished writer who published mainly in Irish. The survey of the most recent writing in Irish by Alan Titley has been written specially for this second edition; and both chapters are a most necessary preliminary to the bulk of the dictionary, which treats Irish writing in English.

The first edition of this book contained 470 entries on authors who wrote mainly in the English language. The entries contained biographical data, critical evaluation, and a bibliography. This edition contains about 1,000 such entries and about 200 short entries, mainly of very recent authors, which give only bibliographical and sometimes biographical information. Most of the new entries are devoted to the extraordinary number of new writers who have appeared in the Irish publishing explosion of the last fifteen years. However, the number of writers from the eighteenth and nineteenth centuries has been considerably expanded also.

The choice of authors to be included has been basically the decision of the editor, although he has availed himself of the oral suggestions of so many people and of the written opinions of so many more, that the final choice probably approaches a consensus. Most of the authors included are obvious choices, authors whose omission would have been ridiculous from the standpoint of either literature or history. The choice, however, of the most recent authors, those who appeared from 1980 to 1995, has been the most difficult, not only because there have been so many of them but also because one is too close to them to see clearly. I fully expect that the next fifteen years will witness the flowering of some reputations that seem at the moment unimpressive and whose authors I may not have included. I hasten to offer my mea culpas in advance. In the first edition I remarked that I fully expected to be asked, ''Why did you leave out the brilliant A_____ and include that poetaster X_____?'' My answer must still be the same: ''The reason is probably attributable to ignorance, bias, lack of taste, and human fallibility.''

Still and all, in this area of minimal excellence and excellent potential, there is no thoroughly satisfactory solution. One arbitrary solution adopted in the first edition was to limit the entries almost exclusively to authors who have published a book, no matter how slim. I have not entirely been able to keep to that criterion in this second, much expanded edition. Another arbitrary criterion was to lend a tolerant ear to new writers who are still establishing themselves. There are so many new writers that I fear I have not entirely been able to keep to that criterion either.

I have again included a few Irish writers—among them Congreve and Goldsmith and Sheridan and even George Darley—who hardly wrote of Ireland at all. My reasons are partly an intractable bias in their favor and partly pure chauvinism. A few foreign authors were included in the first edition, because of the rich and lasting contribution they had made to Irish literature. Such volumes as, for instance, Robin Flower's *The Western Island* or Richard Ellmann's *James Joyce* or J. P. Donleavy's *The Ginger Man* or J. G. Farrell's *Troubles* seem classics of Irish literature, and to have omitted their remarkable authors from this company would have been chauvinistic indeed. In this edition, the number of foreign authors has been somewhat expanded to include, for instance, from the nineteenth century, Trollope and Thackeray, and from the twentieth, Thomas Flanagan and Nina Fitzpatrick (even though a prestigious award to Fitzpatrick was withdrawn because she was not Irish).

I hope that no author of outstanding achievement has been omitted. However, that was what I wrongly hoped about the first edition, and I daresay that I am still wrong. If so, perhaps some other, and younger, editor will make amends at some future date.

The length of the alphabetical entries varies from about 25 words to about 10,000, and obviously the length of an entry implies some judgment about the author's work as it at present appears. However, this is only a very rough judgment, and the reader is cautioned not to regard Author A, who is discussed in 250 words, as one-sixth less admirable than Author B, who is discussed in 1,500. Also, the length of the articles has not entirely been my editorial judgment. There are many entries longer than my personal judgment of an author's worth might have allowed, and this is particularly so in the case of the recent writers. However, there is a received general critical opinion about the literary worth of nearly every author discussed here. Although I think that a good deal of contemporary Irish literary criticism is gushingly hyperbolic, it would be editorially arrogant to ignore it.

The Irish are, possibly with good reason, fond of the term "begrudgery," which means a snidely vicious condemnation. This is not a begrudger's book. The authors of the individual entries have been chosen not only for their taste and knowledge but also for their enthusiasm about their author. Some few comments in this volume strike me as more book-blurbish than critical, but the glumness of much recent Irish writing may have affected my own aging and increasingly sour critical view, and so I have, of course, welcomed my commentators' enthusiasms. Some other comments—among them possibly a few of my own—are doubtless hard-hitting, but the reason, I trust, is not begrudgery, but judicious judgment, which must be the chief criterion for a volume such as this. As Richard Stanyhurst well remarked in 1584, "I have no stomach for decrying anyone with stinging insults nor do I consider it to be in keeping with my dignity (insofar as it exists) to insinuate myself into the ear with bland, emollient words."

The body of the dictionary also contains a handful of general articles on topics such as folklore and children's literature. At one time, I contemplated a larger number of these articles, which would deal with historical writing, travel writing, biographies, memoirs, journalism, broadcasting, and other endeavors whose best examples have strong claims to literary worth. After much consideration, however, I decided that comprehensive surveys of such fields would not only extend the book greatly but also dissipate its major impact by including much that was tangential or transitory. On the other hand, individual entries for major historians, political writers, editors, orators, journalists, and the like have been expanded. The dictionary also contains a number of entries for important organizations or publications, such as the Abbey Theatre, the Cuala Press, and *The Nation.*

The original entries from the first edition have been in every instance reconsidered, revised, corrected, and frequently expanded. In nearly all instances, the revision has been made by the original writer. However, since the first edition of this book, some of its most distinguished authors have died: Helmut Gerber, Richard M. Kain, Liam Miller, Sven Eric Molin, John Nemo, John O'Donovan ("Andrew Marsh"), Seamus O'Neill, Raymond J. Porter, George Brandon Saul, and Terence de Vere White. In every instance, their original entries seemed sound enough to stand, with only an occasional sentence or two appended to add significant new matter. In a few instances, I have not been able to contact the original writers, and often I have allowed those sound entries to stand also.

The particular articles have been signed by their authors, and any unsigned entries have been written by the general editor. Finally, a person's name or topic or organization followed by an asterisk has its own separate entry in the appropriate alphabetical place in the dictionary.

Perhaps a third to a half of this book consists of bibliographies. The bibliographies of specific writers or topics follow their individual entries. Most have been compiled by the author of the entry, although the editor is responsible for the bibliographical form of the citations and has frequently made additions and, occasionally, deletions. In the case of the important and complicated W. B. Yeats bibliography, however, the original compiler was deceased; and the revised and expanded bibliography has been entrusted to the leading authority, K.P.S. Jochum. The individual bibliographies list all of the author's significant work, and "significant work" has usually been taken to mean every individual book publication and the important fugitive material. In many instances, it has been possible to list practically everything an author is known to have written. However, in the case of an extremely important or prolific writer, such as Shaw or Yeats, a complete listing has been impossible. Even so, a diligent attempt has been made to list everything of primary or even secondary importance.

The individual bibliographies are divided into two sections. The first section lists the writer's works in the order in which they were published. Usually, American editions as well as British and Irish ones are listed. The second, and usually shorter, section lists the major critical, biographical, and bibliographical works about the writer and is arranged alphabetically by the last names of the authors, editors, or compilers. To conserve space, the name of the publisher has been shortened to its essential components: thus, Maunsel and Company appears simply as "Maunsel," the Dolmen Press simply as "Dolmen," and so on (though "Press" is retained in university presses). The subtitles of books have usually been retained.

Although the limitations of space and human energy have prevented an exhaustive or complete listing, I believe that these bibliographies as a whole constitute the most comprehensive listing of Irish literature that is in print or is likely to be in print for many years.

The Chronology of historical and literary events given at the end of the dictionary is intended not as a substitute for a basic grasp of Irish history and literature but as a simple chart for the neophyte traveler in moments of occasional bafflement. For more precise knowledge, the reader is directed to the excellent volumes of history and literary history cited in the general Bibliography. The latter is a concise listing of the best general books on Ireland, its geography, its climate, its history, its economics, its architecture, its customs, and, particularly, its literature.

A dictionary or an encyclopedia does not always have an index. This volume does, and I trust that the reader will quickly appreciate its utility. Irish literature has emerged from a small and close-knit society. One Irish wit remarked that a literary movement occurred when a number of writers lived in the same place and did not speak to each other. There is a deal of justice in that remark, but in Ireland the writers do always speak about each other. They also necessarily work together, and they inevitably influence one another. For instance, the most pervasive influence in modern Irish literature has been W. B. Yeats, who is discussed at considerable length in the entry by Richard M. Kain. However, Yeats was of crucial importance for the careers of scores of writers, and additional information about him appears throughout this book. To a lesser extent, that same point is valid for many other writers. Hence, judicious readers will not only read the article about the author they are interested in but also consult the Index for other citations.

To save space, there are no separate entries for individual works in the text, unless the author is unknown. Thus, a discussion of *Ulysses* or *Juno and the Paycock* will be found under the entries for their authors, Joyce and O'Casey. If the reader knows the work and not the author, he may quickly find a discussion of the work by referring to its title in the Index. An anonymous work like *The Táin,* which is not entered separately in the dictionary but is discussed in Seamus O'Neill's chapter on Gaelic literature, can also be located through use of the Index. The Index does not cite information from the bibliographies, but everything cited in the text proper—both in the introductory material and in the alphabetical entries—is noted.

Not every Irish author or magazine or literary society has been thought important enough to be accorded a separate listing in the body of the work. However, a glance at the Index will indicate that many of these individuals or organizations have been discussed somewhere in the dictionary. For instance, Richard Lovell Edgeworth is cited only in the Index but will be found briefly discussed in the entry on his very important daughter, Maria; the magazine *Threshold* is cited only in the Index but will be found in the entry on its parent organization, the Lyric Players Theatre of Belfast.

An editor of such a volume as this must feel like the captain of a ship manned by many and much more knowledgeable sailors than he. As I have that feeling quite strongly, I should like to mention my particular gratitude to the late Richard M. Kain, the late John O'Donovan, the late Seamus O'Neill, and the late

Sven Eric Molin, whose erudition, kindness, and generous labors contributed immensely to the first edition of this work. To Zack Bowen, Mary Rose Callaghan, William J. Feeney, and James Kilroy I am indebted for their continuing contributions, and to their names I must add those of Anne Colman, Peter Costello, Maryanne Felter, Bernard McKenna, Cóilín Owens, Marguerite Quintelli-Neary, and Alan Titley. To them and to a host of others, particularly to Mervyn Wall and to Lis Pihl, who called my attention to errors and omissions, my deepest and most abiding thanks.

Dr. Johnson said, "A man will turn over half a library to make one book." Of the half a library that was turned over in the making of this book, there were some volumes to which I constantly returned and to which every student of Irish literature must remain indebted. I have particularly in mind D. J. O'Donoghue's *The Poets of Ireland,* Stephen J. Brown's *Ireland in Fiction,* Richard Best's *Bibliography of Irish Philology* and its sequel, Patrick Rafroidi's *Irish Literature in English: The Romantic Period,* Brian McKenna's *Irish Literature, 1800–1875,* and *The Field Day Anthology* of Seamus Deane and others. I have constantly had recourse to the annual bibliographies printed by the Modern Language Association of America and to those in the *Irish University Review* and *Études Irlandaises;* and my copies of Anne M. Brady and Brian Cleeve's *A Biographical Dictionary of Irish Writers* and of Anne Owens Weekes's *Unveiling Treasures: The Attic Guide to the Published Works of Irish Women Literary Writers* have become well thumbed.

It was momentarily gratifying to hear that several Irish librarians referred to the first edition as "the bible." It was, however, a bible with missing pages. In correcting that edition, I was chagrined to discover more errors than I had thought possible to be there. I am certain that errors of fact have undoubtedly found their way in here also, and I will be most grateful if readers will bring them to my attention. I hope that this new edition might also be thought worthy enough to be termed a bible, for a bible has its "Revelations." Undoubtedly, this volume also has some heresies of opinion, and I am happy enough with them too. If they prove, finally, errors of judgment, let Time be the judge, for he is much more judicious than I and considerably less vulnerable.

Robert Hogan
Bray, Co. Wicklow
November 30, 1995

ACKNOWLEDGMENTS

For permission to quote published material, the editor and publisher gratefully make the following acknowledgments: to the Blackstaff Press for lines from Norman Dugdale's *Running Repairs.* Belfast: Blackstaff, 1983 and from Michael Foley's *The Go Situation.* Dundonald, N. I.: Blackstaff, 1982, and *Insomnia in the Afternoon.* Belfast: Blackstaff, 1994; to John and Patricia Coffey for various lines by Brian Coffey; to Colin Smythe, Ltd. for quotations from Austin Clarke's *Collected Poems;* to Anthony Cronin for lines from several poems; to the Dedalus Press for lines from Chris Agee's *In the New Hampshire Woods,* for lines from Padraig J. Daly, for lines from "Corc's Gold Vessel" and "Setting the Type" from Greg Delanty's *Southward,* for lines from Conleth Ellis's *Darkness Blossoming,* for lines from "Joyce Cycling to Oughterard and Vico" from John Ennis's *Down in the Deeper Helicon,* for lines from "During the Illness of Dolores Ibarruri" from John Jordan's *Collected Poems,* for lines from Hugh Maxton's *The Engraved Passion,* and for lines from *Personal Places* in Thomas Kinsella's Peppercanister volume; to Gill & Macmillan for lines from "After Love," "Goodbye," "Ploughman and Kestrel," and "West of Here" from Conleth Ellis's *Under the Stone;* to Graywolf Press and Eamon Grennan for lines from various poems: "A Closer Look" copyright 1989 by Eamon Grennan. Reprinted from *What Light There Is* with the permission of Graywolf Press, Saint Paul, Minnesota and "Breaking Point," "Sea Dog," "The Cave Painters" copyright 1991 by Eamon Grennan. Reprinted from *As If It Matters* with the permission of Graywolf Press, Saint Paul, Minnesota; to Faber and Faber Ltd for quotations from *Wintering Out, North, Station Island, The Haw Lantern,* and *Seeing Things* by Seamus Heaney, Faber and Faber Ltd; selections from *Selected Poems* 1966–1987 by Seamus Heaney. Copyright © 1990 by Seamus Heaney. Reprinted by permission of Farrar, Straus & Giroux, Inc.; selections from *Seeing Things* by Seamus Heaney. Copyright © 1991 by Seamus Heaney. Reprinted by permission of Farrar, Straus & Giroux, Inc.; to James Liddy for lines from *In a Blue Smoke;* to Michael Longley for lines from "Letters" and "Wounds" from *An Exploded View;* to Michael Longley and Wake Forest University Press: lines from "Northern Lights" and "Laertes" by Michael Longley are reprinted from *Gorse Fires* with the permission of Wake Forest University Press; to Martin Secker & Warburg Ltd; for Michael Longley, *Gorse Fires,* London: Martin Secker & Warburg Ltd; to The Lilliput Press for lines from "Winter Landscape" from Bryan Guinness's *On a Ledge;* to Roy McFadden and Chatto & Windus for lines from *The Garryowen.* London: Chatto & Windus, 1971; to Mercier Press for permission to use lines from Sigerson Clifford's "The Boys of Barr na Sraide," Cork: Mercier, 1989; to Faber and Faber Ltd for *Quoof* and *Meeting the British* by Paul Muldoon, Faber and Faber Ltd; lines from "Gathering Mushrooms" from *Quoof,* "Meeting the British," and "7, Middagh Street" from *Meeting the British* by Paul Muldoon are reprinted with the permission of Wake Forest University Press. To Richard Murphy for lines from *Sailing to an Island, High Island, The Price of Stone* and *The Mirror Wall;* to Máire Cruise O'Brien for lines from Sean MacEntee's *The Poems of John Francis MacEntee;* to Faber and Faber Ltd for *Seize the Fire, The Strange Museum* and *Liberty Tree* by Tom Paulin, Faber and Faber Ltd; to Dennis O'Driscoll for lines from "Someone" from his volume *Kist;* to R. Dardis Clarke, 21 Pleasants Street, Dublin 8, for lines from *Night and Morning* and *Ancient Lights* by Austin Clarke; to Salmon Publishing, Ltd., for lines of Nuala Archer from *Two Women, Two Shores* and from *The Hour of Pan Ama,* for lines of Roz Cowman from *The Goose Herd,* for lines of Rita Ann Higgins from *Goddess & Witch,* from *Witch in the Bushes,* and from *Philomena's Revenge,* and for lines of Desmond O'Grady from *Tipperary.* To Carcanet Press Limited, for permission to quote the remarks on Austin Clarke from Thomas Kinsella's *The Dual Tradition: An Essay on Poetry and Politics in Ireland* (1995). To Bloodaxe Books Ltd for permission to use material by Åke Persson.

DICTIONARY OF
IRISH LITERATURE

M

Mac ANNA, FERDIA (1955–   ), novelist and playwright. Mac Anna was born in Dublin on August 17, 1955, the son of Tomás Mac Anna, the Abbey Theatre* director. For six years, under the inspired name of Rocky de Valera, Mac Anna traveled Ireland as a rock singer with the Gravediggers and the Rhythm Kings. However, he was plagued with ill health, suffered a brain hemorrhage, and survived a bout with cancer, which he describes in his short book *Bald Head* (1988). He has been arts editor of the *Evening Herald* and is now a television producer and director with RTÉ. He is married to Kathryn Holmquist.*

Both of his comic novels deal with eccentric families living in a village like Howth. The first, *The Last of the High Kings* (1991), is the more extravagant and farcical and tells of a summer in the life of seventeen-year-old Frankie Griffin, who is certain that he has failed his Leaving and so, unable to enter university, will have to run away to California. His actor father, who is off shooting a movie, his patriotic and religious mother, his young brother, who writes western novels of about six pages, his other brother, Noelie, who is charmingly not all there, his intense American cousin, who falls in love with him, and the barmy family dog, Parnell, are but a few of the well-etched, lovingly caught characters who are drawn into Frankie's successively disastrous encounters with life. When all seems at its bleakest, and Frankie, at his mother's behest, is being exorcised by a whiskey-sodden priest for dating a Protestant girl, his successful Leaving Cert results arrive and save the day. The writing is tight, light, and full of witty sentences like "her [piano] playing sounded like suet pudding being hurled into a wall." Or this parody/pastiche of pulp writing from one of the brother's novels: "Luke Odell stood up, the empty whiskey bottle dangling monstrously from his venomous hand."

The Ship Inspector (1994) is similar in tone, but more somber in theme. It is again about a young male hero with a kooky family, engaging friends, and lots of problems. In the present plot, however, Daniel Buckley is older than Frankie and works as a ship inspector at Dublin Airport. Some years earlier, the family's much-loved father had simply disappeared. His mother, who looks like Elizabeth Taylor, becomes a Fianna Fail T.D. before going ga-ga. His brother becomes a manic and usually off-key rock singer with the Silent Screams. His girlfriend leaves him. An older colleague at work has a terminal illness. In fact, the destinies of most of the characters end in failures that should be glumly depressing, and the book is rather more than the broad Saroyan entertainment of *The Last of the High Kings.* Again, though, the story is told with a wealth of comic observation and witty writing that is effectively at odds with the sadness of the action. A sad volume full of lines like, "I remember Maisie Dorney as a dour, stooped, religious maniac with a face like a boiled squirrel" is more comic-tragedy than mere entertainment.

A play, *Big Mom,* about a traveling rock group, appeared for two weeks in April 1994, at the Project.

WORKS: *Bald Head: A Cancer Story.* [Dublin]: Raven Arts, [1988]. (Nonfiction); *The Last of the High Kings.* London: Michael Joseph, 1991. (Novel); *The Ship Inspector.* London: Michael Joseph, [1994]; ed., *An Anthology of Irish Comic Writing.* London: Michael Joseph, 1995.

MACARDLE, DOROTHY [MARGARET CALLAN] (1899–1958), historian, novelist, and playwright. Macardle was born in 1899 to Anglo-Irish parents. Nevertheless, she became an avid Republican and a close acquaintance of Éamon de Valera. She was educated at University College, Dublin, and taught at Alexandra College, where she is said to have been arrested by the British. Between the wars, she served as a journalist at the League of Nations in Geneva. Following World War II, she worked for the cause of displaced and refugee children, producing the documentary *Children of Europe: A Study of Liberated Countries, Their War-time Experiences, Their Reactions and Their Needs* (1949).

Macardle's most important historical work is *The Irish Republic* (1937), a carefully documented, massive account of the political aspects of the Revolution, concentrating on the 1912–1923 era. While admitting that the narrative is written from the viewpoint of an Irish Republican, Macardle has consulted non-Republican and British authorities in an attempt at fairness and accuracy. In his preface to the work, de Valera heralds it as a "complete and authoritative record." He notes further that Macardle's "interpretations and conclusions are her own" and are sometimes at variance with his. A related political work is *Without Fanfares: Some Reflections on the Republic of Éire* (1946).

The human impact of the revolutionary period is studied by Macardle in several short stories written in Mountjoy and Kilmainham prisons and later collected in *Earth-Bound: Nine Stories of Ireland* (1924). The realistically portrayed situations include the midwinter cross-country evasion of the Black and Tans by two escaped prisoners, a young rebel's sacrifice of his life to prevent the capture of his "Chief," the hallucinatory experiences of a hunger-striking prisoner, and the troubling premonitions of a revolutionary's wife. Frequently, the ghosts of recent companions or heroes from former Irish uprisings make mystical interventions, saving the day. Supernatural visions also intrude into Macardle's nonpolitical stories about rural parish priests, a child nearly lost to the fairies, and a selfish, eccentric painter—a character type that reappears in Macardle's novels.

Macardle's plays include *Atonement* (1918), *The Old Man* (1925), *Witch's Brew* (1931), *The Loving Cup* (1943), and *Ann Kavanagh* (1937). The last-named drama, about the Rising of 1798, was first produced at the Abbey Theatre* on April 6, 1922. Like several of her stories, this play demonstrates the psychological stresses that revolutions impose on women. In this case, the heroine's compassion for the fugitive—be it her rebel husband or the spy he hunts—is stronger than political allegiances.

In her novels *The Uninvited* (1942; also filmed), *The Unforeseen* (1946; also published under the title *Fantastic Summer*), and *Dark Enchantment* (1953), Macardle places her characters in lonely situations, indulges extensively in the supernatural, an interest already detected in her stories, and manages to quiet the haunting forces and unite young couples in matrimony by the conclusion. An uninitiated heroine and a young hero concerned for her safety are usually featured characters. *The Uninvited* is a rather strung-out tale of double exorcism set in a haunted house on the North Devon cliffs. In *The Unforeseen,* the author explores a woman's gift of "precognition"—the power to have visions of future events—and the effects of this power on her own psyche and the lives of her daughter and their acquaintances. Macardle, aware of American research into ESP, hinges her plot on the difficulty of interpreting and acting on premonitions. This novel is set mostly in the Dublin hills near Glencree, near where Macardle spent much of her life. One of its strengths is the author's apparent interest in the Irish countryside, including the stone thrones of the Sugar Loafs, the churches of Glendalough, the woodland birds, and the itinerant tinkers. In *Dark Enchantment,* a busy novel set in the fictional village of St. Jacques in the Maritime Alps, Macardle studies the effects of a supposed sorceress on a superstitious village that seems at first to offer only relaxation and charm to a visiting Irish girl, her father, and a young student of forestry. All of Macardle's mystical mysteries are entertaining, but need not be taken as weighty fiction. Seemingly supernatural events often evoke very melodramatic reactions.

She died on December 23, 1958, in Drogheda.

BONNIE KIME SCOTT

WORKS: *Earth-bound: Nine Stories of Ireland.* Worcester, Mass.: Harrigan, 1924. (Short stories); *Tragedies of Kerry,* 1922–23. Dublin: Emton, [1924]; *Witch's Brew.* London: H. F. W. Deane, [1931]. (One-act play); *Ann Kavanagh.* New York: Samuel French, [1937]. (Play); *The Irish Republic.* London: Gollancz, 1937. (History); *The Children's Guest.* London: Oxford University Press, 1940. (One-act children's play); *Uneasy Freehold.* London: Peter Davies, [1942]/as *The Uninvited* in the United States, Garden City, N.Y.: Doubleday, Doran, 1942. (Novel); *The Loving-Cup.* London: Nelson, 1943. (One-act children's play); *The Seed Was Kind.* London: Peter Davies, 1944. (Novel); *Fantastic Summer.* London: Peter Davies, [1946]/as *The Unforeseen* in the United States, Garden City, N.Y.: Doubleday, 1946. (Novel); *Without Fanfares, Some Reflections on the Republic of Eire.* Dublin: Gill, 1946. (Pamphlet); *Children of Europe, A Study of the Children of Liberated Countries* . . . London: Gollancz, 1949/Boston: Beacon, 1951; *Shakespeare, Man and Boy.* George Bott, ed. London: Faber, 1961.

McARDLE, J[OSEPH] ARDLE (1934–   ), novelist. McArdle was educated in Monaghan, Limerick, and Dublin and has been barrister, lecturer, and business consultant. He was a founder of Co-op Books, which published his first novel, *Closing Time* (1982). Leland Bardwell* called it ''[a] worthy successor to *Under the Volcano,*'' which is a considerable overstatement, but this study of the alcoholic headmaster of a seedy private school in London is tightly written and effective, even though its many chapters are often as short as one page. There is nothing short about his 1987 novel, *Sin Embargo,* which is well over 300,000 words. It is ambitious, often well written, sprawls over decades, ranges from Ireland to Switzerland and Africa, and addresses portentous questions. Its greatest drawback is a lack of narrative thrust that has the reader frequently calculating how many hundred pages are left to go.

WORKS: *Closing Time.* Dublin: Co-op, 1982; *Sin Embargo.* [Dublin]: Odell & Adair, [1987].

Mc AUGHTRY, SAM (1921–   ), novelist, short story writer, and journalist. Mc Aughtry was born in Belfast and left school at the age of fourteen. During the war, he served in the Royal Air Force and afterward worked as a builder's laborer in London. He joined the Ministry of Agriculture in Belfast in 1947 and eventually retired as deputy principal. His stories and sketches contain many drolly entertaining vignettes of working-class Belfast.

WORKS: *The Sinking of the Kenbane Head.* Belfast: Blackstaff, 1977. (Autobiographical anecdotes); *Play It Again, Sam.* [Belfast]: Blackstaff, [1978]. (Stories); *Blind Spot and Other Stories.* [Belfast]: Blackstaff, [1979]. (Short stories); *Belfast Stories.* Belfast: Ward & River, 1981. (Stories); *Sam Mc Aughtry's Belfast.* Belfast: Blackstaff, 1981. (Stories and sketches); *Mc Aughtry's War.* Belfast: Blackstaff, 1985. (Autobiographical anecdotes); *Down in the Free State.* Belfast: Blackstaff, 1987. (Travel); *Touch and Go.* [Belfast]: Blackstaff, [1993]. (Novel); *Hillman Street High Roller: Tales from a Belfast Boyhood.* Belfast: Appletree, 1994. (Stories).

McAULEY, JAMES J[OHN] (1935–   ), poet. McAuley was born in Dublin and became a professor of English at Eastern Washington University in the United States. The pieces in his rather large collection *Recital* (1982) have a high percentage of real successes in them. The more formal poems, such as ''Identikit,'' ''Making an Impression,'' and ''Timepiece,'' stick in the mind, and the book is one to return to.

WORKS: *Observations. A Collection of Fourteen Poems.* Blackrock: Mount Salus, 1960; *A New Address.* Dublin: Dolmen, 1965; *Draft Balance Sheet. Poems 1963–1969.* Dublin: Dolmen, 1970; *After the Blizzard.* Columbia: University of Missouri Press, 1975; *Recital. Poems 1975–1980.* [Dublin]: Dolmen, [1982]; *The Exile's Book of Hours.* Lewiston, Idaho: Confluence, [ca. 1982]; *Coming and Going: New and Selected Poems.* Fayetteville: University of Arkansas Press, 1989.

McBREEN, JOAN (1946–   ), poet. McBreen was born in Sligo and has been a primary school teacher. With her family, she lives in Tuam, County Galway.

WORKS: *The Wind beyond the Wall.* Brownsville, Oreg.: Story Line, 1990; *A Walled Garden in Moylough.* [Galway]: Salmon, [1995]. REFERENCE: Brandes, Rand. "Interview with Joan McBreen." *Colby Quarterly* 28 (December 1992): 260–264.

McCABE, EUGENE (1930–   ), stage and television playwright, short story writer, and novelist. Eugene McCabe might be described as a writer's writer. Although the body of his work is small, he is held in high regard by his contemporaries. Born on July 7, 1930, in Glasgow, where his family lived until the outbreak of World War II, McCabe was mainly educated at Castleknock College and University College, Cork, where he began to write short stories. The London publisher Rupert Hart-Davis read one of the stories and invited McCabe to write a novel. Although the novel was a failure, he discovered he could write dialogue and wrote his first play, *A Matter of Conscience* (later adapted for television), which Hilton Edwards of the Gate Theatre* admired but did not stage. In 1954, McCabe took over management of the family farm outside Clones, County Monaghan, and thereafter combined farming with writing.

In the 1964 Dublin Theatre Festival, McCabe shared the critical honors with Brian Friel* when his first major play, *King of the Castle,* attracted a good deal of attention. A rugged, naturalistic piece, it remains McCabe's best play. It tells the story of Scober MacAdam, a powerful farmer, his wife, Tressa, who is childless because of his impotence, and Matt Lynch, a traveling farm laborer hired for the harvest and hired also by Scober to impregnate his wife. The result is tragic. With its frank treatment of a sexual theme, the play broke new ground in the Irish theater. *Breakdown* (1967) marked a shift to the bourgeois world of the new Ireland and to a sharp, satirical exposure of corruption. *Swift* (1969) was a major event at the Abbey Theatre,* marking not only McCabe's debut on the main stage but also the first and only time Sir Tyrone Guthrie directed there. Micheál Mac Liammóir* played Dean Swift. In spite of all of this talent, the production was a failure and may have arrested McCabe's theatrical career. His only other stage plays are *Gale Dale* (1979), written as pendant to *Pull Down a Horseman* (1966), both one-act plays exploring the character of the Irish poet-revolutionary Patrick Pearse.*

In 1972, *Swift* was successfully rewritten as an expressionistic study of Swift's madness that challenges comparison with Lord Longford's* *Yahoo.* In 1976, RTÉ also screened a much-admired trilogy on the violence in Northern Ireland, *Victims,* based on his stories "Cancer" and "Heritage" and his novella *Victims.* In 1979, his successful adaptation of Thomas Flanagan's* *The Year of the French* as a major drama series for RTÉ/Channel 4 enhanced McCabe's reputation further.

McCabe's fiction, the short stories, the novella, and the children's story *Cyril* culminated in the powerful novel *Death and Nightingales* (1992). Set in County Fermanagh in the early 1880s, the novel depicts Catholic–Protestant relations in a tale of love, murder, and revenge and may be read as an allegory of the conflict in Northern Ireland. "What I always have in mind when I write is the political situation." McCabe's voice is distinctive: penetrating, clear, and forthright. His honest style and unflinching confrontation of the violence inherent in the Irish character provide a refreshing antidote to the marketable charm of much Irish writing.

CHRISTOPHER MURRAY

WORKS: *Victims: A Tale from Fermanagh.* London: Gollancz/Cork: Mercier, 1976. (Novella and the stories "Cancer" and "Heritage"); *Heritage and Other Stories.* London: Gollancz, 1978/Dublin: O'Brien, 1985; *King of the Castle.* [Dublin]: Gallery/[Newark, Del.]: Proscenium, [1978]. (Play); *Pull Down a Horseman/Gale Day.* [Dublin]: Gallery, [1979]. (One-act plays); *Roma.* [Dublin]: Turoe & RTE, [1979]. (Television play with the short story from which it was adapted); *Cancer.* Newark, Del.: Proscenium, [1980]. (Television play with the short story from which it was adapted); *Cyril: The Quest of an Orphaned Squirrel.* Dublin: O'Brien, 1986 (Children's story); *Death and Nightingales.* London: Secker & Warburg, 1992. (Novel); *Christ in the Fields.* London: Minerva, 1993. (Novel). REFERENCES: "Eugene McCabe." In *Education and the Arts.* Daniel Murphy, ed. Dublin: Trinity College, 1987, pp. 175–182; Simion D. " 'This Place Owns Me': Eugene McCabe in Conversation with Simion D." *Irish Studies Review* 7 (Summer 1994): 28–30.

McCABE, PATRICK (1955–   ), novelist and playwright. McCabe was born in Clones, County Monaghan, and has worked as a remedial teacher in Balbriggan. One of his short stories received a Hennessy Award in 1979. He has also written a children's story and has had plays broadcast on the BBC and RTÉ. In 1992, his best-known novel, *Butcher Boy,* was short-listed for the Booker McConnell Prize and won the *Irish Times*/Aer Lingus Prize. A play based on it, *Frank Pig Says Hello,* was premiered at the 1992 Dublin Theatre Festival. Another play, *Loco County Lonesome,* was premiered with less success at the 1994 festival.

McCabe's first novel, *Music on Clinton Street* (1986), tellingly explores the effect of the modern world, with its rock music and drug culture, on rural Ireland and of how older values as embodied in the boys' school that the adolescent hero attends seek and fail to accommodate themselves to the new. Although a short novel, the theme is explored from several vantage points—that of the boy who hits a priest, that of the priest himself, who is dissatisfied with the old ways, that of the boy's older brother, who is battered into a zombielike state by the worlds of New York and London, that of the boy's father and friends, who are clinging nostalgically to a earlier time. The complex but controlled plot presents a vividly condemnatory picture of the Irish brave new world of the 1960s and 1970s. Even in this first book, McCabe appears as a frightening herald of a new generation of writers who are chronicling a very different generation of Irishmen in a rapidly changing society.

Carn (1989) is a novel about a handful of people who live in the small town of Carn near the Ulster border. In 1959, the town had gone into a decline when the railway closed down its branch line. In 1965, however, an entrepreneur gave new life to the town by opening a meat-processing plant and a glossy modern pub. Some of the characters still attempt to escape from Carn but are inevitably drawn back and, in various ways, have their lives blighted by the place. When the meat-processing plant closes, the town sinks back into decay and hopelessness. The novel is a strong, glum indictment of life in a small Irish town of yesterday, but the individual characters quickly fade from memory.

Butcher Boy (1992) is, on the other hand, a very arresting novel, and its vivid title character has been fairly described by the *New York Times* as "Part Huck Finn, part Holden Caulfield, part Hannibal Lector." At the beginning, Francie Brady is a childish boy who reads the *Beano* and retains much of a boyish innocence. Without quite ever losing those qualities, though, he grows more and more monstrous. In the reform school to which he has been sent, for instance, he is so little perturbed by a priest molesting him that he, in effect, controls the priest and extorts candy from him. The first-person narrative is a lively, funny, profane re-creation of his thoughts, without much punctuation but never without clarity and vividness:

I needn't have worried for they met the other girl and some of her friends hi! shouts the one and then they all went off together let them what did I care about them I had my own business to take care of right Francie I said let's mosey and in I went to the shop, I was just wondering what Joe was saying to her, maybe he was talking to her about music he was hardly talking to her about John Wayne—for fuck's sake!

McCabe's style is not basically clear and flat, however, for he inserts many striking comparisons that accurately reflect Francie's clever mind and sordid world: "Every two seconds Leddy'd draw in this big deep breath with the sound of snots like paper tearing." More important than the book's racy style, however, is its accurate depiction of the rough beast that has slouched into the 1990s to be born.

The Dead School (1995) is written in a flip, breezy, and highly individual conversational voice. It begins:

Boys and girls and I hope you are all well. The story I have for you this morning is all about two teachers and the things they got up to in the days gone by. It begins in the year of Our Lord 1956 in a maternity hospital in Ireland when a wee fat chubby lad by the name of Malachy fell out of Cissie who was married to Packie Dudgeon the biggest bollocks in town.

The chapters are quite short, even as short as a third of a page, but the action often continues uninterrupted from one chapter to another, and so this is really a stylistic strategy. It and the rather cutesy chapter titles—such as "Hello There," "Little Chubbies," and "Chirpy Chirpy"—quite reinforce the prose style.

The story is about two interwoven lives—that of Raphael Bell, who became headmaster of a school in Dublin, and that of Malachy Dudgeon, who, for a time, taught in the school. The deterioration of their lives, which leads to Raphael's madness and suicide and to Malachy's descent into drugged aimlessness, is full of sordid and depressing details that are in stark contrast to some chirpy and happier early incidents. The theme would seem to be twofold: the changing of traditional Irish values during the 1970s and the dying of love. With its accumulating grimness and yet cheery style, the book rises to some sadly moving moments. It will be few people's favorite novel, but there is much to be admired in it.

WORKS: *The Adventures of Shay Mouse, The Mouse from Longford.* [Dublin]: Raven Arts, [1985]. (Children's story); *Music on Clinton Street.* Dublin: Raven Arts, [1986]; *Carn.* London: Aidan Ellis, 1989; *Butcher Boy.* London & Basingstoke: Pan, 1992; *The Dead School.* [London & Basingstoke]: Picador, [1995].

McCALL, P[ATRICK] J[OSEPH] (1861–1919), poet and humorist. McCall was born in Dublin on March 6, 1861, and was educated at the Catholic University. He contributed both fictional sketches and poetry to the popular press around the turn of the century. As a popular writer, McCall was hardly considered a member of the Literary Revival, and some of his humorous retellings of the heroic stories were utterly opposed to its spirit. Nothing could be further from the manner and tone and spirit of Yeats'* misty and beautiful "The Wanderings of Oisin" (1889) than McCall's retelling of the stories in contemporary low dialect in *The Fenian Nights' Entertainment* (1897):

"Well, me lad," says Fan, stoopin' for another [stone] as big as a hill, "I'm sorry I have to bate you; but I can't help it," sez he, lookin' over at the Prencess Maynish, an' she as mute as a mouse watchin' the two big men, an' the ould king showin' fair play, as delighted as a child. "Watch this," sez he, whirlin' his arm like a windmill, and away he sends the stone, buzzin' through the air like a peggin'-top, over the other three clochauns, and then across Dublin Bay, an' scrapin' the nose off ov Howth, it landed with a swish in the say beyant it. That's the rock they calls Ireland's Eye now!

McCall's verses are smoother than much popular verse, but that is about all that can be claimed for them. He wrote the song "Herself and Myself," which O'Casey* used in "Nannie's Night Out." His most popular song is "Boulavogue." He died in 1919.

WORKS: *In the Shadow of St. Patrick's.* Dublin: Sealy, Bryers & Walker, 1894; *Irish Nóiníns (Daisies).* Dublin: Sealy & Bryers, 1894; *The Fenian Nights' Entertainments.* Dublin: T. G. O'Donoghue, 1897; *Songs of Erinn.* London: Simpkin, Marshall, 1899; *Pulse of the Bards.* Dublin: Gill, 1904; *Irish Fireside Songs.* Dublin: Gill, 1911.

McCANN, COLUM (1965–   ), novelist and short story writer. McCann was born in Dublin, the son of Sean McCann, a well-known journalist. He himself graduated from the journalism course at Rathmines College of Commerce and worked as a journalist in New York and Dublin. He spent two years bicycling all around the United States. He won two Hennessy Awards in 1990, and his collection of stories, *Fishing the Sloe-Black River,* won the Rooney Prize in 1994. He lives in Dublin and New York, and his stories are set both in Ireland and the United States. His collection is a very uneven one, in which the weaker stories tend to be propped up by a racy prose style, although even that can be a bit mechanical. The arresting phrase ''[a] dirge of girls'' in one story becomes ''[a] dirge of blind children'' in another. Nevertheless, in the best of the stories—''Step We Gaily, On We Go,'' ''Through the Field,'' and the superb ''Around the Bend and Back Again''—the racily colloquial writing vividly supports the characterization of the narrators. In these pieces, the praises of the book blurb do not really seem too fulsome.

McCann's novel, *Songdogs* (1995), tells of an unsuccessful Irish photographer who marries a beautiful Mexican woman and takes her to San Francisco, to Wyoming, and finally to Mayo. After she eventually disappears, their son attempts unsuccessfully to find her. The present action—or situation, really, for it has little action—shows the son visiting his scruffy and aging father in Mayo. The details, both in the present and in the past, are squalid, sordid, and sleazy, but overall the book has a sweetness about it, for its maimed characters have finally a tolerance and even love for each other. The prose is excellent.

WORKS: *Fishing the Sloe-Black River.* London: Phoenix House, [1994]. (Short stories); *Songdogs.* London: Phoenix House, [1995]. (Novel).

McCANN, JOHN (1905–1980), playwright and politician. McCann was born in Dublin on June 17, 1905, and educated by the Christian Brothers of Synge Street. He became a journalist and also wrote plays for Radio Éireann. In 1939, he was elected to the Dail, and in 1946–1947, he served as lord mayor of Dublin. In 1954, he lost his Dail seat, but by then his plays were being regularly produced by the Abbey Theatre.* Such pieces as *Twenty Years A-Wooing* (1954), *Blood Is Thicker than Water* (1955), *Early and Often* (1956), and *Give Me a Bed of Roses* (1957) were among the Abbey's biggest box-office draws during its long exile in the Queen's Theatre. The plays present a genial picture of lower-middle-class Dublin families, with stock comic characterization, topical allusions, a plot usually revolving around money, and a platitudinous theme. While much akin to today's television situation comedies, the plays do show a command of conventional stagecraft. The best of them, *Early and Often,* a well-observed study of Irish political machinations, may take an honorable place beside such worthy previous studies as William Boyle's* *The Eloquent Dempsy,* Edward McNulty's* *The Lord Mayor,* and John MacDonagh's* *The Irish Jew.* McCann died in Dublin in February 1980. The well-known actor Donal McCann is his son.

WORKS: *War by the Irish.* Tralee: Kerryman, [1946]. (Historical memoir); *Twenty Years A-Wooing.* Dublin: James Duffy, 1954; *Early and Often.* Dublin: P. J. Bourke, 1956; *I Know Where I'm Going.* Naas: Printed for the Author by the Leinster Leader, 1965.

MacCANN, PHILIP (ca. 1965–   ), short story writer. A character in MacCann's *The Miracle Shed* (1995) remarks, ''Then all of a sudden, nothing happens,'' and the point seems applicable to most of the stories and sketches in the book. One is left with the impression of a sleazy and sordid world in which sad characters named Fish and Vomit wander aimlessly about, "sigh putridly," suffer from the "hottest stink" of their lives, and reflect upon "the filth of our flesh" and the "piss and juice and the sweat between his sweet dirty arse." There is some talented, cutesy writing, such as "his jittery eyes, blue moons that typed on the day and bumped back every so often like somebody ironing the day with moons or tennis balls." The final story, "Naturally Strange," about an abandoned, pregnant wife who is contemplating abortion and coping with her randy adolescent son, is quite able, but MacCann's clever pen is so far solely in the service of the theme "Life's evil, Paula, that's my opinion."

The book won the first Kerry Ingredients Book of the Year Award at the 1995 Listowel Writers' Week.

WORK: *The Miracle Shed.* London & Boston: Faber, [1995]. (Short stories).

MacCARTHY, CATHERINE PHIL (1954–   ), poet. Born in Crecora, County Limerick, MacCarthy received an honours degree in English literature from University College, Cork, and did postgraduate work in drama at Trinity College, Dublin, and the Central School of Speech and Drama in London. She was the 1990 winner of the National Women's Poetry Competition and a Patrick Kavanagh* prizewinner in 1992. Eavan Boland* remarks of her book, *This Hour of the Tide* (1994), that the poems have "the sort of music that reaches outwards and into the memory." The diction of the poems is simple, terse, and unadorned, and the pieces are usually arranged in regular stanzas of two, three, four, or more lines. However, there seems no attempt at either rhythm or music, so, despite the stanzaic patterns, there is little formally to help the poems cling in the memory.

WORK: *This Hour of the Tide.* [Dublin]: Salmon, [1994].

MacCARTHY, DENIS FLORENCE (1817–1882), poet and translator. MacCarthy, the translator of Calderón, was born in Dublin in 1817 and died in Blackrock, County Dublin, on April 7, 1882. Today unread and unreadable, he was saluted by his contemporaries as Ireland's own Poet Laureate, the only true successor of Thomas Moore.* He contributed to Irish magazines with the copiousness that one would expect from a breadwinner for a wife and nine children. This burden can be regarded as an extenuating circumstance for his acceptance of the professorship of English literature in the local Catholic university and for his more frequent verse:

> An uncountable assemblage
> All recumbent in the fire:
> Through their bodies and their members
> Burning spikes and nails were driven . . .
> Vipers of red fire the entrails
> Gnawed of some; while others lying,

With their teeth in maniac frenzy
Bit the earth.

(From MacCarthy's translation of Calderón's *The Purgatory of Patrick*.)

ANDREW MARSH

WORKS: ed., *The Book of Irish Ballads*. Dublin: Duffy, 1846; *The Poets and Dramatists of Ireland*. Dublin: Duffy, 1846; trans., *Justina, a Play by Calderón de la Barca*. London: J. Burns, 1848; *Ballads, Poems and Lyrics, Original and Translated*. Dublin: J. McGlashan, 1850; trans., *Dramas of Calderón, Tragic, Comic, and Legendary*. London: C. Dolman, 1853; *The Bell-Founder, and Other Poems*. London: D. Bogue, 1857; *Underglimpses and Other Poems*. London: D. Bogue, 1857; *Irish Legends and Lyrics*. Dublin: McGlashan & Gill, 1858; trans., *Mysteries of Corpus Christi by Calderón de la Barca*. London: Duffy, 1867; trans., *The Two Lovers of Heaven*, by Calderón de la Barca. Dublin: John F. Fowler, 1870; *Shelley's Early Life from Original Sources*. London: J. C. Holten, [1872]; *The Centenary of Moore. May 28th, 1879. An Ode*. London: Privately printed, 1880; *Poems*. Dublin: Gill, 1882.

MacCARTHY, J[OHN] BERNARD (1888–1979), playwright and short story writer. A Cork realist,* MacCarthy (sometimes McCarthy) was born in Crosshaven, County Cork, on June 24, 1888. He worked most of his life as a postman in Crosshaven and was active in amateur theatrics there.

Although MacCarthy wrote of land-hunger and concern for reputation, the staples of Cork realism, he expanded its range to include seafaring life in plays such as *Wrecked* (1922), *The Sea-Call* (1917), and *The Long Road to Garranbraher* (1928). His fundamental tragic situation is a family caught in an ethical dilemma, a theme typified by the powerful *Crusaders* (1918): Father Tom Moran must choose between abandoning his successful temperance campaign or ruining his father's tavern business.

With one exception MacCarthy's best drama was produced by the Abbey*: *Kinship* (1914), *The Supplanter* (1914), *Crusaders* (1918), and *Garranbraher* (1923). The exception is *The Sea-Call,* a poignant tragedy of a man in love with the sea, and his childless wife who left the green quiet of inland Cork for the endless tumult of the Atlantic Coast.

Of MacCarthy's numerous farces written for amateur companies, *Dead Men's Shoes* (1919) is representative. Friends and relatives of Timothy Conroy, hearing a false report of his death, are squabbling over his possessions when he returns.

MacCarthy's poetry and fiction are more significant in quantity than in artistic merit. His legacy to Irish literature is a few strong, tightly wound tragedies. He died on January 18, 1979.

WILLIAM J. FEENEY

WORKS: *Wrecked*. Dublin: Gill, 1912. (Tragedy in one act); *The Sea-Call*. Dublin: Talbot, [1916]. (Tragedy in one act); *Crusaders*. Dublin: Maunsel, 1918. (Play in two acts); *The Shadow of the Rose*. Dublin: Talbot, 1919. (Poems); *The Romantic Lover*. Dublin: Gill, 1922. (Comedy in one act); *Cough Water*. Dublin: Gill, 1922. (Farce in one act); *The Men in Possession*. Dublin: Gill, 1922. (Farce in three acts); *The Rising Generation*. Dublin: Duffy, [1922?]. (Comedy in three acts); *Covert*. London: Hutchinson, [1925]. (Novel); *Possessions*. London: Hutchinson, [1926]. (Novel); *Exile's Bread*. London: Hutchinson, [1927]. (Novel); *The Able Dealer*. Dublin: Gill, 1928. (Farcical comedy in three acts); *The Down Express*. Dublin: Gill, 1928. (Farcical comedy in three acts); *Fine*

Feathers. Dublin: Gill, 1928. (Farcical sketch); *The Long Road to Garranbraher.* Dublin: Gill, 1928. (Play in one act); *Old Acquaintance.* Dublin: Gill, 1928. (Farcical comedy in one act); *Poachers.* Dublin: Gill, 1928. (Comedy in one act); *All on One Summer Day and Julia Josephine Goes First.* Dublin: Catholic Truth Society of Ireland, [1928]. (Stories); *Heirs at Law and Donny Takes a Wife.* Dublin: Catholic Truth Society of Ireland, [1928]. (Stories); *The Magic Sign and Allotments.* Dublin: Catholic Truth Society of Ireland, [1928]. (Stories); *The Crossing and The Six Months' Corner.* Dublin: Catholic Truth Society of Ireland, [1929]. (Stories); *The Life of Trade and At the Show.* Dublin: Catholic Truth Society of Ireland. [1929]. (Stories); *A Marriage of Convenience and The Betrayal.* Dublin: Catholic Truth Society of Ireland, [1929]. (Stories); *Rope Enough and Julia Maud Goes to the Races and The Passing of the Torch.* Dublin: Catholic Truth Society of Ireland, [1929]. (Stories); *The Valuation and A Musical Interlude.* Dublin: Catholic Truth society of Ireland, [1929]. (Stories); *Verbatim and The End of a Holiday.* Dublin: Catholic Truth Society of Ireland, [1929]. (Stories); *Wheels o' Fortune and Those Who Smile before Dawn.* Dublin: Catholic Truth Society of Ireland, [1929]. (Stories); *The Wooing of Michael and His Royal Highness.* Dublin: Catholic Truth Society of Ireland, [1929]. (Stories); *Who Will Kiss Cinderella?* [London]: George Roberts, 1929. (Romantic comedy in three acts); *Andy Takes an Outing.* Dublin: Catholic Truth Society of Ireland, [1930]. (Story); *Annie All-Alone.* Dublin: Catholic Truth Society of Ireland, [1931]. (Story); *Easy Money.* Dublin: Catholic Truth Society of Ireland, [1931]. (Story); *The Fiddle Men.* Dublin: Catholic Truth Society of Ireland, [1931]. (Story); *The Grain of the Wood.* Dublin: Gill, [1931]. (Comedy in three acts); *The Partition.* Dublin: Catholic Truth Society of Ireland, [1931]. (Story); *A Test of Intelligence.* Dublin: Catholic Truth Society of Ireland, [1931]. (Story); *Until Dawn.* Dublin: Catholic Truth Society of Ireland, [1931]. (Story); *The Valley Farm.* Dublin: Gill, [1931]. (Drama in three acts); *Bridget's Biddy.* Dublin: Gill, [1932]. (Play in one act); *Dead Men's Shoes.* Dublin: Duffy, [1932]. (Comedy in one act); *Over Cassidy's Counter.* Dublin: Catholic Truth Society of Ireland, [1932]. (Story); *Wheel of Fortune.* Dublin: Gill, [1932]. (Comedy in one act); *When a Man Marries.* Dublin: Gill, [1932]. (Comedy in two acts); *The Missing Prince.* Dublin: Gill, [1934]. (Fairy play in four scenes); *A Change in Partners and A Midsummer Knight's Dream.* Dublin: Catholic Truth Society of Ireland, 1935. (Stories); *The White Souls and A St. Patrick's Day Presentation and The Sweeterie.* Dublin: Catholic Truth Society of Ireland, 1935. (Stories); *Murtagh's Monument and The Skipper Strikes his Flag.* Dublin: Catholic Truth Society of Ireland, [1936]. (Stories); *Plays.* Dublin: Gill, [1936]. (Includes "Watchers for the Dawn," "Kinship," "Green Leaves," "Rolling Stones," "Widows are So Fascinating," "The Ugly Duckling," and "The Man for Mannarue"); *Green Leaves.* Dublin: Gill, [1936]. (Farce in one act); *The Man from Mannarue.* Dublin: Gill, [1936]. (Comedy in three acts); *Rolling Stone.* Dublin: Gill, [1936]. (Comedy in one act); *A Disgrace to the Parish and A Quiet One.* Dublin: Catholic Truth Society of Ireland, [1937]. (Stories); *Old Times and Toys.* Dublin: Catholic Truth Society of Ireland, [1937]. (Stories); *The Playboy of the Seven Worlds.* Dublin: Gill, 1944. (Comedy in four acts); *The Duplicity of David.* Dublin: Duffy, 1945. (Farce in one act); *The Gold Train.* Dublin: Gill, [1947]. (Farcical thriller in three acts); *Crime Comes to Ballyconeen.* Dublin: Gill, [1947]. (Drama in four acts); *You Might Call It a Day.* Dublin: Catholic Truth Society of Ireland, 1948. (Story); *Master of the House.* Dublin: Gill, [1950?]. (Play in three acts); *The Wide Open Spaces.* Dublin: Duffy, [ca. 1950]. (Comedy in one act); *The Town Museum.* Dublin: Duffy, [ca. 1950]. (Farce in one act); *Fair Play's Bonnie Play.* Belfast: Carter, 1951. (Comedy in one act); *The Land Where Dreams Come True,* with music and lyrics by B. Walsh MacCarthy. Dublin: Gill, 1952. (Comedy in one act); *One Day You'll Find It.* Dublin: Gill, 1953. (Comedy in three acts); *Marriage Is a Lottery.* Dublin (Farcical comedy in one act); *Ladies, Take Your Partners,* with music and lyrics by B. Walsh MacCarthy. Belfast: Carter, 1953. (Light comedy in two acts); *Mister Storm Along.* Dublin: Gill, 1960. (Drama in one act); *The White Jackdaw.* Dublin: Gill, [1960?]. (Comedy in one act).

McCARTHY, JIM (1954–), short story writer. McCarthy was born in Dublin and won a Hennessey Award for one of his stories in 1983.

WORK: *Sinead's Head.* Dublin: Brodir Books, 1994.

McCARTHY, JUSTIN (1830–1912), journalist, historian, and novelist. McCarthy was born in Cork on November 22, 1830, and became an incredibly prolific writer whose many books are now quite forgotten. Perhaps the most popular was his four-volume *A History of Our Own Times* (1879), which went into many editions. McCarthy was not an original writer, but a fluent and pleasant popularizer. He was a member of Parliament in the Irish party during the Parnell divorce case, and it was through him that Gladstone put pressure on Parnell to retire from the leadership. After the famous debate on the subject in Committee Room 15, McCarthy led the majority of the members out. Nevertheless, through all of the acrimony, McCarthy is said to have retained Parnell's friendship and, indeed, to have made no enemies at all. In 1904, he published a ten-volume anthology, *Irish Literature,* for which he enlisted the aid of Standish O'Grady,* W. B. Yeats,* Douglas Hyde,* AE,* Lady Gregory,* and others. Despite a preponderance of dross in its many pages, the work is still of interest and utility. McCarthy left public life in 1900 but continued to write by dictation up to 1911. He died at Folkestone on April 24, 1912.

PRINCIPAL WORKS: *A History of Our Own Times.* 4 vols. London: Chatto & Windus, 1879; *Reminiscences.* London: Chatto & Windus, 1899; *An Irishman's Story.* New York & London: Macmillan, 1904; ed., *Irish Literature.* 10 vols. Chicago: De Bower-Elliott, [1904].

McCARTHY, THOMAS (1954–   ), poet and novelist. Born in County Waterford, Thomas McCarthy has lived in Cork since the early 1970s. He was educated locally at Cappoquin, County Waterford, and later at University College, Cork, where John Montague* and Sean Lucy* were among his lecturers and where, with Seàn Dunne,* Bill Wall, and others, he organized a poetry workshop. He won the Patrick Kavanagh* Award in 1977 for his collection *The First Convention.* The book was published in 1978 and was admired by many reviewers. Other books of poems followed. He was a fellow of the International Writing Program at the University of Iowa in 1978–1979. In 1984, he won the Irish-American Foundation's literary award and in 1991 received the O'Shaughnessy Poetry Prize of the Irish-American Cultural Institute. For many years, he has worked as a library assistant with the Cork City Library, and he has also guided a number of workshops for aspirant writers, most significantly at Listowel Writers Week. In 1991, his first novel, *Without Power,* was published. Another, *Aysa and Christine,* appeared in 1992.

From the start, Thomas McCarthy's work has been seen mainly as an exploration of politics, society, and the self in contemporary Ireland. Reviewing *The First Convention,* Eavan Boland* declared: "This is that rare and long-awaited advent in Irish poetry: a glimpse of de Valera's Ireland, through the eyes of a poet born into the officially-declared Irish Republic. Here is a scrutiny of the dream in the punishing light of reality." The reality, for McCarthy, is linked with the internal workings of the Fianna Fail Party. His work constitutes an exploration of constituency politics as much as of idealism, and he has brought an essentially lyric impulse to bear on what might seem a mundane world of internal arguments, disappointments, and vituperative jostling. The characters in his poems include local party members and others who hold more senior positions in government, such as the benign health minister, spreading "his balsam of care." Other poems look at figures who combined politics and writing in various ways: Frank O'Connor,* Vladimir Nabokov, Andre Gide, Arthur Koestler. To twist a phrase of Philip Larkin, politics are for McCarthy what daffodils were for Wordsworth.

The political emphasis of his work has, perhaps, limited the way in which it has been examined, in the sense that it has allowed critics to ignore some of his other themes. He is a strong love-poet, for example, and also a considerable elegist: the title poem of *The Sorrow-Garden* (1981), a sequence for his late father, is among his strongest poems. He has also celebrated places—Waterford, Cork, and America—and in his first work there is a combination of intimacy and literary strength. His weaker poems tend to rely too much on anecdote or on the power of single lines, and they can sometimes display a prosaic slackness. It came as no surprise, then, that he should turn to prose as well. His novels also present vignettes from the world of party politics. In *Without Power,* local stalwarts face the prospect of losing power. In *Aysa and Christine,* the family life of a politician merges with the public world of politics in insidious and often damaging ways. Each has many memorable vignettes. As in all of McCarthy's work, there is a strong social awareness, driven perhaps by a memory of the "countless humiliations" his mother and others endured in an Ireland marked by a strong housing policy but also by poverty and emigration. As a novelist, he belongs to the tradition of Canon Sheehan* and Charles Kickham* rather than to a more purely literary canon. Such writers work from the particular manner in which politics and life can combine in the Irish countryside. In McCarthy's work, the Dail (the Irish Parliament) is as much a metaphor for human behavior as it is a present-day reality.

SEÁN DUNNE

WORKS: *Shattered Frost.* Cork: Miro, 1975. (Poems); *The First Convention.* Dublin: Dolmen, 1978. (Poems); *The Sorrow-Garden.* London: Anvil, 1981. (Poems); *The Non-Aligned Story-Teller.* London: Anvil, 1984. (Poems); *Seven Winters in Paris.* London: Anvil, 1989. (Poems); *Without Power.* [Swords, Co. Dublin]: Poolbeg, [1991]. (Novel); *Aysa and Christine.* [Swords, Co. Dublin:] Poolbeg, [1992]. (Novel). REFERENCE: Naiden, James. "Orphaned like Us: Memory in the Poetry of Thomas McCarthy." *Éire-Ireland* 26 (Summer 1991): 104–119.

McCRORY, MOY

WORKS: *The Water's Edge and Other Stories.* London: Sheba Feminist, 1985; *The Fading Shrine.* London: Flamingo (HarperCollins), 1991. (Novel); *Those Sailing Ships of His Boyhood Dreams.* London: Jonathan Cape, 1991. (Novel).

MacDERMOTT, W[ILLIAM] R[OBERT] (1838–1918), novelist. MacDermott was born in County Monaghan, educated at Trinity College, Dublin, and practiced medicine in Armagh, where he died. His *Foughilotra: A Forbye Story* (1906) is described by Stephen J. Brown as "[a] memorial of the Ulster handloom weavers. A sociological study, in form of a novel, of the history and development of a family.''

WORKS: As A.P.A. O'Gara: *The Green Republic: A Visit to South Tyrone.* London: T. Fisher Unwin, 1902. As MacDermott: *Foughilotra: A Forbye Story.* Dublin: Sealy, Bryers & Walker, [1906].

MacDONAGH, DONAGH (1912–1968), poet and playwright. MacDonagh was born on November 22, 1912, the son of Thomas MacDonagh,* one of the executed leaders of the 1916 Rising. About a year after his father's death, his mother drowned in a swimming accident. He received his early education at Belvedere College and then went to University College, Dublin, where he and his contemporaries—Niall Sheridan,* Denis Devlin,* Cyril Cusack the actor, Brian O'Nolan,* Charlie Donnelly* the young poet, and Mervyn Wall*—made up one of the liveliest student generations since the time of James Joyce.* Already in college, his main literary preoccupations were emerging. He and Sheridan published a joint volume, *Twenty Poems,* and with Liam Redmond, who was to become his brother-in-law, he staged the first Irish production of Eliot's *Murder in the Cathedral.*

He practiced at the bar from 1935 until 1941 when he was appointed a district justice, a position he retained until his death. He became a popular broadcaster on Radio Éireann which provided him a platform for his lifelong interest in folk ballads. His own plays are either poetic dramas or ballad operas in which, like John Gay, he wrote new words to traditional tunes. His most successful play was *Happy as Larry* (1946) which in a good production is an enchanting piece of theatre. It received a highly successful production in London, and an elaborate and extremely unsuccessful production by Burgess Meredith in New York. His ballad opera *God's Gentry* (Belfast Arts, 1951) about tinkers remains unpublished, but his excellent verse treatment of the Deirdre story, *Lady Spider,* appeared posthumously. His *Step-in-the-Hollow* (Gaiety, 1957) is a broad comedy of intrigue and mistaken identity with a Falstaffian main character. However, this work (and really all of MacDonagh's plays) are essentially theatrical rather than literary. Their language requires the immediacy of spoken speech or the extra dimension of song to lift them into a transient wit and eloquence. His words per se are too often flat and pedestrian, and even trembling on the verge of doggerel. In *Happy as Larry,* he will sometimes in the same passage use exact rhyme in a definite pattern and then suddenly shift into irregularity for no apparent reason. That is, he will rhyme exactly, then give an off-rhyme or an assonance, and then drop any similarity of sound entirely.

A similar thinness is noticeable in MacDonagh's small output of verse, though a few lyrics such as ''The Hungry Grass'' and ''Dublin Made Me'' will always find their places in anthologies. He was personally a quick and witty man; he died in Dublin on January 1, 1968.

WORKS: *Veterans and Other Poems.* Dublin: Cuala, 1941; *Happy as Larry.* Dublin: Maurice Fridberg, 1946/Dublin: Fridberg & Dolmen, 1967/included in *Modern Verse Plays,* E. Martin

Browne, ed. Harmondsworth, Middlesex: Penguin, 1958. (Play); *The Hungry Grass.* London: Faber & Faber, 1947. (Poems); *The Oxford Book of Irish Verse,* ed. with Lennox Robinson. Oxford: Clarendon, 1958; *Step-in-the-Hollow* in *Three Irish Plays.* Harmondsworth, Middlesex: Penguin, 1959. (Play); *Lady Spider,* edited and annotated by Gordon M. Wickstrom. *Journal of Irish Literature* 9 (September 1980): 3–82. (Play). REFERENCE: Hogan, Robert. *After the Irish Renaissance.* Minneapolis: University of Minnesota Press, 1967.

MacDONAGH, JOHN (?–1961), playwright and play director. MacDonagh was a versatile man of the theatre—producer, actor, author of plays and revues, a pioneer in the Irish motion picture industry, and productions director for Radio Éireann.

Because of his experience in English and American theatre he was appointed producer of the Irish Theatre in 1914. During the 1916 Rising he was with his brother Thomas* in the Jacob's Biscuit Factory garrison; afterwards he was interned for a few months in England. In addition to taking roles in most of the Irish Theatre plays, MacDonagh wrote two one-act comedies, *Author! Author!* (1915), a satire on peasant drama, and *Just Like Shaw* (1916), a mocking commentary on British officialdom in Ireland. *Weeds* (1919) was a serious three-act study of Irish landlordism.

Leaving the Irish Theatre in 1919, he worked with the Film Company of Ireland and later with Irish Photoplays. Among the pictures he directed were *Williy Reilly and his Colleen Bawn, Cruiskeen Lawn, The O'Casey Millions,* and *Wicklow Gold.*

MacDonagh's four-act comedy *The Irish Jew* was first performed at the Empire Theatre, Dublin, on December 13, 1921, and frequently revived. Its hero, Abraham Golder, Lord Mayor of Dublin, prevents an attempted swindle by members of the Corporation. For the commercial theatre MacDonagh wrote several revues, among them *Dublin To-night* (1924), *All Aboard for Dublin* (1931), and *Dublin on Parade* (1932), which offered home-grown talent and topicality as an alternative to the material presented by British touring companies.

As productions director of Radio Éireann from 1938 to his retirement in 1947, he created the popular quiz game "Question Time," wrote a satirical play *Attempted Murder* (the victim is the Stage Irishman), and on January 16, 1947, gave a short talk on his remembrances of Edward Martyn* and the Irish Theatre, as a prelude to a radio adaption of Martyn's *The Heather Field* on January 19.

Born in Cloughjordan, County Tipperary, MacDonagh died in Dublin on July 1, 1961.

WILLIAM J. FEENEY

WORKS: "Enterprise at the Irish Theatre." *New Ireland,* III (March 10, 1917), 293–295; *Just Like Shaw: A Play in One Act. The Dublin Magazine,* I (September 1923), 141–148; "Edward Martyn." *The Dublin Magazine,* I (January 1924), 465–467; *Author! Author! The Dublin Magazine,* I (February 1924), 621–628; "Film Production in Ireland in the Early Days." *Cinema Ireland 1895– 1976.* Dublin Arts Festival, 1976. REFERENCE: Boyd, Ernest. "The Work of the Irish Theatre." *The Irish Monthly,* XLVIII (February 1919), 71–76.

MacDONAGH, PATRICK (1902–1961), poet. MacDonagh was born in the North of Ireland in 1902. From the middle 1920s to the late 1950s, he published many poems in periodicals and in a few short volumes. The best of his work is gathered in the 1958 volume *One Landscape Still.* A comparison of that book with a collection of nearly thirty years earlier, *A Leaf in the Wind,* is rather instructive. The poems in *A Leaf in the Wind* seem for their day anachronistically conventional, and, if any poetic presence broods over the book, it is the spirit of Wordsworth (although John Hewitt* discerns Yeats,* AE,* and Richard Rowley*). Romantic in diction, conventional in technique, and full of nostalgic yearning for lost love, the book nevertheless manages a number of lines of compressed strength. *One Landscape Still* of thirty years later is discernibly by the same poet. The rue, the nostalgia, and the romance are still present, but so also are some satire and some bitterness. More impressive is the improvement in technique. There are still gaffes and failures, but in nearly half of the poems MacDonagh moves easily and impressively from the tight three-stressed line to the usually cumbersome six-stressed, from deft couplets and quatrains to fluent blank verse and even free verse. In any good subsequent anthology of modern Irish poetry, MacDonagh must be represented; the anthologist might do well to consider "One Landscape Still" or "Feltrim Hill" or the very impressive "The Bone-Bright Tree."

WORKS: *Flirtation, Some Occasional Verses.* Dublin: G. F. Healy, 1927; *A Leaf in the Wind.* Belfast: Quota, [1929]; *The Vestal Fire, a Poem.* Dublin: Orwell, 1941; *Over the Water and Other Poems.* Dublin: Orwell, 1943; *One Landscape Still.* London: Secker & Warburg, 1958.

MacDONAGH, THOMAS (1878–1916), patriot, poet, and man of letters. MacDonagh was born in Cloughjordan, County Tipperary, on February 1, 1878. Educated at Rockwell College, Cashel, he decided at an early age to enter the Holy Ghost Order, but gave up his vocation after a personal religious crisis, which is the subject of his first book of poems, *Through the Ivory Gate* (1902), an otherwise unremarkable volume. Like many of his generation, he joined the Gaelic League and held offices in league branches in Kilkenny and Fermoy, where he taught, respectively, at St. Kieran's and St. Colman's Colleges. Continuing to write poetry, he published *April and May* (1903), which in part echoes his first book and also Gaelic League nationalism, and *The Golden Joy* (1906), a volume influenced by his readings in Plotinus and Walt Whitman.

The year 1908 marked a turning point in his life. He came to Dublin and joined Patrick Pearse* at St. Enda's, a school founded on Gaelic League principles. St. Enda's introduced him to an expanding circle of acquaintances— Martyn,* Hyde,* and Yeats,* among many others—and the production of his first play, *When the Dawn Is Come,* by the Abbey* in October 1908 established him as a minor literary figure. In its earliest drafts, *Dawn* was a play about a poet/patriot who, by means of his poetry, inspires the Irish to rebellion and freedom from a foreign power. Much revised on guidelines suggested by Yeats and Synge,* the play in its final form has stilted dialogue, a lopsided construction, and, ironically, a purely nationalist message. The Abbey production left MacDonagh embittered. More disappointment followed, in the form of a frustrated love affair with Mary Maguire* (later Mrs. Padraic Colum*), and in the late spring of 1910, he left Dublin for a summer of isolation in Paris.

MacDonagh returned from Paris in September 1910 and moved to Grange House Lodge, determined to live a hermit-like existence in the foothills of the Dublin mountains. But, as James Stephens* has said in his introduction to *The Poetical Works of Thomas MacDonagh* (1916), "he fled into and out of solitude with equal precipitancy." Rejoining Pearse at nearby St. Enda's, he commenced studies toward the M.A. at University College, Dublin. His Master's thesis, *Thomas Campion and the Art of English Poetry* (published in 1913), contains a fairly unoriginal study of Campion's life and work, and then, by MacDonagh's own admission, it digresses into a treatise on English prosody, dividing poetry into "speech verse" and "song verse." During this period he also wrote a play, *Metempsychosis* (produced by the Theatre of Ireland in April 1912), in which Yeats is satirized as Earl Winton-Winton de Winton, a visionary type who believes in the transmigration of souls. *Metempsychosis* shows considerably more talent than *Dawn* in that it is an amusing, and very actable, drawing room comedy. Poems of this period, *Songs of Myself* (1910), also show signs of advance in MacDonagh's literary capabilities. "John-John" is straightforward and colloquial in language, a rejection of the stilted, conventional manner of his earlier work.

The happiest period of MacDonagh's adult life began with his marriage to Muriel Gifford on January 3, 1912. Now steadily employed at University College and working with Stephens and Colum (and, later, Joseph Plunkett*) in editing *The Irish Review,** he seemed destined for the life of an academic, and one with literary aspirations. *Lyrical Poems* (1913) contained healthy revisions of earlier work and some new pieces—"The Yellow Bittern," "The Man Upright," and "The Night Hunt"—which indicate, as did "John-John," that he had found an original poetic voice. He also began a study of Anglo-Irish literature, the result of which was *Literature in Ireland,* published posthumously in 1916. A very uneven book, *Literature in Ireland* is nonetheless significant because it is the acknowledgment of an Irish Catholic nationalist that Anglo-Irish literature, and language, had arrived as the literature and speech of the Irish people. MacDonagh concluded that the Irish language had caused a "prose intonation" and "conversational tone" in the poetry written in English, i.e., Anglo-Irish, in modern Ireland. He called this influence "the Irish Mode."

All the manuscript evidence suggests that MacDonagh never had enough time, or scholarly discipline, to devote to the book: as much as a third of the material had been published previously as book reviews or articles. With the formation of the Irish Volunteers in November 1913, he entered the last, fateful phase of his life. Ever a joiner of idealistic causes, he embraced Volunteer activities to such an extent that literature became a minor part of his life. The years 1914 and 1915 saw piecemeal work on *Literature in Ireland,* some poetry (including some very jingoistic marching songs), a realistic play, *Pagans,* done as part of Edward Martyn's ill-fated Irish Theatre* venture, and a great deal of organizing, speaking, and parading for the Volunteer movement. Despite these latter activities, there is no evidence to prove that he was a confidant in the planning of the Easter Rising. As Marcus Bourke has suggested (*Irish Sword,* summer 1968), he probably became involved at the last moment as an intermediary between Pearse and Eoin MacNeill, when MacNeill attempted to abort the Rising.

MacDonagh commanded the garrison at Jacob's Biscuit Factory—a post which saw little action—during the Rising itself, and for his part was executed on May 3, 1916. His participation in the Rising has, over the years, distorted the meaning of his literary work. It is doubtful that he was, as Loftus has suggested in *Nationalism and Modern Anglo-Irish Poetry* (1964), a Messianic idealist, or that the Easter Rising was, for him, a "blood sacrifice." Rather, he was a fairly ordinary man, one who could never give to any single aspect of his life the concentration it deserved. He loved literature and life but was, finally, a victim of his enthusiastic nature.

JOHANN A. NORSTEDT

WORKS: *Through the Ivory Gate.* Dublin: Sealy, Bryers & Walker, [1902]; *April and May, with Other Verses.* Dublin: Sealy, Bryers & Walker, [1903]; *When the Dawn Is Come.* Dublin: Maunsel, 1908/Chicago: De Paul University, 1973. (Play); *Songs of Myself.* Dublin: Hodges Figgis, 1910; *Lyrical Poems.* Dublin: Irish Review, 1913; *Thomas Campion and the Art of English Poetry.* Dublin: Hodges Figgis, 1913. (Criticism); *Literature in Ireland: Studies Irish and Anglo-Irish.* Dublin: Talbot, 1916. (Criticism); *The Poetical Works of Thomas MacDonagh.* James Stephens, ed. Dublin: Talbot/London: Unwin, 1916; *Pagans.* London: Talbot/London, Unwin, 1920. (Play); *Poems,* selected by his sister. Dublin: Talbot, [1925]. REFERENCES: MacDonagh, Donagh. "Plunkett and MacDonagh." In *Leaders and Men of the Easter Rising: Dublin 1916.* F. X. Martin, ed. London: Methuen, 1967; Norstedt, Johann A. *Thomas MacDonagh, A Critical Biography.* Charlottesville: University of Virginia Press, 1980; Parks, Edd Winfield & Aileen Wells Parks. *Thomas MacDonagh: The Man, the Patriot, the Writer.* Athens: University of Georgia Press, 1967.

MacDONNELL, ENEAS (1783–1858), novelist and political pamphleteer. MacDonnell was born in Westport, County Mayo, and educated at Tuam and Maynooth. He edited the *Cork Chronicle* in 1816 and was jailed for six months for one of his articles. He was a prolific pamphleteer for Catholic rights. He died in Laragh, County Wicklow.

LITERARY WORK: *The Hermit of Glenconella.* London: G. Cowie, 1820.

McDONNELL, GERRY (1950–), poet. Born in Dublin and educated at Trinity College, McDonnell edited the college literary magazine, *Icarus,* and for a time coedited the satirical magazine *Blazes.* He completed an M. A. at Dublin City University and is currently research and publications officer with the National Council of Education Awards, in Dublin.

His poems have appeared in *The Honest Ulsterman, Salmon,* and *The Journal for the Irish Forum for Psychoanalytic Psychotherapy* and have been anthologized. His first collection, *From the Shelf of Unknowing and Other Poems*

(1991), contains a Foreword in which Brendan Kennelly* remarks that the book "moves constantly between poles of loneliness and connection." He also describes the poems as "quietly impressive." In essence, the poems are reflective, combining images and personalities from childhood and early adulthood with philosophical speculation. Always, the city of Dublin plays an essential part.

McDonnell has also written a radio play based on the life of James Clarence Mangan,* as well as the libretto for a chamber opera about Mangan, with music by John Byrne.

FRED JOHNSTON

WORK: *From the Shelf of Unknowing and Other Poems.* Dublin: Cluain, [1991].

MacDONNELL, RANDALL WILLIAM (1870–?), novelist and poet. MacDonnell was born in Dublin, educated at University College, Dublin, became an engineer, and between 1895 and 1905 wrote several treatises on steam engines and locomotives. His historical novels often use for verisimilitude the device of a memoir or diary written by the leading character. His popular *Kathleen Mavourneen* of 1898 had, by 1935, gone into its eighth impression.

WORKS: *Kathleen Mavourneen: A Memory of the Great Rebellion.* London: T. Fisher Unwin, 1898; *The Perfect Rest and Other Verses.* Dublin: M. H. Gill, 1903; *When Cromwell Came to Drogheda: A Memory of 1649, Edited from the Record of Clarence Stranger, a Captain in the Army of Owen Roe O'Neill.* Dublin: M. H. Gill, 1906; *The Irish Squireens, and Other Verses.* Dublin: Sealy, Bryers & Walker, M. H. Gill, 1906; *My Sword for Patrick Sarsfield. A Story of the Jacobite War in Ireland. Edited from the Memoirs of Phelim O'Hara (1668–1750), a Colonel in Sarsfield's Horse.* Dublin: M. H. Gill, 1907; *Ardnaree: The Story of an English Girl in Connaught Told by Herself and Edited from the Original MSS.* Dublin & Waterford: M. H. Gill, 1911; *A Study in Starlight, and Other Poems.* Dundalk: W. Tempest, Dundalgan, 1919; *Songs of Seaside Places, and Other Verses.* Dublin & Cork: Talbot, [1932].

McDONNELL, VINCENT (1951–   ), novelist. McDonnell worked as a service engineer in London for many years and now lives near Swinford, County Mayo, with his family. In 1978, he won the *Ireland's Own* short story competition and published several stories in that popular magazine. His novel *The Broken Commandment* (1988) was short-listed for the Guinness Peat Aviation Award in 1989, but most of the judges favored John Banville's* *The Book of Evidence,* which did receive the prize. One judge, Graham Greene, held out strongly for McDonnell's novel, and so a special prize, the Guinness Peat First Fiction Award, was given to it. It is easy to see why the novel would appeal to Greene, for it is generally about a man's tormented rejection of God. In its first 100 pages, the novel depicts the wrenching situation of a man whose terrible wife has had an auto accident after storming out of the house after a quarrel. The accident necessitated the amputation of a leg, and the husband's dilemma is whether to consent to a possibly fatal operation to save the other leg or to consent to its amputation. The situation is complicated by his mistress, Barbara, and by his two children. The novel fails not so much in the intensity with which McDonnell depicts the husband's increasing guilt but by a succession of incidents that pile horror upon horror—the disappearance of one of the children, the wife's attempted suicide, the mistress's leaving pills where the wife can reach them, the wife's being reduced to a vegetable, the husband's confession that he left the pills, the pregnant mistress's death in an auto accident, and the husband's final smothering the wife to death in the hospital. It would take an extraordinary talent to pull off such a Grand Guignol plot, but McDonnell in his writing constantly descends to portentous writing, so that the effect is finally that of an extravagant Jacobean blood tragedy without the compensating per-fervid genius of a Webster, a Ford, or a Tourneur. The book is certainly striking, but not finally the masterpiece its talented author was striving for.

Imagination of the Heart (1995) is better written, although many paragraphs are pervasively, pejoratively slanted in their diction, imagery, and figurative language. To cite one typical instance: "Her face powder was flaking, and re-sembled the scales of skin my father used to scrape from the soles of his feet with his cut-throat razor." Despite a mildly upbeat ending, the novel is basically a grisly and graphic account of child molestation in a western town. Much of the authorial tone and attitude is symbolically suggested by an overwhelming stench from the local sewer. Although the protagonist has a pervading sense of disgust at himself and others, the book is not without some moments of com-passion. They are much needed in this strong and horrendous volume.

WORKS: *The Broken Commandment.* London: Reinhart Books in association with Viking, 1988; *Imagination of the Heart.* [Dingle, Co. Kerry]: Brandon, [1995].

MacDONOGH, STEVE (1949–   ), poet and publisher. MacDonogh was born in Dublin and educated at Rugby. He was a cofounder of the Irish Writers' Co-op in 1976 and also of Brandon Books in 1984.

WORKS: *York Poems.* York, 1972; *My Tribe.* Dublin: Beaver Row, 1982. (Poetry); *Green and Gold: The Wren Boys of Dingle.* Dingle, Co. Kerry: Brandon, 1883; *By Dingle Bay and Blasket Sound.* [Dingle, Co. Kerry]: Brandon, [1991].

McDOWELL, PATRICIA AAKHUS (fl. 1990s), novelist. McDowell is an American with Cherokee, as well as Irish, blood.

WORKS: *Daughter of the Boyne.* Dublin: Wolfhound, 1992; *The Voyage of Mael Duin.* Dublin: Wolfhound, 1993; *The Sorrows of Tara.* Dublin: Wolfhound, 1995.

McELDOWNEY, EUGENE (fl. 1990s), novelist. McEldowny was born in Bel-fast and is now an assistant editor with the *Irish Times* and lives with his family in Howth. His first novel, *A Kind of Homecoming* (1994), is the first of a pro-jected series of thrillers set in contemporary Belfast. Its protagonist, Superinten-dent Cecil Megarry, is a middle-aged man who drinks too much, is separated from his wife, and is full of guilt for his daughter's anorexia. He has become a workaholic policeman to assuage his guilt about his own father's having been killed by a bomb meant for him. This is a thoroughly professional story, leanly written, and with lots of dialogue and dramatized scenes. However, in finding his own version of the popular thriller, McEldowney breaks no new ground. Dick Francis has exploited his formula for horse-racing thrillers for over thirty best-selling books, but Francis's endings are upbeat and jolly. McEldowney's debut, with its mainly two-dimensional characters and particularly with its sourly disillusioned tone, à la John le Carré, does not augur well for such popularity.

WORKS: *A Kind of Homecoming.* London: Heinemann, [1994]; *A Stone of the Heart.* London: Heinemann, [1996].

MacENTEE, SEÁN (1899–1984), politician and poet. MacEntee was born in Belfast and educated at St. Malachy's College there and at the Belfast College of Technology. He was sentenced to death for his part in the Easter Rising, but that sentence was commuted to life imprisonment. He was released in the general amnesty of 1917 and elected as Sinn Féin member for Monaghan in 1918. He became a prominent Fianna Fail politician and served as Tanaiste (deputy prime minister) from 1959 to 1965 and also, at various times, as minister for health, for industry and commerce, and for local government. He retired in May 1969, and he died on January 9, 1984.

In 1917, a collection of his poems appeared with the title *The Poems of John Francis Mac Entee.* In content, it is romantic, patriotic, and pious; in diction, it is generally quite old-fashioned, using words like "hath" and "hast," "saist," "perchance," "guerdon," and "gyves." The opening apostrophe of "To Her Who Is Most Beautiful and Beloved" is not untypical:

> Rose of Love's coronal! flaming, perfervid,
>   Red-hearted passionate flower of the morn,
> Torch of Astarte! lambent and splendid. . . .

On occasion, however, MacEntee could be simple and effective, as in this first stanza of "The Vagabond":

> The long white road, the open road
> With the wind swept in from the sea,
> The bending trees and the shivering corn
> And the fight with the rain for me.

Indeed, the final poem in the collection, "Retrospection," is both simple and eloquent. He was the father of Máire Mhac an tSaoi, the Irish-language poet.

WORK: *The Poems of John Francis Mac Entee.* Dublin: Talbot, [1917].

McFADDEN, ROY (1921–   ), poet and editor. McFadden was born in Belfast on November 14, 1921, the son of an Irish bank official and an English mother. He was educated at Regent School House, Newtownards, County Down, and graduated to become a solicitor from Queen's University, Belfast, in 1944. He has lived for most of his life in Belfast, which may account for his stoical fortitude, and the troubled city is the source of much of his poetry. Since Belfast, like all Irish urban districts, is invincibly interpenetrated by the country, the poet's eye is not entirely focused on "insouciant streets" but takes in the sad beauties of Antrim and Down as well. Unlike MacNeice,* he is only confessionally "banned from the candles of the Irish poor," being manifestly aware of their crucifixion by history.

Any artist who has lived in Ulster for the lifetime of its separate state— McFadden's birth year is full of gnomic significance—has to face a political provincialism more stultifying than any comparative regionalism. The one-third nationalist underclass could at least feel themselves whole and part of a future reunited Ireland. A man of McFadden's temper could neither take this cozy line nor yet accept the ingrowing paranationalism of Orangeism. He can feel in the tribal drumming "a masturbation struggling for release" and be appalled at the underlying violence. Philip Hobsbawn called him a "war poet," and Ulster kept him supplied with material.

One is conscious of a man steeped in a European culture, wishing to slough off his state of being "oxtered by history" and yet finding himself responsive to the numinous pull of place. It is very possible that the twenty-four-year gap between his collection *The Heart's Townland* (1947) and his next substantial collection, *The Garryowen* (1971), was ended by the province's turmoil; he might well have been hurt into poetry. Certainly, the title poem of the new collection, a celebration of the game that makes Ireland united, seeks in some such fusion "an Irish remedy for rout." The paradox continues that McFadden, who is a quiet, perhaps even introverted man and whose poetry is often about himself, his family, the sweet sadness of children's growing up and away, should have been one of the least rhetorical but most effective delineators of "the hostile territory . . . symbolised / By the bricked-up hotel / Inside a cage to keep the bombers out." As this is being written, peace in Ulster is beginning to toddle. Possibly, McFadden's is the voice to look out for in the future: its vatic utterances should have most virtue—and grace.

A sequence of poems, "Sketches of Boz," in *Letters to the Hinterland* (1986) about "the abandoned unforgiving boy," in which Maria Beadnell is justly accused that "she brought it on herself," shows an impressive appreciation of Dickens and gives a hint of what the poet's preoccupations might have been if he could have lived elsewhere in the world.

As well as poetry, McFadden has written short stories for various periodicals and been editor and coeditor of several anthologies of Irish writing. He and Barbara Hunter edited *Rann,* a poetry quarterly, from 1948 to 1953. Now retired from his legal practice, he continues to write; a volume of collected poems is due in 1996.

SEAN McMAHON

WORKS: *Three New Poets,* with Alex Comfort & Ian Serrailier. Billericay, Essex: Grey Walls, 1942; *A Poem: Russian Summer.* Dublin: Gayfield, 1942. (Pamphlet poem); *Swords and Ploughshares.* London: Routledge, 1943; ed., with Robert Greacen. *Ulster Voices.* Belfast: Ulster Voices, 1943; ed., with Robert Greacen. *Irish Voices.* Belfast: Ulster Voices, 1943; *Flowers for a Lady.* London: Routledge, 1945; *The Heart's Townland.* London: Routledge, 1947; ed., with Barbara Hunter. *Rann.* Lisburn, Co. Antrim: Lisnagarvey, 1948–1953. (Literary magazine); *Elegy for the*

Dead of the Princess Victoria. Belfast: Lisnagarvey, 1953. (Pamphlet poem); *The Garryowen.* London: Chatto & Windus, 1971; *Verifications.* Belfast: Blackstaff, 1977; *A Watching Brief.* Belfast: Blackstaff, 1978; *The Selected Roy McFadden.* John Boyd, ed. Belfast: Blackstaff, 1983; *Letters to the Hinterland.* Dublin: Dedalus, 1986; *After Seymour's Funeral.* Belfast: Blackstaff, 1990; *Collected Poems.* Belfast: Lagan, 1995. REFERENCES: Brown, Terence. *Northern Voices.* Dublin: Gill & Macmillan, 1975, pp. 128–140; Longley, Michael. In *Causeway: The Arts in Ulster.* Belfast: Arts Council of Northern Ireland, 1971.

McGAHERN, JOHN (1934–   ), novelist, short story writer, and dramatist. Born on November 12, 1934, the son of a police officer and a schoolteacher, McGahern was raised in Ballinamore and Cootehall, County Leitrim. He was educated at Presentation College, Carrick-on-Shannon, at St. Patrick's College, Drumcondra, and at University College, Dublin. He taught at St. John the Baptist Boys National School in Clontarf for seven years until he won a Macauley fellowship in 1964 for his novel *The Barracks* (1963), the early chapters of which had won him the first AE* Memorial Award in 1962. His second novel, *The Dark,* appeared in 1965, and that same year he married the Finnish theatrical producer Annikki Laaksi.

The Irish Censorship Board banned *The Dark* in June 1965, and its author was dismissed, without explanation, from his teaching post that autumn. When his dismissal became publicly known the following spring, there was a furious controversy, and futile attempts were made to have McGahern reinstated. He moved to London and lived for a time in Spain and the United States before returning to a small farm in County Leitrim in 1974 with his American wife, Madeline Green. He has been a visiting professor at many universities, including Colgate (United States), Durham (U.K.), Victoria (Canada), and University College, Dublin. Since 1971, all of his work has been translated into French. He has won the Irish-American Foundation Award (1985), the title of Chevalier des Arts et Lettres (France, 1989), the *Irish Times*/Aer Lingus Fiction Prize (1990), and an honorary doctorate from Trinity College, Dublin (1991).

McGahern's poetic vision is grim. His mode of existentialism intellectualizes his melancholic temperament and the defeatist culture in which it immerses its characters. Within these confines and brooding over a black hole of inner silence, his characters, incapable of emotional intimacy, allow the rituals of social, familial, and religious life to thwart their need to love one another. His rural poor or their city cousins take little or no comfort from community relations, and impervious to the consolations of art or religion, they merely get along with one another. His highly disciplined fiction registers the dissonances between generations, sexes, and classes, appalled by the enclosed and enclosing silences. His characters move through a predatory clime, victims and victimizers, driven by greed, hatred, and want of feeling, but most of all by an existential fear of their own annihilation. They grope for frayed material consolations or flay their dependents, collapsing back upon themselves in desperate acceptance of their approaching ends. Thus, a modish despair pervades McGahern's fiction; and the usual enemies—naively devoted females, benighted clerics, fatuous bourgeoisie—form the pathetic opposition. What rescues McGahern's vision from bathos is his technical mastery of narrative. Within its chosen limits, McGahern's fiction, at its best, is uniquely powerful in Irish writing. He requires slow reading.

In *The Barracks,* Elizabeth Reegan has returned to a small Irish village to marry the local police sergeant, a widower with a young family. Already oppressed by the monotonous provinciality and her husband's truculent grappling with his servile rounds, she discovers that she is dying of cancer. Against a background of the indifferent sounds of the countryside, the church rituals, the comings and goings at the barracks, punctuated by ritual dark humor and occasional fumbling affection, she does quiet, heroic battle with death and despair. McGahern's portrait of Elizabeth is a triumph: she is marvelously observed, thoughtful, sympathetic, and entirely credible. Her relationship with Reegan, however, lacks the same clarity. The domestic interiors, dialogue, and local color of this dull Shannon backwater are unerringly rendered. The major achievement of the novel is its technical control: the spare, cool, narrative style; the disciplined, unsentimental management of descriptive detail; and the assured handling of interior monologue and flashback. The tension between the desire for security and the fear of petrifaction is a major theme, but, more profoundly, *The Barracks* redefines the impact of a not quite articulate agnosticism on an imagination shaped by the mores of provincial Irish Catholicism.

In the story of a tortured adolescent, *The Dark* commits to confessional form essentially the same vision, yet without the flashes of mystical joy of *The Barracks.* The anonymous protagonist is emotionally thwarted by the loss of his mother, an ambiguous relationship with his father, repressive religious training, poverty, and an examination-ridden school. The conflicts among his emotional needs, ambitions, and these constrictions make for a bleak and desperate farce. The banning of this novel—no doubt because of its frank depiction of masturbation and suggestions of homosexuality in father and priest—may have dramatized its relevancy in Ireland, but it also deflected attention from McGahern's achievement: the grim, humorless, spartan narrative and the depiction of the hero, caught between hopelessly irreconcilable needs, as depersonalized. The effect, however, tends to undermine the reader's belief in the hero's final realization of his personal independence despite the encircling futility.

The "leave" in the title of McGahern's third novel, *The Leavetaking* (1974) is taken from the guilt and repression of Ireland to the commitment of adult human love. Much of this work is a review of the road traveled in the first two, resolved by Patrick's idyllic love affair and marriage to an American (who is escaping her debilitating past). Although the first half contains some of McGahern's most lyrical prose, the rest—depicting the American businessman, his daughter, the tryst—is singularly mawkish. The novel is not an advance over the earlier works, where the sense of loss is modulated by a poised phrase or a measured silence. Here the commitment takes shape in a language that, for all its passionate overtones, springs from relative emotional shallows.

The Pornographer (1979) interweaves the stories of a writer of low-grade pornography with those of his characters. For all the humor of its parodic sexuality, this portrait of a writer's moral confusion is not successful. The reader is not made to care about the fate of so detached a figure. The eleven-year wait for McGahern's next novel, *Amongst Women* (1990), was amply justified: by general account, his finest work. Michael Moran, a former member of the old Irish Republican Army, has soured on what he and his comrades have delivered. Disdaining a part in the new political order, he ruthlessly overmasters his own family. He manipulates his wife, deflates his daughters' aspirations, and with obscene violence descends on his sons. It is at once an exposé of patriarchy, a postcolonial fable, an archetypal tale of generational change, and another existential meditation in McGahern's characteristic mode. For all his inscrutable silences and authoritarianism, Moran is slowly revealed to us as a self-made, willful man who defies conventional expectations and derives no solace from the rituals of family, society, or sect: a true existential hero. In bringing this complex figure to life, McGahern exercises his many gifts of narrative organization, poetic language, and symbol, with consummate skill. Moran's epiphany of acceptance—not blessedness—is profoundly touching.

Collected Stories (1992) compiles his three volumes, *Nightlines* (1970), *Getting Through* (1978), and *High Ground* (1985), along with a brief, late story, "The Creamery Manager," and a novella, "The Country Funeral": thirty-four stories in all. As in his novels, his steely keen sketches of rural Ireland show him at his best. Speech rhythms are always true; symbols are cunningly chosen; and the prose oscillates between unflinching objectivity and guarded lyricism. These devices reveal the void beneath the joviality of Irish life: in the words of one of his characters, he "refines our ignorance." The choices here—"Korea," "All Sorts of Impossible Things," "Gold Watch," and "The Country Funeral"—are sterling examples of his fine observation, economy, understatement, carefully weighed diction, and well-crafted meshing of psychology and symbol. The effect of these miniature, grim pastorals is indelible.

In all of McGahern's work, the subject is the same: "the soul's incurable loneliness." Conciliations are private matters: Moran's epiphany in *Amongst Women* or Philly's in "A Country Funeral." In each case, the truce is with the silent landscape of home, with Moran's fields or Philly's Gloria bog. John McGahern's postreligious imagination has translated the hedgerows and waterways of the upper Shannon and the accents of Breffni into chilling existential metaphors.

CÓILÍN OWENS

WORKS: *The Barracks.* London: Faber, 1963/New York: Macmillan, 1964; *The Dark.* London: Faber, 1965/New York: Knopf, 1966; *Nightlines.* London: Faber, 1970/Boston & Toronto: Little, Brown, 1971. (Short stories); *The Leavetaking.* London: Faber, 1974/Boston & Toronto: Little, Brown, 1975; *Getting Through.* London: Faber, 1978/London: Quartet, 1979/Dublin: Poolbeg, 1979/ New York: Harper & Row, 1980. (Short stories); *The Pornographer.* London: Faber/New York: Harper & Row, 1979; *High Ground.* London: Faber, 1985/New York: Viking, 1987. (Short stories); *The Rockingham Shoot.* BBC-TV, September 1987. (Television play); *Amongst Women.* London: Faber/New York: Harper & Row, 1990; *The Power of Darkness.* London: Faber, 1991. (Play); *The*

Collected Stories. London: Faber, 1992/New York: Knopf, 1993. REFERENCES: Carlson, Julia, ed. *Banned in Ireland: Censorship & The Irish Writer.* London: Routledge/Athens: University of Georgia Press, 1990, pp. 53–67; Freyer, Grattan. "Change Naturally: The Fiction of O'Flaherty, O'Faolain, McGahern." *Eire-Ireland* 18 (Spring 1983): 138–145; Garfitt, Roger. "Constants in Contemporary Irish Fiction." In *Two Decades of Irish Writing.* Douglas Dunn, ed. Chester Springs, Pa.: Dufour, 1975, pp. 207–211, 221–224; Kamm, Jurgen. "John McGahern." In *Contemporary Irish Novelists.* Rüdiger Imhof, ed. Tübingen: Gunter Narr Verlag, 1900, pp. 175–191; Kennedy, Eileen. "The Novels of John McGahern: The Road Away Becomes the Road Back." In *Contemporary Irish Writing.* James D. Brophy & Raymond J. Porter, eds. Boston: Iona College Press/ Twayne, 1983, pp. 115–126; Kennedy, Eileen. "Sons and Fathers in John McGahern's Short Stories." In *New Irish Writing.* James D. Brophy & Eamon Grennan, eds. Boston: Iona College Press/ Twayne, 1989, pp. 65–74; Parette, Henri-D. "Conflicts in a Changing World: John McGahern." In *The Irish Novel in Our Time.* Patrick Rafroidi & Maurice Harmon, eds. Lille: Publications del'Universite de Lille, 1976, pp. 311–327; O'Connell, Shaun. "Door into the Light: John McGahern's Ireland." *Massachussetts Review* 25 (Summer 1984): 255–268; Sampson, Denis, ed. Special John McGahern Issue, *Canadian Journal of Irish Studies* 17 (July 1991): 1–101. (Contains pieces by McGahern, an interview with him, articles, and a checklist by Sampson; Sampson, Denis. *Outstaring Nature's Eye: The Fiction of John McGahern.* Washington, D.C.: Catholic University of America Press/Dublin: Lilliput, [1993]; Schwartz, Karlheinz. "John McGahern's Point of View." *Éire-Ireland* 19 (Fall 1984): 92–110; Sheehy-Skeffington, Owen. "The McGahern Affair." *Censorship* 2 Spring 1966): 27–30.

McGEE, THOMAS D'ARCY (1825–1868), politician, journalist, and poet. McGee was born in Carlingford, County Louth, on April 13, 1825. He emigrated to America when he was seventeen and made such a reputation as a dynamic and forceful speaker that he was made editor of *The* [Boston] *Pilot* when only nineteen. He returned to Ireland, became strongly involved in Nationalist activities, and worked on *The Nation** under Gavan Duffy.* After the 1848 Rising, he escaped to America where he edited journals, and in 1858 he moved to Canada, quickly becoming prominent in Canadian politics. His own Irish revolutionary fervor had by then died down, and on visits to Ireland he was highly critical of the young Fenian movement. He was assassinated, possibly by an Irish revolutionary, on the streets of Ottawa on April 7, 1868. His poems are thoroughly fluent and show an easy control of form. However, they are unoriginal popular poems, lacking individuality or real literary taste. They are full of shamrocks, tears, patriotism, death, and the other preoccupations of the sea-divided Gael. McGee is probably seen at his conventional best in a sentimental but still somewhat effective poem like "Death of the Homeward Bound." Despite some fluency and vigor, he was always liable to slip into lines like:

A cypress wreath darkles now, I ween,
Upon the brow of my love in green.

WORKS: *Historical Sketches of O'Connell and his Friends.* Boston: Donahoe & Rohan, 1844; *Gallery of Irish Writers: The Irish Writers of the XVIIth Century.* Dublin: Duffy, 1846; *A Memoir of the Life and Conquest of Art McMurrough.* Dublin: Duffy, 1847; *Memoir of Charles Gavan Duffy.* Dublin: W. Hogan, 1849. (Pamphlet); *Poems.* Dublin: reprinted for *The Nation,* 1852; *Canadian Ballads and Occasional Verses.* Montreal: Lovel, 1858; *A Popular History of Ireland.* Glasgow: Cameron & Ferguson, 1862; *The Poems of Thomas D'Arcy McGee.* London, New York,

Montreal: Sadlier, 1869. REFERENCES: Brady, A. *Thomas D'Arcy McGee.* Toronto: Macmillan, 1925; Coleman, James. *Bibliography of Thomas D'Arcy McGee.* Dublin: [Bibliographical Society of Ireland], 1925; Phelan, J. *The Ardent Exile: The Life and Times of Thomas D'Arcy McGee.* Toronto: Macmillan, 1951; Skelton, I. M. *The Life of Thomas D'Arcy McGee.* Gardenvale, Canada: Garden City, 1925.

MacGILL, PATRICK (1891–1963), novelist and poet. MacGill was born in 1891 in the Glen of Glenties, County Donegal. The eldest of eleven children of a small farmer, he received his only formal education at the National School of Mullanmore. He left school at twelve and hired out for six months at a time as a farm laborer for a fee of £5. When he was fourteen, he emigrated to Scotland to work in the potato fields and then as an itinerant navvy. In 1911, while working on the Glasgow-Greenock Railway Line, he published at his own expense a volume of verse entitled *Gleanings from a Navvy's Scrapbook.* He sold the book from door to door in Greenock, and, incredible as it may seem, it reportedly sold eight thousand copies. *Gleanings* was followed quickly by *Songs of a Navvy* and *Songs of the Dead End,* and his work came to the attention of London critics who were both amused and impressed. Some of the verses in these books were conventionally romantic, but the more characteristic were bitter and realistic portrayals of the navvy's life. The books achieved considerable popularity for several reasons—the novel and appalling picture of the laborer's life; the utter, burning sincerity of the social indictment; and, among working people, the simple attraction of the writing. The long and heavily rhythmic lines and the emphatic end and internal rhymes had a particular charm for the untutored ear. To the well-read, the verses were simply reminiscent of the jingles of Robert W. Service, although their actual literary provenance owes much to folk poetry.

MacGill was a skilled versifier in this popular poetry and was occasionally strong in his diction and imagery, but it is as a novelist that he compels serious attention. In 1914 and 1915, respectively, he published his two interlocking novels *Children of the Dead End* and *The Rat Pit.* These books caused a literary sensation, and the first sold ten thousand copies within fifteen days of publication. With these books, MacGill became the spokesman for a mute and ignored section of society. As a self-taught writer, the author was lionized much as Sean O'Casey* was in the 1920s. However, World War I intervened, and MacGill served throughout as a private with the London Irish Rifles. His experiences were the basis for the account of his personal experiences in *The Amateur Army* (1915) and in some blistering fictional accounts of life in the ranks. MacGill continued to write into the 1930s, drawing on his memories of Ireland and of his laboring days, and always as the voice of the forgotten people at the bottom of society. He was little, if at all, influenced by the writers of the Irish literary renaissance. What literary influence he had came from the social realism of Emile Zola in novels such as *Germinal.* Nor was he interested in Irish nationalism; for him the one burning social issue was the plight of the underprivileged who scrambled for existence at the bottom of society.

MacGill's fiction is much of a piece then, but time seems to have winnowed out his first two novels as his best. These books are parallel accounts of a boy and a girl from a Donegal village who, like thousands of others in real life, made the long journey to Scotland's potato fields. The lives of the two diverge and then coalesce, and MacGill makes effective use of some nearly identical scenes in both novels. *Children of the Dead End* follows Dermod in his harrowing experiences as an itinerant navvy to his first steps in journalism, while *The Rat Pit* charts the ever-downward path of Norah through seduction, abandonment, prostitution, and death. *Children of the Dead End* is the better book because it depicts the immense vigor and even humor of life in the work camps, and because of the memorable portrait of Moleskin Joe. The book contains a few romantic flights and some savage moralizing, but the point of view and the power of the narrative sustain these merely literary flaws, if indeed they be flaws at all. The books have their crudities, but their power and compassion have little dissipated over the years. MacGill's poems may be the lowbrow stuff of popular literature, but his novels at their best have much of the strength of Zola, as well as MacGill's own horrific eloquence. Almost totally forgotten, he died in November 1963 and is buried in Fall River, Massachusetts. However, a half dozen of his books were reissued in the early 1980s by Caliban Books of London, and there is now a Patrick MacGill summer school in the Glenties.

WORKS: *Gleanings from a Navvy's Scrapbook.* Derry: Printed by the Derry Journal, 1911; *Songs of a Navvy.* Windsor: P. MacGill, [1911]; *Songs of the Dead End.* London: Year Book Press, 1912; *Children of the Dead End.* London: Herbert Jenkins, 1914; *The Amateur Army.* London: Herbert Jenkins, 1915; *The Rat Pit.* London: Herbert Jenkins, 1915; *The Great Push, an Episode of the Great War.* London: Herbert Jenkins, 1916; *The Red Horizon.* London: Herbert Jenkins, 1916; *The Brown Brethren.* London: Herbert Jenkins, 1917; *Soldier Songs.* London: Herbert Jenkins, 1917; *The Diggers: the Australians in France.* London: Herbert Jenkins, 1919; *The Dough-boys,* by John O'Gorman, Pseud. London: Herbert Jenkins, 1919; *Glenmornan.* London: Herbert Jenkins, 1919; *Maureen.* London: Herbert Jenkins, 1920; *Songs of Donegal.* London: Herbert Jenkins, 1921; *Lanty Hanlon: a Comedy of Irish Life.* London: Herbert Jenkins, 1922; *Moleskin Joe.* London: Herbert Jenkins, 1923; *The Carpenter of Orra.* London: Herbert Jenkins, 1924; *Sid Puddiefoot.* London: Herbert Jenkins, 1926; *Black Bonar.* London: Herbert Jenkins, 1928; *Suspense: a Play in Three Acts.* London: Herbert Jenkins, [1930]; *The Glen of Carra.* London: Herbert Jenkins, 1934; *Tulliver's Mill.* London: Herbert Jenkins, 1934; *The House at the World's End.* London: Herbert Jenkins, 1935; *Helen Spenser.* London: Herbert Jenkins, [1937].

McGINLEY, PATRICK (1937–), novelist. Born in County Donegal, McGinley was educated at St. Enda's College, Galway, and at University College, Galway. He spent four years teaching in Ireland before taking up a career in publishing in London. He now lives in Kent, with his wife and son.

Between 1978 and 1988, McGinley published seven novels. His third novel, *Bogmail,* was published first (1978), followed by *Goosefoot* (1982), which was filmed as *The Fantasist* and reissued under the film title. After that there followed *Fox Prints* (1983), *Foggage* (1984), *The Trick of the Ga Bolga* (1985), *The Red Men* (1987), and *The Devil's Diary* (1988).

There is a thin line between farce and tragedy in all of his novels, with sex (of the more deviant kind) and death (by accident, suicide, or murder) at the center of his tales. Both are treated with a mixture of macabre and grotesque humor. In tenor, style, and purpose, McGinley can be compared to Flann O'Brien (Brian O'Nolan*), to whom *The Trick of the Ga Bolga* is dedicated. Using the techniques of distortion and caricature, McGinley, with frivolous detachment, debunks Irish values, life, and institutions. In his stories, one is never quite on safe ground because nothing is what it seems to be. The innocent usually suffer, and the wicked get away; liars are given more credence than those telling the truth. His protagonists range from "philosophizing" drinkers and schemers, raunchy country women, land-grabbing farmers, ineffectual policemen, spoiled priests-turned-tramp or publican, and ludicrous teachers, to psychopathic killers. All of them are prone to blathering a good deal. We also come across traces of absurd de Selbian theories (particularly in *The Fantasist*), myth and folklore (in *The Trick of the Ga Bolga* and *The Red Men*), and historical allusions. Like O'Brien's protagonists, McGinley's frequently take to bed, either because they are afflicted with some kind of disease and are close to death or because they are in pursuit of sexual pleasure.

McGinley's novels are entertaining, full of suspense in the old-fashioned "whodunit" style, and deliberately unsettling.

BARBARA FREITAG

WORKS: *Bogmail.* London: Martin Brian & O'Keeffe, 1978; *Goosefoot.* London: Weidenfeld & Nicolson, 1982/reissued as *The Fantasist.* London: Flamingo, 1987; *Fox Prints.* London: Weidenfeld & Nicolson, 1983; *Foggage.* New York: St. Martin's, 1983/London: Jonathan Cape, 1984; *The Trick of the Ga Bolga.* London: Jonathan Cape, 1985; *The Red Men.* London: Jonathan Cape, 1987; *The Devil's Diary.* London: Jonathan Cape, 1988. REFERENCES: Imhof, Rüdiger. "Patrick McGinley." In *Contemporary Irish Novelists.* Tübingen: Narr, 1990, pp. 193–206.

McGRATH, EAMON (1929–   ), novelist. McGrath was born in a small farming community in County Wexford and in 1952 received a B.A. from University College, Galway, in English and Irish literature. He lives in Clonakilty, County Cork, where he taught.

McGrath's first novel, *Honour Thy Father* (1970), is the story of several years in the life of a boy who grows up on a farm and then is sent away to school. In the first chapter, the boy is repelled by his boorish and drinking father, but McGrath falls into no simplicities of characterization. "There were times," the boy muses, "when I did not hate my father at all." Indeed, by the end of by book, when the boy is about to leave school, he has come to appreciate and love his father. McGrath has a large cast of characters, but in the main they are beautifully observed, and the details of life on the farm and at the school are exactly caught. For instance:

My father picking clover from the pasture and smelling it. My father pointing to the white flower on spring nettles, with simple astonishment that God should take such trouble with weeds. My father showing us how to suck honey from purple fuchsia bells. My father placing his boot on a dozen daisies and announcing the arrival of spring.

There was a hiatus of twenty years between *Honour Thy Father* and *The Charnel House* of 1990. That novel is set in a tuberculosis sanitarium in the 1950s, when that disease was still a major cause of death in Ireland, as well as a social disgrace for a family. The book is set at the time when streptomycin was just being developed as a cure and is dedicated to Dr. Noel Browne, minister of health from 1948 to 1951, whose efforts are credited with largely eradicating the disease. McGrath uses a large, well-delineated cast of patients, nurses, and doctors and draws a persuasive picture of the emotional trauma of people gripped by a well-nigh incurable disease. Often the picture of suffering and anguish is most poignant and moving, but in his large canvas he finds room for some effective and telling comedy, particularly in the series of letters that one patient, Arty, writes to impress a young woman, posing as a devil-may-care adventurer. Then when she proposes a visit, he attempts to fend her off with ludicrous reports of his death in a racing car or with his impending marriage to the daughter of a Venezuelan millionaire. The style is lean and vigorous, and the book is a superb reincarnation of a once-terrible facet of Irish life.

The Fish in the Stone (1994) is a powerful study, probably the first one, of a significant and fairly widespread fact of Irish life: incest. The four main characters are the sexually frustrated father, the frigid and religious mother, their teenage daughter, and a sympathetic young clerk in the father's grocery. The great strength of the book lies not merely in its subject, but in its characterization. As the father's obsession grows, his actions become horrifically brutal, but McGrath draws him with understanding and even compassion. There is no two-dimensional characterization. The events push the mother from a self-absorbed religious fanaticism into compassion and the beginnings of love and drive the young girl into an hysterical maturity. Also, the novel is not merely the exploration of a ghastly situation or an ambling narrative. It is plotted, and its effective arrangement of incidents rise ever more tensely to an awful climax. Subject and characterization and plot all combine to evoke the power of this almost tragic book. One of the real misfortunes of recent Irish literature is that McGrath has written so little of it.

WORKS: *Honour Thy Father.* Dublin: Allen Figgis, 1970; *The Charnel House.* Belfast: Blackstaff, [1990]; *The Fish in the Stone.* Belfast: Blackstaff, [1994].

MacGREEVY, THOMAS (1893–1967), poet and critic. MacGreevy was born at Tarbert, County Kerry, the son of a policeman and of a schoolteacher. He fought in World War I, was twice wounded, and after being demobilized was educated at Trinity College, Dublin. In the late 1920s and early 1930s, he lived in Paris and became much influenced by the modernist movement. He introduced Samuel Beckett* to James Joyce* and was a contributor to *Our Examination round His Factification for Incamination of Work in Progress,* the early examination of what was eventually to become *Finnegans Wake.* These years saw also the publication of his one book of poetry, his two monographs of literary criticism (about his friends T. S. Eliot and Richard Aldington), and much fugitive work for *The Dial, The Criterion,* and *transition.* In 1933, he moved to London, lectured at the National Gallery, and translated some de Montherlant. In 1941, he returned to Dublin and in 1950 was appointed director of the National Gallery, a post that he held until his retirement in 1963. He died in Dublin on March 16, 1967. He had been a friend of James Stephens,* Stephen MacKenna,* Denis Devlin,* and Brian Coffey* and was the executor of the wills of Joyce and Jack B. Yeats.* In later years, he corresponded with the American poets Wallace Stevens, Babette Deutsch, and Marianne Moore, who greatly admired his generally neglected work.

MacGreevy's poetry faithfully reflects the avant-garde writing of the 1920s and 1930s, being written in free verse that often, as in Eliot's poems of the 1920s, is recondite and obscure in its frequent allusions. His most recent editor, Susan Schreibman, has produced a heavily annotated edition, which is not only useful but utterly necessary in understanding what MacGreevy was up to. With the allusions explained, the basic content of the poems is not usually too complicated. Like the work of Devlin and Coffey, however, MacGreevy's work is probably destined to remain caviar to the general public.

PRINCIPAL WORKS: *Richard Aldington: An Englishman.* London: Chatto & Windus, 1931. (Critical monograph); *Thomas Stearns Eliot. A Study.* London: Chatto & Windus, 1931. (Critical monograph); *Poems.* London: William Heinemann, 1934; *Jack B. Yeats. An Appreciation and an Interpretation.* Dublin: Victor Waddington, 1945. (Pamphlet); *Pictures in the Irish National Gallery* [Reprinted from *The Capuchin Annual*]. London: B. T. Batsford, [1946]. (Pamphlet); *Nicholas Poussin.* Dublin: Dolmen, 1960. (Pamphlet); *Collected Poems,* edited by Thomas Dillon Redshaw, with a Foreword by Samuel Beckett. Dublin: New Writers', 1971; *Collected Poems of Thomas MacGreevy: An Annotated Edition,* edited by Susan Schreibman. Dublin: Anna Livia/Washington, D.C.: Catholic University of America Press, 1991. REFERENCES: Cronin, Anthony. "Thomas MacGreevy: Modernism Not Triumphant." In *Heritage Now.* Dingle: Brandon, 1982, pp. 155–160; Smith, Stan. "From a Great Distance: Thomas MacGreevy's 'Frames of Reference.' " *Lace Curtain,* No. 6 (Autumn 1978): 47–55.

McGUCKIAN, MEDBH (1950–   ), poet. Born a Catholic in Belfast on August 12, 1950, Medbh McGuckian was educated at Holy Family Primary School in Newington and the Dominican Convent in Fortwilliam Park. Recipient of a Sullivan Scholarship to Queen's University in Belfast, she earned a B.A. in 1972 and an M.A. in Anglo-Irish literature in 1974. She taught English for several years and, from 1986 to 1988, was the first woman poet in residence at Queen's. Married to John McGuckian in 1977, she is the mother of three boys and a girl and divides her time between her home in Belfast and a cottage in Ballycastle.

Winner of a national poetry competition in 1979, McGuckian published two pamphlets, *Single Ladies* and *Portrait of Joanna,* before her first volume, *The Flower Master,* was released by Oxford University Press in 1982. The recipient of both the Alice Hunt Bartlett Award and the Rooney Prize, *The Flower Master* introduced readers to the highly original and often controversial style McGuckian has become known for. Three subsequent volumes, *Venus and the Rain* (1984), *On Ballycastle Beach* (1988), and *Marconi's Cottage* (1991), confirmed her growing reputation and fueled the debate on her distinctive style.

"Womanliness" in its many dimensions is the subject of most of Mc-Guckian's work. As woman, mother, and poet, she writes about female sexuality, gender roles, the relationship between woman and poet. Woman as artist is a recurring subject in her work; the links between the artistic and other aspects of a woman's life are the focus of many of her poems. Motherhood is an important subject in each volume, with some poems, like "The Seed-Picture," suggesting the similarities between the work of the mother and that of the poet. Images of houses, rooms, furniture, windows, doors, gardens, and colors recur in her poems.

The experimental nature of McGuckian's poetry, however, suggests that she is challenging both conventional views of the female and traditional poetic language and form. Unusual syntax, startling images, ambiguous pronouns, shifts in tense and person create multiple voices within poems, voices often at odds with one another. Reflecting both poststructuralist and contemporary feminist theory, her poetry illustrates the unstable subject and multiple meanings described by Jacques Derrida's *différence* and Hélène Cixous' *écriture féminine*. Some critics see McGuckian as challenging patriarchal discourse, a view suggested by her own statement that her language has its own logic, "which may be the opposite of men's."

McGuckian's imagery is perhaps the unique aspect of her poetry, with numerous connotations embedded in single images. Venus, the major figure in *Venus and the Rain,* appears as the classical goddess of love, the form born from the sea, and the second planet from the sun, enveloped in thick clouds. Issues of gender, authority, dependence, and independence and images of conception, birth, and rebirth in the life of a woman, mother, and poet continually appear in these poems.

McGuckian's later volumes, *On Ballycastle Beach* and *Marconi's Cottage,* refer to Ballycastle, the birthplace of McGuckian and her father, and to Ballycastle Beach, where she purchased a cottage Marconi was reputed to have visited. The first of these volumes is concerned with the concept of home, defined in both a personal and political sense. Poems on time, territory, language, art, and gender are placed in the broader landscape of Northern Ireland, where questions of language, borders, and boundaries take on added significance. The relationship of art to politics surfaces in poems like "Little House, Big House," which suggests that the Irish, described in this poem as "half-people, each with his own separate sky," might be brought together in a new house, with a "new arrangement of doorways." Connecting the political and the personal in "Woman with Blue-Ringed Bowl," McGuckian alludes to her own mother to suggest the ways in which women maintain homes while the Troubles swirl around them. A deepened appreciation of the effects of time and of change, whether in personal, political, or artistic life, is a central concern of *On Ballycastle Beach.*

Marconi's Cottage, which was short-listed for the *Irish Times*/Aer Lingus Award, touches on similar ideas, the death of a father and the birth of a daughter providing a cyclical structure for poems that deal with the poet's struggle to communicate. Many of the poems illustrate the parallels between the conception and birth of a child and the start and finish of a poem. Like those in her other volumes, some of the poems in *Marconi's Cottage* allude to artists and take their images from painting and writing. Using the traditional representation of winter as death and spring as rebirth, McGuckian suggests that art is often the offspring of suffering. At the end of the volume, a woman who has confronted death and come through an arduous process of writing tells us that "[w]hen spring hesitates," we have to wait for it ("The Watch Fire").

McGuckian is a difficult poet, challenging not only gender roles and traditional ideas about women but also conventions of poetic language, syntax, and image. Placing the woman poet and artist within the larger context of the multiple roles women play, she has created a poetry to express the complexity of women's lives, merging the private and public, the personal and political, the domestic and artistic. Calling McGuckian one of "the most original and compelling" poets writing in English, Calvin Bedient also describes her as "the most *white*-hot poet since Yeats." McGuckian's fifth volume, *Captain Lavender,* appeared in late 1995.

PATRICIA BOYLE HABERSTROH

WORKS: *Single Ladies*. Budleigh Salterton: Interim, 1980; *Portrait of Joanna*. Belfast: Ulsterman, 1980; *The Flower Master*. Oxford & New York: Oxford University Press, 1982/*The Flower Master and Other Poems*. [Oldcastle, Co. Meath]: Gallery, [1993]; *Venus and the Rain*. Oxford: Oxford University Press, 1984/rev. ed., [Oldcastle, Co. Meath]: Gallery, [1995]; *On Ballycastle Beach*. Oxford: Oxford University Press/Winston-Salem, N.C.: Wake University Press, 1988; *Two Women, Two Shores, Poems by Medbh McGuckian and Nuala Archer*. Baltimore, Md.: New Poets Series, 1989/Galway: Salmon, 1989; *Marconi's Cottage*. [Oldcastle, Co. Meath]: Gallery, 1991; *Captain Lavender*. [Oldcastle, Co. Meath]: Gallery, [1995]; *The Flower Master and Other Poems* [Oldcastle. Co. Meath]: Gallery. [1994]. REFERENCE: McCracken, Kathleen. "An Attitude of Compassion." *Irish Literary Supplement* 9 (Fall 1990): 20–21. (Interview).

McGUINNESS, FRANK (1953–   ), playwright. Born in Buncrana, County Donegal, on July 29, 1953, the eldest of three children, McGuinness was educated locally and at Carndonagh College before going to University College, Dublin, in 1971, to study arts. Upon graduation, he specialized in Old and Middle English, took his M.Phil. in 1976, and pursued an academic career while developing as a writer. In 1984 he was appointed full-time lecturer in modern English at St. Patrick's College, Maynooth.

Factory Girls, written to satisfy the demands of a drama workshop attended at University College, Galway, was McGuinness's first play and was staged at the Peacock Theatre in 1982. In the light of his subsequent work, which is mainly experimental, *Factory Girls* is chiefly distinguished by its straightforward naturalism and its strong theme or thesis. Set in a shirt factory in Donegal, the play shows how women take the initiative when male management tries to enforce new conditions. When the women occupy the manager's office, a battle for leadership exposes flaws and strengths within their own ranks, until a new leader emerges, and guilt is put aside. As a play about women and women's rights, *Factory Girls* broke new ground and has been enduringly popular on the Irish stage. It does not rank beside *Observe the Sons of Ulster Marching towards the Somme,* however, which premiered in 1985 and won many prizes in Ireland and Britain. Set in Northern Ireland in 1916, this is an extraordinary imaginative achievement, being a study of the Northern Unionist mind by a Southern Catholic. Whereas it is a history play, focused on the fate of eight men in World War I, it is also a study of identity, both sexual and national, dramatized with great skill and compassion, and is therefore a strong political play also. Indeed, *Observe the Sons* merits a place alongside O'Casey's* *The Silver Tassie* (1929). McGuinness, however, is more interested in exploring states of feeling and conditions of individual integrity than was O'Casey the socialist. Where he does employ actual political themes in his plays, McGuinness makes them form a background against which psychological and social questions are defined, as happens in the plays written for TEAM, *Borderlands* and *Gatherers* and *The Bread Man,* and produced during the Dublin Theatre Festival of 1990. Each of these has a political agenda. *The Bread Man,* for instance, is set in a border town in 1970 just after the outbreak of hostilities in Northern Ireland but concentrates on interrelationships brought into crisis by the political context. *Carthaginians,* which premiered at the Peacock in 1988, moves rather more closely to a straightforward political theme, namely, Bloody Sunday in Derry (1972), and yet it is a play in which parody, pastiche, and comic characterization direct attention to the dangers of manipulated feeling and the necessity for each individual, as the homosexual Dido says at the end, to "watch yourself." McGuinness has said that "resurrection" is a theme that interests him profoundly, and one must see this as a possibility in many of his plays, which often end in an upbeat way, signifying hope. This may be seen both in *Innocence* produced in 1986, a play about the artist Caravaggio, and *Mary and Lizzie,* a strange fantasy involving Marx, Lenin, and two Irishwomen in Manchester. In particular, this emphasis on hope is the key to McGuinness's most successful play to date, *Someone Who'll Watch over Me,* which premiered at the Hampstead Theatre Club in 1992, transferred to the West End, and had a three-month run at Broadway's Booth Theatre in 1992–1993. Whereas the situation in this play is based on the experiences of hostages in Lebanon, notably, Brian Keenan (to whom the play is dedicated) and John McCarthy, McGuinness's strength is seen in his imaginative understanding of psychic pressure and survival. In this play the weakest turns out to be the strongest spiritually. Using wit, fantasy, games, and routines, the prisoners, as universal as Beckett's,* act out the human need to overcome a sense of degradation and to reach instead a sense of community and endurance. This play won many international awards.

McGuinness has also adapted plays by Ibsen, Chekhov, Lorca, Brecht, and others for both the Irish and English stages. In 1994, his version of *Peer Gynt* (which premiered at the Gate Theatre* in 1988) was directed by Yukio Ninegawa in Oslo and went on tour in Britain before opening in Tokyo. Several times McGuinness has worked on an adaptation of Ibsen or Chekhov while also writing a new play, and these adaptations must therefore be seen as significant contributions to his development as a dramatist. *Baglady* (Peacock, 1985), a one-woman play, shows McGuinness in another light again, poetic and tragic. The focus on a woman's history, however, is a reminder of how much of McGuinness's work is gender-based. Homosexuality is dealt with as an issue in his latest play, *The Bird Sanctuary* (Abbey, 1994), but revealingly, in the context of the Irish family and its coercive norms. McGuinness is a prolific and constantly developing playwright who has already expanded the horizons of Irish theater but who is young enough to contribute a great deal more yet to the distinguished body of plays he has written in his first twelve years.

CHRISTOPHER MURRAY

WORKS: *The Factory Girls.* Dublin: Monarch Line, 1982/revised ed. Dublin: Wolfhound, 1988; *Observe the Sons of Ulster Marching towards the Somme.* London & Boston: Faber, 1986; *Innocence: The Life and Death of Michelangelo Merisi, Caravaggio.* London & Boston: Faber, 1987; *Borderlands* in *Three Team Plays.* Martin Drury, ed. Dublin: Wolfhound, 1988; *Carthagenians and Baglady.* London & Boston: Faber, 1988; *Mary and Lizzie.* London & Boston: Faber, 1989; *Henrik Ibsen's Peer Gynt: A New Version by Frank McGuinness: From a Literal Translation by Rose Cullen.* London & Boston: Faber, 1990; *Someone Who'll Watch over Me.* London & Boston: Faber, 1992. *Booterstown.* [Oldcastle, Co. Meath]: Gallery, [1994]. (Poems). REFERENCES: Cave, Richard Allen & McLoone, Martin. "J'Accuse." *Theatre Ireland* 21 (December 1989): 58–62; Jordan, Eamonn Martin. "The Plays of Frank McGuinness: Form and Vision." Diss., University College, Dublin, 1993; Lojek, Helen. "Myth and Bonding in Frank McGuinness's *Observe the Sons of Ulster Marching towards the Somme.*" *Canadian Journal of Irish Studies* 14 (1988): 45–53; Lojek, Helen. "The Drama of Frank McGuinness and Anne Devlin." *Éire-Ireland* 25 (1990): 56–68; O'Toole, Fintan. "Innocence Uprooted." *Magill* 10 (November 1986): 48–54; Pine, Richard. "Frank McGuinness: A Profile." *Irish Literary Supplement* 10 (Spring 1991): 29–30; Wilcox, Angela. "The Temple of the Lord Is Ransacked." *Theatre Ireland* 8 (Winter 1984): 87–89; Wilcox, Angela. "The Memory of Wounds." *Theatre Ireland* 16 (September–November 1988): 6–8.

McHENRY, JAMES (1785–1845), novelist, poet, and playwright. McHenry was born in Larne and educated in Dublin and in Glasgow, where he obtained a medical degree. He emigrated to the United States in 1817, practicing medicine in Philadelphia and editing *The American Monthly Magazine.* In 1842, he became U.S. consul in Derry, and he died in Larne on June 21, 1845. D. J. O'Donoghue thought his poetry prosaic, but his historical novel *O'Halloran; or, The Insurgent Chief* (1824) was popular for at least a quarter of a century.

WORKS: *The Bard of Erin and Other Poems.* Belfast: Smythe & Lyons, 1808; *Patrick: A Poetical Tale.* . . . Glasgow: McKenzie, 1810; *The Pleasures of Friendship.* Pittsburgh: Author, 1822. (Poetry); *Waltham: An American Revolutionary Tale. In Three Cantos.* New York: Bliss & White, 1823; *The Wilderness; or, Braddock's Times.* New York: Bliss & White, 1823. (Novel); *The Spectre of the Forest.* . . . New York: Bliss & White, 1823. (Novel); *O'Halloran; or, The Insurgent Chief.* Philadelphia: Carey & Lea, 1824/Belfast: Henderson, 1847. (The Belfast edition includes the author's notes); *The Hearts of Steel, An Irish Historical Tale of the Last Century.* Philadelphia: Poole, 1825; *The Usurper, An Historical Tragedy.* Philadelphia: Harding, 1829. (Five-act play); *The Betrothed of Wyoming.* Philadelphia: n.p., ca. 1830. (Novel); *Feelings of Age, to Which Is Added the Star of Love.* Philadelphia: Banks, ca. 1830. (Poetry); *Meredith; or, The Mystery of the Meschianza.*

Philadelphia: n.p., 1831. (Novel); *The Antediluvians; or, The World Destroyed.* London, 1839. (Poetry); *Britannia, An Ode.* London, 1839.

McHUGH, MARTIN J. (?–1951), playwright and short story writer. McHugh wrote short stories for the popular press and several short plays, three of which were performed by the Abbey Theatre* in the second decade of the twentieth century. His many unpublished letters to Joseph Holloway* are incredibly garrulous and so mind-bogglingly boring that, if printed (which they should not be), they would prove something of an antiliterary comic masterpiece. He was for a while employed by *The Irish Times,* but later moved to England. The best-known of his daughters is Mary Frances McHugh.* His multitudinous comic stories in the popular press in the first decade of the century are no better than those of George Fitzmaurice* or Maurice Walsh,* who at that time were also writing Stage Irish stories of little merit. Of his several broad farces, however, *A Minute's Wait* (Abbey, 1914) is a small, sweetly silly theatrical gem. It was one segment of John Ford's film *The Rising of the Moon* and featured the eminent Irish comedian Jimmy O'Dea. Sean O'Casey* utilized precisely the same situation for his late one-act *The Moon Shines on Kylenamoe.* McHugh died on November 11, 1951.

WORKS: *Straws in the Wind.* Aberdeen: Moran, 1896; *A Modern Mage,* with Henry T. Hunt Grubb. London: Simpkin, Marshall, 1904; *A Minute's Wait.* Dublin: Duffy, [1922]. (One-act play); *The Philosopher.* Dublin: Duffy, [1922?]. (One-act play); *Tommy Tom-Tom.* Dublin: Duffy, [1922?]. (One-act play); *A Girl Like Mary.* Dublin: Duffy, [1935]; (One-act play); *The Trifler.* Dublin: Duffy, [1946]. (One-act play).

McHUGH, MARY FRANCES (fl. first half of the twentieth century), woman of letters. McHugh was the daughter of the playwright and popular short story writer Martin J. McHugh.* A typical work is her *Thalassa* (1931), which is subtitled "A Story of Childhood by the Western Wave" and which is a memoir of her childhood in the west of Ireland. The book is written in stiff, English-composition-prizewinning prose. Clouds are "[s]mall, tossed, white"; hills are "limpid"; cottages "nestle"; and the sea is "murmuring and melancholic." In sum, "every moment changed to something more indescribable and entrancing, until it seemed one's heart would break with beauty." McHugh's evocation of the scenery is a barrier to enjoyment, but when she forgets about beauty and simply describes the people who lived around her, the little book becomes an engrossing and valuable social record of life in the west of Ireland at the beginning of the century.

Her poems are as literary as her prose and quite conventional.

MARY ROSE CALLAGHAN

WORKS: *Poems.* Dublin: Martin Lester, [1919]; *Thalassa.* London: Macmillan, 1931/Dublin: Parkside, 1945; *The Bud of Spring.* London: Macmillan, 1932.

McHUGH, ROGER [JOSEPH] (1908–1987), critic, scholar, and playwright. McHugh was born in Dublin on July 14, 1908, and became professor of Anglo-

Irish literature and drama at University College, Dublin. He edited several useful books on Anglo-Irish literature, wrote a short life of Henry Grattan,* and with Maurice Harmon wrote the excellent *Short History of Anglo-Irish Literature from Its Origins to the Present Day* (1982). Two of his plays were performed by the Abbey Theater*: *Trial at Green Street Courthouse* in 1941 and *Rossa* in 1945. Neither was memorable, but both were worthy. A third play, in collaboration with Alfred Noyes, about Roger Casement, has not been published. He died in Dublin on January 1, 1987.

PRINCIPAL WORKS: *Henry Grattan.* Dublin: Talbot/London: Duckworth, 1936; *Trial at Green Street Courthouse.* Dublin: Browne & Nolan, [1946]; *Rossa.* Tralee: Kerryman, [1946?]; ed., *Letters to Katharine Tynan.* New York: McMullen, [1953]; ed., *Dublin, 1916.* London: Arlington Books/ New York: Hawthorn Books, [1966]; ed. with Philip Edwards. *Jonathan Swift 1667–1967.* [Dublin]: Dolmen, 1967; ed., *Ah, Sweet Dancer: W. B. Yeats, Margot Ruddick, a Correspondence.* London: Macmillan/[Dublin]: Gill & Macmillan, 1970; ed., *Jack B. Yeats. A Centenary Gathering.* Dublin: Dolmen, 1971; with Maurice Harmon. *Short History of Anglo-Irish Literature from Its Origins to the Present Day.* Dublin: Wolfhound/Totowa, N.J.: Barnes & Noble, 1982.   REFERENCE: Harmon, Maurice, ed. *Image and Illusion: Anglo-Irish Literature and Its Contexts: A Festschrift for Roger McHugh.* Portsmouth: Wolfhound, 1979.

McILROY, ARCHIBALD (1860–1915), novelist and short story writer. McIlroy was born in County Antrim, worked in insurance and in banks, and was drowned on the *Lusitania.* He often wrote in dialect, as in *The Humour of Druid's Island* (1902) which is set in Islandmagee, County Antrim.

WORKS: *When Lint Was in the Bell.* Belfast: M'Caw, Stevenson & Orr, 1897; *The Auld Meetin'-hoose.* Belfast: M'Caw, Stevenson & Orr, 1898/Toronto: P. H. Revell, 1899; *By the Lone Craig-Linnie Burn.* London: T. Fisher Unwin, 1900; *A Banker's Love Story.* London: T. Fisher Unwin, 1901; *The Humour of Druid's Island.* Dublin: Hodges, Figgis, Belfast: Mullan, 1902.

MacINTYRE, TOM (1931–   ), man of letters. MacIntyre was born in 1931 in County Cavan. He was educated at University College, Dublin, and has taught at Clongowes Wood College and creative writing at the University of Michigan and at Williams College in Massachusetts. In 1978, he received an Arts Council bursary and in 1991 was elected to Aosdána.* He has has written a novel, short stories, plays, poems, and reportage, as well as having made some translations from the Irish. He is one of the more experimental of contemporary Irish writers.

His novel, *The Charollais* (1969), a short, fantastic story reminiscent of Joyce,* Beckett,* and Flann O'Brien, (Brian O'Nolan*) is told in a highly individual, freewheeling style. For instance:

In short, Drumgoon was over the barrel—they knew it, and so, by the cut of him, did he. A pimpled, pock-marked, prepubescent omadhaun could tell him that he might as well accept a situation he couldn't alter, nor would it alter, not—C lammed the table— not if he went down on his knees and washed that floor with a mixture of his own annointed spittle, oil, chrism, and/or diced carrots to the full-dress accompaniment of the *Diocesan Chapter* chaunting *Ecce Sacerdos Magnus* in catatonic thirds, diatonic fifths, galvanic sevenths, macaronic—.

This excerpt is typical of the style and, indeed, the quality of imagination in the book, which predictably begin to pall after about fifty overripe pages. Character is sacrificed to fantasy, fantasy is camouflaged by style, and the style finally becomes more clever than funny, as the author more often than not opts for the easy gag, the half pun, and the quip.

The Word for Yes (1991) contains some stories from two previous collections as well as seven new pieces. The earlier stories from the collection *Dance the Dance* (1969) are fairly conventional in form but somewhat uneven in quality. If there is a common situation, it might be that of fate or of people playing bad jokes on other people. Some of the pieces are so short—two or three or four pages—that they are really only sketches. Several, nevertheless, do cling in the memory, particularly "Stallions," "Willie Wynne, Con Moto," "An Aspect of the Rising," and, most particularly, the long "Epithalamion," which MacIntrye did not reprint in the 1991 collection. All of the pieces are, like the novel, notable for their quirky prose. For instance:

Heavy traffic, thunder and lightning, holding that child in his arms, sheltering, a good feeling and a bad, mind the child, mind the child, ever walk a cobbled yard a wine-glass tied to your ankle, the child a fragile old dog for the hard road had been pulled out of ditches, quagmires, marl-holes and midden-humps, indestructible, breath, clay, open hand, and telegram-boy.—*Frog needs no hammer in the rainy season.*

The last, longest, and most ambitious story in *The Word for Yes* is "Rise Up Lovely Sweeney," but its prose is so clever-clever that it severely strains the patience.

Many of MacIntyre's plays have been presented at the Peacock and in the 1980s often were directed by Patrick Mason and featured the actor Tom Hickey. Although highly admired by Dublin critics as avant-garde, the productions seemed little more than acting-school exercises or, at best, versions of what such groups as the Living Theatre had been doing in the 1960s. Like the Living Theatre productions, the Mason-Hickey-MacIntyre pieces relied on thoroughly choreographed action and minimal dialogue. Thus, an adaptation of Patrick Kavanagh's* poem *The Great Hunger* (1983) could, at best, claim to reproduce only the spirit of the poem, for it relied more on grunts than on words. *The Bearded Lady* (1984) was nominally a depiction of Swift,* Stella, and Vanessa, but so simplistic in its characterizations that they could have been given any other names, while the use of actors ferociously clomping around on five-inch hooves was an appropriation from *Equus,* and the scowling actors bore no relation whatsoever to Swift's rational and benevolent Houyhnhnms. In their underwriting, MacIntyre's plays are a startling contrast to his heady prose. They have not been, and hardly could be, published, for there is little to read in them. They may possibly serve as outlines for theatrical performances but have little to do with the drama as literature or indeed with literature itself.

MacIntyre's *Fleurs-du-Lit* (1990) is typical of his poetry, a collection of short pieces in short line lengths but with hardly the vaguest rhythmical pattern apparent. The punctuation is eccentric and various but does not hinder the sense, despite quite a lot of sentence fragments. There is an immediacy to this writing, but very little art.

WORKS: *The Charollais.* London: Faber, 1969. (Novel); *Dance the Dance.* London: Faber, 1969. (Short stories); *Through the Bridewell Gate.* London: Faber, 1971. (Reportage); *Blood Relations.* [Dublin]: New Writers', [1972]. (Translations of Irish poems); *The Harper's Turn.* [Dublin]: Gallery, [1982]. (Short stories); *I Bailed Out at Ardee.* Dublin: Dedalus, 1987. (Poems); *Fleurs-du-Lit.* [Dublin]: Dedalus, [1990]. (Poems); *The Word for Yes: New and Selected Stories.* [Oldcastle, Co. Meath]: Gallery, [1991]; *A Glance Will Tell You and a Dream Confirm.* [Dublin]: Dedalus, [1994]. (Poems).

MacKAY, WILLIAM (1846–?), novelist. MacKay was born in Belfast and worked as a journalist.

WORKS: *The Popular Idol.* 2 vols. London: Richard Bentley, 1876; *Pro Patria: The Autobiography of an Irish Conspirator.* 2 vols. London: Remington, 1883; *Beside Still Waters.* London: Remington, 1885; *Unvarnished Tales.* London: Sonnenschein, 1886. (Short stories); *A Mender of Nets.* London: Chatto & Windus, 1905.

MACKEN, WALTER (1915–1967), playwright, novelist, and actor. Macken was born on May 3, 1915, in the city of Galway. He wrote his first story at the age of twelve, and when he was seventeen he joined the Taibhdhearc, the Irish language theatre in Galway. For the Taibhdhearc he not only acted and directed, but also wrote several plays in Irish. In the 1940s and 1950s, he was a prominent Abbey* actor, and he also played leading roles on Broadway in Michael J. Molloy's* *The King of Friday's Men* and in his own *Home Is the Hero* in 1954. He also played leading roles in the film versions of *Home Is the Hero* and of Brendan Behan's* *The Quare Fellow.* Early in 1966, he became artistic director and manager of the Abbey Theatre in its last days at the Queen's, but he gave up the job after a few months to devote full time to writing. He died on April 22, 1967, in Galway.

Macken's four published plays are *Mungo's Mansion* (Abbey, 1946), *Vacant Possession* (produced only by amateurs), *Home Is the Hero* (Abbey, 1952), and *Twilight of a Warrior* (Abbey, 1955). The first two plays are somewhat larger-than-life attempts at doing for Galway City what O'Casey* had done in his first plays for Dublin. Macken's plays, however, hang between O'Caseyan tragicomedy and a broader farcical-melodrama, but they do have considerable theatrical vitality. *Home Is the Hero* is probably Macken's best, and certainly most produced, play. Its central character is a figure of the father as outcast, as in John B. Keane's* later *The Year of the Hiker;* the play somewhat suffers for insufficient sympathy with this simple, though brutal, man. *Twilight of a Warrior* is an intriguing character study of the type of man who created de Valera's new Ireland—a hero of the Troubles grown into a successful businessman. Macken's Dacey Adam is not quite arresting enough to hold the play together, but, like Macken's later study of alcoholism, *The Voices of Doolin* (Dublin Theatre Festival, 1960), the play shows a lessening concern with easy theatricality and an increasing interest in character drawing.

Macken's greater growth as a dramatist was limited mainly by his considerable success as a novelist and his increasing fascination with fiction. Some of his books found a wide audience in America, and many of them are kept in print by an English popular market paperback firm. Macken's fiction, like his plays, hangs between entertainment and art—say, between the excellent popular novels of a Maurice Walsh* and the serious work of a Liam O'Flaherty.* Macken's books are what is sometimes called a good read; they have usually well-drawn, if somewhat simple, characters, strong plotting, and an easy and often evocative style. At his best, as in his study of Claddagh fishermen, *Rain on the Wind,* Macken is not only powerful but memorable. His most ambitious work is an historical trilogy comprising *Seek the Fair Land* about Cromwellian Ireland, *The Silent People* about the Famine years of the nineteenth century, and *The Scorching Wind* about the Troubles of the twentieth century. The first novels are effective recreations of their time, but the last seems hurried and thin. Macken's work in both fiction and drama has force, energy, and a confident craftsmanship. At its best, it only narrowly misses lasting excellence.

WORKS: *Mungo's Mansion.* London: Macmillan, 1946. (Play); *Quench the Moon.* London: Macmillan, 1948/New York: Viking, 1948. (Novel); *Vacant Possession.* London: Macmillan, 1948. (Play); *I Am Alone.* London: Macmillan, 1949. (Novel); *Rain on the Wind.* London: Macmillan, 1950. (Novel); *The Bogman.* London: Macmillan, 1952. (Novel); *Home Is the Hero.* London: Macmillan, 1953. (Play); *Sunset on the Window-Panes.* London: Macmillan, 1954. (Novel); *The Green Hills and Other Stories.* London: Macmillan, 1956; *Twilight of a Warrior.* London: Macmillan, 1956. (Play); *Sullivan.* London: Macmillan, 1957. (Novel); *Seek the Fair Land.* London: Macmillan, 1959. (Novel); *God Made Sunday and Other Stories.* London: Macmillan, 1962; *The Silent People.* London: Macmillan, 1962. (Novel); *The Scorching Wind,* London: Macmillan, 1964; *Island of the Great Yellow Ox.* London: Macmillan, 1966; *Brown Lord of the Mountain.* London: Macmillan, 1967; *The Coll Doll and Other Stories.* Dublin: Gill & Macmillan, 1969; *The Flight of the Doves.* London: Pan, 1971. REFERENCES: Drees, Roswitha. "Die Darstellung irischer Geschichte im Erzählwerk Walter Mackens." Diss., Wuppertal, 1982; Hogan, Robert. *After the Irish Renaissance.* Minneapolis: University Press, pp. 65–70

McKENNA, JAMES (1933–   ), playwright and sculptor. McKenna was born in Dublin in June 1933. He spent five years studying at the College of Art, after which he received a Macaulay Fellowship in sculpture. In the same year, his Dublin "Teddy-Boy" musical, *The Scatterin',* was presented at the Theatre Festival in a lively production by Alan Simpson; it eventually moved to London's Theatre Royal, Stratford East. The play is in the vein of Brendan Behan's* *The Hostage,* except that it is less comic than romantic-realistic. It has a strong plotline, but the writing and characterization are thin; hence *The Scatterin'* remains "theater" rather than literature. In its time, it was effective theater. A second play, *At Bantry,* won a prize in the 1916 Commemoration Competition and was produced at the Peacock in 1967. The play is a stylized treatment of the attempted landing of the French at Bantry Bay. It is written in unmemorable verse and was originally played in masks designed by the author. McKenna has also published a volume of verse. None of his later plays has been published, although *The Battering Ram* in 1976 and *A Dance of Time* in 1979 won prizes.

In recent years, McKenna has devoted himself more to sculpture and for his sculpture is a member of Aosdána.*

WORKS: *At Bantry.* Dublin: Sceptre Books, [1968]; *Poems.* Curragh, Co. Kildare: Goldsmith, 1973; *The Scatterin'.* [Curragh, Co. Kildare]: Goldsmith, 1977.

MacKENNA, JOHN (1952–), novelist and short story writer. MacKenna was born in Castledermot, County Kildare, and works as a commissioning editor for RTÉ. He won a Hennessy Award in 1983, a C. Day-Lewis Fiction Award in 1989 and 1990, and an *Irish Times* Literature Prize for a first book in 1993.

His novel, *Clare* (1993), is a beautiful evocation of the life and character of John Clare, the extraordinary nineteenth-century English poet who, despite practically no formal education, wrote one volume of poems, *The Shepherd's Calendar,* that Ian Jack thought "ranks with all but the greatest in our language." MacKenna's novel stays close to the facts of Clare's life but depicts him mainly from the outside, through accounts by his sister, wife, daughter, and a pompous and amorous patron. Their characters, as well as Clare's own gradual descent into madness, are persuasively caught in clear and tight prose. Eschewing the dramatic rhetorical high jinks of some of his notable contemporaries, McKenna has produced a quiet but thoroughly realized and even lyric book.

MacKenna has also produced two admired volumes of short stories, *The Fallen* (1992) and *A Year of Our Lives* (1995), but despite frequent cleverness in combining two or more points of view in several stories, the stories tend to fuse in the memory. Perhaps a reason is that most of them share a glum similarity in their depiction of gray lives, failure, unhappiness, and death. The narrowness of scope is especially evident in the two brief stories, "The First Epistle" and "The Second Epistle," which seem little more than exercises. The second story repeats not only the action of the first but much of its actual wording, the main difference being that in the first the priest is making a train journey to meet a widower with whom he had an adolescent affair, and in the second the widower has become a widow. Many other pieces stay firmly within the protagonist's thoughts, and some, such as "Landscape with Three Figures," require a rereading to discern which of the three figures is talking in which paragraph. MacKenna's most successful pieces, such as "Streets," are ones in which the stories are dramatizations rather than internal monologues. The style is generally simple and unadorned, often made up of repetitive sentence fragments, and only occasionally is there a descent into such floridness as, "Sometimes I'd bury my hands in the silken ashes of the morning."

WORKS: *The Occasional Optimist.* Winter Wood Books, 1976; *Castledermot and Kilkea.* Winter Wood Books, 1982; *The Lost Village: Portrait of an Irish Village in 1925.* Dublin: Stephen Scroop, 1985; *The Fallen and Other Stories.* Belfast: Blackstaff, 1992; *Clare.* Belfast: Blackstaff/Chester Springs, Pa.: Dufour, [1993]. (Novel); *A Year of Our Lives.* [London & Basingstoke]: Picador, [1995]. (Short Stories).

MacKENNA, STEPHEN (1872–1934), translator. MacKenna is known for his eloquent translation of Plotinus, a labor which occupied him for many difficult years. His importance for Irish literature lies in his personality and his friendships. Among the writers who esteemed his vivid conversation and qualities of mind were AE,* J. M. Synge,* and James Stephens.* MacKenna was born on January 15, 1872, but did not attend university. In the late 1890s, he led a penurious bohemian life in Paris, during which he was Synge's best friend. "How do those two young men live?" said an inquisitive person. "Oh, Synge lives on what MacKenna lends him, and MacKenna lives on what Synge pays him back." MacKenna joined the Greek side in the war between Greece and Turkey in 1897, later apparently visited New York, and then became the continental representative of *The New York World.* For a time he was a prosperous journalist, covering, for instance, the 1904–1905 Russian revolution and visiting Tolstoy. However, thoroughly disenchanted with journalism and refusing to act as personal valet to the visiting Joseph Pulitzer, who owned the paper, he resigned in 1907. He then returned to Dublin, becoming a leader writer for *The Freeman's Journal,* commencing his Plotinus, and gathering around him a group of interesting young men such as J. M. Hone,* Edmund Curtis,* the Celtic scholar Osborn Bergin, Padraic Colum,* Thomas MacDonagh,* Seumas O'Sullivan,* and James Stephens. His translating was hampered by his own ill health, and the long and lingering illness of his wife. After her death and after his disillusionment about the Anglo-Irish Treaty, he lived in England, working intermittently and living in some poverty. He died on March 8, 1934. His letters, particularly the whimsical and loosely written later ones, are still a delight to read, but, as he once wrote to AE: "I am not a man of the pen. I can say more in five minutes with my little tongue than with the longest fountain-pen in the world."

(He is not to be confused with the English novelist Stephen McKenna.)

WORKS: *Plotinus,* translator. 5 vols. London: P. L. Warner, 1917–1930; *Journal and Letters,* ed. with a Memoir by E. R. Dodds and a Preface by Padraic Colum. London: Constable, 1936/New York: William Morrow, [1937]. REFERENCE: Ó Rinn, Liam. *Mo Chara Stiofán.* Baile Átha Cliath: Óifig an tSoláthair, 1939. (Biography).

MACKLIN, CHARLES (1699?–1797), playwright and actor. With the exception of David Garrick, Charles Macklin was possibly the most considerable actor on the English stage during the eighteenth century. As a playwright, some critics claim that he is excelled only by his countrymen Sheridan,* Goldsmith,* and Farquhar.*

Macklin is sometimes said to have been born in 1690, and there is a story that his mother spirited him away from the Battle of the Boyne where his father was fighting for King James. However, the most reliable commentators, as well as Macklin himself, assert that he was born in 1699. His family name was probably originally Melaghlin or MacLoughlin, and most scholars believe that he was born at Culdaff on the Inishowen peninsula, County Donegal. Very little is known about him until he made his way upon the English stage in 1733. There, he had a long and distinguished career, playing over two hundred roles and being particularly admired in such forceful characters as Macbeth, Shylock, and Sir Pertinax Macsychophant in his own best play, *The Man of the World.* Of his realistic performance as Shylock, Pope, according to legend, said, "This is the Jew that Shakespeare drew."

Macklin seems to have been Irish enough in his temper, and in 1735 in a quarrel over a wig in the greenroom of Drury Lane, he plunged the tip of his cane into another actor's eye. When the actor died, Macklin was arraigned, ably conducted his own defense, and was sentenced to be branded—but only with a cold iron. He seems to have been a blunt, outspoken, honest man, somewhat given to litigation to protect his rights. He was an advocate of a more realistic style of acting, as opposed to the somewhat artificial declamatory style of James Quinn and others, and he was an effective teacher of actors. In 1789, his memory finally failing, he broke down in his old part of Shylock and thereafter appeared no more on the stage. In his last years he was somewhat senile; he died on July 11, 1797, and was buried in St. Paul's, Covent Garden.

As a playwright, Macklin does not rank with Goldsmith or Sheridan, but his character drawing is usually strong, and his best work would bear revival today. His most famous characters were not Irishmen but Scotsmen, such as the superb Sir Pertinax and Sir Archy Macsarcasm in *Love à la Mode.* That quite funny play has a querulous and family-proud Scotsman, a booby of a fox-hunting English squire, a Jewish dandy named Beau Mordecai, and a warlike Irishman named Sir Callaghan O'Brallaghan, all contesting for the hand of the heroine. The Irishman, being naturally the noblest, wins. Sir Callaghan is something of a Stage Irishman, but Macklin's other Irish hero, Murrough O'Dogherty, is quite solidly drawn. In *The True-born Irishman,* O'Dogherty is realistically cynical about politicians, but he avoids misanthropy and is firmly level-headed and concerned for the welfare of his country. His opinions are grafted onto a conventional, yet effective, plot in which a good deal of fun is poked at the foppish Englishman and at the Irish foolishly aping English customs. At its most recently known revival, by the Theatre of Ireland in Dublin in 1910, the play was very successful.

WORKS: *King Henry VII, or, The Popish Imposter.* London: Dodsley, 1746. (Play); *The Fortune Hunters.* London: McCulloh/Dublin: Powell, 1750. (Play); *The Man of the World and Love à la Mode.* London: Bell, 1793. (Plays); *The True-born Irishman; or, The Irish Fine Lady.* Dublin: Jones, 1793. (Play); *Four Comedies.* J. O. Bartley, ed. Hamden, Conn.: Archon Books/London: Sidgwick & Jackson, 1968. (Contains *Love à la Mode, The True-born Irishman, The School for Husbands,* and *The Man of the World*); *A Will and No Will or a Bone for the Lawyers* in *Eighteenth Century Drama: Afterpieces.* Richard W. Bevis, ed. London, Oxford & New York: Oxford University Press, 1970. (Two-act farce). REFERENCES: Appleton, William W. *Charles Macklin, An Actor's Life.* Cambridge: Harvard University Press, 1960; Cooke, W. *Memoirs of Charles Macklin, Comedian.* . . . London: J. Asperne, 1804; Kirkman, James Thomas. *Memoirs of the Life of C. Macklin. . . .* 2 vols. London: Lackington, Allen, 1799.

Mac LAVERTY, BERNARD (1942–), novelist and short story writer. Mac Laverty was born in Belfast on September 14, 1942. He worked for ten years as a medical technician before entering Queen's University, where he received an honours degree in English and a diploma in education. He taught English at St. Augustin's High School in Edinburgh from 1975 to 1978 and on the Isle of Islay from 1978 to 1981. Since then he has been a full-time writer. In 1975, the Northern Arts Council awarded him a bursary for his stories, which had appeared in various magazines and anthologies. A first collection, *Secrets,* was published in 1977 and was the winner of a book award from the Scottish Arts Council. He has since written three more collections of stories and two novels and written and illustrated children's stories.

His first novel, *Lamb* (1980), is a powerful story about a Christian brother, Michael Lamb, who flees from a repressive home for difficult boys, taking one young boy with him. The boy, Owen Kane, is a tough but vulnerable child from Dublin's inner city, with epilepsy as well as a frightening background. As their money runs out in London, and the certainty of their apprehension increases, Michael's love for the boy grows, and he realizes that Owen's only possible escape from a horrible life ahead is to die. The boy once explained that the onset of an attack was the most beautiful experience he had ever had, and so Michael exchanges the pills that control the boy's attacks for aspirin. When the fit comes on, Michael drowns him. This bald summary does little justice to the beautiful evocation of the two characters and to the horrendous and moving conclusion. The book was made into a successful film.

Also filmed was Mac Laverty's 1983 novel, *Cal,* an absorbing story about a Catholic youth in the North. Cal is on the dole and has been reluctantly persuaded to drive a car on several Irish Republican Army missions. In one, a man was killed, and his father gravely wounded. Later, Cal meets the man's wife, a local librarian, and comes to work on her in-laws' farm. Indeed, he stays on the farm after his father's house has been gasoline-bombed and destroyed. Despite his guilt about her husband's death, Cal and Marcella become lovers, but he is apprehended by the police and finds himself "grateful that at last someone was going to beat him to within an inch of his life." The main thrust of the story is a condemnation of hatred in the North, but its main excellence is characterization. Without being in the least stupid, Cal's education and interests are very different from those of the ten years' older Marcella. He likes rock music and is bored by books. However, even this cultural gap underscores the possibility of love among the most disparate kinds of people, and this thwarted possibility gives the story its point and strength.

Strong as his novels are, Mac Laverty's best work is probably in the short story. In *Secrets,* he writes, like William Trevor,* detached observations of quite different types of people—children, university students, housewives, men on the dole, a man who artificially inseminates cattle, old ladies who are dying. Unlike Trevor's work, however, Mac Laverty's stories are meant to produce different kinds of effects, ranging from a Trevorian study of accumulating failure in "Hugo" to the jokey fantasy of "The Miraculous Candidate." Some characters lose in Mac Laverty, but some people win: the husband and wife in "The

Pornographer Woos'' do go happily to bed. But more interestingly, even Mac Laverty's losers can win a battle. In "A Present for Christmas," the down-and-out McGettigan accidentally comes across a sackful of drink to lighten a few days of his wretched life. In "The Bull with the Hard Hat," the depressed and even ineffectual artificial inseminator does still have his Walter Mitty fantasies. Mac Laverty's view of the world can be as gray as Trevor's or Aidan Higgins's* or John McGahern's,* but for Mac Laverty gray is not the the only color on his palette.

In A Time to Dance (1982), most of the pieces are static sketches of character rather than stories. As sketches, they are generally successful and provocatively contrasting both in subject and in tone. The best are probably "A Time to Dance," in which the boy's eye patch becomes a telling symbol of what his mother does not want him to see about life; "Life Drawing," in which the dead relations between an artist and his father are neatly summarized by the artist's failure to realize his father has died while being sketched; "Phonefun Limited," in which two middle-aged ex-prostitutes carry on their business of glamorous titillation from their most unglamorous flat; and "Language, Truth and Lock-jaw," in which a husband more interested in abstract analysis than emotion gets his jaw locked. Some pieces, such as the too-short "Father and Son" or "The Beginning of Sin," which is about a drunken priest, have predictably Trevorian endings. Others, however, such as "The Daily Woman," are either amusing or upbeat. The one developed story is "My Dear Palestrina," about a talented boy and his music teacher and how a narrow Northern society pulls them apart.

In his collection The Great Profundo (1987), Mac Laverty's characterization is again stronger than his plotting. The longest story, with the most action, "End of Season," is not as arresting as several of the shorter pieces that portray a situation or develop a character. Indeed, the characters of some of MacLaverty's sketches are distinctly memorable—particularly "the sad sword swallower" of the title story and the kind calligrapher of "Words the Happy Say." Even more effective are the pairings of disparate characters: the cardinal and his father, who has lost his faith, in "The Break," the photographer and his bigoted and yet not monstrous Unionist father in "Some Surrender," and especially the irascible blind painter who uses his secretary to paint his new pictures in "The Drapery Man." Mac Laverty's most recent work, Walking the Dog (1994), is a collection of nine stories divided by occasionally very funny and more often rather inexplicable vignettes. A couple of the stories seem slight and nearly pointless, but "The Grandmaster," about a mother's relation with her teenage, chess-playing daughter, and "Just Visiting," about a man sneaking drink in to his dying friend in hospital, are as strong as Mac Laverty's best. All are written in tight, beautifully crafted prose.

WORKS: Secrets and Other Stories. [Belfast]: Blackstaff, [1977]/New York: Viking, 1984; A Man in Search of a Pet. Belfast: Blackstaff, 1978. (Children's story); Mochua the Monk. Belfast: Blackstaff, 1978. (Children's story); Lamb. London: Jonathan Cape/New York: George Braziller, 1980. (Novel); A Time to Dance and Other Stories. London: Jonathan Cape/New York: George

Braziller, 1982; *Cal.* London; Cape/New York: George Braziller, 1983. (Novel); *The Great Profundo and Other Stories.* London: Jonathan Cape, 1987/New York: Grove, 1988; *Andrew McAndrew.* London: Walker, 1989. (Children's story); *Walking the Dog and Other Stories.* Belfast: Blackstaff, [1994].   REFERENCE: Saxon, Arnold. "An Introduction to the Stories of Bernard MacLaverty." *Journal of the Short Story* 8 (Spring 1987): 113–123.

McLAVERTY, MICHAEL (1904–1992), novelist and short story writer. McLaverty was born in Carrickmacross, County Monaghan, on July 5, 1904, but lived part of his childhood on Rathlin Island off the northern coast of County Antrim. Later, he lived and was educated in Belfast, first at St. Malachy's College and then at Queen's University where he read science and was awarded his M.Sc. in 1933. Until his retirement, he was a teacher of mathematics and later headmaster in the northern capital, during which time he maintained a steady output of novels and stories.

A great deal of McLaverty's fiction depicts the North of Ireland during the years between the two world wars when the decline of the small farmer, rural depopulation, and the accompanying growth of the industrial working class of Belfast began to accelerate. In such novels as *Call My Brother Back* (1939), *Lost Fields* (1941), and *In This Thy Day* (1945), he shuns direct treatment of public and political issues for the more local and urgent concerns of his characters: the conflicts between an individual and the rural community, within families and between generations, and, of course, poverty. Although one senses that they belong to a social and religious minority, rarely do McLaverty's people question either their Catholic faith or the larger social system that is the essential backdrop to their conflicts. Their vague dissatisfaction with their lot, not in society or in Northern Ireland, but in the world at large lends them an innocence that reminds one of Hardy's peasants.

His chief characters' broken relationship with the ancestral fields is the upshot of most of these conflicts and might be said to be McLaverty's principal theme in whichever of his favorite locales—Rathlin Island, the shores of Strangford Lough, the damp country rimming Lough Neagh, or the back streets of Belfast— a particular work may be set. In *Call My Brother Back,* his first and perhaps finest novel, McLaverty couples this theme with a blurred account of the sectarian outrages in Belfast during the creation of Northern Ireland. In addition, since both themes are presented in the strange and dreamlike currency of boyhood (a thirteen-year-old Rathlin islander is the central character), it is a troubled and poetic song of the awakening adolescent heart. McLaverty returned to Rathlin Island for his fictional setting in a later novel, *Truth in the Night* (1952).

The writing in *Call My Brother Back* represents McLaverty at his best. The limpness of style is at first glance almost childlike: large brushstrokes and broad, primary effects. But the untutored appearance of McLaverty's prose, as well as suiting the novel's point of view, barely disguises the author's deliberate attempt to isolate the subject matter by draining the style of affectation. At its worst, McLaverty's prose sinks with a leaden pathos; at its best, it is as single-minded and elemental as a mountain stream.

At the expense of a certain vigor, McLaverty has continued to cultivate quiet, even delicate powers of observation whose results are recorded on a restricted canvas. The short story, of which he is close to being a master, is probably his true *métier,* though he has not been prolific in the form. Whether he is writing about country people, as in "The Wild Duck's Nest," or of first-generation Belfast people, as in "The Game Cock," McLaverty tends to achieve a poignant and meditative quality that is hardly threatened by subdued irony or rueful humor. "The Game Cock," "Pigeons," and "Six Weeks On and Two Ashore" are among the best of his very fine stories.

McLaverty died in County Down on March 20, 1992.

JOHN WILSON FOSTER

WORKS: *Call My Brother Back.* London & New York: Longmans, Green, 1939/reissued Dublin: Allen Figgis, 1970; *Lost Fields.* New York & Toronto: Longmans, Green, 1941; *The White Mare and Other Stories.* New York: Devin-Adair, 1947; *The Three Brothers.* London: Jonathan Cape, 1948; *Truth in the Night.* New York: Macmillan, 1951; *School for Hope.* London: Jonathan Cape, 1954; *The Choice.* London: Jonathan Cape, 1958; *The Brightening Day.* New York: Macmillan, 1965; *The Road to the Shore and Other Stories.* Dublin: Poolbeg, [1976]; *Collected Short Stories.* Dublin: Poolbeg, [1979]; *Billy Boogles and the Brown Cow.* Dublin: Poolbeg, 1982. (Children's book); *In Quiet Places.* [Dublin]: Poolbeg, [1989]. Sophia Hillan King, ed. (Uncollected stories, letters, and critical prose). REFERENCES: Foster, John Wilson. *Forces and Themes in Ulster Fiction.* Dublin: Gill & Macmillan/Totowa, N.J.: Rowman & Littlefield, 1974, pp. 36–47, 59–63; King, Sophia Hillen. *The Silken Twine: A Study of the Works of Michael McLaverty.* Dublin: Poolbeg, 1992.

MacLIAMMÓIR, MICHEÁL (1899–1978), playwright, actor, and man of letters. Although he professed to have been born in Cork, MacLiammóir was actually born of English parents in London on October 15, 1899, and his name was Alfred Willmore. His adoption of Irishness was sincere and enthusiastic. He learned the language and wrote several books and plays in it, and Dublin remained his theatrical base. As a child actor, he played in London in *Peter Pan* and with Beerbohm Tree. For sixty years, however, he was one of the sights and delights of Dublin. He was one of the ablest modern actors, with a range from light romantic comedy to darkest tragedy. His Robert Emmet in Denis Johnston's* *The Old Lady Says "No!"* is considered an Irish classic; he was a preeminent interpreter of Oscar Wilde* and toured his own one-man show, *The Importance of Being Oscar,* all over the world; he played with much success roles as disparate as Hamlet and Liam O'Flaherty's* Gypo Nolan. In 1928, he and his English partner, Hilton Edwards, founded the Dublin Gate Theatre.* For it, he was involved as actor, director, author, set designer, and costume designer in over 300 productions. Few of his many plays have been published, but his several volumes of theatrical reminiscences are, in their graceful and witty mandarin style, a delightful re-creation of theatrical history and gossip. In 1977, he published a thinly disguised autobiographical novel, *Enter a Goldfish.* His panache and brio, his sweetness and urbanity, were notable in a city so seldom associated with such qualities. His literary taste was perhaps bounded by the English fin de siècle, and, consequently much of his writing seems only charmingly lightweight. His theatrical taste, however, was healthily eclectic, and the Gate Theatre, although hardly in the vanguard of theatrical experiment, has been healthily various and long vigorous. MacLiammóir died on March 6, 1978, nearly fifty years after the theater's first performance.

PRINCIPAL WORKS: *Diarmuid agus Grainne.* Baile Atha Cliath: Oifig Dialta Foilseachain Rialtais, 1935. (Play); *All for Hecuba.* London: Methuen, 1946/revised, Dublin: Progress House, 1961. (Memoir); *Put Money in Thy Purse: The Filming of Orson Welles' Othello.* London: Routledge & Kegan Paul, 1952; *Each Actor on His Ass.* London: Routledge & Kegan Paul, 1961. (Memoir); *Where Stars Walk.* Dublin: Progress House, 1962. (Play); *The Importance of Being Oscar.* Dublin: Dolmen/London: Oxford, 1963. (Text of one-man show); *Ill Met by Moonlight.* Dublin: Duffy, 1954. (Play); *Theatre in Ireland.* 2d ed., with sequel: Dublin: Three Candles, 1964; *An Oscar of No Importance.* London: Heinemann, 1968. (Memoir); with Eavan Boland, *W. B. Yeats.* London: Thames & Hudson, 1971/New York: Viking, 1972; *Enter a Goldfish.* London: Thames & Hudson, 1977. (Autobiographical novel).   REFERENCES: Fitz-Simon, Christopher. *The Boys: A Double Biography.* London: Nick Hern, [1994]; Luke, Peter, ed. *Enter Certain Players: Edwards, Mac Liammóir and the Gate.* [Dublin]: Dolmen, [1978]; Ó hAodha, Micheál. *The Importance of Being Michael.* [Dingle, Co. Kerry]: Brandon, [1990].

MacLOCHLAINN, ALF (1926–   ), novelist and librarian. MacLochlainn was born in Dublin in 1926 and graduated from University College, Dublin. He joined the National Library of Ireland in 1949 and worked with R. J. Hayes on the eleven-volume *Manuscript Sources for the History of Irish Civilisation* (Boston: G. K. Hall, 1965). In 1976, he was appointed director of the National Library and in 1982 was appointed librarian of University College, Galway, from which position he has now retired. In addition to many scholarly papers, he has published *Out of Focus,* which is described as a novella, but which would appear to be four short reflections of Flann O'Brien's (Brian O'Nolan*) de Selby as dictated to Samuel Beckett.*

WORK: *Out of Focus.* Dublin: O'Brien, 1977.

MacLYSAGHT, EDWARD [ANTHONY EDGEWORTH] (1887–1986), farmer, genealogist, and man of letters. MacLysaght was born in Nailsea, Somerset, on November 6, 1887. His father, Sydney Royce Lysaght* (the Gaelic form was his son's later adoption) was independently wealthy and the author of *My Tower in Desmond* and other novels. He was educated at Rugby, briefly at Oxford, and at the National University of Ireland. From 1909, he raised cattle, farmed, and market-gardened in Clare, Tipperary, and County Dublin. He was a partner with J. M. Hone and George Roberts in the Maunsel* press. This firm published his autobiographical novel, *The Gael* (1919), which chronicled the hero's increasing identification with the Irish and his growing unease with the Anglo-Irish. He was a member of the Irish Convention in 1917 and 1918 and a senator from 1922 to 1925. During 1929, 1930, 1936, and 1938, he was in South Africa, about which he later wrote a book in Irish. He was an inspector for the Irish Manuscripts Commission from 1939 to 1943, a member of the commission from 1949 to 1973, and its chairman from 1956 to 1973. He was made chief herald of Ireland, an appointment by de Valera, in 1943. He was keeper of manuscripts in the National Library from 1945 to 1955 and a member of the governing body of the School of Celtic Studies from 1942 to 1976. As chairman of the Manuscripts Commission, he did an immense amount of work, but to a wider readership he was known as the author of *Irish Life in the Seventeenth Century* (1939) and for his series on Irish family names. He wrote an appealing, though not overly revealing, autobiography, *Changing Times* (1978), which reflects his enthusiasms, his kindness, and his lifelong generosity. To MacLysaght's delight, a London publisher regretfully declined his memoirs, explaining that he could withstand one libel action, but not forty. Active until nearly the end of his long life, he died in Blackrock on March 4, 1986.

PETER COSTELLO

PRINCIPAL WORKS: *The Gael*. Dublin & London: Maunsel, 1919. (Novel); *Cursai Thomais: shios seal a's shuas seal*. Baile Atha Cliath: Hodges Figgis, 1927/translated by E. O'Clery and published as *The Small Fields of Carrig*. London: Heath Cranton, 1929. (Novel); *Poems*. Dublin: Hodges, Figgis/London: George Roberts, 1928; *Irish Life in the Seventeenth Century: After Cromwell*. 2d ed, revised & enlarged. Cork: Cork University Press/Oxford: Basil Blackwell, 1950; *Irish Families*. Dublin: Hodges Figgis, 1957; *More Irish Families*. Galway & Dublin: O'Gorman, 1960; *Supplement to Irish Families*. Dublin: Helicon, 1964; *A Guide to Irish Surnames*. Dublin: Helicon, 1964; *The Surnames of Ireland*. Shannon: Irish University Press, [1969]; *Forth the Banners Go. Reminiscences of William O'Brien as told to Edward MacLysaght*. Dublin: Three Candles, 1969; *Changing Times: Ireland since 1888*. Gerrards Cross: Colin Smythe, 1978. (Memoir); *More Irish Families: Incorporating Supplement to Irish Families, with an Essay on Irish Chieftainries*. Rev. & enlarged ed. Dublin: Irish Academic, [1982]. REFERENCE: Lysaght, Charles. *Edward MacLysaght, 1887–1986*. [Dublin]: Cumann Leabharlann Naisiunta na hÉireann, [1988].

MacMAHON, BRYAN (1909–   ), man of letters. Although he has written novels, plays, poems, memoirs, and children's books, as well as making ballads and translating from the Irish, MacMahon's chief allegiance as a writer has been to the short story. He is generally acknowledged to be one of the few Irish masters of that form to appear after Frank O'Connor* and Sean O'Faolain.*He was born on September 29, 1909, in Listowel, County Kerry, in a rich, rural environment that also produced George Fitzmaurice,* Maurice Walsh,* and John B. Keane.* He attended St. Michael's College in Listowel, and one of his early teachers was the writer Seamus Wilmot (1902–1977). Later, he attended St. Patrick's College in Drumcondra and qualified as a national teacher. For forty-five years he taught in the National Parochial School in Listowel. He also ran a bookstore and was a moving spirit in the town's amateur dramatic society.

MacMahon's first poems and stories were published in *The Bell** and were much admired by O'Connor and O'Faolain. His first collection of stories, *The Lion-Tamer* (1948), immediately established his reputation as a fresh and vital new voice in Irish fiction. If there is any serious fault in this excellent collection and in its successor, *The Red Petticoat* (1955), it probably stems from Mac-Mahon's own strong personality. He is a man of great enthusiasms and boundless energy, and his early prose sometimes romantically reflects that fact.

The dozen stories of *The Sound of Hooves* (1985) retain a high level of quality, with perhaps only two being rather slight and with three or four being notably strong. The most complex in form is "The French Cradle," which uses the framing device of an American graduate student writing a dissertation on "The Cult of the Severed Head in Celtic Mythology." Her studies uncover a story from 1691 that is passionate, bizarre, and also factual. "The Right to Be Maudlin," about a woman who has to give up her adopted child to its natural parents, is told in the first person and told with a rigid restraint, until its powerful final action, after the baby is taken away. In part, it concludes:

Smash, shatter and break. Moan, yell and howl. Through profanities and blasphemies I sob my thanks to the nuns who damned my emotions. Meanwhile, writhe, sway, seethe, bay, rave and wreck. Rage and again rage! Rage and vent the radiant obscenities that I have harboured and treasured and nursed against the transfiguration of this single fucking hour.

In his later work, MacMahon has become generally less florid in his prose, but as this passage shows, he is one of the few modern Irish story writers capable of unleashing a real bolt of rhetoric. The use of the language's most potent participle in this passage is unique in MacMahon, but its contrast to the Elizabethan rhetoric before it is explosive and a perfect example of what is meant by *le mot juste*.

The Tallystick (1994) is a very mixed bag of short pieces, ranging from character sketches or revealing encounters to developed stories such as "Testament of a Sewer Rat," "The House of Silence," and the title piece. Their tone ranges from the humorous to the effectively sad, as in "The Rich Fields of Meath," and sometimes combines both qualities, as in "The End of an Era," about the funeral of an old Anglo-Irish Lady. They are always impelled by a catchy idea that sets the point of view of the telling. Sometimes they are a bit romantically exuberant, as in "The Crossing," which is told entirely in dialogue about a bumptious sexual nonencounter. Much more effective in the same line are "Apples for Sale" and "The Cloak of Fire." However, the best pieces are those in which the author shrewdly observes others, rather than speaks through a MacMahon-like persona. There is still the occasional gorgeous word or phrase, such as "mythofacient" or "blepharitic eyes," but they can be forgiven for the many evocative descriptions, such as this terse snapshot of a workshop: "the whirr, hiss, thock and whine of the place."

MacMahon is steeped in rural tradition. This knowledge pervades his work and is particularly evident in *The Honey Spike* (1967), which is probably both his finest play and his finest novel. This picaresque tale of a young tinker couple traveling through Ireland is much enriched by MacMahon's intimate knowledge of the Traveling People, including an acquaintance with their secret language, Shelta. The story is, by turns, humorous, melodramatic, and full of local color and at the end is movingly eloquent. The fictional version perhaps loses something of the dramatic intensity of the play, but the play is probably one of the half-dozen best pieces to appear on the Irish stage since World War II. Its closest rival among MacMahon's own work is *The Song of the Anvil,* a blend of folklore, fantasy, and romance that, nevertheless, retains a firm grip on reality. MacMahon has also written a handful of short plays, the best of which—probably *Jack Furey* or *The Death of Biddy Early*—would not be out of place in an anthology that began with "Riders to the Sea."

Although in his middle eighties at this writing, MacMahon has remained productive, publishing not only the volume of stories *The Tallystick* but two volumes of memoirs that summarize the two main strands of his career, as teacher and as writer. *The Master* (1992), which won the 1993 American Ireland Literary Award, describes MacMahon's life as schoolmaster in Listowel (and, as a coda, as lecturer in creative writing at the University of Iowa). He writes of the appallingly primitive conditions of the first building he taught in, of his sane and humane thoughts about how to teach, of his experiences with students and parents and, being a gregarious man, with his fellow townsmen. The book is anecdotal, thoughtful, and wise. Nor, considering that MacMahon is something of a showman, is it lacking in razzmatazz—as in the story of how he introduced a baby elephant into the classroom. *The Storyman* (1994) is a companion volume that describes his writing career as budding poet, ballad maker, novelist, playwright, and, especially, short story writer. In it, he develops his notion of the basic ingredient of a story, the coupling of opposites, an idea that germinated from a lunch he had as a young man with O'Connor and O'Faolain. He asked how one wrote a short story and was told by one of them: "You get a male idea and a female idea and you couple them. The children are short stories." Perhaps as valuable are his description of how he cuts and rewrites and the discussion of how some of his own stories were first suggested. As the book makes clear, the main source and value of his writing derive from a canny observation of people, and the book, among other things, is the reflective autobiography of a boy sucking in observation and of a man mulling it over. Throughout there are striking vignettes of ordinary people and of some extraordinary ones, such as George Fitzmaurice.

MacMahon is a member of the Irish Academy of Letters and of Aosdána.* He was also a chief organizer of the Writers' Week in Listowel, and in 1972 he was awarded an LL.D. from the National University of Ireland for his services to Irish writing.

WORKS: *The Lion-Tamer and Other Stories.* Toronto: Macmillan, 1948/New York: E. P. Dutton, 1949, 1958/London: Dent, 1958; *Jack O'Moora, and the King of Ireland's Son.* New York: E. P. Dutton, 1950. (Children's book); *Children of the Rainbow.* New York: E. P. Dutton/London & Toronto: Macmillan, 1952. (Novel); *The Red Petticoat and Other Stories.* New York: E. P. Dutton/ London: Macmillan, 1955; *Brendan of Ireland.* London: Methuen, 1965/New York: Hastings House, 1967. (Children's book); *The Honey Spike.* New York: E. P. Dutton/London: Bodley Head/Toronto: Clarke, Irwin, 1967. (Novel); *The Song of the Anvil* in *Seven Irish Plays, 1946–1964.* Robert Hogan, ed. Minneapolis: University of Minnesota Press, 1967; *Patsy-O and His Wonderful Pets.* New York: E. P. Dutton, 1970. (Children's book); *Here's Ireland.* New York: E. P. Dutton/London: Batsford, 1971. (Travel); "The Death of Biddy Early." *Journal of Irish Literature* 1 (May 1972): 30–44.

(One-act play); "Jack Furey." *Journal of Irish Literature* 1 (May 1972): 45–62. (One-act play); trans., *Peig: The Autobiography of Peig Sayers of the Great Blasket Island.* Dublin: Talbot, 1974; *The End of the World and Other Stories.* Dublin: Poolbeg, 1976; *The Sound of Hooves, and Other Stories.* London: Bodley Head, 1985. (Short stories); *The Master.* [Swords, Co. Dublin]: Poolbeg, [1992]. (Memoir); *Mascot Patsy-O.* [Swords, Co. Dublin]: Poolbeg, [1992]. (Children's book); *The Talleystick and Other Stories.* [Dublin]: Poolbeg, [1994]; *The Storyman.* [Dublin]: Poolbeg, [1994]. (Memoir).   REFERENCES: Henderson, Gordon. "An Interview with Bryan MacMahon." *Journal of Irish Literature* 3 (September 1974): 3–23; Henderson, Joanne L. "Four Kerry Writers: Fitzmaurice, Walsh, MacMahon, Keane, a Checklist." *Journal of Irish Literature* 1 (May 1972): 112–118.

MacMANUS, CHARLOTTE ELISABETH (ca. 1850–1941), novelist.

MacManus, who usually published as L. MacManus, was active in the Gaelic League and wrote serials for newspapers and also patriotic historical novels.

WORKS: *The Red Star.* New York: G. P. Putnam's Sons, 1895/London: T. Fisher Unwin, 1896; *The Silk of the Kine.* London: T. Fisher Unwin, 1896/as *Silk.* New York: Harper, 1896; *In Sarsfield's Days: A Tale of the Siege of Limerick.* Dublin: M. H. Gill, 1906; *Lally of the Brigade.* London: T. Fisher Unwin/Boston: L. C. Page, 1899; *Nessa.* Dublin: Sealy, Bryers & Walker, [1902]; *The Wager.* New York: F. M. Buckles, [1902]; *Nuala: The Story of a Perilous Quest.* Dublin: Browne & Nolan, 1908; *The Professor in Erin.* Dublin: M. H. Gill, 1918; *Within the Four Seas of Fola.* Dublin: M. H. Gill, 1922; *White Light and Flame. Memories of the Irish Literary Revival and the Anglo-Irish War.* Dublin & Cork: Talbot, [1929].

MacMANUS, FRANCIS (1909–1965), novelist.

MacManus was born in Kilkenny on March 8, 1909. He was educated at the local Christian Brothers school, at St. Patrick's Teacher Training College in Dublin, and at University College, Dublin. He taught for eighteen years in the Synge Street Christian Brothers school in Dublin before joining Radio Éireann in 1948 as general features editor. He traveled widely in Europe, was a member of the Irish Academy of Letters, and was a moving force in introducing the Thomas Davis lecture series on Radio Éireann. His genial and helpful disposition endeared him to many writers. He died suddenly of a heart attack in Dublin on November 27, 1965.

MacManus wrote eleven novels and two interesting biographies, *Boccaccio* (1947) and *St. Columban* (1963). The novels begin with an historical trilogy based on peasant life in eighteenth-century Ireland: *Stand and Give Challenge* (1934), *Candle for the Proud* (1936), and *Men Withering* (1939). Unity is given to the trilogy by the central character, Donnacha Ruadh Mac Conmara, a hedge-schoolmaster and Gaelic poet.

From imaginative recreation of his racial past, "the hidden Ireland" of Daniel Corkery,* MacManus turned to depiction of the contemporary rural scene. The Drombridge trilogy, comprising *This House Was Mine* (1937), *Flow On, Lovely River* (1941), and *Watergate* (1942), is the first result. Dombridge is the fictional town in MacManus' native County Kilkenny. *This House Was Mine* concerns the self-destructive effects of land greed. *Flow On, Lovely River* is the diary of a schoolmaster thwarted by circumstances from marrying the girl he loves. Its title, a snatch from a popular song, is given Dantesque overtones; for the river is human life and unhappy human willing which flow to the sea of eternity and to God. *Watergate* (which has absolutely no connection with Richard M. Nixon) is the tale of a woman who returns to Ireland from the states and gradually finds her native rural Kilkenny not quite "the land of heart's desire."

MacManus was most prolific in the early 1940s, when he also composed *The Wild Garden* (1940), *The Greatest of These* (1943), and *Statue for a Square* (1945). The last-mentioned is MacManus' only true failure. Its parody of the small-town bumptiousness involved in erecting a public memorial is quite boring. Perhaps lighthearted satire was not an appropriate genre for so morally serious a writer. *The Wild Garden,* on the other hand, evokes brilliantly the fears and joys of childhood, and *The Greatest of These* is a fine delineation of a pre-Vatican II Irish bishop grappling with the psychological problems involved in practicing the highest theological virtue. Like Thomas Kilroy's* novel *The Big Chapel* (1971), *The Greatest of These* is based on the ecclesiastical conflicts in the town of Callan, County Kilkenny, during the 1870s.

The Fire in the Dust, MacManus' chief novel, appeared in 1950. The "fire" is the fire of normal sexual appetite, wrongly identified by the novel's puritans as the fire of lust. The "dust" is human mortality, especially the adolescents of Kilkenny City. Strongly autobiographical in flavor, the novel courageously attacked the Jansenistic tendencies of Irish Catholicism through affirming the sane humanistic values of the *philosophia perennis. American Son* (1959), the last MacManus novel, explores these values in the dramatic conflicts between New Mexican Indian Catholic religiosity, American capitalism, beatnik Franciscanism, and middle-class Irish Catholicism.

MacManus' *oeuvre* is best viewed, like Paul Claudel's, as the fruit of a mind which accepted willingly and liberatingly the dogmas of orthodox Catholic scholasticism. In this religious acceptance, as in his benign acceptance of the Irish race and language (as witness his U.S. travel book, *Seal Ag Rodaiocht/On the Road for a Time* of 1955), MacManus is the diametric opposite of James Joyce* and is also estranged from his acerbic contemporaries—O'Flaherty,* O'Faolain,* and O'Connor.* An absence of overt sexual detail, dictated only by artistic preference, ensured that, unlike those contemporaries, none of his works was banned by the Irish Censorship Board. His literary achievement, however, is often quite as high as theirs, and certainly needs reevaluation.

DENIS COTTER, JR.

WORKS: *Stand and Give Challenge.* Dublin: Talbot, 1934; *Candle for the Proud.* Dublin: Talbot, 1936; *This House Was Mine.* Dublin: Talbot, 1937; *Men Withering.* Dublin: Talbot, 1939; *The Wild Garden.* Dublin: Talbot, 1940; *Flow On, Lovely River.* Dublin: Talbot, 1941; *Watergate.* Dublin: Talbot, 1942; *The Greatest of These.* Dublin: Talbot, 1943; *Statue for a Square.* Dublin: Talbot, 1945; *Boccaccio.* London: Sheed and Ward, 1947; *The Fire in the Dust.* London: Jonathan Cape, 1950; *Seal Ag Rodaiocht/On the Road for a Time.* Baile Atha Cliath: Sairseal agus Dill, 1955; *American Son.* London: Jonathan Cape, 1959; *St. Columban.* Dublin: Clonmore & Reynolds, 1963. REFERENCES: Kiely, Benedict. "Praise God for Ireland." *The Irish Monthly* 76 (September 1948): 402–406. An extended version of this article appears in *The Kilkenny Magazine,* No. 14

(Spring–Summer 1966): 121–136; MacMahon, Sean. "Francis MacManus's Novels of Modern Ireland." *Eire-Ireland* 5 (1970): 116–130.

McMANUS, LIZ (1947–), novelist, short story writer, and journalist. McManus was born in Montreal, Canada, on March 23, 1947, the daughter of an Irish diplomat. Educated at convent school, she subsequently attended University College, Dublin, qualifying as an architect in 1968. A columnist with the *Sunday Tribune,* she served for nine years as a county councillor before being elected to the Dail in 1992. An early short story won a Hennessy Award in 1981. Her novel, *Acts of Subversion* (1991), set in the early 1970s, tells the story of Oran Reidy, a Dublin working-class youth who joins the republican movement in Galway.

IVY BANNISTER

WORK: *Acts of Subversion.* Dublin: Poolbeg, 1991.   REFERENCE: Claffey, Una. *The Women Who Won: Women of the 27th Dail.* Dublin: Attic, 1993, pp. 23–31.

MacMANUS, M[ICHAEL] J[OSEPH] (1888–1951), man of letters. MacManus was born in County Leitrim and died in County Donegal. He was educated at London University, taught in Lancashire, and was a freelance journalist in London. He returned to Ireland in 1916 and from 1931 until his death was literary editor of the *Irish Press.* MacManus was a devoted bibliophile, and his essays and light verse are pleasant but slight.

WORKS: *A Green Jackdaw. Adventures in Parody.* Dublin & Cork: Talbot, [1925]. (Light verse); *Connacht Songs.* Dublin: Talbot, 1927. (Poetry); *"So This Is Dublin."* Dublin & Cork: Talbot, 1927; *Dublin Diversions.* Dublin & Cork: Talbot, 1928; ed., *Irish Cavalcade, 1550–1850.* London: Macmillan, 1939; *Rackrent Hall and Other Poems.* Dublin: Talbot, 1941; ed., *Thomas Davis and Young Ireland.* Dublin: Stationery Office, 1945; *Adventures of an Irish Bookman.* Francis MacManus, ed. Dublin: Talbot, 1952. (Essays); *Eamon de Valera: A Biography.* rev. ed., with additional chapters by David O'Neill. Dublin: Talbot, 1957. For *The Dublin Magazine,* MacManus compiled a number of bibliographies of Synge,* Tom Moore,* Wolfe Tone,* and others, and some were reprinted as pamphlets.

MacMANUS, SEUMAS (ca. 1868–1960), man of letters. MacManus, a prolific writer of popular stories, verse, and plays, was born James MacManus in County Donegal and was the son of a poor farmer. Joseph Holloway* and other early commentators give his birthdate as December 31, 1868, although other authorities have cited 1869, 1870, and even 1860. At eighteen years of age, he became a National School teacher in the school where he himself had been taught. He soon began contributing pieces to many Irish papers, and he published his first book, *Shuilers from Healthy Hills,* in 1893. He was a contributor to the Belfast Nationalist magazine *The Shan Van Vocht,* and in 1901 he married one of its editors, the poet Anna Johnston who wrote under the name of Ethna Carbery* (died 1902). One of MacManus' early plays, *The Townland of Tamney,* was presented by the Irish National Theatre Society in January 1904. When the Abbey* first toured America in 1911, MacManus was one of the most virulent detractors of Synge's* *Playboy of the Western World;* Lady Gregory* referred to MacManus as "Shame-Us MacManus." For more than fifty years after his first wife's death, MacManus divided his time between America and Donegal. He continued to write prolifically, his most popular work possibly being his autobiography *The Rocky Road to Dublin* (1938) and a very long history of Ireland.

MacManus' conventional, sentimental, and patriotic verse has its banalities (see, for instance, the second saccharine stanza of "Lullaby," which Padraic Colum* anthologized), but has occasional small excellences (see, for instance, the fourth tight stanza of the otherwise piffling "A Stor, Gra Geal Mochree"). His plays are usually too simple and too broad, but one drama, *The Townland of Tamney,* might work if played with restraint instead of gagged as it was by the pre-Abbey players. His stories and retellings of folktales are often, despite his patriotism, an exaggeration for a foreign audience. Nevertheless, despite their Mr. Dooleyish broguing, they do contain many authentic and racy turns of phrase and even some eloquent writing. For instance, this passage from *The Humours of Donegal:*

He was as merry as a mouse in a cornstack, but as roguish as a rat that grew gray in mischief and morodin'. The lark herself didn't sing sweeter, nor rise earlier, nor think less of the troubles of the morra. The hare hadn't a lighter foot scuddin' from the corn, the throstle of Murvagh Wood a lighter heart, nor the *Bacach Beag* [little beggarman] a lighter purse. Barney wrought to any man in the parish—or the next to it—by day, and he attended every spree in the parish—or the next to it—by night. No wake missed Barney; no weddin' missed Barney; no berral missed Barney; no christenin' missed him. If there was a fair, Barney was the second man at it; if there was a raffle, Barney was the first; if there was a dance, Barney was there; if there was a scuffle, me brave Barney was everywhere. He owned as much clothes as was on his back, as much land as stuck to the soles of his brogues, and as much motherwit as would dower a townland. As for the amount of thickery in his head, there's no tellin' of it. Och, it's Barney was the boy out an' out!

MacManus died at about age ninety in New York City on October 23, 1960, as a result of a fall out of the seventh-story window of his nursing home.

WORKS: *Shuilers from Healthy Hills,* by "Mac." Donegal: G. Kirke, 1893; *The Leadin' Road to Donegal, and Other Stories,* by "Mac." London: Digby, Long, ca. 1895; *'Twas in Dhroll Donegal,* by "Mac." 2d ed. London: Downey, 1897; *The Bend of the Road,* by James MacManus ("Mac"). London: Downey, 1898; *The Humours of Donegal,* by James MacManus ("Mac"). London: Unwin, 1898; *In Chimney Corners, Merry Tales of Irish Folk-lore.* New York: Doubleday & McClure, 1899/many other editions, the latest, Garden City, N.Y.: Doubleday, Doran, 1935; *Through the Turf Smoke,* by "Mac." New York: Doubleday & McClure, 1899/London: Unwin, 1901; *The Bewitched Fiddle and Other Irish Tales.* New York: Doubleday & McClure, 1900; *Donegal Fairy Stories.* New York: McClure, Phillips, 1900/London: Isbistor, 1902/Garden City, N.Y.: Doubleday & Page, 1910/New York: Doubleday, 1912/Garden City, N.Y.: Doubleday, 1943; *A Lad of the O'Friels.* New York: McClure, Phillips, 1903/various other editions, the latest, New York: Devin-Adair, 1947; *The Red Poacher.* New York: Funk & Wagnalls, 1903; *Ballads of a Country Boy.* Dublin: Gill, 1905; *The Hard-Hearted Man.* Dublin: Gill, 1905. (Play); *Doctor Kilgannan.* Dublin: Gill, 1907; *Yourself and the Neighbours.* New York: Devin-Adair, [1914], 1944;

Ireland's Curse. New York: Irish Publishing Co., ca. 1917; *Lo, and Behold Ye!* New York: Frederick A. Stokes, [1919]; *Tales That Were Told.* Dublin: Talbot/London: Unwin, 1920; *Top o' the Mornin'.* New York: Frederick A. Stokes, [1920]; *The Story of the Irish Race.* New York: Irish Publishing Co., 1921/New York: Devin-Adair, 1945, 1955; *The Donegal Wonder Book.* New York: Frederick A. Stokes, 1926; *O, Do You Remember. . . .* Dublin: Duffy, 1926; ed., *The Four Winds of Eirinn,* Poems of Ethna Carbery, 25th Anniversary edition. Dublin: Gill, 1927; *A Short Story of the Irish Race.* Dublin: Browne & Nolan, [1928]; *Bold Blades of Donegal.* New York: Frederick A. Stokes, 1935/London: Marston, [1937]; *The Rocky Road to Dublin.* New York: Macmillan, 1938/New York: Devin-Adair, 1947; *Dark Patrick,* New York: Macmillan, 1939; *The Well o' the World's End.* New York: Macmillan, 1939/New York: Devin-Adair, 1949, 1954; *Woman of Seven Sorrows.* Dublin: Gill, 1945. (Play); *Tales from Ireland.* London: Evans [1949]; *We Sang for Ireland, Poems of Ethna Carbery, Seumas MacManus, Alice Milligan.* New York: Devin-Adair, 1950: *Heavy Hangs the Golden Grain.* New York: Macmillan, 1950/Dublin: Talbot, [1951]; *The Bold Heroes of Hungry Hill, and Other Irish Folk Tales.* New York: Ariel Books, [1951]/New York: Pellegrini & Cudahy, 1951/London: Dent, [1952]; *The Little Mistress of the Eskar Mór.* Dublin: Gill, 1960; *Hibernian Nights.* New York: Macmillan, 1963. (There is also an early volume, apparently from the 1890s: *Barney Brean and Other Boys.* Dublin: "Irish Nights" Office, n.d.) Most of MacManus' plays were issued from about 1905 by D. O'Molloy of Mount Charles, County Donegal. These were paperback editions for amateur actors, and included: 1. *The Leadin' Road to Donegal;* 2. *The Resurrection of Dinny O'Dowd;* 3. *The Lad from Largymore;* 6. *The Townland of Tamney,* reprint, Chicago: De Paul University, 1972; 7. *Orange and Green;* 8. *Nabby Heron's Matching; Bong Tong Comes to Balruddery;* 10. *Rory Wins;* 11. *Mrs. Connolly's Cashmere;* 12. *The Miracle of Father Peter;* 13. *The Rale True Doctor;* 14. *The Bachelors of Braggy.*

Mac MATHUNA, SEÁN (1936–   ), short story writer.

WORK IN ENGLISH: *The Atheist and Other Stories.* Dublin: Wolfhound, 1987.

McNALLY, LEONARD (1752–1820), playwright.

The infamous, though fascinating, Leonard McNally was born in Dublin in 1752, and was admitted to the Irish bar in 1776 and to the English bar in 1783. He edited *The Public Ledger,* and several of his plays were successfully performed at Covent Garden. He was counsel for Napper Tandy in 1792 and was one of the original members of the United Irishmen. Indeed, he even fought a duel with Sir Jonah Barrington* to defend the honor of the United Irishmen. However, from at least 1794, he was in the pay of Dublin Castle from which he received a substantial yearly stipend of £300 until his death. Thoroughly trusted by the United Irishmen, he was in the habit of entertaining them and then reporting their conversations to the authorities. He put the finger on Lord Edward Fitzgerald in 1797, and he sold Emmet* in 1803 for £200. However, he was the defense counsel for the most prominent men of '98 and his defense of Emmet in 1803 was thought brilliantly eloquent. He is also said to have consoled Emmet in his death cell by pointing out that the young patriot would soon be united with his mother in Heaven. He died in Harcourt Street, Dublin, on February 13, 1820, and was buried in Donnybrook church, his villainies still undetected.

McNally was a personally brave man who fought several duels, and he was the most engaging company. His plays and comic operas have not held up and were not Irish in subject, but they were droll and entertaining in their day.

Several are available on microprint from the Larpent collection, and his five-act comedy *Fashionable Levities* (1785) is available in the reprint of Mrs. Inchbald's *Modern Theatre*. The popular song "The Lass of Richmond Hill" is his. He adapted *Tristram Shandy* to the stage (1783), and he also wrote a fictional parody of Sterne* in his *Sentimental Excursions to Windsor* (1781). As a writer, he would repay examination.

WORKS: *The Apotheosis of Punch*. London: J. Wenman, 1779. (Satirical masque); *Sentimental Excursions to Windsor and Other Places*. London: J. Walker, 1781; *Retaliation*. London: F. Blythe, 1782. 2d ed./Dublin: Printed by R. Marchbank, for the Company of Booksellers, 1782. (Farce in two acts); *Tristram Shandy*. London: S. Bladon, 1783. ("a sentimental, Shandean bagatelle in two acts"); *Fashionable Levities*. London: G. G. F. & J. Robinson, 1785/also in Mrs. Inchbald's *The Modern Theatre*, Vol. 10; *Richard Coeur de Lion*. London: Debrett, 1786. (Play); *Critic upon Critic*. London: G. Brand, 1788. ("a dramatic medley in three acts"); *Cottage Festival*. London: G. Brand, 1796. (Play).   REFERENCES: Pitcher, E. W. "Leonard McNally: A Few Facts on a Minor Author of the Eighteenth Century." *Notes and Queries* 28 (August 1981): 306–308.

MacNAMARA, BRINSLEY (1890–1963), novelist, short story writer, and playwright. MacNamara was born John Weldon on September 6, 1890, in Ballinacor, Hiskinstown, Delvin, County Westmeath, one of seven children of the local schoolmaster, James Weldon. In 1910, while in Dublin ostensibly to study for a career in the excise, young Weldon joined the Abbey Theatre* company as a stagehand and actor. He adopted or was assigned the stage name "Brinsley MacNamara" and eventually went with the company in 1911 on the first Abbey tour of America. He remained in America until 1913, attempting to make a career in New York, but he was unsuccessful and returned to Ireland. From 1913 until 1918, he retired to Delvin, from where he published numerous derivative poems and stories in Dublin newspapers and magazines. His burgeoning talent gradually evidenced a peculiar turn, a whimsical, ironic, curious eye for reality as he perceived it—a patiently refracting vision of human experience and knowledge.

This period of apprentice work was disrupted by the 1918 publication of his classic novel, *The Valley of the Squinting Windows,* a young man's scathing demythologizing of Irish village life. MacNamara's milestone was chronologically analogous to America's *The Spoon River Anthology, Winesburg, Ohio,* and *Main Street.* This was the first of seven novels he was to write as "Brinsley MacNamara"; and, although not his finest literary achievement, the book and its title entered Ireland's national consciousness.

The resultant notoriety of the novel provoked several disastrous effects for MacNamara: in best medieval fashion the book was publicly burned in Delvin's square; James Weldon's school was boycotted (eventually, he unsuccessfully sued the parish priest and several parishioners, correctly citing a conspiracy that affected his pension); and MacNamara was driven from Delvin in fear of his life, ever after to consider himself an outsider, an exiled man of the country compelled to live in Dublin.

A decade after its publication, Andrew E. Malone* correctly perceived the novel's essential provocation: "Unerringly the novelist struck at the weakest spot in the Irish rural social system—its treatment of women. . . . *The Valley of the Squinting Windows* is the story of an entire village—but it is mainly the story of two much-wronged women." Intentionally or not, Malone also stigmatized MacNamara as the originator of the "squinting windows" school of realistic Irish fiction. This unfortunate misnomer forever compounded Mac-Namara with lesser lights, redundant recorders of "authentic" wakes, weddings, and emigrations.

MacNamara's life became a continual distancing, an enduring alienation, from that legacy he most loved and hated. The acrimonious Ireland that Dublin epitomized for James Joyce* was typified for MacNamara by his own Irish Midlands. They are the true center of his Ireland. No Irish novelist had ever so painstakingly, nor with such incisive, quixotic compassion, delineated the self-righteous intolerance and rancor of rural Ireland's insensibilities. MacNamara's novels and stories preserve a people whose only traditions are those of orthodoxy, avarice, and prideful ignorance; set where, ominously and always, the major antagonist is a benighted Catholic Church and its *a priori,* bumptious clergy.

MacNamara had determined not to succumb to the bleak anomaly of this life. He became its master, its historian, and its savior. Inevitably, youthful idealism led to stoic disbelief and still later, to mature submission, a chilling sense of the tragicomic—which he pensively called "the long, low chuckle of the mind."

In the summer of 1920, he married Helena Degidon in Quin, County Clare. Their only child, Oliver Weldon, was born there in May 1921. By this time, two of MacNamara's plays had been produced at the Abbey Theatre, *The Rebellion in Ballycullen* (1919) and *The Land for the People* (1920). He had also published three additional novels: *The Clanking of Chains* (1920), in which, given the frantic, insurgent times, he far more dangerously pursued his indictment of the apathetic Irish village, especially in its conservative political indecision; *The Irishman* (1920), under the pseudonym "Oliver Blyth," wherein he delineates his evolving literary aesthetic, reveals how *The Valley of the Squinting Windows* came to be written, and satirizes the pomposity and personae of the Irish literary renaissance; and the hauntingly beautiful and Hardy-esque *The Mirror in the Dusk* (1921), in which he finally comprehends the absurdity of bearing his redeemer's mirror into a world of the smugly, wretchedly, gratefully blind.

MacNamara never again experienced years of such progress in his work (including an impressive series of twenty-three articles entitled "Books and Their Writers" for *The Gael,* 1920–1921). The period between 1916 and 1922 was the years of Ireland's descent from the idealism of the few to the vulgarity of a majority, and during this era of rampant nationalism MacNamara struggled heroically to proclaim the truths others would exploit in retrospect. The unrequited struggle proved too much for one man. The dedicated novelist who worked so arduously to produce four novels, several plays, and dozens of stories in less than six years produced only three additional novels in the remaining forty years of his life—and two of them, *The Various Lives of Marcus Igoe* (1929) and *Return to Ebontheever* (1930), were partially written during this same chaotic period.

MacNamara was appointed temporary registrar to the National Gallery in 1925, succeeding James Stephens.* The position was made permanent in 1926.

Between 1919 and 1945, MacNamara had nine plays produced at the Abbey, the most memorable and powerful of which is *Margaret Gillan* (1933), a stark, fantastic, Ibsen-like study of a woman's frustrated love, repressed passions, and revenge. It was awarded the Casement Prize as the best Irish play of the year, as well as the Harmsworth Literary Award. *The Master*, a drama based on the boycotting of Master Weldon's school in Ballinvalley, was first produced at the Abbey in 1928. MacNamara's comedies, the best of which are *The Glorious Uncertainty* (1923) and *Look at the Heffernans!* (1926), confirm that he did artistically compromise himself to produce commercially successful Abbey formula plays. Remarkably, despite his lifelong association with the Abbey, he was never truly a man of the theater, although he served briefly in 1935 on the Abbey's Board of Directors. Shortly after his appointment by W. B. Yeats* (together with F. R. Higgins* and Ernest Blythe, men of even less or no theatrical acumen), he impetuously resigned in protest over production details in Sean O'Casey's* *The Silver Tassie*. MacNamara was later a drama critic for the *Irish Times*, but his reviews clearly disclose a man who did not consider drama a serious form of literature.

Following the financial success of his frequently revived comedies, *The Glorious Uncertainty* and *Look at the Heffernans!*, both fashioned from far less amusing short stories, MacNamara's life was more devoted to being a literary raconteur and fashionable dramatist about town than to the more exacting, secluded, and purposeful life of enfant terrible of Irish fiction. Nevertheless, he was a founding member of the Irish Academy of Letters in 1932.

In 1929, MacNamara had produced his finest novel, *The Various Lives of Marcus Igoe*, an intensely personal, self-evaluative, tragicomic dialectic. In the multiplicity of its concerns and in its undeniably existential musings, the book emerges as his masterpiece: a profoundly original and challenging work and a too-long-neglected gem worthy of MacNamara's boon companion, Flann O'Brien (Brian O'Nolan*). It is also anticipatory of Aidan Higgins's* *Langrishe, Go Down* or Benedict Kiely's* *Nothing Happens in Carmincross* and a precursor to John Banville's* metafictional canon. MacNamara's primary concerns here are the envisioned immortality of the artist in his own work and man's dilemma of defining himself between the celestial and the secular, the ephemeral and the eternal. He vigorously asserts the supremacy, reliability, and immutability of characters in literature over the inconstancy, mutability, and enigma that he ascertained were modern man.

The year 1929 also saw the publication of a collection of short stories, *The Smiling Faces*, mostly reworked, familiar materials and methods from an earlier period. In 1930, he published *Return to Ebontheever,* a melancholy, disquieting, but beautifully written novel of life imitating art, shadowing Shakespeare's *Othello.*

A long silence in his fiction (although *The Grand House in the City* [1936] and *The Three Thimbles* [1941] had been inauspiciously produced at the Abbey) was broken in 1945 with the publication of a book of stories entitled *Some Curious People.* The stories are vintage MacNamara, unhurried, ironic, poetically idiomatic, sad, and often brilliantly humorous.

His final novel, *Michael Caravan* (1946), is in a lighter, perhaps forgiving, dreamlike mood, but more sentimental, concerned with life-replacing fantasies. It is a comedy of rural manners and affectations, by turns touching naive and nostalgic, and set in a remote, more innocently sincere time than the post-World War II world.

The Whole Story of the X. Y. Z. (1951), a novella, deals with a man's absorption in his inspiriting fantasies and the necessities for illusions in a world mad enough to pass him by. With the exception of a few stories, an anthologized poem, and the belated publication of *The Glorious Uncertainty* in 1957, MacNamara did not appear in print again until the charmingly reminiscent "Growing Up in the Midlands" appeared posthumously in *The Capuchin Annual 1964.* Crippled by arthritis and old age, MacNamara retired from a distinguished thirty-five-year career in the National Gallery in 1960, only a few years before his death in 1963.

Today, MacNamara must be acknowledged as a pioneer of iconoclastic, postmodern Irish fiction. He may have been driven to the whimsy of his Abbey comedies for relief from financial burdens; from the disillusionment of being a prophet in his own country; from a rural man's desire for recognition in his capital city; or, more likely, from his sense of the futility of any artistic endeavor.

Whatever his impetus, MacNamara discovered the milieu that best suited his idiosyncratic, curious talents. With *The Various Lives of Marcus Igoe,* he produced the work that is his most demanding accomplishment and the cornerstone of his distinctive, innovative achievement.

MICHAEL McDONNELL

WORKS: *The Valley of the Squinting Windows.* London: Sampson Low, Marston, 1918; as "Oliver Blyth," *The Irishman.* London: Everleigh Nash, 1920; *The Clanking of Chains.* Dublin: Maunsel, 1920; *The Mirror in the Dusk.* Dublin & London: Maunsel & Roberts, 1921; *Look at the Heffernans!* Dublin & Cork: Talbot, n.d. (Play); *The Smiling Faces.* London: Mandrake, 1929. (Short stories); *The Various Lives of Marcus Igoe.* London: Sampson Low, Marston, 1929; *Return to Ebontheever.* London: Jonathan Cape, 1930/reissued in paper edition as *Othello's Daughter,* 1942; *Margaret Gillan.* London: George Allen & Unwin, 1934. (Play); *Marks and Mabel.* Dublin: James Duffy, 1945. (Play); *Some Curious People.* Dublin: Talbot, 1945. (Short stories); *Michael Caravan.* Dublin: Talbot, 1946; "The Master's Holiday." *The Bell* (August 1947); *Abbey Plays, 1899–1948.* Dublin: At the Sign of the Three Candles, 1949. (Pamphlet listing Abbey plays and first productions, with Introduction); "The World and Garrett Reilly." *Irish Writing* (January 1950); *The Whole Story of the X. Y. Z.* Belfast: H. R. Carter, 1951. (Novella); "Mullally's Reverie." *The Bell* (1954); *The Glorious Uncertainty.* Dublin: P. J. Bourke, 1957. (Play); "On Seeing Swift in Laracor." *The*

Oxford Book of Irish Verse. Donagh MacDonagh & Lennox Robinson, eds. Oxford: Clarendon, [1958]; "Growing Up in the Midlands." *The Capuchin Annual 1964:* 149–170. (Autobiographical article). REFERENCES: Boyd, Ernest. *Ireland's Literary Renaissance.* New York: Barnes & Noble, 1922; Costello, Peter. *The Heart Grown Brutal.* Dublin: Gill & Macmillan, 1977; Cronin, John. *The Anglo-Irish Novel.* Vol. 2. Belfast: Appletree, 1990; Deane, Seamus. *A Short History of Irish Literature.* Notre Dame, Ind.: University of Notre Dame Press, 1986; Fallis, Richard. *The Irish Renaissance.* Syracuse, N.Y.: Syracuse University Press, 1977; Flanagan, Thomas. "The Night the Book Was Burned." *Irish Evening Press* (July 18, 1964); Fleischmann, Ruth. "Brinsley Mac-Namara's Penny Dreadful." *Éire-Ireland* (Summer 1983): 53–74; Foster, John Wilson. *Fictions of the Literary Revival.* Syracuse, N.Y.: Syracuse University Press, 1987; Gonzalez, Alexander G. "The Novels of Brinsley MacNamara's Later Period." *Irish University Review* (Autumn 1989): 272–286; Kiely, Benedict. *Modern Irish Fiction.* Dublin: Golden Eagle Books, 1950; Malone, Andrew E. "Brinsley MacNamara: An Appreciation." *Dublin Magazine* (July 1929); McDonnell, Michael. "Brinsley MacNamara: A Checklist." *Journal of Irish Literature* 4 (May 1975): 79–88; McDonnell, Michael. "Stereotypes and Caricatures of the Abbey Theatre (1910) in *The Irishman* by 'Brinsley MacNamara.' " *Éire-Ireland* (Fall 1989): 53–64; McMahon, Sean. "A Reappraisal: *The Valley of the Squinting Windows.*" *Éire-Ireland* (Spring 1968): 106–117; O'Farrell, Padraic. *The Burning of Brinsley MacNamara.* Dublin: Lilliput, 1990.

MacNAMARA, DESMOND (1918–   ), sculptor, retired lecturer in art, and novelist. MacNamara was born in Dublin but moved to London in the 1950s. He has designed costumes for Olivier's film of *Henry V,* worked for the Gate* and Abbey* theaters, and reviewed books for *The New Statesman, Studies,* and *The Tablet.* His own works include books on the use of papier-mâché in sculpture, on puppetry, on picture framing, and on de Valera and, in 1994, a novel, *The Book of Intrusions.*

Its title is a semipun on the Irish medieval *Book of Invasions,* and the novel itself is a spin on Flann O'Brien's (Brian O'Nolan*) *At Swim-Two-Birds,* the innovative novel in which the author is dominated by his own characters, who eventually take over the plot. But, while O'Brien's work includes pookas, Finn MacCool, and leftover characters from American westerns, MacNamara's encyclopedic parody deals with the problem of leftover or discarded characters from unfinished or unpublished literary works. The "book-begotten" (characters) wage war on the "bed-begotten" (writers), as an encorpified Owen Mountmellick and his servant, MacGilla, carryovers from an unfinished Lever* novel, hatch a scheme to escape from literary Limbo and enjoy earth a bit before ascending to Parnassus, the heavenly abode for fictional types. After capturing a scribe, Mountmellick, in whom MacNamara parodies pedantry, springs Loreto Amargamente, a second-generation literary discard as the offspring of characters from an unfinished F. Scott Fitzgerald short story, releasing her from her life as a "particle." He next releases Liadin, from George Moore's* unpublished historical novel (but only after the reader is treated to a forty-page rendition of the medieval saga of Curither and Liadin, Moore's source work). His troupe of renegades also includes the unsummoned Eevell of Craglee, Queen of the Munster Hosts of Fairy. She is an eight-foot-tall feminist who has been brought to earth by the scribe himself, whom she dubs "Scribbles." Unfortunately, Eevell has a predilection for the rhetoric of Brendan Behan,* for she turns out to be his conception of Eevell and not the original queen of the *sidhe.*

MacNamara's escapees assume control of a publishing house and make their host a hostage as they seek to release other characters from discriminating works of fiction. Literary redemption or immortalization would reward the long-suffering creatures who have merely existed on the pen pusher's page. But in a dramatic reversal of power, the scribe, aided by James Stephens's* canine character, Bran, registers the tricky characters' names on chapters sealed in milk bottles containing a plea for help. With publication, Mountmellick and company will ascend to Parnassus, and the writer will be freed.

MacNamara uses this imaginative and digressive novel to poke fun at the traditions of Celtic folklore, the fate of the novel, and academic research (offering a paper entitled "The Prostrate Gland in Anglo-Irish Literature"), as well as his own friendship with J. P. Donleavy* and Brendan Behan. The labyrinthine style of Gaelic narrative, incomprehensible to the Fitzgerald character, provides the framework for this intricate comic novel.

MARGUERITE QUINTELLI-NEARY

WORKS: *A New Art of Papier-Mâché.* London: Arco, 1963; *Puppetry.* London: Arco, 1965; *Picture Framing: A Practical Guide from Basic to Baroque.* Newton Abbot & North Pomfret, Vt.: David & Charles, 1986; *Eamon de Valera: President of Ireland.* New York: Chelsea House, 1988. (Juvenile biography); *The Book of Intrusions.* Normal, Ill.: Dalkey Archive, 1994. (Novel). REFERENCE: Jacobsen, Kurt. "Desmond MacNamara, An Interview." *Journal of Irish Literature* 10 (January 1981): 61–73.

MacNAMARA, GERALD (1865–1938), playwright and actor. Gerald Mac-Namara was the pen and stage name of Harry C. Morrow, who was born on August 27, 1865, and died in Belfast on January 11, 1938. He became the head of the family firm of Belfast house painters, decorators, and renovators. Two of his brothers, Fred and Jack, were involved in stage production, costuming, and design. Three other brothers became well-known illustrators. MacNamara himself became one of the most important actors and writers for the Ulster Literary Theatre.* Like his colleague Rutherford Mayne,* he was a brilliant amateur actor, and he excelled in comic character parts. As a writer, he contributed about eleven slight but quirky comedies to the Ulster Theatre. His plays tended to be burlesques, satires, or fantasies, and his most popular piece, *Thompson in Tir-na-n-Og,* was constantly revived after its first production in 1912 and was rivaled in popularity only by Mayne's *The Drone. Thompson* is an Irish equivalent of *A Connecticut Yankee in King Arthur's Court,* and in it a rather dense Orange-man is transported, with incongruous results, back into the Land of Youth. Among MacNamara's most popular other plays were *The Mist That Does Be on the Bog* (1909), a satire of the Abbey Theatre* peasant play, and *Suzanne and the Sovereigns* (1907), an historical burlesque about Orangemen and Catholics, written with Lewis Purcell.* Toward the end of his life, a few short pieces and closet dramas appeared in *The Dublin Magazine,** and in 1988 Kathleen

Danaher collected five of his plays, including three previously unpublished ones. Only about half of his plays have thus far come to light, and to judge by them and by contemporary reactions to the others, one would have to conclude that he was a minor but very individual comic talent—if not perhaps, as his colleague Rutherford Mayne called him, "one of the finest comic geniuses that the Irish dramatic revival has produced."

WORKS: *Thompson in Tir-na-n-Og*. Dublin: Talbot, 1918; "Stage Directions for a play called *William John Jamieson*." *Dublin Magazine* 1 (1923–1924); "trans. from the Norwegian of Gibson's *Babes in the Woods*" in *Dublin Magazine* 1 (1924); "Tcindrella." *Dublin Magazine* 2 (1924); "Little Devil Dought." *Dublin Magazine* 2 (1925); "The Plays of Gerald MacNamara," edited by Kathleen Danaher. *Journal of Irish Literature* 17 (May–September 1988), and containing *Suzanne and the Sovereigns, The Mist That Does Be on the Bog, Thompson in Tir-na-n-Og, No Surrender,* and *Who Fears to Speak?* REFERENCES: Danaher, Kathleen. op. cit. "Introduction" and Introductions to the individual plays; Mayne, Rutherford. "Gerald MacNamara." *Dublin Magazine* 12, New Series (1938): 53–56.

McNAMARA, LINDA

WORK: *Drinker at the Spring of Kardaki*. Dublin: Wolfhound, 1992.

McNAMEE, BRENDAN (1955–), fiction writer.

McNamee was born in County Donegal and now lives in London. His *The Man Who Lived in Sorcy Wood* (1987) is a fable of novella length, told in simple, unadorned storyteller's prose, without a word wasted. It is a tale about a schoolteacher who goes to live in a wood, a priest who wants to level the wood and build an airport for a local shrine, and a businessman who wants to level the wood for an Irish Disneyland. Something of a fairy tale or a wonder tale, the book is a stinging yet uplifting comment on life and values in modern Ireland and could become something of a minor classic.

WORK: *The Man Who Lived in Sorcy Wood*. Dublin: Raven Arts, [1987].

McNAMEE, EOIN (1961–), fiction writer.

McNamee was born in Kilkeel, County Down, and his fiction is about sex and violence, often graphically depicted, in the North. Dermot Bolger,* who published his novella *The Last of Deeds* (1989), later referred to his "stark and exquisite prose." In the novella, the similes and metaphors strain too much for the striking effect and often become either ludicrous, as in "She had a big nose like a vegetable covered in broken veins and blackheads," or poetically vague, as in "The man's voice was soft like bad meat" or "he smiled the wide, blue smile of a drought in the cornbelt." Or simply awful as in "the unimaginable lingerie of death" or "birth-stretched breasts lolling like tongues out of rubber bras, and cunts like something you'd find on the dump." Much of the literal description, as on the first page of Chapter 2, refers to "toe rot and other diseases," crabs feeding on a corpse, and a young man who "always had six inches of snot hanging from his sleeve and a chinful of pimples on the verge of busting."

By *Resurrection Man* (1994), McNamee developed an effectively terse dialogue, although its strength mainly relies on a profuse use of the usual four-letter words. The descriptive passages, however, are even more florid and portentous, and there are many phrases like "the cleansing lustre of selfishness," "the strange architecture of their loathing," "the flawed verities of his life," "the artifacts of desolation," "the edge of the disconsolate," "the momentous dark," "the intricate landscapes of memory," and "the lonely and vigilant dead." Indeed, the overwriting sometimes tends to smother the meaning, as in "The cracked nail polish and period pains symptoms of the inept and needy self." Or as in "it was almost night, if night described the fraught blackness closing from the mountains and the freezing lough in the first coming of another governance of light which was infallible and cold," in which the more portentous words seem out of focus.

The Last of Deeds was short-listed for the 1989 *Irish Times*/Aer Lingus Prize for Literature, and in 1990 McNamee received the Macauley Fellowship for Irish Literature, facts that may suggest something about the state of Irish literary criticism at the end of the twentieth century.

WORKS: *The Last of Deeds.* Dublin: Raven Arts, [1989]. (Novella, printed with "The Lion Alone" and "Radio 1974")/republished with "Love in History," an expanded version of "The Lion Alone," [London]: Penguin, [1992]); *Resurrection Man.* [London & Basingstoke]: Picador, [1994]. (Novel); *The Language of Birds.* Dublin: New Island, [1995]. (Poetry).

McNAMEE, JOHN

WORK: *New and Selected Poems.* Dublin: Weaver, 1990.

MacNEICE, LOUIS

MacNEICE, LOUIS (1907–1963), poet. MacNeice was born in Belfast on September 12, 1907, the third child of the Reverend John Frederick MacNeice who was to become Church of Ireland bishop of Down and Connor and Dromore. MacNeice was educated at Sherbourne, Marlborough, and at Merton College, Oxford, where he read classics and philosophy. From 1930 to 1939, he lectured in classics in Birmingham and London.

MacNeice's name was linked in the 1930s with those of W. H. Auden, Stephen Spender, and C. Day-Lewis.* It was assumed that he shared the ideological commitment of those left-wing poets, but in fact his work at that period, while conscious of contradictions in the social order, lacked any distinctive political faith, expressing rather melancholy, fear of the future, and a heightened apprehension of transience. At this point in his career, his work focused on exploitation of cliché or rhythms drawn from popular songs and was remarkably sensitive to sensory experience. *Autumn Journal* (1939) is both representative of this work and a culmination of his art to that date. A long journalistic poem, it records the impressions, fears, and hopes of a young intellectual in London in the months surrounding the Munich crisis, assessing a middle-class education, a childhood and past in Ireland, and an adult experience of sexual relations, political and social realities, and human values tested in the crucible of civil war in Spain. The poem is a *tour de force,* brilliantly evoking the life of a city and the particulars of a period. It manages readability and seriousness of purpose, combining a journalistic ease of metaphor and simile with structural completeness.

In 1940, MacNeice returned to England from the United States where he was lecturing, so that he could be part of the war effort. He entered the BBC features department in May 1941 where he revealed a considerable talent for radio drama. His play *The Dark Tower* (first broadcast in January 1946) is an acknowledged classic of the genre.

In the 1940s, MacNeice's poetic ambitions deepened. His effort to comprehend the work of the Irish poet W. B. Yeats* (his book *W. B. Yeats* appeared in 1941) allowed his own interest in folklore, myth, and dreams to break through the superficial colors and sequinned elegance of his style to suggest depths and heights of experience that he had hitherto ignored. The poet's temperamental melancholy deepened during the war and its anticlimactic aftermath, becoming something altogether more metaphysically troubled. "Brother Fire," written around 1943 about the German blitz on London, is representative of these sombre poems which, while maintaining a realistic grasp on external events, reach down into folk memory and dream.

The 1950s were a difficult time for MacNeice. His most ambitious work to date, *Ten Burnt Offerings* (1952), was received without much enthusiasm by the critics, while his long journalistic poem *Autumn Sequel* (1954) did not, in the main, achieve the same level as his earlier journal poem. The writing in *Autumn Sequel* is slack, often superficially attractive but without the sense of real personal involvement in the contemporary scene that made *Autumn Journal* so readable a work.

MacNeice's last three volumes, *Visitations* (1957), *Solstices* (1961), and *The Burning Perch* (published shortly after his death in 1963), reflected a resurgence of poetic energy. The earlier lyrical zest and panache are present but are now directed to the treatment of bleak truths. The passage of time, the imminence of death, the loss of love and ambition, and the degradation of the spirit in a mean-spirited time are treated with a ghoulish glee and a laconic, slangy offhanded wit, which suggest emotional and metaphysical despair acknowledged but not yet allowed final victory.

MacNeice's poetic involvement with Ireland is an important aspect of his work. In the 1930s, his poems impatiently dismissed a country he felt had little to offer the modern world. In the 1939–1944 war years, his distaste for Ireland's neutrality was expressed in "Neutrality." As he grew older, however, and as the contemporary city world in which he had early found excitement and inspiration began to pall in postwar enervation, the Irish countryside came increasingly to occupy an area in his imagination related to his developing interest in myth and folktale. MacNeice began to consider his own identity in terms of his Irish background, seeking some adequate means of relating to the country despite his alienation from the actual political and social facts of North and

South. Ireland became for him an image of human imaginative possibilities remote from the squalor and compromises of modern social experience, a world of ultimate belonging.

MacNeice was an extraordinarily prolific writer. His *Collected Poems* runs to six hundred pages; his output of literary journalism was prodigious; he wrote plays, radio dramas, features, film scripts, and three full-length critical works; he did translations of Aeschylus and Goethe; and he was a competent travel writer. His final claim to remembrance must be as a poet, however, and it is as a poet whose work captures the tang and texture of living while suggesting depths as yet unplumbed by human consciousness, that he commends himself to our attention. The zest and energy of life, the fear of death and loss, are the poles of his imagination. It is in his very fine love poems ("The Sunlight On The Garden," "Meeting Point") that we encounter the essential MacNeice— elegant, controlled, formally accomplished to an admirable degree, attentive to surfaces, to the passing moment, but conscious of significances beyond the moment, celebratory, with a Horatian grasp of sufficiencies, of the gifts of life, which are all life has to offer.

TERENCE BROWN

WORKS: *Blind Fireworks*. London: Gollancz, 1929; *Roundabout Way* by Louis Malone (pseudonym). London & New York: Putnam, [1932]. (Novel); *Poems*. London: Faber, [1935]; *The Agamemnon of Aeschylus*. London: Faber, [1936]. (Translation); with W. H. Auden, *Letters from Iceland*. London: Faber, [1937]; *Out of the Picture*. London: Faber, [1937]. (Verse play); *Poems*. New York: Random House, [1937]; *The Earth Compels*. London: Faber, [1938]; *I Crossed the Minch*. London, New York, Toronto: Longmans, Green, [1938]. (Prose); *Modern Poetry*. Oxford: Oxford University Press, [1938]. (Criticism); *Zoo*. London: Michael Joseph, [1938]. (Prose); *Autumn Journal*. London: Faber, [1939]/New York: Random House, 1940; *The Last Ditch*. Dublin: Cuala, 1940/Shannon: Irish University Press, 1971; *Selected Poems*. London: Faber [1940]; *Plant and Phantom*. London: Faber, [1941]; *Poems 1925–1940*. New York: Random House, [1941]; *The Poetry of W. B. Yeats*. London, New York, Toronto: Oxford University Press, 1941; *Meet the U.S. Army*. London: His Majesty's Stationery Office, [1943]. (Prose pamphlet); *Christopher Columbus*. London: Faber, [1944]. (Radio play); *Springboard. Poems 1941–1944*. London: Faber, 1944/New York: Random House, [1945]; *The Dark Tower and Other Radio Scripts*. London: Faber, [1947]; *Holes in the Sky. Poems 1944–1947*. London: Faber, [1948]/New York: Random House, [1949]; *Collected Poems 1925–1948*. London: Faber, 1949/New York: Oxford University Press, [1963]; *Goethe's Faust, Parts I and II*, with E. L. Stahl. London: Faber, [1951]/New York: Oxford University Press, 1952; *Ten Burnt Offerings*. London: Faber, [1952]/New York: Oxford University Press, 1953; *Autumn Sequel*. London: Faber, [1954]; *The Other Wing*. London: Faber, [1954]. (Four-page poem); *The Penny That Rolled Away*. New York: Putnam's 1954/as *The Sixpence That Rolled Away*, London: Faber, [1956]. (Children's story); *Visitations*. London: Faber, [1957]/New York: Oxford University Press, 1958; *Eighty-Five Poems*. London: Faber, 1959/New York: Oxford University Press, [1961]; *Solstices*. London: Faber/New York: Oxford University Press, 1961; *The Burning Perch*. London: Faber/New York: Oxford University Press, 1963; *Astrology*. London: Aldus Books in association with W. H. Allen/New York: Doubleday, 1964. (Prose); *The Mad Islands and The Administrator*. London: Faber, [1964]. (Radio plays); *Selected Poems of Louis MacNeice*, selected and introduced by W. H. Auden. London: Faber, [1964]; *The Strings Are False*. E. R. Dodds, ed. London: Faber, [1965]/New York: Oxford University Press, 1966. (Autobiography); *Varieties of Parable*. Cambridge: Cambridge University Press, 1965. (Criticism); *The Collected Poems of Louis MacNeice*. E. R. Dodds, ed. London: Faber, [1966]/New York: Oxford University Press, 1967; *One For the Grave*. London: Faber/New York: Oxford University Press, 1968. (Play); *Persons from*

Porlock. London: British Broadcasting Corp., [1969]. (Radio plays); *The Revenant: A Song Cycle for Hedli Anderson.* Dublin: Cuala, 1975. *Selected Poems.* Michael Longley, ed. London & Boston: Faber, 1989; *Selected Prose of Louis MacNeice.* Alan Heuser, ed. Oxford: Clarendon, 1991; *Selected Plays of Louis MacNeice.* Alan Heuser & Peter McDonald, eds. Oxford: Clarendon, 1993. REF-ERENCES: Armitrage, Christopher. *A Bibliography of the Works of Louis MacNeice.* London: Kaye & Ward, 1973; Brown, Terence. *Louis MacNeice: Sceptical Vision.* Dublin: Gill & Macmillan/New York: Barnes & Noble, 1975; Brown, Terence, & Alec Reid, eds. *Time Was Away: The World of Louis MacNeice.* Dublin: Dolmen, 1974; Coulton, Barbara. *MacNeice in the BBC.* London & Boston: Faber, 1980; Elton, Edward Smith. *Louis MacNeice.* New York: Twayne, 1970; Longley, Edna. *Louis MacNeice: A Study.* London & Boston: Faber, 1989; McKinnon, William T. *Apollo's Blended Dream.* London: Oxford University Press, 1971; Marsack, Robyn. *The Cave of Making: The Poetry of Louis MacNeice.* Oxford: Clarendon, 1982; Moore, D. B. *The Poetry of Louis MacNeice.* Leicester: Leicester University Press, 1972; Stallworthy, John. *Louis MacNeice: A Biography.* London: Faber, 1995.

McNEILL, JANET (1907–), novelist. McNeill was born in Dublin on September 14, 1907, the daughter of a minister, and was educated in England and later in St. Andrew's University, from which she received an M.A. in 1929. She worked as a journalist on the *Belfast Telegraph* from 1929 to 1933, before marrying Robert Alexander and becoming the mother of four children. From 1956 to 1957, she was chairman of the Belfast Centre of Irish P.E.N. and from 1959 to 1964, she served on the Advisory Council of the BBC. She has written novels, a great number of children's books, and two stage plays, one of which, *Signs and Wonders,* was produced in Belfast in 1951. She is now living in Bristol.

McNeill's novels mainly examine the disillusions and compromises of middle age. In *A Child in the House* (1955), her first novel, Maud and Henry's dead and barren marriage is interrupted by a visit from Maud's niece Elizabeth. With this child comes the past. The one redeeming feature of Henry's life has been his love for Grace, the child's mother, who is now dying. But Henry's failure is one of action. Even now he cannot shake off conventional notions of propriety and visit the dying woman. When the child makes the painful choices necessary for a moral life, Henry feels for her and so becomes involved in humanity. But Maud, whose love preys on Henry and who believed the child's presence would heal their marriage, is isolated further through her irrational jealousy.

Aubrey and Alice, the married couple in *Talk to Me* (1965), are bound together through pity as well as convention. Alice is blind and sits in the dark imagining a golden past, while Aubrey has imaginary talks with the TV announcer. Their lives run on parallel lines which seldom touch. Aubrey flirts ineffectually with the girls in his chemist shop and runs from any real encounters. From behind his counter, he has a goldfish's view of the world:

For all their blatancy, he believed that most of the young girls who came into the shop were looking for a defence against sex, preferring the ideal to the reality; they took their mirrors to bed with them and laid them down at the last possible moment, replacing the dream lover reluctantly with flesh and blood and sharing as little as they were able. He had sympathy with them. When he made love to Alice he had sometimes, just before the final anonymous moment, resented the fact that she was there.

This unwillingness to face reality plagues most of the characters in the novel, except Aubrey and Alice's practical, phlegmatic daughter. For the others, real encounters are too threatening, and Aubrey even finally upholds Alice in her refusal to believe that her cat has been killed.

Middle age is still the subject of *The Maiden Dinosaur* (1964). Sarah is a spinster school mistress who has been frightened into frigidity and tentative lesbianism by a sexual shock in childhood. She is the center of a group of friends whose middle-aged marriages are in various stages of collapse. When Helen, the object of Sarah's devotion, deserts her for her ex-husband, Sarah is bereft and has to face life on her own. She is at first miserable, but before the novel ends, she feels the first stirrings of adult sexuality. Contrasted to Sarah is Sally, a schoolgirl who has a painful infatuation for Sarah. When Sarah unwittingly repulses the child's affections, Sally goes out with a boy who sexually molests her. But it is with Sally that Janet McNeill sees hope for the future, as well as with a girl idly playing with her baby whom Sarah observes from her window. These young people will not be prisoners of their milieu as their middle-aged elders have been.

The Small Widow (1967) examines the complexity of character as well as the incompatibility of fantasy with reality. The novel opens with Julia widowed and lost without the physical presence of her husband Harold. All her life she had wanted passion from him, but believing the marriage happy because she satisfied him, she settled for children and security. She is shocked and outraged when she learns that Madge, Harold's dotty naive cousin, has been his lifelong passionate love. Unable to live without Harold, Madge commits suicide. Julia finally comes to accept the idea that she supplied something Harold needed, as he did her. The novel ends with Julia looking for a stamp and reflecting that "Harold had been unfailingly good at stamps."

McNeill has much to say about human loneliness, the generation gap, the roles society imposes on men and women, and their methods of coping with those roles. She is a tough, adult novelist who charts the complex, mundane territory of middle age with perception and intelligence. For Protestant Belfast, she is the counterpart and often the equal of Brian Moore.* Over the years, her style has tightened into the excellence of *The Maiden Dinosaur,* which is her best novel and deserves to be much better known.

MARY ROSE CALLAGHAN

WORKS: *Gospel Truth.* Belfast: H. R. Carter, [1951]. (Play); *A Child in the House.* London: Hodder & Stoughton, 1955; *My Friend Specs McCann.* London: Faber, 1955; *The Other Side of the Wall.* London: Hodder & Stoughton, 1956; *A Pinch of Salt.* London: Faber, 1956; *Tea at Four O'Clock.* London: Hodder & Stoughton, 1956; *A Light Dozen.* London: Faber, 1957. (Stories); *A Finished Room.* London: Hodder & Stoughton, 1958; *Specs Fortissimo.* London: Faber, 1958; *Search Party.* London: Hodder & Stoughton, [1959]; *This Happy Morning.* London: Faber, 1959; *As Strangers Here.* London: Hodder & Stoughton, 1960; *Special Occasions.* London: Faber, 1960.

(Stories); *Various Specs.* London: Faber, 1961; *The Early Harvest.* London: Geoffrey Bles, 1962; *Finn and the Black Hag,* libretto by McNeill, music by Raymond Warren, children's opera in two acts. London: Novello, [1962]; *Try These for Size.* London: Faber, 1963; *The Maiden Dinosaur.* London: Geoffrey Bles, 1964; *Talk to Me.* London: Geoffrey Bles, 1965; *Tom's Tower.* London: Faber, 1965; *I Didn't Invite You to My Party.* London: Hamish Hamilton, 1967; *The Small Widow.* London: Geoffrey Bles, 1967/New York: Atheneum, 1968; *Switch-On, Switch-Off, and Other Plays.* London: Faber, 1968; *A Helping Hand.* London: Hamilton, 1971; *Much Too Much Magic.* London: Hamilton, 1971; *The Prisoner in the Park.* London: Faber, 1971; *The Nest Spotters.* London: Macmillan, 1972; *Wait for It, and Other Stories.* London: Faber, 1972; *A Fairy Called Andy Perks.* London: Hamilton, 1973; *The Other People.* London: Chatto & Windus, 1973; *The Snow-Clean Pinny.* London: Hamilton, 1973; *Umbrella Thursday and a Helping Hand.* Harmondsworth, Middlesex: Puffin, 1973; *The Family Upstairs.* London: Macmillan, 1974; *The Magic Lollipop.* London: Knight Books, Brockhampton Press, 1974; *We Three Kings.* London: Faber, 1974; *Ever After.* London: Chatto & Windus, 1975; *Go On, Then.* London: Macmillan, 1975; *Growlings.* London: Macmillan, 1975; *My Auntie.* London: Macmillan, 1975; *Just Turn the Key, and Other Stories.* London: Hamilton, 1976; *Billy Brewer Goes on Tour.* London: Macmillan, 1977; *The Day Mum Came Home.* London: Macmillan, 1977; *The Hermit's Purple Shirts.* London: Macmillan, 1977; *Look Who's Here.* London: Macmillan, 1977; *The Three Crowns of King Hullaballoo.* London: Knight Books, Brockhampton Press, 1977. REFERENCE: Foster, John Wilson. *Forces and Themes in Ulster Fiction.* Dublin: Gill & Macmillan, 1974, pp. 228–243.

McNULTY, [MATTHEW] EDWARD (1856–1943), playwright and novelist.

McNulty, born in Antrim in 1856, was a classmate of Bernard Shaw* at a day school in Dublin and a friend of Shaw's sister Lucy. The young men shared an interest in music and writing. In John O'Donovan's* biographical play *The Shaws of Synge Street,* staged at the Abbey* in 1960, naive, goodhearted McNulty is one of the characters. A bank manager, novelist, and playwright, McNulty died on May 12, 1943. His remembrances of Shaw, in manuscript at the time of McNulty's death, are a warm, if not entirely accurate, account of their friendship.

Two McNulty plays were performed at the Abbey. *The Courting of Mary Doyle* (1921) is a broad comedy in which a domestic servant is wooed because of her supposedly large bank account. *The Lord Mayor* (1914) is somewhat more substantial theatre. Jimmy O'Brien is forced into politics by his wife, manipulated into office by a self-serving faction with its eye on lucrative municipal contracts, and is offered a baronetcy by the Castle if he formally welcomes a visiting monarch. His sudden change from puppet to leader is unconvincing, but the play uproariously uncovers the hinder parts of Irish political and social life.

WILLIAM J. FEENEY

WORKS: *Misther O'Ryan.* London: Edward Arnold, 1894. (Novel); *The Son of a Peasant.* London: Edward Arnold, 1897. (Novel); "George Bernard Shaw as a Boy." *The Candid Friend* (July 6, 1901); *Maureen.* London: Edward Arnold, 1904. (Novel); *Mrs. Mulligan's Millions.* London: Hurst & Blackett, 1908. (Novel); *The Lord Mayor.* Dublin: Talbot, 1914. (Play); *Mrs. Mulligan's Millions.* Dublin: Maunsel, 1918. (Play); *The Courting of Mary Doyle.* Dublin: Gill, 1944. (Play). REFERENCES: Coolidge, Olivia. *George Bernard Shaw.* Boston: Houghton Mifflin, 1968; Ervine, St. John. *Bernard Shaw, His Life, Work, and Friends.* New York: William Morrow, 1956; O'Donovan, John. *The Shaws of Synge Street.* Dixon, Calif.: Proscenium, 1966. (Play).

McNULTY, TED (ca. 1930–), poet. McNulty was cited as the "new Irish writer of 1991" in the *Sunday Tribune*/Hennessy Literary Awards. He was raised in New York City, was a teacher, and began writing in the 1950s. He now lives in Dalkey and London. He is a free-verse poet whose strength is the simplicity of his plain style and the vivid clarity of his terse descriptions.

WORK: *Rough Landings.* [Galway: Salmon, 1992].

MACREADY, WILLIAM (1755?–1829), playwright and actor. Macready was born in Dublin and acted in Smock Alley before moving to England. He acted from 1786 to 1798 at Covent Garden and then managed, with small success, various provincial theaters. He wrote three plays, including the two-act farce *The Irishman in London* (1793). He is the father of the eminent tragedian William Charles Macready.

WORKS: *The Village Lawyer.* 5th ed. Dublin: P. Byrne, 1801; *The Irishman in London; or, The Happy African.* London: T. N. Longman, 1793; *The Bank Note; or, Lessons for Ladies.* London: T. N. Longman, 1795. REFERENCES: Bartley, J. O. *Teague, Shenkin and Sawney. Being an Historical Study of the Earliest Irish, Welsh and Scottish Characters in English Plays.* Cork: Cork University Press, 1954; Downer, Alan S. *The Eminent Tragedian William Charles Macready.* Cambridge: Harvard University Press, 1966; Duggan, C. C. *The Stage Irishman.* Dublin: Talbot, 1937; Kavanagh, Peter. *The Irish Theatre.* Tralee: Kerryman, 1946; Macready, William Charles. *The Journal of William Charles Macready, 1832–1851.* Abridged & edited by J. C. Trewin. Longon: Longmans, 1967.

MacSWINEY, TERENCE (1879–1920), patriot and playwright. MacSwiney was a nationalist leader who, while lord mayor of Cork, underwent a lengthy seventy-four day hunger strike when he was interned in Brixton Prison. As a result of it, he died on October 25, 1920. His suffering and death received widespread sympathetic attention throughout the world.

MacSwiney was born in Cork on March 28, 1879. He received the B.A. from the Royal University there in 1907, and he subsequently became a fervent nationalist, taught himself Irish, and was interned in 1916. While MacSwiney is more significant to the history than the literature of Ireland, he has some importance as a playwright and polemicist.

At the end of 1908, with Daniel Corkery,* he founded the Cork Dramatic Society, and produced a number of his plays. Of these, only one has been published, and that is *The Last Warriors of Coole* (1910), a "hero play in one act." The piece takes place, of course, in the Irish heroic period, but it is extremely static and is written in correct but quite undistinguished blank verse. His other early plays include *The Holocaust* (1910), a one-act patriotic tragedy, and *The Wooing of Emer* (1911), a three-act heroic play. A political play, *The Revolutionist,* was produced posthumously at the Abbey* in 1921; it is long, vague, high-minded, and dull. Also published posthumously was a collection of fugitive pieces, *Principles of Freedom* (1921)—patriotic exhortations and theorizing which are lucidly written but of only historical interest.

Although MacSwiney was not a good writer, he was an intensely earnest, utterly idealistic, and personally brave and noble man. The dramatic society which he helped to found gave first productions to such notable writers as Daniel Corkery, Lennox Robinson,* T. C. Murray,* Con O'Leary,* and J. Bernard MacCarthy.* That in itself was an achievement.

WORKS: *The Music of Freedom.* Cork: Risen Gaedheal, 1907; *The Revolutionist.* Dublin & London: Maunsel, 1914. (Play); *Battle-cries.* San Francisco: Rank and File, 1916. (Poems); *Principles of Freedom.* Dublin: Talbot/New York: E. P. Dutton, 1921. (Essays); *Despite Fool's Laughter.* B. G. MacCarthy, ed. Dublin: Gill, 1944. (Poems); "The Last Warriors of Coole." *George Spelvin's Theatre Book* 6 (Spring 1984): 61–77. (One-act play). REFERENCES: Chavasse, Moirin. *Terence MacSwiney.* Dublin: Clonmore & Reynolds/London: Burns & Oates, 1961; Costello, Francis J. *Enduring the Most: The Life and Death of Terence MacSwiney.* Dingle: Brandon, 1995; O'Hegarty, P. S. *A Short Memoir of Terence MacSwiney.* Dublin: Talbot, 1922.

Mac UISTIN, LIAM (1929–   ), playwright. Born in Dublin and educated at University College, Dublin, Mac Uistin has written widely in English and Irish for the stage, for radio, and for television. His two-act *Post Mortem* (Peacock, 1971) is a richly moving study of emigration from an imaginary village in the west. A quotation from his work was engraved in Dublin's National Garden of Remembrance.

WORKS IN ENGLISH: *Post Mortem.* Newark, Del.: Proscenium/Dublin: Society of Irish Playwrights, [1977]; *The Glory and the Dream* in *4 Irish Plays* (also called *4 One-Act Plays*). Newark, Del.: Proscenium, [1982].

MADDEN, AODHAN (1954–   ), playwright and short story writer. Madden was born in Dublin, educated at the Christian Brothers School in North Brunswick Street, and studied journalism at Rathmines College. He then joined the *Irish Press* as subeditor, feature writer, and drama critic and has also worked for *New Hibernia* and the *Evening Press.* His theatrical productions include four plays produced at the Peacock Theatre—*The Midnight Door* (1983), *Sensations* (1986), *Remember Mauritania* (1987), and *Josephine in the Night* (1988). He has had four plays produced during the Dublin Theatre Festival—*The Dosshouse Waltz* (1985), *Private Death of a Queen* (1986), *Sea Urchins* (1988), and *Candlemas Night* (1991). He has had five plays on RTÉ—*Remember Mauritania* (1985), *Obituaries* (1991), *Ladies in Waiting* (1993), and *Searching for Gentleman Joe* (1995). He has also had numerous stories broadcast on RTÉ and published a collection of stories entitled *Mad Angels of Paxenau Street* (1990), a collection of verse called *Demons* (1981), and two of his plays. He has won the O. Z. Whitehead Award three times, the Francis MacManus Radio Short Story Competition three times, and was nominated by the *International Herald Tribune* as the best new playwright of the 1985 Dublin Theatre Festival.

Mad Angels of Paxenau Street contains fourteen stories that focus on the repressed urges endemic to Ireland's Catholic culture. More than simply a subtle representation of sexuality, homoeroticism, the hypocrisy of religious devotion, the hypocrisy of the clergy, death, and the physical decay associated with old age, Madden's stories portray in sometimes graphic detail the sexual, emotional, and intellectual obsessions associated with a culture of subjugation and denial. As an alternative to Ireland, Greece functions as a kind of metaphorical and literal brothel. Priests, young homosexuals, and starved intellectuals fly to Athens and the outlying islands for an experience of sexual license or of a culture with an obvious connection with its mythic pasts. Indeed, the young Greeks do not exist as people but as ideals, as sometimes luminous manifestations of the gods. Even the Western Europeans seem, at first, godlike and free. However, upon closer inspection, their human qualities—age, physical imperfection, emotional immaturity—reveal themselves. The narrative, subsequently, acquires an air of desperation and even panic in the realization of the futility of idealization. The rhythm of the language and the series of Madden's images reveal characters trapped in depression. They and even the narrative voice seem to value the veneer of an imaged Orient, sensuous and alive, or of a postcolonial Ireland trapped by its desire for outward respectability, whether rigid Catholicism or outward Englishness. Significantly, the Irish characters are frequently mistaken for English colonial archetypes. They are seen as older men, defeated and desperate, searching for the sexual comfort of boys or young girls. In this sense, Madden is very much a writer of the Irish East. Madden's Northern and Western contemporaries can take comfort in an easy communion with an Irish mythic past, easy because of the Troubles or because of a cultural geography alive with mythic resonance. But writers from the former Pale, even in this third generation since independence, suffer from the same sense of postmodern existential angst present in the other nations of the industrialized West.

Sensations, published with *The Midnight Door* in 1986, explores many of the same themes of Madden's stories. However, the play details not so much the aftermath of disillusionment as disillusionment's final moments. A tabloid newspaper serves as a microcosm for mid-1980s Irish society. A battle between liberals who joined the paper in the 1960s and want it to return to its roots as a serious journal and the conservative chief editor who desperately pushes forward a reactionary conservative Catholic agenda plays itself out over a news story about a young girl's death as a consequence of an illegal abortion. Each side argues about the underlying causes of the girl's death. The conservative editor uses the story to destroy her liberal father's political career. The liberal staff suggests that society's restrictive morality bears the ultimate guilt. To their credit, some members of the liberal staff seem to want to address the real tragedy of a young girl's desperate loss. However, for the most part, each side tends to manipulate the story for its own political agenda. At the end of the play, though, each side seems defeated and to find little hope or value in its position. The dramatic necessity of staged drama lends a sense of energy absent from Madden's stories. Nevertheless, it is easy to see the characters from *Sensations* later vacationing in Madden's Greece. Madden's only other published play, *The Midnight Door,* addresses the issues of alcoholism and desperation in the lives of aging former writers who cannot remember their works and have lost the enthusiasm and optimism of their youth.

BERNARD McKENNA

WORKS: *Demons and Other Poems*. Gorey: Gorey Arts Centre, 1981; *Sensations* and *The Midnight Door*. Dublin: Society of Irish Playwrights, 1986; *Mad Angels of Paxenau Street*. Dublin: Kildanore, 1990.

MADDEN, DEIRDRE (1960–   ), novelist. Born in Belfast on August 20, 1960, Deirdre Madden is from Toomebridge, County Antrim, and graduated from Trinity College, Dublin, with a B.A. (with honors) in 1983 and from the University of East Anglia with an M.A. (with distinction) in 1985. She won the Hennessy Award in 1980, the Rooney Prize in 1987, and the Somerset Maugham Award in 1989. Madden first came to international attention when her novel *Hidden Symptoms* was published in Faber's *First Fictions: Introduction 9* in 1986. Since then, she has earned a well-deserved reputation as one of Ireland's better young novelists. She is married to the Irish poet Harry Clifton.*

Hidden Symptoms is the story of Theresa Cassidy, a college student who struggles to come to terms with the death of her brother and the challenges in her own life. The setting is a contemporary Belfast still very much maligned by the Troubles. For Theresa, who is Catholic, the murder of her twin brother, Francis, by a group of Protestant assailants has a great impact. The novel is a story about loss, in particular Theresa's fight to understand why her brother was killed and what her religion means to her. The difficulty of remaining true to her religion and forgiving and loving those who killed Francis constantly troubles her. The book is an impressive debut. Not only does Madden tell a harrowing story with great insight into the heroine's emotional state, but she also has a writing style rare in contemporary fiction. Nearly every reviewer of Madden's works comments on the "beautiful" or "poetic" or "passionate" prose, and that skill is indeed evident in her first novel.

The Birds of the Innocent Wood (1988) received the Somerset Maugham Award. The novel actually contains three stories: the story of Jane, who grew up an orphan, married a man she did not really love, and in general had an unhappy and unfulfilled life; and the stories of Catherine and Sarah, Jane's daughters, who must deal with their mother's past and their own desires. Madden alternates the stories of mother and daughters throughout the work; and, as in *Hidden Symptoms,* the major themes are loss and isolation. *The Birds* is an important work because of the way Madden examines the social pressures on women in Ireland. It is a dark novel, yet its despair reflects the hopelessness of the characters.

In *Remembering Light and Stone* (1992), the protagonist is again a young woman. This time, however, the setting is Italy, and the novel focuses on the experiences of an Irish immigrant, Aisling. The core of the book is the classic Irish theme of exile. Aisling, who is fiercely independent, is most concerned with discovering what she wants out of life. Her having lived for five years in a small Italian village illustrates her determination. Both the topography of Italy and Aisling's inner makeup play important roles. While Aisling is easily able to note the beauty of Italy, the fact that she cannot fully describe the physical presence of her own country symbolizes her inability to understand herself. In the end, however, when Aisling returns to Ireland and understands what the country means to her, she is able to end her exile, and her search for meaning in her own life is over. By writing in the first person, Madden is able to create a bond with the reader that makes a memorable novel of maturation and discovery, as Aisling comes to terms with her self-exile, her ties to her estranged family in Dublin, her relationship with an American boyfriend, and the suicide of a friend suffering from cancer.

Nothing Is Black (1994) is set in Donegal, and the story focuses on three women: Nuala, a recent mother in her thirties, who runs a successful restaurant and is a kleptomaniac; Claire, a meditative woman in her thirties, who is an artist; and Anna, a summer visitor from Holland, who is alienated from her adult daughter. All of the women are searching for explanations about their lives, what they have experienced, and what they want. By the novel's end, there is a closure of sorts: after spending time in Donegal at Claire's, Nuala is able to return to her family in Dublin; Claire is able to devote all of her energy to the one thing that means most to her, art; and Anna begins to see that her daughter's rejection is based more on fear than spite. *Nothing Is Black* is a continuation of Madden's investigation of the quest for personal happiness; and, as in her previous works, her depth and insight make for astute observations.

SHAWN O'HARE

WORKS: *Hidden Symptoms.* Included in *First Fictions: Introduction 9.* London: Faber, 1986/ Boston & New York: Atlantic Monthly, 1986/London: Faber, 1988; *The Birds of the Innocent Wood.* London: Faber, 1988; *Remembering Light and Stone.* London: Faber, 1992; *Nothing Is Black.* London: Faber, 1994.

MAGEE, HENO (1939–   ), playwright. Magee was born into a typical Dublin working-class background. At fourteen, he quit primary school to take a job as a messenger boy. For five years, he served abroad in the British Royal Air Force; drawn back to Dublin, he found work in a tobacco factory.

Always a "voracious but indiscriminate reader," Magee started writing on impulse one rainy Sunday afternoon, sitting at a tenement window. The first words he wrote were: "I'm getting out of this kip"; these words formed the title of his first play in 1968. Since then, he has written several more plays, poetry, and character sketches, and for some years, he was drama critic on the Dublin weekly newspaper, *The Catholic Standard.*

His plays explore with bawdy humor, poetic insight, and deep compassion the manners, mores, and morals of Dublin's working-class ghettos. If one treats Brendan Behan's* theatrical cartoons as a case apart, not since O'Casey* have the denizens of the backstreets been put on the stage with such truth and accuracy. Magee's characters speak a rich, low-life vernacular which has been sieved through a shrewd intelligence.

Magee's is a shabby, sedimentary world which festers with an ingrowing energy and frustration: a world which the city's affluent middle class, secure and complacent in the fat of contentment, is happy to ignore. There are no evil men or women in Magee's plays, but there are blighted and befuddled victims of birth and circumstances. These characters articulate their condition through sex, booze, and violence, for no other antidotes are available to them against the sameness, sullenness, and lethargy of life and against the poverty and its pains. Each of the plays enshrines an eloquent, anguished plea to understand— and to be understood. Blind force leads to blinder futility.

If Magee's people are maimed and marred by original sin, they are also blessed with a sanctifying grace. To power his dramatic motor, Magee allows them to carry within themselves the seeds of their own salvation. He provides flickering visions of other attainable worlds and says that to acquiesce is to go down in leaden defeat. His common theme is the struggle to survive with dignity.

To date, one of his plays has been published, and three have been produced: *I'm Getting Out of This Kip* (1972), *Hatchet* (Abbey, 1972), and *Red Biddy* (Abbey, 1974). In 1976, Magee won the Rooney Prize in Irish Literature and was awarded the Abbey Theatre bursary.

JAMES DOUGLAS

WORK: *Hatchet.* [Dublin]: Gallery/[Newark, Del.]: Proscenium, 1978.

MAGENNIS, PETER (1817–1910), poet and novelist. Magennis was born and died in County Fermanagh, where he was a national school teacher.

WORKS: *The Ribbon Informer: A Tale of Lough Erne.* London: F. Bell, 1874. (Novel); *Poems.* London: Roper & Drowley, 1899.

MAGINN, WILLIAM (1793–1842), journalist and man of letters. Maginn, that prodigy of wit, erudition, humor, energy, and genial dissipation, was born in Cork on July 10, 1793. At the early age of twelve, he entered Trinity College. On graduating, he assisted at his father's private school in Cork and then ran the school for several years after his father's death. At the same time, he was making a reputation for his humorous Irish sketches; in 1823, he went to London and continued his prolific writing for journals such as *Blackwood's.* In 1830, he was involved in the founding of *Fraser's Magazine,* for which Carlyle and Maginn's friend Thackeray wrote. His *Noctes Ambrosianae* and *Homeric Ballads* won vast audiences, and his clever Irish sketches and adroit verses are well worth a modern edition. His startling fluency may be seen in the following stanza from "The Wine-Bibber's Glory," which is quite as amusing in his Latin version "Toporis Gloria."

> Fair Sherry, Port's sister, for years they dismissed her
>   To the kitchen to flavour the jellies—
> There long she was banish'd, and well nigh had vanished
>   To comfort the kitchen maids' bellies;

Till his Majesty fixt, he thought Sherry when sixty
  Years old like himself quite the thing;
So I think it but proper, to fill a tip-topper
  Of Sherry to drink to the king.

Huic quamvis cognatum, Xerense damnatum,
  Gelatâ culinâ tingebat,
Vinum exul ibique dum coquo cuique
  Generosum liquorem praebebat.
Sed a rege probatum est valdè pergatum
  Cum (ut ipse) sexagenarium—
Largè ergo implendum, regique bibendum
  Opinor est nunc necessarium.

Maginn was imprisoned for debt in 1840. When finally released in 1842, he was broken in health and died on August 21.

WORKS: *Whitehall, or the Days of George the Fourth.* London, 1827. (Novel); *Miscellaneous Writings of the Late Dr. Maginn.* R. Skelton Mackenzie, ed. 5 vols. New York: Redfield, 1855–1857; *Noctes Ambrosianae,* by Maginn, Lockhart, Hogg & others. R. Skelton MacKenzie, ed. 5 vols. New York: W. J. Middleton, 1863–1865; *Miscellanies: Prose and Verse.* R. W. Montague, ed. 2 vols. London: Sampson, Low, 1885; *Ten Tales.* London: Partridge, 1933. REFERENCES: Kenealy, Edward Vaughan Hyde. "Our Portrait Gallery, no. 34: William Maginn L.L.D." *Dublin University Magazine* 23 (1844): 72–101; Thrall, Miriam M. H. *Rebellious Fraser's: Nol Yorke's Magazine in the Days of Maginn, Thackeray, and Carlyle.* New York: Columbia University Press, 1934; Wardle, Ralph Martin. "William Maginn and Blackwood's Magazine." Diss., Harvard University, 1940.

MAGLONE, BARNEY. *See* WILSON, ROBERT ARTHUR.

MAHAFFY, JOHN PENTLAND (1839–1919), scholar and wit. Even at this late date, one hesitates to call Mahaffy a Dublin character; let us rather call that formidable individual a figure on the Dublin scene. He was born at Chapponnaire, near Vevey in Switzerland, on February 26, 1839. He was educated at Trinity College, Dublin, where he remained as tutor, professor, vice-provost, and provost for fifty-five years. As a major scholar of his day, he published books on Kant and Descartes, and on Greek and Egyptian history, and he was knighted in 1918. As a prominent feature of the life of Dublin, he founded the Georgian Society and was a president of the Royal Irish Academy, but, more memorably, he was an inveterate diner-out and a conversationalist with something of the force of a Dr. Johnson. Despite an overwhelming snobbery, he was a famous wit and raconteur, who wrote a monograph, *The Art of Conversation,* and whose most successful pupils were Oscar Wilde* and Oliver Gogarty.* He is credited with the classic definition of an Irish Bull ("An Irish Bull, Madam, is always pregnant"), as well as such memorable epigrams as, "Ireland is a place where the inevitable never happens, and the unexpected often occurs."

When asked the difference between a man and a woman, he is said to have replied, "I can't conceive." Shane Leslie* remarked of his conversation:

Until you heard Mahaffy talk, you hadn't realised how language could be used to charm and hypnotise. With this gift, there were no doors which could not be opened, no Society which was proof against its astonishing effect. Kings and Queens, famous men and beautiful women, all must come under its powerful and compelling spell.

Mahaffy was most contemptuous of Celtic studies and once proscribed a meeting at Trinity College at which "a man called Pearse*" was scheduled to speak. Although he ably directed the defense of Trinity College against the rebels in 1916, he did propose in 1917 that Ireland should have a federal constitution with Ulster as an autonomous province—a solution which still seems the only workable one. Mahaffy was something of a throwback to, not so much the nineteenth century, as the eighteenth. He died on April 30, 1919, thereby making Dublin considerably less habitable by civilized man.

PRINCIPAL WORKS: *The Decay of Modern Preaching.* London: Macmillan, 1882; *A History of Classical Greek Literature.* 2d ed. revised. 2 vols. London: Longmans, Green, 1883; *The Principles of the Art of Conversation.* London: Macmillan, 1887/2d ed., enlarged. London: Macmillan, 1888; *Greek Life and Thought.* 2d ed., corrected and enlarged. London: Macmillan, 1896; *An Epoch in Irish History, T.C.D. Its Foundation and Early Fortunes, 1591–1660.* London: T. Fisher Unwin, 1903; *The Plate in Trinity College, Dublin: A History.* London: Macmillan, 1918. REFERENCE: Stanford, William Bedell. *Mahaffy.* London: Routledge & Kegan Paul, 1971.

MAHER, JOHN (fl. 1980s–1990s), short story writer. Maher's stories have been read on BBC radio and on RTÉ, and the title story of his impressive first collection, *The Coast of Malabar* (1988), won RTÉ's Francis McManus Award. That story is a strong, short piece set in a pub and divided between the memories of Dillon, who has lost both friend and girlfriend, and the telling of his story by an old busybody at a nearby table. Effective use is made of song and sentence fragments, and the story has been admired by James Plunkett.* Several other stories are as impressive. "The Doppler Effect" is about a political prisoner let out of Portlaoise for a day to attend his son's confirmation and has also a bleakly powerful conclusion. The most ambitious pieces are "When the Sun Bursts" and "The Women by the Window." The first is about a retired woman folklorist giving a lecture at the Royal Irish Academy; the second is about a woman journalist, at the time of Bobby Sands's* hunger strike, interviewing the widow of an old patriot who had once been on hunger strike. These pieces are slow, reflective, even a trifle ambling rather than dramatic. Nevertheless, Maher's subjects are intriguing and make significant social points, and his details are as exact and evocative as William Trevor's.* Indeed, these accomplished stories are reminiscent of Trevor in both tone and craftsmanship.

WORK: *The Coast of Malabar.* Dublin: O'Brien, [1988].

MAHER, MARY (fl. 1960s–1990s), novelist and journalist. Born in Chicago, Maher joined the *Irish Times* in 1965 and has written widely on women's affairs.

WORK: *The Devil's Card.* [Dingle, Co. Kerry]: Brandon/New York: St. Martin's, 1992.

MAHER, SEÁN (1932–   ), memoirist. Maher was born on January 15, 1932. in the County Home in Tullamore. As he wrote in his fascinating memoir, *The Road to God Knows Where* (1972):

My parents were out-and-out travellers, as were their parents and grandparents before them. My father, when sober, was a great hand at making a living on the road, my mother being the expert at begging and fortune-telling. Unlike my father, she never drank in her life, a rare thing on the road.

As a bright lad of twelve, Maher ran away from his parents and succeeded in getting himself four years of schooling and in learning how to read and write. He has put his schooling to very good account in his book, which ably and fully depicts the traveler's life and customs and the camaraderie of the road and makes good use of the rich store of tales and stories he has heard. His style is clear and direct, but his effective use of many words from the traveler's cant, Shelta, will send his readers frequently to the Glossary at the end of the book. For instance:

Well, there was the finest shindig I have seen for many a year at the molly that night. There was a big roaring stick fire and everyone had a hearty peck of fé, cunnions and salery. To make it even better he had the finest of grunter's carnish pickled with salen.

Although nostalgic and even a trifle sentimental in places, Maher does not romanticize or glamorize the traveler's hard life. Although proud of his heritage, he does not gloss over the drinking, the fighting, and the squalor. For its straightforward authenticity, the book deserves a place on the shelf with the memoirs of the Blasket and Aran Islanders.

WORK: *The Road to God Knows Where.* Dublin: Talbot, 1972.

MAHON, BRID (1922–   ), novelist, children's writer, folklorist, and journalist. Mahon was born on July 14, 1922. As a schoolgirl, for pocket money she wrote a forty-minute script dramatizing the history and music of County Cork. It was accepted by Radio Éireann and led to twenty-six such dramatizations and eventually to over 500 scripts for Radio Éireann and many more for the BBC. In the 1950s, she became the Irish theater critic for *Sunday Express* and from 1960 to 1970 was women's editor of the *Sunday Press.* In 1949, she had joined the Irish Folklore Commission and on its demise was transferred to University College, Dublin, where she was senior research lecturer in the Department of Irish Folklore. She has also taught at the University of California at Berkeley and at Los Angeles.

Her children's story, *The Search for the Tinker Chief,* sold about 48,000 copies and was optioned by Disney. Her adult novels are enjoyable historical romances. The first, *A Time to Love* (1992), is a picaresque story based on the life of Peg Woffington, the famous eighteenth-century actress. It is a great read with touches of Georgette Heyer and is full of authentic historical detail about the theater and the city of Dublin, especially the Liberties.

MARY ROSE CALLAGHAN

WORKS: *The Search for the Tinker Chief.* Dublin: Allen Figgis, 1968. (Children's book); *The Wonder Tales of Ireland.* Dublin: Folens, 1975. (Children's textbook); *Irish Dress.* Dublin: Folens, 1976. (Nonfiction); *Irish Food.* Dublin: Folens, [1976?]. (Nonfiction); ed., *My Favourite Stories of Ireland.* Guilford: Lutterworth, 1977; *Irish Folklore.* Tallaght, [Co. Dublin]: Folens, [1981?] *A Time to Love.* Dublin: Poolbeg, 1992. (Novel); *Dervorgilla.* Dublin: Poolbeg, 1994. (Novel).

MAHON, DEREK (1941–   ), poet. Mahon was born in Belfast on November 23, 1941, and grew up in Glengormley. He was educated at the Royal Belfast Academical Institution and at Trinity College, Dublin, where he received a B.A. in 1965. He lived for some years in London, working as a freelance journalist and screenwriter. For television, he adapted works by Elizabeth Bowen,* Jennifer Johnston,* and John Montague.* He has taught at the University of Ulster in Coleraine and at New York University and in 1986 was writing fellow at Trinity College, Dublin. He has translated two plays by Molière as well as produced a version of Euripides' *Bacchae* and of Racine's *Phaedra.* He has also translated Gerard de Nerval, and his *Selected Poems of Philippe Jaccottet,* the Swiss-French poet, won the Scott-Moncrief Prize. He also received the American Ireland Fund Literary Award, the Denis Devlin Award, and the Martin Toonder Award. He is a member of Aosdána.*

Of the poets who began to make their reputations after Kinsella,* Montague, and Heaney* had established themselves, probably Mahon and Desmond O'Grady* appear to be the most impressive. Mahon has a tight, precise style that is often enhanced by the memorable phrase. He has an accurate eye and a deft satiric sense, and, as language, the best of his work is as interesting as any poetry written in Ireland today. Like O'Grady and perhaps Richard Murphy,* he appears to have more awareness of form than many of his contemporaries; and his more recent work particularly has its considerable formal successes.

Of his earlier work, perhaps his most significant and controlled long piece is *Beyond Howth Head* (1970), a somber, light-verse jeremiad that owes something, both good and bad, to W. H. Auden. Yet Auden, whatever his occasional thematic triviality, was a poet's poet who never abandoned form. In *Beyond Howth Head,* the form consists of rhymed or off-rhymed couplets. The couplets appear meterless, but some of the rhymes are clever and effective.

The poems in *The Snow Party* (1975) are formally a highly diverse melange. There is, for instance, a shaped verse called "The Window"—a shaped verse is a poem like George Herbert's "Easter Wings" or "The Altar," in which the typographical arrangement of the words visually resembles the subject. It is a tricky feat to pull off, its chief danger probably being that the content may sound, as does that of "The Window," rather puerile. The book also contains various examples of free verse, such as "A Hermit" and "The Apotheosis of Tines," various faulty examples of meter and rhyme, and finally an almost total formal achievement in "September in Great Yarmouth."

At this writing, the diversity and frequent excellence of Mahon's achievement are best seen in *Selected Poems* (1991). There are still many poems in which the content warps the form, for instance, the first poem in the book, "In Carrowdore Churchyard," which is a kind of elegy for Louis MacNeice.* The poem has a few iambic pentameter lines, but most of the lines vary greatly from this form; really, all one can note is that the lines are about the same length; nevertheless, they range from ten to thirteen syllables. The rhyme scheme of the first stanza is ABBCAC, of the two middle stanzas ABACCB, and of the last AABCCB. Further, some of the rhymes are extremely tenuous: "lie" with "peninsula" and the feminine "perspective" with the masculine "live." If a poet allows himself such formal latitude, he is but flirting with form rather than controlling it.

Nevertheless, there are many pieces in which the poet is in absolute formal control. The villanelles, "The Andean Flute," "The Dawn Chorus," and "Antarctica," not only perfectly hold their tight form but also manage to fill it—as many villanelles do not—with a significant statement. "The Hunt by Night" has six stanzas of six lines each. The first and sixth lines have two feet; the second and fifth, three; and the third and fourth, four. Further, the first and sixth lines rhyme, as do the second and fifth, and the third and fourth. There are enough such finely controlled examples in the collection to indicate that Mahon has ceased to conduct his prosodic education in public; he is now a polished practicing graduate.

In content and in tone, the poems have an intriguing range. There is, for instance, the superb, four-page jeu d'esprit called "The Joycentenary Ode," in which Mahon wittily pastiches Joyce's portmanteau diction. There are fine pieces on Brecht and Knut Hansum, and "The Kensington Notebook" is an effectively allusive statement about Ford Madox Ford, Ezra Pound, and Wyndham Lewis. Indeed, there are so many excellently wrought poems that one can overlook such jottings from the poet's notebook as "Light Music."

On the dust jacket of this book, some of Mahon's most notable Northern colleagues make such remarks as Montague's "a living classic," Heaney's "work of the highest order," and Michael Longley's* "gloriously gifted." A less hyperbolic but probably more accurate assessment is Denis Donoghue's, "He is one of the very good poets writing in English."

WORKS: *Twelve Poems.* Belfast: Festival, 1965; *Night-Crossing.* London: Oxford University Press, 1968; *Ecclesiastes.* Manchester: Phoenix Pamphlet Poets, 1970; *Beyond Howth Head.* Dublin: Dolmen, 1970; *Lives.* London: Oxford University Press, 1972; *The Man Who Built His City in Snow.* London: Poem-of-the-Month Club, 1972; ed., *Modern Irish Poetry.* London: Sphere, 1972; *The Snow Party.* London: Oxford University Press, 1975; *Light Music.* Belfast: Ulsterman, 1977; *The Sea in Winter.* Dublin: Gallery/Old Deerfield, Mass.: Deerfield, 1979; *Poems 1962–1978.* Oxford: Oxford University Press, 1979; *Courtyards in Delft.* Dublin: Gallery, 1981; *The Chimeras.* Dublin: Gallery, 1982. (After de Nerval); *The Hunt by Night.* [Oxford]: Oxford University Press, 1982/Winston-Salem, N.C.: Wake Forest University Press, 1983; *A Kensington Notebook.* [London]: Anvil Press Poetry, [1984]. (Poetry pamphlet); *Antarctica.* Dublin: Gallery, 1985; *High Time.* Dublin: Gallery, 1985. (After Molière); *The School for Wives.* Dublin: Gallery, 1986. (After Molière); ed. & tr., *Philippe Jaccottet, Selected Poems.* Harmondsworth: Penguin/Winston-Salem, N.C.: Wake Forest University Press, 1988; ed., with Peter Fallon. *The Penguin Book of Contem-*

porary Irish Poetry. London: Penguin, 1990; Bacchae, After Euripides. [Oldcastle, Co. Meath]: Gallery, [1991]; Selected Poems. [Oldcastle, Co. Meath]: Gallery, [1991]/London: Penguin, 1993; The Yaddo Letter. [Oldcastle, Co. Meath]: Gallery, [1992]; Racine's Phaedra. [Oldcastle, Co. Meath]: Gallery, [1995]. REFERENCES: Murphy, James J., McDairmid, Lucy & Durkan, Michael. "Q. and A. with Derek Mahon." Irish Literary Supplement 10 (Fall 1991): 27–28; Tinley, Bill. "International Perspectives in the Poetry of Derek Mahon." Irish University Review 21 (Spring–September 1991): 106–117.

MAHONEY, ROSEMARY (1961–   ), diarist. Mahoney was born in Boston to a large Irish-American family. While an undergraduate at Harvard, she won the Charles E. Horman Prize in fiction writing. Later she received an M.A. from Johns Hopkins University and was the winner of a Henfield/*Transatlantic Review* Award for creative writing.

Her first book, *The Early Arrival of Dreams* (1990) is an account of a year spent as a teacher in China, just one year before the student uprisings at Tian'an Men Square. She writes in the first person, splendidly and succinctly re-creating experience. Although material conditions at the university were in a deplorable condition following the Cultural Revolution, she found her students, though shy, eager to learn English, and she delighted in getting to know many of them socially. The title of the book does not refer to the author's dream of teaching abroad but rather to a Chinese student's forlorn wish to study in the United States, although her father had cautioned her that it is foolish to wish for "the early arrival of dreams."

Back in America after the student uprisings, the author is concerned for her former students and received a reply to a letter of inquiry. Her student asked her not to write too many letters to her Chinese friends, to avoid unnecessary and unexpected troubles for them. "I can feel your love forever, and love is not measured by the number of letters."

Whoredom in Kimmage (1993) is an account of the year 1991, which the author spent in Ireland. Although the book is subtitled "Irish Women Coming of Age," its appeal is largely through the author's ability to conjure up the scene, whether of a raucous night at an Irish pub, an encounter with a proper gentleman while hitchhiking in the country, or a description of fifteenth-century Ballyportry Castle, where she lived for some months. Dutifully, however, she interviewed women prominent in the Irish feminist movement, from President Mary Robinson to Ruth Riddick, as well as writers Mary Dorcey* and Mary O'Donnell* and the poet Eavan Boland.* She concluded that Irish society, although still more restricted than in many parts of the world, is charting a more liberal pathway to the future.

JEAN FRANKS

WORKS: The Early Arrival of Dreams. New York: Ballantine, 1990; Whoredom in Kimmage. Boston: Houghton Mifflin, 1993.

MAHONY, FRANCIS SYLVESTER. *See* PROUT, FATHER.

MAHONY, MARTIN FRANCIS (1831–1885), novelist. A nephew of Father Prout,* Mahony was born in Cork and wrote, sometimes under the pseudonym of Matthew Stradling, satirical novels that retain a bit of bite.

WORKS: *Checkmate*. London: Richard Bentley, 1858; as Matthew Stradling. *The Bar Sinister*. Dublin: McGlashan & Gill, 1871. (Nonfiction); as Matthew Stradling. *The Misadventures of Mr. Catlyne, Q. C.* 2 vols. London: Tinsley, 1873; *A Chronicle of the Fermors: Horace Walpole in Love*. 2 vols. London: Sampson Low, Marston, Low & Searle, 1873; *Jerpoint, An Ungarnished Story of the Time*. 3 vols. London: Chapman & Hall, 1875; *A Westminster Night's Dream*. London & Dublin, 1877.

MALONE, ANDREW E. (1888–1939), drama critic and journalist. Andrew E. Malone was the pen name of Laurence Patrick Byrne who was born in Dublin in 1888 and died there on April 13, 1939. He was a journalist, author, and probably the best Dublin drama critic of the twentieth century to date. While he was an honest and conscientious writer who had fortified himself with uncommonly wide reading in world drama, he was unable to shake off entirely the bonds of the ultra-conservative and narrow cultural attitudes in the Dublin of his time. His criticisms contain a few odd judgments, and his praises of the newly arrived Sean O'Casey* are niggardly, a consequence of his fastidious tastes in humor and of his tendency to view every work of man *sub specie aeternitatis*. But his book *The Irish Drama* (1929) is authoritative, invaluable, and still highly readable. His forecast in this book about the Abbey Theatre* was devastatingly accurate:

The pioneer directors of the Abbey have grown weary of pioneering, and it seems that the Abbey Theatre is to settle down to the repertory work of a State Theatre, where the "great plays" of the Masters will be presented at suitable intervals, and the works of expatriate Irishmen, from Farquhar to Shaw, O'Neill and Munro, will be claimed for the greater glory of Ireland . . . very useful and necessary work, but it is not quite the work for which the Irish National Theatre was founded: it is the work of the Irish Literary Theatre revived after thirty years, and a triumph for Edward Martyn* long after his death.

ANDREW MARSH

WORK: *The Irish Drama*. London: Constable, 1929.

MALONE, EDMOND (1741–1812), editor. Malone was the last and perhaps the greatest of the eighteenth-century editors of Shakespeare. Born into a family of lawyers on October 4, 1741, in Dublin, he seemed destined to follow in the family line and did, in fact, study at the Inner Temple, London, from 1763 to 1767, after taking his A.B. degree at Trinity College, Dublin, in 1761. When he returned to Ireland in 1767, however, he found briefs few and far between. Meanwhile, he had made a number of literary and theatrical acquaintances in London, having met Dr. Samuel Johnson in 1765, and he began writing essays and articles for Irish newspapers. In 1776, he started work on his edition of Goldsmith's* poetical and dramatic works, which was published in 1780.

In 1777, he returned to London to live permanently as a man of letters, becoming a member of Dr. Johnson's club. Among his many intellectual and artistic friends were Sir Joshua Reynolds, who painted his portrait, and Johnson's biographer, James Boswell, who dedicated his *Tour to the Hebrides* to him in 1786. Malone soon turned his attention to Shakespeare criticism and was at first encouraged by George Steevens. He worked on Shakespeare's biography and established the chronology of his plays, which for long was generally accepted, although scholarship has since made modifications. In 1780, he published a supplement to Johnson's edition of Shakespeare, which included reprints of Arthur Brooke's *Romeus and Juliet,* Shakespeare's poems, *Pericles* and several of the apocryphal plays, such as *Locrine.* Although Shakespeare's sonnets had been reprinted several times since 1609, Malone was the first to edit them, hitherto neglected by editors as reflecting an alien sensibility.

Perceiving a rival editor in Malone, Steevens eventually quarreled with him, whose edition in ten volumes (eleven, actually, since one volume was in two parts) appeared in 1790. Unlike many previous editors except Capell, Malone used as his copy texts many of the earliest editions, such as the quartos and the folio of 1623, which are now seen as more authoritative than the later folios. His notes encompassed those of earlier editors, supplemented or modified by his own.

Malone was an indefatigable researcher in Elizabethan drama, and his notes frequently point out parallels not only to other plays by Shakespeare but to plays by his contemporaries, early and late. He also examined many original documents, such as the books of the corporation of Stratford and Chancery rolls. His *Life* is a running commentary on Rowe's, the first that had appeared, in 1709, and that editors had subsequently followed. Throughout, he corrected error, destroyed myths, and broke new ground. His edition includes *An Historical Account of the English Stage,* the first true work of stage history. It showed later editors the importance of recognizing Shakespeare's plays in the context of the drama of their time.

In 1798, Malone exposed the forgeries of Samuel Ireland, earning the praise of even George Steevens; and the value of his edition of John Dryden (1800) later earned the praise of Sir Walter Scott. In 1798, Oxford awarded Malone a D.C.L., and in 1801 the University of Dublin gave him a D.D.L. He died on April 25, 1812, and was buried in the family mausoleum in Kilbixy churchyard, near Baronstown. The victim of an early unsuccessful love affair, he never married. His extensive library was left to his brother, who gave the Shakespearean materials to the Bodleian Library in Oxford, where they remain to this day.

JAY L. HALIO

PRINCIPAL WORK: *The Plays and Poems of William Shakespeare . . .* 21 vols. London: F. C. & J. Rivington, 1790. This edition, brought out by James Boswell the younger, is generally known as the Third Variorum and was the standard complete edition for the rest of the nineteenth century.

MANGAN, JAMES CLARENCE (1803–1849), poet. In reassessments of Irish literary history of the nineteenth century, Mangan emerges as the central figure.

Thomas Moore* and Thomas Davis* gained more popular appeal and were given credit for establishing a distinctive Irish poetry in English, but this odd, idiosyncratic writer now seems the real formulator of a distinctive Irish literary voice. Not that he was unknown until recently; both James Joyce* and W. B. Yeats* devoted early critical efforts to his work, and his patriotic verse has attracted a broad audience ever since it first appeared.

Mangan's life was one of almost unrelieved misery. He was born on May 1, 1803, into a poor Dublin family. His life was plagued by a variety of physical weaknesses and later by his addiction to alcohol and to opium. He was an eccentric character who dressed in the bizarre style of his literary idol, Maturin*; his only social contacts seem to have been with a small circle of literary acquaintances. The most important event of his adult career was his association with Petrie,* John O'Donovan,* and O'Curry* in the work of the Ordnance Topographical Survey. His clerical assistance brought him in contact with the rich lore of early Irish poetry and folklore, which he was to mine for the few remaining years of his life. He wrote little, but the few poems and prose pieces are startling in their literary techniques and in the force of convictions they contain. He died of cholera in Dublin on June 20, 1849.

Most of Mangan's poems and stories were published in *The Dublin University Magazine,* and the most popular of them are rousing patriotic exhortations. He wrote a number of poems based on the translations by others of Old Irish originals; their complicated rhyme schemes and long lines are striking. "Dark Rosaleen" is the best known of them—a forceful statement expressed in a driving melodic scheme; "O'Hussey's Ode to the Maguire" is nearly as fine. In such poems, Mangan revives the spirit of early verse, making it immediate and urgent and free from the antiquarian dust of many translations. His original patriotic verses are passionate, but their elaborate verse forms and prosodic devices bring a level of control and sophistication that raise them above the usual patriotic verse of the time—far better than most entries in the immensely popular *The Spirit of the Nation.*

Mangan has frequently been compared with his American contemporary Edgar Allan Poe, not only because of resemblances in their lives and personalities but because their literary productions are so similar. The comparison is instructive, for both experimented extensively with verse techniques, investigating the effects of multiple rhymes, refrains, and elaborate prosodic schemes. Both were fascinated by extreme states of psychological distress, and some of their best prose pieces describe states of anxiety with such precision that they are assumed to be autobiographical. There are specific resemblances that have caused some to claim that one author knew the other's work. Their productions and comments on their own intentions lead one to conclude that Mangan would even have agreed with Poe's published theories on literature.

But Mangan's interest in Continental literature extends beyond Poe's. His verse translations of nineteenth-century German poems are both accurate and reflective of the subtle musical effects of the originals. In addition, he published "versions" of Spanish and Islamic poems, based on translations by others. Some, such as the Oriental fantasies, are probably not authentic, but many of these poems reveal ingenuity and considerable poetic skill.

His prose tales reflect the taste of the times; they are Gothic stories, humorous observations, and fantasies. His incomplete *Autobiography* is expressed with such narrative skill that it is now regarded as the best of his prose writing, although it is largely fictional.

Mangan was a genius, one Irish poet of the nineteenth century whose work cannot be overlooked. He wrote about Ireland with a fervor that no subsequent writer has matched, and he was a consummate craftsman of poetic forms and techniques. As David Lloyd points out, to relegate Mangan's work to a category of "minor literature" is to reveal more about the cultural aspect of literary criticism than about literature itself.

JAMES KILROY

WORKS: *Anthologia Hibernica: German Anthology.* 2 vols. Dublin: Curry, 1845. (Translations); *The Poets and Poetry of Munster.* Dublin: O'Daly, 1849; *Poems by James Clarence Mangan.* Introduction by John Mitchel. New York: P. M. Haverty, 1859; *Essays in Prose and Verse.* C. P. Heehan, ed. Dublin: James Duffy, 1884; *Poems of James Clarence Mangan.* D. J. O'Donoghue, ed. Dublin: M. H. Gill, 1903; *Prose Writings of James Clarence Mangan.* D. J. O'Donoghue, ed. Dublin: M. H. Gill, 1904; *Autobiography.* James Kilroy, ed. Dublin: Dolmen, 1968.   REFERENCES: Clifford, Brendan. *Dubliner: The Lives, Times, and Writings of James Clarence Mangan.* Belfast: Athol, 1988; Donaghy, Henry J. *James Clarence Mangan.* New York: Twayne, 1974; Kilroy, James. *James Clarence Mangan.* Lewisburg, Pa.: Bucknell University Press, 1970; Lloyd, David. *Nationalism and Minor Literature: James Clarence Mangan and the Emergence of Irish Cultural Nationalism.* Berkeley: University of California Press, 1987; Mangan, Ellen Shannon. *James Clarence Mangan: A Biography.* Dublin: Irish Academic, 1995; O'Donoghue, D. J. *The Life and Writings of J. C. Mangan.* Edinburgh: P. Geddes, 1897.

MANNIN, ETHEL (1900–1984), novelist, autobiographer, and travel writer. Mannin was born on October 6, 1900, in a London suburb, went to local council schools till the age of fifteen, and very early went into journalism. The *London Times* justly remarks, "She would have been a success in daily journalism and it seems likely that its merciless discipline would have done her good. As it was, she remained to some extent the victim of her own precocity and facility. She wrote too much and was insufficiently critical of her work." Book after book, often two a year, flowed from her indefatigable pen, but few retain much interest today. She may be called an Irish writer by virtue of her Connemara residence, her *Connemara Journal,* her best-selling novel *Late Have I Loved Thee,* and her *Two Studies in Integrity,* which is about Gerald Griffin* and Father Prout.* She is also reputed to have had a brief affair with the elderly W. B. Yeats.* She died on December 5, 1984.

Late Have I Loved Thee (1948), a study of a late vocation to the priesthood, for years held an exalted position in Irish convent libraries, and thus in the mind of every Irish Catholic schoolgirl of a certain generation. The aristocratic and cynical Francis Sable is brought to his knees by God in a manner predictable from page two. In spite of a rather good evocation of Paris and of the west of

Ireland, the novel is superficial and plastic and often sinks into the appalling sentimentality that Mannin mistakes for feeling. Although the novel sentimentalizes religion, it was responsible for many vocations to the Catholic Church. In her autobiographical journals, however, the author states that the book was written without any belief in that church.

In her journals, Mannin goes on about (at considerable length) her cat, vegetarianism, and the Arab Cause. (She also wrote a novel about the last-named subject.) Apparently, she can turn her hand to anything. *Two Studies in Integrity* (1954) compares the depressing Gerald Griffin, who somehow contrived to write the admired novel *The Collegians,* with the waggish and scholarly Francis Mahoney who created Father Prout. The book is interesting for the specialist, but not sufficiently well written to retain the interest of the average reader.

                                                                MARY ROSE CALLAGHAN

WORKS: *Martha.* London: Leonard Parsons, 1923/revised, London: Jarrolds, 1929; *Hunger of the Sea.* London: Jarrolds, 1924; *Pilgrims.* London: Jarrolds, [1927]; *Green Willow.* London: Jarrolds, [1928]; *Crescendo.* London: Jarrolds, [1929]; *Forbidden Music,* with *Martyrdom* by Warwick Deeping and *The House Behind the Judas Tree* by Gilbert Frankau. London: Readers Library, [1929]; *Children of the Earth.* London: Jarrolds, [1930]; *Confessions and Impressions.* London: Jarrolds, [1930]. (Autobiographical); *Bruised Wings and Other Stories.* London: Wright & Brown, [1931]; *Commonsense and the Child.* London: Jarrolds, [1931]; *Green Figs.* London: Jarrolds, [1931]. (Stories); *Ragged Banners.* London: Jarrolds, [1931]; *The Tinsel Eden, and Other Stories.* London: Wright & Brown, [1931]; *All Experience.* London: Jarrolds, 1932; *Linda Shawn.* London: Jarrolds, [1932]; *Love's Winnowing.* London: Wright & Brown, [1932]; *Dryad.* London: Jarrolds, 1933. (Stories); *Venetian Blinds.* London: Jarrolds, 1933; *Forever Wandering.* London: Jarrolds, 1934. (Travel); *Men Are Unwise.* London: Jarrolds, 1934; *Cactus.* London: Jarrolds, 1935/revised, London: Jarrolds, [1944]; *The Falconer's Voice.* London: Jarrolds, 1935. (Stories); *The Pure Flame.* London: Jarrolds, 1936; *South to Samarkand.* London: Jarrolds, 1936. (Travel); *Commonsense and the Adolescent.* London: Jarrolds, [1937]; *Women Also Dream.* London: Jarrolds, 1937; *Darkness my Bride.* London: Jarrolds, [1938]; *Rose and Sylvie.* London: Jarrolds, [1938]; *Women and the Revolution.* London: Secker & Warburg, 1938; *Privileged Spectator.* London: Jarrolds, 1939/revised, London: Jarrolds, [1948]. (Autobiographical); *Julie.* London: Jarrolds, [1940]; *Rolling in the Dew.* London: Jarrolds, [1940]; *Christianity—or Chaos?* London: Jarrolds, [1941]; *Red Rose.* London: Jarrolds, [1941]; *Captain Moonlight.* London: Jarrolds, [1942]; *Castles in the Street.* London: Letchworth, [1942]; *Commonsense and Morality.* London: Jarrolds, [1942]; *The Blooming Bough.* London: Macdonald, [1943]; *No More Mimosa.* London: Jarrolds, [1943]; *Bread and Roses.* London: Jarrolds, [1944]; *Proud Heaven.* London: Jarrolds, [1944]; *Lucifer and the Child.* London: Jarrolds, 1945; *The Dark Forest.* London: Jarrolds, 1946; *Selected Stories.* Dublin, London: Maurice Fridberg, 1946; *Comrade, O Comrade; or, Low-Down on the Left.* London: Jarrolds, [1947]; *Connemara Journal.* London: Westhouse, 1947; *Sounding Brass.* London: Jarrolds, [1947]; *German Journey.* London: Jarrolds, [1948]. (Travel); *Late Have I Loved Thee.* London: Jarrolds, [1948]; *Every Man a Stranger.* London: Jarrolds, [1949]; *Jungle Journey.* London: Jarrolds, [1950]. (Travel); *Moroccan Music.* London: Jarrolds, 1951. (Travel); *At Sundown, the Tiger.* London: Jarrolds, 1951; *The Fields at Evening.* London: Jarrolds, 1952; *This Was a Man. Some Memories of Robert Mannin, by His Daughter.* London: Jarrolds, 1952; *The Wild Swans, and Other Tales Based on the Ancient Irish.* London: Jarrolds, 1952; *Love under Another Name.* London: Jarrolds, 1953; *So Tiberius. . . .* London: Jarrolds, 1954; *Two Studies in Integrity: Gerald Griffin and the Rev. Francis Mahony.* London: Jarrolds, 1954; *Land of the Crested Lion.* London: Jarrolds, 1955. (Travel); *The Living Lotus.* London: Jarrolds, 1956; *The Country of the Sea.* London: Jarrolds, 1957. (Travel); *Pity the Innocent.* London: Jarrolds, 1957; *Fragrance of Hyacinths.* London: Jarrolds, 1958; *Ann and Peter in Sweden.* London: Frederick Muller, [1959]; *The Blue Eyed Bay.* London: Jarrolds, 1959; *Brief*

Voices. London: Hutchinson, 1959. (Autobiographical); *Ann and Peter in Japan.* London: Frederick Muller, 1960; *The Flowery Sword.* London: Hutchinson, 1960. (Travel); *Sabishisa.* London: Hutchinson, 1961; *Ann and Peter in Austria.* London: Frederick Muller, 1962; *Curfew at Dawn.* London: Hutchinson, 1962; *With Will Adams through Japan.* London: Frederick Muller, 1962; *A Lance for the Arabs.* London: Hutchinson, 1963. (Travel); *The Road to Beersheba.* London: Hutchinson, 1963. (Travel); *Aspects of Egypt.* London: Hutchinson, 1964. (Travel); *Bavarian Story.* London: Arrow Books, 1964; *Rebel's Ride.* London: Hutchinson, 1964; *The Burning Bush.* London: Hutchinson, 1965; *The Lovely Land.* London: Hutchinson, 1965. (Travel); *Loneliness: a Study of the Human Condition.* London: Hutchinson, 1966; *An American Journey.* London: Hutchinson, 1967. (Travel); *Bitter Babylon.* London: Hutchinson, 1968; *The Midnight Street.* London: Hutchinson, 1969; *Practitioners of Love.* London: Hutchinson, 1969; *The Saga of Sammy-cat.* Oxford: Pergamon, 1969; *England at Large.* London: Hutchinson, 1970; *My Cat Sammy.* London: Joseph, 1971; *Young in the Twenties.* London: Hutchinson, 1971. (Autobiographical); *The Curious Adventures of Major Fosdick.* London: Hutchinson, 1972; *England My Adventure.* London: Hutchinson, 1972; *Sounding Brass.* London: Hutchinson, 1972; *Mission to Beirut.* London: Hutchinson, 1973; *Stories from My Life.* London: Hutchinson, 1973; *Kildoon.* London: Hutchinson, 1974; *An Italian Journey.* London: Hutchinson, 1975; *Pity the Innocent.* London: Hutchinson, 1975; *The Late Miss Guthrie.* London: Hutchinson, 1976; *Sunset over Dartmoor.* London: Hutchinson, 1977.

MANNING, KITTY (1936–   ), novelist. Manning was born in England of Irish parents but moved to Northern Ireland when she was five.

WORK: *The Between People.* Dublin: Attic, 1990.

MANNING, MARY (1906–   ), playwright and novelist. Manning was born in Dublin on June 30, 1906. She was educated at Morehampton House School and Alexandra College in Dublin and later studied art in London and Boston. She also studied acting at the Abbey school and played small parts with the Irish Players in England and with the Abbey* in Dublin before joining the Gate,* where she was publicity manager and editor of *Motley,* the theater's amusing, short-lived magazine. Micheál MacLiammóir* has written that during this period Manning's ''brain, nimble and observant as it was, could not yet keep pace with a tongue so caustic that even her native city . . . was a little in awe of her.'' That satiric wit was beautifully displayed in the finest of her three Gate plays, *Youth's the Season———?* (1931). This is a sardonic, yet moving and wittily written study of a group of young, middle-class Dubliners caught just at that moment before their lives are set in a permanent pattern. In it, the curious character of Egosmith was suggested by her friend Samuel Beckett.* It was one of the most accomplished first plays ever to be seen in Dublin. Her two other Gate plays, *Storm over Wicklow* (1933) and *Happy Family* (1934), were less successful and have not been published.

In the mid-1930s, Manning married Mark De Wolfe Howe, Jr., the authority on Justice Holmes, and left Dublin for Boston. She wrote no more plays for several years, but in the interval of raising a family she published two novels in America, *Mount Venus* (1938) and *Lovely People* (1953). The better of the two, *Lovely People,* is a stylish entertainment about the upper middle class of Boston and Cambridge. She was one of the founders of the Cambridge Poets'

Theatre, which gave the first production of her adaptation of Joyce's* *Finnegans Wake* in April 1955. The play, called variously *Passages from Finnegans Wake* and *The Voices of Shem,* is a successfully theatrical adaptation of enormously recalcitrant material. After her husband's death, she returned to Ireland; and in the 1970s she was a perceptive, if astringent, theater critic for *Hibernia.* She also returned to playwriting, her most effective piece being a comic but moving adaptation of Frank O'Connor's novel *The Saint and Mary Kate* (Abbey, 1968). In 1978, there appeared *The Last Chronicles of Ballyfungus,* a volume of short stories so nicely interconnected that they grow into a novel. The book is a droll and accurate satiric caricature of quickly changing modern Ireland, but the satire is leavened by sympathy, and the glum conclusion is unfortunately appropriate.

In 1979, she returned to America and remarried. One of her daughters is Fanny Howe, the American novelist and poet.

WORKS: *Youth's the Season——?* In *Plays of Changing Ireland.* Curtis Canfield, ed. New York: Macmillan, 1936; *Mount Venus.* Boston: Houghton Mifflin, 1938. (Novel); *Lovely People.* Boston: Houghton Mifflin, 1953. (Novel); *Passages from Finnegans Wake by James Joyce.* Cambridge: Harvard University Press, 1957. Also published as *The Voices of Shem.* (Play); *Frank O'Connor's The Saint and Mary Kate.* [Newark, Del.]: Proscenium, [1970]. (Play); *The Last Chronicles of Ballyfungus.* Boston: Houghton Mifflin/London: Routledge & Kegan Paul, 1978. (Short stories); I *Remember It Well. Journal of Irish Literature* 15 (September 1986): 17–41. (Autobiographical sketches). REFERENCE: "Let's Be Dublin." *Journal of Irish Literature* 15 (September 1986): 3–17. (Interview by Mary Rose Callaghan).

MARCUS, DAVID (1924–) editor and fiction writer. Marcus was born in Cork City on August 21, 1924. He was educated by the Presentation Brothers, at University College, Cork, and at King's Inns, Dublin, and then practiced law for some years in Dublin. As editor and publisher, his work has given immense impetus to modern Irish writing. He was founder-editor of the important literary magazine *Irish Writing** from 1946 to 1954. In 1948, he founded *Poetry Ireland,* which he edited until 1954. Then, after thirteen years in London, he returned to Dublin and became literary editor of the *Irish Press,* for which in 1968 he inaugurated a New Irish Writing page to publish new poetry and short stories. In 1976, he formed Poolbeg Press, which initially published distinguished volumes by such established writers as Michael McLaverty,* Bryan MacMahon,* Benedict Kiely,* and James Plunkett,* as well as able work by such new writers as Maeve Kelly,* Helen Lucy Burke,* Emma Cooke,* Gillman Noonan,* and many others. In 1986, he retired from the *Irish Press* in order to devote more time to his own writing. Nevertheless, he has continued to proselytize for the Irish short story by editing many anthologies of new writing. Indeed, the roll call of new writers whom Marcus has published is nearly a list of all that is best in modern Irish fiction.

As a writer himself, Marcus has published a very slim volume of poems and an able translation of Brian Merriman's *The Midnight Court.* A novel, *To Next Year in Jerusalem,* did appear in 1954, but not until more than thirty years later with the publication of *A Land Not Theirs* in 1986 and *A Land in Flames* in

1987 did he make a popular impact as a novelist. *To Next Year in Jerusalem* is set in a small western town in the winter of 1947–1948, in the days leading up to the foundation of the state of Israel. The town has a very small Jewish community, only, in fact, the ten necessary males needed to maintain a congregation. The problem of the young protagonist, Jonathan Lippman, is "how could he be both Irish and Jewish?" He is fluent in Irish; with the backing of a priest friend, he is elected chairman of the St. Mary's Parish Club's Central Council; and, most important, he is in love with a Catholic girl. Nevertheless, his deepest desire is, as soon as he is freed by the death of one of the ten males in the little Jewish community, to go to Israel and to help in the formation of the new state. This is a solid, well-developed book, but an overly leisurely one. The paragraphs are long and unnecessarily circumstantial, and some of the scenes are stretched much too far. The first scene with the priest, for instance, goes on for about thirty-five pages, although its content probably merits only about fifteen or twenty.

The two novels of the 1980s are also long, but the writing has become so leanly professional, and the scenes so much more throughly dramatized, that the reader gallops effortlessly through them. Both deal with Ireland in the troubled years of the early century. Both are excellently characterized and plotted. *A Land Not Theirs* depicts the Jewish community in Cork city with knowledge and deep sympathy and succeeds in reclaiming for literature a facet of life in Ireland that had hardly, despite the rather assimilated Leopold Bloom, been touched upon. *A Land in Flames* is not a Jewish novel but is set in Kerry in the summer of 1920 and depicts in microcosm the buildup of disruption and violence between the republicans and the British military. Like *A Land Not Theirs,* it has a large cast of well-etched characters, but its plot, which culminates in the burning of a Big House, is even more effectively structured. Marcus's novels have been described as "easy reads." They, of course, are that, but the term suggests a rather dismissive popular commercialism. That is, Marcus is more on the level of a Maeve Binchy* than of a John McGahern* or a John Banville.* The truth is that these serious books are easy reads because they are well and traditionally crafted.

In 1988, Marcus published a slim volume of short stories called *Who Ever Heard of an Irish Jew?*, whose title accurately describes the subject matter. Like the late novels, the stories are traditional in form and very professionally done. The most substantial story, "Monty's Monday," is a fine character sketch of a young Waterford man, a traveling salesman for his father's fancy goods business, who ineffectually tries to stave off the boredom of provincial life by picking up girls on his travels. The lesser pieces are leavened by considerable quiet humor.

Marcus is married to the novelist Ita Daly* and is the brother of Louis Marcus, the documentary filmmaker.

PRINCIPAL WORKS: *Six Poems.* Dublin: Dolmen, 1952; trans., *The Midnight Court* by Brian Merriman. Dublin: Dolmen, 1953; *To Next Year in Jerusalem.* London: Macmillan/New York: St.

Martin's, 1954. (Novel); *A Land Not Theirs.* London: Bantam, 1986. (Novel); *A Land in Flames.* London: Bantam, 1987. (Novel); *Who Ever Heard of an Irish Jew? and Other Stories.* London, New York, Toronto, Sydney & Auckland: Bantam, [1988].

MARTELLA, MAUREEN

WORK: *Bugger Bucharest.* Dublin: Basement, 1995. (Novel).

MARTIN, [WILLIAM] DAVID McCART (1937–   ), novelist. Martin was born in July 1937 in Belfast and was educated locally. From 1951 to 1952, he worked at various jobs, like apprentice electrician, and from 1955 to 1962 he served in the Royal Navy. From 1967 to 1971, he attended the University of Keele and received a B.A. in English and philosophy. After lecturing in English from 1971 to 1975 at the Northern Ireland Polytechnic in County Antrim, he attended the University of Warwick and received an M.A. in English literature. After 1976, he was for several years senior lecturer at Northern Ireland Polytechnic. His novels deal with the violence occasioned by Irish politics in this century, particularly during the civil war and during the recent troubles in the North. *The Task* (1975) and *The Ceremony of Innocence* (1977) are both set in modern Belfast, and their realism, authenticity, and strength have been much admired. *The Task* is technically interesting for its attempt to tell the story from different points of view, but that technique clogs the progress of the narrative considerably. A tauter narrative is *The Road to Ballyshannon* (1981), which is set during the Irish civil war in the days after Partition. A republican soldier and a boy escape from a prison ship moored in Lough Larne. They meet an Royal Ulster Constabolary sergeant and a constable, and the man kills the constable and takes the sergeant hostage. During their trek across the North to the Free State border, the sergeant acknowledges that the constable who has been killed was his son, and the trek becomes something of a struggle for the moral allegiance of the boy but culminates in the killing of the man and boy just across the border. The characters are humanly drawn and memorable. For some reason, Martin stitches this same story into his longer and most ambitious work, *Dream* (1986). That novel traces the fortunes of an Ulster family and their friends from the days of the Ulster gunrunning before World War I, through the war, the Easter Rising, and the civil war, and up to the German bombing of the North in World War II. As in *The Task* and *The Road to Ballyshannon,* Martin frequently switches his point of view; but, as he largely stays with the character of Harry, this technique does seem a little unbalanced. Martin writes a basically clear prose, but he does repeat certain catch phrases and, à la Thomas Wolfe, often repeats certain lyrical refrains. This and a tendency to slip into loose romantic writing at emotional moments certainly sometimes hurt his pace. For instance:

And so the ritual continued and continued in a time without end or beginning either, passionately, wantonly, somnolently, the musk scent of the night which was the land and their own bodies and the brisk breezes from the bay and the beasts from land and sea secret sharers in a marriage feast.

Nevertheless, these are strong novels with nicely explored and plausible characters, and the latest two are ones of some accomplishment.

WORKS: *The Task*. London: Secker & Warburg, 1975; *The Ceremony of Innocence*. London: Secker & Warburg, 1977; *The Road to Ballyshannon*. London: Secker & Warburg, [1981]; *Dream*. London: Secker & Warburg, [1986].

MARTIN, JAMES (1783–1860), poet. Martin was born in Millbrook, County Meath, and was a small farmer, a millworker, and a farm laborer. He wrote copiously about the issues of the day and has been described as an unrecognized genius and as a mediocrity. He is not usually a mediocrity, but occasionally he can rise to it.

WORKS: *Translations from Ancient Irish MSS and Other Poems*. London: Sherwood, Neely & Jones, 1811; *Poems*. Cavan, 1813; *Poems on Various Subjects*. Cavan: For the Author, 1816; *Man's Final End: A Vision of the Last Judgment*. ca. 1823; *Ireland's Dirge: An Historical Poem*. Dublin: For the Translator, 1827; *A Poetical Letter Addressed to the Independent Electors of the County*. Knockbrack, 1831; *Cottage Minstrelsy; or, Poems on Various Subjects*. Kells: Henderson, 1832; *Miscellaneous Verses*. Ca. 1833; *Reformation the Third, or the Apostate N-L-N, and the Perverts of Athboy*. . . . Dublin: For the Author, 1838; *The Medal and Glass: A Poetical Dialogue*. Kells: Henderson, 1841; *The Wounded Soldier, a Tale of Waterloo, with Other Poems, on Temperance*. Kells: Henderson, k1841; *The Truth Teller, or, Poems on Various Subjects*. Kells: Henderson, 1842; *The Repealer or the Bane and Antidote of Ireland*. . . . Dublin: For the Author, 1844; *A Dialogue between John Bull and Granna Uille; or, Ireland in 1845*. . . . Dublin: For the Author, 1845; *A Dialogue between an Irish Agent and Tenant*. Dublin: For the Author, 1848; *Edmund and Marcella, A Tale of Waterloo*. . . . Kells: Henderson, 1949; *An Answer to the Objections of the Ven. the Archdeacon of Meath against the Sacrifice of the Mass*. . . . Navan: Kelly, 1850; *An Inquiry Whether the Roman Catholics Separated from Protestants, or Protestants from Roman Catholics*. . . . Kells: Henderson, 1851; *The Mass Shewn to Be Real Sacrifice*. . . . Dublin: For the Author, 1853; *John and Mary, a Modern Irish Tale*. . . . Trim: Henderson, 1855; *The Immaculate Conception of the Blessed Virgin*. . . . Trim: Henderson, 1855; *The Campaign in the Crimea*. . . . Kells: Henderson, 1856; *Death and the Poet, A Dialogue*. . . . Kells: Henderson, 1857; *Silas and Actea, A Story of Christian Martyrdom*. . . . Kells: Henderson, 1858.

MARTIN, JOY (1937–), novelist. Martin was born and educated in Limerick and has worked as a journalist in Ireland and South Africa.

WORKS: *A Wrong to Sweeten*. London: Weidenfeld & Nicholson, 1986; *The Moon Is Red in April*. London: Weidenfeld & Nicholson, 1989; *Ulick's Daughter*. London: Grafton, 1990; *A Heritage of Wrong*. London: Grafton, 1991; *Image of Laura*. London: HarperCollins, 1992.

MARTIN, MARY LETITIA (1815–1850), novelist. Martin was born on August 28, 1815, at Ballinahinch Castle, County Galway. She was the granddaughter of "Humanity Dick" Martin, the animal lover and duelist, and the only daughter of Thomas Barnewall Martin, MP. The estate she inherited was about 200,000 acres, but her father had mortgaged it. The further expenses she incurred by supporting the peasantry during the Famine earned her the title of "the Princess of Connemara" but left her landless and impoverished. She retired with her husband, Arthur Gonne Bell, to Belgium and endeavored to support herself by writing. Her second novel, *Julia Howard* (1850), is set partly in Ireland, and the descriptions of landscape and peasantry have been thought truthful and picturesque. She and her husband later sailed for New York, but she was prematurely confined on ship and died on November 7, 1850, only ten days after her arrival in the New World.

WORKS: *St. Etienne: A Romance of the First Revolution.* 3 vols. London: T. C. Newby, 1845; *Julia Howard.* 3 vols. London: Richard Bentley, 1850.

MARTYN, EDWARD (1859–1923), playwright. Martyn was born in Tulira, Ardrahan, County Galway, on January 30, 1859. After studying without distinction at preparatory schools and at Oxford, he returned to his ancestral home. His first writing, *Morgante the Lesser,* published pseudonymously in 1890, was a mixture of Rabelaisian satire and utopianism. With his neighbor Lady Gregory* and W. B. Yeats,* he became in 1899 a co-founder of the Irish Literary Theatre, to which he contributed *The Heather Field* and *Maeve* and paid whatever financial deficits were incurred during the group's three-year existence.

Partly because of personality conflicts with Yeats and George Moore,* and partly because of his dislike of "peasant" plays and Celtic Twilight romanticism, Martyn broke away from the main movement of Irish drama which evolved into the Abbey.* In 1906, he helped to organize the Theatre of Ireland, and in 1914, he, Thomas MacDonagh,* and Joseph Plunkett* founded the Irish Theatre.* At a small building in Hardwicke Street, Dublin, they presented continental masterpieces in translation, nonpeasant plays by Irish authors, and a few works in Irish. Despite limited facilities and the death or imprisonment of several members of the company after the 1916 Rising, the theatre remained in operation until early 1920.

Martyn's interests were not confined to literature. Initially a conservative landowner, he swerved into ardent, though not revolutionary, nationalism. From 1904 to 1908, he was president of Sinn Féin. His devout Catholicism was manifested in the endowment of a choir in the Dublin Pro-Cathedral and in his crusade to improve the quality of ecclesiastical art in Ireland.

In his final years, failing health and disturbances in rural Galway during the Troubles forced his retirement from active life. He died at Tulira on December 5, 1923, the last of a family that had resided in Ireland since the twelfth century.

The major influences on Martyn were continental writers, particularly Ibsen. As a straight-line moralist, Martyn did not subscribe to the specific ideas of the Norwegian master, but he did admire the craftsmanship and intellectual fiber of Ibsen's plays.

The influence of Ibsen's dramas of municipal corruption is apparent in Martyn's comic satires, although much of the humor lies in the topical allusions and the flimsy concealment of actual persons as characters. Political patronage and the servility of "West Briton" Irishmen are ridiculed in *The Tale of a Town* (1905), *The Place-Hunters* (printed in 1902, not staged), and the unpublished

The Privilege of Place, performed in 1915. The comic history of *The Tale of a Town,* and its revision by George Moore as *The Bending of the Bough,* is told with malicious glee in Moore's *Hail and Farewell. The Dream Physician* (1914) and *Romulus and Remus* (1916) are allegories of the activities and personalities of the Irish Literary Theatre. Yeats is portrayed as an extravagant poseur, Moore as an egotistical hack writer, and Lady Gregory as a sensible person mesmerized into silliness by Yeats. Martyn casts himself as a slightly bemused gentleman remaining calm in the midst of chaos and lunacy.

The standard plot of Martyn's serious drama is a conflict between an idealistic, reclusive man (not unlike Martyn himself) and an aggressive, unscrupulous woman. Typical is his best and earliest play, *The Heather Field,* performed by the Irish Literary Theatre in 1899. Carden Tyrrell and his wife Grace both violate laws of nature—he by cultivating a heather field, she by demanding that her dreamy husband become a socialite and a prudent manager. Nature retaliates. The field reverts to its wild state, and the bankrupt, insane Tyrrell reverts to living in the happy days of his youth.

Realistic-idealistic roles are reversed in *Maeve* (1900). The O'Heynes, an impoverished Irish chief, expediently offers his daughter Maeve in marriage to a wealthy Englishman. The play is an allegory of the Norman invasion of Ireland, but it is also a variation on *The Heather Field. Maeve* finds in death what Tyrrell found in madness: retreat from a world too full of weeping into one of unfading beauty.

In *An Enchanted Sea* (1904), which owes much to Ibsen's *The Lady from the Sea,* Rachel Font's matchmaking of her daughter Agnes and Lord Mask is frustrated because her eerie young nephew Guy Font has infected Mask with his mystical obsession with the sea. Like Martyn's other tough-minded women, Mrs. Font lets nothing stand in her way. She murders Guy, Mask drowns himself, and as the law closes in, Mrs. Font commits suicide.

Michael Colman, a melancholy widower in *Grangecolman* (1912), falls in love with his young secretary. His daughter Catharine, embittered by her failure as a wife and as a physician, destroys the match with a vindictive, suicidal gesture. She disguises herself as the family ghost, a figure in white, knowing that the secretary, an expert marksman, will show her scorn for the ghost by firing a pistol at it.

The unpublished *Regina Eyre* (1919) was hooted even by critics friendly to the Irish Theatre. Only a mountaintop set designed by young Micheál Mac Liammóir* was applauded. In this play, Martyn reverses the gender of the *Hamlet* characters, changes the scene from Elsinore to Kerry, and superimposes on Shakespeare an Ibsenite ending: a symbolic mountain-climb in which puresouled Regina attains the summit and her vicious stepmother (like Claudius she poisons people) plunges to her death.

Martyn was a loser in everything he attempted. His taste in liturgical music drove the gross-eared faithful away from the Pro-Cathedral. The violence engendered by Ireland's struggle for independence greatly distressed him. The

Theatre of Ireland and the Irish Theatre failed, although their concepts were embodied successfully in the Gate Theatre.* He never again matched the high level of craftsmanship and intellectual control displayed in *The Heather Field,* nor did he ever learn to write believable, free-flowing dialogue.

To his credit, this high-minded, pleasantly eccentric gentleman chose not to take the easy road to popularity. He was ever ready to advance his artistic, political, and social beliefs, whatever the cost, with all his resources and full-spirited dedication.

WILLIAM J. FEENEY

WORKS: *Morgante the Lesser, His Notorious Life and Wonderful Deeds,* under the pseudonym of Sirius. London: Swan Sonnenschein, 1890; *The Heather Field: A Play in Three Acts and Maeve: A Psychological Drama in Two Acts.* Introduction by George Moore. London: Duckworth, 1899. (*The Heather Field* was reprinted in Vol. 1, Irish Drama Series, Chicago: De Paul University, 1966. *Maeve* was reprinted in Vol. 2, 1967.); "A Plea for a National Theatre in Ireland." *Samhain,* No. 1 (October 1901): 14–15; *The Place-Hunters: A Political Comedy in One Act. The Leader,* July 26, 1902; *The Tale of a Town: A Comedy of Affairs in Five Acts and An Enchanted Sea: A Play in Four Acts.* Kilkenny: Standish O'Grady/London: Fisher Unwin, 1902; *Romulus and Remus, or The Makers of Delights: A Symbolist Extravaganza in One Act.* Christmas supplement to *The Irish People,* December 21, 1907, 1–2; *Grangecolman: A Domestic Drama in Three Acts.* Dublin: Maunsel, 1912; *The Dream Physician: A Play in Five Acts.* Dublin: Talbot, 1914/reprinted in Vol. 7, Irish Drama Series, 1972; "A Plea for the Revival of the Irish Literary Theatre." *The Irish Review* 4 (April 1914): 79–84; "*The Cherry Orchard* of Tchekoff." *New Ireland* 8 (June 21, 1919): 108–109; *Selected Plays by George Moore and Edward Martyn.* David Eakin & Michael Case, eds. Washington, D.C.: Catholic University of America Press, 1995. REFERENCES: Courtney, Sr. Marie-Therese. *Edward Martyn and the Irish Theatre.* New York: Vantage, 1956; Ellis-Fermor, Una. *The Irish Dramatic Movement.* London: Methuen, 1939; Fallis, Richard. *The Irish Renaissance.* Syracuse, N.Y.: Syracuse University Press, 1977; Feeney, William J. *Drama in Hardwicke Street: A History of the Irish Theatre Company.* Rutherford, Madison, Teaneck, N.J.: Fairleigh Dickinson University Press/London & Toronto: Associated University Presses, [1984]; Feeney, William J., ed. *Edward Martyn's Irish Theatre. Lost Plays of the Irish Renaissance.* Vol. 2. Newark, Del.: Proscenium, 1980. (Contains Martyn's "Romulus and Remus"); Gwynn, Denis. *Edward Martyn and the Irish Revival.* London: Jonathan Cape, 1930; Hall, Wayne. "Edward Martyn: Politics and Drama of Ice." *Éire-Ireland* 15 (Summer 1980): 113–122; MacDonagh, John. "Edward Martyn." *Dublin Magazine* 1 (January 1924): 465–467; McFate, Patricia. "*The Bending of the Bough* and *The Heather Field.*" *Éire-Ireland* 8 (Spring 1973): 52–61; Moore, George. *Hail and Farewell.* 3 vols. London: Heinemann, 1937; Nolan, J.C.M. "Edward Martyn and Guests at Tulira." *Irish Arts Review* 10 (1994): 167–173; O'Connor, Ulick. *All the Olympians.* New York: Atheneum, 1984; Setterquist, Jan. *Ibsen and the Beginnings of Anglo-Irish Drama.* II. *Edward Martyn.* Upsala: Lundquist, 1960.

MATHEW, FRANK [JAMES] (1865–1920), novelist. Mathew was a nephew of Father Theobald Mathew, the apostle of temperance, whose life he wrote.

WORKS: *Father Mathew, His Life and Times.* London: Cassell, 1980; *At the Rising of the Moon: Irish Stories and Sketches.* London: McClure/New York: Tait, 1893; *The Wood of the Brambles.* London: John Lane/Chicago: Way & Williams, 1896; *A Child in the Temple.* London & New York: John Lane, 1897; *The Spanish Urn.* London: & New York: John Lane, 1897; *The Spanish Wine.* London & New York: John Lane, 1898; *One Queen Triumphant.* New York & London: John Lane, 1899; *Defender of the Faith.* London & New York: John Lane, 1899; *Love of Comrades.* London & New York: John Lane, 1900.

MATHEWS, AIDAN CARL (1956–   ), poet, fiction writer, and playwright. Born into a Dublin medical family, Mathews was educated first by the Jesuits at Gonzaga College and later at University College, Dublin, where his literary talent was early recognized. After his graduation, he was accepted by Donald Davie into his Seminar in Creative Literature at Stanford University, after which he joined RTÉ as a producer in sound radio. Quite early, Mathews was winning prizes and awards: the Macaulay Fellowship Award in 1978–1979, the Ina Coolbrith Poetry Prize at Stanford in 1981, and the Academy of American Poets Award in 1982. His first book of poems, *Windfalls* (1977), winner of the Patrick Kavanagh* Award of 1976, showed remarkable technical finesse joined to a grievous apprehension of life and death—such as had impelled their creator to a stint as a mortuary technician in Dublin in 1975. This experience issued in some of the most memorable poems in *Minding Ruth* (1983)—"Heart Failure," "Infanticide," "Mortuaries," and "Still Birth," side by side with lyrics of poignant sensitivity, the book's exquisite title poem.

His first volume of short stories, *Adventures in a Bathyscope* (1988), with its curious blend of fantasy and realism, established him as one of the more original and challenging fictionists of his generation, combining the sensuous curiosity of a Joyce* with the crabbed euphuism of a Flann O'Brien (Brian O'Nolan*). Neil Jordan* wrote, "The lucid prose, the metaphysical ironies, the vision and fidelity of the observation make *Adventures in a Bathyscope* an absolute delight, a unique event in Irish fiction." Mathews's next work of fiction was a novel, *Muesli at Midnight* (1990), a macabre and startling exercise in the postmodern picaresque, with two kinky lovers circling the roads of Ireland with the skeleton of an archbishop as their traveling companion. In *Lipstick on the Host* (1992), Mathews returned to the short story form and to his obsessive themes of death, love, and religion. In "Train Tracks," surely among the most painful fables of childhood, he returns to his earlier boy-hero Timmy to focus and universalize the horrors of the Holocaust. The long title story, which explores his central obsession with love, sex, and religion, has as its heroine Meggie, one of the most vibrant female characterizations in modern Irish fiction, as memorable as Joyce's Molly Bloom or the Nell of Edna O'Brien's* *Time and Tide*.

Mathew's work in the theater has been equally daring and experimental. *The Diamond Body,* which opened at Dublin's Project in 1984, provided a spectacular vehicle for the acting talents of Olwen Fouere in the androgynous central role. *The Antigone,* which also premiered at the Project in 1984 and subsequently toured, made the theater itself the focus of its theme. His more conventional *Exit/Entrance,* a grave and witty exploration of suicide and euthanasia, received wide critical acclaim on its premiere at Dublin's Peacock Theatre and later when it removed to London.

It is difficult to say in what mode or genre Mathews's mercurial talent excels or where it may take him next. Apart from his memorable characterizations of dotty women, eccentric priests, and precocious children, his skill with language—at turns zany, poetic, and sensuous—perhaps constitutes his most vivid resource. Both his narrative and his dialogue carry a remarkable infusion of the writer's personality. This individuality of voice, with its intense, varied range from the profound to the hilarious, is perhaps the truest measure of his genius and its promise.

AUGUSTINE MARTIN

WORKS: *Windfalls*. Dublin: Dolmen, 1977. (Poetry); *Minding Ruth*. Dublin: Dolmen, 1983. (Poetry); ed., *Immediate Man. Cuimhni ar Chearbhaill O Dalaigh*. Dublin: Dolmen, 1983; *Adventures in a Bathyscope*. London: Secker & Warburg, [1988]. (Short stories); *Muesli at Midnight*. London: Secker & Warburg, 1990. (Novel); *Lipstick on the Host*. London: Secker & Warburg, 1992. (Short stories).

MATURIN, CHARLES ROBERT (1780–1824), novelist and playwright. In many respects *Melmoth the Wanderer* is the classic Gothic novel, complete with complex plot and eerie effects. Its author, Charles Robert Maturin, was as strange as his title character. He was born in Dublin on September 25, 1780, graduated from Trinity College, and was ordained a minister, serving first in Loughrea and then in St. Peter's, Dublin. He was eccentric in dress and manner, and in the later part of his life he became a strange, reclusive figure.

Maturin's first novel, *Fatal Revenge* (1807), reminds one of novels by Radcliffe in its contorted revenge plot and its reliance on shocking events. Like other Gothic novels, it includes instances of unmotivated cruelty and a strong anti-Catholic bias. His next two novels, *The Wild Irish Boy* (1808) and *The Milesian Chief* (1812), are, as the titles indicate, efforts to treat native subjects, but the plots are strained, and the prose is lifeless. Maturin's principal drama, *Bertram*, was produced in 1816 and brought him some popular acclaim, particularly because Edmund Kean played the title role.

Maturin's masterpiece is undoubtedly *Melmoth the Wanderer* (1820). A long novel, it contains numerous digressions and a confusing narrative line, but at its center is a strong and explicit moral concern: no one would willingly sell his or her soul at any price. Despite the didactic tendency of the whole, the book abounds with instances of cruelty, masochism, even satanism, so strong that they threaten the moral theme. Later in the nineteenth century such diabolical elements found special appeal; English writers of the decadence praised the book, and Baudelaire once proposed to translate it. Like many Gothic novels, this work promotes republicanism, including a rejection of civil authority and an exposure of the decadence of the aristocracy. Likewise, the subject of religious belief is treated seriously. Calvinism is weighed against Catholicism, and the entire subject of faith is explored intelligently. The plot is complicated, but its very confusion may suggest the inner tumult of the human mind. There are multiple plots, all leading to the same conclusions: we cannot escape death, and the misery of life is unavoidable. Although some critics praise the novel for its investigations of psychology, the cases studied are surely instances of the most abnormal kind. As a whole, the novel succeeds through its evocation of extreme feelings and its unbridled indulgence in terror. There is no novel quite like it:

a highly colored, shocking account of a variety of perverse experiences. Although it relies on theatrical effects, such as coincidences and stock characters, it conveys its subject so boldly that the effect is irresistible. The author's attitude toward life is so negative that the overstatement and excesses of the whole seem justifiable.

Balzac wrote a sequel to *Melmoth* called *Melmoth Réconsilié,* and Oscar Wilde* adopted the name of Sebastian Melmoth after his release from prison.

Although Maturin wrote another novel, *The Albigenses* (1824), he never again achieved the startling effects of his one great novel. He died in Dublin after an accidental poisoning on October 30, 1824.

JAMES KILROY

WORKS: *Fatal Revenge; or, The Family of Montorio.* 3 vols. London: Longman, Hurst, Rees & Orme, 1807; *The Wild Irish Boy.* 3 vols. London: Longman, Hurst, Rees & Orme, 1808/New York: Arno, 1977; *The Milesian Chief.* 4 vols. London: Henry Colburn, 1812; *Bertram; or, The Castle of St. Aldobrand.* London: John Murray, 1816. (Play); *Manuel.* London: John Murray, 1817. (Play); *Woman; or, Pour et Contre.* 3 vols. Edinburgh: Constable/London: Longman, Hurst, Rees, 1818; *Fredolfo.* London: Constable, 1819. (Play); *Sermons.* Edinburgh: Constable/London: Longman, Hurst, 1819; *Melmoth the Wanderer.* 4 vols. Edinburgh: Constable/London: Hurst & Robinson, 1820/London: Bentley, 1892 (with a bibliography containing a full listing of Maturin's reviews & critical pieces)/Lincoln: University of Nebraska Press, 1961/Douglas Grant, ed. London: Oxford University Press, 1968; *The Albigenses.* 4 vols. London: Hurst, Robinson/Edinburgh: Constable, 1824/New York: Arno, 1974; *Five Sermons on the Errors of the Roman Catholic Church....* Dublin: Folds, 1824; "Leixlip Castle, an Irish Family Legend." In *The Literary Souvenir; or, Cabinet of Poetry and Romance.* London: Hurst & Robinson, 1825. (Story); Fannie Elizabeth Ratchford & William Henry McCarthy, eds. *The Correspondence of Sir Walter Scott and Charles Robert Maturin, with a Few Other Allied Letters.* Austin: University of Texas Press, 1937. REFERENCES: Fierobe, Claude. *Charles Robert Maturin (1780–1824), L'homme et l'oeuvre.* Paris: Editions Universitaires, 1974; Harris, Charles B. *Charles Robert Maturin: The Forgotten Imitator.* New York: Arno, 1980; Henderson, Peter Mills. *A Nut between Two Blades: The Novels of Charles Robert Maturin.* New York: Arno, 1980; Hinck, Henry William. *Three Studies on Charles Robert Maturin.* New York: Arno, 1980; Idman, Nilo. *Charles Robert Maturin: His Life and Works.* London: Constable, 1923; Kiely, Robert. *The Romantic Novel in England.* Cambridge: Harvard University Press, 1972, pp. 189–207; Kramer, Dale. *Charles Robert Maturin.* New York: Twayne, 1973; Lougy, Robert E. *Charles Robert Maturin.* Lewisburg, Pa.: Bucknell University Press, 1975; Monroe, Judson. *Tragedy in the Novels of the Reverend Charles Robert Maturin.* New York: Arno, 1972; Scholten, Willem. *Charles Robert Maturin: The Terror Novelist.* Amsterdam: H. J. Paris, 1933/New York: Garland, 1981; Scott, Shirley. *Myths and Consciousness in the Novels of Charles Maturin.* New York: Arno, 1973.

MAUNSEL AND COMPANY (later MAUNSEL AND ROBERTS) (1905–1925), publishing house. Maunsel and Company Limited was founded in 1905 by Joseph Maunsel Hone,* George Roberts, and Stephen Gwynn.* Roberts was interested in all aspects of book production and design, and from 1910 he printed over one hundred books for the firm—between 1910 and 1916 under the imprint of "Maunsel and Co. Ltd."; between 1917 and 1920 under the imprint of "George Roberts"; and between 1920 and 1925 under the imprint of "Maunsel and Roberts, Ltd." Several of the books which Roberts designed and printed, such as the 1910 de luxe edition of Synge's* Collected Works, are highly regarded even today as examples of good book design.

By the autumn of 1906, Maunsel and Company's publications were already being extensively distributed by several London booksellers. One of the firm's most successful and widely known publications, *The Shanachie,* a quarterly literary magazine edited by Hone, appeared in 1906. This magazine counted Yeats,* Shaw,* Synge, and Lady Gregory* among its contributors, although it only lasted for six issues. In its early years, Maunsel concentrated on publishing literary works, especially poetry and drama, although it also published some novels and volumes of essays. It gradually broadened its publishing ventures to include books in Irish and school editions.

In 1906 and 1907, Maunsel and Company published two books by Yeats in conjunction with A. H. Bullen—*Poems 1899–1905* and *Deirdre.* In 1908, Bullen arranged for special title pages to be printed for fifty sets of the Collected Edition of Yeats' Works, with Maunsel's name on the title pages. Synge, however, was Maunsel's most important author and the firm is remembered by many as Synge's publisher. Several different editions of Synge's works were published by Maunsel; his plays under the title *Dramatic Works* were also published for the first time by Maunsel in December 1914.

In the years after 1910, Maunsel and Company, having already established itself as the most important publishing firm in Ireland, went on to consolidate that position and to acquire a reputation outside Ireland. In the spring of 1912, it opened a London office, and henceforth the firm began to publish a number of books about non-Irish subjects and by non-Irish authors. Morever, around 1912 Maunsel and Company made arrangements for distributing its most important books in America through the Boston publishing house of John W. Luce.

In July 1915, Maunsel made an arrangement with George Allen and Unwin, Ltd., a London publishing house, whereby Maunsel undertook to stock George Allen and Unwin's publications on a sale or return basis. It is probable that some kind of reciprocal arrangement was made whereby George Allen and Unwin undertook to stock Maunsel's publications on a similar basis. For about this time Maunsel closed its own London office at Oakley House, Bloomsbury, and from then until the firm closed in 1925, Maunsel's London address was 40 Museum Street, which was and still is George Unwin's office. This would indicate that George Unwin was acting as Maunsel's London representative in some capacity. In fact, George Allen and Unwin benefited much more from the arrangement than did Maunsel. In time they managed to persuade several of Maunsel's established authors, such as St. John Ervine* and the trustees of the Synge estate, to transfer their publishing rights from Maunsel to themselves, whereas many of the George Allen and Unwin books stocked by Maunsel were, in the words of George Allen and Unwin's managing director, ''only fit for waste paper!''

In January 1916, Dr. Edward MacLysaght* joined Maunsel as a junior director. Shortly thereafter, the firm was destroyed in the Easter Week Rising. Maunsel was fortunate for once because it had done much to foster the climate which produced the events of Easter Week 1916. In fact, much material on the premises at the time was semi-treasonable, including the manuscript of the first volume of Pearse's* Collected Works, which had been entrusted by Pearse, shortly before Easter Week, to George Roberts for safekeeping and subsequent publication.

By 1920, Maunsel and Company was in financial difficulty. Roberts, never a good businessman, had lost all sense of proportion when the firm received its vastly overassessed compensation from the British government for the destruction of its Dublin premises. Roberts used Maunsel's sudden affluence to overproduce and publish books and pamphlets. From May 1916 to December 1919, in two and one-half years, the firm published 117 new books and pamphlets, of which Roberts printed 66 himself. Another 30 books and pamphlets were set up and reached page proof stage, before coming to grief at the hands of the press censor. Unfortunately, the financial difficulties of 1920 continued for Roberts until his firm's demise in 1925. Toward the end of its existence, Maunsel and Roberts published very few books, and those often by little known authors of small merit.

Maunsel and Company is perhaps best remembered today for George Roberts's timidity about publishing James Joyce's* Dubliners. Indeed, Roberts finally caused the printed sheets to be destroyed. The entire business was justifiably satirized by Joyce in his amusing and savage poem "Gas from a Burner."

RICHARD BURNHAM

MAXTON, HUGH (1947–   ), poet. Hugh Maxton is the pseudonym of William John McCormack, the critic, who was born in County Wicklow. He was educated at Trinity College, Dublin, and has taught at the New University of Ulster, Leeds, Antwerp, Clemson, and University College, Dublin.

In an appreciation at the end of his *The Engraved Passion* (1991), Gerald Dawe* asserts that Maxton's poetic experimentation has "transformed the terms by which we should read poetry in Ireland." It is true enough that Maxton essays new forms or new versions of old forms in a most fertile fashion. His success and his poetic influence, however, are more dubious. For instance, the first poem in *The Engraved Passion* is called "Sonnet at King's Cross," but it is an unrhymed poem written in syllabic verse, and its only real connection with the sonnet form is that it has fourteen lines. "Invitation to a Beheading" on the next page is composed of five prose paragraphs, and the three succeeding pieces are also mainly in prose. The next poem is titled "Ode." However, an ode is fairly described as "a lyric poem usually marked by intensity of feeling and style, varying length of line, and complexity of stanza form." There seems little exaltation of feeling and style in such lines as "or, high on dynamite, / they industrialize old dreads" or in conversational clauses like "you'd think" or "Yet truth is." The line lengths do vary, but not by much. The four stanzas each have five lines. Later poems attempt other devices, such as the effectively flip side notes in "South Carolina Night" or combinations of prose and poetry in "The Enlightened Page," in which the poetic stanzas, for some reason, are sometimes printed flush with the left margin and sometimes with the right.

Maxton's language is frequently oblique or densely clotted, and there are many lines like "Surplusage / of alienated subjectivity" or "to here aured by a chit of / profession" or "Whatever the case they wheeled / they pavilion worst want." Even the long essay in satiric doggerel, "The Last Irish Hooker," seems a perverse attempt to make a silk purse out of a perfectly respectable sow's ear, but such rhymes as "needed" and "knee-deep," or "corset" and "forced" simply mangle the necessities of doggerel. What one finds in Maxton are inventiveness, many striking lines, often admirable coinages, a deal of cleverness, and some wit. What is not yet there is one totally successful poem.

As W. J. McCormack, this author is a highly regarded critic. Possibly his most substantial book is *Sheridan Le Fanu and Victorian Ireland* (1980), which is excellent on Le Fanu's* Irish background as well as meticulous and ingenious on *Uncle Silas*. On Le Fanu's other novels, he is much more cursory, and the finely comic *All in the Dark* is completely dismissed. *Dissolute Characters: Irish Literary History through Balzac, Sheridan Le Fanu, Yeats and Bowen* (1993) and *From Burke to Beckett* (1994) are also well worth perusal, although, like the Le Fanu volume, they are rather heavy academic criticism.

WORKS: *Stones*. Dublin: Allen Figgis, 1970; *The Noise of the Field, 1970–1975*. Dublin: Dolmen, 1976; *Jubilee for Renegades: Poems 1976–1980*. Dublin: Dolmen, 1982; *At the Protestant Museum*. Dublin: Dolmen, 1986; *The Puzzle Tree Ascendant*. Dublin: Dedalus, 1988; *Between*. Dublin: Dedalus/Budapest: Corvince, 1988. (Translation of Agnes Nemes Nagy's Hungarian poems); *The Engraved Passion: New and Selected Poems 1970–1991*. [Dublin: Dedalus, 1991]. As W. J. McCormack: *Sheridan Le Fanu and Victorian Ireland*. London: Oxford University Press, 1980; *Ascendancy and Tradition: Anglo-Irish Literary History from Burke to Yeats*. London: Oxford University Press, 1985; *The Battle of the Books*. Gigginstown, Co. Westmeath: Lilliput, 1987; *Dissolute Characters: Irish Literary History through Balzac, Sheridan Le Fanu, Yeats and Bowen*. Manchester & New York: Manchester University Press, [1993]; *From Burke to Beckett: Ascendancy, Tradition and Betrayal in Literary History*. [Cork]: Cork University Press, [1994]. (A revised edition of *Ascendancy and Tradition*).

MAXWELL, CONSTANTIA [ELIZABETH] (1886–1962), historian. Maxwell was born in Dublin and educated at Trinity College, Dublin, and at Bedford College, London. She taught at Trinity College and in 1939 became professor of economic history, the first woman to be appointed to a chair in Trinity. In 1945, she became Lecky Professor of History. She was also a member of the Irish Academy of Letters. She retired in 1951 and died in Kent, England, on February 6, 1962.

PRINCIPAL WORKS: *A Short History of Ireland*. Dublin & Belfast: Educational Company of Ireland/London: T. Fisher Unwin, 1914; ed., *Irish History from Contemporary Sources. 1509–1610*. London: G. Allen & Unwin, 1932; *Dublin under the Georges: 1714–1830*. London: G. G. Harrap, 1936/rev. ed., London: Faber, 1956; *Country and Town under the Georges*. London: G. G. Harrap, 1940/rev. ed., Dundalk: W. Tempest, 1949; *A History of Trinity College, Dublin*. Dublin: University

Press, 1946; *The Stranger in Ireland. From the Reign of Elizabeth to the Great Famine.* London: Cape, [1954].

MAXWELL, WILLIAM HAMILTON (1792–1850), novelist and writer of sketches. Maxwell was born in 1792 at Newry, County Down, and was educated at Trinity College, Dublin. Apparently as "Hamilton Maxwell," he obtained a captaincy of foot in 1812 and served in the Peninsular campaigns and at Waterloo. He later took Holy Orders somewhat against his inclinations and in 1820 was presented a living at Ballagh in Connemara. His duties were light in that little-tenanted district, and he was able freely to indulge his taste for hunting and to write his popular fictions on sporting and military subjects. His more serious pieces have a quaint nineteenth-century stiffness, but his comic sketches are well done, particularly in the easy dialogue. He is credited with popularizing the rollicking Harry Lorrequer kind of hero, and, although he is not quite of Lever's* calibre, he is nonetheless a pleasant read. He died at Musselburgh, near Edinburgh, on December 29, 1850.

WORKS: *O'Hara; or 1798.* 2 vols. London: J. Andrews, 1825; *Stories of Waterloo, and Other Tales.* 3 vols. London: H. Colburn, 1829; *Wild Sports of the West.* 2 vols. London: R. Bentley, 1832; *The Field Book; or, Sports and Pastimes of the United Kingdom.* London: Effingham Wilson, 1833; *The Dark Lady of Doona.* London: Smith, Elder, 1834; *My Life.* 3 vols. London: R. Bentley, 1835; *The Bivouac; or, Stories of the Peninsular War.* 3 vols. London: R. Bentley, 1837; *The Victories of the British Armies.* 2 vols. London: R. Bentley, 1839; *Life of Field-Marshall His Grace the Duke of Wellington.* 3 vols. London: A. K. Baily, 1841; *Rambling Recollections of a Soldier of Fortune.* Dublin: W. Curry, 1842; *The Fortunes of Hector O'Halloran and His Man Mark Antony O'Toole.* London: R. Bentley, n.d.; *Wanderings in the Highlands and Islands.* 2 vols. London: A. H. Baily, 1844; *Hints to a Soldier on Service.* 2 vols. London: T. C. Newby, 1845; *History of the Irish Rebellion in 1798.* London: Baily Brothers, Cornhill, 1845; *Peninsular Sketches by Actors on the Scene.* 2 vols. London: H. Colburn, 1845; *Captain O'Sullivan; or, Adventures, Civil, Military, and Matrimonial of a Gentleman on Half-Pay.* 3 vols. London: H. Colburn, 1846; *Hill-Side and Border Sketches.* 2 vols. London: R. Bentley, 1847; *Brian O'Linn; or, Luck Is Everything.* 3 vols. London: R. Bentley, 1848; *The Irish Movements: Their Rise, Progress and Certain Termination.* London: Baily Brothers, 1848; *Erin Go Bragh; or, Irish Life Pictures,* with a biographical sketch by Dr. Maginn. 2 vols. London: R. Bentley, 1859.

MAYNE, RUTHERFORD (1878–1967), playwright and actor. Rutherford Mayne, born Samuel Waddell in Japan in 1878, was to Ulster theatre what Yeats,* Robinson,* and Lady Gregory* were to the Abbey,* a person of many parts. Between 1906 and 1923, he contributed nine plays to the Ulster Literary Theatre,* Belfast, including *The Turn of the Road* (1906), *The Drone* (1908), and *The Troth* (1909). An amateur actor, Mayne performed in Belfast, Dublin, and English cities, sometimes in his own plays. Withdrawing from his long association with the Literary Theatre in 1930, he wrote *Peter* (1930) and *Bridgehead* (1934) for the Abbey. His study of engineering and his employment with the Irish Land Commission before and after the Treaty are reflected in his writing. In 1960, at age eighty-two, he was appointed a trustee of the Lyric Players

Theatre* of Belfast. He died in Dublin on February 25, 1967. His sister was Helen Waddell,* the scholar.

Mayne's early plays examine the life of rural County Down. The Ulster work ethic enters seriously into *The Turn of the Road* and humorously into the kitchen comedy *The Drone*. In the former, Robbie John Granahan leaves home rather than yield to the stern demand of his parents that he throw away his violin and dedicate himself to farming. Easygoing Daniel Murray, the drone, forced by Northern mores to do something, spends his time puttering at a worthless mechanical invention. *The Troth* is a harrowing account of an agreement between a Catholic and a Protestant farmer, fellow sufferers at the hands of an unfeeling landlord, to murder their oppressor. If either is killed or apprehended, the other will care for both families. Implicit in *The Troth* is a call for unity and social justice.

Mayne shifts the locale to Galway for his one-act agrarian tragedy *Red Turf* (1911). Martin Burke, goaded by his termagant wife, kills a neighbor in a dispute over a tiny patch of land.

Peter, dedicated in part to Lennox Robinson,* may have been influenced by Robinson's dramatic experiments. The prologue and epilogue take place while Peter Grahame is awake. The rest is a dream in which he fails in his engineering studies and goes to work as an entertainer-gigolo in a hotel patronized by eccentrics and owned by boorish Sam Partridge. Mayne subtly disciplines the comedy by his understanding of the insecurity of a young man preparing for entry into the real, competitive world.

Distilled from Mayne's experience with the Land Commission, *Bridgehead* is a triumph of dramatic art over material better suited to a novel or a documentary movie. It is essentially a character study of plain, dogged Stephen Moore, who must plan for Ireland's future even as he is adjudicating the conflicting land and money claims of the old Ascendancy, hungry have-nots, and ruthless grabbers.

For many years, Mayne's cottage dramas were sentimental favorites, especially in Belfast. Today they suffer from association with an overworked and confined genre, although their muffled lyricism and a sympathy for the characters not always evident in the Cork realists* or St. John Ervine* gain for them a measure of distinctiveness. Modern audiences are more likely to respond to the skillful unconventionality of *Peter* or *Bridgehead*.

WILLIAM J. FEENEY

WORKS: *The Turn of the Road: A Play in Two Scenes and an Epilogue.* Dublin: Maunsel, 1907/ reprinted, Dublin: Duffy, 1950; *The Drone: A Play in Three Acts.* Dublin: Maunsel, 1909; *The Troth: A Play in One Act.* Dublin: Maunsel, 1909; ''The Freeholder.'' *The Irish Review* 1 (November 1911): 432–434. (Short story); ''A Prologue.'' *The Dublin Magazine* 2 (June 1925): 723–725. (A play in one act); *Bridgehead: A Play in Three Acts.* London: Constable, 1939. Also in *Plays of Changing Ireland.* Curtis Canfield, ed. New York: Macmillan, 1936; *Peter: A Comedy in Three Acts and a Prologue and Epilogue.* Dublin: Duffy, 1964. REFERENCES: Bell, Sam Hanna. *The Theatre in Ulster.* Dublin: Gill & Macmillan, 1972; Kane, Whitford. *Are We All Met?* London:

Elkins, Mathews & Marrot, 1931; McHenry, Margaret. *The Ulster Theatre in Ireland.* Philadelphia: University of Pennsylvania, 1931.

MAYNE, THOMAS EKENHEAD (1867–1899), short story writer.

WORK: *The Heart o' the Peat. Irish Fireside and Wayside Sketches.* London: Simpkin, Marshal, [1900].

MEADE, ELIZABETH THOMASINA (1854–1914), novelist. Of all of the highly productive nineteenth-century women novelists, Meade was undoubtedly the most amazingly prolific, turning out something like 280 books. She was born in Bandon, County Cork, the daughter of the Reverend R. T. Meade, and she wrote her first book when she was seventeen. In 1879, she married Toulmin Smith. She moved to London, worked at the British Museum, and studied East London life. From 1887 to 1898, she edited *Atalanta,* a magazine for girls that numbered H. Rider Haggard and Robert Louis Stevenson among its contributors. She wrote adventure novels, medical novels, novels about East London, and a few novels about Irish life, but mainly she wrote novels for girls and young women. She popularized the girl's school story, which still exists in such comics as *Bunty.* Her girls were not quite hoydens, but distinctly tomboyish; however, they all matured into quite proper young ladies. She died on October 26, 1914.

TYPICAL WORKS: *A World of Girls.* London: Cassell, 1886; *The Medicine Lady.* London: Cassell, 1901.

MEDBH, MAIGHREAD (1959–   ), poet. Medbh was born and educated in County Limerick and now lives in Belfast with her two children.

WORK: *The Making of a Pagan.* Belfast: Blackstaff, 1990.

MEEHAN, PAULA (1955–   ), poet. Meehan was born into a large family on Dublin's north side. She was expelled from the Holy Faith Convent in Finglas, where her family had moved, and had a rebellious adolescence. Nevertheless, she studied successfully on her own for her Intermediate Certificate and, after her Leaving Certificate, was involved in street theater in Dublin. She received a B.A. from Trinity College and later a master of fine arts from Eastern Washington University in America. She received bursaries from the Arts Council in 1987 and 1990 and has been writer in residence at Trinity. She has published four volumes of verse and has been warmly admired by Brendan Kennelly,* Eavan Boland,* Ferdia Mac Anna,* and Paul Durcan,* who exuberantly described her work as "cavewoman music." Although she is an effective reader of her verse, it is difficult to discover much rhythmical pattern in her earlier collections, other than the loose prose rhythm determined by content and syntax. She does once or twice use rhyme, but, except for the poem "Insomnia," not usually in any pattern. "Insomnia," however, is in four stanzas of six lines each with the rhyme scheme of ABCABC, but its evanescent rhythm arises as usual from syntactical breaks of various lengths determined by content. She is good at describing people, as in "Buying Winkles" or "The Pattern," and she is always clear and specific and sometimes even arresting in diction. *Pillow Talk* (1994), too, has its striking phrases but also contains a number of actual prose passages as well as some pieces distinguishable from prose only by their cutoff lines. Nevertheless, some poems, such as "Hearth" and "Full Moon," gain interesting effects from a mixture of rhyme and near-rhyme and from a mixture of iambs and anapests. A last line like "first of the steep drop, the six dark feet" gains much power from its heavy stresses. With its frequent and sometimes successful attempts to find a form for her statement, *Pillow Talk* must be seen as a considerable advance for Paula Meehan.

WORKS: *Return and No Blame*. Dublin: Beaver Row, 1984; *Reading the Sky*. Dublin: Beaver Row, 1986; *The Man Who Was Marked by Winter*. [Oldcastle, Co. Meath]: Gallery, [1991]; *Pillow Talk*. [Oldcastle, Co. Meath]: Gallery, [1994]. REFERENCE: Dorgan, Theo. "Interview with Paula Meehan." *Colby Quarterly* 28 (December 1992): 265–269.

MELDON, MAURICE (1926–1958), playwright. Meldon was born in Dublin in 1926, became a civil servant, and died most prematurely in a traffic accident on November 12, 1958. His best work seems reminiscent of an expressionistic Gerald MacNamara,* satiric and relying strongly on Irish history and myth. The best of his three published plays is *Aisling* (37 Theatre Club, 1953). An Aisling is a dream-vision, and the play is a free-wheeling social and political satire set during a highly stylized time of the Troubles but with much obvious contemporary relevance. Meldon's use of allusion to, as well as parody and pastiche of, various styles of Irish writing, make this a trenchant, eminently witty, and unfortunately neglected play. Indeed, Hugh Leonard* referred to Meldon as "probably our most neglected author."

WORKS: "Purple Path to the Poppy Field," in *New World Writing, Fifth Mentor Selection*. New York: New American Library, 1954; *Aisling*. Dublin: Progress House, 1959; *House under Green Shadows*. Dublin: Progress House, 1962.

MERCIER, PAUL (1958–   ), playwright. Born in Dublin, Mercier is best known as the founder and artistic director of the Passion Machine Theatre Company. He has directed not only the six plays—*Drowning* (1984), *Wasters* (1985), *Studs* (1986), *Spacers* (1986), *Home* (1988), and *Pilgrims* (1991)—that he has written for the company but also Roddy Doyle's two plays, *Brownbread* and *War*. Mercier's plays have won the Harvey's Theatre Award, the *Sunday Independent* Arts Award, the *Sunday Tribune* Arts Award, the Rooney Prize for Irish Literature, and the Edinburgh Fringe First Award. In addition, he has received numerous grants from An Chomhairle Ealaion, the Irish Arts Council. Mercier's theater company is known for its energetic ensemble work, imaginative designs, and innovative texts. Anne Gately, the company's designer and director and Mercier's wife, deserves much of the credit for Passion Machine's creative sets and staging. In 1990, the company courageously refused to participate in the Dublin Theatre Festival because of the festival's policy of not paying local theater companies for their contributions, although paying companies from outside Ireland. In March 1994, Passion Machine produced its own festival, staging ten original works. ''Songs of the Reaper,'' the festival's title, focused on plays examining various aspects of the environmental issue.

Currently, Mercier's only published work is *Home.* The play depicts a remarkably sensitive and naive young man who moves from Westmeath in the Irish Midlands to Dublin, possessing a newly won degree in hotel management and many American self-help and positive thinking manuals. Michael, the play's protagonist, becomes involved in a cycle of disappointments and disappointing relationships. He begins by attempting to ingratiate himself, in the style of his manuals, with other residents of the dilapidated house in which he takes a room. Most of the other characters ignore him or, when they do notice him, take advantage of his kindness and sensitivity. When he does achieve a degree of intimacy with each of his fellow tenants, they ultimately disappear or leave. His search for work fares no better. After many rejections, he finally gets a job as a waiter in a hotel restaurant. However, the position offers no potential for advancement, and, as the play closes, he is left in his bedsit staring blankly at the television, defeated and alone. The play stages rather well, with an imaginative set and skillful manipulation of lighting techniques and stage design.

Of Mercier's nonpublished work, *Drowning* is a rock opera focusing on the surreal dream world of Luke, a young man who fantasizes about a fame and fortune far removed from the mundane, ordinary lifestyle of his Dublin family. *Wasters,* substantially revised between its premiere in 1985 and its revival in 1990, shows a group of young adults who try to infuse their lives with some sense of meaning and joy on a reunion retreat. The play, although finally bitter and hopeless, maintains a consistently humorous tone. *Studs* explores the activities of a football team that consistently loses until approached by a mysterious individual who volunteers to be the coach and promises to bring them to victory. *Spacers,* about a theater company, is a quite funny play that puts up the actor as ''artiste'' and follows the adventures of the production company in the various stages of rehearsal. *Pilgrims* explores the lives of nine people on a beach vacation who reflect on the viability of reality as compared to their dreams, past and present.

The Passion Machine has published *Breaking Up* by Brendan Gleason, *Going Places* by Aidan Parkinson, *War* by Roddy Doyle, and Mercier's *Home.* It plans to bring out Mercier's other plays, but he tends to downplay the publications as companions to the performances. However, each volume is a handsome, professional production containing extensive notes on scene design and sometimes pictures of the more intricate sets.

BERNARD McKENNA

WORK: *Home.* Dublin: Passion Machine, 1992.

MERCIER PRESS, THE (1945–), publishing house. This Cork-based publishing house was founded by Captain John Feehan, late of the Irish army, and in its first fifty years proved to be a prolific purveyor of inexpensive paperbacks for the general market. Its products ranged from current affairs to folklore to joke books. Its best and most popular literary author has been John B. Keane,* with whom the press has had a long association, bringing out many of his plays, stories, essays, and novels.

MICHELBURNE (or MICHELBURNE or MICHELBORNE), JOHN
(1647/1648–1721), playwright. Michelburne was born on January 8, 1647 or 1648, at Horsted Keynes, Sussex. The governor of Londonderry, he defended the city during the siege of 1689, but his wife and seven children lost their lives. He commanded a corps at the Battle of the Boyne and served at the siege of Sligo, taking possession of the city on September 19, 1691. A prose tragicomedy, *Ireland Preserv'd: or the Siege of London-Derry* (1705), in two parts of five acts each, was based on his experiences. He died in Derry on October 1, 1721.

WORK: *Ireland Preserv'd: or the Siege of London-Derry.* 2 pts. London: [Privately printed], 1705.

MILLAR, FLORENCE NORAH (1920–), fiction writer and playwright.
Millar was born in County Dublin and studied music at the Royal Irish Academy of Music.

WORKS: *Fishing Is Dangerous.* London: John Gifford, 1946. (Novel); *Grant's Overture.* London: John Gifford, 1946. (Novel); *The Lone Kiwi.* Dublin: Dawson, 1948. (Boys' story).

MILLAR, RUDDICK (1907–1952), playwright and poet. Born in Belfast.

WORKS: *The Dream of Things: Poems.* Belfast: Quota, 1929; *Johnny Comes Marching Home: An Ulster Comedy in Three Acts.* Belfast: Quota, 1946; *The Land Girl: An Ulster Comedy in Three Acts.* Belfast: Quota, 1946; *'Tapsy Toosey': A Comedy in Three Acts.* Belfast: H. R. Carter, 1950; *One Minute from Sea: An Ulster Comedy in Two Acts.* Belfast: H. R. Carter, 1951; *Collected Poems.* Belfast: Quota, 1951; *Fair Exchange: A Comedy in One Act.* Belfast: H. R. Carter, 1951.

MILLER, AINE (fl. 1990s), poet. Miller won the Kavanagh Prize in 1992 for
an unpublished collection of poetry.

WORK: *Goldfish in a Baby Bath.* [Dublin]: Salmon, [1994].

MILLIGAN, ALICE (1866–1953), poet, novelist, and dramatist. Milligan was
born in Omagh, County Tyrone, on September 14, 1866. She studied history at King's College, London, and afterward traveled through Ireland, under the auspices of the Gaelic League, lecturing on Irish history. From 1896 to 1899, she and Ethna Carbery* edited the nationalist and literary magazine *The Shan Van Vocht* in Belfast. In 1898, she was involved in what was apparently the first production of a play in Irish, in the town of Letterkenny.

Milligan's early verse dealt with scenery and legend. *Hero Lays* (1908) and most of her subsequent poems were historical and nationalistic, ranging in subject from pre-Christian figures to the heroes of the 1916 Rising.

A Royal Democrat, a novel written in 1892, begins with an unusual plot line: a shipwrecked English prince lands in Ireland and becomes, incognito, an Irish patriot. But the story dwindles into stock love-and-honor romanticism.

Milligan's one-act play, *The Last Feast of the Fianna,* the beginning of a trilogy on the adventures of Oisin, was the earliest specimen of Celtic Twilight drama to emerge from the Irish theatre movement. The slender, graceful work was staged in 1900 by the Irish Literary Theatre. *The Daughter of Donagh,* a stilted historical melodrama set in Cromwellian Ireland, was published serially in *United Irishman* in 1909.

Most of Milligan's work, impressive in volume if not always in quality, was done before 1922. Saddened by the division of her native Ulster and the Free State, she wrote little after the Treaty. She died at Omagh on April 13, 1953.

WILLIAM J. FEENEY

WORKS: *A Royal Democrat.* London: Simpkin, Marshall/Dublin: Gill, 1892; *The Life of Theobald Wolfe Tone.* Belfast: J. W. Boyd, 1898; *The Last Feast of the Fianna.* London: David Nutt, 1900/reprinted, Chicago: De Paul University, 1967; *The Daughter of Donagh, a Cromwellian Drama in Four Acts,* in *United Irishman* (December 5, 12, 19, 26, 1903)/reprinted, Dublin: Lester, 1920; *Hero Lays.* Dublin: Maunsel, 1908; "Oisin in Tir nan Og," *Sinn Fein* (January 23, 1909). (One-act play); "Oisin and Padraic," *Sinn Fein* (February 20, 1909). (One-act play); with W. H. Milligan. *Sons of the Sea Kings.* Dublin: Gill, 1914; with Ethna Carbery & Seumas MacManus. *We Sang for Ireland.* Dublin: Gill, 1950; *Poems by Alice Milligan,* edited with an Introduction by Henry Mangan. Dublin: Gill, 1954. (Mangan's introduction is a good source of biographical information); *The Harper of the Only God: A Selection of Poetry by Alice Milligan.* Sheila Turner, ed. [Omagh, Co. Tyrone: Colourprint, [1993]. REFERENCES: Johnston, Sheila Turner. *Alice, A Life of Alice Milligan.* [Omagh, Co. Tyrone]: Colourpoint, [1994]; MacDonagh, Thomas. "The Best Living Irish Poet." *Irish Review* 4 (September–November 1914): 287–293; Racine, Carl. "Alice Milligan and Irish Nationalism." *Harvard Library Bulletin* 3 (Spring 1992): 47–52.

MILLIGAN, SPIKE (1918–   ), humorist and actor. Milligan was born Terence Alan Milligan, of Irish parents, on April 16, 1918, at Ahmadnager, India. He first attended school in a tent in the Hyderabad Sindh Desert. From there he went to various Roman Catholic schools in India and England and then on to Lewisham Polytechnic. After starting his career as a band musician, he became a founding member of the Goon Show, and his *The Goon Show Script Book* became a best-seller. He has frequently appeared on stage, on television, and in small parts in films, and he has been a prolific writer of children's books, poetry, and comic novels, such as the popular *Adolf Hitler—My Part in His Downfall.* His chief contribution to Irish literature is his first novel, *Puckoon* (1963), which "bursts at the seams with superb comic characters involved in unbelievably likely troubles on the Irish border" (*Observer*). Though the hero, Dan Milligan, is forced to live "of his pension and his wits, both hopelessly inadequate," he seems to accept those deficiencies. But what he doesn't like are his legs. As a newly created character, he has never seen his legs before. (They are really only "two thin white hairy affairs of the leg variety.") So, when he does see them, his first response is "Holy God! Wot are dese den? Eh?" He looks around for an answer, then repeats the question angrily, "Wot are dey?" The reader expects the question, which can only be rhetorical, to disappear into the Irish mist. But instead, an answer comes: "Legs." Without thinking who the speaker might be, Milligan instantly cries out, "Legs? LEGS? Whose legs?" And the conversation continues:

"Yours,"
"Mine? And who are you?"
"The Author."
"Author? Author? Did you write these legs?"
"Yes."
"Well, I don't like dem. I don't like 'em at all at all. I could ha' writted better legs meself. Did you write your legs?"
"No."
"Ahhh. *Sooo!* You got some one else to write your legs, some one who's a good leg writer and den you write dis pair of crappy old legs fer me, well mister, it's not good enough."
"I'll try and develop them with the plot."
"It's a dia-bo-likal liberty lettin' an untrained leg writer loose on an unsuspectin' human bean like me."

The comedy is not limited to the author's unconventional conversations with his main character. There is a wake scene that is more fully orchestrated than the most elaborate version of Finnegan's wake. Another scene is so packed with marvelous slapstick that it is reminiscent of the hot chestnut fiasco of *Tristram Shandy.* The final scene brings all elements crashing together and leaves Dan Milligan hanging from a tree with a rusty organ pipe lodged over his head, crying "You can't leave me like this!" to which the author replies, "Oh, can't I?" And the book ends.

Between the major scenes, the author continually provides the reader with descriptions that guarantee hearty and audible laughter. For example, "The pub door opened, and in bore a podgy police uniform carrying the body of Sgt. MacGillikudie," or "Peering intently from behind a wall was something that Milligan could only hope was a face. The fact that it was hanging from a hat gave credulity to his belief." Spike Milligan is such a gifted comedian that he even sees comic potential in a single moment: "There was a short pause, then a longer one, but so close were they together, you couldn't tell the difference."

His 1987 Irish novel, *The Looney,* serves up pretty much the same ingredients.

KATHLEEN DANAHER

IRISH WORKS: *Puckoon.* London: Anthony Blond, 1963; *The Looney: An Irish Fantasy.* London: Joseph, 1987.

MILLIKEN, RICHARD ALFRED (1767–1815), poet. Milliken was born at Castlemartyr, County Cork, on September 8, 1767. He was an attorney, painter, and musician, though not very successful in any of these areas. With his sister, who was a very minor novelist indeed, he founded *The Casket, or Hesperian Magazine* in 1797. *The Casket* lasted only a year, until the Rebellion of 1798, which Milliken helped to put down. He wrote poems and plays, but is remembered only for his poem "The Groves of Blarney," a pastiche of a popular ballad which has been widely reprinted. Geoffrey Taylor in *Irish Poets of the Nineteenth Century* notes that the meter is derived from the Gaelic and that "The parade of learning, the inconsequence, and the decorative use of words not fully understood, hark back to the proverbial grandiloquence of the hedge-schoolmasters." The popularity of the poem undoubtedly derives from its ear-arresting meter and its charmingly inane rhyming, but its imagery is sometimes scarcely less remarkable, and the description of "comely eels in the verdant mud" deserves some sort of immortality. The poem was attractive enough for Father Prout* to add a stanza. Milliken, although no patriot, was a convivial and lovable man who earned the sobriquet "Honest Dick." He died on December 16, 1815.

WORKS: *The River-Side, a Poem in Three Books.* Cork: J. Connor, 1807; *The Slave of Surinam; or, Innocent Victim of Cruelty.* Cork: Mathews, 1810. (Novel); *Poetical Fragments of the Late Richard Alfred Milliken, with an Authentic Memoir of His Life.* London: Longman, 1823.

MILLS, JOHN FITZMAURICE (1917–   ), novelist and art critic. Mills wrote art criticism for the *Irish Times* for ten years and has done BBC documentaries on collecting and on fakes and forgeries. He lives now in Wales. His novel *Top Knocker* (1990) is a soundly plotted, excellently characterized, and extremely knowledgeable entertainment about chicaneries in the art and antiques trade. Among its many pleasures are several mouth-watering descriptions of food.

WORK: *Top Knocker.* [Dublin]: Wolfhound, [1990].

MILNE, EWART (CHARLES) (1903–1987), poet.

Born Dublin 1903. Student teacher, seaman; works-clerk; journalist; estate manager. Poet and writer of letters and essays. Published 14 volumes of poetry, four in Dublin, the rest in England, the last being *Drift of Pinions* and *Cantata Under Orion.* Contributor to Irish and British national press, and to leading Irish, British, and American literary magazines over forty years. Mem. Society of Authors and British Interplanetary Society. Recreations: reading science fiction and watching television.

This is Milne's summary of himself, characteristically wry about the self and studied about the poetry. Born in Dublin of an Anglo-Irish family, he grew into leftist politics as the political split in his family and his nation became more pronounced. Perhaps the early rejection of his father fostered his marriage to an Irish girl, as it did his years of wandering rather than accept his father's pro-British politics.

After the death of their first-born, the Milnes returned to Dublin, though Ewart intended to go to sea. He published poems in *Comment* and wrote letters to the newspapers about the problems in Spain. At the same time, his developing antipathy to "Gaelicism" kept him from supporting de Valera. He drifted back to London to work for the Spanish Medical Aid; in 1937, he followed his friend Charles Donnelly* to Madrid, only to find Donnelly had been killed.

Milne's pro-Republican affiliation cooled, and he returned to London in 1941 to work for Edward Sheehy's *Ireland Today* before again moving to Ireland. By the time he moved to England, he had published three volumes of poetry. Curiously, even these early volumes have a post-Yeatsian ring and an Anglo-Irish hauteur, though no single style then or later characterizes Milne's poetry. During the war, he worked on a farm, continued his publishing, and met Thelma Dobson, whom he married in 1948. During the war years and through the 1950s, he was very pro-Irish and published *Galion,* a mock epic at Liam Miller's* Dolmen Press* in 1953. By 1962, the Milnes were living in Dublin, and he published his nationalistic *A Garland for the Green* (1962), which found no favor with the new circle of poets and critics who formed literary Dublin.

Milne's wife died in 1964. In going through her papers, he discovered her involvement with (or victimization by, as Milne sees it) a close friend of theirs. He then began a period of withdrawal and self-examination that resulted in *Time Stopped* (1967), a book-length study in poetry and prose in which he presented his love and accepted his Anglo-Irish background. That he would continue to write after such a strong statement seemed unlikely, but he has since published two volumes of poetry.

The writing of poetry has been the major force in Milne's life. Always poetry led him to consider his relationship with Ireland, which has changed with the circumstances of his life. Perhaps that is why he has restlessly changed styles.

Milne was born on May 25, 1903, was educated at Christ Church Cathedral Grammar School in Dublin, served as a merchant seaman from 1920 to 1935, and from 1946 to 1962 was a farmer in Suffolk. He died in Bedford, England, on January 14, 1987.

FRANK KERSNOWSKI

WORKS: *Forty North Fifty West.* Dublin: Gayfield, 1938; *Letter from Ireland: Verses.* Dublin: Gayfield, 1940; *Listen Mangan: Poems.* Dublin: Sign of the Three Candles, 1941; *Jubilo: Poems.* London: Mullter, 1944; *Boding Day.* London: Muller, 1947; *Elegy for a Lost Submarine.* Burnham-on-Crouch, Essex: Plow Poems, 1951; *Diamond Cut Diamon: Selected Poems.* London: Bodley Head, 1953; *Galion: A Poem.* Dublin: Dolmen, 1953; *Life Arboreal: Poems.* Tunbridge Wells: Pound, 1953; *Once More to Tourney: A Book of Ballads and Light Verse, Serious, Gay, and Grisly.* Introduction by J. M. Cohen. London: Linden, 1958; *A Garland for the Green: Poems.* London: Hutchinson, 1962; *Time Stopped: A Poem-Sequence with Prose Intermissions.* London: Plow Poems, 1967; *Cantata under Orion.* Isle of Skye: Aquila Poetry, 1976; *Drift of Pinions.* Isle of Skye: Aquila & Wayzgoose, 1976; *Deus Est Qui Regit Omnia.* Mornington, Co. Meath: St. Bueno's, 1980; *Spring Offering.* Portree, Isle of Skye: Aquila, 1981; *The Folded Leaf: Poems 1970–1980.* Portree, Isle of Skye: Aquila, 1983; *Drums without End.* Portree, Isle of Skye, 1985. (Stories). REFERENCES: Ford, Hugh D. *A Poet's War: British Poets in the Spanish Civil War.* Philadelphia: University of Pennsylvania Press, 1965; Green, J.C.R., ed. *Ewart Milne: For His 80th Birthday: A Festschrift.*

Portree, Isle of Skye: Aquila, [ca. 1983]; Kersnowski, Frank. *The Outsiders.* Fort Worth: Texas Christian University Press, 1975.

MITCHEL, JOHN (1815–1875), journalist and historian. Mitchel, the Irish patriot, was born on November 3, 1815, at Camnish, near Dungiven, County Londonderry, the third son of a Presbyterian minister. He matriculated at Trinity College, Dublin, in 1830, and according to one biographer took his degree in 1834, although his name does not appear in the Catalogue of Graduates. He was intended by his father for the ministry but began life as a bank clerk in Londonderry before entering a solicitor's office at Newry. When he was nineteen, he eloped with Jane Verner, a school girl of sixteen, but they were caught at Chester, and Mitchel was taken back to Ireland in custody. A year later they eloped again, and this time got married.

In 1842, Mitchel met Thomas Davis* who "filled his soul with the passion of a great ambition and a lofty purpose." In 1843, he qualified as a lawyer and joined the Repeal Association, and in 1845, he began writing for *The Nation.** He soon emerged as one of the most effective Irish journalists of the century, but, as *The Nation* was not radical enough for Mitchel in its political stand, he found *The United Irishman* in 1848. In this paper, he advocated armed insurrection to achieve an Irish republic which would secure "the land for the people." In May 1848, he was arrested, convicted of treason by a packed jury, and sentenced to fourteen years' transportation. He was first shipped to Bermuda where he spent ten awful, asthmatic months and nearly died in close confinement. From there he sailed to South Africa, but an uprising of the colonists prevented the convicts from landing, so the ship sailed on to Tasmania. There Mitchel sent for his wife and children and lived happily as a farmer until 1853 when he escaped to America. He worked as a journalist in America for twenty years and gained notoriety during the Civil War for his defense of slavery. His bad eyesight prevented him from fighting, but he accepted the editorship of *The Enquirer,* a semi-official organ of President Jefferson Davis. Two of his sons were killed fighting for the Confederate side, and the third lost an arm. After the war, Mitchel went to New York where he became editor of *The Daily News.* He was arrested by the military authorities and imprisoned for nearly five months because of his articles defending the South. He retained an interest in Irish politics of the more extreme variety, and in February 1875 he was elected to a Tipperary seat after he indicated he would not go to Westminster. He was unseated as a convicted felon but returned again in March. He traveled to Ireland for the election but died at Newry within a few days of his success on March 20, 1875.

Mitchel was a prolific journalist and historian, but today is remembered mainly for the *Jail Journal,* a record of his time in captivity. Although a sacred cow of Irish literature, this book makes fairly dull reading. Occasionally, however, a striking phrase does break through the Carlylean prose: "Dublin city, with its bay and pleasant villas—city of bellowing slaves, villas of genteel dastards—lies now behind us." The journal's chief interest is political rather than literary. Mitchel's hatred of England spilled out in bloodletting prose which influenced Pearse,* and his ideas for a complete restructure of society filtered through to Connolly.*

Nevertheless, the patriot's concern for social justice did not quite extend to criminals or to blacks:

Not that I think it wrong to flog convicted felons for preservation of discipline . . . but I had rather as a matter of personal taste be out of hearing.

Or:

What to do with all our robbers, burglars and forgers? Why hang them, hang them.

Or:

Jails ought to be places of discomfort; the sanitary condition of miscreants ought not to be cared for more than the health of honest industrious people, and for "ventilation" I would ventilate the rascals in front of the country jails at the end of a rope.

Or, as he remarked about Tasmania:

Here a freeman is a king; and the convict class is regarded just as the negroes must be in South Carolina; which indeed is perfectly right.

In domestic life he is said to have been the gentlest of men, but one shudders to think of the social consequences had this champion of liberty ever come to power in Ireland.

MARY ROSE CALLAGHAN

PRINCIPAL WORKS: *The Life and Times of Aodh O'Neill, Prince of Ulster.* Dublin: Duffy, 1846; *Jail Journal; or, Five Years in British Prisons.* [New York: *The Citizen,* 1854]/New York: P. M. Haverty, 1868/Dublin: Gill, 1913/Thomas Flanagan, ed., Dublin: University Press of Ireland, 1982; *The Last Conquest of Ireland (Perhaps).* Dublin: *The Irishman* Office, 1861; *The History of Ireland from the Treaty of Limerick to the Present Time.* Glasgow: Cameron & Ferguson/London: C. Griffin/Dublin: Duffy, 1869; *An Ulsterman for Ireland, Being Letters to the Protestant Farmers, Labourers and Artisans of the North of Ireland.* Dublin: Candle, 1917; *An Apology for the British Government in Ireland.* Dublin: M. H. Gill, 1920. REFERENCES: Dillon, W. *Life of John Mitchel.* 2 vols. London: Kegan Paul, Trench, 1888; MacCall, S. *Irish Mitchel: A Biography.* London: T. Nelson, 1938; O'Hegarty, P. S. *John Mitchel: An Appreciation, with Some Account of Young Ireland.* Dublin & London: Maunsel, 1917.

MITCHELL, JULIE (fl. 1980s), novelist. Mitchell was born in Cheshire, England but moved with her family to Northern Ireland when she was seven. She was educated at Bristol University.

WORK: *Sunday Afternoon.* London: Penguin, 1988.

MITCHELL, SUSAN [LANGSTAFF] (1866–1926), poet and editor. Mitchell was born at Carrick-on-Shannon on December 5, 1866. She stayed with relatives in Ireland and with the Yeats* family in London, before becoming, in 1901, assistant editor for George William Russell (AE)* on *The Irish Homestead* and its successor, *The Irish Statesman.** Unmarried, she lived quietly with a sister. Despite frail health, she was noted for her wit and charm, as J. B. Yeats,* AE, and Seumas O'Sullivan* testify. Nostalgia, sentiment, and mystical feeling pervade *The Living Chalice* (1908). Her religious poetry, muted in tone, is slightly reminiscent of Emily Dickinson. Her humor appears in her contributions to the parody on the *Playboy* riots, *The Abbey Row, Not Edited by W. B. Yeats* (1907), and to *Secret Springs of Dublin Song* (1918). Her satires were appropriately entitled *Aids to the Immortality of Certain Persons in Dublin: Charitably Administered* (1908). The cover of the first edition of *Aids* has a delightful caricature of Dublin celebrities. Though dated by topicality, these poems evoke the issues of the time, viewed with gaiety. George Moore's* pretensions were also a favorite target, both in verse and in her mocking study *George Moore* (1916). She died in Dublin on March 4, 1926.

RICHARD M. KAIN

WORKS: *Aids to the Immortality of Certain Persons in Ireland: Charitably Administered.* Dublin: New Nation, 1908/enlarged, Dublin: Maunsel, 1913; *The Living Chalice.* Dublin: Maunsel, 1908/ enlarged, 1913; *Frankincense and Myrrh.* Dublin: Cuala, 1912; *George Moore.* Dublin: Maunsel, 1916; *Secret Springs of Dublin Song.* Dublin: Talbot, 1918. Contributed to *The Abbey Row, Not Edited by W. B. Yeats.* Dublin: Maunsel, 1907.   REFERENCE: Kain, Richard M. *Susan L. Mitchell.* Lewisburg, Pa.: Bucknell University Press, 1972.

MOFFET (or MOFFETT), WILLIAM (fl. 1716). Moffett, a schoolmaster, is usually credited with the extremely popular long poem *Hesperi-neso-graphia: Or, a Description of the Western Isle* (1716), which eventually came to be known as *The Irish Hudibras* and was frequently reprinted even into the nineteenth century. D. J. O'Donoghue* regarded it as virulent satire, but it is closer to jaunty doggerel. O'Donoghue also asserted that the true author was Walter Jones.*

WORK: *Hesperi-neso-graphia: Or, a Description of the Western Isle. In Eight Cantos.* London: J. Baker, 1716/Dublin, 1724. Also published as *The History of Ireland in Verse* and *The Irish Hudibras.*

MOLLOY, CHARLES (ca. 1690–1767), playwright and journalist. Molloy was born probably at Birr, King's County (now County Offaly). He was educated in Dublin and later was a student at Gray's Inn. He had several plays performed at Lincoln's Inn Fields: *The Perplex'd Couple; or, Mistake upon Mistake* (1715), after Molière's *Cocu Imaginaire; The Coquet; or, the English Chevalier* (1718), and *The Half-Pay Officers* (1720), partly after Davenant's *Love and Honour.* The last piece was his most successful, running for seven nights, but the reason was partly that an eighty-five-year-old actress from the time of Charles II, who had not appeared on the stage for fifty years, both acted well in it and danced a jig. Molloy edited *Fog's Weekly Journal* beginning in October 1728 and then edited and mainly wrote, although with some contributions from Lord Chesterfield, Lord Lyttleton, and others, *Common Sense, or the Englishman's Journal.* His own contributions have been described as "remarkable for their bright style, knowledge of affairs, and closeness of reasoning." He died in London on July 16, 1767.

WORK: *Common Sense, or the Englishman's Journal*. 2 vols. London, 1738. (Reprinted from the periodical).

MOLLOY, FRANCES (1947–1991), novelist and short story writer. Molloy was born in County Derry, left school at fifteen to work in a local factory, and was for a time a nun. She lived in Lancashire for eighteen years and published stories in English magazines. Her *No Mate for the Magpie* (1985) is a comic-tragic novel written in Derry dialect. It follows the life of Ann Elizabeth McGlone, a stoic girl who has her own fanciful way of dealing with the ups and downs of Catholic living in the 1950s and 1960s. Eventually, she works in a factory, goes on "the sick," becomes an embryo nun, spends a while in "the mental," becomes a parish priest's housekeeper, a nurses' assistant, a shroud maker in a Dublin undertaker's, and a business lady with radical tendencies. While accomplishing all that and more, she develops an illuminating skill at irony. The astonishment of Frances Molloy's work lies not only in the art of storytelling but also in the meticulous use of the written word as spoken. It is possible to say that this has hardly been achieved with such accuracy in Ireland before. When Ann goes to school, she enters not just the classroom but a place of moral standards previously unnoticed:

The first thing the teacher taught me was mortal sins—sins of the flesh, stealing, lyin', cursin', cheatin' an' breakin' all the Commandments. She taught me the Commandments, too, but somehow I managed to grasp the sins better. . . . A was lucky, a suppose, that a went te school at all . . . just think a could have been sittin' there at home in blissful ignorance, sinnin' away to me heart's content an' damnin' me soul te hell.

With that stark observation, the author invites us to collude with her in her quirky way of viewing the world, a view that could have been fashioned behind a purdah.

Frances Molloy is so witty that it can nearly be forgotten how serious are the matters that have just made you laugh. She tackles the issues of bigotry, class prejudice, and misogyny in such a subversive way that she has to be read and reread for the full import of her work to be understood.

In 1988, she returned to Ireland and was working on a second novel. In March 1991, she died, leaving behind two as yet unpublished volumes, a collection of stories called *Women Are the Scourge of the Earth* and a novel called *Only Talk to the Sea.*

EVELYN CONLON

WORKS: *No Mate for the Magpie*. London: Virago/New York: Persea Books, 1985; "An Irish Fairy Tale." In *The Female Line: Northern Irish Women Writers*. Ruth Hooley, ed. Belfast: Northern Ireland Women's Rights Movement, 1985. (Story); "Women Are the Scourge of the Earth." In *Wildish Things*. Ailbhe Smythe, ed. [Dublin]: Attic, [1989]. (Story).

MOLLOY, M[ICHAEL] J[OSEPH] (1917–1994), playwright. Molloy was born on March 3, 1917, in Milltown, County Galway. He trained for the priesthood until illness forced him to discontinue his studies, and for most of his adult life he worked a small farm outside Milltown. Molloy's plays, whether historical or modern, are steeped in the tradition, customs, folklore, and language of the west of Ireland. The modern plays show characters fighting to stave off the death of a culture, and the historical plays show characters fighting to stave off the literal and metaphorical deaths that the culture caused. The rich texture of the best Molloy plays has sometimes occasioned comparisons to J. M. Synge,* but, because Molloy's plays of country people have a more mournful note than Synge's—especially such plays as *Old Road* or *The Wood of the Whispering* or *The King of Friday's Men*—there may be a tendency to forget that he was as capable as Synge of grotesque comedy and sudden violence. His best characters are often mournful eccentrics, droll, fatalistic, and ultimately just a bit too resilient to be quite totally defeated. The thick Western texture of his plays and his overelaborate plots have probably militated against any great popularity of the plays outside of Ireland, but, with Synge and Fitzmaurice,* he must be accounted the most individual of modern Irish dramatists.

His first play, *The Old Road* (Abbey, 1943), is about emigration and the depopulation of the West, and shows many of Molloy's continuing characteristics: barmy character parts, young lovers, a complicated plot, a fight scene, and rich dialogue. *The Visiting House* (Abbey, 1946) combines these qualities with the elaborate playmaking of an old-time Visiting House. In the Merryman or Master of the Visiting House and in his two ancient cronies, the Man of Learning and the Man of Education, Molloy has created a rare trio of eccentrics to stand for the values of the traditional past. The plot of the play is one of the most snarled of any Irish play, but some of the long speeches contain passages of great eloquence.

Molloy's masterpiece, *The King of Friday's Men* (Abbey, 1948), is an historical play set in the late eighteenth century; it contains both his faults and his virtues in abundance. Indeed, a rich abundance is the best way to describe this play that in its many well-drawn and memorable characters, in its tangled plot, in its grotesquerie and violence, and, especially, in its noble melancholy, must rank among the most densely textured, difficult to produce, and potentially rewarding pieces of folk drama since García Lorca.

The Wood of the Whispering (Abbey, 1953) has none of the violence of *The King of Friday's Men,* but its genial comedy and quaint ruefulness give it a pervasive and attractive charm. It is set in modern times and is a reprise of the themes of *Old Road,* romantic love and emigration. It must be taken at its own pace to work, and its pace is meandering and leisurely. A venue, such as it received in its English production at Joan Littlewood's Stratford East, is utterly wrong. This is one of the most appealing of Molloy's plays, but it is in a muted minor key and all the richer for it.

Although *The Paddy Pedlar* (Abbey, 1953) is a one-act play, it must stand with Molloy's best work. Like much of his work, it is based on a story that he has heard, and tells of how a ne'er-do-well attempts to rob a pedlar of the contents of his sack, only to discover therein the corpse of the pedlar's mother. The play is a unique blend of the macabre and, amazingly, the sweet. It must rank with the best half-dozen one-act plays of the Irish drama.

Molloy's later work, such as *The Will and the Way* (1955), *Daughter from Over the Water* (1962), the arrestingly bizarre *Petticoat Loose* (Abbey, 1979), and several professionally unproduced pieces, may have more of Molloy's characteristic faults than his qualities, but they are so individual that they could have been written by no other Irish dramatist. After fifty years, the Irish theatrical movement finally produced an authentic folk dramatist. In fact, a late and lengthy book on Irish folklore he withdrew from publication in order to revise. He was always a meticulous reviser and an indefatigable worker, and there are a number of interesting unproduced Molloy plays. Indeed, but a week before his death he wrote that the Abbey had rejected his latest play, saying it "contained enough plot and dramatic action for two plays." Considering the plotless wonders that the Abbey had lately been producing, in which six people sit around and bicker about their past for two hours, the theater might well have taken Molloy's and contributed to their new authors some of his rich surplus of plot.

He was a member of Aosdána,* and he died on May 27, 1994.

WORKS: *The King of Friday's Men.* Dublin: James Duffy, 1953; *The Paddy Pedlar.* Dublin: James Duffy, 1954; *The Will and the Way.* Dublin: P. J. Bourke, n.d.; *Old Road.* Dublin: Progress House, 1961; *The Wood of the Whispering.* Dublin: Progress House, 1961; *Daughter from Over the Water.* Dublin: Progress House, 1963; *The Bitter Pill.* In *Prizewinning Plays of 1964.* Dublin: Progress House, 1965; *The Visiting House.* In *Seven Irish Plays, 1946–1964.* Robert Hogan, ed. Minneapolis: University of Minnesota Press, 1967; *Three Plays by M. J. Molloy.* Newark, Del.: Proscenium, 1975. (Contains *The King of Friday's Men, The Paddy Pedlar,* and *The Wood of the Whispering*); "The Making of Folk Plays." In *Literature and Folk Culture.* Alison Feder & Bernice Schrank, eds. St. John's, Newfoundland: Memorial University of Newfoundland, 1977, pp. 58–80; *Petticoat Loose.* Newark, Del.: Proscenium/Dublin: Society of Irish Playwrights, 1980. REFERENCES: Hogan, Robert. *After the Irish Renaissance.* Minneapolis: University of Minnesota Press, 1967/London: Macmillan, 1968; Kennedy, Maeve. "Maeve Kennedy Talked to M. J. Molloy." *Irish Times* (May 19, 1979); Maxwell, D.E.S. *A Critical History of Irish Drama 1891–1980.* Cambridge: Cambridge University Press, 1984.

MONAHAN, NOEL (fl. 1990s), poet. Monahan was born in Granard, County Longford, graduated from Maynooth, and lives in County Cavan.

WORK: *Opposite Walls.* [Galway: Salmon, 1992]: *Snowfire.* [Galway]: Salmon, [1995].

MONCK, MARY (ca. 1678–1715), poet. Monck was the second daughter of Robert, Viscount Molesworth, of Edlinton, Yorkshire, and of Brackenstown, County Dublin. Her mother was Laetitia, the daughter of Richard, Lord Coote of Coloony. Viscount Molesworth was an author, politician, and diplomat who served as ambassador to the Court of Denmark until 1694, when he offended the court and had to depart.

Mary was born about 1678 in County Dublin. As a child, she pursued an education without the approval of her family, and she excelled at languages, particularly Latin, Spanish, and Italian. She became the wife of George Monck (or Monk) of Stephen's Green, Dublin, about 1700. George Monck represented Philipstown in the 1703–1713 Irish Parliament. The couple had two daughters and one son but remained somewhat financially dependent upon Viscount Molesworth after their marriage. George Monck appears to have suffered a mental breakdown about 1712, and Mary was reported to be living separately from him by 1714. She was thirty-eight years old when she died in 1715 at Bath, following a lengthy illness.

None of Monck's literary efforts were published during her lifetime, but she left a sizable collection of manuscripts containing original poetry and translations. Her father edited and wrote the preface for her collection *Marinda: Poems and Translations* (1716). Lord Molesworth said that his daughter's poems were found primarily "in her Scrittore after her Death, written in her own hand, little expecting and as little desiring the Publick should have any opportunity either of applauding or condemning them" (Preface). As she was not writing for publication, her verses are often personal and reflective, although she appears to have enjoyed the occasional foray into satire.

ANNE COLMAN

WORK: *Marinda: Poems and Translations on Several Occasions.* London: Tonson, 1716. REFERENCES: Blackburne, E. Owens. *Illustrious Irishwomen.* Vol. 2. London: Tinsley, 1877; Lonsdale, Roger. *Eighteenth-Century Women Poets.* Oxford: Oxford University Press, 1989.

MONTAGUE, JOHN (1929–   ), poet, short story writer, and essayist. Montague was born in Brooklyn, New York, on February 28, 1929. His childhood was spent in New York and County Tyrone. He was educated at University College, Dublin, lived in Paris, taught at University College, Cork, and is now a distinguished professor at the State University of New York at Albany.

Montague began as a Southern writer, a young man in Dublin's difficult literary circles of the 1950s. He made his debut in its magazines. His early poems were published in 1958 by the Dolmen Press*; MacGibbon and Kee published a second, more ambitious collection in 1961. Here the poet is beginning to take a long look at his Northern background. Village and town land experiences are already being assessed and assorted into folk imagery that wears a Jungian aspect. Montague has always been serious about his work; he has none of the casualness of Patrick Kavanagh* or the devil-may-care subversion of Austin Clarke.* *Tides* (1970), a mixture of lapidary styles and short-lined poetry exploring a moonscape of love, serves as an overture to Montague's gradual return to Ulster themes. In *The Rough Field* (1972), he planned a book that would take in the Northern conflict in its parameters of consciousness. The work, elaborate in its sectioning and epic in its attempted range, includes poems written during a ten-year period. Montague retells the history of the truncated province, edging back to its roots in the plantation. The least successful section is "Hymn to the New Omagh Road," where a confused medley of comment, quotation, and halfhearted real lines obscures every facet of the poem except its intent. The use of marginalia gives an artificial ambience to parts of the book. What remains brilliant about it is the series of family vignettes and anecdotes; memories of a divided and, in many ways, betrayed family haunt Montague. His father and uncle appear as Virgilian characters in Hades: his exorcisms of them evoke the wonder of art.

The steel of the political temper in Montague shines in an ideological poem like "Penal Rock/Altamuskin." At least to Irish readers, Montague's tribalism must be fascinating. In *A Slow Dance* (1975), Montague has his eyes wide open, especially in the pieces dealing with the North. "Falls Funeral" reports with deadly accuracy the burial of a murdered Catholic child, while "Northern Express" hits at the center of the terrorism that involves the most average citizen. In his later poems Montague grips the fear of Ulster. There are no panaceas, no ways to accept or sublimate what is occurring. In this atmosphere, Montague represses what had been a feature of his early work, especially in his love poems: coy gestures. He begins to make good on Hugh MacDiarmaid's encouragement in *Agenda* (Spring–Summer 1973): "How far we are here from anything savouring of the Celtic Twilight!"

Montague's career in the 1980s and 1990s has been an ambiguous one. He is regarded as a major writer but remains neglected (though not by himself). The longer *Selected Poems* (1982) is unwieldy; the streamlined *New Selected Poems* (1989) offers Montague's work stripped to its core. It is a Montague primer, notable for the inclusion of a fine prose poem, "Luggala." In *The Dead Kingdom,* the poet pours out family history on his readers; his past is illuminated, if repeated. One gets the feeling that the histories are plotted almost in a prose sense.

Prose is a mark of the late Montague—from a concise novella, *The Lost Notebook* (1987), to a book of essays, *The Figure in the Cave* (1989). In the latter, the pieces on Joyce* and MacNeice* are the best; the accusing ghost of Patrick Kavanagh is not totally confronted. The more recent *Born in Brooklyn* (1991), subtitled "John Montague's America," is a loose anthology (thirty-seven poems, two essays, and three short stories) of the author's personal and cultural connection to the United States. The touch is not always light: the master's domination is sometimes dissipated by the considerable charm. But the sense of pilgrimage remains real. Montague can be summed up as a prolific writer in whom the reader can sometimes recognize a great voice—at whose birth W. B. Yeats* and William Carlos Williams acted as midwives.

JAMES LIDDY

WORKS: *Forms of Exile.* Dublin: Dolmen, 1958; *Poisoned Lands and Other Poems.* London: MacGibbon & Kee, 1961/Chester Springs, Pa.: Dufour, 1963/Dublin: Dolmen/London: Oxford University Press, 1977; *Death of a Chieftain.* London: MacGibbon & Kee, 1964/Chester Springs, Pa.:

Dufour, 1967/Swords, Co. Dublin: Poolbeg, 1978. (Short stories); *Home Again*. Belfast: Festival, 1966; *Patriotic Suite*. Dublin: Dolmen, 1966; *A Chosen Light*. London: MacGibbon & Kee, 1967/ Chicago: Swallow, 1969; *Tides*. Dublin: Dolmen, 1970/Chicago: Swallow, 1971; *The Wild Dog Rose*. London: MacGibbon & Kee, 1970; *The Rough Field*. Dublin: Dolmen/Winston-Salem, N.C.: Wake Forest University Press, 1972/Belfast: Blackstaff, 1984; ed., *The Faber Book of Irish Verse*. London: Faber, 1974/ as *The Book of Irish Verse*. New York: Macmillan, 1976/rev. ed., 1988; *A Slow Dance*. Dublin: Dolmen/London: Oxford University Press/Winston-Salem, N.C.: Wake Forest University Press, 1975; *The Great Cloak*. Dublin: Dolmen/London: Oxford University Press/Winston-Salem, N.C.: Wake Forest University Press, 1978; *Selected Poems*. Dublin: Dolmen/London: Oxford University Press/Winston-Salem, N.C.: Wake Forest University Press/Toronto: Exile Editions, 1982; *The Dead Kingdom*. Dublin: Dolmen/London: Oxford University Press/Winston-Salem, N.C.: Wake Forest University Press/Belfast: Blackstaff, 1984; *The Lost Notebook*. Cork & Dublin: Mercier, 1987. (Novella); *Mount Eagle*. Dublin: Gallery/Winston-Salem: Wake Forest University Press/Newcastle upon Tyne: Bloodake, 1989; *The Figure in the Cave and Other Essays*. Dublin: Lilliput, 1989; *New Selected Poems*. Dublin: Gallery, 1989; *Born in Brooklyn*. Fredonia, N.Y.: White Pine, 1991; *The Love Poems*. 1992; *Time in Armagh*. [Oldcastle, Co. Meath]: Gallery, [1993]; *Collected Poems*. [Oldcastle, Co. Meath]: Gallery, [1995].   REFERENCES: Allen, Michael. "Celebrations." *Irish Review* 7 (1989); Brown, Terence. *Northern Voices: Poets from Ulster*. Dublin: Gill & Macmillan, 1975; Dillon-Redshaw, Thomas. *Hillfield: Poems and Memoirs for John Montague*. Minneapolis: Coffee House/Co. Meath: Gallery, 1989; Dunn, Douglas, ed. *Two Decades of Irish Writing*. Cheadle: Carcanet, 1975; Higgins, Aidan. "Paradiddle and Paradigm." *Irish Review* 5 (Autumn 1988); *Irish University Review* 19 (Spring 1989, John Montague Issue); Kersnowski, Frank. *John Montague*. Lewisburg, Pa.: Bucknell University press, 1975.

MONTGOMERY, LESLIE ALEXANDER. *See* DOYLE, LYNN.

MOONEY, MARTIN (1964–   ), poet. Mooney was born in Belfast and graduated from Queen's University in 1986. He is a member of the faculty of the Poets' House at Portmuck, County Antrim, and his poems have been published widely and anthologized. *Brecht and an Exquisite Corpse: Two Long Poems* was published by Lapwing Pamphlets in 1992, and *Honest Ulsterman* published his pamphlet *Escaping with Cuts and Bruises* in the same year. *Grub* of 1993 was a humorous and intelligent first collection that dealt imaginatively with politics, history, and Irish alienation in 1980s Britain. Also in 1993 Mooney was short-listed for the Ruth Hadden Memorial Award. Mooney's work is a mixture of humor and social comment, ranging from the immediate to the universal and historical. One of the most interesting and wide-ranging of the younger Northern poets, Mooney's work reveals an intelligent and informed grasp of the use of satire and social commentary. Mooney is now an editor with *the big spoon* magazine.

FRED JOHNSTON

WORKS: *Brecht and an Exquisite Corpse: Two Long Poems*. Belfast: Lapwing Poetry Pamphlets, 1992; *Escaping with Cuts and Bruises: Poems*. Belfast: Honest Ulsterman, 1992. (Poetry pamphlet); *Grub*. Belfast: Blackstaff, 1993; *Bonfire Makers*. [Dublin]: Dedalus, [1995].

MOORE, BRIAN (1921–   ), novelist. Moore, by using his successive countries of residence as settings for his novels, has set critics the problem of assigning him a literary nationality. Despite this difficulty, he can perhaps be claimed with least argument as one of the best novelists Ulster has produced. His first novel, *Judith Hearne* (1955), has been hailed as a minor masterpiece in its incisive portrayal of a pathetic Belfast spinster. *The Feast of Lupercal* (1957) attempts less successfully the similar theme of a social failure ironically regarded by the community as a threat to its puritanical, Irish-Catholic virtues. Moore's partly comic *bildungsroman, The Emperor of Ice-Cream* (1965), re-creates Belfast during the World War II German "Blitz," whose effects precipitate the hero into manhood. *An Answer from Limbo* (1962) is the author's very fine *künstlerroman,* whose central figure has been strong enough to escape Ulster's provincialism, philistinism, and sectarianism only to discover in America the perplexing moral problems of his craft. In these four novels the city of Belfast is evocatively drawn.

Since *The Luck of Ginger Coffey* (1960), his third novel and a work of comic pathos that follows the harrowing adventures in Canada of an Irish immigrant, Moore's fiction has become more cosmopolitan. Subsequent novels have mirrored, with the expected refractions and reversions, the author's own movements. Born in Belfast on August 25, 1921, into a Catholic family that had recently converted from Protestantism, Moore left Northern Ireland twenty-two years later when he joined the British Ministry of War Transport during World War II and was stationed briefly in North Africa, Italy, and France. In 1948, he emigrated to Canada and there took out citizenship. He spent several years as a journalist and struggling fiction writer in Montreal, the setting for *Ginger Coffey*. Following the publication of this novel, the Canadian writer and critic Jack Ludwig wrote an article entitled "Brian Moore: Ireland's Loss, Canada's Novelist." Moore was regarded for a few years as Canada's most promising writer and in 1960 received the Governor General of Canada's Award for Fiction. In 1959, the author moved to the United States, first to Long Island and then to New York City, the setting for *An Answer from Limbo,* which is in part an energetic, bitter portrait of that city's literary and bohemian scene. Later he moved to Malibu, California, which provided him with the motive and material for *Fergus* (1970), a novel that is an equally bitter portrait of Hollywood's literary side-industry in which Moore has been involved, writing motion picture scripts. On the strength of such novels, Moore has been acclaimed a prominent United States writer.

Through a tyrannizing memory stirred by guilt, remorse, or depression, Moore's Irish-born Americans vainly try to exorcise the Ireland they thought they had left behind. Moreover, their solution to an Irish problem itself becomes merely a new American problem and a new theme: thus, the escape from provincialism leads to the dreadful freedom of the cosmopolis, and the escape from religion becomes the new problem of faithlessness. For Moore America is Ireland's probable future, but in the provocative and fable-like *Catholics* (1972), a late twentieth-century Ireland becomes the hideously bureaucratic and faithless future of both. And when there is no continuity of theme and crisis between Ireland and America, Moore senses analogies. The sectarianism of Ulster, no doubt, as well as his knowledge of Quebec, supply him with the idea and necessary insights for a book on the Quebec separatist kidnapping and murder of a cabinet minister. This work, *The Revolution Script* (1972), has been called documentary fiction in the manner of Norman Mailer.

The realistic surfaces of Moore's novels derive as much from English and American as from Irish models, but there is a preoccupation with ritual in the novels that may be attuned to the primitive echoes of Irish society. From his fellow-countryman James Joyce* (also an uncompromisingly urban writer), Moore has learned the technique of internalizing at length his characters' thoughts and feelings. His most psychologically revealing successes with it are his vivid portraits of women under sexual stress: the titular heroines of *Judith Hearne, I Am Mary Dunne* (1968), and *The Doctor's Wife* (1976). Moore has a seductive storytelling ability, great honesty, and profound sympathetic identification with his heroes. He is unwilling, however, to explore the complexity of ethical and theological issues in addition to dramatizing their psychological causes and effects. A certain flatness of diction and a marked thinning of fictional texture developed after *I Am Mary Dunne.* That novel, alongside *Judith Hearne* and *An Answer from Limbo,* represents Moore's finest writing.

JOHN WILSON FOSTER

Moore's novels have continued to appear regularly at two-or three-year intervals and have continued to sell well because of their crafted plots, brisk pacing, and lucidly readable style. To critics, however, they have seemed something of a disappointment after the superb characters, such as Judith Hearne and Ginger Coffey, of the first books and also after the finely evoked backgrounds of Belfast, Montreal, and New York, which were drawn from personal experience. Up to *I Am Mary Dunne* of 1968, one Moore novel had a comfortable similarity to another. His recent books, however, have been disconcertingly various in genre, and one does not really know what to expect from the next Moore book except that it will probably differ considerably from the previous one. Although it might seem that the recent work depends on idea and imagination because the vein of memory and personal experience has dried up, it might more plausibly seem that the recent books, so seemingly disparate, have the underlying similarity of tracing and investigating contradictory and clashing moralities.

The Mangan Inheritance (1979) is about James Mangan, a sometime poet whose wife, a well-known actress, leaves him and is shortly killed with her lover in a car crash. Mangan has been struck by his remarkable resemblance to a daguerrotype of the poet James Clarence Mangan* and journeys to an Irish village to investigate a possible family connection. He discovers two previous Mangan poets, the later one still living, with his face and with a ghastly personal story to tell. The characters are excellently drawn, the prose very readable, and the plot well structured, but what it all means is another matter. The production of poetry is itself a kind of morality, but the various Mangan *poetes maudites* live selfish, even appallingly selfish, lives; and the hero at the end seems to opt for humane responsibility rather than for art.

Cold Heaven (1983) appears initially a sort of spooky thriller about the heroine's husband, who has been pronounced dead after a boating accident in France but who disappears from the hospital morgue and returns to America, where he has physical relapses into death or near-death. The real story, however, concerns the wife, a Catholic-educated atheist who has for a year refused to announce an apparition of the Blessed Virgin who wants a shrine on a rock off the California coast. The plight of the husband appears as a divine attempt to put pressure on the wife, but eventually God lets the heroine off the hook by having a nun see the apparition also. This allows the wife to leave her husband for her lover and to live more happily ever after. This seems an outlandish and even silly framework of plot, but it is well told and has some excellent minor characters. Why Moore devised it would seem, possibly, an attempt to continue his investigation of moral action, which is the crux of his recent books and which is distinctly an antidote to the moral simplicities of most fiction.

Black Robe (1985) is an account of a canoe journey from Quebec by a Jesuit missionary accompanied by a band of Algonquin Indians in the seventeenth century. The book is the most violent and harrowing of Moore's works and is full of murder, rape, cannibalism, and the grisliest depiction of torture. The primitive life with its hazards, hardships, and ferocious sufferings is graphically caught, and Moore is particularly successful in his evocation of the Indian character. In part, he accomplishes this by devising a language for them both simple and pervasively profane. His underlying message seems to be the depiction "of the strange and gripping tragedy that occurred when the Indian belief in a world of night and in the power of dreams clashed with the Jesuits' preachments of Christianity and a paradise after death."

The Colour of Blood (1987) is partly a John Buchanish thriller with lots of exciting chases. However, it is also a late cold war thriller with, as its intriguing hero, the Roman Catholic cardinal of a country in the Eastern bloc. Even more interesting is that the opposition is not between communist bad guys and Western good guys. The cardinal is attempting to avert a great public demonstration against the puppet government, a demonstration being incited by patriots and even patriotic elements among his own clergy. Seeing little reason to look to the West for help, the cardinal fears that antigovernment protests will cause violence, deaths, and a much more repressive regime for his country than that now in power. Changing world events have, to an extent, dated the political background, but the book remains a thoroughly taut and thoughtful read that seems to suggest that the best moral view is pragmatic. Perhaps the one drawback of this short book is that most of its many characters are a bit thinly drawn.

Lies of Silence (1990) is about the Northern Troubles and set in contemporary Belfast and London. The protagonist is Michael Dillon, a hotel manager who is planning to leave his wife. Before he can tell her, their home is invaded by masked Irish Republican Army (IRA) men who plan to keep his wife hostage while he delivers a bomb to his hotel. Accidentally, Dillon sees one of their faces and, to avert the massacre of many people, seizes an opportunity to alert the police to the bomb. His subsequent and well-dramatized problem is whether to opt for safety and refuse to identify the IRA man and live a contented life in England with his mistress, whom he loves, in a job that he likes. Much pressure is put on him by his mistress, his wife, and a priest who is an uncle of the IRA man to remain silent. After several times refusing, he at length decides not to testify, but it is too late, and the IRA burst into his London flat to kill him. This is a tautly plotted novel, full of incident. More important, it poses, as many modern Irish novels do not, a moral choice that is not clear-cut.

So also does *No Other Life* (1993), which is laid in a Caribbean country much like Haiti, and its action parallels recent political developments there. More important, it is an excellently, even excitingly dramatized story of the clash of morality with, or possibly the perversion of morality by, politics. The story details the rise of a brilliant and even saintly young black priest who comes to political power on a swell of popular anger against the years-long social and economic repression of the people by wealthy businessmen and the army. It is a story of how goodness does not merely temporize with expediency but even verges itself into tyranny and possibly finally does more harm than good.

What Moore seems attempting in his recent work is the concoction of fables investigating the complex vagaries of morality, rather than the traditional black and white simplicities of fiction. He has grown from a depicter of individual tragedies into a provocative novelist of ideas. The ideas are much more unsettling than the straightforward simplicities of 1930s social novelists like Dos Passos or Steinbeck. Nor is he to be really compared with a more complicated artistic polemicist such as Shaw,* for in Moore the moral view is distinctly and most un-Shavianly not clear-cut. In actuality, his recent work can hardly be regarded as a falling-off, but rather as an exciting advance into little-charted territory.

WORKS: *Judith Hearne.* London: Andre Deutsch, 1955/reprinted as *The Lonely Passion of Judith Hearne.* Boston & Toronto: Little, Brown, 1956/reprinted as *The Lonely Passion of Miss Judith Hearne.* Harmondsworth: Penguin, 1959; *The Feast Lupercal.* London: Andre Deutsch/Boston & Toronto: Little, Brown, 1957/reprinted as *A Moment of Love.* London: Panther Books, 1965; *The Luck of Ginger Coffey.* London: Andre Deutsch/Boston & Toronto: Little, Brown, 1960; *An Answer from Limbo.* London: Andre Deutsch/Boston & Toronto, 1962; *The Emperor of Ice Cream.* New York: Viking, 1965; *I Am Mary Dunne.* New York: Viking, 1968; *Fergus.* New York: Holt, Rinehart & Winston, [1970]; *Catholics.* New York: Holt, Rinehart & Winston/London: Jonathan Cape, 1972; *The Revolution Script.* London: Jonathan Cape, 1972; *The Great Victorian Collection.* New York: Farrar, Straus & Giroux, [1975]; *The Doctor's Wife.* New York: Farrar, Straus & Giroux/London: Jonathan Cape, [1976]; *The Mangan Inheritance.* London: Jonathan Cape, [1979]; *The Temptation of Eileen Hughes.* London: Jonathan Cape, [1981]; *Cold Heaven.* New York: Holt, Rinehart & Winston, 1983; *Black Robe.* New York: Dutton/New York: Jonathan Cape, 1985; *The Colour of Blood.* London: Jonathan Cape/Toronto: McClelland & Stewart, 1987; *Lies of Silence.* London: Bloomsbury, 1990; *No Other Life.* London: Bloomsbury, 1993; *The Statement.* London: Bloomsbury, 1995. REFERENCES: Dahlie, Hallvard. *Brian Moore.* Toronto: Copp Clark, 1969; Flood, Jeanne. *Brian Moore.* Lewisburg, Pa.: Bucknell University Press, 1974; Foster, John Wilson. *Forces and Themes in Ulster Fiction.* Dublin: Gill & Macmillan/Totowa, N.J.: Rowman & Littlefield, 1974, pp. 122–130, 151–185; Foster, John Wilson. ''An Interview with Brian Moore.'' *Irish Literary*

Supplement (Fall 1985): 44–45; Ludwig, Jack. "Brian Moore: Ireland's Loss, Canada's Novelist." *Critique: Studies in Modern Fiction* 5 (Spring–Summer 1962): 5–13; McSweeney, Kerry. *Four Contemporary Novelists.* Kingston, Ontario: McGill-Queen's University Press, 1983; Murray, Christopher, ed. *Irish University Review* (A Brian Moore Special Issue) 18 (Spring 1988).

MOORE, F[RANK] FRANKFORT (1855–1931), novelist, playwright, and poet. Moore was born in Limerick on May 15, 1855, and educated at the Royal Academical Institution, Belfast. From 1876 to 1892, he traveled widely in South and East Africa, India, the West Indies, and South America as a journalist, and later he sometimes utilized such backgrounds for his novels. His first book was a volume of verse, *Flying from a Shadow,* in 1875. Between 1876 and 1895, he wrote many plays, several of which enjoyed considerable success in productions in London and elsewhere. He was a prolific writer, largely of novels in every typical period vein—light, almost fantastic historical romances. His early novels, however, are sea adventures in the mode of Russell Clarke and Stevenson. His greatest success was *The Jessamy Bride,* a 1897 best-seller that included Dr. Johnson, Burke,* Sheridan,* Garrick, Boswell, and an amusingly drawn Goldsmith* among its characters. For many years he lived in a house inside the castle of Lewes, Sussex, where he could display a magnificent collection of antiques to advantage. He died there on May 11, 1931.

WORKS: *Flying from a Shadow.* London, 1875 (Poetry); *Sojourners Together.* London: Smith, Elder, 1875; *Where the Rail Runs Now.* London: Marcus Ward, 1876; *Told by the Sea.* London: Marcus Ward, 1877. (Short stories); *Daireen.* London: Smith, Elder, 1879; *Mate of the Jessica.* 2 vols. London, 1879; *Coral and Cocoa-Nut. The Cruise of the Yacht" Fire-Fly" to Samoa.* London: Christian Knowledge Society, 1890; *A Gray Eye or So.* 3 vols. London: Hutchinson, 1883; *The Fate of the "Black Swan."* London: Christian Knowledge Society, [1885]; *The Great Orion.* London: Christian Knowledge Society, [1886]; *Will's Voyage.* London: Christian Knowledge Society, [1886]; *Tre, Pal, and Pen.* London: Christian Knowledge Society, [1887]; *Fire-Flies and Mosquitoes.* London: Christian Knowledge Society, [1888]; *Highways and High Seas: Cyril Harley's Adventures on Both.* London: Blackie, [1889]; *The Slaver of Zanzibar.* London: Christian Knowledge Society, [1889]; *Under Hatches.* London: Blackie, 1889; *The Ice Prison.* London: Christian Knowledge Society, 1891; *The Silver Sickle.* London: Griffith, Farran, 1891; *Sailing and Sealing.* London: Christian Knowledge Society, [1892]; *From the Bush to the Breakers.* London: Christian Knowledge Society, [1893]; *"I Forbid the Banns".* 3 vols. London: Hutchinson, 1893; *A Journalist's Notebook.* London, 1894; *One Fair Daughter.* 3 vols. London: Hutchinson, 1894; *Phyllis of Philistia.* London: Hutchinson, [1895]; *The Sale of a Soul.* London: Hutchinson, [1895]; *The Secret of the Court.* London: Hutchinson, 1895; *They Call It Love.* London: Hutchinson/Philadelphia: J. B. Lippincott, 1895; *Two in the Bush, and Others Elsewhere.* London: A. D. Innes, 1895. (Short stories); *Dr. Koodmadhi of Ashantee.* London: Constable, 1896; *In Our House of Ease.* London: Mentz, 1896; *The Jessamy Bride.* London: Hutchinson, 1897; *The Impudent Comedian and Others.* London: C. A. Pearson, 1897. (Short stories); *The Millionairess.* London: Hutchinson, 1898; *The Fatal Gift.* London: Hutchinson, 1898; *Well, After All—.* London: Hutchinson, 1899; *Nell Gwynn, Comedian.* London: C. A. Pearson, 1900/rev. ed., 1926. (Novel); *A Nest of Linnets.* London: *According to Plato.* London: Hutchinson, 1901; *A Damsel or Two.* London: Hutchinson, 1902; *Shipmates in Sunshine.* London: Hutchinson, 1903; *Castle Omeragh.* Westminster: A. Constable, 1903; *The Original Woman.* London: Hutchinson, 1904; *Sir Roger's Heir.* London: Hodder & Stoughton, [1904]; *The Other World.* London: Eveleigh Nash, 1904. (Short stories); *Rachel's Escape.* London: "Daily Mail," [1904]; *He Loved but One: The Story of Lord Byron and Mary Chaworth.* London: Eveleigh Nash, 1905; *The White Causeway.* London: Hutchinson, 1905; *The Artful Miss Dill.* London: Hutchinson, 1906; *Captain Latymer*. London: Cassell, 1907; *The Marriage Lease*. London: Hutchinson, 1907; *The Messenger*. London: Hodder & Stoughton, 1907; *An Amateur Adventuress*. London: Hutchinson, 1908; *A Georgian Pageant*. London: Hutchinson, 1908; *Love and the Interloper*. London: Hutchinson, 1908; *The Food of Love*. London: Eveleigh Nash, 1909; *Priscilla and Charybdis*. London: Constable, 1909; *The Commonsense Collector*. London: Hodder & Stoughton, 1910. (On antique furniture); *The Discoverer and In the Queen's Room: Dramas in Metre*. London: Elkin Mathews, 1910; *The Laird of Craig Athol*. London: Constable, 1910; *The Life of Oliver Goldsmith*. London: Constable, 1910; *The Marriage of Barbara*. London: Constable, 1911; *The Keeper of the Robes*. London: Hodder & Stoughton, [1911]. (Life of Fanny Burney); *The Narrow Escape of Lady Hardwell*. London: Constable, 1912; *The Red Man's Secret*. London: Hutchinson, 1912; *The Rescue of Martha*. London: Hutchinson, 1913; *Fanny's First Novel*. London: Hutchinson, 1913; *The Lighter Side of English Life* . . . London & Edinburgh: T. N. Foulis, 1913; *The Truth about Ulster*. London: Eveleigh Nash, 1914. (Nonfiction); *The Ulsterman*. London: Hutchinson, 1914; *The Lady of the Reef*. London: Hutchinson, 1915; *The Romance of a Red Cross Hospital*. London: Hutchinson, 1915; *A Friend Indeed*. London: Hutchinson, 1916; *The Rise of Raymond*. London: Hutchinson, 1916; *The Fall of Raymond*. London: Hutchinson, 1917; *The Conscience of Coralie*. London: C. Arthur Parsons, 1920; *The Courtship of Prince Charming*. London: W. Collins, [1920]; *The 9.15*. London: Hutchinson, [1921]; *A Few Hours in Lewes. An Itinerary*. Lewes: Farncombe, [1921]; *The Hand and Dagger*. London: E. Nash & Grayson, 1928; *That Holy Kiss*. London: E. Nash & Grayson, 1928; *The Awakening of Helen*. London: E. Nash & Grayson, 1929; *Kitty Clive, and Other Plays in One Act*. London: A. & C. Black, 1929; *A Mixed Grill*. London: Hutchinson, [1930]. (Nonfiction). As F. Littlemore: *A Garden of Peace*. London: W. Collins, [1919].

MOORE, GEORGE (1852–1933), novelist and man of letters. For all practical purposes, the Moore family had its vague beginnings as English Protestants who settled in County Mayo in the seventeenth century, asserted an unproved claim of descent from Sir Thomas More, made a fortune in the wine trade in Spain during the period of Catholic disabilities in Ireland, and married into a Spanish Catholic family for political and commercial advantage. In about 1790, George Moore, the merchant, returned to Ireland, acquired some twelve thousand acres of land, and built Moore Hall. One of the merchant's three sons, a studious man with a taste for literature and history, married into a Protestant family, let his strong-willed wife manage practical affairs, and retired to his library to read and write. His eldest son, the novelist's father, distinguished himself at the Roman Catholic college of Oscott, went to Cambridge, turned his interests to racing, hunting, and women, traveled in the East, including Palestine, and kept the notebooks which his son, Colonel Maurice Moore, incorporated into a biography (*An Irish Gentleman: George Henry Moore*, 1913). George Henry successfully bred and raced horses, saw his estate threatened by economic disasters, became concerned about the political and economic welfare of Ireland, entered politics, and married a lady from the Catholic gentry.

By this point in the family's history, all the diverse interests and temperaments that seem to have been absorbed by the novelist had been established: the Catholic and Protestant lines, the shrewd landlord-businessman and the contemplative writer, the man of action and the dreamer, the sensualist and the austere moralist, the indecisive and the strong-willed mentality.

George Augustus Moore was born on February 24, 1852, at Moore Hall,

County Mayo. He was tutored locally, and as a child he heard romantic tales of adventures in the East, his mother's redactions of episodes from the novels of Walter Scott, and the tales the servants and the local storytellers told. He also spent much of his time around his father's racing stables. In the winter of 1861, he was sent to Oscott, an experience he later recalled with much bitterness (*Salve,* 1912). At Oscott, George was regarded as a dunce, at least in the conventional studies, and later wrote of himself as the "boy that no schoolmaster wants" (*Confessions of a Young Man,* 1888). However, he developed an instinct for literature, read ardently whatever happened to attract him, and determined only to "know what he wanted to know" (Hone, *Life,* p. 25). He read some history, Miss Braddon's *Lady Audley's Secret,* and *The Doctor's Wife,* which in turn led him to his obsession with Shelley. Without the aid of Shelleyan ideas, however, George had already openly expressed his doubts about supernatural religion. In about 1867, George was permitted, probably even urged, to withdraw from Oscott. His father sided with the land reformers against the landlords and won election to Parliament in 1868; in 1869, he moved his family to London. During this period, young George was interested primarily in horse racing and betting, reading Dickens fairly systematically, and learning about art from the painter Jim Browne.

This first phase of Moore's life ended with the death of his father in April 1870. Although grief-stricken, Moore also saw his father's death as liberation from the threat of continued formal cramming for a career in one of the gentlemanly professions. He painted, visited art galleries, spent too much money on scent and clothes, and generally imitated the life of a sophisticated young man about town. However, he also read or at least sampled Godwin, Buckle, Mill, Lecky,* George Eliot, Berkeley,* and Plato. The early years in Ireland and in London always remained vivid in his memory; hence, their importance should not be overshadowed by the much-discussed French period and the influence of French artists and writers.

The second phase of Moore's development began in 1873 when his attaining legal maturity freed him to go to Paris. In Paris, Moore studied at the Beaux Arts and at Jullian's Academy. In 1874, he briefly took a studio in London, where he was visited by Millais, painted, came to know Whistler, overspent on amusements, and again returned to Paris. In 1875, he saw his first major Impressionist exhibition and, like others at the time, disliked their work. Although he had some ability as a painter, Moore himself decided his talent was not great enough. In 1876, he connived to get introductions to influential hostesses, which eventually led to his meeting Degas, Ludovic Halévy, Fromentin, and others.

In the mid-1870s, Moore had met Bernard Lopez, the dramatist; had probably written *Worldliness* (1874?), a comedy of which no copies have survived; began *Martin Luther* (1879), a tragedy in collaboration with Lopez; and moved to the apartment in Montmarte which he describes in *Confessions.* He read Baudelaire, Gautier, probably Poe, and others, and began to write poems. He frequented the Nouvelle Athènes, a café where most of the avant-garde painters and writers of the time gathered. The café became, as he was to say, his university. Here he met Villiers de l'Isle Adam, Mallarmé, Manet, Monet, Degas, Pissarro, Renoir, Sisley, and perhaps Zola. "With the patience of a cat before a mouse-hole," he later wrote in *Confessions,* "I watched and listened." The watching and listening soon bore fruit. He published his first slim volume of poems, *Flowers of Passion* (1878 [1877]), which was viciously reviewed by Edmund Yates under the heading "A Bestial Bard," and his play, *Martin Luther.* Around this time, he reversed his earlier attitude toward the Impressionists, capitulating to the art and personalities of Manet and Degas. He acclaimed Zola, whom he knew only slightly, and Paul Alexis, whom he knew much better.

Moore's residency in Paris ended abruptly and unexpectedly early in 1880. The Moore estates in Ireland were in a disastrous state. Rents were uncollectable, Michael Davitt's Land League was becoming a threat to the landlords, and Moore's credit was overextended. He recorded his first supposed reaction in his usual *épater-les-bourgeois* manner in *Confessions.* "That some wretched farmers and miners should refuse to starve, that I may not be deprived of my *demitasse* at Tortoni's, that I may not be forced to leave this beautiful retreat, my cat and my python—monstrous!" However, this moment may have been one of the most crucial in the record it left on his waxplate. He did return to England, he did, if impatiently, put his affairs in order, he did begin to inform himself about legal, political, and economic conditions in Ireland, and he did commit himself to becoming a professional writer. In fact, he became a highly self-disciplined person, a shrewd businessman, perhaps discovering in himself some of the qualities of that forebear, the wine merchant, who founded the Moore fortune. Moore patched up his financial condition and probably worked briefly on the *Examiner.*

Within the next few years, Moore published work reflecting both the Irish and the French experiences: *Pagan Poems* (1881), a total critical failure in its barely being noticed at all; *A Modern Lover* (1883), a three-volume novel indebted to Henry James, Balzac, the Goncourts, and Zola, respected for its candor and realism but suppressed by Mudie's, the ubiquitous lending library; *A Mummer's Wife* (1885 [1884]), a one-volume novel intended to circumvent the lending libraries and undoubtedly his best work in the Zolaesque vein; *Literature at Nurse; or Circulating Morals* (1885), his polemic against the lending libraries; *A Drama in Muslin* (1886), a satirical treatment of Irish society and politics and like most of his work pervaded with autobiographical allusions; *A Mere Accident* (1887), a novel in which Zolaesque naturalism gives way to French symbolism and the influence of J.-K. Huysmans; and *Parnell and His Island* (1887), a collection of satirical essays on Irish society. From the mid-1880s on, Moore had as much difficulty keeping Ireland and boyhood experience out of his work as Dick Babley in Dickens' *David Copperfield* had in keeping King Charles I out of his Memorial.

The major landmark between Moore's return from France in 1880 and the publication of *Esther Waters* in 1894 is undoubtedly *Confessions.* Year by year until 1888, Moore published on a wide range of subjects in various newspapers and periodicals, including portions of his *Confessions.* It is a delightful record of what Walter Pater had called "mind-building," the progress of an artist's soul, a mixture of penetrating self-analysis, outrageous effrontery to "good taste," flamboyant but highly quotable phrase-making, comic and pathetic self-portraiture, and shrewd observations on art and life. The book contains beautifully controlled passages of reverie as well as clumsy rhetoric.

Spring Days (1888) and *Mike Fletcher* (1889), in various ways related to *A Mere Accident* and *A Drama in Muslin,* were in nearly every way critical failures. In 1891, however, Moore brought together a large body of essays, reviews, and sketches in *Impressions and Opinions.* The essays, however inaccurate in details or wrong-headed in critical stances, are, like *Confessions,* remarkable revelations of a vigorous, curious, sensitive, and highly independent mind. As a result of this book, Moore became a regular art critic for the *Speaker.*

Vain Fortune (1891), although certainly not among Moore's better performances, is markedly superior to *A Mere Accident, Spring Days,* and *Mike Fletcher.* As his three failures in a decadent or aesthetic mode suggest a partial rejection of the naturalist mode, so *Vain Fortune* suggests a partial rejection of the decadent mode and prepares the way for *Esther Waters.* Hubert Price, the hero of *Vain Fortune,* voices Moore's own indecisiveness about artistic means and goals as well as Moore's fear of waning artistic energy, and his concern about his economic circumstances. Moore's participation in founding the Independent Theatre in 1890–1891 and his efforts to write an Ibsenian play, which became *The Strike at Arlingford* (1893), are also reflected in the greater emphasis on dialogue and scenic development and the diminished character analysis and authorial intrusion of various kinds.

Moore's reputation as an art critic advanced rapidly between 1888 and 1893, when he was publishing essays on drama and art and reviews of exhibitions and the like in the *Speaker.* This activity was capped by *Modern Painting* (1893), a volume which introduced to many generations of readers the innovative work of the French Impressionists and the New English Art Club. Although this book will not satisfy the modern scholarly art historian, it is a highly readable, often perceptive, and imaginative personal view of one of the most important and exciting movements in the pictorial arts. (For the family background and Moore's life and career to about 1895, see Joseph Hone's *The Life of George Moore* [1936] and *The Moores of Moore Hall* [1939]; Malcolm Brown's *George Moore: A Reconsideration* [1955]; E. Jay Jernigan's dissertation, "George Moore's 'Re-tying of Bows': A Critical Study of the Eight Early Novels and Their Revisions" [1966]; and Milton Chaikin's dissertation, "The Influence of French Realism and Naturalism on George Moore's Early Fiction" [1954].)

Esther Waters is a brilliant climax to Moore's productive career to 1894. In this novel, he brought together in a coherently structured form and with a masterfully restrained style nearly everything he had learned. What he had learned from the pictorial arts, Flaubert, and Zola, is remarkably demonstrated in the

Derby Day chapters, a brilliant verbalization of W. P. Frith's painting, "Derby Day"; his memories of the racing stables and betting are assimilated in his depiction of Woodview; his fondness for Dickens is reflected in such caricatures as Swindles, the Demon, Ginger, and others, though these figures are functionally integrated into the novel; his now more calculated watching and listening are reflected in his use of visits to pubs, his interview with a wet-nurse, and his reading of contemporary journalism (Bartlett and Sporn, in *English Literature in Transition,* 1966 and 1968, respectively). The novel is also especially interesting insofar as it brings to a head Moore's lifelong distaste for Hardy's novels. *Esther Waters* is an anti-*Tess* novel and makes for fruitful comparison with *Tess of the d'Ubervilles* and George Eliot's *Adam Bede* (Gregor and Nicholas, *The Moral and the Story* [1962]).

In *Celibates* (1895), Moore's first collection of short stories, some of his developing artistic interests were sharpened and new directions tentatively indicated. Moore had dealt with celibacy in *A Drama in Muslin* and in *A Mere Accident.* In *Celibates,* however, the psychological studies are far more penetrating and probably influenced by his study of Dostoevski and Turgenev.

With the success of *Esther Waters,* Moore apparently felt he had exhausted what he could do in the realist vein. At this point in his career, he seems to have been particularly concerned about the possibility of declining talent, and he began to flounder in search of new subject matter and new techniques. Clearly, a break in his artistic stride had occurred. His involvement in censorship controversies, his anger over the British prosecution of the Boer War, and, in the late 1890s, Edward Martyn's,* Arthur Symons', and Yeats'* appeals that he help them launch an Irish drama movement—all combined to develop in Moore considerable hostility to the British cultural scene.

That Ireland was on his mind between 1895 and 1901 is at least covertly evident in *Evelyn Innes* (1898) and *Sister Teresa* (1901). It is evidenced by the dedication of *Evelyn Innes* to Yeats and Symons, by the likelihood that AE* and Yeats were partly models for the character of Ulick, by his advising Yeats in 1898 on the structure of *The Countess Cathleen,* by references in letters to Yeats and in *Evelyn Innes* to the Irish heroine Grania, and by his writing a preface to two of Edward Martyn's plays. In addition, Maud Burke, the one woman whom Moore seems genuinely to have loved, married; he quarreled with Pearl Craigie, a collaborator with whom Moore also seems to have had a more personal relationship; and his relationship with his publisher, T. Fisher Unwin, became increasingly more strained toward the turn of the century. Further, *Evelyn Innes* and *Sister Teresa* had been particularly difficult to write, and he was fearful that his creative energies had dried up. By 1901, therefore, circumstances compounded to make the move to Ireland, his "messianic mission," as he called it, very attractive.

The next phase of Moore's career (1901–1910) was undoubtedly one of the richest and most invigorating periods for his artistic renewal and development. In Ireland, Moore took charge: he organized play productions, wrote plays, gave speeches, and defended and propagandized on behalf of the theatre movement. By about 1904, he appears to have quarreled with nearly everyone and to have given up much hope for an effective cultural revival anywhere in the Western world—a melancholy view that was to deepen during the rest of his life. The Irish landscape, the old ruins, the myths, even the Irish language, however, revitalized his imagination, markedly influenced the development of what he came to call his "melodic line," and gradually turned his attention away from contemporary life to explorations of the past.

Out of his "messianic mission" came the stories of *The Untilled Field* (1903); *The Lake* (1905), his symbolic novel of the "swimming priest"; his remarkable imaginative autobiography, *Hail and Farewell* (1911, 1912, 1914); the stories of *A Story-Teller's Holiday* (1918); and the short novel *Ulick and Soracha* (1926). Although he left Ireland in 1911, Ireland and Irish speech rhythms colored much of his work thereafter. (For Moore's career from about 1894 to about 1911, see H. E. Gerber's *George Moore in Transition* [1968] and Jack Wayne Weaver's dissertation, "A Story-Teller's Holiday: George Moore's Irish Renaissance, 1897 to 1911" [1966].)

In 1911, Moore set up residence in a modest house in London; kept in touch with Irish, French, and English friends; visited France frequently; and traveled to Palestine in preparation for the writing of *The Brook Kerith* (1916). On the whole, however, he devoted most of his energies to his art, to publication of new works for "subscribers only," and to the preparation of collected editions and revisions of his works. Although this last phase of Moore's career has received much less attention than the period of the naturalist-realist novels (1880–1895) or the Irish period (1901–1911), it was a time of rich productivity. He developed a finely honed style at this time and amalgamated much that he had learned from extraordinarily diverse authors and from several arts and genres: Pater, Zola, Turgenev, Dostoevski, Dickens, Wagner, the Dolmetsch circle, D'Annunzio, even Schopenhauer and Nietzsche, Yeats and Edward Martyn, Dujardin, the Impressionist painters, authorities on history, myth, and Biblical exegesis. In 1912, in a statement that has an unexpectedly modest ring, he said with both conviction and a touch of wonder, "I am a little nearer the summit of Parnassus" (letter to Dujardin, February 12, 1912). His perhaps premature self-assessment was to be justified by his recreation of Biblical history in *The Brook Kerith*, biography in *Héloise and Abélard* (1921), myth in *Daphnis and Chloe* (1924), and Irish history in *Ulick and Soracha*. Despite declining creative energies and frequent illness between 1927 and 1933, he wrote short stories, wrote and had two plays produced, recreated the Greece of the fifth century B.C. in *Aphrodite in Aulis* (1930), and worked on *Madeline de Lisle*, the novel about convent life and the religious temperament which he left unfinished upon his death on January 21, 1933. (For Moore's career from about 1910 to 1933, see H. E. Gerber's *George Moore on Parnassus* and Hone's *Life*.)

Moore will be acclaimed in cultural history for his contributions to the naturalist-realist movement in English fiction; his lifelong attacks on censorship;

his contributions, as writer, critic, and apologist, to candor in realistic drama and to the beginnings of the Irish dramatic movement; his contributions to the development of the modern short story, with emphasis on symbolism, penetrating psychological character studies, and the revival of the oral narrator; his brilliant models for modern imaginative autobiography; his introduction of the French Impressionist painters and Symbolist poets to the English-speaking world; his amalgamation of pictorial arts, music, history, myth, and autobiography in imaginative fiction; and his contributions to the structure and style, to the painstaking artistry, of the modern novel. He is not only a writer's writer, but a reader's writer.

Moore could undoubtedly be difficult in personal relationships. He could be arrogant, he could be foolish, he could be troublesome to his publishers and agents, but to the last day of his life he remained profoundly devoted to his one enduring mistress—his art. Many left their marks on his imagination, but he, too, left his mark on cultural history.

HELMUT E. GERBER

WORKS: Collected Editions—There is no complete collected edition, but the first two items, below, are generally regarded as the best. Moore's multiple revisions of nearly every major title should make one wary of any title in one of the collected editions (see Gilcher's bibliography for notes on variant editions). Carra Edition. 21 vols. New York: Boni & Liveright, 1922–1924. Plus 2 supplementary vols., 1925, 1926; Uniform Edition. 20 vols. London: Heinemann, 1924–1933. (Reissued as the Ebury Edition.) Poetry—*Flowers of Passion* (1878), *Pagan Poems* (1881). Plays— *Worldliness* (1874?), *Martin Luther* (1879, with Bernard Lopez), *The Strike at Arlingford* (1893), *The Bending of the Bough* (1900, a rewriting of Edward Martyn's *The Tale of the Town*), *The Apostle* (1911; rewritten, 1923; revised as *The Passing of the Essenes,* 1930), *Esther Waters* (1913), *Elizabeth Cooper* (1913; rewritten as *The Coming of Gabrielle,* 1920), *The Making of an Immortal* (1927), and *Diarmuid and Grania* (produced, 1901; published, 1951; with W. B. Yeats). Critical Essays, Reviews, and Polemics (some with autobiographical significance)—*Literature at Nurse; or Circulating Morals* (1885), *Parnell and His Ireland* (1887; in French, 1886), *Impressions and Opinions* (1891), *Modern Painting* (1893), *Reminiscences of the Impressionist Painters* (1906, a pamphlet), *Memoirs of My Dead Life* (1906), *Avowals* (1919), and *Conversations in Ebury Street* (1924). Imaginative Autobiographies—*Confessions of a Young Man* (1888), *Hail and Farewell (Ave.,* 1911; *Salve,* 1912; *Vale,* 1914), *A Communication to My Friends* (1933). Short Stories—*Celibates* (1895; includes revision of *A Mere Accident* as "John Norton"; rewritten and rearranged with varying contents as *In Single Strictness* [1922] and *Celibate Lives* [1927]), *The Untilled Field* (1903; in Irish, 1902), *A Story-Teller's Holiday* (1918); *In Minor Keys: The Uncollected Stories of George Moore.* David B. Eakin & Helmut E. Gerber, eds. [Syracuse, N.Y.]: Syracuse University Press, 1985. Novels—*A Modern Lover* (1883; rewritten as *Lewis Seymour and Some Women,* 1917), *A Mummer's Wife* (1885), *A Drama in Muslin* (1887; rewritten as *Muslin,* 1915), *A Mere Accident* (1887; rewritten and condensed as "John Norton" for *Celibates,* 1895), *Spring Days* (1888), *Mike Fletcher* (1889), *Vain Fortune* (1891), *Esther Waters* (1894), *Evelyn Innes* (1898), *Sister Teresa* (1901), *The Lake* (1905), *The Brook Kerith* (1916), *Héloise and Abélard* (1921), *The Pastoral Loves of Daphnis and Chloë* (1924), *Ulick and Soracha* (1926), *Aphrodite in Aulis* (1930). Miscellaneous—*Pure Poetry* (1924, an anthology). Collections of Letters—Additional letters and excerpts have been published in various books and articles (see Gilcher's bibliography and Gerber's chapter in *Anglo-Irish Literature: A Review of Research*). *Letters from George Moore to Ed. Dujardin, 1886–1922,* selected, edited and translated by John Eglinton. New York: Crosby Gaige, 1929. (124 letters); *Letters of George Moore,* "with an introduction by John Eglinton, to whom they were written." Bournemouth: Sydenham & Co., 1942. (119 letters); *George Moore: Letters to Lady Cunard, 1895–*

1933. Rupert Hart-Davis, ed. London: Hart-Davis, 1957. (247 letters); "The Letters of George Moore to Edmund Gosse, W. B. Yeats, R. I. Best, Miss Nancy Cunard, and Mrs. Mary Hutchinson." Ph.D. thesis, University of Maryland, 1958. (302 letters); *George Moore in Transition: Letters to T. Fisher Unwin and Lena Milman, 1894–1910,* ed., with a commentary, by Helmut E. Gerber. Detroit: Wayne State University Press, 1968. (298 letters); "Letters of George Moore (1852–1933) to His Brother, Colonel Maurice Moore, C. B. (1857–1939)." Seamus mac Donncha, ed., National University of Ireland (Galway) thesis, 1972–1973. (94 letters). *George Moore on Parnassus: Letters (1900–1933) to Secretaries, Publishers, Printers, Agents, Literati, Friends and Acquaintances.* Helmut Gerber, ed. Newark, Del.: University of Delaware Press/London: Associated University Presses, 1988. (1,214 letters). REFERENCES: Biographical: Cunard, Nancy. *GM: Memories of George Moore.* London: Hart-Davis, 1956; Hone, Joseph. *The Life of George Moore.* New York: Macmillan, 1936. (The standard life; supplemented by Hone's *The Moores of Moore Hall.* London: Jonathan Cape, 1939); Noel, Jean C. *George Moore: L'Homme et l'oeuvre (1852–1933).* Paris: Didier, 1966. (A critical biography, the fullest and most scholarly to date). Critical: Blissett, William F. "George Moore and Literary Wagnerism." *Comparative Literature* 13 (Winter 1961): 52–71; Brown, Malcolm. *George Moore: A Reconsideration.* Seattle: University of Washington Press, 1955; Cave, Richard. *A Study of the Novels of George Moore.* Gerrards Cross: Colin Smythe/New York: Barnes & Noble, 1978; Dunleavy, Janet, ed. *George Moore in Perspective.* Gerrards Cross: Colin Smythe/ Totowa, N.J.: Barnes & Noble, 1983; Farrow, Anthony. *George Moore.* Boston: Twayne, 1978; Firth, John. "George Moore and Modern Irish Autobiography." *Wisconsin Studies in Literature* 5 (1968): 64–72; Gerber, Helmut E. "From Pure Poetry to Pure Criticism." *Journal of Aesthetics and Art Criticism* 25 (Spring 1967): 281–291; Gettman, Royal A. "George Moore's Revisions of *The Lake,* 'The Wilde Goose,' and *Esther Waters.*" *PMLA* 69 (June 1944): 540–555; Grubgeld, Elizabeth. *George Moore and the Autogenous Self: The Autobiography and Fiction.* Syracuse, N.Y.: Syracuse University Press, 1994; Hough, Graham. *Image and Experience.* Lincoln: University of Nebraska Press, 1960, pp. 177–199, 200–210; Hughes, Douglas, ed. *The Man of Wax: Critical Essays on George Moore.* New York: New York University Press, 1971; Jeffares, A. Norman. *George Moore.* London: Longmans, Green [Writers and Their Work], 1965; Kennedy, Eileen. "Turgenev and George Moore's *The Untilled Field.*" *English Literature in Transition* 18 (3) (1975): 145–159; Nye, Francis L. "George Moore's Use of Sources in *Heloise and Abelard.*" *English Literature in Transition* 18 (3) (1975): 161–180; Owens, Graham, ed. *George Moore's Mind and Art.* London: Oliver & Boyd, 1968/New York: Barnes & Noble, 1970; Shumaker, Wayne. *English Autobiography: Its Emergence, Materials, and Form.* Berkeley & Los Angeles: University of California Press, 1954, pp. 185–213; Stevenson, Lional. "Introduction." *Esther Waters.* Boston: Houghton Mifflin, 1963; Temple, Ruth Z. *The Critic's Alchemy.* New York: Twayne, 1953. Part V, pp. 231–271; Uslenghi, Rafaella M. "Una prospettiva di unita nell'arte di George Moore." *English Miscellany* 15 (1964): 213–258. Bibliographical: Gilcher, Edwin. *A Bibliography of George Moore.* Dekalb: Northern Illinois University Press, 1970; Gilcher, Edwin. "George Moore Bibliography: Problems That Remain." *English Literature in Transition* (Special Series, 3 (1985): 30–41; Gilcher, Edwin. *Supplement to a Bibliography of George Moore.* Westport, Conn.: Meckler, 1988; Langenfeld, Robert. *George Moore, An Annotated Secondary Bibliography of Writings about Him.* New York: AMS, 1988.

MOORE, THOMAS (1779–1852), poet. In his lifetime Thomas Moore was the most popular of his generation of Irish writers, particularly to the English audience. Such enormous popularity has not been sustained, and he is now remembered primarily as the friend and biographer of Lord Byron. But if the public does not remember the man, his poems have entered popular culture to such an extent that some measure of fame is assured. Many of his songs, contained in *Irish Melodies,* are classics, including "Believe Me, If All Those Endearing Young Charms" and "The Last Rose of Summer."

Moore's cheerful disposition and love of society made him a much admired figure in upper-class society, but that facade of tranquility masked a life of frequent suffering. He was born in Dublin on May 28, 1779, and lived his early years above his father's grocery shop. Well loved by his family, he was given a solid education in the classics and even attended Trinity College, which only recently had begun admitting Catholics. There he began the long project of translating poems attributed to Anacreon, which he published in 1800.

The next year, a collection of his own verse, *The Poetical Works of Thomas Little, Esq.*, was published. The pseudonym fooled no one, and the public received this set of light verse with such enthusiasm that his reputation was secured.

With no independent income, Moore required regular employment, and through his connections he secured an appointment as registrar of the Admiralty Prize Court in Bermuda. However, he spent only a few months there in 1804 before returning to England.

His next collection, *Epistles, Odes and Other Poems* (1806), added to his popular reputation, partly because some of its contents were considered risqué. His satiric skills were becoming evident, and in occasional political lampoons, he became a formidable spokesman for the opposition.

Moore next turned to his most ambitious and successful project, composition of the *Irish Melodies,* a series of volumes in which his own verse compositions were set to Irish folk airs. Ten volumes in all were published, beginning in 1808 and concluding in 1834. The fame he derived from these works was immediate and lasting, for the verses are by far his best lyrics. Moore had a sure knowledge of music, and the fact that he himself sang some of his pieces in London salons surely helped win them popularity.

In 1817, he published *Lalla Rookh,* a series of four verse narratives sung by an Indian prince disguised as a court minstrel in praise of the title character, an Indian princess. The poem's exotic subject and its elaborate descriptions appealed strongly to Moore's audience, which was then developing a taste for Oriental decor. But like the Royal Pavilion at Brighton, where cast iron is painted to look like bamboo and where Chinese decoration is oddly juxtaposed with Indian, *Lalla Rookh* is stocked with decorations that are more profuse than authentic. The atmosphere is lush indeed, and the music of the verse is in places intoxicating, but the whole bears little resemblance to the Near or Far East. The poem's exoticism is somewhat counterbalanced by its satire. One of the tales, "The Veiled Prophet of Khorassan," attacks the demagoguery of actual contemporaries, including Daniel O'Connell, for whom Moore had a long-standing contempt. Throughout this exotic piece, Moore's love of Ireland and even his patriotism are often expressed.

The satiric impulse dominates the best of Moore's later poems, such as *Intercepted Letters, or the Two-Penny Post Bag* (1813) and *The Fudge Family in Paris* (1818). In these works, Moore's mastery of light musical effects leavens the more acerbic content of his satire. Despite the appearance of polite banter, he took on bold subjects, and his satire can be sharp. His own convictions were quite firm. In *Travels of an Irish Gentleman in Search of a Religion* (1834), he even defended Catholicism at a time and within a society that found such a view surprising.

Before his death, Lord Byron gave to his close friend Moore his memoirs, but when Moore found himself in need of cash, he used the memoirs as collateral for a loan from the publisher, John Murray. After Byron's death, he was sued by Lady Byron and by the poet's half-sister Augusta Leigh, who claimed that Moore should not publish the memoirs, which they feared would be incriminating. As a result, the draft memoirs were burned, although Moore did publish *The Letters and Journals of Lord Byron, with Notices of His Life* in 1830. As the title indicates, the work is based on documentary material, but Moore's comments on Byron's writings are so perceptive that critics still regard Moore's work as important for scholarly study.

Personal trials continued to plague Moore's life, including the deaths of each of his children. His journals and letters, works of considerable literary merit in themselves, reveal the strain he long experienced. Toward the end of his life he turned to a four-volume *History of Ireland* (1835–1846), a project for which he was unsuited; his accounts are based on careful research but nevertheless are superficial and dull. He died on February 25, 1852.

As sources of literary history, Moore's letters and journals are important documents, and the author's engaging personality and eventful life make them lively reading. He was an exceptionally influential writer. The *Melodies,* for instance, created a taste for songs of a definite kind, and they remain popular. Although scholars demonstrated that *Lalla Rookh* was not an authentic version of an Oriental romance, its popularity did not wane. For the modern reader, Moore's fame is likely to rest on his satiric verse, in which his comic and musical skills function so well.

JAMES KILROY

WORKS: *Odes of Anacreon.* London: John Stockdale, 1800; *Poetical Works of Thomas Little Esq.* London: J. & T. Carpenter, 1801; *Epistles, Odes, and Other Poems.* London: Carpenter, 1806; *Corruption and Intolerance.* London: Carpenter, 1808; *Irish Melodies.* 2 vols. London: James Power/Dublin: William Power, 1808; *The Sceptic: A Philosophical Satire.* London: Carpenter, 1809; *Irish Melodies.* Vol. 3. London & Dublin: J. & W. Power, 1810; *A Letter to the Roman Catholics of Dublin.* London: Carpenter, 1810; *Irish Melodies.* Vol. 4. London & Dublin: J. & W. Power, 1811; *M.P., or The Blue-Stocking.* London: J. Power, 1811; *Intercepted Letters, or the Two-Penny Post-Bag,* by "Thomas Brown the Younger." London: J. Carr, 1813; *Irish Melodies.* Vol. 5. London & Dublin: J. & W. Power, 1813; *Irish Melodies.* Vol. 6. London & Dublin: J. & W. Power, 1815; *Sacred Songs.* Vol. 1. London & Dublin: J. & W. Power, 1816; *Lalla Rookh, An Oriental Romance.* London: Longman, Hurst, Orme & Browne, 1817; *The Fudge Family in Paris,* by "Thomas Brown the Younger." London: Longmans, 1818; *Irish Melodies.* Vol. 7. London: J. Power, 1818; *National Airs.* Vol. 1. London & Dublin: J. & W. Power, 1818; *The Works of Thomas Moore.* 7 vols. Paris: Galignani et Cie, 1819; *Irish Melodies.* Dublin: W. Power, 1820. (First collection); *National Airs.* Vol. 2. London & Dublin: J. & W. Power, 1820; *Irish Melodies.* Revised ed. with Prefatory Letter on Music. London: J. Power, 1821; *Irish Melodies.* Vol. 8. London: J. Power, 1821; *National Airs.* Vol. 3. London: J. Power, 1822; *National Airs.* Vol. 4. London: J. Power, 1822; *Fables for the Holy Alliance,* by "Thomas Brown the Younger." London: Longmans, 1823; *The Loves of the*

Angels. London: Longmans, 1823; *Irish Melodies.* Vol. 9. London: J. Power, 1824; *Memoirs of Captain Rock, the Celebrated Irish Chieftain, with Some Account of his Ancestors.* London: Longmans, 1824; *Sacred Songs.* Vol. 2. London: J. Power, 1824; *Memoirs of the Life of the Right Honourable Richard Brinsley Sheridan.* London: Longmans, 1825; *Evenings in Greece.* London: J. Power, 1826; *National Airs.* Vol. 5. London: J. Power, 1826; *The Epicurean. A Tale.* London: Longmans, 1827; *National Airs.* Vol. 6. London: J. Power, 1827; *Legendary Ballads.* London: J. Power, 1828; *Odes upon Cash, Corn, Catholics, and Other Matters.* London: Longmans, 1828; *Letters and Journals of Lord Byron: with Notices of His Life.* London: John Murray, 1830; *Evenings in Greece: The Second Evening.* London: J. Power, 1831; *The Life and Death of Lord Edward Fitzgerald.* London: Longmans, 1831; *The Summer Fête.* London: J. Power, 1831; *Travels of an Irish Gentleman in Search of Religion.* London: Longmans, 1833; *Irish Melodies.* Vol. 10. London: J. Power, 1834; *The Fudge Family in England.* London: Longmans, 1835; *The History of Ireland.* Vol. 1. London: published jointly by Longman, Rees, Brown, Green & Longman of Paternoster Row, & John Taylor, 1835; *Alciphron: A Poem.* London: John Macrone, 1839; *The History of Ireland.* Vol. 2. London: Longmans, & Taylor, 1840; *The History of Ireland.* Vol. 3. London: Longmans, & Taylor, 1840; *The Poetical Works of Thomas Moore,* Collected by Himself. 10 vols. London: Longmans, 1841; *The History of Ireland.* Vol. 4. London: Longmans, & Taylor, 1846; *The Memoirs, Journal and Correspondence of Thomas Moore.* Lord John Russell, ed. 8 vols. London: Longmans, 1853–1856; *Poems and Verse, Humourous, Satirical and Sentimental, with Suppressed Passages from the Memoirs of Lord Byron, and Including Contributions to the Edinburgh Review between 1814 and 1834.* London: Chatto & Windus, 1878; *The Poetical Works of Thomas Moore.* A. D. Godley, ed. London: Henry Frowde, 1910; *The Letters of Thomas Moore.* Wilfred S. Dowden, ed. 2 vols. Oxford: Clarendon, 1964; *The Journal of Thomas Moore.* Wilfred S. Dowden, ed., with Barbara Bartholomew & Joy L. Linsley. 6 vols. Newark, Del.: University of Delaware Press/London & Toronto: Associated University Presses, 1983–1991. REFERENCES: Brown, Terence. "Thomas Moore: A Reputation." In *Ireland's Literature: Selected Essays.* Mullingar, Co. Westmeath: Lilliput, 1988; de Ford, Miriam Allen. *Thomas Moore.* New York: Twayne, 1967; Gwynn, Stephen L. *Thomas Moore.* London: Macmillan, 1905; Jones, Howard Mumford. *The Harp That Once.* New York: Henry Holt, 1937; Jordan, Hoover H. *Bolt Upright: The Life of Thomas Moore.* 2 vols. Salzburg, 1975; Martz, Louis L. *Thomas Moore: The Search for the Inner Man.* New Haven, Conn.: Yale University Press, 1990; Strong, L.A.G. The *Minstrel Boy, A Portrait of Tom Moore.* New York: Knopf, 1937; Tessier, Thérèse. *La Poesie lyrique de Thomas Moore (1779–1852).* Paris: Didier, 1975; Tessier, Thérèse. *The Bard of Erin. A Study of Thomas Moore's "Irish Melodies" 1808–1834.* Salzburg: Salzburg Studies in English Literature/Atlantic Highlands, N.J.: Humanities, 1981; Welch, Robert. *Irish Poetry from Moore to Yeats.* Gerrards Cross: Colin Smythe, 1980; White, Terence de Vere. *Tom Moore: The Irish Poet.* London: Hamish Hamilton, 1977.

MORAN, LYNDA (1948–   ), poet. Moran was born on April 8, 1948. In her collection, *The Truth about Lucy* (1985), she writes in free verse, and about half of the poems are quite straightforward but with frequently striking phrases and lines, like "tea-dipped words," "the worn censure of wood," or "Apples autograph the trees." In others, the diction becomes even more distinctive, if not precious: "exwomb," "ushabti," "wombroom." Some verge on the baffling: "wine-rust scented earth," "Some reptilian aspersorium," "unsexed seaweed," "you ochre my studied scenario," and "the peradventure / of his spare coins."

WORK: *The Truth about Lucy.* [Dublin]: Beaver Row, [1985].

MORAN, MICHAEL. *See* ZOZIMUS.

MORGAN, LADY (1776?–1859), novelist and woman of letters. The birth date of Sydney Owenson, Lady Morgan, must be an assumption, for she carefully kept it a secret. However, she was probably born in 1775 or 1776. Her father, Robert Owenson (born MacOwen), was an Irishman and a Protestant derived from a line of Catholics. He was an actor—a stage Irishman—and a failed producer. Her mother was an English Methodist. Sydney Owenson herself personified everything that was essentially Irish in her time; in her were met all the contradictions that identified Irish conflicts and troubles.

The future Lady Morgan received a sound education, relieved the family penury by serving as a governess, began her writing career with a volume of poetry in 1801, published two probationary novels, and became famous with *The Wild Irish Girl* in 1806. Other works, such as *O'Donnell, Florence Macarthy, The O'Briens and the O'Flahertys,* and *Dramatic Scenes from Real Life,* were extremely popular in their day and made her a good deal of money.

She married Sir Charles Morgan in 1812. Until 1837 she lived in Dublin, and then removed to London. She steeped herself in Irish life by moving about the country in childhood and youth, knew English and aristocratic life well, and traveled in France, Italy, and Belgium in order to write books about them.

Lady Morgan fought all her life for two goals: liberty for all and the emancipation of Ireland. The Emancipation of Catholics Act of 1829 was in no small part the result of her persistent, strident, and energetic work, chiefly by means of her novels. In her four national tales, she depicted Irish struggles and troubles in realistic detail. Her solution was to bring Catholic and Protestant together in amity, submerge the romantic past in the realistic present, give the Irishman opportunity for labor and reward for his work, and free Ireland from English domination. Her goals were generous, but her style was often flamboyant and careless. She died in London on April 13, 1859.

JAMES NEWCOMER

WORKS: *Poems.* Dublin: Printed by Alex. Stewart . . . , 1801. *St. Clair; or, The Heiress of Desmond.* London: Harding/Dublin: J. Archer, 1803. (Novel); *A Few Reflections.* Dublin: Printed by J. Parry, 1804; *The Novice of St. Dominick.* 4 vols. London: R. Phillips, 1805. (Novel); *Twelve Original Hibernian Melodies.* London: Preston, [1805]; *The Wild Irish Girl.* 4 vols. London: Phillips, 1806. (Novel); *The Lay of an Irish Harp; or, Metrical Fragments.* London: R. Phillips, 1807; *Woman, or, Ida of Athens.* 4 vols. London: Longman, 1809. (Novel); *The Missionary, an Indian Tale.* 3 vols. London: J. J. Stockdale, 1811. (Novel); *O'Donnell, a National Tale.* 3 vols. London: H. Colburn, 1814. (Novel); *France.* 2 vols. London: Colburn, 1817; *Florence Macarthy, an Irish Tale.* 4 vols. London: H. Colburn, 1818. (Novel); *Italy.* 2 vols. London: H. Colburn, 1821; *The Life and Times of Salvator Rosa.* 2 vols. London: H. Colburn, 1824; *Absenteeism.* London: H. Colburn, 1825; *The O'Briens and the O'Flahertys, a National Tale.* 4 vols. London: H. Colburn, 1827. (Novel); *The Book of the Boudoir.* 2 vols. London: H. Colburn, 1829; *France in 1829–30.* 2 vols. London: Saunders & Otley, 1830; *Dramatic Scenes of Real Life.* 2 vols. London: Saunders & Otley, 1833; *The Princess; or, the Beguine.* 3 vols. London: R. Bentley, 1835. (Novel); *Woman and her Master.* 2 vols. London: H. Colburn, 1840. (A study of woman through the ages); with Sir Charles Morgan, *The Book Without a Name.* 2 vols. London: H. Colburn, 1841; *Letter to Cardinal Wiseman.* London: Westerton, 1851; *Passages in My Autobiography.* London: R. Bentley, 1859; *Lady Morgan's Memoirs. Autobiography, Diaries and Correspondence.* W. Hepworth Dixon, ed. 2 vols. London: W. H. Allen, 1862. REFERENCES: Dunne, Tom. "Fiction as 'the Best History of

Nations': Lady Morgan's Irish Novels." In *The Writer as Witness: Literature as Historical Evidence*. Tom Dunne, ed. Cork: Cork University Press, 1987, pp. 133–59; Fitzpatrick, William John. *The Friends, Facts, and Adventures of Lady Morgan*. Dublin: W. B. Kelly, 1859; Fitzpatrick, William John. *Lady Morgan, Her Career, Literary and Personal*. London: Charles J. Skeet, 1860; Flanagan, Thomas. *The Irish Novelists 1800–1850*. New York: Columbia University Press, 1959; Newcomer, James. *Lady Morgan the Novelist*. Lewisburg, Pa.: Bucknell University Press, 1990; Stevenson, Lionel. *The Wild Irish Girl*. New York: Russell & Russell/London: Chapman & Hall, 1936.

MORRISON, DANIEL GERARD "DANNY" (1953–   ), former Sinn Féin spokesperson and novelist. Morrison was born in Belfast and became a prominent member of Sinn Féin and for a time editor of *An Phoblacht*. He was often on television during the 1981 hunger strike in Maze Prison as the external spokesman for the fasting prisoners. At the Sinn Féin Ard Fheis in 1981, he made the notable remark that "with an Armalite in one hand and a ballot in the other, we will take power in Ireland." He was arrested in 1982 trying to enter the United States from Canada, and in December of that year he was banned from entering Great Britain. He was runner-up in the 1984 European election, gaining over 13% of first-preference votes. After serving half of an eight-year sentence in Maze Prison, where he wrote his second novel, he was released in May 1995. In September 1995 he was awarded an Arts Council bursary of £3,500.

His first novel, *West Belfast* (1989), is about a young man growing up in a Catholic area of Belfast in the 1960s. At first a bildungsroman, it develops into an account, from a Catholic and nationalist point of view, of the street fighting in Belfast during the late 1960s and early 1970s. That long latter portion is too thinly developed but has effective moments. There is a strong attempt to stress the humanity of the nationalists, as in the concluding diary entries of the protagonist's scrupulous younger brother, who is killed. Nevertheless, many readers would have difficulty with these reflections on the British soldier whom the speaker has just killed:

I curse the life that has brought me to this; then I focus in on the British government. I think of the corporal who might have hated his job, who might have been buying himself out of the army.
I'll live for him and in some sort of communion with him.
One thing is for sure.
I'll think about him more often than his commanding officer.
I'll maybe even be still thinking about him when his widow has stopped.

On the Back of the Swallow (1994) tells of Nicky Smith, who is devastated at age fifteen by the death of a childhood friend. As a young man, he has an affair with a volatile girl who leaves him and also leaves him devastated. He next commences a romantic attachment with a fifteen-year-old boy and is wrongfully arrested for having sex with the boy. Eventually, he dies while attempting to escape from prison. This is a very mixed bag of a book. Early on, there is some "literary" overwriting, such as "the mighty rolling cymbals of the sea" and "the gelid water, its sheerness, ran its protean blade up to and over their belly-buttons." However, Nicky's interrogation scenes with the police and also the bleak scenes of prison life are done economically and convincingly. As an attempt to write a tragedy arising from social pressures about homosexual love, the book is not entirely unsuccessful.

WORKS: *West Belfast.* Cork & Dublin: Mercier, [1989]; *On the Back of the Swallow.* Cork: Mercier, 1994.

MORRISSEY, MARTIN (ca. 1940–), memoirist. Morrissey was born in West Clare, emigrated to New York in the late 1950s, returned to Ireland in the early 1970s, and is now a travel agent living in Clare.

WORKS: *Land of My Cradle Days.* Dublin: O'Brien, 1990; *The Changing Years.* Dublin: O'Brien, [1992].

MORRISSY, MARY (1957–), fiction writer. Morrissy was born in Dublin and won the Hennessey Award in 1984 and the $50,000 Lannan Literary Award in 1995. Her first collection, *A Lazy Eye* (1993), is a consistently well-written but very uneven book. Although the pieces have usually an arresting idea behind them, many remain rather undeveloped sketches. Of the others, "Divided Attention" has the striking idea of a woman being plagued by an obscene phone caller, although she herself is so obsessed with a married man that she makes anonymous calls to his house and even hides outside in the garden to see what is going on. The most powerful and realized story is "A Curse," about a teenage baby-sitter who gets a crush on the father of the family she sits for, collapses in tears on his chest, and later—embarrassed by hearing the family discuss her at a christening party—stabs the new baby in the hip with a diaper pin and flees the house, now conscious of humanity's enduring albatross, guilt.

WORKS: *A Lazy Eye.* London: Jonathan Cape, [1993]. (Short stories); *Mother of Pearl.* New York: Scribner's, 1995/London: Jonathan Cape, 1996. (Novel).

MORROW, JOHN (1930–), novelist and short story writer. Morrow, who is about the only comic writer to emerge from the Northern Ireland Troubles of the past twenty-five years, was born in Belfast. He left school at age fourteen to work in the shipyards. He later served an apprenticeship in the linen trade and worked as a unskilled laborer, furniture salesman, and insurance agent. He has done considerable writing and broadcasting for radio and in 1975 was awarded a bursary by the Arts Council of Northern Ireland.

Morrow's fiction deals with the disrupted contemporary North but treats the subject in a manner quite his own: by means of comic exaggeration. The best quality of his novel *The Confessions of Proinsias O'Toole* (1977) is a cynical eye that lights gleefully on venality, opportunism, self-serving attitudes, and corruption among the combatants, and this attitude is a refreshing antidote to the bloated idealism of public rhetoric. He has been admired for his prose style,

which is reminiscent of the American humorist S. J. Perelman, being characterized by quips, gags, and satiric exaggerations. The witticisms are most various
in quality, however, ranging from the highly imaginative to the simply puerile.
Moreover, there are so many witticisms that they clog virtually every sentence,
considerably impeding the narrative. The characters are constantly engaged in
heroic bouts of drink and sex, and his humor often seems less out of Rabelais
than out of *Playboy* magazine and quickly becomes adolescent and tedious.

Sects and Other Stories (1987), although verging from sketches and even
squibs like "Tommy Carlisle" or "Oul Cruelty," to stories of some length and
complexity like "The Gandhi Gong," seems more mature. The command of
Belfast speech remains self-assured, but the prose has become less clotted with
wordplay. Nevertheless, it retains its many caustic and extravagant delights:

the "General Salute" richocheted off the sweating walls of the church hall like the
unsynchronised laments of six mortally wounded elephants.

you'd have sworn it was some BBC producer from around the corner taking his ulcer
for a walk.

I caught a whiff of that sweaty-sheep smell that arises from Long Johns at that stage of
fission just before they have to be amputated.

yesterday, for the umpteenth time, a car-bomb had brought the windows cascading into
the street like crumbling teeth in a *Tom & Jerry* cartoon.

With dozens of such delights, Morrow must be accounted something of a
Northern national treasure.

WORKS: *The Confessions of Proinsias O'Toole*. [Belfast]: Blackstaff, [1977]; *Northern Myths*.
Belfast: Blackstaff, 1979. (Short stories); *The Essex Factor*. Dundonald: Blackstaff, 1982. (Novel);
Sects and Other Stories. Belfast: Blackstaff/[London]: Black Swan, [1987].

MORTON, MAY (1876–1957), poet. Mary (May) Elizabeth Morton was born
and raised in County Limerick, before moving to Belfast when she was twenty-
four years of age. In Belfast, she became vice principal of the Girls' Model
School and was a founding member of the Young Ulster Society. She had a
long association with the Belfast P.E.N., serving first as secretary and later as
chairperson. She was one of the Quota Press poets and a contributor to *Rann*,
Lagan, and *Poetry Ireland*. *Spindle and Shuttle* (1951) won the Festival of Britain, Northern Ireland Award for poetry.

Morton frequently used the typography of her poems to illustrate the content.
Masque in Maytime (1948) is a particularly experimental work, where the
typestyle, line length, variations in stanza length, and poetic styles all contribute
to make the poem function as a musical score. The inside front cover of *Masque
in Maytime* gives this definition of the volume's intent: "In it the author has
tried, by the use of a variety of metres, to capture the colour and rhythm, the
accompanying music and the underlying theme of a natural ballet produced on
an Ulster landscape by the caprice of the Ulster climate."

ANNE COLMAN

WORKS: *Dawn and Afterglow.* Belfast: Quota, 1936; *Masque in Maytime.* Lisburn: Lisnagarvey, 1948; *Spindle and Shuttle.* Festival of Britain Committee for Northern Ireland, Prize Poems, 1951; *Sung to the Spinning Wheel.* Belfast: Quota, 1952.

MOYLAN, THOMAS KING (1885–1958), playwright.

Moylan, who was chief clerk to the Grangegorman Mental Hospital near Dublin, began his writing career in 1909 with an amateur production of *Paid in His Own Coin* by the Metropolitan Art Students League. His work, which may be typified by such plays as *Tactics, Naboclish, The Curse of the Country,* and *Oh Lawsy Me!,* was either farcical or broadly comic. It remained popular among amateur dramatic societies but had little literary merit and retains insufficient theatrical merit to warrant revival today. In November 1917, however, Sean O'Casey* organized a concert at the Empire Theatre in Dublin that included *Naboclish* and was highly successful.

WORKS: *Paid in His Own Coin and Tactics.* Dublin: James Duffy, n.d.; *The Curse of the Country.* Dublin: James Duffy, n.d.; *The Naboclish and Uncle Pat.* Dublin: James Duffy, 1913; *Oh Lawsy Me! and Movies.* Dublin: James Duffy, 1917; *Dopey Dan.* Dublin: James Duffy, n.d.; *A Damsel from Dublin.* Dublin: James Duffy, 1945.

MULCHINOCK, WILLIAM PEMBROKE (ca. 1820–1864), poet.

Mulchinock was born in Tralee, County Kerry and, after an unhappy love affair, became a war correspondent during the British war on Afghanistan. In Ireland, he contributed poems to *The Nation.** Living in America from 1849 to 1855, he became literary editor of *The Irish Advocate.* His *Ballads and Songs* appeared in 1851. His famous poem is "The Rose of Tralee." He died in Tralee in 1864.

PRINCIPAL WORK: *Ballads and Songs of William Pembroke Mulchinock.* New York: T. W. Strong, 1851. REFERENCE: Caball, J. T. *The Rose of Tralee: The Story of a Tradition.* Tralee: Kerryman, 1964.

MULDOON, PAUL (1951–   ), poet.

Muldoon was born near Moy in County Armagh on June 20, 1951, the son of a commercial mushroom grower. After graduating from Queen's University, Belfast, he worked for several years as a producer for BBC Northern Ireland radio, then moved to the Kerry Gaeltacht. He taught at Cambridge and Columbia before becoming chairman of the Creative Writing Program at Princeton. He won the Eric Gregory Award in 1972 and the Geoffrey Faber Memorial Prize in 1982. He is married to the writer Jean Korelitz, and they have a daughter, Dorothy.

"In a way," says Harry Clifton,* "Muldoon is not so much an Irish poet as a poet who happens to have been born in Ireland. What is real about him is not his Irishness but the intensity of his imaginative synthesis, wherever it is applied." From the airy, enigmatic quietness of his published first poems to the incompletely colonized theoretical vocabulary in the later *Madoc,* Muldoon's work does often seem, again in Clifton's words, "more American than Irish in the eclecticism of its myths, its imaginative homelessness." Yet Muldoon's references to Northern Ireland are persistent and telling. Even in the self-absorbed game playing of *The Prince of the Quotidian* (a book advertised as itself a key to Muldoon's own *Annals of Chile*), his thinking of a New Jersey region, the Oranges, can suddenly leave him dismayed by thinking of two murders in Northern Ireland.

In the early poems of *New Weather* (1973), he began combining distant allusion and local reference. "Good Friday, 1971, Driving Westward" takes him through Gallygawley, Omagh, Strabane, and John Donne to a perhaps imagined collision in Donegal. "Dancers at the Moy" portrays a town "coloured" by "one or other Greek war." Various kinds of combination abound in Muldoon's second major volume, *Mules* (1977), which "concerns," he has said, "mixed marriages—between delicacy and bestiality, Grace and Will, humble and heavenly, jackass and mare." *Why Brownlee Left* (1980) considers what is perhaps the quintessential Muldoonian institution, "the Boundary Commission," but its most characteristic set of juxtapositions comes in the remarkable "Cuba," in which the Cuban missile crisis prompts an Irish family drama, suggesting a new version of Kavanagh's* question in "Epic": "Which was more important?" The poem ends with a young girl's enforced confession that a boy once touched her. In response to the priest's asking whether the touch was immodest, she elaborates that he brushed against her, very gently. Declan Kiberd* has described the extraordinary adequacy of Muldoon's "tentative and irresolute" closing images or phrases, which often seem to be the poems' whole reasons for being. The poems issue in a kind of "balancing act, by which extremes may meet and be aligned." The intensity and inconclusiveness of that aligning in "Cuba" mark it as one of the most important Irish poems written in the 1970s. The same volume also includes "Anseo," which means "here and now" and which was the first word of Irish he spoke. In recollection of the word, he connects his attendance first in primary school and later at a camp of paramilitaries across the mountain." The word stands as an indicator, like Muldoon's poem, of a kind of presence.

"Gathering Mushrooms," in *Quoof* (1983), makes a kind of psychedelic companion piece to Derek Mahon's* "A Disused Shed in Co. Wexford." Reaching back via psilocybin to Troy and then moving forward to "the fire-bomb / that sent Malone House sky-high / and its priceless collection of linen / sky-high," the poem proceeds by "blowing your mind." *Meeting the British* (1987) presents Muldoon's vision of his homeland in "Christo's," with all of Ireland being under wraps in black polythene. His approach to Irish history is well represented by the volume's title poem, which records a Native American encounter that yields for its speaker "six fishhooks / and two blankets embroidered with smallpox"—a wholly non-Irish encounter and yet a discomfiting analogue. Muldoon's decisive and characteristically mediated comment on the public role of poetry is spoken in the persona of W. H. Auden, quoting and then responding to Yeats,* in the New York artistic milieu of "7, Middagh Street":

"Did that play of mine
send out certain men (*certain*men?)

the English shot . . . ?"
the answer is "Certainly not."

If Yeats had saved his pencil-lead
would certain men have stayed in bed?

By the time of *Meeting the British,* Muldoon was established as one of the most important of contemporary Irish poets.

Edna Longley* in *The Living Stream* describes *Madoc* (1990) as "a satire, a *Dunciad,* whose miscegenations mock native modes, . . . an in-joke, with Southey and Coleridge representing Heaney and Muldoon in America. . . . In *Madoc* one thing alarmingly leads to another: not only image, word, rhyme, but idea, cultural practice, politics, literature." Each page is headed with the name of a Western philosopher, but the name's command of what comes below, often no more than a single line, is tenuous at best. "Anselm" watches over a page that reads in its entirety, "De dum, Te Deum, de dum, Te Deum, de dum." If Lacan might think himself affirmed by the " 'joyance everywhere' " over which he looks, Mill would hardly be reassured to find on one of his pages the suggestion "that *Madoc* means 'the greatest, greatest good.' " The thinkers' names "preside," as Longley says, "over much satirical negation of their attempts to establish cognitive (and thereby ethical, political, and literary) order." If the thirty-something mostly empty pages of *The Prince of the Quotidian* (1994) provide a promised order for the baffled reader of *The Annals of Chile* (1994), they must do so through a self-reflexive account of Muldoon's life among "the Princeton heavy hitters," in which Muldoon's meeting Langston Hughes' biographer Arnold Rampersand at a party gives Muldoon the license to insert himself "like an ampersand" between the novelist Joyce Carol Oates & the boxer Ingemar Johansson. But the slim volume does offer familiarity and lucidity by duplicating a terrific poem from *The Annals of Chile,* "The Sonogram," which ends with an image of Muldoon's yet unborn child doing figuratively what his poems never have at all.

VICTOR LUFTIG

WORKS: *Knowing My Place.* [Belfast]: Honest Ulsterman, 1971; *New Weather.* London: Faber, 1973; *Spirit of Dawn.* [Belfast]: Ulsterman, [1975]; *Mules.* London: Faber/Winston-Salem, N.C.: Wake Forest University Press, 1977; ed., *The Scrake of Dawn, Poems by Young People from Northern Ireland.* Belfast: Blackstaff, 1979; *Single Ladies: Sixteen Poems.* Devon: Interim, 1980; *Why Brownlee Left.* London & Boston: Faber/Winston-Salem, N.C.: Wake Forest University Press, 1980; with Ted Hughes, *Ted Hughes and Paul Muldoon.* London: Faber, 1983. (Poetry cassette); *Quoof.* London: Faber/Winston-Salem, N.C.: Wake Forest University Press, 1983; *Mules and Early Poems.* Winston-Salem, N.C.: Wake Forest University Press, 1985; ed., *The Faber Book of Contemporary Irish Poetry.* London & Boston: Faber, 1986; *Selected Poems, 1968–1986.* London: Faber, 1986/New York: Ecco, 1987/New York: Noonday, 1993; *Meeting the British.* London: Faber/Winston-Salem, N.C.: Wake Forest University Press, 1987; ed., *The Essential Byron.* New York: Ecco, 1989; *Madoc: A Mystery.* London: Faber, 1990/New York: Farrar, Straus & Giroux, 1991;

with Czeslaw Milosz, *Czeslaw Milosz and Paul Muldoon Reading Their Poems.* Washington, D.C.: Library of Congress, 1991. (Recording); trans., *The Astrakhan Cloak.* [Oldcastle, Co. Meath]: Gallery, [1992]/Winston-Salem, N.C.: Wake Forest University Press, 1993. (From the Irish of Nuala Ní Dhomhnaill); *Shining Brow: An Opera in Two Acts.* London: Faber/Boston: ECS, 1993. (Libretto for Daron Hagen); *The Annals of Chile.* London: Faber/New York: Farrar, Straus & Giroux, 1994; *The Prince of the Quotidian.* [Oldcastle, Co. Meath]: Gallery/Winston-Salem, N.C.: Wake Forest University Press, 1994; *Six Honest Serving Men.* [Oldcastle, Co. Meath]: Gallery, [1995]. (Play); *Ambient Starlight.* [Oldcastle, Co. Meath]: Gallery, [1995].

MULKERNS, VAL (1925–   ), short story writer and novelist. Mulkerns was born on February 14, 1925, in Dublin, and educated at Dominican College in Eccles Street. She worked initially as a civil servant, then moved to London, where her early novels were published, and then returned to Dublin in 1952 to serve as associate editor of *The Bell** under Peadar O'Donnell.* From 1968 to 1983, she was a weekly columnist for the *Irish Press.* After a hiatus of nearly a quarter of a century, she again began writing books, and the novels and volumes of stories she has published since *Antiquities* of 1978 are a striking advance over her early work and, indeed, are among the important contemporary works of Irish fiction.

Her first novel, *A Time Outworn* (1951) is a rather conventional story of young love but contains many nice bits of observation about young girls. A second novel, *A Peacock Cry* (1954), was no great advance, and both books are distinctly pre-Edna O'Brien* in their romantic view. *Antiquities,* however, and its successor, *An Idle Woman* (1980), are quite post-O'Brien in attitude, in maturity, and in quality. The difference is not a matter of one writer's influence upon another but of the influence of a changed world.

Antiquities contains several loosely connected stories about several generations of a single family, and its best pieces are more controlled and distanced than anything in Mulkerns's early novels. *An Idle Woman* breaks into two halves. In the first and poorer part, there are stories of vital, brittle women and gentle, ineffectual men. The women love to plunge ecstatically into the chilling waters of the Atlantic, while the men wade out a few feet, hastily return, and shiver on the shore. The women bound over bogs from tussock to tussock or lithely leap from rock to rock; the men either sink in up to their ankles or scuttle breathlessly around. These stories are conventionally well done and conventionally depressing.

The second half of the book is really impressive. "The Birthday Party" is a horrendous little fable about some tinker children being invited to a birthday party for a middle-class child and being run down by the mother's automobile. Although specifically realistic, it has some allegorical resonance. "Phone You Some Time" is a lighthearted comic triumph. "Home for Christmas" is a brief, brutal vignette, seen through a child's eyes, of unnecessarily penurious living. "Memory and Desire" is a study of middle-aged loneliness contrasted with the making of a television film by bright, virile young people—and the protagonist is a man. Unlike Edna O'Brien, Mulkerns shows healthy signs of escaping the confines of liberated woman's fiction.

A Friend of Don Juan (1988) reprints some of the best of Mulkerns' earlier stories and adds some telling new ones, such as the very moving "End of the Line." Some pieces, such as "Still Life," are thin in plot but compensate by fine characterization. Indeed, Mulkerns' forte is characterization, and in a short space she is remarkably effective in catching it—so effective that her stories must rank with Bryan MacMahon's* and James Plunkett's* as among the very best in the generation after O'Flaherty,* O'Connor,* and O'Faolain.*

The Summerhouse (1984) is a gem of a short novel; perhaps its one notable flaw is that the reader would like it longer and more developed. *Very like a Whale* (1986) is a quiet, accomplished story about Dublin in the 1980s. Also a rather short book, it nevertheless takes in a rather broad panorama. There is a broken, middle-aged, middle-class marriage. The overtly considerate but basically self-protecting man drives away a young girl who adores him. His wife, who has left him, decides that she wants him back and repulses the nice man who wants her—but then accepts him back when the husband repulses her. Their daughter has a happy yuppie marriage, although her au pair is raped and later assaulted for not paying drug debts. Their son takes a job in an inner-city school that has all of the horrors of any school in any poor urban area. He does some good in it, although he is not able to save his own girlfriend, a drug addict. The social problems and behavior Mulkerns describes are light-years away from her own Irish novels of twenty-five years earlier but are a true and telling depiction of contemporary Irish behavior. Her characters, often a blend of goodness and selfishness, are persuasively observed portraits of the people who inhabit this sad new world.

In 1984, Mulkerns shared the Allied Irish Banks Prize for Literature. She is a member of Aosdána.*

WORKS: *A Time Outworn*. London: Chatto & Windus, 1951/New York: Devin-Adair, 1952. (Novel); *A Peacock Cry*. London: Hodder & Stoughton, [1954]. (Novel); *Antiquities*. London: Andre Deutsch, 1978. (Stories); *An Idle Woman and Other Stories*. [Swords, Co. Dublin]: Poolbeg, [1980]; *The Summerhouse*. London: John Murray, 1984. (Novel); *Very like a Whale*. London: John Murray, 1986. (Novel); *A Friend of Don Juan*. London: John Murray, 1988. (Stories).

MULLEN, MICHAEL

WORK: *The Midnight Country*. London: HarperCollins, 1995. (Novel).

MULVIHILL, MARGARET

WORK: *St. Patrick's Daughter*. London: Hodder, 1993. (Novel).

MURDOCH, IRIS (1919–   ), novelist, philosopher, dramatist, and poet. Born of Anglo-Irish parents in Dublin, Murdoch was raised in London and educated at the Badminton School and Somerville College, Oxford. She spent time in the British civil service during World War II and taught philosophy at Oxford during a career that has seen her concentrating her energies increasingly on her writing. Widely regarded as one of the more prolific and important British novelists of her time, she visited Ireland during the summers of her youth and occasionally returns there in her fiction, especially in her one "historical novel," *The Red and the Green* (1965), and, to a lesser, mostly atmospheric extent, in *The Unicorn* (1963) and *The Sea, The Sea* (1978).

While not considered one of Murdoch's most notable works, *The Red and the Green* reflects many of her preoccupations as novelist and thinker. She has frequently associated herself with the nineteenth-century realistic tradition in the English, European, and Russian novel, citing George Eliot and Henry James as major influences. Acknowledging that her fiction moves beyond conventional realism, particularly in the areas of narration, plot, and characterization, she has termed it "transcendental realism." While her methods of exploring such concerns as the complexity of sexual relationships, the nature of good and evil, and the conflict between the sacred and profane deny easy categorization, she does depict middle- and upper-middle-class life with considerable verisimilitude and frequently with a richly comic tone.

The Red and the Green is set in Dublin and its vicinity during the week preceding the Easter Rising of 1916, though it spends relatively little time referring in detail to major historical figures and events. Instead, the historical context informs the portrayal of such characters as Pat Dumay, a fervent patriot who embraces the Rising but desires to protect his younger brother Cahal from the harm he might experience by participating. While the novel climaxes with the Rising, it foregrounds several complicated, interconnected lives: Dumay; Cahal; Millie, a sexually uninhibited widow; Andrew, a much-maligned relation serving as a British officer; and Barnabas Drum, a would-be priest who left the seminary years before because of his inability to suppress his sexuality. The novel's sense of time and place is vivid enough for the reader's understanding of a major period in Irish history to be enhanced.

PETER DREWNIANY

WORKS: *Sartre: Romantic Rationalist.* Cambridge: Bowes & Bowes/New Haven, Conn.: Yale University Press/2d ed. Brighton: Harvest/New York: Barnes & Noble, 1980; *Under the Net.* London: Chatto & Windus/New York: Viking, 1956; *The Sandcastle.* London: Chatto & Windus/New York: Viking, 1957; *The Bell.* London: Chatto & Windus/New York: Viking, 1958; *A Severed Head.* London: Chatto & Windus/New York: Viking, 1961; *An Unofficial Rose.* London: Chatto & Windus/New York: Viking, 1962; *The Unicorn.* London: Chatto & Windus/New York: Viking, 1963; with J. B. Priestley. *A Severed Head.* London: Chatto & Windus, 1964. (Play); *The Red and the Green.* London: Chatto & Windus/New York: Viking, 1965; *The Time of the Angels.* London: Chatto & Windus/New York: Viking, 1966; with James Saunders. *The Italian Girl.* London & New York: Samuel French, 1968. (Play); *The Nice and the Good.* London: Chatto & Windus/New York: Viking, 1968; *Bruno's Dream.* London: Chatto & Windus/New York: Viking, 1969; *A Fairly Honourable Defeat.* London: Chatto & Windus/New York: Viking, 1970; *The Sovereignty of Good.* London: Oxford University Press/New York: Schocken Books, 1971. (Philosophy); *An Accidental Man.* London: Chatto & Windus/New York: Viking, 1971; *The Black Prince.* London: Chatto & Windus/New York: Viking, 1973; *The Three Arrows and The Servants in the Snow.* London: Chatto & Windus, 1973/New York: Viking, 1974. (Plays); *The Sacred and Profane Love Machine.* London:

Chatto & Windus/New York: Viking, 1974; *A Word Child.* London: Chatto & Windus/New York: Viking, 1975; *Henry and Cato.* London: Chatto & Windus, 1976/New York: Viking, 1977; *The Fire and the Sun: Why Plato Banished the Artists.* London: Oxford University Press, 1977. (Philosophy); *The Sea, The Sea.* London: Chatto & Windus/New York: Viking, 1978; *Nuns and Soldiers.* London: Chatto & Windus, 1980/New York: Viking, 1981; *The Servants.* London: Oxford University Press Music Department, 1980. (Adaptation of *The Servants and the Snow* as libretto for opera by William Mathias); *The Philosopher's Pupil.* London: Chatto & Windus/New York: Viking, 1983; *The Good Apprentice.* London: Chatto & Windus/New York: Viking, 1986; *Acastos: Two Platonic Dialogues.* London: Chatto & Windus, 1985; *The Book and the Brotherhood.* New York: Viking, 1988; *The Servants and the Snow; The Three Arrows; The Black Prince: Three Plays.* London: Chatto & Windus, 1989; *The Message to the Planet.* New York: Viking, 1990; *Metaphysics as a Guide to Morals.* New York: Penguin, 1993; *The Green Knight.* New York: Viking, 1994.   REFERENCES: Bagnal, Kate. *Iris Murdoch: A Reference Guide.* Boston: G. K. Hall, 1987; Baldenza, Frank. *Iris Murdoch.* New York: Twayne, 1974; Bove, Cheryl K. *Understanding Iris Murdoch.* Columbia: University of South Carolina Press, 1993; Byatt, A. S. *Degrees of Freedom: The Novels of Iris Murdoch.* London: Chatto & Windus/New York: Barnes & Noble, 1965; Conradi, Peter J. *Iris Murdoch: The Saint and the Artist.* New York: St. Martin's, 1986; Dipple, Elizabeth. *Iris Murdoch: Work for the Spirit.* London: Methuen/Chicago: University of Chicago Press, 1982; Gerstenberger, Donna. *Iris Murdoch.* Lewisburg, Pa.: Bucknell University Press/London: Associated University Presses, 1975; Phillips, Diana. *Agencies of the Good in the Work of Iris Murdoch.* New York: Peter Lang, 1991; Ramanathan, Suguna. *Iris Murdoch: Figures of Good.* New York: St. Martin's, 1990; Todd, Richard. *Iris Murdoch.* London & New York: Methuen, 1984; Todd, Richard. *Iris Murdoch: The Shakespearian Interest.* London: Vision/New York: Barnes & Noble, 1979; Tucker, Lindsey, ed. *Critical Essays on Iris Murdoch.* New York: G. K. Hall, 1992; Wolfe, Peter. *The Disciplined Heart: Iris Murdoch and Her Novels.* Columbia: University of Missouri Press, 1966.

MURPHY, AIDAN (1952–   ), poet. Murphy was born in Cork and in recent years has lived in London. His free-verse poems have their line and stanza lengths determined, sometimes tellingly, by the dramatic effect of the content. His first volume, *The Restless Factor* (1985), has occasional puzzlements of syntax or of imagery. For instance, in the last stanza of "Unpunctual Mercy," the word "Glazed" makes little sense if attached to its nominal noun, "years," and possibly refers to "us" in the previous sentence. Or, in "Conversation with a Wall," one can understand a greasy finger or even an ethereal finger, but how could the finger be both greasy and ethereal? Despite such problems, in *The Way the Money Goes* (1987), the formlessness of his generally short, flat statements is often jerked into interest by dramatic phrasing or an arresting idea that does much to compensate for the general casualness.

WORKS: *The Restless Factor.* Dublin: Raven Arts/Bucks.: Colin Smythe, [1985]; *The Way the Money Goes.* Dublin: Raven Arts/London & New York: Allison & Busby, [1987].

MURPHY, ARTHUR (1727–1805), playwright. Murphy was born at Cloonyquin, County Roscommon, on December 27, 1727. Because his father died when Murphy was but two, he was educated principally in France at the English Jesuit school at St. Omar, where he was an outstanding student of the classics. His maternal uncle intended him for a career in business and sent him to Cork for a two-year apprenticeship. He disliked the work but enjoyed the hospitality.

When he returned to London against his uncle's will, he was disinherited. Soon after, Murphy originated a newspaper column and then a separate weekly paper called *The Gray's Inn Journal* (1752–1754), modeled on *The Spectator.* Under the name of Charles Ranger, he commented frequently on theatrical matters. To earn money, at the suggestion of his friend the mimic Foote, he became an actor for two seasons, one at Covent Garden and the second at Drury Lane under David Garrick, who produced his first play, the longlived farce *The Apprentice,* in 1756. He left acting for a spate of political journalism and then studied law, which he practiced successfully for most of his life, carrying on a double career as a playwright. *The Apprentice, The Way to Keep Him* (1761), *Three Weeks After Marriage* (1776), and *Know Your Own Mind* (1777), all comedies or farces, were produced well into the nineteenth century. *The Orphan of China* (1759) and *Zenobia* (1768) established him as a writer of tragedy as well. He favored laughing rather than sentimental comedy, and *The Way to Keep Him* holds up favorably to the best of Goldsmith* and Sheridan.* He published translations of Sallust and of Tacitus; his translation of Tacitus, with notes, was long the standard version. He wrote brief, rather informal, but well-informed biographies of his close friends Dr. Johnson (whom he was responsible for introducing to the Thrales) and of David Garrick, with whom his personal and professional relationship was long and sometimes explosive. He was noted for his informed and amiable conversation. He died in London on June 18, 1805.

SVEN ERIC MOLIN

WORKS: *The Works of Arthur Murphy, Esq.* 7 vols. London: T. Cadell, 1786. (Collected edition of his plays and essays. There are many editions of his most famous plays: *All in the Wrong, The Apprentice, The Citizen, The Grecian Daughter, Know Your Own Mind, The Old Maid, The Orphan of China, Three Weeks after Marriage,* and *The Way to Keep Him)*); *New Essays.* Arthur Sherbo, ed. [Ann Arbor]: Michigan State University Press, 1963; *Eighteenth Century Drama: Afterpieces.* Richard W. Bevis, ed. London, Oxford & New York: Oxford University Press, 1970. (Contains Murphy's *The Upholsterer* and *The Way to Keep Him*); *The Plays of Arthur Murphy.* Richard B. Schwartz, ed. 4 vols. New York & London: Garland, 1979. (Facsimiles of texts published in London, 1786–1798); *Plays by Samuel Foote and Arthur Murphy.* George Taylor, ed. Cambridge: Cambridge University Press, 1984. (Contains Murphy's *The Citizen, Three Weeks after Marriage,* and *Know Your Own Mind*). REFERENCES: Dunbar, Howard Hunter. *The Dramatic Career of Arthur Murphy.* New York: Modern Language Association/London: Oxford University Press, 1946; Emery, John Pike. *Arthur Murphy.* Philadelphia: University Press for Temple University, 1946; Spector, Robert Donald. *Arthur Murphy.* Boston: Twayne, 1979. For comments on the attributions of Sherbo's *New Essays,* see H. K. Miller in *Bulletin of the New York Public Library* 69 (1965).

MURPHY, DERVLA (1931–   ), travel writer. Murphy was born on November 28, 1931, in Lismore, County Waterford, where she still lives. She was the daughter of two teachers, Fergus Murphy and his wife, the former Kathleen Rochefort-Dowling. Murphy was educated at the Ursuline Convent, Waterford, and at Trinity College, Dublin. She made her name with her first exuberant book, *Full Tilt* (1965), about her trip to India on a bicycle. She has since followed the success of that book with many others, creating an oeuvre remarkable for her sympathy with diverse cultures that she attempts to meet on common ground, with little of the Western sense of superiority that mars much travel writing. She has also written an impassioned book about the nuclear arms race and another about the racial groups in English cities, a sort of travel book in Britain. She was won several prizes, among them the American Irish Foundation Literary Award in 1975, the Christopher Ewart-Biggs Memorial Prize in 1978, and the Irish-American Cultural Institute Literary Award in 1985. She has one daughter, Rachel, the companion on many of her recent trips.

PETER COSTELLO

WORKS: *Full Tilt: Ireland to India with a Bicycle.* London: John Murray, [1965]; *Tibetan Foothold.* London: John Murray, [1966]; *The Waiting Land: A Spell in Nepal.* London: John Murray, [1967]; *In Ethiopia with a Mule.* London: London: John Murray, 1968; *On a Shoestring to Coorg: An Experience of South India.* London: John Murray, 1976; *Where the Indus Is Young: A Winter in Baltistan.* London: John Murray, 1977; *A Place Apart.* London: John Murray, 1978; *Wheels within Wheels.* London: John Murray, 1979. (Autobiography); *Eight Feet in the Andes.* London: John Murray, 1983; *Race to the Finish?: The Nuclear Stakes.* London: John Murray, 1981; *Changing the Problem: Post-Forum Reflections.* Mullingar: Lilliput, 1984. (Pamphlet); *Ireland.* London: Orbis, 1985; *Muddling through in Madagascar.* London: John Murray, 1985; *Tales from Two Cities.* London; John Murray, 1987; ed., *Embassy to Constantinople: The Travels of Lady Mary Wortley Montague.* London, 1988; *Cameroon with Egbert.* London: John Murray, 1989; *Transylvania and Beyond.* London: John Murray, 1992; *The Ukimwi Road: From Kenya to Zimbabwe.* London: John Murray, 1993; *South Africa.* London: John Murray, 1995.

MURPHY, GERRY

WORK: *Rio de la Plata and All That . . .* [Dublin]: Dedalus, [1993]. (Poetry); *The Empty Quarter.* Dublin: Dedalus, [1995]. (Poetry).

MURPHY, JAMES (1839–1921), novelist. Murphy was born in Glynn, County Carlow. He became professor of mathematics in Catholic University, Dublin. Some of his historical novels were several times reprinted, and some were translated into Irish. His prose tends to an old-fashioned stiffness, but there are considerable dialogue and incident.

WORKS: *Hugh Roach, the Ribbonman. A Story of Thirty Years Ago.* Dublin: Duffy, [187?]; *The Fortunes of Maurice O'Donnell: An Irish-American Story.* Dublin: J. Falconer, [1877]/New York: A. E. & R. E. Ford, [1887]; *The Forge of Clohogue: A Story of the Rebellion of '98.* Dublin: Sealy, Bryers & Walker, 1885; *The Shan Van Vocht. A Story of the United Irishmen.* Dublin: Forster, 1886; *The Haunted Church.* London: Spencer Blackett, 1889; *Lays and Legends of Ireland.* Dublin: J. Duffy, [1911]; *In the Days of Owen Roe.* Dublin: M. H. Gill, 1920; *The Priest Hunters.* Dublin: Talbot, [1926]; *In Emmet's Days: The Story of Eamon Revelle.* Dublin: Talbot, n.d.

MURPHY, JOHN [JOSEPH] (1924–   ), playwright. Murphy was born in Charleston, County Mayo, on May 21, 1924. His one play, *The Country Boy,* was staged by the Group Theatre in Belfast in April 1959 and by the Abbey* in May 1959. This play, about emigration and the contrast of visiting "Yanks" with those who stayed home, is soundly observed and well constructed and hit such a responsive chord that it has constantly been revived by amateurs. Indeed, its most recent professional revival was in Dublin's Andrews Lane Theatre in May 1995, thirty years after Murphy himself emigrated to Los Angeles.

WORK: *The Country Boy.* Dublin: Progress House, [1960].

MURPHY, KATHARINE MARY (1840–1885), poet. Murphy was born in 1840, at Ballyhooley, County Cork. The birthdate of 1825 has also been suggested, but 1840 seems more likely, for she was reported to have died relatively young. She was the daughter of a coal merchant on Pope's Quay, Cork, and her mother was Miss Foley, of Ballyhooley. The family moved from Ballyhooley to Cork when she was about three years of age. Her only sister died in infancy, and her brother later emigrated to Australia. Following her parents' death, Murphy opened a shop, which proved unsuccessful. She then turned to writing as a means of supporting herself. She was a regular contributor to *The Nation** and *Young Ireland* under the pseudonym of Brigid, and her work also appeared in the *Cork Examiner, Sharp's London Magazine,* and several American periodicals. Her most famous poem, "Sentenced to Death," was frequently reprinted in *The Nation,* but her work has yet to be collected into a volume. Her health deteriorated about 1884, and she died in the South Cork Infirmary.

ANNE COLMAN

REFERENCES: Russell, Matthew. "Our Poets, No. 14: Katharine Murphy (Brigid)." *Irish Monthly* 13 (1885): 433–440; Sherlock, Thomas. "Kate Mary Murphy (Brigid)." *Young Ireland* 11 (1885): 320–321.

MURPHY, MICHAEL J[OSEPH] (1913–1996), folklorist and playwright. Murphy was born in Liverpool of Irish parents on July 2, 1913, but educated at Dromintee National School in South Armagh. He left school at age fourteen to work for local farmers. In a few years, he began broadcasting for the BBC and Radio Éireann, in 1942 joined the Irish Folklore Commission, and was later a member of the Department of Irish Folklore at University College, Dublin. The Belfast Group Theatre staged his *Dust under Our Feet* in 1953, and the Abbey* staged his *Men on the Wall* in 1961. He died on May 18, 1996, at Walterstown, County Louth.

WORKS: *At Slieve Gullion's Foot.* Dundalk: W. Tempest, 1940; *"The Hard Man."* Belfast: H. R. Carter, 1950. (One-act play); *Culprit of the Shadows.* Belfast: H. R. Carter, 1955. (One-act play); *Mountain Year.* Dublin: Dolmen, 1964. (Essays); *Tyrone Folk Quest.* Belfast: Blackstaff, 1973; *Mountainy Crack: Tales of Slieve Gullioners.* Belfast: Blackstaff, 1975; *Now You're Talking—: Folk Tales from the North of Ireland.* Belfast: Blackstaff, 1975.

MURPHY, RICHARD (1927–   ), poet. Born August 6, 1927, at Milford House, County Mayo, Murphy spent some of his early childhood in Ceylon, now Sri Lanka, where his father was the last British mayor of Colombo. Educated at Magdalen College, Oxford, where he studied English language and literature under C. S. Lewis, he received his B.A. in 1948 and his M.A. in 1965. He has taught widely at universities in England and the United States. In addition to a number of private and limited editions, Murphy's major collections include *Sailing to an Island* (1963), *The Battle of Aughrim* (1968), *High Island* (1974), *Selected Poems* (1979), *The Price of Stone* (1985), *The Price of Stone and Earlier Poems* (1985), *The Mirror Wall* (1989), and *New Selected Poems* (1989). Among the awards he has received are the A.E.* Memorial Award, the Guinness Poetry Award, the British Arts Council Award, the American Irish Foundation Literary Award, and the Marten Toonder Award.

The problematic relationship between the poet and his places has always figured strongly in Murphy's work. In his first major collection, *Sailing to an Island,* his places are the sea and the rocky coasts and islands of the west of Ireland. He explores the interaction—or oftentimes the collision—between place and consciousness. Again and again, the indifferent otherness of the sea or the indomitable absoluteness of stone attracts, rejects, and sometimes overwhelms the poet and his personae. Thus, the long poem "The Cleggan Disaster" recounts the devastation wrought on a small group of fishing boats by a sudden storm. In the title poem, Murphy writes:

> Seven hours we try against wind and tide,
> Tack and return, making no headway.
> The north wind sticks like a gag in our teeth.

One feature of *Sailing to an Island* that has drawn a lot of comment is Murphy's attempt to construct a verse that adequately corresponds to the strenuous physicality of his surroundings. Especially in the poems of the sea, he employs accentual rhythms reminiscent both of Austin Clarke's* experiments with Irish sound patterns in English verse and of Anglo-Saxon poetry. For example, in his note to "The Last Galway Hooker," a poem about a fishing boat that he bought and restored, Murphy explains that each line is meant to have four stresses with a long caesura. Frequently, however, the verse comes across as labored, with a heavy-handed insistence on its form. The result is a poetry of hard surfaces without any deeper resonance. Nevertheless, Donald Davie's opinion in the *New York Review of Books* should certainly be noted:

Only the bare style of the later Murphy could have risen to the splendid and marmoreal lines which give to this poem a conclusion among the most memorable, for dignity and poignancy combined, of any in modern English:

> Old men my instructors, and with all new gear
> May I handle her well down tomorrow's sea-road.

Murphy's sense of struggle and conflict plays out on a cultural level as well. Here the conflict is between his Anglo-Irish heritage and the dominant culture of his country. Poems such as "Woman of the House" and "Droit de Seigneur" address these concerns explicitly. But even when he is not overtly focusing on the cultural division, Murphy's ambivalence about his own place comes through, as, for example, when he asks in "Sailing to an Island,"

> Am I jealous of these courteous fishermen
> Who hand us ashore, for knowing the sea
> Intimately . . . ?

Elsewhere Murphy has commented on his awareness of a sense of difference between himself and those whom he calls "truly Irish": "They seemed sharper, freer, more cunning than we were. Stones, salmon-falls, rain clouds and drownings had entered and shaped their minds, loaded with ancestral bias."

Murphy examines his consciousness of this "ancestral bias" in its historical context in *The Battle of Aughrim*. Originally commissioned as a BBC radio piece, the poem mixes dramatic monologues, bits of historic documents, and short lyrics to meditate on the complex entanglements of Irish identity and of a battle that, Murphy writes, "[h]as a beginning in my blood." Many of the short lyrics that make up the work are deftly handled and hint at the psychological complexity of the speaker. But the overall effect of the rapid development of multiple points of view is that of a montage of disembodiment without a convincing emotional center. In the words of one critic, the work is too "programmatic." More successful is the other long poem in the volume, "The God Who Eats Corn." In memory of Murphy's father, who had retired to Rhodesia and had served there temporarily as acting governor-general, the poem again explores Murphy's own sense of involvement in, and detachment from, the colonial legacy of his class. It is a legacy he finds troubling and troubled. Maintaining gardens, establishing a school for African children, Murphy's father upholds "the manners of a lost empire" where "[t]ime has confused dead honour with dead guilt" and where "[p]lyres kindle under *Pax Britannica*."

The sense of cultural ambivalence and of occasionally overwrought rhythms in these first two volumes is pared back in *High Island*, where a number of the poems are more intimate, more quietly personal. But the strongest poems in this book are those like "Seals at High Island," "Stormpetrel," and the title poem, in which the speaker is either self-effacing ("I watch from a cliff-top, trying not to move") or absent. In these poems, Murphy demonstrates control over his material, showing, more than insisting upon, the starkness of the natural world:

> The calamity of seals begins with jaws.
> Born in caverns that reverberate
> With endless malice of the sea's tongue
> Clacking on shingle, they learn to bark back
> In fear and sadness and celebration.
> The ocean's mouth opens forty feet wide
> And closes on a morsel of their rock.

Lines like these lead Seamus Heaney* to say that in *High Island* "the effort of making is subsumed into the pleasures of saying."

The Price of Stone continues with Murphy's characteristic themes, while it also shows him working more thoroughly than before in tighter forms. Indeed, the title section of the volume is a sequence of fifty sonnets. In them, Murphy's personae are the buildings and locales that shaped him. Detached from himself but self-reflective, Murphy explores the process by which the writer is shaped by, and shapes, his environment: "Fear makes you lock out more than you include / By tackling my red brick with Shakespeare's form / Of love poem." While some of the poems in the sequence try too hard and suffer from what one critic calls "ostentatious verbal chiselling," when they are successful, the compact form of the sonnet conveys a satisfying solidity that echoes with delicate subtleties.

Murphy's most recent collection, *The Mirror Wall,* again gives voice to the inanimate, and again, Murphy assumes the stance of an outsider. Returning to Sri Lanka after an absence of fifty years, Murphy approaches his subject looking not at a colonial or postcolonial milieu but at a precolonial one. The volume consists of poems inspired by, and adapted from, Sinhala songs from the eighth through tenth centuries. The original songs, carved on the polished plaster of a parapet wall (the "mirror wall"), celebrate the mysterious paintings of women that decorate the rock above this wall, women who, Murphy says, "seem to be dancing in the clouds." Many of the poems are short, haikulike evocations of these women "whose beauty / Irradiates the silence of the rock." The volume is redolent of tropical sensuousness and sensuality. But along with this there are many characteristics that link *The Mirror Wall* to Murphy's other work: the irreducible absoluteness of stone, the questing, questioning consciousness, the multiplicity of voices, the entanglement of public and personal. Again, as in *The Price of Stone,* many of the poems display Murphy's concern with the poet's role as maker and mediator of experience:

> The moon rose
> > when I was on the mountain
> > > looking closely
> at those eyes like a forest gazelle's.
>
> Climbing down
> > I resolved to lure them
> > > nightly to gleam
> across my memory's water-hole.
>
> Their small elliptical
> > dying-of-thirst flame
> > > made all seem dark
> until this poem came to light.

Murphy's departures in these recent volumes indicate a continuing deepening in his work. In one of the sonnets in *The Price of Stone,* he uses the image of a waterfall as a metaphor for his poetry:

> Still flowing steadfast in a flagstone cleft
> Of stunted alders clinging on, it pours

With resonant gravity, bringing the gift
Of widespread raindrops crafted to great force.

In the contrast between stillness and motion, between rocky solidity and fluid evanescence, in the precarious tenacity of the alders, in the gathering and crafting of disparate experience into something of "great force," we have a rich collection of the ingredients and methods that inform Murphy's best work and that hold forth the promise of continuing rewards.

CHRISTOPHER PENNA

WORKS: *Sailing to an Island.* London: Faber/New York: Chilmark, 1963; *The Battle of Aughrim.* London: Faber/New York: Knopf, 1968; *High Island.* London: Faber/New York: Harper & Row, 1974. (This edition contains most of the previous volumes in addition to the London edition of *High Island*); *Selected Poems.* London & Boston: Faber, 1979; *The Price of Stone.* London & Boston: Faber, 1985; *The Price of Stone and Earlier Poems.* Winston-Salem, N.C.: Wake Forest University Press, 1985; *The Mirror Wall.* Winston-Salem, N.C.: Wake Forest University Press/ Newcastle upon Tyne: Bloodaxe, 1989; *New Selected Poems.* London & Boston: Faber, 1989. (Reprint of *The Price of Stone and Earlier Poems*).   REFERENCES: Brown, Terence. "Poets and Patrimony: Richard Murphy and James Simmons." In *Ireland's Literature.* Mullingar: Lilliput, 1988, pp. 189–202; Heaney, Seamus. "The Poetry of Richard Murphy." In *Richard Murphy: Poet of Two Traditions.* Maurice Harmon, ed. Dublin: Wolfhound, 1978, pp. 18–30. (This book is a reprint of the *Irish University Review* special issue on the poetry of Murphy [7.1 (1977)]. It includes a useful biographical note and a bibliography covering Murphy's work through 1977); Longley, Edna. "Searching the Darkness: The Poetry of Richard Murphy, Thomas Kinsella, John Montague and James Simmons." In *Two Decades of Irish Writing.* Douglas Dunn, ed. Manchester: Carcanet Chester Springs, Pa.: 1975; Swann, Joseph. "The Historian, the Critic and the Poet: A Reading of Richard Murphy's Poetry and Some Questions of Theory." *Canadian Journal of Irish Studies* 16 (July 1990): 33–47.

MURPHY, THOMAS [BERNARD] (1935–   ), playwright and novelist. Murphy was born in Tuam, County Galway, on February 23, 1935. While he taught metalwork, math, and religion at Mountbellew Vocational School from 1957 to 1962, he participated in amateur drama. From 1962 until 1970, he lived in London, where his writings included plays for the BBC. He moved to Dublin with his wife, Mary Hippisley, and his two children in 1970. From 1971 to 1973, he worked on the International Committee for English in the liturgy. In 1972, he received the Irish Academy of Letters Award for distinction in literature, and in 1973, he became a director on the board of the Abbey Theatre.* He is a member of Aosdána.*

Tom Murphy's first professional production, *A Whistle in the Dark,* launched his career, yet it was staged not in Ireland but in London, on September 11, 1961. The Carneys fight the world and each other with a ferocity born of inner emptiness, frustration, and bitterness. In *The Observer,* Kenneth Tynan called the play "the most uninhibited display of brutality that the London theatre has ever witnessed. This is not American 'Method' violence, slowly burning through understatement; it is naked, immediate, and terrifying." *Whistle* showed the stereotype of the Irish immigrant in England that many Irish people detest. It is one thing for a theater to show a nation an unflattering, disturbing image of some of its people, but it is another to show that image to an "enemy" nation. Originally rejected by the Abbey, *Whistle* became in 1986 its thirteenth production of a Murphy play.

In *Famine,* Murphy managed Brechtian scenes with over thirty characters to depict the social issues, moral dilemmas, and modern consequences of the 1840s trauma. Contradictory situations range from the tribal responsibility of John Connor to the option of landlord-sponsored emigration. Exile seemed as much a form of cultural genocide as starvation. In these dramas, Murphy expressed his own ambivalence and that of his compatriots about the wrenching dilemmas of emigration and exile. *The Orphans,* produced at the Peacock in 1968, tediously portrays a group of "limbo" people who, at a time when people can reach the moon, still cannot reach each other.

A Crucial Week in the Life of a Grocer's Assistant, earlier called *The Fooleen* (1969), deals with the ambivalence of John Joe's desire to leave his hometown: "It's not just a case of staying or leaving." He desires to escape but fears the alienation of exile. In John Joe's final liberating aria, he roars: "Forced to stay or forced to go. Never the freedom to decide and make the choice for ourselves. And then we're half-men here, or half-men away, and how can we hope to do anything." His mother complains: "Leaving us here in the lurch. Deserting us. Leaving his manny and daddy and uncle that's good to him. That's gratitudiness. Seeking his independence." In *Crucial Week,* another young man home from England expresses his wish to return, buy out the town, and "burn it to the ground." Another voice warns, "[W]oe . . . to the fooleen that goes Holyhead way-woe, and leaves himself behind."

In *The Morning after Optimism* (1971), Murphy stretched further than he had in any previous play and opened up psychic territory that would be explored later in *The Sanctuary Lamp* (1975) and *The Gigli Concert* (1983). The fact that these (anti?) religious plays were premiered at Ireland's national theater signifies that this returned exile was reflecting his compatriots' new questionings, doubts about the old eternal verities, Ireland's spiritual vulnerability in the age of anxiety, and new forms of conflict between Ireland's past and present. Such productions as *The Morning after Optimism* also reflected an openness in Ireland's mainstream theater to a more vigorous, imaginative, experimental theatricality not confined to a naturalistic "Abbey style." *Morning* is a perverted fairy tale that shows the dangers of feeding the heart on fantasies. In a surrealistic forest, a soiled couple meet and kill their ideal counterparts. Murphy's plays are part of Antonin Artaud's "theatre of cruelty."

In *The White House* (1972), J. J. Kilkelly, a publican inspired by John F. Kennedy, has hopes of "a people reeling and chattering away irredeemable time now becoming a cultured and settled community." However, his country town pub does not become the vital center for a fulfilling, joyful town life. Another disillusioned exile argues with equally disappointed friends who stayed. *The White House* was rewritten as a one-act play, *Conversations on a Homecoming* (1985), and the Druid* production toured Ireland and abroad. Similar plays about the frustrations of small-town life were *On the Outside,* his first play, produced in 1975 with a new companion piece, *On the Inside.*

The Sanctuary Lamp (1975) could hardly have been written, never mind produced, in Ireland before the 1960s. The two main questions that it provoked were religious and artistic: Is the play blasphemous or truly spiritual? and Is it a masterpiece or merely a pretentious, bombastic, boring tirade? During its first week at the 1975 Dublin Theatre Festival, spectators left the Abbey in protest. The critic of the *Irish Times* regarded the play as "profoundly religious" but called it "the most anti-clerical play ever staged by Ireland's national theatre, which makes it politically important." Perhaps more daring than the play itself was the real-life epilogue when President Cearbhall Ó Dalaigh, despite the public outcry, declared from the Abbey stage: "I would think that this play, which I do not require to see a second time as some critics have said, ranks in the first three of the great plays seen in the Abbey Theatre—*The Playboy of the Western World, Juno and the Paycock, The Sanctuary Lamp.*" To Patricia Coby in the *Educational Times,* the play's daring was mere posturing: "In a less religiously neurotic society, it would be seen for what it is: emotional bombast."

The J. Arthur Maginnis Story (1977) and *The Blue Macushla* (1980) were broad satirical romps. But in *The Gigli Concert* (1983), Murphy returned to "the audacity of despair," the driving force in his drama. In the successful *Gigli Concert,* one character says, "I longed to take myself captive too and root myself, but you came in that door, with the audacity of despair, wild with the idea of wanting to soar, and I was the most pitiful of spiritless things." Spiritual despair and formal audacity also combine in *Too Late for Logic* (1989). Murphy's fruitful collaboration with Galway's Druid Theatre produced *Bailegangaire* (1985), written especially for Siobhan McKenna. A woman bedridden in a thatched house tries to finish narrating a story to her two granddaughters, who are in despair about their own lives. The story is eventually recollected in full; it also became Murphy's *A Thief of Christmas* (1985). Most of Tom Murphy's plays are both rooted in the past and responsive to the present, of potential interest both in Ireland and internationally.

In 1994, Murphy's first novel, *The Seduction of Morality,* was published to reasonably good reviews. The central character is a woman (incredibly, a prostitute in America) who returns to a web of troubled family relationships in her country town.

CHRISTOPHER GRIFFIN

WORKS: *The Fooleen.* Dixon, Calif.: Proscenium, [1968]. (An early version of *A Crucial Week in the Life of a Grocer's Assistant*); *A Whistle in the Dark.* New York: Samuel French, [1970]/ [Dublin]: Gallery, [1984]; *The Morning after Optimism.* Dublin & Cork: Mercier, [1973]; *The Orphans.* Newark, Del.: Proscenium, [1974]; *The Sanctuary Lamp.* Dublin: Poolbeg, [1976]; *On the Outside/On the Inside.* [Dublin]: Gallery, [1976]; *Famine.* [Dublin]: Gallery, [1977]; *A Crucial Week in the Life of a Grocer's Assistant.* [Dublin]: Gallery/[Newark, Del.]: Proscenium, [1978]; *The Gigli Concert.* [Dublin]: Gallery, [1984]; *Bailegangaire.* [Dublin]: Gallery, [1986]; *Conversations on a Homecoming.* [Dublin]: Gallery, [1986]; *Too Late for Logic.* London: Methuen, 1989; *A*

Whistle in the Dark and Other Plays. [London]: Methuen, [1990]; *Plays: One.* [London]: Methuen, [1992]. (Contains *Famine, The Patriot Game* & *The Blue Macushla*); *Plays: Two.* [London]: Methuen, [1993]. (Contains *Conversations on a Homecoming, Bailegangaire* & *A Thief of Christmas; Plays: Three.* [London]: Methuen, [1994]. (Contains *The Morning after Optimism, Sanctuary Lamp* & *The Gigli Concert*); *The Seduction of Morality.* London: Abacus, 1994. (Novel). REFERENCES: Grene, Nicholas. "Talking, Singing, Storytelling: Tom Murphy's After Tragedy." *Colby Quarterly* 27 (December 1991): 210–224; Griffin, Christopher. "The Plays of Thomas Murphy." Master's thesis, University College, Dublin, 1976; Griffin, Christopher. "Produced, Praised, and Hammered: The Career of Thomas Murphy." *Theatre Ireland* 4 (1984); Lane, Mark. "Theatrical Space and National Place in Four Plays by Thomas Murphy." *Irish University Review* 21 (Autumn–Winter 1991): 219–228; Murray, Christopher, ed. Thomas Murphy Issue. *Irish University Review* (Spring 1987); O'Toole, Fintan. *The Politics of Magic: The Work and Times of Tom Murphy.* Dublin: Raven Arts, 1987/revised ed., Dublin: New Island/London: Nick Hern, [1994].

MURRAY, JOHN FISHER (1811–1865), novelist, essayist, and poet. Murray was born in Belfast on February 11, 1811. He was educated there and at Trinity College, Dublin, taking a degree in medicine. A Young Irelander, he contributed to *The Nation,* * *Dublin University Magazine, Blackwood's,* and many other journals. His amusing *Blackwood's* sketches of London life were reprinted in two volumes, and D. J. O'Donoghue* called his 1841 novel, *The Viceroy,* a "scathing description of life in fashionable Dublin at the beginning of the [nineteenth] century." He died in Dublin on October 20, 1865.

WORKS: *The Viceroy.* London: Murray, 1841. (Novel); *Environs of London.* Edinburgh & London: Blackwood, 1842. (Essays); *The World of London.* Edinburgh & London, 1843. (Essays). REFERENCE: Russell, Matthew. "John Fisher Murray: An Irishman of Letters." *Irish Monthly* 40 (1912): 257–261.

MURRAY, MELISSA

WORK: *Changelings.* Dublin: Attic, [1987]. (Short stories).

MURRAY, PAUL (1947–), poet. Murray was born in Newcastle, County Down, educated at St. Malachy's College, Belfast, and joined the Dominican Order in 1966. He has published three volumes of poetry—*Ritual Poems* (1971), *Rites and Meditations* (1982), and *The Absent Fountain* (1991). His first two volumes are slim collections of free verse, take as their subjects death, sexuality, and relationships, and have an undercurrent of mysticism and faith. They are moving pieces and show the promise that was fulfilled, to a certain extent, in his most recent work, *The Absent Fountain.* That collection explores themes familiar to readers of Murray's earlier work but does so with more maturity and understanding. In addition, Murray turns his attention to his heritage as a Northern writer. Particularly moving is a series of thirteen poems that come under the title of "Homage to the Void." These works explore what mystical philosophers call the silent center of man, the Christic experience, the cosmic consummation. In addition, Murray has published a book of spiritual reflections called *The Mysticism Debate* (1978), a short narrative tale called *Culann and* *the Leprechauns* (1987), and a study of T. S. Eliot titled *T. S. Eliot and Mysticism* (1991).

BERNARD McKENNA

WORKS: *Ritual Poems.* Dublin: New Writers', 1971; *The Mysticism Debate.* Chicago: Franciscan Herald, 1978; *Rites and Meditations.* [Mountrath, Co. Laois]: Dolmen, [1982]; *Culann and the Leprechauns: A Tale of Ireland.* Cork: Mercier, 1987; *The Absent Fountain.* Dublin: Dedalus, 1991; *T. S. Eliot and Mysticism.* London: Macmillan, 1991.

MURRAY, T[HOMAS] C[ORNELIUS] (1873–1959), playwright. Murray was born in Macroom, County Cork, on January 17, 1873. In addition to writing plays, he taught at St. Patrick's College, Dublin, and was headmaster of the model school at Inchicore, County Dublin, from 1915 until his retirement in 1932. He served as director of the Authors' Guild of Ireland and was a member of the Irish Academy of Letters. He died on March 7, 1959, at Ballsbridge, Dublin.

Murray's plays of life in rural Cork reflect the countryman's acquisitive hunger and his fear of poverty and disgrace. *Birthright* (1910), his first Abbey* play, ends with brothers fighting to the death over a patch of farmland. The title character of *Maurice Harte* (1912) continues to study for the priesthood, and suffers a mental breakdown, because his family has gone into debt for his schooling and will be humiliated if he leaves the seminary. In *The Briery Gap* (1917), a man delays marriage to a pregnant girl until he can obtain a farm; she counters by appealing to the ultimate voice of public opinion, the priest. *Spring* (1918) depicts a woman embittered by penury trying to force her aged father-in-law into the workhouse. Even a matchmaking comedy, *Sovereign Love* (Cork, 1909, titled *The Wheel of Fortune;* Abbey, 1913), darkens when a girl is virtually auctioned to the highest bidder.

Incompatible marriage is a recurring theme in Murray's middle period. In *Aftermath* (1922) and *Michaelmas Eve* (1932), a man, prompted by his mother, forsakes the woman he loves and marries the woman with land. *Autumn Fire* (1924) deals with the May–December union of widower Owen Keegan and young Nance Desmond. As gossipers predict, Owen's son Michael is drawn into a love rivalry with his father. *Autumn Fire* is strikingly similar to Eugene O'Neill's tragedy *Desire Under the Elms* (which opened two months after *Autumn Fire*) and does not emerge badly when compared with O'Neill's better known play.

Most of Murray's late efforts were devoted to reworking earlier material. Although he sets *The Blind Wolf* (1928) (afterward titled *The Karavoes*) in Hungary and *A Stag at Bay* in England, he does not expand his dramatic range. *Illumination* (1939) is the *Maurice Harte* theme with a happy ending. Only *The Pipe in the Fields* (1927) is a departure from Murray's basic realism: Peter Keville creates beautiful music and experiences visions when he plays a "magic" fife. But this play, too, contains a veteran Murray character, the well-intentioned, domineering mother. *Spring Horizon* (1937) is a gently paced autobiographical novel of growing up in a Cork village. A planned sequel never materialized.

Although Murray worked with combustible material—murder, insanity, families in conflict (how often the old disable the young), clerical influence, incest—he was not a controversialist. Primeval passions are disciplined by his intense Catholicism, and the result is a darkly brooding view of life. It is enhanced by lyrical passages influenced by Synge,* sad as Synge's can be but never joyfully surging. The comic muse was not his friend; his comedy *A Flutter of Wings* (1929, Gate) was rejected by the Abbey. Of his tragic plays, *Autumn Fire* and *Maurice Harte* have an enduring place in Irish dramatic literature.

WILLIAM J. FEENEY

WORKS: *Birthright*. Dublin: Maunsel, 1911; *Maurice Harte*. Dublin: Maunsel, 1912/reprinted with *A Stag at Bay,* London: Allen & Unwin, 1934; *Spring and Other Plays (Sovereign Love* and *The Briery Gap)*. Dublin: Talbot, 1917; *Aftermath: A Play in Three Acts*. Dublin: Talbot, 1922; *Autumn Fire: A Play in Three Acts*. London: G. Allen & Unwin, 1925; *The Pipe in the Fields: A Play in One Act,* in *The Dublin Magazine* 2 (April–June 1927): 7–30. Reprinted with *Birthright*. London: G. Allen & Unwin, 1928; *Michaelmas Eve: A Play in Three Acts*. London: G. Allen & Unwin, 1932; *Spring Horizon*. London: T. Nelson & Sons, 1937. A typescript of *Illumination* is in the Boston College Library. REFERENCES: Connolly, Terence L. "T. C. Murray, The Quiet Man." *The Catholic World* 190 (March 1960): 364–369; Fitzgibbon, T. Gerald. "The Elements of Conflict in the Plays of T. C. Murray." *Studies* 64 (Spring 1975): 59–65; DeGiacomo, Albert J. "Remembering T. C. Murray." *Irish University Review* 25 (Autumn/Winter 1995): 298–307; Hogan, Thomas. "T. C. Murray." *Envoy* 3 (November 1950): 138–148; Macardle, Dorothy. "The Dramatic Art of T. C. Murray." *The Dublin Magazine* 2 (January 1925): 393–398; Ó hAodha, Micheál. "T. C. Murray and Some Critics." *Studies* 47 (Summer 1958): 185–191.

MURRAY, WILLIAM [MARTIN] COTTER (1929–), novelist. Murray was born in Miltown Malbay, County Clare, on June 18, 1929. He emigrated to the United States in 1949, served in the Korean War, and became a naturalized U.S. citizen in 1952. He received a B.S. from Southern Connecticut State College in 1956, an M.A. from the University of Iowa in 1959, and a Ph.D. from Iowa in 1964. In 1956 he joined the University of Iowa Writers Workshop, and since 1970 he has been a professor of English at Iowa. His first novel, *Michael Joe* (1965), is set in the small town of Corrigbeg in County Clare and persuasively depicts the effects of pre-European Union Ireland on the shopkeeper Michael Joe McCarthy and those close to him. Authentic and compulsively readable, it is one of a long line of modern novels and plays—from Brinsley MacNamara* and T. C. Murray* to Patrick McCabe* and Brian Friel*—that have flayed the narrowness of Irish village life. Michael Joe is large, handsome, sensual, good-natured, an able shopkeeper, and a canny cattle dealer. Rebuffed by a young woman he has tried to seduce, he then falls in love with her and is about to marry her when he discovers that she once had a child out of wedlock in England. He drops her instantly but goes through torments of jealousy when she marries a bank clerk. He himself marries a farmer's daughter whom he does not love and who is repelled and frightened by sex. His mother and his increasingly religious wife indoctrinate his son so thoroughly that the boy becomes a narrow and self-centered priest, while Michael Joe becomes ever more an unhappy and drunken lout. As a parable of blighted lives caused by the mores of an insular village, the book is both eminently glum and eminently plausible.

WORKS: *Michael Joe*. London: Muller, 1965; *A Long Way from Home*. Boston: Houghton Mifflin, 1974.

N

na gCOPALEEN, MYLES. *See* O'NOLAN, BRIAN.

NALLY, T[HOMAS] H[ENRY] (ca. 1869–1932), playwright. Nally was born in County Mayo around 1869. He is known (though probably only to historians) for his play *The Spancel of Death,* which was to have been produced at the Abbey Theatre* during Easter Week 1916. After the Rising, no attempt was made to produce the play, which was thought to be too gloomy for the times. In fact, it was never produced, nor should be, although a modern editor has reassembled most of it from the actors' "sides." In 1917, Nally's Irish fairy pantomime, *Finn Varra Maa,* was produced for matinees at the Theatre Royal and was rather successful. During the war years, he also wrote the books for a few Irish musical revues, such as *The King of Dublin.*

WORKS: *Finn Varra Maa.* Dublin: Talbot, 1917; *The Aonach Tailteann and the Tailteann Games.* Dublin: Talbot, 1923. (History); Adele Dalsimer, comp. & ed., *The Spancel of Death.* [Holbrook, N.Y.: Irish Studies]: 1983. REFERENCES: Dalsimer, Adele. "Introduction." In *The Spancel of Death.* [Holbrook, N.Y.: Irish Studies]: 1983, n.p.

NATION, THE (1842–1892), periodical. *The Nation,* probably the most famous Irish periodical, was founded by Sir Charles Gavan Duffy,* Thomas Davis,* and John Blake Dillon (1816–1866) in 1842. It was initially the mouthpiece of the Young Ireland movement, and its policy of idealistic and vehement nationalism quickly made itself felt. After the collapse of Daniel O'Connell's proscribed mass meeting at Clontarf in 1843, the fervently patriotic spirit of the paper grew ever more inflammatory, and it aroused the enthusiasm of thousands. When Lord Plunket was asked to describe the tone of the paper, he simply and aptly replied "Wolfe Tone." However, the reclamation of the patriotic past was done to inflame a revolutionary future and to ensure complete separation from England.

The Nation was primarily political, but it also attempted to raise the national consciousness of the country by fostering a cultural awareness as well as an historical pride. Through the publisher James Duffy,* the paper disseminated over twenty volumes of its "Library of Ireland." These books, issued cheaply at a shilling in paper wrappers, were widely circulated. They contained collections of ballad poetry and songs, novels by Carleton,* essays by Davis, biographical sketches of earlier Irish writers, as well as lives of great Irishmen such as Aodh O'Neill and Curran and several works of history.

The writers for the journal itself constitute a Who's-Who of Irish literary talent at midcentury—Davis, Mitchel,* Mangan,* Lalor,* and a huge group of new ballad writers and poets, the most famous of whose work was published in *The Spirit of the Nation* and *The New Spirit of the Nation.* However, apart from a handful of poems mainly by Davis and Mangan, the poetry of *The Nation* is conventional, imitative popular poetry in which much more emotion than ability is apparent. Still, many of the pieces by John de Jean Frazer,* Denis Florence MacCarthy,* John Kells Ingram,* and Richard D'Alton Williams* have remained in the consciousness of several generations of readers. Many of the poets were women who wrote under pseudonyms, the most famous being Speranza, Mary, Eva, Thomasine, and Finola. Speranza was Jane Francesca Elgee, later Lady Wilde*; Mary was Ellen Mary Patrick Downing (1828–1869); Eva was Mary Anne Kelly (ca. 1825–1910); Thomasine was Olivia Knight, later Mrs. Hope Connolly (ca. 1830–1909); and Finola was Elizabeth Willoughby Treacy who married the Cork poet Ralph Varian. Both Mary and Eva were in love with Young Irelanders who were exiled. Eva was in love with Kevin Izod O'Doherty who could have been pardoned had he admitted his guilt. When he asked Eva's advice, she said, "Be a man and face the worst. I'll wait for you however long the sentence may be." The sentence was ten years; two days after his return they were married. Mary was in love with another *Nation* poet, Joseph Brennan (1828–1857), but, as A. M. Sullivan* writes, "Less happy was the romance of Mary's fate. . . . Alas! in foreign climes he learned to forget home vows. 'Mary' sank under the blow. She put by the lyre, and in utter seclusion from the world lingered for a while; but ere long the spring flowers blossomed on her grave." Actually, Mary entered the North Presentation Convent in Cork in 1849, taking the name of Sister Mary Alphonsus, and she did not die until twenty years later.

In 1848, the Young Irelanders had an ineffective Rising, the only military engagement being, as Conor Cruise O'Brien* puts it, "under the chivalrous and incompetent leadership of William Smith O'Brien." The Rising was swiftly put down, *The Nation* was quashed, and the principal leaders transported to Australia. A new series of *The Nation* was begun in 1849, and, under one editor or another, the journal continued until 1896. It was the initial volumes, however, which fomented, as Edmund Curtis* put it, "a revival of the Gaelic, militant, and aristocratic spirit, and the cult of 'the Dark Rosaleen', formerly expressed in the native tongue but now poured into the new mould of the English language which was steadily spreading among the common people.'' It was also the initial volumes and the writings of Davis, Mitchel, Lalor, and the rest that kept alive for succeeding generations the spirit of revolt and of national pride in the country's history and culture. What is called the Literary Renaissance, that astonishing movement which began at the end of the century and that fostered Yeats,* Hyde,* Synge,* and Stephens,* most assuredly had its seeds in the simple verses of the poets of *The Nation.*

WORKS: *The Spirit of the Nation.* Dublin: J. Duffy, 1843; *The Spirit of the Nation, Part II.* Dublin: J. Duffy, 1843; *A Voice from the Prison, or, The Voice of the Nation.* Dublin: J. Duffy, 1844. (Prose); *The New Spirit of the Nation,* ed. with an Introduction by Martin Mac Dermott. London: T. Fisher Unwin/Dublin: Sealy/New York: Kennedy, 1894.

NELSON, DOROTHY (1952–   ), novelist. Nelson was born on December 15, 1952, in Bray, County Wicklow, and educated there. She worked as secretary and receptionist in Dublin and London. Her two short novels treat of the brutality of life in two working-class families and are told from various points of view. *In Night's City* (1982) is the more obliquely told but powerfully depicts the plight of a mother and daughter who are terrorized, beaten, and sexually abused by their husband and father. The story ends with the mother's funeral and the daughter's imaginary alter ego saying to the girl, ''Remember this. All men are bastards.'' The last paragraph is the daughter's poignant cry:

My Ma was a good woman. Da beat us sometimes but that's because we were bad. He loved us all the same. And my Ma loved me. My Ma LOVED ME. Someday I'll get married and have children just like she did. Everything will be all right then. I don't hate being a woman. I don't. I don't.

The novel was televised by Channel 4 and won the Rooney Prize in 1983.

Nelson's second novel, *Tar and Feathers* (1987), is no less ferocious in subject matter and concerns a father who exposes himself to children, rapes and batters a woman, and is finally jailed for an Irish Republican Army murder; a mother who retreats into alcoholism; and a fourteen-year-old son who at the end happily joins an amateur rock band. Although he fantasizes about how the pearly teeth of one of the members ''cut into my flesh and then he sucked lovingly on his dinner,'' the book concludes two lines later with his remark, ''I could hear the sweet sounds of my voice soaring like a bird over the rooftops.'' Part of Nelson's point seems to be that people can find some warped hope and happiness even in hopelessness and misery, and much of the strength of the book derives from her tolerance, understanding, and sympathy for her characters. The book is probably less quirkily told and more accessible than her first and is narrated by internal monologues of the three main characters. These are seemingly simple, seemingly ambling reflections with a good deal of blackish humor and brackish charm that effectively counterpoint the horrific action. For instance, as the mother says:

I never managed to give up the tablets or the cigarettes. My only success was with humans. I have learned to ignore them. I fall asleep in the middle of a chat.

Or:

They all go to mass and take an interest in religion, including my sons. I am the only sane one left here, the rest have long since been bought off lock, stock and barrel. A splash of water on their foreheads and they're booking their flights to heaven. A blessing from the priest and they're sitting on God's lap in their best bib and tucker. God give me patience.

Or:

God spits on the innocent. He hates babies, they give him the creeps. After all he's a man, what does a man want a baby for. He doesn't want a baby, that's it in a nutshell. . . . It's the same all over the world, who is the arsehole in the sky to tell us what to do?

Nelson's two savage and moving novels are, both in matter and in manner, accomplished and highly distinctive work.

WORKS: *In Night's City.* [Dublin]: Wolfhound, [1982]; *Tar and Feathers.* [Dublin]: Wolfhound, [1987].

NEW WRITERS' PRESS (1967–), publishing house. This press was founded by Michael Smith,* Irene Smith, and Trevor Joyce* and has published about fifty volumes of poems. It introduced such writers as Paul Durcan,* Augustus Young,* Gerard Smith,* Leland Bardwell,* and MacDara Woods* as well as Smith and Joyce. It published neglected avant-garde poets of the 1930s, notably, Thomas MacGreevy* and Brian Coffey.* It also published translations of notable poets like Mallarmé, Borges, and Machado; and it utilized such Irish translators as Pearse Hutchinson,* Tom MacIntyre,* and Coffey. In 1969, the press initiated a lively literary magazine, *The Lace Curtain.* Edited by Smith and Joyce, it appeared sporadically into the early 1970s.

NEWMAN, JOAN (1942–), poet.

WORK: *Coming of Age.* Belfast: Blackstaff, 1995.

NÍ CHUILLEANÁIN, EILÉAN (1942–), poet. Ní Chuilleanáin was one of three children of the novelist and critic Eilis Dillon* and Cormac Ó Chuilleanain, a professor of Irish at University College, Cork. Raised in a home at the university, Ní Chuilleanáin recalls a happy and intellectually stimulating childhood. Educated at the local Ursuline Convent, she moved on to earn a B.A. in literature and history in 1962 and an M.A. in literature in 1964 at Cork. Early influences, including the watery landscape of her native city and an interest in history, continue to have a strong impact on her work.

Study in Elizabethan literature at Oxford from 1964 to 1966 was followed by a return to Ireland, where Ní Chuilleanáin joined the faculty at Trinity College. Active in Irish poetry circles, she was one of four founding coeditors of the literary magazine *Cyphers*. In 1973, she won the Patrick Kavanagh* Award for her first volume of poems, *Acts and Monuments*.

Ní Chuilleanáin's early volumes all challenge traditional images of heroic action. Alluding to John Foxe's martyrology, *Acts and Monuments* (1972) focuses on the darker side of survival, confronting a conventional Christian emphasis on the importance of human will and the value of an afterlife with a folkloric response to fate, death, and natural disaster. Filled with images of islands and boats, the poems contrast the uncontrollable and mysterious sea with the solidity of land.

The Second Voyage (1977, 1986) includes many of the poems from *Acts and Monuments* and others from a 1975 collection, *Site of Ambush*. Odysseus is a major figure in *The Second Voyage,* portrayed as a frustrated hero, trapped by his need to control his ultimately uncontrollable surroundings. "Site of Ambush" also develops this theme in a long poem set in the Irish Troubles of the early 1920s, where a group of soldiers die as they execute a carefully planned military strategy. In many of these poems, figures like Noah, John the Baptist, and Odysseus are humanized and, by extension, appear as victims rather than as heroes. Male voyagers and adventurers are sometimes contrasted to females, like the one in "The Lady's Tower" who is anchored to a domestic and natural landscape. Ní Chuilleanáin has suggested that this poem be read as a response to Yeats'* poem "The Tower," with the female figure in her poem, unlike Yeats' persona, integrated into the landscape around her.

Two other volumes, *Cork* (1977) and *The Rose-Geranium* (1981), fuse Ní Chuilleanáin's interest in history with meditations on personal experiences. The poems in *Cork,* intended to complement Brian Lalor's drawings of Cork City, describe the changing face of what Lalor calls a "city reeling from the cataclysm of 'urban renewal.'" *The Rose-Geranium* contains some revised poems from *Cork* and an eighteen-poem title sequence on love, time, and loss. The tone of this sequence is decidedly pessimistic, as seen in the four lines of "Waters Between."

Ní Chuilleanáin's 1989 volume, *The Magdalene Sermon,* focuses almost exclusively on female subjects and personae. Catholic saints, *sheela-na-gigs,* mythic goddesses, and contemporary women coexist in a volume in which female voices and values are preeminent. "The Informant" contrasts the world of folklore with that of contemporary technology as a young man's tape recorder, symbol of modern forms of communication, breaks down while he listens to an old woman, the repository of traditional wisdom. In this volume, Mary Magdalene, who, according to legend, preached in Marseilles after the death of Christ, is a "voice glittering in the wilderness," one of the many female voices we hear. Short-listed for the *Irish Times*/Aer Lingus Award and nominated for the European Literature Prize, *The Magdalene Sermon* was recognized by critics as a significant contribution to Irish poetry.

Ní Chuilleanáin is noted for her intellectually rigorous poetry and for her sharp, complex images, like those in "Fallen Tree in a Churchyard," an elegy for the writer John Jordan,* which compares the uprooted tree roots to the dead man. Ní Chuilleanáin's poems often grow from narrative or dramatic scenes. Her lyrics contain little direct statement, and her later poems increasingly develop voices in monologues and dialogues. In a review of *The Magdalene Sermon* in the Spring 1991 issue of the *Irish Literary Supplement*, Jonathan Allison suggests that Ní Chuilleanáin "seems incapable of writing a superfluous line."

In addition to her poetry, Ní Chuilleanáin has edited a volume of essays, *Irish Women: Image and Achievement* (1985), and an edition of Maria Edgeworth's* *Belinda* (1993); she has coedited, with J. D. Pheifer, *Noble and Joyous Histories: English Romances, 1375–1650* (1993). A lecturer in English and fellow of Trinity College, Ní Chuilleanáin lives in Dublin with her husband, the poet MacDara Woods,* and their son, Niall. A new volume of poems, *The Brazen Serpent*, appeared in late 1994.

PATRICIA BOYLE HABERSTROH

WORKS: *Acts and Monuments.* [Dublin]: Gallery, [1972]; *Site of Ambush.* [Dublin]: Gallery, [1975]; *The Second Voyage.* [Dublin]: Gallery, [1977], [1986]/Winston-Salem, N.C.: Wake Forest University Press, 1977; *Cork.* [Dublin]: Gallery, [1977]; *The Rose-Geranium.* [Dublin]: Gallery, [1981]; ed., *Irish Women: Image and Achievement.* Dublin: Arlen House, 1985; *The Magdalene Sermon.* [Dublin]: Gallery, [1989]; *The Magdalene Sermon and Earlier Poems.* Winston-Salem, N.C.: Wake Forest University Press, 1991; ed., *Belinda* by Maria Edgeworth. London: Everyman, 1993; ed., with J. D. Pheifer. *Noble and Joyous Histories: English Romances, 1375–1650.* Dublin: Irish Academic, 1993: *The Brazen Serpent.* [Oldcastle, Co. Meath]: Gallery, [1994]. REFERENCE: McWilliams Consalvo, Deborah. "Interview with Eileán Ní Chuilleanáin." *Irish Literary Supplement* 12 (Fall 1993): 15–17.

NÍ DHÓMHNAILL, NUALA (1952–   ), poet.

Ní Dhómhnaill was born in England to Irish parents but educated in Ireland. She received a B.A. from University College, Cork, in 1972, and spent several years abroad in Turkey and Holland. Although she writes in Irish, many of her poems have been translated into English.

WORKS IN TRANSLATION: *Selected Poems.* Dublin: Raven Arts, 1986. Translated by Michael Hartnett; *Selected Poems/Rogha Danta.* Dublin: Raven Arts, 1988. Translated by Michael Hartnett; *Pharaoh's Daughter.* [Oldcastle, Co. Meath]: Gallery, 1990]. Various translators; *The Astrakhan Cloak.* [Oldcastle, Co. Meath]: Gallery, [1992]. Translated by Paul Muldoon.

NÍ DHUIBHNE, EILÍS (1954–   ), short story writer, novelist, poet, children's writer, and playwright.

Born on February 22, 1954, Ní Dhuibhne grew up in Dublin, receiving her early education through Irish. For a decade, she pursued a passion for folklore at University College, Dublin, earning B.A., M.Phil., and Ph.D. degrees and spending a year researching in Denmark. She lectures on Irish folklore, and for some years she has worked as an assistant keeper in the National Library of Ireland. Her debut collection, *Blood and Water* (1988), draws upon her rich knowledge of folklore in tales like "Midwife to the Fairies" and the splendidly gruesome "Fulfilment." Yet these stories also reflect the angst of contemporary Ireland, offering a bittersweet perception of what has been lost as the old Ireland has given way to the new. This sense of loss is treated more explicitly in the second collection, *Eating Women Is Not Recommended* (1991). In "The Flowering," Ní Dhuibhne writes:

A real language has crept into the sound archives of linguistic departments and folklore institutions, and it has faded away from people's tongues. In one or two generations. In *her* generation. It has been a time of endings. Of deaths, great and small.

A novel, *The Bray House* (1990), ventures into uncharted territory, as a Swedish archaeologist sets sail for an Ireland devastated by nuclear disaster. Ní Dhuibhne received an Arts Council Bursary in 1987 and has won awards for poetry and for her children's books written under the pseudonym of Elizabeth O'Hara. In 1994, she became chairperson of the Irish Writers' Union.

IVY BANNISTER

WORKS: *Blood and Water*. Dublin: Attic, 1988. (Short stories); *The Bray House*. Dublin: Attic, 1990. (Novel); *The Uncommon Cormorant*. Dublin: Poolbeg, 1990. (Children's book); *Eating Women Is Not Recommended*. Dublin: Attic, 1991. (Short stories); *Hugo and the Sunshine Girl*. Dublin: Poolbeg, 1991. (Children's book); ed., with Seamas O Cathain. *Viking Ale*. Boethius, 1991. (Festschrift for Professor Bo Almqvist).

NOLAN, CHRISTOPHER (1965–   ), man of letters. Nolan was born on September 6, 1965, at County Hospital Mullingar. Severely brain-damaged because of a difficult birth, he grew up with virtually no control over his body. Nevertheless, like Christy Brown* and Davoren Hanna,* he had an acute and receptive mind, a supportive family, intelligent teachers, and caring friends. He also had an indomitable spirit and an exuberant love of words. He was educated in Dublin at the Central Remedial School, Mount Temple Comprehensive, and Trinity College. His first collection, *Dam-Burst of Dreams* (1981), was issued by an English publisher when he was only sixteen and contains his writings from age eleven to age fourteen. Perhaps the most notable of them is the first, "My Autobiography Entitled A Mammy Encomimum," which, in its richness of expression, would have been remarkable no matter who had written it, however healthy, and at whatever age. The volume also contains poems, letters, and a couple of plays. Nolan's full-length autobiography, *Under the Eye of the Clock,* received the 1987 Whitbread Book of the Year Award, and its rich and frequently eloquent style earned him comparisons with such modern wordsmiths as Joyce* and Dylan Thomas. In modern Irish literary criticism, the word "brilliant" has become debased by its constant and often feckless use; it does, however, without exaggeration, describe Nolan's talent.

A demurrer must also be recorded. Like Brown and Hanna, Nolan's giddy and gaudy use of words can attain an individual eloquence. It can also be floridly, unreadably bad. Its excess of alliteration, for instance, can rival that of the astonishingly awful Amanda M'Kittrick Ros.* For a random example:

Years budded hushed, bubbling bubbly bubbles, but bubbles burst and leave no trace. The father tried to nylon-thread his love for his broken breastplate boy by rescuing history in plonk of poetic but nomdeplumed, headgritted charting.

It seems terribly harsh to criticize what Nolan has aptly described as "the surrealism of a creativity which had, chaos-like, nearly clung forever to the lip of the abyss of hell." However, if Nolan is going to be a brilliant writer, rather than a brilliant, appallingly handicapped person who writes, it is a criticism to be made. An even more difficult problem to grapple with is that of widening the author's subject matter to a horizon beyond the wheelchair. This was a problem that Christy Brown struggled with not very successfully in his later books. However, Christopher Nolan is used to struggling with problems.

WORKS: *Dam-Burst of Dreams: The Writings of Christopher Nolan.* London: Weidenfeld & Nicolson, [1981]; *Under the Clock: The Life Story of Christopher Nolan.* London: Weidenfeld & Nicolson, 1987.

NOONAN, GILLMAN (1937–   ), short story writer. Noonan was born in Kanturk, County Cork, in 1937. He graduated from University College, Cork, and then spent several years working on a German newspaper in Hamburg. His first collection of stories, *A Sexual Relationship* (1976), has five or six quite striking pieces—the title story, "Goodbye Gran," "Dear Parents, I'm Working for the EEC!" "Money for the Town," "The Wedding Suit," and the fantastic sequences of "Writer Story." He does not entirely escape the occupational blight of being a modern Irish writer, and the first story, "Between the Cells," is the quintessence of Irish dreariness. The pejorative connotations of the writing equal anything in McGahern* or Broderick* or Trevor.* For instance, from only ten lines on page 8:

a thousand paunchy insects all carrying bags of stout . . . dry flaking skin . . . closing in . . . tormented . . . slow decay beneath the mucus of a smelly cubicle . . . slime eddying around my feet while men prowled and grunted outside at the urinals.

The stories range from simple and static character sketches to rather complicated studies such as the excellent title story. Despite some tendency to the essay rather than the dramatic style, several of the stories are technically inventive, humorously observed, and whimsically imaginative. *Friends and Occasional Lovers* (1982) does not extend or develop the good qualities of Noonan's first book. It is mainly about varieties of sexual nonexperience, in which things never happen or stop happening or happen without being important. In one of the best stories, "Haiku and High Octane," the interesting leading character is not even quite sure what did happen; and most of the stories are rather embalmed in the main characters' ruminations. One notable exception is "Excerpts from the Journal of a Confirmed Bachelor," in which Noonan develops a distinctive narrative voice.

WORKS: *A Sexual Relationship and Other Stories.* Dublin: Poolbeg, [1976]; *Friends and Occasional Lovers.* [Swords, Co. Dublin]: Poolbeg, [1982].

NORTON, CAROLINE ELIZABETH SARAH (1808–1877), poet and novelist. Brilliant, beautiful, an able editor, a prolific poet, a writer of lengthy novels, a playwright, and a political pamphleteer who effected some major legislation about the relations of Victorian men and women, Caroline Norton was the most dynamic of Tom Sheridan's* children. Her facility with both her pen and tongue reminded everyone that she was a true granddaughter of Richard Brinsley Sheridan.* Yet she had one of the unhappiest lives of all the Sheridans. She was born in London on March 22, 1808, the younger sister of the future Lady Dufferin.* After her father, Tom, died in 1816, she moved with her mother and six brothers and sisters into Hampton Court, an accommodation arranged by the duke of York, a friend of her grandfather. Although her two sisters married brilliantly, Caroline was not so fortunate. Her husband, George Chapple Norton, was as brutal a cad as anything that Victorian fiction could envisage, and the couple separated in 1836. In that year Norton cited Lord Melbourne, the prime minister, as correspondent in a divorce suit, although Norton had actually encouraged Melbourne's friendship with Caroline in order to secure his own advancement. The suit was defeated, but the publicity caused Caroline to be hounded all her life by scandal-mongering journalists. For the next six years, Norton refused to let her see her children and relented only after the youngest died. Her sufferings led her to write pamphlets that helped to change British law about the custody of infants and the legal rights of married women.

Despite a hasty temper, Caroline was a loving and witty woman who inspired the lifelong friendships of many brilliant men. Melbourne died protesting her innocence, but the stuffy Victorians always suspected her. Even George Meredith in his novel *Diana of the Crossways,* for which she was the inspiration, implied that she had betrayed government secrets. Her husband mercifully died in 1869, and in spring of 1877 Caroline married an old friend, Sir W. Stirling-Maxwell. However, she died only a few months later, on June 15.

The publication when she was eleven of *The Dandies Rout,* a pastiche of a famous series called *The Dandy Books,* by her and her sister Helen, began a prolific writing career. Her poetry, which often touched on the condition of women, children, and factory workers, was as highly regarded as Elizabeth Barrett Browning's, and Hartley Coleridge referred to her as "the Byron of Modern Poetesses." Some of her poetry is remembered today, and, although hardly literature, it is always fluent and sometimes fun, for instance, "The Arab's Farewell to his Steed" or "Bingen on the Rhine," which begins with marvelous panache and triteness:

A soldier of the Legion lay dying in Algiers,
There was lack of woman's nursing, there was dearth of woman's tears.

Her lengthy novels—*The Wife and Woman's Reward* (1836), *Stuart of Dunleath* (1851), *Lost and Saved* (1865), and *Old Sir Douglas* (1867)—are much alike and forgotten today. They resemble those of her mother, Henrietta, and of her great-grandmother Frances.* Her heroines are women of impregnable virtue who, either by the machinations of others or their own overscrupulousness, are made to suffer and suffer. Her villains are usually brutal husbands or scheming sisters-in-law. Her greatest faults as a novelist are that she insufficiently dramatizes and that she is given to intruding into her narrative long, sententious moral essays. She does have some successes of characterization, but the novels were too influenced by her own unhappy life and lack the wit and humor for which she was renowned.

She occasionally visited Ireland to see her sister.

WORKS IN PRINT: *Selected Writings of Caroline Norton.* Delmar, N.Y.: Scholars' Facsimiles & Reprints, 1978. (Contains selections from *The Sorrows of Rosalie and Other Poems, The Undying One and Other Poems, A Plain Letter to the Lord Chancellor on the Infant Custody Bill . . . , The Dream and Other Poems, The Child of the Islands, English Laws for Women in the Nineteenth Century, A Letter to the Queen on Lord Chancellor Cranworth's Marriage and Divorce Bill,* and the novel *Lost and Saved.* There are an introduction and notes by James O. Hoge and Jane Marcus.) REFERENCES: Acland, Alice. *Caroline Norton.* London: Constable, 1948; Perkins, Jane Gray. *The Life of Mrs. Norton.* London: John Murray, 1909. Margaret Foster has a chapter on Norton from a feminist view in *Significant Sisters: The Grassroots of Active Feminism, 1839–1939.* London: Martin Secker & Warburg, 1984.

O

O'BEIRNE, CHARLES

WORK: *The Good People.* [Belfast]: Blackstaff, [1985]. (Novel).

O'BRIEN, CHARLOTTE GRACE (1845–1909), poet, dramatist, novelist, and emigrant rights activist. O'Brien was the daughter of William Smith O'Brien and his wife, the former Miss Gubbert of High Park, County Limerick. She was born on November 23, 1845, at Cahirmoyle, County Limerick, one of five sons and two daughters. The O'Brien family held a somewhat unusual position, for they were both wealthy Protestant landlords and members of the native Irish aristocracy, claiming genealogical connections back to Brian Boru. Charlotte was three years old when her father was convicted of high treason and exiled to Tasmania. In 1854, he was allowed to return to Europe, and the family joined him in Brussels. They were allowed to return to Ireland in 1856, when Charlotte was eleven years old.

Following the death of his wife in 1861, Smith O'Brien took his daughters to live in Killiney, near Dublin. Later, Charlotte returned to her brother Edward's home at Cahirmoyle to finish her education under the instruction of a Miss D'Arcy. She joined her father and brother William at Bangor in Wales, where her father died in 1864. Charlotte accompanied his body back to Dublin before returning to Cahirmoyle. Mary O'Brien, Edward's wife, became a close friend, and Charlotte wrote a series of poems in her honor.

Deafness appears to have been a hereditary trait for Smith O'Brien's children. Stephen Gwynn,* Charlotte's nephew, recalls that all seven were afflicted to some degree with hearing problems. Charlotte's hearing began rapidly to deteriorate in 1866. By the age of thirty-five, she was nearly deaf.

In 1868, Mary O'Brien died, leaving the care of her husband and three children to Charlotte. For the next ten years, she was fully occupied with that task. When Edward's children left for boarding school, she moved to a home of her own, Ardanoir, near Mt. Trenchard. The famine of 1879–1880 directed her attention away from her previous interest in archaeology toward the Land League. She determined to make Irish emigration her primary concern, particularly the shipboard conditions for female emigrants. She founded an emigrant home in Queenstown, where she provided lodging for 105 people at a time. About 3,000 emigrants a year stayed in her boardinghouse. Through her efforts, the shipboard conditions were greatly improved. Horses were no longer stabled with the steerage passengers, and sleeping berths were rearranged to separate married couples, unmarried men, and unmarried women. After closing the Queenstown home in 1882, Charlotte lived quietly at Ardanoir, caring for her pet dogs. In later life, she converted to Catholicism. She died on June 3, 1909, and is buried at Knockpatrick.

Stephen Gwynn's selections from his Aunt Charlotte's work include a lengthy memoir, plus a selection of poems and essays. The poetry is generally commemorative of people or events. Charlotte occasionally wrote several poems on, or to, the same subject over several years, such as her four "Gladstone" poems, written from 1869 to 1886. Her essay "The Feminine Animal" explores the relationship between male and female, especially noting Darwin's theories and the development of engendered roles. Her comment on the nature of the spinster is self-revealing: "A woman is herself, and by herself alone, is required to be as hard and as well able to combat with the world as man." Her final advice to mothers is to teach their daughters to forsake the whims of fashion in preference to "work and cleanliness, truth, modesty, and pure womanhood."

ANNE COLMAN

WORKS: *Light and Shade*. London: Kegan Paul, 1878; *A Tale of Venice: A Drama and Lyrics*. Dublin: M. H. Gill, 1880; *Lyrics*. London: Kegan Paul, 1886; *Cahirmoyle, of the Old Home*. Limerick, 1888; *Charlotte Grace O'Brien, Selections from Her Writings and Correspondence, with Memoir by Stephen Gwynn*. Dublin: Maunsel, 1909. REFERENCES: Coleman, James. "From South and West." *Irish Book Lover* 1 (September 1909); 21–22; Keogh, M. C. "Charlotte Grace O'Brien." *Irish Monthly* 38 (May 1910): 241–245; O'Kennedy, Richard. "With the Emigrant." *Irish Monthly* 38 (May 1910): 661–672; Russell, Matthew. "Our Poets, No. 20: Charlotte Grace O'Brien." *Irish Monthly* 16 (December 1888): 728–733.

O'BRIEN, CONOR CRUISE (1917–   ), politician, historian, and man of letters. O'Brien was born on November 3, 1917. His father was a well-known journalist, and his mother was Kathleen Sheehy, who appears as Miss Ivors in Joyce's* story "The Dead." O'Brien received a Ph.D. from Trinity College, Dublin.

Where other men have been content to lead but one life, it sometimes appears that O'Brien has been determined to live five. He has been an academic administrator (at vice chancellor level), a journalist (editor of *The Observer*), a politician (an Irish Cabinet minister from 1973 to 1977), a diplomat (the representative of the United Nations secretary-general in Katanga in 1961 and author of a brilliant book based on the experience), and playwright whose work has appeared in Dublin and on Broadway. This achievement is all the more spectacular when it is recalled that his most enduring achievements lie in a different field yet again—his many books of literary and historical comment on Irish and other affairs.

Yet, in fact, O'Brien's career had a relatively slow start. He did not publish his first book, *Maria Cross* (1952, under the pseudonym of Donat O'Donnell), until he was thirty-five. He followed this five years later with *Parnell and His Party* (1957), a meticulous study of the Home Rule Party of the 1880s. Until this point, O'Brien had had a spell as a schoolteacher in the north of Ireland before joining the Department of External Affairs in 1944, where he was to specialize in anti-Partitionist propaganda.

In the 1970s, O'Brien emerged as one of the outstanding figures of the academic New Left; as Albert Schweitzer Professor at New York University from 1965 to 1969, he was well known for his opposition to the Vietnam War. His book on Albert Camus (1969) made much of his subject's colonial mentality. Even then, however, O'Brien was hardly a typical "movement" intellectual. He had no real interest in Marxist theory. His analysis of the Easter Rising of 1916, at the moment of its fiftieth anniversary in 1966, appeared both in the conservative *Spectator* and *New Left Review,* a unique feat. O'Brien's intellectual love affair with conservative philosopher Edmund Burke* and his determination to flesh out Burke's Irish context began in his 1969 introduction to the Penguin *Reflections on the Revolution in France.* It was 1992 before he achieved one of his life's great ambitions and produced his empathic and intriguing full-length study of Burke. The warm style of *The Great Melody* is in marked contrast to his equally brilliant *Parnell and His Party,* in that the earlier work is characterized by a rather cold, detached, even uncurious attitude toward his subject's personality, political or otherwise.

In short, O'Brien's gifts for heterodoxy were already well established before his great apostasy in Irish nationalist eyes. His steady adoption of a more or less openly Ulster Unionist position following the publication of his *States of Ireland* (1972), a book based partly on his wide historical learning but also on his political experiences as the Northern crisis continued, provoked anger and debate in Dublin. By this time, O'Brien was undoubtedly nationalist Ireland's best-known intellectual and man of affairs; given his broad civil rights and "progressive" profile, his "conversion" was, for many, all the harder to take. Yet his refusal to act as a fellow traveler for terrorism did more to preserve the ties of affection between Belfast and Dublin in a difficult time than any other single act. With *Negotiations,* his Ewart-Biggs lectures given in 1977, O'Brien signaled that there could be no turning back and pressed on with this new course.

Throughout the 1980s, O'Brien continued to comment on events in a decidedly nonnationalist spirit. He was an opponent of the Anglo-Irish Agreement in 1985, and in 1993–1994 he was highly suspicious of the Hume-Adams peace process. In the view of some, he was disoriented and even discomfited by its apparent success. He was perhaps the victim of his own moral seriousness. O'Brien's hero, Edmund Burke, spoke polemically of "a species of men to whom a state of order could become a sentence of obscurity,'' adding that it is ''no wonder that, by a sort of sinister piety, they cherish in their turn the disorders which are the parents of all their consequences.'' O'Brien viewed the Irish Republican Army in this light. He could not imagine or accept the media triumphs that the Sinn Féin leadership was allowed to substitute for the bitter realities of armed struggle. More profoundly, if—as others allege and not without reason—several key republican tenets were abandoned in 1994, if revisionism had broken out even in the republican movement, then part of the credit must lie with one of its arch critics, Conor Cruise O'Brien.

Above all, O'Brien appears as perhaps the greatest of a distinguished generation at Trinity College, Dublin. A restless intellectual curiosity—fueled by regular pit stops as a visiting professor at top American universities—combined with a vigorous, witty, and durable prose style meant that he retained the capacity to influence both public and intellectual debate well into the 1990s.

He is married to Maire Mhac an tSaoi, the Irish-language poet, and the father of the fiction writer Kate Cruise O'Brien.*

PAUL BEW

PRINCIPAL WORKS: As Donat O'Donnell: *Maria Cross: Imaginative Patterns in a Group of Modern Catholic Writers.* New York & Toronto: Oxford University Press/London: Chatto & Windus, 1952; *Parnell and His Party, 1880–1890.* Oxford: Clarendon/London & New York: Oxford University Press, 1957; ed., *The Shaping of Modern Ireland.* London: Routledge & Kegan Paul, [1960]; *To Katanga and Back: A U.N. Case History.* London: Hutchinson, 1962/New York: Simon & Schuster, 1963; *Writers and Politics.* London: Chatto & Windus/New York, Pantheon, 1965; *The United Nations: Sacred Drama.* London: Hutchinson/New York: Simon & Schuster, 1968; *Murderous Angels.* Boston: Little, Brown, 1968/London: Hutchinson, 1969. (Play); ed., *Reflections on the Revolution in France* by Edmund Burke. Harmondsworth, Middlesex: Penguin/Baltimore: Penguin, 1969; ed., with William Varech. *Power and Consciousness.* London: University of London Press/New York: New York University Press, 1969; *Camus.* London: Fontana, Collins, 1969/ as *Albert Camus of Europe and Africa.* New York: Viking, 1970; with Maire Cruise O'Brien, *A Concise History of Ireland.* London: Thames & Hudson, 1972; *The Suspecting Glance.* London: Faber, [1972]; *States of Ireland.* London: Hutchinson/New York: Pantheon, 1972; *Herod: Reflections on Political Violence.* London: Hutchinson, [1978]. (Essays and three short plays); *Neighbours.* London & Boston: Faber, [1980]. (Ewart-Biggs Memorial Lectures); *The Siege, the Saga of Israel and Zionism.* London: Weidenfeld & Nicolson, 1986/New York: Simon & Schuster, 1987; *Passion and Cunning, and Other Essays.* London: Weidenfeld & Nicolson, 1988; *God Land: Reflections on Religion and Nationalism.* Cambridge: Harvard University Press, 1988; *The Great Melody. A Thematic Biography and Commented Anthology of Edmund Burke.* London: Sinclair-Stevenson, 1992. O'Brien's uncollected fugitive pieces are legion. Joanne L. Henderson's checklist in Young-Bruehl & Hogan in References is good up to 1973. REFERENCES: Akenson, Donald Harman. *Conor: A Biography of Conor Cruise O'Brien.* Montreal & Kingston: McGill-Queen's University Press, [1994]; Jordan, Anthony J. *To Laugh or To Weep: A Biography of Conor Cruise O'Brien.* [Dublin]: Blackwater, [1994]; Lysaght, D. R. O'Connor. *End of a Liberal: The Literary Politics of Conor Cruise O'Brien.* [Dublin: Plough Books, 1976]; O Glaisne, Risteard. *Conor Cruise O'Brien agus an Liobralachas.* Baile Atha Cliath: Clodhanna Teo, [1974]; Young-Bruehl, Elisabeth & Hogan, Robert. *Conor Cruise O'Brien, an Appraisal.* Newark, Del.: Proscenium, [1974].

O'BRIEN, EDNA (1930?–   ), novelist and short story writer. O'Brien grew up on a farm near the village of Tuamgraney, County Clare. She attended the

National School in Scarriff and the strict Convent of Mercy in Loughrea, County Galway. She graduated from the Pharmaceutical College of Ireland, Dublin, in 1950. In 1952, she married Dublin-born novelist Ernest Gebler* and was divorced from him in 1964. O'Brien's older son, Carlos Gébler,* is also a novelist. O'Brien has lived in England since 1958.

O'Brien's novels honor one great theme, one that she cannot or will not renounce, one that she herself calls an obsession: the bleak lives—specifically, the desperate love lives—of Irishwomen. The typical O'Brien plot is about an Irishwoman who devotes her life to her children and to demeaning affairs before and after an acrimonious divorce from a dominating older man. First established by the Caithleen Brady story line in the "Girls" cycle (*The Country Girls,* 1960, *The Lonely Girl,* 1962, and *Girls in Their Married Bliss,* 1964), this story is repeated in full, or several of the Brady episodes are extracted and expanded upon, in all of O'Brien's novels. Her American publishers hailed the plot of the latest novel, *House of Splendid Isolation* (1994), as a "departure" for O'Brien; nonetheless, it revolves around yet another Caithleen who regrets that she sacrifices her will to each man who enters her life. O'Brien compounds the sense of sameness by borrowing identical subplots, characters, and details from book to book—for instance, infatuation with a handyman, seduction by a middle-aged bachelor, a drunken father's binges, a teacher's breakdown, stolen shoes, a trip to the Mediterranean or New York, a child's death, misdirected love letters, a childhood riddle, the colors fawn and mauve. Though her talent in reconstructing her archetype sentence by sentence protects O'Brien from parody, her single-mindedness opens her to unflattering comparisons to the Ancient Mariner, particularly when her attempts to tell any other novel-length tale deteriorate into the same old story. (Even O'Brien's attempt at biography, *James and Nora: A Portrait of Joyce's Marriage,* (1981) is transformed into an O'Brien tale.) O'Brien's persistence in returning to this formula might account for why her work has generated comparatively little scholarly analysis.

Nevertheless, critics should not dismiss O'Brien's work on the grounds that her novels are simplistic or that she writes only autobiographies, for readers are drawn to O'Brien by her acuity and writing, not her storytelling.

O'Brien's strength, readily noticeable in her short stories, is her braiding of realistic dialogue, realistic situations, and realistic women characters. In half a sentence, O'Brien can explain why male–female relationships fail: "[My friends and I] believed that there was a species of gent quite different from the ones we knew who would charge into town and carry us off" (*Johnny I Hardly Knew You,* 1977). Many readers have met people who could be characters from "A Scandalous Woman," such as the outraged neighbor who is so eager to confront a young girl's impregnator that she organizes a buffet for that purpose, or the mother who serves a visiting priest a grapefruit for dinner because she is accustomed to feeding him breakfast. The advantage of having spent thousands of words on one topic is that O'Brien can, for example, masterfully isolate the five minutes when a relationship began to deteriorate ("Epitaph," *Lantern Slides,*

1990). First-time readers should seek out *A Fanatic Heart* (1984) for the best of O'Brien's short stories and possibly the best of her work.

Another of O'Brien's notable talents—but an albatross at times—is her willingness to discuss sex. Passages about foreplay and self-induced abortions in the "Girls" cycle led to a banning of O'Brien's books in Ireland almost as soon as she began to be published. While O'Brien's descriptions of heterosexual and homosexual intercourse have earned her praise for a liberating frankness, they also have made her vulnerable to charges of blatant exploitation.

A willingness to test narrative voice and language is also an O'Brien trademark. O'Brien wrote *A Pagan Place* (1970) in the second person and in staccato sentences to compel the reader to live a girlhood spent in rural Ireland. More and more of O'Brien's attention has shifted to describing internal thought patterns. For example, *Night* (1972) records the coherent yet rambling thoughts of a woman drifting in and out of sleep, and an extended passage in *Time and Tide* (1992) tries to duplicate the reeling thoughts of a drug user. O'Brien's adeptness with language lets her use feminine pronouns ambiguously in "Baby Blue" to clarify that a betrayed wife and a betrayed mistress are both intruders in relationships. O'Brien pleasantly waylays a reader with well-chosen words and phrases: frost "starches" grass, ice "bevels" a pothole, bracelets "barnacled" an arm, unmarried pregnant girls join the "sodality of scandalous women." O'Brien's facility with language and character has earned her comparisons to Virginia Woolf, Dylan Thomas, and her acknowledged idol, James Joyce.*

O'Brien's drive to write has also produced poetry, plays, four children's stories, four filmed screenplays (three adapted from her own works), and an anthology of favorite passages on her favorite topic, *Some Irish Loving: A Selection* (1979). In addition, she wrote the text to accompany photographs in *Mother Ireland* (1976) and *Vanishing Ireland* (1986); the former is noteworthy for O'Brien's thoughts on leaving Ireland (see Chapter 7). O'Brien frequently contributes to *The New Yorker*.

PRISCILLA GOLDSMITH

WORKS: *The Country Girls*. London: Hutchinson, 1960/New York: Knopf, 1960; *The Lonely Girl*. London: Jonathan Cape/New York: Random House, 1962/reprinted as *The Girl with Green Eyes*. London: Penguin, 1964; *Girls in Their Married Bliss*. London: Jonathan Cape, 1964/New York: Simon & Schuster, 1968; *August Is a Wicked Month*. London: Jonathan Cape/New York: Simon & Schuster, 1965; *Casualties of Peace*. London: Jonathan Cape, 1966/New York: Simon & Schuster, 1967; *The Love Object*. London: Jonathan Cape, 1968/New York: Knopf, 1969. (Short stories); *A Pagan Place*. London: Weidenfeld & Nicolson/New York: Knopf, 1970; *Zee & Co*. London: Weidenfeld & Nicolson, 1971; *Night: A Novel*. London: Weidenfeld & Nicolson, 1972/New York: Knopf, 1973/revised as *Night*. New York: Farrar, Straus, Giroux, 1987; *A Pagan Place: A Play*. London: Faber, 1973; *A Scandalous Woman: Stories*. London: Weidenfeld & Nicolson, 1974/printed as *A Scandalous Woman and Other Stories*. New York: Harcourt Brace Jovanovich, 1974; *Mother Ireland*. New York: Harcourt Brace Jovanovich, 1976/Harmondsworth, Middlesex: Penguin, 1978. (Nonfiction); *Johnny I Hardly Knew You*. London: Weidenfeld & Nicolson, 1977/printed as *I Hardly Knew You*. New York: Doubleday, 1978; *Mrs. Reinhardt and Other Stories*. London: Weidenfeld & Nicolson, 1978/ten of the twelve stories plus two substitute stories were published as *A Rose in the Heart*. Garden City, N.Y.: Doubleday, 1979; *Some Irish Loving: A Selection*. London: Weidenfeld & Nicolson/New York: Harper & Row, 1979. (Anthology); *Virginia: A Play*. London: Hogarth/New York: Harcourt Brace Jovanovich, 1981; *James and Nora: A Portrait of Joyce's Marriage*. Northridge, Calif.: Lord John, 1981; *Returning: A Collection of Tales*. London: Weidenfeld & Nicolson, 1982; *A Fanatic Heart: Selected Stories of Edna O'Brien*. New York: Farrar, Straus, Giroux, 1984. (Twenty-five previously collected stories plus four uncollected ones); *The Country Girls Trilogy and Epilogue*. New York: Farrar, Straus, Giroux, 1986; *Vanishing Ireland*. London: Jonathan Cape/New York: C. N. Potter, 1986. (Seventeen-page introduction to photos by Richard Fitzgerald); *Tales for the Telling: Irish Folk & Fairy Stories*. New York: Atheneum, 1986. (Children's book); *The High Road*. London: Weidenfeld & Nicolson/New York: Farrar, Straus, Giroux, 1988; *On the Bone*. Warwick: Greville, 1989. (Poem); *Lantern Slides: Stories by Edna O'Brien*. New York: Farrar, Straus, Giroux, 1990; *Time and Tide*. London: Viking/New York: Farrar, Straus, Giroux, 1992; *House of Splendid Isolation*. London: Weidenfeld & Nicolson/New York: Farrar, Straus, Giroux, 1994. REFERENCES: Eckley, Grace. *Edna O'Brien*. Lewisburg, Pa.: Bucknell University Press, 1974; Guppy, Shusha. Interview with Edna O'Brien. *Paris Review* 92 (Summer 1984): 22–50; Haule, James M. "Tough Luck: The Unfortunate Birth of Edna O'Brien." *Colby Library Quarterly* 23 (December 1987): 216–224; O'Brien, Peggy. "The Silly and the Serious: An Assessment of Edna O'Brien." *Massachusetts Review* 28 (Autumn 1987): 474–488; O'Hara, Kiera. "Love Objects: Love and Obsession in the Stories of Edna O'Brien." *Studies in Short Fiction* 10 (1993): 317–25.

O'BRIEN, FITZ-JAMES (1828–1862), short story writer and poet. O'Brien was born in County Cork and spent his early years in Baltimore. Although his family was well-to-do, he was appalled at the suffering caused by the Famine and in his teens wrote a poem about it that was published in *The Nation*.* In the next few years, many more poems appeared in Irish periodicals, but one critic has described his poetry as a "mere tinkle." In 1849, he inherited £8,000 left by his father and grandfather and left for London, where in two and a half years he ran through his inheritance. At the end of 1851, he sailed to America, where he wrote stories and poems and journalism and lived the Bohemian life. He enlisted in the Union army at the outbreak of the Civil War and was promoted to captain. Severely wounded in February 1862, he lingered until April. O'Brien's small reputation rests on a very slim handful of ghostly tales, particularly "The Diamond Lens," "What Was It?," and "The Wondersmith." Although his ideas were sometimes ingenious, his writing was frequently florid. Had he lived longer and worked harder, he might have become more than a third-rate Poe.

WORKS: *The Poems and Stories of Fitz-James O'Brien*. William Winter, ed. Boston: Osgood, 1881; *The Fantastic Tales of Fitz-James O'Brien*. Michael Hayes, ed. London: John Calder, [1977]. REFERENCE: Wolle, Francis. *Fitz-James O'Brien: A Literary Bohemian of the Eighteen-Fifties*. Boulder: University of Colorado Studies, 1944.

O'BRIEN, GEORGE (1945–   ), memoirist and critic. Born in Enniscorthy, County Wexford, on February 14, 1945, O'Brien, after his mother's early death, was raised in Lismore, County Waterford, by his paternal grandmother. Having received his secondary education at St. Augustine's College, a boarding school in Dungarvan, he went in 1962 to live with his father and stepmother in Dublin, where he was apprenticed to an electronics engineer, attended night classes at Kevin Street College of Technology from 1962 to 1964, and worked for a short time as an apprentice photographer. In 1965, he emigrated to England, working in London as a barman, an invoice clerk, and an encyclopedia salesman. Throughout these vagaries of economic exile, his chief ambition was to go to university, and his economic difficulties were removed in 1968 by a special scholarship to Ruskin College, Oxford, which he attended for two years, proceeding from there to the University of Warwick, where he graduated with a B.A. in English and American literature in 1973 and a Ph.D. in 1980. His teaching experience began as a tutor at the University of Birmingham in 1974 and as an English tutor at Clare College, Cambridge, in 1975. In 1976, he became a lecturer in English at Warwick, a post he held until 1980, when he left for a position of visiting assistant professor of English at Vassar College, where he remained until 1984. Since 1984, he has taught English at Georgetown University, where he is currently an associate professor. He married Pam Henderson in 1969, and they have two sons and live in Arlington, Virginia.

Aside from some short stories, O'Brien's writing has been divided between literary criticism and the work for which he is best known, a memoir of his life to age twenty-five in three volumes.

O'Brien's doctoral dissertation, "Life on the Land: Identity and Community in Three Nineteenth-Century Irish Novelists," was his first extended engagement with a subject, nineteenth- and twentieth-century Irish fiction, which has remained a chief intellectual preoccupation. Firmly anchored in an extensive knowledge of modern Ireland, O'Brien's criticism is distinguished by its regard for facts, its evenhanded good sense, its ability to combine plain language with subtlety of intellect and to join pragmatic textualism to a keen awareness of the fashions and factions of contemporary theory. In his excellent introductory study of Brian Friel's* stories and plays, O'Brien showed how Friel's drama extends the Irish literary tradition and fashions valuable analyses of modern Irish life and culture. As a critic, O'Brien is capable of muscular generalization that is always rooted and organic, growing out of a deep, various, and complex grasp of facts. Always aware of the linguistic status of a text, it is to his subtle understanding of language as instrument and subject that he owes his stimulating accounts of Friel, Banville, Joyce, and Irish "Literary Criticism since 1960." Independent of mind, scrupulous in feeling, unswayed by factional considerations, O'Brien is an exemplary figure in what he calls, in remarks on the Field Day* enterprise and its anthology, an emergent Irish intelligentsia.

O'Brien's gifts as literary and cultural critic are beautifully deployed in the three volumes of his memoirs of growing up in Ireland and England in the 1950s and 1960s. Here, however, such gifts are responsible for only part of the picture. The pages of the widely admired *The Village of Longing* (1987), *Dancehall Days* (1988), and *Out of Our Minds* (1994) are marked by shrewd, witty, sympathetic, and critical "readings" of Irish and English cultural reality during these two decades, with particular attention to the politics of unemployment and emigration, the stranglehold of institutional conservatism, residual imprints of colonial power, and the psychological and sociological implications of popular music. What especially distinguishes these volumes, however, are the richness of O'Brien's recall and the vivid, immediate, spoken quality of his language, his companionable voice. Telling his life in thematic swirls, not chronological lines, he creates a stream of associations that can swerve, in the space of a paragraph, from piano lessons to pigs' heads to football pools to wireless programs; or in a page or two touch on the brotherhood of trade unions, north-country accents and working-class argot, the political connection between working-class and being Irish, Ping-Pong games and E. P. Thompson and libraries, pan-fried pork chops, civil coffee, and sociability with the girls of Stoke House. Although the twenty-year journey from Lismore to Oxford is painful, its main stages a series of major or minor humiliations, there are never a moment of self-pity in the emotional charge and never a trace of self-importance in the writing. In ways both convincing and delightful, his chapters show us that "complexity is more nourishing to the spirit than reverie." The whole performance is light on its feet and endlessly allusive, at once knowing and innocent, gauche and sophisticated, skeptical and affectionate. It is an anatomy of family and the familiar, a fulfilling "poetics of the prosaic" (a term he used about Joyce) in the "blessed secular spirit of the everyday." It is, finally, a joyous celebration of the persistent wonder of consciousness itself, the redemptive power of which—in the absence of those comforts that come from familial and institutional ties—enables this émigré villager of longing to become an independent man of the world. At a certain point the narrator wonders of a character's delight in local talk: "Loved it yes, but did he make anything of that love and of the something he has made of it." In this singular work, in a style apt to its occasions, by means of his critical intelligence, emotional and factual memory, his social, political, and cultural insight, and deep moral seriousness, O'Brien achieves the creative equilibrium that belongs only to the genuine and inimitable work of art.

                                                                        EAMON GRENNAN

WORKS: *The Village of Longing: An Irish Boyhood in the Fifties.* Gigginstown, Co. Meath: Lilliput, 1987/Belfast: Blackstaff, 1993; *Dancehall Days; or, Love in Dublin.* Dublin: Lilliput, 1988/ Belfast: Blackstaff, 1994; *The Village of Longing/Dancehall Days.* London: Viking, 1989/New York: Viking, 1990; *Brian Friel.* Boston: Twayne/Dublin: Gill & Macmillan, 1990; *Out of Our Minds.* Belfast: Blackstaff, 1994.

O'BRIEN, KATE (1897–1974), novelist, playwright, journalist, critic, and travel writer. O'Brien was born in Limerick on December 3, 1897. She was educated by French nuns at Laurel Hill Convent, Limerick, and in the autumn of 1916, she went to Dublin to continue her education at University College. The height of the Irish Renaissance was an exciting time to be in school in Dublin, but O'Brien maintained a detachment from it.

While a governess in Bilboa, Spain, in the early 1920s, she began to write and continued to do so when she returned. She took up residence in England and began to work for the *Manchester Guardian.* Her first efforts were plays; *A Distinguished Villa,* produced in 1926, won critical acclaim. However, she soon turned to novels, which, she said, you could "carry on your back" (*New York Times,* December 4, 1949, p. 22), avoiding the extensive collaboration involved in producing a play.

Her first novel, *Without My Cloak* (1931), a chronicle of an Irish family through three generations, won two of the leading British literary prizes: the Hawthornden Prize and the James Tait Black Prize. The theme of family, so-cietal, and religious solidarity and restraint versus individual freedom, which had already been manifested in her plays and is central here, continues through-out all of her work. Her characters struggle against consuming parental love, the constraints of society, and the dictates of the Church. Their bids for freedom often fail, but the failure is not always seen as totally negative. For, although her novels are profoundly Catholic, her characters often make decisions based on responsibility toward and love of others as much as on the regulations of society and the Church. However, there are exceptions to this failure. In *Mary Lavelle,* a book which was banned in Ireland in 1936 under the Censorship Act, the heroine learns to be an individual and in the process abandons the moral strictures of her youth. In *As Music and Splendour* (1958), the two heroines also break with their Irish Catholic backgrounds, but here the results are not as positive. Some of O'Brien's novels narrow the conflict with society, focusing on the battle between the individualism and imagination of the artist and the restraining religious and societal codes.

Except for *Pray for the Wanderer* (1938), the major protagonists of all of O'Brien's novels are women, and the stories often deal with their attempts to overcome the rigid roles defined for them by society. In *Mary Lavelle, The Land of Spices,* and *The Flower of May,* women have to fight for the opportunities of travel and education which act as catalysts for the development of the indi-vidual.

O'Brien's greatest popular success was a sixteenth-century Spanish historical romance, *That Lady* (1946; published in the United States as *For One Sweet Grape*). She adapted it for the stage for Katharine Cornell, who starred in the 1949 Broadway production.

Besides plays and novels, O'Brien wrote two travel books, *Farewell, Spain* (1937) and *My Ireland* (1962). Both are personal, idiosyncratic views which nevertheless capture the essence of those two countries. *Teresa of Avila* (1951) is a portrait of St. Teresa as a "women of genius" rather than as a canonized saint, again reflecting the interests of the author.

O'Brien's work is occasionally marred by overanalysis of her characters' emotions and motives. Such lapses lead to an unnecessary obscurity. For the most part, however, hers is a fluid style which is not obtrusive. This is mirrored by the contrast in many of her works between the internal world of the emotions and the external world of appearances. The surface smoothness of the lives of her characters is set off against the passion, tension, and conflict of their inner lives. She shows a deep understanding of her characterization, and an ability to create atmosphere by her acute observation of detail. She deserves to be ranked with the important novelists of the twentieth century.

After her return from Spain, O'Brien lived in England for twenty years. Then, after a long interim in Ireland, she returned to Britain in 1965. She died in Faversham, Kent, August 13, 1974.

BARBARA DiBERNARD

WORKS: *Distinguished Villa.* London: E. Benn, 1926. (Play in three acts); *Without My Cloak.* London: Heinemann/Garden City, N.Y.: Doubleday, Doran, 1931; *The Anteroom.* London: Heinemann/Garden City, N.Y.: Doubleday, Doran, 1934; *Mary Lavelle.* London: Heinemann/Garden City, N.Y.: Doubleday, Doran, 1936; *Farewell, Spain.* London: Heinemann/Garden City, N.Y.: Doubleday, Doran, 1937; *Pray for the Wanderer.* London: Heinemann/Garden City, N.Y.: Doubleday, Doran, 1938; *The Land of Spices.* London: Heinemann/Garden City, N.Y.: Doubleday, Doran, 1941; *English Diaries and Journals.* London: Collins, 1943; *The Last of Summer.* London: Heinemann/Garden City, N.Y.: Doubleday, Doran, 1943; *That Lady.* London: Heinemann, 1946/published in the United States as *For One Sweet Grape.* Garden City, N.Y.: Doubleday, 1946; *That Lady.* New York: Harper, 1949. (Play); *Teresa of Avila.* London: Max Parrish/New York: Sheed & Ward, 1951; *The Flower of May.* London: Heinemann/New York: Harper, 1953; *As Music and Splendour.* London: Heinemann/New York: Harper, 1958; *My Ireland.* London: Batsford/New York: Hastings House, 1962. (Guide to country); *Presentation Parlour.* London: Heinemann, 1963. (Biographical sketches). REFERENCES: Dalsimer, Adele. *Kate O'Brien.* New York: Twayne/Dublin: Gill & Macmillan, 1990; Reynolds, Lorna. *Kate O'Brien: A Literary Portrait.* Gerrards Cross: Colin Smythe/Totowa, N.J.: Barnes & Noble, 1987; Walshe, Eibhear. *Ordinary People Dancing: Essays on Kate O'Brien.* [Cork]: Cork University Press, [1993]; Weekes, Ann Owens. "Kate O'Brien: Family in the New Nation." In *Irish Women Writers: An Uncharted Tradition.* [Lexington]: University Press of Kentucky, [1990], pp. 108–132.

O'BRIEN, KATE CRUISE (1948–   ), short story writer and novelist. O'Brien, daughter of writer and diplomat Conor Cruise O'Brien,* was born in Dublin on June 25, 1948, and graduated in English from Trinity College in 1972. She has worked as a columnist with the *Irish Independent* and is at present literary editor at Poolbeg Press. She is married, with a son, and lives in Dublin.

O'Brien's first published short story, "Henry Died," appeared in 1971 in the *Irish Press.* It won the Hennessy Award and was included in her subsequent collection *A Gift Horse* (1978). Many stories in this collection examine the effects of differing normalities within the one, conventional society. Sarah, in "Sackcloth," is aware of being "SOMETHING UNUSUAL." In choosing to attend a series of tradition-laden schools, Sarah tries to come to terms with the embarrassment of a mother who goes barefoot and who is not religious. In "Some Rain Must Fall," the focus is on the married life of Gerald and Margaret and on the compromises and misunderstandings necessary to keep them together despite the difference in their upbringings. The invisible difference between the two is summed up by Gerald: "Our lot don't *have* tax returns, we just pay tax." Throughout these stories there is a clarity of dialogue that creates an understanding of the situations and relationships in which the characters find themselves. Always there is an acknowledgment that what is eccentric for some is normal for others. Sarah, rushing in panic from her latest school, is unconcerned at how strange this flight might seem. "Sarah's mother accepted it and because she did that, it was natural to Sarah."

This concept is carried into O'Brien's first novel, *The Homesick Garden* (1991). Antonia is the teenage protagonist. She goes to lengths to understand the peculiarities of the adults in her life. Her refuge is in the chaos created by an eccentric mother, a pregnant, unmarried aunt, and a manipulative grandmother. Her father is a chef who cannot cook at home. Each character is defined through his or her refusal to be conventional and his or her reaction to the lack of convention in others.

RACHEL DOUGLAS

WORKS: *A Gift Horse and Other Stories.* [Swords, Co. Dublin]: Poolbeg, [1978]; *The Homesick Garden.* [Swords, Co. Dublin]: Poolbeg, [1991]. (Novel).

O'BRIEN, MARY (fl. 1790s), poet and playwright.

WORKS: *The Political Monitor, or Regent's Friend.* Dublin: W. Gilbert, 1790. (Poetry); *The Fallen Patriot.* Dublin: W. Gilbert, 1794. (Play).

O'BRIEN, PHIL

WORK: *Memories of the Irish-Israeli War.* London: New Futurist Books, 1995. (Novel).

O'BRIEN, RICHARD BAPTIST (1809–1885), novelist. O'Brien was born at Carrick-on-Suir, County Tipperary. He became a priest and later dean of Limerick. He wrote three novels and some religious works and contributed poems to *The Nation.**

WORKS: *Ailey Moore, A Tale of the Times; Showing How Evictions, Murder, and Such-like Pastimes Are Managed and Justice Administered in Ireland. . . .* Dublin: Duffy, 1856; *Jack Hazlitt, A Hiberno-American Story. . . .* Dublin: Duffy, 1875; *The D'Altons of Crag: A Story of '48 and '49.* Dublin: Duffy, 1882. REFERENCE: Egan, Michael J. *Life of Dean O'Brien, Founder of the Catholic Young Men's Society.* Dublin: Gill, 1949.

O'BRIEN, WILLIAM (1852–1928), novelist, editor, and nationalist politician. O'Brien was born in Mallow, County Cork, on October 2, 1852, and though a Catholic, was educated at Cloyne Diocesan College and later at Queen's College, Cork. In 1869, he took up a career in journalism, working for the *Freeman's Journal* until Parnell appointed him editor of the Land League journal, *United Ireland,* in 1881. Under his editorship, it became the voice of militancy and was quickly suppressed. O'Brien was arrested to suffer the first of nine prison terms. In Kilmainham, on the instructions of his fellow prisoner Parnell, he worded the "No Rent" manifesto that was to be the main item of the Land League's highly effective "plan of campaign" that he elaborated with John Dillon in 1886. Released in 1882, he resumed editorship of *United Ireland* and became MP for Mallow. His agrarian agitation led to a six-month term in Tullamore jail in 1887, during which he went naked rather than wear prison garb. The last incarceration was in Galway during the Parnell crisis.

As Parnell's most senior deputy, he strove to handle the O'Shea crisis by making Dillon a temporary leader of the party in the hope that the split might be healed by time and common sense, but Parnell would yield only to O'Brien himself, who refused the mantle. Elected as MP for Cork in 1892, O'Brien changed tack. He believed that a reconciliation between Unionist and nationalist was the only solution to the Irish question, and it was mainly due to his efforts that Wyndham's Land Act of 1903, the measure that finally ended the land agitation, became law. His "All for Ireland" League, faithful to its motto of "conference, conciliation, consent," found itself overtaken by the rise of the new Sinn Féin after 1916. It took no part in the crucial 1918 elections, and O'Brien retired to a life of reminiscence and literary pursuits. He died suddenly in London on February 25, 1928, and was buried in Mallow.

O'Brien's writing is consciously literary, witty, and of an unimpeachable patriotic and moral quality. His account of the Kilmainham treaty in *Recollections* (1905) contains no mention of Mrs. O'Shea. His main work of fiction, *When We Were Boys* (1890), meant as the first volume of a diptych, is 500 pages long, the possible charge of its being overlong extenuated by its author's terms of imprisonment, "which left such an abundance of weary time on my hands." The novel, with its great vitality and humor, is still very readable. It is full of such *aperçus* as "that wildly romantic being the British shareholder" and "Most of their lordships [of the Catholic see of Clonard] had to make shift with a mountain cave for a palace, and some with a gallows for a pulpit." Set in Glengarriff, County Cork, during the period, as the title suggests, of the active Fenianism of the 1860s, its romantic hero, Ken Rohan, first glimpsed as he sets off to attend St. Fergal's, a seminary clearly based on Cloyne, is essentially a portrait of O'Brien's older brother, Jim. There are similarities to the work of Maria Edgeworth,* but the authentic sense of the politics of the period is O'Brien's unique contribution. The religious clash between Monsignor McGruder, who condemns the movement, and Father O'Harte, who sympathizes with the brotherhood's ideals, is a fictionalized version of the struggle between the Rome-trained anti-Garibaldist, Cardinal Cullen, and Archbishop Croke, who did so much to continue the work of *The Nation** in re-creating Irish patriotic self-esteem. The unwritten second volume would have, in O'Brien's words, portrayed "the wondrous sea-change after the bold lead of Archbishop Croke . . . in what promised to be an unbreakable alliance. Parnell's party and Croke's Church seemed an unconquerable combination."

O'Brien's only other novel was *A Queen of Men* (1898), based on the career of the "most famous feminine sea-captain," Grainne Ní Mhaille, who fought such an effective rearguard action against Elizabeth I's forces in County Mayo.

SEAN McMAHON

PRINCIPAL WORKS: *When We Were Boys*. Dublin: Maunsel, 1890. (Novel); *The Influence of the Irish Language on Irish National Literature and Character*. Cork: Gay, 1892; *Irish Ideas*.

London & New York: Longmans, Green, 1893; *A Queen of Men.* London: T. Fisher Unwin, 1898. (Novel); *The Irish National Question and the Land Acts.* Dublin: Irish People Office, 1903; *Recollections.* London: Macmillan, 1905; *An Olive Branch in Ireland and Its History.* London: Macmillan, 1910; *Sinn Fein and Its Enemies.* Dublin: Maunsel, 1917; *The Downfall of Parliamentarianism: A Retrospect for the Accounting Day.* Dublin: Maunsel, 1918; *Evening Memories; Being a Continuation of "Recollections."* Dublin & London: Maunsel, 1920; *The Responsibility for Partition Considered with an Eye to* Ireland's *Future.* Dublin: Maunsel & Roberts, 1921; *The Irish Revolution and How It Came About.* Dublin: Maunsel & Roberts, 1923; *Edmund Burke as an Irishman.* Dublin: Gill, 1924; *The Parnell of Real Life.* London: T. Fisher Unwin, 1926. REFERENCES: Meehan, P.J. *Life of John Dillon, M.P., and William O'Brien, M.P., Ireland's Patriots.* New York: Law & Trade Printing, n.d.; Murphy, James H. "William O'Brien's *When We Were Boys:* A New Voice from Old Conventions." *Irish University Review* 22 (Autumn–Winter 1992): 298–304; O'Brien, J. V. *William O'Brien and the Course of Irish Politics 1881–1918.* Berkeley: University of California Press, 1976; Warwick-Haller, Sally. *William O'Brien and the Irish Land War.* Dublin: Irish Academic, 1990.

O'BYRNE, BRENDAN (1912–   ), novelist, born in Dublin.

WORK: *The Song They Sang.* Haywards Heath, West Sussex: Two Heads, 1994.

O'BYRNE, KEVIN (1934–   ), poet, artist, and educator. O'Byrne was born on November 1, 1934, and brought up in Dublin's East Wall. After being expelled from a number of schools, he attended the National College of Art and Design and studied pottery and sculpture. At about the age of thirty, he entered University College, Dublin, and graduated with a B.Sci. He has been a docker and a dress designer, has run an art gallery, and has been an alderman in Dublin Corporation. In 1986, he founded Saor-Ollscoil na hÉireann, the Free University of Ireland. His volume of poems, *The Clocks of Time* (1992), is written in clear and unpretentious free verse and profusely illustrated by his attractive black and white drawings.

WORK: *The Clocks of Time.* Dublin: Saor-Ollscoil, [1992].

O'CALLAGHAN, CONOR (1968–   ), poet. Callaghan was born in Newry, County Down, and grew up in Dundalk, County Louth. He is married and lives in Dublin. In 1990, he was awarded a bursary from the Arts Council; in 1992, he won the Cloverdale Prize for Poetry; and in 1993, his *The History of Rain* won the Patrick Kavanagh* Poetry Award. That book chiefly uses literal statement or description and wastes few words. The writing is clear, and the diction never exactly flat, but this is not a singing voice. The poet does often use a loose pattern of sound at the end of lines. Occasionally he rhymes, but more often uses assonance or consonance or sometimes merely a loose similarity, as in "rotten" and "broken," or a very loose one, as in "bed" and "world," or a quite tenuous one, as in "dawn" and "pigeons." His pattern, for instance, in "Postcard" quite disappears in the third stanza, in which he pairs "feelings" and "questions," and "unkind" and "changed." Often also, he arbitrarily changes his pattern so that the scheme of the first stanza is ABBA and of the second, ABAB. A yet more ineffective looseness is his meter, which often just disappears, a fault particularly noticeable in his "Three Villanelles in California." O'Callaghan's is more a flirtation with form than a use of it, a pretending to eat a nonexistent cake.

WORK: *The History of Rain.* [Oldcastle, Co. Meath]: Gallery/Chester Springs, Pa.: Dufour, [1993].

O'CALLAGHAN, JULIE (1954–   ), poet. Born in the United States, O'Callaghan works at Trinity College, Dublin.

WORKS: *Edible Anecdotes.* Portlaoise: Dolmen, 1983; *Taking My Pen for a Walk.* London & New York: Orchard Books, 1988. (Children's verse); *What's What.* Newcastle upon Tyne: Bloodaxe, 1991.

O'CALLAGHAN, SEAN

WORK: *Down by the Glenside.* Cork: Mercier, 1992.

Ó CANAINN, TOMÁS (1930), novelist and poet. Born in County Derry.

WORKS: *Home to Derry.* Belfast: Appletree, 1985; *Melos.* [Cork]: Clog, [1987]. (Poetry).

O'CASEY, SEAN (1880–1964), playwright. Sean O'Casey was born John Casey in Dublin on March 30, 1880, into a poor Protestant family. He was the last of thirteen children, only five of whom reached adulthood. With the early death of his father, Michael Casey, the fortunes of the family declined further. O'Casey's lifelong eye trouble may probably be traced to early poverty. This enduring affliction began in early youth and made his attendance at school sporadic. Indeed, he only learned to read in his early teens. His first autobiographies, *I Knock at the Door* (1939) and *Pictures in the Hallway* (1942), recreate his early life with Dickensian gusto and poignance.

O'Casey spent his young manhood as an ordinary laborer, but the evenings were, as Lady Gregory* said of her own life, "a succession of enthusiasms." He entered with great fervor into the life of his church, St. Barnabas; into the Orange Lodge, the Gaelic League, and the Irish Republican Brotherhood; and, most importantly, into the labor movement as embodied in Jim Larkin's recently formed Irish Transport and General Workers' Union, and into its political arm, the Irish Citizen Army of which he was the first secretary. His initial idealistic enthusiasms were often dampened by disillusionment, and he so often truculently withdrew from active participation in causes he had once espoused that the patriot Tom Clarke dismissed him as simply "a disgruntled fellow."

At the same time, he was with wonder and delight discovering the world of books. His reading was excited, diverse, and unmethodical, but he was particularly enchanted by Shakespeare and the Elizabethan dramatists, by Shelley, Ruskin, and Shaw.* Their influence may be seen in his early prose and verse, and in the later self-portraits of Donal Davoren in *The Shadow of a Gunman* (1923) and of Ayamonn Breydon in *Red Roses for Me* (1943). In his Citizen

Army days, he had written much rather florid journalism for the labor paper, *The Irish Worker;* then, although somewhat estranged from his former associates, he wrote a short history of the Citizen Army (1919) as well as an unpublished Ruskinian treatise, *Three Shouts from a Hill.* He had also been writing poems and greeting card verse for a small Dublin publisher, as well as dramatic sketches for his branch of the Gaelic League. As his interest in the theatre grew, he took part in an amateur production at the Empire Theatre, and he attempted several short plays which he submitted to the Abbey Theatre.* Finally, in 1923, his two-act play *On the Run* was accepted by the Abbey and was produced at the end of the season under the title *The Shadow of a Gunman.* This play was the first effective representation of Dublin slum life on the Irish stage, although, earlier, A. Patrick Wilson* and Oliver St. John Gogarty* had also written slum plays. However, it was probably the genial satiric comedy of the piece and the brilliant acting of the Abbey players, as well as the novelty of the subject, that gave the play its immediate popularity.

In the next year, 1924, the Abbey produced O'Casey's three-act play, *Juno and the Paycock,* which treated the Civil War and which was a considerable extension of the techniques of the *Gunman.* The major male roles of *Juno* were brilliantly created by Barry Fitzgerald and F. J. McCormick. To this day the play remains one of the most revived and popular of all Abbey plays.

O'Casey's next major production was *The Plough and the Stars* (1926). Although as great an artistic advance over *Juno* as *Juno* had been over the *Gunman,* the *Plough* at first shared none of their popularity, but instead caused a week of riotous disturbances in the theatre, as had John Synge's* *The Playboy of the Western World* nearly twenty years before. The motives of the rioters were precisely those of twenty years before. The national self-esteem had once again been insulted, and an Irish writer had once again held up to ridicule Irish patriotism, Irish chastity, and indeed the whole Irish character. O'Casey's view, of course, was that the play was a fair and just representation which cut through much cant and humbug. If it laughed at fustian and hypocrisy, it was also profoundly sympathetic to suffering and sacrifice. This is the view that later audiences, in Ireland and elsewhere, have come to take. W. B. Yeats* delivered his view from the stage to the 1926 audience in a superb short tirade:

You have disgraced yourselves again. Is this to be an ever-recurring celebration of the arrival of Irish genius? Synge first and then O'Casey. The news of the happenings of the past few minutes will go from country to country. Dublin has once more rocked the cradle of genius. From such a scene in this theatre went forth the fame of Synge. Equally the fame of O'Casey is born here tonight. This is his apotheosis.

Bewildered, angered, and hurt at the denunciations in the theatre and in the press, O'Casey went to London shortly after the production, to receive the Hawthornden Prize for *Juno* and to look over that play's West End production. Except for a few brief visits, he never returned to Ireland.

In London, he was immediately recognized as an original personality, a rough genius from the working class, and he was feted and acclaimed. His first years in London were heady and exciting times. He was encountering an entirely new world. He was making friends with brilliant personalities, such as Bernard Shaw and Augustus John. His plays were produced in the West End to great acclaim and were published by the distinguished firm of Macmillan's, and in 1927, he married a young Irish actress who had played in them.

In the meantime, he was working on a new play, *The Silver Tassie*. This time, the subject was not merely Irish but international—the trauma of World War I—and the technique was in part (particularly in the lyricism and satire of the expressionistic second act) an unexpected divergence from that of the slum plays. The play was submitted first to the Abbey, and O'Casey confidently expected its acceptance, but in an often recounted literary brouhaha, it was rejected by Yeats, Lennox Robinson,* and Lady Gregory. Angered and cha- grined, O'Casey sent the correspondence to the press, and for a while the matter was a cause célèbre. A London production was arranged by the unlikely person of C. B. Cochran, an English Ziegfeld who specialized in musical comedies. With Charles Laughton somewhat miscast in the leading role, but supported by a number of distinguished Irish players, and also with a striking second act set by Augustus John, the play was a critical but not quite a popular success. The play's high production costs also made a fairly early demise inevitable. With this commercial failure and with O'Casey's slow gestation of a new play, his reputation as genius and money-spinner was somewhat deflated. O'Casey tended to think that it was the Abbey rejection which harmed him commercially. If anything, however, the publicity given the Abbey rejection simply whetted in- terest in the Cochran production. The real reasons for the decline in O'Casey's fortunes on the commercial stage were the tenor of the times and the expense involved in producing large, complicated, and somewhat experimental plays with rather unpalatable themes. The three early plays had certainly been fero- cious enough in their statement, but they also had more memorable comic char- acterizations that evoked a lot of laughter. If it looked profitable, a commercial management might take a chance on art once, but, as a character in a later O'Casey play remarked, "Business is business."

In the next several years, O'Casey wrote a good deal of casual journalism and worked on *Within the Gates;* in 1928, he saw the birth of his first son. Despite a film of *Juno,* his income was declining, and so the production of *Gates* in 1934 was most welcome. The unsuccessful London production further harmed his commercial reputation, but another production, initiated by the en- thusiasm of the influential American critic George Jean Nathan, opened in New York in the fall. With help from rich friends, O'Casey was able to travel to New York for rehearsals. Rather predictably, as with the *Tassie,* the play was not a commercial success, although the mixed notices contained much laudatory comment.

O'Casey now found it difficult to get important commercial productions, and the next years saw a good deal of miscellaneous writing. His frustrations with the commercial theatre were reflected in his lively, funny, and acid collection of theatrical comment, *The Flying Wasp,* of 1937. Then, in 1939, the first volume of his lengthy autobiography appeared, and five more volumes followed at intervals until 1954.

In 1935, his second son was born, and in 1938, at Shaw's suggestion, he moved to Devon to be near the experimental school, Dartington Hall, which all of his children subsequently attended. His last child, a daughter, was born in 1939.

In 1940, his communist extravaganza *The Star Turns Red* was given an amateur production in London by the Unity Theatre, and in 1943, Shelagh Richards presented his *Red Roses for Me,* a partial return to his first dramatic manner, in Dublin. Productions of later plays—*Purple Dust* in Liverpool in 1945, *Oak Leaves and Lavender* in Hammersmith in 1947, and *Cock-a-Doodle Dandy* in Newcastle-upon-Tyne in 1949—only showed that for the moment he was a back number in the commercial theatre.

His next important production, and one which heralded an upswing in his fortunes, was that of *The Bishop's Bonfire* in Dublin in 1955. Produced by Cyril Cusack and directed by Tyrone Guthrie at the Gaiety Theatre, it was the first new O'Casey play in Dublin in years and occasioned a good deal of interest in Ireland and abroad. Ireland in the middle 1950s, before the advent of television, was still in the grip of the provincial insularity, bourgeois stuffiness, and clerical puritanism that O'Faolain* had railed at a decade before in *The Bell.** O'Casey, because of his communism and his occasional combatively critical letters to the Irish press, had become anathema to the more hidebound sections of the community. Consequently, there was a mild pother about the production, and the Irish critics reviewed it with a more strident denunciation than either the play or the production warranted. Nevertheless, O'Casey's fortunes were finally on the mend. The English notices of the *Bonfire* were rather favorable, and then in 1956 there began a long-running off-Broadway production of *Purple Dust.* However, 1956 was not a happy year: O'Casey's second son, Niall, died of leukemia.

O'Casey's deteriorating relations with Ireland received wide publicity in 1958 over his new play, *The Drums of Father Ned.* O'Casey had been begged to allow a production of the play for the Dublin Theatre Festival. However, when John Charles McQuaid, the archbishop of Dublin, refused to say an inaugural Mass for a festival containing works by O'Casey, Beckett,* and Joyce,* the Festival director hastily canceled the production of *Bloomsday,* an adaptation of *Ulysses.* O'Casey and Beckett then withdrew their works, and the Festival for that year was abandoned. *Drums* received its first production by amateurs in Lafayette, Indiana, in 1959.

In 1960, a couple of academic books appeared on O'Casey, heralding a new critical attention that was to burgeon, particularly after the playwright's death, into a spate of books, articles, and even a *Sean O'Casey Review.* In 1962, his last long play received its initial production at an American university, and in the same year an American university press published a collection of his early fugitive material, *Feathers from the Green Crow*. Whether this academic acceptance spurred any of the increasing interest in his plays by the commercial theatre is debatable, but at least it belatedly confirmed his acceptance into the hierarchy of modern letters.

In 1963, O'Casey issued a collection of essays, *Under a Coloured Cap*. After the *Father Ned* affair, he had banned professional productions of his plays in Ireland, but he rescinded the ban for the Abbey productions of *Juno* and *The Plough* at the World Theatre Festival in London in 1964. He was now all but nearly blind, and on September 18, 1964, after a second heart attack, he died in Devon.

Despite his long and extraordinary autobiography and a mass of miscellaneous writing, O'Casey will be remembered primarily as a playwright. For many years, critical opinion about his plays asserted that the three early slum plays were lasting achievements of rough genius, but that, after his departure from the Abbey Theatre and Dublin, his work deteriorated. There was little consensus about the value of individual late plays, but they were generally regarded as flawed experiments. A demurrer to this view was taken by the Irish critics who almost unanimously denounced all of the late plays as hopeless failures. However, elements other than a calmly critical judiciousness impelled their strident comment. If the condemnation of Ireland may be explained by religiosity and rancor, the apathy of England and America may be explained by a basic law of the modern theatre, which is that critical adulation almost invariably follows rather than precedes successful commercial production. Conversely, when O'Casey failed commercially, he had, therefore, failed artistically.

In the dismissal of the late plays, it was customary to look back to the slum plays as unqualified masterpieces; even the recent academic discussion of O'Casey has accepted this view. Still, even in the initial praise for the earliest productions, there were dissenting voices from several notable Irish men of letters. Indeed, to this day some members of the Dublin intelligentsia speak disparagingly of the early work. The reason usually given is poor construction. There is some accuracy in this stricture, although recent academic apologists persist in thinking that everything in a masterpiece must be masterly. A more judicious view would probably be that O'Casey's first long plays are flawed, but contain such striking virtues that the flaws, particularly in a good production, are overwhelmed. This seems a sounder conclusion than simply viewing the Dublin "trilogy" as ever more skillful versions of Chekhovian tragicomedy. By such a standard, the *Gunman* and *Juno* are saved from structural catastrophe only by arbitrary and illogical surprises of genius.

Both the *Gunman* and *Juno* illustrate O'Casey's great strengths: his brilliantly comic observation, his rich dialogue, and his striking and mordant technique of shifting abruptly from the comic to the tragic. In both plays, however, the comic is the more pervasive and powerful element. The *Gunman* is mainly a succession of illustrative comic dialogues, in which examples of cowardice are sometimes subtly and sometimes broadly exposed. These illustrations are threaded together by a thin strand of plot. Indeed, the plot is so tenuous that two major characters of the action, the gunman and the girl, are only sketchily indicated, while the comic characters of the illustrations are much more fully developed. Then, after the illustrative characters have been developed, the plot is arbitrarily, swiftly, and shockingly concluded.

The comedy of *Juno* is more brilliant, and the tragedy is more developed. When they are merged in the extraordinarily ironic final scene, we have a memorable rather than a momentary eloquence. However, the vividness of the dialogue, the strikingness of the characterization, and the intensity of the ending are so remarkable that the play's intrinsic conventionality is forgiven or forgotten. The main strand of plot is a variation on the legacy or Cinderella theme, and one minor plot, that of the daughter, is even more well-worn in its depiction of the seduced and abandoned heroine. In addition, Mary's reading of such "advanced" writers as Ibsen must make her the very last of the nineteenth century's new women. It has been noted that Captain Boyle and Joxer Daly are but new representations of the braggart soldier and the parasite, whose provenance stretches back through the Elizabethans to the Romans and even the Greeks. However, such loving detail has been expended on these two cronies that their individuality is etched in the memory. The daughter, the son, and even, despite her eloquent third act speech, the mother are not developed far beyond stage types.

If Elizabethan tragedies are often punctuated with short scenes of comic relief, O'Casey's first two tragedies are overwhelmingly scenes of comedy, interrupted by short, shocking fragments of tragic relief. The most extended scene in *Juno* is the second act party which does not advance the plot, but which is so superbly comic that it creates its own necessity. The death of Tancred which arbitrarily concludes this hooley is a theatrical shock, but no less arbitrary than the conclusion of the *Gunman*. In the unforgettable conclusion of the third act, however, O'Casey has moved from the arbitrary to the inevitable, and the extent of our surprise at the inevitable is what makes the conclusion of *Juno* literature as well as drama. Also in this third act, the characters of Boyle and Joxer are both darkened, and O'Casey has begun to move from the static illustration of his first plays toward the fluid development of *The Plough and the Stars*.

The *Plough* has no comic characters as memorable as Boyle and Joxer, but in every other way it represents such an advance in technique, and therefore in power, that it is regarded as O'Casey's early, and possibly his only thoroughgoing, masterpiece. The significant technical achievement is the mastery of a large cast in a much more complex plot than O'Casey had previously attempted. At the same time, the terms of the statement are broader, and the particularizing texture of the dialogue is rarely sacrificed to the theme.

As in Chekhov's major plays, the story is told by means of a broad plot and many individual illustrative plots. The broad plot charts the 1916 Rising—its gestation, its gathering momentum, its actuality, and its defeat. Simultaneously, the individual stories of the Clitheroes, of Bessie, Fluther, Mollser, and the other tenement dwellers, are worked out in reaction to the broad social drama. And, at the end of the play, as in Chekhov, the small strands and the large one are knitted together in a tragicomic irony of devastating power.

The play has flaws. The most brilliant comic scene, that in the pub of the second act, has a static and illustrative quality about it; indeed, the scene was originally the basis for a one-act play. However, like the hooley scene in *Juno,* the pub scene does not depend merely on its comic verve to sustain it, but it has emphatically underlined counterpoints to the ongoing broad plot. It has a thematic relevance and is therefore a part of the plot, as the joyous *Juno* scene is not.

There are a few minor blemishes. The young married couple tends to be a trifle mawkish, while the tubercular girl is too sketchily developed to be more than simply a stark illustration, and the Lady from Rathmines needs more development if she is not to be merely a satiric joke. Even some major characters, such as Bessie and Fluther, could stand further development, so that their nobility under stress could be dramatized rather than merely asserted. And certainly the madness of Nora in the last act needs more preparation to keep it from merely arbitrary shock and melodramatic coloring.

Despite these flaws, many of which can be minimized in production, the play has a development of plot and a darkening of tone that sweeps it towards a conclusion blackly comic, tragically ironic, and ferociously harrowing.

The plays of O'Casey's middle period have been lumped together as experiments in expressionism, but it would be more apt to call them modern versions of the Morality and Miracle plays. Expressionism emphasizes technique, but the medieval plays emphasized statement. In the last act of *Juno* and in most of the *Plough,* O'Casey had already tended to stress statement more than characterization or comedy. For the most part, the middle plays are yet more emphatic attempts to underline some general statement about society rather than to illustrate some aspects of human nature.

The mingling of styles in *The Silver Tassie* has occasioned some casuistical defenses from O'Casey's purely aesthetic apologists. Probably the fact is simply that O'Casey thought it much more urgent to indict mankind for the mad masochism of creating its own agonies than to create a tidily unified work of art. To him, the unity of the play lay in its statement rather than in its mode of statement, or even the coherence of its plot.

Nevertheless, the expressionistic second act, startling though it was in context, was less of a novelty for O'Casey than was immediately apparent. In 1923, the Abbey had produced a minor one-act play of his, *Kathleen Listens In,* in which he attempted broad statement by type characters. Of course, in both *Juno* and the *Plough* he had already utilized a basically illustrative act which nearly halts the progress of the plot. The great difference of Act II of the *Tassie* is that its language strikingly differs from the rest of the play. *The Wasteland* of Eliot and the *Ulysses* of Joyce set a precedent for startling variations in levels of language, but the theatre as the most public of literary arts is also the most conventional and the slowest to change its conventions. Readers of O'Casey's neo-Biblical chants have trouble accepting the repetitive simplicities. Yet, in a well-produced staging the language does not only hold, but even rivets, the attention with much of the sardonic eloquence which O'Casey desired. The value of *Juno* and the *Plough* can be easily appreciated on the page, but the value of the *Tassie* and the other middle plays can most fully be appreciated on the stage. The paradox of these plays is that, in trying to stress statement, O'Casey was pushed deeper into technique and the technique was often more theatrical than literary. Whether the technique was always successful is another question and one to be answered by production. Recent revivals of the *Tassie* by the Royal Court and the Abbey suggest that, in this instance, the strength of the play's theme and the savagery of its tone are cohesive enough to draw the play's disparate elements together into a moving theatrical experience.

Unlike the *Tassie, Within the Gates* (1934) was in one style, and its theatricality was, if anything, more inventive. Moreover, its statement and scope were as ambitious as those of the *Tassie*. Nevertheless, *Gates* has not been commercially revived and is generally much less highly regarded. The reason is probably that for three acts of the *Tassie* O'Casey held to a semirealism which worked more or less conventionally. In *Gates,* he opts entirely for a stylized plot and type characters in order, of course, to emphasize his statement. However, on the page the morality play baldness of plot, language, characterization, and, finally, statement is particularly daunting, and a reader is tempted to dismiss the play as an experiment which misfired. While the inventiveness of the play is of a high order, it resides less in the literary elements than in the theatrical ones. This is an aural and visual play which is couched in demanding theatrical terms. Even more than the *Tassie,* the question about this modern morality for the urban world is how fully in production do the theatrical virtues compensate for the lack of literary ones. To judge by reports of the play's only notable production, the theatricality in that instance did not altogether overcome the simplicity. Like other so-called flawed O'Casey plays, *Gates* probably remains a score which has never found its conductor.

The Star Turns Red (1940) is generally considered O'Casey's weakest long play. It has the morality play simplicity of *Gates,* although there are a couple of scenes of mere funning and a symbolic theatrical use of costume and decor. Its strength of statement, coupled with its weakness of invention, make it seem more propaganda than art.

Red Roses for Me (1943) is regarded with some nostalgic benevolence by many critics but has never proved itself upon the stage. The critics' gentle treatment of the play may stem from the first two acts which resemble, albeit palely, the early manner of the Dublin trilogy. But although somewhat realistic, these first two acts are little more inventive than the stylized *Stars Turns Red.* The hero, Ayamonn Breydon, is, like Donal Davoren of the *Gunman,* largely autobiographical. However, where Davoren was admired for his lyricism but condemned for his cravenness, Breydon is presented as so thoroughly admirable that he seems no more individual than the type characters of *Gates* or the *Star*. The play has a lyric third act of much theatrical potential, but its illustrative power is somewhat lessened by the first two acts, which in their own way have also been little more than illustration. In these acts of static exposition, O'Casey's most intrusive characteristic is his language which here has become gaudy and bloated and tends toward self-parody. Most of the plot is huddled up unsatisfactorily in the first scene of the last act. The lyric coda of the last scene is more theatrical and has a haunting final song. If this last scene does save the play from disaster, it probably does not compensate for the lack of drama.

The self-indulgent lyricism of *Red Roses* is less evident in *Purple Dust* (1945). In it, O'Casey is making a less broad, less urgent, and less personal statement. Primarily, he is contrasting old rural Irish virtues practiced mainly by the young to modern urban decadence which belongs mainly to the old. He is no less involved with his opinions, which indeed will become the major themes of his last work, but his tone is less frantic. This ease seems to allow his fancy a freer play, and this relaxed geniality makes even his villains more absurd than evil. *Purple Dust* is aimed with a smaller, less taut bow and so does not travel as far or hit as hard as the other middle plays, but it is much closer to the center of its target.

Oak Leaves and Lavender, its successor, is no major work but is probably one of the more undervalued of O'Casey's plays. Taking for its subject the British war effort, it was produced in 1947 when the issue was dead. To war-weary Britons, it must have seemed rather like yesterday's newspaper. Now, when the subject has receded, like World War I of *The Silver Tassie* into history, this play might well repay revival. It has the thematic urgency and strong simplicities of the middle plays before *Purple Dust,* some of *Purple Dust's* warmth, as well as a provocative theatrically in its set and sound effects.

The last group of long plays, of which *Purple Dust* seems a harbinger, consists of *Cock-a-Doodle Dandy* (first produced in 1949), *The Bishop's Bonfire* (1955), *The Drums of Father Ned* (1959), and *Behind the Green Curtains* (1962). These last plays are closely connected in both theme and technique. All of them have at their center the opposition of youth and age. If the plays of the middle period can be regarded as patterns of the medieval Morality play, the plays of the last period can be seen as versions of the Pastoral. In them, O'Casey posits a symbolic Golden Age which is either defeating the materialistic world of the present or being defeated by it. Yet, unlike the middle plays, these are less didactic than opinionated. The difference between the Morality and the Pastoral is not that the Pastoral is divorced from opinion, but that its opinions are less overtly expressed and more fancifully embroidered.

There is a contrast in tone among the last four plays. The first and the third, *Cock* and *Father Ned,* are gay; the second and the fourth, *Bonfire* and *Green Curtains,* are glum. The gay and optimistic plays, in which the Golden Age triumphs, are much the more successful—richer in situation, dialogue, whimsical invention, and comic theatricality. The glum plays, in which the Golden Age is defeated, have moments of inspired feeling, but definite arid passages where O'Casey's pessimistic feelings pull him back to the didactic exhortation of the middle plays. It is in these moments also that, perhaps in compensation, his theatricality becomes emphatic and exaggerated rather than effective.

The conclusion of *The Bishop's Bonfire* and the whole last two acts of *Behind the Green Curtains* are cases in point. Both passages seem rather frantically bolstered by an almost operatic melodrama which is extraordinarily difficult to rise to. With inspired direction, these passages might be made to work, but in the original productions they appeared as major flaws in the plays.

Such dead passages hardly exist in *Cock* and *Father Ned*, which have a comic exuberance and facility of invention rare outside of the most inspired musical comedy. Indeed, in technique both plays seem trembling on the verge of that form. Music pervades the background while characters in gaudy costumes repeatedly burst into song, lyric declamation, or dramatic dance. With these two plays, O'Casey concluded his career with a flamboyant originality as fine as the best of his early work.

O'Casey's one-act plays have received little critical attention, but quite a few productions. In all, they form a body of work much less flawed and quite as various in form as his full-length work. They range from the tragicomedy of his first manner in *Nannie's Night Out,* to the farcical music hall sketch of *A Pound on Demand,* and even to the dancing pastoral of *Time to Go.* Like Strindberg, Shaw, and Tennessee Williams, O'Casey has worked consistently in the short form, and like them he is a master of it.

O'Casey's dramatic criticism has been collected mainly in *The Flying Wasp* (1937), *The Green Crow* (1956), *Under a Coloured Cap* (1963), and in the posthumous *Blasts and Benedictions* (1967). Like D. H. Lawrence's *Studies in Classic American Literature,* O'Casey's criticism is slapdash but vital. The best of it has an infectious verve and a pervasive sense of the author's character. Occasionally, it sinks into a repetitive thinness and stridency, but its freshness is a welcoming antidote to a multitude of dry commentaries.

The six volumes of autobiography were published over a long period, from 1939 to 1954, and then collectively in America in 1954 under the title of *Mirror in My House,* and again in England in 1963 under the simple title of *Autobiographies.* They form a massive and characteristic work. The many facets of O'Casey's personality are luminously apparent, and the chapters vary eclectically in tone, style, and technique. The books do not form a precise and factual account, but an impressionistic, and even sometimes a fantastic one. The best volumes are the first three or four, which treat of O'Casey's youth and manhood in Dublin. The last two volumes, *Rose and Crown* (1952) and *Sunset and Evening Star* (1954), are more diffuse, garrulous, and occasionally shrilly combative. All of the books range fascinatingly in tone from the noble to the whining, from the satiric to the lyric. They range in style from passages of inordinate eloquence to ones of bad semipuns, gushy fervor, and what Orwell called "basic

Joyce.'' They might, however, stand as a full testament of the faults and qualities of one of the most individual and brilliant figures of contemporary Irish writing. O'Casey's reputation, which had begun to rise again in the last five or ten years of his life, has since continued to grow. Many of his neglected plays have now received belated attention. For instance, in recent years the Abbey Theatre has done interesting revivals of the *Tassie, Red Roses for Me, Purple Dust,* and *Cock-a-Doodle Dandy.* A great spate of critical attention has continued. Many full-length critical or biographical studies have appeared; there have been several collections of criticism; a full-scale bibliography and also a four-volume edition of his letters have appeared. The current O'Casey boom is probably an over-reaction to the years in which he was neglected, and some final reassessment and deevaluation may be looked for in the years ahead. Whatever that reassessment may determine, he will remain, at the very least, one of Ireland's major dramatists and most vivid individuals.

WORKS: *Windfalls.* London: Macmillan, 1934. (Stories, poems & plays); *The Flying Wasp.* London: Macmillan, 1937. (Essays); *Collected Plays.* 4 vols. London: Macmillan/New York: St. Martin's, 1949–1951. A fifth volume, containing previously uncollected plays, both late and early, was issued by the same publishers in 1984; *Mirror in My House: The Autobiographies of Sean O'Casey.* New York: Macmillan, 1956. A collection of the six separately published volumes, originally issued in London by Macmillan from 1939 to 1954; reprinted as *Autobiographies.* 2 vols. London: Macmillan, 1963; reprinted in London by Pan Books in 1980 in six volumes, and in 1981 in two; *The Green Crow.* New York: George Braziller, 1956. (Essays); *Feathers* from *the Green Crow.* Robert Hogan, ed. Columbia: University of Missouri Press, 1962/London: Macmillan, 1963. (Early essays, poems & plays); *Under a Coloured Cap.* London: Macmillan/New York: St. Martin's, 1963. (Essays); *Blasts and Benedictions.* Ronald Ayling, ed. London: Macmillan/New York: St. Martin's, 1967. (Essays); *The Letters of Sean O'Casey, 1910–41.* David Krause, ed. New York: Macmillan/London: Macmillan, 1975; *The Letters . . . 1942–54.* David Krause, ed. New York: Macmillan/London: Macmillan, 1980; *The Letters . . . 1955–58.* David Krause, ed. Washington, D.C.: Catholic University of America Press, 1989; *The Letters . . . 1959–64.* David Krause, ed. Washington, D.C. Catholic University of America Press, 1992; *Niall: A Lament.* London: Calder, 1991. (Memoir). REFERENCES: Armstrong, William A. *Sean O'Casey.* London: Published for the British Council & the National Book League by Longmans, Green, 1967; Atkinson, Brooks. *Sean O'Casey: From Times Past.* London: Macmillan, 1981/Totowa, N.J.: Barnes & Noble, 1982; Ayling, Ronald. *Continuity and Innovation in Sean O'Casey's Drama: A Critical Monograph.* Salzburg: Institut für Englische Sprache und Literatur/New York: Humanities, 1976; Ayling, Ronald, ed. *Sean O'Casey: Modern Judgements.* London: Macmillan, 1969; Ayling, Ronald & Durkan, Michael J. *Sean O'Casey, a Bibliography.* [London & Basingstoke]: Macmillan/Seattle: University of Washington Press, 1978; Benstock, Bernard. *Sean O'Casey.* Lewisburg, Pa.: Bucknell University Press, [1970]; Benstock, Bernard, ed. *James Joyce Quarterly* 8 (Fall 1970), O'Casey issue; Benstock, Bernard. *Paycocks and Others: Sean O'Casey's World.* Dublin: Gill & Macmillan/New York: Barnes & Noble, [1976]; Cowasjee, Saros. *Sean O'Casey: The Man behind the Plays.* Edinburgh & London: Oliver & Boyd, 1963/New York: St. Martin's, 1964; Cowasjee, Saros. *Sean O'Casey.* Edinburgh & London: Oliver & Boyd, [1966]; Da Rin, Doris. *Sean O'Casey.* New York: Frederick Ungar, 1976; Fallon, Gabriel. *Sean O'Casey: The Man I Knew.* London: Routledge & Kegan Paul/Boston: Little, Brown, 1965; Frayne, John P. *Sean O'Casey.* New York: Columbia University Press, 1976; Goldstone, Herbert. *In Search of Community: The Achievement of Sean O'Casey.* Cork & Dublin: Mercier, [1972]; Greaves, C. Desmond. *Sean O'Casey: Politics and Art.* London: Lawrence & Wishart/ [Atlantic Highlands, N.J.]: Humanities, 1979; Hogan, Robert. *The Experiments of Sean O'Casey.* New York: St. Martin's, 1960; Hogan, Robert. *"Since O'Casey"* and Other Essays on

Irish Drama. Gerrards Cross: Colin Smythe/Totowa, N.J.: Barnes & Noble, 1983; Hogan, Robert & Burnham, Richard. *The Years of O'Casey, 1921–1926: A Documentary History.* Newark: University of Delaware Press/Gerrards Cross: Colin Smythe, 1992; Hunt, Hugh. *Sean O'Casey.* Dublin: Gill & Macmillan, 1980; Kilroy, Thomas, ed. *Sean O'Casey: A Collection of Criticism.* Englewood Cliffs, N.J.: Prentice-Hall, 1975; Kleiman, Carol. *Sean O'Casey's Bridge of Vision: Four Essays on Structure and Perspective.* Toronto, Buffalo, London: University of Toronto Press, [1982]; Koslow, Jules. *The Green and the Red: Sean O'Casey, the Man and His Plays.* New York: Golden Griffin, 1950; Kosok, Heinz. *O'Casey the Dramatist.* Gerrards Cross: Colin Smythe/Totowa, N.J.: Barnes & Noble, 1985; Krause, David. *A Self-Portrait of the Artist as a Man: Sean O'Casey's Letters.* [Dublin]: Dolmen, [1968]; Krause, David. *Sean O'Casey and His World.* London: Thames & Hudson/New York: Scribner's, 1976; Krause, David. *Sean O'Casey: The Man and His Work.* London: MacGibbon & Kee/New York: Macmillan, 1960/2d ed. New York: Macmillan/London: Collier Macmillan, 1975; Krause, David & Lowery, Robert G., eds. *Sean O'Casey Centenary Essays.* Gerrards Cross: Colin Smythe/Totowa, N.J.: Barnes & Noble, 1981; Lowery, Robert, G., ed. *Essays on Sean O'Casey's Autobiographies.* London: Macmillan/Totowa, N.J.: Barnes & Noble, 1981; Lowery, Robert G. *Sean O'Casey's Autobiographies: An Annotated Index.* Westport, Conn. & London: Greenwood, [1983]; McCann, Sean, ed. *The World of Sean O'Casey.* London: New English Library, 1966; Malone, Maureen. *The Plays of Sean O'Casey.* Carbondale & Edwardsville: Southern Illinois University Press/London & Amsterdam: Feffer & Simons, [1969]; Margulies, Martin B. *The Early Life of Sean O'Casey.* [Dublin]: Dolmen, [1970]; Metscher, Thomas. *Sean O'Caseys dramatischer Still.* Braunschweig: Georg Westermann, 1968; Mikhail, E. H. *Sean O'Casey and His Critics: An Annotated Bibliography, 1916–1982.* Metuchen, N.J. & London: Scarecrow, 1985; Mikhail, E. H. & O'Riordan, John, eds. *The Sting and the Twinkle: Conversations with Sean O'Casey.* [London & Basingstoke]: Macmillan, [1974]; Mitchell, Jack. *The Essential O'Casey: A Study of the Twelve Major Plays of Sean O'Casey.* New York: International/Berlin: Seven Seas, 1980; Murray, Christopher, ed. *Irish University Review* 10 (Spring 1980), Special Issue, "Sean O'Casey: Roots and Branches"; Nathan, George Jean. *My Very Dear Sean: George Jean Nathan to Sean O'Casey, Letters and Articles.* Rutherford, Madison, Teaneck, N.J.: Fairleigh Dickinson University Press/London & Toronto: Associated University Presses, [1985]; O'Casey, Eileen. *Cheerio, Titan: The Friendship between George Bernard Shaw and Eileen and Sean O'Casey.* New York: Scribner's, [1989]; O'Casey, Eileen. *Eileen.* London: Macmillan, 1976; O'Casey, Eileen. *Sean.* London: Macmillan/Dublin: Gill & Macmillan, 1971/New York: Coward, McCann & Geoghegan, 1972; Ó hAodha, Micheál, ed. *The O'Casey Enigma.* Dublin & Cork: Radio Telefís Éireann & Mercier, [1980]; Pauli, Manfred. *Sean O'Casey: Drama, Poesie, Wirklichkeit.* Berlin: Henscheiverlag Kunst und Gesellschaft, 1977; Rollins, Ronald G. *Sean O'Casey's Drama: Verisimilitude and Vision.* University: University of Alabama Press, 1979; Scrimgeour, James B. *Sean O'Casey.* Boston: Twayne, [1978]; Simmons, James. *Sean O'Casey.* London & Basingstoke: Macmillan, 1983; Smith, B. L. *O'Casey's Satiric Vision.* [Kent, Ohio]: Kent State University Press, [1978]; Volker, Klaus. *Irisches Theater II: Sean O'Casey.* Velber: Friedrich Verlag, 1968; Widmer, Urs, ed. *Sean O'Casey: Eine Auswahl aus den Stücken, der Autobiographie und den Aufsätzen.* Zurich: Diogenes, 1970; Wilson, Donald Douglas. *Sean O'Casey's Tragi-Comic Vision.* New York: Revisionist, 1970; Winkler, Burchard. *Wirkstrategische Verwendung popularliterarischer Elemente in Sean O'Caseys dramatischen Werk unter besonderer Berücksichtigung des Melodramas.* Göppingen: Alfred Kümmerle, 1977; Wittig, Kurt. *Sean O'Casey als Dramatiker: Ein Beitrag zum Nachkriegsdrama Irlands.* Leipzig: Fritz Scharf, 1937; Zaslawski, Heinz. *Die Werke Sean O'Caseys, unter Besonderer Berücksichtigung Seiner Zweiten Periode.* Wien, 1949. In addition, Robert G. Lowery edited and published from Holbrook, New York, *The Sean O'Casey Review,* which lasted from 1974 to 1980. It was succeeded by the *O'Casey Annual,* also edited by Lowery, which appeared from 1982 to 1985, and was published by Humanities Press of Atlantic Highlands, N.J.

O'CONNELL, CHARLES C[HRISTOPHER] (fl. 1940s–1960s), novelist. O'Connell wrote four novels with a religious bent, which are rather generously considered remarkable by Brady and Cleeve.

WORKS: *Light over Fatima.* Cork: Mercier, 1947; *The Vanishing Island.* Dublin: Talbot, 1957; *The Miracle Maker.* Dublin: Talbot, 1960; *The Stubborn Heart.* Dublin: Talbot, 1964.

O'CONNOR, BRIDGET (1961–   ), short story writer. Born in London to Irish parents on January 18, 1961, O'Connor took a B.A. in English literature at Lancaster University. She has worked as a writer in residence and a community publisher and in adult education. Her collection, *Here Comes John* (1993), was short-listed for the *Irish Times* First Fiction Award. It is a heady cacophony of the 1990s, a jangle of mostly young, urban voices, gritty, greedy, obsessional, and occasionally violent. At their best, O'Connor's characters, from the knowing manipulator of the title story to the self-centered teenager of "I'm Running Late," spring from the darker realities of the here and now, provoking a shudder of recognition. If some of the stories are slight, they engage nonetheless through a zest for language and their coruscating black humor.

IVY BANNISTER

WORK: *Here Comes John.* London: Jonathan Cape, 1993. (Short stories).

O'CONNOR, CLAIRR (1951–   ), novelist, poet, and playwright. Born in Limerick, O'Connor received a B.A. from University College, Cork, in medieval history and English in 1972. In 1982 she received a master's in education and in 1986 a diploma in Japanese studies from St. Patrick's College, Maynooth. Since 1972, she has taught in England and in Ireland. She has published short stories, and her as yet unpublished plays have been performed in Cork, on RTÉ, and on BBC Radio 4. She lives with her family in Dublin.

Her *When You Need Them* (1989) is a book of short, free-verse poems, straightforward, often descriptive, usually about motherhood and housewifery, and none really too striking. Her novel, *Belonging* (1991), however, is quite a considerable accomplishment. The heroine, Deirdre, is initially a rather hysterical and dissatisfied young woman who returns to Ireland from her university teaching job in New York for the funeral of her parents. Her insecurity is increased by the apparent revelation in her father's papers that she is really the daughter of a Hungarian refugee and also by her childhood friend's becoming pregnant by her New York lover. Up to about halfway in the book, the reader is somewhat irked by Deirdre's cloying self-pity. However, the good counsel of good friends and the discovery that she is really her parents' daughter slowly help her to pull herself together, to write a book on Emily Dickinson, and to decide to keep her parents' house, which she now treasures, and to renovate it as a small country house hotel. The change in Deirdre necessarily comes slowly, and the book is a leisurely one. Its characters, however, are excellently realized, and it is a mature, intelligent, and very satisfying volume.

Love in Another Room (1995) is a crisply written, page-turning account of the interwoven lives of perhaps forty people—wives, new wives, old husbands, children, friends, children's friends, servants. Some characters are nicely caught, but others are necessarily more skimpily developed. Thus, one often wonders at the beginning of a new scene—Robert? Connie? Now who are they? The story is told in many somewhat short scenes, rather like a television soap opera. It eventually comes to a cursory winding up of several of the main plot strands, but there was no reason it could not have been extended, like a soap opera, for many more episodes. The strength of the book is the persuasiveness of some of the characterization. What it all means is something else again. But what did "Dallas" mean, or "The Riordans," or "Glenroe"?

WORKS: *When You Need Them.* [Galway]: Salmon, [1989]. (Poetry); *Belonging.* Dublin: Attic, [1991]. (Novel); *Love in Another Room.* [Dublin]: Marino, [1995]. (Novel).

O'CONNOR, CONLETH (1947–   ), poet. O'Connor was born in Newbridge, County Kildare. His first slim volume of verse and poetic prose, *Trinities* (1976), is interesting in language but seldom, even on its own terms, approaches effective poetic form. By his third volume, *Behind the Garden Gnomes* (1982), it seemed clear that a major influence was e. e. cummings. The effects depended on striking phrasing, arbitrary line lengths, and eccentric positioning of words and lines on the page. Some of the phrasing and ideas are extremely striking, such as a farmer dosing his cows with valium to protect them from "the indignity of milk." In the best of cummings, however, there is a discernible and effective reason for his arrangement of words on the page. In O'Connor, the reasons are usually inexplicable, and pieces like "still life" or "Pensketches" would be difficult to defend as poetry or, indeed, anything.

WORKS: *Trinities.* Clondalkin, Co. Dublin: Profile, 1976; *The Judas Cry.* [Dublin: Raven Arts, 1979]; *Behind the Garden Gnomes.* [Dublin: Raven Arts, 1982].

O'CONNOR, FRANK (1903–1966), short story writer and man of letters. Frank O'Connor, a pseudonym for Michael O'Donovan, is known primarily for his short stories but claims an equally high place in Anglo-Irish literature for his translations from Irish verse. He also wrote novels, biography, criticism, poetry, and autobiography. Michael O'Donovan was a person of fierce sympathies; his idealism was often too buoyant, his bitterness too heavy; his personal affairs swirled in a maze of conflicting impulses. But in his writing Frank O'Connor was a model of discipline and self-control. Everything he wrote displays his contending spirit, but his stories and translations in particular reveal his struggle for artistic integrity and personal freedom.

Michael O'Donovan was born on September 17, 1903, in Cork, where he was raised in impoverished conditions. These early years are brilliantly drawn by O'Connor in *An Only Child* (1964). Being frail and sensitive as well as poor, Michael found escape in his books and his dreams. Formal schooling ended when he was twelve, though not before he had come under the tutelage of Daniel Corkery,* who introduced him to the Irish language and the richness of his native past and showed him the breadth of European culture. Corkery's nationalistic fervor led Michael to enlist with the Volunteers and eventually to stand adamant with the Republicans in the Civil War. For this activity he was imprisoned at Gormanstown. Much of his early writing emanates from the unrestrained idealism of those troubled times; his first volume of stories, *Guests of the Nation* (1931), indulges the romanticism of ambushes, guns, and flying-columns. The brilliance and appeal of the title story are beyond question. Abstract "duty" forces three Irish rebels to execute their two English hostages after a long night of cards, drink, and talk. The narrator's response to what he had done sounds that note of tragic disaffection which O'Connor himself carried away from prison; the same lonely voice is heard again in story after story. It is heard, too, in his biography of Michael Collins, *The Big Fellow* (1937), a strident and uncompromising book which says as much about Michael O'Donovan as Michael Collins. It represents O'Connor's most extreme attitude toward the Revolution; disillusioned by the Catholic-nationalist establishment of de Valera, he asserted that the heat of genius had been replaced by the chill of normality.

After his release from prison, O'Connor taught Irish, started a theatre group in Cork, and earned his living as a librarian in Sligo, Wicklow, and Cork. While serving in Wicklow he met AE* and began publishing in *The Irish Statesman* under the name "Frank O'Connor" (his middle name and his mother's maiden name). During the short life of that influential magazine, O'Connor contributed over seventy-five pieces (poems, articles, reviews, and stories) and became a prominent figure in Dublin literary circles. He sketched these productive years in *My Father's Son* (1967), including his friendship with AE and Yeats* and his tumultuous tenure on the Board of Directors of the Abbey Theatre.* During that decade in Dublin, he published two volumes of stories, *Guests of the Nation* (1931) and *Bones of Contention* (1936); a novel, *The Saint and Mary Kate* (1932); the biography of Collins; a volume of poetry, *Three Old Brothers* (1936); three volumes of verse translations from the Irish; and even a few plays. By his own admission he was "fumbling for a style" during these years. In the two novels *The Saint and Mary Kate* and *Dutch Interior* (1940), he not only experimented with an unfamiliar form but also explored his past. The young people in both novels seek escape from the provincial narrowness of Cork—from poverty or boredom or loneliness. Like the poems he had been writing for over ten years, the novels were improvisational and imbalanced. But where the poems of *Three Old Brothers* present a detached and mannered voice, the novels are serious and personal. Still, the poetry is as direct and unpretentious as his finest prose; the novels are as dramatic and intense as his stories. Which is to say, these early improvisations on the theme of the writer creating himself help to explain why O'Connor inevitably stayed with the short story. He was a lyric poet ill at ease with the formal limitations of poetry. He was a storyteller interested more in the flash points of human experience than in sustained artifice. As flawed as they are, the novels and poems deal with most of the issues which dominate O'Connor's stories, particularly the burden of loneliness.

By 1939, O'Connor had resigned from the Abbey Theatre after a bitter feud, resigned his library post, married a young Welsh actress, and moved to Wicklow to write. By any reckoning, 1940 marks a dividing line for all Irish writers:

Yeats was dead and Joyce* soon would be; a new international war had broken out, testing Ireland's political strength, to say nothing of its intellectual integrity. Censorship and shrinking markets in Britain and America closed the usual publishing channels to writers of O'Connor's generation. Some followed Joyce into exile; O'Connor stayed. In 1940, a new magazine, *The Bell,** appeared in Dublin, edited by O'Connor's old Cork friend Sean O'Faolain.* For the first few years O'Connor was the poetry editor. O'Connor and O'Faolain and the other "strayed revellers" of the Literary Revival sought to clear the air of "convention, imitation, traditionalism, wishful thinking." They also needed an outlet for their work. *The Bell,* literally and figuratively, kept writers and their work alive during those lean years; it stimulated the second wave of significant literary activity in Ireland in this century. O'Connor's role was substantial. In addition to his essays, reviews, and stinging letters to the editor, he contributed some of his best stories ("Bridal Night," "Long Road to Ummera," and "Uprooted") and translations, including "The Midnight Court."

Both O'Faolain and O'Connor believed that the esoteric and elitist forms used by Yeats and Joyce failed to touch the majority of Irishmen. Thus, they took their concerns directly to the "common reader." O'Connor's struggle with Irish provincialism during these years took the form of a campaign to preserve that heritage held in the monasteries, castles, and megalithic sites scattered about the country. The first skirmishes appeared in *The Bell;* more articles appeared in *The Irish Times* and *The Sunday Independent. Irish Miles* (1947) was the culmination of this campaign, which established O'Connor as one of the abrasive voices of conscience in Ireland. It is a travel book only to the extent that *The Big Fellow* is biography; as with everything else he wrote it is more like autobiography, for O'Connor believed that a writer's works are an allegory of his life. In the account of the cycling trips he and his wife had been taking around the Irish countryside in search of ruins and other antiquities, *Irish Miles* is vintage O'Connor. It is also Michael O'Donovan playing himself—effusive and restless, lyrical and irascible. Above all, it reveals a storyteller in hot pursuit of stories. These cycling trips kept his curious and contentious spirit alive, but his writing was insufficient to support his growing family. He therefore resorted to broadcasting readings of his stories and of Irish poetry, personal reminiscences, and literary opinions for the BBC. What is striking about his broadcasting and journalistic endeavors is that he did not see them as alien to his artistic commitment. To him a story required the voice of a man speaking. Literature—fiction, poetry, or drama—he considered to be nothing less than the art of collaboration.

By the time he published his third volume of stories, O'Connor had not only explored the limits of the story but had begun to expand them. Consequently, *Crab Apple Jelly* (1944) is at once the most varied and disciplined collection he was to produce. As the title implies, its voice is both sweet and tart, entertaining and serious. O'Connor was at a sufficient distance from his subjects to observe and accept without casting blame or becoming involved. Such stories as "Bridal Night," "Michael's Wife," and "Uprooted" leave little doubt about the power of his prose to evoke highly poetic visual images. Like his translations from the Irish, however, these stories are "lyrical" not because of static description but because the sound of the voice is heard within a supremely resonant environment. The stories of *Crab Apple Jelly* represent the refinement of his technique of exploiting the speaking voice, the voice of the broadcaster or the *shanachie*. Nowhere is this oral quality more evident than in "The Long Road to Ummera," a simple tale about an old woman's wish to be buried in the mountain home of her people. In the same volume were O'Connor's first stories about sexual repression within Irish life; "The Mad Lomasneys," however, was really more subtle than shocking. Still, O'Connor's name gradually became associated with sexual impiety and unpatriotic complaint. *Dutch Interior* (1940) was officially banned as were his translations of "The Midnight Court" and, later, *The Common Chord* (1948) and *Traveller's Samples* (1951).

Thus, by 1950, O'Connor had created a vacuum for himself in Ireland. The pressures of war and his extended absences had complicated his personal life. It was probably inevitable that in 1951, unable to support himself in Dublin or to cope with the turmoil of censorship and his own divorce, O'Connor accepted invitations to teach in the United States. This "exile" was both a personal and a professional necessity; he was able to heal his personal life and to plunge into his writing again. His stories and autobiographical sketches drew great acclaim as they appeared with increasing frequency in American magazines. Readers were more than likely charmed by the deceptively simple manner of his writing, particularly those stories of childhood and adolescence for which he is best known ("My Oedipus Complex," "The Drunkard," "My First Confession"). As his writing became more personal, O'Connor attained a kind of detachment by way of technique. Emotion and lyrical expressiveness were dropped in favor of formal control. A strategy of containment (scaling down of issue, situations, and language) had always been the mark of an O'Connor story. But the stories of the 1950s, particularly those in *Domestic Relations* (1956), are rather too simple, too balanced, too smooth. It is not without significance that O'Connor was also writing his most extensive literary criticism at this time.

O'Connor had always seen life through a veil of literature, and from his first reviews in *The Irish Statesman* to his last articles in *The New York Times Review of Books,* O'Connor's literary opinions were assumptive and flamboyant, revealing as much about him as what he happened to be writing about. *The Mirror in the Roadway* (1956) and *The Lonely Voice* (1962) both grew out of his American teaching experiences. O'Connor took literature seriously, and these books stand not only as explorations of the novel and the short story but also as a defense of literature. In the one, he is an audacious amateur, reading such giants as Dickens, Flaubert, and Tolstoy. What one hears in *The Lonely Voice* is one great writer of short stories collaborating with other great writers of short stories. It is a defense of the writer himself. Shortly after that book, O'Connor turned his hand to the book suggested thirty years before by Yeats—a history of Irish literature. *The Backward Look* (1967) is actually a criticism of a larger life, a synthesis of a culture; it is a personal statement because O'Connor was strictly an Irish writer and Irish culture was his only battleground. In the first half of the book, O'Connor the translator is seen at work, talking about Irish literature in Irish. In the second half, the Anglo-Irish short story writer holds forth on Irish literature in English. The backward look is a forward impulse: coming to terms with what you are, you confront what you are becoming. O'Connor's collaboration with Merriman and Swift,* Ferguson* and Yeats, is a magical and improvisational process.

O'Connor married again in 1953 and frequently visited Ireland with his young American wife after 1956. He had kept tenaciously to his writing during the years of separation and exile. Actually, during the last ten years of his life he published more than in any comparable period in his career. Ireland had remained his primary source of imaginative energy and though his return (finally, in 1961 after a stroke) was not accompanied by an infusion of magic, his writing appeared to regain something of its old vigor and audacity. *Kings, Lords, and Commons* (1959) is the culmination of almost forty years of devotion to the translation of Irish poetry into English. *The Backward Look* is an equally mature and considered affirmation of Ireland's rich heritage. *A Set of Variations* (published posthumously), a collection of stories written mainly in the 1960s, shows flashes of the rough intensity found in his early stories. As a whole, the volume displays a range of themes, characters, and styles as extensive as *Crab Apple Jelly*. O'Connor had moved closer to himself while assuming once again the detached narrative voice. The stories about priests at the end of the volume carry a distinct emotional power. Like the title story, they represent O'Connor's last affirmations of the imaginative way of life, or what he called his "lyric cry in the face of destiny."

O'Connor died in Dublin on March 10, 1966. James Plunkett* in *The Gems She Wore* describes O'Connor at the end of his life as having "the air of someone who had found where he belonged, not an easy thing for a writer to achieve in the Ireland of his time." At the graveside oration, Brendan Kennelly* suggested for an epitaph the lines of Yeats about the "life like a gambler's throw." With all the arrogance of the self-taught, Michael O'Donovan/Frank O'Connor had improvised his way to greatness in a "lonely, personal art," producing simple stories of impeccable design carrying sparse revelations about common folks in language direct and alive. He once said that where Yeats, Synge,* and the rest have their "presences" to offer eternity, "I have only my voices." The voice of such books as *Kings, Lords, and Commons, Irish Miles,* and *The Backward Look* will persist, but his stories will inevitably stand as his most enduring contribution to modern literature and to Irish life.

JAMES H. MATTHEWS

WORKS: *Guests of the Nation.* London: Macmillan, 1931. (Stories); *The Saint and Mary Kate.* London: Macmillan, 1932. (Novel); *The Wild Bird's Nest.* Dublin: Cuala, 1932. (Translations from the Irish); *Bones of Contention and Other Stories.* London: Macmillan, 1936; *Three Old Brothers and Other Poems.* London: Nelson, 1936; *The Big Fellow.* London: Nelson, 1937. (Biography of Michael Collins); *The Fountain of Magic.* London: Macmillan, 1939. (Translations from the Irish); *Dutch Interior.* London: Macmillan, 1940. (Novel); *Three Tales.* Dublin: Cuala, 1941; *Crab Apple Jelly.* London: Macmillan, 1944. (Stories); *Towards an Appreciation of Literature.* Dublin: Metropolitan, 1945. (Criticism); *Selected Stories.* Dublin: Maurice Fridberg, 1946; *The Art of the Theatre.* Dublin & London: Maurice Fridberg, 1947. (Criticism); *The Common Chord.* London: Macmillan, 1947. (Stories); *Irish Miles.* London: Macmillan, 1947. (Travel/architecture); *The Road to Stratford.* London: Methuen, 1948. (Criticism); *Traveller's Samples.* London: Macmillan, 1951. (Stories); *The Stories of Frank O'Connor.* New York: Knopf, 1952/London: Hamish Hamilton, 1953; *More Stories by Frank O'Connor.* New York: Knopf, 1954, 1967; *The Mirror in the Roadway.* New York: Knopf, 1956. (Criticism); *Domestic Relations.* New York: Knopf/London: Hamish Hamilton, 1957. (Stories); *Kings, Lords, & Commons.* New York: Knopf, 1959. (Translations from the Irish); *Shakespeare's Progress.* Cleveland: World, 1960. (Revised & enlarged edition of *The Road to Stratford*); *An Only Child.* New York: Knopf, 1961/London: Macmillan, 1962. (Autobiography); *The Lonely Voice.* Cleveland: World, 1962/London: Macmillan, 1963. (Criticism); *Collection Two.* London: Macmillan, 1964. (Stories); *The Backward Look.* London: Macmillan, 1967/published in the United States as *A Short History of Irish Literature,* New York: Putnam, 1967; *My Father's Son.* London: Macmillan, 1968/New York: Knopf, 1969. (Autobiography); *Collection Three.* London: Macmillan, 1969/published in the United States as *A Set of Variations,* New York: Knopf, 1969; *Journal of Irish Literature* 4 (January 1975), a Frank O'Connor Number. James H. Matthews, ed.; with Hugh Hunt, *The Invincibles.* Ruth Sherry, ed. [Newark, Del.:] Proscenium, [1980]. (Play); *The Cornet Player Who Betrayed Ireland.* Swords, Co. Dublin: Poolbeg, 1981. (Stories); with Hugh Hunt, *Moses' Rock.* Ruth Sherry, ed. Gerrards Cross: Colin Smythe/Washington, D.C.: Catholic University of America Press, 1983; "Rodney's Glory." Ruth Sherry, ed. *Irish University Review* 22 (Autumn/Winter 1992): 219–241. (One-act play); *A Frank O'Connor Reader.* Michael Steinman, ed. Syracuse, N.Y.: Syracuse University Press, 1994. REFERENCES: Alexander, James. "An Annotated Bibliography of Works about Frank O'Connor." *Journal of Irish Literature* 16 (September 1987): 40–48; Matthews, James H. *Frank O'Connor.* Lewisburg, Pa.: Bucknell University Press, 1976; Matthews, James H. *Voices: A Life of Frank O'Connor.* New York: Atheneum, 1985; Sheehy, Maurice, ed. *Michael/Frank: Studies in Frank O'Connor.* Dublin: Gill & Macmillan, 1969; Steinman, Michael. *Frank O'Connor at Work.* Syracuse, N.Y.: Syracuse University Press, 1990; Tomory, William. *Frank O'Connor.* Boston: Twayne, 1980; Wohlgelernter, Maurice. *Frank O'Connor: An Introduction.* New York: Columbia University Press, 1977.

O'CONNOR, GEMMA (1940–   ), novelist. O'Connor was born in Dublin on May 3, 1940, and educated in Ireland and France. She has worked as a bookbinder and restorer and edited *Valiant Women,* a biographical series on Irish political women published by Pandora Press. She has published *Back to Work,* a self-help book for women, edited two dramatic anthologies, and written an unpublished play on Swift* and another on Nora Joyce. Her *"Hell!" Said the Duchess or First Lines* (1985) is an engaging collection of first lines from books. Her novel, *Sins of Omission* (1995), is an engrossing psychological thriller. The reader is immediately hooked as a man's body is pulled from the Grand Canal in Dublin. Then we are introduced to Grace Hartfield, whose world in the London suburbs has fallen apart when her husband left her. Grace, a book dealer, finds herself the beneficiary of two unknown women who turn out to be her long-lost sister and her niece. The novel tells the story of these three intertwining lives. The characters of Grace and her niece, Bid, are touching and convincing, as are those of Reggie, the deserting husband, and of Father Crowley. The plot skillfully moves back and forward in time, and it is to O'Connor's credit that she makes believable an unbelievable situation in its resolution. Also, the sense of place is excellent. London comes alive, and the reader can almost smell Dublin's dank canal and its leaf-choked locks.

MARY ROSE CALLAGHAN

PRINCIPAL WORKS: Comp. *"Hell!" Said the Duchess or First Lines.* [Dublin]: Wolfhound, [1985]; *Sins of Omission.* [Dublin]: Poolbeg, [1995].

O'CONNOR, JOSEPH (1963–), novelist and short story writer. Born in Dublin, O'Connor graduated from University College, Dublin, in 1986, and later briefly attended Oxford University and worked for the British Nicaragua Solidarity Campaign. He has been a journalist and has written television and film scripts and a biography of the Irish poet Charles Donnelly.* In 1989, he won the *Sunday Tribune* First Fiction and New Irish Writer of the Year Awards. In 1990, he won the *Time Out* magazine Writing Prize and was short-listed for the Whitbread Prize for his first novel, *Cowboys and Indians.* In 1993, he was awarded the Macaulay Fellowship of the Irish Arts Council. His sister is the well-known pop singer Sinead O'Connor.

The critical reception to O'Connor's first three works—*Cowboys and Indians* (1991), *True Believers* (1991), and *Desperadoes* (1994)—was mixed. While many critics applauded his eye for contemporary life, others chided his works for relying too much on shock value and having, at times, an unpolished writing style. An accurate reading probably lies somewhere in the middle. Undoubtedly O'Connor has a sharp eye for the less glamorous side of life; his is a kind of realism that would make the Irish realist writers of the 1930s and 1940s blush. Yet, the potential for impressive accomplishments to come is obviously there. In *Cowboys and Indians,* O'Connor creates a wonderful character in Eddie Virago, a would-be rock star with a Mohawk hairstyle and a troubled personal life. In many ways, Virago is a 1990s Stephen Dedalus; indeed, the protagonist even draws the comparison himself. While the overall depth and artistry of the book are not on the same level as those of *A Portrait of the Artist as a Young Man,* the parallels exist. In *Cowboys and Indians,* O'Connor does a fine job of illustrating the malaise of what has come to be known as "Generation X"—people born in the mid-1960s to the mid-1970s. Essentially, the novel is about self-discovery and self-definition. Caught up in a world of alcohol and drugs, Virago stumbles through a life of emigration in London, determined to distance himself from Ireland and his past. When he finally decides that what he really wants is a meaningful relationship with his girlfriend, Marion, Virago discovers that the Donegal woman has a past more complex and horrible than his own. As a debut, *Cowboys and Indians* is impressive because of O'Connor's ability to capture realistically the sense of confusion and anguish in the characters' lives.

The opening story of O'Connor's collection entitled *True Believers* features the return of Eddie Virago in "Last of the Mohicans." The collection highlights some of O'Connor's best traits as a writer: realism and a style that breaks from the tightly structured traditional Irish short story. His main theme, however, is traditionally Irish: exile. With a focus on London's Irish émigrés, O'Connor gives a voice to a group of people who have been largely ignored: Nipples (New Irish Professional Person), as they are called in the story "The Wizard of Oz." Again, at times the storytelling and technique could be smoother, but O'Connor's characters and shrewd observations of contemporary life make *True Believers* a fine collection.

O'Connor's second novel, *Desperadoes,* is an ambitious work that shows a development in writing style and storytelling skill. Ostensibly, it is a story about Dubliners Frank and Eleanor Little going to Nicaragua to collect the body of their slain son. The time and setting, 1985 and Managua and a host of small towns caught in the Sandanista-Contra battle for power, give the work a sense of urgency and desperation. O'Connor's realism makes *Desperadoes* an engaging and believable narrative; and the descriptions of the places, the heat, and the people are photographic. Yet, as Frank Little points out a number of times, take away the heat and humidity, and Nicaragua is Ireland: green fields, impressive mountains, an abundance of poor people struggling to make a living, and a dependence on the agricultural past. While the action centers on the arduous process the Littles must go through to find their son, Johnny (who went to Nicaragua to escape his family and "assist" in the fight for freedom), the core of the account is how Frank and Eleanor sort out their failed marriage and the toll it took on each other and their son. O'Connor does a wonderful job of alternating the action in Nicaragua and of tracing the Littles' lives that led to the troubled situation. When they finally discover that Johnny is alive but in prison for transporting drugs for the Contras, father, mother, and son struggle to come to terms with their past. Like *Cowboys and Indians, Desperadoes* offers a collection of entertaining characters, ranging from Johnny's rich American rebel friend and rock-and-roll bandmate Smokes, to Lorenzo, a blind guitar player who sold his soul to the devil to be able to play the blues. The most impressive aspect of the novel, though, is O'Connor's insight into the emotional state of his characters. Some may credit this to a maturation in his writing style or a stronger plot. Regardless, O'Connor continues to prove that his work is among young Ireland's best and that he, along with Roddy Doyle,* Dermot Bolger,* and Colm Toibin,* is the nucleus of the revival of the Irish novel.

SHAWN O'HARE

WORKS: *Cowboys and Indians.* London: Sinclair-Stevenson, 1991/London: Flamingo, 1992; *True Believers.* London: Sinclair-Stevenson, 1991/London: Flamingo, 1992; *Even the Olives Are Bleeding: The Life and Times of Charles Donnelly.* Dublin: New Island Books, 1992; *Desperadoes.* London: Flamingo, 1994; *The Secret World of the Irish Male.* Dublin: New Island Books, [1994]. (Essays); *Red Roses and Petrol.* [London]: Methuen, [1995]. (Play).

O'CONNOR, JOSEPH K. (1878–1961), writer of sketches. O'Connor was born in Ashford, County Limerick, and educated at Clongowes Wood. He became a barrister and later a judge. His *Studies in Blue* (1903), written under the pseudonym of Heblon, was sketches of Dublin slum life, as seen from the police courts. O'Connor also had a minor hand in revising the dialogue of Oliver Gogarty's* play of slum life, *Blight* (1917), which was produced under the pseudonyms of Alpha and Omega.

WORKS: *Studies in Blue.* Dublin: Sealy, Bryers, [1903]; *Blight.* Dublin: Talbot, 1917/rpt. in *The Plays of Oliver Gogarty.* James F. Carens, ed. Newark, Del.: Proscenium, 1971.

O'CONNOR, KATHLEEN (1934–   ), novelist. O'Connor was born in Blackpool near Cork city, joined the Irish Sisters of Charity when she was seventeen, and taught for several years before leaving the convent and marrying.

WORKS: *A Question of Heaven.* Cork: Emperor, 1990; *Stepping Stones.* Cork: Emperor, 1990; *Mags.* Cork: Emperor, 1991.

O'CONNOR, PATRICIA (fl. 1930s–1950s), novelist and playwright.

WORKS: *Mary Doherty.* London & Glasgow: Sands, [1938]. (Novel); *The Mill in the North.* Dublin: Talbot, 1938. (Novel); *Select Vestry.* Belfast: Quota, [1946]; ed., *Four New One-Act Plays.* Belfast: Quota, [1948]; *The Farmer Wants a Wife.* Belfast: H. R. Carter, 1955. (Three-act comedy).

O'CONNOR, ULICK (1928–   ), sportsman and man of letters. Born in Dublin, O'Connor attended St. Mary's College, Rathmines. As a young man, he had a distinguished career as an athlete and later as a sporting journalist. Having been Irish champion pole vaulter in 1947, he then won the welterweight boxing British Universities championship in 1950. A graduate of University College, Dublin, he did postgraduate work at Loyola University in New Orleans. Called to the Irish bar in 1951, he practiced as a barrister for fifteen years. He is now a frequent broadcaster on sport and literature and contributes to *Observer, Scotsman, Spectator, Tablet,* and *Time and Tide.* Though he has written poetry, plays, and a great deal of literary and social criticism, O'Connor's reputation is as a biographer in the Lytton Strachey mold. His aim is to present not a biography in the overly detailed modern style but a rounded, humane portrait of his subjects. He wrote biographies of Oliver St. John Gogarty* and of Brendan Behan,* as well as popular accounts of the Troubles and of the Irish literary revival. Of these, the biography of Gogarty remains the most readable, one where the author matches the subject with fine feeling and warmth. A colorful controversialist with strong opinions on many subjects, he was for years a feature of "The Late, Late Show" on RTÉ.

PETER COSTELLO

WORKS: *Oliver St. John Gogarty: A Poet and His Times.* London: Cape, 1964; *The Gresham Hotel, 1865–1965.* Cork: Printed by Guy & Co., 1965; ed., *The Joyce We Knew.* Cork: Mercier, 1967; *Travels with Ulick.* Cork: Mercier, 1967; *Sputnik and Other Poems.* New York: Devin-Adair, [1967]; *Brendan.* London: Hamish Hamilton, 1970/Englewood Cliffs, N.J.: Prentice-Hall, [1971]; *Life Styles.* Dublin: Dolmen, 1973. (Poetry); *A Terrible Beauty Is Born: The Irish Troubles, 1912–1922.* London: Hamish Hamilton, 1975; *The Fitzwilliam Story, 1877–1977.* [Dublin: Fitzwilliam Lawn Tennis Club, 1977]; *Three Noh Plays.* Portmarnock: Wolfhound, 1980; *Irish Tales and Sagas.*

London: Granada, 1981; ed., *Skylark Sing Your Lonely Song: An Anthology of the Writings of Bobby Sands.* Dublin & Cork: Mercier, 1982; *Celtic Dawn: A Portrait of the Irish Literary Renaissance.* London: Hamish Hamilton, 1984. (Literary history); *A Critic at Large.* Cork: Mercier, 1984; *Sport Is My Lifeline.* London: Pelham, 1984. (Collection of sporting journalism); ed., *The Campbell Companion: The Best of Patrick Campbell.* London: Pavilion, 1987; *Brian Friel: Crisis and Commitment, the Writer and Northern Ireland.* Dublin: Ely, 1989. (Pamphlet); *Biography as an Art.* Dublin: Wolfhound, 1991/London: Quartet, 1993; *One Is Animate.* Dublin: Beaver Row, 1991. (Poetry); ed., *The Yeats Companion.* London: Mandarin, 1991; *Executions.* [Dingle, Co. Kerry]: Brandon, [1992]. (Play); tr., *Baudelaire: Poems of the Damned.* Dublin: Wolfhound, 1995.

O'CURRY, EUGENE (1796–1862), scholar. O'Curry was born in Dunaha, County Clare, in 1796. He was self-educated, and in 1834 was employed in the topographical and historical section of the Ordnance Survey. This employment brought him into contact with such learned contemporaries as George Petrie* and John O'Donovan* and made him aware of the rich collections of Irish manuscript material in Dublin, London, and Oxford. With Petrie and O'Donovan, O'Curry laid the foundations of modern scholarship in Irish, by his prodigious cataloguing and voluminous transcribing of Irish manuscripts, as well as his translations of a number of them. On the foundation of the new Catholic University, O'Curry became professor of Irish History and Archaeology and gave his first lectures in 1855. These lectures, published in 1861, ran to over seven hundred pages and gave a full account of the chief Irish medieval manuscripts and their contents. He died in Dublin on July 30, 1862.

WORKS: *The Sick Bed of Cuchulainn and The Only Jealousy of Emer. The "Tri Thruaighe na Scéalaigheachta": The Three Most Sorrowful Tales of Erinn.* Dublin: J. F. Fowles, 1858; *Lectures on the Manuscript Materials of Ancient Irish History.* Dublin: J. Duffy, 1861; *On the Manners and Customs of the Ancient Irish.* 3 vols. London: Williams & Norgate/Dublin: W. B. Kelly/New York: Scribner's, 1873.

O'DOHERTY, BRIAN

WORK: *The Strange Case of Mademoiselle P.* London: Chatto, 1992. (Novel).

O'DOHERTY, SHANE

WORK: *The Immaculate Deception.* Dublin: Down to Earth, 1994. (Novel).

O'DONNELL, HUGH (1951–   ), poet. O'Donnell is a Salesian priest who was born in Dublin.

WORKS: *Mrs. Moody's Blues See Red.* 1980; *Roman Pines at Berkeley.* Galway: Salmon, 1990. (Poems).

O'DONNELL, JOHN FRANCIS (1837–1874), poet and fiction writer. O'Donnell was born in Limerick and, when only fourteen, began to publish verses in *The Kilkenny Journal.* A fluent and prolific poet and prose writer, he contributed to, or edited, many journals—*The Nation,* * *The Lamp, The Irish People, The Shamrock, The Dublin Review,* Dickens's *All the Year Round, Duf-*

fy's Hibernian Magazine, and others. His two serialized novels and broadly amusing sketches are now forgotten, but his poetry has had some modern champions, among them Geoffrey Taylor,* John Betjeman, and Seamus Deane.* He has his occasional nineteenth-century poetic mannerisms, and some of his nature poetry is a little dimly focused. Nevertheless, he can be as tersely exact as:

> Then crew the cocks from echoing farms,
>   The chimney-tops were plumed with smoke,
> The windmill shook its slanted arms,
>   The sun was up, the country woke!

He has also, no matter what formal problem he sets for himself, a smooth metrical command. This stanza from "Limerick Town," for instance:

> "Pshaw! you're prosy." Am I prosy? Mark you then this
>   sunward flight:
> I have seen this street and rooftops ambered in the
>   morning's light,
> Golden in the deep of noonday, crimson on the marge of
>   night.

Or these two stanzas from "A Spinning Song":

> My love to fight the Saxon goes
>   And bravely shines his sword of steel,
> A heron's feather decks his brows,
>   And a spur on either heel;
> His steel is blacker than the sloe,
>   And fleeter than the falling star;
> Amid the surging ranks he'll go
>   And shout for joy of war.
>
> Tinkle, twinkle, pretty spindle, let the white wool drift and dwindle,
>   Oh! we weave a damask doublet for my love's coat of steel.
> Hark! the timid, turning treadle crooning soft, old-fashioned ditties
>   To the low, slow murmur of the brown round wheel.

O'Donnell has his dull patches, but he can do so much so well that he is nigh irresistible to quote. Both his poetry and his prose would repay scrutiny. He died in London in May 1874.

PRINCIPAL WORKS: *The Emerald War: A Fireside Treasury of Legends, Stories.* . . . Dublin: Duffy, 1864. (Prose and verse under the pseudonym of Caviare); *Memories of the Irish Franciscans.* Dublin: Duffy, 1871; *The Flight of the Earls.* Dublin, n.d.; *Poems.* London: Ward & Downey, 1891. REFERENCES: Dowling, Richard. "Introduction" to *Poems;* Taylor, Geoffrey. "The Best Nation Poet." *The Bell* 6 (1943): 237–241.

O'DONNELL, MARY (1954–   ), fiction writer and poet. O'Donnell was born in County Monaghan. She studied German and philosophy at Maynooth College and lives in Kildare with her husband and daughter. A poet, fiction writer, and critic, she is one of the most stylistically sophisticated and adventurous of the generation of Irishwomen who began writing in the 1970s.

She has published two collections of poetry, *Reading the Sunflowers in September* (1990) and *Spiderwoman's Third Avenue Rhapsody* (1993). Her poetry celebrates the power of the senses and the natural world; mythological motifs, childhood, love, motherhood, femininity are some of the themes. The poetry is striking for its combination of sensuality and convincingly intense emotion with an intellectual clarity. Her use of language is exceptionally deft, and her structures often perfect. She is one of the most imaginative and original of the younger Irish poets.

Her prose is also strong and exhibits many of the qualities of the poems; the same judicious use of language, elegance of structure, and essential intelligence are evident in both the short stories, *Strong Pagans* (1991), and the novel, *The Light-Makers* (1992). The stories, like those in most first collections, vary in thematic significance; several are concerned with marriage, illicit love, childhood experiences. These include some well-written and memorable explorations of feminine emotion, ''The Adulteress'' being particularly striking. This title story, which is the best harbinger of O'Donnell's mature voice, examines childhood wildness and relates it to adult nonconformity: the main male character is a transvestite.

The Light-Makers is a naturalistic novel whose heroine has confronted the problem of childlessness and now finds herself separated from her husband. Her childhood and early relationships are explored and successfully meshed with the experiences of her adult life. She is a photographer, and the role of art in life, particularly in her self-development and salvation, is examined. Although, in many ways, a conventional novel, *The Light-Makers* is structurally interesting: all the action occurs within one twenty-four-hour period, and the entwining of past and present, art and life, is dextrously achieved.

O'Donnell has not been beguiled by the pressure to be accessible and easy. She almost always avoids clichéd language or clichéd thought. Even her few flaws—for instance, occasional overexplication in the prose—are personal and original, rather than commonplace.

She has won a Francis MacManus Award for a short story and Listowel Writers' Week Awards for poetry. *Reading the Sunflowers in September* was nominated for the *Irish Times*/Aer Lingus Award in 1990.

EILÍS NÍ DHUIBHNE

WORKS: *Reading the Sunflowers in September*. Galway: Salmon, 1990. (Poetry); *Strong Pagans and Other Stories*. Dublin: Poolbeg, 1991; *The Light-Makers*. [Swords, Co. Dublin]: Poolbeg, [1992]. (Novel); *Spiderwoman's Third Avenue Rhapsody*. Dublin: Salmon/Poolbeg, 1993. (Poetry).

O'DONNELL, PEADAR (1893–1986), novelist, short story writer, editor, and social reformer. O'Donnell was born on February 22, 1893, on a farm at Meenmore, County Donegal, obtained his teaching credentials at St. Patrick's College,

Dublin, and taught for several years before espousing socialist views and becoming an organizer for the Transport and General Workers' Union in 1918.

In 1919, he participated in the Irish Republican Army's (IRA) guerrilla warfare against the British. He sided with the anti-Treaty forces against the Free Staters. When the civil war broke out, he was seized in July 1922 and imprisoned for almost two years. His first novel, *Storm,* appeared in 1925; and his second, *Islanders* of 1928, attracted considerable literary attention. For several years, he edited both *An t'Oglach* and *An Poblacht,* and in 1932 he published *The Gates Flew Open,* the first of three perceptive autobiographical commentaries. He continued to combine both political and literary concerns, breaking away from the IRA in 1934 to help form the Republican Congress, and in 1936 he began organizing support against Franco. From 1946 until it finally ceased publication in 1954, *The Bell** was edited by O'Donnell. He continued his campaign to improve economic conditions in western Ireland, served as a delegate to the World Peace Congress, and protested American involvement in the Vietnam War. He also worked diligently for nuclear disarmament and continued his social and political activism until his death in Dublin on May 13, 1986.

O'Donnell's most persistent theme is his concern for the poor farmers and fisherfolk who live in the west of Ireland, where hunger is omnipresent. Mary Doogan in *Islanders* must starve herself so that her children will have enough to eat. *Ardrigoole* is based on a true tragedy involving the death by starvation of a mother and child while the husband is imprisoned. The family had been shunned by neighbors because of the support it had given to the anti-Treaty group in the civil war.

In western Ireland, even hard work does not bring security, because of the rocky, nonfertile soil, the uncertainty of fishing catches, and the storms that oppress the fishermen. To endure, the peasants must hire out their children or take seasonal employment in Scotland. The emigrant laborers then force down the wages and amount of work for the Scottish poor. When Brigid Gallagher in *The Knife* remarks to a Scotswoman working beside her, ''Over at home we blame the Scotch for takin' the land we should be on,'' her coworker responds, ''It's a pickle, an' it's naw you an' me can put it right, lassie.''

O'Donnell's lifelong goal was to ''put it right''—to improve economic conditions for the poor by freeing the land from British domination and from the avarice of the shopkeepers and the well-to-do. Idealistically, he advocated the creation of worker-oriented cooperatives, socialist trade unions, and a government controlled by the working class.

As a novelist, O'Donnell's strongest qualities are his exceedingly realistic descriptions, his mastery of dialogue (which is enhanced by his firsthand command of Gaelic speech rhythms and phraseology), and his penetrating character portrayals. On the negative side, his novels and stories are frequently too slow-paced, often overly detailed, and too obviously, at times, tinged with social and political propaganda. Nevertheless, in his narratives, journalism, and autobiographical studies, O'Donnell has presented a painfully comprehensive picture of Ireland in one of its most turbulent eras.

PAUL A. DOYLE

WORKS: *Storm.* Dublin: Talbot, [1925]; *Islanders.* London: Jonathan Cape, 1928/published in the United States as *The Way It Was with Them.* New York: Putnam's, 1928/published later as *Irelanders.* Chester Springs, Pa.: Dufour, 1988; *Ardrigoole* London: Jonathan Cape/New York: Putnam's, 1929; *The Knife.* London: Jonathan Cape, 1930/published in the United States as *There Will Be Fighting.* New York: Putnam's, 1931/published later as *The Knife.* Dublin: Irish Humanities Centre & Chester Springs, Pa.: Dufour, 1980; *The Gates Flew Open.* London: Jonathan Cape, 1932. (Autobiography); *Wrack.* London: Jonathan Cape, 1933. (Play); *On the Edge of the Stream.* London: Jonathan Cape, 1934; *Salud! An Irishman in Spain.* London: Methuen, 1937. (Autobiography); *The Big Windows.* London: London: Jonathan Cape, 1955/reprinted London: Allison & Busby & Dublin: O'Brien, 1983/reprinted Dublin: O'Brien & Chester Springs, Pa.: Dufour, 1988; *There Will Be Another Day.* Dublin: Dolmen, 1963. (Autobiography); *Proud Island.* Dublin: O'Brien, 1975, 1988/ Chester Springs, Pa.: Dufour, 1988.   REFERENCES: Cahalan, James M. "Peadar O'Donnell and Michael McLaverty." In *The Irish Novel.* Boston: Twayne, 1988, pp. 191–196; Doyle, Paul A. "Peadar O'Donnell: A Checklist." *Bulletin of Bibliography* 28 (January–March 1971): 3–4; Freyer, Grattan. *Peadar O'Donnell.* Lewisburg, Pa.: Bucknell University Press, 1973; McInerney, Michael. *Peadar O'Donnell: Irish Social Rebel.* Dublin: O'Brien, 1976; Gonzalez, Alexander G. "Peadar O'Donnell's Short Stories." *Journal of Irish Literature* 17 (January 1988): 544–556; O'Leary, Philip. "The Donegal of Séamus Ó Grianna and Peadar O'Donnell." *Éire* 23 (Summer 1988): 135–149.

O'DONOGHUE, BERNARD (1945–   ), poet and scholar. O'Donoghue was born in Cullen, County Cork, and teaches medieval literature at Oxford. His first collection, *The Weakness* (1991), contains many poems about rural Cork and is written in a clean, easy, conversational style. It is thoughtful, realistically descriptive, and often quietly moving, as in "Lesser Deaths," or quietly resigned, as in the acceptance of inevitable failure in "The Dandy Dolls," a poem written from the viewpoint of Roger Carmondy, George Fitzmaurice's* Dandy doll maker. Much of the book is a low-key but frequently moving reflection on the past. Nevertheless, as Brian Lynch* remarks about his second book, *Gunpowder* (1995), "O'Donoghue's verse is sadly metre-less; awkward enjambments are everywhere; and the only rhymes are accidental."

WORK: *The Weakness.* London: Chatto & Windus, [1991]; *Gunpowder.* London: Chatto & Windus, [1995].

O'DONOGHUE, D[AVID] J[AMES] (1866–1917), scholar and editor. O'Donoghue was born in London on July 22, 1866, of Cork parents. In 1896, he came to Dublin and became a bookseller and then, in 1909, librarian to University College, Dublin. Like his friends W. J. Lawrence* and Joseph Holloway,* he was a self-taught scholar of prodigious industry and incredible learning. He did much valuable editing, including a Life and Writings of Mangan* and a six-volume edition of Lover.* He also wrote the first biography of William Carleton,* and his *The Poets of Ireland: A Biographical Dictionary* is still an impressive compilation, to which "this Dictionary owes much." He died in Dublin in 1917.

WORKS: ed., *The Humour of Ireland*. London: Walter Scott, 1894; *The Life of William Carleton*. 2 vols. London: Downey, 1896; *The Life and Writings of James Clarence Mangan*. Edinburgh: P. Geddes, 1897; *Life of Robert Emmet*. Dublin: Duffy, 1902; *The Geographical Distribution of Irish Ability*. Dublin: O'Donoghue, 1906; *The Poets of Ireland. A Biographical Dictionary*. Dublin: Hodges, Figgis/London: Henry Frowde, Oxford University Press, 1912.

O'DONOGHUE, JOHN (1900–1964), novelist. O'Donoghue was born in Kerry in 1900, the son of a small farmer. From 1924 to 1931, he served in the Irish police force, the Garda Siochana. Later he joined a monastery, and then he emigrated to England where he worked as a common laborer. His three published volumes are highly autobiographical, and the first and most successful, *In a Quiet Land* (1957), is perhaps the most typical. Nominally a novel, the book is really a simple, straightforward, and vivid evocation of a primitive society that in the author's youth was already dying but that had its roots in centuries past. Perhaps much more than the literary embroideries of Synge,* O'Donoghue's simple, naive, and eloquent books bring alive the rural Ireland of yesterday. He died in London in 1964, while he was working on his fourth book.

WORKS: *In Kerry Long Ago*. London: B. T. Batsford, 1950; *In a Quiet Land*. London: B. T. Batsford, 1957; *In a Strange Land*. London: B. T. Batsford, 1958.

O'DONOGHUE, ROBERT (1929–   ), poet, playwright, and journalist. O'Donoghue was born and educated in Cork and later worked for many years at *The Cork Examiner* where, among other ventures, he was a theater critic and also edited an idiosyncratic magazine page that gave a forum and a check to many Irish writers, including Paul Durcan,* Pearse Hutchinson,* Seán Dunne,* MacDara Woods,* and Patrick Galvin,* all of whom were weekly columnists. In 1986, with Professor John Barry, he coedited a lengthy series on the history of Cork. His plays include *The Long Night* and *Hate Was the Spur*. He has also written for radio.

It is as a poet, however, that he is best known now. He has written poems for many decades, and his early work appeared in the early issues of *Irish Writing*, edited in Cork by David Marcus* and Terence Smith. The journal *Cyphers* also became a forum for his work, and its first issue, in June 1975, contained five of his poems. This publication marked the end of a silence and led to a number of new poems. His collection *The Witness* was published in 1990, and he has said of it: "The poet as witness is central to this collection. . . . He is required to be detached, to 'still the variable in a trance of words.'" O'Donoghue uses words in a musical yet disjunctive manner that carries echoes of Beckett's* cadences—Beckett, in fact, is the subject of one of his poems—and that is similar, too, to the work of his friend Patrick Galvin. When it works, it is a technique that carries both music and meaning; when it fails, one or the other is lost. His best poems have a voice that is wholly his own, and the figures who inhabit his work—old women, lovers, characters from myth and history, people on the edge of events—are often isolated figures. Despite their modernist modes, there is an elegiac quality to many of his poems.

SEÁN DUNNE

WORK: *The Witness*. Dublin: Raven Arts, 1990.

O'DONOVAN, GERALD (1871–1942), novelist. O'Donovan, the intimate friend of Rose Macauley, the English novelist, was born Jeremiah O'Donovan on July 15, 1871, in County Down, far from his family's native Cork. His father was a builder who moved from place to place erecting piers. As a child, O'Donovan attended schools in Cork, Galway, and Sligo. He obtained a poor education, as he later recalled that he even obtained a pass in agriculture—a subject about which he knew nothing.

He entered a seminary to study for the priesthood and then Maynooth College in September 1889. His academic career was unremarkable, though his Irish teacher was Father Eugene O'Growney, a pioneer of the Gaelic League.

In June 1895, O'Donovan was ordained a priest for the diocese of Clonfert. His first appointment was as a curate for Kilmalinoge and Lickmassy, and he lived in Portumna in Galway. In 1896, he was moved to Loughrea as a curate. In that year Dr. Healy, who had been co-adjutor since 1884, became bishop of Clonfert. Under his administration, O'Donovan flourished as an active, socially minded priest of a type unusual in Ireland at that date. His sympathies were liberal, and his theology veered towards the ideas of modernism; reform, improvement, and progress were his watchwords. During these years, he published articles on progressive themes, such as workhouse reform, practical education for girls, village libraries, and the Celtic Revival.

In about 1897, he joined the Irish Agricultural Organisation Society (IAOS), which was spreading the ideas of cooperation in rural Ireland, under the leadership of Sir Horace Plunkett and George Russell.* In June 1901, O'Donovan was elected along with Edward Martyn* as representatives of Connaught on the IAOS committee.

By now he had become administrator in Loughrea and was deeply involved in the building and decorating of the new cathedral of St. Brendan. Jack B. Yeats* and Sarah Purser were among the artists who worked on this church, the one great architectural achievement of the Revival.

O'Donovan invited the theatrical company which was soon to become the Abbey* down to Loughrea in 1901, their one and only provincial visit at this time. Years later, Maire Walker recalled his excited enthusiasm over the visit. O'Donovan also brought John McCormack, then only a schoolboy, down from Sligo to sing in the cathedral. In Dublin, O'Donovan was on friendly terms with writers and artists. George Moore* based the priest in "Fugitives" in *The Untilled Field* on O'Donovan.

During these years, O'Donovan was also active in the Gaelic League, and in 1902, after a visit to America, he gave for the Gaelic League the O'Growney Memorial lecture in Dublin.

In 1903, the bishop of Tuam died, and Dr. Healy was appointed to the post. Thomas O'Dea became the new bishop of Clonfert and chose to live in Loughrea rather than in Ballinasloe as Healy had. Very quickly relations between O'Dea and O'Donovan became difficult. The reasons have never been fully elucidated, but it seems quite certain that O'Donovan had been the diocesan clergy's choice for the new bishop, but that the Vatican passed over him either because he was too young or for political reasons.

O'Donovan went to America again in November 1903 with some members of the IAOS, where he lectured on the artistic side of the Irish Revival and on the cooperative movement. However, on his return to Loughrea his relations with Dr. O'Dea reached a crisis. In about September 1904, O'Donovan left both Loughrea and the priesthood.

He went first to Dublin, and then to London, taking with him a letter of introduction to various publishers from George Moore. Moore was curious about his character, and O'Donovan's departure from Loughrea was the initial inspiration for Moore's writing of *The Lake*.

At this time, he began to sign himself Gerald O'Donovan, marking a complete break with his past. From London, where he was grubbing for work on the fringes of publishing, he tried to keep up his interest in the IAOS. But this interest lapsed about 1909. In the spring of 1910, he was appointed subwarden of Toynbee Hall in the east end of London.

In October 1910, he married Beryl Verschoyle, the daughter of an Irish Protestant colonel, who had been brought up in Italy. In the years to come, his wife's family was to provide much support for O'Donovan and his family. Three children were born, a boy and two girls, one of whom died tragically young.

In July 1911, O'Donovan left Toynbee Hall, which his wife was beginning to find something of a strain. He now began writing seriously. In the spring of 1913, Macmillan (then publishers in ordinary to the Irish Literary Revival) brought out *Father Ralph,* the first and most effective of his six novels. It was largely autobiographical, drawing on his own experiences as a priest. The crisis in the novel is brought about by the young priest's refusal to submit to the terms of the papal encyclical on modernism (*Paschendi Gregis*), which destroyed the liberal movement within the Church. Deeply felt and vivid in its sketches of rural Ireland, the novel made a sensation and is the work by which O'Donovan will be remembered.

Father Ralph was followed in 1914 by *Waiting,* which deals with the difficulties for a young liberal-minded couple made by the papal decree *Ne Temere* concerning the intermarriage of Catholics and non-Catholics. Again O'Donovan was writing about an area of Irish life which many writers neglected (or knew nothing about), and once again one of his books made a distinct impact. Frank O'Connor* recalls being given a copy of the novel in his teens by a workmate who told him it would show him what Ireland "was really like."

During the Great War, O'Donovan worked in the Italian section of the British Department of Propaganda, where his wife's family connections were of use to him. In 1918, he became head of the section, and it was at this period that he first met Rose Macauley.

After the war, he was involved with the establishment of the London office of the publishers William Collins, for whom he worked as a reader. He himself brought out four more novels, two of which had been written during the war. One was *Conquest,* which deals with events in Ireland down to 1919. This interesting book is marred by the many earnest debates which dominate it, but it gives the modern reader a liberal view of the divided nation during that heady period.

Also published in 1920 was *How They Did It,* which focuses on the "Home Front" in Britain during the war. In his last two novels, *Vocations* (1921) and *The Holy Tree* (1922), O'Donovan returned to his earlier material and to the one theme which asserts itself in all of his work, the search for real love. Grace in his last novel was based on Rose Macauley, with whom he had established a special friendship. In her short story "Miss Anstruther's Letters" written after bombs had destroyed her flat and all his letters to her, Rose Macauley gives an idea of what O'Donovan meant to her. Her precise relationship to him is less clear; for he stayed with his wife and children, but Rose was a frequent visitor, godmother to his son's child, and a traveling companion of his daughter.

O'Donovan exerted great influence over Macauley and her literary work, but after he met her, his own creative urge declined. Indeed, what O'Donovan actually did for a living between the wars is not clear even to his children. His daughter Brigid recalls him lying on the sofa all afternoon reading his way through the *Cambridge Ancient History* and endless detective stories, one a day. He rarely mentioned Ireland, and one senses a loss of real purpose in his life.

In 1938, the O'Donovans became involved with helping Czech refugees. On June 26, 1939, while on a holiday in the Lake District with Rose Macauley, he and Macauley were involved in an accident in which he fractured his skull. His already failing health was further weakened. A long illness set in, during which O'Donovan consoled himself by reading Somerville and Ross,* and his old friend George Moore.

On July 26, 1942, O'Donovan died of cancer and was buried in Albury, Surrey, where he had lived for some years. A fortnight later, Rose Macauley writing as "A friend" published a short obituary notice in *The Times.* She concluded the polite formalities with a sudden personal note: "To know him was to love him."

Though now almost forgotten, O'Donovan's novels give a good picture of the progressive and liberal movements in Ireland before 1916, which were to be swamped by the rising nationalism of the new state. They portray a forgotten Ireland that is becoming of increasing interest to readers tired of the clichés that often pass for Irish history.

PETER COSTELLO

WORKS: *Father Ralph.* London: Macmillan, 1913; *Waiting.* London: Macmillan, 1914; *Conquest.* London: Constable, 1920; *How They Did It.* London: Methuen, 1920; *Vocations.* London:

Martin Secker, 1921; *The Holy Tree.* London: Heinemann, 1922. REFERENCES: Candy, Catherine. *Priestly Fictions: Popular Irish Novelists of the Early 20th Century.* Dublin: Wolfhound, 1995; Costello, Peter. *The Heart Grown Brutal.* Dublin: Gill & Macmillan/Totowa, N.J.: Rowman & Littlefield, 1978; O'Connor, Norrys. "The Irish Uncle Tom's Cabin." In *Changing Ireland.* Cambridge: Harvard University Press, 1924.

O'DONOVAN, JOHN (1809–1861), scholar. O'Donovan, the great topographer and Celtic scholar, was born in Attateemore, County Kilkenny, on July 9, 1809. In 1829, he was appointed to a post in the historical department of the Ordnance Survey, where he worked under Petrie* and later with O'Curry,* whose sister he married. O'Donovan's task was to examine old Irish records and manuscripts, in order to decide the nomenclature for maps. As part of his work, he visited every part of Ireland, taking profuse notes. Many of his findings originally appeared in essays on topography and history written for *The Dublin Penny Journal* and *The Irish Penny Journal.* Like O'Curry, he was a diligent transcriber and translator of manuscripts, and he also published *A Grammar of the Irish Language* (1845). Of his many works, his masterpiece is *The Annals of the Four Masters* (1848–1851), which he edited and translated. For his enormous contributions to Irish scholarship, he was awarded an LL.D. by the University of Dublin. He died on December 9, 1861, in Dublin.

PRINCIPAL WORK: *Annala Rioghacta Éireann, Annals of the Kingdom of Ireland by the Four Masters.* 7 vols. Dublin: Hodges, Smith, 1848–1851.

O'DONOVAN, JOHN [PURCELL] (1921–1985), playwright, journalist, historian, and wit. O'Donovan was born on January 29, 1921, in Dublin, and educated at the Synge Street Christian Brothers school and by himself. After the war, which he spent working at the Royal Victoria Hospital in Belfast, he drifted into journalism and eventually became the avuncular but formidable subeditor of the *Irish Press.* His impressive erudition may be indicated by a story of his managing editor Douglas Gageby, who introduced him to a young man who was applying for the position of second-string drama critic:

"Well, Mr. So and So," said O'Donovan, "you are interested in drama, I hear. Suppose we take *Coriolanus,* Act II, and you will remember where in the second scene . . . perhaps you will give me your opinion on that and on another passage with which you are no doubt familiar."

After about five years, O'Donovan went into full-time freelancing, at which he was eminently successful. Under the pseudonym of "Andrew Marsh," he wrote a droll weekly column for the *Evening Press* about Ireland's past, and his encyclopedic knowledge of that past was the basis of his companionable posthumous book, *Life by the Liffey* (1986). He was an able music critic, and that interest, combined with his fascination about Bernard Shaw,* led to his book on Shaw's musical mentor Vandeleur Lee, *Shaw and the Charlatan Genius* (1965), and to his short biography of Shaw, *G. B. Shaw* (1983), both of which volumes uncovered much new information about Shaw's background and early life. He wrote prolifically for Irish radio, including *The Fiddler and the Dean,* an intriguing dialogue between Swift* and Handel. He also had, for years, his own radio program, "Dear Sir or Madam," in which he commented jovially and sometimes acidly about letters people had written him on issues of the day. He was a governor of the Royal Irish Academy of Music and its vice president. He was a founder member and first chairman of the Society of Irish Playwrights.

His most memorable work, however, was as a playwright, and his plays were done by the Abbey* mainly between 1957 and 1963, when the theater was in residence at the Queen's, a period usually conceded to be one of the low points of its long history. The chief of those plays are *The Less We Are Together* (1957), a satirical cartoon about Partition, *The Shaws of Synge Street* (1960), a superbly evocative portrait of the eccentric family background of Bernard Shaw, and *Copperfaced Jack* (1963), an historical play about John Scott, the first earl of Clonmell. That character is portrayed with a Rabelaisian gusto far in advance of its Irish day, and the play is a splendid antidote to the plethora of popular patriotic melodramas about the 1798 period. His last play, the unproduced *Carlotta,* is a witty sequel to *The Shaws,* in which the characters are Shaw, his wife Charlotte, his sister Lucy and his "Liza Doolittle," Mrs. Patrick Campbell. O'Donovan's witty plays hardly received the productions that they deserved, and the best of them cry for revival. He died on August 26, 1985.

PRINCIPAL WORKS: *Shaw and the Charlatan Genius.* Dublin: Dolmen, 1965. (Biography); *G. B. Shaw.* [Dublin]: Gill & Macmillan, [1983]. (Biography); *Life by the Liffey: A Kaleidoscope of Dubliners.* [Dublin]: Gill & Macmillan, [1986]. (History); *Jonathan, Jack, and GPS: Four Plays about Irish History and Literature.* Robert Hogan, ed. Newark: University of Delaware Press/London & Toronto: Associated University Presses, [1993]. (Contains *Copperfaced Jack, The Fiddler and the Dean, The Shaws of Synge Street,* and *Carlotta*).

O'DRISCOLL, CIARAN (1943–   ), poet. Born in County Kilkenny.

WORKS: *Gog and Magog.* [Galway]: Salmon, [1987]; *The Poet and His Shadow.* Dublin: Dedalus, 1990; *The Myth of the South.* [Dublin]: Dedalus, [1992]. (Poetry pamphlet); *Listening to Different Drummers.* [Dublin]: Dedalus, [1993].

O'DRISCOLL, DENNIS (1954–   ), poet and critic. O'Driscoll was born in Thurles, County Tipperary, in 1954, and was educated at the local Christian Brothers school. Later, he attended the Institute of Public Administration in Dublin and University College, Dublin. He has worked for many years as a civil servant in Dublin, and the world of the office worker is among his themes, most notably in his sequence *The Bottom Line* (1994).

His reputation as a poet has, at the very least, been matched by his reputation as a reviewer and critic. His reviews and essays in such publications as *The Poetry Ireland Review* (Dublin), *Krino* (Dublin), and the *Poetry Review* (London) have been marked by an ability to assess a text and a reputation coolly and to do this from the words that lie before him rather than from the general air of unformed or fashionable opinion that surrounds the arts. In Ireland, good poetry critics are few, but O'Driscoll is undoubtedly among them; the depth of his response is a creative act in itself. His reading and his standards have served not only to confirm the worth of established writers such as Thomas Kinsella* or W. S. Graham but also to keep before our mind the reputations of writers who, for one reason or another, may not be as well known as they should be. He championed Eastern European poets such as Miroslav Holub long before the work of such writers became intellectually fashionable. He has also helped to spread the good news about the worth of writers such as George MacKay Browne. For many years, he has edited a collection of quotations on the subject of poetry for the *Poetry Ireland Review,* a journal of which he was himself the editor for a time.

His own poems were distinguished from the start by a sense of morality. Reviewing his first book, *Kist,* Seamus Heaney* pointed to the way in which "the stylist in him gets into step with the griever, and the poetry hits its full emotional stride." The poem "Someone" from that collection became one of those poems that lift themselves from books and become part of the public air:

> Someone is dressing up for death today, a change of skirt or tie
> eating a last feast of buttered pan, tea
> scarcely having noticed the erection that was his last . . .

One of the distinguishing and most welcome features of O'Driscoll's work is the manner in which he assumes an almost deliberate lack of poeticizing. There is no sense in his work that only certain subjects are fit for poetry; if anything, his work makes poetry out of areas and experiences that others might regard as unpoetic, and the sense of pressure within his writing ultimately proves the rightness of his approach. He once wrote: "To live my life, no matter how plain and eventful on the surface, is to undergo a range of emotions and experiences which would stretch any poetic talent to the full. . . . We don't need to seek out experience."

In his work, the everyday is more often a matter of record rather than a mode of revelation. Offices, journeys, work, Thurles—all of these find their way into his poems and are recorded in a measured manner. If his work records a quotidian office life, it is not from any mandarin contempt but from an exactitude and honesty that refuse to treat office workers as mindless ants and likewise to romanticize them. In doing this, he makes his office workers as typical of his time as farm laborers or mariners were in the poetry of earlier centuries.

While his work is marked by a sense of mortality, O'Driscoll can also be very funny, and this aspect of his work too many reviewers tend to miss. His comedy can be black, but it is not forced, and it is a natural constituent of the voice in many of his poems. As his work has developed, his eye has sharpened, too, and his sense of form has widened to include both tiny observation and long sequence.

SEÁN DUNNE

WORKS: Ed., with Peter Fallon, *The First Ten Years*. Dublin: Dublin Arts Festival, 1979; *Kist.* Mountrath, Co. Laois: Dolmen, 1982; *Hidden Extras*. Dublin: Dedalus/London: Anvil, 1987; with others, *Five Irish Poets*. New York: White Pine, 1990; *Long Short Story*. Dublin: Dedalus, 1993; *The Bottom Line*. Dublin: Dedalus, 1994. REFERENCES: "Interview with Isabelle Cartwright." *Cobweb* (Maynooth College) 10 (1994); "Poet as Civil Servant." *Poetry Ireland Review* 33 (Winter 1991).

O'DRISCOLL, KATHLEEN (1941–   ), poet and short story writer. O'Driscoll was educated at University College, Galway, and has worked as a teacher.

WORKS: *Goodbye Joe*. Dublin: Caledon, 1980. (Poetry); *Ether*. Dublin: Caledon, 1981. (Short stories).

O'DUFFY, EIMAR [ULTAN] (1893–1935), novelist and satirist. O'Duffy, who has been called "modern Ireland's only prose satirist," was born on September 29, 1893, in Dublin. The son of a well-to-do dentist, he attended Stonyhurst in England and then University College, Dublin, where he wrote light verse and facetious stories, and edited the student magazine. After graduating with a Bachelor of Dental Surgery degree, he became increasingly involved in the Irish nationalist and cultural movement. He had some plays produced at Edward Martyn's* Irish Theatre* in Hardwicke Street, and he joined the Irish Republican Brotherhood, became a captain in the Irish Volunteers, and wrote frequently on military tactics for the group's newspaper. It was O'Duffy and J. J. O'Connell who alerted Bulmer Hobson and then Eoin MacNeill on Holy Thursday, 1916, that a Rising was imminent. O'Duffy was then sent by MacNeill to Belfast to quash any insurgency there. O'Duffy's deep disillusionment with the Rising was reflected in his novel *The Wasted Island* (1919), which was more bitterly critical than even O'Casey's* later *The Plough and the Stars.* Naturally, there was little place in the new Free State for a man with such opinions. Even so, O'Duffy worked in Ireland as a teacher and at the Department of External Affairs until 1925. During these years, he published several novels and other books under Bulmer Hobson's "Martin Lester" imprint but made little money by them. Losing his post in External Affairs, O'Duffy moved his family to England in 1925 and spent some of that year free-lancing and working for an American newspaper in Paris. In 1926, the first novel of his Cuandine trilogy, *King Goshawk and the Birds,* was published and was a critical, if not a financial, success. In 1928, the second volume, *The Spacious Adventures of the Man in the Street,* appeared. In the following year, he published a revised version of *The Wasted Island.* In his last years, O'Duffy was much attracted to the social credit theories of Major Douglas and others, and wrote *Life and Money,* a book on economics which went through three editions. He also wrote three potboiling novels, but he managed to complete, albeit faultily, his Cuandine trilogy with *Asses in Clover* (1933). He died in Surrey in 1935 of duodenal ulcers.

Plagued by ill health and little money, O'Duffy nevertheless produced a substantial body of work that ranges in quality from the trivial to the masterly. His many early verses are local and facetious, and yet show a playful facility with words. His early plays—*The Walls of Athens, The Phoenix on the Roof,* and particularly *Bricriu's Feast*—indicate a strong talent for satiric comedy. His major early work, however, was the novel *The Wasted Island* (1919, revised 1929), which is both *bildungsroman* and intellectual history of the years leading up to the Rising. Despite some awkwardness of style, it is one of the best fictional introductions to its era.

In the decade after the Rising, O'Duffy published several minor works of considerable charm and excellence. The most important is an historical novel of the Munster Confederation, *The Lion and the Fox* (1922), which in sweep and power recalls Dumas and which must be accounted one of the finest examples of the genre in modern Irish writing. Two other volumes, *Printer's Errors* (1922) and *Miss Rudd and Some Lovers* (1923), have a lightheartedness which O'Duffy was never to recapture. *Printer's Errors* is a genial satire about Irish cultural life before the Rising, and *Miss Rudd* is a disarming comic love story set incongruously during the Black and Tan War.

O'Duffy's major accomplishment is the Cuandine trilogy composed of *King Goshawk and the Birds, The Spacious Adventures of the Man in the Street,* and *Asses in Clover.* These books are a scathing, funny, and highly inventive satire of modern life, half Erewhonian adventure and half science fiction. The first two volumes range from the mordant to the frivolous in their criticism and embody a flamboyant range of ironic and rhetorical techniques that bear comparison to James Stephens* or Flann O'Brien (Brian O'Nolan*) or, indeed, to James Joyce* himself. The second volume, *The Spacious Adventures,* is perhaps the most integrated of the trilogy, and the final volume, *Asses in Clover,* composed while gravely ill, is the least successful. However, even this work has superb moments, as in the muted, bleakly savage ending.

In the 1930s, O'Duffy wrote three unimportant detective stories, evidently to make money, and was much impressed by theories of social credit as remedies for the worldwide Depression. This extreme commitment, plus undoubtedly an increasingly sardonic view, erased from his work the lightness, fancy, frivolity, and satiric detachment that were its great strengths. Despite his failures, his false starts, and his potboilers, he is a unique and extraordinary figure in modern Irish literature.

WORKS: *The Walls of Athens.* Dublin: Irish Review, 1914. (Play); *A Lay of the Liffey, and Other Verses.* Dublin: Candle, 1918; *Bricriu's Feast.* Dublin: Martin Lester, [1919?]. (Play); *The Wasted Island.* Dublin: Martin Lester, 1919/revised ed., London: Macmillan, 1929. (Novel); *The Lion and the Fox.* Dublin: Martin Lester, [1922]. (Novel); *Printer's Errors.* Dublin: Martin Lester, 1922/ London: Leonard Parsons, [1922]. (Novel); *Miss Rudd and Some Lovers.* Dublin: Talbot, 1923. (Novel); ''The Phoenix on the Roof'' in *The Irish Review* 1 (1923): 75–82. (One-act play); *King Goshawk and the Birds.* London: Macmillan, 1926. (Novel); *The Spacious Adventures of the Man in the Street.* London: Macmillan, 1928. (Novel); *The Bird Cage.* London: Geoffrey Bles, 1932. (Mystery novel); *Life and Money.* London & New York: Putnam's, 1932/2d ed., revised & enlarged, 1933/3d ed., revised, 1935; *The Secret Enemy.* London: Geoffrey Bles, 1932. (Mystery novel); *Asses in Clover.* London: Putnam's, 1933. (Novel); *Heart of a Girl.* London: Geoffrey Bles, [1935].

(Mystery novel); *The Journal of Irish Literature* 7 (1978), reprints *Printer's Errors, Bricriu's Feast,* and some fugitive material.   REFERENCE: Hogan, Robert. *Eimar O'Duffy.* Lewisburg, Pa.: Bucknell University Press, 1972.

O'DWYER, MICHAEL

WORK: *Drowning the Hullaballo Blues.* Dublin: Basement, 1995. (Novel).

O'FAOLAIN, JULIA (1932–   ), novelist and short story writer, is considered one of the most Irish accomplished writers of her generation and one of the few with a truly international background. At her best in some darkly comic short stories concerned with the position of women, she cannot be categorized easily. Her novels range from the burlesque adventures of a young girl in Paris, to a brilliant evocation of sixth-century Gaul, to the story of three generations of a modern Irish political family, to the latest—a portrait of nineteenth-century Italy.

The daughter of writers Sean O'Faolain* and Eileen Gould, she was born in London on June 6, 1932, and grew up in a house "buzzing with stories." She was educated in Dublin by the Sacred Heart nuns and, after taking a B.A. and an M.A. at University College, Dublin (UCD), continued her education at the University di Roma and the Sorbonne, University of Paris. In Italy she met and married Lauro Martines, an American Renaissance historian, and they have one son. She has worked as a teacher of languages, an interpreter, and a translator.

Her first collection of short stories, *We Might See Sights* (1968), established her as an important new voice in Irish fiction. The book is divided into Irish and Italian stories, reflecting her youth in both countries. The biting sardonic tone of the Irish stories hits hard at sexual hypocrisies and repressions, while the Italian stories are milder in tone and less concerned with sexual attitudes. However, the Irish stories have an authenticity of time and place, Dublin of the 1950s, and "Chronic" is particularly fine on student life at UCD.

O'Faolain's first novel, *Godded and Codded* (1970), which had to be withdrawn because of a threatened libel suit, is set in Paris and is the burlesque account of a young girl's sexual adventures. Indeed, almost the entire action is spent in various beds; and the main character, Sally, is rather shallowly and unconvincingly portrayed. Again Irish religious and sexual hypocrisies are satirized. Characters like Sally's pious father undoubtedly did, and still do, exist, but he is portrayed too broadly to engage the sympathy of the reader. The other characters, with the exception of an old man and an aging mistress, are not particularly memorable.

Not in God's Image (1973), coedited with Lauro Martines, is a fascinating documentary history of women from Greek to Roman times. However, her next collection of stories, *Man in the Cellar* (1974), confirmed O'Faolain's reputation. The title story is again set in Italy, where Una, a brutalized wife, locks her husband in the cellar to get revenge for his beatings but also to demonstrate that she is a person. In this story, O'Faolain is at her best and most blackly comic.

She inquires into the unequal battle of the sexes and the nature of marriage, leaving us in no doubt as to who the real victim is.

Women in the Wall (1975), her second novel, further explores the position of women in history. This is a departure from her previous work and brilliantly evokes sixth-century Gaul. This powerful novel is not so much a study of mysticism as a study of its failure to help humanity. Structurally and thematically, it is O'Faolain's most accomplished book and has been highly praised by the critics.

O'Faolain's next novel, *No Country for Young Men* (1980), which was shortlisted for the Booker Prize, is set in modern Dublin and tells the story of the O'Malley family through three generations, from the civil war to today. The most sympathetic character, a young American, is tragically murdered as a result of his curiosity about a past secret. Through great-aunt Judith, a memorably drawn senile nun, this secret is revealed. Although a compelling read, this novel is decidedly glum and sour in tone: it is nearly always raining; characters are constantly described by their rotting teeth; the older members of the family live in a dead past that the young are eager to embrace. O'Faolain, who has not lived in Ireland for most of her adult life, indicates that the past can affect the present. However, she has written that this is often a mistake: "Time stops for the remembering expatriate, and the past becomes his native land."

O'Faolain now divides her time between Los Angeles, where her husband teaches, and London, where they own a house. Although she never writes from an American viewpoint, her fourth novel, *The Obedient Wife* (1982), is set in California, where Carla, the Italian heroine, becomes involved with a priest called Leo. While he is the product of a trendy, watered-down Catholicism, she represents a highly civilized and secular code. The best scenes in the book are between these two. The relationship eventually fails, however, not because Carla feels guilty but because lust as an abstraction holds little attraction for her.

Daughters of Passion (1982) confirmed O'Faolain's versatility as a writer of short stories. The stories range from a feminist fairy tale, to the study of a young woman caught up in terrorism, to an academic wife who entertains a lonely Indian in London. Again O'Faolain inserts the disturbing dental detail, and in "Found" a character has "huge corpse-like" teeth, whatever they may be. However, in "Mad Marge," she brilliantly engages our pity for an unforgettable revolutionary activist from middle America.

The Irish Signorina (1984) is a Gothic novella, set in modern-day Italy. A young Irishwoman is invited for the summer and finds herself drawn into her mother's murky past. It is a page-turner, with terrorists, mad strangers in the attic, eccentric aristocrats, and secrets galore.

The Judas Cloth (1992) is set in nineteenth-century Italy and the strife-torn papacy of Pope Pius IX, Pio Nono, famous for having had himself declared infallible. The unification of Italy and the decreasing power of the church are seen through the eyes of several young Jesuit students who are imagined characters, particularly Nicola Santi, a bastard who becomes a bishop. O'Faolain is particularly good on young men, but with her penchant for disturbing detail, she describes an older man as having a mouth like a chicken's anus. Covered with feathers? The main focus of the plot concerns Nicola's illegitimate but illustrious parentage. Although the novel comes brilliantly to life in some scenes—especially one in which a hot-air balloon gets lost along with a dangling horse and a transsexual bareback rider—it is generally a difficult slog. Like the creaking papacy itself, the story sinks under the weight of historical fact. There are too many peripheral characters and references made without explanation. However, it does depict an age that, with its autocratic pope and rash of visionaries, parallels our own increasing secularism.

O'Faolain admits that her father was a great influence on her life and self-mockingly refers to herself as ''Daddy's girl.'' Her work, however, has its own distinct and important voice. If some of her Irish fiction hits hard in depicting a cruel, nasty, and sexually repressed race, it is because she is such an astute and honest observer; her hard edge finally has to be admired. Also her style is always a joy, and there are compassion and mature humor in her later work.

MARY ROSE CALLAGHAN

WORKS: Tr. as Julia Martines. *Two Memoirs of Florence: The Diaries of Buonaecorso Pitti and Gregorio Dati.* New York: Harper & Row, 1967; tr. as Julia Martines. *A Man of Parts,* by Piera Chiara. Boston: Little, Brown, 1968/London: Barrie & Rockliff, 1969; *We Might See Sights and Other Stories.* London: Faber, 1968; *Godded and Codded.* London, Faber 1970/published in United States as *Three Lovers.* New York: Coward, McCann & Geoghegan, 1971. (Novel); ed., with Lauro Martines, *Not in God's Image: Women in History from the Greeks to the Victorians.* London: Temple Smith, 1973; *Man in the Cellar* London: Faber, 1974. (Short stories); *Women in the Wall.* 1975. London: Faber 1975/London: Virago, 1985/New York: Carroll & Graf, 1988. (Novel); *Melancholy Baby and Other Stories.* Dublin: Poolbeg, 1978. (A selection from her first two collections); *No Country for Young Men.* London: Allen Lane, 1980/New York: Carroll & Graf, 1986. (Novel); *The Obedient Wife.* [London]: Allen Lane, [1982]/New York: Carroll & Graf, 1985. (Novel); *Daughters of Passion.* [Harmondsworth, Middlesex]: Penguin, 1982. (Short stories); *The Irish Signorina.* Harmondsworth, Middlesex & New York: Viking 1984. (Novel); *The Judas Cloth.* [London]: Sinclair-Stevenson, [1992]. (Novel). REFERENCES: Imhof, Rüdiger "Julia O'Faolain." In *Contemporary Irish Novelists.* Rüdiger Imhof, ed. Tübingen: Narr, 1990, pp. 159–174; Weekes, Ann Owens. "Julia O'Faolain: The Imaginative Crucible." In *Irish Women Writers: An Uncharted Tradition.* [Lexington]: University Press of Kentucky, [1990], pp. 191–211.

O'FAOLAIN, SEAN (1900–1991), short story writer and man of letters. To Sean O'Faolain, the literary culture of Ireland owes a tremendous debt. In an age of provincialism, censorship, prudery, and factionalism, he remained a cosmopolitan, reasonable, cool-headed, witty humanitarian who spoke his mind and challenged the irrational whenever he encountered it. His works, whether they are his carefully crafted short stories, his novels, his literary criticism, or even his travel books, attest to his lifelong humanitarian and rational habit of mind and further express his firm belief that a watery-eyed nostalgia for a mythic past is the one obstacle preventing Ireland from joining the modern world.

Born John Whelan on February 22, 1900, in Cork, the youngest of three boys in a family of, as he called them in *Vive Moi,* ''shabby genteels,'' O'Faolain grew up in a repressed and repressive household. He attended the Presentation Brothers secondary school in Cork ("if no one mentioned sex organs, we would not notice we had them") and later University College, Cork, where he received his B.A. in modern literature. In 1917, a visit to Gougane Barra, the valley west of Cork in the heart of the Gaeltacht region, and his sympathies with the republicans moved him to Gaelicize his name and to join the Irish Republican Army (IRA). He served as an "irregular" for six years, an experience that provided him with his first literary theme—the tension between fear and the need for liberty.

Between 1921 and the outbreak of civil war, O'Faolain worked as a traveling book salesman, a job allowing him to wander through and absorb the Irish countryside. However, in 1922, he returned to the IRA, worked in a bomb shop, and was appointed director of publicity for the Dublin division. Disaffection with the republican cause—a sense that one tyranny was simply replacing another—resulted in his resignation from the IRA. He returned to Cork, reenrolled in the University for an M.A. in English, taught at a Christian Brothers school in Ennis for a year, obtained a second M.A. in Irish, and published his first short story, "Lilliput," in *The Irish Statesman.** This story won him the Harkness Commonwealth Fellowship to study in the United States. In 1926, he set out for Harvard University to study philology under George Lyman Kitteredge and lived in Bohemian penury in Cambridge, Massachusetts, where he was joined by his fiancée, Eileen Gould, in 1927. They married, honeymooned by camping across the country, and returned to Cambridge. In 1929, they left for London, where O'Faolain taught at St. Mary's College while completing his first collection of stories, *Midsummer Night Madness.*

This first collection, heavily dependent on his intellectual and spiritual experiences during the rebellion and civil war, was immediately banned in Ireland, not because of its politics but because it acknowledged that men and women were sexual beings, possessed desires and fantasies, and occasionally acted on them. Further, O'Faolain was called a traitor for writing in English, a criticism leveled against many Irish writers in this period of early nationhood and search for national identity.

Rather than becoming embittered by these experiences, O'Faolain decided to return to Ireland to struggle against the forces of prudery and provincialism. Although he was outranked by Daniel Corkery* for a teaching position at the University of Cork, he and Eileen and their baby daughter, Julia,* returned to Ireland in 1933, settling in Wicklow.

That he was denied the security of a teaching position in which he could presumably have lived out his days was an enormous stroke of good luck. Freelancing for *The Spectator* and *The New Statesman,* he worked on his first novel, *A Nest of Simple Folk,* and joined the next postrenaissance generation of Irish writers.

The year 1934 saw the publication of two works: the novel *A Nest of Simple*

Folk and a biography of Constance Markievicz. Although very different in genre and technique, these two works are alike in their celebration of romantic rebellion. Leo Foxe-Donnell, the lecherous, self-destructive protagonist of *A Nest of Simple Folk,* may come to patriotism late, but he does, at sixty, join the Volunteers, only to be slain in the Easter rebellion. Markievicz was famous (or infamous) for her wild, aristocratic revolutionary activity. The heroism O'Faolain celebrates is neither patriotic nor political and is quite the opposite of a nostalgic longing for the past. Heroism is simply a metaphor for self-expression. These two works are only too clear in their message that expressing the self was becoming increasingly problematic in an Ireland that had become dull, patently bourgeois, and intolerant of any act of nonconformity. In fact, O'Faolain's other two novels, *Bird Alone* (1936) and *Come Back to Erin* (1940), are variations on the same theme: the former, the story of Corkman Corney Crone and his one unrepentant act of sexuality, for which he is punished for life; and the latter, the story of the romantic Irish American, cherishing an idealized version of holy Ireland until he arrives on the "auld sod" and experiences devastating disillusionment. Sixteen years later, O'Faolain was to pick up this theme again in the Christian Gauss Lectures at Princeton University, in which he comments on the works of Virginia Woolf, Graham Greene, James Joyce,* William Faulkner, Evelyn Waugh, and Ernest Hemingway. In these lectures, published in 1956 as *The Vanishing Hero,* O'Faolain argues that each of these writers has replaced the traditional hero of fiction with a doomed and desperate creation of his own, because society no longer admits personal heroism in this era of the "modern desiccation of feeling."

The years 1937 to 1939 were enormously productive, seeing the publication of four rather disparate works: *She Had to Do Something,* a farce about a lively Frenchwoman "trapped" in puritanical Ireland, which put him in the excellent company of Yeats* and Synge,* as he was booed and hissed at the curtain call; *The Silver Branch,* translations of old Irish poetry; *King of the Beggars,* a biography of Daniel O'Connell; and *De Valera,* a somewhat more subdued version of the biography he had written in 1933. *De Valera* yields an interesting insight into O'Faolain's definition of leadership in that it praises de Valera for his vision and passion but criticizes him as a man not practical enough to lead the nation.

While working on the novel *Come Back to Erin* and the lyrical and evocative travel book *An Irish Journey,* O'Faolain established one of Ireland's finest literary magazines, *The Bell.* In the six years he was editor and manager of this publication, he encouraged and coached many young Irish writers, including Brendan Behan,* James Plunkett,* and Bryan MacMahon.* His monthly editorials hammered hard at the stuffed shirts, the Censorship Board, and the Celtophiles, with the hope that in forcing the Irish to look at themselves and modify their religious and political backwardness, they might develop enough sophistication to enter the modern world. His tone is assertive and provocative. Here, for example, is a selection from a diatribe against the Celtophile movement:

It is plain that our generation has lost all sense of its origins. The healthy, generous, human sweep of feeling that we associate with the traditions of our countryside no longer runs through society or political life. The very history being pumped into our children in the schools and the image of life being offered to them is all alien alike to our nature and to fact. . . . The main notion of it is that we have, since the dawn of history, been united here in our efforts to eject all foreign ways, peoples, manners, and customs—which is, of course arrant nonsense: on this fancy there has been piled up a gospel of sanctity of the West and the evil of the East, the generative power and utter purity of all native custom and tradition, as handed down by an army of mainly legendary saints and heroes (*The Bell* 6 [June 1943]: 189).

O'Faolain's editorials may have been harsh, but they grew out of "tough love" for a country in which he saw so much potential and so much self-destruction. This is the theme of his cultural study, *The Irish* (1947), which is sharply critical of what needs change and supportive of what is positive. This carefully balanced relationship is also evident in perhaps his finest collection of short fiction, *Teresa, and Other Stories* (1947, published in the United States as *The Man Who Invented Sin*). These stories show a maturity, an ability to laugh, and a satire that, far from vicious or destructive, moves us to change those things lending themselves to satire. For instance, the title story of the American edition is the tale of two monks and two nuns who have traveled to the Gaeltacht to improve their Irish. There they are denounced by a local curate who accuses them of immorality, when, in fact, all they had been doing was singing joyfully in a boat. The curate is, of course, the "man" who has invented the sin that eventually destroys innocence.

Travel to Italy in 1949 resulted in two more evocative essay/travel books, *A Summer in Italy* (1949) and *South to Sicily* (published in the United States as *An Autumn in Italy,* 1953). In his late forties, O'Faolain uses this sojourn as a metaphor for a spiritual journey, the discovery of inner joy, and the distinction between values that are illusory and those that are permanent. These themes—or, more precisely, meditations—are explored more fully in the autobiography *Vive Moi!* (1964) and in the last four collections of short fiction, *I Remember! I Remember!* (1961), *The Heat of the Sun* (1966), *The Talking Trees* (1971), and *Foreign Affairs and Other Stories* (1976), and, to some extent, in a final novel, *And Again?* (1979). These later works are more personal, reflecting on the process of aging and the connection of the "boy within" to the man "who enfolds him," as he remarked in *Vive Moi!* Through them, O'Faolain seeks to give wholeness and harmony to his life and his life's work.

In retirement, O'Faolain lived with Eileen in Dun Laoghaire, watched his daughter become an accomplished writer, and continued to read, write, and encourage young writers. In 1989, he entered Alcare House, a nursing home in Dublin, where he died after a brief illness in 1991.

Although O'Faolain wrote in many genres, he is most accomplished as a writer of short stories and joins (if he does not surpass) James Joyce,* Elizabeth Bowen,* Frank O'Connor,* and Mary Lavin,* to name a few. All the stories from the first collection, *Midsummer Night Madness,* to the last, *Foreign Affairs,* show the same cosmopolitan, entirely unsentimental approach to human frailty. As one of his characters puts it: "This famous experience of ours, what else is it but the lamentable record of our carefully concealed mistakes," and these "concealed mistakes" are, more often than not, more specifically defined as acts emerging from repressed sexuality. From the aging celibate Aloysius Gonzaga O'Sullivan in *A Purse of Coppers,* whose experience of the Russian ballet and a subsequent encounter with the Catholic censorship squad are his undoing, to Mary Anne Gorgan in *The Talking Trees,* the fifty-year-old spinster who takes up with an Italian lover, O'Faolain's characters either wither away, sexually unfulfilled, or throw all caution to the winds with either disastrous or gratifying results. The only difference in the treatment of this theme between the earlier and later works is that, as O'Faolain matured, he replaced anger and censure with good humor and, like Chekhov, was able to understand even that which he most condemned. This is O'Faolain's greatest gift of spirit, this ability to balance anger and disapprobation with irony, wit, and, ultimately, acceptance of things as they are.

The technique of the stories is also reminiscent of Chekhov. The relatively simple plots (nothing much "happens") are attended by an array of techniques. Symbolism, dream, flashback, memory, and a complex narrative point of view (the narrator of many of the later stories is "Sean," an integral part of the narrative fabric) weave in and out of the tales to create a rich and complex tapestry. In "The Trout," for example, a young girl whose parents have a habit of turning everything into a moral, gets out of bed in the dead of night to rescue a trout caught in a woodland pool. Although the darkness of the wood frightens her, she overcomes her fear, reaches the pool, catches the trout, and releases it into the river, thus achieving her own secret freedom through this tiny rebellion. The story itself is insignificant except as symbol, imagery, and a subtle glimpse into the heart of a child and the meaning of freedom. This habit of mind characterizes O'Faolain as an impressionist rather than a realist.

In an interview, O'Faolain once said, "As I see it, a short story, if it is a good story, is like a child's kite—a small wonder, a brief, bright moment." Indeed, when O'Faolain is at his frequent best, once his story gets off the ground, it soars effortlessly, seemingly unattached to the string that plays it out and pulls it in.

M. KELLY LYNCH

WORKS: *Midsummer Night Madness and Other Stories.* London: Jonathan Cape, 1932; *The Life Story of Eamon de Valera.* Dublin: Talbot, 1933; *Constance Markievicz, or The Average Revolutionary, A Biography.* London: Jonathan Cape, 1934; *A Nest of Simple Folk.* New York: Viking, 1934. (Novel); *There's a Birdie in the Cage.* London: Grayson & Grayson, 1935. (Short stories); *Bird Alone.* London: Jonathan Cape, 1936. (Novel); *The Autobiography of Theobald Wolfe Tone.* London: Thomas Nelson, 1937. (Biography); *A Purse of Coppers: Short Stories.* London: Jonathan Cape, 1937; *King of the Beggars, A Life of Daniel O'Connell.* London: Thomas Nelson/New York: Viking, 1938; *She Had to Do Something: A Comedy in Three Acts.* London: Jonathan Cape, 1938; *De Valera.* Harmondsworth, Middlesex: Penguin, 1939; *Come Back to Erin.* New York: Viking,

1940. (Novel); *An Irish Journey.* London: Longmans, Green, 1940. (Travel); *The Great O'Neill, A Biography of Hugh O'Neill, Earl of Tyrone.* New York: Duell, Sloan & Pearce/London: Longmans, Green, 1942; *The Story of Ireland.* London: William Collins, 1943; *Teresa, and Other Stories.* London: Jonathan Cape, 1947/as *The Man Who Invented Sin, and Other Stories.* New York: Devin-Adair, 1949; *The Irish.* West Drayton, Middlesex: Penguin, 1947/New York: Devin-Adair, 1948; *The Short Story.* London: William Collins, 1948; *A Summer in Italy.* London: Eyre & Spottiswoode, 1949/New York: Devin-Adair. (Travel); *Newman's Way, The Odyssey of John Henry Newman.* London: Longmans, Green, 1952; *South to Sicily.* London: William: Collins, 1953/in United States as *An Autumn in Italy,* New York: Devin-Adair, 1953. (Travel); *With the Gaels of Wexford.* Introduced and compiled by O'Faolain. Enniscorthy, 1955; *The Vanishing Hero, Studies in Novelists of the Twenties.* London: Eyre & Spottiswoode, 1956; *The Finest Stories of Sean O'Faolain.* Boston: Little, Brown, 1958; *I Remember! I Remember!* Boston: Little, Brown, 1961. (Short stories); ed., *Short Stories, A Study in Pleasure.* Boston: Little, Brown, 1961; *Vive Moi!* Boston: Little, Brown, 1964. (Autobiography); *The Heat of the Sun, Stories and Tales.* London: Rupert Hart-Davis/Boston: Little, Brown, 1966; *The Talking Trees and Other Stories.* London: Jonathan Cape, 1971; *Foreign Affairs and Other Stories.* London: Constable/Boston: Little, Brown, 1976; *And Again?* London: Constable, 1979. (Novel); *The Collected Short Stories of Sean O'Faolain.* 3 vols. London: Constable, 1980–1982/Boston: Little, Brown, 1983. REFERENCES: Butler, Pierce. *Sean O'Faolain: A Study of the Short Fiction.* New York: Twayne, 1993; *The Cork Review: Sean O Faolain, 1990–1991.* Cork: Cork Review, 1991; Doyle, Paul A. *Sean O'Faolain.* New York: Twayne, 1968; Harmon, Maurice. *Sean O'Faolain: A Critical Introduction.* South Bend, Ind.: University of Notre Dame Press, 1966; Harmon, Maurice, ed. *Irish University Review* 6 (Spring 1976), Sean O'Faolain Special Issue; Harmon, Maurice. *Sean O'Faolain: A Life.* London: Constable, 1994; O'Donnell, Donat (pseudonym of Conor Cruise O'Brien). "The Parnellism of Sean O'Faolain." In *Maria Cross.* Oxford: Oxford University Press, 1952, pp. 87–105.

Ó FARACHÁIN, ROIBÉARD (1909–1984), poet and critic. Roibéard Ó Farachái was born Robert Farren in Dublin in 1909. He was very much a product of de Valera's Ireland, and from that milieu of the 1930s, 1940s, and 1950s, he derived his strengths and his considerable weaknesses. He was trained as a teacher at St. Patrick's College, Drumcondra, and later took an M.A. at the National University. He was a teacher for ten years and then became associated with Radio Éireann. In 1940, he became a member of the Board of the Abbey Theatre,* and in 1943 the theater presented his verse plays *Assembly at Druim Ceat* and *Lost Light.* His more than thirty years with the theater did little to mitigate the somewhat stultifying influence of the Gaelophile ex-politician Ernest Blythe, who was the theater's managing director for most of that time. However, also in 1940, Austin Clarke* and Ó Farachái formed the Dublin Verse-Speaking Society, which grew into the Lyric Theatre. He died in Dublin in 1984.

Ó Farachái's preoccupation with poetic technique is apparent in his book *How to Enjoy Poetry* (1948). This is an adequate explanatory introduction as well as a small anthology, but the author seems to assume that he is not writing for, but talking to, an audience of bored morons. In addition, many readers will find his chatty jocularity irritating, if not painful. His *The Course of Irish Verse* (1947) is a short introduction for the interested and intelligent reader, and so much of the grating bonhommie is absent. At times, a rather narrow Catholicism and jingoistic patriotism are evident, but Ó Farachái never becomes as rabid as Daniel Corkery,* and he does have some appreciative remarks about writers with whom he is not thoroughly in sympathy. The later pages on the moderns (up to F. R. Higgins* and Austin Clarke) have enough analyses to be of some persuasiveness, but the earlier pages on the nineteenth-century poets are general, skimpy, and journalistic. Like the slightly older Clarke, he mounts the hobby horse of assonance, but unlike the mature Clarke, he feels that assonance may be sprayed over a poem more or less like salt—and the saltier the better.

Ó Faracháin's own poems are a mixed bag of curate's eggs; they range from damp light-verse squibs to a book-length poetic life of Colmcille. At his most serious, he is a religious poet, but at his most serious he is also a dull poet. His language is usually neither particularly visual nor figurative, and he seems mainly interested in sound and form. His Colmcille poem (or series of poems in a variety of forms and nonforms) lacks drama or any urgent narrative thrust or strong imagery or even much distinction of language. Among his shorter poems, the religious pieces are rather innocuous, as if emotion or piety were being substituted for technique. However, if one rummages through any of his books of lyrics, one may find four or five tight, strong, and controlled pieces. For instance, from *Time's Wall Asunder* (1939), one must single out "Where is an Eye, is Beauty," "After the Fianna," and "Yeats." The pity is that there is not enough of such excellent work for him to rank with Clarke or even with Patrick Kavanagh* or Fred Higgins.

WORKS: *Thronging Feet.* London: Sheed & Ward, 1936; *Time's Wall Asunder.* London: Sheed & Ward, 1939; *The First Exile.* London: Sheed & Ward, 1944; *Rime, Gentlemen, Please.* London: Sheed & Ward, 1945; *The Course of Irish Verse.* New York: Sheed & Ward, 1947/London: Sheed & Ward, 1948. (Critical history); *Towards an Appreciation of Poetry.* Dublin: Metropolitan, 1947. (Essay); *How to Enjoy Poetry.* New York: Sheed & Ward, 1948; *Selected Poems.* London & New York: Sheed & Ward, 1951.

O'FARRELL, KATHLEEN (fl. 1990s), novelist.

WORKS: *Kilbroney.* [Dingle, Co. Kerry]: Brandon, [1992]; *The Fiddler of Kilbroney.* [Dingle, Co. Kerry]: Brandon, [1994].

O'FLAHERTY, CHARLES (ca. 1794–1828), poet. According to D. J. O'Donoghue,* O'Flaherty was the son of a pawnbroker in Ross Lane, Dublin. He was apprenticed to a bookseller in Parliament Street and wrote verse for the *Morning Post.* After being, for several years, on the staff of that journal, he went to Wexford in 1826 and edited the *Evening Post.* He wrote various once-popular songs, including "The Humours of Donnybrook Fair," with its engaging detail and rollicking rhythm.

WORKS: *Poems. Dedicated to Thomas Moore, Esq.* Dublin: Printed for the Author, 1813; *Trifles in Poetry, Including Hermit's Minstrelsy.* Dublin: R. Carrick, 1821; *Poems and Songs.* Dublin, 1821; *Retrospection, or A Lover's Lapses and a Poet's Love. . . .* Dublin: J. Carrick, 1824.

O'FLAHERTY, LIAM (1896–1984), novelist and short story writer. O'Flaherty was born on August 28, 1896, at Gort na gCapall, Inishmore, the largest Aran island. He was the ninth child and second son of Michael O'Flaherty who worked fifteen acres of barren land. The family cottage stands within sound of the sea, the ruined fort of Dun Aengus rising on the high cliffs beyond. The islanders speak Irish, but young William (or Billy) was educated in English until the age of eleven at Oatquarter School, across the fields. A visiting priest from the Holy Ghost Order offered him a place at the Order's junior seminary at Rockwell College, County Tipperary. At the age of sixteen he moved on to Blackrock College, County Dublin. With a scholarship he completed one year at University College, Dublin, for the first two months of which he was enrolled as a Dublin diocesan seminarian. His vocation to the priesthood evaporated, and claiming he was "tired of waiting for the Irish revolution," he volunteered for the Irish Guards in 1915 under his mother's maiden name of Ganly.

All of his life, O'Flaherty was aware of his twofold temperamental heritage. He was proud of his fierce O'Flaherty blood—"the only princely thing I possess"—but he also inherited a gentler side from his mother Margaret Ganly, descended from Plymouth Brethren from County Antrim, who had settled on Aran two generations before to build lighthouses. His mother was forty when Liam was born, and his second autobiographical volume, *Shame the Devil,* shows how close to her in spirit he remained. From her he learned his love of nature, and from his father came a restless independence and a hatred of restriction and repression. The beauty and the hardship of his childhood both bit deep.

O'Flaherty's service in the Irish Guards also left its lifelong mark. First, he received the intensive initial training which the Guards recruits traditionally receive as an elite corps; then he experienced the mud and blood of the Somme; and finally, in 1917, he was shellshocked and discharged after a year's medical treatment. O'Flaherty's war experience, overlaying his physically tough childhood and religiously disciplined education, left him, at age twenty-one, psychologically disoriented.

Then, still as Bill Ganly, he set off for a period of odd jobs and wandering which was eventually recorded in his first autobiographical volume *Two Years* (1930). During this period, he worked at almost every kind of unskilled job on three continents and claimed he had "developed contempt for dirt, and ceased to think or to be sensitive about myself." In fact, all his life he was to remain hypersensitive about himself, intuitively aware of the feelings of others.

While wandering he visited his elder brother Tom, who had emigrated to Boston years before. Tom urged him to write, and Liam, who had already started writing stories during his convalescence on Aran, wrote more in Boston but after reading Maupassant burned his work in disgust. During this period, he became a communist and stopped using the name of Ganly.

In 1921, O'Flaherty, styling himself "Chairman of the Council of the Unemployed," led a group of unemployed dockers, seized the Rotunda in Dublin, hoisted the red flag, and held the building for several days. On the outbreak of the Civil War, he joined the Republicans against the Free Staters and wrote for Republican papers such as *The Plain People.* He then returned to London and in September 1922 started to write "definitively." In a few weeks he produced a novel and several stories, all of which have been lost. His first published short story was "The Sniper," which appeared on January 12, 1923, in the British socialist weekly *The New Leader.* It was noticed by the critic Edward Garnett (1868–1937). At Garnett's recommendation, O'Flaherty's next attempted novel, *Thy Neighbour's Wife* (1923) was accepted by Jonathan Cape. This flawed book contains O'Flaherty's most detailed description of peasant life on Aran.

O'Flaherty's next novel, *The Black Soul* (1924), was written under Garnett's tutelage. At the same time Garnett, whose wife Constance was a well-known Russian translator, directed O'Flaherty's attention to writers such as Gogol and Dostoyevsky. The correspondence between Garnett and O'Flaherty during this period reveals how close their relationship had become.

Throughout the later 1920s and early 1930s, O'Flaherty continued to form his basic values. During this period his literary output was high. He married Margaret Barrington* and became a father. He was restless, moving to Dublin, to rural isolation in Wicklow, to London, and France, and visiting Russia. In spite of his success, he had financial difficulties, recurring fears of insanity, and two nervous breakdowns, caused perhaps by the aftermath of shellshock and by conflicts within and around him, some of which emerge as satire in works such as *A Tourist's Guide to Ireland* (1929).

In 1932, now separated from his wife and disillusioned with communism, O'Flaherty became one of the founding members of the Irish Academy of Letters. During the 1930s, though much of his work was banned in Ireland, three of his novels were filmed—two in the United States and one in France. He continued to travel and write. During World War II, he moved to the Caribbean and South America and settled temporarily in Connecticut where he wrote more stories. When the war ended he returned to Europe. Between 1946 and 1957, he broadcast several stories in Irish and English over Radio Éireann. He was finally persuaded to record some of his work in 1976 to celebrate his eightieth birthday. O'Flaherty avoided publicity, refusing television and press interviews. The latter part of his life was spent mostly in Dublin, with trips to London and France. He visited Aran once, when in his eighties. His last short stories date from the early 1960s. In old age, he struggled but failed to complete a last novel, *The Gamblers,* the plot of which is summarized in an appendix to his collected letters. He died in St. Vincent's Hospital, Dublin, on September 7, 1984.

O'Flaherty's work is variable in tone, style, and quality. He is not an easy writer to pigeonhole by exterior criteria, and it would be entirely false to do so. He had difficulty maintaining consistency in his novels, which tend to become episodic; his best work is to be found in his short stories. He is very Irish in temperament, especially in his use of what Yeats* called "tragic-farce," and as a result, has been accused of being melodramatic. His abrasive sense of humor stems from disappointed idealism. He said: "No ideal is practical, but all ideals are the mothers of great poetry, and it is only from the womb of an ideal that a great race, or a great literature, or a great art can spring."

O'Flaherty formulated his ideal in *The Ecstasy of Angus* (1931), an allegory in which Angus, the Celtic god of love, mates with Fand the earth fairy. Awakening, Angus finds he has lost his youth and beauty, killed the gods, and sown enmity in nature. Behind him has risen the Tree of Knowledge guarded by the warlike Genius of Unrest. The offspring of his union is Man with divine capacity but whose love will always be as unstable as nature herself. O'Flaherty's man, unlike Adam, is not given domination over nature but is part of it. His capacity for thought is both curse and blessing. By this mating of the ideal and the physical, O'Flaherty proclaims the inescapable tension within man's nature.

The allegory was written after a series of novels in all of which the central male character is persecuted by circumstances or by his own neuroticism. *The Black Soul* and *Thy Neighbour's Wife* are both set on Aran; Fergus, the hero of *The Black Soul,* is a projection of the author himself. O'Flaherty said that Dostoyevsky, as well as Gogol and James Joyce,* affected him deeply. The influence of the first can be detected in *Mr. Gilhooley* (1926), *The Assassin* (1928), and *The Puritan* (1931), all three of which are about lost urbanized man. His most acclaimed early novel, *The Informer* (1925), he called "a sort of high-blown detective story and its style based on the technique of the cinema." In spite of its plot and setting, this novel is not a serious attempt to write about Irish politics or the secret Irish revolutionary organization. It is about Gypo Nolan's struggle as "a human soul, weak and helpless in suffering, shivering in the toils of the eternal struggle of the human soul with pain."

By the end of the 1920s, O'Flaherty's work shows that he had started to pass beyond his own sufferings, projected into one central character and into the sufferings of others. *The House of Gold* (1929) has four main characters and a complex plot. As suggested by the title, which is culled from the litany to the Blessed Virgin Mary but also stands for gold as an image of cupidity, the work contains a good deal of symbolism, and the weight of social criticism overpowers the characters.

Didactic idealism also manipulates artistic expression in *The Wilderness* (1927). Here O'Flaherty illustrates that, though man is incapable of rising above his human limitations, there is necessity and even beauty in his struggle for integration. Lawless, Macanasa, and Stevens, the three principal characters, imperfectly represent man's will to immortality, beauty, and power which O'Flaherty was to introduce as a ground-theme in two later novels, *Land* (1946) and *Insurrection* (1954). In all three books, the artistic impact is marred by a too-explicit message. In *Insurrection,* the three characters of *The Wilderness* are redefined: the mystical Lawless becomes the poet Stapleton; the peasant Macanasa becomes the soldier Madden; and the scientific freethinker Stevens becomes the monklike but pragmatic Kinsella who once dreamed of becoming a famous chemist. The thesis also involves social criticism of the specifically Irish situation.

Though novels such as *The Informer, The Assassin, The Martyr, Land, Insurrection,* and *Famine* are related to crucial events in Irish history, the basic human reactions of the characters predominate over the historic setting. *The Martyr* satirizes all civil wars; *The Return of the Brute,* calling on O'Flaherty's experience in the Irish Guards, describes war's bestial effects; the quasi-historic situation of *The Assassin* lends the plot authenticity, but the human reactions described are timeless; *Insurrection* is about the Irish struggle but also suggests that the contradictory forces within man should not weaken themselves in strife but should unite in the face of moral defeat—that common enemy.

O'Flaherty gave his best answer to his question "What is man for?" not in those novels in which he makes the most explicit attempt to do so, but in *Skerrett* (1932) and *Famine* (1937), in both of which the theme grows out of the action rather than the other way around. Skerrett, the Aran schoolmaster, and the Kilmartin family in the 1845–1847 famine fight against outward circumstances, but their true enemy is within themselves. Skerrett and the Kilmartins die undaunted as they had lived; both novels are paeans of praise to endurance. That Skerrett ends in the padded cell of a lunatic asylum and that Thomsy Kilmartin's dead body is savaged by dogs is of lesser importance. In *Famine,* O'Flaherty also created his only full-blown female character, Mary Kilmartin.

O'Flaherty experimented unsuccessfully with drama in *Darkness* (1926) and wrote two good Irish poems, two amusing autobiographical volumes which reveal his volatile temperament, and a good deal of satire in which must be included the novel *Hollywood Cemetery* (1935) and the travelogue *I Went to Russia* (1931). As a writer he will ultimately be remembered, however, for his work in the short story. He is at his best when his gifts as a raconteur are disciplined, when he forgets his sense of frustration or his concern for man at large, and keeps within the limits of either a concentric moment or a dramatic situation. Without the expansiveness of the novel form, however, into which he put his main effort, the artistic economy of his best short stories might never have been achieved.

His best stories tell of Aran, peasants and fishermen, the sea and wildlife. They are based on observation and the memories nearest his heart. He wrote over one hundred and fifty short stories. As in any artist's output, their subject matter, quality, and style vary considerably. Some were written as potboilers, some to a tailored length to suit a specific market; in others, he is careless or allows his subjective feelings to intervene inappropriately. His best stories are based on transposed, well-objectivized, personal experience, such as "The Cow's Death," a story about twelve hundred words long, in which a frenzied cow, after giving birth to a stillborn calf whose body has been thrown over the cliffs, flings herself after it. Other stories as varied as "The Sniper," "The Child of God," and "The Fairy Goose" fall into this category. He writes best when he does not attempt to preach but instead creates a faithful picture of life as he sees it, of human feelings which are universal, of an Aran life-style which has disappeared with the advent of tourism, electricity, and the mass media.

In spite of his vivid visual imagination, illustrated, for example, in "The Mountain Tavern" or "The Touch," there remains something of the oral "sean-chai," or Gaelic storyteller, in O'Flaherty. To flavor his entirety, one should read those stories originally written in Irish or later translated by him. His English is often subconsciously affected by Gaelic speech patterns and by the patterns of storytelling he heard as a child when groups used to gather round the O'Flaherty hearth. These influences emerge most strongly in works such as "The Black Mare" and "The Mermaid"—both of which contain formulaic repeated phrases, proverbs, hyperbole, anticipation, and a typical Christian/pagan mixture of imagery.

The O'Flaherty praise of courage which emerged so clearly in *Skerrett* and *Famine* is repeated in short stories such as "The Hawk," "The Landing," and "Red Barbara." For O'Flaherty life is no pastel-colored affair but rather a joyful acceptance of struggle, without which the lyrical aspect of nature, of life, has no meaning.

For O'Flaherty, immortality or godliness consists of an indomitable spirit rather than the perpetuation of an individual soul after death. The defeat or sickness of the spirit during life which he finds so prevalent in modern society he reveals in stories such as "Unclean," "The Tramp," or "Mackerel for Sale." As struggle against defeat is so important, so is the overcoming of fear by love, for the two cannot coexist.

In later stories such as "The Post Office," which is a dramatic mixture of irony and comedy, the world comes to a remote western Ireland village; the rapidly shifting and subtle dialogue represents the juxtaposed trains of thought which these two worlds embody. In this story, the foretaste of the physical disintegration of the old society, shown earlier in "Going into Exile," becomes a cultural certainty.

Apart from their literary pleasure and value, therefore, O'Flaherty's peasant stories also form a valuable record of Irish social change.

                                                                                                    A. A. KELLY

WORKS: *Thy Neighbour's Wife*. London: Jonathan Cape, 1923/New York: Boni & Liveright, 1924. (Novel); *The Black Soul*. London: Jonathan Cape, 1924/New York: Boni & Liveright, 1925/ Bath: Lythway, 1972. (Novel); *The Informer*. London: Jonathan Cape/New York: Alfred A. Knopf, 1925. (Novel); *Darkness*. London: E. Archer, 1926. (Tragedy in three acts); *Mr. Gilhooley*. London: Jonathan Cape, 1926/New York: Harcourt, Brace, 1927. (Novel); *The Wilderness*. London: *The Humanist*, 1927 (serialized in six parts)/Dublin: Wolfhound, 1978/New York: Dodd, Mead, 1986. (Novel); *The Assassin*. London: Jonathan Cape/New York: Harcourt, Brace, 1928. (Novel); *The House of Gold*. London: Jonathan Cape, 1929/New York: Harcourt, Brace, 1930. (Novel); *The Return of the Brute*. London: Mandrake, 1929/New York: Harcourt, Brace, 1930. (Novel); *A Tourist's Guide to Ireland*. London: Mandrake, 1929; *Two Years*. London: Jonathan Cape/New York: Harcourt, Brace, 1930. (Autobiography); *The Ecstasy of Angus*. London: Joiner & Steele, 1931/ Dublin: Wolfhound, 1978; *I Went to Russia*. London: Jonathan Cape/New York: Harcourt, Brace, 1931. (Autobiography cum travel book); *The Puritan*. London: Jonathan Cape, 1931/New York: Harcourt, Brace, 1932/Bath: Lythway, 1973. (Novel); *Skerrett*. London: Gollancz/New York: Long

& Smith, 1932/Dublin: Wolfhound, 1977. (Novel); *The Martyr.* New York: Macmillan, 1933/London: Gollancz, 1935. (Novel); *Shame the Devil.* London: Grayson & Grayson, 1934. (Autobiography); *Hollywood Cemetery.* London: Gollancz, 1935. (Novel); *Famine.* London: Gollancz/New York: Random House, 1937. (Novel); *The Short Stories of Liam O'Flaherty.* London: Jonathan Cape, 1937; *Land.* London: Gollancz/New York: Random House, 1946. (Novel); *Two Lovely Beasts.* London: Gollancz, 1948/New York: Devin-Adair, 1950. (Short stories); *Insurrection.* London: Gollancz, 1950/Boston: Little, Brown, 1951. (Novel); *Duil.* (Desire). Dublin: Sairseal agus Dill, 1953. (A collection of stories in Irish); *The Stories of Liam O'Flaherty.* New York: Devin-Adair, 1956; *The Pedlar's Revenge.* Dublin: Wolfhound, 1976. (Stories).   REFERENCES: Cahalan, James M. *Liam O'Flaherty: A Study of the Short Fiction.* Boston: Twayne, 1991; Jefferson, George. *Liam O'Flaherty: A Descriptive Bibliography of His Works.* Dublin: Wolfhound, 1991; Kelly, A. A. *Liam O'Flaherty, the Storyteller.* London: Macmillan, 1976; Kelly, A. A., ed. *The Collected Letters of Liam O'Flaherty.* Dublin: Wolfhound, 1994; Sheeran, Patrick. *The Novels of Liam O'Flaherty.* Dublin: Wolfhound, 1976; Zneimmer, John N. *The Literary Vision of Liam O'Flaherty.* Syracuse, N.Y.: Syracuse University Press, 1970.

O'FLANAGAN, JAMES RODERICK (1814–1900), historian and novelist. O'Flanagan was born in Fermoy, County Cork, on September 1, 1814. He was educated at Fermoy, at Trinity College, Dublin, and at King's Inn. Called to the Irish bar in 1838, he practiced on the Munster circuit. He wrote on Irish rivers for *The Dublin University Magazine,* collaborated on a history of Dundalk, and wrote several very readable anecdotal histories of the Irish bar as well as three novels. His fine sense of detail may be seen in this brief extract from *The Irish Bar* (1879), in which he characterizes Harry Deane Grady, a member of the Irish Parliament for Limerick and a strong supporter of the government and of the Act of Union.

"What!" cried his indignant remonstrator, "do you mean to sell your country?"
"Thank God," cried this pure patriot, "that I have a country to sell."
He was very coarse in his expressions, and when reminded that he owed his position to his constituents, he said, "I care nothing for my constituents, I get nothing good from them. Begad, if I only shake hands with them they give me the itch."

WORKS: *Impressions at Home or Abroad, or Year of Real Life.* London, 1837; *The Blackwater in Munster.* London: J. How, 1844; *Gentle Blood, or the Secret Marriage.* Dublin, 1861. (Novel); with John D'alton. *The History of Dundalk, and Its Environs. . . .* Dublin: Hodges, Smith, 1864; *The Lives of the Lord Chancellors and Keepers of the Great Seal of Ireland, from the Earliest Times to the Reign of Queen Victoria.* 2 vols. London: Longmans, Green, 1870; *Captain O'Shaughnessy's Sporting Career. An Autobiography.* 2 vols. London: Chapman & Hall, 1873. (Novel); *The Irish Bar: Comprising Anecdotes, Bon-mots and Biographical Sketches of the Bench and Bar of Ireland.* London: Sampson Low, Marston, Searle & Rivington, 1879; *The Munster Circuit.* London: Sampson Low, Marston, Searle & Rivington, 1880; *Through North Wales with My Wife. An Arcadian Tour.* London: Burns & Oates, [1884]; *Annals, Anecdotes, Traits, and Traditions of the Irish Parliament, 1172 to 1800.* Dublin: M. H. Gill, [1893]; *An Octogenerian Literary Life.* Cork: Guy, 1896. (Autobiographical); *The Life and Adventures of Bryan O'Regan, an Irish Sporting Tale.* Dublin: P.C.D. Warren, n.d. (Novel).

O'FLYNN, CRIOSTOIR (1927–   ), man of letters. O'Flynn (Ó Floinn in Irish) was born in Limerick on December 18, 1927, and was educated there and at the National University and Trinity College, Dublin. He worked in Ireland

and England as teacher, broadcaster, journalist, publicity writer, and lecturer and is a noted and formidable controversialist. He married in 1952, has seven children, and lives in Glenageary, County Dublin.

O'Flynn's home language was English, but he writes in both English and Irish. He began to learn Irish in school at the age of four, and his knowledge of it is now both fluent and scholarly. Certain themes and materials are common to his main work in both languages. They turn most notably upon a coalescence of realism and fantasy, and a highly independent reading of the Irish scene, rural and urban.

To English-speaking audiences, O'Flynn is best known for his collection of short stories *Sanctuary Island* (1971) and his two plays *Land of the Living* and *The Order of Melchizedek*. *Land of the Living* modulates between two styles, a naturalistic and a poetic speech. The present of a marriage of convenience between two old people intermingles with the past of a legendary, magical love, mysteriously reenacted. *The Order of Melchizedek* confronts a priest with a young girl who persuades him to believe her a reincarnation of the Virgin Mary. The play ends in a tragic resolution with her and her infant's death, by her own hand, in exile. The priest, by these strange paths, remains in his priesthood.

Sanctuary Island surveys contemporary Ireland with a largely satirical, at times affectionately humorous, regard. It emerges as a land of victims, buffoons, poseurs; capable of a savagery which does not exclude moments of communion between people or between people and their land; moments, too, of richly comic extravagance. *Sanctuary Island,* by its diversity of subject, mood, and manner, sets out prospects inviting O'Flynn's continued exploration. Whatever the form of exploration, its character is essentially dramatic and sustained by a lively sense of the absurdity of the received facts of life.

D.E.S. MAXWELL

As poet, O'Flynn may be fairly judged by his chatty and companionable volume, *A Poet in Rome* (1992). It is flavored with occasional poeticisms like "o'erflows" or old-fashioned inversions like "words obscene." But such usages are in close proximity to modern slang like "odd-balls" or "puts you off." Also, the poet frequently uses the clichés of conversation. In "La donna e mobile," for instance, there is "[b]ringing home the bacon," "daily bread," and "count one's blessings," all in the first three lines. One even finds old saws such as, "When in Rome do as the Romans do" or "All work and no play makes Jack a dull boy" or "Music hath charms to soothe a savage breast." Yet there are passages of fluency and vigor, as, for instance, the brilliantly bigoted quote overheard in a bar, in the second to fourth stanzas of "Immigrazione-Discriminazione / Lavori agli Italiani." This is, however, a casual, curious, and uneven volume with some poems, such as "Direzioni," about so little as to seem almost pointless.

A prolific writer in many genres, O'Flynn is a member of Aosdána.*

PRINCIPAL WORKS: *Lá Dá bhFaca Thú.* Dublin: Cló Marainn, 1955. (Novel); *Éirí Amach na Cásca.* Dublin: Sáirséal agus Dill, 1966. (Poems); Learairí Lios an Phúca. Dublin: F.N.T., 1968.

(Novel); Oineachlann. Dublin: An Gúm, 1968. (Stories); *Ó Fhás go hAois.* Dublin: Sáirséal agus Dill, 1969. (Poems); *Sanctuary Island.* Dublin: Gill & Macmillan. (Stories); *Aisling Dhá Abhainn.* Dublin: F.N.T., 1977. (Poems); *Banana.* Dublin: Obelisk, 1977. (Poems); *At Dun Laoghaire Lighthouse.* [Dun Laoghaire: C. O. Floinn, 1978]. (Poems); *Summer in Kilkee.* Limerick: Treaty, 1984; *A Poet in Rome.* [Blackrock, Co. Dublin]: Four Courts, [1992] (Poetry); *The Obelisk Year.* [Dun Laoghaire, Co. Dublin]: Obelisk, [1993]; *When Dasher Died.* Dublin: Obelisk, 1994. (Translations from the Irish); ed. & trans., *Irish Comic Poems.* Indreabhan, Conamara: Cló Iar-Chonnachta, [1995].

O'GAORA, COLM (1966–   ), short story writer. O'Gaora was born in Dublin and now lives in London. His collection of stories, *Giving Ground* (1993), is thoroughly glum, the pieces generally being about loss, parting, and death. There is not a great deal of action in most of them, but they are written in a clean and beautifully lucid prose.

WORK: *Giving Ground.* London: Jonathan Cape, [1993].

O'GORMAN, MICHAEL (ca. 1950–   ), novelist. O'Gorman was born on the outskirts of Ennis, County Clare. At eighteen, he moved to Australia for several years, and in 1974 he moved to London, where he supported his writing by such jobs as bartending and window cleaning. His novel, *Clancy's Bulba* (1983), is mainly a broadly comic account of three Mayo men training their cock, Taurus Bulba, for a fight with the most formidable cock in Ireland, Satan the First. The large cast is distinctively drawn, and the novel is packed with well-structured incidents, such as cock fights, fistfights, and a broadcast of the Grand National at Aintree. Its chief quality, however, is its faintly exaggerated, richly profane language. Also, the book is not entirely an entertainment with a happy ending. When the sickly son of Stallion O'Casey dies, O'Gorman puts his hitherto comic language to powerful use in a ferocious diatribe against God:

Ya're the mother of a cunt that took him from me! He's your responsibility! Seein' as I don't stand a ghost of a chance of gettin' past yer fuckin' doors when my time comes, and seein' as how I'll never lay eyes on me darlin' again, then 'tis you that's got the fuckin' job whether ya like it or not! So take care of him, ya king of shits! Ya murderer of cripples! Ya widow-maker! Ya famine-maker you!

WORK: *Clancy's Bulba.* London: Hutchinson, 1983.

O'GRADY, DESMOND [JAMES BERNARD] (1935–   ), poet. O'Grady was born in Limerick on August 27, 1935, and spent most of his childhood in West Clare and in the Irish-speaking districts of Kerry. He was educated by Jesuits and Cistercians. In the mid-1950s, he lived in Dublin and then in Paris and published a small collection of poems called *Chords and Orchestrations* (1956). After a brief stay on Caldey Island off the Welsh coast, he moved to Rome, and in 1961 a long collection of poems, *Reilly,* appeared. In the early 1960s, he did postgraduate work at Harvard and in 1964 received an M.A. in Celtic studies. He then acted as senior English master at the Overseas School of Rome until 1974 and became the friend and secretary of Ezra Pound in the poet's last years. After 1974, he held a number of teaching positions: at the American University in Cairo, at Tabriz University in Iran, and at the University of Alexandria. In the fall of 1980, he returned to Harvard, studied with John Kelleher, and in 1982 received a Ph.D. in Celtic languages and literature and in comparative literature. He is a member of Aosdána* and lives in Kinsale, County Cork.

O'Grady's fine early collection, *The Dark Edge of Europe* (1967) displays great technical proficiency. The rhythms often have a base of anapests and dactyls, varied felicitously by iambs, trochees, and even spondees; as a result, even in long lines, the artificial "rocking chair" motion of mere mechanical expertise is avoided. The poem "His Bath" particularly indicates these qualities, as well as an effective use of alliteration and assonance. The most technically complex poem in the book is the remarkable "Land," but "Years Ending," the sequence entitled "Sea," and perhaps half a dozen other pieces in this volume show an impressive formal control, some rhetorically effective long sentences, and some occasional echoes of Hopkins and Dylan Thomas.

In other collections of the late 1960s and 1970s, such as *The Dying Gaul* (1968) and particularly in *Separations* (1973), O'Grady loosens his form and becomes merely fluently chatty or sometimes even phlegmatic, as in "Back to Our Mountains." If some of this middle work is much more relaxed, it is immeasurably much less accomplished than *The Dark Edge of Europe*. The late collection *Tipperary* (1991) well illustrates O'Grady's curious verging from relaxed looseness to tight formal control. Parts of "An Irish Exile in Liege" are so casual that they slide into prose. In other poems, the chattiness disappears into the scrunched-up syntax of a Hopkins: "It possesses a fearsome force revitalizes" or "Conger-faced, their snouts / whole ferrets, they fang ferocious." In some poems, much is made of alliteration, as in "his dare-days' / dodgems." Sometimes too much is made of it:

> . . . may pilot the hard hurt heart
> home to a harboured honour.

More than many of his contemporaries, however, O'Grady realizes the poetic resources of sound and rhythm, takes chances, and sometimes pulls off brilliant effects, as in the last line of "Spring": "I start this fresh blank page." Perhaps the most effective pieces in this richly talented and uneven book are "My Rites" and "Tipperary," but there are other strong contenders.

WORKS: *Chords and Orchestrations.* Limerick: Echo, 1956; *Reilly.* London: Phoenix, 1961; *Professor Kelleher and the Charles River.* Cambridge, Mass.: Carthage, 1964; *Separazioni.* Rome: Edizioni Europei, 1965. (Poems with Italian translations); *The Dark Edge of Europe.* London: MacGibbon & Kee, 1967; *The Dying Gaul.* London: MacGibbon & Kee, 1968; *Off Licence.* Dublin: Dolmen, 1968. (Translations from Irish, Armenian & Italian); *Hellas.* Dublin: New Writers', 1971; *Separations.* Dublin: Goldsmith, 1973; *Stations.* Cairo: American University in Cairo, 1976; *The Gododdin.* Dublin: Dolmen, 1977. (Translations from the Welsh); *Sing Me Creation.* Dublin: Gallery, 1977; *The Headgear of the Tribe.* London: Martin Brian & O'Keeffe, 1978/Dublin: Gallery, 1979; *A Limerick Rake: Versions from the Irish.* Dublin: Gallery, 1978; *His Scaldcrane's Nest.*

Dublin: Gallery, 1979; *Crecian Glances: Versions from the Classical Anthology.* Cambridge, Mass.: Inkling, 1981; *The Wandering Celt.* Dublin: Gallery, 1984; *These Fields in Springtime.* Dublin: Gallery/Deerfield, Mass.: Deerfield, 1984; *Alexandria Notebook.* Dublin: Raven Arts, 1989; *Seven Arab Odes: An English Verse Rendering.* London: Agenda/Dublin: Raven Arts, 1990; *Tipperary.* [Galway: Salmon, 1991]; *Ten Modern Arab Poets: Selected Versions.* Dublin: Dedalus, 1992; *Alternative Manners.* Galway: Salmon, 1992. (Versions from the Greek of C. P. Cavafy); *Trawling Tradition: Translations 1954–1994.* Salzburg: University of Salzburg, 1994; *My Fields This Springtime.* Belfast: Lapwing Poetry Pamphlets, 1994.

O'GRADY, HUBERT (1841–1899), playwright and actor. Born in Limerick, O'Grady became, during the last quarter of the nineteenth century, an actor-manager who specialized in Irish comic roles à la the Shaughraun, but mainly of his own devising. He wrote at least eight Irish patriotic melodramas, but they might be described as Boucicault*-and-water, and their transient merits were theatrical rather than literary.

WORKS: "A Hubert O'Grady Number." Stephen Watt, ed. *The Journal of Irish Literature* 14 (January 1985): 3–49. (Contains "Emigration" and *The Famine* and an Introduction by Watt.)

O'GRADY, STANDISH (1846–1928), novelist. Although the revival of interest in Irish culture and the development of a distinctive new national literature early in the twentieth century resulted primarily from the linguistic, historic, and literary research of Petrie,* O'Donovan,* O'Curry,* and such scholars, credit for directly stimulating the effort goes to Standish O'Grady. Yeats* and AE* considered him the real father of the Irish literary revival.

O'Grady was born on September 18, 1846, in Castletown Berehaven, County Cork. After graduation from Trinity College, he practiced law while pursuing an interest in Irish history and mythology, which were to dominate the rest of his life. His discovery of the rich store of ancient Irish history and his reading of the early Irish legends and sagas prompted him to write his two-volume *History of Ireland* (1878–1880). Included in this work are the versions of the mythological tales and the heroic cycle that were the sources of much of the literature on such subjects at the turn of the century. His version of the Cuchulainn cycle was particularly fascinating to Yeats and others. Although he attempted to be faithful to the tone of the early texts, while adapting them to the tastes of modern readers, O'Grady tends to domesticate the rough tales and make gentlemen and ladies of the heroic characters. Because the sources from which he worked were fragmentary, some of his revisions were inevitable, but his versions hardly resemble the vigorous, pagan tone of the originals. To correct what he saw as his own inaccuracies in those volumes, O'Grady followed them with his *History of Ireland: Critical and Philosophical* (1881), which is a genuine contribution to our knowledge of Irish history and culture.

O'Grady's deepest interest was in the literary artifacts, the heroic tales and legends, and he devoted his attention in the years following to the dissemination of them. Presupposing his readers' lack of knowledge of the original tales, O'Grady proceeded to rewrite them as adventure novels. Cuchulainn became the hero of a trilogy: *The Coming of Cuculain* (1894), *In the Gates of the North* (1901), and *The Triumph and Passing of Cuculain* (1920). He treated Fionn macCumhaill similarly in *Finn and His Companions* (1892). In these and in all his fiction, the characters are superficial and wooden, and a strong moral tone is imposed on what had been lively, amoral tales. Also, his descriptions tend to be extensive, and his prose overwrought.

He wrote several other historical novels on Irish history, particularly on the Tudor period. In them the historical description and even analysis are sure, and the plots lively and engaging. *The Flight of the Eagle* (1897) presents the story of Red Hugh O'Donnell, one version of an Irish epic hero. But the novels resemble children's adventure stories, packed with action but thin on characterization.

Unlike most of his literary associates, O'Grady remained true to the cause of Unionism, and he wrote extensively on the subject, particularly in the effort to reform landlords in their treatment of the farming class. In *Toryism and the Tory Democracy* (1886), he proposed a coalition of peasant and landlord classes to revive Ireland's economy. He was frustrated in his political efforts, and after the failure of his journal, the *All-Ireland Review* in 1907, he withdrew from active political affairs. He left Ireland in 1918 and died on the Isle of Wight on May 18, 1928.

Although his political and economic theories were not adopted, O'Grady's influence on Irish writers is indisputable. Major writers such as Yeats and AE built on his research, discovering through his novels and historical writings sources for their own superior creations. The broader audience of readers learned from him about their own heritage, at a time when such an assertion of national identity was being cultivated. He was a powerful advocate of the Ascendancy class and a positive force on that population; "the last champion of the Irish aristocracy," AE called him. Yeats found such a role particularly attractive. As editor of the weekly *All-Ireland Review,* O'Grady advanced both the formulation of political theory and the development of indigenous Irish art, and he personally gave support to many of the leading young writers of the time. His personality and dedication to high standards of literary and historical work were so powerful that, through his influence, more than through his own writings, he is assured an important place in Ireland's history.

JAMES KILROY

WORKS: *History of Ireland: The Heroic Period.* London: Sampson Low, Searle, Marston, & Rivington/Dublin: E. Ponsonby, 1878; *Early Bardic Literature, Ireland.* London: Sampson Low, Searle, Marston, & Rivington/Dublin: E. Ponsonby, 1879; *History of Ireland: Cuculain and His Contemporaries.* London: Sampson Low, Searle, Marston, & Rivington/Dublin: E. Ponsonby, 1880; *History of Ireland: Critical and Philosophical.* London: Sampson Low/Dublin: E. Ponsonby, 1881; *The Crisis in Ireland.* Dublin: E. Ponsonby/London: Simpkin & Marshall, 1882; *Cuculain: An Epic.* London: Sampson Low, Searle, Marston, & Rivington/Dublin: E. Ponsonby, 1882; *Toryism and the Tory Democracy.* London: Chapman & Hall, 1886; *Red Hugh's Captivity.* London: Ward & Downey, 1889; *Finn and His Companions.* London: T. Fisher Unwin, 1892; *The Bog of Stars.* London: T. Fisher Unwin/Dublin: Sealy, Bryers & Walker/New York: P. J. Kennedy, 1893; *The Coming of*

Cuculain. London: Methuen, 1894; *Lost on Du-Corrig*. London, Paris, & Melbourne: Cassell, 1894; *The Story of Ireland*. London: Methuen, 1894; *The Chain of Gold*. London: T. Fisher Unwin, 1895; *Ulrick the Ready*. London: Downey, 1896; *In the Wake of King James*. London: J. M. Dent, 1896; *The Flight of the Eagle*. London: Lawrence & Bullen, 1897; *All Ireland*. Dublin: Sealy, Bryers, & Walker/London: T. Fisher Unwin, 1898; *The Queen of the World*. London: Lawrence & Bullen, 1900; *In the Gates of the North*. Kilkenny: Standish O'Grady, 1901; *Hugh Roe O'Donnell*. Belfast: Nelson & Knox, 1902; *The Masque of Finn*. Dublin: Sealy, Bryers & Walker, 1907; *The Triumph and Passing of Cuculain*. Dublin: Talbot/London: T. Fisher Unwin, 1920; *Standish O'Grady: Selected Essays and Passages*. Ernest A. Boyd, ed. Dublin: Talbot, n.d. REFERENCES: Hagan, Edward A. *"High Nonsensical Works": A Study of the Works of Standish James O'Grady*. Troy, N.Y.: Whitston, 1986; Marcus, Phillip. *Standish O'Grady*. Lewisburg, Pa.: Bucknell University Press, 1970; O'Grady, Hugh Art. *Standish James O'Grady: The Man and the Work*. Dublin: Talbot, 1929.

O'GRADY, TIMOTHY E. (fl. 1980s), novelist. O'Grady's novel *Motherland* won the David Higham Award in 1989. This accomplished novel is a quest in which the hero, accompanied by his mentor grandfather, his grandfather's dog, and an affectionate, nameless monkey travel around Ireland. The fat, awkward, middle-aged hero, who has webbed fingers and a gift of clairvoyance, is searching for his mother, who occasionally, in fits of madness, disappears. His grandfather is nominally looking for some missing pages of a twelfth-century family journal. However, after his grandfather has been killed, the hero learns that "he had invented Hugh's missing manuscript and its fevered prophecy in order to keep me by his side, to give me his gifts of thought and love and history." The hero finally finds his dying mother and in the process comes to some sort of peace after long torment. The details of the novel are half realistic and half surreal: "I began to dream. Rocks walked and the walls of houses rippled. . . . I saw bats flying at the windscreen." Even when the hero is not dreaming, the details are striking and bizarre:

On the far bank of one of these rivers, I believe it was the Urrin, I saw a violinist standing in some brown mud under a tree, playing his violin and screaming.

Or:

Somewhere I heard a wild, reverberating roar, strange and vast like the call of a beast, and when I looked round me I saw far below at the base of the ravine a solitary trombonist playing up to the echoing mountainside.

The opening of the novel is, "My mother's rooms smelled of the jungle and of death. I could see, from the doorway, a deep green fungus spreading across the ceiling from the cracked skylight." This would suggest yet another Irish novel replete with depressing details, sordid images, and glum conclusions. There is plenty that is depressing and sordid in O'Grady, but basically this is an exuberant, affirmative, and highly individual volume.

WORKS: With Kenneth Griffith, *Curious Journey: An Oral History of Ireland's Unfinished Revolution*. London: Hutchinson, 1982; *Motherland*. London: Chatto & Windus, 1989/New York: Henry Holt, 1990; with photos by Steve Pyke. *Acts of Memory*. London: Chatto & Windus, 1995.

O'HAGAN, JOHN (1822–1890), poet and translator. O'Hagan was born in Newry on March 19, 1822. He was educated at Trinity College, Dublin, and contributed much verse to *The Nation** under the pseudonym mainly of Sliabh Cuilinn. His most popular pieces were "Ourselves Alone" and "Dear Land." After having been active in the Young Ireland movement, he later had a successful career at the bar. He also published a translation of *Le Chanson de Roland* before his death on November 12 or 13, 1890. His best known Irish songs are reprinted in *The Spirit of the Nation.*

WORKS: *Afternoon Lectures on English Literature: Chaucer.* Dublin: Hodges, 1864; *The Song of Roland.* Translated into English Verse. London: Kegan, Paul, 1880; *The Poetry of Sir Samuel Ferguson.* Dublin: Gill, 1887; *The Children's Ballad-Rosary.* London, 1890; *Joan of Arc.* London: Kegan, Paul, 1893. (Biography).

O'HAGAN, SHEILA (fl. 1990s), poet. O'Hagan was educated at Birkbeck College and has won prizes at Listowel Writers' Week, as well as the Goldsmith Award in 1988, the Patrick Kavanagh* Award in 1991, and the Hennessy/*Sunday Tribune* New Poet of the Year Award in 1992. Brian Lynch* has justly described her language as "very peculiar" and has remarked about her technique: "As for metre or rhyme, neither is here found. The technique has more to do with visual design than prosody."

WORK: *The Peacock's Eye.* Galway: Salmon, 1992; *The Troubled House.* [Galway]: Salmon, [1995].

O'HANLON, HENRY B. (1886–1967), playwright. O'Hanlon was born in March 1886, the son of Henry O'Hanlon, rate collector, Dalkey. He was educated at Blackrock College, qualified as a solicitor, and practiced in Dublin. He was also a master mariner and well-known yachtsman and a great friend of de Valera and his family. He was appointed taxing master in 1919 and held that post until he retired in 1957. He was much involved in public affairs. For instance, he was appointed by the government in 1955 as chairman of a committee to examine the possibility of a voluntary health insurance scheme; and when the Voluntary Health Insurance Board was set up in 1957, he was one of its first members. He died on November 18, 1967.

Although he gave up playwriting because of the pressure of business, Edward Martyn* considered him the most important of the Irish dramatists who wrote for the Irish Theatre,* Hardwicke Street, in its 1914–1920 life span. His opinion is difficult to evaluate, since only two O'Hanlon plays are extant.

To-morrow, a Maeterlinckish "nightmare in one act," performed at the Irish Theatre on December 18–23, 1916, is set in a morgue. The drunken caretaker, who hears or thinks he hears the corpses talking of what their lives had been and of what their eternity will be, suffers a fatal heart attack.

Martyn's favorite, *The All-Alone,* a four-act tragedy, was presented at the Irish Theatre* on June 17–22, 1918. It markedly resembles Ibsen's *The Lady from the Sea.* Esmond Everard, son of a seafaring man whose ship was named "The

All-Alone,'' must choose between sweet, sensible Sheila Cleary and the "spirit of the sea" embodied in the mysterious, alluring Syra. He and Syra are last seen in a tiny boat headed into the open sea.

The unpublished *Her Second Chance* was staged at the Abbey* on May 19, 1914, by the Dramatic Society of St. Mary's College, Rathmines. In this social melodrama, a repentant wastrel commits suicide so that his wife may have a second chance. Knowledge of *Speculations,* a three-act tragedy offered by the Irish Theatre on November 19–24, 1917, must be pieced together from reviews. Lucien Westray, blinded by congenital disease, is dependent on his sister Mary. When she dies, doctors persuade Mary's friend Constance Beaumont to impersonate the dead woman. To the supposed sister, Westray confides his love for Constance just before he too dies. Of the three-act comedy *Norah's Birthday,* only the title survives. This play was taken on a tour of the west of Ireland in August 1915 as a benefit for Red Cross hospitals.

Like Martyn, O'Hanlon was interested in transplanting Ibsenite themes to Irish soil. Possibly at the time there was a surfeit of discussion drama; at least reviewers complained that O'Hanlon's plays were garrulous to the point of fogging over the plot line. Read today, *The All-Alone* and *Tomorrow* seem worthwhile experiments, marked by a competent, if not triumphant, blending of the mundane and the eerie, and a refreshing departure from standard cottage drama.

WILLIAM J. FEENEY

WORKS: "To-morrow." *Studies* 6 (March 1917): 48–57/in *Edward Martyn's Irish Theatre.* William J. Feeney, ed. [Newark, Del.]: Proscenium, [1980], pp. 107–114; *The All-Alone.* Preface by Edward Martyn. Dublin: Thomas Kiersey, 1919.

O'HANRAHAN, MICHAEL or Ó HANNRACHAIN, MICHEÁL (1877–1916), novelist. O'Hanrahan was born in New Ross, County Wexford, on March 17, 1877. His family moved to Carlow, and he was educated by the Christian Brothers and at Carlow College Academy. He became a freelance journalist and a member of the Irish Volunteers and of the Gaelic League. His father had been involved in the 1867 Rising, and in 1916 O'Hanrahan fought in Jacob's Biscuit Factory. He was executed on May 4, 1916. His published historical novels are *A Swordsman of the Brigade* (1914) and the posthumous *When the Normans Came* (1918).

WORKS: *A Swordsman of the Brigade.* Edinburgh & London: Sands, [1914]; *When the Normans Came.* Dublin: Maunsel, 1918.

O'HARA, KANE (1714?–1782), writer of musical burlesques. O'Hara was born at Temple House, County Sligo, and educated at Trinity College, Dublin, where he received a B.A. in 1732 and an M.A. in 1735. He settled in Dublin and interested himself in music. Success came with his travesty of the newly popular Italian burlettas, entitled *Midas* (Capel Street, Dublin, 1761; Covent Garden, London, 1764). Similar was *The Golden Pippin* (Covent Garden, 1773) and several other burlettas as well as an opera of Fielding's *Tom Thumb* (Covent

Garden, 1780). O'Hara became blind and was so tall that he was described as "St. Patrick's steeple." His work, which had nothing Irish about it, was popular well into the nineteenth century, and he was wrongfully credited with the Dublin ballad "The Night That Larry Was Stretched." He died in Dublin on June 17, 1782.

WORKS: *Midas, an English Burletta.* London, 1764/Los Angeles: William Andrews Clark Memorial Library, 1974. Introduction by P. T. Dircks; *The Two Misers, a Musical Farce.* London, 1775. (An adaptation from the French of C. J. Fenouillot de Balbaire de Quingey); *The Golden Pippin: An English Burletta, in Three Acts.* Dublin: W. Sleater, 1776; *April-Day, a Burletta in Three Acts.* London: G. Kearsly, 1775; *Tom Thumb, Altered.* In *Cawthorne's Minor British Theatre,* Vol. 1. London: John Cawthorn, 1806. (After Fielding). There were many later editions of these plays.

O'KEEFFE, JOHN (1747–1833), playwright and actor. O'Keeffe was born in Abbey Street, Dublin, on June 24, 1747. He acted at the Smock Alley Theatre for twelve years, and there began writing his many farces and comic operas, such as *Tony Lumpkin in Town* (Haymarket, 1778), which was a sequel to Goldsmith's* *She Stoops to Conquer,* and *The Agreeable Surprise* (Haymarket, 1781), which Hazlitt much admired. Indeed, Hazlitt called O'Keeffe "the English Molière. . . . In light, careless laughter, and pleasant exaggerations of the humorous, we have no one to equal him." There is little of Irish interest in O'Keeffe, and nothing that has held the stage. However, one might cite *The Wicklow Gold Mine,* an opera of 1796 (later revised as *The Wicklow Mountains*), and the unpublished *The Shamrock; or, St. Patrick's Day* of 1777. In the mid-1970s, one of his last popular plays, *Wild Oats* (1791), was revived with much success in London. A lame production, somewhat Irished by Tom MacIntyre,* was then done at the Abbey* in 1977; much more stylish acting is needed to raise the convoluted plot to success. O'Keeffe retired early from the stage because of blindness, but he continued to write prolifically. His *Recollections,* first published in 1826, are well worth perusal. He died in Southampton on February 4, 1833.

WORKS: *The Dramatic Works of John O'Keeffe, Esq.* 4 vols. London: Printed by T. Woodfall, 1798; *Recollections of the Life of John O'Keeffe.* 2 vols. London: H. Colbourn, 1826; *O'Keeffe's Legacy to His Daughter, Being the Poetical Works of the Late John O'Keeffe.* Adelaide D. O'Keeffe, ed. London, 1834; *Wild Oats; or, The Strolling Gentleman.* Clifford Williams, ed. London: Heinemann Educational, 1977; *The Plays of John O'Keeffe.* Frederick M. Link, ed. 4 vols. New York: Garland, 1981. (A modern reprint). REFERENCES: Anderson, Phillip Bruce. "The Genius of Nonsense: A Study of the Later Eighteenth Century English Farce." Diss., Duke University, 1976; Besset, Julian. "John O'Keeffe et William Shield: la collaboration d'un dramaturge et d'un musicien de théâtre en Angleterre au 18e Siècle." Diss., Lille, 1972; Harvey, Karen J. & Pry, Kevin B. "John O'Keeffe as an Irish Playwright within the Theatrical, Social and Economic Context of his Time." *Éire-Ireland* 22 (Spring 1987): 19–43; Kavanagh, Peter. "John O'Keeffe." In *The Irish Theatre.* Tralee: The Kerryman, 1946, pp. 346–361; Kosok, Heinz. " 'George My Belov'd King, and Ireland My Honor'd Country': John O'Keeffe and Ireland." *Irish University Review* 22 (Spring–Summer 1992): 40–54.

O'KELLY, SEUMAS (ca. 1875–1918), playwright, novelist, short story writer, and journalist. O'Kelly, once called "Ireland's most neglected genius," was the son of Michael and Catherine Kelly. He was born on an unestablished date (?1875–?1878) at Mobhill, Loughrea, whose lake and "Meadow of the Dead" were to enter his fiction. Scantily educated, he began his main editorial and journalistic career in 1903 on the Skibbereen *Southern Star.* He ended it on *Nationality,* in whose office he died of a cerebral hemorrhage on November 14, 1918, during a rowdy incursion of the premises by anti-Sinn Féin celebrators of the World War I armistice. A huge procession attended his body to its grave in Glasnevin.

Though never robust in health, especially after the rheumatic fever which struck about seven years before his death, O'Kelly managed to produce an amazing amount of journalism, drama, prose fiction, and verse, contributing widely to such journals as *The Irish Rosary,* the *Irish Weekly Independent,* the *Weekly Freeman, Sinn Féin,* and the *Manchester Guardian,* and leaving much for posthumous issue. All this creative work is richly reflective of his Galway youth and often based on literal experience, firsthand or reported. The verse (*Ranns and Ballads,* 1918), however, is unimpressive, being technically defective and rarely evocative or exciting; its finest exemplar is an untitled piece embedded in "The Gray Lake."

The short fiction, though highly variable in quality, is O'Kelly's soundest claim to distinction. The apprentice work of the parochially overpraised first collection, *By the Stream of Killmeen* (1906), published while O'Kelly was editor of the *Leinster Leader,* was no prophecy of the remarkable work to come. That later work is concentrated mainly in *Waysiders, The Golden Barque and The Weaver's Grave,* and *Hillsiders. The Leprechaun of Killmeen* (n.d.;?1918) and the uncollected tales are negligible.

As Forrest Reid* remarks in *Retrospective Adventures* (1942), "the effect of his [O'Kelly's] finest stories is infinitely richer than the sum of their recorded happenings." This is achieved through a warm handling of country (especially Galway) people, a pastoral-dramatic tone, a realistic approach (sometimes weakened by sentimentality or melodrama), and a frequently poetic concept, though O'Kelly could never rise to a great love story. From his best collections emerge preeminently "The Can with the Diamond Notch," a delightful account of tinker trickery; "The Gray Lake," a memorable tale of the faery drowning of a town; and "The Weaver's Grave," in which a young widow warms to incipient love while it is argued where her late husband should properly be buried. The last-named is a novella that can stand with the finest in English.

Of the novels, *The Lady of Deerpark* is a melodramatic tale of a "Big House" with a grotesquely contrived ending. Nevertheless, as Seumas O'Sullivan* maintains (*Essays and Recollections,* 1944), it has "elements of greatness in it." In contrast, *Wet Clay* (1922) is almost incredibly bad, with its melodramatic sentimentality, clichés, and perverse character manipulations.

The published plays (sometimes transformed short stories) are a mixed lot: nine one-acters (counting a collaboration); one two-acter, *The Shuiler's Child;* and two three-acters, *The Bribe* and *The Parnellite* (n.d.; 1919), the last being basically propaganda. Of these, *The Shuiler's Child* and *The Bribe* (not alone in being well received in production) are enough to give O'Kelly an important place among Irish Renaissance dramatists. *The Shuiler's Child,* involving child desertion followed by a pathetic effort at reclamation, is a moving piece of character presentation, as is *The Bribe,* with its sad complications centering in a retiring dispensary doctor's snaring his job for his incompetent son.

GEORGE BRANDON SAUL

WORKS: *The Shuiler's Child.* Dublin: Maunsel, 1909/Chicago: De Paul University, 1971. (Play); *The Bribe.* London: Maunsel, 1914/Dublin: James Duffy, 1952. (Play); *The Lady of Deerpark.* London: Methuen, 1917. (Novel); *Waysiders.* Dublin: Talbot/London: Unwin, [1917]/New York: Stokes, 1919. (Stories); *Ranns and Ballads.* Dublin: Candle, 1918; *The Golden Barque and the Weaver's Grave.* Dublin: Talbot/London: Unwin, 1919. (Stories); *The Leprechaun of Kilmeen.* Dublin: Martin Lester, 1920; *Hillsiders.* Dublin: Talbot/London: Unwin, 1921. (Stories); *Wet Clay.* Dublin: Talbot/London: Unwin, 1922. (Novel); *The Matchmakers.* Dublin: Talbot, 1925. (One-act play); *Meadowsweet.* Dublin: Talbot, 1925. (One-act play); *The Weaver's Grave.* Dublin: Talbot, 1925; *The Land of Loneliness and Other Stories,* selected & with Introduction by Eamon Grennan. Dublin: Gill & Macmillan, 1969; *Seumas O'Kelly's The Weaver's Grave,* dramatized by Mícheál Ó hAodha. [Newark, Del.]: Proscenium, [1984]. (One-act play). REFERENCES: Clune, Anne. "Seumas O'Kelly." In *The Irish Short Story.* Patrick Rafroidi & Terence Brown, eds. Gerrards Cross: Colin Smythe/Atlantic Highlands, N.J.: Humanities, 1979; Foster, John Wilson. *Fictions of the Irish Literary Revival.* Dublin: Gill & Macmillan/Syracuse, N.Y.: Syracuse University Press, 1987; Saul, George Brandon. *Seumas O'Kelly.* Lewisburg, Pa.: Bucknell University Press, 1971.

O'LEARY, CON (1887–1958), journalist and novelist. O'Leary was a well known journalist on London's Fleet Street. He was described by *The Times* as "a warm and lovable personality" with a "mercurial temperament . . . a craftsman with style and, at his best, an individual artist." He was born in Cork in 1887. He attended University College, Cork, and while a student there became involved with the Cork Dramatic Society whose leading spirits were Daniel Corkery* and Terence J. MacSwiney.* He acted for the society, and two of his own plays were produced. One of these, *The Crossing,* was later produced by the Abbey* in 1914, as was his one-act *Queer Ones* in 1919. His plays were not too well received and have not been published, but he was described as much influenced by Synge.*

O'Leary worked on *The Freeman's Journal* in Dublin, and then under C. P. Scott on *The Manchester Guardian* and edited its weekly edition. He was brought to London by T. P. O'Connor, and was an assistant editor of *T. P.'s Weekly.* At his death on November 11, 1958, he was working in the London office of *The Irish Press.* He published a charming volume of Irish sketches, *An Exile's Bundle,* in 1923 and probably his best novel, *Break o' Day,* in 1926. His other novels include *This Delicate Creature* (1928) and *Passage West* (1945). He wrote a history of the Grand National and one of the more engaging of the multitudinous travel books on Ireland. He was probably always too much engaged in daily journalism ever to develop fully his undeniable creative talents.

WORKS: *An Exile's Bundle.* London & New York: Andrew Melrose, 1923. (Stories); *Break o' Day.* London: Cassell, 1926. (Novel); *This Delicate Creature.* London: Constable, 1928. (Novel);

A Hillside Man. London: Lovat Dickson, 1933. (Novel); *A Wayfarer in Ireland.* London: Methuen, 1935. (Travel); *Grand National.* London: Rockliff, 1945/revised ed., London: Rockliff, 1947. (Racing history); *Passage West.* London: Rockliff, 1945.

O'LEARY, ELLEN (1831–1889), poet. O'Leary was the sister of the Fenian John O'Leary,* who was much admired by W. B. Yeats.* Of her poetry, Yeats's judgment is both gentle and discerning:

Poetry such as hers belongs to a primitive country and a young literature. It is exceedingly simple, both in thought and expression. Its very simplicity and sincerity have made it, like much Irish verse, unequal; for when the inspiration fails, the writer has no art to fall back upon. Nor does it know anything of studied adjective and subtle observation. To it the grass is simply green and the sea simply blue; and yet it has, in its degree, the sacred passion of true poetry.

WORK: *Lays of Country, Home and Friends.* Dublin: Sealy, Bryers & Walker, 1890. REFERENCES: Mulholland, Rosa. "Some Recollections of Ellen O'Leary." *Irish Monthly* 39 (1911): 456–462; Rollestan, T. W. "Introductory Notice" to *Lays of Country, Home and Friends;* Yeats, W. B. "Ellen O'Leary, 1831–1889." In *Uncollected Prose by W. B. Yeats.* Vol. 1. John P. Frayne, ed. New York: Columbia University Press/London: Macmillan, 1970. pp. 256–258.

O'LEARY, JOHN (1830–1907), Fenian and journalist. O'Leary was born in Tipperary on July 23, 1830. He joined the Young Ireland movement, and later was a prominent Fenian and edited the Fenian journal *The Irish People.* Arrested after the Fenian uprising, he was imprisoned for nine years and exiled from Ireland for a further eleven. When he returned, he became the friend and mentor of the young W. B. Yeats,* who wrote of "O'Leary's noble head." Indeed, everyone who knew O'Leary in his old age was impressed by his lofty character. His chief work is a memoir, *Recollections of Fenians and Fenianism* (1896), which is now little read but which is written with an urbane lucidity and a calm good sense. O'Leary's account of how he was awakened to a national consciousness by reading Thomas Davis* might be taken as a paradigm of how several generations of young men were affected by Davis. His account of his fellow Fenians is refreshingly lacking in hero worship, and he is worth consulting on C. J. Kickham.* He died in Dublin on March 16, 1907.

PRINCIPAL WORKS: *Young Ireland: The Old and the New.* Dublin: Dollard, 1885; *What Irishmen Should Know: What Irishmen Should Feel.* Dublin: Cahill, 1886; *Recollections of Fenians and Fenianism.* 2 vols. London: Downey, 1896/facsimile rpt., Shannon: Irish University Press, 1969. REFERENCE: Bourke, Marcus. *John O'Leary: A Study in Irish Separatism.* Tralee: Anvil Books, 1967.

O'LOUGHLIN, MICHAEL (1958–   ), poet and short story writer. O'Loughlin was born in Dublin and was closely involved with Dermot Bolger* in setting up the Raven Arts Press in 1979. More recently, he has lived in Barcelona and Amsterdam. His poems are mainly glum, sour, critical, and clear; a line like "Pristine, orphic; obmutescent" is a rarity. Sometimes he plays casually with form, as in "Declassé Memory," which employs very loose slant rhymes—

muffled, wood/doorway, today/Gracia, nostalgia, and so on—to make couplets. The rhyming seems paralleled by the rhythmic looseness, with any line often bearing very little resemblance to the one before or after. "An Irish Requiem" makes an effective refrainlike use of the line "Born in another country, under a different flag," which appears at varying intervals. Mainly, however, it seems that the matter more than the manner is primary in O'Loughlin's poems.

The Inside Story (1989) is a slim but impressive volume of sketches and stories. The most developed as a story is the effective, if rather far-fetched, "The Language of Stones," about one of Michael Collins's gunmen, a Jew named Goldfarb, who is run down on the Aran Islands. Among the more telling sketches are "Traditional Music" and "What Can You Do?" The first is about an Irish folksong festival in Germany; the second, about an Irish businessman, makes a sardonic contrast between a growing European homogeneity and the nationalistic Irish past.

WORKS: with Phyl O'Donnell & others. *Urban Voices*. Dublin: Raven Arts, [1980]. (Poetry); *Stalingrad: The Street Dictionary*. Dublin: Raven Arts, 1980. (Poetry); *Atlantic Blues*. [Dublin]: Raven Arts, [1982]. (Poetry); *The Diary of a Silence*. Dublin: Raven Arts, 1985. (Poetry); *After Kavanagh: Patrick Kavanagh and the Discourse of Contemporary Irish Poetry*. Dublin: Raven Arts, 1985. (Prose pamphlet); with Dermot Bolger. *A New Primer for Irish Schools*. [Dublin]: Raven Arts, [1985]. (Poetry booklet); tr., *Hidden Weddings*. Dublin: Raven Arts, 1987. (Translations of German poems by Gerrit Achterberg); *Frank Ryan: Journey to the Centre*. Dublin: Raven Arts, 1987. (Prose pamphlet); *The Inside Story*. Dublin: Raven Arts, [1989]. (Short stories).

O'MAHONY, T. P. (1939–   ), novelist, journalist, and religious and social commentator. O'Mahony was born in Cork and became a columnist for the *Irish Press* on religious affairs. In addition to several nonfictional books such as a biography of Jack Lynch, he was written some broadly comic novels.

WORKS: *The Politics of Dishonour: Ireland, 1916–1977*. Dublin: Talbot, 1977; *The New Pope: The Election, the Man and the Future*. Dublin: Villa Books, 1978; *Sex and Sanctity*. [Swords, Co. Dublin]: Poolbeg, [1979]. (Novel); *The Vatican Caper*. Dublin: Ward River, 1981. (Novel); *The Klondyke Memorial*. [Swords, Co. Dublin]: Poolbeg, [1983]. (Novel); *The Lynch Years, a Political Fantasy*. Mountrath, Co. Laois: Dolmen, 1986. (Novel); *Jack Lynch—A Biography*. Dublin: Blackwater, 1991.

O'MALLEY, EARNAN ("ERNIE") BERNARD (1897–1957), memoirist. Ernie O'Malley was born in Castlebar, County Mayo. When he was eight, his family moved to Dublin. He studied at O'Connell Schools and University College, Dublin (UCD), focusing his studies on medicine. While a student at UCD, he joined the Irish Volunteers and fought for Irish independence during the Easter Rising of 1916. He became an organizer for Michael Collins during the War for Independence. During the campaign, he was wounded, imprisoned, and tortured before engineering an escape. During the civil war, he fought on the anti-Treaty side and was again imprisoned and then sentenced to death. His death sentence was ultimately revoked, but not before he went on a forty-one-day hunger strike and was elected as a Sinn Féin representative to the Dail. He never took his seat, however, as he refused to take the oath of allegiance to the Crown. Released from prison in 1924, he traveled to Spain to fight for the Basque separatists. Subsequently, he traveled to the United States and settled in New York. Returning to Ireland, he was elected to the Irish Academy of Letters in 1947. He died in Howth, County Dublin, in March 1957.

In his volumes of reminiscences about the War for Independence and the civil war—*On Another Man's Wound,* published in 1936, and *The Singing Flame,* posthumously published in 1978—O'Malley wrote valuable historical documents that also make for entertaining reading. In them, he refers to an Irish mythic past as a context for the struggle, beginning the first volume with a reference to Cuchullain. In 1991, O'Malley's son Cormac, with the assistance of Richard English, published his father's letters written from November 1922 to July 1924, when he was a prisoner during the civil war. The letters speak in tender and vivid prose of the post-Treaty years. They are also highly autobiographical, speaking of the writer's hopes for his future and his reflections on his past.

BERNARD McKENNA

WORKS: *On Another Man's Wound.* Dublin: Three Candles, 1936/as *Army without Banners: Adventures of an Irish Volunteer.* Boston: Houghton Mifflin, 1937; *The Singing Flame.* Tralee: Anvil, 1978; *Prisoners: The Civil War Letters of Ernie O'Malley.* Richard English & Cormac O'Malley, eds. [Swords, Co. Dublin]: Poolbeg, [1991].

O'MALLEY, MARY (fl. 1990s), poet. O'Malley was born in Connemara, educated at University College, Galway (UCG), and lives in the Moycullen Gaeltacht with her husband and two children. After taking her degree from UCG, she taught at the New University of Lisbon for eight years, and her poetry shows the influence of Portuguese landscapes and architecture. Since her return to Galway, she has taught at UCG, served as a director of the Galway Arts Centre, and been a strong influence on the organizing committee of the CÚIRT Festival of Literature. She has received a Hennessy Award and bursaries from the Irish Arts Council. Her poetry has appeared in *Krino, Fortnight, The Salmon Magazine, Poetry Ireland,* and *The Sunday Tribune* and has been featured on RTÉ radio and television and on BBC radio. She has published two volumes of verse, *A Consideration of Silk* (1990) and *Where the Rocks Float* (1993).

O'Malley's work speaks of the transforming and revitalizing power of language, of self-actualization, of the quest for identity. It speaks of keeping, losing, finding, and growing in understanding of self through interaction with the outside, the other. She writes of her native Irish West, of her sense of feminine identity as sexual being and as mother, of her vocation as artist, and of the Northern war. Indeed, careful analysis of her work reveals a montage of various stages of self-discovery, of reclamation of identity, of growing understanding of self and of mission in the world. Although the form of her work does not arrange itself as conveniently as traditional texts of spiritual pilgrimage, the work does share common motifs with such earlier texts. The convention is simply a method of presentation, something to make the ascent more understandable. Our age may no longer use the same spiritual or epic conventions and vocabulary, but O'Malley's poetry suggests that our age does share like sentiments.

Specifically, O'Malley details seven stages of self-discovery that culminate in a celebration of the certainty of identity and the poetic vocation. The stages begin with (1) an intuitive discomfort in place. There is a sense that the home no longer provides the seeker with what is necessary to understand self. There is a sense or intuition that journey is necessary and imminent. (2) Subsequently, on the eve of journey, the pilgrim attempts ritual to placate the fear and trepidation surrounding departure. Sadly, the ritual fails, and the pilgrim finds only despair. (3) After the pilgrim leaves home, a sense of longing for it emerges. The pilgrim, through longing, reclaims the inheritance left behind. (4) After the longing, the pilgrim catches glimpses of true identity and self-actualization but discovers that these moments cannot be sustained because the pilgrim remains reliant on external forces to give form to internal sentiment. (5) Because the moments fall away, the pilgrim is left to despair and must confront unpleasant aspects of self to grow in self-understanding. The pilgrim then merges these aspects with self in a realization of complete identity. (6) Subsequently, the pilgrim experiences a physical union that literally merges the realized aspects of self into one identity. (7) The final stage details full self-actualization and its attendant joys and responsibilities. Again, O'Malley's distinctive contemporary voice finds more randomness to these movements than the writers of spiritual or epic texts, but she does find the same type of moments, and she does detail the same sort of themes along the pilgrimage of self-discovery.

BERNARD McKENNA

WORK: *A Consideration of Silk.* [Galway: Salmon, 1990]; *Where the Rocks Float.* [Dublin]: Salmon, [1993].

O'MEARA, JOE

WORK: *The Singing Masters.* Dublin: Lilliput, 1991.

Ó MUIRÍ, PÓL (1965–), poet. Born in Belfast, Ó Muirí publishes in both Irish and English.

WORK: *D-Day.* Belfast: Lagan, 1995.

O'NEILL, J. M.

WORK: *Commissar Connell.* London: Hamish Hamilton, 1992. (Novel).

O'NEILL, JOAN (?–), novelist. Joan O'Neill was born in Dublin probably in the mid-1940s and grew up in Dun Laoghaire. She was educated at the Dominican Convent, Sion Hill, Dublin, and studied piano at the Royal Academy in Dublin and at the Royal Academy in London. Before marriage, she worked as a secretary and now lives with her family in Bray. Her very popular

Daisy Chain War (1990) and its sequel, *Bread & Sugar* (1993), are "young adult" novels that tell the story of the Doyle family during the late 1930s and 1940s. Both books are packed with action, and the story lines flow. The background rings true, and the author knows the Ireland of the period well, but her characters remain two-dimensional. *Promised* (1991) is the story of a young Irish girl who enters a convent, falls in love with a young priest, loses his baby in an accident, and ends up a reverend mother happy in her chosen vocation. As a "modern" book, it has everything—rape, incest, child abuse, and fairly explicit sex. But again none of the characters seem real, and the book seems designed more as a page-turner rather than as a work of literary art.

DOROTHY ROBBIE

WORKS: *Daisy Chain War.* Dublin: Attic, [1990]; *Promised.* Dublin: Attic, [1991]; *Bread & Sugar.* [Dublin]: Poolbeg, [1993]; *Goodbye, Summer, Goodbye.* Dublin: Attic, 1994. (Young people's novel).

O'NEILL, JOHN (1777–1858), poet. O'Neill was born in Waterford, became a shoemaker in Carrick-on-Suir, and then moved to London, where he wrote some temperance poetry, notably the popular *The Drunkard,* which Cruikshank illustrated.

PRINCIPAL WORKS: *The Drunkard.* London, 1840/London: W. Tweedie, 1842; *The Blessings of Temperance.* London: E. Wilson, 1849; *The Triumph of Temperance; or, The Destruction of the British Upas Tree.* London: W. Tweedie, 1852; *Handrahan, the Irish Fairman; and Legends of Carrick.* London: W. Tweedie, 1854. (Tales).

O'NEILL, JOSEPH [JAMES] (1878–1953), novelist. O'Neill was born in Tuam, County Galway, on December 18, 1878, but spent much of his boyhood on the Aran Islands, where his father, a member of the Royal Irish Constabulary, had been stationed. He returned to the mainland in 1893 to attend St. Jarlath's College in Tuam, and later, from 1898 to 1901, Queen's College, Galway, from which he received his B.A. and M.A. in modern literature. O'Neill's years on Aran, and his upbringing in a household where Irish was the language spoken, contributed to his interest in the revival of Irish language and literature. In 1903, he left a teaching position at Queen's College to enroll in Kuno Meyer's School of Irish Learning. His first scholarly work, a translation of *"Cath Boinde"* published in *Eriu,* secured him a scholarship to Victoria College in Manchester where he studied under John Strachan, the classical and Celtic scholar (1862–1907). In 1907, he studied comparative philology at the University of Freiburg where he formed a close friendship with his fellow-student Osborn Bergin (1872–1950).

Although O'Neill was considered a promising scholar, he abandoned Irish studies for civil service when, in 1908, his former teacher, William Starkey, then resident commissioner of education, offered him a job as second class inspector of primary schools. After his marriage to Mary Devenport,* a student at the National College of Art, on June 29, 1908, O'Neill rose quickly in the

Department of Secondary Education and was appointed its permanent secretary in 1923, a post he held until his retirement in 1944.

O'Neill always had literary interests. He had published poetry regularly in *The Freeman's Journal* under the pseudonym "Oisin" and some articles on cultural and philological subjects for the *Irish Statesman*. His first book-length work, however, was *The Kingdom-Maker* (1917), a verse play set at the beginning of the Christian Era in Ireland; the wars between the Firbolgs and the Gaels provided him with a metaphor through which to comment on both World War I and Ireland's suit for independence. By the 1920s, the O'Neills had bought their house at 2 Kenilworth Square, Rathgar, and established a Thursday evening salon, which AE,* Bergin, Yeats,* Lennox Robinson,* and Austin Clarke,* among many other distinguished writers, attended.

The company he kept encouraged O'Neill to begin writing in earnest, although his first novel, *Wind from the North,* took ten years to complete and was not published until 1934. The novel is a historical romance that often achieves a chilling epic quality through the conflict that rages within its protagonist. The protagonist, a nameless Dublin clerk, is hit by a tramcar and wakes as one of the principal participants in the turmoil that has beset the eleventh-century Norse town of Dyflin in the weeks preceding Brian Boru's invasion. The theme of the novel is based on Karl Jung's doctrine of man's search for his Ancestral Self and on AE's belief that every man lives through repeated reincarnations. In O'Neill's protagonist, the world of twentieth-century Dublin and eleventh-century Dyflin vie for possession of his soul, and the novel ends with this conflict unresolved. *Wind from the North* won the Harmsworth Award of the Irish Academy of Letters in 1934.

How man thinking and man acting can function in accord became O'Neill's persistent theme. The two novels that followed, *Land Under England* (1935) and *Day of Wrath* (1936), develop this theme in the tradition of the counter-utopian novels of Huxley and the later H. G. Wells. The first is a political and psychological allegory of a young Englishman trapped in a horrifying world beneath the Yorkshire countryside. The area is inhabited by dehumanized automatons, the descendants of the last Roman legionnaires to occupy England, and the hero attempts to fathom the source of man's Oedipal drives and fears of miscegenation. The second, a futuristic political polemic responding to the European political situation of 1936, shows how man will behave when the thin crust of civilization that separates him from his primitive self is broken by a worldwide war. Both novels are structurally and stylistically flawed, *Land Under England* being an exciting but unimpressive work of the imagination, and *Day of Wrath* a total failure in style and conception.

Philip (1940), a return to historical fiction, is the story of a physician, half-Greek, half-Jew, who returns to Israel to seek his Ancestral Past. Set in the teeming, brawling, politically and religiously chaotic streets of Jerusalem in the few months preceding Christ's Crucifixion, the novel is remarkably evocative and structurally flawless and marks the high point in O'Neill's literary achieve-

ment. Short historical sketches for *The Dublin Magazine** followed; two in particular, "An Evening with Ben Jonson" and "Audience with Gloriana," served
as preparation for his final full-length work, *Chosen By the Queen* (1947). The
historical information O'Neill amassed for this study of Robert Devereaux, second earl of Essex, his ignominious fall from Elizabeth's favor, and his execution
in the Tower, is not as well controlled as that of *Philip*. Still, the novel projects
much of the bustle, intrigue, and grandeur of Elizabeth's court and of an England
just emerging into nationhood.

Beset with financial difficulties and having lived long enough to survive most
of his friends, O'Neill sold the Kenilworth Square residence and all its furnish-
ings in August 1949 and, with his wife, moved to Nice. The move was disastrous. Not only was living in southern France far more expensive than he had
anticipated, but also in a fall, he broke his kneecap which would not knit properly. Fearing that he would become an invalid in a foreign and, for him, un-
congenial country, O'Neill returned to Ireland in April 1950. They rented a
house in Wicklow where O'Neill began to recover and work on his final project,
"Pages from the Journal of Edmund Shakespeare," published serially in *The
Dublin Magazine* between 1951 and 1952. Whether this series of journal entries
made between 1596 and 1598 by the sixteen-year-old brother of William Shakespeare was another work in progress is uncertain. Walking in the Wicklow Hills
in the early spring of 1952, O'Neill suffered a cerebral hemorrhage and was
brought to St. John of God's Nursing Home in Stillorgan, where he died on
May 3, 1953.

M. KELLY LYNCH

WORKS: *The Kingdom-Maker: A Verse Play in Five Acts*. Dublin: Talbot, 1917; *Wind from the
North*. London: Jonathan Cape, 1934. (Novel); *Land under England*. London: Gollancz/New York:
Simon & Schuster, 1935. (Novel); *Day of Wrath*. London: Gollancz, 1936. (Novel); *Philip*. London:
Gollancz, 1940. (Novel); *Chosen by the Queen*. London: Gollancz, 1947. (Novel).   REFERENCE:
Lynch, M. Kelly. "The Smiling Public Man: Joseph O'Neill and His Works." *Journal of Irish
Literature* 12 (May 1983): 3–72.

O'NEILL, MARY DEVENPORT (1879–1967), poet. Mary Devenport was
born on August 3, 1879, in Loughrea, County Galway, the daughter of a sub-
constable. After convent school, she attended the National College of Art in
Dublin and, while a student, began a correspondence with Joseph O'Neill,*
whose poetry in the *Freeman's Journal* she had admired. They eventually married on June 19, 1908.

In 1917, O'Neill wrote the lyrics for her husband's verse play *The Kingdom-
Maker*, which was followed by her only published book, *Prometheus and Other
Poems* (1929), a collection of lyrics, the single, long title poem, and a one-act
verse play, *Bluebeard*. Influenced profoundly by Pound, Peguy, and Proust, the
shorter poems show a writer with a keen lyric gift, a sensitivity to tone, and a
sharp eye for color, image, and detail. "Prometheus," however, a longer and
more ambitious "dialogue" between reality and imagination, tends to lapse into
occasional tedium.

During the 1920s and 1930s, Mary O'Neill kept a highly respected salon in Rathgar, a "Thursday at home," attended by many famous writers of the day. She was a particular friend of W. B. Yeats* during the time he was writing *A Vision,* a sounding board and a respondent to his theories and ideas. In fact, Yeats kept a diary-notebook of these weekly conversations (National Library of Ireland, Ms. 13576) and included one of her poems in his *Oxford Anthology of English Verse,* much to the disapproval of other, better-known poets who had not been included.

Although O'Neill published only a single collection, she remained an active and influential voice in Dublin's literary world. *Bluebird* was performed by Austin Clarke's* Lyric Theatre Company in 1933, and *Cain,* another verse play, in 1945. Single poems appeared regularly in the *Irish Times, The Bell,** and *The Dublin Magazine,** which also published several of her plays and verse plays. These are very much in the tradition of the Celtic Twilight and draw their subject matter principally from Irish and German myth and legend.

After her husband's death in 1953, her own health began to fail. She lived with relatives in Dublin until her death in 1967.

M. KELLY LYNCH

WORKS: "Three Poems." *The Irish Statesman* 4 (August 1, 1926):650; *Prometheus and Other Poems.* London: Jonathan Cape, 1929; "Cain." *The Dublin Magazine* 13 (Spring 1938):30–48. (Verse play); "Dead in Wars and in Revolutions." *The Dublin Magazine* 16 (Winter 1941):7. (Poem); "Scene-Shifter Death." *The Dublin Magazine* 19 (Spring 1944):40. (Poem); "Valhalla." *The Dublin Magazine* 19 (Winter 1944):3. (Poem); "Out of Darkness." *The Dublin Magazine* 22 (Summer 1947):20–39. (Play); "The Visiting Moon." *The Dublin Magazine* 23 (Spring 1948):35–46. (Verse play); "Lost Legions." *The Dublin Magazine* 24 (Spring 1949):16. (Poem).

O'NEILL, MOIRA (1865–1955), poet. Moira O'Neill was the pen name of Agnes Nesta Shakespeare Higginson, who married Walter Clarmont Skrine and lived for a while in Canada and in County Antrim and on country estates in Kildare and Wexford. Despite being an Anglo-Irish lady of the Big House, she wrote popular dialect poems about country people. A pallid Irish version of Burns, she used a variety of heavily stressed rhythms and complicated rhyme patterns. Her subjects were the usual ones of the popular Irish poet: nostalgia, patriotism, and occasional mild comedy. Nevertheless, for a popular poet, she was not without quality; and sometimes, as in the refrain to "Corrymella," she uses euphony and rhythm with considerable effect. Occasionally, as in "Marriage," she can even manage characterization as well as the young Padraic Colum.* Her daughter is Molly Keane,* the novelist and playwright.

PRINCIPAL WORKS: *An Easter Vacation.* London: Lawrence & Bullen, 1893/New York: E. P. Dutton, 1894; *The Elf-Errant.* London: Lawrence & Bullen, 1893/New York: E. P. Dutton, 1894; *Songs of the Glens of Antrim.* Edinburgh & London: Blackwood, 1901; *More Songs of the Glens of Antrim.* Edinburgh & London: Blackwood, 1921; *From Two Points of View.* Edinburgh & London: Blackwood, 1924; *Collected Poems of Moira O'Neill.* Edinburgh & London: Blackwood, 1933.

O'NOLAN, BRIAN (1911–1966), novelist, journalist, and humorist. Brian O'Nolan (or Ó Nuallain), author of novels, plays, and short stories, was much

better known as Flann O'Brien or Myles na gCopaleen, but he had other pseu-
donymic incarnations: Brother Barnabas, George Knowall, Count O'Blather, and
John James Doe. An intensely private man in many ways, he seems to have felt
the need to disguise his personality behind a series of "elaborate façades" and
once described as "horrible" the type of biography that lifts the veil on the true
man. The real Brian O'Nolan was born on October 5, 1911, in Strabane, County
Tyrone, the third of twelve children. His father, an Irish speaker, was an officer
in the Customs and Excise Service and was moved so often around the country
(from Strabane to Dublin to Tullamore) that it was not until the family settled
in Dublin again, in 1923, that he went to school. He attended first the Christian
Brothers school in Synge Street, which he didn't like, and then Blackrock College. In 1929, he entered University College, Dublin, where he took a B.A.
degree in English, Irish, and German, followed by an M.A. with a thesis on
Irish poetry. During his years at University College, O'Nolan was renowned as
a debater, winning a gold medal for impromptu debate in the 1932–1933 session
and challenging, albeit unsuccessfully, Vivian de Valera, for the auditorship of
the College's Literary and Historical Society. In the college magazine *Comhth-
rom Féinne* and in his own magazine *Blather,* he began to write articles in Irish
and English which clearly indicated his tendency towards parody, satire, and
fantasy.

In 1935, O'Nolan entered the local government section of the Irish civil service where he was to remain for eighteen years until his retirement in 1953. His
first novel, *At Swim-Two-Birds,* published in 1939, was not a success, and *The
Third Policeman,* completed in 1940, was refused by the publishers and remained unpublished until after his death. His disappointment was slightly alle-
viated by an invitation to write a column for *The Irish Times. Cruiskeen Lawn*
by Myles na gCopaleen became famous (or infamous) and remained so for its
more than twenty-five years' duration. The next few years saw O'Nolan at a
peak of creativity. In 1941, *An Béal Bocht* (trans. *The Poor Mouth*) appeared
and was an instant success among the Irish-speaking "establishment" which it
mercilessly parodied. In 1943, three plays, *Faustus Kelly, The Insect Play,* and
Thirst, were produced. Thereafter there was a decline, and until the reissue of
At Swim-Two-Birds in 1960, there were many years of frustration, poverty, and
hack journalism. The success of the reissue led to a period of renewed activity.
The Hard Life appeared in 1961, and *The Dalkey Archive* in 1964. There were
many television scripts, plays, and short stories, and seven chapters of a new
novel *Slattery's Sago Saga* had been completed by the time of his death, after
a painful illness, on April 1, 1966.

O'Nolan's output, then, was varied and plentiful. There was a slow deterioration in standards over the years, and certainly the best work was produced
before 1945. The two novels written after 1960 were, respectively, a rehash of
much of the material which had proved so successful in *Cruiskeen Lawn,* and
a rewrite of *The Third Policeman,* sunnier in vision but less structurally coherent.
His best works are *At Swim-Two-Birds, The Third Policeman, An Béal Bocht,*

and *Cruiskeen Lawn.* To a great extent, the characteristics of the *Cruiskeen Lawn* newspaper column are those of the novels as well, where they are, of necessity, distilled and compressed.

O'Nolan's column appeared approximately triweekly from 1940 to 1966. It was written in Irish and English and occasionally in hybrid languages of O'Nolan's own invention. It was full of elaborate puns, linguistic jokes, nonsense, satire, fantastic inventions, unforgettable characters (the Brother and Myles), verbatim reports of the deliberations of local councils and courts of law (often more fantastic than his own wildest imagination!), and analyses of the debasement of language and the clichéd jargon of the various professions. O'Nolan was bilingual and had a more than competent knowledge of several other languages; in a manner characteristic of many Irish writers, he was in love with words. One of his greatest talents was an ear for dialogue, especially for that of bourgeois Dubliners—repetitive, opinionated, boring, misinformed, and brilliant. He loved the weight and color of words and linguistic games of all kinds. He was acutely aware of the way different grammatical forms could affect the perception of the people who used them. Many of his statements about language are serious and penetrating, though he had, of course, an incurable habit of immediately undercutting any even semiserious thought by elaborating or exaggerating it until it became nonsense.

The obsession with words is one of the notable features of the novels. Both *At Swim-Two-Birds* and *An Béal Bocht* can be said to be "about" style. In many ways, O'Nolan's work is typical of the twentieth-century Irish writer, but whereas many of his contemporaries were poised uneasily between the two cultures, the two literary and linguistic traditions, O'Nolan was able to move with confidence within each tradition and to create, from parodied versions of both, his own strange, fantastic world. At once conservative and ultramodern, his first three novels are based, in part, on versions of medieval Irish tales but have recognizable affinities with the worlds of Joyce* and Beckett* as well as Sartre, the Theatre of the Absurd, and the *nouveau-roman.* In his best work, O'Nolan emerges as a writer of real originality, a satirist, parodist, and fantasist whose main creative impulse arose from the desire to reconcile two opposing urges. On one hand, he wanted to deflate the pretensions of intellectuals and fanatics of all kinds in favor of the common sense of the "Plain People of Ireland." But the forms he chose in which to embody this deflation resulted in the creation of fantasy worlds, of situations that had an often disturbing, sideways relationship to reality but in which "the possibilities [were] endless." O'Nolan delighted in the creation of such worlds, where the imagination could roam at will. He exulted in the boundless creativity of the human mind, where there were no limits to supposition. At the same time he feared it, for the overthrowing or transcending of the ordinary world could lead to the hell of *The Third Policeman* or to the merciless violence that is everywhere represented in all its comic horror in his work. Nevertheless, he had little patience with the limitations of formal realism. In eschewing the realistic, mundane, and overtly moralistic tradition of English novelists, O'Nolan was consciously returning to the Gaelic models he admired while paradoxically fitting very well into some of the main patterns of contemporary European writing.

ANNE CLUNE

WORKS: *At Swim-Two-Birds.* London: Longmans, Green, 1939/New York: Pantheon, 1951/London: MacGibbon & Kee, 1960/New York: Viking, [1967]. (Novel); *An Béal Beacht.* Dublin: An Press Náisiúnta, 1941/Dublin: Dolmen, 1964/as *The Poor Mouth.* London: Hart-Davis, MacGibbon, [1973]. Patrick C. Power, tr. (Novel); *Cruiskeen Lawn.* Dublin: Cahill, 1943. (Selections from his *Irish Times* column); *Faustus Kelly.* Dublin: Cahill, 1943. (Play); tr., *Mairead Gillan.* Dublin: Stationery Office, 1953. (Translation of a play by Brinsley MacNamara); *The Hard Life: An Exegesis of Squalor.* London: MacGibbon & Kee, 1961/New York: Pantheon, [1962]. (Novel); *The Dalkey Archive.* London: MacGibbon & Kee, 1964/New York: Macmillan, [1965]. (Novel); *The Third Policeman.* [London]: MacGibbon & Kee/New York: Walker, [1967]. (Novel); *The Best of Myles: A Selection from "Cruiskeen Lawn."* Kevin O'Nolan, ed. London: MacGibbon & Kee/New York: Walker, [1968]/New York: Penguin, 1983; *Stories and Plays.* London: Hart-Davis, MacGibbon, [1973]/New York: Penguin, 1979; "A Flann O'Brien-Myles na Gopaleen Number." *Journal of Irish Literature* 3 (January 1974). Anne Clissman & David Powell, eds.; *The Various Lives of Keats and Chapman and The Brother.* Benedict Kiely, ed. London: Hart-Davis, MacGibbon, 1976; *Further Cuttings from Cruiskeen Lawn.* Kevin O'Nolan, ed. London: Hart-Davis, MacGibbon, 1976; *The Hair of the Dogma: A Further Selection from "Cruiskeen Lawn."* Kevin O'Nolan, ed. London: Hart-Davis, MacGibbon, 1977/London: Grafton, 1987; *A Flann O'Brien Reader.* Stephen Jones, ed. New York: Viking, 1978; *Myles Away from Dublin.* Martin Green, ed. London: Granada, 1985; *Myles before Myles.* John Wyse Jackson, ed. London: Paladin, Grafton Books, [1988]; *Rhapsody in Stephen's Green: The Insect Play.* Robert Tracy, ed. [Dublin]: Lilliput, 1994. REFERENCES: Asbee, Sue. *Flann O'Brien.* Boston: Twayne, 1991; Clissmann [Clune], Anne. *Flann O'Brien: A Critical Introduction to His Writing.* Dublin: Gill & Macmillan, 1975; Costello, Peter & Van de Kamp, Peter. *Flann O'Brien: An Illustrated Biography.* London: Bloomsbury, 1987; Cronin, Anthony. *Dead as Doornails.* Dublin: Dolmen, 1975; Cronin, Anthony. *No Laughing Matter: The Life and Times of Flann O'Brien.* London: Grafton, 1989; Hopper, Keith. *Flann O'Brien: A Portrait of the Artist as a Young Post-Modernist.* Cork: Cork University Press, 1995; Imhof, Rüdiger, ed. *Alive-alive O! Flann O'Brien's At Swim-Two-Birds.* Dublin: Wolfhound/ Totowa, N.J.: Barnes & Noble, 1985; Ó Conaire, Breandán. *Myles na Gaeilge: Lámhleabhar ar Shaothar Gaeilge Bhrian Ó Nuallain.* Dublin: An Clóchomhar, 1986; O'Keeffe, Timothy, ed. *Myles: Portraits of Brian O'Nolan.* London: Martin Brian & O'Keeffe, [1973]; Ó Nualláin, Ciarán. *Óige an Dearthár. i. Myles na gCopaleen.* Baile Atha Cliath: Foilseachain Naisiunta Teo, 1973; Shea, Thomas F. *Flann O'Brien's Exorbitant Novels.* Lewisburg, Pa.: Bucknell University Press, 1992; Wäppling, Eva. *Four Irish Legendary Figures in "At Swim Swim-Two-Birds": A Study of Flann O'Brien's Use of Finn, Suibhne, the Pooka and the Good Fairy.* Uppsala: Almqvist & Wiksell, 1984.

O'RAHILLY, EOIN

WORK: *Sybil: A Tale of Innocence.* Dublin: Argenta, 1992. (Novel).

O'REILLY, J. B.

WORK: *The Cry of Dreamers and Other Poems.* Drogheda: Breeda Tuite, 1990.

O'REILLY, JOHN BOYLE (1844–1890), Fenian, journalist, poet, and novelist. O'Reilly was born at Dowth Castle, County Meath, on June 28, 1844. A soldier in the British Army, he was transported to Australia for disseminating Fenianism but escaped to America where he edited *The* [Boston] *Pilot.* He published a novel, *Moondyne* (1879), about the Australian convict settlements, as well as several volumes of polished popular verse of the usual sentimental and patriotic kind. He died in Boston on August 10, 1890.

WORKS: *Songs from the Southern Seas, and Other Poems.* Boston: Roberts, 1873; *Songs, Legends, and Ballads.* Boston: Pilot Publishing Co., 1878; *Moondyne.* Boston: Pilot Publishing Co., 1879. (Novel); *The Statues in the Block, and Other Poems.* Boston: Roberts, 1881; *The King's Men.* New York: Scribner, 1884. Written in collaboration with several friends. (Novel); *In Bohemia.* Boston: Pilot Publishing Co., 1886. (Poems); *Watchwords from John Boyle O'Reilly.* Katherine E. Conway, ed. Boston: Cupples, 1892; *Selected Poems of John Boyle O'Reilly.* New York & Boston: Caldwell, 1904; *Selected Poems by John Boyle O'Reilly.* Mary J. A. O'Reilly, ed. New York: Kenedy, 1913. REFERENCE: Roche, James Jeffrey. *Life of John Boyle O'Reilly Together with his Complete Poems and Speeches.* Mrs. John Boyle O'Reilly, ed. New York: Mershon, 1891.

O'RIORDAN, CONAL (1874–1948), novelist and playwright. O'Riordan, one of the most extraordinary modern Irish writers, is also one of the most neglected. In his own day, his work was compared to that of Balzac and Dickens, but today every one of his twenty-seven volumes is out of print.

He was born Conal Holmes O'Connell O'Riordan on April 29, 1874, in Dublin, the younger son of Daniel O'Connell O'Riordan, Q.C. Like James Joyce,* he was educated at Belvedere College, but he left school early to prepare for a military career. This hope was dashed when a fall from a horse caused a permanent spinal ailment. He then went on the stage and was involved in London with J. T. Grein's Independent Theatre, playing Engstrand in the first English production of Ibsen's *Ghosts.* He also began to write plays with some success and to publish novels under the pseudonym of F. Norreys Connell. Yeats* and Lady Gregory* chose him to replace J. M. Synge* on the board of the Abbey Theatre* after Synge's death. Among the plays he produced at the Abbey was the first revival of *The Playboy of the Western World,* a production that occasioned some protests. His own Abbey plays were short curtain-raisers, but one of them, *The Piper* (1908), seemed about to cause another *Playboy*-like riot until Yeats placated the audience by the explanation that the play was a patriotic political allegory. After a few months, O'Riordan resigned from the Abbey, impatient with the constant interference of Miss Horniman, the theatre's financial backer. Because of his small stature and physical disabilities, O'Riordan was rejected by the British Army in 1914, but he made his way to the front as head of a YMCA rest hut.

After the war, O'Riordan wrote under his own name. He had some success again with plays which were mainly breezy light comedies, especially *Napoleon's Josephine* produced at the Fortune Theatre, London, in 1928. However, his major achievement was a series of twelve novels which traced the fortunes of several connected Irish families from the Napoleonic wars to about 1920. O'Riordan lived the rest of his life in London and among his friends were many of the important writers of the day—Dowson, Yeats, Conrad, Galsworthy, Wilfrid Owen, and a multitude of others. He was small, frail, seemingly crippled, and yet a convivial and witty conversationalist. In an obituary in *The London*

Times, John Brophy remarked that courage was one of his lifelong characteristics: "He needed it to overcome his physical disabilities and to endure professional disappointments without rancor or self-pity." Most of his last years were spent in seclusion, and he died at his home in Ealing on June 18, 1948.

O'Riordan's prewar writing was less than successful. His first book, *In the Green Park* (1894), is a group of fancifully connected short stories. Although the book went into a second edition, it is a sophomoric bit of facetiousness by a clever young man facile with words but possessing little taste or judgment. *The House of the Strange Woman* (1895), a novel about love and marriage, is romantic, sardonic, and jejune. The book's main strength is the terse and dramatic fluency of the dialogue, a quality that grows increasingly evident in all of O'Riordan's later work. The descriptive and narrative passages are much stiffer, and the baby-talk of the opening chapter is deplorable. The pervasive disillusionment is both more realistic and less mature than what would be found in conventional books of the day. *The Fool and His Heart* (1896), a sweeter version of *The House of the Strange Woman,* is rather autobiographical and contains some ineffective satire of the bohemian life in *fin de siècle* London. O'Riordan's later prewar work has considerably more technical facility. While none of it is superb, the callowness of the early books has disappeared. For instance, most of the stories in *The Pity of War* (1906) are rather Kiplingesque and suggest a soldier morality of bravery which is often nobler than the cause in which it is engaged. The style is simple and lucid. Some of the stories are too pat, but the book is a creditable advance over *In the Green Park.*

O'Riordan's major work was produced after the war—a twelve-volume cycle which began to appear in 1920 and which was concluded in 1940. The cycle was not written in chronological order but commenced with the "Adam" novels that conclude the story. The chronological beginning is with the four "Soldier" novels: *Soldier Born* (1927), *Soldier of Waterloo* (1928), *Soldier's Wife* (1935), and *Soldier's End* (1938). It is difficult to find an exact literary parallel to this tetralogy. In one sense, in its hero's picaresque wanderings over Europe and America, it is an unfacetious relative of the recent Flashman novels. Or perhaps a better comparison would be to Thackeray's *Henry Esmond,* whose hero O'Riordan's David Quinn in many ways resembles. David Quinn becomes involved with many historical personages and events, such as Princess Charlotte and the battle of Waterloo, Daniel O'Connell and the Irish Potato Famine, Lincoln and the American Civil War, and he finally dies in the Franco-Prussian War. Both the public and personal stories of the tetralogy—and, indeed, of the whole cycle—are extraordinarily complex, and the relations of the characters are occasionally an inextricable tangle. *Soldier of Waterloo,* perhaps the best of the David Quinn stories, has been ranked by some critics with *Adam of Dublin* (1920) as O'Riordan's best work. Its tone, however, is typically uneven: it is in part conventional and somewhat stilted romance, in part a vivid depiction of Dublin and London, and in one chapter a brilliantly impressionistic and hideous view of the battle of Waterloo from the vantage point of one individual soldier.

The entire cycle is at its weakest in depicting the relations between men and women. The poorest volumes—*The Age of Miracles* (1925) and its sequel *Young Lady Dazincourt* (1926), and *Judith Quinn* (1939) and its sequel *Judith's Love* (1940)—are, in a pejorative sense, little better than woman's fiction. Indeed, one of the novels is subtitled "A Novel for Women." The conversations are often witty, but the analysis of motives goes on interminably; as a result, the novels seem to be written by a jocular Henry James in collaboration with Mrs. Henry Wood. The characters in these volumes also exhibit a priggish diffidence about sexual love. Judith Quinn, for instance, is so foggy about the two sexual encounters she has over a period of some thirteen years that she does not really know what happened. More importantly, neither does the reader; for one of the most peculiar aspects of the entire cycle is that in several crucial instances it is difficult to know who is whose parent. Indeed, the genealogy of the dozens of important characters in the cycle is almost hopelessly confused.

The Adam novels which conclude the series chronologically are enormously better than the female fiction of the central books. The initial volume, *Adam of Dublin,* is one of the finest evocations of the city ever written by anyone, including Joyce. The portrait of the Jesuit school, Belvedere College, deserves to be set beside the Joyce passages in *Portrait of the Artist,* and the hilarious scene at the Abbey Theatre during the first revival of Synge's *Playboy* is memorable. The comparison to *Portrait of the Artist* is particularly apt, except that the Adam volumes carry O'Riordan's young artist into exile, marriage, and maturity. If the Adam books do not satisfactorily resolve the tangled threads of this 120-year cycle, they are more controlled than the Soldier books and as consummate a recreation of the past. The entire cycle is flawed, wavering in intention and varying in execution from the bathetic to the eloquent. Nevertheless, its scope is so vast and its virtues so many that its rediscovery must establish O'Riordan as one of the major Irish writers of his day.

WORKS: *In the Green Park; or, Half-Pay Deities.* London: Henry, 1894. (Stories); *The House of the Strange Woman.* London: Henry, 1895. (Novel); *The Fool and His Heart.* London: Leonard Smithers, 1896. (Novel); *How Soldiers Fight.* London: James Bowden, 1899; *The Nigger Knights.* London: Methuen, 1900; *The Follies of Captain Daly.* London: Grant Richards, 1901. (Novel); *The Pity of War.* London: Henry J. Glaisher, 1906. (Stories); *The Young Days of Admiral Quilliam.* Edinburgh & London: William Blackwood, 1906; *Shakespeare's End, and Other Irish Plays.* London: Stephen Swift, 1912; *Rope Enough.* Dublin & London: Maunsel, 1914. (Play); *Adam of Dublin.* London: Collins, [1920]. (Novel); *Adam and Caroline.* London: Collins, [1921]. (Novel); *In London: The Story of Adam and Marriage.* London: Collins, [1922]; *Rowena Barnes.* London: Collins, [1923]. (Novel); *Married Life.* London: Collins, [1924]. (Novel); *The Age of Miracles.* London: Collins, [1925]. (Novel); *His Majesty's Pleasure.* London: Ernest Benn, 1925. (Play); *Young Lady Dazincourt.* London: Collins, [1925]. (Novel); *Soldier Born.* London: Collins, [1927]. (Novel); *Soldier of Waterloo.* London: Collins, [1928]. (Novel); *The King's Wooing.* London & Glasgow: Gowans & Gray, 1929. (One-act play); *Napoleon Passes.* London: Arrowsmith, 1933. (History); *Captain Falstaff and Other Plays.* London: Arrowsmith, 1935; *Soldier's Wife.* London: Arrowsmith, 1935. (Novel); *Soldier's End.* [London]: Arrowsmith, 1938. (Novel); *Judith Quinn: A Novel for Women.* Bristol: Arrowsmith, 1939; *Judith's Love.* Bristol: Arrowsmith, 1940. (Novel). REFERENCE: O'Riordan, Judith, ed. "A Conal O'Riordan Number" of *Journal of Irish Literature* 14 (September 1885). Contains the editor's Introduction and a Chronology of O'Riordan's life, as well as O'Riordan's horoscope by Yeats. The O'Riordan material consists of two one-act plays, a story, and five autobiographical pieces.

O'RIORDAN, KATE. O'Riordan won the 1991 *Sunday Tribune*/Hennessy Best Emerging Writer Award.

  WORK: *Involved.* London: Flamingo, 1995. (Novel).

ORMSBY, FRANK (1947–   ), poet and editor. Ormsby was born in Enniskillen, County Fermanagh, on October 30, 1947. He received a B.A. from Queen's University, Belfast, in 1970, and an M.A. in 1971. Since 1971, he has taught English at the Royal Belfast Academical Institution. In 1974, he received an Eric Gregory Award. His two principal collections have been choices of the Poetry Book Society. He succeeded James Simmons* as editor of *The Honest Ulsterman,* which published four of his early poetry pamphlets. From them, he salvaged a few poems for his first collection, *A Store of Candles* (1977). His early work was characterized by clarity of statement and some sporadic attempts toward form. For instance, his ''Poem for Paula'' was meterless and rhymed ABABCC in its first stanza; its second stanza of five lines was also meterless but did not attempt to rhyme. However, he was capable of an effective image, as in one of his early poems ''McQuade,'' in which cancer is pictured as a football match. Generally, the poems in *A Store of Candles* are factual and small in scope and take few chances of either language or emotion. Any strivings toward poetic form are rather tentative, but two pieces, ''At the Reception'' and ''Aftermath,'' are very good. *A Northern Spring* (1986) is no real advance. The pieces are mainly terse, flat statement with little adornment or figurative language and only the most austere imagery. Except for the ironic, loose doggerel of ''My Careful Life'' and the equally loose iambic pentameter of an occasional piece like ''Survivors,'' the poems are fairly rhythmless. Other than their content—most of them being about the experiences of American soldiers in the Second World War—few have little reason to cling in the memory.

  As well as a number of anthologies, Ormsby has continued to edit *The Honest Ulsterman,* which is now second only to Seumas O'Sullivan's* *Dublin Magazine* as modern Ireland's longest-running literary periodical. The *Ulsterman,* however, has little resemblance to O'Sullivan's genteel journal, for it possesses a slapdash liveliness unique in Irish literary periodicals. It has also provided a forum for the Northern writer and is particularly receptive to new poets. Its many poetry pamphlets have included work by Seamus Heaney,* Derek Mahon,* Paul Muldoon,* Tom Paulin,* and many others.

  WORKS: *Knowing My Place.* Belfast: Ulsterman, 1971. (Poetry pamphlet); *Ripe for Company.* Belfast: Ulsterman, 1971. (Poetry pamphlet); *Spirit of Dawn.* Belfast: Ulsterman, 1973. (Poetry pamphlet); *Business as Usual.* Belfast: Ulsterman, 1973. (Poetry pamphlet); *A Store of Candles.* Oxford, London, New York: Oxford University Press, 1977; ed., *Poets from the North of Ireland.* Belfast: Blackstaff, 1979; *A Northern Spring.* London: Secker & Warburg/Dublin: Gallery, 1986; ed., *The Long Embrace: Twentieth-Century Irish Love Poems.* Belfast: Blackstaff, 1987; ed., *Northern Windows: An Anthology of Ulster Autobiography.* Belfast: Blackstaff, 1987; ed., *The Col-*

lected Poems of John Hewitt. Belfast: Blackstaff, [1991].   REFERENCE: Marken, Ronald. " 'A Line's Trail in the Water': The Poetry of Frank Ormsby." *Irish University Review* 14 (Autumn 1984): 221–227.

ORR, JAMES (1770–1816), poet. Orr was born at Broad Island, County Antrim, in 1770. He was the only son of a weaver with a few acres of land, and he followed his father's profession. In his teens, he became a United Irishman and contributed verse to the movement's periodical, *The Northern Star.* After fighting heroically in the battle of Antrim, on June 7, 1798, he was jailed and then sent to America. When he returned to his native village of Ballycarry in the early 1800s, he continued to write verse, and a collection of his work appeared in 1804. After this, however, he took to drink, and he died in Ballycarry on April 24, 1816.

Orr's poem "The Irishman" was his most popular, but its undoubted sincerity is defeated by its utterly conventional phrasing. Orr has no totally admirable poems, but portions of certain poems are quite striking. For instance, the early stanzas of "Song of an Exile" are reminiscent of Goldsmith's* "The Deserted Village," and do not quite wither by the comparison. More interesting, because it is more authentic, is "Death and Burial of an Irish Cotter," with its realistic observation and its effective if not thorough-going use of dialect. A handful of critics, from D. J. O'Donoghue* to John Hewitt,* have found much to admire in Orr. Perhaps the most judicious view is that Orr had few opportunities for education, and so never developed a discriminating literary judgment commensurate with his considerable native abilities.

WORKS: *Poems on Various Subjects.* Belfast: Smyth & Lyons, 1804; *The Posthumous Works of James Orr, of Ballycarry with a Sketch of his Life.* Belfast: Finlay, 1817; *Poems on Various Subjects.* Belfast: Mullan, 1935. (A new edition of the two previous volumes).   REFERENCES: Akenson, Donald Harman, & Crawford, W. H. *Local Poets and Social History: James Orr, Bard of Ballycarry.* Belfast: Public Record Office of Northern Ireland, 1977; Hewitt, John. *Rhyming Weavers and Other Country Poets of Antrim and Down.* Belfast: Blackstaff, 1974; Lunney, Linde Connolly. "Attitudes to Life and Death in the Poetry of James Orr, an Eighteenth-Century Ulster Weaver." *Ulster Folklore* 31 (1985): 1–12.

ORRERY, LORD (1707–1762), biographer and translator. John Boyle, fifth earl of Cork, fifth earl of Orrery, second Baron Marston, was born on January 2, 1707, and died on November 16, 1762. Although the Cork peerage was the more ancient of the two earldoms united in Boyle, he remains known as Orrery, the title he preferred. Educated at Christ Church, Orrery's limited time in the English Parliament was spent opposing Walpole, and this opposition helped to cement his friendship with Swift.* This relationship also helped to secure Orrery's name in the world of letters, though largely in a light unfavorable to the earl, whose acerbic and often unsubstantiated slanders of the dean in his *Remarks on the Life and Writings of Dr. Jonathan Swift* (1752) made the book an instant best-seller. The book also provoked lengthy, better-argued, and usually more eloquent replies from Swift's friends, most notably that of Patrick Delany's* *Observations upon Lord Orrery's Remarks on the Life and Writings of Jonathan Swift* (1754). Nevertheless, Orrery's friendship with Swift allowed his book to be taken seriously by any scholars and curiosity seekers wishing to highlight Swift's misanthropic and melancholic tendencies, thus helping to secure the industry that still surrounds Swift.

Orrery's reputation has too long been that of a half-competent dilettante for any other portrait to gain a hearing. Succeeding to his father's title in 1731, he was soon obliged to return to Ireland to restore the fortunes of the family estates. His acquaintance with Swift was made soon after that. Lonely, politically distrusted, and offering a glimpse of the society Swift both scorned and wanted to be a part of, Orrery was a natural companion of the dean when in Dublin. In December 1732, Swift wrote of "Lord Orrery . . . who seems every way a most deserving person, a good scholar, with much wit, manners, and modesty." Few others shared Swift's opinion of Orrery's scholarship; most famously, Samuel Johnson called Orrery a "feeble-minded" man who "tried to pass for a better talker, a better writer, and a better thinker than he was." Among those skeptical of Orrery's abilities seemed to have been his father, who left his extensive library to Christ College, citing his son's "want of taste for literature." Johnson, in a more generous mode, thought the donation a consequence of the son's refusing to let his wife socialize with his father's mistress, a story that reflects upon Orrery's reputation for honesty and familial duty. It was to Orrery that Swift entrusted his copy of *A History of the Four Last Years of the Queen* for delivery to William King, principal of St. Mary Hall, Oxford, and the last significant spokesman for the Jacobite movement. Swift showed few people this potentially incendiary manuscript. Although Deane Swift, his cousin, was a student at St. Mary Hall, he chose Orrery to be the messenger, suggesting a mutual trust that has often been overlooked.

Although most famous for his Swift biography, Orrery also produced articles for the *World* and the *Connoisseur,* as well as various prologues and some verse. He translated the letters of Pliny the Younger (2 vols., 1951), as well as *An Essay on the Life of Pliny* (1751). He edited the *Memoirs of Robert Carey, Earl of Monmouth* (1754), and his "Letters from Italy in 1754 and 1755" were posthumously published by the Reverend John Duncombe in 1774, who also included a "life" that remains the only significant biography. In later life, he received some recognition from august bodies, among them Oxford, which invested him as a D.C.L. in 1743, and the Royal Society, which made him a fellow in 1740.

CHRISTOPHER FAUSKE

PRINCIPAL WORKS: *A Poem, Sacred to the Memory of Edmund Sheffield, Duke of Buckingham.* . . . London: J. Brindley, 1736; *The First Ode of the First Book of Horace.* Dublin: G. Faulkner/ London: C. Bathurst & G. Hawkins, 1741; *Pyrrha; An Imitation of the Fifth Ode of the First Book of Horace.* London: R. Dodsley, 1741; *Pliny's Epistles. Book I.* [London, 1746]; *The Letters of Pliny the Younger, with Observations on Each Letter; and an Essay on Pliny's Life . . .* 2 vols. London: P. Vaillant/Dublin: G. Faulkner, 1751; *Remarks on the Life and Writings of Dr. Jonathan Swift.* London: A. Millar/Dublin: G. Faulkner, 1752; *Letters from Italy, in the Years 1754 & 1735.*

... London: B. White, 1733. (With notes by John Duncombe). REFERENCES: The bulk of Or-
rery's papers are held at Harvard. There is a study of Orrery in Phillip S. Y. Sun's dissertation,
"Swift's Eighteenth-Century Biographers" (Yale University, 1963). Sir Harold Williams makes
some remarks on Orrery in his essay in the *festschrift, Pope and His Contemporaries* (New York:
Oxford University Press, 1949, pp. 114–128). Irvin Ehrenpreis's biography, *Swift: The Man, His
Works, and the Age,* has much on Orrery from the view of a Swift partisan, especially in vol. 3,
Dean Swift (Cambridge: Harvard University Press/London: Methuen, 1983).

O'SIADHAIL, MICHEAL (1947–   ), poet. One of Ireland's leading poets,
O'Siadhail was born in Dublin and educated at Clongowes Wood College, at
Trinity College, Dublin, and at the University of Oslo. In 1982, he was awarded
the Irish-American Cultural Institute Literary Prize for his poetry. Recognized
as a stylistically courageous, humorous, and experimental poet, his work has
been set to music and broadcast by RTÉ, and he has been widely anthologized.
At twenty-two, he was one of the youngest lecturers ever to teach at Trinity
College, and he has also worked at the Dublin Institute for Advanced Studies.
He is also recognized as an authority on the Irish language and gave the Vernan
Hull lecture at Harvard in 1985 and, at Yale University, the Trumbull lecture.
However, he left academic life after four years and is now a full-time writer.
He has been quoted in a *Sunday Independent* interview by Patricia Deevy as
saying, "My whole life revolves around my work." He is a member of the Arts
Council and of Aosdána* and has edited *Poetry Ireland Review.*

"Poetry," says O'Siadhail in an *Irish Times* interview with Katie Donovan,*
"is the process of trying to catch the wind with nets—it's the art of the impossible." Using a varied selection of poetic forms, O'Siadhail's work ranges
over diverse topics. Always linguistically skillful, he initially wrote in Irish;
three collections were published, and some later poems are reworked versions
in English of some of these. *Hail! Madam Jazz* (1992) is a compendium of work
from five books published over a long period, coupled with a new sequence,
"The Middle Voice," and "The Chosen Garden." The former sequence announces the more mature poetry of middle age.

Many of O'Siadhail's poems, particularly the earlier ones, have a great dramatic vigor of statement, as is apparent from the use of such words as "numb-
skull," "nitwit," "damn," "lousy," and "bitch." In "Work," he superbly uses
the figure of a passionate woman as a metaphor for his topic. Less conversa-
tionally direct but as notable are the arresting phrases liberally sprinkled
throughout the later work. See, for instance, the poems "Freedom" and "Return." O'Siadhail is hardly yet in Yeats'* league as a phrasemaker, but he can
fashion a phrase that sticks in the mind.

O'Siadhail has less concern than Yeats for form, and usually his form is very
free, even when he attempts, as he fairly often does, a pattern as rigid as the
sonnet. His concern is most apparent in his end rhymes. These usually appear
in a consistent pattern, although not always. See, for instance, "The Umbrella,"
which for four of its five stanzas rhymes ABBA but which in its second stanza
switches to ABAB, the only reason apparently being that in this stanza he was

unable to reconcile the necessities of his statement with his formal pattern. Also, O'Siadhail's end rhymes are more often than not imperfect ones. He often settles for easy similarities of sound such as slant rhyme, consonance, assonance, or the rhyming of a stressed with an unstressed syllable. In some poems, the mélange is so great that any pattern is all but destroyed. In other poems—such as "Seepage" or "Francis to His Father" or "Absence"—the poet is dead accurate. In most of these poems, nevertheless, the basic and very faulty quantitative meter is at war with the formality of the rhyme. In any event, O'Siadhail's work is some of the most interesting in contemporary Irish poetry, for it demands—and often repays—a close and repeated scrutiny.

FRED JOHNSTON

WORKS: *Coras Fuaimeanna na Gailge.* Dublin, 1977; *The Leap Year.* 1978. (Translation of *An Bhliain Bhisigh.* Baile Atha Cliath: An Clóchomhar, [1978]); *Rungs of Time,* 1980. (Translation of *Runga.* Baile Atha Cliath: An Clóchomhar, [1980]); with Ardnt Wigger. *Belonging.* 1982. (Translation of *Cumann.* Baile Atha Cliath: An Clóchomhar, 1982); *Springnight.* [Dublin]: Bluett, [1983]; *The Image Wheel.* [Dublin]: Bluett, [1985]; *Learning Irish.* New Haven, Conn.: Yale University Press, 1988; *Modern Irish.* Cambridge: Cambridge University Press, 1989; *The Chosen Garden.* [Dublin: Dedalus, 1990]; *Hail! Madam Jazz: New and Selected Poems.* [Newcastle upon Tyne]: Bloodaxe, [1992]; *A Fragile City.* [Newcastle upon Tyne]: Bloodaxe, [1995].

O'SULLIVAN, MICHAEL JOHN (1794–1845), poet, playwright, and journalist. Born in Cork, where he studied under William Maginn,* O'Sullivan took a law degree and at one time edited *The Freeman's Journal.* His play, *Lallah Rookh,* after Thomas Moore,* ran for 100 nights in Dublin in 1815. Of his verses, D. J. O'Donoghue remarked, "[T]hough able to do better, he wished to stultify himself by the writing of meaningless melodies, and has been most successful in the attempt."

WORKS: *The Prince of the Lake. . . .* Cork: J. Bolster, 1815. (Poetry); *A Fasciculus of Lyric Verses by the Late M. J. O'Sullivan.* Cork: W. Scraggs, 1846. "Memoir of the Author." In *A Fasciculus,* pp. 7–15; O'Donoghue, D. J. "Some Minor Irish Poets 6: Michael John O'Sullivan." *Shamrock* 28 (1890): 11–12.

O'SULLIVAN, PATRICK

WORKS: *I Heard the Wild Birds Sing.* (Memoir); *A Country Diary: The Year in Kerry.* Anvil, 1994.

O'SULLIVAN, SEUMAS (1879–1958), poet and editor. Seumas O'Sullivan was born James Sullivan Starkey in Dublin on July 17, 1879. His literary career did not begin until 1902 with the publication of a few poems in *The Irish Homestead, The United Irishman,* and *Celtic Christmas.* With the 1904 publications of *New Songs* edited by George Russell,* five of O'Sullivan's poems were for the first time included in a book. In 1904, O'Sullivan also helped to reestablish the publishing firm Whaley and Company with fellow poet and actor George Roberts (1873–1953), and one year later, in 1905, Whaley and Company published O'Sullivan's first book of poetry, *The Twilight People.* Encouraged by the reception of his verse in *New Songs,* O'Sullivan had decided to put three dozen of his poems into a book. They made delicate use of melody and were concerned more with the establishment of atmosphere than with themes. O'Sullivan's poetry drew the reader into an elemental world populated by waning moons, pale stars, and wandering shades. Many of the moods that infused the early work of W. B. Yeats* and George Russell were resurrected in O'Sullivan: the yearning for the infinite, the turmoil of the soul, the silence and magic of twilight.

Between 1906 and 1908, O'Sullivan co-edited the Tower Press Booklets with James Connolly (not the labor leader). The Tower Press intended to issue monthly booklets of unpublished verse, sketches, and essays by living Irish writers, some established and others less well known—many of whom were personal friends of Seumas O'Sullivan. The first series of booklets originally sold for one shilling, and, with the exception of George Russell's *Some Irish Essays* and George Moore's* *Reminiscences of the Impressionist Painters,* the little booklets were slow to sell. O'Sullivan's own booklets, *Verses: Sacred and Profane,* appeared in 1908. In this poetry, the mood of subjective and tender melancholy, which was so prevalent in *The Twilight People,* was even more prevalent. Here, he was absorbed with the beauty of decay and was immured in sadness. It was only proper for O'Sullivan, the archetypal Celtic poet and incurable idealist, to be depressed since the best that life and nature showed him was meager compared with that unrealized perfection he sought.

In 1909, O'Sullivan's New Nation Press published his third volume of poetry, *The Earth-Lover and Other Verses,* which, like other true lyric verse, expressed a personal mood and not the war-cry of a group. Its delicately wrought verse echoed a mood of calm prevalent in Celtic Twilight poetry. O'Sullivan renounced the energy of sunlight for evening time, which offered the tenderness of the stars and the nirvana of sleep for company. In *The Earth-Lover,* O'Sullivan once again showed an ability to deal simply and directly with life. For the first time, he took impressions of Dublin street life as material for several of his poems: the waif's fondness for the rags and bones man, and the regularity of the organ grinder who came to the street each Monday.

With the 1917 publication of *Requiem and Other Poems,* O'Sullivan's nationalism was apparent for the first time. In the elegy "In Memoriam—T. MacD.," O'Sullivan praised the poet, playwright, and nationalist Thomas MacDonagh* for his ability to learn from the past as well as for his skill to stimulate song in others. In another poem, "Requiem," O'Sullivan exhorted his readers not to greet those who died in the Easter Rebellion with tears; he believed they deserved a more vigorous and noble tribute. Because much of the poetry in this volume was concerned with the feverish period in which it was published, it was not surprising that O'Sullivan's contributions to another 1917 publication, *Aftermath of Easter Week,* edited by Padraic Browne, were also deeply nationalistic and at times almost reverential. O'Sullivan's involvement with Irish nationalism began before and extended beyond the publication of

Requiem and *Aftermath*. When he first met Arthur Griffith,* O'Sullivan established a friendship that was to continue for many years. His rooms became a
favorite place of call for Griffith and for some of those who associated with
him in the early days of Sinn Féin. When Griffith went on his weekend tramps
in the Dublin mountains or occasional excursions to the Continent, he was often
accompanied by O'Sullivan.

When O'Sullivan began to edit *The Dublin Magazine** in 1923, a task that
was to occupy him until his death in 1958, he subordinated his nationalism to
this work, and the magazine assumed an apolitical and eclectic point of view.
O'Sullivan encouraged young writers, and the advent of *The Dublin Magazine*
coincided with the rise of a new generation of Irish writers such as Austin
Clarke,* F. R. Higgins,* and Liam O'Flaherty.* In an awkward period of transition when the so-called Irish Renaissance had already reached its zenith,
O'Sullivan rallied many young Irish writers around himself and *The Dublin
Magazine*. Writers like Samuel Beckett,* Patrick Kavanagh,* Padraic Fallon,*
and Mary Lavin* started their literary careers in the pages of *The Dublin Magazine*. O'Sullivan was unique as an editor because he combined an ability to
attract established writers like W. B. Yeats and George Russell with instant and
repeated generosity to the young and unknown. The pages of *The Dublin Magazine* were not limited to Irish writers: the poetry of R. S. Thomas and Alun
Lewis first appeared there and writers like Paul Valery, Francis Viele-Griffin,
S. S. Koteliansky, and Gordon Bottomley were also given space.

While O'Sullivan edited *The Dublin Magazine* (1923 through 1958), he published few new poems and sketches of his own. He appeared to be more concerned with the careers of those whom he published than with his own creative
talent. Realizing that several of his contributors had more talent and greater
capacity for creative growth than he possessed, he selflessly devoted his life to
the publication and promotion of their work. For this reason, O'Sullivan's contributors developed a strong loyalty toward *The Dublin Magazine*. Padraic Fallon's remark that he would rather see a poem of his in *The Dublin Magazine*
than in any other literary journal was not an uncommon attitude among the
magazine's contributors.

O'Sullivan died in Dublin on March 24, 1958.

RICHARD BURNHAM

WORKS: *The Twilight People*. Dublin: Whaley/London: A. H. Bullen, 1905; *Verses: Sacred and
Profane*. Dublin: Maunsel, 1908; *The Earth-Lover and Other Verses*. Dublin: New Nation, 1909;
under the pseudonym of J. H. Orwell, *Impressions*. Dublin: New Nation, 1910; *Poems*. Dublin:
Maunsel, 1912; *An Epilogue to the Praise of Angus, and Other Poems*. Dublin: Maunsel, 1914;
Mud and Purple. Dublin: Talbot, 1917. (Essays); *Requiem and Other Poems*. Dublin: Privately
printed, 1917. (Poetry pamphlet); *The Rosses and Other Poems*. Dublin: Maunsel, 1918; *The Poems
of Seumas O'Sullivan*. Boston: B. J. Brimmer, 1923; *Common Adventures: A Book of Prose and
Verse*. Dublin: Orwell, 1926; *The Lamplighter, and Other Poems*. Dublin: Orwell, 1929. (Poetry
pamphlet); *Twenty-Five Lyrics*. Bognor Regis, Sussex: Pear Tree Press, 1933. (Poetry pamphlet);
Personal Talk. Dublin: Privately printed, 1936; *Poems . . . 1930–1938*. Dublin: Orwell, 1938. (Poetry
pamphlet); *Collected Poems*. Dublin: Orwell, 1940; *This Is the House, and Other Verses*. Dublin:
Privately printed, 1942. (Poetry pamphlet); *Essays and Recollections*. Dublin: Talbot, 1944; *The

Rose and Bottle. Dublin: Talbot, 1946. (Essays); *Dublin Poems.* New York: Creative Age, [1946]; *Translations and Transcriptions.* Belfast: H. R. Carter, 1950. (Poetry pamphlet). REFERENCES: Miller, Liam, ed. *Retrospect: The Work of Seumas O'Sullivan and Estella F. Solomons.* Dublin: Dolmen, 1973; Russell, Jane. *James Starkey/Seumas O'Sullivan: A Critical Biography.* Rutherford, Madison, Teaneck, N. J.: Fairleigh Dickinson University Press/London: Associated University Presses, [1987].

OTWAY, CAESAR (1780–1842), writer of travel sketches and editor. Otway's most notable contribution to literature was the launching of William Carleton* in his anti-Catholic magazine, *The Christian Examiner.* His own volumes of Irish travel sketches are not really worth reprinting, but they do offer some interesting, if deeply biased, reporting. Otway was born in Tipperary, took his B.A. from Trinity College, Dublin, in 1801, was ordained, and became a notable preacher. He died in Dublin on March 16, 1842.

WORKS: *A Letter to the Roman Catholic Priests of Ireland*... Dublin: Coyne, 1814. (Religious tract); *A Lecture on Miracles*... Dublin: R. M. Tims, 1823. (Religious tract); *Sketches in Ireland, Descriptive of Interesting and Hitherto Unnoticed Districts, in the North and South.* Dublin: W. Curry, Jun., 1827/2d edition corrected, 1839; *A Tour in Connaught, Comprising Sketches of Clonmacnoise, Joyce Country and Achill.* Dublin: W. Curry, Jun., 1839; *Sketches in Erris and Tyrawly.* Dublin: W. Curry, Jun., 1841.

OULTON, WALLEY CHAMBERLAIN (1770?–1820?), playwright and theatrical historian. Oulton was born in Dublin possibly around 1770, although Patrick Rafroidi thinks that it must have been ten years earlier. As a schoolboy, he had plays performed at various Dublin theaters, and about 1786 he went to London and wrote a considerable number of short farces and musical farces. One unpublished piece in the Larpent Collection, *The Irish Tar; or, Which Is the Girl?* of 1797, has some Irish interest. Oulton's real interest, however, lies in his two long histories of the London stage from 1771 to 1817.

PRINCIPAL WORKS: *The Mad House.* Dublin: R. Marchbank, 1786. (Musical farce); *A New Way to Keep a Wife at Home.* Dublin: H. Chamberlaine, 1786. (Adaptation of Fielding's *The Letter Writers*); *As It Should Be.* London: W. Lowndes, 1789. (One-act play); *The Busy Body.* London: C. Stalker, [1789]. (Collection of pieces from a periodical Oulton briefly ran); *All in Good Humour.* London, 1792. (One-act farce); *The Wonderful Story Teller or New Pocket Library of Agreeable Entertainment....* London: C. Johnson, [ca. 1795]; *The History of the Theatres of London...from 1771 to 1795.* 2 vols. London: Martin & Bain, 1796. (A continuation of Benjamin Victor's *History of the Theatres of London*); *Botheration; or, A Ten Years' Blunder.* London: C. Cawthorn, 1798. (Two-act farce); tr., *The Beauties of Kotzebue.* London: Crosby & Letterman, 1800; *The Sixty-Third Letter.* London: Barker, 1802. (Two-act musical farce); tr., *The Death of Abel.* London: Hogg, 1811. (After a German poem by S. Gessner); *The Sleep-walker; or, Which Is the Lady?* London: J. Roach, 1812. (Two-act farce); *My Landlady's Gown.* London: W. Simpkin & R. Marshall, 1816. (Two-act farce); *Frighten'd to Death!* London: W. Simpkin & R. Marshall, 1817. (Two-act musical farce); *A History of the Theatres of London...from 1795 to 1817.* 3 vols. London: C. Chapple, 1818.

OWENSON, SYDNEY *See* MORGAN, LADY.

P

PARK, DAVID (1954–   ), novelist and short story writer. Park was born and educated in Belfast and now teaches in a country school in County Down. His stories in *Oranges from Spain* (1990) all have very different themes, but all in their different ways reflect life in Northern Ireland. ''The Trap'' is the story of a boy who does not want to become a farmer like his father. ''Killing a Brit'' tells of a boy who sees a soldier shot. Perhaps the strongest piece is the title story, in which Park describes a small greengrocer shop and its Catholic owner, Mr. Breen. The detail is beautifully meticulous yet told with disciplined economy. The violence at the end comes to us through the eyes of the young apprentice who tells the story, and the horror of senseless violence leaps from the page. *The Healing* (1992) is the powerful story of a boy who had seen his father shot by terrorists and of an old man who knows that his only son is a terrorist. These two come together when the boy and his mother leave their country home and come to Belfast. The old man believes that the boy is a sacred trust and that through him would come understanding of the great mystery of God, and ''healing would pour down upon a people riven by sickness.'' The writing is again strong, economical, and evocative. There is no humor, but there is a real feeling for the effect of violence upon a people. *The Rye Man* (1994) tells of a man who returns to his old primary school as its new headmaster. He has strong, almost obsessive views about what he wants his school to become. His marriage is going through a crisis caused by his wife's miscarriage. Also, he is haunted by the memory of a young child he had found years before, locked in a shed, starving and naked. This memory affects his feelings about a mentally handicapped girl in the school. Park uses words carefully to create remarkable and disturbing images. He is a writer of great talent.

DOROTHY ROBBIE

WORKS: *Oranges from Spain*. London: Cape, [1990]. (Short stories); *The Healing*. London: Cape, [1992]. (Novel); *The Rye Man*. London: Cape, [1994]. (Novel).

PARKER, [JAMES] STEWART (1941–1988), playwright. Parker was born in the Sydenham area of East Belfast on October 20, 1941, into what he described as "an average Unionist family," close to the Harland and Wolff shipyard, about which Sam Thompson* wrote *Over the Bridge,* a play dear to Parker's heart and edited by him in 1970. He went to school in East Belfast and later to Queen's University in 1959, where he studied English and took an active part in the drama society. In his second year at Queen's, he was diagnosed as having a form of bone cancer, which necessitated the amputation of a leg. Nevertheless, he took his B.A. in 1963 and an M.A. in English in 1965. He subsequently taught in the United States at Hamilton College and at Cornell, before returning to Belfast in 1969 and beginning a career as a professional writer. Parker wrote several radio plays for BBC Northern Ireland before having his first stage success with *Spokesong* at the Dublin Theatre Festival in 1975. Productions in London, New Haven, Connecticut, and New York followed. As Parker's most successful play, it deserves detailed examination. It tells the story of Frank Stock, owner of a small bicycle shop in Belfast, whose attempts to stay in business while the city is torn apart all around him provide an allegory of human endurance. The story, interspersed with music by the composer of "Red Sails in the Sunset" and "South of the Border Down Mexico Way," is told through a choric figure called the Trick Cyclist and goes back and forth in time to include the love and marriage of Frank's grandparents, the founders of the firm. Through Parker's easy style, punning wit, and sense of history, Frank's survival is a telling, if gentle, rebuke to political defeatism. Parker's interest in music, reflected in the column he wrote for the *Irish Times* from 1971 to 1976, was combined with a desire to write a play about the violence in Northern Ireland when *Catchpenny Twist,* his best-balanced play, was staged at the Peacock in 1977. Two Belfast teachers flee south of the border when they lose their jobs and attract death threats for the political ballads they sell commercially. A new career as composers of pop songs leads them to the Eurovision Song Contest, where, however, their political enemies violently catch up with them.

In 1978, Parker went to live in Edinburgh and later moved to London, where he wrote radio and television plays. About Parker's stage plays, there is always a quality of black farce. This quality is seen again in *Nightshade* (1980), which concerns a mortician, Quinn, whose avocation as conjuror hilariously becomes part of his funeral arrangements. By means of farce, Parker explores ways open to people to combat despair and death. His themes are invariably serious, but his plays are entertaining on many levels. In the essay "State of Play," Parker made it clear that for him theater is essentially ludic, "amongst the most civilised and subtle of the public games that we play." "Pratt's Fall" (1983), which is unpublished, was a rare but literal flop in this respect; but the three plays that followed, *Northern Star* (1984), *Heavenly Bodies* (1986), and *Pentecost* (1987), conceived as a trilogy or "triptych" of history plays, bear out well Parker's theory of drama as self-conscious play. *Pentecost,* the most effective, is also perhaps Parker's most serious comment on the Northern situation. Set during the Protestant Workers' Council strike in Belfast in 1974, which resisted the concept and practice of "power sharing," *Pentecost* uses a strong spiritualistic emphasis to suggest that only through love, biblically understood, can reconciliation, or what he called "wholeness," become a political possibility. In a fine production by Patrick Mason for the Field Day Theatre Company,* *Pentecost* proved a fitting finale to Parker's brief career, which was cut short by cancer on November 2, 1988.

CHRISTOPHER MURRAY

WORKS: *The Casualty's Meditation.* Belfast: Festival, 1966. (Poetry pamphlet); *Maw.* Belfast: Festival, 1968. (Poetry pamphlet); "Introduction" to *Over the Bridge* by Sam Thompson. Dublin: Gill & Macmillan, 1970, pp. 7–15; "The Iceberg." *The Honest Ulsterman* 50 (Winter 1975): 4–64. (Radio play); "The Kamikaze Ground Staff Reunion Dinner." In *Best Radio Plays of 1980.* London: Eyre Methuen, 1981; *Spokesong: Music by Jimmy Kennedy: Lyrics by Stewart Parker.* New York & London: Samuel French, 1980; *Catchpenny Twist.* Dublin: Gallery, 1980/New York: French, 1984; *Nightshade.* Dublin: Co-op Books, 1980; "State of Play." *Canadian Journal of Irish Studies* 7 (June 1981): 5–11. (Essay); *Three Plays for Ireland: Northern Star/Heavenly Bodies/Pentecost.* Birmingham: Oberon Books, 1989. REFERENCES: Andrews, Elmer. "The Will to Freedom: Politics and Play in the Theatre of Stewart Parker." In *Irish Writers and Politics.* Okifumi Fomesu & Masaru Sekine, eds. Gerrards Cross: Colin Smythe, 1989, pp. 237–269; Etherton, Michael. *Contemporary Irish Dramatists.* Houndmills: Macmillan/New York: St. Martin's, 1989, pp. 15–25; Harris, Claudia W. "From Pastness to Wholeness: Stewart Parker's Reinventing Theatre." *Colby Quarterly* 27 (December 1991): 233–241; Kurdi, Maria. "The Ways of Twoness: Pairs, Parallels and Contrasts in Stewart Parker's *Spokesong.*" In *A Small Nation's Contribution to the World: Essays on Anglo-Irish Literature and Language.* Donald E. Morse, Csilla Bertha & Istvan Palffy, eds. Gerrards Cross: Colin Smythe/Debrecen: Lajos Kossuth University, 1993, pp. 61–69.

PARNELL, [FRANCES ISABEL] "FANNY" (1849–1882), poet. Parnell was born at Avondale in County Wicklow in 1849 and was the favorite sister of Charles Stewart Parnell. In 1864 and 1865, when still very young; she published poems in *The Irish People.* Moving to America with her mother in 1874, she became busily involved in the Famine Relief Committee, and she founded the Ladies' Land League. These activities, combined with her violently patriotic poetry, made her, in R. F. Foster's* words, "a national figure both in Ireland and America." Indeed, her early death on July 20, 1882, transformed her into an Irish-American cult figure, and for some years pilgrimages were made to her grave.

Of her verse, John Boyle O'Reilly* wrote, "Crushed out, like the sweet life of a bruised flower, they are the very soul cry of a race." A soberer view would find the less vehement poems conventional and poor and the more embattled ones capable of such flamboyant rhetorical flourishes as:

> You, Gladstone, sunk supine to quivering slush—
> You, Forster, with the seal of Cain in breast and eye—
> You, Bright, whose slopping tongue can gloss and gush—

Nevertheless, her vigorous individuality sometimes broke through both the poetic conventions and those of patriotic rhetoric. For instance, in the second stanza of "Hold the Harvest," possibly her most famous poem, she effectively wrote:

> The serpent's curse upon you lies—ye writhe within the dust,
> Ye fill your mouths with beggar's swill, ye grovel for a crust:
> Your lords have set their blood-stained heels upon your shameful heads,
> Yet they are kind—they leave you still their ditches for your beds!

WORKS: *The Hovels of Ireland.* New York: T. Kelly, [1879]; *Land League Songs.* Boston, 1882. REFERENCE: Foster, R. F. "The Muse of Bordentown: Fanny Parnell, 1875–82." In *Charles Stewart Parnell: The Man and his Family.* 2d ed. [Hassocks, Sussex]: Harvester/[Atlantic Highlands, N.J.]: Humanities, [1979], pp. 241–259.

PARNELL, THOMAS (1679–1718), poet. Parnell was a member of a prosperous and well-known family of merchant class status with Cromwellian connections. His father, an alderman from Congleton in Cheshire, refused to take the oath of office under Charles II and emigrated to Ireland after the Restoration. (Charles Stewart Parnell was a descendant of Thomas's younger brother.) Thomas, born in Dublin, was ordained in the Anglican Church in 1703 and served as a minor canon at St. Patrick's, Dublin, and as archdeacon of Clogher from 1706 to 1716. He was active in the Scriblerus Club, which consisted principally of John Gay, Dr. Arbuthnot, the Lord Treasurer Robert Harley (later earl of Oxford), Pope, and Swift,* the latter two particularly close friends of Parnell in the Augustan literary scene. The Scriblerus group satirized literary incompetence, false taste, and useless learning through the guise of the "memoirs" of a fictional pedant named Martinus Scriblerus. Despite Swift biographer Irvin Ehrenpreis's description of Parnell as "mournful," "bibulous," and given to depression, he seemed well attuned to the conviviality, practical joking, and literary foolery associated with the club's activities. Parnell co-contributed with Arbuthnot and Pope the *Essay Concerning the Origin of the Sciences* (1732), in which Martin hilariously argues that all serious learning and science descended to the ancients from pygmies and that their modern counterparts—monkeys, tigers, marmosets, and the like—could be conditioned to continue this passing on of knowledge. He prevailed on a servant to concoct a false report of an outbreak of smallpox at Lord Bathurst's residence to prevent Swift, who was pathological about the disease, from arriving first on a visit and securing the most comfortable bed. He overheard Pope's reading to Swift the famous dressing room scene in Canto I of *The Rape of the Lock,* proceeded to translate the memorized passage into Latin, and the following day accused Pope of plagiarizing from a monkish manuscript—a hoax surely in the class with Swift's own substitution of a mock-serious "meditation" on a broomstick during one of his readings from Robert Boyle's philosophical efforts to Lady Betty Germaine. Like other Scriblerian high jinks, this one had a purpose, in this case, exposing human gullibility. Repeatedly, Swift intervened on behalf of Parnell, trying to advance his ecclesiastical career and associate him with the political successes of the Tory government, apparently to no avail. Swift had praise for Parnell's literary efforts, writing to Stella that his verse "outdoes all our poets here a Barrs length."

At his death in 1718, only nine of Parnell's poems had been published, and Pope prepared a posthumous edition, *Poems on Several Occasions* (1722), and acted as the poet's literary executor. Parnell's modest reputation as a poet, both in the eighteenth century and today, rests largely on this slim volume of twenty poems. But Pope's real motives for publishing his friend's verse are problematic. This should hardly come as a surprise to anyone remembering Dr. Johnson's description of Pope as someone who "hardly drank tea without a stratagem." Among other things, Pope clearly sought the ego boost provided by Parnell's essay on Homer, which prefixed Pope's *Iliad* (1715) and which depicted the translation as a modern classic in its own right. Deprived of a formal university education because of his Roman Catholic faith, Pope relied on Parnell's advice and seemed genuinely in awe of his erudition and knowledge of the classics in other ways apart from the essay itself. "You are a Generous Author," he wrote to Parnell, "I a Hackney Scribler, You are a Grecian & bred at a University, I a poor Englishman of my own Educating."

Parnell's literary reputation over the years has depended largely on two poems. "The Hermit" was his most popular poem during the eighteenth and nineteenth centuries. This may be partly owing to the almost cult status the hermit figure enjoyed during the emergence of a new romantic sensibility. But the themes explored are conventionally moralistic, and the poem is didactic, with heavy Christian emphasis. Today, Parnell's most widely anthologized work is "A Night-Piece on Death," an early example of the so-called Graveyard school of English verse. Such poems find their inspiration in graveyard settings, dark lake scenes, and the contemplation of ruins and mortality and exhibit a preference for melancholic Christian religiosity and Gothic gloom. Notable among such poems are Gray's "Elegy in a Country Churchyard," Blair's "The Grave," Young's "Night-Thoughts," and perhaps even this kind of poem's prototype in Milton's "Il Penseroso." Charles Peake finds Parnell's poem unique in this tradition for its purity of diction, ease of octosyllabic movement, controlled progress of thought, and "intricate religious emotion." Several of its themes and images appear to be proleptic of those developed by Gray in his much better known "Elegy," notably the topos of "mute inglorious Miltons" and "village Hampdens" seemingly anticipated by Parnell's "men half-ambitious, all unknown," as well as similar contrasts between humble and ostentatious burials in both poems. This may be more atmospheric than an example of direct allusion, since Gray contemptuously referred to Parnell as "the dunghill of Irish-Grubstreet," ostensibly for his use of the low word "dung" in the poem "Bacchus; or the Drunken Metamorphosis." Goldsmith,* whose *Life* prefaced the 1770 edition of Parnell's *Poems* and is the repository for much of the information, anecdotal reportage, and critical opinion on Parnell's life and art, found the poem "deserv[ing] every praise" and surpassing all such previous writings. Later, in *The Beauties of English Poetry,* Goldsmith refers to "A

Night-Piece'' as ''natural'' and ''its reflections just,'' although faulting the octosyllabic metric as inappropriate for sublimity.

Parnell's output is representative of the whole gamut of eighteenth-century poetic styles, genres, and themes. There are the de riguer ars poetica, ''An Essay on the Different Styles of Poetry,'' modeled after Horace (or possibly Pope), translations, imitations, pastorals, satire, hymns, pindarics, mock-heroic exercises, epigrams, allegory, occasional verse, elegies (and their mock forms), biblical paraphrases, scatology, and a host of minor verse forms.

Pope's moving dedicatory poem to Harley, the earl of Oxford, prefixed to *Poems on Several Occasions,* opens on an elegiac note, simultaneously lamenting and praising their Scriblerian colleague. But it also furnishes a fitting characterization of Parnell's poetic accomplishment:

> Such were the Notes, thy once lov'd Poet sung,
> 'Till Death untimely stop'd his tuneful Tongue.
>   Oh just beheld, and lost! admir'd, and mourn'd!
> With softest Manners, gentlest Arts, adorn'd!
> Blest in each Science, blest in ev'ry Strain!
> Dear to the Muse, to HARLEY dear—in vain!

The parallel phrasing of ''softest Manners'' and ''gentlest Arts'' suggests the overlapping of life and art in Parnell's case. His sociability, good nature, politeness, and generosity complement the artistic polish, simplicity, sophistication, and ''correctness'' that characterize his versification and tone. The balance of ''Blest in each Science, blest in ev'ry Strain'' might suggest his knowledgeability and classical learning, as well as his poetic versatility and courtly detachment combining classicism, religious sentiment, and moral fervor with Augustan wit, humor, and verbal grace.

The editors of the most recent (and definitive) edition of Parnell's poems, Claude Rawson and F. P. Lock, in addition to printing some 130 new or little-known poems, describe Parnell as ''a minor classic, as a poet of versatility and accomplishment rather than originality.'' The poet-critic Donald Davie, with admirable restraint and uncommon sensitivity, calls Parnell's unique poetic tone and sensibility a ''valuable, a civilized moderation and elegance,'' literary qualities clearly more esteemed in the eighteenth century than in the twentieth.

                                                                                    DONALD C. MELL

WORKS: *Poems on Several Occasions. Written by Dr. Thomas Parnell, Late Archdeacon of Clogher: and Published by Mr. Pope.* London: B. Lintot, 1722; *Works in Verse and Prose of Dr. Thomas Parnell: Enlarged with Variations and Poems Not Publish'd.* Glasgow: R. and A. Foulis, 1755; *The Posthumous Poems of Dr. Thomas Parnell, Containing Poems Moral and Divine, and on Various Other Subjects.* London: B. Gunne, 1758; *Works of the English Poets.* Alexander, Chalmers, ed. Vol. 9. London: C. Whittingham, 1810; *The Poetical Works of Thomas Parnell.* John Mitford, ed. Aldine Edition. London: Bell, 1833; *The Poetical Works of Thomas Gray, Thomas Parnell, William Collins, Matthew Green, and Thomas Warton.* Robert A. Wilmott, ed. London: George Routledge, 1855; *Collected Poems of Thomas Parnell.* Claude Rawson & F. P. Lock, eds. Newark: University of Delaware Press, 1989. REFERENCES: Cruickshank, A. H. ''Thomas Parnell, or What Was Wrong with the Eighteenth Century.'' *Essays and Studies* 7 (1921): 57–81;

Goldsmith, Oliver. *Life of Parnell.* London: T. Davies, 1770; Havens, Raymond D. "Parnell's 'Hymn to Contentment.' " *Modern Language Notes* 59 (1944): 329–331; Jackson, R. Wyse. "Thomas Parnell, The Poet." *Dublin Magazine* 20 (1945): 28–35; Johnson, Samuel. *Lives of the Poets.* G. B. Hill, ed. Oxford: Clarendon, 1905; Rawson, C. J. "Some Unpublished Letters of Pope and Gay: And Some Manuscript Sources of Goldsmith's Life of Parnell." *Review of English Studies* 10 (1959): 371–387; Rawson, C. J. "Swift's Certificate to Parnell's 'Posthumous Works.' " *Modern Language Review* 57 (1962): 179–182; Rawson, C. J. "New Parnell Manuscripts." *Scriblerian* 1 (2) (1969): 1–2; Rawson, C. J. & F. P. Lock. "Scriblerian Epigrams by Thomas Parnell." *Review of English Studies* 33 (1982): 138–157; Starr, Herbert W. "Gray's Opinion of Parnell." *Modern Language Notes* 57 (1942): 675–676; Woodman, Thomas M. *Thomas Parnell.* Boston: Twayne, 1985.

PATTERSON, EVANGELINE (fl. 1990s), poet. Patterson was born in Limavady and grew up in Dublin.

WORKS: *Lucifer, with Angels: New and Selected Poems.* Dublin: Dedalus, [1994].

PATTERSON, GLENN (1961–   ), novelist. Patterson was born in Belfast, the setting for his two ambitious and impressive novels. From 1989 to 1991, he was writer in the community for Lisburn and Craigavon. He now lives in Manchester.

His first novel, *Burning Your Own* (1988), which won the Rooney Prize and a Betty Trask Prize, is on a mainly Protestant housing estate on the outskirts of Belfast in the turbulent summer of 1969. The protagonist is a ten-year-old boy, Mal Martin, and the story is partly about the reconciliation of his mother and his reformed drunkard of a father, who has failed in business but who does finally get a job as a workman on the construction of a new Catholic housing estate nearby. The story also concerns Mal's desire to be accepted as an equal by the gang of boys in the estate. The first half of the novel is much taken up with the amassing of rubbish for a huge bonfire on the eve of July 12, the traditional day for celebrating King William's victory at the Battle of the Boyne. The success of the bonfire is aborted when the one Catholic boy on the estate discovers the center pole around which the bonfire is to be built and destroys it beforehand. This boy, Francey Hagan, is an eccentric, even bizarre, outcast who lives in filth and squalor surrounded by rats in the adjacent dump. Eventually, the inhabitants of the estate, impelled by fear and the increasing troubles in the city and in Derry, drive Francey's parents away, and there is an abortive attempt to burn the rising new estate. As Francey and his father leave, Mal cries to his friend to take him along. What Patterson has written, although rooted in reality, is nearly an allegory of the Troubles in the north, as compelling in story as it is powerful in theme.

In *Fat Lad* (1992), the complex narrative again carries a heavy load of meaning. A young man, Drew, reluctantly returns to Belfast to take up a job as assistant manager of a bookstore owned by a large English chain. The involved action wanders back and forth in time; and, although Drew's plot is its spine, the narrative involves—indeed, sometimes centers on—his parents and relatives and friends and lovers and how they have been variously affected by the ever-present backdrop of troubled Belfast. In construction, the novel reminds one of plays like *The Cherry Orchard* or *The Plough and the Stars*. Although much happens that is glum and troubling, the hero at the end seems to have become a more open and caring person who has now accepted, rather than rejected, the heritage of his past. The writing is extremely able, even if it contains some effectively appalling similes like, "Their leathery tongues entwined, like ancient turtles rubbing necks." Sometimes the word choice is nicely witty, as in this list of guests at a party at the bookstore: "staff from rival shops, publishers' reps, favoured customers, and an intensity of local poets."

With these two solid accomplishments, Patterson must be regarded as an important writer.

WORKS: *Burning Your Own.* London: Chatto & Windus, [1988]; *Fat Lad.* London: Chatto & Windus, 1992. (Novel); *Black Night at Big Thunder Mountain.* London: Chatto & Windus, [1995].

PAULIN, TOM (1949–   ), poet and critic. Paulin was born in Leeds on January 25, 1949, but grew up in Belfast after 1953. He took a B.A. with first-class honours in English at the University of Hull and then did two years' research at Lincoln College, Oxford, taking a B.Litt. in 1973. Since 1972, he has lectured in English at the University of Nottingham. In 1976, he received the Eric Gregory Award and in 1978 the Somerset Maugham Award and in 1982 was joint winner with Paul Muldoon* of the Geoffrey Faber Memorial Prize.

Paulin's primary reputation is as a poet, and he often has great vigor of expression. His *Seize the Fire* (1990), for instance, is a very free adaptation of Aeschylus's *Prometheus Bound* that utilizes such modernisms as "stretched limos" and "brownie points." However, lines like the following succeed in dramatically revitalizing for the modern stage the classical theater's stateliest tragedy:

> Didn't I seize the fire of ideas
> and make them leap, tear, fly, sing—
> the rush and rush and whap of them
> in each split moment!—

Even an early poem like "Pings on the Great Globe" throbs with its energy of expression. For instance:

> Unclean! Unclean! The groan of drains,
> Their whoop and gritty slabber. Down with
> What is done, they glump and splat.

In his early work particularly, Paulin sometimes gets easy effects by lines like "Something made a fuck of things." Sometimes, however, he does not, as in "A buggered sun" or "Perfected girls equipped with cunts and tits." Sometimes his searching for effect creates an imagery as muddled as it is striking, as these lines from "Desertmartin":

> . . . in Desertmartin's sandy light,
> I see a culture of twigs and bird-shit
> Waving a gaudy flag it loves and curses.

Dotted profusely throughout the later poems are esoteric or sometimes possibly coined words: "fremd," "glubbed," "savin," "glooby," "clagged," "skrimshandering," "choggy," "mopane," "elsan," "schisty," "planished," "sangar," "dwammy," "lunk July," "yompy farts," and so on. His syntax is always clear, but his allusions are often a bit too obscure. In "S/He," for instance, the references in the last stanza to Guildhall, Vershinin, and Olga would probably refer to a Field Day production in Derry of Thomas Kilroy's* adaptation of Chekhov's play *The Seagull*—but how many common readers would know that? He does at least provide a footnote to "The Caravans on Lüneburg Heath," and if the brief references to Heidegger would help some readers, the brief discussion of Simon Dach (1605–1659) would be needed by just about everybody. To comment on Paulin's form—in a poem, say, like "I Am Nature"—would be like commenting on the form of wind, not to mention "yompy farts."

Paulin's criticism is well typified by *Ireland & the English Crisis* (1984), a collection mainly of short reviews about literature and politics. Some of the shortest pieces, while they would have been more than perceptive as fugitive reviews, seem a little thin as chapters in a book. Nevertheless, despite an academic tendency to quote a lot, Paulin writes well and is particularly worth reading on Louis MacNeice* and in a long attack on Conor Cruise O'Brien.*

WORKS: *Theoretical Locations*. Belfast: Ulsterman, 1975. (Poetry pamphlet); *Thomas Hardy: The Poetry of Perception*. London: Macmillan/Totowa, N.J.: Rowman & Littlefield, 1975; *A State of Justice*. London: Faber, 1977. (Poetry); *Personal Column*. Belfast: Ulsterman, 1978. (Poetry pamphlet); *The Strange Museum*. London: Faber, 1980. (Poetry); *The Book of Juniper*. Newcastle upon Tyne: Bloodaxe, 1981; *Liberty Tree*. London: Faber, 1983. (Poetry); *A New Look at the Language Question*. Derry: Field Day, 1983. (Essay); *Ireland & the English Crisis*. Newcastle upon Tyne: Bloodaxe, 1984. (Criticism); *The Riot Act: A Version of Sophocles'* Antigone. London: Faber, 1984; *Argument at Great Tew. A Poem*. 1985; ed., *The Faber Book of Political Verse*. London: Faber, 1986; *The Hillsborough Script: A Dramatic Satire*. London: Faber, 1986; *Fivemiletown*. London: Faber, 1987. (Poetry); *Seize the Fire: A Version of Aeschylus's* Prometheus Bound. London: Faber, 1990; ed., *The Faber Book of Vernacular Verse*. London: Faber, 1990; *Minotaur: Poetry and the Nation State*. London: Faber, 1991. (Criticism); *Selected Poems, 1972–1990*. London & Boston: Faber, [1993]; *Walking a Line*. London & Boston: Faber, [1994]. REFERENCE: Haffenden, John. "Tom Paulin." In *Viewpoints: Poets in Conversation*. London: Faber, 1981, pp. 157–173.

PAYNE, BASIL (1928–   ), poet. Payne was born in Dublin on July 22, 1928. He was educated at the Christian Brothers school in Synge Street and at University College, Dublin. He has lectured at various universities and colleges on the Continent, in Canada, and in the United States, and he received the Guinness

Poetry Award at the Cheltenham Festival in 1964 and 1966. He has published three volumes of original verse and a couple of translations from the French and German. He is an easily understood and undemanding writer whose work seems to have moved from conventional form and somewhat pedestrian statement to what is not so much poetry as language to be recited. The work in his most recent volume, *Another Kind of Optimism* (1974), sometimes resorts to the primary devices of poetry, rhyme and meter, but the pieces are basically inflated epigrams or squashed essays. If his longer pieces are difficult to defend and tend to sink into the banal, his shorter ones are sometimes arresting, and practically all of them have a conversational fluency. Thus far, his work does not have enough form or wit to be important light verse, but it is not unpleasant entertainment.

WORKS: *Sunlight on a Square.* Dublin: Augustine, 1961; *Love in the Afternoon.* Dublin: Gill & Macmillan, 1971; *Another Kind of Optimism.* Dublin: Gill & Macmillan, 1974.

PEARSE, MARY BRIGID (1884–1947), novelist. Pearse, the sister of Patrick Pearse,* was born and raised in Dublin, edited a family memoir about her brother, and wrote one novel.

WORKS: *The Murphys of Ballystack.* Dublin: Gill, 1917; *The Home Life of Padraig Pearse: As Told by Himself, His Family and Friends.* Dublin: Browne & Nolan, 1935.

PEARSE, PATRICK [HENRY] (1879–1916), patriot, teacher, and man of letters. Pearse is best known for his involvement in the Easter Rising of 1916 and his subsequent execution by a British firing squad on May 3, 1916. During the two years preceding the Rising, he was the leading public spokesman for Ireland's separatism by physical force. When he read the Proclamation of the Irish Republic on the steps of Dublin's General Post Office, he was the president of the shortlived Republic's provisional government and commander-in-chief of its military forces. Yet, Pearse was not a politician or a military man, nor, looking at his private life and public deeds up to 1912, would one have expected him to have become an adherent of armed rebellion. He was a shy, gentle, and pious man whose main interests were language, literature, and education. These interests were channeled into Ireland's cultural revival; cultural nationalism led Pearse to political nationalism and, ultimately, to the belief that only through the use of arms could his nation wrest independence from England.

Born in Dublin on November 10, 1879, Pearse received his schooling from the Christian Brothers at Westland Row and then went on to earn a B.A. at University College, Dublin (then affiliated with the Royal University), and a B.L. at King's Inns, both in 1901. In 1903, he became the editor of the Gaelic League's weekly newspaper, *An Claidheamh Soluis (The Sword of Light),* continuing in that position until late 1909, when the school he had founded in 1908, St. Enda's, began to make heavy demands upon his time.

Pearse's interests in education, the Gaelic language, and literature are evident in his journalism for *An Claidheamh.* The newspaper played a leading role in the campaign to get Irish spoken in the schools, pulpits, and homes of Ireland, and Pearse argued for the improvement of teaching methods in the schools. In numberless editorials, articles, and book reviews, he discussed literary theory and practice in relation to what had been done by the Gaelic writers of the past and what should be tried by those attempting to build a new literature in the present.

Despite his many activities connected with St. Enda's and the Gaelic League, Pearse found time to write some plays, short stories, and poems. Between 1909 and 1916, he wrote eight dramatic works, six of them in Gaelic, expressly for production at St. Enda's: they include two outdoor pageants based on the *Táin Bó Cualigne,* a passion play, and four one-act plays. All these works had religious or heroic themes, and sometimes both. Although Pearse was not a good dramatist and further limited himself by writing for his students, he did produce playable pieces with moments of dramatic intensity. They have interest as products of the Irish Revival and as revelations of the ideas that motivated their author. *The Singer,* composed in English late in 1915 and dealing openly with rebellion and the theme of blood-sacrificing, is the best known. Despite stilted dialogue, the play contains passages of poetic beauty and rhetorical power. Proclaiming the messianic message that heroic self-sacrificing can free Ireland, *The Singer* is a literary analogue for the event of Easter 1916.

The ten short stories in Irish, published in *Iosagan and Other Stories* (1907) and *The Mother and Other Stories* (1916), are important in the history of the Gaelic language and literature revival. They helped to establish a prose style based on spoken Gaelic rather than the archaic, literary Gaelic of previous centuries, and they provided examples of the modern short story, as opposed to the folktale, in Irish. The first collection, *Iosagan,* is marred by sentimentality and idealization of the Irish-speaking inhabitants of Connemara, particularly the children. In addition, the stories are imperfectly shaped and structured, and the narrative method is often unpolished and lacks sophistication. In four of the stories of the second collection, Pearse moved from the child's world, which had dominated *Iosagan,* to that of the adult, exhibiting improved technique, increased control of structure and form, and a deeper awareness of life's struggles. "The Dearg Daol," with its restrained and reticent narration and open ending, and its view of lives of quiet desperation, is a successful story. With "Brigid of the Songs" and "The Keening Woman," "The Dearg Daol" indicates its author had a developing, though modest, talent for prose narrative.

Pearse's poetry represents his best creative achievement. Between 1905 and 1916, he fashioned ten poems in English and eighteen in Gaelic. "The Fool," "The Rebel," and "The Mother," because of their relevance to the Rising of 1916, are the best known. Composed in late 1915, when *The Singer* was written, these poems convey the idealism, dedication, and determination that characterized Ireland's struggle for freedom. First-person dramatic lyrics in free verse, they derive their rhetorical power from direct statement, sincerity of tone, effective employment of Biblical allusion, and repetitive diction and syntax. The twelve Gaelic lyrics of *Suantraidhe agus Goltraidhe (Songs of Sleep and Sorrow)* (1914) are far superior to the poems in English. Using elements of both the syllabic and accentual systems of Gaelic prosody, Pearse wrote lyrics characterized by simplicity and economy of diction, directness of statement, and careful structuring based on skillfully arranged patterns of word, phrase, sound, and image. The general tone of the collection is quiet, serious, and sad; the themes include the transitory nature of earthly pleasure and beauty, the joy and innocence of youth, the sorrow and experience of adulthood, and the inevitable coming of death. With poems such as "A Woman of the Mountain Keens Her Son," "Why Do Ye Torture Me?" and "Naked I Saw Thee" (sometimes titled "Renunciation" in English translation), Pearse brought Gaelic poetry into the twentieth century and carved a recognized place for himself in the Irish poetic tradition.

With his work in the Irish Volunteers and the Irish Republican Brotherhood, his active involvement in the Gaelic League, his educational experiment at St. Enda's, and his creative efforts in the Irish language, Patrick Pearse made a significant contribution to Ireland's political and cultural life.

RAYMOND J. PORTER

PRINCIPAL WORKS: *Collected Works of P. H. Pearse. Plays, Stories, Poems.* Dublin: Maunsel, 1917; *Political Writings and Speeches.* Dublin: Talbot, 1952; *The Literary Writings of Patrick Pearse,* Sean O Buachalla, ed. Cork: Mercier, 1979. REFERENCES: Deane, Seamus. "Pearse: Writing and Chivalry." In *Celtic Revivals: Essays in Modern Irish Literature.* London & Boston: Faber, 1985, pp. 63–74; Edwards, Ruth Dudley. *Patrick Pearse: The Triumph of Failure.* London: Gollancz, 1977; Moran, Sean Farrell. *Patrick Pearse and the Politics of Redemption: The Mind of the Easter Rising, 1916.* Washington, D.C.: Catholic University of America Press, [1994]; Porter, Raymond J. *P. H. Pearse.* New York Twayne, 1973.

PENDER, MARGARET T. (1865–?), novelist and poet. Pender was born Margaret O'Doherty and was the daughter of a farmer in County Antrim. She was educated at the Ballyrobin National School and at the Convent of Mercy in Belfast. She married soon after leaving school and contributed a stream of stories and popular verse to Irish journals. Her Irish historical novels were full of incident, but of only mild literary importance.

WORKS IN ENGLISH: *The Green Cockade. A Tale of Ulster in 'Ninety-eight.* Dublin: Sealy, 1898/Dublin: Martin Lester, [1920]; *Married in May.* Dublin: Martin Lester, [1920]; *The Bog of Lilies.* Dublin & Cork: Talbot, 1927; *The Spearman of the North.* Dublin & Cork: Talbot, 1931.

PESKETT, WILLIAM (1952–   ), poet. Born in Belfast.

WORKS: *The Night-owls' Dissection.* London: Secker & Warburg, 1975; *Survivors.* London: Secker & Warburg, 1980.

PETRIE, GEORGE (1790–1866), antiquarian, artist, musician, and scholar. Petrie, one of the most distinguished Irishmen of the nineteenth century, was born in Dublin in 1790. Much of his work of reclaiming the Irish past is not overtly concerned with literature, although *The Petrie Collection of the Ancient*

Music of Ireland (1852) is most significant. With Caesar Otway,* Petrie edited *The Dublin Penny Journal,* and he later edited *The Irish Penny Journal* (1840–1841), to which Carleton,* Mangan,* and Ferguson,* as well as his brilliant assistants on the Ordnance Topographical Survey, O'Curry* and O'Donovan,* contributed. He died in Rathmines on January 17, 1866.

WORKS: *On the History & Antiquities of Tara Hill.* Dublin: Printed by R. Graisberry, 1839; *The Ecclesiastical Architecture of Ireland.* Dublin: Hodges & Smith, 1845. (Contains his 1833 essay "The Round Towers of Ireland"); *The Petrie Collection of the Ancient Music of Ireland.* 2 vols. Dublin: University Press, 1855–1882; *Christian Inscriptions in the Irish Language.* 2 vols. Dublin: Royal Historical & Archaeological Association of Ireland, 1872–1878. REFERENCES: Calder, G. J. *George Petrie and the Ancient Music of Ireland.* Dublin: Dolmen, 1968; Dillon, Myles. "George Petrie (1789–1866)." *Studies* (Autumn 1967): 266–276; Hutchinson, J. *The Dynamics of Cultural Nationalism: The Gaelic Revival and the Creation of the Irish Nation State.* London: Allen & Unwin, 1987; Sheehy, J. *The Rediscovery of Ireland's Past: The Celtic Revival 1830–1930.* London: Thames & Hudson, 1980; Stokes, W. *The Life and Labours in Art and Archaeology of G. Petrie.* London: Longmans, 1868.

PHELAN, [JAMES LEO] "JIM" (1895–1966), novelist and short story writer. Phelan was born in Dublin in 1895 into a poor family. Although brilliant in school, he preferred the life of the streets and had little formal education. He held many jobs in a long, wandering career. As a young man, he became an actor in such fit-up companies as Roberto Lena's. He was also a blacksmith, bank clerk, journalist, film technician, scriptwriter, novelist, and tramp. He is said to have been twice sentenced to death and to have spent fourteen years in prison, in Dartmoor and in Parkhurst. He wrote many short stories and some novels as well as factual studies of criminals, gypsies, and tramps. Like Patrick MacGill,* Sean O'Casey,* and Liam O'Flaherty,* he was somewhat outside the literary tradition, and his work is permeated by his strong, forceful personality. At his frequent less than best, he degenerates into the shortcuts of poor slick writing, his themes become simplistic, and his characters become the stereotypes of brutal machismo. Nevertheless, his vigorous talent deserves attention, and his adventurous and obscure life deserves investigation.

WORKS: . . . *Museum.* New York: W. Morrow, 1937; *Green Volcano.* London: P. Davies, [1938]; *Lifer.* London: P. Davies, 1938; *Ten-a-Penny People.* London: Gollancz, 1938; . . . *In the Can.* London: M. Joseph, 1939; . . . *Churchill Can Unite Ireland.* London: Gollancz, 1940; *Jail Journey.* London: Secker & Warburg, 1940; *Ireland—Atlantic Gateway.* London: John Lane, [1941]; *Letters from the Big House.* London: Cresset, 1943; . . . *And Blackthorns.* London: Nicholson & Watson, [1944]/published in America as *Banshee Harvest,* New York: Viking, 1945; *Moon in the River.* New York: A. A. Wyn, [1946]; *Turf-Fire Tales.* London: Heinemann, [1947]; *Bog Blossom Stories.* London: Sidgwick & Jackson, [1948]; *The Name's Phelan.* London: Sidgwick & Jackson, [1948]. (Autobiography); *We Follow the Roads.* London: Phoenix House, [1949]/Longcraft: Country Book Club, 1950; *Vagabond Cavalry.* London & New York: T. U. Boardman, [1951]; *Wagon-Wheels.* London: Harrap, [1951]; *The Underworld.* London: Harrap, [1953]/London: Tandem, 1967; *Tramp at Anchor.* London: Harrap, [1954]; *Tramping the Toby.* London: Burke, [1955]; *Criminals in Real Life.* London: Burke, [1956]; *Fetters for Twenty.* London: Burke, [1957]; *Nine Murderers and Me.* London: Phoenix House, 1967; *Meet the Criminal Class.* London: Tallis, 1969.

PHELAN, TOM (1940–), novelist. Phelan was born in the Irish Midlands and educated at St. Patrick's Seminary, Carlow. Ordained, he worked in England and then emigrated to the United States in 1970. He attended the University of Seattle, left the priesthood, and now lives on Long Island with his wife and two children.

His *In the Season of the Daisies* (1993) is set in a Midland village in 1948, on the eve of a visit by Sean T. O'Kelly and Eamon de Valera for the inauguration of a new wing to the Catholic church. The story is told from several points of view, but most are preoccupied with a grisly Irish Republican Army murder of a little boy and the maiming of his twin brother that occurred years before in 1921. There is considerable overlapping of both past and present actions, but the horrific detail of the murder becomes ever more gruesomely full and clear. The townspeople are divided between the almost fiendishly horrible and the pathetically guilt-ridden. Perhaps the most telling chapters are those seen through the mind of Seanie Doolin, the surviving brother who, now a grown man, lives on the periphery of society, most of his wits gone, frightened, tormented, and haunted by his brother's death. There is something of Faulkner's Benjy from *The Sound and the Fury* in Seanie, and his repetitive, almost incantatory memories catch the quality of his mind and the intensity of his suffering. This is a powerful book, but many of its characters are monsters. One symptom of the disgust and fury with which Irish society of the day is excoriated would seem to be the author's obsession with excrement.

WORKS: *In the Season of the Daisies.* [Dublin]: Lilliput, [1993]; *Iscariot.* Dingle: Brandon, 1995.

PHILIBIN, AN. *See* POLLOCK, JOHN H.

PHILIPS, AMBROSE (1675–1749), poet and pastoralist, playwright, translator, journalist, editor, and essayist. Philips was educated at St. John's College, Cambridge, where he received both a B.A. and M.A. He was elected a fellow in 1699 and held that title until resigning sometime in March 1708. He evidently had varied, intermittent, and minor diplomatic and military careers in Holland, Spain, and at the Battle of Almanza in 1707. He was captured by the French but returned to England. Steele* published Phillips' poem addressed to his patron, the earl of Dorset, dated Copenhagen, March 9, 1709, in *Tatler* No. 12, calling it a *Winter-Piece* worthy of the most skillful painter. It reveals a certain talent for the picturesque and sensitive handling of imagery:

> The ruddy morn disclos'd at once to view
> The face of nature in a rich disguise,
> And brighten'd ev'ry object to my eyes:
> For ev'ry shrub, and ev'ry blade of grass,
> And ev'ry pointed thorn, seem'd wrought in glass;
> In pearls and rubies rich the hawthorns show,
> While through the ice the crimson berries glow.

Philips was, at this point, on friendly terms with Swift,* despite being connected with the Addison-Steele circle of Whig writers and politicians for whom Swift was ambivalent. Later, he became secretary of the Hanover Club, an organization formed to secure the succession of George I, a position that suited his Whiggish sympathies. His notorious *Pastorals* were printed, along with Pope's, in Tonson's *Miscellanies* in 1709, a publishing event that earned him from Swift the playful sobriquet "Pastoral" Philips. It was also an event that had unforeseen consequences in literary history, giving him a reputation as a harmless figure of fun.

Philips had apparent success as a tragic dramatist. His *The Distressed Mother,* adapted from Racine's *Andromaque,* drew a prologue from Steele* and an epilogue by either Addison or Eustace Budgell, a miscellaneous writer satirized by Pope in *The Dunciad* and the *Epistle to Dr. Arbuthnot.* In *Spectator* No. 290, Steele commented on the play that "it is every where Nature," thus invoking the age's most honorific critical term. Noting Phillips's avoidance of the bombastic rhetoric that so often marred heroic tragedy, Steele exclaims, "I congratulate to the Age, that they are at last to see Truth and humane Life represented in the Incidents which concern Heroes and Heroines." Later on Addison describes leaving the playhouse "highly pleased . . . with the Performance of the Excellent Piece," noting the satisfaction the performance had given his companion Sir Roger de Coverley, the fictional old-fashioned country squire: "Why there is not a single Sentence in this Play that I do not know the Meaning of" (*Spectator,* No. 335). Reportedly, Pope was less sanguine about the play's artistic achievement, complaining that the audience was composed of a Whig claque assembled to support Philips.

Philips founded the periodical *The Free-Thinker,* a credible successor to the *Tatler, Spectator,* and *Guardian,* but more blatantly partisan, active in its support of the earl of Stanhope's Whig ministry, of latitudinarianism in religion, and of Cartesian and Lockean philosophies. Thus, the general tenor of the writing was polemical despite the employment of the character mask of Mr. Freethinker, which would suggest, like the mask of Mr. Spectator, a pose of impartiality, objectivity, and political disinterest. It was published twice weekly and ran for 350 issues, between 1718 and 1728. The preface to the collected edition of 1739 speaks of Philips as "the Author of some of these Papers, and Editor of them all." *The Free-Thinker* published some of Philips' prose pieces, some poems, his translations of Fenelon, and a reprint of the 1707 *Persian Tales,* which inspired one of Pope's most scathing couplets: "The Bard whom Pilf'red Pastorals renown, / Who turns a *Persian* Tale for half a crown" (*Epistle to Dr. Arbuthnot*), the cost of an ordinary London prostitute. Among its contributors were possibly Steele himself and other notables in political, ecclesiastical, and literary circles. The most important of these for Philips' future career was Hugh Boulter, who became archbishop of Armagh in 1724. Philips accompanied Boulter to Ireland as his secretary and procured a seat in the Irish House of Commons and later judicial appointments through Boulter's offices.

Philips also came again to the attention of Swift, in circumstances that were, in many ways, a replay of Philips's continual, but seldom successful, search for preferment during the years of the Tory government of Harley and Lord Bolingbroke. At this time Swift and Pope were on more or less amicable terms with the Addison-Steele circle of wits who met at Button's Coffee-House and to which Philips had links. "This evening," Swift wrote to Stella in September 1711, "I met Addison and Pastoral Philips in the Park, and supped with them at Addison's lodgings; we were very good company." A number of references in the *Journal to Stella* attest to Swift's active solicitude in easing Philips' preferment plight. He noted in December 1710 that Addison importuned his help "to make another of his friends Queen's secretary at Geneva; and I'll do it if I can; it is poor Pastoral Philips." In a letter to Philips, Swift indicated his friendship: "Mr. Addison and I drink [your health] often. He loves you very well, and you can hardly have a better Possession, upon every Account imaginable."

But there is another side to this pose of camaraderie and mutual support among Swift, Philips, and Addison. In the context of party divisions and hostilities of the day, such professions of friendship should be viewed somewhat skeptically. Political differences could sour relationships based on shared literary interests. Swift's bitterness at times is notable; as he wrote to Stella in July 1711, "I will do nothing for Philips; I find him more a puppy than ever, so don't solicit for him."

After Philips accompanied Boulter to Ireland, Swift wrote to Pope, "Philips is a complainer, and on this occasion I told Lord Carteret that complainers never succeed at court though railers do." During this period, Philips was writing a series of poems to Daniel Pulteney's and Lord Lieutenant Carteret's infant daughters. These "little Flams," as Swift contemptuously calls them, earned Philips the infamous name of "Namby-Pamby," a term of derision coined in 1726 in a Philips parody by the Dublin wit Henry Carey. These nursery verses, written to court favor, seem by modern standards embarrassingly puerile and hopelessly sentimental. "Dimply damsel, sweetly smiling"; "Little Charm of placid mien, / Miniature of beauty's queen"; "Timely blossom, infant fair, / Fondling of a happy pair"; and so forth. There has been notable critical dissent, however. Samuel Johnson, in his *Life of Philips,* found them Philips's happiest productions: "The numbers are smooth and spritely, and the diction is seldom faulty." Had they been written by Addison, he avers, "they would have had admirers." Indeed, a recent apologist claims for these poems "moments of solidity and insight," especially in describing the development of a child's sexuality.

Philips most likely would be a forgotten figure, his *Pastorals* relegated to the obscure status of so many conventional products of the Augustan pastoral mode, had not Pope written his famous critique. Some critics suggest that Gay may have assisted, but, in any event, *Guardian* No. 40 is one of Pope's wittiest, most mischievous, and skillful satiric put-downs. It is a tour de force of satiric prose, and one wonders why Steele published such a frontal attack on his fellow Whig and literary protégé. It guarantees lasting, but dubious, fame for the feckless Philips, who took such umbrage, so the story goes, that he kept a rod at Button's to use on Pope if he dared to step inside. Like Swift's *Modest Proposal,* it constitutes an exercise in extended irony in which the ironic mask is allowed to drop just enough to signal satiric intentions. In it, Pope seemingly attacks his own way of writing pastoral and praises Philips' method. His clever juxtapositioning of banal passages from Philips with his own sophisticated achievement produces ironic incongruities of hilarious proportions:

With what Simplicity [Philips] introduces two Shepherds singing alternatively.

> *Hobb.* Come, Rosalind, O come, for without thee
> What Pleasure can the Country have for me:
> Come, Rosalind, O come; my brinded Kine,
> My snowy Sheep, my Farm, and all is thine.

Our other Pastoral Writer, in expressing the same Thought, deviates into downright Poetry.

> *Streph.* In Spring the Fields, in Autumn Hills I love,
> At Morn the Plains, at Noon the shady Grove,
> But Delia always; forc'd from Delia's Sight,
> Nor Plains at Morn, nor Groves at Noon delight.

Another effective irony is profusely praising while resolutely blaming. Having compared passages from the two pastoralists, Pope says tongue-in-cheek:

it is a Justice I owe to Mr. Philips, to discover those in which no Man can compare with him. First, That beautiful Rusticity, of which I shall only produce two Instances, out of a hundred not yet quoted.

> O woful Day! O Day of Woe, quothe he,
> And woful, I, who live the Day to see!

That Simplicity of Diction, the Melancholy Flowing of the Numbers, the Solemnity of the Sound, and the easie Turn of the Words, in this Dirge (to make use of our Author's Expression) are extremely Elegant.

These poems did (and still do) have their defenders. In *Spectator* No. 400, for instance, Steele cites the "delicate and careful Spirit of Modesty" and "prevailing gentle Art" of Philips' eclogues; and Addison, in *Spectator* No. 223, approves the realism of the English settings as against the bookish artifice of the Virgilian classical model.

Addison's point raises a number of aesthetic issues with implications beyond the specific debate over pastoral forms and styles. Like the controversy between ancients and moderns, between humanistic learning and scientific rationalism, the quarrel here involves an ongoing dispute in the eighteenth century. Pope espoused the so-called neoclassical perspective of Rapin and the Virgilian image of a pastoral golden age; Philips adopted the "rationalist" attitude of Fontenelle, which demanded rustic realism and simplicity, though highly idealized, rarified, and literary.

Complicating the argument over aesthetics was an interaction of often explosive personal and political biases, including the neglect that Pope felt at the hands of the Whig literary establishment and his outsider status as a Catholic. These writers continually promoted one another's literary careers. A good example is the remark in Philips' preface to his *Pastorals* that "Virgil and Spenser made use of [pastoral] as a prelude to Epic Poetry," an association Thomas Tickell and others cultivated for Philips in the five *Guardian* essays preceding Pope's. This self-aggrandizement infuriated Pope, who was deliberately modeling his own career on the same pattern of genres and heroic ambition. Of course, this famous episode in literary history puts into sharp focus aesthetic considerations, but it also tells something about the complicated political and personal concerns that characterized the literary world of Augustan England.

DONALD C. MELL

WORKS: *A Collection of Old Ballads.* 3 vols. London: J. Roberts, 1723–1725; *Three Tragedies.* London: J. Tonson, 1725; *Pastorals, Epistles, Odes, and Other Original Poems, with Translations from Pindar, Anacreon, and Sappho by Ambrose Philips.* London: J. & R. Tonson, 1738; *A Variorum Text of Four Pastorals by Ambrose Philips.* R. H. Griffith, ed. *Texas Studies in English* 12 (1932); *The Poems of Ambrose Philips.* Mary G. Segar, ed. Oxford: Blackwell, 1937. REFERENCES: *Dictionary of National Biography;* Ehrenpreis, Irvin. *Swift: The Man, His Works, and the Age.* 3 vols. Cambridge: Harvard University Press, 1962–1983; Fogle, S. F. "Notes on Ambrose Philips." *Modern Language Notes* 54 (May 1939): 354–359; *The Guardian.* John Calhoun Stephens, ed. Lexington: University of Kentucky Press, 1983; Johnson, Samuel. *The Lives of the Poets.* George Birkbeck Hill, ed. 3 vols. Oxford: Clarendon, 1905; Joost, Nicholas. "The Authorship of the *Free-Thinker.*" In *Studies in the Early English Periodical.* Richmond P. Bond, ed. Chapel Hill: University of North Carolina Press, 1987, pp. 105–133; Mack, Maynard. *Alexander Pope: A Life.* New York: Norton, 1985; Nokes, David. *John Gay: A Profession of Friendship.* New York: Oxford University Press, 1995; Pope, Alexander. *The Correspondence of Alexander Pope.* George Sherburn, ed. 5 vols. Oxford: Clarendon, 1956; Pope, Alexander. *The Poems of Alexander Pope.* John Butt et al., eds. 11 vols. New Haven, Conn.: Yale University Press, 1939–1969; *The Spectator.* Donald F. Bond, ed. 5 vols. Oxford: Clarendon, 1965; Spence, Joseph. *Observations, Anecdotes, and Characters of Books and Men.* James M. Osborne, ed. 2 vols. Oxford: Clarendon, 1966; Swift, Jonathan. *The Correspondence of Jonathan Swift.* Harold Williams, ed. 5 vols. Oxford: Clarendon, 1963; Swift, Jonathan. *Journal to Stella.* Harold Williams, ed. 2 vols. Oxford: Clarendon, 1948; *The Tatler.* Donald F. Bond, ed. 3 vols. Oxford: Clarendon, 1987.

PHILIPS, WILLIAM (ca. 1675–1734), playwright. Philips was the son of George Philips, the governor of Londonderry, whose warning probably sent the Apprentice Boys to lock the city gates against Lord Antrim's men in 1688. Philips himself became a captain in the army and served on the Continent. He wrote plays from an early age, and his *The Revengeful Queen,* a "bloodbath" tragedy taken from Machiavelli's *History of Florence,* was performed at Drury Lane in 1698. In 1700, his Irish comedy, *St. Stephen's Green,* was performed at the Theatre Royal, Smock Alley, in Dublin. A late Restoration comedy of manners, it looks more forward to the sentimental comedy of Colley Cibber and Richard Steele,* rather than backward to the tougher, more amoral comedy of

Wycherley and Vanbrugh. There is, as Christopher Murray noted, some vigor in the character of Sir Francis Feignyouth, but the play is basically an unoriginal and innocuous piece. It is notable mainly for being nearly the first play to utilize an Irish setting, but if one changed a couple of Irish place-names to English ones, there would be little Irish about it. After an interval of more than twenty years, Philips had an Irish tragedy, *Hibernia Freed,* performed at the Theatre Royal, Lincoln's Inn Fields, on February 13, 1722. This play was about the liberation of Ireland from a Danish invader called Turgesius, and Brian Boru was anachronistically one of the characters. Genest, the stage historian, called it ''a dull Tragedy with little or no incident till the 5th act.'' Philip's final piece, *Belisarius* (1724), a five-act verse tragedy, was admired by Allardyce Nicoll. Philips died on December 12, 1734.

WORKS: *The Revengeful Queen: A Tragedy.* London: P. Buck, 1698; *St. Stephen's Green; Or, the Generous Lovers: A Comedy.* Dublin: J. Brocas, 1700/Christopher Murray, ed. Dublin: Cadenus, 1979; *Hibernia Freed; A Tragedy.* London: J. Bowyer, 1722; *Belisarius: a Tragedy.* London: T. Woodward, 1724. REFERENCE: Murray, Christopher. ''Introduction'' to the Cadenus edition.

PILKINGTON, LAETITIA (1712?–1750), autobiographer and poet. Pilkington's mother (née Meade) was an Irish gentlewoman; her father, Van Lewen, was a man-midwife of Dutch descent. Pilkington's reputation rests on her *Memoirs* (1748–1754), the last volume of which was published posthumously by her son. During the 1730s, Pilkington and her clergyman husband, Matthew,* were part of a literary and social circle centered on Jonathan Swift.* In February 1737/38, the Pilkingtons were divorced in the ecclesiastical courts on the grounds of Laetitia's adultery. She subsequently left Dublin for London, where she made a living through hack writing and a small print shop. Her circumstances were difficult, and at one time she was imprisoned for debt. She returned to Dublin, where she died in August 1750.

The *Memoirs,* a defense of Pilkington's reputation offered as ''a warning'' to other women, also contains poetry by her along with anecdotes of ''several eminent persons.'' The tone of the work is defiant and vigorous, and Pilkington's commentary on her adventures is sharp and witty. Her account of Swift—a rude, wrathful figure, given to obscenities and physical violence—was much exploited by subsequent writers, including Thackeray.* Its accuracy is uncertain. The *Memoirs* also deserves attention for Pilkington's self-conscious presentation of herself as a writer and wit. She recounts how, as a five-year-old, she was surprised reading ''Alexander's Feast'' aloud and comments that from being a reader she ''quickly became a Writer.'' Pilkington's delight in her own creative powers is one of the most attractive elements of her work.

AILEEN DOUGLAS

WORKS: *The Statues; or, the Trial of Constancy.* London, 1739; *The Memoirs of Mrs. Laetitia Pilkington . . . Wherein Are Occasionally Interspersed, All Her Poems, with Anecdotes of Several Eminent Persons, Living and Dead. . . .* 2 vols. Dublin: Printed for the Author, 1748/Vol. 3. London, 1754/London: G. Routledge & Sons, [1928]. REFERENCES: Barry, Iris. Introduction to the 1928 edition of *The Memoirs;* Relke, Diana M. A. ''In Search of Mrs. Pilkington.'' In *Gender at Work:*

Four Women Writers of the Eighteenth Century. Anne Messenger, ed. Detroit: Wayne State University Press, 1990, pp. 114–150; Woolf, Virginia. "The Lives of the Obscure." In *The Common Reader,* 1st series. London: Hogarth, 1925/rpt., London: Hogarth, 1962, pp. 146–167.

PILKINGTON, MATTHEW (1701?–1774), poet and clergyman. Pilkington was the son of a clock maker and was born in Ballyboy, King's County (now County Offaly). He was educated at Trinity College, Dublin, and ordained in the Church of Ireland. He was the husband of Laetitia* and part of Jonathan Swift's* literary circle. The Preface to his *Poems on Several Occasions* (1730) claims that Swift "honour'd [the collection] with his Corrections and Remarks." Swift initially furthered Pilkington's career but later denounced him as "falsest rogue" in the kingdom. Much of Pilkington's poetry is highly conventional, but he could turn an elegant compliment in verse. His poem "The Gift" celebrates Swift as a gift of the gods to "Oppress'd Hibernia," while his "The Invitation to Doctor Delany at Delville" charmingly exploits town/country oppositions. The *Dictionary of National Biography* erroneously states that, after separating from his wife, Pilkington "fell into evil habits and obscurity" and that he is not to be confused with Matthew Pilkington, vicar of Donabate and Portrane and author of *The Gentleman's and Connoisseur's Dictionary of Painters* (1770). In fact, as F. Elrington Ball has established, both are the same person. *The Dictionary* remained a standard work well into the nineteenth century.

AILEEN DOUGLAS

WORKS: *Poems on Several Occasions.* Dublin: G. Faulkner, 1730/*Poems on Several Occasions . . . with several Poems not in the Dublin edition . . . Revised by . . . Dr. Swift.* London: T. Woodward, 1731; *The Gentleman's and Connoisseur's Dictionary of Painters.* London, 1770. (New editions appeared until 1857). REFERENCES: Ehrenpreis, Irvin. *Swift: The Man, His Works and the Age.* Cambridge: Harvard University Press, 1983; Fagan, Patrick. *A Georgian Celebration.* Dublin: Branar, [1989]. (Contains a note on Pilkington and several of his poems); Pilkington, John Carteret. *The Life of John Cartaret Pilkington. . . .* London, 1761. (Also contains some of Pilkington's verse); Pilkington, Laetitia. *The Memoirs of Mrs. Laetitia Pilkington, . . .* 2 vols. Dublin: Printed for the Author, 1748. Pilkington's will, in which he describes his children by Laetitia as "abandoned wretches," is reproduced by F. E. Ball in *Notes and Queries,* 11th series, 6 (July 27, 1912).

PIM, HERBERT MOORE (1883–?), poet, novelist, and nonfiction writer. Born in Belfast and educated as a Quaker, Pim became a Catholic nationalist about 1918 and is later said to have reverted to Unionism.

SELECTED WORKS: *Unknown Immortals in the Northern City of Success.* Dublin: Talbot, 1917. (Belfast sketches); As A. Newman. *The Pessimist: A Confession.* London: David Nutt, 1914. (Autobiographical). *Sayings from an Ulster Valley.* London: Grant Richards, 1920. (Poetry); *New Poems and a Preface.* London: Burns, Oates, 1927. (Poetry).

PIM, SHEILA (1909–1995), novelist and nonfiction writer. Pim was born in Dublin of a well-known Quaker family and was educated at the French School in Bray and at La Casita in Lausanne. She went to Girton College, Oxford, in 1928 and took a modern languages tripos in French and Italian. She worked first as a shorthand typist for the Royal Dublin Society. Illness forced her to leave this post, and while recuperating during the first years of the war, she wrote her first book, *Getting Better* (1945), "a handbook for convalescents" that contained much sensible and amusing advice. For many years she was the honorary secretary of the Dublin branch of Irish P.E.N., and in the 1950s she was honorary treasurer of the Dundrum District Nursing Association and a member of the Council of the Royal Horticultural Association of Ireland. She wrote four detective novels and three lighthearted satirical novels, which now have a certain period charm, drawing on backgrounds in gardening, painting, and cottage industries that she knew well. She has been concerned with social work, especially with the travelers. Another interest is contemporary painting, and in 1951 she provided an introduction to the catalog of Patrick Hennesy's first retrospective exhibition. Her most important work, however, is her biography of the Irish botanist and explorer Augustus Henry, a very important but previously neglected figure in Irish science, who introduced many new varieties of Chinese plants into European gardens. In later years, she was involved with the running of the Society of Friends Historical Library House in Donnybrook, and with a friend she wrote a history of the Friends Meeting House in Eustace Street, *Quakers in Eustace Street* (1985). She died in Dublin on December 16, 1995.

PETER COSTELLO

WORKS: *Getting Better. A Handbook for Convalescents*. London: Faber, 1945; *Common or Garden Crime*. London: Hodder & Stoughton, 1945. (Detective novel); *Creeping Venom*. London: Hodder & Stoughton, 1946. (Detective novel); *Bringing the Garden Indoors*. London: My Garden, 1949; *The Flowering Shamrock*. London: Hodder & Stoughton, 1949. (Novel); *A Brush with Death*. London: Hodder & Stoughton, 1950. (Detective novel); *A Hive of Suspects*. London: Hodder & Stoughton, 1952. (Detective novel); *Other People's Business*. London: Hodder & Stoughton, 1957. (Novel); *The Sheltered Garden*. London: Hodder & Stoughton, 1964. (Novel); *The Wood and the Trees. A Biography of Augustine Henry*. London: Macdonald, 1966/rev. with additional material by Charles Nelson, Kilkenny: Boethius, 1984; with Annelies Becker. *Quakers in Eustace Street*. Waterford: Friendly, 1985.

PLUNKETT, JAMES (1920–   ), novelist, short story writer, playwright, and essayist. Born on May 21, 1920, in the Sandymount area of Dublin, James Plunkett (pseudonym of James Plunkett Kelly) has earned a well-deserved reputation as one of Ireland's finest novelists and short story writers. Plunkett's works are steeped in the realistic tradition of the generation before his, and he carries on the legacy of writers such as Frank O'Connor,* Sean O'Faolain,* and Peadar O'Donnell.*

Plunkett was educated at the Christian Brothers school in Synge Street, Dublin, where his interests in reading and writing were developed at an early age. Plunkett's primary passion, however, was music, and he studied the violin and viola at the Dublin College of Music from the age of eight to twenty-three. At seventeen, Plunkett left school and went to work for the gas company. This was to have a great influence on his life because he became involved with the Workers' Union of Ireland, took on the duties of branch and staff secretary in 1946, and worked for the great labor leader Jim Larkin. Though Plunkett worked with

Larkin for only a year, that experience had an impact on his work, particularly the highly praised novel *Strumpet City.* Throughout the 1940s and 1950s, Plunkett's short stories appeared in *The Bell* and *The Irish Bookman,* and he began to develop a literary reputation. In 1955, he visited the Soviet Union as part of a delegation invited by the Soviet secretary of the arts. The visit resulted in a number of Irish-style McCarthyites calling for his resignation from the Workers' Union. The union withstood the public pressure, but Plunkett joined Radio Éireann as the drama assistant that same year. Four of his radio plays—"Dublin Fusilier" (1952), "Mercy" (1953), "Homecoming" (1954), and "Big Jim" (1954)—had already been broadcast by the station. The move was an important one for him because it surrounded him with people involved in the arts. He later became one of the first television producers for Telefis Éireann.

In 1955, Plunkett's first collection of short stories, *The Trusting and the Maimed,* was published. His approach to the short story was greatly influenced by *The Bell's* two editors, O'Faolain and O'Donnell, and the collection illustrated what had become the Irish tradition in the modern short story—straightforward, svelte, descriptive prose. While Plunkett's stories were reminiscent of O'Faolain's and O'Connor's, his book also had Joycean* echoes. His focus, like Joyce's and O'Casey's,* was the less glamorous side of Dublin. The combination of this subject matter and a lucid style makes *The Trusting and the Maimed* an engrossing, memorable volume. Yet the work is more than a collection of disparate stories, for the twelve stories capture the stages of one's life. Four stories focus on childhood, four deal with young adulthood, and four address old age. Plunkett also writes in a variety of modes—from the humor of "The Scoop," to the savvy of "The Wearin' of the Green," to the sympathy and tenderness of "Weep for Our Pride." *The Trusting and the Maimed* remains one of the best volumes of short stories of the twentieth century and served as a striking debut. In 1977, Plunkett's second volume of stories, *Collected Short Stories,* appeared and revealed that his skill as a storyteller had continued to develop. While this volume contained only six stories written after *The Trusting and the Maimed,* those stories, particularly "Ferris Moore and the Earwig," show a break from the traditional storytelling methods, as Plunkett moves into stream-of-consciousness techniques.

After *The Trusting and the Maimed,* Plunkett turned his attention to revising his radio play "Big Jim." In 1958, a new play based on it, *The Risen People,* premiered at the Abbey Theatre.* Its successful run led to the idea of reworking the theme into a novel, and in 1969 *Strumpet City* appeared. The novel differs from its early dramatic incarnations because Larkin is more of a background character. Plunkett purposely did this because, as he once noted, "you can't mix a huge heroic figure with the ordinary life. You can hint at him alright, like a shadow looking over things, but you can't have him as true flesh and blood." *Strumpet City* is arguably Plunkett's masterpiece and was a tremendous success worldwide. The novel has since become a staple of the Irish canon.

The novel is a detailed, sweeping account of Dublin from 1907 to 1914 and the labor problems that arose in the years leading to World War I. For Plunkett, the Dublin lockout of 1913 was, in many ways, more important than the 1916 Rising, because, as he once said, "it introduced the element of organized labor which was very, very badly needed. . . . I had a desire [in *Strumpet City*] not to applaud trade unions as a system, but to show the Irish, the Dublin people, in action and the bravery they had." Plunkett's Dublin in the novel is very much a character, yet it differs from Joyce's seedy city or O'Casey's poorest-of-the-poor depiction. Plunkett's version accurately portrays the degrees of the two main social classes, the poor and the wealthy: from the pitiful Rashers Tierney to the working-class Fitz, to the isolated Father O'Connor, to the refined Bradshaws. The genius of the novel is the way in which Plunkett weaves a number of stories and connects characters from such disparate backgrounds. The details, in particular the descriptions of the decaying tenements and the often-appalling living conditions, provide *Strumpet City* a sense of historical verisimilitude. Plunkett's commitment to features of the naturalist and realist ideals makes the book one of the best Irish novels of the century.

Plunkett's next book, *The Gems She Wore: A Book of Irish Places,* was a candid observation of his homeland. The book, he once said, was "not just a travel book, but Ireland and the state of mind of Ireland, and the churches, and mythology." Frank O'Connor, who was doing a series on early Irish monasticism for Irish television, was a frequent companion who served as Plunkett's mentor about Irish architecture and myth, and *The Gems She Wore* is in the manner of O'Connor's *Irish Miles.*

In 1977, Plunkett's second novel, *Farewell Companions,* begins where *Strumpet City* ended and covers the 1920s through the mid-1940s. *Farewell Companions* is semiautobiographical, and the main character, Tim McDonagh, may be Plunkett's most endearing character. As in the first novel, Plunkett strings together a number of connecting stories. The focus, however, is on personal relationships, in particular the friendship of Tim, Brian, and Cunningham. The book is essentially about loss and how one must deal with misfortune and move on. For Tim, the losses are so great—his father dies, his good friend Cunningham dies in the war, and his girlfriend, Anna, emigrates with her family to the United States—that he finally seeks refuge in the Roman Catholic Church. *Farewell Companions* is clearly the most personal of Plunkett's novels, and indeed that is one of the book's great strengths.

The Boy on the Back Wall and Other Essays (1987) is a selection of essays that Plunkett wrote from the late 1960s to the mid-1980s. They cover some of his favorite themes: Dublin, Irish literature, and what makes good writing. Whether he is talking about Jim Larkin, Frank O'Connor, or how to write a short story, Plunkett's essays are full of insight and characteristic of an artist who has spent his life considering Ireland. His experience in radio and television gives his musings the "man-on-the-street" approach, and they well illustrate his expository talent.

Plunkett's third novel, *The Circus Animals* (1990), focuses on Ireland's struggling economy during the postwar years. The action, though, centers on a young married couple, Frank and Margaret McDonagh, and their struggle to mesh modern situations and young emotions with an inhibiting Roman Catholic Church. Plunkett underscores the generational difference of prewar and postwar Ireland in the form of Lemuel Cox, a Jonathan Swift* admirer who befriends the McDonaghs. The book again shows Plunkett's great talent of creating complex and genuine characters. While his writing style is similar to that of realists such as O'Faolain and O'Flaherty,* Plunkett's works have a distinguishing emotional depth. Through his novels, stories, plays, and essays, James Plunkett has proved a most worthy successor to *The Bell*-era writers and is certainly one of the important artists in twentieth-century Irish literature.

SHAWN O'HARE

WORKS: "Homecoming." *The Bell* (June 1954). (Radio play); *The Eagle and the Trumpets, and Other Stories.* Dublin: The Bell, 1954. (Published in August 1954 in place of Vol. 19, No. 9 of *The Bell*); *Big Jim.* Dublin: Martin O'Donnell, 1955. (Radio play); *The Trusting and the Maimed, and Other Irish Stories.* New York: Devin Adair, 1955/London: Hutchinson, 1959; *Strumpet City.* London: Hutchinson/New York: Delacorte, 1969. (Novel); *The Gems She Wore: A Book of Irish Places.* London: Hutchinson, 1972/New York: Holt Rinehart, 1973. (Travel); *Collected Short stories.* Dublin: Poolbeg, 1977; *Farewell Companions.* London: Hutchinson, 1977/New York: Coward, McCann & Geoghegan, 1978. (Novel); *The Risen People.* Dublin: Co-Op Books, 1978/revised in *Journal of Irish Literature* 21 (January 1992). (Play); *The Boy on the Back Wall and Other Essays.* Dublin: Poolbeg, 1987; *The Circus Animals.* London: Hutchinson, 1990. (Novel).

PLUNKETT, JOSEPH MARY (1887–1916), patriot and poet. Plunkett, one of the executed leaders of the Easter Rising, was born in Dublin in November 1887. He was the son of George Noble Plunkett, a poet and a papal count. For much of his life, Joseph Plunkett was in ill health, and for this reason he traveled a good deal in Europe and North Africa. He became a close friend of Thomas MacDonagh* with whom he studied Irish; they also exchanged poems and criticisms of each other's work. Plunkett was one of the founders of the Irish Volunteers and a member of the first Executive. He was also a member of the Irish Republican Brotherhood, which sent him on missions to Germany and to America. In 1916, he was director of military operations and drew up the detailed plans for the Rising. On Good Friday of 1916, he was in a nursing home recuperating from an operation, but he still took part in the fighting in the General Post Office. On the eve of his execution, he married Grace Gifford, the artist, and he was executed on May 4, 1916.

In 1911, Plunkett was associated with David Houston, James Stephens,* Padraic Colum,* and MacDonagh in the founding of the distinguished magazine *The Irish Review.** In 1913, he became its editor until its demise in 1914. Also in 1914 he was engaged with Edward Martyn* and MacDonagh in the formation of the Irish Theatre* in Hardwicke Street. He later disassociated himself from the theatre because he disapproved of the group producing Strindberg's *Easter.*

Plunkett published only one volume of poems during his lifetime: *The Circle and the Sword* (1911). A posthumous volume of the best of those poems and his later work was edited by his sister Grace, also a poet, in 1916. Plunkett is a difficult poet to assess. William Irwin Thompson wrote, "The poems show talent, but it is anybody's guess if their baroque and chryselephantine lusciousness could ever be brought under control, and once under control, directed toward greatness." It is easy to see why a critic would veer away from Plunkett's romanticism of love and even of God, and from a diction that is sometimes both conventional and florid. However, Plunkett did have a consciousness, albeit intermittent, of form. And, too, he did have some partial successes. To argue analogously, the firmly architectured sentences of his prose might be cited, as in the essay "Obscurity and Poetry" reprinted in his posthumous poems. He also is aware of the Gaelic use of assonance in poetry, as in the pieces printed on pages xiii–xv of his *Poems* (1916). Sometimes, too, he works in an interesting stanza form (in basically iambic trimeter and rhymed ABAAB), which he uses to good effect as in "The Spark." But more important than his awareness of technique is the number of startlingly effective, if romantic, lines in his work. To be sure, they are often buried in language like "Your innocence has stabbed my heart" or "the secrets of your eyes," from "The White Feather," but that poem also has some remarkable lines. So also does "Your Fear" in which he works interestingly with varied line lengths and internal rhyming. He is not even always florid; in a poem like "1841–1891" he is utterly simple. In sum, there is much of interest in Plunkett, so much so that one suspects he might have become a more considerable poet than either Pearse* or MacDonagh.

WORK: *Poems*. Dublin: Talbot, 1916.   REFERENCE: Thompson, William Irwin. *The Imagination of an Insurrection: Dublin, Easter 1916*. New York: Oxford University Press, 1961, 131–139.

POEKRICH (or POCKRICH, POKRICH, POKERIDGE, or PUCK-RIDGE), RICHARD (1690–1759), poet and promoter. Poekrich was born in Monaghan, swiftly went through a large inheritance, and spent most of his life in poverty, which he attempted to alleviate by a fertile succession of eccentric schemes including growing grapes on bogs, supplying his countrymen with wings, and rejuvenating old people by blood transfusions from the young. His one successful scheme was the invention of musical glasses that he filled with various levels of water and then produced tunes from them by rubbing his moistened fingers around the rims. This "Angelic Organ," as he called it, had a brief vogue, and he gave a number of concerts in London.

He published one volume of verse entitled *The Miscellaneous Works of Richard Poekrich. Vol. I.* This is a genial, if sometimes technically awkward, collection of mainly light verse that tends toward the bawdy, particularly in the epigrams at the end, but that rarely rises to great wit, despite being adorned with occasional puns, as in the quatrain:

> A Brisk young Fellow and a Maid,
>   Beneath a Gate were *tete a tete;*

B'ing ask'd his business there, he said,
His business was to *prop-a-gate*.

He was suffocated by a fire in his London lodgings in 1759.

WORK: *The Miscellaneous Works of Richard Poekrich. Vol. I.* Dublin: Printed for the Author, by James Byrn, 1775. REFERENCES: Newburgh, Brockhill. *Essays Poetical, Moral and Critical.* Dublin, 1769; O'Donoghue, D. J. *An Irish Musical Genius (Richard Pockrich). The Inventor of the Musical Glasses.* Dublin: M. H. Gill, 1899; Pilkington, John Carteret. *The Life of J. C. Pilkington.* Dublin, 1762; Somerville-Large, Peter. *Irish Eccentrics.* London: Hamish Hamilton, 1975.

POLLOCK, JOHN H. (1887–1964), poet, novelist, and playwright. John Hackett Pollock was born in Dublin of a mixed marriage in 1887, and his awareness of the separate streams pervading the Irish nation is apparent in his books. The son of Hugh Pollock, a barrister who was later registrar to the Land Commission, by his wife, Mary Donnelly, the boy was educated at Catholic University School, Leeson Street, and the medical school in Cecilia Street, taking the M.B. and B.Ch. from the National University in 1913.

He specialized in pathology and was assistant to Richmond Hospital, from where in the 1916 rebellion he ventured fearlessly into the streets wearing a Red Cross armlet to help the wounded. Believing he had a late vocation for the church, he resigned his post and entered Buckfast Abbey but left it to resume his career in pathology. His early papers included "Blood Culture in Diagnosis" and "Observations upon Scarlatina," but before long his interest in pathology appears to have taken second place to the attractions of literature.

His output was large: he was a poet, critic and author of an early monograph on W. B. Yeats,* novelist, and playwright—his one-act *Tristram and Iseult* was staged at the Peacock Theatre by Edwards and Mac Liammóir* in 1929. A contemporary reviewer found in his writings a "strange quality which lifts his prose so far above that of most leading Irish writers, a quality which is almost Meredithian in its sustained lyrical flow." A love of nature and appreciation of landscape are apparent in his novels. Repeatedly, he praises the beautiful Vale of Shanganagh, covered over now by housing estates.

The Lost Nightingale is a romance based on the life of John Dowland, the sixteenth lutanist and poet, who is said to have lived in Dalkey. *Peter and Paul* is the story of identical twins of rather different temperaments; its main interest today is a comparison between Dublin's universities: "Was the somewhat parochial outlook of the National University in reality a primitive condition which by virtue of its very primitiveness might promise a future development beyond the delightful but final limits to which Trinity had already attained?"

Toward the end of his career in pathology, to the discomfiture of the prolific author, a dynamic, American-trained pathologist was appointed director of the department. One day Pollock called a junior, Dr. Patrick Bofin, into his room and showed him a sheaf of laboratory reports. "Look at those, Bofin!" "Yes, Dr. Pollock," the junior replied, impressed by the wealth of descriptive microscopy. "But those aren't yours, Dr. Pollock." "Certainly not, Bofin," thrusting a report under the young man's nose. "Have you ever seen anything like that? A whole page without a comma, a paragraph without a full stop, and sentences without verbs." "He was trained in America, Dr. Pollock." "Even Americans use verbs, Bofin."

Pollock sometimes used a pen name, "An Philibin" (the Plover). His complex and extraordinary mind was open to all facets of life from the most simple to the scholarly. By his marriage to Anna Waters in 1926, there were four children. He died on December 11, 1964.

J. B. LYONS

WORKS: *The Secret Altar.* Dublin: Martin Lester, n.d. (Poems); *Autumn Crocus.* Dublin: Talbot, n.d. (Poems); *Hills of Dublin.* Dublin: Talbot, 1917. (Poems); *Athens Aflame.* Dublin: Martin Lester, 1923. (Poems); *The Sun-child, A Poem.* Dublin: Talbot, 1925; *Grass of Parnassus.* Dublin: Three Candles, 1936. (Poems); *Irish Ironies.* Dublin: Talbot, 1930. (Short stories); *The Valley of the Wild Swans: A Romance.* Dublin: Talbot, 1932; *Peter and Paul.* Dublin: Talbot, 1933. (Novel); *W. B. Yeats.* Dublin: Talbot, 1935; *The Moth and the Star.* Dublin: Talbot, 1937. (Novel); *Mount Kestrel.* Dublin: Gill, 1945. (Novel); *The Lost Nightingale.* Dublin, 1951. (Novel).

POOLBEG PRESS (1979–   ), publishing house. Poolbeg was founded in 1979 by David Marcus* and Philip MacDermott initially to publish new authors appearing in Marcus's New Irish Writing Page in the *Irish Press* and to reprint some established authors. Among its many new writers were Helen Lucy Burke,* Emma Cooke,* Kate Cruise O'Brien,* Maura Treacy,* and Gillman Noonan,* and it republished good work by Bryan MacMahon* and Michael McLaverty.* After Marcus's departure, the firm has been led by MacDermott into more mainstream publishing. Its first commercial success was *The Boss* in 1984, a biography by Joe Joyce and Peter Murtagh of the Irish politician Charles J. Haughey, which sold 50,000 copies. There were popular successes with some early Maeve Binchy* short stories, but most particularly with Patricia Scanlan's* *City Girl,* which has sold over 100,000 copies since 1990, an extraordinary number for Ireland. Since the late 1980s, Poolbeg has also been developing an extensive children's list, and the firm's commercial success may be measured by a turnover of over £1 million in 1994. The press has not, however, abandoned literary publishing. Poolbeg's literary editor is now Kate Cruise O'Brien, and in 1994 under her wing the press brought out books by Sheila Barrett,* Kathleen Ferguson,* Briege Duffaud,* John F. Deane,* and Adrian Kenny.*

REFERENCE: Kelly, Shirley. "Reaching for the Stars." *Books Ireland,* No. 185 (April 1995): 73–74.

PORTER, JAMES (1753–1798), satirist. Porter was a farmer, schoolteacher, and the Presbyterian minister of Greyabbey, County Down. His satire on local dignitaries, *Billy Bluff and Squire Firebrand* (1796), became extremely popular and was seen by the authorities as an attack on British rule in Ireland. When the government ordered a fast day of thanksgiving for the storm that dispersed the British fleet in Bantry Bay, Porter wrote *Wind and Water* (1797), satirizing the order. These works made Porter's a household name in Ulster, and when the 1798 rebellion broke out, a reward was offered for his capture. Although not a United Irishman—indeed, he was an advocate of peaceful reform—Porter was apprehended and hanged before his meetinghouse on July 2, 1798.

WORKS: *Billy Bluff and Squire Firebrand.* . . . Belfast, 1796; *Wind and Water.* . . . Belfast, 1797.

POWER, BRIAN (1930–), short story writer. Power was born on August 18, 1930, holds an M.A. in sociology from Boston University, and is a Roman Catholic priest who has been chaplain to University College, Dublin, and is now the parish priest in Sandymount. He won a Hennessy Award for his short story "Requiem," and in 1977 he published a collection of stories entitled *A Land Not Sown.* The collection is extremely readable, alternately moving and funny, and is written in several styles and techniques. Perhaps the most successful stories are a novella, *Two Hundred Greeners,* told from the viewpoint of an ignorant fifteen-year-old slum boy; "The Godmother," told from the viewpoint of a clever middle-class boy of about the same age; and "Games Children Play," told from the viewpoint of a stuffy academic researcher. *The Wild & Daring Sixties* (1980) is similarly eclectic in both subject and technique. The title story is a dialogue that contrasts the true and the false idealism of the mild Irish university student revolution of the late 1960s with the complacency of material success a decade later. "Pyromaniacs" is a short comic story about three children lighting candles in church. "Mary, Maureen and Angelina" is a quietly mordant piece about nuns living outside the convent. "The Pursuer" is a reflection in the form of a letter about the death of a charmingly hypocritical and perfectly monstrous teenager. "Kyrie Boom-Boom-Boom" effectively contrasts a reactionary canon and a young curate who leaves the priesthood and marries. In his varied and generally successful short stories, Power shows an ability to catch broadly diverse characters and a fine control of technique. He needs to publish more of them.

WORKS: *A Land Not Sown.* [Dublin]: Egotist, [1977]; *The Wild & Daring Sixties and Other Stories.* [Enniskerry, Co. Wicklow: Egotist, 1980].

POWER, M[AURICE] S. (1935–), novelist. Power was born in Dublin and educated in Ireland and France. He worked as a television producer in the United States, and he won a Hennessy Short Story Award in 1983, the year he published his first novel, *Hunt for the Autumn Clowns.* That book is set on a not very well realized island off the west coast but is peopled by at least half a dozen very well realized characters indeed. The adolescent idiot Pericles Stort is the most emphasized. Normally gentle and amiable, he allows his grandfather to drown for killing a fox the boy was fond of. He also hides the body and, after it is found, mutilates it with his knife. When his mother sends him to cut the throat of a chicken, he vaguely starts to cut the throats of all the chickens. He breaks the neck of his schoolteacher, whom he has lured into the woods to make love to. Most of the other characters, including the schoolteacher, are obsessed with sex. The priest usually stumbles about in a drunken stupor but does rally to try to pull away the dogs that have been set upon Pericles and is killed by them himself. As a catalog of lust, rape, incest, and murder, the novel makes the characteristics of Synge's western peasants seem mere pecadilloes. The book slides constantly and effectively from one character to another and achieves considerable strength from a constant repetition of details and motifs. Occasionally, the style is more convoluted than that of Power's later thrillers. For instance, an eleven-line sentence on pages 9 and 10 has no less than three parenthetical elements and concludes with italics. In general, however, Power creates a memorably bizarre world, somewhat reminiscent of Faulkner or Flannery O'Connor.

The Killing of Yesterday's Children (1985) describes the amoral machinations of the Irish Republican Army (IRA) and the British in recent-day Belfast. Its buildup is leisurely, stressing the characterization of an enigmatic and saintly old man who has suffered torture and violence in Mexico and also of an IRA killer who derives a sensual thrill from murder but whom Power refuses to depict as a total monster. Their world is not one of clear-cut issues, but of deal making between opposing sides. It is a bleak world, violent and sordid; and the saintly Mr. Apple, who almost succeeds in saving the killer, Martin Deeley, is himself done in by it. Power is rather more than a thriller writer. Although he has his amoral villains, for some of his trapped and blighted people he evokes a real sympathy. The book is the first of a trilogy called *Children of the North.* Like the later volumes, *Lonely the Man without Heroes* (1986) and *A Darkness in the Eye* (1987), its plot is complete and self-contained. Nevertheless, several important characters in the first book appear in the later two—notably, Stephen Reilly, the IRA godfather, and Inspector John Asher of the Royal Ulster Constabulary, who often find themselves pragmatically cooperating; and Colonel Matthew Maddox, the benevolent and bewildered and untypical representative of the British army. More typical are the ruthless and devious Brigadier General Brazier and Colonel Guy Sharman of Army Intelligence. Again, Power devises well-constructed plots, full of intrigue, that move to a strong climax. Again, his values are the same. The disruptive force for him is mainly the British army or, in the final volume, a fanatical splinter group of republicans who plant a bomb in the Grand Hotel in Brighton at the Tory Party conference. There is, particularly in the final volume, a growing disenchantment with violence; and even the coldhearted Reilly has come to accept the necessity for political action, before he himself is killed by his associates. One may question the values Power assigns to his various factions and also his need to write three basically similar novels to make his point. One can hardly, however, question his professional writing skills. The three novels were dramatized for a television series.

Bridie and the Silver Lady (1988) is told by Bridie's interviews with a psychiatrist, which are interrupted by dramatized flashbacks. Bridie proves to be a coolly monstrous little girl who adored her father's cuddling her but who smothered her baby brother, pushed an old lady off a bicycle and smashed her head in with a stone, and finally knifed her mother in the back. There is quite a bit about demonic possession in the book, but Bridie is another of Power's all-too-plausibly human gallery of near-fiends and semimonsters. It has much in common with *Crucible of Fools* (1990), a rather short and powerful novel about a farmer who goes mad after the death of his young retarded son and the suicide of his wife. Depicted as a rather amiable man, he nevertheless kidnaps a woman, whom he treats kindly but keeps tied up until she dies. He also commits several murders of neighbors who had beaten him up. The climactic scene in which he is shot is horrific in its details.

An early book like *The Killing of Yesterday's Children* had many long passages of description or internal reflection. They have not disappeared in *Come the Executioner* (1991), but patches of terse dialogue have become more prominent. *Come the Executioner* is something of a reprise of the *Children of the North* trilogy, another J. S. le Carré-like version of Brits versus Provos. Power's sympathies are clearly on the side of the Provos, whose commandant is portrayed as pragmatic and ruthless if necessary, but essentially idealistic and honest. The British army and the politicians governing it are depicted as thoroughly dishonest and capable of killing one of their own officers and blaming it on the Provos, the act that triggers the action when the murdered captain's journalist brother decides to find out what really happened. Another whitewashing of the Provos is their willingness to raise funds by leasing slot machines, but their total refusal to have anything to do with drug dealing or protection rackets. Without agreeing with Power's view, it is possible to admire the construction of a leanly plotted, easily read, and serious thriller, as well as to be impressed by the world of disillusionment, deal making, and compromise that he evokes.

The Stalker's Apprentice (1993) has all of Power's best qualities, especially strong plotting and characterization, a lean and unclichéd style, and much terse dialogue. The main character, a publisher's reader, is a psychological study of an arrogant and conscienceless young murderer. To call it a mere thriller and lump it together with works by Tom Clancy or Jack Higgins is to do it a disservice; and to call Power's Marcus Walwyn a second cousin twice removed of Raskolnikov is not to denigrate Power's achievement.

WORKS: *Hunt for the Autumn Clowns*. London: Chatto & Windus, 1983; *The Killing of Yesterday's Children*. London: Chatto & Windus-Hogarth, [1985]; *Lonely the Man without Heroes*. London: Heinemann, [1986]; *A Darkness in the Eye*. London: Heinemann, [1987]. (The last three novels constitute the "Children of the North" trilogy); *Bridie and the Silver Lady*. London: Heinemann, [1988]; *The Crucifixion of Septimus Roach*. London: Bloomsbury, 1989; *Crucible of Fools*. London: Hamish Hamilton, [1990]; *Come the Executioner*. London: Hamish Hamilton, [1991]; *Skating round the Poppy*. Edinburgh: Mainstream, 1992; *The Stalker's Apprentice*. Edinburgh & London: Mainstream, 1993; *A Sheltering Silence*. Edinburgh & London: Mainstream, [1994].

POWER, MARGUERITE, LADY BLESSINGTON (1789–1849), woman of letters. Margaret was the daughter of Edmund and Ellen Sheehy Power. She was born on September 1, 1789, at Knockbrit, County Tipperary. At the age of fourteen, she was forced by her father to marry Maurice St. Leger Farmer. Her

husband proved to be a brutal man, and she returned home after three months of marriage. Several years later, she became involved with Captain Thomas Jenkins and set up housekeeping with him. When she and the earl of Blessington developed a relationship, the earl paid Jenkins for her release. When her first husband died, Margaret changed her name to Marguerite and married the earl of Blessington. During that marriage, she was a prominent social figure and influential hostess. The countess was readily accepted by the powerful men of her social circle, but never by their wives, who found her past unacceptable. After the earl's death, she lived with Count D'Orsay, her son-in-law from her second marriage. This new living arrangement was the cause of great speculation, particularly in regard to their sexual relationship. Whether she was the count's lover or a maternal figure remains unknown. The scandal of their relationship occasioned their departure from London to Paris, where Marguerite's novels and travel writings supported their household. She published anonymously, and as the countess of Blessington, for several years prior to her death. She died in Paris on June 4, 1849. Lady Blessington was best known for *Conversations of Lord Byron,* published in 1834. She had reportedly met Byron in Genoa in 1823.

ANNE COLMAN

WORKS: *Journal of a Tour through the Netherlands to Paris in 1821.* London: Longman, Hurst, Rees, Orme & Brown, 1822; *The Magic Lantern.* London: Longman, Hurst, Rees, Orme & Brown, 1822; *Sketches and Fragments.* London: Longman, Hurst, Rees, Orme & Brown, 1822; *Rambles in Waltham Forest.* London: Printed by J. L. Cox, 1827; *Ella Stratford.* London, 1830/Philadelphia: T. B. Peterson, [1830?]; *Grace Cassidy; or, The Repealers.* 3 vols. London: R. Bentley/Philadelphia: Carey, Lea & Blanchard, 1833; *Conversations of Lord Byron with the Countess of Blessington.* London: Henry Colburn, 1834/rpt., Princeton, N. J.: Princeton University Press, 1969; *Two Friends.* 3 vols. London: Saunders & Otley/Philadelphia: Carey, Lea & Blanchard, 1835; *The Confessions of an Elderly Gentleman.* 8 vols. London: Longman, Rees, Orme, Brown, Green & Longmans/ Philadelphia: Carey, Lea & Blanchard, 1836; *Galeria.* London, 1836; *Gems of Beauty.* London: Longman, Rees, Orme, Brown, Green & Longmans/New York: Appleton, 1836; *The Honeymoon.* London, 1837/Philadelphia: E. L. Carey & A. Hart, 1837; *The Victims of Society.* 3 vols. London: Saunders & Otley/Philadelphia: Carey, Lea & Blanchard, 1837; *The Works of Lady Blessington.* 2 vols. Philadelphia: E. L. Carey & A. Hart, 1838; *The Confessions of an Elderly Lady.* London: Longman, Rees, Orme, Brown, Green & Longmans, 1838; *Desultory Thoughts and Reflections.* London: Longman, Orme, Brown, Green & Longmans, 1839; *The Idler in Italy.* 3 vols. London: H. Colburn/Philadelphia: Carey & Hart, 1839; *The Governess.* 2 vols. London: Longman, Orme, Brown, Green & Longmans/Philadelphia: Lea & Blanchard, 1839; *The Belle of a Season.* London: Published for the Proprietor by Longman, 1840; *The Idler in France.* 2 vols. London: H. Colburn/ Philadelphia: Carey & Hart, 1841; *Veronica of Castille.* London, 1842; *The Lottery of Life.* 3 vols. London: H. Colburn/New York: A. Winchester, 1842; *Meredith.* 3 vols. London: Longman, Brown, Green & Longmans, 1843; *Strathern.* 4 vols. London: H. Colburn, 1845; *The Memoirs of a Femme de Chambre.* 3 vols. London: R. Bentley, 1846; *Marmaduke Herbert; or, The Fatal Error.* 3 vols. London: R. Bentley/New York: Burgess, Stringer, 1847; *The Book of Beauty or Regal Gallery.* London: David Bogue/New York: Appleton, 1849; *Country Quarters.* 3 vols. London: W. Shobere, 1850; *A Journal of the Correspondence and Conversations between Lord Byron and the Countess of Blessington.* London, 1851/rev. ed., London: R. Bentley, 1893; *One Hundred Valuable Receipts for the Young Lady of the Period.* 1878; *The Blessington Papers.* [London]: Printed for private circulation, 1895. (Letters to Lady Blessington.) REFERENCES: Madden, Richard Robert, ed. *The Literary Life and Correspondence of the Countess of Blessington.* 3 vols. London: Woking printed, 1855; Molloy, Joseph Fitzgerald. *The Most Gorgeous Lady Blessington.* 2 vols. London: Downey, 1896.

POWER, RICHARD (1928–1970), novelist. Richard Power (Risteard De Paor in Irish) was born in Dublin on February 2, 1928. In 1945, he entered the Irish civil service in Dublin, where he lived (apart from periods on the Aran Islands and in the United States) until his early death in 1970. On leave from the civil service, he took a degree in English and Irish at Trinity College, Dublin, in 1952, and he also studied Gaelic on the Aran Islands. His book about his experiences on the islands, *Úll i mBarr an Ghéagáin,* was awarded the Gaelic Book Club Award in 1959. He spent 1958–1960 teaching and studying at the Writers' Workshop at the University of Iowa. His one-act plays in Gaelic were presented at the Abbey Theatre,* Dublin, in 1955 (*Saoirse*) and 1958 (*An Oidhreacht*). He also wrote scripts for Radio Éireann for documentary films.

Power is best remembered for his two completed novels in English. *The Land of Youth* (1964, 1966) is an extended saga of frustrated sexuality and enmity set, in the main, on the Aran island of Inishheever before and after the War of Independence. The central character is Barbara Nora whose failed relationship with a young man destined for the priesthood is the source of a protracted series of emotional savageries played out against the background of wild natural scenery and physical privation. The novel, traditional in narrative form and uncomplicated in structure, has been admired for its sombre reflective sense of emotional currents running, inevitably, deep in the psyche. Power's second novel, *The Hungry Grass* (1969), is structurally much more compact. The last year of a country priest in the post-revolutionary period is treated with a gravely compassionate sense of idealism perverted and family life and affections contaminated by vulgar material and social opportunism. The novel, a haunting study in loneliness, suggests how much Irish writing lost in the early death of its author.

He died in Bray on February 12, 1970.

TERENCE BROWN

WORKS: *The Land of Youth.* New York: Dial, 1964/London: Secker & Warburg, 1966; *The Hungry Grass.* London: Bodley Head, 1969. REFERENCE: Brown, Terence. "Family Lives: The Fiction of Richard Power." In *The Irish Novel in Our Time.* Patrick Rafroidi & Maurice Harmon, eds. Villeneuve-d'Ascq: Publications de l'Université de Lille III, [1975–1976], pp. 245–253.

POWER, TYRONE (1797–1841), actor and author. The son of an itinerant actor, William Grattan Tyrone Power was born in Kilmacthomas, County Waterford on November 2, 1797 (some accounts say 1795). His acting career began on the Isle of Wight, as Alonzo in R. B. Sheridan's* *Pizarro,* in 1815. Seven years later he was performing in London. Although he took on Shakespearean roles, such as Romeo, Power was most successful as an interpreter of Irish characters such as Major O'Flaherty in Richard Cumberland's *The West Indian*

and Sir Lucius O'Trigger in Sheridan's *The Rivals*. Famous abroad as in England, Power toured America in the 1830s. His published account of these visits
is mostly appreciative, even if some theaters were better suited to agriculture
than to drama. Returning from New York on March 21, 1841, at the end of a
tour, he was lost at sea when the steamer *President* sank. He and his wife, née
Annie Gilbert, had four sons and four daughters. Frederick Tyrone Power
(1869–1931), the distinguished American actor, was his grandson, and Edmund
Tyrone Power (1914–1958) of cinema fame was his great-grandson.

Ebullient Irishmen were the central figures in the comedies of which Power
was both author and performer. They descended to the Handy Andy level of
the blundering servant Pat Rooney in *The Omnibus* (ca. 1833) and rose to the
unsophisticated dignity of Major O'Dogherty in *St. Patrick's Eve* (1837). No
little ingenuity was required to steer these characters into and out of comic
predicaments. Paudeen O'Rafferty in *Born to Good Luck* (1832) by mistake
boards a ship bound to Naples. There he is caught in the middle of a volatile
romantic rivalry. Major O'Dogherty, in the service of Frederick the Great, is
sentenced to death for a well-intentioned violation of the Order of the Day. The
title character in *Paddy Carey* (produced in 1833) and his rival—each without
the other's knowledge—enlist in the Royal Irish Hussars and offer their bonus
payment to free from debt the father of the woman they love. They do so aware
that she is bound by her mother's deathbed injunction never to marry a soldier.
Fortunately, Power's characters are fundamentally good-natured or at least per-
suadable, even Frederick the Great and the hard-hearted landlord in *How to Pay
the Rent* (1840). Early Victorian audiences went home assured by the genial
Irish actor-dramatist that all was right with the world.

WILLIAM J. FEENEY

WORKS: *The Lost Heir* and *The Prediction*. London: E. Bull/New York: J. & J. Harper, 1830.
(Novels); *Married Lovers: A Petite Comedy in Two Acts*. Baltimore: J. Robinson, 1831; *The King's
Secret*. 3 vols. London: E. Bull, 1831. (Novel); *Born to Good Luck: The Irishman's Fortune, A
Farce in Two Acts*. London: T. H. Lacy, [ca. 1832]; *The Omnibus, A Farce in One Act*. New York:
Clinton DeWitt, n.d.; *Impressions of America during the Years 1833, 1834, and 1835*. 2 vols.
London: R. Bentley/Philadelphia: Carey, Lea & Blanchard, 1836/rpt., New York: Benjamin Blom,
1971; *St. Patrick's Eve, or The Order of the Day*. London: Chapman & Hall, 1838. (Three-act
play); *How to Pay the Rent*. London: Sherwood, Gilbert & Piper, [ca. 1840]. (One-act play); *The
Gipsy of the Abruzzo*. London: J. Clements, 1846. (Novel); *Paddy Carey, or the Boy of Clogheen*.
New York: Samuel French, [ca. 1876]. (One-act play).   REFERENCES: Downer, Alan. *The Emi-
nent Tragedian: William Charles Macready*. Cambridge: Harvard University Press, 1966; Hornblow,
Arthur. *A History of the American Theatre*. 2 vols. New York: J. B. Lippincott, 1919/rpt., New
York: Benjamin Blom, 1965; Hughes, Glenn. *A History of the American Theatre, 1700–1950*. New
York: Samuel French, 1951; Ireland, Joseph N. *Records of the New York Stage from 1750 to 1850*.
2 vols. New York: T. H. Morrell, 1866; Murdoch, James E. *The Stage*. Philadelphia: J. M. Stoddart,
1880; Watson, Ernest B. *Sheridan to Robertson: A Study of the Nineteenth Century Stage*. Cambridge: Harvard University Press, 1926; Wemyss, Francis Courtney. *Twenty-Six Years in the Life
of an Actor and Manager*. New York: Burgess, Stringer, 1847; Winter William. [Frederick] *Tyrone
Power*. New York: Moffat, Yard, 1913/rpt., New York: Benjamin Blom, 1972; Young, William C.,
ed. *Famous Actors and Actresses on the American Stage*. Vol. 2. New York: R. R. Bowker, 1975.

POWER, UNA

WORK: *The Spellbinder.* London: Century, 1993. (Novel).

POWER, VICTOR (1930–1987), playwright and short story writer. Power was born in Dublin on October 16, 1930. His career included the priesthood (ordained 1954, left 1968), study at the University of Iowa Writers' Workshop from 1966 to 1971, teaching at King Abdulazziz University in Saudi Arabia from 1971 to 1972, employment in the Department of Human Services in Chicago from 1972 to 1980, and, after a two-year writing sabbatical, teaching at Cochise College, Bisbee, Arizona, until his death on September 28, 1987. He was married to Marybel Killian in 1968. They had no children.

As a parish priest in County Waterford, Power wrote comedies in Irish for an amateur company. Most of his work, however, though set in Ireland, was staged and published in America. Short stories collected in *The Town of Ballymuck* (1984) form an autobiographical account of a boy's meager life in slum Dublin and rural Ireland after the death of his father. The plays, ingeniously crafted for performance with limited facilities, set modern ideas on a collision course with the way things have always been. Typical is *The Escape* (produced in 1970). Its central figure, an iconoclastic young Irish priest, clashes with stand-pat fellow clergymen. Power's allegiance is with rebels, but he avoids sociological melodrama by giving an admirable tenacity to those who resist the uncertainties of a new order. His writing is characterized by dialogue that makes few concessions to gentility, by shaggy realism, and by robust humor.

WILLIAM J. FEENEY

WORKS: *The Mud Nest* in *Story, The Yearbook of Discovery/1969.* New York: Four Winds, 1969. (Play); *The Town of Ballymuck.* Tallahassee, Fla.: Swallow's Tale, 1984. (Short stories); *The Escape.* Bisbee, Ariz.: Mule Mountain, 1984. (Play); *Johnnie Will.* Bisbee, Ariz.: Mule Mountain, 1985. (Play); *Mother Jones.* Bisbee, Ariz.: Privately printed, 1987. (Docudrama of Mary Harris Jones, Irish-born American labor leader, 1830–1930). REFERENCES: Feeney, William J. "Portrait of the Artist as a Survivor: Victor Power's Short Stories." *Éire-Ireland* 18 (Fall 1983): 127–135; Feeney, William J. "The Stage as Catalyst: The Plays of Victor Power." *Éire-Ireland* 25 (Fall 1990): 79–95.

POWER, VICTOR O'D[ONOVAN] (fl. late nineteenth and early twentieth centuries), short story writer, novelist, and playwright. Power, a native of County Wexford, was a vastly prolific writer of popular fiction for the young and also of broadly comic and melodramatic plays. His stories appeared in all of the popular family journals in the first quarter of this century and were staples of *Ireland's Own* and *Our Boys,* in which they still continue to be reprinted. The best known are a series of comic or romantic or melodramatic tales related by Kitty the Hare, a wandering woman of the roads. Power's plays were produced mainly in the provinces by fit-up companies, such as the O'Brien and Ireland Company, and, in the 1920s, by Power's own company. One of his plays, *David Mahony,* was presented by the Abbey* with mild success in 1914.

WORKS: *Bonnie Dunraven.* 2 vols. London: Remington, 1881. (Novel); *The Heir of Liscarragh.* London: Art & Book, 1891. (Novel); *A Secret of the Past.* London: Ward & Downey, 1893. (Novel); *Flurry to the Rescue.* Dublin: Duffy, 1918. (One-act play); *When the Cat's Away the Mice Can Play . . . and Dinny Donoghue's Damsel.* [Dublin]: Duffy, [1927]. (Two one-act farces); *The Footsteps of Fate.* Dublin: Ireland's Own, [1930]. (Novel); *Some Strange Experiences of Kitty the Hare, the Famous Travelling Woman of Ireland.* Dublin & Cork: Mercier, [1981].

PRAEGER, ROBERT LLOYD (1865–1953), botanist and librarian. Praeger was born on August 26, 1865, at Holywood, County Down, the son of William Emil Praeger, a Dutch linen merchant, and Maria Patterson, daughter of the Belfast scientist Robert Patterson. He was the brother of the artist Rosamund Praeger. He was early attracted to botany, joining the Belfast Field Club at the age of eleven. He was educated at the Belfast Academical Institution and at Queen's College, Belfast, and he started his active life as a civil engineer with the City and District Water Commissioners. He read his first scientific paper on geology in 1886. In 1891, he was elected to the Royal Irish Academy. He was a founder of the important journal *The Irish Naturalist,* which for a time he edited. His *Flora of the County Armagh* appeared in 1893, and that year he joined the staff of the National Library in Dublin under the famous W. P. Lyster, rising to chief librarian in 1920. He took advantage of the terms of the Anglo-Irish treaty respecting civil servants retiring on full pension at the age of fifty-nine and at once set out to research in the field in the Canary islands. He made numerous scientific contributions in the fields of botany, geology, and other sciences, but his general fame rests on *The Way That I Went,* an accepted classic. His other important books for the general reader are *The Botanist in Ireland* (1934) and *The Natural History of Ireland* (1950).

Praeger was a pioneer of the kind of total study of man and landscape that was continued by E. E. Evans* and others and in which the long tides of historical cultures in Ireland are investigated. His writings, like those of many Protestant scientists, are devoid of the controversy that surrounds the subject of Irish culture. He died at Belfast on May 5, 1953.

PETER COSTELLO

PRINCIPAL WORKS: *Belfast and County Down Railway Company: Official Guide to County Down and the Mourne Mountains.* Belfast: Marcus Ward, 1898: *Aspects of Plant Life.* London: [Nature Lover's Series], 1921; *Beyond Soundings.* Dublin: Talbot, 1930. (Essays); *The Botanist in Ireland.* Dublin: Hodges, Figgis, 1934; *The Way That I Went.* Dublin: Hodges, Figgis/London: Methuen, 1937; *A Populous Solitude.* London: Methuen, 1941. (Irish essays); *Some Irish Naturalists.* Dundalk: W. Tempest, 1949; *Natural History of Ireland.* London: Collins, 1950; also many scientific papers detailed in Collins, following.   REFERENCE: Collins, Timothy, with David Bellamy. *Floreat Hibernia, A Bio-Bibliography of Robert Lloyd Praeger.* Dublin: Royal Dublin Society, 1985.

PRESTON, WILLIAM (1753–1807), poet and playwright. Preston was born in Dublin and educated at Trinity College and at the Middle Temple. He was a judge in the Court of Appeal and, for more than twenty years, secretary of the Royal Irish Academy. Although a member of the establishment, he was against the Union and in favor of Catholic emancipation. A learned and prolific author, he died in Dublin on February 2, 1807.

PRINCIPAL WORKS: *Offa and Ethelbert; or, The Saxon Princess.* Dublin: J. Archer, 1791. (Verse tragedy); *Democratic Rage; or, Louis the Unfortunate.* London: For the Author, 1793. (Verse tragedy); *The Poetical Works.* 2 vols. Dublin: J. Archer, 1792; *The Siege of Ismail; or, A Prospect of War.* Dublin: Graisberry & Campbell, 1794. (Verse tragedy); *The Posthumous Poems of William Preston, Esq.* Dublin: Wilkinson & Courtney, 1809.

PRICE, K[ATHLEEN] ARNOLD (1893–1989), novelist, short story writer, and poet. Price was born in County Mayo in 1893 into a Church of Ireland family but spent her childhood in the Shannon-side country of County Limerick. Her mother, Augusta, was the daughter of Thomas Arnold, professor of English at University College, Dublin ("Philip Hewson" in Arthur Hugh Clough's *The Bothie of Tober-na-Vuolich*), and a granddaughter of Thomas Arnold, the reforming headmaster of Rugby College, and a sister to Mrs. Humphrey Ward. Her father, William Robert Price, a teacher by profession, was (in Miss Price's words) "a mathematician, golfer, fisherman and rugby player" by vocation. She was educated privately and entered Trinity College, Dublin, in October 1913 to read modern languages. She graduated in December 1917 with a B.A. in English and French and then spent a year at King's College in London and another at the University of Lyons. After this she spent some enjoyable times climbing in the Alps above Grenoble and living in Athens and Crete. Her "semischolarly peregrinations" also took in other parts of France, the Basque country, and England, as she sketched and studied local architecture and furniture. An unpublished story deals with a youthful love affair in Paris. She claimed to have begun writing in the early 1940s, but poems appeared in *The Dublin Magazine* as early as the summer of 1925. This was followed by a hiatus until 1943, when both poetry and prose began to appear under her unusual, nonspecific form of name in newspapers and periodicals in Ireland and Britain, especially in the *Irish Press, The Kerryman, Dublin Magazine,* * *Envoy,* and *Irish Writing.** Only later in life with the publication of her impressionistic short novel *The New Perspective* in 1980 did her work come to wider notice. That book dealt with the revelation to a working librarian in a provincial town, after her son's wedding, that her own long years of marriage to an estate agent had been, in fact, loveless. The stories collected in *The Captain's Paramour,* though published in 1985 (when the author was ninety-two, a fact well disguised at the time), date from 1949 and later and cover the experiences of both growing up and the problematic relations of adults. The connected tales in the first part form almost a short novel. She wrote of a now-vanished Ireland—Limerick, Tipperary, and Kerry—of ordinary common life invested with often mysterious elements. In 1980, William Trevor* found her work "arrestingly good" and saw her novel as "one of the most skilful to come out of Ireland for many years."

Despite her wide travels, Price lived, for many years after the war, at Muckross Cottage, Delgany, County Wicklow. This had been the home of her grandmother Helen Adelaide Arnold and of her father and mother, all of whom are buried in Delgany churchyard. Later, Price moved to a flat in Lansdowne Road, Dublin, where she continued to pursue her interests in baroque music and Celtic archaeology. Much of her work remains uncollected in various literary magazines. She died in June 1989 and was buried on June 12 in the family grave in Delgany (No. 834, unmarked). A curious unsocial person with many, with some she was more open, but always unrevealing. She remains a unique literary personality.

PETER COSTELLO

WORKS: *The New Perspective.* [Swords, Co. Dublin]: Poolbeg, [1980]. (Novel); *The Captain's Paramour.* London: Hamish Hamilton, 1985. (Short stories).

PRONE, TERRY (1949–   ), fiction writer. Prone was born in Clontarf, County Dublin, on October 11, 1949. She attended University College, Dublin, but left to act with the Abbey Theatre.* In 1980, she became managing director of Carr Communications, a media consulting agency that often advises Irish politicians about how to improve their public image. In the 1980s, she was in a horrific automobile accident that nearly killed her but from which she finally recovered. In addition to several self-help books, such as *Write and Get Paid for It* and *Just a Few Words,* on public speaking, she has written two books of fiction. *The Scattering of Mrs. Blake and Related Matters* (1986) is a novelette about the difficulties of an idealistic young priest being outmaneuvered by a canny publican in a rural parish. It is more mordant than comic in its evocation of modern country life, and its writing is often lean and telling: "Do you know what schizophrenia is? It's emigration without leaving home." Most of the stories in *Blood Brothers, Soul Sisters* (1994) are less memorable, because so little happens in them: a woman lashes out at her sister, a sister tearfully accuses her brother, a bum walks along a big city street, a man watches people dance in a bar, a woman sits by a swimming pool at a posh resort. One better story is really the recycled first chapter of her novelette. The brief "Butterfly Christmas," however, is an effective depiction of a badly disabled woman coming to some acceptance of her condition; and the best and most dramatized story is the rather long "Captiva Blues," which charts the short, aborted affair of an amiable politician and a young businesswoman and the effect upon the politician's wife.

PRINCIPAL WORKS: *The Scattering of Mrs. Blake and Related Matters.* London & New York: Marion Boyars/Dublin: Arlen House, [1986]. (Novella); *Blood Brothers, Soul Sisters.* [Dublin]: Poolbeg, [1994].

PROSCENIUM PRESS (1964–1994), publishing house. This American-based press was founded by Robert Hogan primarily to publish plays. Of its nearly 100 volumes, many are Irish and include three volumes of Joseph Holloway's* journal, an uncompleted but five-volume life and works of Boucicault,* four volumes of "Lost Plays of the Irish Renaissance," and an eighteen-volume Irish play series. It published collections of plays by Gogarty* and M. J. Molloy* and individual plays by such dramatists as Fitzmaurice,* Carroll,* Brendan Behan,* Keane,* Friel,* and Leonard.* It also published two magazines, *The Journal of Irish Literature** and *George Spelvin's Theatre Book,* the latter often containing Irish material, such as Ria Mooney's autobiography. In appearance, its books ranged from the handsome to the extraordinarily tatty.

PROUT, FATHER (1804–1866), humorist and journalist. Using his pseudonym of Father Prout, Francis Sylvester Mahony was a central figure in English literary circles, respected and loved for his quick wit. Born in Cork on December 31, 1804, he enrolled in a Jesuit seminary in France and later studied in Rome. Although his native intelligence surely qualified him for the priesthood, he was discouraged from pursuing ordination, probably because his temperament was unsuitable for such a life. The most widespread story of the reasons for his dismissal was that he led a group of seminarians on a drunken spree. Although he was expelled from the Jesuits, he was eventually ordained, in Italy, in 1832. However, after years of stubborn effort to become a priest, he practiced for only a few years. After serving in his native Cork during the time of a cholera epidemic, he moved to London and began work as a journalist. Although he was referred to as a priest, he seems to have been relieved of his official duties.

Mahony soon began to contribute to *Fraser's,* which was, at the time, the most lively and influential of literary journals. Thackeray* and Carlyle contributed to it, as had Southey and Coleridge. Under the name of Father Prout, whom Mahony described as the child of Jonathan Swift* and Stella, he wrote short, humorous pieces on a wide variety of subjects. Prout was fictional, of course, but he was characterized as a simple priest from County Cork. To complicate the matter, Mahony invented an editor of Prout's writings, Oliver Yorke. These contributions were collected as *The Reliques of Father Prout* in 1836, with illustrations by Daniel Maclise. The essays reveal comprehensive learning and an endearing humor. Some are less humane; one even purported to prove that Thomas Moore* was a plagiarist. For the occasion, Mahony went to the trouble of translating various of Moore's *Melodies* into Greek, Latin, and Old French simply to prove that they had been stolen. In this essay, entitled "The Rogueries of Tom Moore," Mahony included a poem, "The Shandon Bells," which was to become immensely popular. Although it has entered the canon of sentimental songs, it is clear that Mahony intended it to be ironic. Elsewhere in the collection, Father Prout attacked Daniel O'Connell, whom he mocked as Dandeleon. *The Reliques* contains parodies of scholarly criticism that are still amusing, as well as a store of verse translations. At times his satire is precious and academic, as he tends to exhibit the exceptional breadth of his knowledge too frequently. But when we put his essays next to the work of his friend Thomas Carlyle, particularly *Sartor Resartus,* the quality of his work becomes clearer. For all his personal contacts with the literary lights of his time, Mahony still seems a minor figure, for he never attempted a sustained work or even a very serious one.

The facts of Mahony's life are obscure, but the few autobiographic references and comments by others indicate that behind his merry facade he led a troubled life. He died in Paris on May 18, 1866.

JAMES KILROY

WORKS: *The Reliques of Father Prout late P.P. of Watergrasshill in the County of Cork, Ireland.* 2 vols. London: James Fraser, 1836; *The Tour of the French Traveller M. de la Boullaye le Gouz in Ireland.* T. Crofton Croker, ed., with Notes and Illustrative Extracts Contributed by James Roche, F. Mahony, T. Wright, and the Editor. London: T. & W. Boone, 1837; *Facts and Figures from Italy.* By Don Jeremy Savanarola, Benedictine Monk [pseud. for Mahony]. London: R. Bentley, 1847; *The Final Reliques of Father Prout.* Blanchard Jerrold, ed. London: Chatto & Windus, 1876; *The Works of Father Prout.* Charles Kent, ed. London & New York: G. Routledge, 1881. REFERENCE: Mannin, Ethel. *Two Studies in Integrity. Gerald Griffin and the Rev. Francis Mahony ("Father Prout").* London: Jarrolds/New York: Putnam, 1954.

PURCELL, DEIRDRE (1945–   ), novelist. Deirdre Purcell, born in Dublin in 1945, is an actress and journalist as well as a novelist. As a result of appearances on the Dublin amateur stage, she was invited to join the Abbey Theatre's* permanent company of actors. In 1968, she moved to Chicago to take a position as actor in residence at Loyola University. Returning to Dublin in 1973, she worked as a radio announcer for RTÉ and as a television journalist. In 1983, she began writing for the *Irish Press* and the *Sunday Tribune.* Having won two prestigious Irish journalism awards, the Benson and Hedges Award and the A. T. Cross Award, Purcell turned to fiction, with three novels following in rapid succession. *A Place of Stones* (1991), almost Hardyan in its reliance on coincidence, is the tale of two families whose paths cross in the person of a child lost at sea. *That Childhood Country* (1992) is a Big House novel, tracing the decline of an aristocratic family whose daughter becomes involved with the gatekeeper's son. *Falling for a Dancer* (1993) examines the life of a woman in a small Irish town in the 1930s and 1940s. Purcell's journalism is reflected in her writing. As chief feature writer for the *Sunday Tribune,* she covered many contemporary events, including the Enniskillen bombings, the drought in Ethiopia and the Sudan, the Stava Dam disaster in Northern Italy, and the royal wedding of the duke and duchess of York. Purcell's fiction relies, to some degree, on potboiling sensationalism; she fills her novels with incest, violent deaths, alcoholism, illegitimate pregnancies, attempted fratricide, murder, air and sea crashes, and spiritualism. The plots make for a good read, and her well-drawn and engaging characters make these books impossible to put down. Although *A Place of Stones* and *That Childhood Country* are set in Ireland, North America, and England, it is not Purcell's aim to examine cultural differences or even to explore Irish culture by contrasting it with other cultures. Her focus is on Irish life, particularly life in the small towns and on the barren island of Inishmann. Her descriptions are penetratingly alive, evoking the beauties as well as the devastating isolation of the countryside. She examines as well some issues that have particular significance in Ireland: pregnancy out of wedlock, the effect of drink, emigration, and the influence of the church.

The Catholic tradition is also explored in her book *On Lough Derg* (1988), written in conjunction with Liam Blake's photography, in which Purcell follows the rituals of pilgrims who make the three-day retreat to this holy shrine in the west of Ireland. Purcell's talent for characterization is evident as she probes the minds and emotions of the pilgrims as they wind their sleepless way through the shrine, fasting, praying, and meditating. Her ability to cut to the heart of her characters—fictional as well as, in this case, actual—is one of Purcell's strongest traits, one that is also useful in her ghostwritten autobiography of Gay Byrne (1989).

Purcell is currently working on her fourth novel, a sequel to *Falling for a Dancer,* a part of a projected trilogy that will follow the family through the generations.

MARYANNE FELTER

WORKS: *The Dark Hunger.* Dublin: Magill, 1984; *On Lough Derg.* Dublin: Veritas, 1988; with Gay Byrne. *The Time of My Life: An Autobiography.* Dublin: Gill & Macmillan, 1989; *A Place of Stones.* Dublin: Town House & Country House, 1991. (Novel); *That Childhood Country.* Dublin: Town House & Country House, 1992. (Novel); *Falling for a Dancer.* Dublin: Town House & Country House/London: Macmillan, 1993. (Novel); *Francey.* Dublin: Town House/London: Macmillan, 1994. (Novel); *Sky.* Dublin: Town House & Country House, 1995.

PURCELL, PATRICK [JOSEPH] (1914–   ), novelist. Born in County Kilkenny, Purcell was educated at University College, Dublin, and became a sports journalist in Dublin. His nonfictional works included an account of the Gaelic Athletic Association, *Sixty Glorious Years* (1945), and a collaboration on *The Guinness Book of Hurling Records* (1965). He also published four novels: *Hanrahan's Daughter* (1942), *A Keeper of Swans* (1944), *The Quiet Man* (1945), and *Fiddler's Green* (1949). These were fluent entertainments, and *The Quiet Man* was an Alternate Selection of the Book of the Month Club in the United States.

LITERARY WORKS: *Hanrahan's Daughter.* Dublin: Talbot, [1942]/New York: G. P. Putnam's Sons, [1944]; *A Keeper of Swans.* Dublin: Talbot, [1944]; *The Quiet Man.* Dublin: Talbot, [1945]/ New York: G. P. Putnam's Sons, [1946]; *Fiddlers' Green.* Dublin: Talbot, 1949.

Q

QUIGLEY, PATRICK (1953–   ). Born in Monaghan.

WORK: *Borderland.* [Dingle, Co. Kerry]: Brandon, [1994]. (Novel).

QUINN, BOB (1935–   ), filmmaker and fictional memoirist. Quinn has made approximately 100 films, and his work has represented Ireland at various film festivals. For this work, he is a member of Aosdána.*

WORKS: *Atlantean.* London: Quartet, 1986; *Smokey Hollow: A Fictional Memoir.* Dublin: O'Brien, 1991.

QUINN, JUSTIN (fl. 1990s), poet.

WORK: *The O'o'a'a' Bird.* Manchester: Carcanet, 1995.

QUINN, NIALL (?–   ), novelist and short story writer. Quinn was born in Dublin possibly in the 1950s and worked as a seaman in the merchant navies of several countries. He received the 1983 Brendan Behan* Memorial Fellowship Award. His collection of stories, *Voyovic,* is set in Paris, Pakistan, and London, as well as in Ireland, and takes as subjects the lives of laborers, the unemployed, and the underpaid. The characters inhabit a bleak, harsh world, and their solaces are sex, drugs, and drink. These remedies often afford insufficient solace, and the protagonists of both the first and last stories, the Polish worker Voyovic and the Irish girl Brigitte, seek the final solace of suicide. In quality, the stories are extremely uneven. "Fixing" is an impressive study of drug addiction. "Fates," about sympathy and sex, is marred by some perfectly awful writing that ranges from a Desmond Hogan* cutesiness to a romantic Mills and Boon lushness. "The Search" is a static Krapp's-Last-Tape-Revisited, but "Marchpast" is a telling account of bombing raids, while Brigitte's collisions with bigotry in Ireland and England result in a nearly Swiftian* indictment of living.

Quinn's style is also uneven. It is more descriptive or phlegmatically lyric than dramatic. The sentences are often long, sometimes quite long, and more than lightly salted with words like "mathesis," "pneumatism," "macled," "zoomorphism," "triune," "limbic," and, just on page 149, "parsonics," "bascule," "abscissions," and "adytum." Frequently, the style becomes more notable than the content, as in the mannered: "Sometimes, maybe, a freak combination illuminates a nubile insight and the nymph of meaning is had, pulsating, and truth ejaculates." Such characteristics make for an often irritating read, but more than occasionally Quinn rises to some eloquence. The disparity may be suggested by the last two lines of "Brigitte":

Thoughts of infinite beauty, questionless and needless of answers, weaved through a brightening gem of consciousness. She slept, and consciousness passed from her and disappeared into the universe.

Quinn's *Stolen Air* (1988) is called a novel but is really three situations—set in South America, somewhere in the American Southwest, and in London—that possibly detail a bleak journey of a young sailor, bum, and factory worker into renunciation, apathy, and defeat. Not much happens, but any narrative thrust is clotted by the author's continuing fascination with such words as "vestural," "featous," "sthenic," "retuse," "mascaron," "graticule," "phatic," and "pesade." Not to mention his penchant for romantic phrases such as "the Cycladic silent face of oblivion," "the milieu of the heart," "the lagoon of her soul," "the normal specularities of new lovers," "the graticule of clichés," and "the fractional gap of attuition." Whether or not Quinn's sentences emerge from, as he puts it, "a deeply etched, deep-structured, imitative yet uniquely juggled, regenerative matrix of clichés" is perhaps debatable. What is certain is that the prose of his second book remains portentously unreadable.

Quinn's 1991 novel, *The Cafe Cong,* is about a young Irishman who winds up in Paris at about the time of the student unrest in 1968. The first paragraph contains the typical Quinnisms of "the amoeba of their consciousness" and "the gore of their senility." The final paragraph is Quinnianly romantic:

Goodbye, Inga, goodbye. And by this goodbye the sadness of each of my future goodbyes, the sadness, too, of death, is of all grief now bereft.

In between, it is business as usual. Of this book, Feargal Murphy perceptively remarked:

Liam O'Flaherty is a good writer not because of the greatness of [his] ideas . . . but because he could convey the ideas in well crafted sentences that one doesn't have to read a few times in order to unknot. Niall Quinn should think about this.

He certainly should have thought about the craft of writing because, as his books indicate, talent and sensibility are not enough.

WORKS: *Voyovic and Other Stories.* Dublin: Wolfhound, 1980/rpt. as *Voyovic, Brigitte and Other Stories,* 1983; *Stolen Air.* [Dublin]: Wolfhound, [1988]. (Novel); *The Cafe Cong.* [Dublin]: Wolfhound, [1991]; *Welcome to Gomorrah.* [Dublin]: Wolfhound, [1995]. (Novel).

R

RAY, R. J. (fl. first quarter of the twentieth century), playwright. R. J. Ray was the pseudonym of Robert Brophy, who worked on newspapers in Kilkenny, Cork, and Dublin. Between 1909 and 1922, he wrote five unpublished plays for the Abbey.* In *The Story of the Abbey Theatre,* Peter Kavanagh surmises that the plays were not printed because Yeats* did not like them. However, this theory ignores several long and helpful letters from Yeats to Ray, as well as evidence in one of them that Yeats arranged for a revival of Ray's work.

The Casting-Out of Martin Whelan, a three-act play (1910), may be derived from Canon P. A. Sheehan's* novel *Glenanaar.* In both works, a decent person is ostracized because a long-departed relative (Whelan's grandfather in the play) was an informer. *The Gombeen Man,* a play in three acts (1913), deals with a type once common in rural Ireland—a man who acquired wealth and power by lending money to ignorant farmers at exorbitant interest. *The Strong Hand,* a tragedy in two acts (1917), is a reworking of Ray's first Abbey drama, the three-act *The White Feather* (1919). Michael John Dillon, the strong hand seemingly capable of every form of violence, is actually a coward. He shrinks from clearing a man he knows to be innocent of a murder charge, and he must prime himself with drink before killing an unpopular landlord, after which he dies of a heart attack. Ray's final work, *The Moral Law,* a play in one act (1922), is a melodrama of divided loyalties. A retired policeman is certain that his son has killed a district inspector and is ready to turn him in, but at the last moment paternal feeling prevails over duty.

Lennox Robinson,* who like Ray was a Cork realist, comments in *Ireland's Abbey Theatre* (1951) that Ray's works are "undeservedly overlooked." Newspaper reviews are less favorable: they concede his raw power but complain of faulty construction, outworn themes, and straining for picturesque dialogue. Andrew Malone,* in *The Irish Drama* (1929), writes that Ray's characters are "almost incredibly brutal types of humanity." One may conclude that Ray's shortcoming is not his preoccupation with violence, which was far from uncommon in early Abbey drama, but a failure to go beyond it and offer insight into his characters and their environment.

WILLIAM J. FEENEY

RAYMO, CHET (ca. 1935–), novelist. Raymo is professor of physics and astronomy at Stonehill College, Massachusetts. He has written eight volumes of nonfiction, which explore the relationships among nature, science, and the humanities. He and his family live part of each year in Ventry, County Kerry.

His two novels have little in common except brilliance. *In the Falcon's Claw* (1990) is set around the year 1000 and tells the story of the Irish monk Aileran, his friend Gerbert, who becomes Pope Sylvester II, and his lover, Melisande. It is a story of sensual attraction, of church politics, and principally of a good man's growth toward a skeptical definition of God. The characters are nicely realized, as is the sense of the past, particularly the sections set on Skellig Michael off the Dingle Peninsula. The taut narrative, which goes backward and forward in time, is developed by memoirs and letters. This is a sad, thoughtful, accomplished, and highly individual novel.

The Dork of Cork (1993) is equally individual but quite different. Set in modern Cork, its hero is Frank Bois, who writes a best-selling book on astronomy and the people in his life. Frank is the dork (a mispronunciation of dwarf) of the novel, "forty-three years old and forty-three inches tall. Balding, square-jawed, thick lipped. My ears are florescences on the side of my head, my nose might have been struck a blow by a hurley, my spine has a twist that I must consciously correct by turning my body to the right." Like *In the Falcon's Claw,* the story moves backward and forward in time, but the half-dozen principal characters are more eccentrically vivid than those of the earlier novel. The intelligence and poise of Frank Bois, despite the sexual and emotional frustration caused by his dwarfed body, are beautifully done. His abstracted, yet sensual, mother and her lovers—a Church of Ireland curate and a Missouri hillbilly—cling in the memory. The tone of the book, however, is its most remarkable facet. Like many modern Irish novels, its details are often sordid, but while an Eoin McNamee,* a Patrick McCabe,* or a Philip McCann* uses such details to condemn life, Raymo uses them as but a part of life that is controlled by the humane, sane, and intelligent view of the protagonist. The happy ending is also a rarity in modern Irish novels, but it is not only aesthetically satisfying, but also an affirmation of sanity and goodness amid the cultural squalor of the modern world.

WORKS: *In the Falcon's Claw.* New York: Viking Penguin, 1990/[Dingle, Co. Kerry]: Brandon, [1995]; *The Dork of Cork.* London: Bloomsbury, 1993.

READ, CHARLES ANDERSON (1841–1878), editor and novelist. Read was born on November 10, 1841, at Kilsella House, near Sligo. After failing in business through an excess of kindness, he moved to London, where he wrote many forgotten poems and nine hack novels on Irish themes. The novels were serialized in magazines, but at least two of them, *Savourneen Dheelish* (1869) and *Aileen Aroon* (1870), were published in book form. He began the compilation of *The Cabinet of Irish Literature,* which was a large anthology of Irish writing in English with some biographical and critical commentary. Although Read's taste is—to put it mildly—democratic, this is still an eminently useful compilation. Justin McCarthy's* anthology, *Irish Literature,* leans heavily on Read's work, and much of the criticism is simply quoted from Read. Read died in Surrey on January 23, 1878, and the last volume of his anthology was completed by T. P. O'Connor.

WORKS: *Aileen Aroon.* London: People's Pocket Story Books, 1867. (Novel); *Savourneen Dheelish.* 3d ed. London: People's Pocket Story Books, 1867. (Novel); *The Cabinet of Irish Literature,* ed. with T. P. O'Connor. 4 vols. London: Blackie, 1879–1884/new ed., revised and greatly extended, ed. by Katharine Tynan Hinkson. London: Gresham, 1902–1903.

REDDIN, KENNETH. *See* SARR, KENNETH.

REDMOND, LAR (1919–1995), novelist. Redmond was born in the Liberties area of Dublin and educated at the Christian Brothers school in James's Street. He lived in England and in Australia, where he studied at the University of Adelaide. Returning to Ireland, he became a frequent broadcaster, commenting on working-class culture, and is most noted for his novels about life in the Liberties, *Emerald Square* (1987) and *A Walk in the Alien Corn* (1990). He died in Dublin on October 13, 1995.

WORKS: *Emerald Square.* London: Corgi, 1987; *Show Us the Moon: The Dublin Days of Lar Redmond.* [Dingle]: Brandon, [1988]; *A Walk in the Alien Corn.* Dublin: Glendale, 1990.

REDMOND, LUCILE (1949–), short story writer. Redmond was born in Dublin and educated in England, Ireland, and the United States. She has received a Hennessy Award, an Allied Irish Banks Award, and an Arts Council Bursary. Her volume of stories, *Who Breaks Up the Old Moon to Make New Stars* (1978), has one impressive piece but is generally swamped by sensitivity.

WORK: *Who Breaks Up the Old Moon to Make New Stars.* Enniskerry, Co. Wicklow: Egotist, 1978.

REID, CHRISTINA (1942–), playwright. Reid was born in Belfast on March 12, 1942, and educated at Everton Primary School, Girls Model School, and Queen's University. Her productions for the theater include *Tea in a China Cup,* which was produced by the Lyric Theatre* in Belfast in 1983; *Joyriders,* produced at the Tricycle Theatre in Kilburn on February 13, 1986; *Did You Hear the One about the Irishman . . . ?* produced, after a reading by the Royal Shakespeare Company in New York in 1985, at the King's Head Theatre in London in 1987; and *The Belle of Belfast City,* produced in Belfast in May 1989 by the Lyric. Her radio plays include *The Last of a Dyin' Race* (1986), *My Name, Shall*

I Tell You My Name (1987), *The Unfortunate Fursey* (1989), and *Today and Yesterday in Northern Ireland* (1989). In addition, *The Last of a Dyin' Race* was performed on television in 1987, and she has written an adaptation of *Les Miserables,* which was produced in Nottingham in 1992.

Of her unpublished works, the best include *My Name, Shall I Tell You My Name* and *Today and Yesterday in Northern Ireland.* The former play, originally written for the radio, although it was produced at the Dublin Theatre Festival in 1989, details the relationship between a veteran of the Battle of the Somme and his granddaughter. The relationship plays itself out between the early 1960s and the mid-1980s. The granddaughter, who is imprisoned for her part in an antinuclear rally, writes letters to her grandfather and draws sketches in an effort to come to terms with her independent identity and her relationship with her grandfather. The play surveys her growth from girlhood during the beginning of the Troubles, through young adulthood at university in England during the Falklands War, through her days as a graduate and young adult. *Today and Yesterday in Northern Ireland* is a radio play for children and details a life of a young girl in the Ardoyne in the 1950s. The premise of the play is to rally against a question by a reporter about a ''deprived'' childhood. Through the course of the play, life in Northern Ireland reveals itself as fairly typical of life in the industrialized, postwar West. In addition, the underlying violence and hatred of society also reveal themselves in the lives of the children and their games.

Of her published work, *Did You Hear the One about the Irishman . . . ?* studies the relationship between a Protestant girl and a Catholic boy whose ''starry-eyed romantic'' ideals cloud their rational judgment. Both their families have members in Long Kesh. The boy's father was murdered, and each family speaks against the relationship. Nevertheless, the young couple pursues a relationship, and the play builds toward a tragic conclusion. *Tea in a China Cup* was the runner-up in the *Irish Times* Women's Play Competition and earned Reid her position as resident playwright at the Lyric Players Theatre in Belfast. Many of the play's themes will be familiar to readers of feminist literature and literature that discusses the plight of women in Northern Ireland. The play explores the lives and relationships of three generations of Protestant women in Belfast. Set during the days surrounding the Twelfth of July celebrations, the play highlights the conditions of women in Belfast trying to preserve some sense of community and family continuity by passing down traditions and possessions and struggling with relationships of seemingly inept men who brutalize and ignore the women, treating them as possessions like the china of the play's title. *Joyriders* studies the lives of Catholic teenagers in Belfast. It focuses on four young people growing up in the Divis Flats who are placed in a youth training program. The two boys and two girls represent distinctive character types who are all destroyed by their society and the violence and hopelessness of their world, despite the temporary happiness and joy of the training program and their youthful ''games.'' *The Belle of Belfast City,* winner of the George Devine Award in

1987, also explores relationships in the context of a violent Belfast, specifically a community of women who struggle to live in a society in which sectarian hatred and gendering tropes are ingrained in the consciousness of the male and female population.

BERNARD McKENNA

WORKS: *The Last of a Dyin' Race* in *Best Radio Plays of 1986*. London: Methuen, 1986; *Joyriders* and *Tea in a China Cup*. London: Methuen, 1987; *Did You Hear the One about the Irishman . . . ?* and *The Belle of Belfast City*. London: Methuen, 1989. REFERENCES: Bort, Eberhard. "Female Voices in Northern Irish Drama: Anne Devlin, Christina Reid, and Charabanc Theatre Company." In *"Standing in Their Shifts Itself . . ." Irish Drama from Farquhar to Friel*. Vol. 1. Bremen: European Society for Irish Studies, 1993; Henderson, Lynda. "Two New Plays from Belfast." *Theatre Ireland* 5 (December/March 1984): 97–98; Nightingale, Benedict. *"Joyriders." New Statesman* 111 (February 28, 1986): 31; Roll-Hanson, Diderik. "Dramatic Strategy in Christina Reid's *Tea in a China Cup*." *Modern Drama* 30 (September 1987): 389–395.

REID, FORREST (1875–1947), novelist. Few Irish writers have written as lucidly or stylishly as Forrest Reid, author of some sixteen novels, several critical studies, and two volumes of autobiography. He was born on June 24, 1875, in Belfast of Presbyterian stock and, except for an education at Cambridge, lived there inconspicuously until his death on January 4, 1947. His father was a firm's manager who had had to begin again after bankrupting himself as a mercantile shipowner; from this side of the family, Reid may have inherited a Protestant liking for self-reliant democracy but also, in reaction, a loathing of middle-class, commercial values. His mother was a last survivor of the Shropshire Parr family that appeared in *Burke's Peerage* and traced itself back to the last wife of Henry VIII. The declining fortunes of this side of the family may have reinforced Reid's fear of social descent and promoted the faint snobbery of decayed gentility that lightly taints the sensibilities of his boy-heroes.

"The primary impulse of the artist springs, I fancy, from discontent, and his art is a kind of crying for Elysium," wrote Reid in the first paragraph of his excellent first autobiography, *Apostate* (1926). This notion of art as inspired nostalgia may have had family origins, or it may have originated in part with the disappearance of the semi-rustic nineteenth-century Belfast in which Reid grew up and which he mourned beautifully, after the inexorable urban sprawl, in *Apostate*. That book breaks off with Reid's apprenticeship to the tea-trade which he later abandoned in favor of Cambridge. He described his time at the university as a "rather blank interlude." Yet, his life and art can be fully understood only if they are set at least partly within the context of the liberal, humane, Hellenistic Cambridge of Lowes Dickinson, who admired Reid's work, and E. M. Forster, who became a lifelong friend and supporter. Stylistically, too, Reid belongs to no peculiarly Irish tradition, even though he influenced a few younger Ulster writers. During his productive but quiet years in Belfast, after having come down from Cambridge, Reid enjoyed the friendship of Forster, Edwin Muir, and Walter de la Mare who all thought highly of his fiction.

Reid, with a deceptive modesty that resembled that of his friend E. M. Forster, was aware of his limitations as a novelist. "I alone knew, how much, as an author, I resembled Mr. Dick," he noted in his second autobiography, *Private Road* (1940). "I could get on swimmingly until I reached my King Charles's head—the point where a boy becomes a man. Then something seemed to happen, my inspiration was cut off, my interest flagged, so that all became a labour, and not a labour of love." Mediocre at portraying adults and heterosexual relationships, Reid cultivated instead his own strength—the depiction of friendship between older children, especially boys. Though he dared not, or did not wish to, go farther in his novels than a Greek conception of friendship between males as a platonic love or tutelage, he incurred the displeasure of Henry James, to whom he had dedicated his second novel, *The Garden God* (1905), the story of a love affair between two boys. Reid furnishes an account of his rift with the revered master in *Private Road.*

AE* and Edmund Gosse considered Reid a realist, and certainly there are flashes of harsh realism in *The Kingdom of Twilight* (1904), Reid's first novel, and *At the Door of the Gate* (1915), his sixth, especially forthcoming when Reid wishes to portray the squalor of working-class Belfast. But one could with more justification call Reid a gentle fantasist—"he who dreamed," as Forster remarked, "and was partly a dream." Much of Reid's best fiction can be found in the Tom Barber trilogy: *Uncle Stephen* (1931), *The Retreat* (1936), and *Young Tom* (1944), the last volume of which won Reid the James Tait Black Memorial Prize. The trilogy is an exploration, without benefit of Jung or Freud, of the relationship between myth and dream, but it can also be read simply as a work that gives voice to the simple joys of discovery that animate boyhood. *Peter Waring* (1937), however, may be Reid's best novel, free as it is from the narcissism and preciosity that occasionally mar the trilogy and beautifully combining as it does realism and dream. This novel, a deft recreation of a sensitive Protestant adolescence in the North of Ireland in the 1890s, follows its young hero through the confusions of art, sexuality, and religion in a style that is rich, fluent, and assured.

Though primarily a novelist, Reid wrote nonfiction that must not be overlooked. Especially important are *W. B. Yeats: A Critical Study* (1915), *Illustrators of the Sixties* (1928), and *Walter de la Mare: A Critical Study* (1929).

JOHN WILSON FOSTER

WORKS: *The Kingdom of Twilight.* London: Unwin, 1904; *The Garden God.* London: David Nutt, 1905; *The Bracknels.* London: Edward Arnold, 1911/rewritten as *Denis Bracknel,* London: Faber, 1947; *Following Darkness.* London: Edward Arnold, 1912/rewritten as *Peter Waring,* London: Faber, 1937/Belfast: Blackstaff, 1976; *The Gentle Lover.* London: Edward Arnold, 1913; *At the Door of the Gate.* London: Edward Arnold, 1915; *W. B. Yeats, a Critical Study.* London: Martin Secker, 1915; *The Spring Song.* London: Edward Arnold, 1916; *A Garden by the Sea.* Dublin: Talbot/London: Unwin, 1918. (Stories and sketches); *Pirates of the Spring.* Dublin: Talbot/London: Unwin, 1919; *Pender among the Residents.* London: Collins, 1922; *Apostate.* London: Constable, 1926/London: Faber, 1947. (Reminiscences); *Demophon.* London: Collins, 1927; *Illustrators of the Sixties.* London: Faber & Gwyer, 1928; *Walter de la Mare: A Critical Study.* London: Faber, 1929; *Uncle Stephen.* London: Faber, 1931; *Brian Westby.* London: Faber, 1934; *The Retreat; or, the Machinations of Henry.* London: Faber, 1936; *Private Road.* London: Faber, 1940. (Autobiography);

Retrospective Adventures. London: Faber, 1941. (Articles); *Notes and Impressions.* Newcastle, County Down: Mourne, 1942. (Essays); *Young Tom; or, Very Mixed Company.* London: Faber, 1944; *The Milk of Paradise, Some Thoughts on Poetry.* London: Faber, 1946. REFERENCES: Bryan, Mary. *Forrest Reid.* Boston: Twayne, 1976; Burlingham, Russell. *Forrest Reid: A Portrait and a Study.* London: Faber, 1953; Forster, E. M. *Abinger Harvest.* London: Arnold, 1936; Forster, E. M. *Two Cheers for Democracy.* London: Arnold, 1951; Foster, John Wilson. *Forces and Themes in Ulster Fiction.* Dublin: Gill & Macmillan/Totowa, N.J.: Rowman & Littlefield, 1974.

REID, J. GRAHAM (1945–   ), playwright. Reid was born in Belfast and raised in the Protestant Donegal Road area. He left school at age fifteen, after his father's suicide, and worked in a variety of jobs, including lamplighter. He was involved at least marginally in the vigilante groups formed by the Ulster Defense Association. He returned to school, the Belfast College of Business Studies, at age twenty-six. He then took a degree in education from Queen's University, Belfast, and taught for three years at the Gransha Boys' School in County Down. In 1980, he left teaching to devote himself to writing on a full-time basis. His stage productions include *The Death of Humpty Dumpty* (1979), *The Closed Door* (1980), *Dorothy* (1980), *The Hidden Curriculum* (1982), *Remembrance* (1984), and *Callers* (1985). His first plays for television, broadcast on the BBC between 1982 and 1984, include the *Billy* trilogy—*Too Late to Talk to Billy, A Matter of Choice for Billy,* and *A Coming to Terms for Billy.* A fourth play in the *Billy* series, *Lorna,* was broadcast by the BBC in 1987. The *Ties of Blood* series of plays was produced by BBC television in November and December 1985. In addition, some of his works for the stage have been adapted and broadcast on radio and television. *Remembrance* was broadcast by BBC Radio in 1986, and *The Hidden Curriculum* was broadcast by Ulster television in 1984 and in 1985 by Channel 4. His numerous awards include a Jacobs Award in 1984 and the first Royal Court Theatre/Faber and Faber/Channel 4 Samuel Beckett Award in 1982.

Reid's early stage productions were put on by the Peacock Theatre. In fact, he is part of a group of playwrights known as the "Peacock Playwrights"—a group that includes Frank McGuinness,* Neil Donnelly,* Bernard Farrell,* and Martin Boylan*—whose work is particularly suited to the smaller, intimate stage of the Peacock and whose writings were cultivated by the then-Abbey script editor Sean McCarthy and the Abbey's artistic director Joe Dowling. Reid's first production, *The Death of Humpty Dumpty,* was produced in 1979 on the Abbey stage but had been originally staged as *Humpty Dumpty* at the Peacock that same year. The play studies the psychological deterioration of a domineering schoolteacher following an attack that leaves him largely paralyzed; he has lost control over his body from the neck down. The play contrasts the dependent, bitter patient's current condition with his prior self-reliance and supreme confidence. In his injured state, the protagonist makes life so miserable for those around him, particularly his family, that his son eventually kills him. The play's dialogue is fast-moving and hard-hitting in a way reminiscent of David Mamet. In addition, the play's theme speaks to the potential for brutality and cruelty resident in each person. Reid's second staged production, *The Closed Door,* was put on in 1980 by the Peacock. It is a play about cowardice. A man refuses to open his door for a friend who is being pursued by a terrorist gang. The friend is tortured and murdered on the doorstep. The last of Reid's three early plays, *Dorothy,* carries forward his themes of violence and brutality. In this work, the civilized veneer of society is stripped away in favor of a dark, violent, and brutal society. Reid's next play, *The Hidden Curriculum,* was presented in 1982 by both the Peacock, in a production directed by Sean McCarthy, and the Lyric Theatre* in Belfast. The play explores the relationship between formal education and the life of sectarian violence outside the classroom. Drawing on his own experiences as a teacher, Reid details the difficulties of educating students whose classroom lives seem largely irrelevant and far removed from their daily lives. This theme comes across clearly in the thwarted efforts of one teacher to revise the curriculum to seem more relevant to the students' lives. In addition, the play explores the life and conflicts of Protestant children growing up in the face of violence, an aspect of Northern Irish life often ignored. Reid's next play, *Remembrance,* was first performed in 1984 at the Lyric Theatre in Belfast and is, perhaps, his most successful stage production, having been revived numerous times, including at the Riverside Theatre in Coleraine in October 1990, at the Irish Arts Center in New York also in October 1990, and at the John Houseman Theatre in New York in 1992. *Remembrance* details the relationship between a Protestant man and a Catholic woman who meet in a cemetery, both having buried sons who were victims of sectarian violence. The play, in contrast to Reid's earlier work, speaks to the ability of individuals to transcend the violence of society through affection and love. The play also details the reactions of each family to the liaison. Predictably, the response is far from sympathetic. The woman's daughters oppose the match, particularly one whose husband, an Irish Republican Army (IRA) gunman, is in prison. The father's remaining son feels that his father would rather that he had died in his brother's place. Reid's remaining Abbey/Peacock play, *Callers,* is as yet unpublished. The play explores the motives and influences of two IRA men as they plan the assassination of a Royal Ulster Constabulary detective. It was presented at the Peacock from September 30 to October 21, 1985.

Reid's two series of plays for television, *The Billy Plays* and *Ties of Blood,* have been published by Faber and Faber. *The Billy Plays* details the experiences of the Martin family and the effect on their lives and relationships of the violence surrounding life in Belfast. *Ties of Blood* further explores these themes but from the perspective of British soldiers involved in the occupation, members of the Royal Ulster Constabulary, and civilians trapped within the Troubles.

BERNARD McKENNA

WORKS: *The Death of Humpty Dumpty.* [Dublin]: Co-op Books, [1980]; *The Closed Door.* [Dublin]: Co-op Books, [1980]; *The Plays of Graham Reid: Too Late to Talk to Billy, Dorothy, The Hidden Curriculum.* [Dublin]: Co-op Books, [1982]; *Remembrance.* London: Faber, 1985; *Ties of Blood.* London: Faber, 1986. (Contains *McCabe's Wall, Out of Tune, Going Home, Attachments,*

Invitation to a Party, and *The Military Wing*); *The Billy Plays: Too Late to Talk to Billy, A Matter of Choice, A Coming to Terms for Billy,* and *Lorna*). REFERENCES: Andrews, Elmer. "Graham Reid's *Ties of Blood*—a Failure of Realism." *Honest Ulsterman* 83 (Spring 1987): 73–86; Campbell, Paul. "Graham Reid, Professional—the Playwright Talks to Paul Campbell." *Linenhall Review* 1 (2) (1984): 4–7; Etherton, Michael. *Contemporary Irish Dramatists.* London: Macmillan, 1989; Henderson, Lynda. "The Violent Curriculum of Graham Reid." *Fortnight* (June 1983): 21–22; Herbert, Hugh. "The Mask of Violence." *Guardian* (November 12, 1985); "The Hidden Curriculum." *Theatre Ireland* 1 (September–December 1982): 15–17; Lynch, Martin. "Beyond O'Casey: Working-Class Dramatists." *Irish Literary Supplement* 3 (Spring 1984): 35; Macken, Ultan. "Prolific Northern Pen." *Irish Times* (November 12, 1985): 10; O'Toole, Fintan. "Graham Reid's Hearts of Darkness." *In Dublin* (April 1983): 14–16; O'Malley, Conor. *A Poet's Theatre.* Dublin: Elo, 1988; Osmond, John. "Clash of Identities: The Ulster Theatre of Graham Reid and Martin Lynch." In *"Standing in Shifts Itself" . . . Irish Drama from Farquhar to Friel.* Bremen: European Society for Irish Studies, 1993, pp. 243–261; Pilkington, Lionel. "Violence and Identity in Northern Ireland: Graham Reid's *The Death of Humpty Dumpty.*" *Modern Drama* 33 (March 1990): 15–29.

REID, CAPTAIN [THOMAS] MAYNE (1818–1883), novelist and adventurer. Born on April 4, 1818, at Ballyroney, County Down, the eldest son of a Presbyterian minister, Reid was supposed to follow his father's calling. However, though he distinguished himself at college in many subjects, theology was not one of them. He "ran away to sea," shipping out to New Orleans at the age of twenty. He traveled widely in the interior of what was then the Wild West, working as a storekeeper and eventually as a journalist. A long poem, "La Cubana," and a five-act tragedy belong to this period. He knew Poe in Philadelphia and, though he did not admire him as a poet, was later prepared to defend his character. Commissioned in the U.S. Army as a captain in the Mexican War of 1845, he took part in the siege of Chaupultepec in 1847. He was wounded and began his first novel, *The Rifle Rangers* (1850), while recuperating. In 1849, he settled in London, where that novel, the first of over forty, was published with success the following year. He joined Kossuth and the Hungarian rebels for a time. In 1853, he met a thirteen-year-old girl, Elizabeth Hyde, whom he married two years later. She was the inspiration of his novel *The Child Wife* (1868). His literary career was successful until 1866, when he suffered financial reverses. An infection of the foot picked up on a tour of the United States left him crippled for the rest of his life. His ill health affected his writing, and his popularity waned. The last years of his life were difficult. He gave an account of his life in *Ran Away to Sea* (1858), and his wife, who survived him for many years, wrote two books about her gallant and dashing captain. A contemporary of Verne, Ballantyne, and Marryat, he drew on his early life to create a long series of adventure novels, which have dash and vitality and a great deal of color, if little psychology. His own inner life and sexuality were strangely concurrent with the sentimental notions of Dickens, Ruskin, and Poe (who also married a child wife). Though *The Rifle Rangers* remained a boys' favorite well into the middle of this century, his reputation has now faded, though not beyond recovery. He virtually invented the "Wild West" as a literary genre. The plot of his rather more serious *The Quadroon* Boucicault* appropriated for his play

The Octoroon. Robert Louis Stevenson described him as "that cheerful, ingenious, romantic soul," and Vladimir Nabokov remembered being impressed by *The Headless Horseman* in his Russian youth. Reid died in London on October 22, 1883.

PETER COSTELLO

REPRESENTATIVE WORKS: *The Rifle Rangers.* 2 vols. London: W. Shoberl, 1850; *The Scalp Hunters.* 3 vols. London: C. J. Skeet, 1851; *The Boy Hunters.* London: D. Bogue, 1853; *The Quadroon.* London: G. W. Hyde, 1856; *The War Trail.* London: J. & C. Brown, [1857]; *Ran Away to Sea: An Autobiography for Boys.* Boston: Ticknor & Fields, 1858/London: W. Kent, 1859; *Croquet.* Boston: J. Redpath/London: C. J. Skeet, 1863; (Handbook); *The Boy Slaves.* Boston: Ticknor & Fields, 1865/London & New York: G. Routledge, [1865?]; *The Headless Horseman.* London & New York: G. Routledge, [1866?]; *The Child Wife.* London: Ward, Lock & Tyler, 1868/ New York: Sheldon, 1869; *The Free Lances.* London: Remington, 1881/New York: Hurst, n.d. REFERENCES: Dorset, Gerald. "The Wonderful World of Captain Mayne Reid." *Journal of Irish Literature* 15 (January 1986): 43–49; Reid, Elizabeth Mayne. *Mayne Reid, A Memoir of His Life.* London: Ward & Downey, 1890; Reid, Elizabeth Mayne, with C. H. Coe. *Captain Mayne Reid, His Life and Adventures.* London: Greening, 1900; Steele, Joan. "Mayne Reid, a Revised Bibliography." *Bulletin of Bibliography* 19 (July–September 1972): 95–100; Steele, Joan. *Captain Mayne Reid.* New York: Twayne, 1977.

RICE, DAVID (fl. 1970s–1990s), novelist. Rice has been a Dominican friar, a Catholic priest, and a journalist in the United States, China, and Ireland. His novel, *Blood Guilt* (1994), begins in Ireland before the real outbreak of the recent Northern Troubles but shows a young student, Connor Emmet, killing three people after an aborted Irish Republican Army raid on a police barracks. He is sent from Ireland and told not to return, and most of the action takes place in the United States. In Carbondale, Illinois, Emmet becomes a journalist and eventually a nationally syndicated columnist. The death of his new bride, as well as his guilt for the three killings in Ireland, plunges him into alcoholism. He finally emerges from the bottle to work on a small paper in Washington state and finds himself more involved in the plight of illegal Mexican workers than in the now heated-up struggle in Ireland. Although the theme is about coming to terms with overwhelming guilt, the novel is not more than a serious entertainment. As such, it is readable and well observed. Its plot, except for a lengthy debate about values toward the end, gallops right along.

Rice has also published several nonfictional books: *Shattered Vows: Exodus from the Priesthood, The Dragon's Brood: Conversations with Young Chinese,* and *The Rathmines Stylebook: Guidelines for Writing.*

WORK: *Blood Guilt.* Belfast: Blackstaff, [1994].

RICHARDS, MAURA (1939–   ), novelist. Richards was born and educated in Mitchelstown, County Cork. She came to Dublin in 1968, and the birth of a daughter out of wedlock provided the experience for her first novel, *Two to Tango* (1981). In 1972, she helped to found Cherish, an association of single parents. In 1977, she married and moved to Kent in England, where she now works as a child counselor. *Two to Tango* is a graphic account of what one must assume was the author's own pregnancy. She writes well of her feelings and can be both moving and cynical in describing the events of the nine months. Possibly, this book was a kind of catharsis, as it cannot have been easy—to say the least of it—to discover you are pregnant and unmarried in Catholic Ireland of 1969. With the skill displayed in this book, it would have been reasonable to hope that the writer would next look further afield and write a book rich in characters other than herself. However, *Interlude* of 1982 is a rubbishy novella that purports to tell the story of a sudden lesbian affair between two unlikely ladies who meet in a cubicle in a Grafton Street department store. The women's dialogue reads like a very bad Mills and Boon novel, the sex is graphically explicit, and the denouement reveals that one of them is an ex-nun who had lesbian affairs in the convent. The publishers may have assumed that the book would have had some sale as "soft porn," for as a psychological exploration of a genuine lesbian relationship, it fails utterly.

DOROTHY ROBBIE

WORKS: *Two to Tango*. Dublin: Ward River, [1981]; *Interlude*. [Dublin]: Ward River, [1982].

RIDDELL, CHARLOTTE ELIZA LAWSON (1832–1906), fiction writer. Mrs. J. H. Riddell was born Charlotte Cowan in Carrickfergus, County Antrim, on September 30, 1832, and died in Middlesex, England, on September 24, 1906. A vastly prolific and fairly popular writer, she occasionally used Ireland as her setting, but she is mainly remembered as an author of spooky tales, and some of these are now and then republished. She often has engaging ideas, but she is no M. R. James. Her story "The Banshee's Warning," for instance, is narrated rather than dramatized, and she is given to inserting long essayistic paragraphs like the one that begins:

Even supposing a man's springtime to have been a cold and ungenial one, with bitter easterly winds and nipping frosts, biting the buds and retarding the blossoms, still it was spring for all that—spring with the young green leaves sprouting forth, with the flowers unfolding tenderly, with the songs of the birds.

PRINCIPAL WORKS: *Which, the Right or the Left*. New York: Garrett, 1855; As Rainey Hawthorne. *The Ruling Passion*. 3 vols. London: Bentley, 1857; *City and Suburb*. New ed. London: Gall & Inglis, [1860?]; as F. G. Trafford. *The Moors and the Fens*. Rev. ed. London: Smith Elder, 1863; *George Geith of Fen Court*. London: Warne, [1865?]/Boston: T.O.H. P. Burnham, 1865/New York: O. S. Felt, 1865; as F. G. Trafford. *Maxwell Drewitt*. London: Tinsley, 1865/New York: Harper, 1866; as F. G. Trafford. *Phemie Keller*. London: Tinsley/New York: Harper, 1866; *The Race for Wealth*. 3 vols. London: Tinsley/New York: Harper, 1866; *Too Much Alone*. London: Warne, 1866/Boston: Estes & Lauriat, [187?]; *Far above Rubies*. 3 vols. 2d ed. London, 1867; as Rainey Hawthorne. *The Rich Husband*. London, 1867/Philadelphia: T. B. Peterson, [1867?]; *Austin Friars*. 3 vols. London: Hutchinson, 1870; *A Life's Assize*. 3 vols. London: Tinsley/New York: Harper, 1871; *The Earl's Promise*. 3 vols. London: Tinsley, 1873; *Home, Sweet Home*. 3 vols. London: Tinsley, 1873; *Frank Sinclair's Wife, and Other Stories*. London: Tinsley, 1874; *Montmorley's Estate*. 3 vols. London: Tinsley, 1874; *Above Suspicion*. 3 vols. London, 1876/Boston: Estes & Lauriat, [1876?]; *Her Mother's Darling*. 3 vols. London: Tinsley, 1877/New York: G. Munro, 1880; *Alaric Spenceley, or, A High Ideal*. 3 vols. London: C. J. Skeet, 1881; *The Mystery in Palace Gardens.* 3 vols. London: Bentley, 1880/New York: G. Munro, 1881; *The Senior Partner.* London: Bentley, 1881/New York: Harper, [1882]; *Daisies and Buttercups.* London: R. Bentley/ New York: G. Munro, 1882; *The Prince of Wales's Garden-Party, and Other Stories.* New York: G. Munro, 1882/London: Chatto & Windus, 1884; *A Struggle for Fame.* London: Bentley/New York: Harper, 1883; *Berna Boyle. A Love Story of the County Down.* 3 vols. London: Bentley, 1884; *Susan Drummond.* 3 vols. London: Bentley/New York: Harper, 1884; *Weird Stories.* London: J. Hogg, [1884]/London: Home & Van Thal, 1946; *Fairy Water.* New ed. London: Chatto & Windus, 1885; *Mitre Court.* 3 vols. London: Bentley, 1885; *The Government Official.* London: R. Bentley, 1887; *Miss Gascoigne.* London: Ward & Downey/New York: D. Appleton, 1887; *The Nun's Curse.* 3 vols. London: Ward & Downey/New York: G. Munro, 1888; *Idle Tales.* London: Ward & Downey, 1888; *Princess Sunshine and Other Stories.* 2 vols. London: Ward & Downey, 1889/New York: J. W. Lovell, [1890]; *A Mad Tour: or, A Journey Undertaken in an Insane Moment through Central European Foot.* London: Bentley/New York: J. W. Lovell, 1891; *My First Love.* London: Hutchinson, [1891]/*My First Love, and My Last Love* [A sequel]. New York: J. W. Lovell, [1891]; *The Rusty Sword; or, Thereby Hangs a Tale.* London: Christian Knowledge Society, [1893]; *A Silent Tragedy.* London: F. V. White, 1893; *The Banshee's Warning and Other Tales.* 2d ed. London: Remington, 1894; *A Rich Man's Daughter.* New York: International News, [1895?]/ London: White, 1897; *Did He Deserve It?* London: Downey, 1897; *Handsome Phil and Other Stories.* London: F. V. White, 1899; *The Head of the Firm.* 3 vols. London: Heinemann, 1892/New York: J. W. Lovell, [1892?]; *Joy after Sorrow.* New ed. London: Hutchinson, [19??]; *Poor Fellow!* London: F. V. White, 1902. REFERENCE: Ellis, Stewart M. *Wilkie Collins, Le Fanu, and Others.* London: Constable, 1931.

RIORDAN, MAURICE (1953–   ), poet. Riordan was born in Lisgoold, County Cork. His first collection was a choice of the Poetry Book Society.

WORK: *A Word from the Loki.* London: Faber, 1995.

ROBBIE, DOROTHY (1923–   ), playwright. Robbie was born on October 25, 1923, at Abercynon, South Wales. She graduated from the University of London with a B.Sci. in zoology and taught for a number of years at Alexandra College in Dublin. For many years she has lived in Greystones, County Wicklow, where her involvement in amateur dramatics led to her two published plays. She wrote the book and lyrics for a charming musical version of *Alice in Wonderland* (1970), which has several times been performed in the United States. Her *Ribbon with Gold* (1977) is an effective, if somewhat hagiographical, dramatization of the life of Countess Markievicz.

WORKS: *Lewis Carroll's Alice in Wonderland.* Dixon, Calif.: Proscenium, [1970]. (Music by Desmond Hand); *Ribbon with Gold.* Newark, Del.: Proscenium, [1977].

ROBERTSON, OLIVIA (1917–   ), novelist and writer of stories and sketches. Robertson was born in London on Friday, April 13, 1917. She was educated at Heathfield School in Ascot and Alexandra College in Dublin, and then at the Grosvenor School of Modern Art in London and the Royal Hibernian Academy in Dublin. From 1941 to 1945, she worked as a slum playground leader for Dublin Corporation, an experience that was the basis for her first book, *St. Malachy's Court* (1946). This collection of sketches, basically of slum life, is told from the view of an accepted outsider. The book is funny, macabre, poignant, and a good deal more convincing than the steamy glamorizations done by an insider like Paul Smith.* Robertson's writing career lasted a scant ten years, but she is firmly in the tradition of Maria Edgeworth* and Somerville and Ross,* and anyone who reads one of her books will probably search all of the others out and regret there are no more. Among the best of the others is a whimsical and satirical novel, *Miranda Speaks* (1950), but even a simple collection of essays like *It's an Old Irish Custom* (1953) is pervaded by her engaging individuality. For some years, she has lived in a castle near Enniscorthy as a priestess in the Fellowship of Isis, which she and her brother, Lawrence Durdin-Robertson, Baron Strathloch, founded on March 21, 1976. This transformation of a gently humorous writer into a devoted priestess of Isis is perhaps an unusual development, but as she writes:

So you see the transformation of a modest, intellectual(?) tweed-suited Anglo-Irish woman, very factual, possibly a little politically to the left, a Liberal, and not interested in religion into . . . I'm not really sure what, but something more like a Harry Clarke or AE Painting. . . . It would be meaningless, this Pre-Raphaelite Art Nouveau revival, this sudden change to crowns and robes like a Waite Tarot pack, unless we were totally committed and we are. Luckily we are so sure of the reality of the psychic world that we can actually have a sense of humour.

    WORKS: *St. Malachy's Court.* London: Peter Davies, 1946/New York: Odyssey, 1947. (Stories); *Field of the Stranger.* London: Peter Davies, 1948/New York: Random House, [1948]. (Novel); *The Golden Eye.* London: Peter Davies, 1949. (Novel); *Miranda Speaks.* London: Peter Davies, 1950. (Novel); *It's an Old Irish Custom.* London: Denis Dobson, 1953. (Essays); *Dublin Phoenix.* London: Jonathan Cape, 1957. (On Dublin); and the following religious pamphlets published in Enniscorthy by Cesara: *The Call of Isis,* 1975; *The Isis Wedding Rite,* 1976; *Ordination of a Priestess,* 1977; *Rite of Rebirth,* 1977; *Dea: Rites and Mysteries of the Goddess,* 197?; *Urania: Ceremonial Magic of the Goddess,* 1983?. REFERENCE: Lanters, Jose. "The Mythicizing of Napper Tandy Street: The Novels of Olivia Robertson." *Journal of Irish Literature* 22 (September 1993): 17–24.

ROBINSON, LENNOX (1886–1958), playwright. From the staging of his first play in 1908 until his death in 1958, Lennox Robinson was associated with the Abbey* as writer, producer, and director. This service, interrupted only from 1914 to 1919, exceeds in length the time devoted to the theatre by Yeats* or Lady Gregory.*

    Esme Stuart Lennox Robinson was born in Douglas, County Cork, on October 4, 1886, the son of a Church of Ireland clergyman. Because of poor health he had little formal schooling. An interest in drama developed when he saw the Abbey players on tour in Cork in 1907. His literary career was oriented mostly to playwriting, although he also wrote fiction, biography, autobiography, essays, and a history of the Abbey.

    In 1909, Robinson accepted an offer from Yeats and Lady Gregory to work as play director and manager of the theatre. Bernard Shaw* invited him to London to gain theatrical experience. Robinson's decision not to close the Abbey in mourning for the death of Edward VII in 1910 caused a dispute between the directors and their English benefactress Miss A.E.F. Horniman. Following an unsuccessful Abbey tour of the United States in 1914, Robinson resigned from the company but came back in 1919. He was appointed to the Board of Directors in 1923, a post he held until his death, and he doubled as director-producer until 1935. On September 8, 1931, he married Dorothy Travers Smith. They had no children. Robinson frequently traveled to the United States with the Abbey company or as a guest lecturer. In 1956, he went to China to take part in a commemoration of the centenary of Shaw. He died in Dublin on October 14, 1958.

As playwright, Robinson made no territorial conquest as O'Casey* did in tenement drama or Lady Gregory in Kiltartan farce. Instead, he ranged widely, from realism to expressionism, from problems of Irish life before and after the Treaty to easy social comedy.

Robinson's early Abbey plays, set in rural Cork—*The Clancy Name* (1908), *The Cross Roads* (1909), and *Harvest* (1910)—were blemished by unpersuasive didacticism and contrived endings, but they were typical of the shift from the romantic realism of Synge* toward a realism strongly critical of Irish life. The best of his early work is *Patriots* (1912), in which a revolutionary comes home from prison to continue his activity, only to find that negotiation and business as usual are the order of the new day.

Robinson's first important comedy was *The Whiteheaded Boy* (1916). The older Geoghegan children grudgingly sacrifice their futures to provide Denis Geoghegan with a medical education for which he has neither the aptitude nor the desire. Yet, when he sets off on his own as a common laborer, the grumblers unite to prevent him from disgracing the family. The play can be read as an allegory of England's willingness to do everything for Ireland but set it free: however, this family format of workers and drones appears in other of Robinson's plays without apparent political ramifications. *The Round Table* (1922) and *The White Blackbird* (1925) involve a family member exerting himself to support his feckless relatives. *The Far-Off Hills* (1928) inverts the plot of *The Whiteheaded Boy*. Marian Clancy delays entrance into the religious life so that she can care for her father and younger sisters, who only want to escape her well-meaning tyranny. And the father in *Bird's Nest* (1938) slaves to educate children who prefer to live according to their own wishes.

In the 1920s and early 1930s, Robinson sometimes moved the locale from Cork to English, or at least not definitely Irish, settings. It was not, on the whole, a fruitful change. Among the plays of this period are *Portrait* (1925), a study of a loser in the rat race; *Ever the Twain* (1929), on the difference between Englishmen and Yanks; *Give a Dog* (1929), a muddled confrontation of creativity and orthodoxy; and *All's Over, Then?* (1932), a melodrama of mother–daughter rivalry.

Robinson's plays with Irish locales and themes are more deeply rooted. *The Big House* (1926), something of a chronicle play, forcefully asserts the right of the Protestant Ascendancy to a proper place in post-Treaty Ireland. *Killycregs in Twilight* (1937) continues the theme of keeping alive Ascendancy tradition.

Church Street (1934), technically perhaps the most interesting Robinson play, is influenced by Pirandello; at the same time, it is an admission that Ireland is Robinson's ultimate source of strength. A writer of superficial comedies in London pays a duty visit to his Irish home and discovers vital raw material in his seemingly drab townsfellows. *Drama at Inish* (1934) makes another kind of confession. Its plot is the visit of a highbrow drama company to a seaside village for a summer of Serious Theatre; too serious, it fills the residents with all manner of guilt complexes. This play may be self-mockery of Robinson's own efforts, first at the Abbey, then beginning in 1918 with the forming of the Dublin Drama League, to perform exotic foreign masterpieces for Dubliners who preferred the comedies of William Boyle* or Martin J. McHugh.*

Robinson's late work—*Forget Me Not* (1941), *The Lucky Finger* (1948), *The Demon Lover* (1954)—adds nothing to his stature as a dramatist.

Of his nondramatic writing, a history of the Abbey and its predecessors from 1899 to 1951 is pleasantly reminiscent but useful mostly as a catalogue of plays and players. His other work is characteristically graceful, craftsmanlike, candid, and unpretentious when he is the subject, but it is largely overshadowed by his contributions to Irish drama.

In comedy and tragedy alike, Robinson was an intellectual playwright. Even Robert Emmet,* so often turned into a caricature of romantic patriotism, was portrayed as a thinking man in *The Dreamers* (1915). There is, however, no consistent philosophical motif in the plays, and sometimes after delineating a problem Robinson would not stay for an answer. In *The Lost Leader* (1918), this indecisiveness is effective. One cannot be sure that the seemingly demented Lucius Lenihan is not a resurrected Parnell. Generally, however, the uncertainty is a flaw.

Robinson's chief merits are a penetrating wit edged with enough malice to nick the unwary, a sureness of dialogue, and a gift for characterization. His best works are among the Abbey's best works. His failures are evidence that the law of averages lies in wait for any prolific, boldly experimenting writer.

WILLIAM J. FEENEY

WORKS: *The Cross-Roads: A Play in a Prologue and Two Acts.* Dublin: Maunsel, 1909. (Prologue subsequently deleted); *Two Plays: Harvest: A Play in Three Acts* and *The Clancy Name: A Tragedy in One Act.* Dublin: Maunsel, 1911; *Patriots: A Play in Three Acts.* Dublin: Maunsel, 1912; *The Dreamers: A Play in Three Acts.* Dublin: Maunsel, 1915; *A Young Man from the South.* Dublin: Maunsel, 1917. (Autobiographical novel); *Dark Days.* Dublin: Talbot, 1918. (Political sketches); *The Lost Leader: A Play in Three Acts.* Dublin: Kiersey, 1918; *Eight Short Stories.* Dublin: Talbot, 1919; *The Whiteheaded Boy: A Comedy in Three Acts.* London: Putnam's, 1921; *Crabbed Youth and Age: A Little Comedy.* London: Putnam's, 1924; *The Round Table: A Comic Tragedy in Three Acts.* London: Putnam's, 1924; *Never the Time and the Place: A Little Comedy in One Act,* in *The Dublin Magazine* 1 (May 1924): 856–867/reprinted in Belfast: Carter, 1953; *The White Blackbird: A Play in Three Acts* and *Portrait: A Play in Two Sittings.* Dublin: Talbot, 1926; *The Big House: Four Scenes in Its Life.* London: Macmillan, 1928; *Give a Dog—: A Play in Three Acts.* London: Macmillan, 1928; *Plays.* London: Macmillan, 1928; *Ever the Twain: A Comedy in Three Acts.* London: Macmillan, 1930; *Bryan Cooper.* London: Constable, 1931. (Biography); *The Far-Off Hills: A Comedy in Three Acts.* London: Chatto & Windus, 1931; *Drama at Inish: An Exaggeration in Three Acts* (retitled *Is Life Worth Living?*). London: Macmillan, 1933; *More Plays: All's Over, Then?: A Play in Three Acts* and *Church Street: A Play in One Act.* London: Macmillan, 1935; *Killycreggs in Memories* and *Poems and Memories.* Spoken Arts Recordings; "A Lennox Robinson Number." Lloyd Worley & Gary Phillips, eds. *Journal of Irish Literature* 9 (January 1980); *Selected Plays of Lennox Robinson.* Christopher Murray, ed. Gerrards Cross: Colin Smythe/Washington, D.C.: Catholic University of America Press, 1982. REFERENCES: Dorman, Sean (Robinson's nephew). *Limelight over the Liffey.* Fowey: Raffeen, 1983; Everson, Ida G. "Young Lennox Robinson and the Abbey Theatre's First American Tour, 1911–1912." *Modern Drama* 9 (1966): 74–89; Everson, Ida G. "Lennox Robinson and Synge's *Playboy,* 1911–1930: Two Decades of America's Cultural Growth." *New England Quarterly* 44 (March 1971): 3–21; Ferrar, Harold. "Robert Emmet in Irish Drama." *Éire-Ireland* 1 (Summer 1966): 19–28; Murray, Christopher. "Lennox Robinson: The Abbey's Anti-Hero." In *Irish Writers and the Theatre.* Masaru Sekine, ed. Gerrards Cross: Colin Smythe/Totowa, N.J.: Barnes & Noble, 1987; Murray, Christopher. "Lennox Robinson, *The Big House, Killycreggs in Twilight,* and 'the Vestigia of Generations.' " In *Ancestral Voices: The Big House in Anglo-Irish Literature.* Otto Rauchbauer, ed. Hildesheim: Olms, 1992; Ó hAodha, Micheál. *Pictures at the Abbey: The Collection of the Irish National Theatre.* Mountrath, Portlaoise: Dolmen, 1983; O'Neill, Michael J. *Lennox Robinson.* New York: Twayne, 1964; Peterson, Richard F. "The Crane and the Swan: Lennox Robinson and William Butler Yeats." *Journal of Irish Literature* 9 (January 1980): 69–76; Spinner, Kaspar. *Die Alte Dame Sagt Nein! Drei Irische Dramatiker, Lennox Robinson, Sean O'Casey, Denis Johnston.* Bern: Franche Verlag, 1961; Worth, Katharine. "A Place in the Country." *Times Literary Supplement* (September 2, 1983): 929. (Comparison of Robinson and O'Casey).

ROBINSON, TIM (1935–   ), cartographer and historian of Aran. Robinson was born in London and grew up in Yorkshire. He studied mathematics at Cambridge and taught Turkish students on the Bosporus. He practiced painting in Vienna and in London and in 1972 moved to Aran, where he and his wife lived until 1980. His two-volume *Stones of Aran* (1986 and 1995) has been described by Shirley Kelly as "an encyclopedia with soul, a skilfully organised mass of information enriched by the author's poetic touch." J.C.C. Mays has called it "one of the most significant pieces of prose, from a literary point of view, written in Ireland in the past quarter-century."

WORKS: *Stones of Aran: Pilgrimage.* Dublin: Lilliput in association with Wolfhound, 1986; *Stones of Aran: Labyrinth.* Dublin: Lilliput, 1995. REFERENCE: Kelly, Shirley. "Self-Made Man of Aran." *Books Ireland,* No. 188 (September 1996): 193–196.

ROCHE, BILLY (1949–   ), novelist, playwright, actor, and composer. Roche was born in Wexford on January 11, 1949, the youngest of six children. He was educated by the Christian Brothers but left school at seventeen to work in his father's waterfront pub, the Shamrock. A self-taught musician, Roche played the folk clubs of London and later formed a new-wave pop group, the Roach Band. "The Shamrock Shuffle," recorded in the late 1970s, was inspired by characters who frequented his father's pub.

These characters reappear—arguing, telling stories, betting on the horses, and especially singing—in the novel *Tumbling Down* (1986). Roche's writing is drenched in music: the lyrics of ballads, hymns, and pop favorites; the entire act of a busker named Johnny Sligo; and even "the music of the streets" as performed by hawkers and tradesmen. Set in the mid-1960s, *Tumbling Down* sketches a year of Wexford life as seen and experienced by Davy Wolfe, seventeen, an aspiring musician who works in his father's pub, the Rock. The autobiographical story, in Davy's own witty and lyrical telling, is interwoven with omniscient passages that look more deeply and sadly into other lives.

Davy Wolfe is earnest and ambitious. Jimmy Brady—the young protagonist of Roche's first play, *A Handful of Stars* (1988)—is destructive and self-destructive, a would-be rebel turned petty criminal. Yet in his refusal to conform, he transcends his depressed environment, which is crystallized in the play's single set, a seedy pool hall. In *Poor Beast in the Rain* (1989), the single set depicts a betting shop during the weekend of the All Ireland Hurling Final, when the town is half deserted. Drawing on the myth of Oisín, the action converges on the return of an exile, a man who, ten years earlier, had run away with the shop owner's wife. But the play's real subject is the longing of those left behind. *Belfry* (1990) uses a double set, representing both the belfry and vestry of a church, and breaks the fourth wall by means of a narrator: Artie, a sacristan in love with a married woman. The story of their giddy and sad affair illuminates the lives of six people.

After each of these plays won critical awards in London, they were published together—and adapted for BBC television—as "The Wexford Trilogy." Although the plays have no recurring characters, they are linked by tones of rough humor and broad compassion.

Novelistic description in *Tumbling Down* had evoked the six hills of Wexford, the "Bull Ring" (town square), the twin churches on Rowe and Bride Streets, the world of the waterfront, and the barren and uninhabited Ballast Bank, reconceived as "Useless Island." In the Wexford trilogy, however, the setting is fairly generic—*A Handful of Stars* takes place in "a small town somewhere in Ireland"—but Roche's next play, *Amphibians* (1992), brings much of Wexford on stage through multiple sets, traditional music, and eleven fully drawn characters. Several of the characters are former fishermen, now reduced to working in a cannery. The last holdout, Eagle, tries to keep the old rituals alive, and the story narrows to a day once sacred to the fishing folk of Wexford: November 10, St. Martin's Eve.

Amphibians defines time sharply while keeping stage space flexible and imaginative. *The Cavalcaders,* produced in 1993, does just the opposite. Within a single realistic set—an old shoe repair shop—the play wanders freely through the memories of Terry, the leader of a barbershop quartet. The atmosphere, heightened by Roche's original songs, is laden with Terry's nostalgia and guilt.

The Cavalcaders epitomizes several features of Roche's dramatic style: expressive music, a story focusing on sexual betrayal, and important secondary characters who never appear on stage yet seem to hover just beyond it. In theater, as in fiction, Roche summons up the shared life of a community. His acknowledged influences include Chekhov, O'Casey,* Friel,* and Tom Murphy.*

Roche's first five plays, in their fusion of the local and the universal, pay worthy tribute to these masters.

Among Roche's credits as a professional actor are supporting roles in *A Handful of Stars* and *The Cavalcaders.*

KEVIN KERRANE

WORKS: *Tumbling Down.* Dublin: Wolfhound, 1986. (Novel); *A Handful of Stars, Poor Beast in the Rain,* and *Belfry,* published as *The Wexford Trilogy.* London: Nick Hern Books, 1992. (Plays); *Amphibians.* London: Warner Chappell, 1992. (Play); *The Cavalcaders.* London: Nick Hern Books, 1994. (Play).   REFERENCE: Battersby, Eileen. "The Boy from Wexford." *Irish Times* (March 2, 1995): 13.

ROCHE, REGINA MARIA (ca. 1764–1845), novelist. Roche was born Regina Dalton in County Waterford about 1764 and became a very popular Gothic and sentimental novelist. *The Children of the Abbey* (1796), her best-known book, was read well into the nineteenth century. She sometimes used Irish settings, and she was known and deplored by Jane Austen. She died in Waterford on May 17, 1845.

WORKS: *The Vicar of Lansdowne; or, Country Quarters.* 2 vols. London: J. Johnson, 1789; *The Maid of the Hamlet.* London, 1793?/Dublin: G. Burnett, 1802; *The Children of the Abbey.* 4 vols. London: Minerva, 1796; *Clermont.* London: W. Lane, 1798. 4 vols./London: Folio Society, 1968. (As Vol. 6 of *The Northanger Set of Jane Austen Horrid Novels*); *The Nocturnal Visit.* 4 vols. London: W. Lane, Minerva, 1800; *The Discarded Son; or, Haunts of the Banditti.* 5 vols. London: Lane, Newman, 1807; *The House of Osma and Almeria; Or, The Convent of St. Ildefonso.* 3 vols. London: A. K. Newman, 1810; *The Monastery of St. Colomb; Or, The Atonement.* 5 vols. London: A. K. Newman, Minerva, 1813. (Probably first published as early as 1810); *London Tales; Or, Reflective Portraits.* 2 vols. London: J. Booth, 1814; *The Munster Cottage Boy.* 4 vols. London: A. K. Newman, 1820; *The Bridal of Dunamore; And Lost and Won, Two Tales.* 3 vols. London: A. K. Newman, 1823; *The Tradition of the Castle; Or, Scenes in the Emerald Isle.* 4 vols. London: A. K. Newman, 1824; *The Castle Chapel.* 3 vols. London: A. K. Newman, 1825; *Contrast.* 3 vols. London: A. K. Newman, 1828; *The Nun's Picture.* 3 vols. London: A. K. Newman, 1836.

RODDY, MOYA (ca. 1960–   ), novelist. Roddy was born in Dublin and earned a first-class honours degree from Central London Polytechnic in media studies in 1983. She has worked for Channel 4 and has written several screenplays, some short stories, and one novel. She lives in Dublin.

WORK: *The Long Way Home.* Dublin: Attic, 1992.

RODGERS, W[ILLIAM] R[OBERT] (1909–1969), poet. Rodgers was born on August 1, 1909, in Belfast, where he was educated at the Queens University and at the Presbyterian Theological College. There he prepared for his ordination as a Presbyterian minister which took place in 1935. He served as minister at Loughgall, County Antrim, from 1935 to 1946. In 1941, his first collection of poems appeared. Entitled *Awake! And Other Poems,* the volume collected most of the poems he had written while ministering to his congregation in Loughgall. It was widely praised; critics responded to its exurberant relishing of verbal sound patterns. It was assumed that Rodgers' verbal practices owed something to Gerard Manley Hopkins' example. It is clear, however, that, while other English poets of the 1930s unsuccessfully attempted to emulate Hopkins' experiments, Rodgers managed to endow his diction with an energy and bravura reminiscent of Hopkins without having in fact read that poet's work. The verbal effects of Rodgers' poetry are more properly to be related to his perennial zest for word play, pun, and alliteration, to his almost Joycean awareness of linguistic possibilities. The themes of his early poetry, however, do suggest that he experienced a tension between the priestly role and poetic ambition much as Hopkins did. *Awake! And Other Poems* was also notable for an exact scrupulous intensity in rendering Rodgers' awareness of the physical world—its motions, its comings and goings, its explosions of energy and its moments of stillness. A heightened moral awareness of clash and conflict in the social and political world was expressed in a tendency to employ parable and homiletic rhetoric in a distinctly 1930s English mode.

In 1946, Rodgers resigned from the ministry and settled in London where he made many contributions to the BBC features department. Among his excellent radio programs were "The Return Room" broadcast in 1955, an evocation of life in East Belfast, and his collections of spoken reminiscence on the major figures of the Irish Literary Revival (posthumously published in 1972 as *Irish Literary Portraits*).

In 1952, Rodgers published *Europa and the Bull,* his second collection of poems. This volume reflects a considerable development in thematic range. Myth, religion, sexual relations, as well as landscape and social issues, are treated with a new capacity for fulfilled as well as tense celebration. Poems like "The Net" and "Europa and the Bull" are frank, delightfully cavalier celebrations of sexual experience, while "Lent" is one of the most remarkable poems on a Biblical/Christian theme by an Irish poet in this century.

In 1966, Rodgers accepted a post as writer in residence at Pitzer College, in Claremont, California. None of the poems he wrote in this later period maintained the standard achieved in *Europa and the Bull,* though the verbal dexterity and wit, as in *"Home Thoughts From Abroad,"* occasionally flair into moments of characteristic life.

Rodgers died in Los Angeles on February 1, 1969, and he was buried in Loughgall, County Armagh, in March of that year.

Rodgers' contribution to Irish letters was marked by his election to the Irish Academy of Letters in 1951 and by an Irish Arts Council annuity in 1968. As a whole, his work, through its use of baroque verbal effects and of alliterative and assonantal textures, is memorable chiefly as a revelation of exciting, if not always revelatory, linguistic possibilities.

TERENCE BROWN

WORKS: *Awake! and Other Poems.* London: Secker & Warburg, 1941; *Europa and the Bull.* London: Secker & Warburg, 1952; *Collected Poems.* London: Oxford University Press, 1971; *Poems.* [Oldcastle, Co. Meath]: Gallery, [1993]. REFERENCES: Brown, Terence. "The Poetry of W. R. Rodgers and John Hewitt." In *Two Decades of Irish Writing.* Douglas Dunn, ed. Cheadle

Hulme: Carcanet, 1975, pp. 81–97; Brown, Terence. *Northern Voices: Poets from Ulster.* Dublin: Gill & Macmillan, 1975, pp. 114–127; O'Brien, Darcy. *W. R. Rodgers.* Lewisburg, Pa.: Bucknell University Press, 1970.

ROLLESTON, T[HOMAS] W[ILLIAM HAZEN] (1857–1920), poet and translator. Rolleston was born in 1857 near Shinrone. He was educated at St. Columba's College, Rathfarnham, and at Trinity College, Dublin. He was a prolific and erudite writer who published *The Teachings of Epictetus* (1886) and *A Life of Lessing* (1889); translated Whitman's *Leaves of Grass* into German; and made some loose translations into English of Wagner. He was much involved in the Irish literary movement and was first honorary secretary of the London Irish Literary Society. Padraic Colum* thought highly of his translations from the Irish; indeed, Rolleston does make some attempt to find equivalents for Irish verse techniques in English. Nevertheless, in both his translations and original verse, he still appears to have been a captive of outmoded English poetic conventions. He died in Hampstead on December 5, 1920.

PRINCIPAL WORKS: *Imagination and Art in Gaelic Literature, Being Notes on Some Recent Translations from the Gaelic.* Kilkenny: Library of the Nore, 1900; *Sea Spray. Verses and Translations.* Dublin: Maunsel, 1909; *The High Deeds of Finn and Other Bardic Romances of Ancient Ireland.* London: Harrap, 1910; trans., *The Teaching of Epictetus.* London: Camelot Classics, W. Scott, 1886/Chicago: Donohue, Henneberry, 1892; *Life of Gotthold Ephraim Lessing.* London: W. Scott, 1889/rpt. Port Washington, New York & London: Kennikat, 1972; *Imagination and Art in Gaelic Literature.* Kilkenny: Kilkenny Moderator, 1900; ed., with Stopford A. Brooke, *A Treasury of Irish Poetry in the English Tongue.* London: Smith, Elder/New York: Macmillan, 1900; *Myths and Legends of the Celtic Race.* London: Harrap/New York: Crowell, 1911; *Whitman and Rolleston: A Correspondence,* ed. Horst Frenz. Bloomington: Indiana University, 1951/Dublin: Browne & Nolan, [1952].   REFERENCE: Rolleston, Charles Henry. *Portrait of an Irishman.* London: Methuen, 1939.

RONAN, FRANK (1963–   ), novelist. Ronan lives in Ireland and in France and is the author of four novels. His first, *The Men Who Loved Evelyn Cotton* (1989), won the *Irish Times*/Aer Lingus Irish Literature Prize. In it, the author's leisurely depiction of the changes in human relations makes him seem something of a Henry James who writes more overtly about sex. His style, however, is always fluent and often striking. For instance: "She could see his magenta thatcher's hands closing around Julius's thin neck, and Julius's lashless eyes batting like the eyes of a dying chicken." The chief problem of the novel is probably characterization. There were half a dozen men who loved Evelyn Cotton, and the story is narrated by one of them. Not all—even the narrator—are developed at any length. Indeed, most of the space is devoted to just one, Hugh Longford, a young Irish thatcher who is roofing the barn. Some of the lesser characters, such as Evelyn's foolish, selfish, and weepy husband, Julius, are mildly memorable, and there are nice satiric touches about others. Generally, though, the characterization is so bland that the reader keeps forgetting, even when reading the book, just who some of the characters are.

A Picnic in Eden (1991) much resembles *Evelyn Cotton.* It has a large cast of some notable minor characters and many others who are instantly forgettable. Also, despite a minute and convincing account of the changing relations of the three principal characters, they remain curiously amorphous. Perhaps it is partly that Ronan pays little attention to establishing them physically. In any event, this meticulous chronicle of the feelings of Adam Parnell and his wife and of Adam's Scottish friend Dougie Miller is as absorbing in the reading as it is evanescent in the memory when the page has been turned. Again, Ronan makes good and effectively chatty use of the first-person narrator, and again the writing is sometimes striking.

Ronan's last two novels, *The Better Angel* (1992) and *Dixie Chicken* (1994), have none of the earlier books' problems of characterization. *The Better Angel,* which is possibly Ronan's best novel, is set mainly in rural Ireland but, without ever losing its main focus, ranges off to Limerick and Dublin, Italy, and Australia. Mainly, it is an absorbing account of two young men, one a tormented farmer's son and the other from a most impoverished Anglo-Irish family. The balance between normality and madness of John G. and the shaky hold that his friend Smallgods has on normality are both beautifully caught, and their characters are complex and memorable. The whole novel, in fact, is richly peopled with finely individualized and usually eccentric characters who stick in the memory—even the briefly glimpsed Limerick painter who paints only cows and who is but briefly seen hitchhiking off with a large, two-dimensional silhouette of a cow under his arm. The large cast consists of people rooted in the Irish past or of people, like John G.'s Aunt Dervla, who are changing or of the two main characters, who are changed. Dervla has sacrificed her career to look after John G. and his father after the mother's death. When the father dies, she is offered the traditional way out: a safe but loveless marriage. Instead, she turns security down and plans to return to Dublin to resume her studies. If Dervla is an instance of an Irish person's growing out of the old ways, John G. and Smallgods are young Irishmen whose collision with modernity has put them worlds apart from Patrick Kavanagh's* farmer in *The Great Hunger.*

In *Dixie Chicken,* Ronan has solved the problem of characterization so well that his central figure, the charismatic Rory Dixon, dies at the novel's beginning when his car sails over a cliff into the Irish Sea. The large and richly drawn group of family and friends who survive him are drawn into a complex and engrossing web of murder, attempted murder, sex, and corruption. The narrative voice, intermittently at least, is a sometimes whimsical and sometimes satirical God the Father, who concludes resignedly in the book's final sentence, "I am only God and I didn't make the rules." Each of Ronan's books is a compelling read; the last two are also original, crafted, and accomplished work.

WORKS: *The Men Who Loved Evelyn Cotton.* [London]: Bloomsbury, [1989]; *A Picnic in Eden.* [London]: Bloomsbury, [1991]; *The Better Angel.* [London]: Bloomsbury, [1992]; *Dixie Chicken.* London: Hodder & Stoughton, [1994].

ROONEY, PADRAIG (1956–   ), novelist and poet. After teaching in Paris for six years, Rooney now teaches at Chulalongkorn University in Bangkok. He has received two bursaries from the Arts Council, and his volume of poems, *In the Bonsai Garden* (1988), won the Patrick Kavanagh* Award. In his well-written earlier novel, *Oasis* (1982), practically nothing happens. The hero, who thinks a lot about his past, lives in a brothel in North Africa with a deformed boy. An excursion to find some prehistoric cave paintings is made into the desert with the boy, a priest named Cu-Cu (pronounced "cuckoo") and an alcoholic doctor called Namon (spelled backward "No man"). The hero on his way out of the country stays at a hotel where he meets a girl to whom, although her name is Helen, he is not attracted. In the swimming pool, he meets a boy to whom he is attracted. There are long paragraphs of meticulous description, and Anthony Burgess remarked that Rooney was "about his proper business . . . the rendering of the external world in the right words." Burgess also remarked that Rooney would be a considerable credit to Irish letters; but, on the basis of this book, one would think that rather more evidence might be needed.

The single poem in Rooney's *In the Bonsai Garden* with meter and rhyme, "Gide's Scissors," is so mordantly effective a piece of light verse that one would wish for more in the same Audenesque vein. The other pieces are full of allusions to pop culture—King Kong, Robin the Boy Wonder, Rin-Tin-Tin and the Lone Ranger, the Daleks and the Tardis—as well as literary allusions to Robert Musil, Céline, Sartre, Proust, Dante, and Simenon. The scathing "A Supplement to the American-Vietnamese Dictionary" makes its point by a pejorative list of modern terms like "acid trip," "aureomycin," "body count," "consciousness-raising," "cluster bombs," "mind expanding," "paramedic," "paranoia," and "peanut butter." Strong as it is, if recast in conventional form, it could have been brilliant.

WORKS: *Oasis*. [Swords, Co. Dublin]: Poolbeg, [1982]. (Novel); *In the Bonsai Garden*. [Dublin]: Raven Arts, [1988]. (Poetry).

ROONEY, PHILIP (1907–1962), novelist and radio playwright. Rooney was born at Collooney, County Sligo, in 1907. He worked as bank clerk in the Midlands for fifteen years, writing short stories in his spare time. He published his first novel, *All Out to Win*, in 1935 and subsequently published several others. In 1953, he became head of the script writing department for Radio Éireann and wrote or adapted many radio plays. In 1961, he transferred to Irish television but died shortly after in Dublin in 1962.

Rooney's forte is the Irish historical novel with a good deal of action and a dash of romance. Perhaps his best books are *Captain Boycott* (1946), which was made into a film, and *The Golden Coast* (1947). There is a level of competent professionalism in his work, but it is the professionalism of the purveyor of popular entertainment. Even his best work is full of stock characters and tired, slick writing.

WORKS: *All Out to Win.* Dublin & Cork: Talbot, 1935/as Frank Phillips, London: Mellifont, [1941]; as Frank Phillips, *Overnight Entry.* London: Mellifont, [1938]; *Red Sky at Dawn.* Dublin: Gill, 1938/New York: P. J. Kenedy, 1939; *North Road.* Dublin: Talbot, 1940; *Singing River.* Dublin & Cork: Talbot, 1944; *Captain Boycott.* Dublin: Talbot/New York & London: Appleton-Century, 1946; *The Golden Coast.* Dublin: Talbot, 1947; *The Quest for Matt Talbot.* Dublin: Talbot, 1949. (Radio play); *The Long Day.* Dublin: Talbot, 1951. (There is said to be another published novel, *Dark Road.*)

ROPER, MARK (fl. 1990s), poet.

WORK: *The Hen Ark.* Galway: Salmon, 1991.

ROS, AMANDA M'KITTRICK (1860–1939), novelist and poet. Ros was born Anna Margaret M'Kittrick on December 8, 1860, near Ballynahinch, County Down. She claimed that her mother had named her after the heroine of *Children of the Abbey,* a novel by Regina Maria Roche, and that her full name was Amanda Malvina Fitzalan Anna Margaret McLelland M'Kittrick. This claim was to be typical of the extravagance which characterized much of Amanda M'Kittrick Ros's life and work.

Her father, Edward Amlane M'Kittrick, was head teacher of Drumaness High School near Ballynahinch. Anna Margaret was also a teacher, receiving her training at Marlborough Training College in Dublin in 1884–1886 and afterwards obtaining a post at Larne. There she met Andrew Ross, the stationmaster; they were married on August 30, 1887. Although she told friends that she had been writing since the age of four and that her first novel had been completed before she was sixteen and then locked away until 1897, when it was revised and printed, her biographer, Jack Loudan, believes that she wrote *Irene Iddesleigh* between 1892 and 1896. In any case, as a tenth anniversary present her husband gave her enough money to pay the cost of printing her first novel. In it the author was given as Amanda M'Kittrick Ros, the name by which she was to be known from that time on. She built a house in Larne with the proceeds of the novel and named it ''Iddesleigh.'' Her second novel, *Delina Delaney,* was published in 1898.

In 1908, Amanda M'Kittrick Ros inherited a lime kiln from a friend. This embroiled her in a legal battle which lasted for more than five years. She was finally forced to sell the kiln because of legal costs, and the experience permanently embittered her toward lawyers and the legal profession.

The added responsibilities of the stationmaster during World War I destroyed Andrew Ross's health, and in 1915 he was forced to retire. He never fully recovered and died in August 1917. Ros married a well-to-do farmer, Thomas Rodgers, on June 12, 1922, and she began to write again. A volume of poems, *Fumes of Formation,* was published in 1933. Soon after its publication, her second husband died, and she herself died on February 3, 1939. *Helen Huddleson,* her last novel, was never finished, but it was published in 1969, edited and revised by Jack Loudan, who also added a final chapter.

The works of Amanda M'Kittrick Ros are uniquely dreadful. The style is

ROS, AMANDA M'KITTRICK 1069

floaty, artificial, and overdone. For instance, eyes are described as "orbs of
blinded brilliancy," and passion for one of an inferior class is called a "deceptive demon of deluded mockery." Her titles give some indication of her love
of alliteration. Meaning is often lost in a torrent of descriptive phrases. This
style has been viewed both positively and negatively by critics. According to
her biographer, "She writes with a burning imagination that will disregard sense
should it hinder the intensity of her invention" (Loudan, *O Rare Amanda,* p.
28). Mark Twain welcomed one of her books as an addition to his collection
of "hogwash literature."

The events in a Ros novel complement the style. Noble gentlemen fall in
love with peasant girls at first sight, and people often drop dead of shock upon
hearing bad news. Coincidence is carried to the point of absurdity, and time and
possibility are ignored.

Ros's writing is also the vehicle of revenge. "All the rancour in her writing
is strictly personal" (Loudan, *O Rare Amanda,* p. 46). The lawyers who she
felt wronged her appear in her works as Mickey Monkeyface McBlear and
Barney Bloater, and her works include tirades against the profession. *Helen
Huddleson* contains a completely extraneous digression on a lawyer who is
convicted of forgery and kills a servant rather than pay her wages. *Poems of
Puncture* (1913), written during the lime kiln controversy, contains many poems
which are fierce in their denunciation of lawyers.

Ros is not a satirist; her attacks are direct and unsubtle. There is no desire to
improve or instruct. An attack on *Irene Iddesleigh* by Barry Pain on February
19, 1898, in *Black and White* hurt Ros deeply and created her lasting enmity
towards critics. She could not be charitable even at Pain's death; in a poem
entitled "The End of 'Pain' " in *Fumes of Formation,* she calls him a "rodent
of State." In fact, many of the poems in this collection are vicious attacks on
the critics. She ridiculed W.B. Wyndham Lewis in a ten thousand word essay,
St. Scandalbags (1954); and *Donald Dudley: Bastard Critic* (1954) is the first
episode of a long unfinished work, tentatively entitled *Six Months in Hell,* in
which she made sketches of all the people she felt had wronged her.

Despite ridicule and derision, Amanda M'Kittrick Ros took her writing seriously. She has some staunch defenders, and since her death, several of her works
have been printed for the first time, including extracts from her letters (*Bayonets
of Bastard Sheen*). While there is much—if not everything—that is ludicrous
in her writing, there is also a sense of life, a Rabelaisian vigor, that cannot be
suppressed.

BARBARA DiBERNARD

WORKS: *Irene Iddesleigh.* Belfast: W. & G. Baird, 1897/London: Nonesuch, 1926/New York:
Boni & Liveright, 1927. (Novel); *Delina Delaney.* Belfast: R. Aickin, 1989/London: Chatto &
Windus, 1935. (Novel); *Poems of Puncture.* London: Arthur H. Stockwell, 1913; *Fumes of For-
mation.* Belfast: R. Carswell, 1933. (Poems); *Bayonets of Bastard Sheen.* Thames Ditton, Surrey:
Privately published, 1949. (Letters); *Donald Dudley, The Bastard Critic.* Thames Ditton, Surrey:
Merle, 1954. (Fragment of a novel); *St. Scandalbags together with Meet Irene by D. B. Wyndham
Lewis & At the Sign of the Harrow by F. Anstey,* ed. by T. Stanley Mercer. Thames Ditton, Surrey:

Merle, 1954. (Criticism); *Helen Huddleson,* ed. & with a final chapter by Jack Loudan. London: Chatto & Windus, 1969. (Novel); *Thine in Storm and Calm: An Amanda McKittrick Ros Reader,* ed. & with an Introduction by Frank Ormsby. Belfast & St. Paul, Minn.: Blackstaff, [1988].   REFERENCES: Huxley, Aldous. "Euphues Redivivus." In *On the Margin.* London: Chatto & Windus, 1923; Loudan, Jack. *O Rare Amanda!* London: Chatto & Windus, 1954. (Biography).

ROSCOMMON, LORD (ca. 1633–1684 or 1685), poet.

Wentworth Dillon, fourth earl of Roscommon, was born in Ireland, educated at the Protestant University of Caen, and was, as James Sutherland, remarked, "A good deal more learned than most of his fellow peers." After traveling on the Continent, he returned to England following the Restoration and was favorably received at the court of Charles II. Although given to gambling and involved in some duels, he projected a literary academy to "refine and fix the standard of our language." Despite mild interest by Dryden, it came to nothing, although Roscommon wrote his best-known work, "Essay on Translated Verse." That work has little original about it but was influential in its day and well enough written, for Roscommon could turn a good heroic couplet. As Dr. Johnson remarked, "[H]e improved taste, if he did not enlarge knowledge." Of his morality as a poet, Pope added, "[I]n all Charles's days/ Roscommon only boasts unspotted lays." Nevertheless, he was distinctly a minor poet, and his work is hardly ever included in the anthologies.

PRINCIPAL WORKS: *Poems by the Earl of Roscommon.* London: J. Tonson, 1717; *The Poetical Works of Wentworth Dillon, Earl of Roscommon. With the Life of the Author.* London: J. Bell, 1780.   REFERENCE: Johnson, Samuel. *The Works of the English Poets.* Vol. 10. London: J. Nichols, 1779.

ROSENSTOCK, GABRIEL (1949–   ), poet.

WORK: *Cold Moon: The Erotic Haiku of Gabriel Rosenstock.* [Dingle, Co. Kerry]: Brandon, [1993].

ROSS, JOHN (1917–1987), novelist.

Ross was born in London in 1917 and brought to Ireland in 1919. He was a nephew of Arthur Shields and Barry Fitzgerald and as a child appeared occasionally at the Abbey* and the Gate.* From 1936 to 1941, he published nine thrillers, which were translated into several languages. He then went into film scriptwriting with the Rank organization, and in 1953 he joined Radio Éireann on the news desk. He died on January 27, 1987.

WORKS: *The Moccasin Men.* London: Hodder & Stoughton, 1936; *The Black Spot.* London: Hodder & Stoughton, 1936; *The Drone-Man.* London: Hodder & Stoughton, 1937; *Bless the Wasp.* London: Hodder & Stoughton, 1938; *The Major.* London: Hodder & Stoughton, 1938; *The Major Steps Out.* London: Hodder & Stoughton, 1939; *The Man from the Chamber of Horrors.* London: Hodder & Stoughton, 1939; *The Tall Man.* London: Collins, 1940; *Federal Agent.* London: Collins, 1941.

ROSS, MARTIN. *See* SOMERVILLE AND ROSS.

ROTHERY, BRIAN (1934–   ), novelist. Rothery was born in Dublin and became communications officer for the Institute for Industrial Research and Standards. In addition to nonfictional works such as the popular *How to Organize Your Time and Resources* (1972), he has written two novels.

LITERARY WORKS: *The Crossing*. London: Constable, [1970]/Philadelphia: Lippincott, 1977; *The Storm*. London: Constable, 1972.

ROWLEY, RICHARD (1877–1947), poet, playwright, and publisher. Richard Rowley was the pseudonym of Richard Valentine Williams, who was born in Belfast on April 2, 1877. Williams went into the family firm, McBride and Williams, which made cotton handkerchiefs, and became its managing director. His first book of poems, *The City of Refuge* (1917), attracted critical attention largely for the wrong reasons. As the *Times Literary Supplement* wrote, "The sound of a great Northern manufacturing city . . . vibrates through these poems." Today we look rather to the dialect poems that Rowley put in the mouths of working-class Belfast people and of country men and women from Mourne who appeared in this and later collections.

Rowley's firm collapsed in the crisis of 1931. From 1934 to 1943, he was chairman of the Northern Ireland Unemployment Assistance Board. During World War II, he ran the Mourne Press from his Newcastle home. The press brought out six titles, including work by Forrest Reid* and himself, before going under in 1942 from lack of support. Rowley died at Drumilly, Loughgall, County Armagh, on April 25, 1947.

Ironically, the best poems about ordinary Ulster folk are by the industrialist Richard Rowley. Ironically, too, he needed the mask of dialect to speak clearly; his work in standard English, in his own voice, is rhetorical and derivative. His dialect work comprises Mourne poems and Belfast poems. The Mourne poems tend to be light and humorous, with considerable folksy charm, but they can show tragic awareness, as in "Thinkin' Long." The Belfast poems are long, free monologues put into the mouths of working people, like "The Stitcher" or "Oul Jane."

Rowley also wrote stories (*Tales of Mourne*, 1937) and plays (including the popular *Apollo in Mourne*, 1926). The latter is a kind of wistful *Playboy* in which the god Apollo, banished from Olympus and coming to earth in Mourne, plays the role of Christy. He wins and renounces the love of Mary Blane, who is left contemplating her earthy lover Paddy Soye, whose mind is taken up with "a rare jewel o' a wee pig." *Apollo* reconciles Rowley's grandiloquent manner, put into the mouths of gods, and his dialect realism. He regarded it as his best work, but the working-class monologues are superior in one respect. As AE* wrote in his review of *Workers* (*The Irish Homestead*, May 12, 1933), "[T]here are no illusions about the life he depicts."

VICTOR PRICE

WORKS: *The City of Refuge*. Dublin: Maunsel, 1917; *Songs, and Others*. Dublin: Maunsel, 1918; *Workers*. London: Duckworth, 1923; *The Old Gods*. London: Duckworth, 1925; *Apollo in Mourne*.

London: Duckworth, 1926; *Selected Poems*. London: Duckworth, 1931; *Tales of Mourne*. London: Duckworth, 1937; *Ballads of Mourne*. Dundalk: Dundalgan, 1940; *One Cure for Sorrow, and Other One-Act Plays*. Newcastle, Co. Down: Mourne, 1942; *Sonnets for Felicity*. Newcastle, Co. Down: Mourne, 1942; *The Piper of Mourne*. Belfast: Derrick MacCord, 1944; *Final Harvest*. Belfast: Carter, 1951; *Apollo in Mourne*. Edited & with an Introduction by Victor Price. Belfast: Blackstaff, 1977. (A selection of poems, plays, and stories).   REFERENCE: Price, Victor. "Richard Rowley— 100." *Honest Ulsterman*, No. 53 (November–December 1976).

ROWLEY, ROSEMARIE (1942–   ), poet. Rowley was born in Dublin and, with the help of a Dublin Corporation scholarship, earned a degree in English, philosophy, and Irish from Trinity College in 1969. After teaching in Birmingham and working with the BBC and with the European Parliament in Luxembourg, she returned to Trinity and graduated with a master's in literature, writing her thesis on Patrick Kavanagh.*

In each of her interesting books, she is not entirely in control of her poetic form; but, unlike many of her contemporaries, she is interested in form. In *The Broken Pledge* (1985), she even essays some complicated French verse forms. In this first collection, her metrical or rhyming pattern will occasionally push her into awkward inversions of syntax or into archaic poetic language like " 'neath" or "fain." Often, too, she will set up a stanzaic or a rhyming pattern and not be able to keep to it. This fault is particularly noticeable in the ambitious "Broken Pledge" poem, in which the Envoi degenerates into doggerel. Nevertheless, this first volume has its real successes. "My Mind Will Never Be Aisy," "The Salamanca Reel," "The Fair-Haired Boy," and "I'm a Man in Myself like Oliver's Bull" are almost good enough to be anthology pieces.

The Sea of Affliction (1987) is full of portentous phrasing like "the plectrum's imbroglio" or of vague comparisons like comparing "indigenous truth" to an alabaster cliff. The problem of diction is compounded by the casual and inconsistent punctuation, even in the same poem. There are many tight lines and couplets, but again form often gives way to easier phrasing. A rhyming pattern will be established and then capriciously varied; a metrical pattern will become lost in the constant variations from it. A pity, for even a trifle more care could easily set things right.

Flight into Reality (1989) is an ambitious long poem in twenty rather brief cantos. It is not a narrative, which might have helped, but rather a reflection on the contemporary applicability of the Isis-Osiris myth. Each canto is written in a series of three-line stanzas with the rhyme scheme of ABA, BCB, CDC, and so on. The meter is basically iambic pentameter. As is usual with Rowley, the rhymes are often forced—"spirit," "levirate," "inspirit"—while the meter is constantly watered down to accommodate the sense. When a Yeats* goes against his metrical form, he has a reason and usually does it with powerful effect. With Rowley, the effect is generally lameness. Her diction, as in previous volumes, is sometimes arresting, but more often cutely opaque. Her punctuation is again erratic: sometimes, for instance, she avoids end stops, and sometimes she uses them, and the effect is usually to make the reader reread to puzzle out the syntax.

Rowley is an extremely talented poet, but thus far her interest in traditional form is more a flirtation than a commitment.

WORKS: *The Broken Pledge and Other Poems.* [Dublin]: Martello, [1985]; *The Sea of Affliction.* Dublin: Rowan Tree, [1987]; *Flight into Reality.* An Clophreas Caorthainn: Rowan Tree, 1989.

RUSSELL, GEORGE W. *See* AE.

RUSSELL, T[HOMAS] O'NEILL (1828–1908), man of letters. Russell was born in Lissanode, Moate, County Westmeath. A Quaker, he learned Irish and enthusiastically promoted the revival of the language. Fearing imprisonment because of his involvement with the nationalist paper *The Irishman,* he went to America and worked for thirty years as a commercial traveler. He returned to Ireland in 1895, and his many writings included translations from the Irish, essays and poems, a once-popular novel, *Dick Massey,* and two plays. Russell was a competent and even fluent writer. However, as his blank verse tragedy, *Red Hugh* (1905), reveals, he was also a conventional and traditional one:

> Hugh, thou hast now forstalled me. This great battle
> That thou hast won upon the Corlieu hills,
> Where full two thousand of the slaughtered foe,
> And their own general, did bite the dust,
> Crowns thee with glory for all time to come.
> O! 'that I had been with thee in the fight!
> No man would then have 'scaped the sword's keen edge,
> Of those who fought upon the Saxon side.

Such a typical passage is far distant from the fustian of a Whitbread,* but even farther from the contemporary writing of a Yeats* or Synge.* Russell died in Dublin, on June 15, 1908.

PRINCIPAL WORKS: *The Struggles of Dick Massey; or the Battles of a Boy.* Dublin, 1860. (Novel); *The Last Irish King* Dublin: M. H. Gill, 1904. (Three-act verse play); *Red Hugh or Life and Death of Hugh Roe O'Donnell.* Dublin: M. H. Gill, 1905. (Three-act verse play).

RUTHERFORD, JANET

WORKS: *Leaving Karman.* Belfast: Hunter House, 1992; *Signing the Way: A Play in One Act.* Belfast: Hunter House, 1992.

RYAN, FREDERICK (1873–1913), journalist and editor. Ryan was born in Dublin on October 12, 1873. He became secretary of the Irish National Theatre Society, wrote for several journals (sometimes under the pen names of ''Irial'' and ''Finian''), formed the Dublin Philosophical Society in 1906, and founded two monthly journals, *Dana* with John Eglinton* and the *National Democrat* with Francis Sheehy-Skeffington.* He spent some time in Egypt and edited Mustapha Kemel's *Egypt,* and he was also a secretary to Wilfrid Scawen Blunt. His only play, a two-act comedy *The Laying of the Foundations,* was performed

by the Irish National Drama Company on October 29, 1902. Its theme is the conflict between labor and the corrupt alliance of business and municipal government, and it was the first realistic social drama of the modern Irish stage. Curiously, W. B. Yeats* thought highly of the play, calling it "excellent" and "a really astonishing piece of satire." That is far too much praise for this rather bald and stiff piece, and Ryan was more interested in fostering liberal opinions than in writing great drama. Socialist, humanist, internationalist (*Sinn Féin* wrote of him, "The suffering Egyptian had no less claim on him than his own countrymen"), he was widely respected as an honest voice of social conscience, despite his unorthodox opinions. He died in England on April 7, 1913, at the age of thirty-nine.

WILLIAM J. FEENEY

WORKS: *Criticism and Courage.* Vol. 6 of the Tower Press Booklets. Dublin: Maunsel, 1906; "The Laying of the Foundations." In *Lost Plays of the Irish Renaissance.* Robert Hogan & James Kilroy, eds. Newark, Del.: Proscenium, 1970. (Act II only; Act I has been lost). REFERENCE: Sheehy-Skeffington, F. "Frederick Ryan, an Appreciation." *Irish Review* 3 (May 1913): 113–119.

RYAN, HUGH FITZGERALD (1941–   ), novelist. Ryan was born in Skerries, County Dublin, and educated there by the De La Salle Order, with which he now teaches, and at University College, Dublin. His first book, *The Kybe* (1983), is an historical novel set in the village of Skerries during the Napoleonic Wars. At the center of the novel is a love affair between Eileen Mullen, the wife of the local carter, and Peter Howlett, an English sergeant stationed with a small detachment in the nearby Martello Tower. The anguish of the lovers is well caught, but the larger society of the village is also fully portrayed—from the people in the nearby Big House, to the village priest, to the local fisherman. There are a number of effective set scenes—a shipwreck, the Wren boys at the dance on St. Stephen's night, the drowning of Peter Mullen, and especially the scenes farther afield at the Battle of Waterloo. Ryan draws character well and has a fine eye for telling detail in this solidly constructed first book.

Reprisal (1989) is also set in the area around Skerries and Balbriggan and is also an historical novel. It commences on the eve of the First World War and depicts the next troubled years, which included the Easter Rising and which in this book culminate in the ferocious sacking of Balbriggan by Black and Tans in September 1920. Like *The Kybe,* the novel has a large cast that covers the social scale and all shades of political opinion. Again, the characters are not mere mouthpieces for attitudes but engrossingly drawn as people. Ryan's own sympathies are not withheld from the English and the Anglo-Irish, and one of the best characters is the perceptive and tolerant police Sergeant Duffy. The concluding chapter shows a patriotic celebration some years later, the unveiling of a statue to a man killed during the Troubles. A particularly wry touch is that the former Sergeant Duffy, who has come to pay his respects and who had done everything possible to avert trouble, was not taken into the new Free State police force. Instead, he is regarded with suspicion and dislike, while the mythmaking distorts and inflates the memory of others: "[T]hey had indeed known heroes and had walked with titans."

On Borrowed Ground (1991) is a novel about how the modern world has affected Irish life. Much of it describes a boy growing up in rural Ireland in the 1950s, and the details are well and evocatively chosen:

One of the labourers went past, taking the cattle indoors. The hooves made sucking sounds as they squelched through the mud. The man cursed absentmindedly and slapped the hindmost animal with an ash plant. Splatters of dung belied their elegant gait and lady-like demeanour.

There is considerable effective contrast between the characters and qualities of the traditional life and the younger people affected by the movies and motor-bikes of a changing present. The last third of the novel, when the protagonist has grown into a successful architect in Dublin, is not as rich, but a strong plot involving mystery and romance carries it. By this time, the pace of change has accelerated:

As a nation we settled for commercial television. The great pageant of human life pre-sented on the flickering screen has to be fragmented to fit in between the advertisements. The continuity announcers try to keep us in touch with what went before, smiling gamely through stories of war and natural disaster. The news-readers finish with the mandatory smirk as if trying to redress the damage they have done to our spirits. Even the weath-erman assumes a ghastly rictus at the end of his dismal tale. American dramas end with a joke and an explanation for the feeble-minded among us. . . . British dramas end just when you think the story is about to make some sense.

The book, nevertheless, is not entirely a satirical condemnation. The heroine has become a musician who travels to Australia and America with a trendy folk group, and the point would seem to be that some not entirely awful compromise has been made with the present. In any event, it is refreshing to find a book about modern Ireland that has a happy ending.

Ancestral Voices (1995) is also rooted in history and depicts a man attempting to write a novel about the Wexford Rising of 1798. A weakness is the present plot, which mainly concerns the breakup of his marriage for a few years after the accidental death of his young son. Unconnected with this action and also rather undeveloped is the story of a painter who killed two thugs twenty years before. The painter, who is thought to be dead, makes but one fleeting appear-ance; and his story seems included to set up the book's climax in which the protagonist barely stops himself from killing two thugs. The point would seem to be an attempt to dramatize the savagery buried in everybody and thus to explain certain ferocious events in the Wexford Rising. Nevertheless, it all makes for Ryan's most ungainly plot.

Ryan's are serious, conventional, and rewarding mainstream novels. They are suffused by a sense of the past, and, like Maeve Binchy's* novels, they are also suffused by a sense of place. They handle their large casts with ease, and their fluent prose makes for absorbing reading.

WORKS: *The Kybe*. [Dublin]: Wolfhound, [1983]; *Reprisal*. [Dublin]: Wolfhound, [1989]; *On Borrowed Ground*. Dublin: Wolfhound, 1991; *Ancestral Voices*. [Dublin]: Wolfhound/[Arlington, Va.]: Vandamere, [1995].

RYAN, JAMES (1962–   ), novelist. Ryan grew up in County Laois and graduated from Trinity College, Dublin, in 1975. He teaches English and history in a comprehensive school in Dublin. His novel, *Home from England* (1995), treats the important social problem of the Irish emigrant who yearns to return home and cannot.

WORK: *Home from England*. London: Phoenix House, [1995].

RYAN, JOHN (1925–1992), painter, editor, and author. Ryan was born in comfortable circumstances: his father, Senator Seamus Ryan, founded the Monument Creamery chain of shops (which his mother continued), and his brother ran the Monument Bakery. While he was young, the family lived in Burton Hall in County Dublin, where Ryan had his first base for his cultural activities. From his student days, he painted and designed for the stage and, through his support, financial and otherwise, gave rise almost by himself to the culture of midcentury Dublin between 1945 and 1965. This was a culture largely based on the city pubs, especially the Bailey in Duke Street, which he owned for a time in the late 1960s, and nearby McDaid's in Harry Street. Though he wrote and broadcast on a regular basis and even produced about forty plays, it was as an editor, first of *Envoy* and later of the renewed *Dublin Magazine,* that he particularly made his mark. *Envoy* ran for twenty numbers, from December 1949 to July 1951, and published work by Patrick Kavanagh,* J. P. Donleavy,* Brendan Behan,* and many others. *The Dublin Magazine* ran from 1970 to 1975. Ryan's memoir of the period, *Remembering How We Stood* (1975), gives vivid impressions of Kavanagh, Myles na Gopaleen, Behan, and Gainor Crist, the model for "the Ginger Man." When writing retreated into the academy in the mid-1960s, Ryan's style of culture went out of fashion. But the achievements of his circle remain a memorial to his quiet and profound influence on a whole generation. J. P. Donleavy spoke for many of them: "John was also an ardent Joycean long before it became popular, while his broad mind and natural kindness united many disparate friends in the dark 1950s." It was typical of Ryan that, as secretary of the Irish Academy of Letters,* founded by Yeats,* he maintained that institution in nominal existence from a sense of cultural piety, long after its influence had been eclipsed. Twice married, he had three sons and three daughters. His sister was the actress Kathleen Ryan, who appeared in *Odd Man Out* and other films. Aside from his design work, he painted and exhibited on a regular basis. He died after a long illness on May 1, 1992.

PETER COSTELLO

WORKS: Ed., *Envoy,* 1949–1951; ed., *The Dubliner,* later *The Dublin Magazine,* 1970–1975; ed., *A Bash in the Tunnel: James Joyce by the Irish*. Brighton: Clifton Books, [1970]; *Remembering How We Stood: Bohemian Dublin at the Mid-Century*. [Dublin]: Gill & Macmillan, [1975]; *A Wave of the Sea.* [Swords, Co. Dublin]: Ward River, [1981].   REFERENCES: *Irish Times,* May 2 & 6, 1992; *The Times* (London), May 14 & 18, 1992; Costello, Peter. "John Ryan." *Irish Literary Supplement* (Spring 1993); Cronin, Anthony. *Dead as Doornails.* Dublin: Dolmen, 1975; Donleavy, J. P. *Ireland: In All Her Sins and in Some of Her Graces.* London: Michael Joseph/New York: Viking, 1986; Donleavy, J. P. *The History of the Ginger Man.* London: Viking, 1994; Jacobsen, Kurt. "An Interview with John Ryan." *Journal of Irish Literature* 17 (January 1988): 3–14; O'Connor, Ulick. *Brendan.* London: Hamish Hamilton, 1970.

RYAN, MARY (1945–   ), novelist. Ryan was born in County Roscommon and educated in convent schools there and in Dublin. She received a B.A. from University College, Dublin, and taught in England. Returning to Ireland in 1968, she worked for RTÉ, then studied law and was admitted as a solicitor in 1976. She lives in Dublin.

WORKS: *Whispers in the Wind.* Dublin: Attic, 1990; *Glenallen.* Dublin: Attic, 1991; *Into the West.* London: Headline, 1992; *Mask of the Night.* London: Headline, 1994; *Shadows from the Fire.* London: Headline, 1994.

RYAN, RICHARD (1946–   ), poet. Ryan was born in Dublin and was educated at University College, Dublin. He has published two slim collections of verse, *Ledges* (1970) and *Ravenswood* (1973). The pieces in both volumes are straightforward in statement but technically, rather formless. Many of them are written in stanzas of two, three, or four very short lines with no recognizable rhythmical pattern. However, the very shortness of the lines does emphasize the importance of individual words. The imagery in the first volume ranges from the commonplace to, once or twice, the extraordinarily striking. In the second volume, the remarkable quality of imagery is more pervasive, and the images have become surrealistic or even science fictional. Whatever its technical deficiencies, Ryan's writing in the second volume is terse, vivid, and frequently quotable. A few fugitive pieces appeared in the early 1980s, and some others were translated into Hungarian in 1988.

WORKS: *Ledges.* Dublin: Dolmen, 1970; *Ravenswood.* Dublin: Dolmen, 1973.

RYAN, W[ILLIAM] P[ATRICK] (1867–1942), journalist and social and literary critic. Ryan was born in Templemore, County Tipperary. He worked as a journalist in London but returned to Ireland in 1905 to edit the *Irish Peasant.* After Cardinal Logue caused the closure of that paper, Ryan edited the *Irish Nation* in Dublin from 1908 to 1910. Upon its failure, he returned to London to become assistant editor of the *Daily Herald.* Ryan wrote a fluent and forceful prose and was a trenchant critic of the influence of the clergy on Irish life. Seamus Deane* remarks that much of what he wrote in his 1912 volume *The Pope's Green Island* "was still perfectly applicable ten and even twenty years later." One might go further and say that some of it is still applicable today. Ryan wrote in both English and Irish, and he wrote some fiction and some plays, but his important works are probably *The Irish Literary Revival* (1894), *The Pope's Green Island,* and *The Irish Labour Movement* (1918). He died in

London on December 31, 1942. His son, Desmond Ryan (1893–1964), wrote biographies of Pearse, Connolly, and de Valera as well as an interesting autobiography, *Remembering Sion* (1934).

PRINCIPAL WORKS: *The Heart of Tipperary. A Romance of the Land League*. London: Ward & Downey, 1893. (Novel); *The Irish Literary Revival*. London: Ward & Downey, 1894; *Starlight through the Thatch*. London: Downey, 1895; *Literary London: Its Lights and Comedies*. London: L. Smithers, 1898; *Sidheoga ag Obair*. Dublin: Conradh na Gaeilge, 1904; *The Romance of a Motor Mission. With General Booth on His White Car Crusade*. London: Salvation Army, 1906; *The Plough and the Cross*. Dublin: The Irish Nation, 1910; *The Pope's Green Island*. London: James Nisbet, 1912; *Daisy Darley; or, the Fairy Gold of Fleet Street*. London & Toronto: J. M. Dent, 1913. (Novel); *The Labour Revolt and Larkinism*. London: *Daily Herald*, 1913; *Caomhin Ó Cearnaigh*. Dublin: Dublin Gaelic League, 1913; *The Celt and the Cosmos*. London: David Nutt, [1914]. (Pamphlet); *The Irish Labour Movement*. Dublin: Talbot, 1918/London: T. Fisher Unwin, 1919; *Eden and Evolution*. London: Noel Douglas, 1926; *From Atlantis to Thames*. London: Theosophical Publishing House, 1926. (Verse drama); *Patria Poetica*. London: J. M. Watkins/Dublin: Hodges, Figgis, [1928]; *Poets in Paradise*. Dublin: At the Sign of the Tree Candles, 1931. (Poetry); *Gaelachas i gCein*. Dublin: Oifig Díolta Foillseacháin Rialtas, 1933; *King Arthur in Avalon*. London: A. S. Curtis, [1934]. (Play).

RYVES, ELIZABETH (1750–1797), woman of letters. Isaac Disraeli claimed that Ryves was descended from a distinguished Irish family, and Elizabeth Owens Blackburne* suggests that Disraeli was referring to Jerome Ryves, D.D., dean of St. Patrick's Cathedral in the early eighteenth century. Ryves was born in 1750 and apparently inherited substantial property while young but lost it through legal chicanery. Thereafter, her only income came from her writings, and her economic difficulties began. She moved to London and started her literary career by writing first drama, then poetry for various periodicals. None of her efforts paid well enough to support her, and she left London for Islington. She studied French, hoping to earn her living as a translator. She did translate several works but again failed to support herself. Her health began to deteriorate, and she never fully recovered. Her novel, *The Hermit of Snowdon* (1790), contains autobiographical elements. Ryves also worked as manager of the historical and political departments at the Annual Register, again at less than subsistence wages. She died in poverty at her Store Street lodgings in London on April 29, 1797.

ANNE COLMAN

WORKS: *Dialogue in the Elysian Fields between Caesar and Cato*. London, 1784; *An Epistle (in Verse) to the Rt. Hon. Lord John Cavendish, Chancellor the the Exchequer*. London, 1784; *The Hastiniad; an Heroick Poem*. 1785; *The Hermit of Snowdon; or, Memoirs of Albert and Lavinia*. 1790; *Ode to . . . Lord Melton, Infant Son of Earl Fitzwilliam*. 1787; *Ode to the Rev. Mr. Mason*. 1780; *Poems on Several Occasions, and The Prude, a Comic Opera*. London, 1777. REFERENCES: Blackburne, E. Owens. *Illustrious Irishwomen*. Vol. 2. London: Tinsley, 1877; Kelly, A. A. *Pillars of the House*. Dublin: Wolfhound, 1987.

S

SADLIER, MARY ANNE (1820–1903), novelist and journalist. Mary Anne Madden was born in Cootehill, County Cavan, on December 31, 1820. She emigrated to Montreal in August 1844, and there she married a Catholic publisher, James Sadlier. In Canada and after 1860 in New York, she pursued her own career as a Catholic journalist and author of patriotic and romantic historical fiction, such as *The Confederate Chieftains* (1859), *Old House by the Boyne* (1865), *The Heiress of Kilorgan* (1867), and about thirty others. Although her fiction is meant to be uplifting, it is mainly innocuous and full of alternate flushes and blushes on the heroines' cheeks. She also wrote plays and religious tracts, and translated prolifically from the French. Her work is of some interest as an indicator of what the unlearned, homesick Irishman was reading during the latter half of the nineteenth century. She died in Montreal on April 5, 1903.

PRINCIPAL WORKS: *The Red Hand of Ulster.* Boston: P. Donahoe, 1850; *The Blakes and the Flanagans.* Dublin: Duffy, [1855]; *The Confederate Chieftains: A Tale of the Irish Rebellion of 1641.* New York: D. & J. Sadlier/London & Glasgow: Cameron & Ferguson, [ca. 1859]; *Elinor Preston.* New York: D. & J. Sadlier, [ca. 1861]; *Old and New; or, Taste versus Fashion.* New York & Boston: D. & J. Sadlier, 1862; *The Hermit of the Rock.* New York, Boston & Montreal: D. & J. Sadlier, 1863; *The Daughter of Tyrconnell.* New York: D. & J. Sadlier, [1863]; *Bessy Conway; or, The Irish Girl in America.* New York: D. & J. Sadlier, 1863; *The Fate of Father Sheehy: A Tale of Tipperary in the Old Times.* New York & Boston: D. & J. Sadlier/Dublin & London: Duffy, 1864; *Confessions of an Apostate.* New York: Sadlier, [1864]; *Con O'Regan; or, Emigrant Life in the New World.* New York: Sadlier, [1864]; *The Old House by the Boyne.* New York: Sadlier, [1865]/Dublin: Gill, 1910; *Aunt Honor's Keepsake.* New York & Boston: D. & J. Sadlier, 1866; *The Heiress of Kilorgan.* New York: D. & J. Sadlier, [1867?]; *MacCarthy More!* New York: D. & J. Sadlier, 1868; *Maureen Dhu, the Admiral's Daughter.* New York: Sadlier, 1870; *The Invisible Hand.* New York: Sadlier, [ca. 1873]. (Two-act play); *The Secret.* London: R. Washbourne, 1880. (Play); *Alice Riordan, the Blind Man's Daughter.* Dublin: Gill, 1884. (Children's story); *The Minister's Wife, and Other Stories.* New York: C. Wildermann, 1898; *O'Byrne; or, The Expatriated.* New York: C. Wildermann, 1898; *Short Stories.* New York: C. Wildermann, [1900].

SALKELD, BLANAID (1880–1959), poet. Salkeld was born in Chittagong (now Pakistan) on August 10, 1880. Her father was in the Indian medical service and was a friend of Tagore. Most of her own childhood was spent in Dublin, but when she was twenty-two she married an Englishman in the Indian civil service in Bombay. (Her older son, Cecil ffrench Salkeld, became a prominent Irish artist.) When she was twenty-eight, Mrs. Salkeld returned to Ireland and joined the second company of Abbey Theatre* players, using the stage name of Nell Byrne. On one occasion, she played the title role of Fitzmaurice's* *The Country Dressmaker* with the first company in London. She wrote many verse plays, but none has been published and only one, *Scarecrow over the Corn,* reached the stage; it was done at the Gate* in the 1930s. Her poems appeared in several small volumes, from the 1930s to the 1950s, and might be described as the sensitive attempts of a highly intelligent amateur. She is usually committed to rhyme, but her sense of rhythm is erratic. Even in a traditional and highly restricting form like the sonnet, she seems to think that any ten higgledy-piggledy syllables compose an acceptable line. In fact, her rhythm, much broken up by dashes, parentheses, and three dots (used not for elision but for some manner of pause), is finally chaotic. In other poems, she utilizes spacing within a line rather than conventional punctuation, and it is difficult to determine what rhythm, if any, she had in mind, without knowing the length of pauses and the strength of emphases. Moreover, her capitalization—or, in some cases, the lack of it—usually seems affected. If Mrs. Salkeld relied more on sensitivity than on technique, she did have her occasional successes, as particularly in the tight and accomplished poems vii, xv, and xvii of . . . *the engine is left running* (1937). Her grand-daughter Beatrice married Brendan Behan,* and, to judge by her grand-daughter's memoir, *My Life with Brendan,* Mrs. Salkeld and her very different grandson-in-law seem to have gotten on just famously. She died in Dublin in 1959.

WORKS: *Hello, Eternity!* London: Elkin Mathews & Marot, 1933; *The Fox's Covert.* London: Dent, [1935]; . . . *the engine is left running.* Dublin: Gayfield, [1937]; *A Dubliner.* Dublin: Gayfield, 1943; *Experiment in Error.* Aldington, Kent: Hand & Flower, [1955].

SALMON PUBLISHING. Salmon is a Galway-based publishing house that deals mainly with poetry. It was founded by Jessie Lendennie, a writer from Arkansas who came to Galway in 1981. A wide variety of Irish and non-Irish writers appears on Salmon's list, including Rita Ann Higgins,* Theo Dorgan,* Eithne Strong,* Fred Johnston,* and Moya Cannon.* For some years, the firm also published *The Salmon,* a magazine of prose and poetry. Auburn House, an imprint of Salmon Publishing, Ltd., publishes on a number of alternative living issues.

FRED JOHNSTON

REFERENCE: Luftig, Victor. "Migrant Mind in a Mobile Home: Salmon Publishing in the Ireland of the 1990s." *Éire-Ireland* 26 (Spring 1991): 108–119.

SANDS, BOBBY (1954–1981), poet. Sands was born in Belfast and became active in the republican movement. In 1977, he was sentenced to his second prison term, one of fourteen years, for being apprehended with three other men in a car containing weapons. As a protest against not being treated as political prisoners, he and others went on hunger strike. He died on May 5, 1981, in the Maze Prison on the sixty-sixth day of his strike, the first of ten republicans to die. His protest and death gave a great momentary spur to republicanism. For instance, before his death, in an April by-election, he was elected to the Westminster Parliament, receiving over 30,000 votes.

WORK: *Skylark Sing Your Lonely Song.* Ulick O'Connor, ed. Dublin & Cork: Mercier, [1982].

SARR, KENNETH (1895–1967), novelist and playwright. Kenneth Sarr is the occasional pen name of Kenneth Shiels Reddin, who wrote two short plays produced by the Abbey Theatre* and who published three readable novels. He was born in Dublin in 1895 and was educated at Belvedere, Clongowes Wood, St. Enda's, and then at University College, Dublin, where his education was interrupted by a prison sentence for his Sinn Féin activities. He was accustomed to a literary milieu from youth, for his mother kept a literary salon in the early years of the century, and he and his brothers were involved in the activities of the Irish Theatre* in Hardwicke Street. His occupation, however, was the law. After being admitted to the bar, he became a District Justice in 1922, serving in that capacity for forty-two years. He died in Dublin on August 17, 1967.

Sarr's two one-act plays, which were produced at the Abbey in December 1924, are both very brief, each playing only about twelve minutes. *The Passing* won the Dramatic Award at the Tailteainn Games earlier in 1924. Although this slum tragedy offers an excellent opportunity for a brilliant actress, the play is theatre rather than literature and assuredly is not as fine as the second prize winner, *Autumn Fire* of T. C. Murray.* *Old Mag* is a portrait of an old Waterford street vendor and her finding most coincidentally her long-lost son. W. J. Lawrence,* the critic, was apparently baffled by the play's lack of a recognition scene; nevertheless, the little piece has some extremely effective dialogue.

Sarr's novels are substantial and quite excellent recreations of Dublin. The best is *Somewhere to the Sea,* which is set at the end of the Black and Tan War and in the early days of the Treaty negotiations. There is a deal of unnecessary recapitulation of the plot, but the real-life characters, such as AE,* James Stephens,* Susan Mitchell,* and the actress Maire nic Shiubhlaigh, who wander around the periphery of the story, do much to create a real and persuasive atmosphere. The passing satire of the Dublin intellectual scene in the early 1920s is also excellent. It is definitively a minor work, but like his slighter *Another Shore* (1945) it is a rewarding one.

WORKS: As Kenneth Reddin: *Another Shore.* London: Cresset, 1945/republished as *Young Man with a Dream.* New York: A. A. Wyn, [1946]. (Novel). As Kenneth Sarr: *Old Mag.* Dublin & Cork: Talbot, 1924. (One-act play); *The Passing.* Dublin & Cork: Talbot, 1924. (One-act play); *The White*

Bolle-Trie, a Wonder Story. Dublin & Cork: Talbot, 1927; *Somewhere to the Sea.* London: T. Nelson/Boston & New York: Houghton Mifflin, 1936. (Novel).

SAVAGE, JOHN (1828–1888), poet and journalist. Savage was born in Dublin on December 13, 1828. He studied art, was involved in the 1848 rebellion, and then emigrated to America, where he worked on the *New York Tribune* and owned *The States,* the organ of Stephen A. Douglas. He received an honorary LL.D. from Fordham, and he died in New York on October 9, 1888. As a poet, his several volumes are romantic, patriotic, and facile, for instance, these bouncing lines from "Shane's Head":

> The Scotch marauders whitened when his war-cry met their ears,
> And the death-bird, like a vengeance, poised above his stormy cheers;
> Ay, Shane, across the thundering sea, out-chanting it, your tongue
> Flung wild un-Saxon war-whoopings the Saxon Court among.

PRINCIPAL WORKS: *Lays of the Fatherland.* New York: Redfield, 1850; *'98 and '48: The Modern Revolutionary History and Literature of Ireland.* New York: Redfield, 1856; *Faith and Fancy.* New York: Kirker, 1864; *Eva: A Goblin Romance, in Five Parts.* New York: Kirker, 1865; *Sybil: A Tragedy in Five Acts.* New York: Kirker, 1865; *Poems: Lyrical, Dramatic and Romantic.* New York: Kirker, 1867; *Fenian Heroes and Martyrs. . . .* Boston: Donahoe, 1868.

SAVAGE, MARMION W[ILME] (1804–1872), novelist. Savage was born on February 22, 1804, in Dublin to the Reverend Henry Savage and Sarah Bewley. He spent his childhood in his father's parish in Ardkeen in County Down, received a B.A. in classics from Trinity College, Dublin, and occasionally wrote articles for *Dublin University Magazine.* In 1828, he studied law at the Inner Temple in London and in 1829 married Olivia Clarke, niece of Lady Morgan.* Their son, Henry Arthur, died some time before his twentieth birthday. Between 1830 and 1847, Savage wrote articles for *The Examiner, The Amulet,* and other journals. He was also appointed as auditor of the Externe Historical Society of Trinity College and served as barrister at King's Inns in Dublin. Subsequently, he took a post as clerk to Council and Usher and keeper of the council chamber at Dublin Castle. His wife died in 1843, and subsequently he published a series of novels, the first three anonymously. In 1855, he married Narissa Rosava, and in 1856 he moved to London to become only the fourth editor of the *Examiner* following Leigh Hunt, Albany Fonblanque, and John Foster. In 1861, he became seriously ill from overwork and moved to Torquay in Devon, where he died on May 1, 1872.

Savage's novels and writings could be read as a series of satires on the excesses of mid-nineteenth-century politics, religion, and sensibilities. They offer as an alternative moderate change and moderate social reforms, showing the influence of earlier Irish writers and satirists from Swift* to Burke.* His first novel, *Falcon Family* (1845), is a highly politicized satire of the "extremes" of the Young Ireland Party and the early Tractarian movement at Oxford. *The Bachelor of the Albany* (1847) satirizes the "narrow self-interest" of certain members of the English and Irish clergy. *My Uncle the Curate* (1849) is set in the Irish countryside and satirizes outdated customs and self-indulgence. *Reuben Medlicott* (1852), also published as *The Universal Genius,* satirizes complacency and sensibility, as the reader follows Medlicott through various careers and professions. *The Woman of Business* was originally serialized but later published in its entirety in London and New York (1870). Although containing some touches of light satire, the novel is really an affirmation of human nature in the face of the seemingly dehumanizing aspects and distortions of Darwin's theories. *Clover Cottage* (1856), a novelette about a bachelor who finally takes a bride, was dramatized as *Nine Points of the Law* by Tom Taylor and performed on April 11, 1859, at the Olympic Theatre in London.

BERNARD McKENNA

WORKS: *The Falcon Family; or, Young Ireland.* London: Chapman & Hall, 1845; *The Bachelor of the Albany.* London: Chapman & Hall, 1847; *My Uncle the Curate.* 3 vols. London: Chapman & Hall, 1849; *Reuben Medlicott; or, The Coming Man.* 3 vols. London: Chapman & Hall, 1852; ed., *Sketches, Legal and Political 1791–1851,* by Richard Lalor Shiel. London: Hurst & Blackett, 1855; *Clover Cottage.* London: Chapman & Hall, 1856; *The Woman of Business; or, The Lady and the Lawyer.* 3 vols. London: Chapman & Hall, 1870.   REFERENCES: Batho, Edith & Dobrée, Bonamy. *The Victorians and After: 1830–1914.* London: Cresset, 1962; Norman, Paralee. "A Neglected Irish Novelist: Marmion W. Savage." *Books at Iowa* 35 (November 1981): 3–13; Norman, Paralee. "Light Satire and Hogarth's Pictorial Composition: Marmion Savage's Novel *The Falcon Family; Or, Young Ireland.*" *Éire-Ireland* 23 (Spring 1988): 129–143; Norman, Paralee. "The Island of Higgledy-Piggledy: Marmion Savage's *My Uncle the Curate.*" *Éire-Ireland* 25 (Winter 1990): 93–110.

SAVAGE-ARMSTRONG, G[EORGE] F[RANCIS] (1845–1906), poet. Savage-Armstrong was born in County Dublin on May 5, 1845, and was the brother of the promising young poet Edmund J. Armstrong (1841–1865). He was educated at Trinity College, Dublin, and in 1871 was appointed professor of English at Queen's College, Cork. He wrote a number of lengthy closet dramas on Biblical subjects and much generally undistinguished verse. His career is a curious contrast in some respects to that of J. M. Synge,* for both did much tramping in Wicklow and on the Continent, and Savage-Armstrong's great poetic inspiration was landscape. Unlike Synge, however, his descriptions even of Wicklow are the most usual of neo-Wordsworthian effusions. His poem "The Scalp," for instance, begins:

Stern granite Gate of Wicklow, with what awe,
What triumph, oft (glad children strayed from home)
We passed into thy shadows cool, to roam. . . .

It is seldom indeed that he can rise to a line of clear and simple description, such as "Old peasants deep-wrinkled, sat clustered and talked/In their gutteral Gaelic. . . ." He died on July 24, 1906, in Strangford, County Down.

WORKS: *Poems.* London: E. Moxon, 1869; *Ugone. A Tragedy.* London: E. Moxon, 1870; *The Tragedy of Israel.* 3 parts. London: Longmans, 1872–1876; *Poems; Lyrical and Dramatic. . . .* London: Longmans, 1873; *A Garland from Greece.* London: Longmans, 1882; *Stories of Wicklow.*

London: Longmans, 1886; *Victoria Regina et Imperatrix.* London: Longmans, 1887; *Mephistopheles in Broadcloth.* London: Longmans, 1888; *One in the Infinite.* London: Longmans, 1891; *Queen-Empress and the Empire.* Belfast: M. Ward, 1897; *Ballads of Down.* London: Longmans, 1901; *Poems: National and International.* Dublin: E. Ponsonby, 1917.

SCALES, AUDREY, poet.

WORK: *The Ephemeral Isle.* [Limavady, Co. Londonderry]: Portmoon, [1983].

SCANLAN, PATRICIA (1956–   ), novelist. Scanlan was born in Ballygall in
Dublin and educated in Ballymun and at the Dominican Convent in Eccles Street. She worked with Dublin Corporation Libraries from 1974 until the considerable success of her novels, including a six-figure contract from America, allowed her to take a five-year break. Her first novel, *City Girl* (1990), achieved a sales of 100,000 in its first eighteen months, an astonishing figure for Ireland. Her later novels, *Apartment 3B, Finishing Touches,* and *City Woman,* have appeared at regular yearly intervals. The books are formula-written, and their appeal would be to the younger Irishwoman looking for an attractive "easy read." Her heroines are clever, attractive, sexy survivors and could come from the pages of Shirley Conran or Danielle Steele. She places her novels in modern Ireland, but the settings are not of undue importance. Her characters remain cardboard figures in a background that is sketchily drawn. These facts do not impede her sales in the least.

DOROTHY ROBBIE

WORKS: *City Girl.* [Swords, Co. Dublin]: Poolbeg, [1990]; *Apartment 3B.* [Swords, Co. Dublin]: Poolbeg, [1991]; *Finishing Touches.* [Swords, Co. Dublin]: Poolbeg, [1992]; *City Woman.* [Swords, Co. Dublin]: Poolbeg, [1993]; *Foreign Affairs.* [Dublin]: Poolbeg, [1994].

SCULLY, MAURICE (1952–   ), poet.

WORK: *Love Poems and Others.* [Dublin: Raven Arts, 1981]; *Over and Through.* Cambridge: Peter Riley, 1992; *The Basic Colours: A Watchman's Log.* Durham, England: Pig, 1994.

SHANE, ELIZABETH (1877–1951), poet. Elizabeth Shane is the pseudonym
of Gertrude Elizabeth Heron Hine, who was born in Belfast in 1877. Her surname occasionally appears as Hind in some anthologies. She was a resident of Carrickfergus, County Antrim, and first violinist for the Belfast Philharmonic Orchestra until her death. She is chiefly noted for writing poems that incorporate folklore from Donegal. Her work abounds with dialect, which she uses in a facile manner. Shane and Moira O'Neill* of Cushendun are Ulster's most prominent dialectical women poets.

ANNE COLMAN

WORKS: *Piper's Tunes.* London: Selwyn & Blount, [ca. 1920]; *Tales of the Donegal Coast and Islands.* London: Selwyn & Blount, 1921; *By Bog and Sea in Donegal.* London: Selwyn & Blount, 1923; *Collected Poems I: Tales of the Donegal Coast and Islands, and By Bog and Sea in Donegal.* Dundalk: W. Tempest, Dundalgan, 1945; *Collected Poems II: Piper's Tunes and Later Poems.* Dundalk: W. Tempest, Dundalgan, 1945.

SHARE, BERNARD (1930–   ), novelist, social historian, editor, and journalist. Bernard Share was born in Chester, England, on May 31, 1930; he moved to Ireland at a very early age. He graduated from Trinity College, Dublin, in 1951 with an honours degree in modern languages and literature (English and Spanish). In 1955, he received a B.Litt. for a thesis on the prose writings of James Stephens. (The only remaining copy of the study was stolen from Trinity College Library.) After working briefly in publishing and advertising, he was appointed lecturer in English at Newcastle University College, New South Wales, Australia, in 1954—the founder member of the English Department and its sole staff member for the first six months. In 1957, he returned from Australia and worked again as an advertising copywriter before setting up a two-man "creative consultancy" with the graphic designer Bill Bolger. Together they produced a series of children's books, *The Bed That Went Whoosh!* (1965). He was the founder editor of *Books Ireland* from 1976 for twelve years. Also in 1976, he was appointed editor of *Cara,* the in-flight magazine of Aer Lingus, and wrote and traveled extensively on its behalf until 1991. He also served a period as secretary of CLÉ, the Irish Book Publishers' Association.

His preoccupation with travel is reflected in two of his books, *The Moon Is Upside Down* (1962) and *Far Green Fields: Fifteen Hundred Years of Irish Travel Writing* (1992). In addition, he has published studies of social history: *And Nelson on His Pillar* (1976), *The Emergency. Neutral Ireland 1939–45* (1978), *The Flight of the Iolar. The Aer Lingus Experience 1936–1986* (1986), and *Shannon Departures. A Study in Regional Initiatives* (1992); and he has written a book of biography, *Irish Lives* (1971).

In his three novels to date, Share is concerned with exploring the possibilities—and impossibilities—of the novel form. In his view, the *nouveau roman* was probably an unhelpful influence. There is something cubist about the novels in the way they disrupt linear discourse, developing a section, breaking it off, then replaying it, but with almost endless variations, and choosing new angles. Material accumulates that gives the impression that several different "stories" are furthered simultaneously, each one striving for the most appropriate manner to come into its own. Readers are constantly made to feel that they are confronting a narrative *in statu nascendi.*

Inish (1966) marks the first effort in this direction. What emerges from Share's procedure is a mosaic of individual units that progress—if that is the term—in circles and spirals. The units weave and spin, leaving a curious tapestry that seems to expand in all directions. Myriad strands come together—druidism, pornography, export-import business, philology, timetables, females in bathing suits. But no clear story is allowed to develop. One meaning of the word "Inish" is "tell." The account deliberately never lets the reader forget that it is the telling that matters, not the tale told.

In Share's second novel, *Merciful Hour* (1970), MacCarthaig Mor, Laoiseach Mac an Bhaird, and the girl Eílís Rua (not to mention the invisible Shay Fayne) have taken over a sixteenth-century Irish castle with a view to renovating it as a display piece for the blue-rinse Tourist Brigade. With the aid of tape recorder and notebook, each is recording the progress of the work—or so it appears, for the characters' thoughts, the dialogue, and the narration also appear on their tapes and in their notebooks, so that the reader is at all times kept in suspense as to what, within the fiction of the novel itself, is a fact or a fiction. The raison d'être of the telling is a kind of recherché. As so frequently in metafiction, conventions of the detective novel are being exploited, as the Sergeant, the Guard, and the Bean Guard try to investigate the case of Shay Fayne's disappearance. The three main characters are present and are being questioned. Notes are read out, tapes listened to. Share keeps up a tightrope act that has the reader continually wondering what is what. There are more questions posed by the book than answered by it. Again—that is the whole point. Everything is shown to be fiction, not only by means of overt commentary. Share runs the whole gamut of metafictional narrative gimmickry. There is no palpable difference between fact and fiction. The whole finally bites its own tail, presents a paradox—a vicious, playful circle.

Aidan Higgins* has called Share an "acerbic hoaxer," and perhaps it is best to consider *The Finner Faction* (1989) a kind of hoax. In the "Author's Note," Share remarks that he came upon this passage in the Mulcahy papers:

In June 1940, the Fine Gael (Opposition) representatives (on the Defense Council) had originated a proposal for a unified command for the defence of the whole island—a French/British/Irish force supplied with material by the United States and operating under a French General with French officers.

Furthermore, he discovered two other documents allegedly written by an individual named "the Ébéniste," and he found himself wondering how and why did they find their way to Ireland and into a nonrelated file. *The Finner Faction* is an attempt to get to the bottom of the mystery, with Share himself featuring in it. The novel is fiction made from history or rather possible, imaginary history. The narrative procedure is reminiscent of "heteroglossia," which is to say a deliberate polyphony of worlds of discourse. The autobiographical and historical worlds are juxtaposed with the fictional world, and a transworld identity between real and fictional entities is established. Additionally, something akin to the concept of "worlds under erasure" is operative, meaning fiction that cancels itself out. Repeatedly, sections are abruptly cut short, or something is delineated that is in patent opposition to points previously established. But despite all the experimenting that smacks of postmodernist tendencies, *The Finner Faction* is, in the final analysis, somewhat disappointing. Share's historical fantasy in the end does not succeed in pulling the individual intentions together into a meaning-providing whole.

RÜDIGER IMHOF

WORKS: *The Moon Is Upside Down.* Dublin: Figgis, 1962; *The Bed That Went Whoosh!* Dublin: Figgis, 1965. (Series of six children's books); *Inish.* Dublin: Figgis, 1966/New York: Knopf, 1967. (Novel); *Merciful Hour.* Dublin: Figgis, 1970. (Novel); *Irish Lives.* Dublin: Figgis, 1971; *And Nelson*

on His Pillar. Dublin: Nonpareil, 1976; *The Emergency. Neutral Ireland 1939–45.* Dublin: Gill &
Macmillan, 1978; *The Flight of the Iolar. The Aer Lingus Experience 1936–1986.* Dublin: Gill &
Macmillan, 1986; *The Finner Faction.* Swords, Co. Dublin: Poolbeg, & Dublin: Odell & Adair,
1989; ed., *Far Green Fields. Fifteen Hundred Years of Irish Travel Writing.* Belfast: Blackstaff,
1992; *Shannon Departures. A Study in Regional Initiatives.* Dublin: Gill & Macmillan, 1992;
Bunratty, Rebirth of a Castle. [Dingle]: Brandon, [1995]. REFERENCE: Imhof, Rüdiger. "How
It Is on the Fringes of Irish Fiction." *Irish University Review* 22 (Spring–Summer 1992): 151–167.

SHAW, [GEORGE] BERNARD (1856–1950), probably the preeminent dramatist in the English language since Shakespeare. There were few indications
during the first three decades of the long life of George Bernard Shaw that he
would take a place beside Shakespeare as England's most widely recognized
man of letters. He was born at 3 Upper Synge Street (now 33 Synge Street) on
July 26, 1856, the third child and only son of George Carr Shaw and Elizabeth
Gurly Shaw. His father, a wholesale grain merchant, was remembered by Shaw
as a heavy drinker and an inadequate head of the family, being far less an
influence on his son than was the strong, dispassionate mother. The nominally
Protestant Shaws held to the values of the Irish Ascendancy without enjoying
any of its perquisites. Shaw's schooling, wasted on a boy who could not afford
to go on to Trinity, left him unprepared for art, trade, or profession. He left
school at fifteen to serve as a clerk in a land agency at 15 Molesworth Street.

The only common interest in the Shaw home was music. Mrs. Shaw, a mezzo-
soprano, received lessons from a teacher and impressario, George John Vandeleur Lee. Following the death of his brother, Lee and the Shaw family shared
a four-story house at No. 1 Hatch Street. This led to perhaps groundless speculation on an affair between Lee and Mrs. Shaw. G.B.S.'s portrait of Lee as a
genius is unconvincing, but Lee directed ambitious musical programs in Dublin;
his single-minded devotion to music and his brisk self-confidence left a mark
on Shaw's personality.

In 1873, Lee moved to London. The departure of Mrs. Shaw and her daughters followed too closely to be coincidental. Her marriage had become meaningless. With Lee's help she could obtain teaching work in London, and her
daughter Lucy might be able to advance her singing career. (The other daughter,
Elinor Agnes, died of tuberculosis in 1876.) Father and son moved into lodgings
at 61 Harcourt Street.

Shaw joined his mother and sister in London in 1876. He left Dublin without
a sentimental tremor and did not return to Ireland, even when his father died in
1885, for thirty years. During his first three years in London, Shaw did nothing
in pursuit of his dimly defined goal of success in the arts. For a few months he
was a ghost-writer for Lee, contributing articles on music to a shortlived weekly,
The Hornet. They remained in casual contact until Lee's death on November
28, 1886, at his residence in the unfashionable end of Park Lane. Much earlier,
Mrs. Shaw had broken off her unromantic connection with the music teacher;
no Shaw attended his funeral.

In 1879, Shaw began to write novels in outmoded early Victorian style: *Im-*

maturity (1879), *The Irrational Knot* (1880), *Love Among the Artists* (1881), *Cashel Byron's Profession* (1882), *An Unsocial Socialist* (1883), and a fragment later titled *An Unfinished Novel.* All but *Immaturity* and the fragment were printed serially in the socialist periodicals *To-Day* and *Our Corner* after publishing houses rejected them. Shaw's fame in other areas eventually led to the publication of the novels in book format. A few other prose works of this period were accepted by various journals and later issues as part of a collected edition. They are of negligible merit.

The novels are of interest mostly for the autobiographical elements and the early intimations of Shaw's hero type. Robert Smith, the young clerk in *Immaturity;* Ned Connolly, the stolid inventive genius in *The Irrational Knot;* Owen Jack, the musician rampant in *Love Among the Artists;* and Sidney Trefusis, doctrinaire socialist and cool philanderer in *An Unsocial Socialist,* all are adumbrations of what Shaw was or wanted to be. Presumably he had no desire to become a prizefighter like Cashel Byron, though he boxed for exercise. Characterization and dialogue were done with care; plotting he regarded as an irksome necessity.

London in the 1880s was bustling with debating clubs and radical societies. In 1879, Shaw joined the philosophical Zetetical Society. Stimulated by his first taste of intellectual life, he responded, at first haltingly because of innate shyness, then, flitting from one society to another, with growing assurance. He was attracted to socialism in 1882 on hearing a lecture by the American economist Henry George. Soon after the Fabian Society was founded in 1884, Shaw became a member. The Fabians differed from other socialist bodies and splinter groups in repudiating violence and in directing their appeals to intelligent, respectable citizens. Few in number but significant in influence, they operated by infiltrating committees of other organizations, lecturing, debating, and issuing a flood of articulate pamphlets. With them Shaw gained direction, friendships, and an outlet for his burgeoning talent. If he lacked the economic background of many Fabians, such as Sidney Webb, he could hold an audience by his audacity and wit, and the content and style of many Fabian pamphlets bore the stamp of G.B.S.

Little compensation was offered or expected for work on behalf of socialism; and Shaw earned his living as a journalist. From 1885 to 1888, he wrote an anonymous miscellany for the *Pall Mall Gazette.* As "Corno di Bassetto," he produced musical criticism from 1888 to 1890 for T. P. O'Connor's *The Star.* This work overlapped his tour of duty as art critic for *The World,* from 1886 to 1889. For the same journal, from 1890 to 1894, he was music reviewer. Turning to drama criticism in 1895, he wrote for the *Saturday Review* until 1898, when income from plays enabled him to concentrate on creativity.

Shaw's articles were candid revelations of his personality and opinions on almost everything. Michelangelo, Beethoven, Wagner, Ibsen, the iconoclasts, the earth-shakers, were the creators against whom other artists were weighed and found wanting. What Shaw observed on the stage infuriated him: mutilated

Shakespeare, mechanistic well-made plays, melodrama which bolstered hypocritical conventionality, sham-Ibsen plays which labored the supposed naughtiness and ignored the social criticism.

There was more to his critical writing than freedom of the press bravado and overstated favoritism or dislike. Afternoons in the National Gallery of Ireland had given him some visual appreciation of painting, though it was not his strongest area. Music he knew intimately; he had grown up with it and was a self-taught pianist. Furthermore, he noted affinities between the composition of a symphony and a drama, between song and speech—an awareness he put to practical use. The coruscating wit and combativeness of the play reviews have tended to obscure his perceptive commentary not only on the art of playwriting but also on costumes, staging, lighting, and other aspects of theatre craft.

As a Dubliner, Shaw had elbowed his way into the Theatre Royal or the Gaiety to watch English actors on tour. In London, his knowledge of theatre was greatly expanded. Nevertheless, he became a playwright almost by chance. In 1885, William Archer suggested that they collaborate on an Ibsenite play; Archer would write the plot and Shaw fill in dialogue. The collaboration lasted for one act. Seven years later the Independent Theatre founded by J. T. Grein was soliciting plays. Shaw dug out the abandoned manuscript. Reworked and entitled *Widowers' Houses* (Mark 12: 38–40), it was staged at the Royalty Theatre on December 9, 1892. This was the first of three dramas published in 1898 under Shaw's designation Unpleasant Plays.

Widowers' Houses and *Mrs. Warren's Profession* dramatize exploitation, not by heartless monsters but by cheerful, pragmatic, well-spoken, otherwise decent and respectable individuals. Responsibility for the evil is not confined to Sartorius, the slumlord in *Widowers' Houses,* and Mrs. Warren, manager of a chain of brothels. It must be shared equally by respectable persons who by acquiescence become a party to the wrong and by a social order which makes exploitation possible. *The Philanderer* (1893) satirizes ladies who emancipate themselves in the fashion of Ibsen's heroines and at the same time insist on being treated as the weaker sex. Awkwardly attached to this plot line is the ridiculing of medical experimenters engaging in vivisection.

Shaw's first plays did not take the theatre by storm. *Widowers' Houses* had a single performance; Grein wisely turned down *The Philanderer*—it was not staged until 1905; and the lord chamberlain unwisely refused to license *Mrs. Warren's Profession,* the best of the lot, for public presentation. A private performance was given by the Stage Society in London on January 5, 1902. A company staging the play in New York on October 30, 1905, was tried for offending public decency and acquitted. Punitive action was threatened, though not carried out, when the Dublin Repertory Company played it at the Little Theatre, 40 Upper O'Connell Street, on November 16, 1914. Not until July 27, 1925, was there a public showing in England, at the Prince of Wales Theatre, Birmingham.

The Unpleasant Plays were followed by a group of Pleasant Plays, also published in 1898: *Arms and the Man, Candida, The Man of Destiny, You Never Can Tell.* They were pleasant in that they dealt with romantic follies.

Arms and the Man, set in Bulgaria during its war with Serbia in 1885, contrasts saber-flailing panache and romantic sensibility to the plain practicality of the Swiss mercenary Bluntschli. On April 21, 1894, it appeared at the Avenue Theatre, London. The curtain-raiser, W. B. Yeats'* *The Land of Heart's Desire,* by chance or intent provided another comparison of sense and sensibility. Both writers looked on a world too full of weeping; Yeats' solution was to escape from it, and Shaw's was to reform the actual world into a land of heart's desire. *Arms and the Man* was the first Shaw play performed in America, at the Herald Square Theatre, New York, on September 17, 1894.

In *Candida,* eighteen-year-old poet Eugene Marchbanks tries to persuade the wife of a robust Christian socialist, the Reverend James Morrell, to leave her unappreciative husband and fly with him to a Yeatsian dreamworld. Candida's decision to stay with Morrell is founded neither on the sacred marriage contract nor on Victorian right thinking; in spite of his charisma, he is the weaker man and needs her. Eugene goes off alone, self-assured, to meet his destiny. The first staging was in Aberdeen on July 30, 1897. In London, the Stage Society offered a private performance on July 1, 1900. Opening at the Princess Theatre, New York, on December 8, 1903, the play was the hit of the season.

A one-act comedy, *The Man of Destiny* is a witty triviality about compromising letters in a stolen dispatch case belonging to Napoleon Bonaparte, on the verge of greatness in 1796. It contains an analytical passage in which, except for a few details, the description of Napoleon fits G.B.S. The first London performance was at the Royal Court Theatre on June 4, 1907, ten years after a staging at the Grand Theatre, Croydon, in July 1897.

You Never Can Tell involves the comic reunion of a husband and his family after an eighteen-year separation and points out the folly of preparing for married life by indulging in romantic courtship. This popular farce was premiered by the Stage Society on November 16, 1899.

Shaw's friendship with Charlotte Payne-Townsend, an Irish heiress, began in 1896. When he became seriously ill in 1898, she was willing to give him better care than he would receive in the indifferent bosom of his family. But where? Though Shaw was a veteran of a few fleshly and several platonic affairs, he would have no part of a live-in with a gracious lady. Royalties from his plays were starting to accumulate, so there could be no whispers of fortune-hunting. On June 1, 1898, they were married in a civil ceremony. A few years later, they moved into an architecturally undistinguished house in Ayot St. Lawrence, a quiet village close to London. Their childless union ended with her death on September 12, 1943. (Shaw's mother died in 1913, and his sister Lucy in 1920.)

G.B.S. turned aside importunities to stand for Parliament, believing that he could accomplish more on the local level. In 1897, running unopposed, he was elected vestryman, and later borough councillor, of the St. Pancras district of London. For six years he worked diligently on its affairs. Speeches in his 1904 campaign to represent St. Pancras on the London County Council offended most of the electorate, and he lost badly.

Recuperating from illness in 1898, Shaw worked on *Caesar and Cleopatra,* the first of a three-play group he called Plays for Puritans. Shaw's own puritanism consisted of abstinence from tobacco, liquor, and meat. Sex he deemed a groveling sort of pleasure. He dressed with simplicity bordering on shabbiness. The title, however, signified his intent to purge that secular temple, the theater, of hypocrisy and bad art.

Caesar is a good representative of Shaw's hero. He is not a lover but a headmaster who chastises Cleopatra whenever she takes her royalty too seriously; he is tolerant of shortcomings and inanities of lesser men; he is calmly ruthless if the occasion demands; and he foresees, unemotionally, the Ides of March, as Napoleon foresees Waterloo. Shaw considered Caesar, as did the "revisionist" historians of the nineteenth century, a reformer tilting at the aristocratic Senate, hence the difference between his character and Shakespeare's marmoreal pontificator. *Caesar* was performed at the Royal Theatre, Newcastle upon Tyne, on March 15, 1899. Later stagings were in Berlin on March 31, 1906; the New Amsterdam Theatre, New York, on October 30, 1906; and the Savoy, London, on November 25, 1907.

Dick Dudgeon, in revolt against his mother's hate-filled perversion of puritanism, preaches "diabolonian ethics" in *The Devil's Disciple.* There is another revolt in progress, that of Americans against British rule. Soldiers come to arrest the Reverend Anthony Anderson, who is to be hanged as an example to the disloyal, and Dick, visiting the Anderson home, assumes the identity of the absent clergyman. No Sidney Carton doing the far better thing, Dick cannot explain his conduct to others or to himself; he is responding to some incomprehensible urge. A last-minute stroke of fortune saves him from the gallows, and he and the minister reverse roles, Dick to become a preacher, Anderson a freedom fighter. General John Burgoyne, one of the most engaging characters in the play, performs with taste and urbanity what he recognizes as a disagreeable duty to the Empire. The American presentation, premiering at the Fifth Avenue Theatre, New York, on October 4, 1897, brought Shaw his first sizable income from writing and gave him artistic heartburn. Actors read a love affair into the relationship between Dudgeon and the minister's wife, an interpretation which Shaw categorically did not intend. This interpretation was beyond his corrective reach, but when his plays were staged in England he meticulously supervised rehearsals.

The philosophical burden of *Captain Brassbound's Conversion,* the last of the Plays for Puritans, is the difference between justice and revenge. More intriguing than the ideas is Cicely Waynflete, who without apparent effort handles an English judge, American naval officers, the English expatriate Brassbound and his rascal gang, and Moroccan sheiks. If this seems an unlikely dramatis personae, Shaw is parodying melodramas in which British soldiers rescue a white lady from primitive tribesmen. Cicely converts Brassbound from his monomaniacal revenge for an injustice done him long ago and sends him off, as Eugene Marchbanks departed, with confidence and a stronger sense of self-identity. Ellen Terry, for whom Shaw created the character of Cicely, did not fancy herself in the role. She reluctantly appeared in the copyright performance at the Court Theatre, Liverpool, on October 10, 1899, but not again until March 20, 1906.

On April 26, 1904, at the urging of actor-director Harley Granville-Barker, *Candida* was revived at the Royal Court Theatre, a 614-seat house (about the size of the Abbey*) remote from the fashionable West End. From the autumn of 1904 to June 29, 1907, this little hall sustained one of the most incandescent periods of English theatrical history. Of the 938 performances, 701 were of eleven plays by Shaw; other writers included Euripides, Maeterlinck, Schnitzler, and Hauptmann. It was a fusion of talents: business manager John Vedrenne, the versatile Barker, a strong company, and the creativity of G.B.S.

John Bull's Other Island, staged on November 1, 1904, was written for the emerging Irish theatre, but, proving unsuited to the dramatic ideas prevailing there, it was given to the Court. Shaw inverts, though not completely, the old Stage Irish formula. Irishman Larry Doyle is the realist, scornful of his dreaming countrymen; Englishman Tom Broadbent is a sentimentalist about round towers and colleens and all that, but businessman enough to see opportunities in Ireland. In this symposium on Anglo-Irish matters, Shaw's spokesman is the unfrocked priest Peter Keegan, who outlines in mystic terms the ideal state, a socialist commonwealth. During a command performance on March 11, 1905, Edward VII laughed so heartily he broke his chair. At the Abbey in September 1916, audiences laughed just as vigorously, though no doubt for different reasons.

Coming almost at midpoint in Shaw's life span, *Man and Superman,* staged on May 23, 1905, explicated his concept of creative evolution. He shared with Samuel Butler the belief that evolution by adjustment to environment "banished mind from the universe." Instead, Shaw reasoned, man rises to higher levels of consciousness, eventually to pure intellect, by assertion of his will. The impetus for this conscious effort is the Life Force, a power man senses but does not understand. A woman, impelled by the Life Force, singles out a man with the right characteristics for the breeding of superior children. This creates a battle of the sexes: philosopher man must avoid fleshly entanglements to fulfill his purpose, and woman must entangle him to fulfill hers.

The idea is dramatized on two levels. John Tanner, a bull-in-china-shop socialist reformer, is efficiently captured by Ann Whitefield, and the two aspects of the Life Force merge—the drive toward betterment and the improvement of the species. On the other level, the third act, occasionally performed as a reading or a play in itself, opens on a barren Spanish plain which is transformed into Shaw's vision of Hell. Tanner, Ann, and the other characters are metamorphosed temporarily into the figures in the Don Juan story. (Shaw's mother sang Donna Anna in Lee's Dublin production of Mozart's *Don Giovanni.*) Satan is a glib hedonist. The occupants of Hell choose to stay there because they are self-indulgent and intellectually lazy. In terms of orthodox morality Don Juan should be in Hell because of his earthly philandering, but he dismisses his escapades as an experiment which he outgrew; he scorns an eternity of lowbrow pleasures and opts for a heaven of philosophical contemplation. Donna Anna, in mortal life the epitome of stony, negative virtue, calls out at the end of the Hell sequence, "A father! A father for the Superman!"

As in *Man and Superman,* the events in *Major Barbara,* first performed on November 28, 1905, build to a discussion scene. The main event is a contest between Andrew Undershaft, a munitions manufacturer, and his daughter Barbara, an officer in the Salvation Army. Undershaft wins by proving that the charity is funded by the very exploiters who create poverty. In his utopian factory-community he has abolished poverty, the deadliest sin. Herein lies a paradox, posed by Barbara's fiancé, classical scholar Adolphus Cusins: "Then the way to life lies through the factory of death?" Undershaft, who may be modeled on the Swedish inventor-philanthropist Alfred Nobel, resembles Caesar in his heroic stance. He ruthlessly scraps the obsolete (weapons in his case) for the new. A leader must be willing to destroy to make his ideas prevail—thus, he resolves Cusins' paradox; killing "is the final test of conviction . . . the only way of saying must." Shaw's socialist order cannot begin in an industrially primitive nation; capitalism develops the resources of the good life, as Undershaft has done, and then socialism commandeers the machinery. This evidently is the function assigned to Cusins when Undershaft hands the factory over to him. In the control of armaments, Cusins recognizes "a power simple enough for common men to use, yet strong enough to force the intellectual oligarchy to use its genius for the common good."

In 1881, Shaw contracted smallpox in spite of inoculation. In 1898, an infection was aggravated by improper medication. He retaliated in *The Doctor's Dilemma,* produced on November 20, 1906, by characterizing doctors as narrow dogmatists, each asserting a single cause, hence a single cure, for every illness. (Shaw had his own dogmatic explanation: unsanitary slum living and malnutrition.) The dilemma for Dr. Colenso Ridgeon is whether to devote his limited time to treating a decent, mediocre fellow practitioner or a tubercular young painter, Louis Dubedat, a man faithful to nothing but his art. Ridgeon's choice is complicated by his infatuation with Dubedat's blindly loyal wife Jennifer. In considering the larger issues related to Dubedat's amorality, Shaw appears to equate leaders and artists. The leader's goal is to create a better society; the artist's is, so John Tanner puts it, "to shew us ourselves as we really are." To achieve these desirable ends, artists and leaders must not be hemmed in by the restraints and responsibilities imposed on lesser men. This interpretation of *The Doctor's Dilemma* would be more persuasive if Dubedat were not, away from his easel, such a grubby little confidence man.

The success of the Court venture led to the leasing of the Savoy Theatre in the West End for the 1907–1908 season. A few Shaw plays were revived, but he had nothing new to offer, and production costs were high. The season ended with a considerable deficit; at its conclusion, Barker and Vedrenne went their separate ways.

Between *The Doctor's Dilemma* and *Pygmalion* (Vienna, 1913; London, April 11, 1914), most of Shaw's plays were lighthearted comedies on the nature of marriage and parent–child relationships: *Getting Married* (1908), *Misalliance* (1910), and *Fanny's First Play* (1912). *Fanny,* a potboiler done for Barker and his actress wife, Lillah McCarthy, at their 278-seat Little Theatre on April 19, 1911, enjoyed the longest run of Shaw's early plays. Generation-gap humor is mixed with an essay on criticism. The wealthy father of Fanny O'Dowda invites four prominent critics to a private performance of an anonymous play (written by Fanny). Much of the fun is in their effort to identify the author. One critic thinks it is Shaw; another says it is too good to be his work. Shaw himself did not admit authorship until *Fanny* was published in 1914. It was not a well-guarded secret.

Only two plays of this relatively fallow period are worth much attention: *The Shewing-up of Blanco Posnet* and *Androcles and the Lion.*

Myopic English censorship of *Posnet* on grounds of blasphemy (it is no more blasphemous than "The Hound of Heaven") gave the play notoriety beyond its merits. It is *The Devil's Disciple* reset in the American West. Like Dick Dudgeon, Blanco Posnet is a pariah who barely escapes hanging. He sees more clearly than Dudgeon the hand of God moving him to do the right thing, helping a mother with a sick child, almost in spite of himself: "He made me because he had a job for me. He let me run loose till the job was ready." Yeats and Lady Gregory,* defying threatened revocation of the Abbey Theatre* patent, staged this very un-Irish play on August 25, 1909, in Dublin. Irish players gave a private performance of *Posnet* at the Aldwych Theatre, London, on December 5–6, 1909, and at the Maxine Elliott Theatre, New York, on November 23, 1911.

Shaw called *Androcles* an entertainment for children. Except for Androcles' romping with the lion, the play is unintelligible to all but frighteningly precocious youngsters. The familiar story is raw material for Shaw's thesis that there always will be Establishment persecutors (here the pagan Romans) and dissenting martyrs (in this case Christians). Shaw is not writing a brief for Christianity. In another historical context, Establishment Christians will persecute the disturbers of their peace. *Androcles* was first performed in Berlin on November 25, 1912, and in London at the St. James Theatre on September 1, 1913.

The play *Pygmalion* has had to compete for attention with movie and musical comedy variations, and with the snickering over Shaw's temporary infatuation with Mrs. Patrick Campbell, for whom the part of Liza Doolittle was written. She played it in the first English production at His Majesty's Theatre on April 11, 1914.

Shaw had an enduring interest in phonetics, but if *Pygmalion* was written only to promote that science, or to demonstrate the superficiality of polite society, it should have ended with Liza's triumph at the ball. What follows is her greater triumph in declaring independence from her domineering teacher, though it is, all told, a modest rise from guttersnipe to shopkeeper and wife of poor Freddy Eynsford-Hill. Shaw's patience again was sorely tried by those who were determined to see a love affair between Liza and Henry Higgins.

The first run of *Pygmalion* was ended by the outbreak of war. During the years immediately preceding, good repertory theatre flourished, but in wartime England, theatre dwindled into easy entertainment for servicemen and production costs soared. Under these conditions, Shaw wrote only a few inconsequential one-act comedies.

As a humanist, he deplored the slaughter; as a socialist, he anticipated no social betterment in the victory of one set of capitalist powers over another. Shaw likened the war to a battle between pirate ships, in which one's allegiance perforce was with the ship he was on board. His writings and other utterances on the conflict seem, in retrospect, sensible and consistent with his overall thinking, but they deeply offended Englishmen who thought even a licensed jester should become a straight man for the duration.

In wartime Dublin, there was almost a Shaw Festival. Between September 25, 1916, and May 26, 1917, six of his plays were staged by Abbey producer J. Augustus Keogh. This was nothing political. Keogh, like his predecessor St. John Ervine,* sought to expand the Abbey repertoire beyond the "peasant play," and he greatly admired Shaw.

Since the time of Parnell, Shaw had written of Irish affairs. He considered himself Irish or English depending on the point he was making. Parnell's tragedy he attributed to inhumane divorce laws. On the broader political issue, Shaw argued that England would have to come to terms: for three decades, Parliament had been tied up in Home Rule debate, and English rule in Ireland had degenerated into armed occupation. However, in a world of superpowers a wholly independent Ireland could not defend itself from invasion or economic competition. Shaw proposed instead an Irish parliament for national affairs, and Irish membership in a federal parliament to deal with mutual interests of the British Isles. Ulster could not survive as a British enclave with its own version of Home Rule, or as an impotent minority in the British parliament. The North was better off by entering the Irish parliament in which it could exert a strong influence. The Ulsterman's fear of Home Rule was unfounded. The Catholic Church in Ireland had been as conservative and autocratic as English authority. Liberated Ireland, taking a page from the history of Catholic France and Catholic Italy, would curtail the power of the Church.

Shaw's observation that more of Dublin should have been destroyed during Easter Week seems another instance of tactless flippancy. Yet, Shaw knew the squalor of Dublin slums, and unless the change of Ireland's political center from Westminster to Dublin was accompanied by social reforms, the slums would remain. Rejecting the impossiblist stance of the Easter Week rebels, he nonetheless protested the British reprisal, particularly the trial of Roger Casement, who as an Irishman would not be guilty of treason against England.

While Europe was blundering into war, Shaw was working on *Heartbreak House*. He would not permit it to be staged until November 10, 1920, by the New York Theatre Guild, which produced a number of his plays in the 1920s and 1930s. The London premiere was at the Court Theatre on October 18, 1921. Shaw called the play "A Fantasia in the Russian Manner on English Themes." Chekovian influence is present in the country house setting and the futile characters, but Shaw's people are more coherent and less wistful. The English themes actually were the themes of any spiritually exhausted people rushing to war for lack of other stimulation.

In *Major Barbara,* Adolphus Cusins united power and culture. Between it and *Heartbreak House* Shaw's vision darkened. Power lacked direction, culture lacked virility. Heartbreak House is a gathering place of defeated and impotent hopes: Victorian idealism, colonialism, big business, bohemian revelry, youthful romance. Young Ellie Dunn is disillusioned first by a romantic dreamer who is already married; then by Boss Mangan, who for all his seeming strength is only a manager of enterprises owned by bigger bosses; and finally by Captain Shotover, retired seafarer, whose sham senility masks resolute character and deep-probing philosophy. Yet, even his flights to higher levels of consciousness are sustained by rum. At the close, warplanes are showering destruction, and Hector Hushabye, the suicidal romantic, turns on the lights of Heartbreak House as a beacon to the bombers. It is he who speaks most eloquently of the fatigue and despair of mankind: "Out of that darkness some new creation will come to supplant us as we have supplanted the animals, or the heavens will fall in thunder and destroy us."

The pessimism of *Heartbreak House,* induced by war and the doldrums of the theatre, quickly was superseded by the fantastic optimism of Shaw's most ambitious work, *Back to Methuselah.* If *Man and Superman* was the Genesis of Shaw's own Bible, the five-play sequence of *Methuselah* was the Pentateuch. It begins in the Garden and ends in 31,920 A.D. Eve responds to the Life Force by mothering Cain, the first fascist, but she also bears the artists, philosophers, and scientists who will inherit the earth. The guiding principle is that the post-Methuselah life span of three score and ten is insufficient for full development of man's capacities. He must, by conscious exertion of will, break through nature's dominion over him. By 31,920, he is hatched from an egg fully grown, beyond the folly and confusion of childhood. His ecstasies are intellectual rather than sensual. As in Plato's Republic, the arts are toys to be discarded when one attains the mature level of pure intellect. Death comes only from accident. The obsolete shortlived creature of 1920 A.D. has perished like the dinosaur.

Back to Methuselah was commercially risky theatre. So it proved when the New York Theatre Guild produced the series beginning February 27, 1922. The Birmingham Repertory Theatre, founded by Barry Jackson, was more successful in 1923, with a good company and better spacing of performances.

In 1920, Joan of Arc was canonized, and at the prompting of his wife, Shaw wrote a play on her. His Joan, incidentally, is a soldier and visionary, primarily the first Protestant in her assertion of the right of private judgment. As in many other Shaw plays, the climax is a trial scene in which the defendant tries the accusers. Members of the ecclesiastical court are on the whole astute and gentle, honestly concerned with the ramifications of Joan's individualism. Joan is simply too far ahead of her times, and her fellow men kill her because they do not know what else to do. The epilogue shows that though the Maid of Orleans has been declared a saint, the world still is frightened by her free spirit. She asks rhetorically, "How long, O Lord, how long?" The first production of *Saint Joan* was at the Garrick Theatre, New York, on December 28, 1923, and in England at the New Theatre, London, on March 26, 1924. Among distinguished actresses who have played Joan are Sybil Thorndyke, Elizabeth Bergner, Katherine Cornell, Celia Johnson, Siobhan McKenna, and Barbara Jefford.

At the age of seventy, Shaw was awarded the Nobel Prize in 1926 for the writing of *Saint Joan.* He consistently declined honors and degrees, but he accepted the Nobel Prize in order to establish a foundation for promoting knowledge of Swedish literature in England. The next few years he devoted to the tedious work of writing *The Intelligent Woman's Guide to Socialism and Capitalism,* published in 1928. In this stout volume, he sums up his economic philosophy in simple, though not patronizing, language.

If what Shaw wrote between *Saint Joan* and his death was largely reiterative, it remained witty and provocative. *The Apple Cart* (1929) sports with constitutional monarchy by portraying an independent-minded king matching strategies with a government of Laborite hacks. King Magnus terrifies them into submission by threatening to abdicate and stand for election as a commoner, a move which would replace nominal hereditary status with popular support.

Too True to Be Good (1931) is a postwar *Heartbreak House.* In an exotic outpost of the Empire, an incongruous assortment of equally feckless civilians and soldiers ponder the question raised in *Pilgrim's Progress,* "What shall we do to be saved?" The answer seems to be provided by Private Meek (modeled on Lawrence of Arabia), a Shaw type of doer. While the others are talking and blundering, Meek takes care of their problems, except those problems caused by lack of will and conviction. Shaw had much better control of his material in *Heartbreak House. Too True,* despite imaginative staging and a few delightfully weird characters, failed to impress audiences in New York, Warsaw, or London.

Sir Barry Jackson began the yearly Malvern Festival in 1929, principally to stage plays by Shaw. A younger G.B.S. might have done for the festival what he had done for the Court Theatre, but on the whole his autumnal work was not very good. The best of it was *In Good King Charles's Golden Days,* presented on August 11, 1939, a sparkling disquisition on religion, government, man and woman, science and art, by the leading intellectuals and nonintellectuals (e.g., Nell Gwynn) of Restoration England. *Geneva,* produced on August 1, 1938, is another trial play. Bombardone (Mussolini), Battler (Hitler), and Flanco de Fortinbras (Franco) voluntarily appear before a world court with no jurisdiction and no authority to answer their accusers. No verdict is given. Dictators, British and Russian observers, a dotty fundamentalist, and a parochial-minded female member of Parliament all depart convinced of their rightness. The judge, echoing Hector Hushabye, sums up: "Man is a failure as a political animal, the creative forces which produce him must produce something better."

While the Shaws toured South Africa in 1932, Mrs. Shaw was injured in an auto accident. Waiting there for her to recover, Shaw wrote *The Adventures of the Black Girl in Her Search for God.* The girl examines all religions and the irreligion of science, intuitively recognizing their falsities. At last she meets Voltaire and his Irish gardener (G.B.S.), who like John Tanner is caught in the grip of the Life Force. He goes on digging; she raises the children.

In 1933 the Shaws briefly visited America as part of a world cruise. Americans who lionized Shaw on the West Coast, as well as those who heard him lecture in New York's Metropolitan Opera House on April 11, generally did not appreciate his mockery of Yankee materialism or his socialistic vision of a Great Society.

Shaw quickly recognized the potential of the motion picture. The development of sound track was, of course, essential to the adaptation of his discussion dramas. He was adamant on what he wanted, the filming of an actual stage production, until Gabriel Pascal persuaded him to revise the texts to take advantage of the flexibility of the camera. Pascal produced in England a romanticized *Pygmalion* (1938), a simplified *Major Barbara* (1941), and a catastrophically expensive and savagely reviewed *Caesar and Cleopatra* (1945). There were sixteen filmings of Shaw plays, including these three, a Czechoslovakian adaptation of *Cashel Byron* (1921), and a British production of *The Millionairess,* a mediocre late Shaw play, in 1961. *Pygmalion* was filmed in German, Dutch, and English. (For this and other useful information, see Donald Costello, *The Serpent's Eye, Shaw and the Cinema.*) Mercifully, the Hollywood vulgarizations of *Androcles* (1953, by Pascal), *Saint Joan* (1957), and *The Devil's Disciple* (a grinning contest held in 1959) were committed after Shaw's death.

The closing years of Shaw's life could not have been very satisfying. His health slowly deteriorated. Like other thoughtful persons who lived through two world wars, he had reason to wonder "when will they ever learn." The postwar Labor government imposed burdensome taxes without solving problems. What could Shaw say that he had not already said? The ancients of his circle were dropping off: Mrs. Shaw and Beatrice Webb in 1943, his old adversary H. G. Wells in 1946, Sidney Webb in 1947. Of the honors extended to him in his advanced age, he accepted only a few, including the Freedom of Dublin (he still disliked the city) on August 28, 1946.

Shaw was not the man for retired ease. He worked constantly, even during the trips he endured because Mrs. Shaw enjoyed traveling. Always accident prone, on foot or in vehicles, Shaw broke his leg in September 1950, when he fell while working in his garden. The injury was complicated by a kidney infection. After a short stay in the hospital, he insisted on going home to die. Among his last visitors was Mrs. Sean O'Casey. When the Abbey directors refused O'Casey's* *The Silver Tassie* in 1928, Shaw sided with O'Casey in the paper war that followed. Early on the morning of November 2, 1950, G.B.S. slipped easily away in his ninety-fourth year. His ashes, mixed with those of his wife, were scattered in the garden of the house called Shaw's Corner. It was turned over to the National Trust. A small portion of his estate was used to encourage the development of a new phonetic alphabet. The rest was distributed equally to the British Museum, which also received a mass of his personal documents, to the Royal Academy of Dramatic Art, and to the National Gallery of Ireland. The British Museum and the British Library became separate organizations in 1973. Income from Shaw's estate continues to be given to the museum, over the protests of those who hold that Shaw's intent, whatever the literal reading of his will, was to benefit the Reading Room of the library, where in his early years in London he read and met his friends.

Between 1879 and 1950 (compare Shakespeare's productive years, which at most were twenty-five), G.B.S. wrote more than fifty plays, five completed novels, a mountain of critical studies, reviews, letters public and private, Fabian pamphlets, and various expansive statements of opinion. A summary and evaluation of his work in the short space available here must undergo agonies of compression. Here Shaw will be considered, briefly, as religious philosopher, political economist, and man of the theatre. The bibliography will direct readers to more ample studies.

Shaw regards Christ as a good man deluded by his followers into thinking himself the Living God. Shaw flatly rejects the concept of vicarious atonement. In his socialist utopia he permits ethical but not religious instruction. Yet, there are numerous references to God in his plays. St. Joan's curtain lines are addressed to Him. In the final stage directions for *Too True to Be Good,* Shaw writes of the Pentecostal flame. The Black Girl's search for God does not end in negation. Major Barbara cries out near the close of the play, "Let God's work be done for its own sake; the work he had to create us to do because it cannot be done except by living men and women." This is close to what Blanco Posnet says. The Life Force, which Shaw equates with Providence in the preface to *Farfetched Fables,* sees to it that leaders, great thinkers, and great men are on hand when they are needed. But it "proceeds experimentally by Trial-and-Error, and never achieves 100 per cent success"; it can be "defeated by the imperfection of its mortal instruments." If man is fallible, God is not omnipotent. Through the instrumentality of the Life Force, man strives for the ultimate triumph of what is highest in him, his intellect. Perhaps Shaw's best statement on man's destiny is made in the preface to *Misalliance,* in answer to his own question, What is a child: "A fresh attempt to produce the just man made perfect; that is, to make humanity divine."

Shaw's thinking on socialism was affected by experience and the sweeping historical developments of his time. Basically, he advocated the nationalization of essential production and services, equality of income, and compulsory employment—no idle rich, no welfare handouts. He opposed revolutionary socialism, more vigorously perhaps in his early Fabian days, because even if it succeeded, the proletariat stood in the rubble wondering what to do next. Fascism only transferred power from the capitalists to the state. Labor unions took from management and gave to themselves. Not until poverty and degradation could be abolished by equalization of income could mankind achieve any meaningful betterment.

The harsher side of Shaw's program is inherent in his position that higher and lower forms cannot co-exist peacefully. Man supplants beast, Superman supplants common man. Even in the arts, new creators war on their predecessors. Shaw supported England in the Boxer Rebellion and the Boer War because the British would bring a higher civilization to China and South Africa. His Caesar shrugs off the burning of the library at Alexandria, for it was a repository of old knowledge; the future will be built on its ruins. Shaw plays which are blueprints of the coming times are characterized by the unfeeling liquidation of anyone who does not fit into the new order. In *The Tragedy of an Elderly Gentleman,* Part IV of *Black to Methuselah,* the Oracle kills the Elderly Gentleman as an act of kindness to an obsolete life-form: "Poor short-lived thing! What else could I do for you?" The worthless are disposed of en masse in *The Simpleton of the Unexpected Isles.* An angel of judgment announces to decadent Europe: "The lives which have no use, no meaning, no purpose will fade out. You will have to justify your existence or perish." To this Prolla, priestess of the Unexpected Isles, adds: "If the angels fail us we shall set up tribunals of our own from which worthless people will not come out alive." And in Part V of *Back to Methuselah* the She-Ancient matter of factly says, "Children with anything wrong do not live here."

Shaw's vision of the future bore a painful resemblance to the Europe of his own age. In Russia and Germany, there were tribunals for dealing with the worthless, as the state defined the term. Mussolini was bringing a higher civilization to primitive Ethiopia, and Spain was a testing ground for conflicting totalitarian ideologies.

An admirer of the unsentimental doer ever since he created Ned Connolly in *The Irrational Knot,* Shaw observed the apparent failure of parliamentary government in postwar Europe and the fact that in Mussolini's Italy the trains were running on time. About the best that can be said, in retrospect, is that Shaw was not the only intellectual who feared the center could not hold and so turned to get-it-done ideologies of the left or right.

However one may be outraged, bewildered, or stimulated by Shaw as philosopher, his place as a consummate man of the theatre is assured. He mastered every phase of dramatic art from writing to the subtleties of the live stage to carefully supervised texts with stage directions as beneficial to readers as to performers. (Bernard F. Dukore, *Bernard Shaw, Director,* is particularly valuable on Shaw's understanding of the techniques of the stage.)

The triumph of the Don Juan in Hell scene as readers' theatre possibly has created the impression that all one needs for an evening of Shaw is reading

desks or stools, the requisite number of mellow speakers, and an audience aus-
terely content with highbrow talk. Actually, Shaw makes imaginative use of the
stage. His sets range from the left flank of the Sphinx to a dentist's office, a
frontier saloon, Eden, the world of 31,920 A.D.—as far as thought can reach.
Major Barbara is made visually as well as thematically effective by stark contrasts in sets—genteel drawing room, drab Salvation Army shelter, ominous gun
emplacement. Shaw was not alone among his contemporaries in achieving emphasis by contrast: Galsworthy did as much in *The Silver Box,* so did J. M.
Barrie in the shift from the elegant in Act I to the primitive in Act II of *The
Admirable Crichton.* But Shaw also can make small details meaningful. The sets
for the first two acts of *The Devil's Disciple,* the Dudgeon and the Anderson
homes, respectively, are plain New England colonial. The difference lies in the
slight decorative touches attempted by Mrs. Anderson, trinkets perhaps, but indicative of a sense of beauty alien to the life-denying spirit of Mrs. Dudgeon.
This is not a case of an academician imposing his own significance on the raw
material of the play. Shaw himself makes the point in the stage directions.

The discussion scenes necessarily are static; vigorous movement or intrusive
stage business could impede communication of ideas in, for example, the final
scene of *Major Barbara.* But before the characters settle down for discussion,
Shaw sets the hook of empathy. The colloquium which opens *The Doctor's
Dilemma* is an exception. Generally, the plays commence with a brisk confrontation of egos—Joan and the bawling soldier Baudricourt, Tanner and the self-
styled progressive Roebuck Ramsden, Dudgeon and his mother. Thus, his
characters are established as personalities and are not permitted to dwindle into
sound-boxes for projecting ideas.

It would be difficult to write fifty-plus plays without some duplication of
characterizations. These are recurring types—the strong woman, the iconoclast,
the affable, pragmatic moneymaker, and so on. Yet, within a type one finds
recognizable distinctions. Candida Morell displays a touch of the feline in amusing herself with young Marchbanks, a quality absent from the makeup of Cicely
Waynflete. Sartorius, Undershaft, and Broadbent have certain general similarities, yet each man is tailored to the context of a particular play. The commanding, faintly boorish, personality of Sartorius would be ill suited to the texture
of *John Bull.* One does have the impression that Shaw played favorites with his
characters, cutting and polishing all the facets in some cases, tossing in the rough
stones in other cases, such as the idle young men and, especially, the ingenues.
He preferred mature women (Candida is thirty-three, Cicely between thirty and
forty, the glamorous Strange Lady in *The Man of Destiny* is thirty) on and off
stage.

Shaw could make good theatre from dramatic forms he candidly regarded as
trashy. What could be more blatantly melodramatic in plot outline than *Brassbound* or *The Devil's Disciple?* Would Boucicault* himself take a pig for an
auto ride, as Shaw does in *John Bull?* His intent, of course, was to kill theatrical
enemies with their own weapons.

The most substantive criticisms of Shaw, aside from fundamental disagreements with his philosophy, are aimed at needlessly intrusive comic turns and indecisive or ambiguous endings.

The first objection is made not to Shaw's blending of comedy and Roman history or religion and farcicality, but rather to comic bit parts which, however amusing, are of doubtful relevance—for example, the microbe made ill by contact with a human in *Too True to Be Good,* the band of squabbling radicals in *Man and Superman,* the inept avenging gunman in *Misalliance.* Shaw conceded that the jesting spirit occasionally descended at inopportune times.

The unwrapped endings are inherent in Shaw's philosophy and dramatic technique. Romance assumes a happy finality, tragedy closes with all passion spent, melodrama justifies the ways of right-thinking men to God. Shaw wrote none of the above. His plots are not built from floor plans, though he could be a craftsman when he chose to be. His plots are, to use his term, organic, shaping themselves as they grow, continuing to grow even after the curtain descends. This approach to play construction is congruent to Shaw's overview of man's lot. As Lilith says at the end of *Back to Methuselah,* life is endlessly expanding and evolving, there is always something beyond. One may agree that real life is a continuum and still ask that an artistic approximation of reality be symmetrical rather than open-ended.

On a less metaphysical level, Shaw gives all the contending forces such articulate spokesmen—even dictators and transparent rascals of the undeserving poor class can make an eloquent shyster case for themselves—that sometimes Shaw appears to be asking "What is truth?" and not staying for an answer. Anyone who has read enough of Shaw's prefaces, essays, and treatises might be able to work out by projection the meaning of a play. Whether he should have to is another matter.

Shaw's ongoing comparative evaluation of himself and Shakespeare began during his tour of duty as drama critic and ended with one of his last plays, a ten-minute Punch and Judy type of puppet show at Malvern on August 9, 1949, *Shakes versus Shav.* The essence of Shaw's judgment is that the true Shakespeare, removed from the blindness of bardolatry and the perversions of his plays by actor-managers like Henry Irving, was an incomparable poet and a second-rate mentality whose high-sounding platitudes masqueraded as wisdom. Shaw rested his claim to superiority on his confrontation with the vital issues of his day and on his advanced, positive thinking.

It is as vain to compare the Globe and the Court Theatres, or prose and blank verse, as it is to fault Elizabethans for not anticipating Darwin and Marx. One really is left with a subjective choice of world-views. Shakespeare's vision is of man's finitude: "Men must endure their going hence, even as their coming hither; ripeness is all." Shaw's vision is, in the universal sense, comic, as it declares the ultimate victory of man, or some species better than man, over finitude. Who is right? In the words of Mr. Doolittle, "I put it to you; I leave it to you."

A comparison of Ibsen and Shaw is somewhat more productive. In the beginning, Shaw preached the gospel according to Ibsen, took lessons from the master, and then outgrew him. Ibsen slowly, inexorably peels away until his characters and their society are fully revealed. His humor is sardonic. Shaw accelerates quickly and keeps moving, not necessarily in a straight line, until everybody is ready to sit down and discuss. His humor is wide-ranging, sophisticated, broadly vulgar, expansive, intrusive, whatever the situation calls for.

When Shaw identified Ibsen as a socialist during a Fabian meeting on July 18, 1890, Ibsen promptly denied any sort of party line. Though he recognizes, as Shaw does, the meanness behind the facade of social respectability, Ibsen proposes no broadly dogmatic solutions. For Nora Helmer, the answer is to close the door as she leaves; for the weakling Hialmar Ekdal, taking refuge in the life-lie is the only way; for Dr. Stockmann, there is whatever satisfaction comes from being right when everybody else is wrong. The showing-up of Pastor Manders may be read as an attack on orthodox Christianity. If it is, Ibsen offers no alternative, unless it is the bellicose honesty of Pastor Brand, and he winds up with a very small congregation. In sum, Ibsen points to the ring around the collar, while Shaw prescribed detergents—socialism, creative evolution. One may or may not want to wear the shirt after Shaw has laundered it.

Samuel Johnson, in the preface to his edition of Shakespeare, wrote that in judging works "of which the excellence is not absolute and definitive, but gradual and comparative . . . no other test can be applied than length of duration and continuance of esteem." So tested, ninety years after *Man and Superman,* seventy years after *Saint Joan,* how will G.B.S. fare?

Social reforms have reduced his more specific problem plays to historical artifacts. Changing mores have blunted what used to be daring. *Mrs. Warren* would not make the front page of *The New York Times* as it did in 1905, no more than a performance of *Ghosts* would shock London critics into writing of an "open sewer" as they did in 1891. On the other hand, Shaw came to grips with problems beyond the reach of legislators, too deeply rooted to be swayed by the light and variable winds of "in" and "out." The link, or confrontation if you will, between man and woman is more than chic contemporary issues of equitable divorce settlements and who gets the credit cards. The most abiding question of all is, who and what is man? To these universal concerns Shaw vigorously addressed himself. The head count of converts to his ideas is not important. What matters is that after one sorts out the potboilers, the plays tossed off as a *jeu d'esprit,* the more grandiose efforts that did not quite come off, a substantial body of master works—live, exciting theatre—remains. Shaw, young man of Dublin, senior citizen of the world, continues to stand before us on his soapbox, Mephistophelian, nimble, provocative, outrageous, teasing, or browbeating us to hear him out.

WILLIAM J. FEENEY

WORKS: *Plays Pleasant and Unpleasant.* 2 vols. London: Grant Richards, 1898; *The Fabian Society, Its Early History.* London: Fabian Society, 1899; *Three Plays for Puritans.* London: Grant

Richards, 1901; *How to Settle the Irish Question.* Dublin: Talbot, 1917; *The Intelligent Woman's Guide to Socialism and Capitalism.* New York: Brentano's, 1928; *Immaturity.* London: Constable, 1931; *The Irrational Knot.* London: Constable, 1931; *What I Really Wrote About the War.* London: Constable, 1931; *Cashel Byron's Profession.* London: Constable, 1932; *Essays in Fabian Socialism.* London: Constable, 1932; *Love Among the Artists.* London: Constable, 1932; *Major Critical Essays: The Quintessence of Ibsenism, The Perfect Wagnerite, The Sanity of Art.* London: Constable, 1932; *Music in London, 1890–1894.* London: Constable, 1932; *Our Theatres in the Nineties.* 3 vols. London: Constable, 1932; *An Unsocial Socialist.* London: Constable, 1932; *The Political Madhouse in America and Nearer Home.* London: Constable, 1933/printed in America as *American Boobs,* Hollywood: E. O. Jones, 1933; *Short Stories, Scraps, and Shavings.* New York: Dodd, Mead, 1934; *London Music, 1888–1889, as Heard by Corno di Bassetto.* London: Constable, 1937; *Sixteen Self Sketches.* London: Constable, 1949; *An Unfinished Novel,* ed. Stanley Weintraub. London: Constable/New York: Dodd, Mead, 1958; *Shaw on Shakespeare.* Edwin Wilson, ed. New York: E. P. Dutton, 1961; *The Matter with Ireland.* Dan H. Laurence & David H. Greene, eds. New York: Hill & Wang, 1962; *The Shaw Alphabet Edition of Androcles.* Harmondsworth: Penguin, 1962. *Complete Plays with Prefaces.* 6 vols. New York: Dodd, Mead, 1963; *Religious Speeches of Bernard Shaw.* Warren S. Smith, ed. University Park, Pa.: Pennsylvania State University, 1963. *Collected Letters, 1874–1897.* Dan H. Laurence, ed. London: Max Reinhardt/New York: Dodd, Mead, 1965; *An Autobiography, 1856–1898.* Selected by Stanley Weintraub. New York: Weybright & Talley, 1969; *An Autobiography, 1898–1950.* Selected by Stanley Weintraub. New York: Weybright & Talley, 1970; *The Bodley Head Bernard Shaw, Collected Plays with Their Prefaces.* 7 vols. London: Max Reinhardt, 1970–1974. (Probably the definitive collection); *Collected Letters, 1898–1910.* Dan H. Laurence, ed. London: Max Reinhardt/New York: Dodd, Mead, 1972; The *Great Composers: Reviews and Bombardments.* Louis Crompton, ed. Berkeley: University of California Press, 1978; *Collected Letters, 1911–1925.* Dan H. Laurence, ed. London: Max Reinhardt/New York: Viking, 1985; *Selected Short Plays.* Dan H. Laurence, ed. Harmondsworth: Penguin, 1988; *Collected Letters, 1926–1950.* Dan H. Laurence, ed. London: Max Reinhardt/New York: Viking, 1988; *Bernard Shaw on the London Art Scene, 1885–1950.* Stanley Weintraub, ed. University Park: Pennsylvania State University Press, 1989; *Shaw: Interviews and Recollections.* A. M. Gibbs, ed. Iowa City: University of Iowa Press, 1990; *Bernard Shaw's Book Reviews.* Brian Tyson, ed. University Park & London: Pennsylvania State University Press, 1991; *Shaw, Lady Gregory and the Abbey: A Correspondence and a Record.* Dan H. Laurence & Nicholas Grene, eds. Gerrards Cross: Colin Smythe, 1993; *The Compete Prefaces,* Vol. 1. Dan H. Laurence & Daniel J. Leary, eds. Harmondsworth: Penguin, 1994; *Bernard Shaw: The Drama Observed.* 4 vols. Bernard F. Dukore, ed. University Park: Pennsylvania State University Press, 1994; *The Complete Prefaces,* Vol. 2. Dan H. Laurence & Daniel J. Leary, eds. London: Allen Lane, 1995.   REFERENCES: Adams, Elsie B. "Bernard Shaw's Pre-Raphaelite Drama." *PMLA* 81 (October 1966): 428–438; Bentley, Eric. *Bernard Shaw.* New York: New Directions, 1957; Berst, Charles R. "The Devil and Major Barbara." *PMLA* 83 (March 1968): 71–79; Bertolini, John B. *The Playwriting Self of Bernard Shaw.* Carbondale: Southern Illinois University Press, 1991; Chesterton, G. K. *George Bernard Shaw.* New York: John Lane, 1909; Coolidge, Olivia. *George Bernard Shaw.* Boston: Houghton Mifflin, 1968; Costello, Donald P. *The Serpent's Eye: Shaw and the Cinema.* Notre Dame, Ind.: Notre Dame University Press, 1965; Crompton, Louis. *Shaw the Dramatist.* Lincoln: University of Nebraska Press, 1969; Dietrich, R. B. *Portrait of the Artist as a Young Superman: A Study of Shaw's Novels.* Gainesville: University of Florida Press, 1969; Dukore, Bernard F. *Bernard Shaw, Director.* Seattle: University of Washington Press, 1971; Ervine, St. John. *Bernard Shaw, His Life, Work and Friends.* London: Constable/New York: William Morrow, 1956; Ferrar, Harold. "The Caterpillar and the Gracehopper: Bernard Shaw's *John Bull's Other Island.*" *Éire-Ireland* 15 (Spring 1980): 25–45; Fromm, Harold. *Bernard Shaw and the Theatre in the Nineties.* Lawrence: University of Kansas Press, 1967; *G. B. Shaw, An Annotated Bibliography of Writings about Him.* Vol. 1, 1871–1930, J. P. Wearing, ed. Vol. 2, 1930–1956, Elsie B. Adams & Donald D. Haberman, eds. Vol. 3, 1957–1979, Donald D. Haberman, ed. De Kalb: Northern Illinois University Press, 1986–1987; Gerould, Daniel C. "George Bernard

Shaw's Criticism of Ibsen.'' *Comparative Literature* 15 (Spring 1963): 130–145; Gibbs, A. M. *The Art and Mind of Shaw.* New York: St. Martin's, 1983; Grene, Nicholas. *Bernard Shaw, A Critical View.* London: Macmillan/New York: St. Martin's, 1984; Harris, Frank. *Bernard Shaw.* London: Gollancz, 1931; Henderson, Archibald. *George Bernard Shaw: Man of the Century.* New York: Appleton-Century-Crofts, 1956; Hogan, Robert. ''The Novels of Bernard Shaw.'' *English Literature in Transition* 8 (1965): 63–114; Holroyd, Michael. *Bernard Shaw.* 4 vols. London: Chatto & Windus/New York: Random House, 1988–1993; Irvine, William. *The Universe of G.B.S.* New York: Whittlesey House, 1949; Joad, C.E.M. *Shaw.* London: Gollancz, 1949; Jenckes, Norma. ''The Rejection of Shaw's Irish Play, *John Bull's Other Island.*'' *Éire-Ireland* 10 (Spring 1975): 38–53; Kaye, Julian B. *Bernard Shaw and Nineteenth Century Tradition.* Norman: University of Oklahoma Press, 1958; Laurence, Dan H. *Bernard Shaw: A Bibliography.* 2 vols. Oxford: Clarendon, 1983; Lawrence, Kenneth. ''Bernard Shaw, The Career of the Life Force.'' *Modern Drama* 15 (September 1972): 130–146; Levin, Gerald. ''Shaw, Butler, and Kant.'' *Philological Quarterly* 52 (January 1973): 142–156; Lowenstein, F. E. *The Rehearsal Copies of Bernard Shaw's Plays.* London: Reinhardt & Evans, 1950; McCarthy, Desmond. *The Court Theatre, 1904–1907.* London: A. H. Bullen, 1907; McDowell, Frederick F. W. ''Spiritual and Political Reality: *The Simpleton of the Unexpected Isles.*'' *Modern Drama* 3 (September 1960): 196–210; May, Keith M. *Ibsen and Shaw.* New York: St. Martin's, 1985; Mercier, Vivian. ''New Wine in Old Bottles: Shaw and the Dublin Theatre Tradition.'' In *Irish Writers and the Theatre.* Masaru Sekine, ed. Gerrards Cross: Colin Smythe/Totowa, N.J.: Barnes & Noble, 1986; Morgan, Margery A. *The Shavian Playground.* London: Methuen, 1972; O'Casey, Sean. *Sunset and Evening Star.* London: Macmillan, 1954/New York: Macmillan, 1955; O'Donovan, John. *Shaw and the Charlatan Genius.* Dublin: Dolmen/Chester Springs, Pa.: Dufour, 1966; O'Donovan, John. *G. B. Shaw.* [Dublin]: Gill & Macmillan, [1983]; O'Donovan, John. ''The Shaws of Synge Street'' and ''Carlotta.'' In *Jonathan, Jack, and GBS.* Newark: University of Delaware Press/London & Toronto: Associated University Presses, 1993. (Two biographical plays about Shaw and his family); Ohmann, Richard. *Shaw, the Style and the Man.* Middleton, Conn.: Wesleyan University Press, 1962; O'Leary, D. J. ''Shaw's Blakean Vision: A Dialectic Approach to *Heartbreak House.*'' *Modern Drama* 15 (May 1972): 89–103; Pearson, Hesketh. *G.B.S., A Full Length Portrait.* London: Collins/Garden City, N.Y.: Garden City, 1942; Pearson, Hesketh. *G.B.S., A Postscript.* London: Collins, 1951; Peters, Margot. *Bernard Shaw and the Actresses.* New York: Doubleday, 1980; Peters, Sally. *Bernard Shaw: The Ascent of the Superman.* New Haven, Conn.: Yale University Press, 1995; Purdom, C. B. *A Guide to the Plays of Bernard Shaw.* New York: Crowell, 1963; Rosset, B. C. *Shaw of Dublin: The Formative Years.* University Park: Pennsylvania State University Press, 1964; Smith, J. Percy. *The Unrepentant Pilgrim, A Study of the Development of Bernard Shaw.* Boston: Houghton Mifflin, 1965; Smith, Warren S. *Bishop of Everywhere: Bernard Shaw and the Life Force.* University Park: Pennsylvania State University Press, 1982; Turner, Tramble T. ''Bernard Shaw's 'Eternal' Irish Concerns.'' *Éire-Ireland* 21 (Summer 1985): 57–69; Wall, Vincent. *Bernard Shaw, Pygmalion to Many Players.* Ann Arbor: University of Michigan Press, 1973; Weintraub, Stanley, gen. ed. *The Annual of Bernard Shaw Studies.* Vol. 1, *Shaw and Religion,* Charles E. Berst, ed. University Park: Pennsylvania State University Press, 1981; Weintraub, Stanley. *Journey to Heartbreak.* New York: Weybright & Talley, 1971; Weintraub, Stanley. *The Unexpected Shaw.* New York: Frederick Ungar, 1982; Wilson, Colin. *Bernard Shaw, A Reassessment.* New York: Atheneum, 1969; Yorks, Samuel A. *The Evolution of Bernard Shaw.* Washington, D.C.: Catholic University Press of America, 1981.

SHEEHAN, CANON (1852–1913), novelist. Canon Sheehan was born Patrick Augustine Sheehan in Mallow on March 17, 1852. He received his higher education at Maynooth Seminary, and he was ordained a Roman Catholic priest in 1875. He worked for a while in Plymouth and in Exeter before returning to Ireland to work in Mallow and Cobh. In 1895, he was appointed pastor in Doneraile, and he served there until his death on October 5, 1913.

Canon Sheehan was a born novelist, but he had the conventional opinions that one might expect in a Roman Catholic cleric of his day. If that fact is the source of all of the weaknesses in his fiction, it is also the source of many of its strengths. For instance, he was such a well-read, learned, and cultivated man that he startles one by speaking of du Maurier's *Trilby* as an "abomination," and he saddens one by being able only to deplore Yeats,* Synge,* and George Moore* as "Neo-Pagans and Aesthetes." Similarly, although his comedy is often too broad, his humor is usually so warmly genial that one is shocked by the cold austerity that frequently manipulates his characters into implausible and inhuman stances. In short, there are more contradictions in Canon Sheehan than appear in the hagiographical accounts of him.

As a novelist, Sheehan wavered between saintly austerity and tolerant humanity; certain of his characteristics and opinions do war most engagingly with his sternly regarded priestly functions. He was a thoughtful Irishman, but he was sometimes a fervent patriot; his heart sometimes beat and his pen sometimes wrote with a most unclerical and martial ardor. Indeed, there is a spiritually autobiographical moment in *The Queen's Fillet* (1911), when the once young and dashing hero, now a pious abbot, is sorely tempted to buckle on his sword again and win the day. In Dumas, that is precisely what the abbot would have done. Like Aramis, he would have done it and repented later, and Canon Sheehan would have had a better novel than the merely quite good novel that he does have.

Still, character was one of Canon Sheehan's real strengths, and the intellectual priest Luke Delmege and the old priest in *My New Curate* (1900) are triumphs. But when Canon Sheehan the priest takes away the pen from Canon Sheehan the novelist, characterization begins to ring false. Then we get tintype villains, purer-than-the-driven-snow heroines, and a gallery of saintly clerical simpletons that would give even a Paul Vincent Carroll* pause. Canon Sheehan is thought to be best on peasants and priests, but he is rather better on intellectuals and on the middle or the upper classes. His peasants tend to be seen from the presbytery window, and, even though he had as much sympathy for them as Edgeworth* or Somerville and Ross,* Canon Sheehan, like Lady Gregory* sometimes, seems to be merely putting the quaint peasantry on exhibition.

His long novels are structured with a firm nineteenth-century control. When he fails, the reason is often a blend of the theme manipulating the plot and of the author unsophisticatedly accepting the clichés of melodrama. A prime case in point would be the subplot of *Lisheen* (1907), with its hanky-panky about a talisman ring, Indian magic, and leprosy. And sometimes he fails, as in the subplot of *Luke Delmege* (1901), when prostitution is regarded with a horror that is more bourgeois than Christlike. Yet, even here the conventional novelist and the conventional saint are contradicted (in one of the essays) by the practical, commonsensical, and unpuritanical commentator on the education of children.

Canon Sheehan is so good that one yearns for him to have been better, and, if his literary excellence had not sometimes been in opposition to his clerical goodness, he might have been. Nevertheless, he has been read and enjoyed by many thousands who do not like books, and, despite all, he can be read profitably by hundreds who do like them.

WORKS: *Geoffrey Austin, Student.* Dublin: M. H. Gill, 1897; *The Triumph of Failure.* London: Burns & Oates, 1899; *Cithara Mea.* Boston: Marlier, Callanan, 1900. (Poems); *My New Curate.* Boston: Marlier, 1900; *Luke Delmege.* London: Longmans, 1901; *Under the Cedars and the Stars.* Dublin: Browne & Nolan, 1903. (Essays); *Lost Angel of a Ruined Paradise.* London: Longmans, 1904; *Glenanaar.* London: Longmans, 1905; *A Spoiled Priest, and Other Stories.* London: Unwin, 1905; *Early Essays and Lectures.* London: Longmans, 1906; *Lisheen.* London: Longmans, 1907; *Canon Sheehan's Short Stories.* London: Burns & Oates, 1908; *Parerga.* London: Longmans, 1908. (Essays); *The Blindness of Dr. Gray.* London: Longmans, 1909; *The Intellectuals.* London: Longmans, 1911; *The Queen's Fillet.* London: Longmans, 1911; *Miriam Lucas.* London: Longmans, 1912; *The Graves at Kilmorna.* London: Longmans, 1915; *Sermons,* ed. M. J. Phelan. Dublin & London: Maunsel, 1920; *The Literary Life, and Other Essays.* Dublin & London: Maunsel & Roberts, 1921; *Poems.* Dublin & London: Maunsel & Roberts, 1921; *Tristram Lloyd,* completed by Henry Gaffney. Dublin & Cork: Talbot, 1929. REFERENCES: Boyle, Francis. *Canon Sheehan of Doneraile.* Dublin: Gill, 1927; Brown, Terence. "Canon Sheehan and the Catholic Intellectual." In *Ireland's Literature: Selected Essays.* Mullingar, Co. Westmeath: Lilliput/Totowa, N.J.: Barnes & Noble, 1988, pp. 65–76; Candy, Catherine. *Priestly Fictions: Popular Irish Novelists of the Early 20th Century.* Dublin: Wolfhound, 1995; Coussens, Arthur. *P. A. Sheehan, zijn leven en zijn werken.* Bruges, 1923; Heuser, H. J. *Canon Sheehan of Doneraile.* New York: Longmans, 1917; Kiely, Benedict. "Canon Sheehan: The Reluctant Novelist." *Irish Writing* 37 (Autumn 1957): 35–45; Linehan, Michael B. *Canon Sheehan of Doneraile: Priest, Novelist, Man of Letters.* Dublin: Talbot, 1952; MacManus, Francis. "The Fate of Canon Sheehan." *The Bell* 15 (November 1947): 16–27.

SHEEHAN, RONAN (1953–), novelist and short story writer. Sheehan was born in Dublin and educated at Gonzaga College and University College, Dublin. In 1974, he won a Hennessy Literary Award for his short story "Optics," and in 1977 he published a novel. That novel, *Tennis Players,* uses three junior tennis tournaments as occasions to contrast the direct amoralities of the young with the more devious hypocrisies of the middle-aged. Despite a few tedious passages, the novel is quite successful, sometimes funny, and often excellently ironic. Sheehan's collection of short stories, *Boy with an Injured Eye,* comprises several short sketches and two interesting stories about Nero's Rome and one about the eighteenth-century surgeon and scholar Sylvester O'Halloran. These latter pieces are not greatly dramatized, and the title story about O'Halloran seems really the précis for a novel; nevertheless, he won the Rooney Prize in 1984. For *The Crane Bag,* Sheehan has interviewed Sean McBride, John Banville,* and Francis Stuart* and edited in 1983 a Latin American issue.

WORKS: *Tennis Players.* [Dublin]: Co-op Books, [1977]; *Boy with an Injured Eye.* [Dingle, Co. Kerry]: Brandon, [1983].

SHEEHY-SKEFFINGTON, FRANCIS (1878–1916), journalist. Francis Sheehy-Skeffington was born Francis Skeffington on December 23, 1878, at Bailieboro, County Cavan. Like many other Irishmen of his time, he combined literary interests with participation in progressive causes, among them women's suffrage, pacifism, and the integrity of small nations.

Primarily a journalist, Skeffington co-edited *The Nationalist* with T. M. Kettle,* *The National Democrat* with Frederick Ryan,* and in 1913 succeeded James H. Cousins* as editor of the feminist weekly *The Irish Citizen*. In June 1915, he was imprisoned for a seditious speech against the conscription and recruiting of Irishmen. Released after a hunger strike, he carried his antimilitarist appeal to America. His wife, née Hanna Sheehy (hence Sheehy-Skeffington), edited *The Irish Citizen* during his absence.

Skeffington went into the streets to prevent looting when the Easter Week Rising began. On the evening of Tuesday, April 25, he was arrested. The next morning, without trial or notice, he was shot on the order of Captain Bowen-Colthurst. The murder of this high-minded pacifist and the subsequent court martial in which the officer was declared insane aroused widespread indignation.

"A Forgotten Aspect of the University Question," Skeffington's essay demanding equal rights for female students, was printed in 1901 together with "The Day of the Rabblement," by a fellow student at University College, James Joyce.* A biography of Michael Davitt (1908) is an idealist's apologia for another idealist. The heroine of Skeffington's one-act play *The Prodigal Daughter* (1914), feminist Lily Considine, is, like the author, undaunted by imprisonment for breaking windows. His novel *In Dark and Evil Days* (1916, posthumously) is a quasi-historical tale of the rebellion of 1798.

Characteristic of his writing is a black-white contrast: Davitt versus opportunistic Parnell and bullying clergymen, Lily Considine versus small-town reactionaries, United Irishmen versus slinking informers. It is an approach better suited to persuasion than to literary art.

WILLIAM J. FEENEY

WORKS: "A Forgotten Aspect of the University Question," with "The Day of the Rabblement" by James Joyce. Dublin: Gerrard Brothers, 1901; *Michael Davitt: Revolutionary, Agitator, and Labour Leader*. London: Unwin, 1908/Boston: Dana Estes, 1909; "More Shavian Prefaces." *Irish Review* 1 (May 1911): 152–155. (Review of *The Doctor's Dilemma, Getting Married,* and *The Shewing-up of Blanco Posnet*); "Frederick Ryan, An Appreciation." *Irish Review* 3 (May 1913): 113–119; *The Prodigal Daughter: A Comedy in One Act*. Dublin, 1915. (First performed April 24– 25, 1914, in Molesworth Hall, Dublin, as a benefit for the Irish Women's Franchise League); *In Dark and Evil Days*. Dublin: Duffy, 1916/reprinted 1919, with introduction by Hanna Sheehy-Skeffington; "A Forgotten Small Nationality." *Century* 91 (February 1916): 561–569. REFERENCES: A.M.W. "Leading Statesmen of the Co-operative Commonwealth." *Leader* (November 15, 1913): 325. (Cartoon and satirical poem on Yeats, AE, and "Skeffy"); Curran, C. P. *Under the Receding Wave*. Dublin: Gill & Macmillan, 1970; Feeney, William J. "The Informers of '98 as Characters in Irish Literature." *Éire* 19 (August 1977): 1–16; Shaw, George Bernard. "In Behalf of an Irish Pacifist." In *The Matter with Ireland*. Dan H. Laurence & David H. Greene, eds. New York: Hill & Wang, 1962.

SHEIL, RICHARD LALOR (1791–1851), politician, orator, and playwright. Sheil was born on August 16, 1791, near Waterford. He was educated at the English Jesuit college at Stonyhurst, at Trinity College, Dublin, and at Lincoln's Inn where he completed his studies for the bar. He wrote a few plays which were produced in Dublin and London with considerable monetary success, but none of them is of either Irish or permanent interest. Sheil's speeches, which grew out of his involvement in Irish and English politics, have some literary merit and are even today dramatic and eloquent. That their effect was largely from Sheil's rhetorical powers seems also evident by Gladstone's remark that Sheil's voice sounded like "a tin kettle battered about." Sheil's reminiscences of his contemporaries are worth remark, particularly his bustling and vivid picture of Daniel O'Connell in *Sketches of the Irish Bar* (1854). He died in Florence, where he was serving as English ambassador to the court of Tuscany, on May 28, 1851.

WORKS: *Adelaide; or, The Emigrants.* Dublin: Coyne, 1814. (Verse tragedy in five acts); *The Apostate.* 3rd ed. London: J. Murray, 1817. (Verse tragedy in five acts); *Bellamira; or, The Fall of Tunis.* London: J. Murray, 1818. (Verse tragedy in five acts); *Evadne; or, the Statue.* London: J. Murray, 1819. (Verse tragedy in five acts); with John Banim, *Damon and Pythias.* London: J. Warren, 1821. (Tragedy in five acts); *The Speeches of the Rt. Hon. R. L. Sheil, M.P.* Thomas Mac Nevin, ed. Dublin: Duffy, 1845; *Sketches of the Irish Bar.* R. S. Mackenzie, ed. New York: W. J. Middleton, 1854. REFERENCE: McCullagh, W. T. *Memoirs of the Rt. Hon. R. L. Sheil.* 2 vols. London: H. Colburn, 1855.

SHEPHERD, SAMUEL (ca. 1701–1785), poet and sermon writer. Shepherd was born in Limerick in 1701 or 1702, the son of John Shepherd, the archdeacon of Limerick. He was educated at Trinity College, Dublin, ordained in the Established Church, and spent most of his career as rector of Celbridge, County Kildare. He was also chaplain to two lord lieutenants, the duke of Dorset and the earl of Chesterfield, and was apparently an eminent preacher. His posthumous *Sermons on Various Subjects* (1790) was over 500 pages long, and his posthumous *Part of the Poetical Works of the Late Samuel Shepherd, A. M.* (1790) ran to a substantial 250 pages. Patrick Fagan finds the poems "for the most part trite and pedestrian" but admires some of the poems to his wife. Despite some traces of humor, even they are conventional, and Shepherd is occasionally capable of quite "limping feet."

PRINCIPAL WORKS: *Leixlip, a Poem.* Dublin: G. Faulkner, 1847; *Part of the Poetical Works of the Late Samuel Shepherd, A. M.* Dublin: W. Sleater, 1790; *Sermons on Various Subjects. . . .* Dublin: W. Sleater, 1790. REFERENCE: Fagan, Patrick. "Samuel Shepherd." In *A Georgian Celebration.* Dublin: Branar, [1989], pp. 98–102.

SHERIDAN, CLARE (1885–1970), novelist, travel writer, sculptor, and journalist. Clare Sheridan was born in London on September 9, 1885, the daughter of the always nearly successful entrepreneur Moreton Frewen (hence his nickname of "Mortal Ruin") and his wife, Clara, the daughter of the flamboyant New York financier Leonard Jerome. Her cousins were Sir Winston Churchill and Sir Shane Leslie.* She married Wilfrid Sheridan, a direct descendant of the eminent writing family, and was herself a descendant of Frances Sheridan's* sister. After her husband's death in World War I, she trained as a sculptor, visited Russia shortly after the revolution, sculpted Lenin, and had an affair with Trotsky. Her accounts of the trip led her into journalism. She interviewed Rory

O'Connor when he was besieged in the Four Courts, and she interviewed Kemal Ataturk, Marie of Roumania, and Mussolini, who tried to rape her. Journalists once discovered her on a camping trip with Charlie Chaplin. Her eccentric novels as well as her travel books and perfervid autobiographies closely reflected her restless and flamboyant life. The first novels were paeans to sexual freedom, and her late autobiographies reflected a strange personal mysticism, which had doubtless been aggravated by the death of her son. The first third of her briefly notorious novel *Stella Defiant* (1924) takes place in Ireland during the Troubles. In one of its silliest situations, the heroine is high in the councils of the revolutionary movement; and the chief plotters, who meet in her house, are thinly disguised silhouettes of W. B. Yeats,* James Stephens,* a kilted Shane Leslie, and H. G. Wells—as weird an Irish revolutionary quartet as was ever assembled. At the same time, a figure resembling Lord Birkenhead (a former lover in real life) is hidden upstairs. Clare Sheridan was not a very good writer, but she was a fascinating individual whose personality pervades her rackety books. As her friend Henry James wrote to her, "Feel, *feel,* I say—feel for all you're worth, and even if it half kills you, for that is the only way to live." She certainly seems to have taken his advice. In the 1950s, she lived for five years in the Spanish Arch in Galway. She died in England on May 31, 1970.

Her daughter Margaret, under the pen name of Mary Motley, wrote two fine reminiscences of Africa, *Devils in Waiting* (London: Longmans, 1959) and *Morning Glory* (London: Longmans, 1961). Her son Richard Brinsley succeeded in losing some of his namesake's manuscripts when his small boat sank on an ill-advised voyage from Africa to England. Richard Brinsley also wrote an engaging account, *Heavenly Hell* (London: Putnam, 1935), about his experiences on one of the last of the sailing ships.

WORKS: *Russian Portraits.* London: Jonathan Cape, 1921; *My American Diary.* New York: Boni and Liveright, 1922; *In Many Places.* London: Duckworth, 1923; *Stella Defiant.* London: Duckworth, 1924. (Novel); *The Thirteenth.* London: Duckworth, 1925. (Novel); *Across Europe with Satanella.* London: Duckworth, 1925; *A Turkish Kaleidoscope.* London: Duckworth, 1926; *Make Believe.* London: Duckworth, 1926. (Novel); *Nuda Veritas.* London: Duckworth, 1927. (Autobiography); *Green Amber.* London: Thornton Butterworth, 1930. (Novel); *El Caid.* London: Thornton Butterworth, 1931. (Novel); *Genetrix.* London: Thornton Butterworth, 1935. (Novel); *Arab Interlude.* London: I. Nicholson & Watson, 1936; *Redskin Interlude.* London: Without End. London: Cassell, 1939. (Memoir of her son); *The Mask.* London: Hutchinson, 1942. (Novel); *My Crowded Sanctuary.* London: Methuen, 1945. (Autobiography); *To the Four Winds.* London: Andre Deutsch, 1957. (Autobiography). REFERENCES: Dolan, Bricriu (Robert Hogan). "Clare Sheridan, an Adventuress and Her Children." *Journal of Irish Literature* 19 (May 1990): 3–46; Leslie, Anita. *Clare Sheridan.* Garden City, N.Y.: Doubleday, 1977.

SHERIDAN, D[OLORES] S. (fl. 1990s), novelist. Sheridan is said to work in London as a psychotherapist. Her novel, *Strange Fruit* (1993), is a curious, sometimes preciously written account of a woman who is haunted by the memory of a young woman who committed suicide while renting her house. Ultimately the heroine finds peace when she decides or discovers that the young woman has now learned there is an afterlife. Despite this plot and little characterization, there is some real strength in the depiction of the heroine's growing hysteria.

WORK: *Strange Fruit.* [Swords, Co. Dublin]: Poolbeg, [1993].

SHERIDAN, F. D. (1929–   ), short story writer. Sheridan was born in Dublin and educated at University College, after which she traveled throughout Europe and lived for many years in Barcelona. Indeed, most of the stories in her collection *Captives* (1980) are set in Spain or in Italy. Benedict Kiely* accurately wrote that she "sees, and writes, with precision." Nevertheless, most of her pieces are rather slight sketches, and only "The Keeper" and "When the Saints Come Tumbling Down" are very dramatic. Even so, Sheridan is adept at character drawing, as may be especially seen in the accomplished piece "Saint Crispian's Day."

WORK: *Captives.* Dublin: Co-op Books, 1980.

SHERIDAN, FRANCES (1724–1766), novelist and dramatist. The wife of Thomas Sheridan the younger* and the mother of Richard Brinsley Sheridan* was born in Dublin in 1724, the daughter of Reverend Philip Chamberlaine, an Anglo-Irish clergyman. Her father disapproved of schooling for women, believing it led to sentimental scribbling, but her eldest brother taught her secretly. By the age of fifteen, she was writing a two-volume novel, *Eugenia and Adelaide,* years later adapted as a comic opera for the Dublin stage by her daughter Alicia LeFanu.* About 1743, she wrote a poem, "The Owls: a Fable," defending the querulous young Thomas Sheridan for his part in the *Cato* riots at the Smock Alley Theatre. He asked to meet her; they fell in love, married in 1747, and lived for several years at 12 Dorset Street, Dublin, where five of their six children were born. During these years, Mrs. Sheridan was too busy with her children and with buoying up the constantly collapsing hopes of her husband to write. However, in 1761, when the family was living at Windsor, she published a three-volume novel, *Memoirs of Miss Sidney Bidulph,* and the next year her play, *The Discovery,* was produced at Drury Lane. With her husband and David Garrick in leading roles, it ran to full houses for seventeen nights. Boswell reports that Goldsmith* at the first night "said many smart acrimonious things" about it, but the young Irish playwright John O'Keeffe* thought that it "gave great delight, and the success was perfect." Her second play, *The Dupe,* was produced by George Colman later in the year and failed. In 1764, the Sheridans moved to Blois, France, to escape creditors, and there Mrs. Sheridan wrote the two-volume second part of *Miss Sidney Bidulph* and also *A Journey to Bath,* a comic play that Garrick rejected. Her son Richard saw more merit in it and borrowed some of her best malapropisms as well as the idea for his own Mrs. Malaprop in *The Rivals.* Also at Blois, she wrote her charming fable *The History of Nourjahad,* which has occasionally been rediscovered and republished. On

September 26, 1766, she died at Blois, to the great grief of her husband and children. According to Dr. Johnson, Samuel Richardson, Sarah Fielding, and others, she was a very clever and lovable woman.

Her most successful works are the first part of *Sidney Bidulph* and her play, *The Discovery*. *Sidney Bidulph* was very popular in its day because it told an engrossing story in generally lean, uncluttered prose, and the story was rather a prototype of female fiction. That is, there is a pair of star-crossed lovers kept apart by misunderstandings and misfortunes, and in consequence the woman suffers and suffers. Although the heroine may seem too much of the ultrascrupulous prude for our day, Dr. Johnson remarked at the time, ''I know not, Madam, that you have a right, upon moral principles, to make your readers suffer so much.'' Garrick thought *The Discovery* the best comedy of the age, and it was several times revived. It is a typical eighteenth-century sentimental comedy with some stock characters and a predictable, if not awfully well-handled, plot. It is saved, however, by flashes of comic brilliance and some superb roles, such as Lord Medway, Sir Anthony Branville, and particularly the quarrelsome newlyweds, Lord and Lady Flutter. In 1924, Aldous Huxley adapted it rather turgidly for the modern stage. There is nothing Irish in Frances Sheridan's work. Indeed, her few references to Ireland appear mainly in letters to English friends where she bemoans having to live there.

MARY ROSE CALLAGHAN

WORKS: *Memoirs of Miss Sidney Bidulph*. 3 vols. London: R. & J. Dodsley, 1761/rpt. London: Pandora, 1987. (Novel); *The Discovery*. London: Thomas Davies/Dublin: George Faulkner, 1763. (Play); *The Dupe*. London: Andrew Millar/Dublin: G. & A. Ewing, 1764. (Play); *The History of Nourjahad*. London: J. Dodsley, 1767/rpt. London: E. Matthews & Marot, 1927. (Tale); *Conclusion of the Memoirs of Miss Sidney Bidulph*. London: J. Dodsley, 1770. (Novel); *Eugenia and Adelaide*. 2 vols. London: C. Dilly, 1791. (Novel); *A Journey to Bath* in *Sheridan's Plays*. W. Fraser Rae, ed. London: David Nutt, 1902. (Three-act fragment of a five-act play); *The Plays of Frances Sheridan*. Robert Hogan & Jerry C. Beasley, eds. Newark: University of Delaware Press/London & Toronto: Associated University Presses, 1984. (Contains *The Discovery, The Dupe,* and *A Journey to Bath*.) REFERENCES: Hogan, Robert & Beasley, Jerry C., op. cit., ''Introduction''; LeFanu, Alicia. *Memoirs of the Life and Writings of Mrs. Frances Sheridan*. . . . London: G. & W. Whittaker, 1824; Sheldon, Esther K. ''Frances Sheridan's Comedies: Three Stages in the Development of Her Comic Art.'' *Theatre Annual* 26 (1970): 7–23.

SHERIDAN, JIM (1949–   ), playwright and film writer and director. Sheridan was born in Dublin in 1949. He worked with the Lyric Theatre* in Belfast, the Abbey* in Dublin, and the English 7:84 Company before becoming director of the Project Arts Center in Dublin. For the project's theater company, Sheridan and his brother Peter* gave lively productions of several plays, including Sheridan's own *Mobile Homes*. This is a realistic social play about the problems of several young families living on a mobile home site in Dublin. The characters are hardly more than sketches, and the social problem is so specific that the piece is little more than theatrical journalism. Nevertheless, the dialogue is authentic and lively, and the terse and compact scenes are nicely theatrical. After leaving the project, Sheridan produced plays at the Irish Arts Center in New

York City. In the 1990s, he has written and directed films with signal success. Indeed, his *My Left Foot* after Christy Brown,* his *The Field* after John B. Keane,* and his *In the Name of the Father* about the Guildford Four, among them, garnered thirteen Academy Award nominations.

WORK: *Mobile Homes.* [Dublin]: Co-op Books, [1978], (Play); *Leave the Fighting to McGuigan: The Official Biography of Barry McGuigan.* Hardmondsworth, Middlesex: Viking, 1985; with Shane Connaughton. *My Left Foot.* London: Faber, 1989. (Screenplay).

SHERIDAN, JOHN D[ESMOND] (1903–1980), novelist and humorist. Sheridan, the humorous essayist, novelist, and light versifier, published many widely read volumes. Cleeve* calls him "one of the most popular and best loved contemporary Irish writers." That probably is true, but a good deal of Sheridan's popularity may have stemmed from his having been insular, inoffensive, low-brow, and Catholic at a time when Ireland was, even more than usual, noted for those virtues. Compared to his contemporary, the comic genius Flann O'Brien (Brien O'Nolan*), Sheridan appears bland, innocuous, and of negligible literary worth. Nevertheless, the judicious reader might well note his quiet and sincere novel, *The Rest Is Silence.* He died in Dublin in 1980.

WORKS: *Vanishing Spring.* Dublin: Talbot/London: Rich & Cowan, 1934. (Novel); *James Clarence Mangan.* Dublin: Talbot/London: G. Duckworth, 1937; *Here's Their Memory.* Dublin: Talbot, 1941; *I Can't Help Laughing.* Dublin: Talbot, 1944. (Sketches); *Paradise Alley.* Dublin: Talbot, 1945. (Novel); *I Laugh to Think.* Dublin: Talbot, 1946. (Essays); *It Stance to Reason: The Intelligent Rabbit's Guide to Golf.* Dublin: Talbot Press, 1947/enlarged, Dublin: Talbot, 1963; *Half in Earnest.* Dublin: Talbot, 1948. (Essays); *Joe's No Saint, and Other Poems.* Dublin: Gill, 1949; *The Magnificent MacDarney.* Dublin: Talbot, 1949; *My Hat Blew Off.* Dublin: Talbot/London: Dent, 1950; *The Right Time.* Dublin: Talbot, 1951/London: Dent, 1952. (Stories); *The Rest Is Silence.* London: Dent, 1953; *While the Humour is On Me.* Dublin: Talbot, 1954. (Essays); *Stirabout Lane.* Dublin: Talbot/London: Dent, 1955. (Children's verse); *Funnily Enough.* Dublin: Talbot/London: Dent, 1956. (Essays); *Bright Intervals.* Dublin: Talbot/London: Dent, 1958. (Essays); *God Made Little Apples.* Dublin: Talbot/London: Dent, 1964. (Essays); *Joking Apart.* Dublin: Talbot/London: Dent, 1964; *Include Me Out.* Dublin: Talbot, 1967.

SHERIDAN, NIALL [JOSEPH] (1912–   ), man of letters. Sheridan was born in County Meath on July 26, 1912, and educated at University College, Dublin, where he was a member of a remarkable student generation that included Brian O'Nolan,* Denis Devlin,* Donagh MacDonagh,* Mervyn Wall,* Cyril Cusack, and Charles Donnelly.* With MacDonagh, he published a verse pamphlet, *Twenty Poems* (1934). His ten poems were fluent and able, and his friend O'Nolan incorporated one of them in toto in *At Swim-Two-Birds.* That novel is Sheridan's great contribution to Irish literature, for he discussed it thoroughly with the author, cut it by about a fifth, and was the inspiration for the hero's friend, Brinsley. Despite his ability, Sheridan wrote little. There were a few stories in American magazines in the 1940s, and there was an unpublished Abbey* play, *Seven Men and a Dog,* in 1958. He worked for the Irish Tourist Board and later for Radio Telefis Éireann. He was married to the writer on cookery, Monica Sheridan.

PRINCIPAL WORKS: With Donagh MacDonagh. *Twenty Poems.* Dublin: Privately printed, 1934; "Brian, Flann and Myles (The Springtime of Genius)." In *Myles: Portraits of Brian O'Nolan.* Timothy O'Keeffe, ed. London: Martin Brian & O'Keeffe, [1973], pp. 32–53.

SHERIDAN, PETER (1952–   ), playwright. Sheridan was born in Dublin in 1952. He had several plays presented at Dublin's Project Arts Center, of which he was the theater director. In 1978, he received the Rooney Prize and in 1979 was awarded an Abbey Theatre* Bursary. In their Project days, Sheridan and his brother Jim* were committed to the idea of drama as a weapon for bettering social conditions. His *The Liberty Suit* (Project theatre, 1978) is an effective realistic play about juvenile prison life. *Emigrants* produced in 1978, however, is a strongly theatrical study of the dispossessed Irish peasants emigrating to England in search of work in the nineteenth century. It played successfully at the Royal Court in London as well as at the Project and featured Shane Connaughton,* Gerard Mannix Flynn,* and sometimes the author in the cast. In recent years, Sheridan has directed plays in Dublin.

WORKS: *The Liberty Suit.* [Dublin]: Co-op Books, [1978]; *Emigrants.* [Dublin]: Co-op Books, [1979].

SHERIDAN, RICHARD BRINSLEY (1751–1816), playwright and politician. Born at 12 Dorset Street, Dublin, and christened Richard Brinsley Butler at St. Mary's, on November 4, 1751, Sheridan came from a well-known family. His grandfather, Thomas Sheridan,* was a friend of Swift.* His father, also Thomas,* was at the time the successful, controversial manager of the Smock Alley Theatre; later, in England, he was actor, pedagogue, teacher of elocution, and friend of Dr. Johnson. His mother, Frances Chamberlaine Sheridan,* was a novelist and playwright. He was educated at Whyte's School in Grafton Street and at Harrow, where he was an indifferent student. He was often separated from his parents who for some time lived in France to avoid debts. His charm and wit first flourished at Bath in the 1770s, where he courted and then married the famous singer Elizabeth Linley, "the Maid of Bath." The courtship involved a rejected suitor, duels, and an elopement, elements which he later used in *The Rivals* and *The Duenna.* After their marriage, he refused to allow her to sing in public.

Sheridan's career as a playwright was spectacular and brief. After an unsuccessful first night (January 17, 1775), his revised and recast *The Rivals* ran for fourteen nights at Drury Lane and established his reputation. In the same year, he wrote a farce, *St. Patrick's Day,* for the actor Clinch who had saved the production of *The Rivals.* In collaboration with his father-in-law, the musician Thomas Linley, he also wrote the comic opera *The Duenna,* which ran for seventy-five nights and became more successful than *The Beggar's Opera.* In 1777, he revised Vanbrugh's *The Relapse* as *The Trip to Scarborough,* and on May 8, *The School for Scandal* opened with a brilliant cast, establishing Sheridan as "the Congreve* of his day." Like Goldsmith* and Arthur Murphy,* he favored the "laughing comedy" of the Restoration, although all three of them were also influenced by the currently popular sentimental comedy. In Sheridan's plays, the sentimental hero is a hypocrite; the true hero is roguish but decent. Like all Irish writers of English comedy of manners from Congreve to Wilde* and Shaw,* Sheridan's dialogue sparkles with witty repartee. His last original play was *The Critic,* a play about the theatre, produced in 1779, when he was twenty-eight.

In 1776, after long and complicated financial negotiations, Sheridan purchased the principal ownership of the Drury Lane Theatre from David Garrick, who was retiring from the stage. From this point on, the theatre's and Sheridan's own financial situations become a maze. He used his income from the theatre to finance his profligate private life and his political career. Using the theatre as a source of income, he was only sporadically attentive to details of management or artistry. Garrick's theatre seated 2,362 people; Sheridan remodeled and enlarged it in 1794 to seat 3,611. He thus helped create the perpetual problem of the theatre in the nineteenth century: both how to fill such a large house and produce plays of dramatic merit. Sheridan followed popular vogues—such as Carlo, the dog who rescued the baby; the false "new" play by Shakespeare, *Vortigern;* and the boy-actor, Master Betty. When the theatre burned down in a spectacular fire in 1809, the new manager, Samuel Whitbread, for financial reasons froze Sheridan out of any participation in the rebuilding, although Sheridan still held the royal patent.

In 1780, Sheridan became a member of Parliament for Stafford and served in Parliament until 1812. A faithful Whig when they were out of power, he was only scantly rewarded when they gained it and, unlike Edmund Burke,* was not rewarded with a pension. He was steadfastly pro-Irish on the question of land reform, Catholic Emancipation, and Home Rule. He was renowned for his wit and his oratory, especially for his speech against Warren Hastings during the extended impeachment trial of Hastings for his governorship of India.

Sheridan's first wife died in 1792. His second, much younger wife, Hester Jane Ogle, lived with him through his final illness when he was beset by creditors. The funeral following his death on July 7, 1816, was spectacular, attended by the highest nobility, and he was buried in the Poet's Corner of Westminster Abbey.

Like Swift and Congreve before him, and like Wilde and Shaw after him, Sheridan gave his best efforts to the literature of England and is only tangentially an Irish writer. There is the fine but broadly comic caricature of Sir Lucius O'Trigger of Blunderbuss Hall in *The Rivals,* and there is the not particularly Irish Lieutenant O'Connor in the short farce *St. Patrick's Day,* which, save for an allusion to shamrocks and another to St. Stephen's Green, has nothing Irish about it.

SVEN ERIC MOLIN

WORKS: *The Plays and Poems of Richard Brinsley Sheridan.* R. Crompton Rhodes, ed. Oxford: Blackwell, 1928; *The Letters of Richard Brinsley Sheridan.* Cecil J. B. Price, ed. 2 vols. Oxford:

Clarendon, 1966; *The Speeches of the Right Honourable Richard Brinsley Sheridan.* 3 vols. New York: Russell & Russell, 1969; *The Dramatic Works of Richard Brinsley Sheridan.* Cecil J. B. Price, ed. 2 vols. Oxford: Clarendon, 1973. REFERENCES: Auburn, Mark S. *Sheridan's Comedies: Their Contexts and Achievements.* Lincoln: University of Nebraska Press, 1977; Ayling, Stanley. *A Portrait of Sheridan.* London: Constable, 1985; Bevis, Richard. *The Laughing Tradition: Stage Comedy in Garrick's Day.* Athens: University of Georgia Press, 1980; Bingham, Madeleine. *Sheridan: The Trail of a Comet.* London: Allen & Unwin, 1972; Davison, Peter, ed. *Sheridan: Comedies: A Selection of Critical Essays.* Basingstoke: Macmillan, 1986; Durant, Jack D. *Richard Brinsley Sheridan.* Boston: Twayne, 1975; Gibbs, Lewis. *Sheridan, His Life and His Theatre.* New York: Morrow, 1948; Hogan, Robert. "Plot, Character, and Comic Language in Sheridan." In *Comedy from Shakespeare to Sheridan.* A. R. Braunmuller & J. C. Bulman, eds. Newark: University of Delaware Press, [1986], pp. 274–285; Hume, Robert D. "Goldsmith and Sheridan and the Supposed Revolution of 'Laughing' against 'Sentimental' Comedy." In *Studies in Change and Revolution.* Menton, Yorkshire: Scolar, 1972, pp. 237–276; Loftis, John. *Sheridan and the Drama of Georgian England.* Oxford: Blackwell, 1976; Mikhail, E. H., ed. *Sheridan: Interviews and Recollections.* New York: St. Martin's, [1989]; Moore, Thomas. *Memoirs of the Life of the Right Honourable Richard Brinsley Sheridan.* 2 vols. London: Longman, Hurst, Rees, Orme, Brown & Green, 1825; Morwood, James. *The Life and Works of Richard Brinsley Sheridan.* Edinburgh: Scottish Academic, 1985; Rae, W. Fraser. *Sheridan.* 2 vols. New York: Holt, 1896; Rhodes, R. Crompton. *Harlequin Sheridan.* Oxford: Blackwell, 1933; Sadlier, Michael T. H. *The Political Career of Richard Brinsley Sheridan.* Oxford: Blackwell, 1912; Sichel, Walter. *Sheridan from New and Original Sources.* 2 vols. London: Constable, 1909.

SHERIDAN, THOMAS (THE ELDER) (1687–1738), poet, translator, punster, and schoolmaster. Sheridan was born at Cavan in 1687. He entered Trinity College, Dublin in 1707, received a B.A. in 1711 and an M.A. in 1714, and then received a B.D. in 1724 and a D.D. in 1726. After Jonathan Swift* returned to Dublin as dean of St. Patrick's, he and Sheridan became constant companions, allies in the Wood's coinage affair, collaborators on *The Intelligencer* papers, and sometimes poetic sparring partners. Sheridan often stayed at the Deanery, and Swift several times visited Sheridan's small estate, Quilca, in County Cavan, where he worked on *Gulliver's Travels.* Swift also took much interest in Sheridan's classical academy in Capel Street and sometimes taught there when its master was ill. According to Swift, Sheridan was a superb schoolmaster. He was also a witty, convivial, and hopelessly feckless fellow who justly wrote of himself, "I am famous for giving the best advice and following the worst." On one occasion Swift persuaded Carteret, the lord lieutenant of Ireland, to give the improvident Sheridan a living in Cork. The vague Sheridan, not noticing that his first sermon was preached on the anniversary of the Hanoverian succession, used the text of "Sufficient unto the day is the evil thereof"—and consequently lost all favor with Dublin Castle.

Sheridan's pseudonym "Tom Pun-sibi," or Tom the Punster, he adopted for his droll pamphlet of 1719, *Ars Pun-ica* or *The Art of Punning.* His wide reading and command of languages resulted more seriously in able translations of Sophocles' *Philoctetes,* of *The Satyrs of Persius,* and of Guarini's *Il Pastor Fido.* He produced at least two frivolous plays of his own. His greatest achievement, however, was in a large body of verse that appeared in journals, broadsides, personal letters, and manuscripts passed to his friends. There has been no collected edition of Sheridan until the present day, but some of his pieces were printed in various editions of Swift's poems, whose editors usually denigrated them as "trifles." His chief poetic achievement undoubtedly was as a writer of light verse. His metrical command, technical inventiveness, and verbal dexterity result frequently in a wit rivaling Swift's, as the dean occasionally discovered in some of the poetic warfares. If Swift might write:

> I'll drive you to Cavan, from Cavan to Dundalk;
> I'll tear all your rules, and demolish your pun talk. . . .

Sheridan was capable of remarking:

> Thy verse, which ran both smooth and sweet,
> Now limp upon their gouty feet. . . .

Some of Sheridan's technical whimsies included stuttering verses, squashed verses without vowels, and verses written in a circle. As an eighteenth-century poet, he has also some didactic pieces, some formal poems for public occasions, and much caustic journalism and polemics. As a friend of Swift, he has predictably a good deal of ironic verse and a few scabrous pieces. There are even a number of love lyrics that add a romantic facet to his character rather unexpected from so accomplished a comedian. Nevertheless, his accomplished and ebullient comedy gives him a strong claim to be the second Irish poet of his day.

Near the end of Sheridan's life, the increasingly irascible Swift quarreled with him, and Sheridan died unreconciled on October 10, 1738, in Rathfarnham. In his life of Swift, however, the younger Thomas Sheridan* reported that the old dean constantly asked his servant:

"William, did you know Doctor Sheridan?" Yes, Sir, very well—and then, with a heavy sigh, Oh I lost my right hand when I lost him.

WORKS: *An Easy Introduction of Grammar in English for the Understanding of the Latin Tongue.* Dublin: D. Tompson, 1714. (Contains also the anthology *A Method to Improve the Fancy*); *Ars Pun-ica, Sive Flos Linguarum: The Art of Punning; or the Flower of Languages; In Seventy-Nine Rules: For the Farther Improvement of Conversation and the Help of Memory.* Dublin: James Carson, 1719; tr., *The Philoctetes of Sophocles.* Dublin: R. Owen, 1725; tr., *The Satires of Persius.* Dublin: George Grierson, 1728; with Jonathan Swift. *The Intelligencer.* London: A. Moor, 1729/ James Woolley, ed. Oxford: Oxford University Press, 1992; ed., *A Poem on the Immortality of the Soul, by Sir John Davis, to Which Is Prefixed An Essay upon the Same Subject. . . .* Dublin: S. Hyde, 1733; *The Faithful Shepherd. A Translation of Battista Guarini's Il Pastor Fido . . .* Edited and completed by Robert Hogan and Edward A. Nickerson. Newark: University of Delaware Press, 1989; *The Poems of Thomas Sheridan.* Robert Hogan, ed. Newark: University of Delaware Press, 1994. REFERENCES: Hogan, Robert. "Introduction." In *The Poems of Thomas Sheridan.* Pp. 29–56; Woolley, James. "Thomas Sheridan and Swift." *Studies in Eighteenth Century Culture* 9 (1979): 93–114.

SHERIDAN, THOMAS (THE YOUNGER) (1719–1788), actor, theater manager, playwright, elocutionist, rhetorician, lexicographer, and educational theorist. The younger Thomas Sheridan is remembered today for two reasons: he was the grumpy father of Richard Brinsley Sheridan,* and he was the subject of Dr. Johnson's devastating quip, "Why, sir, Sherry is dull, naturally dull; but it must have taken him a great deal of pains to become what we now see him. Such an excess of stupidity is not in nature." His clever wife, Frances,* the novelist and playwright, would hardly have agreed; and also his unlucky and protean career shows that he was one of the ablest of the brilliant Sheridan clan and probably the one original thinker.

He was born in 1719, probably in Dublin, the third or possibly the fourth child of Dr. Thomas Sheridan,* and his godfather was Dr. Thomas' great friend Dean Swift,* whose biography he was to write. He was educated at his father's classical academy, at Westminster School, and at Trinity College, Dublin, where he received his B.A. in 1739. He fitted his father's translation of Guarini's *Il Pastor Fido* to the stage, and he wrote, loosely after Molière, a successful short farce called *The Brave Irishman; or, Captain O'Blunder* (1743). He quickly distinguished himself in tragic roles both in Dublin and in London, and for a while he was probably considered as an actor second only to Garrick. He undertook to manage the Smock Alley Theatre, initiated needed theatrical reforms to restrain the rowdiness of the audience, and engaged such brilliant actors—such as Garrick, Spranger Barry, and Mrs. Bellamy—that the 1745–1746 season has been described as unequaled in Dublin until the twentieth century. His reforms, however, made him the butt of several outbursts of public fury. The first was the Kelly riots of 1747, when a drunken young man named Kelly misbehaved all during the play and finally threw an orange at Sheridan. Sheridan stepped out of his part and was thought to have said, "I am as good a gentleman as you are." Two nights later, Kelly's friends broke up the theater in protest at an actor's calling himself a gentleman. Kelly was jailed but released at Sheridan's request, a kindness that lost him the sympathy of the young Edmund Burke* and other Trinity College students. The second outbreak in 1754 was politically motivated, and the audience tore up the theater because the actor West Digges told them that Sheridan had suggested he should not encore a politically interpreted speech in the tragedy of *Mahomet the Imposter.*

Despite these disasters, Sheridan was connected with the theater for economic reasons for much of the rest of his life. His heart was not in it, however, and in 1758 he removed with his family to England and set up as a teacher of elocution. He also became a voluminous writer on elocution and on educational reform and indeed was obsessed with a grand plan of education, of which the foundation would be a thorough grounding in oratory. He developed his ideas in his lengthy *British Education* (1756), and one modern writer has said, "His ideas were often in advance of his age and his work has had an important effect on educational and literary developments in the 19th and 20th century." In 1780, he brought out really the first pronouncing dictionary in the English language, and though it was based on on the dubious idea of a "correct" pronunciation based on that of the era of Queen Anne, W. Benzie is correct in noting that "it was obvious at once that . . . English lexicography had been raised to a new level."

Sheridan was in the Swiftean sense a "projector," and his grand theatrical and academic schemes generally came to nothing. He died in Margate on August 14, 1788, with his hitherto estranged son Richard Brinsley at his side. People who worked with him described him as "Old Bubble and Squeak," "Old Crusty," and "Old Surly Boots." He had the bad luck to have his acting overshadowed by that of Garrick. He had the bad luck to have his important dictionary overshadowed by Johnson's. He had the bad luck to be permanently cast in the shade by the glitter of his son's achievements. Enough to make one surly.

MARY ROSE CALLAGHAN

PRINCIPAL WORKS: *Cibber and Sheridan: Or the Dublin Miscellany.* Dublin: Peter Wilson, 1743; *A Full Vindication of the Conduct of the Manager of the Theatre-Royal.* Dublin: S. Powell, 1747; *Mr. Sheridan's Address to the Town.* Dublin: Martineau & Kinneir, 1753; *Mr. Sh-----n's Apology to the Town: With the Reasons Which Unfortunately Induced Him to His Late Misconduct.* Dublin, 1754; *A Vindication [by himself] of the Conduct of [Thomas Sheridan] the Late Manager of the Theatre-Royal. . . .* Dublin, 1754; *The Brave Irishman: Or, Captain O'Blunder.* Dublin: R. Watts, 1754. Various other printings, the only modern one being in *Ten English Farces,* Leo Hughes & A. H. Scouten, eds. Austin: University of Texas Press, 1948; *Coriolanus: Or the Roman Matron: A Tragedy Taken from Shakespeare and Thomson. . . .* London: A. Millar, 1755; *British Education: Or, the Source of the Disorders of Great Britain. . . .* London: R. & J. Dodsley, 1756; *An Humble Appeal to the Publick, Together with Some Considerations on the Present Critical and Dangerous State of the Stage in Ireland.* Dublin: George Faulkner, 1758; *An Oration, Pronounced before a Numerous Body of the Nobility and Gentry, Assembled at the Musick-Hall in Fishamble-Street. . . .* 3d ed. Dublin: M. Williamson, 1757; *A Course of Lectures on Elocution. . . .* London: A. Miller et. al, 1762; *A Plan of Education for the Young Nobility and Gentry of Great Britain. . . .* London: E. & C. Dilly/Dublin: George Faulkner, 1769; *Mr. Sheridan's Speech Addressed to a Number of Gentlemen Assembled with a View of Considering the Best Means to Establish One Good Theatre in This City.* Dublin: George Faulkner, 1772; *Lectures on the Art of Reading.* 2 parts. London, 1775; *A General Dictionary of the English Language. . . .* London: J. Dodsley, 1780; *The Life of the Rev. Dr. Jonathan Swift, Dean of St. Patrick's, Dublin.* London, 1784; *A View of the State of School-Education in Ireland. . . .* Dublin: M. Mills, 1787. REFERENCES: Benzie, W. *The Dublin Orator, Thomas Sheridan's Influence on Eighteenth-Century Rhetoric and Belles Lettres.* Leeds: University of Leeds, School of English, 1972; Brown, Wallace A. *The Elocutionary Career of Thomas Sheridan (1719–1788). Speech Monographs* 30 (1) (March 1964); Howell, W. S. *Eighteenth-Century British Logic and Rhetoric.* Princeton, N.J.: Princeton University Press, 1971; Sheldon, Esther K. *Thomas Sheridan of Smock Alley.* Princeton, N.J.: Princeton University Press, 1967. There is much other information to be gleaned from the various biographies of Richard Brinsley Sheridan, from *Betsy Sheridan's Journal,* from George Anne Bellamy's *Apology,* from *Boswell's London Journal 1762–63,* and so on.

SHERIDAN, TOM (1775–1817), playwright and poet. Sheridan was born on March 17, 1775, to Richard Brinsley Sheridan* and his wife, Elizabeth Linley, the singer. In many ways, Tom's greatest drawback in life was his brilliant father. As Michael Kelly* relates:

The two Sheridans were supping with me one night after the opera, at a period when Tom expected to get into Parliament.

"I think, father," said he, "that many men, who are called great patriots in the House of Commons, are great humbugs. For my own part, if I get into Parliament, I will pledge myself to no party, but write upon my forehead in legible characters, 'To be let.' "

"And under that, Tom," said his father, "write, 'Unfurnished.' "

Nevertheless, Tom had a wit of his own. When his father was pointing out that the family was Irish and its members therefore entitled to use the prefix "O" before their names, Tom remarked, "We are certainly O'Sheridans, for do we not *owe* everybody?"

Despite the frustrations of trying to hold his prodigal father's Drury Lane Theatre together, Tom wrote a handful of witty verses and two tolerable, unproduced farces, *The Strolling Players* and *The Savage in Europe,* and also a melodrama, *The Russian,* which was produced at Drury Lane in 1813. He was married to Henrietta Callandar, an interesting novelist. His daughter, Lady Dufferin,* wrote wittily; and his daughter, Caroline Norton,* wrote prolifically. He died at the Cape of Good Hope, where he had finally secured a paying job, on September 12, 1817. He hardly fulfilled his promise, but he was intelligent, talented, witty, and perhaps the sunniest of all the Sheridans.

WORK: *The Strolling Players.* Aileen Douglas, ed. *George Spelvin's Theatre Book* 7 (1985): 133–160. REFERENCE: Aileen Douglas. "Introduction" to *The Strolling Players.*

SHIELS, GEORGE (1886–1949), playwright. Born in Ballymoney, County Antrim, on June 24, 1886, Shiels emigrated to Canada as a young man. Crippled in a railway accident in 1913, he returned to Ireland, wrote stories based on his life in Canada, and then turned to drama. His earliest plays, bearing the pen name George Morshiel, were produced by the Ulster Literary Theatre.* In 1921 the Abbey* accepted his one-act comedy *Bedmates.* From then until 1948, it staged one or two of his plays almost every year. He died at Ballymoney on September 20, 1949.

Bedmates and the one-act comedy *First Aid* (1923) are allegories of Ulster-Free State relations. In *Bedmates,* a Catholic and an Ulsterman peacefully share a doss-house bed until a Cockney sharpster creates religious dissension and almost persuades them to saw the bed in half. The "first aid" is administered, by men from the North and the South, to a Little Old Woman who falls into a well.

Paul Twyning (1922) typifies a more familiar Shiels play built on a picaresque character, in this case an itinerant plasterer, who by wit and guile solves a complex of domestic, romantic, and economic problems. In this class are *Professor Tim* (1925), whose title character, a wealthy professor of geology, comes back to Ireland masquerading as a drunken failure; *The Jailbird* (1936), perhaps the weakest of Shiels' plays; and such comedies as *Cartney and Kevney* (1927) and *Grogan and the Ferret* (1933).

Less engaging rascals are key figures in his later plays, such as *The Passing*

Day (1936), *Quin's Secret* (1937), *Give Him a House* (1939), *The Old Broom* (Belfast, 1944), and *The Caretakers* (1948). Their common denominator is wholehearted avarice. The most interesting of these plays, in terms of technique, is *The Passing Day*. It opens with John Fibbs stricken by a heart attack and the usual speculations on who will get his money. The next four scenes flash back to the morning of the same day, tracing Fibbs' loveless, grasping relationships with other characters, most of whom deserve no better than they receive. In one poignant moment, Fibbs talks to the ghosts of his avaricious father and tigress mother, and his warped character becomes understandable.

Shiels' most thoughtful plays deal with the clash of modern and traditional values. Characters in *The New Gossoon* (1930) are divided into "oldsters" who subscribe to the work ethic; the young, who have been exposed to motorcycles and the cinema; and the poacher, Rabit Hamil, whose "I'm all right" ethic defies social change. *The Rugged Path* (1940) and *The Summit* (1941) constitute a two-part unit. The progressive farmers of the valley are pitted against the mountainy Dolis family trying to preserve an outmoded clan society. Another cultural anachronism considered in the play is the hatred of informers. When Irish law was superimposed over English law, the informer was a collaborator. However, Shiels argues, Ireland has its own legal machinery, and blind hostility to informers serves only to protect thugs and bullies. *The Fort Field* (1942) touches on a millennium rather than a generation gap. Work on a World War II airbase is delayed because of superstitious fear of disturbing a circular earthen mound, supposedly the dwelling place of the little people. The bulldozers finally win, abetted by prospects of money coming into the village from the airbase. *The New Regime* (1944) is a battle of wills between an arch-conservative Northern mill owner and a lorry driver who decorates his vehicle with a Russian flag.

In 1969, Shiels's unpublished play *Macook's Corner* was staged in Ireland by Tyrone Guthrie. Macook, by trade a bootlegger, is descended from Shiels's line of unrepentant and resourceful scoundrels.

Some historians of the Irish theatre dismiss Shiels as an entertainer. Within limits the criticism is valid. He shuttles stock characters from play to play, changing little more than the name. To reconcile differences, he sometimes abruptly stiffens mild persons and softens aggressors, at the expense of psychological credibility. Several plays are vulnerable to overly broad treatment by permissive directors or self-indulgent actors. At his best, however, Shiels is no mere purveyor of cotton candy. His comics rarely descend to the Handy Andy level; generally, they are resourceful, pragmatic, and a bit unscrupulous. Contending forces are not always careful of the niceties of statute law or fair play. In his later work, there is an almost disturbing absence of poetic justice, and the tone is sardonic enough to satisfy the most acidulous taste.

WILLIAM J. FEENEY

WORKS: *Bedmates: A Play in One Act.* Dublin: The Gael Cooperative Society, 1922; *Two Irish Plays: Mountain Dew, a Play in Three Acts* and *Cartney and Kevney, a Comedy in Three Acts.*

London: Macmillan, 1930; *The Passing Day: A Play in Six Scenes* and *The Jailbird: A Comedy in Three Acts.* London: Macmillan, 1937; *The Rugged Path: A Play in Three Acts* and *The Summit: A Play in Three Acts.* London: Macmillan, 1942; *Three Plays (Professor Tim, Paul Twyning, The New Gossoon).* London: Macmillan, 1945; *The Fort Field: A Play in Three Acts.* Dublin: Golden Eagle Books, 1947; *Give Him a House: A Comedy in Three Acts.* Dublin: Golden Eagle Books, 1947; *Grogan and the Ferret: A Comedy in Three Acts.* Dublin: Golden Eagle Books, 1947; *Quin's Secret: A Comedy in Three Acts.* Dublin: Golden Eagle Books, 1947; *Tenants at Will: A Play of Rural Ireland in the Young Ireland Period.* Dublin: Golden Eagle Books, 1947; *The Caretakers: A Play in Three Acts.* Dublin: Golden Eagle Books, 1948; *The Old Broom: A Comedy in Three Acts.* Dublin: Golden Eagle Books, 1948. REFERENCES: Casey, Daniel J. "George Shiels, The Enigmatic Playwright." *Irish Renaissance Annual* 4 (1983): 17–41; Feeney, William J. "The Rugged Path: A Modern View of Informers." *Éire-Ireland* 2 (Spring 1967): 41–47; Hogan, Robert. *After the Irish Renaissance.* Minneapolis: University of Minnesota Press, 1967; Kennedy, David. "George Shiels: A Playwright at Work." *Threshold* 25 (Summer 1974): 50–58; Malone, Andrew E. *The Irish Drana.* New York: Benjamin Blom, 1965; Murray, T. C. "George Shiels, Brinsley MacNamara, etc." In *The Irish Theatre.* Lennox Robinson, ed. London: Macmillan, 1939; Simmons, James. "The Humour of Deprivation." In *Irish Writers and the Theatre.* Masaru Sekine, ed. Gerrards Cross: Colin Smythe, 1986/New York: Barnes & Noble, 1987.

SHORTER, DORA [MARY] SIGERSON (1866–1918), poet.

Shorter was born Dora Mary Sigerson in Dublin in 1866, the eldest daughter of George Sigerson* and of Hester Varian (who wrote one novel called *A Ruined Place* in 1889 as well as much fugitive verse and fiction). With her friends Katherine Tynan* and Alice Furlong,* she was one of the better of the many women writers who turned to Irish themes for their verse during the Literary Renaissance. She married the English critic Clement Shorter in 1895 and thereafter lived in London. Douglas Hyde* wrote that "Her very absence from Ireland has made her—a phenomenon which we may often witness—more Irish than if she had never left it. . . ." Her earlier work was suffused with the traditional poet's ubiquitous melancholy, but some of her work after leaving Ireland became more outward-looking. Always a skilled versifier, she frequently managed the deftly phrased fragment to enliven her generally unexciting work. However, a few of her folk poems and simple ballads are quite striking, especially "A Ballad of Marjorie," "The Wind on the Hills," and "The Banshee." She died on January 6, 1918.

WORKS: *Verses.* London: E. Stock, 1893; *The Fairy Changeling and Other Poems.* London & New York: J. Lane, 1898; *Ballads and Poems.* London: J. Bowden, 1899; *The Father Confessor, Stories of Danger and Death.* London: Ward, Lock, 1900; *The Woman Who Went to Hell, and Other Ballads and Lyrics.* London: De La Mare, [1902]; *As the Sparks Fly Upward.* London: Alexander Moring, [1904]; *The Country-House Party.* London: Hodder & Stoughton, 1905; *The Story and Song of Black Roderick.* London: Alexander Moring, 1906; *The Collected Poems of Dora Sigerson Shorter.* London: Hodder & Stoughton, 1907; *Through Wintry Terrors.* London: Cassell, 1907. (Novel); *The Troubadour and Other Poems.* London: Hodder & Stoughton, 1910; *New Poems.* Dublin & London: Maunsel, 1912; *Do-Well and Do-Little.* London: Cassell, [1913] (Fairy tale); *Love of Ireland, Poems and Ballads.* Dublin & London: Maunsel, 1916; *Madge Linsey and Other Poems.* Dublin & London: Maunsel, 1916; *Sad Years and Other Poems.* London: Constable, 1918; *A Legend of Glendalough and Other Ballads.* Dublin & London: Maunsel, 1919; *A Dull Day in London, and Other Sketches.* London: Eveleigh Nash, 1920, (Short stories); *The Tricolour.* Dublin: Maunsel & Roberts, 1922; *Twenty-one Poems.* London: Ernest Benn, [1926].

SHORTLAND, GAYE (ca. 1950–   ), novelist. Shortland was born in Bantry, County Cork. She received a B.A. in Italian and English and also an M.A. from University College, Cork. After a year teaching at the University of Leeds, she taught English at Ahmadu Bello University in Nigeria and spent eighteen years in Africa. She now lives in Cork with her three children. Her novel, *Mind That 'tis My Brother* (1995), has the interesting idea of making the narrator, Tony, a ghost who has died of AIDS in London and whose ashes have been brought back to Ireland for burial. At first, his strong Cork accent is a distraction, but one becomes inured to it. The story involves the efforts of his friends to carry out his dying wishes to be scattered over the grave of Little Nellie of Holy God in the Good Shepherd Convent. However, the successive episodes do not develop into a plot strong enough to sustain a novel. Also, except for Tony, the characters are too exaggerated to be believable. Gay life is depicted as scatologically camp. No doubt, outlandish sex is one aspect of homosexual society, as it is of heterosexual, but it is not the whole story. The only normal character for the reader to identify with, Tony, is dead. Although at the center of the action, he is beyond involvement in it or change or growth. Nevertheless, he, at least, is touching at the very end.

MARY ROSE CALLAGHAN

WORK: *Mind That 'tis My Brother.* [Dublin]: Poolbeg, [1995]. (Novel).

SIGERSON, GEORGE (1836–1925), historian and translator. Thomas MacDonagh's* *Literature in Ireland* is dedicated to George Sigerson, "Patriot and sage, Bard of the Gael and Gall, Teacher and Healer, Ollamh of subtle lore." The tribute is not an exaggeration. Thoroughly Irish, he claimed descent from Sigurd the Norseman who was defeated at the battle of Clontarf; a medical practitioner and neurologist, he had been Charcot's pupil and translated his *Lectures* from the French; the doyen of the Royal University, he was appointed to the chair of zoology in Newman's Catholic University and still held it when the National University was well established. His physical appearance was no less striking than his intellectual versatility. Terence O'Hanlon recalled him as "Big and broad-shouldered and straight as a lance, with forked beard and a wealth of snowy locks . . ." (*Capuchin Annual,* 95–97, 1954–1955).

Sigerson was born at Holy Hill near Strabane on January 11, 1836, the son of William Sigerson of Derry and his wife Nancy Neilson, a relative of the United Irishman Samuel Neilson. He was educated at the Letterkenny Academy and in France, and studied medicine at Queen's College, Cork, graduating in 1859. His career in medicine, though successful, does not concern us. His role in zoology was pedagogic. In the early 1900s, James Joyce* attended his class; Sigerson gained brief mention in both *Ulysses* and *Finnegans Wake.*

During his own student days in Cork, Sigerson's friends included Ralph and Isaac Varian. Ten of his poems were published in Ralph Varian's *The Harp of Erin* (1869) including the still popular "On the Mountains of Pomeroy." He married the Varians' sister, Hester; they lived first in Synge Street and later at

3, Clare Street. They had four children, of whom the elder daughter, Dora,*
married Clement Shorter and published several books of verse.

Modern Ireland (1868) is a representative collection of Sigerson's political
articles, some of which, dealing with the Orange Order, remain apposite today.
His chapter in *Two Centuries of Irish History,* edited by R. B. O'Brien, was
later published as *The Last Independent Parliament of Ireland* (1919). His *History of the Land Tenures and Land Classes of Ireland* (1871) influenced Gladstone, and he carried on an extensive correspondence regarding education with
Lord Acton.

Sigerson's first book, *The Poets and Poetry of Munster* (1860), contains Irish
songs collected by John O'Daly and translated by "Erionnach" (i.e., Sigerson).
The more easily obtainable *Bards of the Gael and Gall* was published in 1897.
Patrick C. Power in *The Story of Anglo Irish Poetry* (1967) credits this work
with a far-reaching effect on Anglo-Irish poetry and suggests that "his translation methods call for careful examination."

Sigerson's books may lack general appeal today, but they have considerable
historical interest. A child when the first number of *The Nation** appeared, he
lived through many phases of Irish political life to become a senator of the Irish
Free State Senate. He died after a few days' illness on February 17, 1925.

J. B. LYONS

WORKS: *The Poets and Poetry of Munster.* 2d series. Dublin: John O'Daly, 1860; *Modern Ireland.* 2d ed. London: Longmans, 1869; *Political Prisoners.* London: Kegan Paul, 1890; *Bards of the Gael and Gall.* 2d ed. London: T. Fisher Unwin, 1907. (The Phoenix Press edition [Dublin, n.d.] contains Douglas Hyde's Memorial Preface.); *The Last Independent Parliament of Ireland.* Dublin: Gill, 1919; *The Easter-Song of Sedulius.* Dublin: Talbot, 1922; *Songs and Poems.* Introduction by Padraic Colum. Dublin: Duffy, 1927; REFERENCE: Lyons, J. B. "Medicine and Literature in Ireland." *Journal of the Irish Colleges of Physicians and Surgeons* 3, No. 1 (1973): 3–9.

SIMMONS, JAMES [STEWART ALEXANDER] (1933–   ), poet. Simmons
was born on February 14, 1933, in Derry. He was educated at Campbell College,
Belfast, and Leeds University. Having taught English at Friends' School, Lisburn, from 1958 to 1963, he lectured in English at Ahmadu Bello University,
Zaria, Nigeria, from 1963 to 1968. From 1968 to 1984, he was lecturer, then
senior lecturer in Anglo-Irish literature and drama at the University of Ulster,
Coleraine, and sometime chairman of the department. He was writer in residence
at Queen's University, Belfast, from 1989 to 1991. He is at present director
emeritus of the Poets' House, Islandmagee, County Antrim.

Simmons is a controversial, award-winning poet, playwright, songwriter,
critic, and founding editor of *The Honest Ulsterman* (1968). He has won the
Gregory Award and the Cholmondely Award for his poetry. In her introduction
to *Poems 1956–1986,* Edna Longley* aptly summarizes his poetry:

In the poetry of James Simmons art and life never look like becoming polite strangers.
Their intimacy declares itself through the effortlessly natural tones of the poet's voice—

at once source and focus of the pervasive vitality. Whether lyrical or plainspoken, confiding or confessional, pointing a moral or telling a tale, the poems have an air of very immediately addressing the reader out of the immediacy of experience.

Simmons the songwriter and Simmons the poet are both connected to the "word of life"; both have the habit of arresting readers and demanding their attention; they provide "profundity without the po-face." Many of his poems are personal; some are set in the political arena; others are literary in subject matter.

Irony is used to effect. Of *Late But in Earnest* (1967), Graham Greene wrote, "Surely this is the most readable volume of ironic poetry since Norman Cameron died." "Written, Directed by and Starring" in this collection is a typical use of the rhymed iambic that Simmons often effectively employs in traditional forms such as the sonnet and the ballad.

The "honesty, great insight, much humour and the ability to describe mundane circumstance and find it poetically exciting," attributed to Simmons by Anthony Cronin,* are best seen in poems such as "Censorship" from *Energy to Burn*. Literary subject matter also often provides his themes, as in "Cordelia's Grave" and "A Speech for the Clown" from *In the Wilderness* (1969) or in "Stephano Remembers" from *Energy to Burn* (1971). In *From the Irish* (1985), he draws on "The Hag of Beare" in his "The Old Woman of Portrush" and on "The Lament for Art O'Leary" in "Lament for a Dead Policeman." At times, as in the sequence of poems *Sex, Rectitude and Loneliness* (1993), the personal and the political are paralleled.

Simmons' achievement as a poet is probably best summarized by Peter Porter, writing in the *Observer:*

To be pro-booze-and-sex, "on the side of life" and the rest of it, and not seem strained, is Simmons' achievement. I suppose that many years from now his handling of the vernacular will seem one of the lasting styles of a very confused literary period.

CELIA de FRÉINE

WORKS: *Ballad of a Marriage.* Belfast: Festival, 1966; *Late But in Earnest.* London: Bodley Head, 1967; *Ten Poems.* Belfast: Festival, 1969; *In the Wilderness.* London: Bodley Head, 1969; *No Ties.* Belfast: Ulsterman, 1970; *Energy to Burn.* London: Bodley Head, [1971]; *No Land Is Waste.* Surrey: Keepsake, 1972; *The Long Summer Still To Come.* Belfast: Blackstaff, 1973; ed., *Ten Irish Poets.* Cheadle: Carcanet, 1974; *West Strand Visions.* Belfast: Blackstaff, 1974; *Memorials of a Tour in Yorkshire.* Belfast: Ulsterman, 1975. (Poetry pamphlet); *Judy Garland and the Cold War.* Belfast: Blackstaff, 1976; *The Selected James Simmons.* Edna Longley, ed. [Belfast]: Blackstaff, [1978]; *Constantly Singing.* Belfast: Blackstaff, 1980; *Sean O'Casey.* London: Macmillan, 1983. (Criticism); *From the Irish.* Belfast: Blackstaff, 1985; *Poems 1956–1986.* Dublin: Gallery/ Newcastle upon Tyne: Bloodaxe, 1986; *Sex, Rectitude and Loneliness.* Belfast: Lapwing, 1993; *Mainstream.* Dublin: Salmon/Poolbeg, 1995

SIMMONS, JANICE FITZPATRICK (1954), poet. Born on May 5, 1954, in Boston, Massachusetts, Simmons received B.A.s from Franconia College in creative writing and classical literature and an M.A. in creative writing and Anglo-Irish literature from the University of New Hampshire. Having worked for eight years as director of the Frost Place in New Hampshire, she is now director of the Poets' House, Islandmagee, County Antrim. In addition to organizing seminars on poetry, Poets' House teaches an M.A. course in creative writing in association with the University of Lancaster.

Simmons' work is evocative and beautifully descriptive. She writes about Ireland and America, shifting seasons and relationships. Her poems feature many seascapes. She is married to James Simmons.*

CELIA de FRÉINE

WORKS: *Leaving America.* Belfast: Lapwing, 1992; *Settler.* Dublin: Salmon/Poolbeg, 1995.

SIRR, PETER (1960–   ), poet. Sirr was born in Waterford and studied at Trinity College, Dublin. A recipient of the Patrick Kavanagh* Award in 1982, he was also an editor of the recently revamped critical magazine *Graph.* Since September 1991, he has been director of the Irish Writers' Centre* in Dublin. He has traveled widely in Europe and now lives in Dublin. He also reviews poetry on occasion for the *Irish Times.*

Sirr is one of the more exciting of a new generation of Irish poets, his work containing marked intellectual as well as stylistic strengths. His never overdone construction of poetic language lends a graceful yet poetically sturdy feel to his poems, whose subject range is wide, but that most often describe and investigate a sense of restlessness and uncertainty of place. Some of his work is distinctly impressionistic, leaning more toward European poetry—that of, say, Italy or Germany—than what is recognized as contemporary Irish poetry. *The Ledger of Fruitful Exchange* (1995) he considers to be quite different from his earlier work.

FRED JOHNSTON

WORKS: *Marginal Zones.* [Dublin]: Gallery, [1984]; *Talk, Talk.* [Dublin]: Gallery, [1987]; *Ways of Falling.* [Oldcastle, Co. Meath]: Gallery, [1991]; *The Ledger of Fruitful Exchange.* [Oldcastle, Co. Meath]: Gallery, [1995].

SLADE, JO (1952–   ), poet and painter. Slade was born in Hertfordshire and attended the Limerick College of Art, the National College of Art in Dublin, and Trinity College.

WORK: *In Fields I Hear Them Sing.* Galway: Salmon, 1989.

SMEDLEY, JONATHAN (1671–?), poet and clergyman. "That rascal Smedley," as Swift* called him, was born in Dublin and educated at Trinity College, where he received a B.A. in 1695 and an M.A. in 1698. He took orders and received a living in County Cork but lived mainly in Dublin and was an outspoken Whig. According to the *Dictionary of National Biography,* he wrote "some rasping verses affixed to the portal of St. Patrick's upon the announcement of Swift's appointment as Dean." They included the telling quatrain:

This Place He got by Wit and Rhime,
    And many Ways most odd;
And might a Bishop be, in Time,
    Did he believe in God.

In September 1718, he was presented the deanery of Killala. His *Poems on Several Occasions* appeared anonymously in 1721, and some of his verses appeared in Concanen's* *Miscellaneous Poems by Several Hands* in 1724. In the same year, he resigned from Killala but in June was instituted as dean of Clogher. There he was visited by Thomas Birch, the future historian and antiquarian, with whom he planned *An Universal View of All the Eminent Writers in the Holy Scriptures,* a grandiose plan ridiculed by Thomas Sheridan the elder* in *The Intelligencer.* Smedley wrote various facile verses, hoping for preferment, and also some attacks against Swift and Pope, particularly in his vicious *Gulliveriana* and his *The Metamorphosis, A Poem, Shewing the Change of Scriblerus into Snarlerus, Or the Canine Appetite Demonstrated in the Persons of P-p-e and Sw--t.* In consequence, Pope inserted him in the mud-diving episode of *The Dunciad,* remarking that he was "a person dipped in scandal, and deeply immersed in dirty work." In 1727, he had resigned his impoverished deanery of Clogher, and in 1729 he sailed for India, after which nothing is known of him. His departure for India occasioned the amusing poem "Dean Smedley Gone to Seek His Fortune," which appeared in Swift's and Sheridan's *The Intelligencer,* and began with the lines:

The very Reverend Dean Smedley
Of Dullness, Pride, Conceit a medley. . . .

When Swift's "A Panegyrick on the D--N" was printed in Faulkner's 1735 edition of the Works, a footnote, probably by Swift, was appended that described Smedley as "[a] very stupid, insolent, factious, deformed, conceited Parson, a vile Pretender to Poetry."

PRINCIPAL WORKS: *Poems on Several Occasions.* London: Printed by S. Richardson, for the Author, 1721; *Gulliveriana: A Fourth Volume of the Miscellanies.* London: J. Roberts, 1728; *The Metamorphosis, A Poem, Shewing the Change of Scriblerus into Snarlerus, Or the Canine Appetite Demonstrated in the Persons of P-p-e and Sw--t.* London: A Moore, 1728. (Broadside); *A Specimen of an Universal View of All the Eminent Writers on the Holy Scriptures. . . .* [London?]: Printed for the Author, 1728.

SMITH, MICHAEL (1942–), poet and publisher. Smith was born in Dublin and educated at O'Connell's School and at University College, Dublin. He has taught English and Latin at St. Paul's College in Dublin. He was a founder of New Writers' Press* and editor of the too short-lived literary magazine *The Lace Curtain.*

A typical Michael Smith poem is very short, has very short lines, is not notably rhythmical, does not rhyme, and is written very tersely. His most recent collection, *Lost Genealogies* (1993), has many descriptive pieces about Dublin, but everything is minimally described, and the effect usually depends on one striking phrase. When, as in "Absence," there is no striking phrase, flatness is the result. Occasionally, one striking word works well for him, as does "dandruffed" in the last line of "The Bird Market." Now and then he gets some effect from repetition, as he does by twice repeating the words "and death" at the end of "Vigil." His poetry is basically that of statement and understatement and often does not avoid the inherent dangers.

He has done a good deal of translating from Spanish poets.

WORKS: *With the Woodnymphs.* Dublin: New Writers', 1968; *Times and Locations.* [Dublin]: Dolmen, [1972]; ed., *Selected Poems of James Clarence Mangan.* Dublin: Gallery, 1973; tr., *Del Camino por Antonio Machado.* Dublin: Gallery, 1974; *Anglo-Irish Poetry for Leaving Certificate.* Dublin: Gill & Macmillan, 1975. (Study guide); *Stopping to Take Notes.* Dublin: New Writers', 1979; *Familiar Anecdotes.* Dublin: New Writers', 1981. (Poetry pamphlet); ed., *Irish Poetry: The Thirties Generation.* Dublin: Raven Arts, in association with New Writers', 1983. (Originally appeared as *Lace Curtain,* No. 4 (1971); tr., *Unceasing Lightning: Versions.* By Miguel Hernandez. Dublin: Dedalus, 1986; *Lost Genealogies and Other Poems.* Dublin: New Writers', 1993.

SMITH, PAUL (1935–   ), novelist. Smith was born in Dublin in 1935, "in a house near a bridge spanning a canal. My education has been rather do-it-yourself. To this day I cannot recite the alphabet or the multiplication tables. . . . I learned to read at pre-school age. I began writing in my twenties." He left school at the age of eight and has followed many jobs in Europe, Australia, and North America, including factory hand, radio actor, sailor, barman, and theater correspondent. In Ireland, he has been a costume maker and designer with the Gate* and the Abbey* theaters. He has written some unpublished plays. His novel *Annie* was a Book of the Month Club choice in 1972. He received the Irish American Cultural Institute Literary Award in 1977. He is a member of Aosdána,* and he lives in Blackrock.

His first novel, *Esther's Altar,* was published in 1959 to enthusiastic critical acclaim in the United States and to widespread moral disapproval in Ireland. His most characteristic work has been in depicting life in the Dublin slums in the 1910s, 1920s, and 1930s. This subject, as well as a frequent boisterousness of style, has often caused him to be compared to Sean O'Casey.* However, Smith is one of the most uneven writers: his books vary in quality from one near-masterpiece to a couple of shoddy imitations of Irishness.

Nearly twenty years after its first publication, *Esther's Altar* was revised and retitled *Come Trailing Blood.* The story is nominally set in a south Dublin slum during Easter Week 1916. However, the historical background is skimpy, false, unconvincing, and quite tangential to the novel's main preoccupations, which would seem to be a catalogue of unconvincing brutalities: lust, rape, incest, betrayal, beatings, murder, transvestism, mutilation, and suicide. Presumably all of this is meant to evoke the earthy vigor of slum life, but it almost totally fails. The characters are either vague or simplified, and the style is deeply influenced by the more excessive portions of William Faulkner and Thomas Wolfe (of Wolfe particularly, there are close verbal echoes). Indeed, the style is so florid that it sometimes becomes incoherent and takes on the overripe exaggerations of soft-core pornography. For instance, one of the many rhapsodic descriptions of sex reads in part: "Around the man's furnace-heated unmerciful thrust her arms and legs wrapped loose for what she knew would be a prolonged siege. Until the loaded dewy richness of the man's thick white wax soaked the parched earth like rain falling." In short, the novel vies with Christy Brown's* *A Shadow on Summer* for being the worst, most pretentiously written modern Irish novel.

Incredibly, the author of *Come Trailing Blood* also wrote *The Countrywoman*. That novel, published in 1962, depicts Dublin slum life in the time of the Black and Tan War and of the Civil War. Its heroine is a Juno-like mother, Molly Baines, who is trying to raise her family despite poverty, disease, illness, civil turbulence, and a brutal drunkard of a husband. Although some of the many minor characters are but thinly depicted, the general portrait of swarming life in the tenement is vividly and, this time honestly, caught. Smith's impressive accumulation of details leads to an ending which is profoundly poignant, and the novel seems a collaboration between a Liam O'Flaherty* and a Sean O'Casey, except that it has little of O'Flaherty's stylistic awkwardness and much more space than an O'Casey play in which to detail its richly abominable milieu and its intensity of suffering. It is unquestionably one of the strongest modern Irish novels and deserves the high praise that Anthony Burgess, Kate O'Brien,* W. R. Rodgers,* and others have heaped upon it.

'Stravaganza! (1963) is a departure in both setting and tone, for it is a semi-satiric novel set in a remote village of the West. Much of the book contrasts the simple warm humanity of the locals with the silly fecklessness of the arty visitors. The satiric portraits are clever but thin, perhaps the best being a flamboyant actress who seems a faintly disguised portrait of a prominent Dublin actor. Actually, the satire is more clever than amusing, and the best parts of the book are its feeling for landscape and the good-heartedness of its closing. As an entertainment, it is passable but not up to the best of Honor Tracy.*

Smith's latest novel was published as *Annie* in the United States in 1972 and as *Summer Sang in Me* in England in 1975. A return to the Dublin slums, the book contains some of the faults of *Come Trailing Blood* and some of the strengths of *The Countrywoman*. The story is a picaresque series of adventures of a young girl and of a younger boy who helps her try to raise money to buy her a huckster's cart, so that she may avoid being put to work in a biscuit factory. The book has some of the steamy floridness of *Come Trailing Blood* and seems in parts a Stage Irish exaggeration for the American market. Nevertheless, *Annie* is Smith's best drawn character since Molly Baines, and the latter parts of the book markedly demonstrate the talents of this considerable but erratic writer.

WORKS: *Esther's Altar*. London, New York: Abelard-Schumann, [1959]/revised as *Come Trailing Blood*. London: Quartet Books, 1977; *The Countrywoman*. New York: Scribner's, [1966]/London: Heinemann, [1962]; *The Stubborn Season*. London: Heinemann, [1962]; 'Stravaganza! London: Heinemann, [1963]; *Annie*. New York: Dial, 1972/retitled *Summer Sang in Me*. London:

Quartet Books, 1975. REFERENCE: Carty, Ciaran. "Battling from Way Back." *Sunday Tribune* (June 28, 1987): 18.

SMITH, SYDNEY BERNARD (1936–   ), poet, playwright, and novelist. Smith was born in Glasgow on August 4, 1936, and brought up in Portstewart, County Derry. He attended Clongowes Wood College and Queen's College, Oxford. He has taught at Clongowes Wood and at the University of Iowa and other American schools. For some years, he lived on the island of Inishbofin, County Galway, a fact that, as he pointed out, made him the "Westernmost Man of Letters in Europe."

Unlike most Irish poets, Smith has a sense of humor, and it is seen to good effect in his light verse, such as "To My Typewriter, on Its 21st, and My 42nd, Birthday." In his more usual manner, Smith writes free verse, eschews initial capitalization in sentences, and often dispenses with punctuation. His early work sometimes fell into the memorable, if unconsciously loopy, phrase, but his later work, such as "I Spake Unto My Soul" or the mordant "The Dying Gladiator's Salute to His Emperor," has an effective breeziness that compensates for its looseness or even absence of form.

Smith describes himself as weighing about 165 pounds and standing about 5'5". The hero of his novel *Flannery* (1991) is a short, dumpy poet who divides his time between a Dublin pub called the Quare Place and an island like Inishbofin. The book has some engaging pub talk, but practically nothing happens, and its fluency begins to pall. Indeed, much of the book is made up of a large number of poems, a fifty-page one-act play, some dialogue by characters from Flann O'Brien's (Brian O'Nolan*) *At Swim-Two-Birds,* and other diversions that are really not diverting enough to compensate for the lack of a story.

He has written a number of plays, and the only published one to date, *Sherca* (1979), is an effective, modern embodiment of the Philoctetes story. He has also written and acted in several one-man shows, such as *The Second Grand Confabulation of Drum Ceat* (Dublin Theatre Festival, 1989). He is a member of Aosdána.*

WORKS: *Girl with a Violin.* Dublin: Dolmen, 1968. (Poems); *Sherca.* [Newark, Del.]: Proscenium, [1979]. (One-act play); *Priorities.* Dublin: Raven Arts, [1979]. (Poems); *Sensualities.* Dublin: Raven Arts, [1981]. (Poems); *Scurrilities.* Dublin: Raven Arts, [1981]. (Poems); *New and Selected Poems.* Dublin: Raven Arts, [1984]. (Poems); *Flannery.* [Dublin]: Odell & Adair, [1991]. (Novel).

SMITHSON, ANNIE M[ARY] P[ATRICIA] (1873–1948), novelist. Smithson was born in Sandymount, Dublin, in 1873. She was a nurse and midwife who became a fervent convert to both Catholicism and nationalism, and who fought in the Civil War on the Republican side. Her more than twenty novels were extremely popular among the poorly educated; they are thickly sweet, wildly patriotic, and romantically melodramatic. Cleeve* finds in them "freshness and innocence," but Eimar O'Duffy* more accurately remarks that her "naive pages are thronged with people who live in a state of chronic patriotic hysteria and

cannot open their mouths without telling us about their 'faith' and 'ideals.' "
Although Smithson is very bad indeed, she is not quite of the classic badness
of Amanda M'Kittrick Ros.* She died in Dublin on February 21, 1948.

WORKS: *Her Irish Heritage.* Dublin: Talbot, 1917; *By Strange Paths.* Dublin: Talbot/London:
Unwin, 1919; *The Walk of a Queen.* Dublin: Talbot, 1922; *Carmen Cavanagh.* Dublin: Talbot,
[1925]. *The Laughter of Sorrow.* Dublin: Talbot/London: Simpkins, Marshall, 1925; *Norah Connor,
a Romance of Yesterday.* Dublin: Talbot, [1925]; *These Things, the Romance of a Dancer.* London:
Unwin, 1927; *Sheila of the O'Beirnes.* Dublin & Cork: Talbot, 1929; *Traveller's Joy.* Dublin &
Cork: Talbot, 1930; *For God and Ireland.* Dublin: Talbot, 1931; *Leaves of Myrtle.* Dublin & Cork:
Talbot, 1932; *The Light of Other Days.* Dublin & Cork: Talbot, [1933]; *The Marriage of Nurse
Harding.* Dublin: Talbot/London: Rich & Cowan, 1935; *The White Owl.* Dublin & Cork: Talbot,
1937; *Wicklow Heather.* Dublin & Cork: Talbot, 1938; *Margaret of Fair Hill.* Dublin & Cork:
Talbot, 1939; *The Weldons of Tibradden.* Dublin: Talbot, 1940; *Katherine Devoy.* Dublin: Talbot,
1941; *By Shadowed Ways.* Dublin: Talbot, 1942; *Tangled Threads.* Dublin: Talbot, 1943; *Myself—
and Others. An Autobiography.* Dublin: Talbot, 1944; *The Village Mystery.* Dublin: Parkside, [1945];
Paid in Full. Dublin: Talbot, 1946.

SMYTH, GERARD (1951–   ), poet. Smyth was born in Dublin and has
worked there as a journalist. He has published poems widely and has gathered
them in several collections, which have received some acclaim. However, poem
after poem contains such tiredly romantic writing as, "when the dawn meets
the sky," "time hasn't changed the words of songs of long ago," "I won't
forget that song," "the night is full of strangers," "the roses in full bloom,"
"peaceful sleep," "net of tears," "cruel wind," "the wild Atlantic," "calm
before the storm," "the stillness of a faded photograph," "the machinery of
time stands still in regions of the heart and mind," and so on. By contrast, he
relies on e. e. cummings' at one time avant-garde punctuation. That is, he practically never uses commas and only sometimes periods, although a new sentence
or fragment of one always begins with a capital letter. Nevertheless, this technique occasions some rereading to figure out his syntax. Whether the scrutiny
is worth discovering his "adamantine mysteries" or "the soul's blessed via-
tiucum" or even "plausible shadows on the golden dungheap" is debatable. So
also is Michael Hartnett's* remark that Smyth "may do for Dublin in verse
what Joyce* did for it in prose."

WORKS: *The Flags Are Quiet.* Dublin: New Writers', 1969; *Twenty Poems.* Dublin: New Writers', 1970; *Orchestra of Silence.* Dublin: Gallery, 1971; *World without End.* Dublin: New Writers',
1977; *Loss and Gain.* Dublin: Raven Arts, 1981; *Eclipse.* Drogheda: Aquila, 1983. (Poetry pamphlet); *Painting a Pink Rose Black.* Dublin: Dedalus, 1986.

SOMERS, DERMOT (1947–   ), short story writer. Sommers was born in
County Roscommon and now lives in the Wicklow mountains. In 1982 and
1983, he made ascents of the six great Alpine north faces and has also climbed
in Yosemite, the Andes, and the Himalayas. His stories are about mountain
climbing and are rich with authentic detail. Indeed, he writes with a style that
almost overpowers the reader with detail. Such a bewildering barrage of facts

and descriptions is probably too rich for the general reader, although possibly not for members of the climbing fraternity.

PETER ROBBIE

WORKS: *Mountains and Other Ghosts*. London: Diadem Books [1990]; *At the Rising of the Moon*. London: Baton Wicks/Cork: Collins, [1994].

SOMERVILLE AND ROSS—E. OE. SOMERVILLE (1858–1949) and "MARTIN ROSS" (1862–1915), novelists and short story writers. No one has described the culture of the Big House as convincingly and amusingly as the pair of writers known as Somerville and Ross. The facts of their lives do not prepare us for the keen analysis conveyed by these two eccentric characters, although it is clear that they knew and enjoyed their own class, the Ascendancy. Edith Somerville and Violet Martin, who took the pseudonym Martin Ross, shared similar backgrounds and artistic tastes. Somerville, born on May 2, 1858, studied art in London and on the Continent, and throughout her life she continued her work as a painter. She began collaborating with her cousin Violet shortly after they met in 1886. Although Ross was younger, born on June 11, 1862, the partnership was an equal one; in fact, the collaboration was so thorough that it is difficult to distinguish the contributions of one author from the other. Their personal bond was so strong that the works seem to derive from a single personality, and after Ross's death on December 21, 1915, Somerville continued to list her as coauthor, claiming that through spiritualist communication they remained collaborators. Later in her life, Somerville wrote, "[I]n all the happy years of our working and living together, there was never a break in the harmony of our work, nor a flaw in our mutual understanding."

Their first novel, *An Irish Cousin* (1889), is a slight exercise in Gothic narrative, but even it reveals their skill in building interesting characters. In their next novel, *Naboth's Vineyard* (1891), they treated Irish village life; but while their sympathies are evident, their knowledge of that class is inadequate to carry the story.

Very quickly, however, they discovered the subject that was to serve them so well. *The Real Charlotte* appeared in 1894 and was recognized at once as the very best Irish novel since the works of Maria Edgeworth.* The novel clearly aspired to be much more than an amusing account of quaint Irish life. Its main character, Charlotte Mullen, is so frustrated, so vindictive, so utterly evil that she becomes a startling character. Conor Cruise O'Brien* remarks, "Evil has often been more dramatically exhibited, but I do not think it has ever been more convincingly worked out in humdrum action, or brought home with such a terrible cumulative effect as an element in everyday life." Not only is Charlotte an impressive creation, but so are all the characters, her tenants and servants, and particularly her victims—the gentle Francie and the only man she ever loved, Roderick Lambert. The entire atmosphere of the Big House is sustained with a mass of realistic detail. Clearly, the world of fashionable Anglo-Irish country gentry is in its demise, but much of its elegance and dignity is preserved and affectionately described.

While literary critics proclaim *The Real Charlotte* as Somerville and Ross's real masterpiece, their popular reputation—and it has been strong indeed—rests on a series of comic short stories. In 1898, the first collection of these, *Some Experiences of an Irish R.M.*, was published, and they were immediately adopted as favored works. The title character, Major Yeates, is an English magistrate attempting to adjust to life in a small Irish town, Skebaun, among a set of crafty and hilarious Irish types. The humor comes as fast as the turns of plot: a series of comic encounters between landlords and tenants, masters and servants and townsfolk, in which roles are often reversed so that English gentility is outwitted by Irish guile. Yeates has as his comic antagonist a stock character, the landlord Flurry, another sterling creation. So popular was the first collection that two more soon followed: *Further Experiences of an Irish R.M.* (1908) and *In Mr. Knox's Country* (1915). No diminution of talent is detected as the two authors continued to dissect English posturing as well as Irish sentimentality in a series of fast-moving and often hilarious accounts. Throughout the stories, the dialect is amusing in itself, but the real effect comes from sharp contrasts and sheer debunking.

After Ross's death, the tone of the novels is less comic, and several are serious indeed. Of these, the best is *The Big House of Inver* (1925), an account of the decline of the aristocratic Prendeville family. Its plot is surely constructed, although the attempts at comic relief seem strained. Edith Somerville continued to publish sketches and reminiscences until her death on October 8, 1949.

Although they lived through the Irish renaissance and on into the modern period, the pair were little involved with the literary set, preferring their quiet life in the country. But their works are very much part of the history of the period. The best of their fictional works, *The Real Charlotte,* has earned comparison with the great novels of the nineteenth century—specifically with *Middlemarch* and *Cousine Bette.* Their depiction of the closed society of the Big House and their accounts of its unavoidable decay remind one of the dramatic treatments of that subject by W. B. Yeats* and Samuel Beckett.* Their ironic observations of the clash of cultures between the Briton and the Celt are good-humored but often insightful. Even in the most comic of their writings, a suggestion of conflict under way in Ireland adds poignancy to the texts. Their works represent a high level of literary achievement and a fascinating study in creative collaboration.

JAMES KILROY

WORKS: E. OE. Somerville, ed. *The Mark Twain Birthday Book.* London: Remington, 1885; E. OE. Somerville as "Geilles Herring" & Martin Ross. *An Irish Cousin.* 2 Vols. London: Richard Bentley, 1889; E. OE. Somerville & Martin Ross. *Naboth's Vineyard.* London: Spencer Blackett, 1891; E. OE. Somerville & Martin Ross. *Through Connemara in a Governess Cart.* London: W. H. Allen, 1893; E. OE. Somerville & Martin Ross. *In the Vine Country.* London: W. H. Allen, 1893; E. OE. Somerville & Martin Ross. *The Real Charlotte.* 3 vols. London: Ward & Downey, 1894; Martin Ross & E. OE. Somerville. *Beggars on Horseback.* Edinburgh & London: William

Blackwood, 1895; Martin Ross & E. OE. Somerville. *The Silver Fox.* London: Lawrence & Bullen, 1898; E. OE. Somerville & Martin Ross. *Some Experiences of an Irish R. M.* London: Longmans, Green, 1899; Martin Ross & E. OE. Somerville. *A Patrick's Day Hunt.* Westminster: Archibald Constable, [1902]; E. OE. Somerville & Martin Ross. *All on the Irish Shore.* London: Longmans, Green, 1903; E. OE. Somerville. *Slipper's ABC of Fox Hunting.* London: Longmans, 1903; E. OE. Somerville & Martin Ross. *Some Irish Yesterdays.* London: Longmans, Green, 1906; E. OE. Somerville & Martin Ross. *Further Experiences of an Irish R. M.* London: Longmans, Green, 1908; E. OE. Somerville & Martin Ross. *Dan Russel the Fox.* London: Methuen, 1911; E. OE. Somerville. *The Story of the Discontented Little Elephant.* London: Longmans, Green, 1912; E. OE. Somerville & Martin Ross. *In Mr. Knox's Country.* London: Longmans, Green, 1915; E. OE. Somerville & (nominally) Martin Ross. *Irish Memories.* London: Longmans, Green, 1917; E. OE. Somerville & (nominally) Martin Ross. *Mount Music.* London: Longmans, Green, 1919; E. OE. Somerville & Martin Ross. *Stray-Aways.* London: Longmans, Green, 1920; E. OE. Somerville. *An Enthusiast.* London: Longmans, Green, 1921; E. OE. Somerville & (nominally) Martin Ross. *Wheel-Tracks.* London: Longmans, Green, 1923; E. OE. Somerville & (nominally) Martin Ross. *The Big House of Inver.* London: William Heinemann, [1925]; E. OE. Somerville & (nominally) Martin Ross. *French Leave.* London: William Heinemann, [1928]; E. OE. Somerville. *The States Through Irish Eyes.* Boston & New York: Houghton Mifflin, 1930/London: William Heinemann, [1931]; E. OE. Somerville & (nominally) Martin Ross. *An Incorruptible Irishman.* London: Ivor Nicholson & Watson, [1932]; E. OE. Somerville & (nominally) Martin Ross. *The Smile and the Tear.* London: Methuen, [1933]; E. OE. Somerville, ed. *Notes of the Horn: Hunting Verse, Old and New.* London: Peter Davies, [1934]; E. OE. Somerville & (nominally) Martin Ross. *The Sweet Cry of Hounds.* London: Methuen, [1936]; E. OE. Somerville & (nominally) Martin Ross. *Sarah's Youth.* London: Longmans, Green, [1938]; E. OE. Somerville & Boyle Townshend Somerville. *Records of the Somerville Family of Castle-haven & Drishane from 1174, to 1940.* Cork: Guy, 1940; E. OE. Somerville & (nominally) Martin Ross. *Notions in Garrison.* London: Methuen, [1941]; E. OE. Somerville & (nominally) Martin Ross. *Happy Days!* London: Longmans, Green, [1946]; E. OE. Somerville & (nominally) Martin Ross. *Maria and Some Other Dogs.* London: Methuen, [1949]; *Selected Letters of Somerville and Ross.* Gifford Lewis, ed. London: Faber, 1991. REFERENCES: Collis, Maurice. *Somerville and Ross.* London: Faber, 1968; Cronin, John. *Somerville and Ross.* Lewisburg, Pa.: Bucknell University Press, [1972]; Cummins, Geraldine Dorothy. *Dr. E. OE. Somerville.* London: Andrew Dakers, [1952]. (Contains Robert Vaughan's "The First Editions of Edith Oenone Somerville and Violet Florence Martin"); Lewis, Gifford. *Somerville and Ross: The World of the Irish R. M.* London: Penguin/New York: Viking, 1985; Powell, Violet. *The Irish Cousins.* London: Heinemann, 1970; Robinson, Hilary. *Somerville and Ross: A Critical Appreciation.* Dublin: Gill & Macmillan/New York: St. Martin's, 1980.

SOUTHERNE, THOMAS (1660–1746), playwright.

Southerne was born at Oxmantown, Dublin, and educated at Trinity College, Dublin, and at the Middle Temple, London. He served in the army and was a friend of Dryden, with whom he collaborated, and with Aphra Behn, whose novels *The Fatal Marriage* and *Oroonoko* he dramatized with considerable success at the time. He also attempted comedy in the bawdy Restoration vein. He was a friend of Swift,* Pope, and Gray, and he died a wealthy man in London on May 22, 1746. There is nothing Irish in Southerne's plays, but *Oroonoko* was popular well into the nineteenth century. Although he continues to receive some scholarly attention and even some respectful critical attention in literary histories, his plays have not held the stage. In 1922, William Archer in *The Old Drama and the New* thought with considerable justice that *The Fatal Marriage* was given up "to despicable comic scenes," that *Oroonoko* was "a piece of unmitigated nonsense," and that Southerne's comedies were "almost incredibly devoid of talent." In the unlikely event of any of Southerne's plays being revived, a modern audience would undoubtedly concur.

WORKS: *Plays . . . Now First Collected.* 3 vols. London: T. Evans, T. Beckett, 1774; *The Plays of Thomas Southerne.* 2 vols. Robert Jordan & Howard Love, eds. Oxford: Clarendon, 1988.   REFERENCE: Dodds, John Wendell. *Thomas Southerne, Dramatist.* New Haven, Conn. & London: Yale University Press, 1933. (Yale Studies in English, No. 81).

SPENSER, EDMUND (1552–1599), poet. Spenser, one of the greatest of English poets, spent nearly twenty years in Ireland. He had considerable effect on English thinking about Ireland, and Ireland had some effect on his own finest work. He was born in London and educated at the Merchant Taylors' School under the learned Richard Mulcaster, who insisted that his charges study English as well as the classical languages. He attended Cambridge as a sizar, or poor scholar, and was influenced by its puritan ambience. His friendship with the Cambridge don Gabriel Harvey was fueled by a mutual interest in poetic theory, particularly in the possibilities for English of classical quantitative meter. Although Spenser presently abandoned this attempt for the native tradition, his experimentation remained. "The Shepheardes Calender," for instance, has thirteen different meters, and Spenser has been justly labeled "the poet's poet."

Graduating with an M.A. in 1576, Spenser held various positions in the retinue of prominent men, among them the earl of Leicester, whose nephew was Philip Sidney. In 1580, he became secretary to the new lord deputy of Ireland, Lord Grey de Wilton, and traveled with him to Ireland. There, save for two visits to England, he spent the rest of his life; and there he wrote his greatest works. He was first an official of the Elizabethan establishment and later a "planter" on a 3,000-acre estate in County Cork. The last years of the 1590s, however, were politically turbulent ones; and in 1598 Spenser's Kilcolman Castle was destroyed, and one of his children was killed. Bearing messages for aid to the planters, he returned to England, where he died in Westminster on January 13, 1599. His grave may be seen in the Poets' Corner in Westminster Abbey.

Spenser's thoughts about how Ireland should be governed were developed in his long prose treatise, *A View of the Present State of Ireland.* Written in 1596 but not published until 1633, the work was widely circulated in manuscript; and, as Nicholas Canny and Andrew Carpenter remark in *The Field Day Anthology:*

Spenser's political importance lies in the fact that he was the first of his nation to advance a coherent argument for the systematic colonization of Ireland by the English people. In taking this stance, he became the prime apologist for the destruction of the Gaelic and Hiberno-Norman civilizations of Ireland; but he also became the most eloquent advocate of the civilizing reform that was meant to follow upon this destruction.

Spenser's position was, broadly, that the Gaelic Irish were but barbarians and that the Hiberno-Norman settlers who had intermarried with them were only dragged down to their uncivilized level. The solution was forcefully to eradicate all trace of the Gaelic past, its language and its culture; to assimilate the Gaels into English ways; and thus to make them productive members of society, not to mention pious Protestants.

Nevertheless, C. S. Lewis' remark should be borne in mind:

He loves Ireland strongly, in his own way, pronouncing Ulster "a most bewtifull and sweete countrie in any is vnder heaven." And he gives free rein to those antiquarian interests so characteristic of his age. The "pleasure" of such studies is a recurrent theme and Eudoxus [in *A View of the Present State of Ireland*] makes it clear that Spenser hoped to publish a substantial prose work on Irish antiquities.

Spenser made some use of Irish myths and landscape in "Colin Clout's Come Home Againe" (1591), although the landscape is conventionally pastoralized. "Epithalamion" (1594) celebrates his own marriage, which was probably in Cork city, and mingles some Irish details with the classical ones. The "Mutability Cantos" of *The Faerie Queene* are set in the mountains near Spenser's own estate in County Cork. There was a multitude of influences on Spenser's work, and the Irish is hardly that pervasive or strong. Nevertheless, as Lewis also remarked, "By December 1591 we find Spenser restored to poetical health, to his own house at Kilcoman, and probably to the *Faerie Queene.*"

WORK: *The Works of Edmund Spenser: A Variorum Edition.* 10 vols. Rudolf Gottfried, ed. Baltimore: Johns Hopkins University Press, 1932–1957. (*A View of the Present State of Ireland* is printed in Vol. 9, 1949).   REFERENCES: Avery, Bruce. "Mapping the Irish Other: Spenser's A View of the Present State of Ireland." *ELH* 57 (Summer 1990): 263–279; Brady, Ciaran. "Spenser's Irish Crisis: Humanism and Experience in the 1590s." *Past & Present,* No. 111 (May 1986): 17–49; Canny, Nicholas. "Edmund Spenser and the Development of an Anglo-Irish Identity." *Yearbook of English Studies* 13 (1983): 1–19; Coughlan, Patricia, ed. *Spenser and Ireland: An Interdisciplinary Perspective.* Cork: Cork University Press, 1989; Judson, Alexander. *Spenser in Southern Ireland.* Folcroft, Pa.: Folcroft Library Editions, 1977; Maley, Willy. "Spenser and Ireland: A Select Bibliography." *Spenser Studies* 9 (1988): 225–242.

SPERANZA. *See* WILDE, LADY.

SQUIRES, GEOFFREY (1942–   ), poet. Squires was born in Derry in 1942, grew up in Raphoe, County Donegal, and studied at Cambridge. He has published a pamphlet and a small collection of poems. The dominant characteristic of his poems is brevity, and many read like the Imagist pieces of H.D. and the early Ezra Pound. If there is statement, it is either a terse, faint irony at the end, or it is implied. The great difference between the best Imagist work and that of Squires is in the quality of the language. Squires is always clear but never vivid, and so his terseness merely focuses the attentive reader on rather unremarkable prose.

In some of his poems, however, there is some slight edging towards a mild and helpful irony. There is also an awareness of levels of language, although the awareness usually consists of the poet's printing alone on some pages jargonish quotes from books like *Programming and Meta-programming in the Human Biocomputer*. Finally, there also seems to be a consistent attitude throughout his work, but these qualities do not compensate for the printing of what are the casual jottings from a writer's notebook.

WORKS: *Sixteen Poems*. Belfast: Ulsterman Publications, 1969; *Drowned Stones*. Dublin: New Writers', 1975.

STACK, EDDIE (fl. late twentieth century), short story writer. Stack was born in County Clare and graduated from University College, Galway, with a degree in engineering. After working in the West of Ireland, mainly in Gaeltacht areas, he emigrated to the United States, where from San Francisco he edited the Irish quarterly *The Island*. All seven tales of his collection of stories, *The West, Stories from Ireland* (1989), are set in the West, a region with which he is intimately familiar. Ranging from fantasy to social realism, with a humorous as well as a subversive streak running through them, Stack's stories are written in a wonderfully flowing style, strongly reminiscent of James Stephens.*

BARBARA FREITAG

WORK: *The West, Stories from Ireland*. San Francisco: Island House, 1989/London: Bloomsbury, 1990.

STACPOOLE, HENRY DE VERE (1863–1951), novelist. Stacpoole was born in Kingstown (now Dun Laoghaire, County Dublin) to the Reverend William Church Stacpoole and the former Charlotte Augusta Mountjoy. He studied at the Irish Public School in Portarlington and later took up the study of medicine at Saint George's and Saint Mary's Hospitals in London, actually going into practice for some years. He was heir to the late-Victorian, Anglo-Irish society that resided on the southern shore of Dublin Bay. Even though his life roughly spans that of Yeats* and Shaw,* Stacpoole avoided political concerns and distanced himself from Irish nationalism and the Irish literary revival. His writings betray a love for an imagined tropics and contributed much to the "Orientalized" impression of life in the Pacific, Asia, Africa, and the West Indies. However, his work is based on some firsthand experience. He traveled fairly extensively early in his career and utilized many of these memories in his imaginative geography of Eastern sunsets and tropical paradises. His work is largely accessible now because of the number of films based on his 1908 novel, *The Blue Lagoon*. The story details the innocent, prelapsarian relationship between two young lovers orphaned and marooned in the South Seas. Stacpoole wrote four other novels in this series: *The Beach of Dreams* (1919), *The Garden of God* (1923), *The Gates of Morning* (1925), and *The Girl of the Golden Reef* (1929). His other more successful works include *The Crimson Azaleas* (1907), set in Japan, and *The Pools of Silence* (1915), set in the Belgian Congo. Earlier in his career, he also attempted verse, comical farce, and naturalistic prose. The early novel, *The Doctor* (1895), details the idealized life of a general practitioner. His final books include two volumes of reminiscences, *Men and Mice*

(1942) and *More Men and Mice* (1945). He also translated Villon and Sappho. He possesses virtually no literary reputation because of the political sensibilities of his contemporary critics, who could never forgive him for his Irish birth or for his prosperity outside Ireland and Irish politics, and also the need for subsequent critics to consider him within easy categories of time and genre. His personal life reads like the plot of one of his novels of Victorian respectability. His first wife, Margaret Robson, died in 1934, and in 1938 Stacpoole married her sister Florence. He lived out his later years in the bucolic paradise of Cliff Dene in Bonchurch on the Isle of Wight. He died on the Isle of Wight on April 12, 1951, a few days after his eighty-eighth birthday.

BERNARD McKENNA

WORKS: *The Intended.* London: John Lane, 1894; *The Doctor.* London: John Lane, 1895; *Pierrot!* London: John Lane, 1896; *Monsieur de Rochefort.* London: G. Newness, 1900; *The Crimson Azaleas.* Philadelphia: Lippincott, 1907; *Blue Lagoon.* New York: Duffield, 1908; *Garryowen.* New York: Duffield, 1909; *The Drums of War.* London: John Murray, 1910; *Poems and Ballads.* London: John Murray, 1910; *The Ship of Coral.* London: Hutchinson, 1911; *The Street of the Flute Player.* London: Hutchinson, 1912; The Children of the Sea. London: Hutchinson, 1913; *The Poems of François Villon.* London: Hutchinson, 1913; *England Expects.* London: Curwen, 1914; *The New Optimism.* New York: John Lane, 1914; *The North Sea and Other Poems.* London: Hutchinson, 1915; *The Pearl Fishers.* New York: John Lane, 1915; *Pools of Silence.* London: T. Fisher Unwin, 1915; *The Reef of Stars.* London: Hutchinson, 1916; *The Good Trail, A Romance of the South Seas.* New York: John Lane, 1916; *Journal d'un Officier Prussian.* Paris: Bloud & Gay, 1916; *Sea Plunder.* New York: John Lane, 1917; *Francis Villon.* New York: Putnam, 1917; *The Man Who Lost Himself.* New York: John Lane, 1918; *The Beach of Dreams.* New York: John Lane, 1919; *The House of Crimson Shadows.* London: Hutchinson, 1920; *The Man Who Found Himself.* New York: John Lane, 1920; *Sappho.* London: Hutchinson, 1920; *Vanderdecken.* New York: R. M. McBride, 1922; *Men, Women and Beasts.* London: Hutchinson, 1922; *The Garden of God.* New York: Dodd, Mead, 1923; *Golden Ballast.* New York: Jacobson, 1924; *The Gates of Morning.* London: Hutchinson, 1925; *In a Bonchurch Garden.* London: Hutchinson, 1927; *Goblin Market.* London: Cassell, 1927; *The Mystery of Uncle Ballard.* Garden City, N.Y.: Doubleday, Doran, 1928; *Eileen of the Trees.* Garden City, N.Y.: Doran, 1929; *The Girl of the Golden Reef.* London: Hutchinson, 1929; *Pacific Gold.* New York: Sears, 1931; *The Book of Francis Villon.* Boston: International Pocket Library, 1931; *The Naked Soul.* London: W. Collins, 1933; *The Vengeance of Mynheer Van Lok.* London: Hutchinson, 1934; *The Longshore Girl.* London: Hutchinson, 1935; *Men and Mice.* London: Hutchinson, 1942; *More Men and Mice.* London: Hutchinson, 1945.

STANDÚN, PÁDRAIG (1946–   ), novelist and priest. Standún was born on February 8, 1946, in Castlebar. He studied for the priesthood in Maynooth, and since his ordination in 1971 he has worked as a curate in the Connemara and Aran Island Gaeltacht. So far he has published six novels in Irish, and four of these have been reissued in English: *Lovers* (filmed as *Budawanny* in 1986 and more recently as *The Bishop's Story* in 1994), *Celibates, The Anvy, A Woman's Love,* and *Stigmata.*

With the exception of *A Woman's Love,* there are priests at the center of Standún's novels. The portrayal of these characters is a far cry from those in Gerald O'Donovan's* *Father Ralph.* Standún's priests swear, drink, urinate, and copulate like the rest of their parishioners. They are earthy, upright men who, rather than wine, dine, and play golf, are out to support the most vulnerable in their parishes: single pregnant girls, the sick, men on the dole. Standún seems to approve neither of clerical celibacy nor of priests who indulge in surreptitious affairs. His priest protagonists come out of the closet to confront parishioners and the church hierarchy alike over their sexual relationships. One of them sees his mission in helping to "undo some of the damage done by priests over the years," thus seemingly expressing Standún's own ideals.

Standún's criticism is not confined to church matters. He relishes lifting the lid on all those aspects of life that Irish society prefers to keep in the dark. He exposes ineffectual schemes hatched behind closed doors by bigoted civil servants and incompetent politicians. He explores the AIDS problem, child abuse, alcoholism, pollution, wife battering, and lesbian relationships. A negative corollary of this is that his protagonists, locked into their fixed role as Standún's mouthpieces, are not allowed to develop into full-blown characters.

BARBARA FREITAG

WORKS IN ENGLISH: *Lovers.* [Swords, Co. Dublin]: Poolbeg, [1991]; *Celibates.* [Swords, Co. Dublin]: Poolbeg, [1993]; *The Anvy.* Indreabhán: Cló Iar-Chonnachta, 1993; *A Woman's Love.* [Swords, Co. Dublin]: Poolbeg, [1994]; *Stigmata.* Indreabhán: Cló Iar-Chonnachta, 1994/Dingle: Brandon, 1995.

STANYHURST (or STANIHURST), RICHARD (1547–1618), historian and translator of Virgil. Stanyhurst was born in Dublin of an Anglo-Irish family prominent in politics and commerce for several generations. His grandfather was lord mayor, and his father was three times speaker of the Irish House of Commons. Stanyhurst was educated at Peter White's grammar school in Kilkenny and at University College, Oxford, where his mentor was Edmund Campion, and also studied law in Furnival's and Lincoln's Inns in London. His contribution on Ireland to Holinshed's Chronicles (1577) relies heavily on previous writers, particularly Giraldus Cambrensis and Campion; and both it and his later Latin work on Ireland, *De rebus in Hibernia gestis libri quattuor* (1584), are not free from error and bias. He calculates, for instance, that Ireland and England are approximately the same size, and his treatment of the mere Irish is vitiated by his own lack of Irish. Stanyhurst wrote from the viewpoint of—a term he once used—the "Anglo-Hiberni," that is, those descendants of the Norman invasion who, like his own family, were prominent in the affairs of the Pale. He disliked the new breed of English overseers, and he hoped that by education and by learning English the "antiqui Hibernici" would be subsumed into one Irish nation. As a historian of his day, Stanyhurst relied much on compiling from previous authorities, but his own personal observation is lively, vigorous, and entertaining, for instance (in Colm Lennon's translation of his Latin), his description of mourning among the native Irish:

They shout dolefully through swollen cheeks, they cast off their necklaces, they bare their heads, they tear their hair, they beat their brows, they excite emotion on all sides, they spread their palms, they raise their hands to the heavens, they shake the coffin, tear open the shroud, embrace and kiss the corpse and scarcely allow the burial to take place.

. . . I can tell of a little old woman who once, not many years ago, had made herself hoarse from long and loud shrieking. Afterwards she turned to her companion and asked what the name of the dead person was.

Stanyhurst's major literary work was his 1582 translation of the first four books of Virgil's *Aeneid*. Despite interesting thoughts about prosody in his initial remarks, his translation into bumptious diction and clumsy hexameters was generally considered ludicrous. As Thomas Nash wrote, "[H]e trod a foule, lumbering, boysterous, wallowing measure"; or, as Barnaby Rich put it, he "stript [Virgil] out of a Velvet gowne, into a Fooles coate, out of a Latin Heroicall verse, into an English Riffe raffe."

Stanyhurst's nephew was the celebrated Archbishop Ussher of Armagh, but, like his mentor, Campion, Stanyhurst eventually embraced Catholicism, spent most of his adult life on the Continent in the pay of Spain, and was also considered learned in medicine, law, and diplomacy. In later years, he entered the Jesuits, wrote a Latin life of St. Patrick, and became court chaplain to Albert, the archduke of Austria, and his wife Isabella, daughter of Phillip II of Spain. He died in Brussels in the summer of 1618.

PRINCIPAL WORKS: "A Plain and Perfect Description of Ireland" and "A History of the Reign of Henry VIII." In *Chronicles of England, Scotland and Ireland*. Raphael Holinshed, ed. London: John Hunne, 1577/both republished as *Holinshed's Irish Chronicle*. Liam Miller & Eileen Power, eds. [Dublin]: Dolmen/[Atlantic Highlands, N.J.]: Humanities, 1979; *The First Four Books of Virgil's Aeneid Translated into English Heroical Verse*. Leyden: John Pates, 1582; *De rebus in Hibernia gestis libri quattuor*. Antwerp: Christopher Plantin, 1584; *De vita S. Patricii libri duo*. Antwerp: Christopher Plantin, 1587.   REFERENCE: Lennon, Colm. *Richard Stanihurst the Dubliner, 1547–1618: A Biography with a Stanihurst Text* On Ireland's Past. [Blackrock, Co. Dublin:] Irish Academic, [1981]. (The translation is from *De rebus*.)

STARKIE, ENID [MARY] (1897–1970), biographer and critic. Starkie was born in Killiney, County Dublin, the daughter of W.J.M. Starkie, the last minister of education under British rule in Ireland and a famous classical scholar. A sister of Walter Starkie,* she was educated at Alexandra College and at the Royal Irish Academy of Music in Dublin, before going to Somerville College, Oxford, with a scholarship in modern languages. Leaving in 1921 with a first, she studied at the Sorbonne, where her work on Verhaeren earned her a doctorate and a prize from the French Academy. After four years of teaching at the University of Exeter, she returned to Somerville and became ultimately reader in French literature and honorary fellow. Her books on Rimbaud and Baudelaire were considered pioneer works, and her short book on her friend André Gide and her critical study *From Gautier to Eliot* (1960) were much admired. Her work on Flaubert, however, was probably her crowning achievement. Her one book of Irish interest is *A Lady's Child* (1941), about her childhood and adolescence in Dublin and Oxford. The *Times* described it as having "a candour both gentle and bold." Personally, she seemed to be lively, energetic, garrulous, strong-willed, and engagingly eccentric. She died on April 21, 1970, in Oxford.

PRINCIPAL WORKS: *Baudelaire*. London: Gollancz, [1933]/London: Faber, 1957; *Arthur Rimbaud*. London: Faber, 1938/rev. London: Hamish Hamilton, 1947; *A Lady's Child*. London: Faber, 1941. (Memoir); *André Gide*. Cambridge: Bowes & Bowes, 1954; *Petrus Borel, the Lycanthrope: His Life and Times*. London: Faber, 1954; *From Gautier to Eliot. The Influence of France on English Literature, 1851–1939*. London: Hutchinson, 1960; *Flaubert: The Making of the Master*. London: Weidenfeld & Nicolson, [1967]; *Flaubert the Master. A Critical and Biographical Study, 1856–1880*. London: Weindenfeld & Nicolson, 1971.

STARKIE, WALTER [FITZWILLIAM] (1894–1976), autobiographer, critic, and translator. Starkie was born in Dublin on August 9, 1894. He was educated at Shrewsbury School, and Trinity College, Dublin, and was professor of language and literature at Trinity from 1926 to 1943. He was also a director of the Abbey Theatre* from 1926 to 1943, and for some years after that a rather nominal director of the Gate Theatre.* As a critic, he has published a study of Jacinto Benavente, another of Luigi Pirandello, and a translation of *Don Quixote*. He is most known, however, for his attractive studies of gypsy life in *Raggle-Taggle* and *Spanish Raggle-Taggle*, both based on his own wanderings. As A. J. Leventhal wrote of him, "He found that he could reach larger audiences by leaning his fleshy chin on his violin and bowing his way into their hearts with the throb of *Ziegeunerweisen* illustrating his comments on Romany culture. Our professor, like Borrow, found his way to Spain, but unlike him took a fiddle instead of a Bible for company. He never regretted it." Starkie spent the World War II years in Spain working for the British government, and many of his last years in Los Angeles where he was professor in residence at the University of California. He received many public honors from various governments. He died in Madrid on November 2, 1976.

WORKS: *Jacinto Benavente*. London: Humphrey Milford, 1924; *Luigi Pirandello*. London & Toronto: Dent, 1926/3d. ed., revised & enlarged, Berkeley & Los Angeles: University of California Press, 1965; *Raggle-Taggle. Adventures with a Fiddle in Hungary and Roumania*. London: J. Murray, 1933; *Spanish Raggle-Taggle. Adventures with a Fiddle in North Spain*. London: J. Murray, 1934; *Don Gypsy*. London: J. Murray, 1936; *The Waveless Plain. An Italian Autobiography*. London: J. Murray, 1938; *Grand Inquisitor, Being an Account of Cardinal Ximinez de Cisneros and His Times*. London: Hodder & Stoughton, 1940; *In Sara's Tents*. London: J. Murray, 1953; *The Road to Santiago*. London: J. Murray, 1957; *Scholars and Gypsies. An Autobiography*. London: J. Murray, [1963]; ed., with A. Norman Jeffares. *Homage to Yeats, 1865–1965*. Los Angeles: University of California Press, 1966.

STEELE, SIR RICHARD (1672–1729), playwright and journalist. Baptized at St. Bride's, Dublin, on March 12, 1672, the child of a family identified with Ballinakill, Steele later was to proclaim, "I am an Englishman born in the City of Dublin." Orphaned while young, he was supported by the Gascoignes, who were prominent in the establishment of the duke of Ormond. He was educated at Charterhouse, where he first met Joseph Addison, and at Oxford, attending Christ Church and Merton. He left without a degree in 1692 to become a Life

Guard and later a Cold Stream Guard, in which he remained for thirteen years. As Captain Steele, he established in London some reputation as a wit, moralist, and writer. He supported Congreve* in the Collier controversy and published an exemplary book, *The Christian Hero* (1701). After three of his farces succeeded on stage—*The Funeral* (1702), *The Lying Lover* (1704), and *The Tender Husband* (1705)—Steele left the Army to become a courtier. He acquired several sinecures and the editorship of *The Gazette,* the official court newspaper. His career was scattered. He founded three successive periodicals, all of them successful—*The Tatler* (1709–1711), *The Spectator,* with Joseph Addison (1711–1712), and *The Guardian* (1713). The literary and financial success of *The Spectator* as it appeared daily and in later bound volumes established the genre of the urbane journalistic essay, reformist in intention but sophisticated and lively in tone, and opened the way for the newspaper. Addison moderated Steele's political enthusiasm, which emerged in *The Guardian.* Steele immersed himself in politics and controversy as a pamphleteer for the Whigs, who, on the accession of George I, knighted him and awarded him a share in the patent for the Drury Lane Theatre.

As the patent makes clear, Steele was appointed one of the managers of Drury Lane partly to carry out his well-known campaign to reform the stage from its Restoration licentiousness, but his foes were partly right in accusing him of neglecting the theatre except as a source of income. He was in continual disputes with the lord chamberlain and his fellow managers. His best known play, *The Conscious Lovers* (1723), carried out his theories of exemplary (rather than satiric) comedy, wherein the lovers are patterns of virtue, and of sentimental comedy, wherein bathos (rather than laughter) combines with the happy ending to provide delight.

Few details of his personal life are known. His personal life is speculative. An amiable and convivial man who lived by his wits and the main chance, he was impetuous and controversial. His friendships included the members of the Whig Kit-Cat Club and of Addison's "little Senate," as well as the philosopher-bishop Berkeley* and Pope and Swift.* (The relationship with Swift developed into personal and political animosity.) Little is known of his first wife. His second wife ("Prue" in *The Spectator,* the recipient of many foolish-fond notes) died in childbirth with their fifth child. He was extravagant and often in debt. Like Congreve and, later, Sheridan,* he aspired to be known as an English gentleman, although he lacked family connections and money. In ill-health, he retired to Wales in his final years, where he died on September 1, 1729.

SVEN ERIC MOLIN

WORKS: *The Letters of Richard Steele.* R. Brimley Johnson, ed. London: John Lane/New York: Dodd Mead, 1927; *The Correspondence of Richard Steele.* Rae Blanchard, ed. London: Oxford University Press, 1941; *Tracts and Pamphlets.* Rae Blanchard, ed. Baltimore: Johns Hopkins, 1944; *Occasional Verse.* Rae Blanchard, ed. Oxford: Clarendon, 1952; *The Englishman: a Political Journal.* Rae Blanchard, ed. Oxford: Clarendon, 1955; with Joseph Addison & others, *The Spectator,* Vols. 1–5, Oxford: Clarendon, 1965; *The Plays of Richard Steele.* Shirley Strum Kenny, ed. Oxford: Clarendon, 1971. REFERENCES: Connely, Willard. *Sir Richard Steele.* New York & London:

Scribner's, 1934; Loftis, John. *Steele at Drury Lane*. Berkeley & Los Angeles: University of California Press, 1952; Winton, Calhoun. *Captain Steele: The Early Career of Richard Steele*. Baltimore: Johns Hopkins University Press, 1964; Winton, Calhoun. *Sir Richard Steele, M. P.: The Later Career*. Baltimore & London: Johns Hopkins University Press, 1970.

STEPHENS, JAMES (1880 or 1882–1950), poet and man of letters. Stephens was in many ways the most engaging of the writers of Irish fantasy. He was witty and sympathetic, a brilliant conversationalist, and a fascinating story-teller—not only spinning tales based on Irish folklore and folklife, but also making up charming, contradictory stories about himself. Throughout his life, Stephens claimed that he was born on February 2, 1882; recently, others have proposed a birthdate of February 9, 1880, based on certain pieces of evidence. The matter remains unresolved.

There is no question about Stephens' birthplace; it was Dublin, where from 1896 to 1912 he served as a clerk-typist in the offices of several Dublin solicitors. His first story, "The Greatest Miracle," was published by Arthur Griffith* in *The United Irishman* on September 16, 1905. He sent his early pieces of writing to Griffith in envelopes without return addresses, but by 1907 they were friends. Griffith printed many of Stephens' poems, essays, and short stories in his newspaper, *Sinn Féin*. As a follower of Griffith's political views and an ardent nationalist, Stephens attended Gaelic League classes and political meetings during the period 1905–1910. His published essays in this period range from comic to serious, but they are most often passionate pleas to the Irish people: to exhibit national pride, to learn the Irish language and customs, and to remember the ancient saga heroes.

In 1907, Stephens met his friend and mentor, George Russell (AE),* who introduced him to George Moore,* W. B. Yeats,* Lady Gregory,* and other Irish writers. According to Stephens, one of the models for his early work was Lord Dunsany,* whose short stories, he explained, contained "great windy reaches, and wild flights among stars and a very youthful laughter at the gods." Another source of inspiration was Oscar Wilde's* *A House of Pomegranates*. By reading "about twenty pages" of Wilde's novel, Stephens reached his first "illuminating" conclusion: "the art of prose-writing does not really need a murder to carry it." This observation led to a second realization that a novel need not be a philosophical treatise. Stephens decided that a work of fiction did not need to be infused by its author with artificial excitement or thought, but rather that it succeeded or fell on its prose style. Having rejected murder and philosophy as necessary topics, Stephens said that he simply began writing "with the idea of doing a something which I conceived that Wilde has tried, and perhaps failed to do."

The work resulting from this challenge, *The Charwoman's Daughter* (1912), is a fantasy with a remarkably harmonious blend of disparate styles. It ranges in tone from whimsy to objectivity, sentimentality, and "philosophizing," and in approach from passages reminiscent of the nineteenth-century novelist to those peculiar to Stephens alone. At various times and in varying degrees, it is a fairy tale about two characters called the Makebelieves, a realistic look at life in the Dublin slums, and a psychological analysis of the relationship between a widowed mother and her daughter. By the end of the novel, happy endings have been provided in keeping with these genres. A mother and daughter have risen above despair through love and understanding of their life roles. Poverty, which has been described with the objectivity of a social worker and treated with the concern of a humanitarian, is no longer viewed as totally evil but more optimistically, as a spur to ambition. Even the aspects of the Märchen are satisfied: the poor but good Makebelieves find wealth and happiness.

Stephens' second novel, like his first, is a fantasy, but *The Crock of Gold* (1912) also contains philosphical debates, slapstick comedy, a romantic triangle consisting of a shepherdess and two gods, and the life stories of two prisoners. It characters range from the mundane (shepherds) to the magnificent (Celtic gods), and its settings from an enchanted mountain to a village jail. Although Stephens rejected violence as a suitable topic for his first novel, this book opens with a robbery and two suicides, and continues with the seduction of a maiden and the abduction of two children. The work is also philosphical in tone, being in part Stephens' commentary on the Blakean notions of the enmity between Reason (male) and Emotion (female), the happy innocence of childhood, and the exploitation of men and women in a society dominated by those representing law, religion, and politics. Stephens' ability to make these divergent elements understandable, even comical, and his combination of them into a cohesive work is indicative of his literary craftsmanship.

The Demi-Gods (1914), Stephens' third novel, does not differ significantly in structure from its predecessors. Symbolism and naturalism are compounded in this story of angels who appear on earth to the bewilderment, delight, and occasional distress of a group who walk the Irish countryside. Demi-gods and tinkers converse and live together in a manner as happy as the relationship among the gods, fairies, leprecauns, and mortals in *The Crock of Gold.* The novel is narrated in the fashion of one who has lived on the road, just as *The Charwoman's Daughter* seems to be a first-hand account of life among the poor people of Dublin. *The Demi-Gods* closes with the attainment of the goals which we find in *The Crock of Gold* and *The Charwoman's Daughter:* the union of man and woman, of gods and men, and of fantasy and reality.

What intervened between Stephens' third and fourth novels was an event of such impact that it changed the lives of all Irishmen—the Easter Uprising of 1916. For no major Irish writer was the impact of the Easter Uprising greater than for James Stephens. The event transformed his writing in a remarkable way—reviving old interests and kindling new abilities. Between 1915 and 1925, Stephens was registrar of the National Gallery of Ireland. He was on his way back to the National Gallery after lunch on Easter Monday 1916 when he learned of the Rising, saw a barricade, and witnessed the shooting of a man. His reactions to the event led to an elegy, *Green Branches* (1916), and a prose account, *The Insurrection in Dublin* (1916).

Beyond these works, the ten-year period after Easter 1916 became one of intense productivity for Stephens, and, it can be argued, the writing of this period was clearly influenced by an intensified patriotic feeling. He joined a class in elementary Irish at the Gaelic League and returned to his early interest in Old Irish literature. His friendship with the scholars Edmund Curtis,* Osborn Bergin (1872–1950), Richard Best (1872–1959), and Stephen MacKenna,* and his readings of the editions of the Irish Texts Society provided him with the background for *Reincarnations* (1918), a collection of poems adapted from the writings of several Gaelic poets, and for his next three books, which he later listed as his best: *Irish Fairy Tales* (1920), *Deirdre* (1923), and *In the Land of Youth* (1924).

There are certain thematic similarities between *Irish Fairy Tales* and the first three novels. Once again, fantasy (magical dwellings, shape-changing, disguised gods) is combined with reality (conflicting emotions of lovers, boasting conversations between rivals, devotion of children). What is different is the emphasis on Irish mythological figures, Fionn in particular. Fionn is an appropriate figure for a Stephens hero because he embraces two worlds. Fionn is a hero, a giant, a descendant of the gods, but he is also, like Stephens, a father, a husband, and a man who loves "the music of what happens."

The story of Deirdre, the Irish Iseult, was popular during the period of the Irish Literary Revival. Unlike his contemporaries, Stephens dealt with the Deirdre story not simply as an isolated legend, but as one of the many related tales which serve as background material in the ancient Ulster saga, *Táin Bó Cualinge* (The Cattle Raid of Cooley). His novel, like the legend, is structured around two questions: what caused the exile of the sons of Uisneac? what caused their death? His respect for his sources did not prevent him from inserting his own material, however. Stephen's Deirdre, like the heroines in his earlier works, converses with birds, hugs a shaggy mare, and loves the sunshine and peace of the Irish countryside. In his last novel, Stephens again injects his whimsical humor into four ancient tales: the Adventures of Nera, the Vision of Angus Óg, the Tale of the Two Swine-herds, and the Wooing of Etain. The highest comic moment in the novel is a daily parade of the most beautiful women of Ireland conjured up by Angus' enthusiastic father to the boredom and depression of his mother.

Stephens wished to write a five-volume version of the *Táin,* but the task was never completed. He discontinued the project after publication of the first two volumes, *Deirdre* and *In the Land of Youth.* The task was overwhelming, the work exhausting, the critical response to his fifth novel discouraging, and he became too ill in mind and body to continue with the work. In his last collection of short stories, *Etched in Moonlight* (1928), which was published after *Deirdre* and *In the Land of Youth,* his mood ranged from irritability to desperation. Stephens' distinctive comic sense had left him, at least momentarily. His whimsical humor had turned sardonic; there was no light touch to relieve the tension.

He turned to fantasy one last time in *How St. Patrick Saves the Irish,* a short story written in 1928. This is the charming tale of a decision made by St. Patrick and St. Brigid that Patrick ask permission to sit in judgment in Heaven on Irishmen, thus allowing the Irish to avoid the "immovable unescapable, terrific" Rhadamanthus.

Stephens moved to London in 1925 and from there began a series of lecture tours in the United States which lasted until 1935. In 1927, he and James Joyce* started a friendship which, at least initially, was the result of Joyce's belief that he and Stephens shared a birthdate and other personal events in common. The relationship blossomed into joint birthday parties and exchanges of gifts, and it also led to Joyce's proposal that Stephens finish *Finnegans Wake* if he could not do so.

Stephens spent the 1930s writing poetry based on his many years of reading Eastern philosophy and literature. Some readers found these works less appealing than earlier ones. The poems published in *Insurrections* (1909), for example, had a vigor and compelling anger not found in *Strict Joy* (1931). Stephens' growing depression permeated his last volume of poems, *Kings and the Moon* (1938); lost love, the coming of winter, the onset of old age became his subject matter. His final occupation was a happy one, however. He gained a new, appreciative audience through his talks on poets and poetry which began on the BBC in 1937 and continued until his death. He died in London on December 26, 1950.

In *A Short History of Irish Literature* (1967), Frank O'Connor* calls Stephens the Irish writer with the "most agile mind. He is a sort of literary acrobat, doing hair-raising swoops up in the roof of the tent." This mental agility is reflected in Stephens' ability to balance a range of emotions, subject matter, and characters in his writing. His first three novels combine fantasy, philosophy, and comedy with characters including tinkers and gods, charladies and queens, warriors and philosophers, precocious children and bewildered parents. The last two cover a vast array of subjects: love, war, heroism, betrayal, intrigue, romance, humorous events, and magical transformations of shape. Stephens is whimsical and coarse, bold and innocent, earthy and profound. His short fiction offers domestic comedy, psychological warfare, and merciless pictures of poverty, inhumanity, and madness. To describe his works as comic recalls the many forms of Irish humor—fantasy, irony, whimsy, satire, parody, word-play, among others.

Throughout his works, the contraries are to be found, but these contraries are a reflection of his life. The terrors recorded in his writing were those he knew personally: dark nights, hunger, illness, the tortuous gropings of the mind, and old age. The joys were familiar, too: childhood games, the love of a man and a woman, the pleasures of dancing, and conversation.

Stephens had a remarkable ability to marry opposites, including those of time and space—the earliest periods of mankind and the modern day, the wild country regions and the cultivated beauty of city parks—but always within an Irish setting, for he was an Irish storyteller. His stories reveal the gaiety and the loneliness of the Irish people: their estrangement from the land which was once theirs and their desire to return to an earlier, pastoral period; their animosities and suspicions; their flights of imagination and their love of words. His fantasies, especially those which were written after Easter 1916, are filled with the sunshine and thunder, lush vegetation and dirty slums, green trees and bloody combats of Ireland.

PATRICIA McFATE

WORKS: *Insurrections.* Dublin: Maunsel, 1909; *The Charwoman's Daughter.* London: Macmillan, 1912; *The Crock of Gold.* London: Macmillan, 1912; *The Hill of Vision.* New York: Macmillan, 1912; *Here Are Ladies.* London & New York: Macmillan, 1913; *The Demi-Gods.* London & New York: Macmillan, 1914; *Songs from the Clay.* London & New York: Macmillan, 1915; *Green Branches.* Dublin & London: Maunsel, 1916; *The Insurrection in Dublin.* Dublin & London: Maunsel, 1916; *Reincarnations.* London & New York: Macmillan, 1918; *Irish Fairy Tales.* London & New York: Macmillan, 1920; *Deirdre.* London & New York: Macmillan, 1923; *In the Land of Youth.* London & New York: Macmillan, 1924; *A Poetry Recital.* New York: Macmillan, 1925; *Collected Poems.* London & New York: Macmillan, 1926/2d ed., 1954; *Etched in Moonlight.* London & New York: Macmillan, 1928; *Julia Elizabeth: a Comedy in One Act.* New York: Crosby Gaige, 1929; *Theme and Variations.* New York: Fountain Press, 1930; *How St. Patrick Saves the Irish.* Privately Printed, 1931; *Strict Joy.* London & New York: Macmillan, 1931; *Kings and the Moon.* London & New York: Macmillan, 1938; *James, Seumas and Jacques: Unpublished Writings by James Stephens.* Lloyd Frankenberg, ed. London & New York: Macmillan, 1964; *Letters of James Stephens.* Richard J. Finneran, ed. London & New York: Macmillan, 1974; *The Uncollected Prose of James Stephens.* 2 vols. Patricia McFate, ed. New York: St. Martin's, 1983. REFERENCES: Huber, Werner. *James Stephens' frühe Roman: Rezeption—Text—Intention.* Frankfurt & Bern: Lang, 1982; McFate, Patricia. *The Writings of James Stephens: Variations on a Theme of Love.* [London & Basingstoke]: Macmillan/New York: St. Martin's, 1979; Martin, Augustine. *James Stephens, a Critical Study.* Dublin: Gill & Macmillan, 1977; Pyle, Hilary. *James Stephens: His Works and an Account of His Life.* London: Routledge & Kegan Paul, 1965.

STERNE, LAURENCE (1713–1768), novelist. It is doubtless chauvinistic to include the great author of *Tristram Shandy* in an Irish literary dictionary, for he spent only the first nine years of his life in Ireland. However, he was born in Clonmel, County Tipperary, on November 24, 1713, and perhaps it is no exaggeration to say that some of his droll spirit may be seen in Flann O'Brien's (Brian O'Nolan*) *At Swim-Two-Birds.* He died in London on March 18, 1768.

WORKS: *The Works of Laurence Sterne.* 12 vols. Wilbur L. Cross, ed. Cambridge, Mass.: Jenson Society, 1906; *The Shakespeare Head Edition of the Writings of Laurence Sterne.* 7 vols. Oxford: Basil Blackwell, 1926–1927; *The Florida Edition of the Works of Laurence Sterne.* Three volumes to date. Gainesville: University Presses of Florida, 1978– ; *Letters of Laurence Sterne.* Lewis Parry Curtis, ed. Oxford: Clarendon, 1935; *The Life and Opinions of Tristram Shandy, Gentleman.* Ian Campbell Ross, ed. Oxford: Clarendon, 1983; *A Sentimental Journey through France and Italy by Mr. Yorick.* Gardner D. Stout, Jr., ed. Berkeley & Los Angeles: University of California Press, 1967. REFERENCES: Cash, Arthur H. *Laurence Sterne: The Early and Middle Years.* London: Methuen, 1975; Cash, Arthur H. *Laurence Sterne: The Later Years.* London & New York: Methuen, 1986; Cash, Arthur H. & Stedmond, John M., eds. *The Winged Skull: Papers from the Laurence Sterne Bicentenary Conference.* London: Methuen, 1971; Cross, Wilbur L. *The Life and Works of Laurence Sterne.* 3d ed. New Haven, Conn.: Yale University Press, 1929; Howe, Alan B. *Sterne: The Critical Heritage.* London & Boston: Routledge & Kegan Paul, 1974; Stedmond, John M. *The*

Comic Art of Laurence Sterne. Toronto: University of Toronto Press, 1967; Traugott, John, ed. *Laurence Sterne: A Collection of Critical Essays.* Englewood Cliffs, N.J.: Prentice-Hall, [1968].

STOKER, [ABRAHAM] "BRAM" (1847–1912), sensational novelist and theatrical manager. Stoker, author of *Dracula,* was born in Dublin on November 8, 1847. He was the son of a mild civil servant and of a Sligo woman of great energy and character who investigated Dublin's social evils with the breathless enthusiasm evinced by the television reporters of a later age, but whose reckless housekeeping kept the family in a perpetual state of bankruptcy. Stoker inherited a passion for the theatre from his father, and in his twenties combined a civil service post with unpaid service as drama critic of *The Evening Mail.* As volunteer public relations man for Henry Irving, he secured the huge success of that actor's visit to Dublin in 1876. This began a friendship with Irving which resulted in Stoker's leaving Dublin in 1878 to throw in his lot with the actor as secretary, business manager of the Lyceum Theatre in London, and what Shaw* contemptuously described as "literary henchman." He remained with Irving through thick and thin for thirty years, and was near at hand when Irving dropped dead in the hall of a Bradford hotel while on tour. In 1878, Stoker married Florence Balcombe, Oscar Wilde's* early beloved, stated by her granddaughter to have become frigid after the birth of her only child; her frigidity is said to have propelled Stoker into womanizing and perhaps to the syphilis which caused his death on April 20, 1912. *Dracula* is the only Stoker novel which has been widely read. His large output includes other weird fiction and even nonfiction, notably *Famous Imposters* (1910), a chapter of which seriously propounds the theory that Queen Elizabeth I of England was really a man in disguise. His justly forgotten novel, *The Snake's Pass* (1891), has to do with Ireland.

ANDREW MARSH

WORKS: *Under the Sunset.* London: Sampson Low, 1882; *The Snake's Pass.* London: Sampson Low, 1891; *The Shoulder of Shasta.* Westminster: A. Constable, 1895; *The Watter's Mou'.* Westminster: A. Constable, 1895; *Dracula.* Westminster: A. Constable, 1897/*The Annotated Dracula.* Leonard Wolf, ed. New York: Potter, 1975/London: New English Library, 1976. Translated into Irish by Sean O Cuirrin, Baile Atha Cliath: Oifig Diolta Faillseachain Rialtais, 1933. Dramatized by H. Dean & J. L. Balderston, New York: Samuel French, [1933]; *Miss Betty.* London: C. A. Pearson, 1898; *The Jewel of the Seven Stars.* London: Heinemann, 1903; *The Man.* London: Heinemann, 1905; *Personal Reminiscences of Henry Irving.* 2 vols. London: Heinemann, 1906; *Lady Athlyne.* London: Heinemann, 1908; *Snowbound, the Record of a Theatrical Touring Party.* London: Collier, 1908; *The Lady of the Shroud.* London: Heinemann, 1909; *Famous Imposters.* London: Sidgwick & Jackson, 1910; *The Lair of the White Worm.* London: William Rider, [1911]; *Dracula's Guest, and Other Weird Stories.* London: George Routledge, 1914; *Shades of Dracula. Bram Stoker's Uncollected Stories.* Peter Haining, ed. London: Kimba, 1982. REFERENCES: Dalby, Richard. *Bram Stoker: A Bibliography of First Editions.* London: Dracula, 1983; Farson, Daniel. *The Man Who Wrote "Dracula."* London: Joseph, 1975; Leatherdale, Clive. *Dracula: The Novel and the Legend.* Wellingborough: Aquarian, 1985; Ludlum, Harry. *A Biography of Dracula. The Life Story of Bram Stoker.* London: Published for Fireside by W. Foulsham, [1975].

STRONG, EITHNE (1923–   ), novelist, short story writer, and poet. Strong was born Eithne O'Connell in Glensharrold, County Limerick. In 1943, she married Rupert Strong,* and they had nine children and founded the Runa Press. Despite a busy domestic life, Mrs. Strong took a four-year degree course at Trinity College, taught in a Dublin school for a dozen years, and has written prolifically: poetry in Irish and English, short stories, and novels.

Her writing is often more straightforward in her poetry than in her prose, which can become a bit clotted. Nevertheless, the poetry is often a bit formless even for free verse. The only nod to form, for instance, in her long poem *Flesh . . . the Greatest Sin* is that most of the stanzas have twelve lines. The individual lines, however, may contain from one up to twelve or fourteen syllables, and there rarely seems any rhythmic relation of one line to another.

In both poetry and fiction, she keeps fairly close to the details of her life: girlhood in the West, marriage, and the difficulties of coping with a large family. The picture she paints is generally a vague one, with the secondary characters being but faintly evoked. Two notable exceptions are the able story "Ages" and the superbly realized "Red Jelly."

Eithne Strong's recent novel, *The Love Riddle* (1993), is probably her best work. The present plot is set in 1942 and concerns a young girl from the West and an altruistic, impoverished Englishman who, although older, is still a student and still seeking his mission in life. At the end, they marry, but much of the book is taken up with their past lives. The girl's life is dramatized in long and usually effective scenes, but the man's is, for the most part, tersely related, and this fact gives the book a certain imbalance. Also, many of the characters remain mere names rather than dramatized creations, even the significant figure of the hero's guru, a character probably based on Jonathan Hanaghan. This character, despite his importance for the theme and even for the story, stays mainly off-stage, and what he stands for remains pretty dim. There are passages of effective writing, especially in the heroine's flashbacks, but Strong can still, at any time, relapse into turgidly portentous prose, such as:

Rather, you thought of her as a solitary, irreversible force, kept on her inexorable, commanding feet, it seemed, by some unquenchable anger, the reason for which there continued divers apocrypha.

Or:

The moment by moment exigence of an unremitting purification, not as selfish achievement ensuring a personal place in Paradise, but as an endowment—according to all the teaching, grace from such a life was, in some miraculous uncomprehended but promised way, to be bestowed upon others.

WORKS: *Poetry Quartos*. Dublin: Runa, 1943–1945; *Songs of Living*. Dublin: Runa, 1961. (Poetry); "Red Jelly." In *Winter's Tales from Ireland 2*. Kevin Casey, ed. Dublin: Gill & Macmillan/Newark, Del.: Proscenium, 1972, pp. 95–110. (Story); *Sarah*. In *Passing*. Dublin: Runa, 1974. (Poetry); "Ages." In *New Irish Writing*. David Marcus, ed. London: Quartet, [1976], pp. 139–147. (Story); *Degrees of Kindred*. Dublin: Tansy, [1979]. (Novel); *Cuirt Oibre*. Baile Atha Cliath: Coisceim, 1980. (Irish poetry); *Flesh . . . the Greatest Sin*. Monkstown, Co. Dublin: Runa, [1980]. (Poetry); *Patterns*. [Swords, Co. Dublin]: Poolbeg, [1981]. (Short stories); *Fuil agus Fallai*. Baile Atha

Cliath: Coiscéim, 1983. (Irish poetry); *My Darling Neighbour*. Dublin: Beaver Row, 1985. (Poetry); *Aoife fé Ghlas*. Baile Atha Cliath: Coiscéim, 1990. (Irish poetry); *An Sagart Pinc*. Baile Atha Cliath: Coiscéim, 1990. (Irish poetry); *Let Live*. Galway: Salmon, 1990. (Poetry); *The Love Riddle*. Dublin: Attic, [1993]. (Novel); *Spatial Nosing: New and Selected Poems*. [Swords, Co. Dublin]: Salmon, [1993]. REFERENCE: Wright, Nancy Means & Hannan, Dennis. "An Interview with Eithne Strong." *Irish Literary Supplement* 13 (Spring 1994): 13–15.

STRONG, L[EONARD] A[LFRED] G[EORGE] (1896–1958), man of letters. Strong was born in Plymouth, England, on March 8, 1896, of a half Irish father and a wholly Irish mother. The summers of his childhood were spent largely in Ireland. He won an open classical scholarship to Oxford, was kept out of World War I by illness, and took his B.A. in 1920. Until 1930, he was a schoolmaster at Summer Fields School, Oxford, and then the success of one of his books persuaded him to live entirely by his writing. He was an extremely prolific and varied writer (the bibliography below is only a selected one). His poetry compels respect, and some of his fiction, admiration (his book *Travellers* of 1945, for instance, won the James Tait Black Prize). He also wrote film scripts, short and full-length plays, children's books, school books, detective stories, and unacademic literary criticism of some distinction.

Strong's serious fiction may be divided into stories with an Irish background, a Devonshire background, and a background of the Scottish Western Highlands. His finest Irish work is in two somewhat interrelated novels, *The Garden* (1931) and *Sea Wall* (1933). Both books are minor classics of modern Irish literature. They lovingly and memorably evoke that five or six miles of the eastern seacoast that stretches from Dun Laoghaire pier to Sandycove and the Forty Foot, past Bullock Harbor and Dalkey Island, around Sorrento Point, and into Killiney Bay. Anyone who knows that small picturesque portion of Ireland will recognize with startled pleasure Strong's still little-changed picture of some sixty years ago. Strong once remarked to R. L. Megroz, "I see a new novel as a landscape first, with hills and perhaps a sea-coast and bays and promontories. There are one or two clouds obscuring features of the picture. Presently the clouds begin to clear away, and then I have the main events, represented by the chief landmarks." The sense of place and a nostalgia for youth distinctively permeate these two novels, but the characterization is rather fine also—down even to the irascible pet monkey of *The Garden*. If there is any authorial forcing in the books, it is in the endings. The death of the autobiographical character in *The Garden* seems a contrived bid for poignance, perhaps appropriate thematically, but certainly disconcerting factually. The ending of *Sea Wall* has the superb idea of an airplane flight giving the hero a panoramic view of his landscape, but onto this Strong attaches a bit of thematic question-begging which hardly rises out of his narrative. Of the two books, *The Garden* is more of an essayistic evocation, while *Sea Wall* is more vigorously fictionized. It has a finely realized scene about the killing of a conger eel, as well as some boxing and swimming matches which the hero usually wins, that could come out of superior boys' fiction and that at least one critic has seen as a kind of anterior wish-fulfillment.

Strong's *The Director* (1944) also has an Irish setting, and is a lesser, but worthy book. His poetry is usually fluent and graceful. At his poorest, he has the bland conventionality of the minor poet, but at his best—as in "A Young Man Drowned" or "The Door"—he is capable of a tight and memorable line. He is probably best known, albeit unfairly, for his little light verse "The Brewer's Man." In 1938, he became a director of the Methuen publishing house. He died in Guildford, Surrey, on August 17, 1958. His posthumous autobiography, *Green Memory* (1961), contains some excellent glimpses of Yeats.*

PRINCIPAL WORKS: *Dublin Days*. Oxford: Blackwell, 1921. (Poems); *The Lowery Road*. Oxford, 1923. (Poems); *Doyle's Rock and Other Stories*. Oxford: Blackwell, 1925; *Difficult Love*. Oxford: Blackwell, 1927. (Poems); *Dewer Rides*. London: Gollancz, 1929; *The English Captain, and Other Stories*. London: Gollancz, 1929; *The Jealous Ghost*. London: Gollancz, 1930. (Novel); *Northern Light*. London: Gollancz, 1930. (Poems); *Selected Poems*. London: Hamish Hamilton, 1931; *The Garden*. London: Gollancz, 1931. (Novel); *The Brothers*. London: Gollancz, 1932. (Novel); *Don Juan and the Wheelbarrow*. London: Gollancz, 1932; *A Letter to W. B. Yeats*. London: Leonard & Virginia Woolf, 1932. (Pamphlet); *Personal Remarks*. London: Peter Nevill, 1933. (Essays); *Sea Wall*. London: Gollancz, 1933. (Novel); *Corporal Tune*. London: Gollancz, 1934. (Novel); *The Seven Arms*. London: Gollancz, 1935; *Tuesday Afternoon, and Other Stories*. London: Gollancz, 1935; *Call to the Swan*. London: Hamish Hamilton, 1936. (Poems); *The Last Enemy*. London: Gollancz, 1936; *The Minstrel Boy, a Portrait of Tom Moore*. London: Hodder & Stoughton, 1937; *The Fifth of November*. London: Dent, 1937; *The Swift Shadow*. London: Gollancz, 1937; *The Open Sky*. London: Gollancz, 1939; *Sun on the Water, and Other Stories*. London: Gollancz, 1940; *The Bay*. London: Gollancz, 1941. (Novel); *House in Disorder*. London & Redhill: Lutterworth, 1941; *John McCormack, the True Story of a Singer*. London: Methuen, 1941; *John Millington Synge*. London: Allen & Unwin, 1941; *Slocombe Dies*. London: Collins, 1942; *The Unpractised Heart*. London: Gollancz, 1942; *The Director*. London: Methuen, 1944. (Novel); *All Fall Down*. London: Collins, 1944; *Travellers*. London: Methuen, 1945. (Stories, winner of the James Tait Black Memorial Prize); *The Sacred River, an Approach to James Joyce*. London: Methuen, 1949; *Darling Tom, and Other Stories*. London: Methuen, 1952; *The Hill of Howth*. London: Methuen, 1952; *John Masefield*. London: Longmans, Green, 1952. (Pamphlet); The *Writer's Trade*. London: Methuen, 1953; *Deliverance*. London: Methuen, 1955; *Dr. Quicksilver, 1660–1742. The Life and Times of Thomas Dover, M.D.* London: Andrew Melrose, 1955; *The Body's Imperfection. The Collected Poems of L.A.G. Strong*. London: Methuen, 1957; *Green Memory*. London: Methuen, 1961. (Autobiography). Also many children's stories and novels.

STRONG, RUPERT (1911–1984), poet and psychoanalyst. Strong was born in London on May 10, 1911. He came to Ireland in 1937 and graduated from Trinity College. He studied psychoanalysis under Jonathan Hanaghan, whose personality made a great impact upon him. He then became a practicing psychoanalyst in 1944 and made an enviable reputation for warmth and kindness. With his wife, Eithne,* he established the Runa Press, which published a few, often handsome volumes, usually of poetry. His own poems are enthusiastic, occasionally witty, and his themes, sometimes on sexual passion, are refreshingly direct. Individuality, however, is small compensation for ability, and it must be said that his work generally has little poetic ability. Nevertheless, to record one dissenting vote, it might be noted that Bertrand Russell found his poems remarkable. He died in Dublin on December 6, 1984.

PRINCIPAL WORK: *Selected Poems*. Monkstown, Dublin: Runa, 1974.

STUART, [HENRY] FRANCIS M[ONTGOMERY] (1902–   ), novelist. Stuart, the son of a prosperous sheep rancher originally from County Antrim, was born on April 29, 1902, in Townsville, Australia. Less than a year later, following the death of his father, he was brought to Ireland. He grew up in Meath, although as a boy he spent considerable time with relatives in the North of Ireland. Stuart was educated at various preparatory schools in England; the last was Rugby, which he left in 1918 without graduating. In 1920, at age eighteen, he married Iseult Gonne, the natural daughter of French deputy Lucien Millevoye and Irish nationalist Maud Gonne. During the Irish civil war, Stuart fought on the republican side until his capture by Free State troops in August 1922. He was held in Maryborough Prison and later in the Curragh compound until November 1923.

The following year, the war over, Stuart published his first book, a privately printed collection of poems called *We Have Kept the Faith,* dated 1923 but released early in 1924. While continuing to write poetry of a decidedly romantic temper during the next several years, Stuart began to sense that his ''real interests,'' as he later put it, were far more in certain experiences—very often personal experiences, human relationships, human activities—which are certainly not best communicated through poetry'' (''An Interview with Francis Stuart,'' *Journal of Irish Literature* [January 1976]). His first novel, *Women and God* (1931), an uneasy mix of lyricism and Hemingwayesque realism, was a failure critically and aesthetically, but his next two books, *Pigeon Irish* (1932) and *The Coloured Dome* (1932), flawed though they are, demonstrated genuine talent and were well received. Yeats,* writing to Olivia Shakespear, called *The Coloured Dome* ''strange and exciting in theme and perhaps more personally and beautifully written than any book of our generation'' (*Letters of W. B. Yeats,* ed. Allan Wade, 1955). In each novel, the author leads his protagonist from a life of safety and staleness though painful, isolating experiences that leave him outcast and, at the same time, provide him with a depth of spiritual insight witheld from those who live protected lives. The same narrative pattern dominates all of Stuart's major fiction. From 1933 through 1940, he published eight more novels and had two plays produced at the Abbey* (neither these plays nor three others have been published). None of the books is of compelling importance, although *Try the Sky* (1933), *The Angel of Pity* (1935), and *The White Hare* (1936) offer important insight into his thought.

In 1940, troubled by a declining career as well as by lingering financial and marital problems and perhaps unconsciously compelled to live out the narrative pattern of his novels, Stuart accepted a position as lecturer in English and Irish literature at the University of Berlin, where he stayed, except for some months in Luxembourg, for the duration of World War II. In November 1945, after the war in Europe ended, he was arrested by French occupation forces and imprisoned first in Bregenz and later in Freiburg until July 1946. Though no formal charges were brought against him, he was detained presumably because of a series of weekly radio broadcasts he had made to Ireland from 1942 to 1944, in which he took a pro-German perspective on world events, commented on Irish literature and domestic affairs, and called for Ireland's continued neutrality. After his release, he lived in Freiburg, Germany, until 1949, when he moved to Paris. In 1951 he went to London, where he lived for seven years. Then, in 1954, following the death of Iseult, who had remained in Ireland, he married Gertrud Meissner, whom he had met at the University of Berlin and with whom he had been imprisoned in Germany. He returned to Ireland in 1958 and lived near Dunshaughlin in County Meath before moving to the Windy Arbour section of Dublin in 1971.

Understandably, Stuart's activities in wartime Germany have raised serious questions about his politics. Although he has consistently disavowed any political intent or interest, his work displays a strong antipathy toward liberal democracy and other hallmarks of modernity such as rationalism, empiricism, materialism, and urban industrialism. Although his Christian-anarchist sensibility kept him from embracing Nazi ideology, he was not immune to its appeal, as it was at least the opposite of many of the values he deplored in modern society. In this, he resembled those radical conservatives described in Fritz Stern's *The Politics of Cultural Despair* (1961; rpt. Berkeley: University of California Press, 1974) who were drawn to Hitler as a great destructive force capable of bringing down the structure of the modern world. Out of the rubble he hoped renewal would come through the recovery of a past very much like the one he imagined to be characteristic of the Apostolic Age—a spiritual community rooted in familial groups, each cohering around a core of shared suffering, compassion, and love.

Stuart's literary reputation will finally rest on the novels that appeared after the war. The narrative pattern that informed the earlier works was largely imaginative and not firmly rooted in lived experience. While remaining essentially the same in outline during the later period, the pattern takes on a new and more intense power, for Stuart himself had now passed through that ritualistic initiation he had mapped out intuitively for the main characters of the early books.

The two novels that open his postwar career, *The Pillar of Cloud* (1948) and *Redemption* (1949), are among Stuart's strongest works and assure him a significant place among Irish writers of his generation. *The Pillar of Cloud* is set in Germany just after the war and records the spiritual journey of Irish poet Dominic Malone, whose own suffering along with that shared by those close to him results in new perceptions about the value of compassion, fraternity, and selfless love. *Redemption,* set in postwar Ireland, focuses on Ezra Arrigho, who has returned to his homeland after spending the war years in Germany. He has brought with him the terrible knowledge of the human capacity for savagery, but this, he believes, is a knowledge of a past left mercifully behind in the blackened rubble of wartime Germany. Subconsciously, he finds comfort in the safe, predictable life he leads in Ireland. But the precarious balance between past and present is upset when a friend of his brutally rapes and murders a young woman. Evil, he is forced to acknowledge, is not something that can be left behind. His anguish and despair, together with the spiritual guidance of Father Mellowes, result eventually, if hesitantly, in insights that are essentially the same as Dominic's.

From 1950 to 1959, Stuart published six more novels; among the best, though flawed, are *The Flowering Cross* (1950) and *Victors and Vanquished* (1958). Then in 1971, after twelve years of silence, he published *Black List, Section H,* a closely autobiographical novel that Lawrence Durrell described as ''a book of the finest imaginative distinction'' (*New York Times Book Review,* April 9, 1972). Here Stuart returns to his German years and traces the psychic quest of his central character, H, whose unsettling and often painful experiences lead him to new depths of personal and spiritual understanding and reveal the necessarily marginal position of the artist in society. *Black List* marks the beginning of a third productive phase in his career. As in the first two periods, however, he is unable to sustain the early impulse, and none of the novels that follow are of as much interest as *Black List,* although *A Hole in the Head* (1977), *The High Consistory* (1981), and *Faillandia* (1985) are of interest, the last particularly for its political implications.

In 1981, Stuart was inducted into Aosdána,* his first significant public recognition in Ireland since he had been invited, nearly a half-century before, to join Yeats's Irish Academy of Letters in 1932. His only other formal recognition was eight years before that when *We Have Kept the Faith* received awards from the Royal Irish Academy and from Harriet Monroe's *Poetry: A Magazine of Verse.*

A year after the death of his wife, Gertrud, in 1986, Stuart married artist Finola Graham; and three years later, at age eighty-eight, he published still another novel, perhaps his last, *A Compendium of Lovers.*

JERRY H. NATTERSTAD

WORKS: *We Have Kept the Faith.* Dublin: Oak, 1923 [1924]. (Poems); *Nationality and Culture.* Baile Atha Cliath: Sinn Fein Ardchomhairle, 1924. (Pamphlet); *Mystics and Mysticism.* Dublin: Catholic Truth Society of Ireland, [1929]. (Pamphlet); *Women and God.* London: Jonathan Cape, 1931. (Novel); *Pigeon Irish.* London: Gollancz/New York: Macmillan, 1932. (Novel); *The Coloured Dome.* London: Gollancz, 1932/New York: Macmillan, 1933. (Novel); *Try the Sky.* London: Gollancz/New York: Macmillan, 1933. (Novel); *Glory.* London: Gollancz/New York: Macmillan, 1933. (Novel); *Things to Live For: Notes for an Autobiography.* London: Jonathan Cape, 1934/New York: Macmillan, 1935; *In Search of Love.* London: Collins/New York: Macmillan, 1935. (Novel); *The Angel of Pity.* London: Grayson & Grayson, 1935. (Novel); *The White Hare.* London: Collins/New York: Macmillan, 1936. (Novel); *Racing for Pleasure and Profit in Ireland and Elsewhere.* Dublin: Talbot, 1937. (Handbook); *The Bridge.* London: Collins, 1937. (Novel); *Julie.* London: Collins/New York: Knopf, 1938. (Novel); *The Great Squire.* London: Collins, 1939. (Novel); *Der Fall Casement.* Translated by Ruth Weiland. Hamburg: Hanseatische Verlag, [1940]. (Pamphlet on Sir Roger Casement); *The Pillar of Cloud.* London: Gollancz, 1948. (Novel); *Redemption.* London: Gollancz, 1949/ New York: Devin-Adair, 1950. (Novel); *The Flowering Cross.* London: Gollancz/Toronto: Longmans, 1950. (Novel); *Good Friday's Daughter.* London: Gollancz/Toronto: Bond Street, 1952. (Novel); *The Chariot.* London: Gollancz/Toronto: Bond Street, 1953. (Novel); *The Pilgrimage.* London: Gollancz/Toronto: Bond Street, 1955. (Novel); *Victors and Vanquished.* London: Gollancz, 1958/Cleveland: Pennington, 1959/London: Martin Brian & O'Keeffe, 1974. (Novel); *Angels of Providence.* London: Gollancz/Toronto: Doubleday, 1959. (Novel); *Black List, Section H.* Carbondale & Edwardsville: Southern Illinois University Press/London & Amsterdam: Feffer & Simons, 1971. (Novel); *Memorial.* London: Martin Brian & O'Keeffe, 1973. (Novel); *A Hole in the Head.* London: Martin Brian & O'Keeffe, 1977. (Novel); *The High Consistory.* London: Martin Brian & O'Keeffe, 1981. (Novel); *We Have Kept the Faith: New and Selected Poems.* Dublin: Raven Arts, 1982. (Poems); *States of Mind: Selected Short Prose.* Dublin: Raven Arts/London: Martin Brian & O'Keeffe, 1984. (Collection of fiction and nonfiction); *Faillandia.* Dublin: Raven Arts, 1985. (Novel); *The Abandoned Snail Shell.* Dublin: Raven Arts, 1987. (Philosophy); *Night Pilot.* Dublin: Raven Arts, 1988. (Poems); *A Compendium of Lovers.* Dublin: Raven Arts, 1990. (Novel). REFERENCES: Elborn, Geoffrey. *Francis Stuart: A Life.* Dublin: Raven Arts, 1990; Honan, Kevin. "Refloating the Ark: Figural Motifs in the Writings of Francis Stuart." *Irish Review* 4 (Spring 1988): 66–72; Maxton, Hugh [W. J. McCormack], ed. *A Festschrift for Francis Stuart on His Seventieth Birthday.* Dublin: Dolmen, 1972; Molloy, Frances. "The Life of Francis Stuart: Questions and Some Answers." *Biography* 10 (Spring 1987): 129–141; Natterstad, J. H. *Francis Stuart.* Lewisburg, Pa.: Bucknell University Press, 1974; Natterstad, J. H., ed. "A Francis Stuart Number." *Journal of Irish Literature* 5 (January 1976); Natterstad, J. H. "Francis Stuart: The Artist as Outcast." In *Studies in Anglo-Irish Literature.* Bonn: Bouvier Verlag, 1982; Natterstad, J. H. "Locke's Swoon: Francis Stuart and the Politics of Despair." *Éire-Ireland* 26 (Winter 1991): 58–75; Rafroidi, Patrick & Harmon, Maurice, eds. *The Irish Novel in Our Time.* Lille: Publications de l'Université de Lille III, 1975–1976, pp. 157–183; Stuart, Madeleine. *Manna in the Morning: A Memoir 1940–1958.* Dublin: Raven Arts, 1984.

SULLIVAN, A[LEXANDER] M[ARTIN] (1830–1884), journalist and historian. Sullivan, the younger brother of T. D. Sullivan,* was born in Bantry, County Cork, in 1830. The brothers' careers were somewhat parallel, both being editors of *The Nation** and active in politics. A. M. was involved with Isaac Butt in the formation of the Home Rule party, and the Grattan statue in College Green was erected with money collected for him when he was in jail for his opinions on the Manchester Martyrs. His minor contribution to literature is a readable history, *The Story of Ireland.* He died on October 17, 1884, in Dublin.

PRINCIPAL WORKS: *New Ireland.* 2 vols. London: S. Low, Marston, Searle & Rivington, 1877; *A "Nutshell" History of Ireland.* London: Sampson Low, 1883; *The Story of Ireland.* Providence, R.I.: H. McElroy, 1883; *Speeches and Addresses.* 4th ed. Dublin: T. D. Sullivan, 1886. REFERENCE: Sullivan, T. D. *A. M. Sullivan. A Memoir.* Dublin: T. D. Sullivan, 1885.

SULLIVAN, BREDA (1945–   ), poet. Born in Athlone, Sullivan trained as a primary teacher. Her *Smell of Camphor* (1992) is composed of clear, short pieces arranged in very short lines, with no rhyme and very little rhythm. It would be difficult to defend many of them as free verse, except that they are very tightly written, with few words wasted. As small squibs of writing, however, they are alternately funny, sardonic, and even luminous. Of a few pieces like "Horizons," one must say that, if this is not poetry, it is the essence of it.

WORK: *A Smell of Camphor.* [Galway: Salmon, 1992].

SULLIVAN, T[IMOTHY] D[ANIEL] (1827–1914), editor, politician, and poet. Sullivan was born on May 29, 1827, in Bantry, County Cork. He wrote for *The Nation** and became its editor on the retirement of his brother, A. M. Sullivan.* He was lord mayor of Dublin in 1886–1887, was associated with

Parnell in the Land League agitation, and was a member of Parliament from 1880 to 1900. He published half a dozen volumes of patriotic verse, all of which is now forgotten save for the rousing "God Save Ireland." He died on March 31, 1914.

WORKS: *Dunboy and Other Poems*. Dublin: J. F. Fowler, 1861; *Green Leaves. A Volume of Irish Verses*. 11th ed. Dublin: T. D. Sullivan, 1887; *"Guilty or Not Guilty?" Speeches from the Dock*, ed., with A. M. Sullivan & D. B. Sullivan. 23d ed. Dublin: T. D. Sullivan, 1882. (This volume was more generally known as *Speeches from the Dock* and went through many editions, a recent one being edited and continued up to 1921 by Sean Ua Ceallaigh and published by Gill in Dublin in 1945); *A. M. Sullivan. A Memoir*. Dublin: T. D. Sullivan, 1885; *Lays of the Land League*. Dublin, 1887; *A Guide to Dublin*. 2d ed. Dublin: T. D. Sullivan, [1888]; *Poems:* Dublin: T. D. Sullivan, [1888]; *Prison Poems*. Dublin: Nation Office, [1888]; *A Selection from the Songs and Poems of T. D. Sullivan*. Dublin: Sealy, 1899; *Recollections of Troubled Times in Irish Politics*. Dublin: Sealy, Bryers & M. H. Gill, 1905; *Evergreen. A Volume of Irish Verses*. Dublin: Sealy, Bryers & Walker, 1907; *Bantry, Berehaven, and the O'Sullivan Sept*. Dublin: Sealy, Bryers, 1908.

SWEENEY, MATTHEW (1952–   ), poet. Sweeney was born in Lifford, County Donegal, and was educated at Gormanstown College and at the University of Freiburg. Since 1973, he has lived mainly in London. In 1982 and 1989, he was awarded Irish Arts Council bursaries and in 1992 a British Arts Council bursary. In 1984, he received the Prudence Farmer Prize, in 1987 the Cholmondely Award, and in 1986 a Henfield Writing Fellowship. He is a member of Aosdána.*

Sweeney usually writes in rather short lines that have no rhyme and not much reason to their rhythm. His poetry generally relies more on statement than on imagery, but the style is tight, lean, and nearly uncuttable. Many of the poems—"No Welcome," for instance—crackle with energy. Many others—"A Round House," "New Year Party," "The Dancehall"—have the dramatic immediacy of a speaking voice. Among minor quirks, he will often use an ampersand in one line, spell out "and" in the next, and revert to the ampersand in the third. Possibly, there is a reason.

WORKS: *A Dream of Maps*. [Dublin]: Raven Arts, [1981]; *A Round House*. Dublin: Raven Arts/London: Allison & Busby, [1983]; *The Lame Waltzer*. Dublin: Raven Arts/London: Allison & Busby, [1985]; *The Chinese Dressing Gown*. 1987. (Children's fiction; *Blue Shoes*. London: Secker & Warburg, 1989; *Casti*. London: Secker & Warburg, 1992; *Flying Spring Onion*. London: Faber, 1992. (Children's poetry); *The Snow Vulture*. 1992. (Children's fiction).

SWEETMAN, ELINOR MARY (1860–?), poet. Sweetman was the third daughter of Michael James Sweetman of Lamberton Park, County Laois, and his wife, the former Miss Powell, of Fitzwilliam Square, Dublin. Her sisters, Mary and Agnes, both were writers. Mary published under the pseudonym of M. E. Francis, while Agnes used her married name, Mrs. Lewis Anthony Egerton Castle. Elinor Sweetman was educated by governesses at home, then in Brussels and London. Her primary interest was music, and Katharine Tynan notes in *The Cabinet of Irish Literature*, "to that she has devoted the greater portion of her life."

ANNE COLMAN

WORKS: *Footsteps of the Gods, and Other Poems*. London: G. Bell, 1893; *Pastorals, and Other Poems*. London: J. M. Dent, 1899; *Palms*. 1911; *The Wild Orchard*. London: Herbert & Daniel, [1911].

SWIFT, JONATHAN (1667–1745), the great prose satirist of the English language. A hero's welcome awaited Jonathan Swift when he arrived in Dublin during August 1726. In the manner of a modern ticker-tape parade, flags, streamers, church bells, and large bonfires marked his return from England. He had earned the grudging respect of his adversary Robert Walpole and the Whig ministers as a forceful and independent spokesman for Irish interests; he had enjoyed the hospitality and attention of Alexander Pope and subsequent reunion with his literary and political friends of the years 1710–1714, when he was a forceful spokesman for Queen Anne and the Tory cause. Not the least, he had successfully arranged for the printing of his greatest work, *Gulliver's Travels*, which was published on October 28, 1726, by Benjamin Motte in London. In a similar show of exuberant affection, according to the *Dublin Journal*, Dubliners observed Swift's sixty-fifth birthday with new fires and other symbols celebrating this authentic "Hibernian Patriot" who had rallied public opinion for the cause of Irish economic and political independence in his role as M. B. Drapier of St. Francis Street. The ringing words of his Fourth Drapier Letter, addressed to the "Whole People of Ireland"—"by the Laws of God, of Nature, of Nations, and of your own Country, you are and ought to be as Free a people as your brethren in England"—have inspired patriots of countless nations of the world.

In our own time, as well as during the nineteenth century, Irishmen have warmly praised Swift and defended his right to the title of patriot. Indeed, the poet William Butler Yeats,* who wrote his own version of Swift's Latin epitaph in 1929 and a writer "haunted," as he said, by Swift's presence and genius, argues that in *The Drapier's Letters* Swift not only discovered his own Irishness but also "created the political nationality of Ireland." As an Irish legendary figure, a whole body of folklore—some of it humorously detrimental, even, at times, scurrilous—has developed around Swift, attesting to the affection and trust of his fellow countrymen. This mixture of fact and fiction has elevated the life of the dean of St. Patrick's Cathedral, Dublin, to a truly mythical status.

All of this praise and recognition was directed, however, toward a most unlikely candidate as Irish hero. Swift writes, "I do suppose nobody hates and despises this kingdom more than myself"; refers to Ireland as "the most miserable country upon earth"; and describes the trip from England to Ireland as "a passage to the land I hate." Instead of the "fat deanery or lean bishopric" he so assiduously but vainly sought near his literary friends in England, he returned, in 1713, as dean of St. Patrick's to make this "wretched Dublin in Ireland" his permanent home, "a poisoned rat in a hole," as he vividly describes his situation to Bolingbroke. In fact, as early as 1709 Swift complained about the prospects of living in Ireland. A rather self-pitying letter to Esther

Vanhomrigh (Vanessa), written from his country vicarage in Laracor, exhibits this incipient moroseness, which he terms "discontent" and "dulness." This correspondence also documents an unsuccessful but tantalizing love affair expressed in Swift's longest, but controversial poem (for some) *Cadenus and Vanessa* (1713, published in 1726), which employs the fiction of an orderly courtroom debate about the reasons for the insufficiency of love in the world that curiously seems at odds with the unresolved nature of the emotional conflicts depicted:

> Whether the nymph, to please her swain,
> Talks in a high romantic strain;
> Or whether he at last descends
> To like with less seraphic ends;
> Or, to compound the business, whether
> They temper love and books together;
> Must never to mankind be told,
> Nor shall the conscious muse unfold.

Swift's correspondence, as well as the *Journal to Stella,* at times displays a similar coyness and evasive tone. But it also reveals Swift's talent for irony, and role playing, traits characteristic of his most effective prose satire. This mixture of melancholy, anger, and exuberance is quite possibly the calculated stance of the satirist. In light of the many positive depictions of his Irish situation, his letters are less than a trustworthy index to his true feelings, hardly the sincere "representations of his mind," in the words of his first but severely critical biographer, Lord Orrery* (John Boyle). While he is expressing deeply pessimistic attitudes to Pope and Bolingbroke, he is simultaneously corresponding with friends such as Patrick Delany,* Mrs. Howard, Thomas Sheridan,* and the Achesons in the North of Ireland; clearly relishing his social life, influence, and fame in Dublin; even praising Irish weather, advocating Irish food and wine, and talking in a self-satisfied manner about his Irish lifestyle—all at the expense of the English counterparts. It is true, we have come to suspect his dark view of Dublin life as the deliberate self-portrait of the archetypal literary exile, as well as the artist sensitive to the expectations of his English friends. Nevertheless, Swift was deeply ambivalent not only about Ireland in general but also about his particular relationship to the Anglo-Irish colonialists of the late seventeenth and early eighteenth centuries.

The Ireland into which Swift was born on November 30, 1667, was politically unsettled, a whipping boy of changing British governments. It was thoroughly colonized by the Stuarts, who created a Protestant ruling aristocracy amid a relatively poor Catholic population and intimidated clergy. A native Irish rebellion in 1641 helped precipitate the English civil wars; and in 1649, sensing the political need for a foreign excursion as a show of strength, Oliver Cromwell attacked Ireland. The infamous Settlement Act of 1652 dispossessed, to some degree, every Irish landowner, and these lands in question were redistributed to Cromwell's sympathizers. After the Restoration of Charles II in 1660, some land reverted to the former owners; but after the Glorious Revolution of 1688, when James II made his last, desperate stand against William of Orange at the Boyne in 1690, the ownership of land was again scrambled, the bulk of the properties going to supporters of the victorious William regardless of prior claim or nationality. By 1700, England repossessed the lands to sell them to the highest bidders. Unlike the successful Scottish union with England in 1707, the Irish petition of the same year was denied and, along with it, great economic benefits, free trade, and representation in the English Parliament. To be sure, Dublin had a respected parliamentary government with a long history, but it was virtually powerless, able to enact only laws agreed on previously by London. Moreover, it was undemocratically self-perpetuating and inbred.

Born of English parents who had recently moved to Dublin, Swift received the best education that the English governing class in Ireland could provide. Graduating from the Kilkenny School, he entered Trinity College, Dublin, in 1682, and received a degree four years later. While pursuing an M.A. at Oxford (which he completed in 1692), political uncertainties in the wake of the revolution of 1688 forced Swift to England. The decade that followed, 1689–1699, affected his future enormously.

During most of these years, Swift was employed as secretary to Sir William Temple of Moor Park, Surrey, a retired Whig diplomat instrumental in forming the Triple Alliance (England, Holland, and Sweden) and in arranging the marriage of William and Mary. Swift read widely, tried his hand at Cowley-style Pindaric odes (which he soon gave up), and met Esther Johnson (Stella), with whom he shared love and friendship until her death in 1728 and to whom he addressed eleven poems, seven of which are birthday greetings notable for their generosity of spirit, sincerity, elegant but direct style, and authenticity of feeling. But most important, Swift began to develop his literary talents by immersing himself in editorial work on Temple's essays and letters. This experience engendered in Swift the social and intellectual attitudes characteristic of an urbane, sophisticated man of letters of the late seventeenth century. It also exposed him to the combination of aristocratic worldliness and hard-nosed antiromantic realism of the politics of the period. These two important qualities—self-assurance and a realistic view of human experience—are, of course, essential ingredients of the satiric temperament.

In 1694, failure to secure preferment in England drove Swift back to Ireland. He was subsequently ordained an Anglican priest and assumed his first parish duty as prebend of Kilroot, north of Belfast. It was during this period that Swift had a relationship with Jane Waring, to whom he proposed marriage. Four years later Swift refused to marry, although she was more than willing. In 1670, because of Temple's importuning and his own dissatisfaction with such a remote parish consisting mostly of Presbyterians, Swift returned to Moor Park in 1696 and remained there until Temple's death in 1699. Little is known of these years in Kilroot, but being situated in the center of Protestant dissent seems to have inspired what, for some, is his most brilliant prose satire, *A Tale of a Tub,* which includes the *Battle of the Books and the Discourse concerning the Mechanical Operation of the Spirit,* written these last years at Moor Park but published in 1704 and in its final form, with the famous "Apology," in 1710. Satirizing the "numerous and gross Corruptions in Religion and Learning," the *Tale* owes much to Temple's own treatise on ancient and modern learning, a late seventeenth-century version of a perennial debate reaching back to the Renaissance. The *Battle* employs a mock-heroic framework popular with the Augustans within which Swift introduces an entertaining and skillful allegory of a bee and a spider to represent this conflict. Swift strikes a blow for "sweetness and light," that is, for the continuities and verities of traditional humanistic culture and the intangibles of faith and wisdom. As a whole, the *Tale* ridicules forms of pride, irrationality, and delusion, especially the brands revealed in the excesses of religious dissent. The mindlessness of "modern" self-importance, self-assertion, and self-exhibition, Swift believed, led to human folly and moral corruption— a satiric theme on which he provided many variations throughout his career. His point about pride is summed up in the hack's assertion that "what I am going to say is literally true this Minute I am writing," as well as by his gleeful boast that "[i]n my Disposure of Employments of the Brain, I have thought first to make *Invention* the *Master,* and give *Method* and *Reason,* the Office of its *Lacquays.*" The paradox at the heart of this complex work is that, while Swift's own parodic art satirizes the insane world of the modern whose imagination has gotten "astride on" his better reason, Swift also demonstrates the extraordinary imaginative energies and anarchic impulses responsible for "modern" insanity itself. Although "Reason" may be "true and just," as Swift writes in his sermon *On the Trinity,* "the Reason of every particular man is weak and wavering, perpetually swayed and turned by his interests, his passions, and his vices." For some, the contradiction at the conceptual core of the *Tale* marks the high point of Swiftian self-realization, giving the work its truth and power, but, for others, these complexities indicate confused satiric purpose, perversity, even psychic instability. The consensus seems to be that the *Tale* exemplifies "the common principle of his comic irony, posing as the embodiment of what he hates, and recommending persons or practices that he detests."

Like so many of his opinions, Swift's political attitudes during this formative period were complex and paradoxical. Under the influence of Temple, he was committed to the Whig concept of rational liberty with its scorn of political absolutes and fear of excessive reliance of the church on the state and vice versa. His *Contests and Dissensions in Athens and Rome* (1701), a response to extreme Tory partisanship, supported the principle of checks and balances in government to ensure political stability, yet tolerance of differences of opinion. Such a position he later praised under the guise of the mixed state republican government of the practical-minded and commonsensical King of Brobdingnag, of Book Two of *Gulliver's Travels.* So important was this idea of rational freedom in his life that he incorporated a reference in his apologia pro vita sua, "Verses on the Death of Dr. Swift":

Fair *Liberty* was all his cry;
For her he stood prepared to die;
For her he boldly stood alone;
For her he oft expos'd his own.

Nonetheless, this political liberalism increasingly conflicted with Swift's innate conservatism and his obligation to defend the Anglican Church against Whig attempts to weaken its authority by accommodating deists, dissenters, and non-conformists of whatever stripe. Swift's *Contests and Dissensions,* written in a straightforward, impersonal manner, is an early example of his ability to deal with ideas and his delight in controversy and also advances his reputation as a political moderate.

In the *Sentiments of a Church-of-England Man,* written about 1708, Swift argues for the independence and integrity of the Anglican Church within the framework of Whig political theory of the late seventeenth century. Its immediate impetus was the Whig desire to broaden the church's constituency by liberalizing the Test Act, which required holders of civil and political offices to be communicants in the Anglican faith. His spokesman assumes the character of a dispassionate, detached observer of controversy, refusing to become drawn in by extremists on either Whig or Tory side. The creation of complex fictional identities, both independent of the author Swift yet a form or mode of self-revelation, was to become characteristic rhetorical strategy for Swift. Here, in a private capacity, this altruistic apologist for the church seeks "to moderate between the Rival Powers." The speaker strikes the stance of the Augustan middle way, shunning extremes and appealing to reason, tolerance, and compromise between church and state interests.

Swift's *Sentiments* and the straightforward reformist piece *A Project for the Advancement of Religion and Reformation of Manners* (1709) indicate how large the concerns of the church loomed in Swift's consciousness during these early years of the eighteenth century. At the same time he is defending Anglican interests within the context of Whig political theory, he is approaching religious controversy in a highly oblique and ironic manner, characteristic of his most famous political and religious writings. His *Argument against Abolishing Christianity* (1708) presents the reader with what was to become the recurring Swiftian dilemma of choosing among unsatisfactory alternatives: the abolition of religion and establishment of a thoroughgoing secular society; the maintenance of nominal Christianity that permits the pursuit of worldly interests; or the return to "real Christianity," the most radical plan, which would entail breaking "the entire frame and constitution of things, to ruin trade, extinguish arts and sciences with the professors of them . . . to turn our courts, exchanges, and shops into deserts." Like the *Tale,* the arguments and style of this brilliant polemic signal Swift's inherent skepticism of reformative impulses in general and his own in particular and take the reader far beyond the immediate occasion of defending the Test Act. Even *Meditation upon a Broom-Stick* (1703), while ostensibly parodying the serious meditations of the scientist Robert Boyle, ironically scrutinizes "the universal Reformer and Corrector of Abuses." The satirist, like man as symbolic broom, is also a "topsy-turvy creature," his "Animal Faculties perpetually mounted on his Rational," revealing corruptions and stirring up a "mighty dust where there was none before; sharing deeply all the while in the very same Pollutions he pretends to sweep away." This self-reflexivity and self-mockery are vintage Swift.

Ironic playfulness and comic sensibility are nowhere better illustrated than in such pieces of this period as the *Bickerstaff Papers* (1708). Here Swift mocks his favorite targets, pretense, hypocrisy, and religious dissent, by means of an elaborate, zany procedure: his fictional astrologer challenges one of the day's best-known practitioners, John Partridge, to a battle involving the accuracy of predictions. Lamenting the corruption of the "art" in his and others' hands, Swift's Bickerstaff predicts the exact date of Partridge's death. The joke is extended into a second installment that describes through a letter the deathbed statement of astrologer Partridge, who confesses to fraud and fakery. The third and final installment, through further extension of the logic, converts the predictable protestations of Partridge that he is indeed alive into proof that he must be dead. Beneath the comic surface is Swift's continuing attack on pseudoscience posing as serious science, but not in the form of a scholarly refutation. Through a comic hoax Swift beats Partridge at his own game, which may indicate, among other things, Swift's lack of faith in rational persuasion.

A number of explanations have been advanced to account for Swift's political conversion to the Tory ministry of Harley and Bolingbroke in 1710. Swift's political beliefs were complex. His strong support of the Anglican Church against incursions on its authority and continuance and his passionate commitment to moderation in political and social realms both hinged on his recognition that man's beliefs and moral principles were subject to taint of human imperfection. Yet, some clues appear, however, in Swift's *Journal to Stella,* a series of letters recounting his daily activities between September 1710 and June 1711. The letters are addressed both to Esther Johnson (Stella) and to her friend Rebecca Dingley, who were settled in Ireland near his vicarage. Lord Treasurer Harley had interceded for Swift in his assignment to represent the Irish bishops before Queen Anne for the purpose of securing a remission to the clergy of the First Fruits and Twentieth Parts, a tax by the Crown on clerical benefices. Despite the playful, childlike nature of this correspondence, Letter VI shows Swift relishing the attention of the Tory Party, especially the assiduous cultivation of friendship by Harley himself, who, according to Swift, "loves the church" and "has a mind to gain me over." Among the possible reasons for Swift's embracing the new Tory government were the refusal, in 1707, of the first Whig minister, Godolphin, to honor requests for payments to the Irish clergy, the government's persecution of Henry Sacheverell for delivering a High Church sermon, and the increasing unpopularity of the War of the Spanish Succession. Whatever precisely triggered his decision, Swift's temperamental conservatism, devotion to the Anglican Church, and fear of Whig intentions both temporal and spiritual made the Tory cause appear increasingly the safer and more comfortable political persuasion.

At any rate, in this political atmosphere Swift contributed to a series of pamphlets entitled the *Examiner,* written from November 1710 to June 1711. The pamphlets were ostensibly designed to keep politicians and the public informed about the new government and to propagandize for the Tory cause. Despite his obvious partisanship, as "Mr. Examiner," Swift professes impartiality and detachment, usually eschewing "the Violences of either Party." With his growing genius for creating fictional identities, Swift maintains a cool, reasonable mask of moderation, breaking into religious indignation only as a calculated response to Whig provocations. His targets included political policy, the new "moneyed" class he held responsible for the long war, deism, or dissent, and individuals he personally despised, especially the earl of Wharton, the lord lieutenant of Ireland, and the duke of Marlborough, the famous Whig general of the Battle of Blenheim and Ramillies, whose death Swift was to memorialize viciously in a satiric mock-elegy. Swift's stance in the *Examiner* is that of the deliberate and objective observer, "convers[ing] in equal freedom with deserving men of both parties." But the partisanship that drove this pamphlet enterprise makes Swift's pose suspect. His best-known essay of this period, *The Conduct of the Allies* (1711), still considered an effective piece of partisan propaganda, became a kind of handbook of Tory arguments, despite occasional distortion of historical fact and a blindness to English international success under the Whigs. One commentator on this Tory tract has accused Swift of advocating "a sterile past," of being a conformist not alive and responsive to a changing society. Whatever their ultimate value, Swift's major and minor Tory apologetics do reveal, in incipient form, some of the literary techniques that would characterize his great satires: a carefully created fictional identity; a detached tone hiding angry concern; joy in an occasional withering denunciation; an ability to catch the flavor and texture of mad modernism, materialist habits of mind, and banal optimism.

In the three-year period immediately before his involvement in the Tory government of Harley and Bolingbroke, Swift produced, while in Ireland, *The Story of the Injured Lady* (1707), an allegorical dramatization of current Irish–English relations seen in the light of the union effected between England and Scotland. Since it was not published until after his death, it is not clear what Swift's intentions were in writing the piece, nor can the political effect, if any, be gauged. At this time, of course, Swift still hoped for a career in England, but his forthright pronouncements on the beleaguered Anglican Church of Ireland ("the Church in danger") would seem to rule out mere opportunism.

Swift's reputation as a so-called Irish patriot in the years 1720 to 1730 is documented and secure, but the ambivalence surrounding his attitudes toward the Irish as far back as the "Lady Injured" allegory is real and has its roots in the circumstances as well as his political, religious, and literary ambitions. In a sense Swift was a colonial, born as he was into an English colony existing in Ireland for nearly 500 years. Caution marked his Whig years in England, and opportunism can explain his Tory associations. He viewed himself as English, and, had he been accepted in England on his own terms, he might never have become a spokesman for the Irish. His return to Ireland in 1713 as dean of St. Patrick's, rather than a joyous fulfillment of a lifelong ambition, seemed at the time more like a calamity. Swift was slow to warm to Irish causes and wrote little of consequence on those matters between 1713 and 1720. He never fully identified with "the savage old Irish," as he described the native population later to Pope. His eloquent and persuasive defense of Irish interests was largely a manifestation of his sensitive colonial pride: "Am I a Freeman in England," he complains, "and do I become a Slave in six hours, by crossing the Channel?"

However mixed his motives and intentions, Swift did react to the tangible effects of English commercial injustices. It should be remembered that he had interceded for the Irish Church regimes, but his sentiments and emotions were apparently not fully engaged, nor was his patriotism aroused. Now that he was dean of St. Patrick's and an Irishman, even if by default, and now that the possibility of an English career was precluded by the change to a new ruling monarchy in 1714, the repressive English laws that prevented the Irish from conducting their own political and economic affairs became for Swift an intolerable price to pay for the nominal protection provided colonials by the mother country. As he does throughout his literary career, Swift again responds to practical human needs and to real, not abstract, moral issues.

The pamphlet *A Proposal for the Universal Use of Irish Manufacture* (1720) strikes a new note, moreover, by scorning automatic assumptions of English superiority and attacking greedy landlords, high rents, and Irish complacency and defeatism. Obviate the need for imports by consuming native products, he argues: "Burn everything English but their coal." The insults and aggressive attacks on both English and Irish in this tract reveal a new urgency of purpose, an immediacy of concern that belie the plainspoken prose style, the clear, direct discourse ("Proper Words in Proper Places") appealing to men's reason and understanding that Swift advocates in *A Letter to a Young Gentleman, Lately Entered into Holy Orders* (1720).

To add insult to injury, two years later, in 1722, while the English Parliament was reaffirming its right to legislate for Ireland, King George I and the Walpole ministry granted William Wood, an English iron manufacturer, a patent to produce a copper halfpence for circulation in Ireland. The decision was controversial on a number of grounds: presumably secured by the intervention of one of George's mistresses, the agreement called for an excessive number of coins, resulting in a huge profit for Wood; there were no provisions to protect against counterfeiting; and the Irish were not consulted on the matter. Over a two-year period, complaints that the debased currency would drive gold and silver from Ireland and further depress the economy grew so shrill that the English Treasury launched an official inquiry. Broadsides, ballads, poems, several by Swift, flooded the scene. In March 1724, at the height of the controversy, Swift published *A Letter to the Tradesmen, Shopkeepers, Farmers, and Common-People in General, of the Kingdom of Ireland,* by M. B. Drapier.

The full title of this first letter is significant. If Swift were indifferent to the native Irish of Roman Catholic persuasion, as has been charged, or if what interest he had shown involved essentially the fortunes of the Anglican Church and the status of English colonials, the publication in 1724 of these five successive letters (two additional ones were not printed) indisputably reflects a new nationalistic spirit and patriotic concern for what he described in the fourth letter as "the Whole People of Ireland." Despite the similarity of subject and theme, these letters differ in tone and style of expression. One and four are addressed to a cross-section of Irish society, the first playing on the prejudices, pieties, and economic self-interest of the ordinary, patriotic citizen and the fourth dramatically asserting Irish political equality with England in unforgettable phrases. The second letter lampoons the character of Wood ("this little impudent Hardware-Man"), and the third, directed to a sober, educated class, sets forth political and constitutional questions. The fifth letter eloquently summarizes the issues raised and examined in the previous four.

Although his ostensible audience may have been largely Anglo-Irish and middle-class, Swift's rhetorical strategies and convincingly maintained fiction of a concerned and sometimes outraged linen merchant, one M. B. Drapier, succeeded in awakening public opinion and rallying opposition to the economic and constitutional threats posed by England. Throughout his literary career, Swift often expressed doubt about the efficacy of satire and its power to reform or improve society. In September 1725, the lord lieutenant announced the cancellation of the patent and the end of the whole Wood affair. What better testimony to the force and influence of his satiric imagination? Of course, Swift was idolized for his successful challenge to Wood's halfpence, and his reputation as a local patriot was surely well deserved. His many efforts on behalf of Ireland during this period were formidable. Pope's tribute in the Horatian Imitation, *Epistle II, i* (To Augustus), sums up his contributions:

> Let Ireland tell how Wit upheld her cause,
> Her Trade supported, and supply'd her Laws;
> And leave on SWIFT this grateful verse engraved,
> The Rights a court attacked, a Poet saved.

But all the polemics and mockery in the world could not halt the continuing deterioration of Ireland's economy. As Swift wrote to Pope, "[t]he kingdom is absolutely undone, as I have been telling often in print these ten years past." In this same letter, moreover, he grimly recounts the failed harvests, starving population, and hopeless destitution brought about by crippling restraints on Irish manufacture and export and by absentee landlords draining off badly needed currency. These external conditions were exacerbated by a recalcitrant population vainly insisting on the luxury of foreign imports, refusing even to consume what they did produce.

Of these miscellaneous writings devoted to the worsening Irish scene, *A Short View of the State of Ireland* (1727) analyzes the economic and sociological causes of the malaise in a straightforward, deliberate manner. Unlike Swift's negative identification with his speaker through extended irony, in this tract when the spokesman is tempted by sarcasm he is instead overcome with emotion, confessing that "my Heart is too heavy to continue this Irony longer." Swift is, of course, presenting the facts as he saw them. Clearly, however, sympathy is mixed with anger and disappointment, a paradoxical reaction to the social and political stalemate in Ireland. *A Short View,* then, provides both the situational and emotional underpinning of Swift's best-known Irish tract and greatest short satire.

An advertisement appeared in the *Dublin Intelligencer* of November 1729 announcing, in a tone of patriotic concern, a "new scheme" to alleviate the serious famine, restore a sense of national purpose, and, not the least, please the English landlords. At the center of this plan was cannibalism—the eating of a fourth of the Irish infants under two years old. The trope registers Swift's anger and desperation that things had gotten so bad that cannibalism might be a humane act in these circumstances.

Swift's *A Modest Proposal for Preventing the Children of Poor People in Ireland from Being a Burden to Their Parents or Country, and for Making Them Beneficial to the Public* (1729) shows Swift at not only his most complex but also his satiric best, and it puts into sharp focus his ambivalent, often contradictory, attitudes toward Ireland. For, unlike much satire in which the satirist as spectator scorns an unsatisfactory state of affairs from an idealized and morally superior position, Swift simultaneously sympathizes with, and detests, "beggars of female sex" and "helpless infants." Like his polite, knowledgeable "proposer," skilled in statistics and economics and desirous of putting forward "a fair, cheap, and easy method of making . . . children sound and useful members of the commonwealth," Swift's satiric objectives are equally patriotic, moral, and Christian. But distinctly unlike his "proposer," who is bent on a scheme that "as it is wholly new, so it hath something solid and real, of no expense and little trouble, full in our own power, and whereby we can incur no danger in obliging England," Swift voices self-doubts and uncertainties about his role as satirist, reformer, and Irish patriot. Swift suggests alleviating one degradation by another equally grim and savage—and thus unrelentingly exposes man's endless capacity for hypocrisy and self-deception. The ostensible target of the work is the professedly concerned and sympathetic narrator, who is motivated by a social conscience but whose casual references to people as commodities expose an egotism and arrogance almost beyond comprehension. This fact, however, should not blind us to Swift's desperate longing for some positive, humane act that will lessen the suffering he now identifies with. But in the words of one acute critic, "[T]he complicated interplay of compassion and contempt is not to be taken as a finely-textured, sensitively judicial blend. . . . It is an explosive mixture," "a fierce, angry compassion." The presence of contrary attitudes is the hallmark of irony, and the sustained ironic procedures of *A Modest Proposal* are expressive of hope and optimism as, at the same time, they remind us of the probability of defeat and despair. The complexity of Swift's attitude toward Ireland is, then, inseparable from his own self-scrutinizing habit of mind, his dubious appraisal of the moral and corrective function of satire, and the unlikelihood of human progress or improvement.

Gulliver's Travels (1726), Swift's best-known and universally admired work, was written during that extraordinary four-year period when his creative energies were devoted largely to agitating and pamphleteering for the cause of Irish economic independence. It is a work of immense complexity, interpretive disagreement, and mixture of genres, variously children's fantasy, travel book, a parody of travel literature, scientific discourse, science fiction, novel, picaresque fiction, illustrated book, philosophical treatise, and probably the most devastating satire in English on man's pride. Like the "modest proposer," Lemuel Gulliver, a ship's surgeon, is a well-intentioned, decent, likable, educated, but often undiscriminating individual. Unlike the various personae of the pamphlets, however, Gulliver is a more complex figure, perhaps lacking the psychological density and consistency of a character in a novel but nonetheless possessing a personality with which one can identify.

His travels take him, in the phrasing of the book's original title, into "Several Remote Nations of the World" where he meets a whole range of people, ideas, and institutions. These imaginary experiences, instead of providing a romantic escape from the world, as in the standard travel book, force Gulliver and his reader to confront the realities of his own physical, political, intellectual, and moral corruption.

In the *Voyage to Lilliput,* the shipwrecked Gulliver visits a nation of extraordinarily resourceful and industrious miniature people (scale 1:12) who care for his needs, provide him transportation, generally respect his desires, and, in fact, award him their highest medal of honor. But their inevitable political intrigues and pretensions, which at first appear innocent to Gulliver, show them in the end to be cruel, treacherous, and vengeful, qualities paradoxically accentuated by their smallness. Despite topical references to the Whig regime of Sir Robert Walpole, to recent French-English diplomacy, and to current as well as seventeenth-century religious and political conflicts in England, the satire broadens, through the use of disproportionate size metaphor, to emphasize disparity between man's illusions of power and importance and his moral pettiness, pomposity, fear, and paranoia. Through it all, Gulliver miraculously remains rather kindly and understanding, and his naïveté is Swift's main instrument of satire.

In Book II, the *Voyage to Brobdingnag,* Gulliver experiences a traumatic readjustment of perspectives. As a Lilliputian among giants, he begins slowly to reassess many of his opinions about the world. "Undoubtedly philosophers are right," he admits, "when they tell us, that nothing is great or little otherwise than by comparison." Although this comment marks a certain improvement in Gulliver's powers of discrimination, he continually fears for his physical well-being. However, counter to his expectations, the King of Brobdingnag turns out to be fascinated by, not hostile to, this articulate *lusus naturae* (thing of nature) and enthusiastically engages Gulliver in a series of five revealing audiences devoted to an "exact account of the government of England." During the sixth interview, Gulliver assumes the role of straight man for Swift, who sets up, as it were, a variety of ideas, practices, and institutions as targets for ridicule and satire. In his most fulsome panegyrical mode, Gulliver has "celebrat[ed] the praise of [his] own dear native country in a style equal to its merits and felicity," only to have this wise and pragmatic king at the conclusion systematically demolish his opinions and veracity. In a memorable passage Swift has the king excoriate human nature (with uncharacteristic Juvenalian fury): "I cannot but conclude the bulk of your natives to be the most pernicious race of little odious vermin that nature ever suffered to crawl upon the surface of the earth." Against the backdrop of his own physical vulnerability, Gulliver's frantic assertions of faith and pride in English institutions and life further deflate his pride. Far from an impossible utopia, this eminently sensible government of Brobdingnag seems to provide a workable norm against which the follies and corruptions of England are to be measured. At the end of the *Travels,* Swift has Gulliver retrospectively remark that among "those remote Nations where *Yahoos* preside . . . the least corrupted are the *Brobdingnagians,* whose wise Maxims in Morality and Government, it would be our Happiness to observe."

The *Voyage to Laputa,* although the last to be written, appears as Book III of the *Travels* and has been described as a catchall. Swift's main targets are theoretical, speculative science, as represented in the proceedings of the Royal Society and ivory-tower political and economic theory. As a narrative, it is less unified than the others, comprising a long journey to the Flying Island with several side trips to Glubbdubdrib, to view heroes of classical and medieval history and philosophy, and to Luggnagg, to marvel at the immortals who have escaped "that universal calamity of human nature." The touch throughout is lighter, the satire funnier and more comic in effect than is usual in the *Travels.* Laputa itself is a brilliant set of variations on the theme of science and politics, one section in particular allegorizing the Irish-English conflicts of the 1720s. In fact, Swift's famous allegory in Book III, Chapter 3, *A Voyage to Laputa,* portrays graphically the successful resistance of the city Lindalino (Dublin) in Balnibarbi to the political oppression of Laputa, or the Flying Island (England), during the controversy over Wood's coin. (Benjamin Motte, Swift's original London publisher, omitted the four sensitive paragraphs for fear of government reprisals. All subsequent editions omitted these passages until an edition of 1899 restored them.) Despite the comedy, what results is a devastating attack both on the enterprising "projector" mentality and the enthusiastic zeal for perfecting human nature that was such an anathema to Swift, as well as on the frenetic search for the new, the modern, and the different. It also provides one of Swift's clearest statements of faith in the notion of the "ancients," the idea of the traditional Virgilian and Horatian virtues of simplicity, frugality, and self-reliance associated with rural life and harmonious union between man and nature. Gulliver praises Lord Munodi, the only sane man in a land of fools, who is content with "the old forms, to live in the houses his ancestors had built, and act as they did in every part of life without innovation."

Book IV, the *Voyage to the Houyhnhnms,* the most complex and problematical, opens with a Gulliver who is thoroughly disillusioned by his confrontation with the immortal but decrepit Struldbruggs, at the end of Book III, and by the mutiny on board ship, symbolic of the breakdown of an ordered society. The inexorable darkening of tone in this voyage has led many readers, especially Victorian critics, to condemn *Gulliver's Travels,* in the unforgettable language of the novelist Thackeray,* as "filthy in word, filthy in thought, furious, raging, obscene," the production of a bitterly degenerate misanthrope and a danger to read. Characteristically, Swift did not help matters by referring, in an often-quoted letter to Pope (September 29, 1725), to the "great foundation of misanthropy" on which his "treatise" was based, "proving the falsity of that definition *animale rationale;* and to show it should be only *rationis capax.*"

Despite a more balanced view and better understanding today of Swift's rhetorical strategies, there is no way of rationalizing or dispelling the shock expressed by Thackeray and others that Swift's indictment of human nature in Book IV is fierce and unrelenting, living up to his own epitaph: a hauntingly accurate self-portrait of savage indignation and lacerated heart. Such phrases do accurately represent attitudes expressed in some of his prose and several of the later poems, and there is no blinking this fact, as the Victorians understood.

When placed in the larger context of his life, beliefs, and the age, however, Swift's denunciations are the inevitable reaction of a conservative in politics and religion to man's fallen state. Moreover, Swift's assumptions about man's corrupt nature were not unique; indeed, they were axiomatic and were shared by his fellow Scriblerians and others who dismissed the meliorist myth, which argued for man's essential goodness and perfectibility and this society's potential for improvement and progress. From the beginning, Swift's targets were deists, utopians, Stoics, religious enthusiasts, philosophical optimists—deluded idealists of whatever form—who denied man's pride and imperfect nature. As he said in the undated *Of Publick Absurdityes,* "It is a mistake of wise and good men that they expect more Reason and Virtue from human nature, than . . . it is in any sort capable of." By the time of *Gulliver's Travels,* Swift had come to despise delusion in any form, even the innocent brand embraced by the uncomplicated naïf. His attitudes and obsessions are therefore understandable. The interpretive crux of the fourth Voyage lies in one's reading of the Houyhnhnms, those serenely rationalistic horses who are remote and stoical but nonetheless strangely attractive. The Yahoos, the only other inhabitants in this caste society, epitomize man's unregenerate animal nature, repulsive physicality, and appetitive habits. To complicate matters, Swift's relation to Gulliver himself, especially toward the end, is uncertain, and the question arises whether Gulliver speaks for Swift, or whether he is the object of Swift's satire, or both.

Some readers view the horses as Swift's ideal of rationality; others consider them quite the opposite—in fact, as representations of a false ideal about human nature perpetrated by the progressivists, freethinkers, and sentimentalists. A close reading reveals a number of clear signals that warn against a literal reading of man as a rational animal. A number of silly scenes, when horse characteristics and rationality prove incompatible, put the reader on guard. Moreover, as one critic phrases it, "[t]he purity of the horses is preternatural," ideal in the abstract but certainly an unlikely ideal for *human* beings. They appear as a symbol of pure reason that man cannot obtain because of his fallen and corrupt nature. In fact, after Gulliver's long litany of the wars, destruction, and chaos infecting European society, the Master Horse's reaction is: "When a creature pretending to reason could be capable of such enormities, he dreaded lest the corruption of that faculty might be worse than brutality itself." Such a response does not, however, erase the existence of the ideal, but renders it more remote.

Gulliver's experiences with the horses prove unsettling. The more he identifies with the Yahoo nature he perceives within himself, the more he tries to emulate the rational horses. His rejection of his patient family and his rescuer, Captain Pedro de Mendez, and his decision to live and converse with his own horses "at least four hours every day" can be viewed as either ludicrous or tragic. Swift refuses to provide an easy moralization, and his respect for the complexity of the human condition and recognition of man's infinite capacity for self-deception make *Gulliver's Travels* a perpetual and formidable challenge and warning to the overconfident interpreter who, like the unfortunate sailor Gulliver mentions at the beginning of Book IV, may be "an honest man . . . but a little too positive in his own opinions." By placing man between the Houyhnhnms and the Yahoos, Swift creates a dilemma of interpretation: as one critic trenchantly remarks, "While the Houyhnhnms are an insulting impossibility, the Yahoos, though not a reality, are an equally insulting possibility." Swift's genius lies in compelling us to face painful ambiguities, the "uncertainties, mysteries, doubts without any irritable reaching after fact & reason," in Keats's famous words. The satirical outlook on life gave him the sharpest focus on the problematical nature of reality itself.

Swift wrote some 280 poems. Many are parochial in conception and topical in the most limiting of sense. Nevertheless, his best poems, by and large, were written during the 1730s, following his brilliant prose achievement as Irish apologist and sea traveler to faraway places. This extraordinary literary activity should lay to rest permanently arguments for Swift's physical, mental, and literary decline during these years and place him among the most accomplished of eighteenth-century poets. "Verses on the Death of Dr. Swift," "The Day of Judgement," "Strephon and Chloe," "The Beasts' Confession to the Priest," "An Epistle to a Lady," "On Poetry: A Rhapsody," "The Legion Club," to mention only a few of his poetic productions at this point, would place Swift near the top of any list of great Augustan poets. These poems were so viewed in his own time and continue to inspire perceptive analyses. Moreover, criticism of Swift's verse has recently become a major industry—certainly an unlikely fulfillment of Samuel Johnson's prediction: "In the Poetical Works . . . there is not much upon which the critic can exercise his powers." A number of editions, including a 1958 revision of Harold Williams's 1937 standard edition and Pat Rogers's superb 1983 Penguin/Yale modern spelling version, a concordance, numerous books and monographs, and scores of articles and conference papers not only attest to this flourishing interest but also immeasurably enhance our appreciation of Swift's poetic art.

Swift would have savored the irony of these recent developments, for he tended to dismiss his poetic endeavors as mere "trifles" of a "man of rhymes" (Letter to Charles Wogan, 1732). Yet, despite his playful experiments in "left-handed" composition, limericks, peasant balladry, humorous parodies, raillery, as well as some scatology, he produced a large body of verse demonstrating an ironic sophistication, precise use of language, versification skills, and moral seriousness that are worthy of critical attention. His denial of "serious Couplets" must be viewed in the context of his insistence that his "Rhimes" were "never without a moral View."

Swift's remarkable, large poetic output has not enjoyed as much critical attention as has that of the other Augustans. He lacks Dryden's broad historical consciousness, capacity to forge meaningful analogies between biblical narrative or prophecy, Virgilian epic practices, and the rough-and-tumble of seventeenth-century politics. He cannot match Pope's rich allusiveness, complexity of tone, verbal sonorities, and professionalism. His poetry does not have the weight and concentration and tragicomic ambivalence of Johnson's best poems.

Swift's poetic achievement is of a more paradoxical order: social while being intensely personal; at once light-textured and harshly condemnatory; didactic and moralistic yet outrageously parodic and full of fun, playing all sorts of games with rhyme, rhythm, and a variety of tones, at the same time coming across as deadly serious satire; sporting throwaway lines, anticlimax, erratic shifts in mood through a texture of contrived artifice. His verse often recoils on itself, constantly challenging its own reason for being by naming itself a fiction in the denial of seriousness. A recent editor of his verse puts the situation in these terms: "It is nearly all in a deep sense oppositional: it unsettles our stock ideas, it affronts established values, it carries round its own canister of salt looking for open wounds." In fact, his rhetorical experimentation makes his verse an ancestor, it would appear, of the fabulator motif of the postmodernist novel, calling attention to poetic artifice by indulging in verbal slackness and poetic incompetence, while, at the same time, rising above it all by outdoing the awful with brio and confidence. Some examples from "On Poetry" illustrate these comic procedures:

And here a simile comes pat in:
Though chickens take a month to fatten. . . .

Or oft when epithets you link,
In gaping lines to fill a chink;
Like stepping stones to save a stride,
In streets where kennels are too wide. . . .

But these are not a thousandth part
Of jobbers in the poet's art,
Attending each his proper station,
And all in due subordination;
Through every alley to be found,
In garrets high, or underground:
And when they join their pericranies,
Out skips a book of miscellanies.
Hobbes clearly proves that every creature
Lives in a state of war by nature.

So, naturalists observe, a flea
Hath smaller fleas that on him prey,
And these have smaller yet to bite 'em,
And so proceed *ad infinitum:*
Thus every poet in his kind,
Is bit by him that comes behind. . . .

Swift's loathing of delusion is often cited to explain his dislike of conventional literary forms and poetic routines, as well as the parlor sentiments and habits of mind informing them. Thus, the mockery of pastoral and georgic, heroic postures in art, love poetry, progress poems, and laureate odes. However, attempts to characterize Swift as an antipoetic realist, satirizing not only pride and pretension but also the poetic forms that dignify them, can obscure the critical norms created internally, through deliberate jumbling of familiar figures, tropes, and images. Upon closer inspection, this so-called realism turns out to be the product of a calculated aesthetic response that converts everyday actuality through imaginative transformations and the mimetic process into the kind of a seriousness associated with the comic mode.

"Verses on the Death of Dr. Swift" provides a fitting summary of his political, clerical, and literary careers. A combination of satiric thrusts and elegiac sentiments, the poem reviews in detail Swift's actual life and times. It compliments his friends, attacks his enemies, and creates through multiple ironies and juxtaposed speaking voices a picture of his ambivalent motives, attitudes, and commitments. Through a series of claims ranging from the purity of his satiric motives to admission of hypocrisy and vanity in keeping with the poem's epigraph from La Rochefoucault, which states that in friends' adversities we find comfort and pleasure, Swift deliberately distorts and exaggerates the "facts" of his life. As a result, he creates, in the words of two insightful critics of the poem, an "attractive and convincing picture" of himself. Swift characteristically sets the record straight by comically undercutting the self-praise so as to win the reader's assent to his real accomplishments:

> [He] showed by one satiric touch,
> No nation wanted it so much:
> That kingdom he hath left his debtor,
> I wish it soon may have a better.

Swift was declared "of unsound mind and memory" on August 17, 1742. On October 19, 1745, he died, leaving the greater part of his estate, as he had promised, to establish a hospital for the insane:

> He gave the little wealth he had,
> To build a house for fools and mad.

Eighteenth-century studies have been sometimes characterized as peculiarly resistant to postmodernist critical theory and feminist inquiry. Leaving aside for the moment the fairness and accuracy of such an assertion, we could describe Swift (like Sterne) as the obvious exception. Indeed, for some modern critics, Swift is a deconstructionist before the fact, proleptic in his distrust of language and the whole logocentric enterprise generally. In the words of one poststructuralist, Swift exemplifies "the highly dramatic encounters between the anarchy of resistance (agraphia) to the written page and the abiding tory order of the page."

This point is not meant in any superficial sense. Granted, Swift was a cultural conservative and authoritarian thinker, championing religious orthodoxy and moral certitude—but through decidedly unorthodox, often ambiguous, and sharply ironic ways. Like Defoe and others, he advocated the establishment of an academy to institutionalize, standardize, and codify English language usage; he wrote, in 1712, a highly politicized treatise arguing for the need to stabilize and "fix" language and meaning into permanency and coherence; he satirized linguistic corruption in the form of tasteless slang, poor puns, and other barbarous usages, in the early *Tatler* No. 230; he mocked the banalities and shallowness of social chitchat obsessively laced with stale proverbs and truisms, in the late *Polite Conversation.* His unforgettable Lagadian word machine spewing out meaningless sentences marks a high point in the satire of linguistic folly and mindlessness.

Nevertheless, this very campaign of Swift's against the corruption of language in whatever form it may take, which results in subversion of meaning and morality, actually betrays, the postmodernist critic would argue, Swift's deep skepticism regarding the capacity of language to communicate truth, as well as his doubts about art's mimetic function. In the "Epistle Dedicatory" to Prince Posterity, in the *Tale,* the modern hack tries to establish his credentials as a writer and assert the incontestable truths of his message by invoking the image of a cloud paradoxically suggestive of the very evanescent, ephemeral, and unsubstantial nature of the linguistic medium itself.

The numerous fictive identities, masks, and voices Swift invents; the multiple and often conflicting points of view and narrative perspectives; his playful use of hiatus and gaps in "manuscripts" and the like; his presenting of a dilemma that compels his reader to choose between two desirable qualities, such as knowledge or happiness or two undesirable ones, being a fool or knave, as Swift does in *A Tale of a Tub;* the plurality of discourses, genres, and perspectives in *Gulliver's Travels* that create the fundamental indeterminacy of meaning, misunderstanding of intention, and misconstruing of purpose that Gulliver himself complains about in his Letter to Sympson—all these devices and rhetorical strategies exemplify the ironic obliquity and indeterminacy of all texts and the truths they purport to impart. A striking instance of such discontinuity and destabilizing is found in "Verses on the Death." At the end of this problematic poem, Swift creates a fiction in which he views himself as he wants the future to view him—that is, positively—through the eyes of a spokesman "indifferent in the cause" or impartial. At the very point where Swift asserts his originality as a poet, he does so through the borrowed phrase of another poet (Sir John Denham on Cowley). Rather than a simple case of self-mockery or ironic undercutting, this, according to one postmodernist critic, suggests not merely that authors are hypocritical and do not tell the truth about themselves but that, given the nature of language, they *cannot* do so. Swift, it is claimed, is not just raising doubts about the truths of panegyric but presciently revealing postmodernist insistence on the fundamental disjunction between sign and signifier, language and reality.

Both Swift and Pope have attracted the hostility of feminist critics, but for different and sometimes contradictory reasons. In Swift's case, however, the ire stems from the charge of misogyny, the result presumably of a series of so-called scatological poems, which, among other things, depict in intense, unrelenting, and fiercely aggressive terms the ugliness of the female body, the grossness and filthiness referred to in "Strephon and Chloe." As has been pointed out by a number of critics, these poems need to be seen less as concerned with body hatred and more in light of Swift's temperamental dislike of elevated styles and lofty postures, his mockery of the language of pastoral, and the routines of love poetry. Nevertheless, once all the rationalizations and intellectual justifications are offered in an effort to mitigate the shocking picture, the reader is still faced with the highly charged and often cruel imagery of ugliness.

The issue is complex, to be sure, as attested by the example of one critic who, at one point, viewed Swift as a misogynist, only to make a sudden 180-degree turn around and view him as a protofeminist. Also, Swift enjoyed the company of women, had many women friends whom he viewed with respect and admiration, and also furthered the writing careers of such women as Mary Barber* and Constance Grierson.* One critic finds Swift "a useful and liberating model" for women authors; another recently points out that Swift has of late attracted women scholars and critics who find a feminine quality present in his sensibility. Surely the "Letter to a Young Lady, on Her Marriage" and the birthday poems to Stella reveal opinions of women that are not only healthy, sensible, and practical but also sensitive to the plight of women of the time and the tendency to view them as ornaments, not as human beings possessing virtues to be cultivated and respected. Even the scatological verse, often cited as an obstacle to feminine appreciation, has been described lately as "exploding certain bourgeois sexual myths," and Swift's use of the scatological tradition as original, not primarily misogynist. Thus, there is no final consensus, it would seem, but the tendency in recent years has been to view Swift's sensibilities as strangely protean and fluid, providing him insight into, and empathic understanding of, female sexual identity. But like his attitudes generally toward all human behavior and life itself, which he once described in a letter as "a ridiculous tragedy, which is the worst kind of composition," Swift's views about women are conflicting, problematical, and often disturbingly ambiguous.

DONALD C. MELL

WORKS: *The Complete Poems.* Pat Rogers, ed. New Haven, Conn.: Yale University Press/ [Harmondsworth, Middlesex]: Penguin, [1983]; *The Correspondence of Jonathan Swift.* Harold Williams, ed. 5 vols. Oxford: Clarendon, 1963–1965; *The Drapier's Letters.* Herbert Davis, ed. Oxford: Clarendon, 1935; *Gulliver's Travels.* Christopher Fox, ed. New York: Bedford Books, St. Martin's 1995; *The Intelligencer.* James Woolley, ed. Oxford: Clarendon, 1992; *Jonathan Swift.* Angus Ross & David Woolley, eds. (The Oxford Authors). New York: Oxford University Press, 1984; *Journal to Stella.* Harold Williams, ed. 2 vols. Oxford: Clarendon, 1948; *The Poems of Jonathan Swift.* Harold Williams, ed. 3 vols. Oxford: Clarendon, 1937/2d ed. 1958; *The Prose Works of Jonathan Swift.* Herbert Davis et al., eds. 14 vols. Oxford: Blackwell, 1939–1968; *Swift vs. Mainwaring: The Examiner and the Medley.* Frank Ellis, ed. Oxford: Clarendon, 1985; *A Tale of a Tub.* A. C. Guthkelch & D. Nicol Smith, eds. Oxford: Clarendon, 1920/2d ed. 1958.   REFERENCES: Bibliography—Landa, Louis A. & Tobin, James E. *Jonathan Swift: A List of Critical Studies Published from 1895 to 1945.* New York: Cosmopolitan Science and Art Service, 1945; Rodino, Richard H. *Swift Studies, 1965–1980: An Annotated Bibliography.* New York: Garland, 1984; Stathis, James J. *A Bibliography of Swift Studies 1945–1965.* Nashville, Tenn.: Vanderbilt University Press, 1967; Teerink, Herman. *A Bibliography of the Writings of Jonathan Swift.* 2d ed., revised by A. H. Scouten. Philadelphia: University of Pennsylvania Press, 1963; Vieth, David. *Swift's Poetry, 1900–1980: An Annotated Bibliography.* New York: Garland, 1982. Biography—*The Account Books of Jonathan Swift.* Transcribed with an Introduction by Paul V. Thompson & Dorothy Jay Thompson. Cranbury, N.J.: Associated University Presses, 1984; Downie, J. A. *Jonathan Swift: Political Writer.* London: Routledge & Kegan Paul, 1984; Ehrenpreis, Irvin. *Swift: The Man, His Works, and the Age.* 3 vols. Cambridge: Harvard University Press, 1962–1983; McMinn, Joseph. *Jonathan Swift: A Literary Life.* [Basingstoke]: Macmillan, 1991; Mahony, Robert. *Jonathan Swift: The Irish Identity.* New Haven, Conn.: Yale University Press, 1995; Murry, John Middleton. *Jonathan Swift: A Critical Biography.* London: Jonathan Cape, 1954; Nokes, David. *Jonathan Swift, A Hypocrite Reversed: A Critical Biography.* Oxford: Oxford University Press, 1985. Collections of Essays— *The Character of Swift's Satire: A Revised Focus.* Claude Rawson, ed. Newark: University of Delaware Press, 1983; *Contemporary Studies of Swift's Poetry.* John Irwin Fischer & Donald C. Mell, eds. Newark: University of Delaware Press, 1981; *Essential Articles for the Study of Swift's Poetry.* David M. Vieth, ed. Hamden, Conn.: Archon, 1984; *Fair Liberty Was All His Cry: A Tercentenary Tribute to Jonathan Swift, 1667–1745.* A. Norman Jeffares, ed. London: Macmillan, 1967; *Focus: Swift.* C. J. Rawson, ed. London: Sphere Books, 1971; *The Genres of* Gulliver's *Travels.* Frederik N. Smith, ed. Newark: University of Delaware Press, 1990; *Jonathan Swift, 1667–*

1745: A Dublin Tercentenary Tribute. Roger McHugh & Philip Edwards, eds. Dublin: Dolmen, 1967; *Jonathan Swift: A Collection of Critical Essays.* Claude Rawson, ed. Englewood Cliffs, N.J.: Prentice-Hall, 1995; *Jonathan Swift: A Critical Anthology.* Denis Donoghue, ed. [Harmondsworth, Middlesex]: Penguin, 1971; *Jonathan Swift's* Gulliver's Travels. Harold Bloom, ed. (Modern Critical Interpretations.) New York: Chelsea House, 1986; *Proceedings of the First Munster Symposium on Jonathan Swift.* Hermann J. Real & Heinz J. Vienken, eds. Munich: Wilhelm Fink, 1985; *Reading Swift: Papers from the Second Munster Symposium on Jonathan Swift.* Richard H. Rodino & Hermann Real, eds. Munich: Wilhelm Fink, 1993; *Swift: A Collection of Critical Essays.* Ernest Tuveson, ed. Englewood Cliffs, N.J.: Prentice-Hall, 1964; *Swift and His Contexts.* John Irwin Fischer, Hermann Real & James Woolley, eds. New York: AMS, 1989; *Swift: The Critical Heritage.* Kathleen Williams, ed. London: Routledge & Kegan Paul, 1970; *Twentieth Century Interpretations of* Gulliver's Travels. Frank Brady, ed. Englewood Cliffs, N.J.: Prentice-Hall, 1968; *The World of Jonathan Swift: Essays for the Tercentenary.* Brian Vickers, ed. Cambridge: Harvard University Press, 1968. On the Prose—Carnochan, W. B. *Lemuel Gulliver's Mirror for Man.* Los Angeles: University of California Press, 1968; Clark, John R. *Form and Frenzy in Swift's* Tale of a Tub. Ithaca, N.Y.: Cornell University Press, 1970; Cook, Richard. *Jonathan Swift as Tory Pamphleteer.* Seattle: University of Washington Press, 1967; Craven, Kenneth. *Jonathan Swift and the Millennium of Madness: The Information Age in Swift's* A Tale of a Tub. New York: E. J. Brill, 1992; Davis, Herbert. *Jonathan Swift: Essays on His Satire and Other Studies.* New York: Oxford University Press, 1964; Donoghue, Denis. *Jonathan Swift: A Critical Introduction.* Cambridge: Cambridge University Press, 1969; Eilon, Daniel. *Factions' Fictions: Ideological Closure in Swift's Satire.* Newark: University of Delaware Press, 1990; Ewald, William Bragg, Jr. *The Masks of Jonathan Swift.* Cambridge: Harvard University Press, 1954; Fabricant, Carole. *Swift's Landscapes.* Baltimore: Johns Hopkins University Press, 1982; Ferguson, Oliver. *Jonathan Swift and Ireland.* Urbana: University of Illinois Press, 1962; Hammond, Brean. *Gulliver's Travels.* Milton Keynes: Open University Press, 1988; Harth, Phillip. *Swift and Augustan Rationalism: The Religious Background of* A Tale of a Tub. Chicago: University of Chicago Press, 1961; Higgins, Ian. *Swift's Politics: A Study in Disaffection.* Cambridge: Cambridge University Press, 1994; Kelly, Ann Cline. *Swift and the English Language.* Philadelphia: University of Pennsylvania Press, 1988; Landa, Louis A. *Swift and the Church of Ireland.* Oxford: Clarendon, 1954; Levine, Joseph M. *The Battle of the Books: History and Literature in the Augustan Age.* Ithaca, N.Y.: Cornell University Press, 1991; Lock, F. P. *The Politics of* Gulliver's Travels. Oxford: Clarendon, 1980; Lock, F. P. *Swift's Tory Politics.* Newark: University of Delaware Press, 1983; McMinn, Joseph. *Jonathan's Travels: Swift and Ireland.* Belfast: Appletree, 1994; Paulson, Ronald. *Theme and Structure in Swift's* Tale of a Tub. New Haven, Conn.: Yale University Press, 1960; Price, Martin. *Swift's Rhetorical Art: A Study in Structure and Meaning.* New Haven, Conn.: Yale University Press, 1953; Probyn, Clive T. *Jonathan Swift:* Gulliver's Travels. (Penguin Critical Studies.) [Harmondsworth, Middlesex]: Penguin, 1987; Quintana, Ricardo. *The Mind and Art of Jonathan Swift.* New York: Oxford University Press, 1936; Quintana, Ricardo. *Swift: An Introduction.* London: Oxford University Press, 1955; Rawson, Claude. *Gulliver and the Gentle Reader: Studies in Swift and Our Time.* London: Routledge & Kegan Paul, 1973; Rawson, Claude. *Order from Confusion Sprung: Studies in Eighteenth-Century Literature from Swift to Cowper.* London: George Allen & Unwin, 1985; Reilly, Patrick. *Jonathan Swift: The Brave Desponder.* Carbondale: Southern Illinois University Press, 1982; Rosenheim, Edward W. *Swift and the Satirist's Art.* Chicago: University of Chicago Press, 1963; Smith, Frederik N. *Language and Reality in Swift's* A Tale of a Tub. Columbus: Ohio State University Press, 1979; Steele, Peter. *Jonathan Swift: Preacher and Jester.* Oxford: Oxford University Press, 1978; Swaim, Kathleen M. *A Reading of* Gulliver's Travels. The Hague: Mouton, 1972; Tippett, Brian. *Gulliver's Travels.* (The Critics Debate.) Atlantic Highlands, N.J.: Humanities, 1989; Williams, Kathleen. *Jonathan Swift and the Age of Compromise.* Lawrence: University of Kansas Press, 1958; Wyrick, Deborah Baker. *Jonathan Swift and the Vested Word.* Chapel Hill: University of North Carolina Press, 1988; Zimmerman, Everett. *Swift's Narrative Satires: Author and Authority.* Ithaca, N.Y.: Cornell University Press, 1983. On the Poetry—Barnett, Louise K. *Swift's Poetic Worlds.* Newark:

University of Delaware Press, 1981; England, A. B. *Energy and Order in the Poetry of Swift.* Lewisburg, Pa.: Bucknell University Press, 1980; Fischer, John Irwin. *On Swift's Poetry.* Gainesville: University Presses of Florida, 1978; Jaffe, Nora Crow. *The Poet Swift.* Hanover, N.H.: University Press of New England, 1977; Johnson, Maurice. *The Sin of Wit: Jonathan Swift as a Poet.* Syracuse, N.Y.: Syracuse University Press, 1950; Pollak, Ellen. *The Poetics of Sexual Myth: Gender and Ideology in the Verse of Swift and Pope.* Chicago: University of Chicago Press, 1985; Schakel, Peter J. *The Poetry of Jonathan Swift: Allusion and the Development of a Poetic Style.* Madison: University of Wisconsin Press, 1978.

SYNGE, [EDMUND] JOHN MILLINGTON (1871–1909), playwright. Synge was born in Rathfarnham near Dublin on April 16, 1871. The youngest son of a lawyer who died the following year, he lived for most of his life with his mother, next door first to his grandmother, and later to his only sister Annie and her family. Robert, his eldest brother, became an engineer and settled in Argentina; Edward became a land agent in Wicklow and the west of Ireland; Samuel, to whom Synge was closest as a child, and who later published reminiscences of his younger brother in *Letters to My Daughter* (1932), became a medical missionary to China. Except for several brief periods, Synge spent all of his time in Ireland surrounded by family; the indomitable old women of his plays and translations owe much to his admiration for his mother, his grandmother, and elderly aunts.

Never strong as a child and solitary by temperament, Synge's self-absorption and independent critical spirit led him as a young adolescent to reject his family's evangelical teaching (inherited from a long line of clergymen) and to evolve painstakingly his own form of worship. Henceforth, a combination of nature mysticism and moral aestheticism informed all his writings and determined the course of his actions and studies. He attended school irregularly, receiving most of his education through private tuition. With a young cousin Florence Ross as companion, then as a member of the Dublin Naturalists' Field Club, he became a confirmed naturalist and later was to attribute his first religious crisis to the shock of reading Darwin when he was about fourteen. A further departure from family orthodoxy occurred in 1887 when he began studying the violin. At the same time as he attended Trinity College, Dublin, from 1889 to 1892, he was also enrolled at the Royal Irish Academy of Music, and whereas he received from Trinity merely a gentleman's or pass B.A., he won scholarships at the Academy in both counterpoint and harmony. When he joined the Academy orchestra in 1891, he decided to become a professional musician.

This ambition was encouraged by his mother's cousin, Mary Synge, a pianist who visited Dublin in 1893 and offered to accompany her relative to Germany, where he could study the German language and continue his musical education. From late July of that year, Synge boarded in Coblenz with his cousin's friends, the von Eicken sisters, the youngest of whom, Valeska, immediately became his special confidante. Here he established, for the first time outside his family circle, the easy conversational relationship he was to enjoy with women for the rest of his life.

In January, 1894, he moved to Wurzburg, studying both piano and the violin and continuing to compose privately. By spring, however, he was devoting half of his time to writing, and it is likely that when he returned to Ireland in June, he had already decided on a literary career. Later, he reasoned that extreme nervousness as a performer stimulated this change, but in his autobiography he admits that his interest in writing and languages, his devotion to nature, and his love of music had always been in uneasy balance: "I wished to be at once Shakespeare, Beethoven and Darwin; my ambition was boundless and amounted to a real torture in my life. . . . When I was fiddling I mourned over the books I wished to read; when I was reading I yearned for all manner of adventures."

Towards the end of his life, in the preface to his *Poems and Translations,* he was to commend "many of the older poets, such as Villon and Herrick and Burns," who "used the whole of their personal life as their material." From his first determination to be a writer, he seems to have consciously prepared his personality for the event. His naturalism led to an interest in Irish antiquities, which in turn encouraged him to what was then still an uncommon pursuit— the study of the Irish language. He also studied Hebrew and won prizes at Trinity College in both, but the only indication of literary ambitions (his weakest subject was English literature) was the publication in the college journal *Kottabos* in 1893 of a poem heavily influenced by his favorite poet, Wordsworth. Now, however, he resumed his writing of poetry, began a play in German, and on January 1, 1895, arrived in Paris. He joined a students' debating club which he attended faithfully for years, studied literature and languages at the Sorbonne, steeped himself in art and art history, did some tutoring in English, and in his reading ranged widely over contemporary literature, ethics, philosophy, and socialism. Except for four months in Italy in 1896 (when he again attempted to write in the language he was studying and may have first experimented with translating from the Italian), he followed this pattern for the next seven years, spending part of each winter in Paris.

Meanwhile he had fallen in love. Cherrie Matheson, a neighbor, spent several weeks of 1894 with the Synges in Wicklow, where Mrs. Synge regularly rented a house for the summer. A member of the Plymouth Brethren, Cherrie could not accept marriage with a nonbeliever, but Synge, formally proposing in both 1895 and 1896 (the second time seeking his sympathetic mother's unwilling advocacy), did not take rejection easily. Even though he contemplated marriage to at least two women students he met in Paris, his anguish and intellectual resentment over Cherrie are reflected in the arguments of his first play, *When the Moon Has Set,* which he began in 1900. The plot is forced and self-conscious—a young Irish landlord recently returned from Paris successfully woos his nursing cousin, a nun of an indeterminate religious order. In this play, however, we find clear expression of the aesthetic creed behind all of Synge's future work:

God is in the earth and not above it. In the wet elm leaves trailing in the lane in autumn, in the deserted currents of the streams, and in the breaking out of the sap, there are joys that collect all the joy that is in religion and art. . . . Every life is a symphony. It is this cosmic element in the person which gives all personal art, and all sincere life, and all passionate love a share in the dignity of the world.

More personal and even less controlled than the play is the record of his spiritual and emotional crises entitled *Vita Vecchia* (1895–1897), a series of fourteen poems connected by prose narrative. This, together with *Étude Morbide* (1899), "an imaginary portrait," he soon rejected as being immature, morbid, and unduly influenced by the decadent movement. All three works were rejected for publication by Yeats* and Lady Gregory* after his death and were not published until the Oxford edition of his collected works (1962–1968).

Synge's political awareness increased as he studied socialism and became a close friend of the nationalist journalist and translator Stephen MacKenna.* His courses in medieval literature and old Irish at the Sorbonne led to an interest in Celtic civilizations, but still from a European point of view. In December 1896, he met William Butler Yeats* and Maud Gonne, and through them many of the Irish nationalists at home and abroad. He joined Maud Gonne's Irish League in Paris, but when he realized that official membership in *l'Irlande Libre* meant advocating a "revolutionary and semi-military movement," he resigned to become a passive observer. Encouraged by MacKenna in Paris and by George Russell (AE)* in Dublin, he also briefly studied Yeats' related interest, the occult. Finally, in May 1898, he followed Yeats' advice to seek creative inspiration in the Aran Islands. Henceforth, his sympathies and literary ambitions sharpened and concentrated, for in the west of Ireland he found that synthesis of natural and supranatural and astringent reality with the shock of raw joy, all evidence of the cosmic rhythm he sensed in music, nature, and the human passions. On the eve of his departure from Aran for the first time, he received an invitation to visit Lady Gregory* at Coole. Yeats also introduced him to Edward Martyn,* their colleague in the Irish Literary Theatre,* and Synge determined to join the movement. Later that year, his first account of Aran appeared in the *New Ireland Review*.

But he did not give up Paris; rather, he settled in permanent rooms there, continued his studies at the Sorbonne, visited Brittany, and wrote an occasional review of contemporary French and Irish writers for various journals. When he returned each summer to Ireland, he continued to join his mother and her friends in County Wicklow, only then moving on to Aran before returning to the Continent. Between 1898 and his last visit in the autumn of 1902, he spent a total of four and a half months on Aran, compared with forty-three months in all living in Paris. But he had been preparing for this return to Ireland all his life, and in *The Aran Islands*, which he later described as his "first serious piece of work," he found not only the appropriate form through which to explore his own place in the universe while maintaining the stance of the uninvolved though sympathetic outsider, but source material for many of his plays. Completed late in 1901 but not published until 1907, the book led to a desire to root out even more primitiveness, in visits to Mayo, Kerry, and the Blasket Islands. A happy collaboration took place in 1905 when *The Manchester Guardian,* through their mutual friend John Masefield, commissioned Synge and Jack Butler Yeats* to do a series of articles on the congested districts of the west of Ireland. Nor did he forget Wicklow, whose paths, mountains, and streams he had explored since childhood: employing the same technique of the wanderer—half drawn into the world he describes, yet distant by temperament and training—he embarked on a series of similar essays distilling the moods, sounds, colors, and movements of the people and their glens.

During the summer of 1902, Synge wrote his two one-act plays, *Riders to the Sea* (based on an incident he had heard of on Aran) and *(In) the Shadow of the Glen* (expressing many of his experiences of the atmosphere of County Wicklow). He also made the first rough draft of his two-act comedy, *The Tinker's Wedding* (originally entitled "The Movements of May," in keeping with his belief in nature's direct impact on man). Instead of going to France, he joined his new theatre colleagues in London the following January, and marked the end of his apprenticeship by moving out of his Paris flat in March 1903. When he returned to Dublin, it was apparent that his fortunes were now tied to the small company of actors led by Willie and Frank Fay who were to form the nucleus of the Irish National Theatre Society. *The Shadow of the Glen* was first produced by them in October 1903, followed by *Riders to the Sea* in February of the next year; he had written both before seeing the company perform. Now, however, he became a member of the group's Reading Committee, accompanied them on various tours, took over the rehearsal of his own plays, and assisted in revising and producing the work of others. By the time the Abbey Theatre* opened in 1904, he was established, with Yeats and Lady Gregory, as one of the leaders of the movement. *The Well of the Saints* was produced in February 1905 and *The Playboy of the Western World,* under riotous circumstances, in January 1907. His last completed play, *Deirdre of the Sorrows,* still not polished to his satisfaction, was performed in January 1910 after his death.

The first indication of the Hodgkins' disease which was to kill Synge was an enlarged gland on the side of his neck which was removed in 1897 (and which, characteristically, Synge made the occasion for an interesting essay, "Under Ether"); similar swellings recurred over the next ten years. Accustomed to walking and bicycling throughout the countryside (and in spite of the asthma he frequently suffered), Synge had an unusually strong constitution. Consequently, he experienced no pain until late in 1907. Many of his poems and translations were written after be began to realize that his illness might be fatal, but at the same time his urge towards a passionate and rich life was strengthened by his love for the Abbey actress Maire (Molly) O'Neill, the younger sister of actress Sara Allgood. For Molly, Synge wrote some of his finest poems and created the roles of Pegeen Mike in *The Playboy of the Western World* and Deirdre in his last play. Sixteen years his junior, she embodied all the qualities Synge most appreciated in life—wayward passion, artistic sensibility, a sensitive response to nature, and romantic natural beauty. He wrote to her almost daily; his letters not only reveal his personal ambitions and his responses to love and nature, but also document his involvement in management and direction of the Abbey Theatre during its formative years.

These letters also throw light on the painstaking craftsmanship with which Synge honed his plays. Obsessed with the idea of perfection and the achievement of a cosmic and artistic synthesis, he refined and polished every speech and action in an effort to establish the delicate balance between reality and joy (the "romantic" and the "Rabelaisian") which he demanded of his work. "In a good play," he wrote in his preface to *The Playboy of the Western World,* "every speech should be as fully flavoured as a nut or apple," and the simile celebrates his endeavor to draw together sound and senses, light and action, meaning and color. Indeed, this very forcing of audiences to taste and directly respond to the experience before them may well be at the root of the early violent reactions to his plays. Synge's characters feel intensely, speak eloquently, and react simply and immediately to all about them. They dream and project those feelings and wishes onto the reality of their daily lives, creating an impossible tension which leads in the play to further action and in the spectator to a truth he may not be prepared to acknowledge. The world of the play is carefully established and its code and truth are undeniably familiar, while at the same time other worlds are found to be not only possible but seductively preferable. His people are rooted, as Synge felt all poetry should be, in "the clay and worms," but, like Old Mahon in *The Playboy,* they are constantly "shying clods again the visage of the stars."

Thus, in his black comedy *The Well of the Saints,* Martin Doul, "a little dark stump of a fellow looks the fool of the world," speaks persuasively of "sitting blind, hearing a soft wind turning round the little leaves of the spring and feeling the sun, and we not tormenting our souls with the sight of the grey days, and the holy men, and the dirty feet is trampling the world." So he and blind Mary turn their backs on the working, seeing world and choose probable death in the mythical south, "where the people will have kind voices maybe, and we don't know their bad looks or their villainy at all." The young lovers of *Deirdre of the Sorrows* put "a sharp end to the day is brave and glorious, as our fathers put a sharp end to the days of the kings of Ireland." As they chose life in the woods, now they seek the safety of the grave and "a story will be told forever." Even Nora of *The Shadow of the Glen* is fully aware of the choice she makes between a sheltered life with her cold, queer, unyielding husband in the lonely mist-ridden Wicklow glen, and walking the roads below with the sweetly talking Tramp: "I'm thinking it's myself will be wheezing that time with lying down under the Heavens when the night is cold, but you've a fine bit of talk, stranger, and it's with yourself I'll go." And in the rollicking, outrageous farce *The Tinker's Wedding* ("too dangerous to be performed in Dublin" for almost fifty years), young Sarah Casey falters in her ambition to be at one with the married orthodox Christian community only when drunken old Mary Byrne proves the impossibility of conforming to the priest and "his like." Only in Synge's tragic tone poem *Riders to the Sea* are there deliberate simplicity and singleness of mood and action; this distillation of the harsh fateful life on Aran reflects the greater rhythm of timeless nature.

In October 1908, while Synge was convalescing in Germany with his old friends the von Eicken sisters, his mother, whose courage and steadfastness he captured so admirably in his first tragedy, died. His own death followed on March 24, 1909, in Dublin. He was correcting the proofs of *Poems and Translations* when he entered hospital for the last time. Much of the poignancy of these late poems and of the speeches of Deirdre bear witness to his increasing appreciation of the "fiery and magnificent, and tender" popular imagination which he discovered in Ireland and celebrated so singlemindedly in his life and his works. After his death, Yeats wrote of Synge in his diaries, "He had that egotism of the man of genius which Nietzsche compares to the egotism of a woman with child. . . . In the arts he knew no language but his own."

ANN SADDLEMYER

WORKS: "Letters of John Millington Synge from Material Supplied by Max Meyerfeld." *Yale Review* (July 1924): 690–709; *Collected Works Volume I: Poems.* Robin Skelton, ed. London: Oxford University Press, 1962; *Collected Works Volume II: Prose.* Alan Price, ed. London: Oxford University Press, 1966; *Collected Works Volumes III and IV: Plays.* Ann Saddlemyer, ed. London: Oxford University Press, 1968 (A new edition of these four volumes, with minor revisions to the volumes of plays, was published by Colin Smythe, Ltd. in 1982); *Letters to Molly: John Millington Synge to Maire O'Neill.* Ann Saddlemyer, ed. Cambridge, Mass.: Belknap, 1971; *My Wallet of Photographs,* selected by L. M. Stephens. Dublin: Dolmen, 1971; *Some Letters of John M. Synge to Lady Gregory and W. B. Yeats.* Ann Saddlemyer, ed. Dublin: Cuala, 1971; "J. M. Synge on the Early Irish Theatre: An Unpublished Article." Ann Saddlemyer, ed., *Modern Drama* 24 (September 1981): 276–281; *Theatre Business: The Correspondence of the First Abbey Directors.* Ann Saddlemyer, ed. Gerrards Cross: Colin Smythe, 1982; *The Well of the Saints.* Nicholas Grene, ed. Washington, D.C.: Catholic University of America, 1982; *When the Moon Has Set.* Mary King, ed. *Long Room* [Trinity College, Dublin], 1982: 24–25; *The Collected Letters of J. M. Synge.* 2 vols. Ann Saddlemyer, ed. Oxford: Clarendon, 1982, 1983.REFERENCES: Bushrui, S. B., ed. *Sunshine and the Moon's Delight: A Centenary Tribute to John Millington Synge.* Gerrards Cross: Colin Smythe, 1972; Gerstenberger, Donna. *John Millington Synge.* New York: Twayne, 1964; rev. ed., 1990; Greene, David H. & Stephens, Edward M. *J. M. Synge 1871–1909.* New York: Macmillan, 1959; Gregory, Isabella Augusta. *Our Irish Theatre.* London: Putnam, 1913; Grene, Nicholas. *Synge; A Critical Study of the Plays.* London: Macmillan, 1975; Harmon, Maurice, ed. *J. M. Synge Centenary Papers 1971.* Dublin: Dolmen, 1972; Hart, William E. *Synge's First Symphony: The Aran Islands.* New Britain, Conn.: Mariel, 1993; Howarth, Herbert. *The Irish Writers 1880–1940.* London: Rockliff, 1958; Johnson, Toni O'Brien. *Synge: The Medieval and the Grotesque.* Gerrards Cross: Colin Smythe, 1982; Johnston, Denis. *John Millington Synge.* New York: Columbia University Press, 1965; Kiberd, Declan. *Synge and the Irish Language.* London: Macmillan, 1979; Kiely, David M. *John Millington Synge, A Biography.* [Dublin]: Gill & Macmillan, [1994]; Kilroy, James. *The "Playboy" Riots.* Dublin: Dolmen, 1971; King, Mary C. *The Drama of J. M. Synge.* London: Fourth Estate, 1985; Kopper, Edward A., Jr., ed. *A J. M. Synge Literary Companion.* Westport, Conn.: Greenwood, 1988; Price, Alan. *Synge and Anglo-Irish Drama.* London: Methuen, 1961; Saddlemyer, Ann. *J. M. Synge and Modern Comedy.* Dublin: Dolmen, 1968; Saddlemyer, Ann. "Synge and the Doors of Perception." *Place, Personality and the Irish Writer.* Andrew Carpenter, ed. Gerrards

Cross: Colin Smythe, 1977, pp. 97–120; Saddlemyer, Ann. "Synge and the Nature of Women." *Women in Life, Legend and Literature.* S. F. Gallagher, ed. Gerrards Cross: Colin Smythe, 1982; Saddlemyer, Ann. "Synge's Soundscape." *Irish University Review* 22 (Spring/Summer 1992): 55–68; Skelton, Robin. *J. M. Synge and His World.* New York: Viking/London: Thames & Hudson, 1971; Skelton, Robin. *The Writings of J. M. Synge.* New York: Bobbs-Merrill/London: Thames & Hudson, 1971; Skelton, Robin & Saddlemyer, Ann, eds. *The World of W. B. Yeats.* Seattle: University of Washington Press, 1965; Stephens, Edward M. *My Uncle John.* Andrew Carpenter, ed. London: Oxford University Press, 1974; Synge, Samuel. *Letters to My Daughter: Memories of John Millington Synge.* Dublin: Talbot, 1932; *The Synge Manuscripts in the Library of Trinity College Dublin.* Dublin: Dolmen for the Library, 1971; Thornton, Weldon. *J. M. Synge and the Western Mind.* Gerrards Cross: Colin Smythe, 1979; Yeats, William Butler. *Autobiographies.* London: Macmillan, 1955.

T

TATE, NAHUM (1652–1715), poet and dramatist. Tate added nothing to Irish and little of value to English literature. His father, a Puritan divine with the remarkable name of Faithful Teate, was briefly provost of Trinity College, Dublin. His second son Nahum was born in Dublin in 1652 and received a B.A. from Trinity (about which he later wrote some deplorable verses) in 1672. He was a prolific writer of poems and plays, but much of his work was adaptation, translation, or collaboration. Sir Walter Scott called him "one of those second-rate bards, who, by dint of pleonasm and expletive, can find smooth lines if anyone will supply them with ideas." And Alexander Pope has derisively immortalized him in *The Dunciad.* Tate wrote most of the second part of Dryden's "Absalom and Achitophel," and his stage work included adaptations of Shakespeare, Chapman and Marston, Fletcher, and Webster. His happy ending version of *King Lear* is notorious; and, although Dr. Johnson liked it and it held the stage for nearly two hundred years, it gave rise to the term "Tateification," which means the debasement of a masterpiece. With Nicholas Brady he published in 1696 *A New Version of the Psalms;* but he did write the libretto for Purcell's *Dido and Aeneas,* and for that much may be forgiven. His only original poem of note is "Panacea—a Poem upon Tea." He was appointed Poet Laureate in 1692, succeeding Shadwell; Southey thought that only Shadwell was a poorer Poet Laureate than Tate. Personally he seems to have been an unprepossessing man. He died in London on July 30, 1715.

PRINCIPAL WORKS: *Poems.* 2d ed., enlarged. London: B. Toole, 1684; *New Version of the Psalms,* with Nicholas Brady. London, 1696; *Panacea: A Poem upon Tea.* London: J. Roberts, 1700; *Dido and Aeneas.* [London]: Boosey & Hawkes, [1961]. (Facsimile of the first edition); *The History of King Lear.* James Black, ed. London: Arnold, 1976. REFERENCES: Golden, S. A. "Nahum Tate, Poet and Dramatist." Diss., Trinity College, 1954; Spencer, Christopher. *Nahum Tate.* New York: Twayne, 1972; Scott-Thomas, H. F. "The Life and Works of Nahum Tate." 2 vols. Diss., Johns Hopkins University, 1932; Scott-Thomas, H. F. "Nahum Tate and the Seventeenth Century." *English Literary History* 1 (1934): 270.

TAYLOR, ALICE (1938–   ), memoirist and poet. Alice Taylor was born in County Cork, educated there, and presently lives there, in Innishannon, in a house attached to the local supermarket and the post office, with her husband and five children. Her three memoirs, *To School through the Fields* (1988), *Quench the Lamp* (1990), and *The Village* (1992) were received in Ireland enthusiastically. The first volume, in fact, brought out by a small Irish publisher, sold a record 175,000 copies in 1988 alone. Now published also in the United States and England, all three volumes continue to sell well. The success of *To School through the Fields* was, for some reviewers, something of a mystery. Taylor rambles on through places and characters of her childhood, evoking clichéd scenes of the bucolic life in a fairly plodding style. The book contains a couple of interesting characters—Old Nell, for example, with her false teeth and her eccentric ways. But otherwise, it would seem that this book appealed to an older generation's sense of a lost world. The American appeal is also understandable, most Irish Americans nursing a nostalgia for the ''old sod'' they never knew but heard about through generations of relatives' storytelling.

The sequels are surprisingly better than the first volume, as Taylor recounts the changing lifestyles of her villages and herself, chronicling Ireland's leisurely move, in the 1950s and 1960s, into a more modern era. Some of the characters from the first book show up again, and there are some redundancies, but not many. *Quench the Lamp* is more alive than the first book; Taylor moves beyond her tranquil recollections of nature to the people and events of Inishannon. Both *Quench the Lamp* and *The Village* are books that invite the reader to sit back and fall into the rambling rhythms of another world. The stories are good, the descriptions are often vivid, and the re-creation of the older order of the small village is much less tired and clichéd. Probably, Taylor's strongest trait is her depiction of her neighbors. She brings them to life deftly and makes them both interesting and sympathetic. At the end of *The Village,* as she chronicles the deaths of her in-laws, she hints at the death of the village as well, showing how Ireland's modernization has, in fact, ushered in a world far different from the one Taylor describes. So although *To School through the Fields* might not have impressed literary critics as a shining example of the memoir as a genre, the three volumes together make for quite a powerful elegy on the death of the old village life.

Taylor's *Close to the Earth* (1989) is a collection of her poetry, some of which she included in *To School through the Fields*. It is also a paean to a simpler life and shares the same closeness to nature and longing for simplicity that marked the first volume of her memoirs.

MARYANNE FELTER

WORKS: *To School through the Fields.* Dingle, Co. Kerry: Brandon, 1988/New York: St. Martin's, 1990/London: Century, 1991; *An Irish Country Diary.* Dingle, Co. Kerry: Brandon, 1988; *Close to the Earth.* Dingle, Co. Kerry: Brandon, 1989. (Poems); *Quench the Lamp.* Dingle: Co. Kerry: Brandon, 1990/New York: St. Martin's, 1991/London: Century, 1991. (Published with *To School through the Fields*); *Secrets of the Oak.* [Dingle, Co. Kerry]: Brandon, [1991]; *The Village.*

[Dingle, Co. Kerry]: Brandon, [1992]; *Country Days*. [Dingle, Co. Kerry]: Brandon, [1993]; *The Night Before Christmas*. [Dingle, Co. Kerry]: Brandon, [1994].

TAYLOR, GEOFFREY BASIL (1900–1956), poet and anthologist. Taylor was born Geoffrey Phibbs in Norfolk, on April 5, 1900. His Sligo Ascendancy family had been in Ireland since 1590. His father was Owen Phibbs, a soldier, who had married an Englishwoman, Rebekah Wilbraham Taylor. Taylor's earliest years were spent idyllically in England, where he absorbed from his mother and nurse a lifelong love of natural history. His father inherited Lisheen, the family home in Sligo, when he was fourteen. The house was filled with Egyptian antiquities and held a poltergeist that even the Jesuits were unable to exorcise. On leaving Haileybury, he was sent to the Officer Training Corps attached to Queen's University, Belfast, a copy of Shelley in his pocket, but the war ended before he saw service. Moving to Dublin, he joined the literary world there, and AE* published his early poems in *The Irish Statesman*. He worked for a time as a demonstrator in the Royal College of Science. Later he worked, along with Frank O'Connor* and Lennox Robinson,* as one of the Carnegie Library organizers in Ireland. In 1924, he fell in love with the artist Norah McGuinness, and they soon married. Though they had a base in Dublin, they spent much of their time in a Wicklow cottage. Geoffrey was full of sexual theories that were not appreciated by Norah, and she refused to have children. They parted in 1928, and in London Taylor became part of the celebrated ménage with Nancy Nicholson, Laura Riding, and Robert Graves. Eventually, he went to live with Nancy at Sutton Verney in Wiltshire, where they ran the Poulk Press. After they parted, he married Mary Dillwyn in 1935. During this time he brought out two volumes of very period poetry, which he came to dislike. Returning to Dublin, he became poetry editor of *The Bell** and met John Betjeman. For a time he was also poetry editor of *Time and Tide*. His early aggressive Darwinism was tempered by an increasingly mystical bent, a love of nature and gardening, and an interest in the obscurer corners of poetic tradition. He has more in common with the neoromantic poets of the 1940s in England than with his Irish peers. His scientific books are of specialized interest, and his poetry has been admired by some critics, but it is as an anthologist that he shall be remembered—not only for the two exceptional books with John Betjeman but also for his *Irish Poets of the Nineteenth Century*. This remains a key book of its period in stimulating a revival of interest in a more varied poetic tradition in Ireland before the rise of the Irish revival. He died in Dublin in 1956.

PETER COSTELLO

WORKS: As R. Fitzurse: *The Withering of the Fig Leaf*. London, 1927; *It Was Not Jones*. London: Leonard & Virginia Woolf, 1928. (Poetry). As Taylor: *A Dash of Garlic*. Sutton Verney: Poulk, 1933. (Poetry pamphlet); *Seven Simple Poems*. Sutton Verney: Poulk, 1937; ed., *Irish Poems of Today, Chosen from the First Seven Volumes of* The Bell. London: Secker & Warburg, 1944; *Insect Life in Britain*. London: Collins, 1945; *Some British Reptiles*. London: King Penguin, 1948; "Introduction." In *No Rebel Word* by John Hewitt. London: Frederick Muller, 1948; ed., *Irish Poets of the Nineteenth Century*. London: Routledge & Kegan Paul, 1951; *Some Nineteenth Century*

Gardeners. London: Skeffington, 1951; *The Emerald Isle.* London: Evans Bros., 1952; *The Victorian Flower Garden.* London: Skeffington, 1952; ed., with John Betjeman. *English, Scottish and Welsh Landscape.* London: Muller, 1944; ed., with John Betjeman. *English Love Poems.* London: Faber, 1957; *A Natural History.* (Unpublished autobiography). REFERENCES: Brown, Terence. *Ireland's Literature.* Gigginstown, Co. Meath: Lilliput/Totowa, N.J.: Barnes & Noble, 1988; Graves, Richard Percival. *Robert Graves: The Years with Laura, 1926–1940.* London: Weidenfeld & Nicolson, 1990; Lycett-Green, Candida, ed. *The Letters of John Betjeman.* London: Methuen, 1993; O'Connor, Frank. *My Father's Son.* London: Macmillan, 1968.

THACKERAY, WILLIAM MAKEPEACE (1811–1863), novelist and man of letters. Thackeray, the great English Victorian novelist, occasionally used Irish characters, perhaps most notably in his picaresque, Smollett-like first novel, *Barry Lyndon* (1844), which is partly set in Ireland. However, his most notable Irish work is *The Irish Sketch Book* (1843). This still eminently readable volume details Thackeray's impressions on a tour all around the country in 1842 and gives a vivid and basically sympathetic picture of pre-Famine Ireland, "this most distracted of all countries . . . this poor disunited country . . . this country of premature ruin." Although Thackeray remarked at the end of his tour, "A man ought to be forty years in Ireland, not three months, to begin to understand it," he had an accurate eye and often made the telling, perhaps even still appropriate, criticism, for instance, "They respect rank in England—the people seem almost to adore it here." Part of the pleasure of the book lies in the author's charming drawings.

WORKS OF IRISH INTEREST: *The Irish Sketch Book 1842.* London: Chapman & Hall, 1843/ Belfast & Dover, N.H.: Blackstaff, 1985. Introduction by John A. Gamble; *The Memoirs of Barry Lyndon.* George Saintsbury, ed. London: Oxford University Press, [1908]. REFERENCES: Collins, Philip, ed. *Thackeray, Interviews and Recollections.* [London & Basingstoke]: [Macmillan, 1983]; Flamm, Dudley. *Thackeray's Critics: An Annotated Bibliography of British and American Criticism, 1836–1901.* Chapel Hill: University of North Carolina Press, 1967; Olmstead, J. C. *Thackeray and His Twentieth-Century Critics: An Annotated Bibliography, 1900–1975.* New York: Garland, 1977; Ray, Gordon N., ed. *The Letters and Private Papers of William Makepeace Thackeray.* 4 vols. Cambridge: Harvard University Press, 1945–1946/New York: Octagon, 1980l; Ray, Gordon N. *Thackeray, The Uses of Adversity, 1847–1863.* London: Oxford University Press, 1955; Ray, Gordon N. *Thackeray, The Age of Wisdom, 1847–1863.* London: Oxford University Press, 1958; Tillotson, Geoffrey & Hawes, Donald, eds. *Thackeray, The Critical Heritage.* London: Routledge & Kegan Paul/New York: Barnes & Noble, 1968.

THOMPSON, KATE, poet.

WORK: *There Is Something.* [Bellingham, Wash.]: Signpost Press/[Galway]: Salmon, [1992].

THOMPSON, SAM (1916–1965), playwright. Thompson was a Belfast working man and, like Brendan Behan* whom he somewhat resembles, a painter. He was born on May 21, 1916, in Belfast. He was encouraged in his early writing by Sam Hanna Bell* who produced several of his early plays, such as *Brush in Hand* (1956), for radio. Thompson's first stage play, *Over the Bridge,* was a realistic study of a sectarian labor dispute. Although basically a plea for good will and religious tolerance, the play was already in rehearsal by the Ulster

Group Theatre* when the theatre's directors withdrew it. The reason given was a determination "not to mount any play which would offend or affront the religious or political beliefs or sensibilities of the man in the street. . . ." However, when Thompson and friends produced it themselves at the Empire Theatre in Belfast in 1960, it had a most successful and highly acclaimed run. *Over the Bridge* is not a great play, but it is craftsmanlike and well observed; it deals with the crucial Northern problem of religious bigotry which probably only St. John Ervine* in *Mixed Marriage* had until that time put so bluntly on the stage. Thompson's later work, all unpublished, included *The Evangelist* (1963), a study of religious fanaticism, and *Cemented with Love* (1965), a television play about political chicanery. He himself was involved in union work and stood unsuccessfully for political office. He also had begun to act for the stage and for television when he died unexpectedly in Belfast on February 15, 1965, of a heart attack. Stewart Parker* described his death as "a grievous loss to Irish drama."

WORK: *Over the Bridge,* edited & introduced by Stewart Parker. Dublin: Gill & Macmillan, 1970. REFERENCE: Mengel, H. *Sam Thompson and Modern Drama in Ulster.* Frankfurt am Main, Bern, New York: Verlag Peter Lang, 1986.

THURSTON, KATHERINE CECIL (1875–1911), novelist. Katherine Cecil Madden was born in Cork, the only daughter of Paul Madden, a former nationalist mayor of Cork. She married Ernest E. Temple Thurston, an English novelist, in 1901. Ernest Thurston's novels are largely anti-Catholic, and in *Ireland in Fiction* Stephen Brown encapsulates his work with the line: "His writings give constant evidence of misconception of Catholic doctrine." His wife's novels have a more tolerant view of religious doctrine. The Thurstons' marriage was not successful, and the couple divorced after a short time. She was described by the *Irish Book Lover* as "tall and graceful, with wonderful charm of manner and personality." She was due to remarry the same month she died in Moore's Hotel in Cork. The official verdict of her death was suffocation during an epileptic fit. There was, however, speculation about other causes, including the hint of suicide.

Katherine Thurston's novels were extremely popular. Her most successful was *John Chilcote, M.P.,* a tale of political suspense. Ernest Thurston scripted the book for a film made in 1905, one year after the novel's publication. Estimates suggest that up to 200,000 copies of the book were sold just in America. Katherine Thurston was an extremely popular speaker after the success of *John Chilcote, M.P.*

Two of her novels have Irish settings, *The Gambler* (1906) and *The Fly on the Wheel* (1908). The latter details the life of Isabel Costello as she is introduced into Waterford's Catholic, middle-class society. Isabel becomes entangled in a triangular relationship with her fiancé, Frank Carey, and his elder brother, Stephen. There have been suggestions that the book contains autobiographical elements, largely due to the Waterford location and the heroine's suicide, although these elements were probably unintentional on the author's part and were fueled by the circumstances of her own death.

ANNE COLMAN

WORKS: *The Circle*. Edinburgh: Blackwood, 1903; *John Chilcote, M.P.* Edinburgh: Blackwood, 1904; *The Gambler*. London: Hutchinson, 1906; *The Mystics*. Edinburgh: Blackwood, 1907; *The Fly on the Wheel*. Edinburgh & London: Blackwood, 1908/rpt., London: Virago, 1987; *Max*. London: Hutchinson, 1910.

TIGHE, MARY (1772–1810), poet. Tighe was the daughter of the Reverend William Blachford and was born in Dublin on October 9, 1772. Her mother founded the Dublin House of Refuge for Unprotected Female Servants. She herself married her cousin, Henry Tighe, a member of Parliament. Her poem *Psyche* (1805), taken from Apuleius, was widely admired and frequently reprinted. To the modern taste, its six cantos of Spenserian stanzas and its more than 200 pages are, despite occasional strong lines, utterly conventional and excessively wearying. One of Tighe's early admirers was the young Keats, but, as one of his editors justly remarked, "It is true that he sometimes took delight in certain mediocre poets like Beattie and Mrs. Tighe; but he quickly outgrew them, . . . turning for permanent satisfaction to the indubitably great." Indeed, what remaining interest attaches to Tighe is concerned with her influence on Keats. Despite a few lines of close resemblance, that influence was neither lasting nor important. She died of tuberculosis on March 24, 1810.

WORKS: *Psyche; Or, The Legend of Love*. London: Printed for James Carpenter by C. Whittington, 1805; *Psyche, With Other Poems by the Late Mrs. Henry Tighe*. London: Longman, 1811; *Mary, A Series of Reflections during Twenty Years*. William Tighe, ed. 1811. (Neither place nor publisher is listed). REFERENCES: Henchy, Patrick. *The Works of Mary Tighe, Published and Unpublished*. Dublin: At the Sign of the Three Candles, 1957; Weller, E. V. *Keats and Mary Tighe. The Poems of Mary Tighe; With Parallel Passages from the Works of John Keats*. New York: Century, 1928.

TOCNAYE, LE CHEVALIER DE LA (ca. 1767–?), travel writer. Jacques Louis de Bougrenet, Le Chevalier de la Tocnaye was a French aristocrat born in Brittany and forced to flee from France during the revolution. Impoverished, he took walking tours around England and Scotland, Ireland, and Sweden and Norway and published accounts of them. His Irish book, *Promenade d'un Français en Irlande* (1797), is an engaging, readable, and fair-minded account of the country, its landscape, and its customs a little before the 1798 Rising.

IRISH WORK: *Promenade d'un Français en Irlande*. Dublin: Imprime aux frais de l'auteur, par M. & D. Graisberry, 1797/*Rambles through Ireland; by a French Emigrant . . . Translated . . . by an Irishman*. 2 vols. Cork: M. Harris, 1798/translated by John Stevenson. Belfast: McCaw, Stevenson & Orr, 1917/reprinted with an introduction by John A. Gamble. Belfast: Blackstaff, 1985.

TODHUNTER, JOHN (1839–1916), poet and dramatist. Todhunter was born in Dublin on December 29 or 30, 1839. He received an M.D. from Trinity College, Dublin, in 1871, and practiced medicine briefly in Dublin, where he also taught English at Alexandra College. In 1874, he left for London, where he became a friend of the Yeats family and a member of the Rhymers' Club. About 1888, he directed his prolific pen away from classical and toward Irish subjects, such as conventionally lamenting lyrics, retelling of portions of the bardic tales, and a life of Sarsfield. Stephen Gwynn* states that Todhunter's poem "Aghadoe" is deservedly found in every anthology of Irish verse but that is a gentle and nowadays incorrect assessment. W. B. Yeats,* who reviewed many of Todhunter's books, later wrote:

In these articles I overrated Dr. Todhunter's poetical importance, not because he was a friendly neighbor with a charming house, a Morris carpet on the drawing-room floor, upon the walls early pictures by my father painted under the influence of Rossetti, but because a single play of his, the *Sicilian Idyll*—I did not overrate the rest of his work— and still more its success confirmed a passion for that other art [of poetic drama].

Todhunter was a fluent technician, but he saw the world through the eyes of previous (and mainly English) poets. Hence, his verse has a generally correct, if academic, dullness and is little read today.

Todhunter's plays are neither modern nor, despite Yeats, particularly good, but they did have some intellectual success in their day. *Alcestis* was done at Hengler's Circus in 1879; Beerbohm Tree appeared in *Helena in Troas* in 1886; at a minor production of *A Sicilian Idyll* in 1890, Yeats first saw Florence Farr; J. T. Grein's Independent Theatre staged *The Black Cat* in 1893; and in 1894, Florence Farr, with the backing of Miss A.E.F. Horniman, produced *A Comedy of Sighs* at the Avenue Theatre. This last-named play failed so signally that Farr replaced it with another new piece, Bernard Shaw's* *Arms and the Man,* and this was Shaw's first semisuccess on the English stage. The curtain-raiser for both the Todhunter play and the Shaw one was *The Land of Heart's Desire,* W. B. Yeats' first staged play. So, in effect, if Todhunter was himself an unsuccessful dramatist, he was something of an accidental John the Baptist to the most notable poetic and prose dramatists in English in the twentieth century. He died on October 25, 1916, in Chiswick, England.

WORKS: *Laurella and Other Poems.* London, 1876; *Alcestis.* London, 1879; *A Study of Shelley.* London: Kegan Paul, 1880; *Forest Songs and Other Poems.* London: Kegan Paul, 1881; *The True Tragedy of Rienzi, Tribune of Rome.* London: Kegan Paul, 1881; *Helena in Troas.* London: Kegan Paul, 1886; *The Banshee and Other Poems.* London: Kegan Paul, 1888; *A Sicilian Idyll.* London: Elkin Mathews, 1890; *The Black Cat.* London: Henry, 1893; *Three Irish Bardic Tales.* London: J. M. Dent, 1896; *Life of Patrick Sarsfield, Earl of Lucan.* London: Unwin/Dublin: Sealy, Bryers & Walker, 1901; *From the Land of Dreams.* Introduction by T. W. Rolleston. Dublin: Talbot/London: Unwin, 1918. (Irish poems); *Essays.* Foreword by Standish O'Grady. London: Elkin Mathews, 1920; *Isolt of Ireland: A Legend in a Prologue and Three Acts; And The Passion Flower.* London & Toronto: J. M. Dent, 1927; *Trivium Amoris, and the Wooing of Artemis.* London & Toronto: J. M. Dent, 1927; *Selected Poems.* E. L. Todhunter & A. P. Graves, eds. London: E. Mathews & Marrot, 1929. REFERENCE: Moriarty, David James. "John Todhunter: Child of the Coming Century." Diss., University of Wisconsin, 1979.

TÓIBÍN, COLM (1955–), novelist and journalist. Born on May 30, 1955, Tóibín first made his reputation as a journalist and columnist for the *Sunday*

Independent in Dublin and as a contributing editor at *Esquire* in London. In 1991, he won the *Irish Times*/Aer Lingus Award for his first novel, *The South,* which was also short-listed for the Booker Prize.

Tóibín's early works have their background in his journalism. In 1985, he edited *Seeing Is Believing: Moving Statues in Ireland,* a work that focused on the miraculous happenings concerning a statue of the Virgin Mary at the Ballinspittle Christian Church in County Cork. Tóibín followed that work with *Martyrs and Metaphors* (1987), an essay that addressed the place and role of politics in Irish literature. Tóibín's first widely noticed work was *Walking along the Border* (1987), a travel book about Northern Ireland that featured photographs by Tony O'Shea. Tóibín and O'Shea teamed again in 1990 for another travel/essay book, *Dubliners.* Also appearing in 1990 was Tóibín's *Homage to Barcelona* (originally titled *Barcelona*), a timely book, as the 1992 Summer Olympics were held in that Spanish city.

Homage to Barcelona is rather more than the traditional travel book. Tóibín lived in the city for a few years after Franco died, and he returned in the late 1980s, and his knowledge goes deeper than the traditional "the traveler should see this" approach. He is intent on giving the feel of what makes Barcelona so special. In a fluid narrative, he is able to bring the city alive; his attention to the architectural styles (Puig i Cadafalch and Gaudi), the rich artistic past (Picasso, Casals, and Dali), and the ebb and flow of the late-night Catalan society makes Barcelona seem more like a character than a place.

Toibin's first novel, *The South* (1990), also has its roots in the author's knowledge of Barcelona and Spain. In this impressive debut, he tells the story of Katherine Porter's escape from an inhibiting family life in Ireland, to the world of art in post-civil war Spain. Along the way she experiences a lifetime of lessons: she must deal with having abandoned her husband and ten-year-old son; she must decide what her path in life should be; she must decide if she is an artist; she must come to grips with her relationship with her mother; she must decide if she loves Miguel, the troubled socialist who may be a great artist; she must decide what her relationship with fellow Irish émigré Michael Graves is; she must decide if her daughter's death in a car accident with Miguel is indeed an accident. In short, she must decide if life is worth all of the hassles.

The South is a great achievement because of Tóibín's considerable insight into the human condition. Nominally, the novel is about exile, a theme in which twentieth-century Irish literature is well steeped, but the work has more to say than that. Indeed, *The South* is a novel about personal relationships and the forces that control the most basic emotions, love and fear. Loneliness and self-imposed isolation are the determining factors in Katherine's relationships with her mother, her deserted husband, her abandoned son, her passionate lover Miguel, and her friend Michael. The universality of such themes makes *The South* a powerful and moving work.

Tóibín's second novel, *The Heather Blazing* (1992), solidified his reputation. The title is taken from an Irish rebel song, and the protagonist is Eamon Redmond, a judge in the Irish High Court. Born and raised in Enniscorthy, County Wexford, Redmond is a complex man who has faced a variety of challenges: the early death of his mother, the stroke of his father, an uncertainty in dealing with women as a young man, the political struggles of establishing his career, an illegitimate grandson, and finally the stroke and eventual death of his wife. In short, the novel is about how a man comes to terms with who he is and what he represents.

If that summary sounds depressing and hopeless, the novel is not. Rather, Tóibín presents an accurate view of the struggles and complexities of late twentieth-century life in Ireland. When Redmond was growing up in the 1940s and 1950s, his life seemed simple. His family were republicans, his father's word was law, and everything else was referred to the church. As an adult in the late 1980s, however, the certainty of Redmond's youth is gone. Now he, as a High Court judge, has the responsibility of making major decisions of the day. The problem is that life in Ireland has changed. To illustrate this, Tóibín provides Redmond with a difficult case. A sixteen-year-old-girl became pregnant and was expelled from her convent school. She is suing the school, and Redmond must decide the outcome. Fifty years earlier there would have been no hesitation— but Ireland has changed. Eventually, however, Redmond does side with the school, much to the chagrin of his progressive-thinking wife and daughter. This decision highlights his grapple with the New Ireland and indeed symbolizes his inability to understand other people. As intelligent and well meaning as Redmond is, he is ultimately a lonely man who has never allowed anyone—not even his wife, Carmel—to get really close to him. Such is the state, Tóibín seems to be saying, of contemporary life in Ireland.

The Heather Blazing is an impressive and important work. Its quiet and introspective story is simply told. Clearly, it is the depth of Eamon Redmond that is so attractive, because he is much an Everyman figure of late twentieth-century Ireland. Tóibín's use of flashbacks—the juxtaposition of the young Eamon in Enniscorthy and the older Judge Redmond in Dublin and Cush—allows the reader to see how and why Redmond is who he is. As in *The South,* Tóibín gives special attention to creating the sense of place, especially the deteriorating cliffs of Cush, which seem to represent Redmond and, to a larger extent, the state of Ireland.

With *The South* and *The Heather Blazing,* Tóibín has proven to be among the best of the impressive group of young Irish novelists to emerge in the early 1990s.

SHAWN O'HARE

WORKS: Ed., *Seeing Is Believing: Moving Statues in Ireland.* Mountrath, Co. Laois: Pilgrim, 1985; *Martyrs and Metaphors.* Dublin: Raven Arts, 1987. (Nonfiction); *Walking along the Border.* London: MacDonald, Queen Anne, 1987. (Nonfiction, with photographs by Tony O'Shea); *Barcelona.* London: Virgin, 1990/as *Homage to Barcelona.* London & New York: Simon & Schuster, 1990/New York: Penguin, 1992. (Travel); *The South.* London: Serpent's Tale, 1990/New York: Viking, 1991/London: Picador, 1992/New York: Penguin, 1992. (Novel); *The Trial of the Generals: Selected Journalism 1980–1990.* Dublin: Raven Arts, 1990; *The Heather Blazing.* London: Picador/

New York: Viking, 1992. (Novel); ed., *New Writings from Ireland.* Winchester, Mass.: Faber, 1994; ed., *Soho Square Six.* London: Bloomsbury, 1994; *Signs of the Cross.* London: Cape, 1994. (Nonfiction).

TOMAN, EDWARD (ca. 1940–   ), novelist. Toman was born in Northern Ireland and graduated from Queen's University, Belfast. In the late 1960s, when a lecturer in further education in Belfast, he was a founder of the civil rights movement. After two years in Zambia, he moved to London and organized Open University courses in Holloway Prison. He also studied for a master's degree at Oxford and now lives in London with his wife and two children.

Toman's novels are highly readable, extravagant, and sardonic satiric comedies. His first, for instance, *Shambles Corner* (1993), is about the devious machinations of Catholic and Protestant clerics and laymen in the North of Ireland. There are a moving statue for the Catholics and a service involving live snakes for the Protestants, and the practice of religion is carried on like warfare. The exaggeration of the incidents is paralleled by a racily incongruous dialogue, as in this interchange between a priest called Schnozzle Durante and the Catholic cardinal who is known as Big Mac:

"The Legion of Mary were on duty . . ." Schnozzle mumbled.

"A crowd who couldn't control a camogie match! In God's name, man, what were you thinking of! A parish like that needs something more than the Legion of Mary if you're ever going to knock the bastards into line! . . . Have we gone soft altogether? Is the whole nation turning into nothing but a crowd of nancy boys?"

Although the satire in both of Toman's books is very broad, there is more than a bit of bite in it.

WORKS: *Shambles Corner.* [London]: Flamingo, [1993]; *Dancing in Limbo.* [London]: Flamingo, [1995].

TOMELTY, JOSEPH (1911–1995), playwright, novelist, and actor. Tomelty was born on March 12, 1911, at Portaferry near Belfast. His was a musical, rather than a bookish, family, and for years the only book he owned was Goldsmith's* *The Deserted Village.* Leaving the local primary school at the age of twelve, he was apprenticed as a house painter and took some classes at the "Tech" in Belfast, where his English teacher encouraged him to write. He was a founding member in 1940 of the Group Theatre in Belfast, as well as one of its leading actors and playwrights. The Group produced some of his local Belfast comedies, such as *Barnum Was Right* and *Right Again, Barnum,* as well as three of best plays: *The End House* (1944), *All Souls' Night* (1948), and *Is the Priest at Home?* (1954). In 1948, he created a vastly popular radio serial for the BBC in Belfast, "The McCooeys," which ran for seven years and for which he wrote about 800,000 words. In 1951, under the direction of Tyrone Guthrie, he appeared in London as John Phibbs in George Shiels's* *The Passing Day;* and, although that production quickly gave way to the still-running Agatha Christie mystery *The Mousetrap,* it brought him to the attention of David Lean, and Tomelty began a successful career as a character actor in films. His versatile and talented productivity was severely truncated by an extremely serious automobile accident in 1954. In 1956, Queen's University, Belfast, awarded him an M.A. for his services to the theater.

His play *The End House* is almost, if not quite, a Belfast equivalent of O'Casey's* *Juno and the Paycock;* his *All Souls' Night* is a tragedy reminiscent, if not the equal, of *Riders to the Sea;* and his *Is the Priest at Home?* is a realistic but sympathetic depiction of the daily life of a cleric. His "The Singing Bird," written in 1948 but produced on television in 1971 with himself in the lead, is a poignant depiction of a half-mad tinker. His unproduced *April in Assagh* (1953) is something of a three-act extension of Lady Gregory's* "Spreading the News." Practically nothing happens, except that a woman loses her cat, and the village pump breaks, but the superb characterization and chat of the villagers are a tour de force that brilliantly carries the play. Tomelty also published two worthy, if not superb, novels, *Red Is the Port Light* (1948) and *The Apprentice* (1953). His accident cut short a remarkable talent.

He died in Belfast on June 7, 1995.

WORKS: *Red Is the Port Light.* London: Jonathan Cape, 1948. (Novel); *Right Again, Barnum.* Belfast: H. R. Carter, [1950]. (Play); *The Apprentice: The Story of a Nonentity.* London: Jonathan Cape, 1953. (Novel); *Mugs and Money (Barnum Was Right.* Belfast: H. R. Carter, 1953. (Play); *Is the Priest at Home?* Belfast: H. R. Carter, 1954. (Play); *All Souls' Night.* Belfast: H. R. Carter, 1955. (Play); *The End House.* Dublin: James Duffy, 1962. (Play); *All Souls' Night and Other Plays.* Damian Smyth, ed. [Belfast]: Lagan, [1993]. (Contains the title play, "The Singing Bird," *April in Assagh,* and *The End House*). REFERENCES: Gray, John. "Joseph Tomelty Talks to John Gray." *The Linenhall Review* 1 (1985) 9–10; Smyth, Damian. "Introduction." *All Souls' Night and Other Plays.*

TONE, [THEOBALD] WOLFE (1763–1798), patriot and autobiographer. Tone was born in Dublin on June 20, 1763, the eldest son of a coach builder of some means. While still a schoolboy, he developed a passion for military life, but his father insisted that he attend Trinity College, Dublin, where he was an able but unwilling student. In 1785, while still at Trinity, he eloped with sixteen-year-old Martha Witherington of Grafton Street and married her, spending the honeymoon in Maynooth. On graduating from Trinity, he read law in Dublin and London and was called to the Bar in 1789. "As to law, I knew exactly as much about it as I did of necromancy," Tone wrote in his *Autobiography.* Politics was his real interest, and in 1791 he was among those who formed the Society of United Irishmen, a movement uniting Catholics and Protestants to secure parliamentary reform. Although an agnostic of Protestant background, he was appointed secretary of the Catholic Committee in the following year. The Relief Act of 1793 was brought about largely through his efforts, and the Catholic Committee awarded him a gold medal and the sum of £1,500.

The concessions granted by the act were by no means adequate, and the United Irishmen began to plan a rebellion. The authorities seized some documents that revealed that Tone was in correspondence with the French, and so he sailed for America with his wife and children. He landed in Wilmington, Delaware, and had just settled to the life of an American farmer in Princeton, New Jersey, when letters arrived from the United Irishmen asking him to go to France to seek aid for Ireland. Although he could hardly speak French and had no letters of introduction, he set out immediately. Astonishingly, he succeeded in getting the French Directory to appoint General Lazarre Hoche as Commander-in-Chief of an Irish expedition. In December 1796, a large fleet with fifteen thousand soldiers aboard set sail for Ireland. Tone sailed with them as an adjutant general. Unfortunately, a hurricane prevented the soldiers from landing. A year later, the French sent their Dutch fleet, but it was defeated at sea. In 1798, the year of the Irish rebellion, two smaller fleets were defeated. Tone was aboard one of the ships of the second fleet and was captured, court-martialed, and sentenced to be hanged, in spite of his request for a soldier's death by shooting. Tone's father, aided by John Philpot Curran, tried to save him by seeking a writ of Habeas Corpus, but while this action was in progress Tone cut his own throat and died of his wounds on November 19, 1798.

If history had been otherwise, Tone might well be remembered primarily as an Irish writer. While a poor student in London, he wrote articles for money and also collaborated on a burlesque novel, *Belmont Castle,* which was a satire of current popular fiction. But, although gifted as a writer, Tone was interested in writing only as a means to communicate his political ideals. Even his *Autobiography,* which is considered an Irish classic, was written to instruct his children. This work was published in Washington in 1826 in a volume entitled *The Life of Theobald Wolfe Tone,* edited by his son William, along with Tone's diaries, autobiographical memoranda, letters, political writings, and accounts by the son of Tone's death and his family. The *Autobiography* is so engaging on Tone's early life and marriage that it is impossible to remain detached from his political beliefs. The clear strong prose is free of the verbal pomposity of John Mitchel* and reveals an affectionate and fun-loving young man. Nevertheless, he grew fanatical and wrote, for instance, of the young French soldiers: "Many fine lads of twenty, who have sacrificed an arm or a leg to the liberty of their country. I could worship them." There are also amusing accounts of his interviews with the leaders of the French Revolution and his impressions of eighteenth-century Paris. Tone's last letters to his wife are so heart-rending in their simple courage that one cannot help wishing that he had remained living happily as an American farmer.

MARY ROSE CALLAGHAN

PRINCIPAL WORKS: *Life of Theobald Wolfe Tone ... Written by Himself and Continued by His Son. . . .* William Theobald Wolfe Tone, ed. Washington, D.C.: Gale & Seaton, 1826/London: Henry Colburn, 1827/abridged by Sean O'Faolain. London: Nelson, 1937; *The Autobiography of Wolfe Tone.* 2 vols. R. Barry O'Brien, ed. London: Fisher Unwin, 1893; *The Letters of Wolfe Tone.* Bulmer Hobson, ed. Dublin: Martin Lester, [1921] *The Best of Tone.* Proinsias Mac Aonghusa & Liam Ó Réagáin, eds. Cork: Mercier, [1972]. REFERENCES: Boylan, Henry. *Theobald Wolfe Tone.* Dublin: Gill & Macmillan, 1981; Butler, Hubert. *Wolfe Tone and the Common Name of*

Irishman. Gigginstown: Lilliput, 1985; de Blacam, A. S. *The Life of Wolfe Tone.* Dublin: Talbot/ London: Rich & Cowan, 1935; Elliott, Marianne. *Partners in Revolution: The United Irishmen and France.* New Haven, Conn.: Yale University Press, 1982; MacDermot, Frank. *Theobald Wolfe Tone and His Times.* London: Macmillan, 1939/rev. Tralee: Anvil, 1968.

TRACY, HONOR (1913–1989), novelist and humorist. Although an English-woman, Honor Tracy is best known for her humorous novels and sketches about contemporary Irish life. She was born Honor Lilbush Wingfield Tracy in Bury St. Edmunds, Suffolk, on October 19, 1913. She was educated privately in London and in Germany, and she spent two years at the Sorbonne. From 1934 to 1937, she worked for a London publisher, and from 1937 until the outbreak of the war she worked as a freelance writer. She served for two years in the British Women's Auxiliary Air Force and then from 1941 to 1945 was attached to the Ministry of Information as a Japanese specialist. She had some Japanese and was fluent in several other languages, including French, German, Italian, and Russian. Following the war, she was a journalist for the *Observer* and the *Sunday Times* and a frequent contributor to the BBC Third Programme. In Ire-land, she worked with Sean O'Faolain,* who became, as the *Irish Times* put it, "her mentor both in writing and in the 'new acerbic Irish Catholicism.' " She also became an editorial assistant on *The Bell* during the editorship of Peadar O'Donnell.* In 1947, the *Observer* sent her to Japan, and her stay resulted in her first book, *Kakemono* (1950), an account of that country during the American occupation. She was later to write several books about Spain, but her identifi-cation with Ireland began with *Mind You, I've Said Nothing!* (1953), a hilarious collection of essays about the mores and manners of postwar Ireland. The wit is often astringent, but it only thinly disguises Tracey's affection for the dottier quirks of the Irish. Her first and probably best-known novel, *The Straight and Narrow Path* (1956), established her as a satirist of note. In this work she handled the Marian frenzy of the 1950s and the litigiousness of the Irish with a malicious tenderness. Her subsequent novels, about a dozen in number, are more or less in the same vein.

Tracy is an enviable stylist, as she was also a brilliant conversationalist, and she satirizes both the Anglo-Irish and the Mere-Irish with equal wickedness. Her characters, although often pushed to caricature, are so gorgeously ridiculous that it is hard to read any of her novels without chuckling out loud. Nevertheless, she does not have the stature of an Evelyn Waugh, for she tilts mainly at quirks and foibles rather than at anything of significant import. Her books are pleasant reading for a rainy day, but neither her characters nor their adventures are finally memorable.

She lived in many parts of Ireland, from Killiney to Achill Island, but she died in an English nursing home in Oxford on June 13, 1989.

MARY ROSE CALLAGHAN

WORKS: *The Conquest of Violence.* Translated from Bartolomeus's *De Overwinning van het gewald.* London: G. Routledge, 1937/New York: E. P. Dutton, 1938; *Kakemono, a Sketch Book of Post-War Japan.* London: Methuen, 1950; *Mind You, I've Said Nothing! Forays in the Irish Re-*

public. London: Methuen, 1953. (Sketches); *The Deserters.* London: Methuen, 1954. (Novel); *The Straight and Narrow Path.* London: Methuen/New York: Random House, 1956. (Novel); *Silk Hats and No Breakfast. Notes on a Spanish Journey.* London: Methuen, 1957/New York: Random House, 1958; *The Prospects Are Pleasing.* London: Methuen/New York: Random House, 1958. (Novel); *A Number of Things.* London: Methuen/New York: Random House, 1960. (Novel); *A Season of Mists.* London: Methuen/New York: Random House, 1961. (Novel); *The First Day of Friday.* London: Methuen/New York: Random House, 1963. (Novel); *Spanish Leaves.* London: Methuen/New York: Random House, 1964. (Travel); *Men at Work.* London: Methuen, 1966/New York: Random House, 1967. (Novel); *The Beauty of the World.* London: Methuen, 1967/American title, *Settled in Chambers.* New York: Random House, 1968; (Novel); *The Butterflies of the Province.* New York: Random House/London: Eyre Methuen, 1970. (Novel); *The Quiet End of Evening.* London: Eyre Methuen/New York: Random House, 1972. (Novel); *Winter in Castille.* London: Eyre Methuen/New York: Random House, 1975. (Travel); *In the Year of Grace.* New York: Random House, 1974/London: Eyre Methuen, 1975. (Novel); *The Man from Next Door.* London: Hamish Hamilton, 1977. (Novel); *The Ballad of Castle Reef.* London: Hamish Hamilton/New York: Random House, 1979. (Novel); *The Heart of England.* London: Hamish Hamilton, 1983.

TRAPMAN, WILLIAM

WORK: *Marisceo's House and Other Stories.* Kilcullen: Kestrel's Nest, 1993.

TREACY, MAURA (1946–   ), short story writer and novelist. Treacy was born in County Kilkenny, was educated locally, and still lives there. She received a Listowel Short Story Award in 1974, two bursaries from the Arts Council, and a grant from the Irish-American Foundation. Her collection, *Sixpence in Her Shoe* (1977), is mainly concerned with farm life and contains fifteen pieces in a short book of about 125 pages. Some, such as "A Time for Growing" or "Sadness Is over the Fields," are descriptions or character sketches rather than stories; but even the legitimate stories have something of the blandness of sketches. Partly, the problem is that her writing is often only sparely, flatly functional. Here, for instance, is a randomly picked paragraph:

Fionnuala and her mother were home from Mass and had the dinner ready but her father still had not come up from the new building. He had let them out of the car there and they had walked the rest of the way home. Another car drew up at the site as they left and before they reached home yet another had arrived. Later her mother sent her down to tell him the dinner was ready.

Now and then she is stronger—as, for instance, in the conclusion of one of her better pieces, "Separate Ways":

There would always be an echo of wonder at the way he re-emerged to carry on the routine of his days, since effort hardly seemed possible without optimism.

But generally the best that can be said of these stories is that they are careful, serious, a little dull, and rather forgettable.

Treacy's novel, *Scenes from a Country Wedding* (1981), is neither dull nor forgettable. Divided into three parts, it describes the doings, the characters, and the conversations of a large family and their friends before a wedding, at the wedding party, and afterward. The writing is a terse and clear vehicle for accurate observation, and the details and the talk have an authentic ring. The fault of the novel is that its cast is so very large for a medium-sized book of about 70,000 words. A greater development, and particularly an attention to physical description, of characters would have prevented some of the minor ones from being simply names. Nevertheless, the book is a solid accomplishment that makes one regret there has been no recent work from this author.

WORKS: *Sixpence in Her Shoe and Other Stories*. Dublin: Poolbeg, [1977]; *Scenes from a Country Wedding*. [Swords, Co. Dublin]: Poolbeg, [1981]. (Novel).

TRENCH, RICHARD CHENEVIX (1807–1886), poet, philologist, theologian, and cleric. Trench was born in Dublin on September 5, 1807, the son of Richard Trench, a barrister, and his wife, Melesina, herself a poet. He was educated at Harrow and Trinity College, Cambridge, and ordained in 1829. He was professor of divinity at King's College from 1846 to 1858. In 1856, he became dean of Westminster and on January 1, 1864, archbishop of Dublin, a post he held until 1884. He died on March 29, 1886, in London and is buried in Westminster Abbey. In addition to many theological works, he translated Calderon, and his *Study of Words* (1851) went into twenty editions. His has been called a "type of moralizing philology," and the reason may been seen from this quotation from *The Study of Words:*

I open the first letter of the alphabet; what means this "Ah," this "Alas," these deep and long-drawn sighs of humanity, which at once encounter us there? And then presently follow words such as these, Affliction, Agony, Anguish, Assassin, Atheist, Avarice, and twenty more . . . it is a melancholy thing to observe how much richer is every vocabulary in words that set forth sins, than in those that set forth graces.

Nevertheless, Trench originated the scheme of the *Oxford English Dictionary*. Trench's poetry was also much read but had little Irish about it. His poems were urbane, crafted, and lacking any great individuality. As Paul Turner in *The Oxford History of English Literature* remarks, "Tennyson's friends Arthur Hallam and R. C. Trench the philologist were merely thinkers who had learned to versify."

PRINCIPAL LITERARY WORKS: *The Story of Justin Martyr and Other Poems*. London: E. Moxon, 1835; *Sabbation, Honor Neale, and Other Poems*. London: Moxon, 1838; *Poems*. London: Privately printed, 1841; *Genoveva: A Poem*. London, 1842; *Poems from Eastern Sources, The Steadfast Prince, and Other Poems*. London: E. Moxon, 1842/2d ed., with additions. London: J. W. Parker, 1851; *Elegiac Poems*. London: E. Moxon, 1843; *On the Study of Words*. London, 1851/19th ed. London: Kegan Paul, 1886; *Alma and Other Poems*. London: J. W. Parker, 1855; *English, Past and Present*. London: J. W. Parker, 1855/14th ed., revised and in part rewritten by E. L. Mayhew. London: Kegan Paul, 1889; tr., *Life's a Dream; The Great Theatre of the World. From the Spanish of Calderon. With an Essay on His Life and Genius*. London: J. W. Parker, 1856/New York: Redfield, 1856; *On Some Deficiencies in Our English Dictionaries*. London: J. W. Parker, 1857; *Poems. Collected and Arranged Anew*. London & Cambridge: Macmillan, 1865; *Poems*. London: Macmillan, 1885; *In Time of War*. London: Kegan Paul, 1900. (Poetry); *Sonnets and Elegiacs*. London: Kegan Paul, 1910. REFERENCES: Bromley, John. *The Man of Ten Talents: A Portrait of Richard Chenevix Trench 1807–1886: Philologist, Poet, Theologian, Archbishop.*

London: S.P.C.K., 1959; De Vere, Aubrey. "Archbishop Trench's Poems." *Nineteenth Century* 23 (1888): 858–880.

TRENCH, WILLIAM STUART (1808–1872), land agent and author. Trench was born on September 16, 1808, at Bellegrove, near Portarlington, County Offaly. He was the fourth son of Thomas Trench, dean of Kildare, and the cousin of Richard Chenevix Trench.* He was educated at the Royal School, Armagh, and at Trinity College, Dublin. He became land agent for the Shirley estate in County Monaghan in 1843. In 1849 he was appointed agent for Lord Lansdowne's estate in Kerry and was later appointed also as agent for the marquis of Bath's property in Monaghan and for Lord Digby's in Offaly. A humane and very practical man, he related his experiences in his 1868 volume, *Realities of Irish Life,* which went into five editions in a year. The most striking portions of the book are his graphic accounts of the suffering and demoralization of the Famine years. Indeed, the picture is all the more graphic because of his spare and unadorned prose. Nevertheless, when Trench is deeply moved, that prose has its moments of considerable power:

Dark whisperings and rumors of famine in its most appalling form began to reach us, but still we could scarcely believe that men, women and children were actually dying of starvation in thousands. *Yet so it was.* They died in their mountain glens, they died along the sea-coast, they died on the roads, and they died in the fields; they wandered into the towns, and died in the streets; they closed their cabin doors and lay down upon their beds, and died of actual starvation in their houses.

In 1871, he published an unsuccessful novel, *Ierne,* based on the same material. He died on August 10, 1872, at Lord Bath's seat, Carrickmacross, County Monaghan.

PRINCIPAL WORKS: *Realities of Irish Life.* London: Longmans, 1868/London: MacGibbon & Key, 1866. (With a preface by Patrick Kavanagh); *Ierne; A Tale.* 2 vols. London: Longmans, Green, 1871.

TRESSELL, ROBERT (1870–1911), novelist. Tressell was the pen name of Robert Noonan, who was born on April 18, 1870, in Wexford Street, Dublin. At age sixteen, he left home and went to Liverpool and then to South Africa. Returning to England about 1902, he lived in Hastings on the south coast, where he worked as a painter and sign writer and became a dedicated socialist. He started work on his one novel, *The Ragged Trousered Philanthropists* about 1906 or 1907, and the writing of the quarter of a million-page book took about four years. His health, however, had rapidly deteriorated, and he determined to move to Canada in hopes that he would improve. He got no farther than Liverpool, where he died on February 3, 1911.

In 1913, his daughter showed his manuscript to Jessie Pope of *Punch,* who passed it on to the publisher Grant Richards. Cut by Miss Pope to about 160,000 words, the book was published on April 23, 1914, and became a working-class classic, selling perhaps 500,000 copies over the years and being frequently dramatized. The full text was not published until 1955. There is little Irish about this depiction of a year in the life of some workers; and, like Ethel Voynich's *The Gadfly,* the book has not entered the academic canon of English literature. Nevertheless, as Jack Mitchell remarks:

No other work of fiction, possibly no other book of any kind, has taken up such secure quarters in the imagination of succeeding generations of militant British workers. It is our one real working-class classic.

WORK: *The Ragged Trousered Philanthropists.* London: Lawrence & Wishart, 1955. (The complete text). REFERENCES: Alfred, David, ed. *The Robert Tressell Lectures.* [Rochester, Kent: Workers' Educational Association, 1988]; Ball, F. C. *Tressell of Mugsborough.* London: Lawrence & Wishart, 1951; Ball, F. C. *One of the Damned: The Life and Times of Robert Tressell.* London: Weidenfeld & Nicholson, [1973]; Mitchell, Jack. *Robert Tressell and the Ragged Trousered Philanthropists.* [London]: Lawrence & Wishart, [1969].

TREVOR, WILLIAM (1928–   ), short story writer, novelist, and playwright. Trevor was born William Trevor Cox on May 24, 1928, in Mitchelstown, County Cork. His father's work as a bank official involved the family in several moves to other provincial towns. As a result, Trevor attended a number of schools, including St. Columba's College, County Dublin, where he came under the influence of the sculptor Oisin Kelly, who taught him art. He graduated from Trinity College with a degree in history and worked for a number of years as a sculptor, supporting himself by teaching. In 1953, the year following his marriage to Jane Ryan, a fellow student at Trinity, he won joint first prize in the Irish section of the Unknown Political Prisoner sculpture competition, and subsequently his work was included in the Irish Exhibition of Living Art. Over the next few years he exhibited in Dublin and in a number of places in England, to which he emigrated in 1954.

In 1958, Trevor wrote *A Standard of Behaviour,* a novel that met with little critical success. Two years later, in need of a steady income and because he felt his work had become too abstract, he abandoned sculpting and became a copywriter in a London advertising agency. There he began writing fiction again. Following the publication of some short stories, a novel, *The Old Boys,* was accepted by the Bodley Head and won the 1964 Hawthornden Prize for Literature. His next novel, *The Boarding-House* (1965), was also awarded the Hawthornden Prize, and a host of other awards followed: Royal Society of Literature Award for *Angels at the Ritz and Other Stories* (1975); Whitbread Award for *The Children of Dynmouth* (1976) and *Fools of Fortune* (1983); Allied Irish Banks Prize for fiction (1976); Heinemann Award for fiction (1976); *Sunday Independent* Arts Award and *Yorkshire Post* Book of the Year Award for *The Silence in the Garden* (1988). Trevor has adapted much of his work for radio and television, and he received the Giles Cooper Award for radio versions of "Beyond the Pale" (1980) and "Autumn Sunshine" (1982). The television adaptation of "The Ballroom of Romance" was perhaps the most popular film of his work and won a BAFTA award in 1983. He has written a number of stage plays, most notably *Scenes from an Album,* which was performed at the Abbey Theatre* in 1981.

Trevor, who lives in Devon, has been a full-time writer since the early 1970s. He is a member of the Irish Academy of Letters and was made an honorary CBE (Commander of the British Empire) in 1977, in recognition of his services to literature.

Although a prizewinning novelist, Trevor describes himself as "a short story writer who likes writing novels." His short stories often follow a Chekhovian pattern. Characters have deeply felt longings but must accept that life will not change, and the inevitable has to be endured. There are fragmentary moments of illumination, but these are soon quenched, and problems prevail. One of the dominant themes in the stories is the difficulty of dealing with truth, of recognizing it, of communicating it, and of accepting it.

The characters in Trevor's work are usually marginalized members of society: children, old people, single middle-aged men and women, or the unhappily married. Those who cannot accept the reality of their lives create their own alternative worlds into which they retreat. A number of the stories use elements of the Gothic convention to explore the nature of evil and its connection with madness. Trevor acknowledges the influence of Joyce* on his short story writing, and "the odour of ashpits and old weeds and offal" can be detected in his work, but the overall impression is not of gloominess, since, particularly in the early work, the author's wry humor offers the reader a tragicomic version of the world.

In his third collection of stories, *Angels at the Ritz,* the writer makes his first reference to the Northern Ireland Troubles, and in the following collections his observations deepens and darkens, especially when the stories illustrate the coercive power of history. Increasingly, the setting is Irish, the atmosphere is nostalgic, and the resonance is of compassion rather than of comedy.

Trevor maintains that, unlike the characters in his stories, those in his novels "cause everything to happen." His early books are peopled by eccentrics who speak in a pedantically formal manner and engage in hilariously comic activities, which are recounted by a detached narrative voice. Instead of one central figure, the novels feature several protagonists of equal importance, drawn together by an institutional setting, which acts as a convergence point for their individual stories. With the exception of *Mrs. Eckdorf in O'Neill's Hotel* (1969), episodes of which illustrate Trevor's admiration of the work of Flann O'Brien (Brian O'Nolan*), the early novels deal with English society, although they may include a minor character who is Irish.

The later novels are thematically and technically more complex. The operation of grace in the world is explored, and several narrative voices are used to view the same events from different angles. Unreliable narrators and different perspectives reflect the fragmentation and uncertainty of modern life. Again, Trevor draws increasingly on his Irish background for setting and character, and *Fools of Fortune* was a new departure in that it was Trevor's first Big House novel.

In recent times, Trevor has revived the novella. The form is ideally suited to him, as it combines the tautness of the short story and the latitude of the novel. It allows the author to develop theme and character and at the same time demonstrates his spareness of style and superb selection of detail. The influence of his former career in sculpting remains in Trevor's splendidly formed characters, his perfectly shaped stories, and his finely chiseled prose.

DOLORES MacKENNA

WORKS: *A Standard of Behaviour*. London: Hutchinson, 1958/London: Sphere, 1967. (Novel); *The Old Boys*. London: Bodley Head/New York: Viking, 1964. (Novel); *The Boarding-House*. London: Bodley Head/New York: Viking, 1965. (Novel); *The Love Department*. London: Bodley Head, 1966/New York: Viking, 1967. (Novel); *The Day We Got Drunk on Cake and Other Stories*. London: Bodley Head, 1967/New York: Viking, 1968; *The Girl*. London: Samuel French, 1968. (Play); *Mrs. Eckdorf in O'Neill's Hotel*. London: Bodley Head, 1969/New York: Viking, 1970. (Novel); *Miss Gomez and the Brethren*. London: Bodley Head, 1971. (Novel); *Penguin Modern Stories*, with others. London: Penguin, 1971; *The Ballroom of Romance and Other Stories*. London: Bodley Head/New York: Viking, 1971; *Going Home*. London: Samuel French, 1972. (Play); *A Night with Mrs. Da Tanka*. London: Samuel French, 1972. (Play); *Elizabeth Alone*. London: Bodley Head, 1973/New York: Viking, 1974. (Novel); *The Last Lunch of the Season*. London: Covent Garden, 1973. (Story); *Marriages*. London: Samuel French, 1974. (Play); *Angels at the Ritz and Other Stories*. London: Bodley Head, 1975/New York: Viking, 1976; *The Children of Dynmouth*. London: Bodley Head, 1976/New York: Viking, 1977. (Novel); *Old School Ties*. London: Lemon Tree, 1976. (Miscellany); *Lovers of Their Time*. London: Bodley Head, 1978/New York: Viking, 1979. (Short stories); *The Distant Past and Other Stories*. [Swords, Co. Dublin]: Poolbeg, [1979]; *Other People's Worlds*. London: Bodley Head, 1980/New York: Viking, 1981. (Novel); *Beyond the Pale and Other Stories*. London: Bodley Head, 1981/New York: Viking, 1982; *Scenes from an Album*. Dublin: Co-op Books, 1981. (Play); *The Stories of William Trevor*. London: Penguin, 1983; *Fools of Fortune*. London: Bodley Head/New York: Viking, 1983. (Novel); *A Writer's Ireland: Landscape in Literature*. London: Thames & Hudson/New York: Viking, 1984. (Travel); *The News from Ireland and Other Stories*. London: Bodley Head/New York: Viking, 1986; *Nights at the Alexandra*. London: Century Hutchinson/New York: Harper, 1987. (Novella); *The Silence in the Garden*. London: Bodley Head/New York: Viking, 1988. (Novel); ed., *The Oxford Book of Short Stories*. Oxford & New York: Oxford University Press, 1989; *Family Sins and Other Stories*. London: Bodley Head/New York: Viking, 1990; *Two Lives: Reading Turgenev and My House in Umbria*. London: Viking, 1991. (Novellas); *Juliet's Story*. Dublin: O'Brien, 1991. (Children's book); *The Collected Stories of William Trevor*. London: Viking, 1992; *Excursions in the Real World*. London: Hutchinson, 1993. (Autobiographical essays); *Felicia's Journey*. London: Viking, 1994. (Novel). REFERENCES: Books: Morrow Paulson, Suzanne. *William Trevor—A Study of the Short Fiction*. New York: Twayne, 1993; Morrison, Kristin. *William Trevor*. New York: Twayne, 1993; Schirmer, Gregory A. *William Trevor: A Study of His Fiction*. London & New York: Routledge, 1990. Articles: Aronson, Jacqueline Stahl. "William Trevor: An Interview." *Irish Literary Supplement* (Spring 1986): 7–8; Gitzen, Julian. "The Truth-Tellers of William Trevor." *Critique* 21 (1979): 59–72; MacKenna, Dolores. "William Trevor." In *Contemporary Irish Novelists*. Rüdiger Imhof, ed. Tübingen, Germany: Gunter Narr Verlag, 1990, pp. 109–123; Morrison, Kristin. "William Trevor's System of Correspondences." *Massachusetts Review* 28 (1987): 489–496; Mortimer, Mark. "The Short Stories of William Trevor." *Études Irlandaises* 9, New Series (December 1984): 161–173; Mortimer, Mark. "William Trevor in Dublin." *Études Irlandaises* 4 (1975): 77–85; Mortimer, Mark. "William Trevor." *Ireland Today* 1031 (September 1986): 7–10; Ralph-Bowman, Mark. "William Trevor." *Transatlantic Review* 53/54 (1976): 5–12; Rhodes, Robert E. "William Trevor's Stories of the Troubles." In *Contemporary Irish Writing*. James D. Brophy & Raymond Porter, eds. Boston: Iona

College Press/Twayne, 1983, pp. 95–114; Stinson, John J. "Replicas, Foils and Revelation in Some 'Irish' Short Stories of William Trevor." *Canadian Journal of Irish Studies* 11 (2) (1985): 17–26.

TROLLOPE, ANTHONY (1815–1882), English novelist. Although among the most important of nineteenth-century English novelists, Trollope spent much time in Ireland and wrote several important Irish works. Born in Bloomsbury, London, on April 24, 1815, he was the fourth of six children, only two of whom survived to adulthood, and he had a most unhappy childhood. His father, Thomas, was a barrister with a modest practice that he ruined through arrogance. Deprived of a practice, he moved his family to Harrow, where his broody and barkish presence kept the household in a constant state of unease. Retreating from reality, he gave himself to the writing of a great ecclesiastical encyclopedia, which remained unfinished when he died years later in his early sixties. Trollope's mother, Frances, had extravagant tastes and no regard for money but conceived various bizarre and futile plans to improve the family fortunes. Two years in America in pursuit of one such plan completely emptied the family coffers, and in desperation, at age fifty-two, she wrote her first book, *Domestic Manners of the Americans*. The book was a success, and the Trollopes, ignoring their debts, lived comfortably until pressure from their creditors forced them to flee to the Continent to escape debtors' prison. Frances went on to write about forty more books, many critical of some aspect of the English social system, and died a very old lady at her villa in Florence.

Anthony was neglected by both his parents. Never taken on the family trips abroad, he was left on his own to look after himself as best he could. He attended Harrow as a day student, then Winchester, then Harrow again. Poorly clad and dirty, he was regarded as a dunce and both avoided, and was tormented by, his schoolfellows. At Winchester, his older brother Thomas, as part of his daily exercise, beat him. Leaving Harrow at nineteen, he briefly taught the classics in Brussels but then, through his mother's influence, obtained a junior clerkship in the post office in London. He was chafed by the constriction of the job, the dull routine, and the kowtowing. For recreation, he read, took long walks, and drank gin. So he remained for seven years, melancholy and morose, until at age twenty-six a vacancy arose for a clerkship in Ireland. Ireland was to change Trollope. He came, sunk within himself, smothering in self-doubt, but "a good roaring fellow" was soon to emerge.

His pay improved, and his travels on horseback to inspect post offices and set up new postal routes showed him many people whose lot was poorer than his own. He was promoted and could then afford the company of gentlemen and riding to hounds, a sport he came to love "with an affection which I cannot myself fathom." On holiday in Kingstown (Dun Laoghaire), he met Rose Heseltine, a banker's daughter, and their marriage produced two sons and—despite his love for an American actress—lasted until his death. Trollope achieved great eminence in the service of the post office, from which he eventually retired in 1867.

His "second profession," writing, he entered into soon after coming to Ireland, but for the first ten years, breaking stones, as he admitted, would have paid him more money. However, the publication of *The Warden* in 1855 brought him prestige, prominence, and the love of his many readers. His energy was prodigious, and he developed great appetites—for food, for company, and for work. Even while at the post office, his literary output was never less than 2,500 words a day.

Trollope wrote four Irish novels. The first and best is *The Macdermots of Ballycloran* (1847). He was to become a master of that form of the novel in which character and its interplay are paramount to the plot. Yet the arrangement of events gives integrity and force to this first novel. The reader's curiosity is cunningly aroused until the achievement of a final and fitting sense of inevitability. *The Macdermots* has at its core the tragic story of Thady Macdermot, who tries and fails to save his house from ruin and his family from disgrace and is unjustly hanged for the accidental killing of his sister's lover. The novel is set in the grim realities of life for the downtrodden Irish under English rule in the early part of the last century. Trollope wrote it when he was fresh to the country, still on rather poor pay, and the closest he would ever be to the pain of the common people. None of his other Irish novels has the same unblinkered vision or freedom from bias and prejudice. Sales, however, were low, and the book suffered a loss of £63.10s.1½d. English readers, perhaps because of a collective guilty conscience about Ireland and an imputation of Ireland's ills to the Irish themselves, did not respond to realistic novels on Irish subjects.

Trollope, however, was promoted to the office of surveyor in Mallow, County Cork, and his prosperity made him grow more distant from the common Irish and garner the facts of the Young Ireland rebellion of 1848 from the columns of the *Times*. The year 1848 also saw the publication of *The Kellys and the O'Kellys; or Landlords and Tenants,* which opens with the trial in 1844 of Daniel O'Connell and seven of his followers for "conspiracy" against the Crown. The main characters are Lord Ballindine, or Frank O'Kelly, a landlord, and Martin Kelly, his distant relation and tenant. Thereafter, neither the trial nor its outcome has any real impact on the progress of the novel; nor, indeed, does the Irish condition from which the artificial events of the story are entirely divorced. The work finds its feet as an amusing novel of manners. Written with pace and smoothness, it alternates between the courtship of Lord Ballindine and Fanny Wyndham, and Martin Kelly and Amy Lynch. In the end, true love conquers all.

The lord, "a very handsome fellow, full six feet high, with black hair and jet-black silky whiskers," was educated at Eton and Oxford; his manners, therefore, and his mode of thought have been tempered through English social usage. This makes him a fitting match for Fanny, that proud but gentle English rose, "whose light burned with so warm a flame, that butterflies were afraid to trust their wings within its reach." Martin Kelly is a handsome enough young fellow, but his brow is somewhat lower than that of Lord Ballindine; and, if there is frankness in his eye, it is mixed with cunning. His Amy Lynch is not the brightest girl in the world nor the prettiest nor the youngest. Yet Martin is but all the more fond of her because she has some money. The novel is memorable for its wryly humorous portraits, particularly those of Lord and Lady Cashel and their daughter Selina. The peasants, however, come out a trifle overdone, conforming more in this second book to English expectation and never speaking of serious matters except in a comic way. Trollope had begun to echo his readers.

Twelve years elapsed before publication of *Castle Richmond*, Trollope's third Irish novel, in 1860. He spends part of the opening chapter on an attempt to make it acceptable to English readers. He wrote the book, set in the Famine years, during which more than 800,000 people died from sickness and starvation, because he was leaving "the Green Isle" and ought to say something about his Irish friends, whom he "could love and cherish—almost as well, perhaps, as though they had been born in Middlesex." No grounds appear for the supposition of an irony.

Sober and prudent Sir Thomas Fitzgerald, life-heir to Castle Richmond and all its broad acres, loves and marries a childless widow so unutterably pure and lovely that she is known as the Dorsetshire Venus. She bears him an heir, Herbert, and two daughters. However, her odious first husband is not dead but busy blackmailing Sir Thomas by threatening his innocent wife with disgrace and his son with disinheritance. Meanwhile, Herbert and that hard-riding country gentleman, his cousin Owen, vie for the hand of the beautiful Lady Clara, daughter of the countess of Desmond. The countess, widow of the reptilian and debauched old earl of Desmond, still young, still beautiful, still sexually unawakened, feels a quickness in her pulse at every sight of the handsome Owen in his riding breeches. *Castle Richmond* fails for the flatness of its characters, the contrivances of its plot, the eking out of its last pages with irrelevant material—but most of all because the Famine, there on the periphery to be editorialized upon at a chosen time, seeps in of its own awful momentum to make seem preposterous Trollope's preoccupations with romance and property. The starving Irish seldom appear except as a whining chorus. Trollope writes of them with a cold remove almost as a species different from, and inferior to, his own. The slow-witted and servile males, their scabby and submissive females always clustered with so many emaciated offspring, cannot understand the true nature of their calamity. But Trollope can: the Famine was sent as a remedy by a merciful God "to disencumber our crowded places."

Trollope's final, unfinished novel, *The Landleaguers* was published in its incomplete form in 1883 and has as its background that period in Ireland between 1879 and 1882 known as the Land War. In 1879, foreign competition and poor crops saw starving tenants being evicted for nonpayment of rent. Landlords batter-rammed cabins and consolidated the cleared areas into bigger farms. Attempts were made on the lives of landlords and their agents. There were maimings and murders, boycotts and burnings. The Land League was a nonviolent organization, set up to secure rights for tenants. It pressed for an end to evictions, an abatement in rents, and a system of tenant purchase. Threatened, the ruling class urged stern measures against these "rebels," but the government made concessions aimed to appease and contain Irish aspirations.

Trollope, enormously grown by this time in reputation, had the ear of statesmen. Fixated with the idea of a place in the world and the property to go with it and describing himself as an "advanced conservative Liberal," he was opposed to the granting of any concessions. To support this view, he tells the story of Mr. Philip Jones, a decent, honest English Protestant gentleman who buys the combined estates of Ballintubber and Morony in County Galway. He and his family work hard at improving the land, and their efforts are successful. But, to survive, Mr. Jones needs the rent of his tenants, to whom he is kind, even permitting them to come to the Castle for port wine and solace when their rheumatism is rife. None among them starves; each can afford his rent.

However, not only do the tenants, Roman Catholics all, formerly so docile and obedient, begin to repudiate "the power of the priest as to their souls, but, in compliance with teaching . . . from America, they claim to be masters of their bodies. Never were a people less fitted to exercise such dominion without control." Pat Carroll, that "pestilent fellow," a Landleaguer, has the temerity to quarrel with his temperate landlord over rent. As a result, Carroll and his Land League cohorts lay ruin to the Castle acres. Mr. Jones is boycotted, his servants desert him, his tenants refuse him his due; and his darling ten-year-old son is shot dead from ambush by the cowardly Lax, a killer seasoned in America and kept by the Land League to enforce its reign of terror. Mr. Jones does have one ally in the manly presence of Captain Yorke Clayton, that stalwart of British justice, in prosecution of which the brave captain carries in his girdle no less than half a dozen pistols. Sight of the intrepid captain flutters the hearts of the Jones girls.

A second plotline is concerned with the efforts of Rachel O'Mahony, a young American singer, to make her way on the London stage. The hackneyed account of her adventures deserves little consideration, although the portrait is a fond one, vastly different from Trollope's usual palpitating heroines and possibly modeled on Kate Field, his American actress friend. Rachel's father is perhaps the real reason for her place in this disparate novel. Gerard O'Mahony, an appealing Irish-American windbag and buffoon, is used to deride Irish political effort and to treat the Irish-American interest in Ireland with ridicule and scorn.

The Landleaguers, what there is of it, is a bad novel: slackly written, showing evidence of a desperate extemporaneousness and with much recourse to those staples of the tired serialist, the "fresh" character and the sensational incident. It is written with a didactic purpose, and Trollope's overweening indignation makes him miss his aim; it distorts the truth, and Trollope lacks the art to sustain the lie.

In addition to these four novels, Trollope wrote two comic Irish tales, "The O'Conors of Castle Conor" and "Father Giles of Ballymoy." But Irish characters and settings are scattered throughout the vast body of his work, principally in *Phineas Finn* (1869), *Phineas Redux* (1874), and *An Eye for an Eye* (1879). A friend once described Trollope as ''crusty, quarrelsome, wrong-headed, prejudiced, obstinate, kind-hearted and thoroughly honest.'' In his Irish work, no one can doubt that he was all of these—or mostly all.

𝓙𝓐𝓜𝓔𝓢 𝓓𝓞𝓤𝓖𝓛𝓐𝓢

WORKS OF IRISH INTEREST: *The Macdermots of Ballycloran.* 3 vols. London: Newby, 1847/ Robert Tracy, ed. Oxford & New York: Oxford University Press, 1989; *The Kellys and the O'Kellys.* 3 vols. London: Colburn, 1848/[Oxford]: Oxford University Press, [1978]; *Castle Richmond.* 3 vols. London: Chapman & Hall, 1860/Oxford & New York: Oxford University Press, 1989; ''The O'Conors of Castle Conor.'' In *Tales of All Countries.* First series. London: Chapman & Hall, 1861/ London: Oxford University Press, 1931; ''Father Giles of Ballymoy.'' In *Lotta Schmidt and Other Stories.* London: A. Strahan, 1867; *Phineas Finn: The Irish Member.* 2 vols. London: Virtue, 1869/ London, Oxford & New York: Oxford University Press, 1973/London: Trollope Society, [1989]; *Phineas Redux.* 2 vols. London: Chapman & Hall, 1874/Oxford & New York: Oxford University Press, 1983/London: Trollope Society, [1990]/*An Eye for an Eye.* 2 vols. London: Chapman & Hall, 1879/New York & London: Garland, 1979; *The Landleaguers.* 3 vols. London: Chatto & Windus, 1883/R. H. Super, ed. Ann Arbor: University of Michigan Press, [1992]; *An Autobiography.* 2 vols. Edinburgh & London: Blackwood, 1883. REFERENCES: Glendinning, Victoria. *Trollope.* London: Hutchinson, [1992]; Hennessy, James Pope. *Anthony Trollope.* London: Jonathan Cape, [1971]; Smalley, Donald, ed. *Trollope, The Critical Heritage.* London: Routledge & Kegan Paul/New York: Barnes & Noble, [1969].

TROY, UNA. *See* WALSH, UNA TROY.

TYNAN, KATHARINE (1861–1931), poet, novelist, and journalist. Tynan was born on January 21, 1861, in County Dublin. In 1868, she moved with her family to Whitehall, the hospitable farm in Clondalkin which was her home until her marriage. From 1869 to 1875, she attended the convent school of St. Catherine of Drogheda, her only formal education. It was during this period that she suffered from an ulcerated eye condition which, though cured, left her severely myopic.

As mistress of her father's house during the 1880s, Kate was hostess of a highly respected literary salon and met W. B. Yeats,* the great friend of her youth. Her first published poems appeared in the first offering of the Irish Literary Revival, *Poems and Ballads of Young Ireland,* in which she was the youngest collaborator. Other poems appeared in the Catholic nationalist magazine *The Irish Monthly,* and her first collection, *Louise de la Valliere* (1885), an immediate success, established her as the most promising young poet of the Irish Renaissance.

In 1893, she married Henry Albert Hinkson, a barrister and a classics scholar. The Hinksons moved to England where he tutored and she began a career in journalism in which she soon became a regular contributor to *The Irish Statesman,* *Sketch, The Illustrated London News, The English Illustrated, The Pall Mall Gazette, The National Observer,* and, in the United States, *The Providence* [Rhode Island] *Journal, Catholic World,* and *The* [Boston] *Pilot.* Her journalistic pieces—some literary interviews, but mostly articles on education, the working conditions of shopgirls, infanticide, and the plight of unwed mothers—as well as the novels of social protest she had begun to write in the 1890s, in which she celebrated the evangelicism of the middle class, endeared her to a large reading public.

When Henry was appointed resident magistrate for County Mayo in 1911, the Hinksons returned to Ireland with their three children. Despite the Tynan family's strong Parnellite and Republican sympathies, by 1911 both Katharine and her husband identified themselves clearly as British subjects. As magistrate during the tragic years of the Rising and its aftermath, Hinkson evinced no discomfort at having to support pro-British policy, and his wife retained a middle-class horror of insurrection. For her the Rising was a "rebellion," and as such a terrible and irreconcilable embarrassment.

With the death of her husband in 1919, Mrs. Hinkson, who had always contributed substantially to the family income, was forced to make her living by writing. Accordingly, the last ten years of her life show an astonishing output. Since her neutrality made residence in Ireland impossible, she lived in England and traveled extensively and intrepidly in politically chaotic Western Europe. With her daughter Pamela as her guide and co-journalist, she wrote articles on the countries she visited and found herself in danger more than once. She continued to write poetry, published at least seventy novels, and many short stories—even though she was nearly blind. She died on April 2, 1931, in London after a brief illness.

Katharine Tynan was once considered the most promising poet of the Irish Renaissance and during her lifetime was immensely popular. Sadly, she ceased to develop her gifts or stifled them by directing her energies to the mass production of works that appealed to the popular taste. (Her *Oeuvre* numbers 105 novels, 12 short story collections, 3 plays, 18 poetry collections, 2 poetry anthologies, 7 books of devotions, 12 collections of memoirs, essays, and criticism, 2 biographies, and countless uncollected articles and stories.) One reason was surely financial necessity, but another was her latent recognition that her inner vision was limited to the celebration of external realities, and that in celebrating these in her poetry, she had gone as far as she could go. Despite her uniqueness among contemporary Irish writers as a spokesman of an unquestioning faith in Catholicism and the champion of the rights of women, the speed at which she was forced to work prevented her from reaching beneath the surface or beyond the middle class for her values. Consequently, the one writer to whom the most space is devoted in the British Museum Catalogue remains a minor poet, albeit of first rank, and a writer without a single epitomizing work.

When she was not being consciously professional and when she spoke most honestly from personal experience—that is, in her poetry—Katharine Tynan excelled. The early verse (*Louise de la Valliere* and *Shamrocks*) culminated in *Ballads and Lyrics* (1891), a collection of descriptive nature poetry which shows the young poet already a master of the lyric. Her poetry continued to advance:

A Lover's Breast-Knot (1896), a celebration of marital love, was followed by her finest collection, *The Wind in the Trees* (1898), which again was almost exclusively nature poetry and evoked that of the early Wordsworth. The deft metrics of this collection were perfected in *Innocencies* (1905), a pre-Freudian celebration of the eros of motherhood. From this point on, her poetry declined noticeably. The two volumes of war poems, *The Holy War* (1916) and *Herb O'Grace* (1918), are remembered only because the first was quoted from Catholic and Anglican pulpits alike, and the second contained a single remarkable poem, ''Comfort,'' in which a bereaved mother is comforted for her son's death by the knowledge that she will never have to share his love with a daughter-in-law.

As Tynan's poetry dwelled on what should endure, her novels, in which she was less artistically successful, showed what needed change. The earlier novels which took their themes from the journalistic pieces are the tales of the villain redeemed. These novels often testify to a strong feminism which is still compatible with motherhood and domesticity. In the later novels, many written with the younger reader in mind, she turned to historical romance and swashbuckling adventure.

Tynan's four volumes of memoirs (*Twenty-Five Years, The Middle Years, The Wandering Years,* and *The Years of Shadow*) contain sketches of literary friends and acquaintances. In addition, they present a sincere and candid self-appraisal of herself as a woman circumscribed by class values, who aspired neither to heroism nor genius, but who in fifty years of writing achieved something of substantial, though selective, worth.

M. KELLY LYNCH

WORKS: *Louise de la Valliere.* London: Kegan Paul, 1885. (Poems); *Shamrocks.* London: Kegan Paul, 1887. (Poems); *Ballads and Lyrics.* London: Kegan Paul, 1891. (Poems); *A Nun, Her Friends and Her Order.* London: Kegan Paul, 1891. (Biography of Mother Mary Xavier Fallon); *Cuckoo Songs.* London: E. Mathews & J. Lane, 1894. (Poems); *An Isle of Water.* London: A. & C. Black, 1895. (Short stories); *Miracle Plays: Our Lord's Coming and Childhood.* London: J. Lane, 1895. (Verse plays); *The Way of a Maid.* London: Lawrence & Bullen, 1895. (Novel); *A Lover's Breast-Knot.* London: E. Mathews, 1896. (Poems); *The Wind in the Trees.* London: G. Richards, 1898. (Poems); *The Queen's Page.* London: Lawrence & Bullen, 1899. (Novel); *A Daughter of Kings.* London: Smith, Elder & Co., 1900. (Novel); *Poems.* London: Lawrence & Bullen, 1901; *The Sweet Enemy.* London: Archibald Constable & Co., 1901. (Novel); *Julia.* London: Smith, Elder & Co., 1904. (Novel); *Innocencies.* London: A. H. Bullen, 1905. (Poems); *The Story of Bawn.* London: Smith, Elder & Co., 1906. (Novel); *Her Ladyship.* London: Smith, Elder & Co., 1907. (Novel); *A Little Book of Twenty-four Carols.* Portland, Me.: T. B. Mosher, 1907. (Lyrics); *Twenty-one Poems.* Dundrum: Dun Emer, 1907. (Poems selected by W. B. Yeats); *The Lost Angel.* London: John Milne, 1908. (Stories); *Mary Grey.* London: Cassel & Co., 1908. (Novel); with Maitland, Francis—*The Book of Flowers.* London: Smith & Elder, 1909. *A Little Book for John Mahoney's Friends.* Portland, Me.: T. B. Mosher, 1909. (Poems); *Peggy the Daughter.* London: Cassell & Co., 1909. (Novel); *Betty Carew.* London: Smith, Elder & Co., 1910. (Novel); *Freda.* London: Cassell & Co., 1910. (Novel); *New Poems.* London: Sidgwick & Jackson, 1911; *The Story of Celia.* London: Smith, Elder & Co., 1911. (Novel); *Princess Katherine.* London: Ward, Lock & Co., 1912. (Novel); *Rose of the Garden.* London: Constable & Co., 1912. (Novel); *Irish Poems.* London: Sidgwick & Jackson, 1913; *A Midsummer Rose.* London: Smith, Elder & Co., 1913. (Novel); *Twenty-Five Years.* London:

ᐧ

Smith, Elder & Co., 1913. (Memoirs); *The Wild Harp.* London: Sidgwick & Jackson, 1913. (Selection of Irish poetry edited by Katharine Tynan Hinkson); *The Flower of Peace.* London: Burns & Oates, 1914. (Devotional poetry); *Flower of Youth.* London: Sidgwick & Jackson, 1915. (Wartime poems); *The Holy War.* London: Sidgwick & Jackson, 1916. (Poems); *Lord Edward.* London: Smith, Elder & Co., 1916. (A study of Edward Fitzgerald); *The Middle Years.* London: Constable & Co., 1916. (Memoirs); *Late Songs.* London: Sidgwick & Jackson, 1917. (Poems); *Herb O'Grace.* London: Sidgwick & Jackson, 1918. (Poems); *Miss Gascoigne.* London: J. Murray, 1918. (Novel); *Love of Brothers.* London: Constable & Co., 1919. (Novel); *The Man from Australia.* London: W. Collins Sons & Co., 1919. (Novel); *The Years of the Shadow.* London: Constable & Co., 1919. (Memoirs); *Denys the Dreamer.* London: W. Collins Sons & Co., 1920. (Novel); *The House.* London: W. Collins Sons & Co., 1920. (Novel); *The Second Wife.* London: John Murray, 1921. (With "A July Rose": nouvelles); *Evensong.* Oxford: Basil Blackwell, 1922. (Poems); *The Wandering Years.* London: Constable & Co., 1922. (Memoirs); *Pat, the Adventurer.* London: Ward, Lock & Co., 1923. (Novel); *They Loved Greatly.* London: E. Nash & Grayson, 1923. (Novel); *The Golden Rose.* London: E. Nash & Grayson, 1924. (Novel); *The House of Doom.* London: Eveleigh Nash & Grayson, 1924. (Novel); *Memories.* London: E. Nash & Grayson, 1924. (Essays); *Life in the Occupied Area.* London: Hutchinson & Co., 1925. (Essays); *Miss Phipps.* London: Ward, Lock & Co., 1925. (Novel); *The Moated Grange.* London: W. Collins Sons & Co., 1926. (Novel, later *The Night of Terror*); *The Face in the Picture.* London: Ward, Lock & Co., 1927. (Novel); *Twilight Songs.* Oxford: Basil Blackwell, 1927. (Poems); *Castle Perilous.* London: Ward, Lock & Co., 1928. (Novel); *The House in the Forest.* London: Ward, Lock & Co., 1928. (Novel); *Lover of Women.* London: W. Collins Sons & Co., 1928. (Novel); *A Fine Gentleman.* London: Ward, Lock & Co., 1929. (Novel); *A Most Charming Family.* London: Ward, Lock & Co., 1929. (Novel); *The Rich Man.* London. W. Collins Sons & Co., 1929. (Novel); *The River.* London: W. Collins Sons & Co., 1929. (Novel); *The Admirable Simmons.* London: Ward, Lock & Co., 1930. (Novel); *Collected Poems.* London: Macmillan, 1930; *Grayson's Girl.* London: W. Collins Sons & Co., 1930. (Novel); *The Playground.* London: Ward, Lock & Co., 1930. (Novel); *Her Father's Daughter.* London: W. Collins Sons & Co., 1930. (Novel); *Irish Stories 1893–1899.* Peter van de Kamp, ed. University of Leiden Press, 1993.   REFERENCES: Alspach, Russell K. "The Poetry of Katharine Tynan Hinkson." *The Ireland America Review* 4 (1940): 121–126; Boyd, Ernest. *Ireland's Literary Renaissance.* New York: Alfred A. Knopf, 1916; Gibbon, Monk, ed. "Foreword," *Poems* [of Katharine Tynan]. Dublin: Allen Figgis, 1963; Hone, Joseph. *W. B. Yeats: 1865–1939.* London: Macmillan, 1943; Maguire, C. E. "Incense and the Breath of Spice." *Bookman* 72 (June 1931): 375–380; Rose, Marilyn Gaddis. *Katharine Tynan [Irish Writers Series].* Lewisburg, Pa: Bucknell University Press, 1973; Russell, George (AE). "Foreword," *Collected Poems* [of Katharine Tynan]. London: Macmillan, 1930; Yeats, W. B. *The Autobiography of William Butler Yeats.* London: Macmillan, 1916; Yeats, W. B. *Letters to Katharine Tynan.* Roger McHugh, ed. New York: McMullen, 1953.

U

ULSTER GROUP THEATRE (1940–1960). The Ulster Group Theatre was formed by three amateur companies—the Ulster Theatre, the Jewish Institute Dramatic Society, and the Northern Irish Players—joining together. The repertoire of the Group consisted of classic or foreign plays by Ibsen, Chekhov, Sheridan,* Maugham, Bridie, Shaw,* Odets, and others, as well as plays by some of the Southern Irish dramatists. This Belfast group was most successful in the production of new work from Ulster. The mainstays of its Northern repertoire were new pieces by St. John Ervine,* George Shiels,* and the actor-author Joseph Tomelty.* However, in its fifty new Ulster productions, the Group also introduced work by Jack Loudan, Hugh Quinn, John Coulter,* Patricia O'Connor,* John Boyd,* Sam Hanna Bell,* and John Murphy.* The theatre's final breakup was hastened by the controversy over producing Sam Thompson's* *Over the Bridge* in the late 1950s. Among the actors the theatre developed were Harold Goldblatt, J. D. Devlin, Joseph Tomelty, Stephen Boyd, and Colin Blakely.

REFERENCE: Bell, Sam Hanna. *The Theatre in Ulster.* [Dublin]: Gill & Macmillan, [1972].

ULSTER LITERARY THEATRE (1902–1934). The Ulster Literary Theatre received its original inspiration from the Irish Literary Theatre* of Yeats,* Moore,* and Martyn.* Its first organizers were Bulmer Hobson, who was a prominent nationalist in the years before the 1916 Rising, and David Parkhill, who wrote several of the theatre's early plays under the pseudonym of Lewis Purcell. Receiving no encouragement from Yeats, Hobson is reported to have said to Purcell, "Damn Yeats, we'll write our own plays."

The first production of the new group, however, in November 1902, consisted of Yeats' *Cathleen Ni Houlihan* and James Cousins'* *The Racing Lug.* Yeats' play was used on the authority of Maud Gonne who said, "Don't mind Willie.

He wrote that play for me and gave it to me. It is mine and you can put it on whenever you want to.'' The principal actors in this first production were two visitors from the Dublin theatre group, Dudley Digges and Maire T. Quinn. The second production was not presented until early 1904 when Yeats' *Cathleen* was repeated on a bill with AE's* *Deirdre.* At this time, the group called itself the Ulster Branch of the Irish Literary Theatre, but George Roberts, the secretary of the Southern group, wrote forbidding the use of the term Irish Literary Theatre. Hence, the name was changed to the Ulster Literary Theatre. From that time, the group began to develop its own distinctively Northern repertoire and its own actors.

The first real production of the new group was on December 8, 1904, when two new Northern plays, Hobson's *Brian of Banba* and Purcell's *The Reformers,* were first produced. At about the same time, the group began publishing an interesting literary magazine, *Uladh* (or Ulster), which, unfortunately, lasted only four issues.

Many able authors, actors, and well-wishers quickly gathered around the new group. Among them were Forrest Reid* the novelist, James Winder Good the journalist, Joseph Campbell* the poet, and the two men who were to be the most popular and successful authors and actors throughout the company's existence, Rutherford Mayne* and Gerald MacNamara.*

From 1904 to its dissolution thirty years later, the group gave the first productions to over fifty new Ulster plays, including work by Joseph Campbell, Lynn Doyle,* Shan F. Bullock,* Helen Waddell,* George Shiels,* and St. John Ervine.* The most popular and frequently revived pieces were the fine Ulster comedy *The Drone* by Rutherford Mayne and the droll short satire *Thompson in Tir-na-nOg* by Gerald MacNamara. For years, the company (which in 1915 shortened its name to the Ulster Theatre) delighted Belfast with its portraits of Northern life, toured successfully in England and Ireland, and even sent a contingent as far afield as New York City. The company did not generate any masterpieces to rank with the best work of the Abbey Theatre,* nor any actors of the stature of the Fays, Sara Allgood, Maire O'Neill, Barry Fitzgerald, or F. J. McCormick.

One reason why the group was finally dissolved, after so many years of dedicated effort, was that it never succeeded, as did the Abbey group, in getting its own theatre building. Consequently, the Ulster Theatre was always limited to a handful of yearly performances by actors who necessarily had to remain amateurs. As with many theatres, even the most distinguished, the problem was always money, and, as Rutherford Mayne said, ''The Ulster Theatre died as it lived—in penury.''

REFERENCES: Bell, Sam Hanna. *The Theatre in Ulster.* [Dublin]: Gill & Macmillan, [1972]; McHenry, Margaret. *The Ulster Theatre in Ireland.* Philadelphia: University of Pennsylvania, 1931.

USSHER, [PERCIVAL] ARLAND (1899–1980), essayist. Ussher was born in Battersea, London, on September 9, 1899, into a family that had lived in Ireland for many generations. He was educated at Abbotsholme School, Derbyshire, at

Trinity College, Dublin, and at St. John's College, Cambridge. He was proficient in Irish and has translated Merriman's *Midnight Court,* but is known primarily for what he describes as "philosophical belles lettres." His best books are probably *The Face and Mind of Ireland* (1949) and *Three Great Irishmen* (1952). *The Face and Mind of Ireland* is half résumé of twentieth-century Irish history until about 1950 and half description of the Irish character which that history has produced. The first half will not greatly enlighten the knowledgeable, but the second half, even after thirty years, is perceptive, provocative, and relevant. An even better work is *Three Great Irishmen* which considers Shaw,* Yeats,* and Joyce.* Confirmed admirers of these three figures will find Ussher's opinions sometimes uncanonical and irritating, but the less committed general reader will find much thoughtful good sense and only occasional startling gaffes, such as the author's preference for Rosie of Somerset Maugham's *Cakes and Ale* to Molly Bloom of Joyce's *Ulysses.*

Ussher's prose has been much admired, but it seems to obfuscate more than to illuminate his thought. He is capable of the trenchant and necessarily epigrammatic insight, such as "the Irishman treats sex as the Englishman treats death." However, he usually buries his epigram in woolly prose and writes, "For it is hardly too much to say that the Irishman treats sex as the Englishman treats death." His most irritating characteristic of style is the habit of spraying parentheses and dashes through at least half of his sentences. For example, in the last paragraph on page 54 of the Gollancz edition of *The Face and Mind of Ireland,* the first sentence has a pair of dashes, the second sentence a pair of dashes, the third sentence a two-line parenthesis, the fourth sentence a pair of dashes, and so on. This habit becomes so intrusive in *Three Great Irishmen* that the general reader would be well advised to skip the material contained in parentheses and between dashes, and to return to it as one might later refer to footnotes. By the time of *Eros and Psyche* (1977), the prose has become almost too much of a chore to wade through. That fact is indeed unfortunate, for beneath the murky presentation lies one of the country's interesting minds. He died in Dublin in 1980.

WORKS: Tr., *The Midnight Court and the Adventures of a Luckless Fellow.* London: Jonathan Cape, 1926. (After Brian Merriman and Denis Macnamara, the Red); *Postscript on Existentialism, and Other Essays.* Dublin: Sandymount/London: Williams & Norgate, 1946; *The Twilight of Ideas, and Other Essays.* Dublin: Sandymount, 1948; *The Face and Mind of Ireland.* London: Gollancz, 1949; *The Magic People.* London: Gollancz, 1950. (On the Jews); *Three Great Irishmen: Shaw, Yeats, Joyce.* London: Gollancz, 1952; *An Alphabet of Aphorisms.* [Dublin]: Dolmen, [1953]. (Pamphlet); with Carl von Metzradt, *Enter These Enchanted Woods, An Interpretation of Grimm's Fairy Tales.* [Dublin]: Sandymount, 1954/Dublin: Dolmen, 1957; *Journey through Dread.* London: Darwen Finlayson, 1955. (Study of Kierkegaard, Heidegger, and Sartre); *The Thoughts of Wi Wong.* [Dublin]: Dolmen, 1956. (Pamphlet); *The Mines of Siberiay. A New Ballad of Rooshian Rodie and Pawnbroker Liz.* Glenageary, Co. Dublin: Dolmen, 1956. (Ballad sheet, after *Crime and Punishment*); *The XXII Keys of the Tarot.* Dublin: Dolmen, 1957; *Spanish Mercy.* London: Gollancz, 1959. (Travel); *Sages and Schoolmen.* Dublin: Dolmen, 1967; *Eros and Psyche.* Dublin: Runa, 1977; *From a Dead Lantern, A Journal.* Robert Nyle Parisious, ed. Dalkey: Co. Dublin: Cuala, 1978; *The Juggler: Selections from a Journal by Arland Ussher: Being the Second Series of From a Dark Lantern.* Mountrath, Co. Laois: Dolmen, 1982.

V

VALENTINE, JEAN (1934–), poet. Valentine was born in Chicago on April 27, 1934, and currently lives in County Sligo. She was educated at the Milton Academy and at Radcliffe College, Harvard. Her poetry has been highly praised. Grace Paley wrote, "After reading a couple of Jean Valentine poems I need to catch my breath." Adrienne Rich wrote, "Looking into a Jean Valentine poem is like looking into a lake: you can see your own outline, and the slopes of the upper world, reflected among rocks, underwater life, glint of lost bottles, drifted leaves." Seamus Heaney* wrote, "Jean Valentine opens a path to a mature place where there is 'no inside wall': rapturous, risky, shy of words but desperately true to them, these are poems that only she could write."

CELIA de FRÉINE

WORKS: *Dream Barker.* New Haven, Conn.: Yale University Press, 1965; *Pilgrims.* New York: Farrar, Straus & Giroux, 1969; *Ordinary Things.* New York: Farrar, Straus & Giroux, 1974; *The Messenger.* New York: Farrar, Straus & Giroux, 1979; *Home Deep Blue: New and Selected Poems.* Cambridge, Mass.: Alice James Books, 1989; *The River at Wolf.* Cambridge, Mass.: Alice James Books, 1992.

VERSCHOYLE, MOIRA (1904–), novelist. Verschoyle was born in County Limerick and educated privately.

WORKS: *So Long to Wait. An Irish Childhood.* London: Geoffrey Bles, 1960; *Children in Love.* London: Hodder & Stoughton, 1961; *Daughters of the General.* London: Hodder & Stoughton, 1963.

VON PRONDZYNSKI, HEATHER. *See* INGMAN, HEATHER.

VOYNICH, E[THEL] L[ILIAN] (1864–1960), novelist. Although little read today in the West, Voynich's romantic novel *The Gadfly* has always been extremely popular in Russia and in Eastern Europe. Indeed, it has been translated into over thirty languages and sold over 5 million copies. It has been dramatized by Bernard Shaw,* and the Russians in 1955 made it into a film with a score by Shostakovich. The *New York Times* called it "[t]hat masterpiece of story-telling," and Bertrand Russell called it "[t]he most exciting novel I have ever read in the English language."

Its author was born Ethel Lilian Boole in Cork on May 11, 1864, the youngest daughter of Professor George Boole, an eminent mathematician and the author of *The Laws of Thought.* Her mother, Mary Everest Boole, has been described as a radical activist and feminist philosopher.

She was educated locally and later in Berlin. She also traveled to Russia, where she met a Polish patriot, Habdank-Woynick, who had been a political prisoner in Siberia but escaped. They married in 1891. In the mid-1890s, she had an affair with Sidney Reilly, the "Ace of Spies," whose biographer, Robin N. Bruce Lockhart, establishes that much of *The Gadfly* was inspired by his early life. It seems also to have been inspired by Voynich's admiration for the Italian republican and revolutionist Guiseppe Mazzini; and, according to Voynich herself, the heroine was based on Charlotte Wilson, the mistress of the anarchist Prince Peter Kropotkin.

Set in the turbulent Italy of the first half of the nineteenth century, the book is wordy but compulsively readable. It has been deservedly acclaimed as an exciting, moving story set against a well-drawn background of intrigue and rebellion. It probably does not deserve the lavish praise that it has occasionally received, but, like *Gone with the Wind,* it is at least a kitsch masterpiece, and the modern reader can easily understand the enthusiasm it engendered.

Voynich's husband Englished his name to Wilfred Voynich and became a well-known bibliographer and antiquarian bookseller in London. In 1916, they moved to New York City, where Voynich lived for the last forty years of her long life. She died in 1960 at the age of ninety-six.

Voynich published four other novels, one of them as late as 1946, but none of them as successful as *The Gadfly.* She also translated from the Russian, translated Chopin's letters, and wrote a number of cantatas, one of which, *Epitaph in Ballad Form,* is dedicated to the memory of Roger Casement.

PRINCIPAL WORKS: *The Gadfly.* New York: Henry Holt/London: William Heinemann, 1897; *Jack Raymond.* London: William Heinemann/Philadelphia: J. B. Lippincott, 1901; *Olive Latham.* London: William Heinemann/Philadelphia: J. B. Lippincott, 1904; *An Interrupted Friendship.* London: Hutchinson/New York: Macmillan, 1910; *Put Off Thy Shoes.* New York: Macmillan, 1945/ London, Toronto: William Heinemann, 1946. REFERENCES: Kettle, Arnold. "E. L. Voynich: Forgotten English Novelist." *Essays in Criticism* 7 (1957); Lockhart, Robin N. Bruce. *Ace of Spies.* London: Hodder & Stoughton, 1967.

W

WADDELL, HELEN [JANE] (1889–1965), scholar, translator, and novelist. Waddell was born on May 31, 1889, in Tokyo, the sister of Samuel J. Waddell ("Rutherford Mayne"*). In 1900, she traveled to her father's native Ulster, where she attended Victoria College and Queen's University, Belfast, receiving a B.A. in English in 1911 and an M. A. in 1912. Care for her invalid stepmother postponed further study at Oxford until 1919, although during this time she wrote children's Bible stories for a Presbyterian weekly; wartime propaganda for *The Manchester Guardian, The Nation,* and *Blackwood's;* and a play, *The Spoiled Buddha,* produced in 1915 by the Ulster Theatre* of which her brother Sam (Rutherford Mayne)* was a member. Her rendering into verse of the 600 B.C. poems from the Court of Soo, *Lyrics from the Chinese* (1915), got flattering notices in London and Dublin.

Helen Waddell entered Oxford at thirty-one years of age. From 1920 to 1922, she taught Latin at Somerville College and in 1921 she was named Casell Lecturer for St. Hilda's College. Her witty, lucid, and popular lectures, and her scholarship in medieval Latin and French influenced the Committee of Lady Margaret Hall to give her a Susette Taylor Travelling Fellowship for two years, which she spent in Paris researching medieval French Literature for a Ph.D.

In 1923, Waddell lectured briefly at Bedford College. She never returned to Oxford to complete her residence; instead she moved to London, supporting her writing through literary odd jobs and free-lance lecturing. Her discipline led to one supremely productive decade.

In 1927, Constable published *The Wandering Scholars* (1927), a history of and translations from the Goliards, for which the Royal Society of Literature awarded her the A. C. Benson Silver Medal and elected her its first woman fellow. The book was a commercial success, bringing her speaking engagements at colleges and universities and on the BBC. For her translation of the Abbé Prévost's *The Chevalier des Grieux and of Manon Lescaut* and her *Book of*

Medieval Latin For Schools, she was given an honorary D. Litt. by the University of Durham and elected (again as a first woman) to the Irish Academy of Letters in 1932. She then joined Constable and Company as a literary advisor.

After *Peter Abelard* (1933), her only novel, was published, Waddell was lionized—in Dublin as "Ulster's darling," and in London as "the most distinguished woman of her generation." *Beasts and Saints* (1934), a translation of extracts from medieval lives of the saints, and *The Desert Fathers* (1936), translations from the *Vitae Patrum,* were equally well received. In 1934, Queen's University, Belfast, and Columbia University conferred two more honorary degrees of D. Litt. A second play, *Abbé Prévost,* was produced by the Croydon Theatre in 1935.

In 1938, Waddell became the assistant editor of *The Nineteenth Century,* which published several patriotic poems which she had written in response to the war effort. During World War II, she was active in the Air-Raid Patrol and coped with the severe bombing of her own house. In her sympathy for the Free French, she translated articles by "Jacques," the pseudonym for a member of the French Resistance operating out of London, and collected them in the popular and moving *A French Soldier Speaks* (1941). Her only scholarly work of the period was a translation of Milton's *Epitaphium Damonis* (1943).

When Waddell retired in 1945, her creative energy had been drained. Otto Kyllmann of Constable attempted to rekindle her interest by bringing out *Stories from Holy Writ* (1949), a collection of the Bible stories she had written thirty years before. Her final major contribution—a brilliant final success—was "Poetry in the Dark Ages" (1947), the W. P. Ker Memorial Lecture she delivered at the University of Glasgow.

Suffering from a progressive neurological disorder, Waddell stopped writing entirely by 1950; by 1955, she was unable to recognize her closest friends and relatives. She lingered until 1965 when she died of pneumonia.

Of Helen Waddell's major publications, three appear to be of lasting value. *The Wandering Scholars* is a study of Europe's "real" Renaissance; of the centers of learning at Chartres, Orleans, and Paris in the twelfth century and of its byproducts, the Ordo Vagorum, the rowdy, ribald, and intellectual *bohêmes* who produced, among many other works, the "Carmina Burana." Although Waddell shows that they represent a striking contrast to the traditional concept of the medieval mind, she occasionally shies from the indelicacies in their work and ascribes emotional characteristics more in keeping with a late Victorian sensibility. *Mediaeval Latin Lyrics* is a collection that explores what happened in literature between the Fall of Rome and the Cluniac Movement. Ironically, the staunch Presbyterian daughter of missionaries points out that the Protestant tradition in European literature had obscured vast traditions of Roman Catholic poetry. *Peter Abelard,* by which she is largely remembered, is flawed for the reason that Waddell was not a novelist. It suffers from a cryptographic allusiveness possible only in the fictional work of a scholar who assumes an equal interest and knowledge in his reading public. Despite its flaws and its failure to face some of the more brutal realities of the tale, the novel is a fair measure of Helen Waddell's accuracy, acumen, spirited scholarship, and love of poetry.

$\mathcal{M}$. $\mathcal{KELLY}$ $\mathcal{LYNCH}$

WORKS: trans., *Lyrics from the Chinese,* by Shih Ching. London: Constable, 1913; *The Spoiled Buddha.* Dublin: Talbot, 1919. (Play); trans., *The Hollow Field,* by M. Aymeé. London: Constable, 1923; *The Wandering Scholars.* London: Constable, 1927; ed., *A Book of Medieval Latin for Schools.* London: Constable, 1929; trans., *The History of the Chevalier des Grieux and of Manon Lescaut,* by Abbé Prévost d'Exiles. London: Constable, 1931; *The Abbé Prévost.* London: Constable, 1933. (Play); trans., *Mediaeval Latin Lyrics.* London: Constable, 1933; *Peter Abelard.* London: Constable, 1933. (Novel); trans., *Beasts and Saints.* London: Constable, 1934; *New York City.* Newtown: Gregynog Press, 1935. (Poem); trans., *The Desert Fathers.* London. Constable, 1936; trans., *A French Soldier Speaks,* by Jacques (pseud.). London: Constable, 1941; trans., *Epitaphium Damonis. Lament for Damon,* by John Milton. London: Constable, 1943; *Poetry in the Dark Ages.* Glasgow: Jackson, 1947. (W. P. Ker Memorial Lecture, delivered at the University of Glasgow); *Stories from Holy Writ.* London: Constable, 1949. (Bible stories for children); *The Princess Splendour and Other Stories.* London: Longmans Young Books, 1969. (Children's stories). REFERENCE: Blackett, Monica. *The Mask of the Maker.* London: Constable, 1973. (Biography).

WALL, EAMONN (1955–   ), poet and critic. Wall was born in Enniscorthy, County Wexford, where his father and mother manage the leading hotel. He was educated at the Cistercian College, Roscrea, and took a B.A. and higher diploma in education at University College, Dublin. He received an M.A. in English from the University of Wisconsin–Milwaukee in 1984 and a Ph.D. from the City University of New York in 1992. A poem of his has appeared in *Wexford through Its Writers* (1993), edited by Dermot Bolger.* He has written reviews for the *Washington Post,* the *Chicago Tribune,* and *The Review of Contemporary Fiction.* His stories have appeared in *Ireland in Exile: Irish Writers Abroad* (1993) and in the *Sunday Tribune* (1994). He is completing a study of Brian Moore,* Edna O'Brien,* John McGahern,* and Aidan Higgins.*

As a writer, Wall is primarily a poet. His first publication was a chapbook of brilliant juvenilia, *The Celtic Twilight,* published by the Gorey Arts Centre, also called the Funge Arts Centre, in 1974. He was a prominent member of the literary group that gave a special flair to this precedent-making arts festival, and he was also coeditor of the literary magazine of the center, *The Gorey Detail.* His first American publication was *Fire Escape* (1988), an extraordinary collection of six poems. The small volume explored the author's imagination and both-sides-of-the-Atlantic background with a steely aesthetic gaze. His language is broken down into distinct, brief images and momentary epiphanies. The conscious design of the pieces confronts the inordinate demands of Celtic time and memory.

His more substantial *The Tamed Goose* (1990) is an accurate looking back into his Irish background and childhood. The title refers to the expression "Wild Geese," the exiles from Ireland of the seventeenth and eighteenth centuries, and is also a reflection of the author's recent marriage. The book is a fine odyssey of nostalgia, a genesis energy at play, reinvoking and reinventing Enniscorthy.

Some of the poems have Sherwood Anderson's quality of describing small Ohio towns. "The Country Doctor" is an engrossing account of the wide ambit of that traditional miracle worker, the local general practitioner. Wall conveys a close affection for the subject he chooses. The strongest writing here is "The Local Farmer," in which a racial psyche, in all of its historical and folkloric ramifications, is examined so dispassionately that Walls seems a core poet of his culture.

JAMES LIDDY

WORKS: *The Celtic Twilight.* Gorey, Co. Wexford: Funge Arts Centre, 1974; *Fragments and Other Poems.* Gorey, Co. Wexford: Gorey Arts Centre, 1981; *Fire Escape.* New York: Sunken-Isle, 1988; *The Tamed Goose.* New York: Hall, 1990; "Four Paintings by Danny Maloney." In *Ireland in Exile: Irish Writers Abroad.* Dermot Bolger, ed. Dublin: New Ireland Books, 1993; *Dyckman-200 Street.* Dublin: Salmon, 1994.

WALL, MERVYN [EUGENE WELPLY] (1908–   ), novelist, playwright, and short story writer. Wall was born in Dublin on August 23, 1908, and was educated in Belvedere College, in Germany, and at the National University, where he received a B.A. in 1928. After what he considered to be fourteen extremely depressing years in the Irish civil service, he was given more congenial employment by Francis MacManus* in Radio Éireann. Then, in 1957, at the instigation of Sean O'Faolain,* he became secretary of the Arts Council, a post he held until his retirement in 1975. He is married to Fanny Feehan, the music critic, and has four children.

Wall's fame rests on two inimitable books about a medieval Irish monk, *The Unfortunate Fursey* (1946) and *The Return of Fursey* (1948). The first is a sunny mélange of whimsy and satire that, in tone, if not in its highly individual content, brings to mind the work of James Stephens* and George Fitzmaurice* among the Irish and of Kenneth Grahame and J.R.R. Tolkien among the English. The lovable and ineffectual antihero of the novels moves through a malignant landscape of myth and marvels, which is peopled by an enchantingly garrulous collection of devils, witches, vampires, bishops, and Vikings. At the end of the first novel, Fursey improbably but delightfully triumphs over all. If the sequel is darker in tone and more somber in theme, Fursey's final failure is nevertheless described with a sympathetic sweetness that most of Wall's later work, probably to its detriment, lacks.

Much more ambitious and serious is Wall's prizewinning novel of 1952, *Leaves for the Burning.* This novel tells how a group of middle-aged friends makes an increasingly drunken, never-completed journey from Dublin to Sligo, to be present at the reinterment of W. B. Yeats.* The book is a sour but solid indictment of the repressive Ireland of the 1930s and 1940s. It is meticulously wrought and has a sullen power that suggests Graham Greene. Among Irish works, it is akin to the later novels of John McGahern* or William Trevor,* for its world is thoroughly delineated from a very glum view. Nevertheless, the hero is allowed at the end one small and pointless, but admirable, triumph.

Wall's *No Trophies Raise* (1956) is similarly glum in theme but is more intricate in plot and more farcical in tone. The smoldering dislike behind the book prevents the farce from blazing into fun, and so, despite some broadly comic invention, it remains more disturbing than satisfying in depicting its 1950s world of business and backslapping.

Wall's last completed novel, *Hermitage,* was serialized in *The Journal of Irish Literature* (1978–1979) and then published separately in 1982. It is a long (nearly 120,000 words) account of an Irish life, written with detachment and perhaps some puzzlement. Though the tone is muted, and the fable dreary, the prose is crystalline and compulsively readable, for Wall has one of the best commands of prose of any writer of his generation.

A collection of rather early short stories, which are engaging but of minor merit, was issued in 1974 under the title *A Flutter of Wings.*

Wall's two published plays were produced with small success by the Abbey*: *Alarm among the Clerks* in 1940 and *The Lady in the Twilight* in 1941. The earlier work reflects Wall's never-quite-stifled resentment of the soul-deadening bureaucracy of the civil service; in content and technique it has much in common with Elmer Rice's *The Adding Machine. The Lady in the Twilight* is a sadly comic, thickly characterized, and complex Chekhovian study of Ireland in the 1930s. Its accomplished and multistranded realism is probably rivaled in Ireland only by *The Moon in the Yellow River* of Denis Johnston,* who was virtually alone among the play's defenders. One character is an acid portrait of the novelist Michael Farrell.*

In 1962, Wall published a pamphlet of local history entitled *Forty Foot Gentlemen Only.* The work is of broad rather than local, interest because it deals with the men's bathing place in Sandycove, which is featured in the early pages of Joyce's* *Ulysses.* In 1988, Wall published *The Garden of Echoes,* a charming and fanciful children's novella. In 1992, he published in a Festschrift for Maurice Craig* the beginning of an uncompleted novel about contemporary Ireland entitled *The Odious Generation.*

If Wall's talents seem to outstrip his very solid achievement, the reason might be that his formative years were the 1930s and 1940s, the bleakest and most provincial years of the Free State. Quite as much as Brian O'Nolan,* whose comic invention he sometimes rivals, Wall seems to have been formed and depressed by his milieu.

WORKS: *Alarm among the Clerks.* Dublin: Richview, 1940; *The Unfortunate Fursey.* London: Pilot, 1946, New York: Crown, 1947/Dublin: Helicon, 1965; *The Return of Fursey.* London: Pilot, [1948]; both Fursey volumes published together as *The Complete Fursey.* Dublin: Wolfhound, 1985; *Leaves for the Burning.* London: Methuen/New York: Devin-Adair, 1952; "Extract from an Abandoned Novel." In *Irish Writing* 29 (December 1954): 17–28; *No Trophies Raise.* London: Methuen, 1956; *Forty Foot Gentlemen Only.* Dublin: Allen Figgis, 1962. (Pamphlet); *The Lady in the Twilight.* Newark, Del.: Proscenium, 1971; *A Flutter of Wings.* Dublin: Talbot, 1974; *Hermitage.* Dublin: Wolfhound, 1982; *The Journal of Irish Literature* (a Mervyn Wall Double Number) 11 (January–May 1982); *The Garden of Echoes.* Dublin: Fingal, 1988; "Work in Progress—Being the First and Second Chapters of an Unfinished Novel Provisionally Entitled 'The Odious Generation.' " In

Decantations: A Tribute to Maurice Craig. Agnes Bernelle, ed. [Dublin]: Lilliput, [1992], pp. 233–239. REFERENCES: Hogan, Robert. *Mervyn Wall.* Lewisburg, Pa.: Bucknell University Press, 1972; Lanters, Jose. "Unattainable Alternatives: The Writing of Mervyn Wall." *Éire-Ireland* 27 (Summer 1992): 16–34.

WALLER, JOHN FRANCIS (1810–1894), poet and editor. Born in Limerick, Waller graduated from Trinity College, Dublin, in 1832 and was called to the bar in 1833. In 1852, Trinity awarded him the honorary degrees of LL.B. and LL.D. He was an important contributor to *The Dublin University Magazine,* frequently using the pseudonyms of "Iota" or "Jonathan Freke Slingsby," and he succeeded Charles Lever* as editor. He supervised an edition of Goldsmith* (1864–1865) and edited *The Imperial Dictionary of Universal Biography* (1857–1863). He was honorary secretary of the Royal Dublin Society and vice president of the Royal Irish Academy. He retired to England, where he died at Bishop's Stortford on January 19, 1894. His poems, such as "Kitty Neal," and his humorous sketches are pleasant enough but hardly require a modern edition.

LITERARY WORKS: *Harlequin Blunderbore; or, The Enchanted Faun. . . .* Dublin, 1843; *Harlequin Fulminoso: or, The Ganders of Glen Fearna; A Grand Christmas Pantomime.* Dublin: Carrick, 1851; *Inauguration Ode, for the Opening of the National Exhibition . . . at Cork.* Cork: Bradford, 1852; *Ravenscroft Hall and Other Poems.* London, 1852; *The Slingsby Papers.* Dublin: McGlashan, 1852. (Prose and verse, also issued in the same year by McGlashan as *St. Patrick's Day in Our Own Parlour*); *Poems.* Dublin: McGlashan/London: William S. Orr, 1854/2d ed., 1863; *The Dead Bridal: A Venetian Tale of the Fourteenth Century.* London, 1856. (Under the Slingsby pseudonym); *Occasional Odes.* Dublin: Hodges, Smith, 1864; *The Revelations of Peter Brown, Poet and Peripatetic, Found in His Black Box.* London: Cassell, Petter & Galpin/Dublin: McGlashan & Gill, 1870; *Pictures from English Literature.* London: Cassell, Petter, Galpin, [1870]; *Festival Tales.* Dublin: McGlashan & Gill, 1873/London & New York: Cassell, Petter & Galpin, 1878. (Stories); *The Adventures of a Protestant in Search of a Religion. By Iota.* New York: D. & J. Sadlier, 1874; *An Irish Welcome . . . to the American Rifle Team. . . .* Dublin: n.p., 1875; *Boswell and Johnson: Their Companions and Contemporaries.* London: Cassell, Petter, Galpin, [1881]; ed., *The Poetical Works of Thomas Moore, with the Life of the Author.* New York: P. F. Collier, 1884.

WALSH, EDWARD (1805–1850), translator. Walsh, one of the earliest and best translators of Irish folk poetry, was born of a County Cork soldier-father, in Londonderry, in 1805. He was taught in the hedge-schools, and his work appeared often in *The Nation.** He had a difficult and impoverished life, being at one time schoolmaster to the convicts on Spike Island and later to paupers in a Cork Workhouse. He died at Cork in August 1850. Robert Farren* writes of him in *The Course of Irish Verse:*

He appreciated several of the formal virtues of his originals, determined to reproduce them in translating, and did, in fact, do this thing, in a certain degree. That is, he fits the words always to the tune, as [Thomas] Moore* did, arriving as did Moore, Callanan* and Ferguson* at the long, sinuous line; and he "vowels" well, employing cross-rhyme and assonance. His chief fault was a stiff, often bookish diction. . . .

At least a half dozen of his translations are memorable, among them "Mo Craoibhin Cno," "Have You Been at Carrick?," "The Dawning of the Day," "Brighiden ban mo Stor," and "From the Cold Sod That's O'er You."

WORKS: *Reliques of Irish Jacobite Poetry; With Biographical Sketches of the Authors, Interlineal Literal Translations and Historical Illustrative Notes by John Daly; Together with Metrical Versions by E. Walsh.* Dublin: Samuel J. Machen, 1844/2d ed., Dublin: M. H. Gill, [1883]; *Irish Popular Songs; With English Metrical Translations and Introductory Remarks and Notes by E. Walsh.* Dublin: J. M'Glashan/London: W. S. Orr, 1847. REFERENCES: Farren, Robert. *The Course of Irish Verse in English.* London: Sheed & Ward, 1948; Kickham, Charles J. "Edward Walsh: A Memoir." In *The Valley near Slievenamon: A Kickham Anthology.* James Maher, ed. Kilkenny: Kilkenny People, 1942, pp. 331–354; Welch, Robert. *A History of Verse Translation from the Irish 1789–1897.* Gerrards Cross: Colin Smythe, 1987.

WALSH, JOHN EDWARD (1816–1869), author of historical sketches. Walsh was born on November 12, 1816, probably in Finglas, County Dublin. He became a barrister of some prominence and died in Paris on October 17, 20, or 25, 1869. His book *Ireland Sixty Years Ago* is made up of fictional sketches, which were originally published in *The Dublin University Magazine.* Its evocation of Ireland before the Act of Union is both plausible and entertaining.

WORK: *Sketches of Ireland Sixty Years Ago.* Dublin, 1847/revised ed. under the title *Ireland Ninety Years Ago,* Dublin: M. H. Gill, 1885/another revised ed. under the title *Ireland One Hundred and Twenty Years Ago,* Dillon Cosgrave, ed. Dublin & Waterford: M. H. Gill, 1911.

WALSH, LOUIS J. (1880–1942), fiction writer, playwright, and memoirist. A brother of Helena Concannon,* Walsh was born in Maghera, County Derry, and became a solicitor. He was politically active in the Anglo-Irish War and interned. After the establishment of the Free State, he was appointed district justice in County Donegal. He died on December 26, 1942. His comedies, such as *The Guileless Saxon* and *The Pope in Killybuck,* were popular among amateur groups, and his genial sketches of Ulster life had some success.

WORKS: *The Guileless Saxon.* Dublin: M. H. Gill, 1917. (Three-play); *Sketches of Life in Rural Ulster.* Dublin: M. H. Gill, 1917; *The Next Time: A Story of 'Forty-eight.* Dublin: M. H. Gill, [1918]. (Novel); *"On My Keeping" and in Theirs. A Record of Experiences . . . in Derry Gaol, and in Ballykinlar Internment Camp.* Dublin: Talbot/London: T. Fisher Unwin, 1921; *Twilight Reveries.* Dublin: M. H. Gill, 1924; *"Our Own Wee Town." Ulster Stories and Sketches.* Dublin & Cork: Talbot, [1928]; *The Deposit Receipt.* Dublin: M. H. Gill, 1928. (One-act play); *Nothing in His Life.* Letterkenny, Co. Donegal: Mary Walsh, 1929; *Old Friends, Being Memories of Men and Places.* Dundalk: Dundalgan, 1934; *John Mitchel.* Dublin & Cork: Talbot, 1934. (Biography); *Equity Follows the Law.* Belfast: Quota, 1935. (Two-act play).

WALSH, MAURICE (1879–1964), novelist and short story writer. Walsh was born at Ballydonoghue, a townland which lies halfway between the literary town of Listowel and the seaside resort of Ballybunion in North Kerry, on May 2, 1879. He was educated at local national schools—Liselton, Gortnaskehy, and Coolard, and later at St. Michael's College, Listowel, a classical school where the accent was on Latin and Greek. His father was a well-read farmer who transmitted a great deal of his own love of learning to his family.

To the northwest of the Walsh homestead, overlooking the mouth of the River Shannon, stood the hill of Knockanore, so-named from the Irish Cnoc an Áir (the Hill of Slaughter or as given in another version, the Hill of the Harvest) which is mentioned in the legends of the Fianna. The area is rich in folklore.

Walsh successfully stood for an examination for the civil service and subsequently spent twenty years as an excise officer in Scotland, mainly in the Highlands. There he came in contact with a life that was sib to his home experience and where also he acquired a Scottish burr which he never quite lost. He married a Scottish girl—a redhead who appears under various guises throughout his works. As a result of his excise days in Scotland, he was recognized on an international level as an authority on whisky [without the Irish e!].

Under the terms of the Anglo-Irish Treaty in 1922, he transferred to the Irish customs and excise. At this time, he seriously took up writing, his early works being featured in Chambers' *Journal*. His first book, *The Key Above the Door* (1926), although it failed to win a competition for which it was entered, was later published by Chambers of Edinburgh and London and sold a quarter of a million copies.

Thereafter, book after book—novels and short stories—appeared, the scene of each was laid in Scotland or in southwest Ireland. The Walsh books are of the open air, of salmon rivers, of farmlands and fairs, some with historical settings. A departure from his usual pattern was evidenced by *Thomasheen James, Man-of-No-Work*, the theme of which was provided by a rare personality who visited Walsh in his Stillorgan home and remained there for years in the nominal role of gardener. *The Quiet Man*, the famous John Ford film with a redheaded heroine and filmed mainly in the Cong area of County Galway, is based on a Maurice Walsh story from *Green Rushes*. There is now a pub of the name in Listowel. *Trouble in the Glen* was also filmed in England.

On a personal level, Walsh was delightful and cordial in every way. Sturdily built, he dressed in tweeds, sometimes with a pale green cape slung across his shoulders while his tweed hat, set at a jaunty angle, carried a brilliant salmon fly or a feather from the blackcock. His eyes, set in a bearded and fresh-complexioned face, carried more than their share of quiet merriment. His visits to his native area in North Kerry were events in the truest sense of the word as he took time out to visit old friends of his youth and "correct his perspective."

In his Stillorgan, County Dublin, home (it was named "Green Rushes" for one of his books), he held an open night once every week. These were attended by all kinds of personalities, and the conversation was vivid and far-ranging. Walsh, a fine host, was seen at his best on such occasions.

He retired from the Irish civil service in 1933, and he died in Dublin on February 18, 1964.

BRYAN MacMAHON

WORKS: *The Key Above the Door*. London & Edinburgh: Chambers, 1926; *While Rivers Run*. London & Edinburgh: Chambers, 1928; *The Small Dark Man*. London & Edinburgh: Chambers,

1929; *Blackcock's Feather.* London & Edinburgh: Chambers, 1932; *The Road to Nowhere.* London & Edinburgh: Chambers, 1934; *Green Rushes.* London & Edinburgh: Chambers, 1935; *And No Quarter.* London & Edinburgh: Chambers, 1937; *Sons of the Swordmaker.* London & Edinburgh: Chambers, 1938; *The Hill Is Mine.* London & Edinburgh: Chambers, 1940; *Thomasheen James, Man-of-No-Work.* London & Edinburgh: Chambers, 1941; *The Spanish Lady.* London & Edinburgh: Chambers, 1943; *The Man in Brown.* London & Edinburgh: Chambers, 1945; *Son of Apple,* London & Edinburgh: Chambers, 1947; *Castle Gillian.* London & Edinburgh: Chambers, 1948; *Trouble in the Glen.* London & Edinburgh: Chambers, 1950; *Son of a Tinker, and Other Tales.* London & Edinburgh: Chambers, 1951; *The Honest Fisherman, and Other Stories.* London & Edinburgh: Chambers, 1954; *A Strange Woman's Daughter.* London & Edinburgh: Chambers, 1954; *Danger under the Moon.* London & Edinburgh, 1956; *The Smart Fellow.* London & Edinburgh: Chambers, 1964. REFERENCE: Matheson, Steve. *Maurice Walsh, Storyteller.* [Dingle, Co. Kerry]: Brandon, 1985.

WALSH, UNA TROY (1918–   ), novelist and playwright. Una Walsh was born in Fermoy, County Cork, the daughter of Judge Troy. She was educated at the Loreto Abbey in Rathfarnham, County Dublin. She married Joseph Walsh, by whom she had a daughter. She was a contributor to *The Bell,* Ireland Today, Mademoiselle,* and other publications. As her father was a public figure, she began her career using the pseudonym of Elizabeth Connor. Her early work consisted of four plays, produced by the Abbey Theatre*—*Mount Prospect* (1940), *Swans and Geese* (1941), *An Apple a Day* (1942), and *The Dark Road* (1947)—as well as some fiction. From 1955, she wrote novels under the pen name of Una Troy. Set mainly in rural Waterford, they are lighthearted and gently satirical, charming rather than realistic, and deal in types rather than in characters. Typical of these racy, simply told narratives is *Esmonde,* an imaginative story of a young girl who rushes into marriage, gets bored, and makes two other liaisons—at the same time—that supplement her "experience." The situation becomes increasingly unreal, and a suitably melodramatic denouement ensues. However, a subtle tone of self-mockery in the voice of the narrator gives a feeling that the issues here—love, romance, self-awareness, self-fulfillment—are more weighty than the story line would seem to imply.

The Elizabeth Connor story "The Apple," which appeared in *The Bell,* is more realistic. It is a simple tale, economically told, of a middle-aged nun who is "given permission" by her reverend mother to visit her home at a time when nuns did not visit their families. The permission extends only to looking at the house from the outside. However, when Mother Mary Aloysius steals up to her bedroom, the action is seen as a symbolic breaking free of the moral indoctrination that has stunted her up to this point and crippled her ability to think and to choose for herself. The telling of the incident is more finely tuned than that of the novel, whose racy, "popular" style may yet conceal sharp insight into the growth of the person.

Her home for many years has been at Bonmahon, County Waterford.

MARY BALL & PETER COSTELLO

WORKS: As Elizabeth Connor: *No House of Peace.* New York & London: D. Appleton-Century, 1937/as *Mount Prospect.* London: Methuen, 1938. (Novel); "The White Glove." *Ireland Today* 2

(9) (September 1937): 49–55. (Short story); *Dead Star's Light.* London: Methuen/New York: Saunders, 1938. (Novel); "The Apple." *The Bell* 5 (1) (October 1942): 35–41. (Short story). As Una Troy: *We Are Seven.* London: Heinemann, 1955/New York: Dutton, 1957; *Maggie.* London: Heinemann, 1958/as *Miss Maggie and the Doctor.* New York: Dutton, 1958; *The Workhouse Graces.* London: Heinemann, [1959]/as *The Graces of Ballykeen.* New York: Dutton, 1960; *The Other End of the Bridge.* London: Heinemann, [1960]/New York: Dutton, [1961]; *Esmonde.* London: Hodder & Stoughton/New York: Dutton, 1962; *The Brimstone Halo.* London: Hodder & Stoughton, [1965]/as *The Prodigal Father.* New York: Dutton, 1965; "The Best Butter." *Kilkenny Magazine* 14 (Spring–Summer 1966): 48–61. (Short story); *The Benefactors.* London: Hale/New York: Dutton, 1969; *Tiger Puss.* London: Hale/New York: Dutton, 1970; *The Castle That Nobody Wanted.* London: Hale/New York: Dutton, 1970; *Tiger Puss.* London: Hale, 1970; *Stop Press!* London: Hale/New York: Dutton, 1971; *Doctor, Go Home!* London: Hale/New York: Dutton, 1973; *Out of the Everywhere.* London: Hale, 1976; *Caught in the Furze.* London: Hale, 1977; *A Sack of Gold.* London: Hale, 1979; *So True a Fool.* London: Hale, 1981.

WALSHE, DOLORES (1949–), playwright, poet, novelist, and short story writer. Born and raised in the Liberties in Dublin, Walshe earned a B.A. from University College, Dublin, and a higher diploma in education from Trinity College. She has lived and worked in Dublin, New York, San Francisco, and Amsterdam. Her work has ranged from teaching English as a second language to being a suicide counselor. She currently lives in Dublin with her husband and two daughters.

Although Walshe did not begin writing until 1986, she has already achieved remarkable success. She started writing poetry and short stories; several stories have been broadcast on RTÉ and BBC. In 1987, she had a story short-listed for the Hennessy Literary Award, won a story competition in the *Sunday Tribune,* and was awarded a place on the Annual National Writers' Workshop, sponsored by the Irish Arts Council. In 1988, she won first prize in the RTÉ Radio One Poetry competition, and in 1990 she received a grant in creative literature from the Irish Arts Council.

Walshe has a long-standing interest in areas of conflict, frequently using such settings to depict her passionate outrage at injustice and inhumanity. South Africa is the setting for several poems, as well as her plays *In the Talking Dark* and *The Stranded Hours Between,* her short story "Body Found on Waste Ground," and her novel *Where the Trees Weep* (1992). As reviewers have noted, she has the rare gift of using small social units, such as the family, to reflect major political issues. She is currently working on a trilogy of novels set in Northern Ireland, the first to be published in 1996.

Because of her concern for humanitarian causes, Walshe's writing often focuses on the darker side of relationships and of social institutions. The pain endured by her characters is, at times, overwhelming, mainly because it is absolutely believable, whether it is the children slaughtered in *Where the Trees Weep,* Kulie's terrifying description of her husband's death in *The Stranded Hours Between,* or the hatred and desperation in the story "The Edge." The power of her writing, however, pulls the reader through the pain into a catharsis of knowledge.

In the Talking Dark, her first play, won the O. Z. Whitehead/Society of Irish Playwrights/PEN Playwriting Literary Award in 1987 and was staged at the Royal Exchange Theatre in Manchester in 1989. Her other plays include *Seeing an Angel in Hades, The Sins in Sally Gardens,* and *A Country in Our Heads,* which was staged in the 1991 Dublin Theatre Festival.

KATHLEEN A. QUINN

WORKS: *Where the Trees Weep.* Dublin: Wolfhound, 1992. (Novel); *Moon Mad.* Dublin: Wolfhound, 1993. (Short stories).

WARD, JAMES (fl. 1714–1724), poet. Patrick Fagan makes a plausible case for Ward being the James Ward (1691–1736) who became dean of Cloyne. Ward published no collection, but sixteen of his poems were printed in Matthew Concanen's *Miscellaneous Poems, Original and Translated, By Several Hands* (1724). Fagan reprints two of the best of them, "The Smock Race at Finglas" and "Epithalamium on the Marriage of Felim and Oonah," in which some excellent realistic, contemporary observation is somewhat blunted by some conventional contemporary poetic mannerisms.

WORK: In *Miscellaneous Poems, Original and Translated, By Several Hands . . . Published by Mr. Concanen.* London: J. Peele, 1724. REFERENCE: "James Ward." In *A Georgian Celebration: Irish Poets of the Eighteenth Century.* Patrick Fagan, ed. Dublin: Branar, [1989], pp. 52–59.

WARNOCK, GABRIELLE (1947–   ), novelist and short story writer. Warnock was born in West Cork and grew up in Cork city and Kilkenny. She did a social studies diploma at Trinity College, Dublin, and has studied at University College, Galway. She won a Hennessy Literary Award in 1981.

WORK: *Fly in a Web.* Dublin: Poolbeg, 1984. (Novel).

WATERS, JOHN (1955–   ), social commentator. Waters was born in Castlerea, County Roscommon, and writes a lively weekly column on public events for the *Irish Times.*

WORK: *Jiving at the Crossroads.* Belfast: Blackstaff, 1991; *Every Day Like Sunday?* [Dublin]: Poolbeg, [1995]: with David Byrne. *Long Black Coat.* Dublin: New Island/London: Nick Hern, [1995]. (Play).

WATTERS, EUGENE [RUTHERFORD LOUIS] (1919–1982), man of letters, in both English and Irish. Watters was born on April 3, 1919, in Ballinasloe, County Galway. He was educated locally and at St. Patrick's Training College, Drumcondra, and at University College, Dublin, where he received an M.A. in European literature and language in 1947. He also studied European languages at the Vocational Educational College in Rathmines and studied woodwork at the Vocational Educational College in Capel Street, Dublin. He was an officer in the Irish army and worked also as a primary school teacher in Dublin until 1961, when he became a full-time writer. His work in Irish was published as Eoghan Ó Tuairisc. From 1962 to 1965, he edited the magazine *Feasta;* he also worked for the publisher Allen Figgis and for the Mercier Press. After the death of his first wife in 1965, he gave up writing entirely for five years. In 1972, he married Rita E. Kelly,* and his next nine years were extremely productive and saw the publication of novels, collections of poetry, the coauthorship of a history of Dan Lowrey's Music Hall, many fugitive stories, poems, and essays, and several plays. He was a member of Aosdána,* and he died in Caim, County Wexford, on August 24, 1982. Among his awards were the Hyde Memorial Award for his Irish novel *L'Attaque* (1962), another Hyde Award for his collection of Irish poems *Lux Aeterna* (1964), and an Arts Council Bursary for his play *Carolan.*

WORKS IN ENGLISH: *Murder in Three Moves.* Dublin: Allen Figgis, 1960. (Novel); *The Week-End of Dermot and Grace.* Dublin: Allen Figgis, 1964. (Poem); *New Passages.* Newbridge, Co. Kildare: Goldsmith, 1973. (Poetry); *The Story of a Hedgeschool Master.* Cork: Mercier, 1974. (Novel); with Matthew Murtagh. *Infinite Variety, Dan Lowrey's Music Hall 1879–97.* [Dublin]: Gill & Macmillan, [1975]; *Sidelines.* Dublin: Raven Arts, 1981. (Poetry): tr., *The Road to Bright City.* [Swords, Co. Dublin]: Poolbeg, [1981]. (From the Irish of Mairtin O Cadhain).   REFERENCES: Ellis, Conleth & Kelly, Rita E., eds. "Special Eugene Watters Issue." *Poetry Ireland Review* 13 (Spring 1985). (Contains a reprinting of "The Week-End of Dermot and Grace," articles by Ellis, Kelly, Sean Lucy, and Colbert Kearney, and a bibliography by Martin Nugent).

WEBER, RICHARD (1932–   ), poet. Weber was born in Dublin and educated in Dublin public schools and in the National College of Art. He has been librarian at the Chester Beatty Library in Dublin and a lecturer at the University of Massachusetts and at Mount Holyoke College in the United States. From the late 1950s to about 1980, he published several poetry pamphlets and two slim volumes of considerable potential. His first notable collection was *Lady and Gentleman* (1963). Much of the book seems a compilation of botched opportunities, as the poet is usually working in a tight form, such as the rhyming couplet, and does not see or care that his flabby meters are undoing the insistence of his rhymes. In some cases, as in "The Young Poet's Letter to Olympus," the effect is to reduce a serious attempt to doggerel. However, there are several real successes, such as "Summa Theologica" or "An Anatomy of Love" or "The Makers" or, especially, "Morality." Weber's best-known volume is *Stephen's Green Revisited* (1968), but the book is a more formally trivial and a more personally indulgent one. The title poem, for instance, contains one neatly witty idea (of ducks knowing a little Latin because they say "aqua, aqua") and a debilitating, sentimental core ("But sadness is surely the secret mother of memory"). A couple of skillful pieces, such as "Roman Elegy V" and "Religious Knowledge," and one pleasant, if not memorable, tribute to Austin Clarke* called "A Visit to Bridge House" do not quite make up for the disappointment that this poet had not improved.

WORKS: *O'Reilly.* Dublin: Dolmen, 1957. (Poetry pamphlet); *The Time Being.* Dublin: Dolmen, 1957. (Poetry pamphlet); *Lady and Gentleman.* Dublin: Dolmen, 1963; *Stephen's Green Revisited.* Dublin: Dolmen, 1968; *A Few Small Ones.* Dublin: Ballyknockan, 1971. (Poetry pamphlet); *Poems.* [Dublin: Printed at the National College of Art & Design, 1980]. (Poetry pamphlet).

WEEKS, JAMES EYRE (fl. 1743), poet. Nothing is known for certain about this Cork poet, but Patrick Fagan argues that he may not be the James Eyre Weeks [*sic*] who published several poems in the 1740s and 1750s. Given the difference in tone and quality between the work of Weekes and Weeks, that conclusion is not at all impossible. In Weekes' one collection, *Poems on Several Occasions* (1743), there are charm, wit, and a fluent tightness of form. For instance, "The Heart Divided":

> Lucia's not handsome, Stella's pretty,
> but Stella's simple, Lucia's witty;
> was one as fair as t'other's wise,
> had this her tongue, or that her eyes,
> I could resign my heart with ease
> To Lucia's wit or Stella's face.
> But as it is I'm held between
> Lucia's sweet tongue and Stella's mien;
> my hapless passion then to smother,
> I'll *look* at one and *hear* the other.

WORK: *Poems on Several Occasions.* Cork: Thomas Pilkington, 1743.   REFERENCE: Fagan, Patrick. "Were There Two James Eyre Weekeses?" In *A Georgian Celebration: Irish Poets of the Eighteenth Century.* Dublin: Branar, [1889], pp. 120–127.

WELCH, ROBERT (1947–   ), critic, novelist, and poet. Born in Cork on November 25, 1947, Welch was educated at University College, Cork, and at the University of Leeds, where he studied under A. Norman Jeffares* and received a Ph.D. for work on verse translations from the Irish. He is professor of English at the University of Ulster at Coleraine. His excellent *Oxford Companion to Irish Literature,* is the principal rival of this book.

WORKS: *Irish Poetry from Moore to Yeats.* Gerrards Cross: Colin Smythe/Totowa, N.J.: Barnes & Noble, 1980; ed., *A History of Verse Translation from the Irish.* Gerrards Cross: Colin Smythe, 1989; *Muskerry.* [Dublin]: Dedalus, [1991]. (Poetry); *Changing States: Transformations in Modern Irish Writing.* London & New York: Routledge, [1993]; ed., *Celtic Twilight: Writings on Irish Folklore, Legend and Myth.* By W. B. Yeats. London: Penguin, 1993; *The Kilcolman Notebook.* [Dingle, Co. Kerry]: Brandon, [1994]. (Novel); *The Oxford Companion to Irish Literature.* Oxford: Clarendon Press, 1996.

WELDON, JOHN. *See* MacNAMARA, BRINSLEY.

WEST, ANTHONY C[ATHCOT MUIR] (1910–1988), novelist and short story writer. West was born on July 1, 1910, in County Down. He went to America in 1930 and spent some years wandering across the country, from New York to the Pacific Northwest, and making his living by a wide variety of temporary jobs. He returned to Europe in 1938, served in the Royal Air Force (RAF) in World War II, and was a navigator in many Mosquito bombing missions over Germany. After the war he lived in Anglesey, North Wales, with his wife and their twelve children and engaged in "creative farming" and writing.

West's early stories and what John Wilson Foster calls his best novel, *The Ferret Fancier* (1963), are so richly written that reviewers have compared him to the Dylan Thomas of "A Child's Christmas in Wales." West's great pre-occupation is with the early years of puberty of a boy in a farming community in the North of Ireland. The sense of place, a ripe description of landscape, and a meticulous delineation of the tortures of young sexuality are done with a poet's eye, and his early work may be lingered over and savored. One weakness is in the progression of plot, and in both short and long works his frequently lush prose tends to bury a tenuous story. Another flaw is that his characters, other than his protagonists perhaps, are not vividly drawn. These failings keep him from being, as Foster avers, "the most fertile and imaginative fiction writer the North has produced since Carleton.*" Despite his fertility and rich prose, West can be excessively tedious, particularly so in innumerable paragraphs of limply Lawrentian psychic probing, such as:

The salmon made him vaguely sad, seeing it as egg in to redd, then fry, parr, smolt, and then the strong young forger in the tumbling wilderness of sea. He tried to see the shape of the symbol behind the fish as if it had some meaning for himself, some warning or conclusion or explanation for his unreconcilement with life and circumstances. He failed, vague memories defeating any symbolic recognition: the roaring weir and the ploughing salmon, the Jamesons, love's wound in graveward days, the safety of detached innocence hazarded by overcoming experience; doubts, loneliness. O where was he now: a parr perhaps drifting down his river, unfit yet for the salt sea and waiting for mere management and strength to brave the bar: the cold courage of a fish.

West's most ambitious novel is *As Towns with Fire* (1968). It is an extremely long account of the young life of Christopher MacMannan, who is trying to be a poet and who gets caught up in World War II as a navigator. With the exception of a forty-page flashback to his youth in Ireland, the first four hundred pages flounder aimlessly through his various love affairs, little realized characters, and a good deal of philosophic discussion about life. When MacMannan joins the RAF and begins flying missions over Germany, the last two hundred pages of narrative gain much more appeal. The philosophic discussions and even all the shadowy minor characters begin to work, and one character, Jane (who is the hero's duck), becomes rather memorable. Nevertheless, despite West's usual facility with words, the book needed a drastic shaping and cutting to make it into a work of art, rather than another wayward, if very talented, amateur fiction.

West was a member of Aosdána* and died in 1988.

WORKS: *River's End and Other Stories.* New York: McDowell, Obolensky, 1958/London: MacGibbon & Kee, 1960; *The Native Moment.* New York: McDowell, Obolensky, 1959/London: MacGibbon & Kee, 1961. (Novel); *Rebel to Judgment.* New York: Ivan Obolensky, 1962. (Novel); *The Ferret Fancier.* St. Albans: MacGibbon & Kee, 1963/New York: Simon & Schuster, 1965/ Dublin: O'Brien, 1983. (Novel); *As Towns with Fire.* London: MacGibbon & Kee, 1968/New York: Knopf, 1970. (Novel); *All the King's Horses and Other Stories.* [Swords, Co. Dublin]: Poolbeg, [1981]. REFERENCES: Eyler, Audrey Stockin. *Celtic, Christian, Socialist: The Novels of Anthony*

C. West. Rutherford, N.J.: Fairleigh Dickinson University Press, [1993]; Foster, John Wilson. *Forces and Themes in Ulster Fiction.* Dublin: Gill & Macmillan/Totowa, N.J.: Rowman & Littlefield, 1974.

WHALLEY, JOHN (1653–ca. 1724–1729), newspaper editor, astrological almanac maker, printer, and purveyor of nostrums. Whalley's *News Letter* appeared in 1714, and R. R. Madden in *Irish Periodical Literature* writes, "The proprietor, editor and publisher of this newspaper, a *quondam* shoemaker, an astrologer, a quack doctor, an almanack maker, a no Popery firebrand, a champion of Protestant principles, a celebrated empiric, was called 'Dr. Whalley.' " Sir John Gilbert adds that he settled in Dublin in 1682 and was placed in the pillory in 1688. John O'Donovan* in *Life by the Liffey* calls him "a nasty customer who fulfilled a promise to provide in his *News Letter* 'a full and particular account of foreign and domestic news' by packing its pages with scandals, reckless libels on prominent citizens, fake prophecies and lickspittle support of the government." Whalley was also a formidable controversialist. Suspecting a fellow almanac maker, Andrew Cumpsty, of plagiarism, he described him as "my sheeps-face antagonist" and "a Mathemaggotty Monster," and in one poem about Cumpsty he attains the ferocity, if not the facility, of Swift:

> A monster in figure, a monster by nature too,
> A monster in arts, all monstrous things can do,
> None e'er did more pretend, or less e'er knew,
> No baboon else, so monstrously divine,
> No ape or monkey ever half so fine;
> and yet in temper ruder than a swine. . . .

Whalley's own death occasioned the broadside called "A Full Account of Dr. John Whalley's Forced Confession and Entertainment in H-11," which concludes:

> The D[evil's] pride, and the world's wonder,
> For perjury and vice doth here lye under.
> A cobbler, doctor, and star gazer, too,
> Methinks he gave the D---l enough to do.
> I beg the favour of you, pond'rous stone,
> To keep secure this wretched dolt and drone.

Whalley's last almanac was published in 1724, and his mantle descended on a Munster astrologer and almanac maker, John Coats or Coates, whose *Vox Stellarum* Madden justly calls one of the most remarkable almanacs published in Ireland.

WHARTON, ANTHONY P. (1877–1943), novelist and playwright. Anthony P. Wharton was the pseudonym of Alister McAllister, who was born in Dublin and educated at Clongowes Wood College and at the Royal University. At the inception of the National University, he was appointed to the chief clerkship. He achieved a considerable London success with his play *Irene Wycherley* in

1907 and some later success with *At the Barn* in 1912. After his World War I service, during which he was twice wounded, he turned to writing novels, also under the pseudonym of Wharton, but was most successful with a series of detective novels written under the pseudonym of Lynn Brock. In March 1943, the Abbey* presented his last play, *The O'Cuddy*. On April 6, he died at Dorchester in England.

WORKS: As Anthony or Anthony P. Wharton: *At the Barn*. London: Joseph Williams/New York: Samuel French, [1912]. (Play); *Nocturne*. London: Lacy/New York: Samuel French, 1913. (One-act play); *13, Simon Street*. London: Lacy/New York: Samuel French, [1913]. (One-act play); *Joan of Overbarrow*. London: Duckworth/New York: George H. Doran, [1922]. (Novel); *The Man on the Hill*. London: T. Fisher Unwin, [1923]. (Novel); *Be Good, Sweet Maid*. London: T. Fisher Unwin/New York: Boni & Liveright, [1924]. (Novel). As Lynn Brock: *The Deductions of Colonel Gore*. London: W. Collins, [1924]/New York & London: Harper, 1925/republished as *The Barrington Mystery*. London: W. Collins, 1932; *Colonel Gore's Second Case*. London: W. Collins, 1925/ New York & London: Harper, [ca. 1926]; *Colonel Gore's Third Case*. London: W. Collins, [1927]/ published as *The Kink*. New York & London: Harper, [ca. 1927]; *Colonel Gore's Cases. No. 4. The Slip-Carriage Mystery*. London: W. Collins/New York: Harper, 1928; *Colonel Gore's Cases. No. 5. The Mendip Mystery*. London: W. Collins, [1929]; *The Dagwort Coombe Murder*. London: W. Collins, 1929/These two 1929 volumes were published in America by Harper as *The Stoke Silver Case* and *Murder at the Inn*, although which was which we have been unable to determine; *Q. E. D.* London: W. Collins, [1930]/republished as *Murder on the Bridge*. London: W. Collins, [1932]; *Nightmare*. London: W. Collins, 1932; *The Silver Sickle Case*. London: Collins, [1938]; *Fourfingers*. London: W. Collins, [1939]/republished in 1939 by Collins for the Crime Club as *The Riddle of the Roost: The Stoat*. *Colonel Gore's Queerest Case*. London: Collins, 1940.

WHITBREAD, J[AMES] W. (1847–1916), playwright and play producer. Whitbread was born in Portsmouth, England, on October 20, 1847, and died in Scarborough on June 9, 1916. Although he began and ended his career in England, where he managed the Scarborough Theatre Royal in the early 1880s, Whitbread was one of the most successful and prolific playwright-managers for the Queen's Royal Theatre in Dublin, which he ran from 1884 until April 1907. He is known to have written and produced the following plays at the Queen's: *Shoulder to Shoulder* (November 15, 1886), *The Nationalist* (December 26, 1891), *The Irishman* (August 1892), *The Spectre of the Past, Or Homeless in the Streets of Dublin* (August 30, 1893), *The Victoria Cross* (September 7, 1896), *Lord Edward, Or '98* (March 22, 1894), *Theobald Wolfe Tone,* often produced as *Wolfe Tone* (December 26, 1898), *Shadowed* (1899), *Rory O'More* (April 15, 1900), *The Ulster Hero* (January 12, 1902), *The Insurgent Chief* (March 31, 1902), *The Sham Squire* (1902, according to Herr; December 26, 1903, according to Kavanagh), *Sarsfield* (January 2, 1905), *The Irish Dragoon* (December 26, 1905), *The French Huzzar* (December 24, 1906), and possibly several others. In addition, Whitbread appears to have written short stories; some, such as "Shoulder to Shoulder," are fictional retellings of the plays while others, such as "My Adventure in New Mexico," are possibly written under the pseudonym Frank Fairfield.

His Irish political melodramas undermined British stereotypes while casting new vision on the events of 1798. In *Lord Edward* not all the patriots are enthusiastic about war, and the play condemns neither those who want peace nor those who will fight. In *Wolfe Tone,* Shane McMahon begins his career as what seems a stage Irishman, but this porter helps Tone financially, rescues him from other scrapes, and becomes a corporal in the French army.

Although he relied heavily on melodramatic conventions and advanced a myth of Irish heroism that would reign for decades in the popular imagination, when Whitbread writes of 1798, he is no longer obsessed by failure. Instead his melodramas, according to Cheryl Herr, "display the diversity of the rebellion/civil war/revolution that contributed to a splintered historical moment; they emphasize the coexistence of success and defeat." He does not seek reconciliation of the English/Irish opposition as Falconer's* *Peep o' Day* does.

In *Lord Edward,* the question is not whether Edward will succeed or fail; instead the play focuses on the machinations of Magan, an informer who eventually brings about Edward's death. Magan schemes not only for money but for Pamela, a Frenchwoman who, in choosing Edward, justifies the Irish cause. In the penultimate scene, Magan attempts to rape her but is prevented and killed by loyal servants.

In *Wolfe Tone,* similarly, the plot revolves around the conspiracy of informers against Tone. They employ devices from *Othello* to arouse Tone's jealousy toward his wife, but Tone never wavers in his fidelity. When the schemers attempt to convince Bonaparte that Tone is a traitor, their plot turns against them. As Joseph Holloway* said, " 'Wolfe Tone' (though cast on melodramatic mould) is a distinct cut above the usual sensational play."

WILLIAM G. DOLDE

WORKS: *Shoulder to Shoulder.* Dublin: W. J. Alley, 1888; *The Nationalist.* Dublin: W. J. Alley, 1892; *Sarsfield.* Dublin: P. J. Bourke, 1986; *Lord Edward* and *Wolfe Tone.* In *For the Land They Loved: Irish Political Melodramas 1890–1925.* Cheryl Herr, ed. [Syracuse, N.Y.]: Syracuse University Press, [1991]; In addition to these published works, the Raymond Mander and Joe Mitchenson Theatre Collection in London owns some Whitbread papers, and various plays are housed in the Lord Chamberlain's plays in the British Library, Manuscript Collection. REFERENCES: Fay, Frank J. *Towards a National Theatre.* Robert Hogan, ed. [Dublin]: Dolmen, [1970]; Kavanagh, Peter. *The Irish Theatre.* Tralee: Kerryman, 1946; Malone, Andrew E. *The Irish Drama.* London: Constable, 1929; Watt, Stephen. *Joyce, O'Casey, and the Irish Popular Theatre.* [Syracuse, N.Y.]: Syracuse University Press, [1991].

WHITE, AGNES ROMILLY (1872–1945), novelist. White was the daughter of a rector and lived much of her life in Dundonald, County Down. She wrote two comic novels of village life.

WORKS: *Gape Row.* London: Selwyn & Blount, [1934]; *Murphy Buries the Hatchet.* London: Selwyn & Blount, 1936.

WHITE, T[ERENCE] H[ANBURY] (1906–1964), novelist and essayist. Although White, known to his friends as "Tim," was thoroughly English in his rearing and values, he spent his most productive years in Ireland in self-imposed exile during World War II, from 1939 to 1945. He was born in Bombay in 1906 of parents in the civil service whose bitter divorce was to color his adult emotional life. He was educated at Cheltenham and Cambridge, where his tutor was L. J. Potts the critic, and he took a Firsts with honors in 1929. After a brief career as a schoolmaster, he became a professional writer, living in a gamekeeper's cottage in Buckinghamshire. He was a man of many enthusiasms and a compulsive learner. "The best thing for being sad," he has Merlyn say in *The Once and Future King,* "is to learn something." He learned to fly an airplane, show horses, plow a field, fish for salmon, train hawks for hunting, and do all the field sports, all of which turned up in his writing. His hobby, listed in *Who's Who,* was "animals." In 1939, he went on a fishing trip to Ireland with his friends the David Garnetts—and stayed throughout the war. He lived at Doolistown, a farm near Trim, County Meath, and visited regularly in Dublin and in County Mayo, where he hunted and fished. He returned to England in 1945, and after the success of the musical "Camelot," which was based on his Arthuriad *The Once and Future King,* he settled on the Channel island of Alderney. Shortly after completing a successful American lecture tour in 1963 (*America at Last,* Putnam, 1965), he died of heart failure in Athens, where he is buried.

White's best known work, *The Once and Future King* (in four books, completed in 1958), concerns the boyhood, maturity, and eventual defeat of King Arthur. The story of the legendary king provided ample room for comment on personal matters, like the Lancelot-Guinevere love triangle and the clan relationship of the Orkneys, and on "the matter of Britain," or idealized conceptions of leadership and the nation, tested by reality. White based his version mainly on Thomas Malory's *Morte D'Arthur.* He deliberately kept scholarly discussion out of the work and was not directly influenced by Celtic variants of the legend. He also decided not to include the Tristan legend or the Grail quest. Rather, he deals with the Orkney clan and the revenge of Mordred on Arthur in psychological terms as an Aristotelian incest tragedy, a tragedy "of sin come home to roost." He was living in Ireland while he wrote the early versions of the last two books, later revised. He also included an impassioned fifth book, *The Book of Merlyn,* which his editor rejected; it was only recently published from the manuscript (University of Texas Press, 1977). His concern in this fifth book was influenced not by Ireland but by what the ongoing war revealed about the nature of man's self-destructiveness.

White wrote two books directly about Ireland—*The Elephant and the Kangaroo* (1948) and *The Godstone and the Blackymor* (1959). *The Elephant,* which is based on his personal experiences at Doolistown, creates the delightful fiction that the Second Flood is coming to Ireland; a Mr. White, and the aging couple he lives with, are chosen to build the ark. The ark finally flounders down the Boyne and the Liffey, bumping into all the bridges, and the book closes with a successful burlesque of Joycean prose. In a fit of remorse, White tried to stop the book's distribution in Ireland, where in Trim its satirical thrust aroused animosity. Long after he returned to England, White wrote up several of his bizarrely whimsical experiences for the most part in the west of Ireland. *The Godstone and the Blackymor* tells of his search for a talismanic stone on Inniskea, his attendance at a wake, and his climbing Croagh Patrick among other matters. White was quintessentially a foreigner, as he was aware, even though he won a Radio Éireann poetry contest in 1940 with his ''Sheskin,'' which was a tribute to the Irish climate and countryside.

While in Ireland, White also wrote *Mistress Masham's Repose* (1946), his delightful (and neglected) novel about the thirteen-year-old Maria, who finds a hitherto unknown colony of Lilliputians on her estate, brought back by Gulliver from his first travel. Like *The Once and Future King,* it contains an eccentric wisdom figure and is concerned with growing up and the moral values that are tested by dealing with other people. Many years later, White completed a similar but deeply flawed children's book, *The Master* (1957), the setting for which first occurred to him in Ireland.

White also worked intermittently on his substantial scholarly work, *The Book of Beasts* (1954), translating medieval manuscripts in the Trinity College library, and he wrote considerable parts of his two books of eighteenth-century studies in eccentricity, *The Age of Scandal* (1950) and *The Scandalmonger* (1952). Driven in part by his loneliness, he wrote hundreds of fascinating letters (*The White/Garnett Letters,* 1968, is only a sample) and kept voluminous journals.

White was an intelligent, widely read, eccentric, lonely, charming man, nervous and driven by the need to overcome his fears, given to crazes and enthusiasms. Typically, while in Ireland he studied Irish history and Gaelic and prepared to become Catholic, only to remain the educated, agnostic Anglo-Saxon he was raised to be. A heavy drinker and suppressed homosexual, he was true to his dogs and his writings. His letters and journals have been only partly published. Sylvia Townsend Warner's *T. H. White,* while authorized by his executors, is unsympathetic in tone and rather sketchy.

SVEN ERIC MOLIN

WORKS OF IRISH INTEREST: *The Elephant and the Kangaroo.* New York: G. P. Putnam's Sons, [1947]/London: Jonathan Cape, 1948; *The Godstone and the Blackymor.* New York: G. P. Putnam's Sons/London: Jonathan Cape, 1959; *The White/Garnett Letters.* David Garnett, ed. London: Jonathan Cape, 1968.   REFERENCES: Crane, John K. *T. H. White.* Boston: Twayne, 1974; Gallix, François. *T. H. White: An Annotated Bibliography.* London: Garland, 1986; Warner, Sylvia Townsend. *T. H. White.* London: Jonathan Cape with Chatto & Windus, 1967.

WHITE, [HERBERT] TERENCE DE VERE (1912–1994), novelist and man of letters. White was born in Dublin on April 29, 1912. His father was a Protestant, solicitor and his mother Catholic. Although some of White's own writings were about the Anglo-Irish, his own family background was that of the not-too-well-off middle-class. He received a Catholic education until he was fifteen, and then became an unpaid solicitor's apprentice while at the same time working for a B.A. and an LL.B., which he received from Trinity College. When he was twenty-three, he established the law firm, originally a one-man operation, from which he retired as senior partner in 1962 in order to become literary editor of the *Irish Times* and to devote himself more fully to writing. By his first marriage, White had three children, and he and Dervla Murphy* also had a daughter, Rachel.

White was active in the cultural life of Dublin for most of his life: he was on the boards of the Gate Theatre* and the National Gallery, and he was a trustee of the National Library. He was a conversationalist and after-dinner speaker of distinction, and a repository of information about Irish writing, history, and politics. He wrote extensively: twelve novels, three volumes of short stories, five biographies, an autobiography, two histories, and two general interest volumes, *Ireland* and *Leinster.*

As a novelist, White moved outside the mainstream of twentieth-century Irish fiction: he wrote comedies of manners. His main characters are usually society types, members of the declined Ascendany or the professional middle classes. White's approach as a writer was to cultivate the role of the detached observer who chronicles passions and intrigue with a penetrating and ironic eye. However, his descriptive and narrative prose too often lacks genuine literary merit. In this connection, it is instructive to contrast him with Jennifer Johnston,* whose treatment of the Irish gentry is so authentic. When White deals with topical subjects, the topicality is somewhat forced. In *The Distance and the Dark* (1973), the Northern Ireland Troubles form the background, and both the evocation of atmosphere and the various attitudes that are voiced about violence rarely rise above the commonplace. The novel's focus is on a sensitive, unhappily married middle-aged man whose growth in self-knowledge is marked toward the novel's close by Polonius's "This above all: to thine own self be true." Instead of using this truism as a starting point to explore his hero's development, White confines himself to it, thus losing the opportunity to involve the reader imaginatively with the character's development.

The March Hare (1970) exemplifies White's strengths and weaknesses as a novelist. Set in early twentieth-century Dublin, the novel displays a good sense of period; the social and physical detail of the city are unobtrusively and interestingly presented. The comic idiom of character types is also well portrayed. The book has some serious defects, however. For example, the descriptive writing is too uniformly pedestrian, while overall credibility of plot is frequently sacrificed to the effectiveness of a single scene. As an illustration of the former, take the start of the love affair between Millie Preston and Alan Harvey. They meet at a ball where Millie's first sight of Alan brings on a "sensation as if some part of her inside had dropped, at the same time she experienced a slight weakening at the knees." Six pages later, White tells us how the occasion had affected Alan: "[W]hen he first saw her his stomach dropped and he had gone weak at the knees." With reference to credibility of plot, it is significant that some of White's later forays into fiction were in the short story, where the strength of specific scenes at the expense of the whole is of much less importance. Some of the short stories provide thinly disguised portraits of prominent cultural figures.

White's first full-length work, *The Road of Excess* (1946), is a biography of Isaac Butt,* the first leader of the Irish Home Rule Party at Westminster. The work is anecdotal, and Butt's historical statue is not examined in depth. The subjects of White's biographies shifted from political figures like Butt and Kevin O'Higgins (1948) to cultural and literary figures, but none of the books are really analytical. When the subtitle of his *Tom Moore: The Irish Poet* (1977) is considered, the lack of any critical appreciation of Moore's* verse is to be regretted.

White's autobiography, *A Fretful Midge* (1959), ranks among his best works. It gives a critically attractive picture of the birth and growth of the new Irish state, and key artistic and political personages are sharply observed in its pages. His other nonfiction includes *The Anglo-Irish* (1972), an attempt to define Ireland's most elusive social phenomenon. His *Ireland* (1968) has an interesting chapter sketching the country's literary history.

White holds a minor place in Irish letters. In future years, his works will likely appeal more to the social or literary historian than to the general reader.

MARTIN RYAN

After leaving the *Irish Times,* White moved to England, where he made a second marriage to the English writer Victoria Glendinning who recently remarked about him:

Terence de Vere White's fiction, seen in perspective, will be a subject for serious reassessment by future critics. Meanwhile something more should be said about Terence at the *Irish Times,* where as literary editor he wrote the influential lead review on the books page for 25 years, and by his choice of other reviewers made the Saturday page essential reading; he was an important part of the literary education of a whole generation, of which in later years he was given ample testimony. He gave many Irish poets their first chance too—he was the first to publish a Seamus Heaney* poem, for example. He was also a repository of information and intimate knowledge not only about Irish and English writing and writers, but about Irish history, Irish politics and Irish politicians, which he was always happy to share with researchers.

He died in England on July 17, 1994. He was a member of Aosdána.*

WORKS: *The Road of Excess.* Dublin: Browne & Nolan, 1946. (Biography of Isaac Butt); *Kevin O'Higgins.* London: Methuen, 1948. (Biography); *The Story of the Royal Dublin Society.* Tralee: Kerryman, 1955; *A Leaf from the Yellow Book, the Correspondence of George Egerton,* ed. London: Richards Press, 1958; *An Affair with the Moon.* London: Gollancz, 1959. (Novel); *A Fretful Midge.* London: Routledge & Kegan Paul, 1959. (Autobiography); *Prenez Garde.* London: Gollancz, 1961. (Novel); *The Remainderman.* London: Gollancz, 1963. (Novel); *Lucifer Falling.* London: Gollancz, 1966. (Novel); *The Parents of Oscar Wilde.* London: Hodder & Stoughton, 1967. (Biography); *Tara.* London: Gollancz, 1967. (Novel); *Ireland.* London: Thames & Hudson, 1968; *Leinster.* London: Faber, 1968; *The Lambert Mile.* London: Gollancz, 1969. (Novel); *The March Hare.* London: Gollancz, 1970. (Novel); *Mr. Stephen.* London: Gollancz, 1970. (Novel); *The Anglo-Irish.* London: Gollancz, 1972. (Nonfiction); *The Distance and the Dark.* London: Gollancz, 1973. (Novel); *The Radish Memoirs.* London: Gollancz, 1974. (Novel); *Big Fleas and Little Fleas, and Other Stories.*

London: Gollancz, 1976; *Tom Moore: The Irish Poet.* London: Hamilton, 1977. (Biography); *Chimes at Midnight.* London: Gollancz, 1978. (Stories); *My Name Is Norval.* London: Gollancz, 1978. (Novel); *Birds of Prey.* London: Gollancz, 1980. (Stories); *Johnnie Cross.* London: Gollancz, 1983. (Novel); *Chat Show.* London: Gollancz, 1987. (Novel).   REFERENCE: Fallon, Brian. "Terence de Vere White: All-round Man of Letters." *Irish Times* (June 18, 1994): 6.

WHITE, VICTORIA (1962–   ), short story writer and journalist. White was born in Dublin and educated there, studying English and Italian in Trinity College. She now works as a journalist on the *Irish Times.* Her volume of short stories, *Raving Autumn,* published while she was still in her twenties, is a well-written but somewhat sad book. Many of the stories are about the impossibility of finding happiness, either in or out of marriage. In "Margaret," an unhappily married woman gets pregnant mysteriously, and although this child gives life meaning for a while, the feeling does not last. In "Mr. Brennan's Heaven," a young woman goes mad on her honeymoon and ends up giggling insanely at a mirror. The longer title story, "Raving Autumn," is an interesting character study of an Irish rebel and her relationship with her captured young Anglo-Irish mistress. If Victoria White finds any hope at all, it is in artistic endeavor, as "Concubine" illustrates, when a ghost appears to an artist. This hope is repeated in "Landscape Painter," where again a happy and normal artist escapes from the severely depressed protagonist. The more intriguing aspects of Victoria White's technique are her use of ghosts and of history. The two historical stories, one set in nineteenth-century Australia, and the other in the Holy Land, were the most enjoyable in the book, and she would make a good historical novelist.

MARY ROSE CALLAGHAN

WORK: *Raving Autumn and Other Stories.* [Swords, Co. Dublin]: Poolbeg, [1990].

WHITE, W[ILLIAM] J[OHN] "JACK" (1920–1980), novelist, playwright, and journalist. White was born in Cork on March 30, 1920, of English parents. At Trinity College, Dublin, he twice won the Vice-Chancellor's Prizes in both verse and prose. From 1942 to 1962, he was a journalist for the *Irish Times,* as well as the Irish correspondent for the *Observer* and the *Manchester Guardian.* In 1962, he was employed by Radio Telefís Éireann, and in 1974 he became controller of television programs. White wrote three novels, two plays, and a study of the place of Protestants in Southern Ireland, entitled *Minority Report.* The novels—*One for the Road* (1956), *The Hard Man* (1958), and *The Devil You Know* (1962)—are studies of the Dublin middle class. *One for the Road* is set during the war years and is something of a whodunit involving a rather young man in the import business. *The Hard Man* has as protagonist an architect who joins the civil service, and it is a markedly more general study of business chicanery. *The Devil You Know* casts the broadest net of all, has a large and varied cast, and studies the effects of love and ambition on a number of people connected with the fictional Dublin Institute for Historical Research. In all of White's novels, the characters behave with the plausibility of life, but with rather more nastiness than one expects in a novel. One senses the author's sour distaste for their various imbroglios and infidelities. However, all of the books are leanly written and compulsively readable, and *The Devil You Know* has some extremely clever writing (''bottle-scarred veterans,'' for instance), as well as some effective satire. All of the novels excellently re-create the milieu of the affluent middle class, which had been little treated in Irish fiction until the 1950s, and one regrets that White did not continue his dissections into the more affluent and satirizable 1960s. Only one of his two plays, *The Last Eleven* (Abbey, 1968) has been published. That sad and clever drama won the Irish Life Drama Award in 1967; it is a quiet, telling study of the much-diminished congregation of a Protestant church. There is an absolutely solid craftsmanship about White's work, and the only reason he does not have a first-rate reputation is his too meager production.

WORKS: *One for the Road.* London: Jonathan Cape, 1956; *The Hard Man.* London: Jonathan Cape, 1958; *The Devil You Know.* London: Jonathan Cape, 1962/reprint, Dublin: Allen Figgis, 1970; *Minority Report: The Protestant Community in the Irish Republic.* Dublin: Gill & Macmillan, 1975; *The Last Eleven.* Newark, Del.: Proscenium, 1978. (Play).

WHITTY, MICHAEL JAMES (1795–1873), short story writer and journalist. Whitty was born in Wexford but made his reputation in England as an editor-journalist and as a chief constable. In 1823, he became editor of the *London and Dublin Magazine.* Its first volume contained his series on Robert Emmet, which he would later publish separately. He continued as editor until 1827. He later contributed articles under various names, including J. B. Whitty, Rory O'Rourke, and Geoffrey K—n. Also in the 1820s, Whitty contributed widely to Irish journals, becoming an outspoken advocate of Catholic emancipation. In 1836, he accepted the post as chief constable of Liverpool. During his tenure, which lasted until 1848, he established a fire brigade and restructured the police force. On retirement, he purchased the *Liverpool Journal* and founded the *Liverpool Daily Post.* He died in Liverpool on June 10, 1873. Whitty's literary reputation rests on his anonymously published volumes, *Tales of Irish Life,* which were printed in London and America and translated into French and German. Printed in 1824 with illustrations by George Cruikshank, the work depicts the customs and traditions of Irish life in the early nineteenth century. It precedes the work of the Banims* and Carleton,* and John Hennig wrote that ''in his tales the Irish peasant came for the first time really alive on paper.''

BERNARD McKENNA

WORKS: *Tales of Irish Life.* 2 vols. London: J. Robins, 1824; *Robert Emmet.* Liverpool: Longmans, 1870. REFERENCE: Hennig, John. ''Michael Whitty.'' *Irish Bookman* 1 (February 1947): 39–44.

WHYTE, LAURENCE (1680s–ca. 1752), poet. Whyte was perhaps born near Ballymore, County Westmeath, sometime in the 1680s. He became a teacher of mathematics in Dublin, was knowledgeable about music, and had some Irish. Although a rather prolific poet and sometimes an ambitious one, he was not even suspected of poetry until the appearance of his *Poems on Various Subjects* in 1740. That book must have had some success, for an enlarged edition appeared in 1742. Whyte's comic poems are more successful than his serious ones, which are generally uninspired and conventional. Some of the comic poems are quite long, such as "The Parting Cup" or "An Essay on Dunning," whose seven cantos run to sixty pages. His realistic details of country life are pleasant enough, and his usual galloping iambic tetrameters occasionally throw up some tight and effective lines, such as these from "The Parting Cup":

> His first-born, Pat—diebus illis,
> wrote an acrostic upon Phyllis
> and then presents her with some lines
> in epigrams and Valentines,
> in such a soft, pathetic style
> as gained the favour of a smile.

On the other hand, he is more usually never far from the doggerel of:

> What Man can ever pine or mutter,
> When he can have good Toast and Butter. . . .

WORKS: *Poems on Various Subjects, Serious and Diverting, Never Before Published.* Dublin: S. Powell, 1740/*Original Poems on Various Subjects, Serious, Moral and Diverting.* 2d enlarged edition. Dublin: S. Powell, 1742.   REFERENCE: Fagan, Patrick. "Laurence Whyte." In *A Georgian Celebration: Irish Poets of the Eighteenth Century.* Dublin: Branar, [1989], pp. 32–42.

WHYTE, SAMUEL (1733–1811), poet and schoolmaster. Whyte was born aboard a ship bound for Liverpool, and he was brought up there and in Dublin. He was a first cousin of Frances Sheridan,* and much information about her and her husband Thomas Sheridan the younger* is to be found in his *Miscellanea Nova* (1800). He was much influenced by the younger Sheridan's theories on education and elocution, as his own writings on these subjects show. Whyte is remembered for the long-lived academy that he founded in Grafton Street in 1758 on the site of the present Bewley's. Among his best-known pupils were the duke of Wellington, Thomas Moore,* John O'Keeffe,* and Richard Brinsley Sheridan* and his sister Alicia, whose mother, Frances, did not think "they [did] their preceptor . . . much credit." Tom Moore, however, attributed to Whyte, "that excellent person all the instruction in English literature [I have] ever received."

Whyte is little remembered as a poet; however, a piece such as "When Love's Sweet Emotions First Dawn in the Mind" is both charming and effectively musical. Whyte never strives for great effects in his poems, but they are so adroit and smooth that a few deserve to be in any full anthology of Irish verse. He died on October 11, 1811.

WORKS: Ed., *The Shamrock; or, Hibernian Cresses.* Dublin: Printed by R. Marchbank, for the Editor, 1772/as *A Collection of Poems, the Productions of the Kingom of Ireland.* London: Printed for S. Bladen, 1773. (About two-thirds of the poems are by the editor, Whyte); *A Collection of*

Poems on Various Subjects. 2d ed. E. A. Whyte, ed. Dublin: Printed by R. Marchbank, 1792/rev. ed., 1795; *Miscellanea Nova.* E. A. Whyte, ed. Dublin: Printed by R. Marchbank for the Editor, 1800; *An Introductory Essay on the Art of Reading, and Speaking in Public.* E. A. Whyte, ed. Dublin: Printed by Robert Marchbank, for the Editor, 1800. REFERENCE: LeFanu, Alicia. *Memoirs of the Life and Writings of Mrs. Frances Sheridan.* . . . London: G. & W. Whittaker, 1824.

WIBBERLEY, LEONARD [PATRICK O'CONNOR] (1915–1983), novelist, journalist, playwright, and children's writer. Wibberley was born in Dublin on April 9, 1915, to an Anglo-Irish father and to a mother who was ''Irish of the Irish.'' The prolific writer (who eventually authored over 100 books, often pseudonymously) attended schools in both Ireland and England. He then worked as an apprentice to a London publisher and eventually became a reporter for the *London Daily Mirror* and editor of various West Indies journals. He emigrated to the United States in 1943, raising six children with his wife, Katherine Hazel Holton, and serving as cable editor for the Associated Press, as U.S. correspondent for the *London Evening News,* and as staff member of the *Los Angeles Times.* His many avocations, which included scuba diving, sailing, painting, music, and violin making, inspired a number of his nonfictional works.

Wibberley is best known for his non-Irish ''Mouse'' series, a political satire that depicts the fictional duchy of Grand Fenwick, a small, impoverished country that dares to wage war against the United States and to launch a space shuttle. *The Mouse That Roared* was filmed by Columbia Pictures in 1958, starring Peter Sellers, and *The Mouse on the Moon* was produced by Lopert in 1963.

Wibberley's memories of Ireland generated several quasi-fictional texts and historical books, beginning with *The Trouble with the Irish* (1956). This anecdotal, often tongue-in-cheek ''history'' of the Irish nation is actually a combined history of Ireland and England. In it, Wibberley celebrates the Irish disdain for the law, their worship of the past, their disorganization, while remarking that their disorder and internecine struggles usually impaired their ability to notice that their lands were gradually being acquired by the English. He notes the English ability to organize and govern efficiently yet comments that they are not exactly civilized and often render stupid judgments. While scarcely any dates are offered, key events and issues are not avoided, and the strength of Wibberley's account lies in his biting sarcasm, wit, and convincing anecdotes.

Wibberley followed this account with a chronicle of Irish emigration to America, in *The Coming of the Green* (1958). The text is filled with encomia for the hardworking emigrants who built the financial strength of the United States, while never forgetting those who remained in Ireland. He defends the Irish involvement in the corrupt Tammany Hall political machine as a necessary move to secure rights of suffrage and to take care of their own. He explains away Irish pro-slavery attitudes as a defense mechanism arising from a fear of job losses, noting that it took Irish soldiers' involvement in the civil war for them to become Yankees in the eyes of other Americans. He also notes the move toward conservative thinking, as the Irish Americans sought restrictions to immigration, clashed with the Chinese over the building of the Union-Pacific Railroad, and performed some heinous crimes in the Molly Maguires. Ultimately, though, *The Coming of the Green* praises Irish loyalty and determination, ending with a catalog of famous Irish Americans.

A return to Irish soil inspired two Hibernian adventures, the first of which, *The Hands of Cormac Joyce* (1960), was made into a television movie. The short novel depicts the hardships and the bravery of three families seeking to hold onto their island homes and lifestyles in Connemara. A violent Atlantic storm drives out the largest family, the Conneeleys, while the oldest couple lose their home and lives. However, Cormac's young son, Jackie, remains with his injured father and proves himself to be an island hero. Wibberley's observation that island fishermen live *in* the sea, while mainland fishermen live *off* it, is probably accurate, although he also notes the increasing difficulty of making a living with the rigors of island life.

A semiautobiographical tale based on a stay in a Connemara coastal village, *The Land That Isn't There* (1960) approaches life in the Gaeltacht with a lighter touch. Wibberley escorts his seven-year-old son, Kevin, and nine-year-old daughter, Tricia, to Ireland, while his wife awaits the birth of their next child and cares for the others. The amusing novel details the embarrassments of traveling with young children, who often speak quite candidly to strangers but who also sometimes prove wiser than their adult guardians. There are entertaining accounts of a court case between the Walshes and the Joyces (whose attorneys are conversely named Joyce and Walsh); of Irish ghosts, such as the fish ghost on the bog, and of a music festival at Lisdoonvarna, at which the performers have to compete with the noisy audience. Wibberley also explains the importance of horse racing in Irish culture, ponders the effectiveness of folk medicine, and bemoans the indifference to prehistoric culture and shame over Ireland's pagan past. He had noted in *The Trouble with the Irish* that his countrymen were happier before they adopted the Christian religion.

In 1971, Wibberley penned an autobiographical account of coming-of-age as an Irish immigrant in Ayrshire, Scotland. *Down the Bath Rocks,* written under the pseudonym of Patrick O'Connor, captures a child's impressions of silent pictures, the indignities of living in poverty as a minority group, and the hypocrisies of some adults—as a hospital patient, he notes that the toys are roped off from the children unless the "delegates" are paying a visit. But life away from Belfast was not all bad, and initiation into a local gang, learning to box, and visiting in Derry with an aunt who runs a sweetshop all provide exciting or pleasant interruptions in an otherwise dreary existence. Once a smugglers' lair, the Bath Rocks themselves are first shown as a private spot where Patrick can answer nature's call, and his use of this treasured location represents escape from adult authority and from the ugly attic apartment. Wibberley demonstrates the power of the imagination through the young boy who escapes from repressive catechism class and boring schoolwork by creating his own fantasy world.

As in the novels, he shows the resourcefulness of the Irish and their ability to survive the harshest conditions.

He died in Santa Monica, California, on November 22, 1983.

MARGUERITE QUINTELLI-NEARY

WORKS: *The King's Beard.* New York: Ariel, 1952. (Children's story); *The Secret of the Hawk.* New York: Ariel, 1952. (Children's story); *The Coronation Book.* New York: Farrar, Straus, 1953. (Children's story); *The Deadman's Cave.* New York: Farrar, Straus, 1954. (Children's story); *The Spies of Everest.* New York: Farrar, Straus, 1954. (Children's story); *Mrs. Searwood's Secret Weapon.* Boston: Little, Brown, 1954. (Novel); *The Wound of Peter Wayne.* New York: Farrar, Straus, 1955. (Children's story); *The Mouse That Roared.* Boston: Little, Brown, 1955. (Novel); *The Life of Winston Churchill.* New York: Farrar, Straus, 1956. (Juvenile biography); *McGillicudy McGotham.* Boston: Little, Brown, 1956. (Biography); *The Trouble with the Irish.* New York: Holt, [1956]. (Nonfiction); *John Barry: Father of the Navy.* New York: Farrar, Straus, 1957. (Juvenile biography); *Kevin Barry and the Light Brigade.* New York: Farrar, Straus, 1957. (Juvenile nonfiction); *Beware of the Mouse.* New York: Putnam, 1957. (Novel); *Take Me to Your President.* New York: Putnam, 1957. (Novel); *Wes Powell: Conqueror of the Grand Canyon.* New York: Farrar, Straus, 1958. (Juvenile biography); *The Coming of the Green.* New York: Ives Washburn, 1958. (Nonfiction); *John Treegate's Musket.* New York: Farrar, Straus, 1959. (Juvenile biography); *The Quest of Excalibur.* New York: Putnam, 1959. (Novel); *No Garlic in the Soup!* New York: Ives Washburn, 1959. (Nonfiction); *The Land That Isn't There.* New York: Ives Washburn, [1960]. (Nonfiction); *Peter Treegate's War.* New York: Farrar, Straus, 1960. (Children's story); *The Hands of Cormac Joyce.* New York: Putnam, 1960. (Novel); *Sea Captain from Salem.* New York: Farrar, Straus, 1961. (Children's story); *Stranger at Killknock.* New York: Putnam, 1961. (Novel); *Yesterday's Land.* New York: Ives Washburn, 1961. (Nonfiction); *The Time of the Lamb.* New York: Ives Washburn, 1961. (Drama); *Treegate's Raiders.* New York: Farrar, Straus, 1962. (Children's story); *The Mouse on the Moon.* New York: Morrow, 1962. (Novel); *Ventures into the Deep.* New York: Ives Washburn, 1962. (Nonfiction); *Thomas Jefferson: Young Man from the Piedmont.* New York: Farrar, Straus, 1963. (Juvenile biography); *A Feast of Freedom.* New York: Morrow, 1963. (Novel); *Ah Julian: A Memoir of Julian Brodetsky.* New York: Ives Washburn, 1963. (Nonfiction); *The Shepherd's Reward.* New York: Ives Washburn, 1963. (Drama); *Thomas Jefferson: A Dawn in the Trees.* New York: Farrar, Straus, 1964. (Juvenile biography); *Fiji: Islands of the Dawn.* New York: Ives Washburn, 1964. (Nonfiction); *Thomas Jefferson: The Gales of Spring.* New York: Farrar, Straus, 1965. (Juvenile biography); *The Island of the Angels.* New York: Morrow, 1965. (Novel); *Thomas Jefferson: The Time of the Harvest.* New York: Farrar, Straus, 1966. (Juvenile biography); *The Centurion.* New York: Morrow, 1966. (Novel); *Towards a Distant Island.* New York: Ives Washburn, 1966. (Nonfiction); *Encounter near Venus.* New York: Farrar, Straus, 1967. (Children's story); *The Road from Toomi.* New York: Morrow, 1967. (Novel); *Something to Read.* New York: Ives Washburn, 1967. (Nonfiction); *Adventures of an Elephant Boy.* New York: Morrow, 1968. (Novel); *The Heavenly Quarterback.* Woodstock, Ill.: Dramatic, 1969. (Drama); *Thomas Jefferson: Man of Liberty.* New York: Farrar, Straus, 1969. (Earlier series of juvenile biographies published as one volume); *Attar of the Ice Valley.* New York: Farrar, Straus, 1969. (Children's story); *The Mouse on Wall Street.* New York: Morrow, 1969. (Novel); *Hound of the Sea.* New York: Ives Washburn, 1969. (Nonfiction); *Gift of a Star.* Woodstock, Ill.: Dramatic, 1969. (One-act play); *Leopard's Prey.* New York: Farrar, Straus, 1971. (Children's story); *Meeting with a Great Beast.* New York: Morrow, 1971. (Novel); *Voyage by Bus.* New York: Morrow, 1971. (Nonfiction); *Black Jack Rides Again.* Woodstock, Ill.: Dramatic, 1971. (Drama); *The Shannon Sailors.* New York: Morrow, 1972. (Nonfiction); *The Red Pawns.* New York: Farrar, Straus, 1973. (Children's story); *The Testament of Theophilus.* New York: Morrow, 1973. (Novel); *Flint's Island.* New York: Farrar, Straus, 1974. (Children's story); *The Last Stand of Father Felix.* New York: Morrow, 1974. (Novel); *Guarneri: Story of a Genius.* New York: Farrar, Straus, 1975. (Juvenile biography); *1776—And All That.* New York: Morrow, 1975. (Novel); *Once, in a Garden.* Woodstock, Ill.: Dramatic, 1975. (Drama); *The Last Battle.* New York: Farrar, Straus, 1976. (Children's story); *The Vicar of Wake-*

field. Woodstock, Ill.: Dramatic, 1976. (Play based on Goldsmith's novel); *Perilous Gold.* New York: Farrar, Straus, 1978. (Children's story); *Little League Family.* Garden City, N.Y.: Doubleday, 1978. (Children's story); *Homeward to Ithaka.* New York: Morrow, 1978. (Novel); *The Good Natured Man: A Portrait of Oliver Goldsmith.* New York: Morrow, 1979. (Biography); *The Crime of Martin Coverly.* New York: Farrar, Straus, 1980. (Children's story); *The Mouse That Poured.* New York: Morrow, 1981. (Novel); *The Mouse That Saved the West.* New York: Morrow, 1981. (Novel). As Patrick O'Connor: *Flight of the Peacock.* New York: Ives Washburn, 1954. (Children's story); *The Society of Foxes.* New York: Ives Washburn, 1954. (Children's story); *The Watermelon Mystery.* New York: Ives Washburn, 1955. (Children's story); *Gunpowder for Washington.* New York: Ives Washburn, 1956. (Juvenile nonfiction); *The Black Tiger.* New York: Ives Washburn, 1956; *The Lost Harpooner.* New York: Ives Washburn, 1957. (Children's story); *Mexican Road Race.* New York: Ives Washburn, 1957. (Children's story); *The Black Tiger at LeMans.* New York: Ives Washburn, 1958. (Children's story); *The Five-Dollar Watch Mystery.* New York: Ives Washburn, 1959. (Children's story); *The Black Tiger at Bonneville.* New York: Ives Washburn, 1960. (Children's story); *Treasure at Twenty Fathoms.* New York: Ives Washburn, 1961. (Children's story); *The Black Tiger at Indianapolis.* New York: Ives Washburn, 1962. (Children's story); *The Raising of the Dubhe.* New York: Ives Washburn, 1964. (Children's story); *Seawind from Hawaii.* New York: Ives Washburn, 1965. (Children's story); *South Swell.* New York: Ives Washburn, 1967. (Children's story); *Beyond Hawaii.* New York: Ives Washburn, 1969. (Children's story); *A Car Called Camellia.* New York: Ives Washburn, 1970. (Children's story); *Down the Bath Rocks.* Dublin: Gill & Macmillan, 1971. (Fictional memoir). As Leonard Holton: *Saint Maker.* New York: Dodd, 1959. (Detective fiction); *A Pact with Satan.* New York: Dodd, 1960. (Detective fiction); *Secret of the Doubting Saint.* New York: Dodd, 1961. (Detective fiction); *The Ballad of the Pilgrim Cat.* New York: Ives Washburn, 1962. (Detective fiction); *Deliver Us from Wolves.* New York: Dodd, 1963. (Detective fiction); *Flowers by Request.* New York: Dodd, 1964. (Detective fiction); *Out of the Depths.* New York: Dodd, 1966. (Detective fiction); *A Touch of Jonah.* New York: Dodd, 1968. (Detective fiction); *A Problem in Angels.* New York: Dodd, 1970. (Detective fiction); *The Mirror of Hell.* New York: Dodd, 1972. (Detective fiction); *The Devil to Play.* New York: Dodd, 1974. (Detective fiction); *A Corner of Paradise.* New York: St. Martin's, 1976. (Detective fiction). As Christopher Webb: *Mark Toyman's Inheritance.* New York: Funk, 1960. (Children's story); *Zebulon Pike: Soldier and Explorer.* New York: Funk, 1961. (Juvenile biography); *The River of PeeDee Jack.* New York: Funk, 1962. (Children's story); *Quest of the Otter.* New York: Funk, 1963. (Children's story); *The Ann and Hope Mutiny.* New York: Funk, 1966. (Children's story); *Eusebius the Phoenician.* New York: Funk, 1967. (Children's story). With Christopher Sergel: *The Mouse on Mars.* Woodstock, Ill.: Dramatic, 1967. (Drama). With Hazel Weberley, ed. *Shamrocks and Sea Silver, and Other Illuminations.* Vol. 8 in *I. O. Evans Studies in the Philosophy and Criticism of Literature.* San Bernardino, Calif.: Borgo, 1985. (Critical study).

WILDE, LADY (1821–1896), poet and woman of letters. Lady Wilde was born Jane Francesca Elgee in Wexford. She claimed 1826 as her birthdate, but Richard Ellmann has established it as December 27, 1821. As a young woman, under the pseudonymn of Speranza, she became a frequent and fervant contributor to *The Nation.** Her patriotic verses are generally of small merit, but they are vigorous and filled with exhortations such as "God! Liberty! Truth!" and "Oh, courage!" and "To Arms! To Arms! for Truth, Fame, Freedom, Vengeance, Victory!" Nevertheless, some lines are striking, such as these from "The Famine Year":

> There's a proud array of soldiers—what do they round your door?
> "They guard our master's granaries from the thin hands of the poor."

Pale mothers, wherefore weeping?—''Would to God that we were dead—
Our children swoon before us, and we cannot give them bread!'' . . .

Oh! we know not what is smiling, and we know not what is dying;
But we're hungry, very hungry, and we cannot stop our crying. . . .''

Or these from ''Related Souls'':

Time was not made for spirits like ours,
Nor the changing light of the changing hours;
For the life eternal still lies below
The drifted leaves and the fallen snow.

Her articles for *The Nation* were as vehement as most of her verse, and one
fiery piece, ''Jacta Alea Est'' (The Die Is Cast), caused the July 29, 1848, issue
to be immediately suppressed. When Gavan Duffy* was brought to trial, the
attorney-general accused him of writing the inflammatory piece, but Speranza
stood up in the public gallery, asserting her own authorship and her right to be
in the dock.

In 1851, she married William Wilde,* and after he was knighted they kept
virtually open house at their home in Merrion Square. After her husband's death
in 1876, Lady Wilde moved to London and conducted a somewhat raffish salon.
She died on February 3, 1896, in much reduced circumstances and during her
son Oscar Wilde's* incarceration. Lady Wilde is remembered more as a fascinating and somewhat bizarre personality than as a writer. Her poems, translations, essays, and journalism have little merit, but her retellings of Irish folktales
were done with simplicity and humor and with none of her usual stylistic oro-
tundity. The best of them are absolutely enchanting.

WORKS: *Ugo Bassi: A Tale of the Italian Revolution,* by Speranza. London, 1857. (Verse);
Poems. Dublin: James Duffy, 1864; *Driftwood from Scandinavia.* London: R. Bentley, 1884; *Ancient
Legends, Mystic Charms, and Superstitions of Ireland.* 2 vols. London: Ward & Downey, 1887.
(Stories); *Ancient Cures, Charms and Usages of Ireland.* London: Ward & Downey, 1890. (Stories);
Notes on Men, Women, and Books. London: Ward & Downey, 1891; *Social Studies.* London: Ward
& Downey, 1893.   REFERENCES: Melville, Joy. *Mother of Oscar: The Life of Jane Francesca
Wilde.* London: John Murray, 1994; White, Terence de Vere. *The Parents of Oscar Wilde.* London:
Hodder & Stoughton, 1967; Wyndham, Horace. *Speranza.* London: T. V. Boardman, 1951.

WILDE, OSCAR [FINGAL O'FLAHERTIE WILLS] (1854–1900), playwright, poet, and wit. Wilde was born on October 16, 1854, at 15 Westland
Row, Dublin, the second son of Sir William Wilde,* eye-surgeon oculist in
ordinary to the Queen, and Jane Francesca (formerly Elgee).* Sir William's first
ancestor to come to Ireland was a builder from Durham whose son became
agent to Lord Mount Sandford in County Roscommon, and the theory that the
Wildes were descended from a Dutch officer in the army of William of Orange
was a fabrication of Lady Wilde. She, too, was descended from immigrant builders, refugees from religious persecution in Scotland. The Elgees' ancestors were

said to be Italians called Algeo, although Lady Wilde claimed descent from Dante.

Lady Wilde was elephantine in build and extravagant in manner, but her salon in Merrion Square was much frequented. Her husband's moral reputation (always suspect, as he had three illegitimate children) was irreparably injured when a patient alleged that he had seduced her under chloroform. The trial in 1864 was given wide publicity.

Oscar, however, does not seem to have suffered from his father's embarrassments. After school at Portora in Northern Ireland, he read a brilliant course in classics in Trinity College, Dublin; then, moving to Oxford, he took a double first and won the Newdigate Prize for a poem, "Ravenna." He was happy and successful and devoted to a beautiful Dublin girl, Florence Balcombe, who later married Bram Stoker,* author of *Dracula.* Wilde was twenty-five years of age when he took rooms with Frank Miles at 13 Salisbury Street, London, and launched himself in London.

As a poet, Wilde would have said that he had no diffidence. He sent his work to the most eminent in the land, he sighed on the doorsteps of Lily Langtry, actress, beauty, and mistress of the future Edward VII, and Ellen Terry, queen of the English stage, was another recipient of open admiration and a poem. He dressed in velvet with flowing bow tie, courtier's knee breeches, and silk stockings. His aesthetic affectations had won him some rough attentions at Oxford; in London they were part of his provocative self-advertisement. He is generally believed to have inspired Bunthorne in *Patience,* Gilbert and Sullivan's comic opera. To collect funds he made a lecture tour in America in 1882. It was a notorious success. But his first play *Vera,* staged in New York, folded after a week's run the following year.

Now a celebrity, Wilde married Constance Lloyd, the good, decorative, but not very interesting daughter of a respectable legal family in Ireland. The young couple set up house in 16 Tite Street, in circumstances of comparative luxury. Wilde was garrulous about the ardency of his passion. He had inherited a small income under his father's will, and his wife had some money, but not enough. As a result, Wilde did some lecturing, and then, in 1887, he took up the editorship of *Woman's World,* which was rather a comedown, but he invited even royalty to contribute. At this time he published the children's stories "The Happy Prince" and "The Portrait of Mr. W. H." The mystery of Shakespeare's sonnets preoccupied him for many years. It marked the first stage of his awareness of his inverted sexual nature, for which discovery Robert Ross, whom he met in 1886, is usually given responsibility. Wilde's second son, Vyvyan, was born that year; Cyril, the elder, had been born in 1885.

In 1891, Wilde met Lord Alfred Douglas, and fell under the malign influence of this petulant, selfish, and conceited son of a mad father, the marquis of Queensberry. Sulkily handsome, with a facility for writing sonnets, Douglas entered Wilde's life when his own genius was coming into full flower. Always self-confident (an inheritance from his mother), Wilde now became hubristic.

The Picture of Dorian Grey, first published in *Lippincott's,* was produced as a novel in 1891. The matrix of his later plays, sparkling with epigrams (some of which were to be put to use again), it was a scarcely veiled acknowledgment of his revolt against conventional morality. Many critics were hostile; Wilde, never loth, poured contumely on them. His four golden years had now begun. His most brilliant and characteristic essays appeared in a volume *Intentions.* Nowhere is Wilde's wit, paradox, and gracefully worn learning better in evidence than in one of them, *The Decay of the Art of Lying.* The sheer fun and intellectual impudence which was to be whipped up into comic magic in *The Importance of Being Earnest* was here in full measure. *The Soul of Man Under Socialism* was a *tour de force* and shows a side of Wilde that is not much in evidence in his writings. As a rule, he was apolitical as well as amoral, and with no inclination towards radical creeds. His life, he said, was devoted to beauty. But within the limitations of a luxury-loving and self-indulgent nature, he was essentially kind and compassionate. Remorse could be extreme and lasted a day.

Lady Windermere's Fan, produced in London early in 1892, made Wilde's reputation as a fashionable playwright. No longer attempting to emulate Racine, he correctly described his venture as "one of those modern drawing-room plays with pink lampshades." It was followed by *A Woman of No Importance, An Ideal Husband,* and *The Importance of Being Earnest.* (The last two were running in London's West End when Wilde was arrested in 1895.) Wit and a sure instinct for what works on the stage characterized all of Wilde's later plays, but to later tastes the sentiment was dated, the morality insincere and almost maudlin. Consequently, the play that has most of this Victorian cant, *A Woman of No Importance,* is nowadays the least often performed. The only one without any moralizing in it, *The Importance of Being Earnest,* is an established classic. As Wilde moved from one success to another in the London theatre, he attempted also to conquer Paris. *Salomé,* which he wrote in French, attracted Sarah Bernhardt's attention as an ideal vehicle. She planned to perform the play in London, but the lord chamberlain refused his license because of the representation of sacred persons on the stage.

Wilde was indignant and threatened to seek French citizenship. As his son was later to remark, it was a pity that his father did not. Infatuated with Douglas, Wilde was leading a reckless life, consorting with male prostitutes, some of them criminal. His wife, who bored him, was neglected. Lady Wilde even wrote pathetically, begging her son to take his wife to the first night of one of his plays.

Fate might have been kept at bay had Douglas not involved Wilde in his perpetual war with his father. On February 18, 1895, Queensberry left a visiting card for Wilde at his club, for all to see, addressed to "Oscar Wilde posing as a somdomite [sic]." Wilde issued libel proceedings. At the trial, Queensberry pleaded justification in the public interest. He was defended by Edward Carson who had been at Trinity with Wilde and was on his way to establishing a great legal and political career. The trial was a disaster for Wilde. As he knew from blackmailers that compromising letters to Douglas were available, it is extraordinary that he took the risk. He had lost all touch with reality. Douglas, seeking only to humiliate his father, must be seen as the principal agent of Wilde's downfall. In any event, after Carson had led Wilde into damaging admissions on the witness stand and after the jury had brought in a verdict of ''Not guilty'' against Queensberry, it was certain that Wilde would be prosecuted for homosexual offenses. The authorities would have been glad enough to let Wilde slip out of the country, and his wife prayed that he would. However, he sat irresolute in the Cadogan Hotel, and was apprehended by the police and brought to trial.

The first trial led to disagreement among the jury, and Wilde was released on bail. Friends now advised him to flee. Frank Harris for one told him a yacht was waiting to take him abroad, but Wilde could not be prevailed upon to move. His mother, who earlier had stood beside her husband in his own humiliation, urged her son to stand his trial. W. B. Yeats* remarked that ''Wilde was an Irish gentleman. It was a point of honour to face the trial. It could not have occurred to him to act otherwise.'' He did stand trial, and he was sentenced to two years penal servitude, a term of frightful hardship for such a man. While he emerged from prison fitter than before, as events proved, he was in no other respect the better for the experience.

Had Wilde avoided his fate, only his legend would have suffered: all of his work, save one poem, had already been written. In prison he wrote *De Profundis* in the shape of a long letter to Alfred Douglas. This elaborate piece of prose had a chequered history. Douglas destroyed what he believed was the only copy, but the original was put in the safekeeping of the British Museum until 1960. Condemnatory of Douglas, the apologia is undermined by a vein of grandiloquence and an unconvincing tone of martyrdom. Wilde compares himself to Jesus Christ, and by implication, Douglas is Judas. The exercise is magnificent in its flamboyant way, but the justification rings rather hollow. After he came out of prison, Wilde struck a more genuine note of true feeling when he substituted another protagonist for himself in *The Ballad of Reading Gaol.* For all its echoes of *Eugene Aram* and *The Ancient Mariner,* this is the verse on which Wilde's status as poet most confidently rests. His other poems, even the ingenious ones like *The Sphinx,* are marred by a preciosity which frequently spoiled even his best prose. In his own words, Wilde was ''a lord of language,'' but only when he wrote in the vein of La Rochefoucauld. He described shallowness as the supreme vice, but his cadences and purple passages all too often suggest winter gardens and hired musicians. There was some uncertainty in his taste.

But his wit and fun—he had both—were perpetual and, at his best, incomparable. In his later life, Wilde, joined by Douglas for a time, lived abroad, often penniless, always borrowing. His last years in Paris were a sad epilogue to his years of fame. His character had not been chastened by misfortune. In general, he deteriorated in health and in fortune; he had been cut by former acquaintances but some friends, notably Ross, remained staunch. His wife settled an income on him which he lost when he took up again briefly with Douglas. Constance Wilde died in 1898.

In the 1890s Wilde was associated in the public mind with John Lane's magazine *The Yellow Book* and with Aubrey Beardsley, its daring illustrator. Beardsley's illustrations for *Salomé* matched the erotic tone of the text, but Beardsley, in fact, disliked Wilde, and Wilde had no connection with Lane's publication other than as an occasional contributor. His disgrace, however, led to Beardsley's dismissal, and the magazine suffered from Wilde's connection, publicized at the trials, with Shelley, a boy in Lane's employment.

Wilde's reputation as a writer rests on a ballad, a few sparkling essays, fairy stories, *De Profundis,* and the four later plays. As plays they are not as skillfully wrought as Pinero's written at the same time or Barrie's later plays, but they survive for the greater intelligence and wit of the writer. *The Importance of Being Earnest* is Wilde's sure claim to immortality. He himself said that he put his genius into his life, his talent into his work. Except for the few who inevitably found something repellent in his personality—his obesity, lardy color, and dowager mannerism (he laughed behind his hand, probably to conceal a discolored tooth)—people who heard Wilde talk came fully under his fascination. Max Beerbohm, who did not care for him, said that he had heard the table talk of Meredith, Swinburne, Gosse, James, Birrell, Balfour, Chesterton, Desmond MacCarthy, and Belloc—all splendid in their ways—but "Oscar was the greatest of them all—the most spontaneous and yet the most polished, the most soothing and yet the most surprising."

Wilde never exhibited his parents' interest in his own country, but his mother's career as a patriot had closed by the time he was growing up. In later years, she sought a pension for her literary work from the British government and wished for a knighthood for her son. Shaw* described Wilde as a "Merrion Square snob." Yeats, who knew him better, said: "He was not a snob. He was an Irishman; and England to an Irishman is a far strange land. To Wilde the aristocrats of England were as the nobles of Baghdad." Wilde died on November 30, 1900, in Paris, at the Hôtel D'Alsace in the Rue des Beaux Arts, where he was living at the time. He is buried in Père Lachaise.

There have been innumerable editions of Wilde, and the list here cites only the best and most accessible. Similarly, works about Wilde, although not as innumerable as works about Joyce* and Yeats,* have enormously proliferated; and this list is somewhat selective.

TERENCE de VERE WHITE

WORKS: *Complete Works of Oscar Wilde.* Introduction by Vyvyan Holland. London & Glasgow: Collins, 1966. (This is a revised and expanded edition of *The Works of Oscar Wilde.* G. F. Maine, ed. London & Glasgow: Collins, 1948); *The Letters of Oscar Wilde.* Rupert Hart-Davis, ed. London: Rupert Hart-Davis/New York: Harcourt, Brace & World, 1962; *More Letters of Oscar Wilde.* Rupert Hart-Davis, ed. London: John Murray, 1985/Oxford: Oxford University Press, 1987; The *Artist as Critic: Critical Writings of Oscar Wilde.* Richard Ellmann, ed. London: W. H. Allen/New York: Random House, 1969; *The Complete Shorter Fiction of Oscar Wilde.* Isobel Murray, ed. Oxford: Oxford University Press, 1979; *The Annotated Oscar Wilde.* H. Montgomery Hyde, ed. London:

Orbis, 1982; *Oscar Wilde.* Isobel Murray, ed. Oxford: Oxford University Press, 1989; *Oscar Wilde's Oxford Notebooks: A Portrait of a Mind in the Making.* Smith, Philip E., II & Holland, Michael S., eds. New York & Oxford: Oxford University Press, 1989. REFERENCES: Amor, Anne Clark. *Mrs. Oscar Wilde: A Woman of Some Importance.* London: Sidgwick & Jackson, 1983; Beckson, Karl, ed. *Oscar Wilde: The Critical Heritage.* New York: Barnes & Noble/London: Routledge & Kegan Paul, 1970; Behrendt, Patricia Beckson. *Oscar Wilde, Eros and Aesthetics.* [Basingstoke & London]: Macmillan/New York: St. Martin's, 1991; Bentley, Joyce. *The Importance of Being Constance.* London: Hale, 1983; Bird, Alan. *The Plays of Oscar Wilde.* London: Vision, 1977; Coakley, Davis. *Oscar Wilde: The Importance of Being Irish.* Dublin: Town House, 1994; Cohen, Ed. *Talk on the Wilde Side: Toward a Genealogy of a Discourse on Male Sexualities.* New York & London: Routledge, [1993]; Cohen, Philip K. *The Moral Vision of Oscar Wilde.* Rutherford, N.J.: Fairleigh Dickinson University Press/London: Associated University Presses, [1978]; Croft-Cooke, Rupert. *The Unrecorded Life of Oscar Wilde.* London: W. H. Allen/New York: David McKay, 1972; Dollimore, Jonathan. *Sexual Dissidence: Augustine to Wilde, Freud to Foucault.* Oxford: Clarendon, 1991; Douglas, Lord Alfred. *Oscar Wilde and Myself.* London: John Long/New York: Duffield, 1914; Ellmann, Richard. *Eminent Domain.* New York: Oxford University Press, 1967; Ellmann, Richard, ed. *Oscar Wilde: A Collection of Critical Essays.* Englewood Cliffs, N.J. & London: Prentice-Hall, 1969; Ellmann, Richard. *Codgers.* New York: Oxford University Press, 1973; Ellmann, Richard. *Oscar Wilde.* London: Hamish Hamilton/New York: Knopf, 1987; Fido, Martin. *Oscar Wilde.* London: Hamlyn/New York: Viking, 1973; Frewin, Leslie. *The Importance of Being Oscar: The Wit and Wisdom of Oscar Wilde Set against His Life and Times.* London: W. H. Allen, 1986; Gagnier, Reginia. *Idylls of the Marketplace: Oscar Wilde and the Victorian Public.* [Aldershot]: Scolar, [1987]; Gagnier, Reginia, ed. *Critical Essays on Oscar Wilde.* New York: G. K. Hall, 1991; Harris, Frank. *Oscar Wilde: Including My Memories of Oscar Wilde* by Bernard Shaw. East Lansing: Michigan State University Press, 1959/London: Panther, 1965/New York: Horizon, 1974. (A revised edition of Harris's 1916 work entitled *Oscar Wilde: His Life and Confessions*); Holland, Vyvyan. *Son of Oscar Wilde.* London: Rupert Hart-Davis/New York: E. P. Dutton, 1954; Holland, Vyvyan. *Oscar Wilde: A Pictorial Biography.* London: Thames & Hudson/New York: Viking, 1960; Kohl, Norbert. *Oscar Wilde: The Works of a Conformist Rebel.* Cambridge: Cambridge University Press, [1989]; Kronenberger, Louis. *Oscar Wilde.* Boston: Little, Brown, 1976; Mason, Stuart. *Bibliography of Oscar Wilde.* New ed. London: Bertram Rota, 1967; Merle, Robert. *Oscar Wilde.* Paris: Perren, 1984; Mikhail, E. H. *Oscar Wilde: An Annotated Bibliography of Criticism.* [London & Basingstoke]: [Macmillan, 1978]; Mikhail, E. H. *Oscar Wilde: Interviews and Recollections.* 2 vols. [London & Basingstoke]: M[acmillan, 1979]; Nassaar, Christopher S. *Into the Demon Universe: A Literary Exploration of Oscar Wilde.* New Haven, Conn.: Yale University Press, 1974; Nelson, Walter W. *Oscar Wilde from Ravenna to Salome: A Survey of Contemporary English Criticism.* Dublin: Dublin University Press, 1987; Nelson, Walter W. *Wilde and the Dramatic Critics: A Study in Victorian Theatre.* Lund: Bloms Boktryckeri, 1991; Pearson Hesketh. *The Life of Oscar Wilde.* 2d ed. London: Methuen, 1954; Pine, Richard. *Oscar Wilde.* Dublin: Gill & Macmillan, 1983; Pine, Richard. *The Thief of Reason: Oscar Wilde and Modern Ireland.* [Dublin]: Gill & Macmillan, [1995]; Powell, Kerry. *Oscar Wilde and the Theatre of the 1890s.* Miami, Fl.: Miami University Press/Cambridge: Cambridge University Press, [1990]; Raby, Peter. *Oscar Wilde.* Cambridge: Cambridge University Press, [1988]; Ransome, Arthur. *Oscar Wilde: A Critical Study.* London: Martin Secker/New York: Mitchell Kennerley, 1912/New York: Haskell House, 1971; Sandulescu, C. George, ed. *Rediscovering Oscar Wilde.* Gerrards Cross: Colin Smythe, 1995; Schroeder, Horst. *Additions and Corrections to Richard Ellmann's Oscar Wilde.* Braunschweig: [Author], 1989; Shewan, Rodney. *Oscar Wilde: Art and Egotism.* London: Macmillan, 1977; Small, Ian. *Oscar Wilde Revalued: An Essay on New Materials & Methods of Research.* [Greensboro, N.C.: ELT, 1993]; Sokolyansky, M. *Oscar Wilde: An Essay on His Work.* Kiev, Odessa, 1990; Symons, Arthur. *A Study of Oscar Wilde.* London: Charles J. Sawyer, 1930; Tydeman, William, ed. *Oscar Wilde: Comedies.* London: Macmillan, 1984; Worth, Katherine. *Oscar Wilde.* [London & Basingstoke]: M[acmillan, 1983].

WILDE, SIR WILLIAM (1815–1876), antiquarian and topographical writer. There have been instances where a young man's career has been hindered by the celebrity of a brilliant father; the reverse, too, can happen, and Sir William Wilde's versatility and achievements have been diminished by Oscar's* success and notoriety. However, Sir William made significant contributions to a developing specialty, aural surgery; his endeavors as assistant census connoisseur were prodigious; an enthusiastic archaeologist, his catalogue of the Royal Irish Academy's collection of antiquities has been described as "a milestone in the history of Irish Archaelogy"; and through his biographical articles (mainly of Irish medical men) and his topographical books, he has gained a place in the annals of Anglo-Irish literature.

William Wilde was born at Kilkeevin, Castlerea, County Roscommon, in 1815, the son of Dr. Thomas Wilde and his wife, Emily Fynne, a native of Ballymagibbon, near Cong, County Mayo. He took the Licentiate of the Royal College of Surgeons in Ireland in 1837 and spent the next nine months on board the "Crusader" as personal physician to a wealthy businessman who was going abroad on a health cruise. Thus, he obtained material for the two-volume *Narrative of a Voyage to Maderia, Teneriffe and along the Shores of the Mediterranean* (1839). For this work he received £250 which enabled him to study diseases of the eye and ear in London, Vienna, and Berlin.

Equipped as a specialist, Wilde set up in practice at 15 Westland Row and opened a dispensary for poor patients (the forerunner of St. Mark's Hospital) in a converted stable. Growing affluent, he moved to 21 Westland Row and later to a commodious mansion at 1 Merrion Square. Meanwhile, he had contributed biographical articles on Sir Thomas Molyneaux and Dr. R. J. Graves to the *Dublin University Magazine,* and during a brief tenure of the editorial chair of the *Dublin Journal of Medical Science* he wrote or edited other biographical articles. Later contributions to this genre were *The Closing Years of Dean Swift's Life* (1849) and a *Memoir of Gabriel Béranger* (1880).

A characteristic feature of Wilde's biographical work is its discursiveness; he lacks the true instinct of a biographer, being less interested in the man than in his achievements. His topographical works, *The Beauties of the Boyne* (1849) and *Lough Corrib, Its Shores and Islands* (1867), make more satisfactory reading.

On November 12, 1851, Wilde married Jane Francesca Elgee ("Speranza"* of *The Nation**), and they had three children, William, Oscar, and Isola. The Wildes may have seemed an ill-suited pair: he was small, untidy, and physically unprepossessing, while she was tall and striking; his mind sought facts and their collation, while hers was imaginative and fantastic. His avocations brought him in touch with many famous people. When Lord Macaulay who was then writing his *History* came to inspect the field of the Boyne, Wilde was his guide. His honors included the Order of the Polar Star bestowed by the king of Sweden and a knighthood conferred in 1864 for his work in connection with the Irish census.

If fortune had singled out Sir William Wilde in the bestowal of gifts, fate decreed that he should repay by being publicly cast down. An indiscretion with a female patient initiated a chain of events ending in a notorious libel action. His accuser won her case, although only a farthing damages, but Wilde's reputation was destroyed.

Wilde took refuge at Moytura House, overlooking Lough Corrib; soon he resumed practice. When the British Medical Association met in Dublin in 1867 (and Lister read an epoch-making paper "On the Antiseptic Principle"), Wilde acted as guide on an excursion to the Boyne Valley. He engaged in the Irish census of 1871 and rejoiced in 1874 when Oscar won the Berkeley Gold Medal at Trinity College.

Wilde's health deteriorated through 1875, and he died on April 19, 1876.

J. B. LYONS

WORKS: "Sir Thomas Molyneaux." *Dublin University Magazine* 18 (1841): 305–327, 470–489, 604–618, 744–763; "Sylvester O'Halloran." *Dublin Quarterly Journal of Medical Science* 6 (1848): 223; *The Beauties of the Boyne and Its Tributary the Blackwater.* Dublin: McGlashan, 1849/ abridged, Dublin: Three Candles, 1949; *The Closing Years of Dean Swift's Life.* Dublin: Hodges & Smith, 1849; *Lough Corrib, Its Shores and Islands.* Dublin: McGlashan, 1867/3d ed., abridged, Dublin: Three Candles, 1936; *Memoir of Gabriel Beranger.* Dublin: Gill, 1880. REFERENCES: Ellmann, Richard. *Oscar Wilde.* New York: Knopf/London: Hamish Hamilton, 1987; Frogatt, P. "Sir William Wilde and the 1851 Census of Ireland." *Medical History* 9 (1965): 302–327; Lyons, J. B. "Sir William Wilde, 1815–1876." *Journal of the Irish College of Physicians and Surgeons* 5 (1976): 147–152; de Paor, Liam. "Wilde the Antiquarian." *Irish Times* (September 14, 1976): 8; White, Terence de Vere. *The Parents of Oscar Wilde.* London: Hodder & Stoughton, 1967; Wilson, T. G. *Victorian Doctor: Being the Life of Sir William Wilde.* London, 1942/rpt., Wakefield: EP, 1974.

WILLIAMS, RICHARD D'ALTON (1822–1862), poet. Williams, the natural son of Count D'Alton, was born in Dublin on October 8, 1822, and was raised in his mother's home at Grenanstown, County Tipperary. While Williams was still a schoolboy, his first published poem, "The Munster War Song," derivative of Thomas Davis's* more celebrated "Lament for Owen Roe," appeared in *The Nation.* His medical studies in Dublin were interrupted by a close association with the Young Ireland movement, and his contributions to the *Irish Tribune* led to his arrest. Defended by the better-known poet Sir Samuel Ferguson,* he was acquitted of the charge of treason-felony.

Williams' poetry had three moods: patriotic, humorous, and religious. His association with St. Vincent's Hospital inspired his moving "Sister of Charity" and "The Dying Girl." Some lines in "The Dying Girl" became proverbial, particularly, "Consumption has no pity/For blue eyes and golden hair."

After graduating from Edinburgh about 1850, Williams worked at Dr. Steevens' Hospital, but verses published in *The Nation* in 1851 mark his decision to emigrate to a freer world, far from "British greed" and the threat of "her dungeon bars": "Come with me o'er Ohio/Among the vines of Indiana." Upon arriving in America in 1851, he taught in a Jesuit College in Mobile and later practiced medicine in New Orleans. He died in Thibodeaux from tuberculosis on July 5, 1862. His most famous poem of the American period was the "Song of the Irish-American Regiments."

J. B. LYONS

WORK: *The Poems of Richard D'Alton Williams.* Ed. with biographical introduction by P. A. Sillard. 2d ed. Dublin: Duffy, 1901. REFERENCE: Lyons, J. B. "Medicine and Literature in Ireland." *Journal of the Irish Colleges of Physicians and Surgeons* 3 (1975) 3–9.

WILLIAMS, RICHARD VALENTINE. *See* ROWLEY, RICHARD.

WILLS, W[ILLIAM] G[ORMAN] (1828–1891), playwright. Wills was born at Blackwell Lodge in Kilmurry, County Kilkenny, on January 28, 1828, to Katherine Gorman and James Wills, the noted biographer and author of the *Lives of Illustrious and Distinguished Irishmen.* Wills was educated at Waterford Grammar School and at Trinity College, Dublin, completing the entire undergraduate curriculum but taking no degree, and at the Royal Hibernian Academy of Art. Initially, he made his reputation and livelihood as a portrait painter, although his more famous works also included scenes from the theater. He never really abandoned painting, although he found his greatest success as a writer. In 1872, he was appointed "dramatist to the Lyceum," and that post provided a steady income of £300 a year and allowed him to cultivate a reputation as a verse playwright. Critics and biographers describe a man of considerable talent defeated by his lapses into "artistic melancholy" and "Bohemian ways." Indeed, descriptions of his studio detail a rodent-infested apartment occupied by various other animals and numerous vagrants. He was notorious for forgetting appointments and ignoring commissions. Apparently, he was haunted by his failure to achieve his artistic and literary promise, as his biographers provide an image of a rather pathetic old man close to death who would read unpublished and affected verse to anyone who would visit him. He died at Guy's Hospital in London on December 13, 1891.

Wills' plays served as star vehicles and included adaptations from non-English productions and English literary classics. His second and probably best play is *Man o' Airlie* of 1867, which details the decay of a man of great gifts and talents due to personal excesses. It was made popular by Lawrence Barrett, who toured extensively in it. *Charles the First,* produced at the Lyceum in 1872, enjoyed a run of over 200 nights and served as a star vehicle for Henry Irving, who also played in a number of Wills' other productions, including *Eugene Aram* (1873), *Faust* (1885), and *Vanderdicken* (1878), a dramatization written with Percy Fitzgerald* of the Flying Dutchman legend. Ellen Terry starred in Wills' rewriting of Goldsmith's* *The Vicar of Wakefield* at the Court Theatre in 1873. Nicoll's *History of English Drama 1660–1900* attributes forty plays to Wills, not all of which were published. His literary reputation was buoyed at the end of the last century by his brother's biography, which details a fascinating and attractive character. His plays are interesting now mainly as cultural relics of popular Victorian society and as commentaries on the tastes and customs of the mid-to-late nineteenth century.

BERNARD McKENNA

WORKS: *Old Times.* London: Saunders & Otley, 1857. (Novel); *Life's Foreshadowings.* 3 vols. London, 1859. (Novel); *Notice to Quit.* 3 vols. London: Hurst & Blackett/New York: Harper, 1861. (Novel); *St. Cyr.* London: Spottiswoode, 1864; *The Wife's Evidence.* New York: Harper, 1864. (Novel); *David Chantry.* 3 vols. London, 1865. (Novel); *The Love That Kills.* 3 vols. London, 1867. (Novel); *Hermann.* London: Samuel French, 1870; *Hinko, or the Headsman's Daughter.* New York: R. M. DeWitt, 1870/London: Diprose & Bateman, 1871; *The Man o' Airlie, a Drama of Affections.* Philadelphia: Ledger Steam & Power Job Printing Office, 1871; *Charles the First, an Historical Tragedy.* New York: Samuel French, [1872]/Edinburgh & London: W. Blackwood, 1873; with the Hon. Mrs. Greene. *Drawing Room Dramas.* Edinburgh: W. Blackwood, 1873; *Marie Street.* London: Samuel French, 1880; *Juanna.* London: Ballantyne, 1881; *A Little Tramp, or Landlords and Tenants in London.* London: A. Andrews, 1884; *Faust.* Edinburgh: W. Blackwood, 1885; *Melchior.* London: Macmillan, 1885; *Whose Hand? or, The Mystery of No Man's Heath.* Bristol: J. W. Arrowsmith, 1886; *Don Quixote.* New York: Harper, 1895; *Olivia, the Vicar of Wakefield.* New York: Readex Microprint, 1974. REFERENCES: Archer, William. *English Dramatists of Today.* London: S. Low, Marston, Searle & Revington, 1888; Booth, Michael. *English Melodrama.* London: Herbert Jenkins, 1965; Davis, Peter. "Lawrence Barrett and the *Man o' Airlie:* The Genteel Tradition in Performance." *Theatre History Studies* 7 (1987): 61–72; Fitzgerald, Percy Hetherington. *Henry Irving.* London: Chapman & Hall, 1893; Wills, Freeman Crofts. *W. G. Wills, Dramatist and Painter.* London: Longmans, Green, 1898.

WILSON, A[NDREW] PATRICK (ca. 1880–?), playwright and producer. Wilson was probably born in Scotland or in England of Scottish parents, sometime in the 1880s. Around 1911, he appeared in Dublin and became involved in Jim Larkin's Irish Transport and General Worker's Union, and became a correspondent for the labor paper, *The Irish Worker.* Under the pseudonym of "Euchan," he engaged in an acrimonious controversy in its pages with Sean O'Casey.* At the same time, Wilson had become involved with the Abbey Theatre,* first as a student actor, then as a member of the second company, and finally as manager and chief play producer. He was a vigorous producer, doing many new plays and, in 1914, two plays of his own. The more important, *The Slough,* dealt with the 1913 Lockout and was the first Irish play to depict Dublin slum life. In the production, Wilson himself played the Jim Larkin role but apparently with little of Larkin's flamboyance. In 1915, after a terrific row with Yeats* over the staging of Synge's* *Deirdre of the Sorrows,* Wilson resigned. For a while, he managed Arthur Sinclair's Irish Players and a similar Scottish group under the name of Andrew P. Wilson, and in the 1930s and 1940s he published a few plays in Scotland. Only two minor Irish pieces of his have reached print. The date of his death is uncertain.

WORK: *Victims and Poached.* Dublin: Liberty Hall Players, [ca. 1916].

WILSON, FLORENCE M[ARY] (ca. 1870–1946), poet. Wilson was born in Lisburn, County Antrim. After her marriage to F.H.G. Wilson, she lived on the Groomsport Road, Bangor, County Down, for most of her life, and the couple had six children. She was a close friend of Alice Milligan* and Alice Stopford Green.* She frequently wrote poems and essays for *The Ulster Guardian, Northern Whig, T. P.'s Weekly,* and *Irish Homestead.* She was an amateur historian, archaeologist, and artist. Wilson published only one delightful pamphlet of verse. "The Man from God-Knows-Where," a ballad based on Thomas Russell's efforts to organize the North for the 1798 Rising, is probably her best-known poem. Her literary efforts were woven around the needs of her family, but the work she produced was deservedly praised in her time.

ANNE COLMAN

WORK: *The Coming of the Earls and Other Verse.* Dublin: Candle, 1918.

WILSON, ROBERT ARTHUR (ca. 1820–1875), journalist and humorist. Wilson was born in Dunfanaghy, County Donegal, in about 1820. Under the name of Barney Maglone, he wrote popular humorous sketches. He was credited with a great mastery of languages. With his slouch hat, capacious cloak, and "necktie of pronounced hue," he was a striking figure on the streets of Enniskillen and Belfast. On April 10, 1875, he was found in his room in Belfast, dying, as one editor put it, "from the effect of his besetting sin. . . . 'Maglone' was one of the most lovable of men, but unfortunately his social qualities were his bane." He left posterity a vivid warning against his "besetting sin" in his poem "The Irish Cry," from which we extract these small gems:

> There's a wail from the glen;
>   There's a groan from the hill;
> 'Tis the cry of the land
>   'Gainst the Fiend of the Still! . . .
>
> The living! the smitten—
>   The blasted—the seared—
> The souls by the slime of
>   The drink-snake besmeared. . . .
>
> For the sake of the soul smitten
>   Slave of the Cup—
> For the sake of his victims—
>   Up! countrymen, up! . . .

Despite the above extract, Wilson's humorous skits and verses had keen and droll power of observation, and he had the ability to have bulked much larger than the minor and forgotten figure that he is.

WORKS: *Barney Maglone's Almeynack for all Ireland.* London, 1871; *The Reliques of "Barney Maglone."* F. J. Bigger & J. S. Crone, eds., with an Introductory Memoir by D. J. O'Donoghue. Belfast: T. Dargan, 1894.

WILSON, ROBERT McLIAM (1964–   ), novelist and filmmaker. Wilson, born on February 24, 1964, was educated at various secondary schools in his native Belfast and at St. Catherine's College, Cambridge. He earned early notice with his first novel, *Ripley Bogle* (1989), which won him the Rooney, Hughes and Betty Trask Prizes and the Irish Book Award and in which he made his mark as a writer of extraordinary verbal and imagistic facility, analyzing the life preoccupations of a twenty-two-year-old tramp on the eve of his death in London. The novel is remarkable for the fact that Bogle's origins in sectarian West Belfast only gradually obtrude into the wider schema of survival and despair and for its author's capacity for mature reflection—in particular, the depiction of genius in extremis. *Manfred's Pain* (1992) once again has impending death as its ostensible theme and also consists of flashbacks set against present-day narrative, suggesting that Wilson may be a formulaic writer with a diminishing imaginative strength, however impressive his ability to describe the actual experience of death. A coauthored book on poverty and a series of BBC documentary films suggest further that Wilson is becoming more interested in, and adept at, the portrayal of social, rather than imagined, reality.

RICHARD PINE

WORKS: *Ripley Bogle.* [London]: André Deutsch/Belfast: Blackstaff, [1989]; with Donovan Wylie. *The Dispossessed.* London: Picador, 1991. (Nonfiction); *Manfred's Pain.* [London]: Picador/Pan, [1992]; *OTG.* London: Secker & Warburg, 1995.

WINGFIELD, SHEILA (1906–1992), poet. Wingfield was born into a wealthy family in Hampshire on May 23, 1906, and through marriage became Viscountess Powerscourt. Although an active writer of poetry from childhood, her first published work did not appear until 1938, when she was thirty-two years old. After that, she published regularly, except for a ten-year period when illness necessitated a series of operations that rendered her an invalid. She died on January 8, 1992.

Since Wingfield has remained somewhat outside the stream of literary activity and influences, her work has probably not received the acclaim it deserves. Most readers will probably remember her for her long, moving war poem *Beat, Drum, Beat, Heart,* which is a two thousand line comparison of the psychological and philosophical states of men at war and women in love. Her first book, *Poems,* reveals an economical, almost stark style which some reviewers have compared favorably to the early Imagist works of H.D. and Pound. *Beat, Drum, Beat, Heart* (1946), while it is more subjective than the earlier efforts, nevertheless retains much of the objective vividness and taut rigor of *Poems.* Herbert Read celebrated this volume "as the most sustained meditation on war that has been written in our time."

A Cloud Across the Sun came out in 1949, followed by *A Kite's Dinner* in 1954 which was a Poetry Book Society Choice. In 1977, *Admissions* was released, and in 1978 a selection from all the poems, 1938 to 1976, appeared under the title *Her Storms.*

G. S. Fraser classifies Wingfield as an objectivist poet, pointing out her interest "in all the wonderful, sad, and glorious detail of the world around her."

She herself has insisted that "what is personally felt must be fused with what is being, and has been, felt by others. But always in terms of the factual. Nothing woolly or disembodied will do." While her poems do display a healthy respect for concrete nouns and a somewhat weaker resolve to avoid "amorphous description," few American readers would immediately comprehend the "objectivist" label Fraser assigns. Some poems do have a hard-eyed detachment and an almost brittle objectivity reminiscent of the early Ezra Pound or of H. D., particularly Wingfield's pre-1938 work. In the more ambitious pieces of some of her later work, Wingfield indulges in a romantic, highly generalized diction that does not so much bring feeling sharply into focus as it wraps it in gauze. Nevertheless, Wingfield's style never stagnates; and her thought, while always anchored to the simple things and events she knows best—country life, courage, pain, love, and even ecstasy—nearly always avoids the sentimental.

THOMAS F. MERRILL

WORKS: *Poems*. London: Cresset, [1938]; *Beat, Drum, Beat, Heart*. London: Cresset, 1946; *A Cloud Across the Sun*. London: Cresset, 1949; *Real People*. London: Cresset, 1952. (Autobiography); *A Kite's Dinner*. Poems 1938–1954. [London]: Cresset, 1954; *The Leaves Darken*. London: Weidenfeld & Nicolson, [1964]; *Sun Too Fast*. London: Bles, 1975. (Memoirs); *Admissions*. Dublin: Dolmen, 1977; *Her Storms*. Dublin: Dolmen, 1978; *Collected Poems: 1938–1983*. London: Enitharmon, 1983.

WINSTANLEY, JOHN (ca. 1677–1750), poet. Winstanley was born in Dublin, the son of a lawyer, and educated at Dr. Jones's school and at Trinity College, Dublin, which apparently he left without a degree. He lived for a time at Cabra and then at Glasnevin, where he died in 1750. In 1742, he issued *Poems Written Occasionally by John Winstanley . . . Interspers'd with Many Others by Several Ingenious Hands,* and in 1751 there appeared a second, posthumous volume. He is an uneven poet with occasional awkward lines, but "Epigram on the First of April" and "Miss Betty's Singing-Bird" are smoothly charming, and "A Familiar Letter from Town to a Collegian in the Country" rises more than once from doggerel to wit. Ignored until recently, he has lately been included by Lonsdale in *The New Oxford Book of Eighteenth Century Verse* (1984), by Fagan in *A Georgian Celebration* (1989), and by Coleborne in *The Field Day Anthology* (1991). Coleborne does attribute to him, however, a poem that Winstanley did not sign in his first collection, "An Inventory of the Furniture of a Collegian's Chamber"; and there seems more reason to assign this witty piece to Thomas Sheridan the elder.*

WORKS: *Poems Written Occasionally by John Winstanley . . . Interspers'd with Many Others by Several Ingenious Hands*. Dublin: Printed by S. Powell, for the Author, 1742; Vol. 2. Dublin: S. Powell, 1751. REFERENCE: Fagan, Patrick, *A Georgian Celebration*. Dublin: Branar, [1989], pp. 14–23.

WOLFE, CHARLES (1791–1823), poet. Wolfe was born in Dublin on December 14, 1791, a cousin of Wolfe Tone.* He was educated at Trinity College, Dublin. He took Holy Orders and died at Queenstown on February 21, 1823. Padraic Colum* calls him a "one-poem poet." That one good poem was "The

Burial of Sir John Moore,'' which Byron rather overrated as ''the most perfect ode in the language.''

WORKS: *The Burial of Sir John Moore.* London: T. Wilson, 1825; *The Burial of Sir John Moore and Other Poems,* with memoir by C. L. Falkiner. London: Sidgwick & Jackson, 1909.

WOLFHOUND PRESS (1974–   ), publishing house. Wolfhound was founded by Seamus Cashman, who had worked as researcher, editor, and managing editor at Irish University Press from 1968 to 1974. He had previously studied at Maynooth College and at University College, Cork, and taught at St. Colman's College in Fermoy and for two years in Southern Tanzania. For its first five years, the press operated from the Cashman home at Portmarnock, with the publisher's wife, Margaret, as the only permanent member of the staff. In 1979, the press moved to its present offices in Mountjoy Square, Dublin, and by 1987 it was well established and had published its 100th title.

Wolfhound publishes fiction, literary studies, history, art books, legal books, books of general Irish interest, and books for young readers. Since 1976, the press has reprinted Liam O'Flaherty's* most notable works of fiction as well as works by Benedict Kiely* and Mervyn Wall* and notable new novels by Niall Quinn,* Dorothy Nelson,* and Dolores Walshe.* Its important children's list includes the best-selling Tom McCaughren, as well as popular works by Michael Scott and Cormac MacRaois. The McCaughren wildlife series, beginning with *Run with the Wind,* won the Bisto Book of the Decade Award for the 1980s.

WOODS, MACDARA (1942–   ), poet. Woods was born on April 9, 1942, and raised in inner-city Dublin. His mother was a Gaelic teacher and a *sean nós,* an unaccompanied singer. In his youth, Woods spent time on his maternal grandfather's farm in County Meath, where, he says, ''imagination and geography met and became indistinguishable.'' ''My people, on both sides, were travellers, of one kind of another,'' Woods explains, ''and from the start I too have been travelling. Even when staying in one place.''

Educated at Gonzaga College and University College, Dublin, Woods published his first poems before he left university. In the 1960s, his travels took him from London to Marrakech, and his poem, ''Curriculum Vitae Coming up to Twenty-seven,'' tells the story of his life as poet, pipe fitter's mate, forester, postman, milkman, and gypsy. Returning to Ireland after six years in London, Woods devoted himself full-time to writing and by 1994 had published six books of poetry. A founding coeditor of the literary journal *Cyphers,* Woods settled in Dublin and married poet and *Cyphers* coeditor, Eileán Ní Chuilleanáin.* They have a son, Niall.

Woods' early work deals primarily with exile and alienation: *Decimal D. Sec. Drinks in a Bar in Marrakech* (1970) records his experiences in a foreign country in the late 1960s; *Early Morning Matins* (1973) expresses a feeling of dislocation, especially for an Irish person living in London.

Woods' later poetry also records his travels, alternating between scenes of

Dublin life and the observations of a man moving through foreign landscapes. These include poems about family life and relationships in Ireland and poems set in Italy, Russia, France, and the United States, reflecting what he calls "unmediated reporting." Many of these poems also focus on alienation, on how, even from those closest to us, we often feel isolated. The serious side of Woods' personae is often undercut by a wry sense of humor and a healthy respect for the foibles and bizarre quirks of human behavior.

Woods' is a very personal voice, and his poems are full of autobiographical allusions, what one poem describes as "stories that we carry with us." In *Stopping the Lights in Ranelagh* (1987), with many of the poems set in the area where he lives, Woods balances the memories of a difficult past with the solidity of his more settled life, what he calls "holding down the present." Images of fate and fortune, card playing, revenants, falling down stairs are offset by the anchoring images of home and local village, family, and neighbors.

Endurance and survival underpin the poems in *The Hanged Man Was Not Surrendering* (1990) and *Notes from the Countries of Blood-Red Flowers* (1994), where a potential fatalism lurks in the speaker's psyche. Introspective poems explore the metaphoric possibilities of travel as the poet-speaker moves through psychological landscapes, continually suggesting that there is nothing else to do but "travel on." A sequence, "Miz Moon," records a meditation on the only constant in the traveling man's life; he imagines the moon as lover/mother who knows everything about him.

Woods' most ambitious volume, *Notes from the Countries of Blood-Red Flowers,* also contains some of his most polished poems. Set in Ireland and Italy, where he was living for a year, these poems supplement his characteristic conversational tone and more open form with a lyric voice and some tightly crafted sonnets, tercets, and couplets. Poems like "Distances and Funeral: Meath December 1991" open his poetry to larger themes of family and race, to ancestors, ancient history, and emigration, to new definitions of "home." The final long poem, "Above Pesaro June 1993," treats not only unifying family mythologies but also the colonized Irish and colonizing English. Scenes from a family past alternate with expressions of regret over wasted years, frustrations over misdirected anger, questions about the poet's life. But as is typical of Woods's poetry, "transient" resolutions come when needed. "Above Pesaro" begins with the statement that moving on is the best thing for clearing the mind, and the volume ends with an affirmative image of a father, a son, and the ghost of a grandfather on a journey together.

Woods uses little punctuation except an occasional dash, and his style is distinguished by what Fred Johnston,* in an *Irish Times* review of *Notes from the Countries of Blood-Red Flowers,* calls "the sharp immediacy of the clipped, staccato lines." The tension between the conversational tone and the carefully crafted patterns of stanza, rhythm, and rhyme creates a musical poetry and what *Fortnight* has described as "one of the most individual voices in Irish poetry."

In addition to writing poetry, Woods works as a freelance journalist and critic.

He has been writer in residence in Kilkenny and has edited *The Kilkenny Anthology* (1991). His 1978 translation of Radwin Abushwesha's *The King of the Dead and Other Libyan Tales* initiated an interest in translation that has continued throughout his career. Acknowledged as a fine reader of his own poetry, Woods has given readings throughout Ireland, as well as in Europe and North America. In 1986, Woods was elected to Aosdána.*

PATRICIA BOYLE HABERSTROH

WORKS: *Decimal D. Sec. Drinks in a Bar in Marrakech.* Dublin: New Writers', 1970; *Early Morning Matins.* [Dublin]: Gallery, [1973]; tr., with Radwin Abushwesha. *The King of the Dead and Other Libyan Tales.* London: Brian & O'Keeffe, 1978; *Stopping the Lights in Ranelagh.* Dublin: Dedalus, 1987; *Miz Moon.* Dublin: Dedalus, 1988; *The Hanged Man Was Not Surrendering.* [Dublin]: Dedalus, [1990]; ed., *The Kilkenny Anthology.* Kilkenny: Kilkenny City Council, 1991; *Notes from the Countries of Blood-Red Flowers.* Dublin: Dedalus, 1994.

WOODS, UNA (ca. late 1940s–), novelist. Woods was born in Belfast and studied for a year at Queen's University in the late 1960s. At that time, she was also a traditional folksinger. After living in London and Dublin, she now resides in Belfast with her two children. Her *The Dark Hole Days* (1984) consists of a novella and four short stories about life in the north of Ireland. The long title piece is mainly made up of alternating diary entries of two nineteen-year-olds, Joe and Colette, in troubled Belfast. Then the author changes gears, perhaps less effectively, into straight narrative and concludes with Joe, hiding beneath the floorboards of his bedroom in fear of reprisal from the Irish Republican Army for running away from the murder of Colette's brother. As a dual portrait of two typical, well-meaning young people on the dole, both trying helplessly to escape from the grip of a society that holds no future for them, the novella makes its points with some poignance. With more development, it might have worked even better. Two of the stories, "Cora's Plight" and particularly "The Quibbler," are both well realized.

WORK: *The Dark Hole Days.* [Belfast]: Blackstaff, [1984].

WOODS, VINCENT (1960–), playwright and poet. Woods was born in County Leitrim. Before devoting himself to writing full-time, he worked as a journalist for RTÉ and served as a presenter for "Morning Ireland." He has won the P. J. O'Connor Award for radio drama for *The Leitrim Hotel,* and Galway's Druid Theatre* has produced his *Tom Hughdy* (1991), *Tom John* (1991), *At the Black Pig's Dyke* (1992), and *Song of the Yellow Bittern* (1994). His most impressive work is *At the Black Pig's Dyke,* winner of the Stewart Parker Memorial Award and the *Belfast Telegraph* EMA Award. The play has toured in Ireland, Northern Ireland, England, Scotland, and Canada. It is extraordinarily well written and incorporates music, dance, and episodes of intense drama. The plot centers around two generations of lovers and the violence and hatred that drive them apart. One partner is Catholic, and the other Protestant. The piece consciously echoes the Irish myth of the valley of the Black Pig and ancient Greek ritual. A choric allegory punctuates the play and makes an explicit connection between violence and these more ancient traditions.

Woods' only published work is a collection of poetry titled *The Colour of Language* (1994). The poems reveal images of the modern, ordinary world and of modern, ordinary actions that are also punctuated by myth, ritual, and a resonance of the past. Woods's imaginative geography varies from Ireland to Australia and is populated by the young and old, men and women. The narrator enters their worlds and relates, in the first person, their reactions to their lives and the surprising appearance of images from the collective conscious—images of horses in the Irish West, of hens and eggs, of the sea. In addition, there are memorial poems to artists like Primo Levi; Bruce Chatwin, the Australian writer; and Maeliosa Stafford, the director of several of Woods' plays for the Druid. The best of the poems is "Woman Washing Discovers Her Stigmata," which humorously details the manifestation of five wounds on an Irish housewife. People react to her with characteristic selfishness and humor. She passes out her cleaning gloves and her tights as relics and is assumed into heaven. Her husband reflects on his predicament of being left with three children and wonders why God would have "put notions" in his wife's head.

BERNARD McKENNA

WORK: *The Colour of Language.* Dublin: Dedalus, [1994].

WYKHAM, HELEN (ca. 1933–   ), novelist. Helen Wykham is the pseudonym of Pamela Evans. She was born in about 1933, grew up in the Irish countryside, and took a degree in archaeology from Newnham College, Cambridge. She is married, has three children, and lives in a remote spot in Wales.

Wykham's first novel, *Ribstone Pippins* (1974), though marred, shows quite remarkable talent, catching beautifully and comically the intensity and sexual confusion of adolescence. Lumpy, teenage "Helen Wykham," the narrator, goes shopping with her flighty mother and sister in Brown Thomas's to prepare for a house party at the San Fes'. Dominic San Fe, a debauched Heathcliff with a face "like an angel of Jaweh," seduces everyone in sight and is soon bedding Helen's attractive sister. Expeditions to the seaside, the pub, the theatre, even a picnic, are all spiced by his irrepressible appetites. Indeed, the convolutions are amazing, and so many undercurrents only distract the reader from Helen's more serious plight, the ambiguous nature of her sexuality. A teenager with less of a flair for the absurd might have been driven insane, but Helen emerges a confirmed lesbian. Another distraction in the work is that many of the characters are mere presences and cannot be visualized in flesh and blood. Helen, her sister, and her mother are well caught, and the funniest scenes in the book rotate round them, but many of the San Fe's jell together. The prose is often dazzling; descriptions of nature leave the reader with a sense of experiencing the place described. However, too many gems appear together; in a simpler, less poetic prose they would be noticed more.

Although *Ribstone Pippins* tends to pretentiousness, it is saved by Helen's comic vision. Not so *Cavan* (1977), Wykham's second novel. With no redeeming, believable character to filter the febrile sexuality, the novel is more than disappointing. Even the prose style seems arty and affected. Cavan, a sort of God-dolly who cannot be looked upon with the naked eye, is introduced, along with a cripple and his child, to the communal home of three sisters. He soon starts a sexual relationship with the youngest and prettiest. When her boyfriend objects, he is raped by Cavan. Far from disliking the experience, the boy is so transported that he falls at Cavan's feet. The cripple who witnessed it all is far from amused, but when he preaches hellfire, Cavan heats up the poker and pierces the cripple's plastic stomach. These are only samples of the novel's tastelessness and waste of a very considerable talent.

Her third novel, *Ottoline Atlantica* (1980), is set in a remote, rat-infested abbey on an imaginary island at the "edge of the vast Atlantic." Here an old woman, Ottoline, lives in vast eccentricity with her scholarly son, Sigerson, and her black servant, Aelebel. They all hate each other. There are many shouting scenes between the two old women, while Sigerson is obsessed with the abbey's founder, a medieval monk called Mihilanus. The plot, as much as there is any, focuses on a visit by a Cambridge anthropologist interested in the abbey's past, whom Sigerson attempts to bed and thus escape his mother's domination. Meanwhile, Ottoline tries to breed prehistoric cattle, with which she seems to have an underlying sadomasochistic relationship: "I'll tease them. I'll taunt them and seduce them and watch them charge!" Open the novel anywhere, and you will find equally incomprehensible silliness. Eccentricity is fine, but there has to be some "normal" character for the reader to relate to. The visiting scholar could have been a ballast, but she is also bats. There is no light in this miasma. It is baffling that the same writer could have produced *Ribstone Pippins.*

MARY ROSE CALLAGHAN

WORKS: *Ribstone Pippins.* Dublin: Allen Figgis/London: Calder & Boyars, 1974; *Cavan.* London: Marion Boyars, 1977; *Ottoline Atlantica.* London & Boston: Marion Boyars, [1980].

WYNNE, FRANCES (1866–1893), poet.

WORK: *Whisper and Other Poems.* London: Elkin Matthews, 1908.

YEATS, JACK B[UTLER] (1871–1957), painter, playwright, and novelist. Yeats, who is probably Ireland's foremost modern painter, was born in London on August 29, 1871, and died in Dublin on March 28, 1957. Like his older brother, W. B. Yeats,* he wrote his own epitaph, and it is quoted by Terence de Vere White* in *A Fretful Midge:*

> I have travelled all my life without a ticket. . . .
> When we are asked about it all in the end,
> we who travel without tickets, we can say
> with that vanity which takes the place of
> self-confidence: even though we went without
> tickets we never were commuters.

His life and work matched his epitaph for quiet and unassertive individuality and unconventionality. Neither he nor his wife Mary Cottenham White, a fellow art student whom he married in 1894, wished to be commuters or seemed to doubt that art was Jack Yeats' proper profession. He never seemed to need to adopt a flamboyant pose to convince himself that he was truly an artist. Nor did he pretend an artistic scorn for business acumen. Synge* noted in a letter to a friend that after their joint tour of the Congested Districts for the *Manchester Guardian,* "Jack Yeats, being a wiser man than I, made a better bargain." He conducted himself as a working professional, starting out as a black and white illustrator, for fifty years without spectacular success, enjoying great recognition only for the last decade and a half of his long life. His biographer, Hilary Pyle, lists sixty-two individual exhibitions of his work from 1897 to his death in 1957, and he contributed to 160 group exhibitions, during the same period. She also notes that he regularly contributed drawings to *Punch* for more than thirty years, under a pseudonym, and edited the monthly *Broadside* for more than seven years, "gathering materials and colouring his illustrations singlehanded." Pyle cites thirty books and gives the titles of more than forty "magazine articles and stories" he is known to have illustrated. Apparently, he had the work habits of a commuter.

Yeats' professed motive for becoming a painter seems to mark him as a traditionalist. Several times in his life he said that he became a painter because he was "the son of a painter." Yet he was the third, not the first, son—William Butler, Susan Mary, Elizabeth Corbett, and Robert Yeats being the elder children of the portrait painter John Butler Yeats* and Susan Pollexfen Yeats. Moreover, he spent very little of his early life with his father, being raised in Sligo by his maternal grandparents. His father deprecates his own possible influence by say- ing of Jack's upbringing: "I think he has received the education of a man of genius. His personality was given its full chance. It has at once the sense of expansion and the instinct for self-control. He has the habits of a man who knows his own mind" (*Christian Science Monitor,* November 20, 1920). Hilary Pyle corroborates his independence: "He worked alone," and "He continued to deny the company of other painters, living or dead . . . until the end of his life." Jack Yeats said of himself, in * letter to his brother W. B., in 1925, "You say my painting is now 'great'. Great is a word that may mean so many different things. But I know I am the first living painter in the world. And the second is so far away that I am only able to make him out faintly. I have no modesty. I have the immodesty of the spearhead." He appears to have written with the same "immodesty," for both his plays and his nondramatic prose are expres- sionistic and as self-confident in their formlessness as only a man convinced of the truth and worth of his personal vision could have written.

Yeats spoke very little of aesthetic theory, convinced that too much fuss was made about it. Perhaps he formed this opinion listening to the prolonged dis- cussions in the Bedford Park home of his youth. In a letter to Joseph Hone (March 7, 1922), he is quoted as saying "No one creates . . . the artist assembles memories." This certainly appears to be what he was doing in his own fiction of the 1930s. *Sligo; Sailing, Sailing Swiftly; The Amaranthers;* and *The Charmed Life* assemble and reassemble memories. At this time he was doing little painting, much public speaking, and some experimentation with what was for him always a mode of communication less direct, and therefore less valuable, than the visual image—the word. Now in his sixties he claimed that he wrote "to jettison some memories."

Ah, Well; And to You Also; and *The Careless Flower,* published in the 1940s, continue the reminiscence. His biographer speaks of Jack Yeats' conversation in this period as varying "between the charming, realistic, down-to-earth and a muddled monotone slipping from subject to subject and even with the greatest concentration from his listeners very difficult to follow. He seemed to be com- pletely self-contained and he did not mind whether he was comprehensible or not" (p. 149). The same could be said of much of his prose. The reminiscences are stream-of-consciousness pieces, full of short tales, with very little plot or character development. There are affinities to the writing of some of his contemporaries, e.g., to Flann O'Brien's (Brian O'Nolan's*) *The Third Policeman* and to characters of Beckett* (Bowsie and Mr. No Matter resemble Vladimir and Estragon of *Waiting for Godot*). The more interesting connections, however, are to Yeats' own great paintings of this period. They are more fruitfully read as aspects of the personal vision of a powerfully original mind. While not as consciously mystical as his brother's vision and not as concerned with a formally symbolic system (although they shared some symbols like the rose, which is important in both of their works), Jack Yeats' vision was metaphysical. His work is concerned with life as flux, with randomness, and with ontological questions. The same Bowsie and Mr. No Matter of the fiction appear and reappear in the paintings and assume roles, under different names, in the plays. They seem, possibly not unlike Vladimir and Estragon, to represent Jack Yeats' own continuing explorations of the halves of the personality which so interested W.B.

The plays, collected by Robin Skelton and published in 1971, show a stronger sense of controlling form than the nondramatic pieces, while retaining their spontaneity, love of words for their own sounds, freshness of vision, and irony. Of the nine "Plays for the Larger Theatre," three (*Harlequin's Positions, La La Noo,* and *In Sand*) were produced by the Abbey Theatre* or Abbey experimental theatres. Jack Yeats himself produced the "Plays for the Miniature Theatre" for the children of his neighborhood in Devon as holiday entertainments; like the later plays, they reflect his love of melodrama, pantomime, circuses, and pirate themes. This material appears in the early illustrations, such as those for the *Broadsides,* and the later paintings. There is an analogy between the early and late use of materials in his plays to their use in painting—straightforward in the early styles and transformed by his powerfully symbolic vision in the late styles. This use of material conforms to his statement of aesthetic theory, "the artist assembles memories."

Viewed as Robin Skelton views them, as anarchic drama, the later plays cast light on the intentions of the fiction, which they embody more aptly, and are clearly related both to his life and to the vision revealed in the paintings:

Jack Yeats' drama is, one might suggest, anarchic in the proper sense. It mocks and teases notions of government and politics. It opposes materialist values. After its beginnings, it frees itself from the conventions of the drama of its time, breaks the laws of unity, and challenges all contemporary preconceptions of what is dramatic. It utilizes inconsequence and chance. . . . Belonging to no school, not even being easily allied to the Irish writers' drama of its day . . . the drama of Jack B. Yeats, especially in his major plays, *The Silencer, La La Noo,* and *In Sand,* is both inimitable and . . . seminal. It challenges orthodoxies and promotes questions, but does so with an affectionate humor and a dazzle of wit that few playwrights have equalled in our time, and to the question "What does it mean?" it gives the calm answer [taken from the prologue to *In Sand, The Green Wave*], "I think it means just to be."

So intensely individual is Yeats' vision, as it is reflected in both his painting and his writing, so profound and yet gentle are his irony and his "anarchy," that his own description of one of the characters in an early, unpublished play, *The Deathly Terrace,* might well fit him: "an Egotist steeped in generosity and seethed in affection."

NORA McGUINNESS

WORKS: *A Broadside.* Dublin: Dun Emer & Cuala, 1908–1915; *Modern Aspects of Irish Art.* Dublin: Cumann Leigheacht & Phobail, 1922; *Sligo.* London: Wishart, 1930; *Sailing, Sailing Swiftly.* London: Putnam, 1933; *The Amaranthers.* London: Heinemann, 1936; *The Charmed Life.* London: Routledge, 1938/reissued in paperback, Routledge & Kegan Paul, 1974; *Ah, Well.* London: Routledge, 1942/reissued in paperback with *And to You Also,* London: Routledge & Kegan Paul, 1974; *And to You Also.* London: Routledge, 1944; *The Careless Flower.* London: Pilot, 1947; *The Collected Plays of Jack B. Yeats.* Robin Skelton, ed. London: Secker & Warburg, 1971; *The Selected Writings of Jack B. Yeats.* Robin Skelton, ed. [London]: André Deutsch, [1991].   REFERENCES: Booth, John. *A Vision of Ireland: Jack B. Yeats.* Nairn, Scotland: Thomas & Lochar, 1995; MacGowran, Jack. "Preface." *In Sand.* Dublin: Dolmen, 1964; MacGreevy, Thomas. *Jack B. Yeats: An Appreciation and Interpretation.* Dublin: Waddington, 1945; McGuinness, Nora A. *The Literary Universe of Jack B. Yeats.* Washington, D.C.: Catholic University of America Press, 1992; McHugh, Roger, ed. *Jack B. Yeats: A Centenary Gathering.* Dublin: Dolmen, 1971; Marriott, E. *Jack B. Yeats: Being a True and Impartial View of His Pictorial and Dramatic Art.* London: Elkin Mathews, 1911; O'Doherty, Brian. "Humanism in Art: A Study of Jack B. Yeats." *University Review* (Summer 1955); O'Driscoll, Robert & Reynolds, Lorna, eds. *Theatre and the Visual Arts: A Centenary Celebration of Jack Yeats and John Synge.* Shannon: Irish University Press, 1972; Pyle, Hilary. *Jack B. Yeats: A Biography.* London: Routledge & Kegan Paul, 1970; Pyle, Hilary. *Jack B. Yeats: His Watercolours, Drawings and Pastels.* Blackrock, Co. Dublin: Irish Academic, 1993; Pyle, Hilary. *The Different Worlds of Jack B. Yeats: His Cartoons and Illustrations.* Blackrock, Co. Dublin: Irish Academic, 1994; Rosenthal, T. J. *Jack Yeats 1871–1957.* London: Knowledge, 1966; Rosenthal, T. J. *The Art of Jack B. Yeats.* London: Andre Deutsch, 1993; J. Rothenstein. "Visits to Jack Yeats." *New English Review* 13, (July 1946): 42–44; White, James, ed. *Drawings and Paintings of Jack B. Yeats.* London: Secker & Warburg, 1971; White, James. "Jack B. Yeats." *New Knowledge* 6, (April 24, 1966): 966–971.

YEATS, JOHN BUTLER (1839–1922), painter, conversationalist, and letter writer. Yeats, who was born in the Rectory of Tullylish, County Down, on March 16, 1839, was the eldest son of the Reverend William Butler Yeats and a grandson of a rector of Drumcliffe, County Sligo. A further link with Sligo was forged by his marriage to his school friend George Pollexfen's sister, Susan, in 1863. He was then a man of property, having inherited a small estate in County Kildare which brought him a modest income, as well as being an arts graduate of Trinity College, Dublin, and a law student at the King's Inns. His father-in-law, joint owner of a small shipping line and flour mill, saw him as a worthy addition to the family; however, though called to the bar in 1866 John Butler Yeats never practiced, and indecisiveness and procrastination played havoc with his career as an artist.

He claimed that through marriage with a Pollexfen he had given a voice to the sea cliffs, but he was far more than a mere transmitter of the genes of genius; a gifted portrait painter, a critic of merit, capable of highly original observations expressed epigramatically in his speech and letters, he neglected the conventional emblems of success in the pursuit of an illusory perfection. Material needs became a secondary consideration. Financial crises were circumvented with the grudging assistance of his father-in-law and by mortgaging his estate.

John and Susan Yeats had five children, one of whom died in childhood of croup. Their sons, William Butler Yeats* and Jack B. Yeats,* achieved early and increasing success as a poet and painter respectively; their daughters, Lily and Lolly, achieved eventual fulfillment in the Dun Emer Press and its successor the Cuala Press.* The family's unsettled years, with a series of homes in Dublin, Sligo, and London, doubtless had creative advantages, but Mrs. Yeats was temperamentally unsuited to an artistic milieu. While still a young woman, she had a stroke and remained in indifferent health until her death in 1900.

Writing to Sarah Purser in 1891, John Butler Yeats said that a sixteen-year-old model told him that someday he might commit suicide. "When she saw me change my mind so often and begin the picture so often and scratch out so constantly, of course she had my measure and thought me mad and on the way to disaster." He never freed himself of this obsessionalism, but had no intention of quitting a life which he continued to hope would surely someday bring recognition, however slow in coming. In 1902 he returned to Dublin where, notwithstanding his indigence, "old Mr. Yeats" commanded widespread respect and affection.

Hugh Lane and some other friends, knowing that he had never been to Italy, raised a fund to send him there, but to their surprise he elected to use the money to accompany Lily to New York, where his many acquaintances included John Quinn, a wealthy lawyer and collector. Manhattan delighted him, and he established himself there in the role of sage, growing old cheerfully and gracefully. "Young people are sad," he wrote to his daughter, "and sometimes commit suicide, but old men are naturally cheerful. Why? Because the first are oppressed by the menace of life, and of the long road before them. We are delivered from that terror." He died from heart failure on February 3, 1922.

His publications include reviews, essays, and collections of letters to family and friends, but it may be fairly said that his books are a credit to the organization of others rather than to his own unsustained ambition.

J. B. LYONS

WORKS: *Passages from the Letters of John Butler Yeats.* Ezra Pound, ed. Churchtown, Dundrum: Cuala, 1917; *Essays Irish and American,* with an Appreciation by AE. Dublin: Talbot/London: T. Fisher Unwin, 1918/reprint, Freeport, N.Y.: Books for Libraries, 1969; *Further Letters.* Lennox Robinson, ed. Dundrum: Cuala, 1920; *Early Memories: Some Chapters of Autobiography.* Dundrum: Cuala, 1923; *J. B. Yeats, Letters to his Son W. B. Yeats and Others,* ed., with a Memoir by Joseph Hone. London: Faber, 1944/New York: E. P. Dutton, 1946; *Letters from Bedford Park: A Selection from the Correspondence (1890–1901) of John Butler Yeats.* William M. Murphy, ed. Dublin: Cuala, 1972. REFERENCES: Archibald, Douglas N. *John Butler Yeats.* Lewisburg, Pa.: Bucknell University Press, 1974; Gordon, Robert. *John Butler Yeats and John Sloan—the Records of a Friendship.* Dublin: Dolmen, 1978; Murphy, William M. *Prodigal Father, The Life of John Butler Yeats (1839–1922).* Ithaca, N.Y. & London: Cornell University Press, [1978]; White, James. *John Butler Yeats and the Irish Tradition.* Dublin: Dolmen, 1972.

YEATS, WILLIAM BUTLER (1865–1939), a foremost poet of the English-speaking world, founder of the Abbey Theatre,* dramatist, spokesman for the Irish Literary Revival, essayist, autobiographer, occultist, member of the Irish Free State Senate, and winner of the 1923 Nobel Prize for literature.

Louis MacNeice,* himself a fine poet, wrote in 1941 that if he were editing an anthology he would include sixty poems by Yeats: "There is no other poet in the language from whom I should choose so many." Throughout a long career Yeats maintained an extraordinary level of excellence, gaining in power and perception to the end. One of his many fine late poems, "The Municipal Gallery Revisited," a valedictory on his life, his friends, and the Ireland he knew, was written after the age of seventy.

A commanding feature of Yeats' poetry is its confessional nature. The poems move from personal experience to public pronouncements or philosophic meditations. Even when based on his esoteric thought they speak to the human condition, as in the oracular "The Second Coming." Opening with a striking figure of the falcon, it reaches the dictum, so often quoted, "Things fall apart; the centre cannot hold." The imminence of the strange desert beast arouses awe and fear. We have all felt that fear; we need not know that the poem is based on a cyclical theory of history.

Yeats displays astonishing metrical skill and creates an almost magical effect through traditional symbols such as swan or unicorn, horseman or dancer. Thus, unity of being is dramatized in the conclusion of "Among School Children":

> O chestnut tree, great-rooted blossomer,
> Are you the leaf, the blossom or the bole?
> O body swayed to music, O brightening glance,
> How can we know the dancer from the dance?

Titles in *The Collected Poems* show Yeats' sense of stages in his career, but they can be misleading. "Crossways" (1889) and "The Rose" (1893) are not book titles, but were used in the 1895 *Poems,* the first to signify the many paths he had tried, and the second as "the only pathway whereon he can hope to see with his own eyes the Eternal Rose of Beauty and of Peace." Other inaccuracies will be noted later.

Despite the poet's misgivings, his early work retains considerable interest. "The Lake Isle of Innisfree" (1890) was popular from the beginning and was anthologized four years later by W. J. Paul in *Modern Irish Poets.* The rose poems and "The White Birds" rise above romantic cliché; there are also fine adaptations of the Irish song "Down by the Salley Gardens" and of Rimbaud's "When You Are Old," as well as vigorous ballads and the patriotic challenge, "To Ireland in the Coming Times."

In the beginning of this century, Yeats found that "All things can tempt me from this craft of verse"—disappointment in love, political and literary controversy. His subjects became more topical, his style more lean: "Now I may wither into the truth'' (''The Coming of Wisdom with Time''). Classical terseness is found in ''A Woman Homer Sung'' or in the ringing conclusion of ''No Second Troy'': ''Was there another Troy for her to burn?'' Confining romantic dreams to his plays, he writes visionary poems like ''The Cold Heaven'' and ''The Magi,'' and praises aristocratic virtues in ''Fallen Majesty'' and ''That the Night Come.''

The great years of 1918 to 1928 include philosophical poems, epigrams, songs, and satires. ''The Wild Swan at Coole'' reflects on life's transitory nature. The eulogy of Major Robert Gregory, the aviator shot down in 1918, hails him as an exemplar of Unity of Being. An expression of his ideals for womanhood is ''A Prayer for My Daughter.'' Now truly a public man, he commemorates the victims of the Rising in ''Easter 1916'' and responds to the terror of war: ''Now days are dragon-ridden, the nightmare / Rides upon sleep'' (''Nineteen Hundred and Nineteen''), ''Death'' celebrates his friend Kevin O'Higgins, vice-president and minister of justice, as ''A great man in his pride / Confronting murderous men'' at his assassination. He contemplates legend and history in ''The Tower,'' and in ''Among School Children'' he speculates on youth and age, symbol and reality. The cycles of history are evoked in ''Leda and the Swan,'' ''The Second Coming,'' and the ominous ''Two Songs from a Play.'' ''Sailing to Byzantium'' itself is one of the ''Monuments of unageing intellect'' it describes. The Crazy Jane poems express desire and defiance. ''The Double Vision of Michael Robartes'' presents hallucinations of a Sphinx, a Buddha, and a ghostly dancer. Yeats undercuts his explanation of ''The Phases of the Moon'' with ironic humor when the character Aherne walks away from the tower where Yeats is studying and remarks ''He'd crack his wits / Day after day, yet never find the meaning.''

These are but a few of the fine poems in *The Wild Swans at Coole* (1917), *Michael Robartes and the Dancer* (1920), *The Tower* (1928), and *The Winding Stair and Other Poems* (1933).

One might expect that Yeats, after he passed sixty, would have experienced a decline in inspiration; yet during this period he explored new themes and wrote some of his finest work. There were more ballads, satires, and songs; and there emerged both a violent sexuality and a rage against infirmity and death. He celebrated the Gore-Booth sisters of County Sligo, the poet Eva and the artist-patriot Constance Markiewicz, as well as Parnell and Casement, and memorialized Lady Gregory's* estate in ''Coole Park, 1929'' (''They came like swallows and like swallows went'') and in ''Coole Park and Ballylee, 1931'' (''We were the last romantics—chose for theme / Traditional sanctity and loveliness''). He glorified the Georgian Ireland of Swift* and Burke* in ''Blood and the Moon'' and ''The Seven Sages.'' He pondered his own career (''Are You Content?,'' ''What Then?,'' and ''The Circus Animals' Desertion'') and asked ''Why Should Not Old Men Be Mad?'' He pleaded for ''An old man's eagle mind'' (''An Acre of Grass''). He reached profound depths in the visionary ''Byzantium'' and in esoteric poems (''A Dialogue of Self and Soul,'' ''Vacillation,''

"The Delphic Oracle Upon Plotinus," "The Gyres," "Meru," "Lapis Lazuli," "The Statues," "News for the Delphic Oracle"). Irish legend returned with poems on Cuchulain and "The Black Tower," his last work, one week before his death. "Under Ben Bulben," a few months earlier, epitomizes his career and much of his thought.

As a meticulous craftsman, Yeats rewrote, retitled, and rearranged many poems after publication. He defended this practice in 1908 in a quatrain he never republished. "It is myself that I remake," he asserted. We can see the poet at work in the many rough drafts he saved; an extreme example is the play *The Player Queen,* written and revised over a twenty-seven year period.

The plays, more than thirty in all, were of great importance to Yeats as experiments in theatre art and as vehicles for his thought, but they enjoyed only limited success on the stage and are now fairly seldom performed. In reaction against the realistic comedy and social drama of his time, Yeats developed a ritualistic form, later to be influenced by the Japanese Noh tradition, where masked actors, formal gestures, and choreographed actions are rendered in a style of incantation, accompanied by music and interpreted by dance. The subjects are from Irish folklore and legend, or from parable and fantasy, and the plays have close affinities to dance drama. Full appreciation depends on highly trained actors and well-schooled listeners or readers.

Though none of Yeats' prose can be neglected by the interested student, the most important works are *Autobiographies* and *A Vision.* The plural title of the autobiography is preferable, since it comprises six volumes, in different styles and with varied emphases. It is also intermittent, the periods covered being the years from childhood to 1902, then 1909, the year of Synge's* death, and, finally, an account of the Nobel Prize award. More personal testament than autobiography, it shows Yeats creating a personality and creating a philosophy, trying out theories of character and of history, preoccupations to be rendered in more schematic form in *A Vision.* His extensive miscellaneous prose reflects the same concerns, making of Yeats an eminent man of letters.

Yeats was born on June 13, 1865, at Sandymount, County Dublin, the eldest child of John Butler Yeats* and Susan Pollexfen Yeats. In the words of Sir William Wilde,* father of Oscar,* the Yeatses were "the cleverest and most spirited people I ever met." On both sides of the family there were strong personalities, and Yeats celebrated them in poems and in his autobiography, building from them a personal mythology and forming an ideal of Anglo-Irish character. In the untitled verses *"Pardon, old fathers,"* he invokes an *"Old Dublin merchant"* and an *"Old country scholar."* These were Jervis Yeats (d. 1712), first of his family in Ireland, and John Yeats (1774–1846), who had come to County Sligo as a most unconventional rector, a lover of wine and racehorses, and a friend of the patriot Robert Emmet.* With the *"Old merchant skipper"* Yeats moves to his mother's family, of which he was equally proud, the skipper being William Middleton (1770–1832) and the *"silent and fierce old man,"* Middleton's son-in-law William Pollexfen (1811–1892), the poet's grandfather, of whom Yeats wrote in his autobiography: "Even to-day when I read *King Lear* his image is always before me and I often wonder if the delight in passionate men in my plays and in my poetry is more than his memory."

To Yeats these were indeed "Half legendary men," as he wrote in another family poem, "Are You Content?" His father, a bit jealous and disdainful of the commercial bent of the Pollexfens, wrote that "In Willie's eyes they appear something grand like the figures at Stonehenge seen by moon-light." With the instinct of a poet, Yeats cherished family traditions, which included associations with Goldsmith* and Swift. In Sligo, there were many old relatives: three grandparents, a great-uncle, and a great-aunt Micky, "full of family history."

John Butler Yeats was a talented painter, known for his portraits of Synge, AE,* Lady Gregory,* and others in the Irish Revival. Of his lively personality and flair for unconventional ideas, we have some record through his letters and a brief memoir. Little is known of Yeats' mother, a quiet, sensitive woman, in later years an invalid. Her worry over her husband's impracticality and her love of Sligo led to prolonged stays in that beautiful area.

Yeats' two sisters, "Lily" (Susan Mary, 1866–1949) and "Lollie" (Elizabeth Corbet, 1868–1940), were artists. Lollie played a role in her brother's career by publishing in the Dun Emer, later Cuala Press,* about sixty titles, half by Yeats, the rest by Lady Gregory, Synge, AE, Dunsany,* Gogarty,* and others. The fourth and youngest child was "Jack"* (John Butler, 1871–1957), who made a reputation as illustrator of peasant scenes, writer of stories and plays, and painter.

The poet's early years were spent in London, except for delightful vacation visits to relatives in Sligo. Sligo is beautifully situated in a river valley, with a harbor on an inlet of the Atlantic Ocean. The steep cliff of Ben Bulben lies to the north, and on the south the hill of Knocknarea is topped by Maeve's Cairn, a huge mound of stones visible for miles, said to commemorate the Irish queen of the first century. Beneath Ben Bulben is Drumcliff, with a fine stone cross and the ruin of a round tower. Inland are the lakes and waterfalls of Yeats' poetry.

"I remember little of childhood but its pain," Yeats recalled in his autobiography, but this view should be modified by the prominence of Sligo landscape and legend in his work, as well as his memories of relatives. Fear of elders was mixed with admiration; his father could be dogmatic and domineering, but his unconventional views were stimulating. No doubt that Yeats was a shy and sensitive schoolboy in London, but the Sligo countryside had the stuff of romance—mountains and sea and the ever-changing sky, "The blue and the dim and the dark cloths / Of night and light and the half-light," as he described it in "He Wishes for the Cloths of Heaven." There were legends of chieftains, stories of seamen, superstitions, and folktales.

After the family's return to Dublin, Yeats entered the Metropolitan School of Art. Here he met the mystic poet George Russell, who took the pen name AE, and encouraged his interest in the occult. His father brought him to the Contemporary Club; members included the Gaelic scholar Douglas Hyde* and the author Stephen Gwynn* who reported that "every one of us was convinced that Yeats was going to be a better poet than we had yet seen in Ireland."

He branched in several directions—"in a form of literature, in a form of philosophy, and a belief in nationality" ("If I were Four-and-Twenty," in *Explorations,* 1962). In literature, his earliest published verse was "Song of the Faeries" (*The Dublin University Review,* March 1885). A rarity is the pamphlet entitled *Mosada: A Dramatic Poem* (1886). In philosophy, he chaired the first meeting of the Hermetic Society on June 16, 1885; his occult studies were to continue throughout his life. In nationalism, his first essay, "The Poetry of Sir Samuel Ferguson" (*Irish Fireside,* October 9, 1886), praised the poet for recovering neglected riches of Irish lore. A month later, he had the effrontery to attack his father's friend Edward Dowden for neglecting "the interests of his own country, but more also . . . his own dignity and reputation" by ignoring Ferguson* (*The Dublin University Review,* November 1886).

Yeats had urged himself to "Hammer your thoughts into unity," seemingly impossible at the time, but by 1919 he felt that literature, philosophy, and patriotism expressed "a single conviction" which "has behind it my whole character." However, he was divided by his Anglo-Irish descent—too English for the Irish, too Irish for the English. His temperamental mixture of caution and defiance undoubtedly alienated friends, especially AE, as well as political and literary associates.

This diversity of interest is apparent in his Dublin friends at the time: the mystic AE; the romantic poet Katharine Tynan;* and the patriot John O'Leary,* a man of noble character with good literary taste. "We protest against the right of patriots to perpetrate bad verses," Yeats announced, an issue which aroused constant quarrels with patriots whose enthusiasm outran their taste.

O'Leary and Yeats, together with Douglas Hyde and Katharine Tynan, were responsible for the *Poems and Ballads of Young Ireland* (1888), of which Ernest Boyd wrote, "This slim little volume, in white buckram covers, will always be regarded with special affection by lovers of Irish literature, for it was the first offering of the Literary Revival."

With the family's removal to London began the "Four Years: 1887–1891" of *The Trembling of the Veil* (1922), a section of the autobiography filled with portraits and subtle analyses of character. Here Yeats is a master of the epigram: "the dinner table was Wilde's event," or, of Madame Blavatsky, "A great passionate nature, a sort of female Dr. Johnson." There were those psychological opposites, the strenuous William Henley and the aesthete-socialist William Morris, and, above all, the beautiful patriot Maud Gonne, whom Yeats met in 1889, wooed for years, and never forgot. "On meeting her," he wrote, "she seemed a classical impersonation of the Spring."

He continued his interest in the occult, wrote numerous book reviews, and began his study of William Blake. His first collection of verse, *The Wanderings of Oisin and Other Poems* (1889), appeared in an edition of five hundred copies and met with favorable response.

Though gradually overcoming his lack of self-confidence, Yeats was tormented by unrequited love for Maud Gonne and was divided between the comforting mysteries of the occult and the attractions of political and literary organization. His activity during the 1890s was unremitting. An important book appeared almost every year: 1891—*John Sherman and Dhoya,* two stories which illustrate his leanings toward escape and rebellion; 1892—*The Countess Kathleen and Various Legends and Lyrics;* 1893—*The Celtic Twilight,* tales and sketches of Irish folklore, as well as the three-volume edition *The Works of William Blake,* done in collaboration with Edwin J. Ellis; 1894—*The Land of Heart's Desire,* a play of enchantment produced in London in the same year; 1895—the collected and revised *Poems* and *A Book of Irish Verse,* a critical selection with an introduction attacking sentimental patriots as well as unsympathetic Anglo-Irish intellectuals who ignored Irish culture; 1897—two books of symbolic and visionary tales, *The Secret Rose* and the privately printed volume *The Tables of the Law. The Adoration of the Magi;* 1899—a third major collection of verse, *The Wind Among the Reeds.* In addition, Yeats edited or contributed to other volumes and published well over a hundred essays, in which he reported current Irish literature for two American newspapers and for the *London Bookman.*

The Irish political scene had been torn by dissension at Parnell's fall, or betrayal as his supporters would have it, when the Irish party rejected his leadership in December 1889 as a result of his involvement with the married Katharine O'Shea. The conflict between political and moral values created the antagonism so vividly depicted in Joyce's* *A Portrait of the Artist as a Young Man.* By coincidence, Yeats met Maud Gonne at Kingstown as she arrived on the boat which was bringing Parnell's body to Dublin in October 1891. Yeats, always distrustful of politics, was later to compare nationalist opinion to "the fixed ideas of some hysterical woman, a part of the mind turned into stone." In the same passage of his autobiography, he recalled nothing but the bitterness of his political involvement.

Yeats had predicted "an intellectual movement at the first lull in politics." He forthwith helped found the Irish Literary Society in London and the National Literary Society in Dublin. Here too, however, he was thwarted, for a projected series of Irish books failed, largely as a result of the selection of inferior works, insisted upon by Sir Charles Gavan Duffy,* a seventy-five-year-old patriot.

In the London Rhymers' Club Yeats found support for his aestheticism, but in his autobiography he sought an explanation for the mental, moral, and physical breakdowns of "The Tragic Generation." One of these English Decadents was an important influence. Arthur Symons, versed in French poetry, introduced Yeats to Verlaine in Paris where Yeats first witnessed symbolic drama in a performance of *Axel's Castle.* Symons also brought Yeats in contact with George Moore* and Edward Martyn* and, through Martyn, with Lady Gregory. As if to complete the story of the beginnings of the Irish theatre, it was with Symons that Yeats visited the Aran Islands in 1896, which eventuated in enlisting Synge into the movement. Yeats tells the dramatic story of meeting Synge in Paris that December. Finding Synge to be a writer without a theme, Yeats advised him to go to the islands to "express a life that has never found expression," for "I had just come from Arran [sic] and my imagination was full of those gray islands, where men must reap with knives because of the stones" (Preface to Synge's *Well of the Saints,* 1905).

Another member of the Rhymers' Club, Lionel Johnson, had introduced Yeats to his cousin, Mrs. Olivia Shakespear, the "Diana Vernon" of the first draft autobiography, recently published as *Memoirs* (1972). Yeats recalled that "she was like the mild heroines of my plays," a sensitive woman trapped in a boring marriage. Still deeply in love with Maud Gonne, he confided in Mrs. Shakespear, wrote several poems to "His Beloved," and hesitantly became her lover. They remained friends up to her death in 1938.

Yeats' eagerness to combine poetry and patriotism motivated his activities in the Theosophical Society and later among the Hermetic Students of the Golden Dawn, then under the leadership of the eccentric MacGregor Mathers. The poet's experiments with visions, symbols, magic, and initiatory rites have embarrassed many admirers, but they were motivated by the desire to establish the primacy of the supernatural and the power of the poetic imagination.

When O'Leary questioned his occult interests, Yeats replied that "The mystical life is the centre of all that I do and all that I think and all that I write" (*Letters,* ed. Wade, p. 211). The Order of the Golden Dawn promoted spiritual regeneration and the perfection of society. In his study of Blake and the Rosicrucian literature, Yeats attempted to fuse esoteric doctrine with poetic symbolism. His aspirations are expressed in many essays, especially in "The Autumn of the Body" (1898); "We are, it may be, at a crowning crisis of the world, at the moment when man is about to ascend . . . the stairway he has been descending from the first days."

These ideals led to a projected "Castle of the Heroes" for adepts. Yeats also hoped to unite political factions in commemorating the centenary of the death of the patriot Wolfe Tone* in 1798. Ever alert for omens, he took as a portent his dream of a female archer shooting at a star. He felt that he had been directionless, or in the cabbalistic term of the autobiography, "Hodos Chameliontos," or "astray upon the Path of the Chamelion."

His meeting with Lady Gregory in 1896 seemed the fulfillment of some mysterious destiny. However we judge such speculations, no one can question the importance of Lady Gregory in his life. A talented woman and capable organizer, she encouraged Yeats in his hopes for an Irish theatre and came to represent the best in Anglo-Irish culture. Her modest home at Coole Park became a haven for creative spirits, serving as Yeats' own refuge for more than thirty years.

In an Irish drama that was both national and mystical, the tension between occultism and patriotism could perhaps be resolved. The theatre could become a sacred place; Yeats called some of his plays Mysteries or Moralities.

In 1894, his first stage venture brought Celtic lore to a London audience. *The Land of Heart's Desire* shared the program with an unsuccessful play by his father's friend John Todhunter* and later with Shaw's* *Arms and the Man*. With Todhunter's play withdrawn, the bill enjoyed a good run in spite of some amusement caused by Yeats' note that "the characters are supposed to speak in Gaelic." On his opening night, Shaw was booed by one person, but retorted that though he shared the opinion, "what can we do against a whole house," whereupon, as Yeats wrote in his autobiography, "Shaw became the most formidable man in modern letters." Nevertheless, Yeats was never very sympathetic to Shaw's work, and once dreamed of him as a smiling sewing-machine.

The production was managed by the actress Florence Farr, whose beauty and expressive voice entranced Yeats. She acted in his *The Countess Cathleen* in 1899, joined him in occultism, and recited his poems accompanied by a psaltery, in an attempt to revive the art of minstrelsy. She became one of Yeats' ideal characters, to be recollected after her death in the poem "All Souls' Night," along with his friends W. T. Horton and MacGregor Mathers who shared his interest in the occult.

The printed text of *The Land of Heart's Desire* (1894) is the earliest attractive Yeats first edition; the Aubrey Beardsley poster design fills the left-hand side of the cover. Beardsley, who created images of the decadent 1890s, died at the age of twenty-six in 1898; his sister Mabel is celebrated for the gallant humor with which she faced death in Yeats' "Upon a Dying Lady," published in 1917.

The idea of the Irish theatre was formulated during the first summer Yeats spent at Coole Park. (The history of the Irish theatre is well known, having been recounted with witty malice by George Moore in *Hail and Farewell* [1911–1914], by Lady Gregory in *Our Irish Theatre* [1913], and by others, notably Yeats in *Dramatis Personae* [1935], part of his autobiography.) George Moore and Edward Martyn, themselves friends and enemies ("bound one to the other by mutual contempt," Yeats wrote), joined Yeats as directors of the Irish Literary Theatre Society, projecting a series of Celtic plays each spring for three years. The first production was to be Yeats' *The Countess Cathleen* on May 8, 1899. From the start there were difficulties. Much of the financial support came from unionists, who opposed Home Rule, and Lady Gregory herself was suspected of unionist leanings. Tableaux from the play had been previewed at a seat of the enemy, the chief secretary's lodge, with Lady Fingall in the leading role. For the public performance, Moore insisted on engaging an English cast; this proved an unpopular move. There were quarrels at the London rehearsals. (Moore describes the tantrums of the leading ladies.) Before the play opened, it was attacked as unorthodox and insulting to the Irish people because of its Faustian theme. *Souls for Gold* was the title of an attack by a disaffected patriot, Frank Hugh O'Donnell, who was to follow in 1904 with a longer diatribe, *The Stage Irishman of the Pseudo-Celtic Revival*. A controversy ensued, interesting in its political and religious entanglements. Martyn threatened to withdraw support and submitted the text to a monk, who found it objectionable. The spectre of censorship infuriated Moore, but Yeats and Lady Gregory went about the task of getting two clerical votes for the play to counter the opposition. It was provisionally condemned by Cardinal Logue, who had not read it, whereupon Arthur Griffith* suggested bringing a claque to "applaud anything the Church did not like." University College students published a protest (Joyce did not sign). Yeats called the police, a tactless move, but the play went on with some hissing, "completely frustrated by enthusiastic applause which drowned their empty-headed dissension," according to Joseph Holloway,* whose diary is an almost day-by-day record of the Dublin theatre.

It was a typical Irish brouhaha, but only the first of many such conflicts, not only with the public, but also among writers, directors, and actors. Yeats, like Whistler, knew the art of making enemies.

Another absurdity was the collaboration of Yeats and Moore on the legendary *Diarmuid and Grania,* a process described by the authors of *W. B. Yeats and His World* (1971) as consisting of "stages of storm, stress, sulks and strained silences." Moore makes the unbelievable claim that Yeats and Lady Gregory proposed that Moore write the text in French, that it be translated into Irish, then retranslated by Lady Gregory into the rural dialect soon to be known as Kiltartan, and given final touches by Yeats. The celebrated actress Mrs. Patrick Campbell asked sensibly, "Oh, Mr. Yeats, why did you not do the whole play yourself?" Although it was performed with indifferent success on October 21, 1901, the text was not printed until 1951.

One moment of triumph occurred when Maud Gonne played the title role in *Cathleen Ni Houlihan* on April 2, 1902. Cathleen, the legendary figure of Ireland as the "Shan Van Vocht," or Poor Old Woman, is described in the last line of the play as "a young girl" with "the walk of a queen." A member of that audience recalled how "the tall figure straightened itself and took on beauty," and saw in that dramatic moment an augury of war (Stephen Gwynn, *Experiences of a Literary Man*).

Despite accusations of scandal and suspicions of her insincerity from O'Leary and others, Yeats had pleaded with Maud Gonne to marry him. He hoped that she would become "the fiery hand of the intellectual movement," as she did on this one evening. Harmony between such strong and divergent personalities was impossible, and Yeats sometimes realized this fact. His confessions of this hopeless love are found in the recently published *Memoirs;* such material was drastically suppressed in the autobiography.

In February 1903, Yeats was shocked to learn of Maud Gonne's marriage to John MacBride, who had led an Irish brigade against the English in the Boer War. The Boer War was England's Vietnam, in that it aroused strong opposition in England itself, both over its purpose and the way it was conducted. Though MacBride's marriage ended in separation two years later, Yeats' bitterness lasted, expressed in unpublished verses of 1909, now included in *Memoirs.* He accused her of having "taught me hate / By kisses to a clown." In "Easter 1916," he made amends to the executed patriot who "had done most bitter wrong / To some who are near my heart, / Yet I number him in my song." Unforgettable is the refrain: "A terrible beauty is born."

In the early part of the century, Yeats encountered the young James Joyce. At the age of nineteen, the arrogant Joyce accused Yeats of bringing about "The Day of the Rabblement" (1901) by catering to popular taste in the theatre, the very thing Yeats hated. A year later Joyce told Yeats, "I have met you too late," that is, too late for Yeats to be influenced by the twenty-year-old. Yet, in *Stephen Hero* Joyce's autobiographical counterpart intones phrases from *The Tables of the Law and The Adoration of the Magi,* phrases "heavy with incense and omens and the figures of the monk-errants." Yeats wrote that he would not have reissued them in 1904 had he not met one "who liked them very much and nothing else that I have written."

Maud Gonne's marriage shook Yeats' spirit and precipitated a crisis in his efforts to reconcile imagination and action. Though an uneasy admirer of an active life he could not espouse, he could make poetry a weapon against the world instead of an escape from the world. This attitude was reinforced by his reading of Nietzsche, his contact with the ideas of Castiglione, the success of his American lecture tour, and the necessity of fighting opponents of the theatre.

Nietzsche was to him "that strong enchanter" who "completes Blake" (*Letters,* p. 379), perhaps because he broadens Blake's satiric aphorisms into a world view. Blake and Shelley had absorbed Yeats during his early studies of poetry, but when these studies were collected in 1903 as *Ideas of Good and Evil,* he already felt Blake and Shelley to be "too lyrical, too full of aspirations after remote things." He now hoped to express himself "by that sort of thought that leads straight to action" (*Letters,* p. 379). As he wrote to AE in 1904, "Let us have no emotions, however abstract, in which there is not an athletic joy." To use the words of Denis Donoghue,* in his short study of Yeats (1971), the poet's "sense of life as action and gesture" indicates his kinship with Nietzsche, "a more telling relation than that between Yeats and Plato, Plotinus, or Blake." Yeats' father warned him: "You would be a *philosophe* and you are really a poet" (Hone, *Life,* p. 221). In writing, however, he cultivated direct utterance, abandoning the hesitation with which he had couched his earlier prose statements and turning away from wavering rhythms and vague diction in his poetry.

It was in the summer of 1903, as Yeats later remembered, that Lady Gregory read to him at Coole Park the Renaissance classic, Castiglione's *The Book of the Courtier.* This work was destined to be immensely important to his thought. He described its setting in his account of the Nobel Prize award, *The Bounty of Sweden* (1925), as "that court of Urbino where youth for certain brief periods imposed upon drowsy learning the discipline of its joy." Coole Park, with its woods and lake, its books and prints, and its Asian souvenirs (Lady Gregory's late husband had been a governor of Ceylon) became for Yeats an image of Urbino, and Lady Gregory an incarnation of the cultivated Duchess Elisabetta

Gonzaga. When Lady Gregory became seriously ill in 1909, Yeats noted in his diary: "All Wednesday I heard Castiglione's phrase ringing in my memory, 'Never be it spoken without tears, the Duchess, too, is dead.' " *The Book of the Courtier,* like much of Yeats' poetry, is an elegy for past glories.

In Castiglione, Yeats found confirmation of several emerging ideas, the most important being that of Unity of Being. The key word in *The Book of the Courtier* is *sprezzatura,* which cannot be translated precisely but can be taken to mean a combination of ease and elegance, of carelessness and confidence, a product of self-discipline and the acceptance of custom. Spontaneity is central to the term. A year before encountering Castiglione's work, Yeats had written that though a line of poetry may take hours, "Yet if it does not seem a moment's thought, / Our stitching and unstitching has been naught" ("Adam's Curse"). He saw this self-confidence in Lady Gregory, in her nephews Hugh Lane and John Shawe-Taylor, in the horseman of "At Galway Races," in the imagined fisherman for whom he wished to write a poem "cold / And passionate as the dawn." Above all, it was exemplified in Lady Gregory's son Robert, who was killed in World War I, "Our Sidney and our perfect man."

The American lecture tour (November 1903 to March 1904) established Yeats' position as a commanding figure in the English-speaking literary world. He made more than forty appearances from New York City to San Francisco and Toronto. His first biographer, Joseph Hone, described his platform manner: "he was sometimes uneasy at the start, and would then stride up and down the platform in a rather surprising manner before he attained to his natural distinction of bearing, his gravity of utterance and his rhythm" (*Life,* p. 213). Here we see an actor entering upon a bravura performance. Hone characterizes his voice as "musical, touched with melancholy, the tones rising and falling in a continuous flow of sound," an effect fortunately preserved on phonograph recordings.

When Yeats returned to Ireland, he found that the theatre troubles had not abated. Moore, Martyn, and AE had dropped out, leaving the management to Yeats, Lady Gregory, and Synge. The company got its permanent home and name when two buildings on Lower Abbey Street were remodeled by the architect and diarist Joseph Holloway,* through the generosity of an English patron, Miss Horniman, who in turn was to withdraw several years later, not without bitterness.

The opening program, December 27, 1904, consisted of two Yeats plays— *On Baile's Strand,* one of his best early dramas, and *Cathleen Ni Houlihan*— together with Lady Gregory's perennially popular comedy, *Spreading the News.*

A new Yeats play was produced almost every year. Already an author-director-manager, he now assumed another role as publicity agent, handling letters to the press, articles, lectures, and three theatre magazines—*Beltaine* (three issues, 1899–1900), *Samhain* (seven issues, 1901–1906 and 1908), and *The Arrow* (five issues, 1906–1907 and 1909). The first two titles are the Irish words for the seasons of production, spring and harvest, but they also suggest their significance as combative manifestos. An "irascible friend" had said that controversy had made a man of Yeats, an observation that Yeats questioned, but remembered for years, mentioning it in a 1931 reprinting of *Plays and Controversies:* "I do not agree with him; I doubt the value of the embittered controversy that was to fill my life for years, but certainly they rang down the curtain so far as I was concerned on what was called 'The Celtic Movement.' "

The Celtic Movement appealed to the public ("harps and pepperpots" was Yeats' term of contempt for the typical Irish cheap souvenir); and the major affront to the sentimental dream of Ireland was Synge's uncompromising vision. Yeats wrote to the patron and collector John Quinn, who had arranged the American lecture tour, that "Synge is invaluable to us because he has that kind of intense narrow personality which necessarily raises the whole issue." Matters reached a climax with the "Playboy Riots" of January 1907, with audience protests continuing throughout the week. Yeats called an open meeting, where he announced to the crowd, "The author of *Cathleen Ni Houlihan* addresses you." He was supported by his father, as the poet was to remember in one of his last poems, "Beautiful, Lofty Things." J. B. Yeats had been in Dublin for several years, under the patronage of Hugh Lane, doing the well-known portraits of Irish celebrities; in 1908, he was to come to New York, where he lived, ever lively, never successful, until his death in 1922.

The Collected Works in Verse and Prose (1908), in eight handsome volumes and bound in quarter vellum, included portraits by Sargent, J. B. Yeats, and others, and contained about two thousand pages of text. It consolidated Yeats' position, though some thought his career was at an end (*Life,* p. 239). The 1,060 sets were underwritten by Miss Horniman for £1500; currently, a single set sells for about £250.

For lovers of book design, Yeats' first editions are unusually attractive, notably, the art nouveau, gold-stamped covers of the 1890s; the simple good taste of the linen bound Cuala Press* books, with title page woodcuts by Robert Gregory, T. Sturge Moore, AE, Elizabeth Yeats, and others; the blind-stamped patterns on covers of later works; the limited signed editions of *The Trembling of the Veil* and *A Vision;* and perhaps most striking of all, the bold green and gold cover of *The Tower.*

Synge's death in March 1909 ended another chapter in Yeats' career. The long fight against critics like Arthur Griffith* left its mark in the bitterness of "Estrangement" and "The Death of Synge" (considerably toned down in the autobiography from the original text in *Memoirs*). More time was now to be spent away from Dublin, though local disputes loom large in his verse. He kept his attractive London flat in Woburn Buildings, his home from 1895 to 1919. (Fortunately, this residence has been preserved.) He visited Maud Gonne in Normandy and spent summers at Coole Park. He made American tours in 1911 and 1914.

During this period, a new influence emerged—that of the brash young Ezra Pound, who undertook to convert Yeats to modernism, revised his verse, and introduced him to Japanese drama. They had met shortly after Pound's arrival in England in 1908, and Pound was to become his secretary during the winters of 1913–1914, 1914–1915, and 1915–1916. In 1913, Yeats won the *Poetry* magazine prize for "The Grey Rock," a tribute to his friends of the Rhymers' Club. Upon accepting, he made the generous suggestion that some of the money be given to Pound: "although I do not really like with my whole soul the metrical experiments he has made for you, I think those experiments show a vigorous creative mind" (*Letters,* p. 585). Pound could be exasperating, but Yeats found him "a learned companion" who "helps me to get back to the definite and concrete" (*Life,* p. 290).

Mrs. Shakespear became a link between Pound and Yeats when her daughter married Pound. Her relation to the woman Yeats married in 1917 was even closer. Miss George Hyde-Lees, whom Yeats first met in 1911, was the step-daughter of Mrs. Shakespear's brother.

The decade after Synge's death was marked by further Dublin controversies, new directions in writing, and a turn toward reminiscence. Though topical, Yeats' verse gained a new authority. Consider his denunciation of a timid donor for Hugh Lane's projected art gallery which would bridge the River Liffey. No matter that there were problems of personality, or policy, and even of site and design; all are swept aside in the poem with its oddly archaic seventeenth-century title "To a Wealthy Man Who Promised a Second Subscription to the Dublin Municipal Gallery If It Were Proved the People Wanted Pictures" (1913). Timid dependence on "what the blind and ignorant town / Imagines best to make it thrive" is contrasted to the aristocratic indifference of Duke Ercole de l'Este of Ferrara who cared not "What th' onion-sellers thought or did" when he staged the plays of Plautus. And when Guidobaldo di Montefeltro established the court described by Castiglione, "That grammar school of cour-tesies / Where wit and beauty learned their trade / Upon Urbino's windy hill," he "sent no runners to and fro / That he might learn the shepherds' will." Thus, history as personal reflection is distilled into unforgettable phrases.

These may be "Poems Written in Discouragement" (the title of the 1913 limited Cuala Press* edition), but the discouragement is far from defeatist. If "Romantic Ireland's dead and gone" ("September 1913"), there's at least one voice unsilenced. In answer to his father's complaint that this poetry seemed to lack vision, Yeats replied, "I have tried for more self-portraiture . . . with a speech so natural that the hearer would feel the presence of a man thinking and feeling." The quality is rare in English poetry, but "Villon always and Ronsard at times create marvellous drama out of their own lives" (*Letters,* p. 583).

Synge was to be joined by Hugh Lane in the pantheon of heroes Yeats was creating. Lane's career is a success story with a tragic end, followed by an epilogue of controversy. It began with the sensational rise of a shrewd art dealer who had started at a pound a week, amassed considerable wealth in a few years, established the Municipal Gallery, and was knighted before his death at the age of forty in the sinking of the "Lusitania." Lane had been antagonized by authorities in London and in Dublin alike, and his bequest of thirty-nine pictures was to become a source of dispute. His intentions were debatable, for he willed them to the London National Gallery but left a codicil which gave them to Dublin. They were on loan in London at the time of his death.

The pictures exemplify Lane's extraordinary artistic taste; they include Corot and Courbet, Daumier and Degas, Manet's "Le Concert aux Tuileries," a delightful *plein air* group, a fine early impressionistic snow scene by Monet, a charming Morisot of two elegant young women in a boat, and, most striking of all, Renoir's large canvas of a colorful group of women and children in a shower, "Les Parapluies." It was one of Lane's favorites, a harmony of line and color; amazingly enough, the London National Gallery officials thought it unworthy of inclusion in their 1914 exhibit.

Lady Gregory championed the attempt to retrieve the Lane pictures for Dublin, and Yeats supported her but neither lived to see the present compromise, which involves a division into two groups, to alternate between Dublin and London every five years. (See Lady Gregory, *Hugh Lane's Life and Achievement,* 1921, and Thomas Bodkin's illustrated *Hugh Lane and His Pictures,* 1956.)

Events were turning Yeats' thoughts to concepts of personality and to family history: the ever-increasing image of Synge; the death of a favorite uncle, the eccentric horseman and astrologer, George Pollexfen, in 1910; the accounts of the Irish literary scene by George Moore, Lady Gregory, and others, between 1911 and 1914; anger at Moore's mockery. At fifty he was ready to write his *Reveries Over Childhood and Youth* (1915) and, characteristically, to have theories at hand. These theories were expressed in the puzzling poetic dialogue "Ego Dominus Tuus" and further elaborated in a forty-five page footnote to the short poem, published as *Per Amica Silentia Lunae* (1918).

To simplify drastically, the theme is one of transcendence of worldly values through conflict within oneself. In the poem, the contrast is between the worldly *Hic* and his adversary *Ille* (Pound dubbed him "Willie"). *Hic* is content with popular acclaim; *Ille* seeks his mysterious double, or antiself, in order to achieve, not success, but vision. Dante "set his chisel to the hardest stone," says *Ille,* and his concept is modified in the title of another important collection of essays, *The Cutting of an Agate* (1912), which presents evolving views of tragic drama. As early as 1907, and again in the 1910 essay on "The Tragic Theatre," Yeats had written of the insight attained by the tragic hero. In the Japanese Noh drama to which Ezra Pound introduced him, Yeats found the purely symbolic dramatic form he had been seeking. *At the Hawk's Well* was performed privately in London in 1916 with costumes and masks by Edmund Dulac and the dance of the hawk presented by Michio Ito. This is the first of *Four Plays for Dancers,* published in 1922, with illustrations of the Dulac costumes and masks which convey something of the spirit of the performance. The illustrations are repeated in editions of *Plays and Controversies* (1923). Dulac worked with Yeats elsewhere, notably in the woodcuts for *A Vision* (1925).

As one of his most successful plays, *At the Hawk's Well* achieves the seemingly impossible union of a presumably Irish hero and an oriental form. It is a triumph of style, an abstract evocation of spiritual energy, and a worthy successor to his earlier treatment of the Cuchulain legend in the 1904 *On Baile's Strand,* a more accurate dramatization of the traditional tale.

To the influence of Pound must be added the experience of reading John Donne in the definitive 1912 edition by H.J.C. Grierson. In thanking his friend the editor, Yeats wrote: "I notice that the more precise and learned the thought the greater the beauty, the passion; the intricacy and subtleties of his imagination are the length and depths of the furrow made by his passion" (*Letters,* p. 570). He was reading Walter Savage Landor too, finding in him an admirable union of violent passion and serenity. Yeats was to become one of the first modern metaphysical poets. The conclusion of "To a Young Beauty," written in 1918, announces: "There is not a fool can call me friend, / And I may dine at journey's end / With Landor and with Donne."

The young beauty was Iseult Gonne, daughter of Maud Gonne and the French patriot Millevoye. After the execution of Maud Gonne's husband in 1916, Yeats renewed his proposals to her (she had never divorced MacBride) and then proposed to her daughter before marrying Miss Hyde-Lees, who proved to be a vivacious, intelligent wife.

Yeats had received a Civil List pension of £150 per annum in 1913, and two years later he was able to do a favor for his fellow-countryman Joyce, who in the summer of 1915 had come almost penniless to neutral Switzerland for the duration of World War I. Forgetting Joyce's earlier rudeness, Yeats, at the instigation of Ezra Pound, recommended Joyce for a grant from the Royal Literary Fund. He wrote the English critic Edmund Gosse that though *Dubliners* seemed "all atmosphere perhaps" it could be "a sign of an original study of life," while the *Portrait,* then being serialized in *The Egoist,* "increases my conviction that he is the most remarkable new talent in Ireland to-day" (*Letters,* p. 599). A grant of £75 was awarded.

The opening of the world war was marked by mounting Irish tension, with three paramilitary groups active—the Ulster Volunteers, the Irish Volunteers, and the Irish Citizen Army. Many were enlisting, but the majority opposed support of England. Lady Gregory's son had joined the Air Force, and Maud Gonne was nursing the wounded. Yeats sparred with the viceroy of Ireland over political matters and impressed him enough to have him declare: "I really believe I could govern Ireland if I had Mr. Yeats' assistance." Yeats seemed not to share this opinion. When asked to write a war poem, he refused but wrote one instead explaining his refusal: "We have no gift to set a statesman right." He also refused an offer of knighthood.

With English, Irish, and American editions, private printings, theatre texts, and books with contributions or prefaces, about half of the three hundred titles published in his life appeared between 1900 and 1920. The poems are grouped under the headings *In the Seven Woods* (1904), actually published in 1903; *The*

Green Helmet and Other Poems (1910); *Responsibilities* (1914); and *The Wild Swans at Coole* (1919), actually published in 1917.

After Yeats' marriage on October 21, 1917, the couple spent several years in England. (Yeats is so closely associated with Ireland that it is surprising to learn how little he actually lived there.) To his delight he discovered his wife's psychic powers and continued work on the elaborate philosophical system to be known as *A Vision* (1925). Before his marriage, he had written his father apologetically about his thought, knowing the artist's distaste for abstractions: "Much of your thought resembles mine . . . but mine is part of a religious system more or less logically worked out, a system which will I hope interest you as a form of poetry." He continued: "I find the setting it all in order has helped my verse" with "a new framework and new patterns" (*Letters*, p. 627). The same idea was apparently transmitted to his wife when the "unknown writer" of her automatic writing sent the message, "we have come to give you metaphors for poetry" (*A Vision*, 1956 ed., p. 8). Concepts from the system lie behind many magnificent poems of this time.

After his daughter's birth, in the winter of 1919–1920, he toured America, seeing his father for the last time whom he found "as full of the future as when I was a child," as he wrote Lady Gregory.

Yeats' impulse to root himself in Ireland was demonstrated by the acquisition of a Norman tower not far from Coole Park, and his purchase of a Georgian house at 82 Merrion Square, his Dublin home from 1922 to 1928. The house was only two doors away from AE's editorial office. A cartoon by Isa MacNie illustrates the Dublin anecdote that Yeats and AE, on the way to meet, crossed paths without noticing one another. Yeats, regarded by Dubliners as a snob, strides on, gazing loftily, his long black tie flowing, while AE trudges by, his bearded head bent in meditation (*The World of Yeats,* Robin Skelton and Ann Saddlemyer, eds., 1965).

From 1919 to 1923, Ireland was a battleground, first with the brutal "Black and Tans" and other English forces in their attacks on the Sinn Féin government, and then the war by the Republicans or Irregulars against the Free State. Despite atrocities, there were feats of derring-do, as in the escape of Yeats' friend and fellow senator Oliver Gogarty* (see his *An Offering of Swans,* 1923). The tragedy of these times is elevated to a philosophical level in poems such as "Meditations in Time of Civil War."

The tower, Thoor Ballylee (Irish "Tur Bail' i Liagh") with its thatched cottages, is beautifully located beside a stream, a bridge at its foot. It has now been restored. Though too damp for the family (Yeats himself was comfortably settled on an upper floor) and far from safe in time of war, as is shown in the poems, the tower was a source of poetic inspiration, with its historic traditions and symbolic associations. In "The Phases of the Moon," Robartes thinks Yeats chose it "Because, it may be, of the candlelight / From the far tower where Milton's Platonist / Sat late, or Shelley's visionary prince: / The lonely light that Samuel Palmer engraved, / An image of mysterious wisdom won by toil."

Other significances are traced by T. R. Henn in *The Lonely Tower* (1950)—as an emblem of ancient ceremony, as symbol of the destructive forces of time and history, as token of night and the infinite universe beyond. In an 1899 essay, "Dust Hath Closed Helen's Eye," Yeats had told of visiting the tower and hearing of the death there sixty years before of the beautiful Mary Hynes, subject of a romantic Gaelic poem by the blind Raftery. Yeats and his family spent only a few summers between 1919 and 1929 at Ballylee, but its associations reverberate through many poems.

Despite long-standing distrust of politics, Yeats consented to serve in the Free State Senate (1923–1928). In addressing a Celtic Festival in 1924, he expressed his doubts: "We do not believe that war is passing away, and we do not believe that the world is growing better and better." A year later, he shocked his colleagues in a debate on divorce by mentioning the private lives of Nelson, Parnell, and O'Connell, "the three old rascals" of the short poem "The Three Monuments." He concluded his speech with an angry identification of himself with the Anglo-Irish Protestant Ascendancy, the long-hated alien overlords of Ireland: "We are one of the great stocks of Europe. We are the people of Burke; we are the people of Grattan; we are the people of Swift, the people of Parnell. We have created the most of the modern literature of this country. We have created the best of its political intelligence." It was not a speech to win the audience, but such pride imparted eloquence to his writing.

Dublin gossip has it that when a journalist telephoned Yeats in 1923 to notify him that he had won the Nobel Prize, the poet's response was to ask how much money was involved. He enjoyed the ceremony with gusto, seeing in the Swedish court an embodiment of his aristocratic ideals.

The first version of *A Vision*, dated 1925, was actually issued in 1926 in a signed edition of six hundred copies. It opens with a fascinating tale by the fictional Owen Aherne, who, with Michael Robartes, had appeared in Yeats' stories years before. Aherne tells of meeting Robartes in the National Gallery and speaking about Yeats, with whom both had quarrelled, because he had not admitted that they were real persons. Robartes tells his friend about finding an old book by one Giraldus that he discovered in Cracow, with "curious allegorical figures" and "many diagrams," including one "where lunar phases and zodiacal signs were mixed with various unintelligible symbols." This text is, of course, that of *A Vision*. Finding similar signs on the Arabian desert, Robartes continued his search, meeting a man of the Judwali sect, whose leader had been Kusta ben Luka. Joining the sect, Robartes learned that though their Sacred Book had been lost, much preserved in oral tradition resembled the thought of Giraldus. After a quarrel, they agree to show the material to Yeats. In an amusing footnote, Yeats questions the accuracy of Aherne's version.

Central to *A Vision* is the lunar cycle of twenty-eight phases, representing periods of history, stages in human life, degrees of subjectivity, and types of human character, each with its Will and Body of Fate, and its true and false Mask and Creative Mind. The ideal phase, Fifteen, has no exemplar; closest are

Fourteen ("Keats, Giorgione, many beautiful women") and Sixteen (Blake, and, surprisingly, Rabelais and Aretino, as well as "some beautiful women"). The intertwining gyres of human life and of history are also essential. There can be no doubt of the importance to Yeats of his system; it sums up a life of speculation and was immediately undergoing further revision. Perhaps the wisest comment upon it was made by AE when questioned by Elizabeth Yeats: "My opinion is that *anything* Willie writes will be of interest now or later on, and a book like this, which does not excite me or you, may be, possibly will be, studied later on when the psychology of the poet is considered by critics and biographers" (*Life*, p. 435). Of special interest is the passage describing Byzantium, where "religion, art and practical life were one," and "The painter and the mosaic worker, the worker in gold and silver, the illuminator of Sacred Books" were impersonally absorbed in "the vision of a whole people." Here is the germ of the magnificent "Sailing to Byzantium" and its sequel "Byzantium," the mosaics having been recalled from a visit to Palermo in 1924.

The Abbey Theatre was again a center of controversy with O'Casey's* *The Plough and the Stars,* when audiences were affronted by a less than idealistic portrayal of some patriots in the Rising. A protest was made on the fourth night, February 11, 1926, whereupon Yeats is reported to have silenced the crowd. Joseph Holloway, however, records that he could not be heard (*Joseph Holloway's Abbey Theatre,* 1967). Peter Kavanagh is probably right in assuming that the newspaper report was based on a script supplied by Yeats: "you have disgraced yourselves again. . . . Synge first and then O'Casey" (*The Story of the Abbey Theatre,* 1950).

Yeats was to meet his match when he rejected *The Silver Tassie* in 1928, commenting that though in the Irish plays "you were excited and we all caught your excitement," the fact is that "you are not interested in the Great War." O'Casey found this statement to be "impudently arrogant" (Kavanagh, pp. 139, 140). Here began O'Casey's long feud with Ireland.

For Yeats the time of farewells had come: to Merrion Square, 1928; to Ballylee, 1929; to Coole Park, 1932.

Lady Gregory's death in 1932 marked the end of an epoch. Of all the figures in the Revival, only Douglas Hyde survived Yeats. Yeats told of a Dublin sculptor who visited Coole Park at the end, gazed at the family heirlooms, then said, "All the nobility of earth." "How much of my own verses has been but the repetition of those words," Yeats exclaimed (*Letters,* p. 796). The house was razed in 1941, but the beech tree remains, with its carved initials such as W.B.Y., AE, and G.B.S.

Despite ill health, Yeats' last years were vigorous ones. He found new friends (Lady Dorothy Wellesley, Ethel Mannin*), and cultivated new enemies. "And say my glory was I had such friends," he concludes in the Municipal Gallery poem, a line quoted by George McGovern in his concession speech after the 1972 presidential election in the United States. Yeats attacked modern bad taste in *On the Boiler,* published after his death. "I wonder how many friends I will have left,'' he mused (*Letters,* p. 910). Wide reading in philosophy (the Upanishads, Plotinus, Berkeley*) deepened his insight, though some work is marred by feverish sexuality or strident glorification of violence (he was briefly attracted to the Irish protofascist Blue Shirts). ''You were silly like us,'' Auden wrote in his noble elegy, ''your gift survived it all.''

During the 1930s, Yeats had the energy to undertake a successful American tour in 1932, edit the idiosyncratic *Oxford Book of Modern Verse* (1936), publish a revised edition of *A Vision* (1937), and broadcast several BBC programs. In addition, he wrote several hauntingly enigmatic plays. Most accessible are *The Words upon the Window Pane* (produced at the Abbey, November 1930), a seance invoking the ghost of Swift, and *The Resurrection* (Abbey, July 1934), on the divinity of Christ. Three fantasies—*The King of the Great Clock Tower* (Abbey, July 1934), *A Full Moon in March* (1935), and *The Herne's Egg* (1938)—were followed by the nightmare intensity of *Purgatory,* on August 10, 1938, which marked his last appearance at the Abbey Theatre. Although these dramas defy analysis, as do some of the last poems, they convey the impression of a great poet's superhuman vision of things beyond mortal understanding.

On January 4, 1939, Yeats wrote from the Riviera that though ''I know for certain that my time will not be long,'' yet ''I am happy, and I think full of an energy, of an energy I had despaired of.'' Then, in words which some may prefer to the dramatic epitaph, he continued, ''It seems to me that I have found what I wanted. When I try to put all into a phrase I say, 'Man can embody truth but he cannot know it.' I must embody it in the completion of my life'' (*Letters,* p. 922). That existential insight seems to have been demonstrated throughout his career.

Yeats died on January 28, 1939. World War II delayed the fulfillment of his desire to be buried ''Under Ben Bulben'' in the Drumcliff churchyard of his great-grandfather, the rector. The grave is marked with his own memorable and enigmatic words:

> Cast a cold eye
> On life, on death.
> Horseman, pass by!

RICHARD M. KAIN

WORKS: *Mosada.* Dublin: Sealy, Bryers, & Walker, 1886. (Dramatic poem); ed., *Fairy and Folk Tales of the Irish Peasantry.* London: Walter Scott/New York: Thomas Whittaker/Toronto: W. J. Gage, 1888; *The Wanderings of Oisin and Other Poems.* London: Kegan Paul, Trench, 1889; ed., *Stories from Carleton.* London: Walter Scott/New York & Toronto: W. J. Gage, [1889]; under the pseudonym of ''Ganconagh,'' *John Sherman and Dhoya.* London: T. Fisher Unwin, 1891. (Novel); ed., *Representative Irish Tales.* 2 vols. New York & London: G. P. Putnam's Sons, The Knickerbocker Press, [1891]; *The Countess Kathleen and Various Legends and Lyrics.* London: T. Fisher Unwin, 1892/Boston: Roberts Bros., [1892]; ed., *Irish Fairy Tales.* London: T. Fisher Unwin/New York: Cassell, 1892; *The Celtic Twilight.* London: Lawrence & Bullen, 1893/New York: Macmillan, 1894. (Poems and essays); ed. with Edwin John Ellis, *The Works of William Blake.* 3 vols. London: Bernard Quaritch, 1893; *The Land of Heart's Desire.* London: T. Fisher Unwin, 1894/Chicago: Stone & Kimball, 1894/revised ed. Portland, Maine: Thomas B. Mosher, 1903. (Play); *Poems.* London: T. Fisher Unwin, 1895/revised ed. London: T. Fisher Unwin, 1899/2d revised ed. London:

T. Fisher Unwin, 1901; ed., *A Book of Irish Verse*. London: Methuen, 1895; *The Secret Rose*. London: Lawrence & Bullen, 1897. (Poems); *The Tables of the Law. The Adoration of the Magi*. Privately printed, 1897/London: Elkin Mathews, 1904. (Poems); *The Wind among the Reeds*. London: Elkin Mathews, 1899. (Poems); ed., *Beltaine, an Occasional Publication. Number One*. London: At the Sign of the Unicorn/Dublin: At the "Daily Express" Office, 1899; ed., *Beltaine, Number Two*. London: At the Sign of the Unicorn, 1900; ed., *Beltaine, Number Three*. London: At the Sign of the Unicorn, 1900; *The Shadowy Waters*. London: Hodder & Stoughton, 1900. (Play); ed., *Samhain*. [Dublin]: Sealy, Bryers & Walker/[London]: T. Fisher Unwin, 1901. (First number of the theatre magazine); *The Celtic Twilight*. Revised & enlarged. London: A H. Bullen, 1902; *Cathleen Ni Houlihan*. London: A. H. Bullen, 1902. (Play); ed., *Samhain*. [Dublin]: Sealy, Bryers & Walker/ [London]: T. Fisher Unwin, 1902. (Second number of the theatre magazine); *Where There Is Nothing*. London: A. H. Bullen, 1903. (Play, written with some help from Lady Gregory and Douglas Hyde, and first printed as a supplement to *The United Irishman*, Nov. 1, 1902); *Ideas of Good and Evil*. London: A. H. Bullen, 1903. (Essays); *In the Seven Woods*. Dundrum: Dun Emer, 1903. (Poems); *The Hour-Glass*. London: Wm. Heinemann, 1903. (Play); ed., *Samhain*. [Dublin]: Sealy, Bryers & Walker/[London]: T. Fisher Unwin, 1903. (Third number of the theatre magazine); *The Hour-Glass and Other Plays*. New York & London: Macmillan, 1904. (Contains also "Cathleen ni Houlihan" and "The Pot of Broth"); *The Hour-Glass, Cathleen Ni Houlihan, The Pot of Broth*. London: A. H. Bullen, 1904/Dublin: Maunsel, 1905; ed., *Samhain*. [Dublin]: Sealy, Bryers & Walker/[London]: T. Fisher Unwin, 1904. (Fourth number of the theatre magazine); *The King's Threshold: and On Baile's Strand*. London: A. H. Bullen, 1904. (Plays); *Twenty One Poems*. Dundrum: Dun Emer, 1904 [actually 1905]; *Stories of Red Hanrahan*. Dundrum: Dun Emer, 1904 [actually 1905]; ed., *Some Essays and Passages by John Eglinton*. Dundrum: Dun Emer, 1905; ed., *Samhain*. [Dublin]: Maunsel/[London]: A. H. Bullen, 1905. (Fifth number of the theatre magazine); ed., *Sixteen Poems by William Allingham*. Dundrum: Dun Emer, 1905; *Poems, 1899–1905*. London: A. H. Bullen/Dublin: Maunsel, 1906; ed., *Poems of Spenser*. Edinburgh: T. C. & E. C. Jack, [1906]; ed., *The Arrow*. (Five short pamphlets issued by the Abbey Theatre in Dublin, from October 20, 1906, to August 22, 1909); ed., *Samhain*. Dublin: Maunsel, 1906. (Sixth number of the theatre magazine); *The Poetical Works of William B. Yeats. Volume I, Lyrical Poems*. New York & London: Macmillan, 1906; *Deirdre*. London: A. H. Bullen/Dublin: Maunsel, 1907. (Play); ed., *Twenty One Poems by Katharine Tynan*. Dundrum: Dun Emer, 1907; *The Poetical Works of William B. Yeats. Volume II, Dramatical Poems*. New York & London: Macmillan, 1907; *Discoveries*. Dundrum: Dun Emer, 1907. (Essays); *The Unicorn from the Stars and Other Plays*, with Lady Gregory. New York: Macmillan, 1908. (Contains the title play by Yeats and Lady Gregory, which is a reworking of *Where There Is Nothing*, and also "Cathleen ni Houlihan" and "The Hour Glass"); *The Golden Helmet*. New York: John Quinn, 1908; *Poems Lyrical and Narrative, Being the First Volume of the Collected Works in Verse and Prose of William Butler Yeats*. Stratford-on-Avon: Shakespeare Head, 1908; *The King's Threshold. On Baile's Strand. Deirdre. Shadowy Waters*. Stratford-on-Avon: Shakespeare Head, 1908. (Vol. II of the Collected Edition); *The Countess Cathleen. The Land of Heart's Desire. The Unicorn from the Stars*. Stratford-on-Avon: Shakespeare Head, 1908. (Vol. III of the Collected Edition); *The Hour-Glass. Cathleen Ni Houlihan. The Golden Helmet. The Irish Dramatic Movement*. Stratford-on-Avon: Shakespeare Head, 1908. (Vol. IV of the Collected Edition); *The Celtic Twilight and Stories of Red Hanrahan*. Stratford-on-Avon: Shakespeare Head, 1908. (Vol. V of the Collected Edition); *Ideas of Good and Evil*. Stratford-on-Avon: Shakespeare Head, 1908. (Vol. VI of the Collected Edition); *The Secret Rose. Rosa Alchemica. The Tables of the Law. The Adoration of the Magi. John Sherman and Dhoya*. Stratford-on-Avon: Shakespeare Head, 1908. (Vol. VII of the Collected Edition); *Discoveries. Edmund Spenser. Poetry and Tradition: & Other Essays*. Stratford-on-Avon: Shakespeare Head, 1908. (Vol. VIII of the Collected Edition); ed., *Samhain*. Dublin: Maunsel, 1908. (Seventh number of the theatre magazine); *Poetry and Ireland, Essays by W. B. Yeats and Lionel Johnson*. Churchtown, Dundrum: Cuala, 1908; ed., *Poems and Translations by John M. Synge*. Churchtown, Dundrum: Cuala, 1909; *Poems: Second Series*. London & Stratford-on-Avon: A. H. Bullen, 1909 [actually 1910]; ed., *Deirdre of the Sor-*

rows: A Play by John M. Synge. Churchtown, Dundrum: Cuala, 1910; *The Green Helmet and Other Poems.* Churchtown, Dundrum: Cuala, 1910; *Synge and the Ireland of his Time.* Churchtown, Dundrum: Cuala, 1911; *The Green Helmet.* Stratford-on-Avon: Shakespeare Head, 1911. (Only separate edition); *Plays for an Irish Theatre.* London & Stratford-on-Avon: A. H. Bullen, 1911. (Contains "Deirdre," "The Green Helmet," "On Baile's Strand," "The King's Threshold," "The Shadowy Waters," "The Hour-Glass," and "Cathleen ni Houlihan"); *The Countess Cathleen,* revised version. London: T. Fisher Unwin, 1912; *Poems,* revised. London: T. Fisher Unwin, 1912; *The Green Helmet and Other Poems.* New York & London: Macmillan, 1912; ed., *Selections from the Writings of Lord Dunsany.* Churchtown, Dundrum: Cuala, 1912; *The Cutting of an Agate.* New York: Macmillan, 1912. (Essays); *A Selection from the Love Poetry of William Butler Yeats.* Churchtown, Dundrum: Cuala, 1913; *Poems Written in Discouragement.* Churchtown, Dundrum: Cuala, 1913; *Responsibilities: Poems and a Play.* Churchtown, Dundrum: Cuala, 1914. (The play is a new version of "The Hour-Glass"); *Reveries over Childhood and Youth.* Churchtown, Dundrum: Cuala, 1915; *Eight Poems.* London: Morland Press, [1916]; *Responsibilities and Other Poems.* London: Macmillan, 1916; *The Wild Swans at Coole, Other Verses and a Play in Verse.* Churchtown, Dundrum: Cuala, 1917. (The play is "At the Hawk's Well"); *Per Amica Silentia Lunae.* London: Macmillan, 1918; *Nine Poems.* London: Privately printed by Clement Shorter, 1918; *Two Plays for Dancers* London: Macmillan, 1921; Churchtown, Dundrum: Cuala, 1919. (The plays are "The Dreaming of the Bones" and "The Only Jealousy of Emer"); *The Wild Swans at Coole.* London: Macmillan, 1919; *Michael Robartes and the Dancer.* Churchtown, Dundrum: Cuala, 1920. (Poems); *Selected Poems.* New York: Macmillan, 1921; *Four Plays for Dancers.* (The plays are "At the Hawk's Well," "The Only Jealousy of Emer," "The Dreaming of the Bones," and "Calvary"); *Seven Poems and a Fragment.* Dundrum: Cuala, 1922; *The Trembling of the Veil.* London: Privately printed for subscribers by T. Werner Laurie, 1922. (Reminiscences); *Later Poems.* London: Macmillan, 1922; *Plays in Prose and Verse, Written for an Irish Theatre, and Generally with the Help of a Friend* [Lady Gregory]. London: Macmillan, 1922; *The Player Queen.* London: Macmillan, 1922; *Plays and Controversies.* London: Macmillan, 1923; *Essays.* London: Macmillan, 1924; *The Cat and the Moon and Certain Poems.* Dublin: Cuala, 1924; *The Bounty of Sweden.* Dublin: Cuala, 1925; *Early Poems and Stories.* London: Macmillan, 1925; *A Vision.* London: Privately printed for subscribers by T. Werner Laurie, 1925; *Estrangement: Being Some Fifty Thoughts from a Diary Kept by William Butler Yeats in the Year Nineteen Hundred and Nine.* Dublin: Cuala, 1926; *Autobiographies.* London: Macmillan, 1926. (Contains "Reveries over Childhood and Youth" and "The Trembling of the Veil"); *October Blast.* Dublin: Cuala, 1927. (Poems); *The Tower.* London: Macmillan, 1928. (Poems); *Sophocles' King Oedipus, a Version for the Modern Stage.* London: Macmillan, 1928; *The Death of Synge, and Other Passages from an Old Diary.* Dublin: Cuala, 1928; *A Packet for Ezra Pound.* Dublin: Cuala, 1929; *The Winding Stair.* New York: Fountain Press, 1929; *Selected Poems, Lyrical and Narrative.* London: Macmillan, 1929; *Stories of Michael Robartes and his Friends: An Extract from a Record Made by his Pupils: and a Play in Prose.* Dublin: Cuala, 1931. (The play is "The Resurrection"); *Words for Music Perhaps and Other Poems.* Dublin: Cuala, 1932; *The Winding Stair and Other Poems.* London: Macmillan, 1933; *The Collected Poems of W. B. Yeats.* New York: Macmillan, 1933; *Letters to the New Island.* Horace Reynolds, ed. Cambridge, Mass.: Harvard University Press, 1934. (Collection of early essays and reviews for American newspapers); *The Words Upon the Window Pane.* Dublin: Cuala, 1934. (Play); *Wheels and Butterflies.* London: Macmillan, 1934. (Contains texts of and introductions to "The Words Upon the Window Pane," "Fighting the Waves," "The Resurrection," and "The Cat and the Moon"); *The Collected Plays of W. B. Yeats.* London: Macmillan, 1934. (Contains the texts of twenty previously printed plays and also the first printing of *Oedipus at Colonus*); ed. with F. R. Higgins, *Broadsides.* Dublin: Cuala, 1935. (Collections of poems issued in twelve monthly broadsides of 4 pages each); *A Full Moon in March.* London: Macmillan, 1935. (Contains the title play as well as a revision in verse of "The King of the Great Clock Tower" and various poems); *Dramatis Personae.* Dublin: Cuala, 1935. (Reminiscences); *Dramatis Personae 1896–1902, Estrangement, The Death of Synge, The Bounty of Sweden.* New York: Macmillan, 1936; *Modern*

Poetry. London: British Broadcasting Corporation, 1936. (Lecture); ed., *The Oxford Book of Modern Verse.* Oxford: Clarendon Press, 1936; ed., and translated with Shree Purohit Swami, *The Ten Principal Upanishads.* London: Faber, [1937]; *Nine One-Act Plays.* London: Macmillan, 1937; *A Vision.* London: Macmillan, 1937. (Contains much new material); ed., with Dorothy Wellesley, *Broadsides.* Dublin: Cuala, 1937. (Issued individually throughout 1937 and as a bound volume in December 1937); *Essays, 1931 to 1936.* Dublin: Cuala, 1937; *The Herne's Egg.* London: Macmillan, 1938. (Play); *New Poems.* Dublin: Cuala, 1938; *The Autobiography of William Butler Yeats.* New York: Macmillan, 1938. (Consisting of "Reveries over Childhood and Youth," "The Trembling of the Veil," and "Dramatis Personae"); *Last Poems and Two Plays.* Dublin: Cuala, 1939. (The plays are "The Death of Cuchulain" and "Purgatory"); *On the Boiler.* Dublin: Cuala, [1939]; *Last Poems and Plays.* London: Macmillan, 1940. (The selection of poems varies from *Last Poems and Two Plays*); *If I Were Four-and-Twenty.* Dublin: Cuala, 1940; *Pages from a Diary Written in Nineteen Hundred and Thirty.* Dublin: Cuala, 1944; *Tribute to Thomas Davis.* [Cork]: Cork University Press/ Oxford: B. H. Blackwell, 1947. (With a foreword by Denis Gwynn and "An Unpublished Letter" by AE); *The Poems of W. B. Yeats.* 2 vols. London: Macmillan, 1949; *The Collected Poems of W. B. Yeats.* London: Macmillan, 1950/New York: Macmillan, 1951; *Diarmuid and Grania,* with George Moore. [Dublin]: Reprinted from the *Dublin Magazine* (April–June 1951).

The Yeats bibliography is immense, as can be seen from the preceding compilation, which lists only major editions. In recent years, Yeats scholarship has started to produce reliable collected editions. Of *The Collected Works of W. B. Yeats,* Richard Finneran & George Mills Harper, general eds. (London: Macmillan/New York: Scribner's), the following have appeared: Vol. 1, *The Poems,* R. J. Finneran, ed. (1989); Vol. 5, *Later Essays,* William H. O'Donnell, ed. (1994); Vol. 6, *Prefaces and Introductions,* William H. O'Donnell, ed. (1988, i.e., 1989); Vol. 7, *Letters to the New Island,* George Bornstein, ed. (1989); Vol. 12, *John Sherman and Dhoya,* R. J. Finneran, ed. (1992). Editions of the poems are affected by quarrels about textual and editorial procedures. The Finneran edition is basic to *The Poems,* Daniel Albright, ed. (London: Dent, 1990), whereas the different editorial principles of Warwick Gold are explained in *Yeats's Poems,* A. Norman Jeffares, ed. (London: Macmillan, 1989). Further arguments about textual problems are put forward in Finneran's *Editing Yeats's Poems: A Reconsideration* (London: Macmillan, 1990). No such effort has gone into the publication of the plays; the Macmillan London edition of *Collected Plays* (1952) is still the best text. The serious student who wants to reconstruct and appreciate the frequent revisions that Yeats undertook must consult *The Variorum Edition of the Poems of W. B. Yeats,* Peter Allt & Russell K. Alspach, eds. (corrected 3d printing, 1966), and *The Variorum Edition of the Plays of W. B. Yeats,* Russell K. Alspach, ed. (corrected 2d printing, 1966). The preceding volumes and all subsequent ones, unless otherwise noted, were published in London and New York by Macmillan.

Much of Yeats's prose has been collected, including *Autobiographies* (1955), *Mythologies* (1959), *The Senate Speeches of W. B. Yeats,* Donald R. Pearce, ed. (Bloomington: Indiana University Press, 1960); *Essays and Introductions* (1961); *Explorations* (1962); *Memoirs* (the early draft of the autobiography), Denis Donoghue, ed. (1972); and *Uncollected Prose,* John P. Frayne & Colton Johnson, eds. (New York: Columbia University Press, 1970–1975, 2 vols.). Yeats's fragmentary novel, *The Speckled Bird,* was edited by William H. O'Donnell (Toronto: McClelland & Stewart, 1976). The first edition of *A Vision* is available as *A Critical Edition of Yeats's* A Vision *(1925),* George Mills Harper & Walter Kelly Hood, eds. (London: Macmillan, 1978); the revised version of 1937 is part of *A Vision and Related Writings,* A. Norman Jeffares, ed. (London: Arena, 1990). Another useful prose selection is *Writings on Irish Folklore, Myth and Legend,* Robert Welch, ed. (London: Penguin, 1993).

The Letters of W. B. Yeats, Alan Wade, ed. (London: Hart-Davis, 1954/New York: Macmillan, 1955) is now being replaced by *The Collected Letters of W. B. Yeats,* John Kelly, general ed. (Oxford: Clarendon); of the projected twelve volumes the first and third, comprising the years 1865–1895 and 1901–1904, were published in 1986 and 1994. This edition will no doubt include letters already printed in such volumes as *Letters on Poetry from W. B. Yeats to Dorothy Wellesley* (London & New York: Oxford University Press, 1940); *Florence Farr, Bernard Shaw and W. B. Yeats,*

Clifford Bax, ed. (Dublin: Cuala, 1941); *W. B. Yeats and T. Sturge Moore: Their Correspondence, 1901–1937,* Ursula Bridge, ed. (London: Routledge & Kegan Paul/New York: Oxford University Press, 1953); *Letters to Katharine Tynan,* Roger McHugh, ed. (Dublin: Clonmore & Reynolds/New York: McMullen, 1953); and *The Correspondence of Robert Bridges and W. B. Yeats,* Richard J. Fineran, ed. (London: Macmillan, 1977). Abbey Theatre affairs are treated in *Theatre Business: The Correspondence of the First Abbey Theatre Directors: William Butler Yeats, Lady Gregory, and J. M. Synge,* Ann Saddlemyer, ed. (Gerrards Cross: Colin Smythe, 1982). Yeats's relationship with Maud Gonne is chronicled in *The Gonne-Yeats Letters 1893–1938,* Anna McBridge White & A. Norman Jeffares, eds. (London: Hutchinson, 1992/New York: Norton, 1993). Three collections of letters *to* Yeats are of interest: John Butler Yeats: *Letters to His Son W. B. Yeats and Others, 1869–1922,* Joseph Hone, ed. (London: Faber, 1944/New York: Dutton, 1946); *Letters to W. B. Yeats,* Richard J. Finneran et al., eds. (London: Macmillan, 1977); and *The Letters of John Quinn to William Butler Yeats,* Alan Himber, ed. (Ann Arbor, Mich.: UMI Research Press, 1983).

Yeats's complex publishing history is given in Allan Wade's *A Bibliography of the Writings of W. B. Yeats,* 3d ed., revised by Russell K. Alspach (London: Hart-Davis/New York: Oxford University Press, 1968); Colin Smythe is at work on a 4th edition. The enormous amount of secondary material is listed in K.P.S. Jochum's *W. B. Yeats: A Classified Bibliography of Criticism,* 2d ed. (Urbana: University of Illinois Press, 1990); it is updated in the annual checklists printed in *Yeats: An Annual of Critical and Textual Studies,* beginning with Vol. 8 (1990). An extensive survey of works about Yeats is provided by Richard J. Finneran, ed., in *Anglo-Irish Literature: A Review of Research,* supplemented by *Recent Research on Anglo-Irish Writers* (both published New York: Modern Language Association, 1976, 1983). Further reference material includes Stephen Maxfield Parrish & James Allan Painter: *A Concordance to the Poems of W. B. Yeats* and Eric Domville: *A Concordance to the Plays of W. B. Yeats* (both published Ithaca, N.Y.: Cornell University Press, 1963, 1972); Edward O'Shea: *A Descriptive Catalog of W. B. Yeats's Library* (New York: Garland, 1985); and Conrad A. Balliet's somewhat preliminary *W. B. Yeats: A Census of the Manuscripts* (New York: Garland, 1990).

A definitive biography is being undertaken by R. F. Foster; at present Joseph Hone's *W. B. Yeats 1865–1939* (London: Macmillan, 1942, i.e., 1943) and Richard Ellmann's *Yeats: The Man and the Masks,* revised ed. (Oxford: Oxford University Press, 1979) can still be read with profit. Recent biographies include Frank Tuohy: *Yeats* (London: Macmillan, 1976); a short popular account by Augustine Martin: *W. B. Yeats* (Dublin: Gill & Macmillan, 1983); and a more extensive work by A. Norman Jeffares: *W. B. Yeats: A New Biography* (London: Hutchinson, 1988). William M. Murphy was written on *The Yeats Family and the Pollexfens of Sligo* (Dublin: Dolmen, 1977), and the massive biography of Yeats's father, *Prodigal Father: The Life of John Butler Yeats* (Ithaca, N.Y.: Cornell University Press, 1978), and also *Family Secrets: William Butler Yeats and His Relatives* (Dublin: Gill & Macmillan, 1995). One of Yeats's most important friends is the subject of John Harwood's *Olivia Shakespear and W. B. Yeats: After Long Silence* (London: Macmillan, 1989). Ann Saddlemyer is at work on the authorized biography of Mrs. W. B. Yeats. Micheal Mac Liammoir and Eavan Boland collaborated on the richly illustrated *W. B. Yeats and His World* (London: Thames & Hudson, 1971). On the poet's background in the art world, see *The World of W. B. Yeats,* Robin Skelton & Ann Saddlemyer, eds. (Dublin: Dolmen, 1965); for Sligo, see Shellah Kirby: *The Yeats Country,* revised ed. (Dublin: Dolmen, 1977); for the Dublin scene, Richard M. Kain: *Dublin in the Age of W. B. Yeats and James Joyce* (Norman: University of Oklahoma Press, 1962). Biographical material is also contained in *W. B. Yeats: Interviews and Recollections,* E. H. Mikhail, ed. (London: Macmillan, 1976); and the late Karin Strand's Ph.D. thesis, "W. B. Yeats' American Lecture Tours" (Northwestern University, 1978), which deserves publication.

Yeats's painstaking craftsmanship is revealed in studies of manuscript drafts by Curtis Bradford, *Yeats at Work* (Carbondale: Southern Illinois University Press, 1965), and by Jon Stallworthy, *Between the Lines: Yeats's Poetry in the Making* and *Vision and Revision in Yeats's Last Poems* (both London: Oxford University Press, 1963, 1969). Recently the manuscript versions of several texts have been published: they include *Druid Craft: The Writing of "The Shadowy Waters,"*

Michael J. Sidnell et al., eds. (Amherst: University of Massachusetts Press, 1971); *The Writing of "The Player Queen,"* Curtis Bradford, ed. (DeKalb: Northern Illinois University Press, 1977); *The Writing of "Sophocles' King Oedipus,"* David R. Clark & James B. McGuire, eds. (Philadelphia: American Philosophical Society, 1989); *The Secret Rose: A Variorum Edition,* revised ed., Warwick Gould et al., eds. (London: Macmillan, 1992). In the Cornell Yeats series of manuscript reproductions (Ithaca, N.Y.: Cornell University Press), the following titles are available: *The Death of Cuchulain,* Philip L. Marcus, ed. (1982); *Purgatory,* Sandra F. Siegel, ed. (1986); *The Early Poetry,* George Bornstein, ed. (1987–1994, 2 vols.); *The Herne's Egg,* Alison Armstrong, ed. (1993); *The Wind among the Reeds,* Carolyn Holdsworth, ed. (1993); *The Hour-Glass,* Catherine Phillips, ed. (1994); and *Michael Robartes and the Dancer,* Thomas Parkinson, ed. (1994). Yeats's and Mrs. Yeats's automatic scripts and notebooks that led to the writing of *A Vision* have been published as *Yeats's "Vision" Papers,* George Mills Harper, general ed. (London: Macmillan/Iowa City: University of Iowa Press, 1992, 3 vols.); these volumes should be used in conjunction with Harper's *The Making of Yeats's "A Vision"* (London: Macmillan, 1986).

Good introductions to Yeats's work are Balachandra Rajan: *W. B. Yeats: A Critical Introduction.* (London: Hutchinson, 1965); Denis Donoghue: *Yeats* (London: Fontana/Collins, 1971); and Richard F. Peterson: *William Butler Yeats* (Boston: Twayne, 1982). Of the many general studies, the following have proved valuable: Louis MacNeice: *The Poetry of W. B. Yeats* (London: Oxford University Press, 1941; Giorgio Melchiori: *The Whole Mystery of Art: Pattern into Poetry in the Work of W. B. Yeats* (London: Routledge & Kegan Paul, 1960); Richard Ellmann: *The Identity of Yeats,* revised ed. (New York: Oxford University Press, 1964); T. R. Henn: *The Lonely Tower: Studies in the Poetry of W. B. Yeats,* revised ed. (London: Methuen, 1965); *An Honoured Guest: New Essays on W. B. Yeats,* Denis Donoghue & J. R. Mulryne, eds. (London: Arnold, 1965); Harold Bloom: *Yeats* (New York: Oxford University Press, 1970); Douglas N. Archibald: *Yeats* (Syracuse, N.Y.: Syracuse University Press, 1983); Edward Engelberg: *The Vast Design: Patterns in W. B. Yeats's Aesthetic,* revised ed. (Washington, D.C.: Catholic University of America Press, 1988); Phillip L. Marcus: *Yeats and Artistic Power* (London: Macmillan, 1992). Of the several periodicals devoted exclusively to Yeats, two current annuals are the most important: *Yeats Annual,* Warwick Gould, present editor (London: Macmillan, 1982ff.), and *Yeats: An Annual of Critical and Textual Studies,* Richard J. Finneran, ed. (1983ff., presently published Ann Arbor: University of Michigan Press).

Noteworthy specialized studies include Frank Kermode: *Romantic Image* (London: Routledge & Kegan Paul, 1957); two books on Yeats and Neoplatonism by F.A.C. Wilson: *W. B. Yeats and Tradition* and *Yeats's Iconography* (both London: Gollancz, 1958, 1960); Donald T. Torchiana: *W. B. Yeats and Georgian Ireland* (Evanston, Ill.: Northwestern University Press, 1966); Mary Helen Thuente: *W. B. Yeats and Irish Folklore* (Dublin: Gill & Macmillan, 1981); Elizabeth B. Loizeaux: *Yeats and the Visual Arts* (New Brunswick, N.J.: Rutgers University Press, 1986); Patrick J. Keane: *Yeats's Interactions with Tradition* (Columbia: University of Missouri Press, 1987); Phillip L. Marcus: *Yeats and the Beginning of the Irish Renaissance,* 2d ed. (Syracuse, N.Y.: Syracuse University Press, 1987); Frank Kinahan: *Yeats, Folklore, and Occultism: Contexts of the Early Work and Thought* (Boston: Unwin Hyman, 1988); Thomas R. Whitaker: *Swan and Shadow: Yeats's Dialogue with History,* 2d ed. (Washington, D.C.: Catholic University of America Press, 1989); Joann Gardner: *Yeats and the Rhymers' Club: A Nineties' Perspective* (New York: Lang, 1989); Brian Arkins: *Builders of My Soul: Greek and Roman Themes in Yeats* (Gerrards Cross: Colin Smythe, 1990). Postmodernism and poststructuralism have finally caught up with Yeats in *Yeats and Postmodernism,* Leonard Orr, ed. (Syracuse, N.Y.: Syracuse University Press, 1991).

There are many studies of influences and contacts, of which the following are important: Hazard Adams: *Blake and Yeats: The Contrary Vision* (Ithaca, N.Y.: Cornell University Press, 1955); George Bornstein: *Yeats and Shelley* (Chicago: University of Chicago Press, 1970); Rupin W. Desai: *Yeats's Shakespeare* (Evanston, Ill.: Northwestern University Press, 1971); Terence Diggory: *Yeats and American Poetry: The Tradition of the Self.* Princeton, N.J.: Princeton University Press, 1983); Peter Kuch: *Yeats and A.E.: "The Antagonism That Unites Dear Friends"* (Gerrards Cross: Colin Smythe, 1986); James Longenbach: *Stone Cottage: Pound, Yeats, and Modernism* (New York:

Oxford University Press, 1988); Ravindran Sankaran: *W. B. Yeats and Indian Tradition* (Delhi: Konark, 1990); Masaru Sekine & Christopher Murray: *Yeats and the Noh: A Comparative Study* (Gerrards Cross: Colin Smythe, 1990); Wayne K. Chapman: *Yeats and English Renaissance Literature* (London: Macmillan, 1991); *Learning the Trade: Essays on W. B. Yeats and Contemporary Poetry,* Deborah Fleming, ed. (West Cornwall, Conn.: Locust Hill, 1993); Peter Th. M. G. Liebregts: *Centaurs in the Twilight: W. B. Yeats's Use of the Classical Tradition* (Amsterdam: Rodopi, 1993).

Basic to the study of Yeats's poetry is A. Norman Jeffares's *A New Commentary on the Poems of W. B. Yeats* (London: Macmillan, 1984). Other useful monographs are Donald A. Stauffer: *The Golden Nightingale: Essays on Some Principles of Poetry in the Lyrics of William Butler Yeats* (New York: Macmillan, 1949); John Unterecker: *A Reader's Guide to William Butler Yeats* (New York: Noonday, 1959; two books by Thomas F. Parkinson of 1961 and 1964, republished in one: *W. B. Yeats Self-Critic: A Study of His Early Verse, and The Later Poetry* (Berkeley: University of California Press, 1971); B. L. Reid: *William Butler Yeats: The Lyric of Tragedy* (Norman: University of Oklahoma Press, 1961); Robert Beum: *The Poetic Art of W. B. Yeats* (New York: Ungar, 1969); Colin Meir: *The Ballads and Songs of W. B. Yeats: The Anglo-Irish Heritage in Subject and Style* (London: Macmillan, 1974); David R. Clark: *Yeats at Songs and Choruses* (Amherst: University of Massachusetts Press, 1983); Hazard Adams: *The Book of Yeats's Poems* (Tallahassee: Florida State University Press, 1990); Jahan Ramazani: *Yeats and the Poetry of Death: Elegy, Self-Elegy, and the Sublime* (New Haven, Conn.: Yale University Press, 1990); M. L. Rosenthal: *Running to Paradise: Yeats's Poetic Art,* which also discusses most of the plays (New York: Oxford University Press, 1994); Feminist and gender studies are represented by Elizabeth Butler Cullingford: *Gender and History in Yeats's Love Poetry* (Cambridge: Cambridge University Press, 1993); deconstructionist approaches by Edward Larrissy: *Yeats the Poet: The Measures of Difference* (Hemel Hempstead: Harvester Wheatsheaf, 1994).

Studies of Yeats's plays may begin with A. Norman Jeffares and A. S. Knowland: *A Commentary on the Collected Plays of W. B. Yeats* (London: Macmillan, 1975). The pioneer study was Peter Ure's *Yeats the Playwright: A Commentary on Character and Design in the Major Plays* (London: Routledge & Kegan Paul, 1963). Subsequent publications include Leonard E. Nathan: *The Tragic Drama of William Butler Yeats* (New York: Columbia University Press, 1965); John Rees Moore: *Masks of Love and Death: Yeats as Dramatist* (Ithaca, N.Y.: Cornell University Press, 1971); James W. Flannery: *W. B. Yeats and the Idea of a Theatre: The Early Abbey Theatre in Theory and Practice* (New Haven, Conn.: Yale University Press, 1976); Richard Taylor: *The Drama of W. B. Yeats: Irish Myth and the Japanese No* (New Haven, Conn.: Yale University Press, 1976); and *A Reader's Guide to the Plays of W. B. Yeats* (London: Macmillan, 1984); Liam Miller: *The Noble Drama of W. B. Yeats* (Dublin: Dolmen, 1977); Andrew Parkin: *The Dramatic Imagination of W. B. Yeats* (Dublin: Gill & Macmillan, 1978); Katharine Worth: *The Irish Drama of Europe from Yeats to Beckett* (London: Athlone, 1978); Anthony Bradley: *William Butler Yeats* (New York: Ungar, 1979); Karen Dorn: *Players and Painted Stage: The Theatre of W. B. Yeats* (Brighton: Harvester, 1984); David R. Clark: *W. B. Yeats and the Theatre of Desolate Reality,* expanded ed. (Washington, D.C.: Catholic University of America Press, 1993).

Serious discussions of Yeats's politics were sparked by Conor Cruise O'Brien's revisionist essay "Passion and Cunning: An Essay on the Politics of W. B. Yeats," in *Excited Reverie: A Centenary Tribute to William Butler Yeats,* A. Norman Jeffares & K. G. W. Cross, eds. (London: Macmillan, 1965). O'Brien's charge that Yeats was a fascist of sorts was discussed and rebutted by Elizabeth Cullingford: *Yeats, Ireland, and Fascism* (London: Macmillan, 1981), and by Grattan Freyer: *W. B. Yeats and the Anti-Democratic Tradition* (Dublin: Gill & Macmillan, 1981). Further accounts of Yeats's politics can be found in Bernard G. Krimm's *W. B. Yeats and the Emergence of the Irish Free State 1918–1939* (Troy, N.Y.: Whitston, 1981); and Paul Scott Stanfield's *Yeats and Politics in the 1930s* (London: Macmillan, 1988).

The prose fiction is ably dealt with in William H. O'Donnell's *A Guide to the Prose Fiction of W. B. Yeats* (Ann Arbor, Mich.: UMI Research, 1983). Treatments of the autobiographical writings include Joseph Ronsley: *Yeats's Autobiography: Life as Symbolic Pattern* (Cambridge: Harvard

University Press, 1968); Daniel T. O'Hara: *Tragic Knowledge: Yeats's Autobiography and Hermeneutics* (New York: Columbia University Press, 1981); Shirley C. Neuman: *Yeats's Autobiographical Prose* (Mountrath, Portlaoise: Dolmen, 1982); and David G. Wright: *Yeats's Myth of Self: The Autobiographical Prose* (Dublin: Gill & Macmillan, 1987). Yeats's occult interests are the subject of George Mills Harper: *Yeats's Golden Dawn* (London: Macmillan, 1974); *Yeats and the Occult,* George Mills Harper, ed. (Toronto: Macmillan, 1975); James Olney: *The Rhizome and the Flower: The Perennial Philosophy—Yeats and Jung* (Berkeley: University of California Press, 1980); Graham Hough: *The Mystery Religion of W. B. Yeats* (Brighton: Harvester, 1984); and, for the initiated, Kathleen Raine: *Yeats the Initiate: Essays on Certain Themes in the Work of W. B. Yeats* (Mountrath, Portlaoise: Dolmen/London: Allen & Unwin, 1986).

RICHARD M. KAIN,
revised and expanded by K.P.S. JOCHUM

YOUNG, AUGUSTUS (1943–   ), poet. Young is the pseudonym of James Hogan, who was born in Cork and now lives in London. He has not published much, but some of his satiric and sardonic poems stick in the mind. His best work is witty, fluent, and usually so sharply individual in its diction that one is nonplussed at the occasional dreadful line, such as one about "pubescent grass" being scratched from the "groin of the skull." Young's chief failure is an utter lack of poetic technique to focus his wit, but his cleverness of conception and terseness of language can sometimes, as in "Inside Story" or "The Advice of an Efficiency Expert," overcome his technical deficiencies. His translations from the Irish do, however, rise to some formal strength. Also, the excerpt from "Mr. Thackeray on Cork," included in Sean Dunne's* *Poets of Munster* anthology, has more than occasionally some tight and witty couplets.

WORKS: *Survival.* Dublin: New Writers', 1969; *On Loaning Hill.* Dublin: New Writers', 1972; *Dánta Grádha: Love Poems from the Irish.* London: Menard Southampton: Advent Books, 1975/ 2d ed., 1980; *Rosemaries.* 1976. (Poetry pamphlet); *Tapestry of Animals.* [London: Menard, 1977]. (Poetry pamphlet); *The Credit: A Comedy of Empeiria.* London: Menard, 1980; *"Adaptations."* Dublin: Hard Pressed Poetry, 1989. (Poetry pamphlet).

YOUNG, ELLA (1865–1951), poet and author of children's stories. Young, whom AE* once called "a druidess reincarnated," was born to a staunch Presbyterian family in County Antrim in 1865. Her family moved to Rathmines in 1880, and Young took her university degree in political science and law in Dublin. Like many other young scholars of her day, Young developed a consuming interest in Ireland's past. While still a college student, she joined the Hermetical Society, whose founder, AE, urged her to pursue her interest in fairy lore. Her friends Standish James and Margaret O'Grady* introduced her to the west of Ireland, where she lived among the peasants for many months over a period of years.

Young's political sympathies were decidedly Republican. She wrote frequently for *Sinn Féin* and in 1912, rented Temple Hill, a farmhouse in Wicklow from which she ran guns and ammunition for the members of the Irish Republican Army. Although she spent most of World War I in Achill, she returned to Dublin in 1916 and resumed her gun-running from a rented room in a staunchly respectable pro-British house. At the time of the Rising, Young was blacklisted and fled to Connemara where she heard of the executions of many of her friends. She returned to Dublin in 1919 and remained through the Civil War.

In 1925, Young left for the United States on a lecturer's passport. Lecturing in the East, she gradually worked her way across the country to California where she finally settled near Berkeley, accepted a modest position at the University of California at Los Angeles, and studied Mexican and Indian folklore. She led a quiet life; she wrote, gardened, tended her cats until her death in 1951.

Although Young has published several collections of poetry, she is known primarily as a writer of children's stories, based on Celtic myth and legend, in which she often ranks with James Stephens.* *The Coming of Lugh* (1909) was quickly followed by *Celtic Wonder-Tales* (1910), a collection of fourteen stories chosen at random out of Irish mythology and ranging from tales of the fantastic Gobhaun Saor to the Etain legend. Even though these tales charm, they are somewhat restricted by Young's worshipful adherence to the traditional subject matter—something that also mars her collection of Fenian tales, *The Tangle-Coated Horse* (1929). When she used the traditional material to launch her imagination, she was at her best, as, for example, in *The Wonder-Smith and His Son* (1927). Dealing with a series of tales less circumscribed by tradition, it records the adventures of Goibniu, originally a kind of Irish Hephaestus, who came to earth as an architect, exchanged a daughter for a son, and through various wiles escaped the evil Formorian Balor. Finally, in her finest work, *The Unicorn with Silver Shoes* (1932), she takes great liberties with figures out of Celtic myth in telling of the adventures of the son of Balor, a unicorn who is calmed only by listening to epic poetry, a djinn who ends up in a Dublin zoo, and a mischievous Pooka. In the gentle irony which gives this book a refreshing freedom from sentimentality, *The Unicorn with Silver Shoes* remains one of the outstanding examples of the lyrical cadences of the Irish imagination.

M. KELLY LYNCH

WORKS: *Poems.* Tower Press Booklet No. 4. Dublin: Maunsel, 1906; *The Coming of Lugh.* Dublin: Maunsel, 1909. (Tales); *Celtic Wonder-Tales.* Dublin: Maunsel, 1910; *The Rose of Heaven.* Dublin: Colm O'Loughlin, 1918. (Poems); *The Weird of Fionavar.* Dublin: Talbot, 1922. (Poems); *The Wonder-Smith and His Son.* New York: Longmans, 1927. (Tales); *The Tangle-Coated Horse.* Dublin: Maunsel, 1929. (Tales); *The Unicorn with Silver Shoes.* New York: Longmans, 1932. (Tales); *Flowering Dusk.* New York: Longmans, 1945. (Memoirs); *Seed of the Pomegranite.* Oceano (9), 1949. (Poems privately printed in an edition of twenty copies); *Smoke of Myrrh.* Oceano (?), 1950. (Poems privately printed in an edition of twenty-five copies).

Z

ZOZIMUS (ca. 1794–1846), ballad singer and composer. Zozimus was the public name of Michael Moran. Sometimes called ''the Last Gleeman,'' he was a composer, singer, and reciter of ballads, street songs, ranns, and quips. Boylan notes: ''He became known as 'Zozimus' owing to his recitation of the history of St. Mary of Egypt. In this metrical tale written by Dr. Coyle, Bishop of Raphoe, Mary is found, after fifty years of penance in the desert, by the Blessed Zozimus.'' He was born in the Liberties of Dublin in about 1794, was blind almost from birth, and in his picturesque and tattered dress became a familiar character in a city already rich in that commodity. In *The Celtic Twilight,* W. B. Yeats* remarks that Zozimus' poem ''Moses'' went a little nearer poetry than much of his work, yet ''without going very near.'' He died on April 3, 1846.

WORKS: Gulielmus Dubliniensis Humoriensis. *Memoir of the Great Original Zozimus (Michael Moran), the Celebrated Street Rhymer and Reciter, with His Songs, Sayings and Recitations.* Dublin: Carraig Books, 1976. Reprint.

CHRONOLOGY

		Political	Literary
A.D.	432	St. Patrick's mission to Ireland	
	795	Viking raids on Ireland	
ca.	800		Book of Kells
	841	Vikings found city of Dublin	
	1014	Battle of Clontarf and death of Brian Boru	
	1170	Landing of Richard, earl of Pembroke ("Strongbow")	
	1172	The pope grants Ireland to Henry II	
	1550		First Irish printing press set up in Dublin by Humphrey Powell
	1649	Shane O'Neill dies; Cromwell comes to Ireland; massacres at Drogheda and Wexford	
	1652		Nahum Tate born
	1667		Jonathan Swift born
	1670		William Congreve born
	1672		Richard Steele born
	1677		George Farquhar born
	1681	Oliver Plunkett executed	
	1689	Siege of Londonderry	
	1690	William III wins Battle of the Boyne	
	1691	Treaty of Limerick	
	1694		Charles Macklin born
	1695	Beginning of Penal Laws	Congreve's *Love for Love*
	1700		Congreve's *The Way of the World*

	Political	*Literary*
1706		Farquhar's *The Recruiting Officer*
1707		Farquhar's *The Beaux Stratagem;* Farquhar dies
1709		Berkeley's *New Theory of Vision*
1715		Nahum Tate dies
1720	Act declares British Parliament to legislate for Ireland	
1724		Swift's *Drapier's Letters*
1726		Swift's *Gulliver's Travels*
1728		Oliver Goldsmith born
1729		Richard Steele dies; William Congreve dies; Swift's *A Modest Proposal*
1738		Turlough O'Carolan dies
1745		Jonathan Swift dies
1751		Richard Brinsley Sheridan born
1756		Burke's *The Sublime and the Beautiful*
1760		Arthur Murphy's *The Way to Keep Him;* MacPherson's *Ossian*
1766		Goldsmith's *The Vicar of Wakefield*
1767		Maria Edgeworth born
1770		Goldsmith's *The Deserted Village*
1773		Goldsmith's *She Stoops to Conquer*
1774		Goldsmith dies
1775		Sheridan's *The Rivals*
1776	American Declaration of Independence	
1777		Sheridan's *The School for Scandal*
1779		Thomas Moore born
1782	Grattan's Parliament	Charles Robert Maturin born
1784	Eoghan Ruadh O'Suilleabháin dies	
1785	Royal Irish Academy founded	
1789	French Revolution	Charlotte Brooke's *Reliques of Irish Poetry*
1790		Burke's *Reflections on the French Revolution*
1791	United Irishmen formed	
1792	Catholic Relief Act eases the Penal Laws	
1794		William Carleton born
1795	Orange Order founded in Armagh; Maynooth founded	
1796	Wolfe Tone's attempted invasion	

	Political	*Literary*
1797		Charles Macklin dies
1798	United Irishmen's Rising; Wolfe Tone's suicide	John Banim born
1800	Act of Union becomes law; Irish Parliament dissolved	Edgeworth's *Castle Rackrent*
1803	Emmet's Rising	James Clarence Mangan born
1805		Brian Merriman dies
1806		Charles Lever born; Lady Morgan's *The Wild Irish Girl*
1808		Moore's *Irish Melodies*
1812		Edgeworth's *The Absentee*
1814		Thomas Davis born; Joseph Sheridan LeFanu born
1815	Battle of Waterloo	
1816		Richard Brinsley Sheridan dies; Maturin's *Bertram*
1817		Moore's *Lalla Rookh;* Edgeworth's *Ormond*
1820	Death of Henry Grattan	Maturin's *Melmoth the Wanderer*
1821		Theatre Royal, Dublin, opens
1823	Daniel O'Connell forms the Catholic Association	
1824		William Allingham born; Charles Robert Maturin dies
1825		Banims' *Tales of the O'Hara Family*
1826		Banims' *The Boyne Water*
1828	O'Connell wins Clare by-election	Charles J. Kickham born
1829	Catholic emancipation	Griffin's *The Collegians*
1830		Carleton's *Traits and Stories of the Irish Peasantry*
1835		The poet Raftery dies
1836		Mahony's *Reliques of Father Prout*
1837	Victoria ascends throne	Lover's *Handy Andy*
1839		John Butler Yeats born; Lever's *Harry Lorrequer;* Carleton's *Fardorougha the Miser*
1840	O'Connell founds National Repeal Association	
1841		Boucicault's *London Assurance;* Lever's *Charles O'Malley*
1842	*The Nation* founded	John Banim dies
1843	Repeal meeting banned at Clontarf	Davis et al., *The Spirit of the Nation*

	Political	**Literary**
1845	First of the potato famines	Thomas Davis dies
1846		Standish O'Grady born; Davis' *Collected Poems*
1847	Daniel O'Connell dies	Carleton's *The Black Prophet*
1848	Smith O'Brien's rebellion	O'Donovan's *Annals of the Four Masters*
1849		Maria Edgeworth dies; James Clarence Mangan dies
1850		Allingham's *Poems*
1852		Thomas Moore dies; George Moore born; Lady Gregory born
1854	Crimean War; Catholic University of Ireland founded	Mitchel's *Jail Journal*
1856		Oscar Wilde born; George Bernard Shaw born
1858	Fenian movement founded	Edith Somerville born
1860		Boucicault's *The Colleen Bawn;* Amanda McKittrick Ros born
1861	American Civil War	Falconer's *Peep o' Day;* O'Curry's *Manuscript Materials of Ancient Irish History*
1862		Violet Martin ("Martin Ross") born
1863		LeFanu's *The House by the Churchyard*
1864		Allingham's *Laurence Bloomfield;* Boucicault's *Arrah na Pogue;* LeFanu's *Uncle Silas*
1865	American Civil War ends	Ferguson's *Lays of the Western Gael;* W. B. Yeats born; J. O. Hannay ("George A. Birmingham") born
1867	Fenian rebellion; Manchester Martyrs executed	George Russell ("AE") born
1869	Church of Ireland disestablished	William Carleton dies; James Connolly born
1870	Gladstone's First Land Act; Butt forms Home Government Association	
1871		J. M. Synge born; Jack B. Yeats born
1872		LeFanu's *In a Glass Darkly;* Ferguson's *Congal;* Charles Lever dies
1874		Conal O'Riordan born
1875		Boucicault's *The Shaughraun*
1876		Forrest Reid born
1877	Parnell assumes leadership of the Irish party	

Political	Literary
	Political — *Literary*

	Political	*Literary*
1878		O'Grady's *Bardic History of Ireland;* Daniel Corkery born; Lord Dunsany born; Oliver Gogarty born
1879	Davitt founds Land League; Land War begins; Isaac Butt dies	Kickham's *Knocknagow;* Patrick Pearse born; J. S. Starkey ("Seumas O'Sullivan") born; Maurice Walsh born
1880	Parnell elected leader of Irish Parliamentary Party; boycotting of Captain Boycott; Royal University of Ireland founded	O'Grady's *History of Ireland: Cuchulain and His Contemporaries;* Sean O'Casey born
1881	Gladstone's second Land Act; Parnell imprisoned	Padraic Colum born
1882	Lord Frederick Cavendish assassinated; de Valera born; University College, Dublin, founded	Charles J. Kickham dies; James Joyce born; James Stephens born
1883		St. John Ervine born
1884	Gaelic Athletic Association founded	George Moore's *A Modern Lover*
1885		George Moore's *A Mummer's Wife*
1886	Gladstone's first Home Rule Bill defeated	George Moore's *A Drama in Muslin;* Lennox Robinson born; George Shiels born
1887	National Library of Ireland founded	
1888		*Poems and Ballads of Young Ireland*
1889		Yeats' *The Wanderings of Oisin*
1890	Parnell–O'Shea divorce case; Parnell loses control of the Irish party	Boucicault dies
1891	Parnell dies	Wilde's *The Picture of Dorian Gray*
1892		Yeats' *The Countess Cathleen*
1893	Gladstone's second Home Rule Bill defeated; Gaelic League founded	Hyde's *Love Songs of Connacht;* Peadar O'Donnell born; Eimar O'Duffy born
1894		George Moore's *Esther Waters;* Somerville and Ross's *The Real Charlotte;* Yeats' *The Land of Heart's Desire*
1895		Wilde's *The Importance of Being Earnest*
1896		Austin Clarke born
1897		AE's *The Earth Breath;* Ferguson's *Lays of the Red Branch;* Ros's *Irene Iddlesleigh;* Sigerson's *Bards of the Gael and Gall;* Stoker's *Dracula;* Voynich's *The Gadfly*
1898		Shaw's *Plays, Pleasant and Unpleasant*

	Political	*Literary*
1899	Griffith founds *The United Irishman*	Hyde's *A Literary History of Ireland;* Martyn's *The Heather Field;* Somerville and Ross's *Some Experiences of an Irish R. M.;* Yeats' *Countess Cathleen* and *The Wind among the Reeds;* first season of Irish Literary Theatre
1900	Queen Victoria autographs the Book of Kells; Moran founds *The Leader*	Oscar Wilde dies; Paul Vincent Carroll born; Sean O'Faolain born
1901	Queen Victoria dies	Denis Johnston born
1902		AE's *Deirdre;* Lady Gregory's *Cuchulain of Muirthemne;* Francis Stuart born; Cuala Press founded
1903		George Moore's *The Untilled Field;* Yeats' *Ideas of Good and Evil;* Teresa Deevy born; Frank O'Connor born
1904	Griffith's *The Resurrection of Hungary*	Birmingham's *The Seething Pot;* Lady Gregory's *Spreading the News;* Synge's *Riders to the Sea;* Yeats' *The King's Threshold* and *On Baile's Strand;* Abbey Theatre opens; Ulster Literary Theatre founded; Patrick Kavanagh born
1905	Griffith founds Sinn Fein movement	Boyle's *The Building Fund;* Colum's *The Land;* George Moore's *The Lake;* Synge's *The Well of the Saints;* Brian Coffey born; Padraic Fallon born
1906		Joseph Campbell's *The Rush Light;* Seumas O'Kelly's *The Shuiler's Child;* Samuel Beckett born
1907		Abbey Theatre riots over Synge's *The Playboy of the Western World;* Birmingham's *The Northern Iron;* Colum's *Wild Earth;* Fitzmaurice's *The Country Dressmaker;* Joyce's *Chamber Music;* Louis MacNeice born
1908	Larkin forms Irish Transport & General Workers' Union; National University established	Birmingham's *Spanish Gold;* Doyle's *Ballygullion;* Dunsany's *The Sword of Welleran;* Fitzmaurice's *The Pie-dish;* Lady Gregory's *Workhouse Ward;* Mayne's *The Drone;* O'Riordan's *The Piper;* Somerville and Ross's *Further Experiences of an Irish R.M.;* Yeats' *Collected Works*
1909		Birmingham's *The Search Party;* Dunsany's *The Glittering Gate;* J. M. Synge dies; Bryan MacMahon born; W. R. Rodgers born; first production of the Cork Dramatic Society

	Political	*Literary*
1910		Childers' *The Riddle of the Sands;* Ervine's *Mixed Marriage;* Murray's *Birthright;* Ray's *The Casting Out of Martin Whelan;* Synge's *Deirdre of the Sorrows* and *Collected Works;* Yeats' *The Green Helmet*
1911		George Moore's first part of *Hail and Farewell*
1912	Third Home Rule bill; Ulster Covenant signed; Larkin forms Irish Labour party	Murray's *Maurice Harte;* O'Kelly's *Meadowsweet;* Stephens' *The Crock of Gold;* Mary Lavin born; Donagh MacDonagh born; Brian O'Nolan ("Flann O'Brien") born; Terence deVere White born
1913	Formation of Ulster Volunteers, Irish Volunteers, and Irish Citizen Army; the "Great Lockout" begins	AE's *Collected Poems;* Fitzmaurice's *The Magic Glasses*
1914	Outbreak of World War I; Curragh Mutiny; gun-running at Howth; Government of Ireland Act suspended	Dunsany's *Five Plays;* Ervine's *John Ferguson;* Fitzmaurice's *Five Plays;* Joyce's *Dubliners;* Yeats' *Responsibilities*
1915		AE's *Imaginations and Reveries;* MacGill's *The Rat Pit;* Somerville and Ross's *In Mr. Knox's Country;* Martin Ross dies
1916	The Easter Rising	Joyce's *A Portrait of the Artist as a Young Man;* Patrick Pearse, James Connolly, Thomas MacDonagh, and Joseph Mary Plunkett executed; Sheehy-Skeffington executed; Casement executed
1917	The Russian Revolution	Clarke's *The Vengeance of Fionn;* Corkery's *The Threshold of Quiet;* O'Kelly's *Waysiders;* Pearse's *Collected Works;* Yeats' *The Wild Swans at Coole*
1918	World War I ends; Sinn Féin wins majority of Irish seats in Westminster	Brinsley MacNamara's *The Valley of the Squinting Windows;* O'Duffy's *The Wasted Island;* Stephens' *Reincarnations*
1919	First Dail meets in Dublin; de Valera becomes president; Anglo-Irish War begins	Brinsley MacNamara's *The Clanking of Chains;* Benedict Kiely born
1920		Robinson's *The Whiteheaded Boy;* Yeats's *Michael Robartes and the Dancer;* Iris Murdoch born; James Plunkett born; W. J. White born
1921	Anglo-Irish War ends, and Anglo-Irish Treaty signed	Roy McFadden born; Brian Moore born

	Political	*Literary*
1922	Treaty approved by the Dail; establishment of Irish Free State; Civil War begins; deaths of Griffith and Collins	Reid's *Pender among the Residents;* Joyce's *Ulysses;* Yeats' *Later Poems;* the House of Maunsel ceases publication
1923	Civil War ends; Ireland joins League of Nations	O'Casey's *The Shadow of a Gunman;* Yeats receives Nobel Prize; AE founds *The Irish Statesman;* O'Sullivan founds *The Dublin Magazine;* Brendan Behan born
1924	*Freeman's Journal* ceases	Gogarty's *An Offering of Swans;* Murray's *Autumn Fire;* O'Casey's *Juno and the Paycock;* O'Flaherty's *Spring Sowing*
1925	Border between North and South confirmed	Higgins' *Island Blood;* O'Flaherty's *The Informer;* Somerville's *The Big House at Inver;* Yeats' *A Vision;* Shaw receives Nobel Prize
1926	de Valera founds Fianna Fail; Radio Éireann begins	Riots in the Abbey Theatre over O'Casey's *The Plough and the Stars;* O'Flaherty's *Mr. Gilhooley;* Walsh's *The Key above the Door;* Yeats' *Autobiographies*
1927	de Valera and Fianna Fail enter the Dail; Kevin O'Higgins assassinated	O'Riordan's *Soldier Born;* Aidan Higgins born; Richard Murphy born
1928		O'Casey's *The Silver Tassie;* O'Donnell's *Islanders;* O'Riordan's *Soldier of Waterloo;* Yeats' *The Tower;* Padraic O'Conaire dies; Standish O'Grady dies; Thomas Kinsella born; John B. Keane born; Hugh Leonard born; William Trevor born; the Gate Theatre opens
1929	Censorship of Publication Act	Johnston's *The Old Lady Says "No!";* O'Flaherty's *The Mountain Tavern;* Brian Friel born; John Montague born
1930		Eugene McCabe born
1931	*The Irish Press* begins	Johnston's *The Moon in the Yellow River;* Manning's *Youth's the Season . . .?;* Kate O'Brien's *Without My Cloak;* O'Connor's *Guests of the Nation;* Reid's *Uncle Stephen;* Strong's *The Garden*
1932	de Valera forms Fianna Fail government	Clarke's *The Bright Temptation;* Colum's *Collected Poems;* O'Connor's *The Saint and Mary Kate;* O'Faolain's *Midsummer Night's Madness;* O'Flaherty's *Skerritt;* Lady Gregory dies; Edna O'Brien born
1933		Strong's *Sea Wall;* George Moore dies

	Political	Literary
1934		Lynch's *The Turf Cutter's Donkey;* O'Faolain's *A Nest of Simple Folk;* Joseph O'Neill's *Wind from the North*
1935		Deevy's *Katie Roche* and *The King of Spain's Daughter;* Yeats' *A Full Moon in March;* Eimar O'Duffy dies; John MacGahern born
1936	IRA declared illegal	Clarke's *The Singing Men at Cashel;* Kavanagh's *Ploughman;* Francis MacManus' *Candle for the Proud;* O'Connor's *Bones of Contention;* O'Faolain's *Bird Alone;* Sayers' *Peig;* Thomas Murphy born
1937	New constitution for the Irish Free State; Douglas Hyde the first president	Carroll's *Shadow and Substance;* Devlin's *Intercessions;* Gogarty's *As I Was Going Down Sackville Street;* O'Flaherty's *Famine;* Reid's *Peter Waring*
1938		Beckett's *Murphy;* Bowen's *The Death of the Heart;* Kavanagh's *The Green Fool;* O'Riordan's *Soldier's End;* Yeats' *Purgatory*
1939	World War II begins; Ireland remains neutral	Carroll's *The White Steed;* Joyce's *Finnegans Wake;* MacNeice's *Autumn Journal;* Francis MacManus' *Men Withering;* Flann O'Brien's *At Swim-Two-Birds;* O'Casey's *I Knock at the Door;* W. B. Yeats dies; Amanda McKittrick Ros dies; Seamus Heaney born
1940	Battle of Britain	Higgins' *The Dark Breed;* O'Casey's *Purple Dust;* O'Sullivan's *Collected Poems;* Shiels's *The Rugged Path;* Wall's *Alarm among the Clerks;* Yeats' *Last Poems and Plays;* O'Faolain founds *The Bell*
1941	Pearl Harbor	Francis MacManus' *Flow on Lovely River;* Myles na Copaleen's *An Beal Bocht;* Kate O'Brien's *The Land of Spices;* Wall's *The Lady in the Twilight;* James Joyce dies; F. R. Higgins dies
1942		Kavanagh's *The Great Hunger;* Lavin's *Tales from Bective Bridge*
1943		O'Faolain's *The Great O'Neill;* O'Casey's *Red Roses for Me*
1944	D-Day	Laverty's *No More than Human;* O'Connor's *Crab Apple Jelly;* Joseph Campbell dies; Eavan Boland born
1945	End of World War II	Bowen's *The Demon Lover*

Political	*Literary*
1946	Kiely's *Land Without Stars;* Mac Liammóir's *All for Hecuba;* Molloy's *The Visiting House;* Kate O'Brien's *That Lady;* Wall's *The Unfortunate Fursey*
1947	Kavanagh's *A Soul for Sale;* Donagh MacDonagh's *Happy as Larry;* Forrest Reid dies
1948 Fianna Fail defeated in general election; coalition government under John Costello	Gibbon's *Mount Ida;* Kavanagh's *Tarry Flynn;* MacMahon's *The Lion Tamer;* O'Flaherty's *Two Lovely Beasts;* Molloy's *The King of Friday's Men;* Robertson's *Field of the Stranger;* Stuart's *Pillar of Cloud;* Wall's *The Return of Fursey;* Conal O'Riordan dies
1949 Independent Republic of Éire proclaimed	Bowen's *The Heat of the Day;* McLaverty's *The Game Cock;* MacNeice's *Collected Poems;* Douglas Hyde dies; Edith Somerville dies; George Shiels dies
1950 Korean War begins	Byrne's *Design for a Headstone;* Kiely's *Modern Irish Fiction;* Macken's *Rain on the Wind;* O'Flaherty's *Insurrection;* Robertson's *Miranda Speaks;* George A. Birmingham dies; Bernard Shaw dies; James Stephens dies
1951 The Mother and Child scheme fails; Costello government falls	Beckett's *Molloy;* the Abbey Theatre fire; Liam Miller founds the Dolmen Press
1952	Beckett's *Waiting for Godot;* O'Connor's *Stories;* Wall's *Leaves for the Burning*
1953	Kiely's *Cards of the Gambler;* Macken's *Home Is the Hero;* Meldon's *Aisling;* Molloy's *The Wood of the Whispering;* the Pike Theatre opens
1954	O'Connor's *More Stories*
1955 Ireland enters United Nations	Brian Moore's *Judith Hearne;* O'Donnell's *The Big Window;* James Plunkett's *The Trusting and the Maimed*
1956 IRA campaign begins in the North and lasts until 1962	Behan's *The Quare Fellow;* Kinsella's *Poems;* O'Flaherty's *Stories*
1957 Sputnik I	O'Faolain's *Finest Stories;* White's *A Fretful Midge;* Lord Dunsany dies; Oliver Gogarty dies; Jack Yeats dies; First Dublin Theatre Festival; Lantern Theatre opens
1958	Behan's *Borstal Boy* and *The Hostage;* Johnston's *The Scythe and the Sunset;* Kinsella's *Another September;*

Political	Literary
1958 (*cont.*)	O'Faolain's *Stories;* White's *The Hard Man;* Seumas O'Sullivan dies; Lennox Robinson dies
1959 de Valera becomes third president	Keane's *Sive;* Lavin's *Selected Stories;* Macken's *Seek the Fair Land;* Denis Devlin dies
1960 Irish troops engage in UN mission in the Congo; J.F. Kennedy elected president of U.S.	Clarke's *Twice Round the Black Church;* Kavanagh's *Come Dance with Kitty Stobling;* Keane's *Sharon's Grave;* MacMahon's *Song of the Anvil;* Edna O'Brien's *The Country Girls;* O'Donovan's *The Shaws of Synge Street;* Thompson's *Over the Bridge*
1961 Irish television begins with great fanfare, followed by the Cisco Kid	Clarke's *Later Poems;* MacMahon's *The Honey Spike;* Montague's *Poisoned Lands;* Thomas Murphy's *Whistle in the Dark*
1962	Friel's *Saucer of Larks;* Kinsella's *Downstream;* Macken's *The Silent People;* Edna O'Brien's *The Lonely Girl;* Flann O'Brien's *The Hard Life;* O'Donovan's *Copperfaced Jack;* Paul Smith's *The Countrywoman*
1963 Brookeborough retires as prime minister of Northern Ireland; is succeeded by Terence O'Neill; J. F. Kennedy visits Ireland	Clarke's *Collected Plays* and *Flight to Africa;* Farrell's *Thy Tears Might Cease;* McGahern's *The Barracks;* West's *The Ferret Fancier;* Teresa Deevy dies; George Fitzmaurice dies; Louis MacNeice dies
1964	Friel's *Philadelphia, Here I Come!;* Kavanagh's *Collected Poems;* Cronin's *The Life of Riley;* Devlin's *Collected Poems;* McCabe's *The King of the Castle;* Flann O'Brien's *The Dalkey Archive;* O'Connor's *Collection Two;* Trevor's *Old Boys;* Brendan Behan dies; Daniel Corkery dies; Sean O'Casey dies; Maurice Walsh dies
1965 Sean Lemass and Terence O'Neill meet to improve North–South relations—fail utterly	Keane's *The Field;* Leitch's *The Liberty Lad;* McGahern's *The Dark;* MacNeice's *The Strings Are False;* Brian Moore's *The Emperor of Ice Cream;* Murdoch's *The Red and the Green*
1966	Boyd's *The Flats;* Heaney's *Death of a Naturalist;* Aidan Higgins' *Langrishe Go Down;* T. deV. White's *Lucifer Falling;* Frank O'Connor dies; Brian O'Nolan dies; new Abbey Theatre opens

Political	*Literary*
1967	Boland's *New Territory;* Montague's *A Chosen Light;* Flann O'Brien's *The Third Policeman;* Desmond O'Grady's *The Dark Edge of Europe;* Patrick Kavanagh dies; Walter Macken dies
1968 Civil rights movement gains strength in Ulster; Bloody Sunday in Derry	Gilbert's *Ratman's Notebooks;* Paul Vincent Carroll dies; Donagh MacDonagh dies
1969 British troops assigned to Northern Ireland to maintain peace	Patrick Boyle's *All Looks Yellow to the Jaundiced Eye;* James Plunkett's *Strumpet City;* Power's *The Hungry Grass;* W. R. Rodgers dies; Beckett receives Nobel Prize
1970 IRA begins campaign of violence in the North	Brown's *Down All the Days;* Mairtin O Cadhain dies
1971 Chichester-Clark resigns as prime minister in North, is succeeded by Brian Faulkner; internment introduced in North	Kilroy's *The Big Chapel;* Lavin's *Collected Stories;* Stuart's *Black List, Section H;* St. John Ervine dies
1972 Faulkner resigns; Westminster suspends Northern Ireland constitution and rules directly	Heaney's *Wintering Out;* Jennifer Johnston's *The Captains and the Kings;* Mahon's *Lives;* Montague's *The Rough Field*
1973 Ireland enters the Common Market; coalition government; end of Vietnam War	Jennifer Johnston's *The Gates;* Leonard's *Da;* Richard Ryan's *Ravenswood;* Elizabeth Bowen dies
1974 Sean MacBride receives Nobel Peace Prize	Clarke's *Collected Poems;* Padraic Fallon's *Poems;* R. Murphy's *High Island;* Austin Clarke dies; Padraic Fallon dies; Kate O'Brien dies
1975 Death of de Valera	Leitch's *Stamping Ground*
1976	Banville's *Dr. Copernicus;* Denis Johnston's *The Brazen Horn;* O'Faolain's *Foreign Affairs;* Simmons' *Judy Garland and the Cold War*
1977 Fianna Fail back in office; Peace women receive Nobel Prize	K. Casey's *Dreams of Revenge;* Plunkett's *Collected Stories*
1978	Michael McLaverty's *Collected Stories*
1979 Pope John Paul visits Ireland	Friel's *Aristocrats;* Leonard's *Home Before Night*
1980	Friel's *Translations,* Field Day's first production
1981 Fine-Gael Labor coalition	Aosdána established; Molly Keane's *Good Behaviour;* Banville's *Kepler;* Christy Brown dies

	Political	Literary
1982	Falklands war	Annamacarraig writers' center opens; Montague's *Selected Poems;* Wall's *Hermitage;* Maeve Binchy's *Light a Penny Candle*
1983		Bernard MacLaverty's *Cal*
1984		Heaney's *Station Island;* Mulkerns' *The Summer House;* Denis Johnston dies; Liam O'Flaherty dies
1985	Anglo-Irish Agreement; Progressive Democrats formed	Frank McGuinness' *Observe the Sons of Ulster Marching Towards the Somme;* Longley's *Poems 1963–1983*
1986	Chernobyl; divorce referendum fails	Hewitt's *Freehold;* Marcus's *A Land Not Theirs;* Peadar O'Donnell dies
1987	Fianna Fail government	Ita Daly's *A Singular Attraction*
1988	Iran–Iraq war ended	Deirdre Madden's *The Birds of the Innocent Wood*
1989	Fall of the Berlin Wall; coalition government of Fianna Fail and Progressive Democrats	Banville's *The Book of Evidence;* Boland's *Selected Poems;* Samuel Beckett dies
1990	East & West Germany reunited; cold war formally ended; Mary Robinson elected president	McGahern's *Amongst Women;* Callaghan's *The Awkward Girl;* Friel's *Dancing at Lughnasa;* Plunkett's *Circus Animals;* McGahern's *Amongst Women* wins *Irish Times*/Aer Lingus Prize; Durcan's *Daddy, Daddy* wins Whitbread Prize; Jim Sheridan's *My Left Foot* wins two Academy Awards; Sam Hanna Bell dies; Hubert Butler dies
1991	Breakup of the Soviet Union; Gulf War; Yugoslavian conflict	*The Field Day Anthology;* Joseph O'Connor's *Cowboys and Indians;* Sean O'Faolain dies
1992	Fighting in Bosnia; famine in Africa; coalition government of Fianna Fail and Labour	Roddy Doyle's *Barrytown Trilogy;* Toibin's *The Heather Blazing;* O Siadhail's *Hail! Madam Jazz*
1993	Downing Street Declaration	Roddy Doyle's *Paddy Clarke Ha Ha Ha* receives Booker Prize; Neil Jordan wins Academy Award for *The Crying Game*
1994	Mandela elected president of South Africa; PLO–Israeli agreement; Sinn Féin and Loyalist cease-fire; coalition of Fine Gael, Labour, and Democratic Left	M. J. Molloy dies, T. de Vere White dies; Eilis Dillon dies
1995	Second divorce referendum passes	Trevor wins Whitbread Prize for *Felicia's Journey;* Heaney wins Nobel Prize in literature
1996	Sinn Féin returns to violence	Mary Lavin dies

BIBLIOGRAPHY

BACKGROUND

Arnold, Bruce. *A Concise History of Irish Art.* New York & Washington, D.C.: Frederick A. Praeger, 1968/London: Thames & Hudson, 1969/revised, 1977.

Bardon, Jonathan. *A History of Ulster.* Belfast: Blackstaff, 1994.

Beckett, J. C. *The Making of Modern Ireland.* New York: Knopf, 1966.

Boylan, Henry. *A Dictionary of Irish Biography.* Dublin: Gill & Macmillan, 1978/2d ed., 1987.

Cahalan, James M. *Modern Irish Literature and Culture, a Chronology.* New York: G. K. Hall, [1993].

Carroll, Joseph T. *Ireland in the War Years, 1939–1945.* Newton Abbot: David & Charles/New York: Crane, Russak, 1975.

Connell, Kenneth Hugh. *Irish Peasant Society.* Oxford: Clarendon, 1968.

Croker, Thomas Crofton. *Fairy Legends and Traditions in the South of Ireland.* 3 vols. London: Murray, 1825–1828.

Cullen, L. M. *An Economic History of Ireland since 1660.* New York: Barnes & Noble, 1973.

Curtis, Edmund. *A History of Medieval Ireland.* Dublin: Maunsel & Roberts, 1923/revised, London, 1938.

———. *A History of Ireland.* London: Methuen, 1950.

de Paor, Maire and Liam de Paor. *Early Christian Ireland.* London: Thames & Hudson, 1958.

Deutsch, Richard R. *Northern Ireland 1921–1974: A Select Bibliography.* New York & London: Garland, 1975.

Dillon, Myles, ed. *Early Irish Society.* Dublin: Sign of the Three Candles, 1954.

Edwards, R. Dudley. *Ireland in the Age of the Tudors.* London: Croom Helm/New York: Barnes & Noble, 1977.

Evans, E. E. *Prehistoric and Early Christian Ireland.* London: B. T. Batsford, 1966.

Fallon, Brian. *Irish Art, 1830–1990.* [Belfast]: Appletree, [1994].

Farrell, Brian, ed. *The Irish Parliamentary Tradition.* Dublin: Gill & Macmillan/New York: Barnes & Noble, 1973.

Fennell, Desmond. *Heresy: The Battle of Ideas in Modern Ireland.* Belfast: Blackstaff/Chester Springs, Pa.: Dufour, 1994.

Filip, J. *Celtic Civilisation and Its Heritage.* Prague: Czechoslovak Academy of Sciences, 1960/2d ed. Prague: Academia, 1977/Wellingborough, Northants: Collets, 1977.

Foster, R. F. *Modern Ireland 1600–1972.* [London]: Allen Lane, Penguin, [1988].

Freeman, T. W. *Ireland, Its Physical, Historical, Social and Economic Geography.* London: Methuen, 1950.

Harbison, Peter. *Pre-Christian Ireland. From the First Settlers to the Early Celts.* London: Thames & Hudson, 1988.

Hayes, R. J. *Manuscript Sources for the History of Irish Civilisation.* 11 vols. Boston: G. K. Hall, 1965/*First Supplement.* 3 vols. 1979.

————. *Sources for the History of Irish Civilisation: Articles in Irish Periodicals.* 9 vols. Boston: G. K. Hall, 1970.

Kee, Robert. *The Green Flag: A History of Irish Nationalism.* London: Weidenfeld & Nicholson/New York: Delacorte, 1972.

Lee, J. J. *Ireland 1912–1985.* Cambridge: Cambridge University Press, [1989].

Lyons, F.S.L. *Ireland since the Famine.* London: Weidenfeld & Nicolson, 1971; revised, 1973.

Macardle, Dorothy. *The Irish Rising.* London: Gollancz, 1937.

MacCurtain, Margaret. *Tudor and Stuart Ireland.* Dublin & London, 1972.

Martin, F. X., ed. *Leaders and Men of the 1916 Rising.* Ithaca, N.Y.: Cornell University Press, [1967].

Moody, T. W. and Martin, F. X., eds. *The Course of Irish History.* Cork: Mercier, 1967.

Moody, T. W., Martin, F. X. and Byrne, F. J., eds. *A New History of Ireland.* 10 vols. Oxford: Clarendon, 1976– .

Murphy, John Augustine. *Ireland in the Twentieth Century.* London: Macmillan, 1975.

Newmann, Kate. *Dictionary of Ulster Biography.* Belfast: Institute of Irish Studies, Queen's University of Belfast, 1994.

O'Brien, Conor Cruise. *States of Ireland.* London: Hutchinson/New York: Pantheon, 1972.

O'Faolain, Sean. *The Irish.* West Drayton, Middlesex: Penguin, 1947.

O Grada, Cormac. *Ireland. A New Economic History, 1780–1939.* Oxford: Clarendon, 1994.

O'Sullivan, Donal. *Irish Folk Music and Song.* Dublin: Cultural Relations Committee, 1952.

Otway-Ruthven, A. J. *A History of Medieval Ireland.* London: Ernest Benn/New York: Barnes & Noble, 1968.

Praeger, Robert Lloyd. *Natural History of Ireland.* New York: Barnes & Noble, 1972.

Thuente, Mary Helen. *The Harp Re-Strung: The United Irishmen and the Rise of Irish Literary Nationalism.* Syracuse, N.Y. Syracuse University Press, 1994.

Woodham-Smith, Cecil. *The Great Hunger.* London: Hamish Hamilton, [1962].

GENERAL LITERARY HISTORY

Best, Richard I. *Bibliography of Irish Philology and of Irish Printed Literature.* Dublin: Stationery Office, 1913.

————. *Bibliography of Irish Philology and Manuscript Literature: Publications 1913–1931*. Dublin: Institute for Advanced Studies, 1942.

Boyd, Ernest A. *Ireland's Literary Renaissance*. Dublin: Maunsel, 1916/revised, New York: Knopf, 1922/ reprinted, New York: Barnes & Noble, 1968; Dublin: Allen Figgis, 1969.

Brady, Anne M. and Cleeve, Brian. *A Biographical Dictionary of Irish Writers*. [Mullingar, Co. Westmeath]: Lilliput, 1985.

Brown, Malcolm. *The Politics of Irish Literature: From Thomas Davis to W. B. Yeats.* Seattle: University of Washington Press/London: Allen & Unwin, 1972.

Brown, Stephen J. *A Guide to Books on Ireland.* Part I. Dublin: Hodges Figgis, 1912/ reprint, New York: Lema, 1970. (No Part II was ever issued.)

Brown, Terence. *Ireland's Literature: Selected Essays*. Mullingar, Co. Westmeath: Lilliput/Totowa, N.J.: Barnes & Noble, 1988.

Cairns, David and Richards, Shaun. *Writing Ireland: Colonialism, Nationalism and Culture.* [Manchester]: Manchester University Press, [1988].

Carpenter, Andrew, ed. *Place, Personality and the Irish Writer*. Gerrards Cross: Colin Smythe, 1977.

Corkery, Daniel. *The Hidden Ireland: A Study of Gaelic Munster in the Eighteenth Century.* Dublin: Gill, 1925/Dublin: Gill & Macmillan, 1979.

Costello, Pater. *The Heart Grown Brutal*. Dublin: Gill & Macmillan/Totowa, N.J.: Rowman & Littlefield, 1977.

Cronin, Anthony. *Heritage Now: Irish Literature in the English Language.* Dingle: Co. Kerry: Brandon/New York: St. Martin's, 1982.

Deane, Seamus. *Celtic Revivals: Essays in Modern Irish Literature 1880–1980.* London: Faber, 1985/Winston-Salem, N.C.: Wake Forest University Press, 1986.

————. *A Short History of Irish Literature*. London: Hutchinson/Notre Dame, Ind.: University of Notre Dame Press, 1986.

de Blacam, Aodh. *Gaelic Literature Surveyed*. Dublin: Talbot, 1929/revised, 1974.

Donoghue, Denis. *We Irish: Essays on Irish Literature and Society*. Brighton: Harvester, 1986/New York: Knopf, 1987.

Fallis, Richard. *The Irish Renaissance*. Syracuse, N.Y.: Syracuse University Press, 1977.

Finneran, Richard J., ed. *Anglo-Irish Literature: A Review of Research*. New York: Modern Language Association of America, 1976.

————. *Recent Research on Anglo-Irish Writers*. New York: Modern Language Association of America, 1983.

Foster, John Wilson. *Colonial Consequences: Essays in Irish Literature and Culture.* [Dublin]: Lilliput, 1991.

Gose, Elliott, B., Jr. *The World of the Irish Wonder Tale: An Introduction to the Study of Fairy Tales.* Toronto: University of Toronto Press/Dingle, Co. Kerry: Brandon, 1985.

Gwynn, Stephen. *Irish Literature and Drama*. New York: Nelson, 1936.

Hall, Wayne E. *Shadowy Heroes: Irish Literature of the 1890s*. Syracuse, N.Y.: Syracuse University Press, 1980.

Healy, Elizabeth. *Elizabeth Healy's Literary Tour of Ireland*. Dublin: Wolfhound, 1995.

Heaney, Seamus. *Preoccupations: Selected Prose 1968–1978*. London: Faber, 1980.

Howarth, Herbert. *The Irish Writers, 1880–1940*. London: Rockliff, 1958.

Hyde, Douglas. *A Literary History of Ireland*. London: T. Fisher Unwin, 1899/revised, London: Ernest Benn, 1967, 1980.

Igoe, Vivien. *A Literary Guide to Dublin.* [London]: Methuen, [1994].

Jeffares, A. Norman. *Anglo-Irish Literature.* [London]: Macmillan/[Dublin]: Gill & Macmillan, 1982.

Kain, Richard M. *Dublin in the Age of W. B. Yeats and James Joyce.* Norman: University of Oklahoma Press, [1962].

Kenner, Hugh. *A Colder Eye: The Modern Irish Writers.* [London]: Allen Lane/New York: Knopf, 1983.

Kiberd, Declan. *Inventing Ireland.* London: Jonathan Cape, [1995].

Mc Cormack, W. J. *Ascendancy and Tradition in Anglo-Irish Literature.* Oxford: Oxford University Press, 1985.

————. *Dissolute Characters: Irish Literary History through Balzac, Sheridan Le Fanu, Yeats and Bowen.* Manchester & New York: Manchester University Press, [1993].

MacDonagh, Thomas. *Literature in Ireland.* London: T. Fisher Unwin, 1916.

McHugh, Roger, and Harmon, Maurice. *Short History of Anglo-Irish Literature from Its Origins to the Present Day.* Dublin: Wolfhound/Totowa, N.J.: Barnes & Noble, [1982].

McKenna, Brian. *Irish Literature, 1800–1875, A Guide to Information Sources.* Detroit: Gale, 1978.

McSweeney, Patrick M. *A Group of Nation-Builders: O'Donovan, O'Curry, Petrie.* Dublin: Catholic Truth Society of Ireland, 1913.

Martin, Augustine, ed. *The Genius of Irish Prose.* Dublin & Cork: Mercier, 1984.

Mercier, Vivian. *The Irish Comic Tradition.* Oxford: Clarendon, 1962.

————. *Modern Irish Literature: Sources and Founders.* Oxford: Clarendon, 1994.

Montague, John. *The Figure in the Cave and Other Essays.* Dublin: Lilliput, 1989.

Moynahan, Julian. *Anglo-Irish: The Literary Imagination in a Hyphenated Culture.* Princeton, N.J.: Princeton University Press, 1995.

Murphy, Daniel. *Imagination & Religion in Anglo-Irish Literature.* [Blackrock, Co. Dublin]: Irish Academic, [1987].

O'Connor, Frank. *The Backward Look. A Survey of Irish Literature.* London: Macmillan, 1967/published in the United States as *A Short History of Irish Literature.* New York: Putnam, 1967.

O'Connor, Ulick. *Celtic Dawn: A Portrait of the Irish Literary Renaissance.* London: Hamish Hamilton, [1984].

O'Driscoll, Robert, ed. *The Celtic Consciousness.* [Dublin]: Dolmen/[Edinburgh]: Canongate, [1982].

Partridge, A. C. *Language and Society in Anglo-Irish Literature.* [Dublin]: Gill & Macmillan/Totowa, N.J.: Barnes & Noble, [1984].

Power, Patrick C. *A Literary History of Ireland.* Cork: Mercier, 1969.

Rafroidi, Patrick. *Irish Literature in English: The Romantic Period.* 2 vols. Gerrards Cross: Colin Smythe/Atlantic Highlands, N.J.: Humanities, [1980].

Seymour, St. John D. *Anglo-Irish Literature 1200–1582.* Cambridge: Cambridge University Press, 1929.

Stewart, Bruce. *Literature in Twentieth-Century Ulster: A Select Bibliography.* [London]: British Council, 1995].

Vance, Norman. *Irish Literature: A Social History.* [Oxford]: Basil Blackwell, [1990].

Warner, Alan. *A Guide to Anglo-Irish Literature.* Dublin: Gill & Macmillan/New York: St. Martin's, [1981].

Weekes, Ann Owens. *Unveiling Treasures: The Attic Guide to the Published Work of Irish Women Literary Writers.* Dublin: Attic, 1993.

Welch, Robert. *Changing States: Transformations in Modern Irish Writing.* London & New York: Routledge, [1993].

———. *The Oxford Companion to Irish Literature.* Oxford: Clarendon Press, 1996.

MYTHOLOGY

Gregory, Lady Augusta. *Cuchulain of Muirthemne.* London: Murray, 1902.

———. *Gods and Fighting Men.* London: Murray, 1904.

Kinsella, Thomas, trans. *The Tain.* Dublin: Dolmen, 1969.

Murphy, Gerard. *Saga and Myth in Ancient Ireland.* Dublin: Cultural Relations Committee, 1955.

O'Grady, Standish. *History of Ireland: The Heroic Period.* London: Sampson Low, 1878.

———. *History of Ireland: Cuchulain and His Contemporaries.* London: Sampson Low, 1880.

Yeats, W. B. *Writings on Irish Folklore, Legend and Myth.* Robert Welch, ed. London: Penguin, 1993.

HISTORY AND CRITICISM OF FICTION

Brown, Stephen J. *Ireland in Fiction.* Dublin: Maunsel, 1915.

Brown, Stephen J. and Clarke, Desmond. *Ireland in Fiction.* Vol. 2. [Cork]: Royal Carbery Books, [1985].

Cahalan, James M. *Great Hatred, Little Room. The Irish Historical Novel.* Syracuse, N.Y.: Syracuse University Press, 1983.

———. *The Irish Novel: A Critical History.* Dublin: Gill & Macmillan, 1988.

Cronin, John. *The Anglo-Irish Novel,* Vol. 1. *The Nineteenth Century.* Belfast: Appletree, 1980.

Flanagan, Thomas. *The Irish Novelists, 1800–1850.* New York: Columbia University Press, 1959.

Foster, John Wilson. *Forces and Themes in Ulster Fiction.* Dublin: Gill & Macmillan/ Totowa, N.J.: Rowman & Littlefield, 1974.

Kiely, Benedict. *Modern Irish Fiction, A Critique.* Dublin: Golden Eagle, 1959.

Kilroy, James F., ed. *The Irish Short Story: A Critical History.* [Boston]: Twayne, [1984].

Krans, Horatio S. *Irish Life in Irish Fiction.* London: Macmillan, 1903.

Rafroidi, Patrick and Brown, Terence, eds. *The Irish Short Story.* [Lille]: Universite de Lille, [1979].

Rafroidi, Patrick and Harmon, Maurice, eds. *The Irish Novel in Our Time.* Lille: Universite de Lille, 1976.

Sloan, B. *The Pioneers of Anglo-Irish Fiction 1800–1850.* Gerrards Cross: Colin Smythe/ Totowa, N.J.: Barnes & Noble, 1984.

HISTORY AND CRITICISM OF POETRY

Alspach, Russell K. *Irish Poetry from the English Invasion to 1798.* Philadelphia: University of Pennsylvania Press, 1959.

Andrews, Elmer, ed. *Contemporary Irish Poetry: A Collection of Critical Essays.* [Basingstoke & London]: Macmillan, [1992].

Brown, Terence. *Northern Voices: Poets from Ulster.* Totowa, N.J.: Rowman & Littlefield, 1975.

Brown, Terence and Grene, Nicholas, eds. *Tradition and Influence in Anglo-Irish Poetry.* [Basingstoke & London]: Macmillan, [1989].

Clarke, Austin. *Poetry in Modern Ireland.* Dublin: Cultural Relations Committee, 1961.

Coughlan, Patricia & Davis, Alex. *Modernism and Ireland: The Poetry of the 1930s.* Cork: Cork University Press, 1995.

Farren, Robert. *The Course of Irish Verse in English.* London & New York: Sheed & Ward, 1957.

Garratt, Robert F. *Modern Irish Poetry: Tradition and Continuity from Yeats to Heaney.* Berkeley: University of California Press, 1986.

Johnston, Dillon. *Irish Poetry after Joyce.* Notre Dame, Ind.: Notre Dame University Press/Dublin: Dolmen, 1985.

Kenneally, Michael, ed. *Poetry in Contemporary Irish Literature.* Gerrards Cross: Colin Smythe, 1995.

Kersnowski, Frank. *The Outsiders: Poets of Contemporary Ireland.* Fort Worth: Texas Christian University Press, 1975.

Loftus, Richard J. *Nationalism in Modern Anglo-Irish Poetry.* Madison & Milwaukee: University of Wisconsin Press, 1964.

Longley, Edna. *Poetry in the Wars.* Newcastle upon Tyne: Bloodaxe, 1986.

Lucy, Sean. *Irish Poets in English.* Cork: Mercier, 1973.

O'Donoghue, D. J. *The Poets of Ireland, A Bibliographical and Bibliographical Dictionary.* Dublin: Hodges Figgis, 1912/reprint, Detroit: Gale, 1968.

Power, Patrick C. *The Story of Anglo-Irish Poetry, 1800–1922.* Cork: Mercier, 1967.

Storey, Mark, ed. *Poetry and Ireland since 1800: A Source Book.* London & New York: Routledge, [1988].

Welch, Robert. *Irish Poetry from Moore to Yeats.* Gerrards Cross: Colin Smythe/Totowa, N.J.: Barnes & Noble, [1980].

———. *A History of Verse Translation from the Irish.* Gerrards Cross: Colin Smythe/Totowa, N.J.: Barnes & Noble, 1989.

Wills, Clair. *Improprieties: Politics and Sexuality in Northern Irish Poetry.* Oxford: Clarendon, 1993.

HISTORY AND CRITICISM OF DRAMA

Bartley, J. O. *Teague, Shenkin and Sawney. Being an Historical Study of the Earliest Irish, Welsh and Scottish Characters in English Plays.* Cork: Cork University Press, 1954.

Bell, Sam Hanna. *The Theatre in Ulster.* Dublin: Gill & Macmillan, 1972.

Clark, William S. *The Early Irish Stage. The Beginnings to 1720.* Oxford: Clarendon, 1955.

———. *The Irish Stage in the Country Towns, 1720–1860.* Oxford: Clarendon, 1965.

Cowell, John. *No Profit but the Name: The Longfords and the Gate Theatre.* Dublin: O'Brien, 1988.

Duggan, G. C. *The Stage Irishman: A History of the Irish Play and Stage Characters from the Earliest Times.* Dublin & Cork: Talbot, 1937.

Ellis-Fermor, Una. *The Irish Dramatic Movement.* London: Methuen, 1939; revised 1954.

Fay, Gerard. *The Abbey Theatre, Cradle of Genius.* London: Hollis & Carter, 1958.

Feeney, William J. *Drama in Hardwicke Street: A History of the Irish Theatre Company.* Rutherford, N.J.: Fairleigh Dickinson University Press/London & Toronto: Associated University Presses, [1984].

Gailey, Alan. *Irish Folk Drama.* Cork: Mercier, [1969].

Genet, Jacqueline and Cave, Richard Allen, eds. *Perspectives of Irish Drama and Theatre.* Gerrards Cross: Colin Smythe, 1991.

Glassie, Henry. *All Silver and No Brass: An Irish Christmas Mumming.* Bloomington: Indiana University Press, 1975/Philadelphia: University of Pennsylvania Press, 1983.

Gregory, Lady Augusta. *Our Irish Theatre.* Gerrards Cross: Colin Smythe, 1973. (The most satisfactory edition.)

Hogan, Robert. *After the Irish Renaissance.* Minneapolis: University of Minnesota Press, 1967/London: Macmillan, 1968.

———. *"Since O'Casey" and Other Essays on Irish Drama.* Gerrards Cross: Colin Smythe/Totowa, N.J.: Barnes & Noble, 1983.

Hogan, Robert and Burnham, Richard. *The Art of the Amateur, 1916–1920.* Vol. 5 of *The Modern Irish Drama.* [Dublin]: Dolmen/[Atlantic Highlands, N.J.]: Humanities, [1984].

———. *The Years of O'Casey, 1921–1926.* Vol. 6 of *The Modern Irish Drama.* Newark: University of Delaware Press/Gerrards Cross: Colin Smythe, 1992.

Hogan, Robert, with Burnham, Richard and Poteet, Daniel P. *The Rise of the Realists, 1910–1915.* Vol. 4 of *The Modern Irish Drama.* [Dublin]: Dolmen/[Atlantic Highlands, N.J.]: Humanities, [1979].

Hogan, Robert and Kilroy, James. *The Irish Literary Theatre, 1899–1901.* Vol. 1 of *The Modern Irish Drama.* Dublin: Dolmen, 1975.

———. *Laying the Foundations, 1902–1904.* Vol. 2 of *The Modern Irish Drama.* Dublin: Dolmen, 1976.

———. *The Abbey Theatre: The Years of Synge, 1905–1909.* Vol. 3 of *The Modern Irish Drama.* Dublin: Dolmen, 1978.

Holloway, Joseph. *Joseph Holloway's Abbey Theatre.* R. Hogan & M. J. O'Neill, eds. Carbondale: University of Southern Illinois Press, 1967.

———. *Joseph Holloway's Irish Theatre.* 3 vols. R. Hogan & M. J. O'Neill, eds. Dixon, Calif.: Proscenium, 1968–1970.

Hunt, Hugh. *The Abbey, Ireland's National Theatre 1904–1979.* Dublin: Gill & Macmillan/New York: Columbia University Press, 1979.

Kavanagh, Peter. *The Irish Theatre: Being a History of the Drama in Ireland from the Earliest Period Up to the Present Day.* Tralee: Kerryman, 1946.

———. *The Story of the Abbey Theatre.* New York: Devin-Adair, 1950.

Krause, David. *The Profane Book of Irish Comedy.* Ithaca, N.Y. & London: Cornell University Press, [1982].

McCann, Sean, ed. *The Story of the Abbey.* London: New English Library, 1967.

Mac Liammóir, Micheál. *Theatre in Ireland.* Dublin: Cultural Relations Committee, 1964.

Malone, Andrew E. *The Irish Drama.* London: Constable, 1929.

Maxwell, D.E.S. *A Critical History of Modern Irish Drama 1891–1980.* Cambridge: Cambridge University Press, [1984].

Mikhail, E. H., ed. *The Abbey Theatre: Interviews and Recollections.* [Basingstoke, Hampshire]: Macmillan, [1988].

Nic Shiubhaligh, Maire and Kenny, Edward. *The Splendid Years.* Dublin: Duffy, 1955.

Ó hAodha, Micheál. *Theatre in Ireland.* Totowa, N.J.: Rowman & Littlefield, 1974.

O'Malley, Conor. *A Poet's Theatre.* [Dublin: Elo, 1988].

O'Malley, Mary. *Never Shake Hands with the Devil.* Dublin: [Elo], 1990.

Robinson, Lennox. *Ireland's Abbey Theatre.* London: Sidgwick & Jackson, 1951.

———, ed. *The Irish Theatre.* London: Macmillan, 1939.

Roche, Anthony. *Contemporary Irish Drama from Beckett to McGuinness.* [Dublin]: Gill & Macmillan, [1994].

Saddlemyer, Ann, ed. *Theatre Business: The Correspondence of the First Abbey Theatre Directors: William Butler Yeats, Lady Gregory and J. M. Synge.* Gerrards Cross: Colin Smythe, 1982.

Schrank, Bernice and Demastes, William W., eds. *Irish Playwrights, 1880–1995: A Research and Production Sourcebook.* Westport, CT: Greenwood, 1996.

Simpson, Alan. *Beckett and Behan and a Theatre in Dublin.* London: Routledge & Kegan Paul, [1962].

Smith, Gus. *Festival Glory in Athlone.* Dublin: Aherlow, [ca. 1977].

Stockwell, La Tourette. *Dublin Theatres and Theatre Customs, 1637–1820.* Kingsport, Tenn.: Kingsport, 1938/New York: Benjamin Blom, 1968.

Trunninger, A. *Paddy and the Paycock: A Study of the Stage Irishman from Shakespeare to O'Casey.* Berne: Francke, 1976.

Worth, Katharine. *The Irish Drama of Europe from Yeats to Beckett.* London: Athlone, [1986].

COLLECTIONS OF CRITICISM

Allen, Michael and Wilcox, Angela, eds. *Critical Approaches to Anglo-Irish Literature.* Gerrards Cross: Colin Smythe, 1989.

Bowen, Zack, ed. *Irish Renaissance Annual.* 4 vols. Newark: University of Delaware Press/London & Toronto: Associated University Presses, [1980–1983].

Brophy, James D. and Grennan, Eamon, eds. *New Irish Writing: Essays in Memory of Raymond J. Porter.* Boston: Iona College Press & Twayne, [1988].

Carpenter, Andrew, ed. *Place, Personality and the Irish Writer.* Gerrards Cross: Colin Smythe/New York: Barnes & Noble, 1977.

Connolly, Peter, ed. *Literature and the Changing Ireland.* Gerrards Cross: Colin Smythe/ Totowa, N.J.: Barnes & Noble, [1982].

Dick, Susan et al., eds. *Omnium Gatherum: Essays for Richard Ellmann.* Gerrards Cross: Colin Smythe, 1989.

Dunne, Douglas, ed. *Two Decades of Irish Writing.* Chester Springs, Pa.: Dufour, 1975.

Gallagher, S. F., ed. *Women in Irish Legend, Life and Literature.* Gerrards Cross: Colin Smythe/Totowa, N.J.: Barnes & Noble, 1983.

Harmon, Maurice, ed. *Image and Illusion.* Dublin: Wolfhound, [1979].

———. *The Irish Writer and the City.* Gerrards Cross: Colin Smythe/Totowa, N.J.: Barnes & Noble, 1984.

Hyland, Paul and Sammells, Neil, eds. *Irish Writing: Exile and Subversion.* [Basingstoke & London]: Macmillan, [1991].

Komesu, Okifumi and Sekine, Masaru, eds. *Irish Writers and Politics*. Gerrards Cross: Colin Smythe, 1989.

McMinn, Joseph, with McMaster, Anne and Welch, Angela, eds. *The Internationalism of Irish Literature and Drama*. Gerrards Cross: Colin Smythe, 1992.

Morse, Donald E., Bertha Csilla and Palffy, Istvan, eds. *A Small Nation's Contribution to the World: Essays on Anglo-Irish Literature and Language*. Gerrards Cross: Colin Smythe/Debrecen: Lajos Kossuth University, 1993.

Porter, Raymond J. and Brophy, James D., eds. *Modern Irish Literature*. New York: Iona College & Twayne, 1972.

Ronsley, Joseph, ed. *Myth and Reality in Irish Literature*. Waterloo, Ontario, Canada: Wilfrid Laurier University Press, 1977.

Schleifer, Ronald, ed. *The Genres of the Irish Literary Revival*. Norman, Okla.: Pilgrim Books/Dublin: Wolfhound, [1980].

Sekine, Masaru, ed. *Irish Writers and Society at Large*. Gerrards Cross: Colin Smythe/ Totowa, N.J.: Barnes & Noble, 1985.

Wall, Richard, ed. *Medieval and Modern Ireland*. Totowa, N.J.: Barnes & Noble, [1988].

Welch, Robert, ed. *Irish Writers and Religion*. Gerrards Cross: Colin Smythe, 1992.

ANTHOLOGIES

Kosok, Heinz. "Anthologies of Anglo-Irish Literature: 1722–1986: A Checklist." *Irish University Review* 18 (Autumn 1988): 251–262.

General

Deane, Seamus, general ed. *The Field Day Anthology of Irish Writing*. 3 vols. Derry: Field Day, [1991].

Dunne, Sean. *The Cork Anthology*. [Cork]: Cork University Press, [1993].

Greacen, Robert. *Northern Harvest: Anthology of Ulster Writing*. Belfast: MacCord, 1944.

Greene, David H. *An Anthology of Irish Literature*. New York: Modern Library, 1954.

McCarthy, Justin and Welsh, Charles. *Irish Authors and Their Writings in Ten Volumes*. Philadelphia: Morris/London: Collier, 1904.

Mercier, Vivian & Greene, David H. *1000 Years of Irish Prose: The Literary Revival*. New York: Devin-Adair, 1952; New York: Grosset & Dunlap, 1961.

Read, Charles A. *The Cabinet of Irish Literature*. 4 vols. London: Blackie, 1879–1880/ new ed. by Katharine Tynan Hinkson. London: Gresham, 1903.

Russell, Diarmuid. *The Portable Irish Reader*. New York: Viking, 1946.

Smythe, Ailbhe. *Wildish Things: An Anthology of New Irish Women's Writing*. [Dublin]: Attic, [1989].

Poetry

Barry, Sebastian. *The Inherited Boundaries: Younger Poets of the Republic of Ireland*. [Mountrath, Portlaoise]: Dolmen, [1986].

Bradley, Anthony. *Contemporary Irish Poetry: An Anthology*. Berkeley, Los Angeles & London: University of California Press, [1980].

Brooks, S. A. and Rolleston, T. W. *A Treasury of Irish Poetry*. New York: Macmillan, 1932.

Colum, Padraic. *An Anthology of Irish Verse*. New York: Boni & Liveright, 1922.

Cooke, John. *The Dublin Book of Irish Verse. 1728–1909*. Dublin: Hodges & Figgis, 1909.

Croker, T. Crofton. *The Popular Songs of Ireland*. London: Coburn, 1839/London: Routledge, 1886.

Crotty, Patrick. *Modern Irish Poetry*. Belfast: Blackstaff, 1995.

Dawe, Gerald. *The New Younger Irish Poets*. Belfast: Blackstaff, [1982].

Duffy, Charles Gavan. *The Ballad Poetry of Ireland*. Dublin: Duffy, 1845.

Dunne, Sean. *Poets of Munster: An Anthology*. [London]: Anvil Press Poetry/[Dingle, Co. Kerry]: Brandon, [1985].

Fiacc, Padraic. *The Wearing of the Black: An Anthology of Contemporary Ulster Poetry*. Belfast: Blackstaff, 1974.

Fitzmaurice, Gabriel. *Irish Poetry Now*. Dublin: Wolfhound, 1993.

Gareth, James. *The Wind That Shakes the Barley: A Selection of Irish Folk Song*. Belfast: Appletree, 1983.

Garrity, Devin A. *New Irish Poets*. New York: Devin-Adair, 1948.

Greacen, Robert and Iremonger, Valentin. *Contemporary Irish Poetry*. London: Faber, [1949].

Greene, David and O'Connor, Frank. *A Golden Treasury of Irish Verse*, A.D. *600 to 1200*. London: Macmillan, 1967.

Hardiman, James. *Irish Minstrelsy; or, Bardic Remains of Ireland; with English Poetical Translations*. 2 vols. London: Robins, 1831; reprint, New York: Barnes & Noble, 1971.

Hewitt, John. *Rhyming Weavers and Other Country Poets of Antrim and Down*. Belfast: Blackstaff, 1974.

Hoagland, Kathleen. *1000 Years of Irish Poetry*. New York: Devin-Adair, 1947.

Irvine, John. *The Flowering Branch: An Anthology of Irish Poetry Past and Present*. Belfast: MacCord, 1945.

Kennelly, Brendan. *The Penguin Book of Irish Verse*. 2d ed. [London]: Penguin, [1981].

Kinsella, Thomas. *The New Oxford Book of Irish Verse*. Oxford & New York: Oxford University Press, 1986.

MacDonagh, Donagh and Robinson, Lennox. *Oxford Book of Irish Verse*. Oxford: Clarendon, [1958].

Mahon, Derek. *The Sphere Book of Modern Irish Poetry*. London: Sphere Books, 1972.

Marcus, David. *Irish Poets, 1924–1974*. London: Pan Books, 1975.

Montague, John. *The Faber Book of Irish Verse*. London: Faber, 1974/as *The Book of Irish Verse*. New York: Macmillan, 1976.

Muldoon, Paul. *The Faber Book of Contemporary Irish Poetry*. London: Faber, 1986.

O'Lochlainn, Colm. *Irish Street Ballads*. Dublin: Three Candles, 1939.

———. *More Irish Street Ballads*. Dublin: Three Candles, 1965.

O'Reilly, John Boyle. *The Poetry and Song of Ireland*. New York: Gay Brothers, 1889.

Ormsby, Frank. *Poets from the North of Ireland*. [Belfast]: Blackstaff, [1979].

———. *The Long Embrace: Twentieth-Century Irish Love Poems*. Belfast: Blackstaff, 1987.

Simmons, James. *Ten Irish Poets*. [Cheadle, Cheshire]: Carcanet, [1974].

The Spirit of the Nation, Ballads and Songs by the Writers of the Nation with Original and Ancient Music. . . . Dublin: Duffy, 1845.

Taylor, Geoffrey. *Irish Poets of the Nineteenth Century.* London: Routledge & Kegan Paul, 1951.

Whyte, Samuel. *The Shamrock: or, Hibernian Cresses. A Collection of Poems, Songs, Epigrams, &c. Latin as well as English, the Original Production of Ireland.* Dublin: Marchbank, 1772.

Yeats, W. B. *A Book of Irish Verse.* London: Methuen, 1895.

Fiction

Barr, Fiona, Walsh, Barbara Haycock and Mahon, Stella. *Sisters.* Dublin: Blackstaff, 1980.

Birmingham, George A. *Irish Short Stories.* London: Faber, [1932].

Blair, Suzi. *Forty Shades of Green: Short Stories by Writers from Northern Ireland.* Peterborough: New Fiction, 1993.

Bolger, Dermot. *The Picador Book of Irish Contemporary Fiction.* [London & Basingstoke]: Picador/Pan, [1993].

Casey, Kevin. *Winter's Tales from Ireland 2.* Dublin: Gill & Macmillan/Newark, Del.: Proscenium, 1972.

Forkner, Ben. *Modern Irish Short Stories.* [Harmondsworth, Middlesex]: Penguin, [1980].

Garrity, Devin A. *44 Irish Short Stories.* New York: Devin-Adair, 1960.

Kiely, Benedict. *The Penguin Book of Irish Short Stories.* [Harmondsworth, Middlesex]: Penguin, [1981].

Madden-Simpson, Janet. *Woman's Part: An Anthology of Short Fiction by and about Irish Women 1890–1960.* Dublin: Arlen House; London & New York: Marion Boyars, [1984].

Marcus, David. *Modern Irish Short Stories.* London: Sphere, [1972].

———. *Modern Irish Love Stories.* London: Pan, [1974].

———. *New Irish Writing.* London: Quartet, [1976].

———. *The Bodley Head Book of Irish Short Stories.* London: Bodley Head, 1980.

———. *State of the Art: Short Stories by New Irish Writers.* Sevenoaks: Sceptre, 1992.

Martin, Augustine. *Winter's Tales from Ireland.* Dublin: Gill & Macmillan, 1970.

Mercier, Vivian. *Great Irish Short Stories.* New York: Dell, 1964.

O'Connor, Frank. *Modern Irish Short Stories.* London: Oxford University Press, [1957].

Trevor, William. *The Oxford Book of Irish Short Stories.* Oxford & New York: Oxford University Press, 1989.

Vorm, William. *Paddy No More: Modern Irish Short Stories.* Dublin: Wolfhound, 1978.

Drama

Barnet, Sylvan, Berman, Morton and Burto, William. *The Genius of the Irish Theatre.* New York: New American Library, 1960.

Canfield, Curtis. *Plays of the Irish Renaissance.* New York: Macmillan, 1929.

———. *Plays of Changing Ireland.* New York: Macmillan, 1936.

Grant, David. *The Crack in the Emerald: New Irish Plays.* London: Nick Hern, 1994.

Harrington, John P. *Modern Irish Drama.* New York & London: W. W. Norton, [1991].

Hogan, Robert. *Seven Irish Plays, 1946–1964.* Minneapolis: University of Minnesota Press, 1967.

Hogan, Robert and Kilroy, James. *Lost Plays of the Irish Renaissance.* Dixon, Calif.: Proscenium, 1970.

Owens, Coilin D. and Radner, Joan N. *Irish Drama, 1900–1980.* Washington, D.C.: Catholic University of America Press, [1990].

Folklore

Colum, Padraic. *A Treasure of Irish Folklore: The Stories, Traditions, Legends, Humour, Wisdom, Ballads and Songs of the Irish People.* New York: Crown, 1954/revised 1967.

Croker, T. Crofton. *Fairy Legends and Traditions of the South of Ireland.* 3 vols. London: Murray, 1836.

Curtin, Jeremiah. *Myths and Folk-Lore of Ireland.* Boston: Little, Brown, 1890/as *Myths and Folk Tales of Ireland.* New York: Dover, 1975.

Hyde, Douglas. *Beside the Fire: A Collection of Irish Gaelic Folk Stories.* London: Nutt, 1890/Dublin: Irish Academic, 1978.

————. *Legends of Saints and Sinners.* London: T. Fisher Unwin, n.d.

Larminie, William. *West Irish Folk-Tales and Romances.* London: Irish Folklore Series, 1893/Shannon: Irish University Press, 1972.

O'Faolain, Eileen. *Children of the Salmon and Other Irish Folktales.* Boston: Little, Brown, 1965/Swords, Co. Dublin: Ward River, 1984.

Wilde, Lady. *Ancient Legends, Mystic Charms, and Superstitions of Ireland: With Sketches of the Irish Past.* London: Ward & Downey, 1888/Galway: O'Gorman, 1971.

Yeats, W. B. *Fairy and Folk Tales of the Irish Peasantry.* London: Scott, 1888.

————. *Irish Fairy and Folk Tales.* New York: Carlton House, n.d.

————. *Fairy and Folk Tales of Ireland.* Gerrards Cross: Colin Smythe, 1973.

INDEX

Boldface page numbers indicate location of main entries.

About the Editor

ROBERT HOGAN is Professor Emeritus of English Literature at the University of Delaware. For 22 years he edited *The Journal of Irish Literature*, and his books include *The Experiments of Sean O'Casey* (1960), *After the Irish Renaissance* (1967), and the six-volume history called *The Modern Irish Drama* (1975–1992). His plays have been produced in Los Angeles, New York, and Dublin, and he has recently published a novel, *Murder at the Abbey Theatre* (1993).

ISBN 0-313-30176-X

HARDCOVER BAR CODE